Halliday

WINE COMPANION

THE BESTSELLING AND DEFINITIVE GUIDE TO AUSTRALIAN WINE
EDITED BY TYSON STELZER

- ESTABLISHED 1986 - WINECOMPANION.COM.AU -

2023

Hardie Grant

BOOKS

Published in 2022 by Hardie Grant Books,
an imprint of Hardie Grant Publishing

Hardie Grant Books (Melbourne)
Wurundjeri Country
Building 1, 658 Church Street
Richmond, Victoria 3121

Hardie Grant Books (London)
5th & 6th Floors
52–54 Southwark Street
London SE1 1UN

hardiegrantbooks.com

The *Halliday Wine Companion* is a joint venture between James Halliday and
HGX Pty Ltd.

The map in this publication incorporates data copyright © Commonwealth of
Australia (Geoscience Australia) 2004. Geoscience Australia has not evaluated
the data as altered and incorporated within this publication and therefore gives
no warranty regarding accuracy, completeness, currency or suitability for any
particular purpose.

Australian wine zones and wine regions data copyright © Wine Australia

Halliday Wine Companion 2023
ISBN 978 1 74379 872 0

Cover design by Pidgeon Ward
Illustration by David Lancashire
Photography by Marie Pangaud and Sherpa
Typeset by Megan Ellis
Printed in Australia by McPherson's Printing Group, Maryborough, Victoria

Hardie Grant acknowledges the Traditional Owners of the country on which we
work, the Wurundjeri people of the Kulin nation and the Gadigal people of the
Eora nation, and recognises their continuing connection to the land, waters and
culture. We pay our respects to their Elders past and present.

Contents

The tasting team

James Halliday

Respected wine critic and vigneron James Halliday is the founder of the *Halliday Wine Companion*. With a wine career spanning over 50 years, he was one of the founders of Brokenwood in the Hunter Valley, and later, Coldstream Hills in the Yarra Valley. James is an unmatched authority on all aspects of the wine industry, and for more than 30 years was among the most senior and active wine judges in Australia. He has won a clutch of awards for his contributions, including the Australian wine industry's ultimate accolade, the Maurice O'Shea Award. In 2010 he was made a Member of the Order of Australia for his services to the wine industry. James has written or contributed to over 80 books on wine since 1970 and has written a weekly wine column for Australian newspapers since 1978.

Regional focus: Langhorne Creek, Currency Creek, Kangaroo Island, Southern Fleurieu

Tyson Stelzer

Tyson Stelzer fell in love with wine more than 20 years ago between the pages of James Halliday's *Australia & New Zealand Wine Companion 2000*. He is now a multi-award-winning wine writer, TV host and producer, and international speaker. He was named The International Wine & Spirit Competition Communicator of the Year in 2015, The Australian Wine Communicator of the Year in 2015 and 2013, and The International Champagne Writer of the Year in 2011. Tyson is the author of 17 wine books, including six editions of The Champagne Guide, and a contributor to Jancis Robinson's *The Oxford Companion to Wine* (3rd edition), and regularly writes for many wine magazines. As an international speaker, Tyson has presented at wine events in 12 countries, and is also a regular judge and chair of wine shows throughout Australia. Tyson also hosts intimate Champagne tours.

Tyson is the chief editor for the *Halliday Wine Companion 2023*.

Regional focus: Tasmania, Queensland

Twitter: @TysonStelzer | Facebook: TysonStelzer | Instagram: @tyson_Stelzer | YouTube: Tyson Stelzer

Website: tysonstelzer.com

Dave Brookes

An established wine journalist, Dave contributes to a range of publications domestically and overseas. Originally from New Zealand, Dave lived in South Australia's Barossa for many years and has almost 30 years' experience working in the wine industry across a range of sectors, including retail, wholesale, wineries, the secondary market and brand management. Dave was awarded Dux of the prestigious Len Evans Tutorial in 2011 and is a sought-after judge and panel chair on the wine show circuit, having judged at more than 70 wine shows around Australia and the world. He is also the chief editor of the Wine100 Challenge in Shanghai and Beijing Fangshan Wine & Food Competition.

Regional focus: Barossa

Twitter: @vino_freakism | Instagram: @vino_freakism

Erin Larkin

Erin is an independent wine writer, judge and presenter based in Perth, Western Australia. She takes an individual, grass-roots approach to her work. Multi-skilled when it comes to the business of wine, she is a regular contributor to *Halliday* magazine, a prolific presenter and educator across multiple platforms, and an Australian wine show judge. Erin is also an active consultant for retail and private clients, with a keen eye for quality and creativity in wine, marrying classic and contemporary perspectives. She has a weekly newspaper column and a YouTube channel where she opens and discusses a vast array of wines, releasing up to two videos a week.

Regional focus: Western Australia, Limestone Coast, Clare Valley and Riverland

Instagram: @erinllarkin | erinlarkin.com.au

Jane Faulkner

Jane is a journalist by training and wine writer by vocation. A long-time contributor and columnist for *Halliday* magazine, she has been reviewing for the *Companion* since 2016. Jane is respected for her honesty, fairness and rigour in her writing and tasting. She started her career in newspapers, later working at *The Age/The Sydney Morning Herald*, and also in TV and radio. She is a sought-after local and international wine judge and chairs numerous shows. On a personal level, Jane is an Italophile, spending considerable time each year visiting Italy's wine regions and dreams of living in Piemonte. She never tires of travelling throughout the wine world in search of stories and bottles from inspirational, thoughtful producers.

Regional focus: Southern NSW including Canberra District; Mornington Peninsula, Macedon Ranges, Sunbury and Gippsland

Twitter: @winematters | Facebook: Jane Faulkner | Instagram: @winematters

Jeni Port

Jeni is a trained journalist, who caught the wine bug when she was a cadet on Melbourne's *The Sun News-Pictorial* newspaper (now *Herald Sun*). She was working in the paper's Women's Section (yes, really) and her first story was on a woman winemaker – a subject that would become a recurring theme over her career. During her time there, she wrote a weekly food market review, which quickly incorporated wine stories, and that was the start of the paper's first wine column. She covered wine in *The Age* for 30 years, and is an author and wine judge here and overseas, including in Germany for Mundus Vini, and in Europe for Concours Mondial de Bruxelles. Jeni has served on various wine bodies, is a founding board member of the Australian Women in Wine awards and has won numerous awards for wine writing over her career.

Regional focus: Geelong and Port Phillip, Central Victoria, North East Victoria, Western Victoria, North West Victoria; Mount Lofty Ranges including Adelaide Hills

Twitter: @jeniport | Instagram @jeniport

Ned Goodwin MW

Born in London, raised in Australia and educated in Tokyo and Paris, Ned splits his time between Tokyo, where he lived for 14 years, and his beloved Sydney. Ned is a Dux of the Len Evans Tutorial, Japan's first master of wine, an educator, consultant, judge, critic and motivational speaker and presenter. He has served as wine director for one of Asia's largest restaurant groups and was also the 'wine face' for All Nippon Airways. In addition, he is an Asian-focused ambassador for a Champagne house, the host of Langton's TV, has had his own TV wine show in Japan, is on the Wine Committee at Italy's illustrious Biondi-Santi, and has his own import company, Wine Diamonds. Before Japan, Ned was a sommelier, including at Michelin-starred Veritas in New York, which had arguably the finest wine list in the world.

Regional focus: Hunter Valley and Central Ranges, NSW; McLaren Vale

Instagram: @NedGoodwinMW | Twitter: @rednedwine

Philip Rich

Philip has more than 25 years' experience as a wine retailer, educator, show judge and writer. In 1996, Philip joined the van Haandels at The Prince of Wales and Stokehouse in Melbourne, where he was responsible for the wine buying, wine lists and sommelier training. Philip also co-founded Melbourne's Prince Wine Store and Bellota Wine Bar and wrote the monthly wine column for *The Australian Financial Review Magazine* for 17 years. Philip has chaired various wine shows, including the James Halliday Chardonnay Challenge, Yarra Valley Wine Show, Margaret River Wine Show, Mornington Peninsula Wine Show and The Australian Pinot Noir Challenge. In addition to tasting for the *Companion*, Philip is general manager of wine at Karen Martini's restaurant Hero, and he consults to wine importers and retailers.

Regional focus: Yarra Valley

Twitter: @jayer78 | Instagram: @psrich

Australia's geographical indications

Regions and subregions marked with an asterisk are not registered but are in common usage.

NEW SOUTH WALES

WINE ZONE		WINE REGION		SUBREGION
Big Rivers	(A)	Murray Darling	1	
		Perricoota	2	
		Riverina	3	
		Swan Hill	4	
Central Ranges	(B)	Cowra	5	
		Mudgee	6	
		Orange	7	
Hunter Valley	(C)	Hunter	8	Broke Fordwich Pokolbin Upper Hunter
Northern Rivers	(D)	Hastings River	9	
Northern Slopes	(E)	New England Australia	10	
South Coast	(F)	Shoalhaven Coast	11	
		Southern Highlands	12	
Southern New South Wales	(G)	Canberra District	13	
		Gundagai	14	
		Hilltops	15	
		Tumbarumba	16	
Western Plains	(H)			

SOUTH AUSTRALIA

WINE ZONE		WINE REGION		SUBREGION
Adelaide Super Zone includes Mount Lofty Ranges, Fleurieu and Barossa wine regions				
Barossa		Barossa Valley	17	
		Eden Valley	18	High Eden
Fleurieu	(J)	Currency Creek	19	
		Kangaroo Island	20	
		Langhorne Creek	21	
		McLaren Vale	22	
		Southern Fleurieu	23	
Mount Lofty Ranges		Adelaide Hills	24	Lenswood Piccadilly Valley
		Adelaide Plains	25	
		Clare Valley	26	Polish River* Watervale*
Far North	(K)	Southern Flinders Ranges	27	
Limestone Coast	(L)	Coonawarra	28	
		Mount Benson	29	
		Mount Gambier	30	
		Padthaway	31	
		Robe	32	
		Wrattonbully	33	
Lower Murray	(M)	Riverland	34	
The Peninsulas	(N)	Southern Eyre Peninsula*	35	

AUSTRALIAN CAPITAL TERRITORY

WINE ZONE	WINE REGION	SUBREGION

NORTHERN TERRITORY

WINE ZONE	WINE REGION	SUBREGION

VICTORIA

WINE ZONE		WINE REGION		SUBREGION
Central Victoria	(P)	Bendigo	36	
		Goulburn Valley	37	Nagambie Lakes
		Heathcote	38	
		Strathbogie Ranges	39	
		Upper Goulburn	40	
Gippsland	(Q)			
North East Victoria	(R)	Alpine Valleys	41	
		Beechworth	42	
		Glenrowan	43	
		King Valley	44	
		Rutherglen	45	
North West Victoria	(S)	Murray Darling	46	
		Swan Hill	47	
Port Phillip	(T)	Geelong	48	
		Macedon Ranges	49	
		Mornington Peninsula	50	
		Sunbury	51	
		Yarra Valley	52	
Western Victoria	(U)	Ballarat*	53	
		Grampians	54	Great Western
		Henty	55	
		Pyrenees	56	

WESTERN AUSTRALIA

WINE ZONE		WINE REGION		SUBREGION
Central Western Australia	(V)			
Eastern Plains, Inland and North of Western Australia	(W)			
Greater Perth	(X)	Peel	57	
		Perth Hills	58	
		Swan District	59	Swan Valley
South West Australia	(Y)	Blackwood Valley	60	
		Geographe	61	
		Great Southern	62	Albany Denmark Frankland River Mount Barker Porongurup
		Manjimup	63	
		Margaret River	64	
		Pemberton	65	
West Australian South East Coastal	(Z)			

QUEENSLAND

WINE ZONE	WINE REGION		SUBREGION
Queensland	Granite Belt	66	
	South Burnett	67	

TASMANIA

WINE ZONE	WINE REGION		SUBREGION
Tasmania	Northern Tasmania*	68	
	Southern Tasmania*	69	
	East Coast Tasmania*	70	

N

0   500 km

Timor Sea

●Darwin

Arafura Sea

Gulf of

Carpentaria

Coral

Sea

Great

Barkly

TABLELAND

NORTHERN

Barrier

Great

DIVIDING

RANGE

TANAMI

DESERT

TERRITORY

Reef

INDIAN

HAMMERSLEY RA.

Great Sandy

Desert

GIBSON

McDonnell Ra.

QUEENSLAND

Tropic of Capricorn

Tropic of Capricorn

DESERT

Simpson

OCEAN

WESTERN

(W)

Desert

67

Kati Thanda–Lake Eyre

(K)

AUSTRALIA

Great Victoria

Desert

●Brisbane

SOUTH AUSTRALIA

66

10

Lake

Torrens

(H)

R

NEW

(E)

9

Lake Gairdner

Darling

SOUTH

(D)

Plain

27

35 (N)

(A)

WALES

6

(B)

(C) 8

NULLARBOR

X

59 58

Perth●

26 17 18

34

5 7

Great Australian Bight

25 24

46 1

15

12

57 (V)

(J)

●Sydney

61

22 21

(M)

3

14 13

CANBERRA

60

23 19

47

2 (R)

A.C.T.

11

64

63

20

4

45

16 (G)

Tasman

Y

65 62

SOUTHERN OCEAN

(S)

(P) 37

43 42

(F)

32

36 38 39

44 41

29

31

54 56 49 40

Sea

33

53 51 Melbourne●

28

55 48 52

(L)

30

(U)

(Q)

(T)

VICTORIA

Bass Strait

68

70 TASMANIA

69 ●Hobart

Introduction

The dynamic world of Australian wine is fast on the move, and 2021–22 certainly delivered another tumultuous and nail-biting year of instability – environmentally, economically and politically.

The lingering ramifications of China's so-called anti-dumping trade tariffs since late 2020 have shrivelled Australia's biggest wine export market by 97%. Australia's next 5 top export markets, the UK, US, Canada, Germany and New Zealand, also dropped slightly in 2021. The only Australian wine exports not to drop in value in 2021 were the over $75/bottle category.

Domestic consumption of Australian wine likewise saw a decline in volume and an even larger decline in value in 2021. The consequences on grape prices were debilitating, with the average price of shiraz falling from $650/tonne in 2020 to just $350/tonne in 2022. Meanwhile, after three lean years, the record national crush of more than 2 million tonnes in 2021 landed at precisely the wrong time. The net effect of this perfect storm has been to overload the national wine stocks to more than 2 billion litres, the highest in 15 years. Set against this backdrop, truncated yields across most regions in the 2022 harvest has perhaps proved to be a blessing in disguise.

At the time of writing, one of the most successful men in Australian wine, John Casella, has put his entire estate of 5 650ha of vineyards on the market, representing more than one 25th of the nation's vineyard surface.

In retail land, the pendulum has swung back to a cycle of wine dumping, and my inbox has been bombarded with a daily parade of discounting. An unusual, and perhaps unprecedented, dynamic is increasingly emerging in which an ocean of wine is being flogged off for a song, while the great wines of the world have never been more highly sought after or more scarce. Australia's most celebrated estates have enjoyed unprecedented demand over the past two years. At the same time, Australian wine imports continue to progressively increase in both volume and value. Champagne alone smashed all records and shipped more than 10 million bottles into Australia in 2021.

The wine world is more competitive and global than ever, and in these unstable times it is vital for Australian wine to continue to raise its game. This is a pivotal era that will set the direction for Australia's wine future.

Given this volatile environment, it has never been more important for you to distinguish the truly great wines from the ocean of ho-hum, to anticipate the top vintages, and to be ready to pounce the instant they land. This is why our expanded tasting team has assessed more than 8000 wines for this edition, and why we are releasing more reviews more often through the *Halliday* magazine and www.winecompanion.com.au.

The great 2021 vintage has landed, with most of Victoria, South Australia and Tasmania flourishing under wonderfully cool, classic conditions reminiscent of the great seasons of the 1980s and 1990s. Harvest 2022 is still underway at the time of writing, but early reports indicate similarly elegant conditions. We have much to look forward to!

Now is the time to sign up to the mailing lists of your favourite producers and to secure your allocations the moment they're unleashed. Build a relationship with a good retailer and make sure you're on their list to be alerted when new arrivals land. Armed with our selections, you'll be set to enjoy all the finest wines in Australia again this year.

The tasting team of regional specialists

Last year we established the regional specialist roles of the *Halliday Wine Companion* tasting team. The success of this model in its first year opened the way for us to extend the team with two new members this year. Experienced writer and judge Dave Brookes was ideally suited to take on the Barossa, having lived in the region for many years. Philip Rich was perfectly positioned to cover the Yarra Valley, not least thanks to his experience in chairing the James Halliday Chardonnay Challenge and the Yarra Valley Wine Show. See pages 4–7 for the other tasters' focus regions.

Awards judging by the tasting team

Judging for the *Halliday Wine Companion* Awards was conducted by the full tasting panel, in the manner established last year. This again served the dual benefit of a rigorously collaborative result and also offered the ultimate context for the team to calibrate and benchmark at the top end.

Each of the eight tasters was invited to nominate their top wine in each of the 18 categories to progress to the trophy judging. In order to ensure that those tasters with multiple key regions had proper opportunity to champion each region, each was offered the option of nominating a second top wine from a different region in the six big categories of Riesling, Chardonnay, Pinot Noir, Shiraz, Cabernet Sauvignon and Cabernet and Family. This permitted those with two key regions to choose one from each (e.g. Margaret River and Coonawarra cabernet sauvignon for Erin Larkin). Each judge was also offered a maximum of three 'wild card' nominations of second (or third) nominations, again from different regions.

There were no points thresholds defined for nomination of top wines, so as not to encourage overscoring in order to qualify. The wines put forward obviously had to be the highest or equal-highest scoring for that variety in that region for that judge. (Nominated wines are marked with ♥ at the end of their tasting notes.) See pages 36–51 for winners of each category. Because each taster was only permitted to submit their single best wine from each region, the judges' nominations did not encompass all the top-scoring wines listed.

Last year we judged the Awards with the labels revealed, with all the detail of viticulture and vinification before us. For the first time this year we judged blind. There are advantages in assessing a wine in the context of its full identity, pedigree, style, region, variety, vintage, producer, history, method, terroir, etc. There is also great benefit in assessing nothing but the wine in the glass. Which is best? We are again delighted with the wines that have come forward, and we'll let you be the judge. But one result this year commends the validity of both methods. In our final taste-off for Chardonnay of the Year – one of the finest and largest classes of all – successive vintages of Penfolds Yattarna and Oakridge 864 came forward as two of the top three wines last year (revealed) and this year (blind). It is certainly encouraging that great wines ultimately triumph, regardless of process.

Members of the tasting panel were given time to taste each flight individually and to write their own notes. At the conclusion of each class, each member cast their vote using the Borda count method (as per wine show best practice). In instances where the results were close, there was a revote on the top two, three or four wines.

In determining our winners for each category, after much deliberation we again maintained last year's decision to uphold individual tasters' scores and reviews for every wine, resisting the temptation to meddle with scores in hindsight to inflate points based on group consensus. Thus, every review can rightly be considered in the context of every other rating from that taster. The winner of each category won the most votes from across the panel, which is why it does not always appear as the highest-scored entry in its category. Scores are individual to each taster, and to highlight this we have introduced the initials of each taster in our Top Rated by Variety lists for the first time (pages 36–51). Just as our reviews carry our own unique voices, so too do we score slightly differently, and this diversity is something that we celebrate.

The collaborative judging of the *Halliday Wine Companion* Awards by the assembled tasting team represents an important embodiment of the increasingly vital role of the team in the evolving story and future of the *Companion*. While an odd number of team members last year precluded the opportunity for tied results, this year the number of equal votes and revotes from an even number of tasters in close finish after close finish was indicative of the calibre of the wines put forward. In many cases, second- and third-place holders were but one or two votes behind the winners, so we have highlighted these in the relevant introductions to the Top Rated by Variety lists. Don't miss these! We are immensely proud of all of our finalists, and our winners fought harder than ever to secure a coveted place in the annals of *Halliday Wine Companion* history!

Tyson Stelzer
Chief Editor, *Halliday Wine Companion*
May 2022

How to use this book

Wineries

Pooley Wines

Butcher's Hill Vineyard, 1431 Richmond Road, Richmond, Tas 7025 **Region** Tasmania
T (03) 6260 2895 **www**.pooleywines.com.au **Open** 7 days 10–5 **Winemaker** Anna
Pooley, Justin Bubb **Viticulturist** Hannah McKay **Est.** 1985 **Dozens** 8500 **Vyds** 18ha
Pooley Wines is a glowing exemplar of a boutique Tasmanian family estate. Three generations
of the family have been involved in its development, with the little hands of the fourth
generation now starting to get involved. The heart of production has historically been the
glorious Campania vineyard of Cooinda Vale (after which the brand was originally named),
planted to 12ha of chardonnay, pinot noir, riesling and pinot grigio, with new plantings
currently underway. In 2003, the family planted pinot noir and pinot grigio (and more
recently chardonnay, riesling and syrah, bringing plantings to 6ha) at Belmont Vineyard
near Richmond, renamed Butcher's Hill. A cellar door was established in the heritage-listed
sandstone barn and coach house of the distinguished 1830s convict-built Georgian home,
standing in pride of place on the heritage property. In 2017 the family acquired the nearby
1830s Prospect House and refurbished it into a glorious private hotel. Wine quality has risen
to dramatic effect, no small feat while doubling production, since the return to Tasmania
of Anna Pooley and husband Justin Bubb to establish the winemaking arm of the estate in
2012. Riesling, pinot noir and chardonnay now rank among Tasmania's finest. Conversion to
organic viticulture is currently underway, with a goal of achieving certification by the 2026
vintage. Pooley is the Wine Companion 2023 Winery of the Year. Exports to the UK, the US
and Sweden. (TS)

Pooley Wines

The producer name appearing on the front label is used throughout the book.

★★★★★

Star ratings provide a highly coveted and oft-quoted snapshot of the calibre of a
winery based on the ratings of its wines in recent years.

Last year we applied a three-year rolling average for the first time. This year we have
returned to James' traditional system of calculating star ratings based primarily on the
wines tasted for this edition.

James writes, 'we look at the ratings for this year and the previous year; if the wines
tasted this year justify a higher rating than last year, that higher rating has been given.
If, on the other hand, the wines are of lesser quality, the winery rating will drop half
a star.'

In total, more than one-quarter of wineries awarded a star rating this year have
achieved the coveted 5-star status.

Of the more than 3000 wineries on www.winecompanion.com.au, 1128 submitted
wines for review this year. Space constraints dictate that not every review and score
can be printed in this book, which means that star ratings are best understood in the
context of the website, where all wine scores appear.

The number at the end of each rating below notes the number of wineries in that category in this year's edition, and the percentage is taken from the total number of wineries who submitted wines this year.

Where no wines were submitted by a well-rated winery with a reliable track record of providing samples, we may roll over last year's rating; these wineries can be found on www.winecompanion.com.au. Only wineries who submitted wines for review this year are in this edition.

★★★★★   Outstanding winery regularly producing wines of exemplary quality and typicity. Will have at least two wines rated at 95 points or above, and has typically held a 5-star rating for the previous three years. 102 wineries, 8.7%

                  Where the winery name itself is printed in red, it is a winery generally acknowledged to have had a long track record of excellence, typically having held a 5-star rating for the previous nine years. Truly the best of the best. 161 wineries, 14.3%

★★★★★   Outstanding winery capable of producing wines of very high quality, and did so this year. Will have at least two wines rated at 95 points or above. 137 wineries, 11.9%

★★★★☆   Excellent winery able to produce wines of high to very high quality, knocking on the door of a 5-star rating. Will have one wine rated at 95 or above, and two (or more) at 90 or above, others 86–89. 185 wineries, 16.4%

★★★★   Very good producer of wines with class and character. Will have two (or more) wines rated at 90 or above (or possibly one at 95 or above). 364 wineries, 32.3%

★★★☆   A solid, usually reliable maker of good, sometimes very good, wines. Will have one wine rated at 90 points or above, others 86–89. 113 wineries, 10%

★★★   A typically good winery, but often has a few lesser wines. Will have wines rated at 86–89 points. 57 wineries, 5.1%

     The vine leaf symbol indicates wineries that are new entries in this year's *Wine Companion*.

Butcher's Hill Vineyard, 1431 Richmond Road, Richmond, Tas 7025 **T** (03) 6260 2895

Contact details are usually those of the winery and cellar door, but in a few instances may simply be a postal address; this occurs when the wine is made at another winery or wineries, and is sold only through the website and/or retail.

Region Tasmania

A full list of zones, regions and subregions appears on page 8. Occasionally you will see 'various', meaning the winery sources grapes from a number of regions, usually without a vineyard or cellar door of its own.

www.pooleywines.com.au

An important reference point, normally containing material not found (for space reasons) in this book.

Open 7 days 10–5

Although a winery might be listed as not open or only open on weekends, many may in fact be prepared to open by appointment. A telephone call will establish whether this is possible or not. For space reasons we have simplified the open hours listed; where the hours vary each day or for holidays, we refer the reader to the website.

Winemaker Anna Pooley, Justin Bubb

In all but the smallest producers, the winemaker is simply the head of a team; there may be many executive winemakers actually responsible for specific wines in the medium to large companies (80 000 dozens and upwards). Once again, space constraints mean usually only one or two winemakers are named, even if they are part of a larger team.

Viticulturist Hannah McKay

Viticulturists have long been the unsung heroes of Australian wine – every winemaker will tell you they can't make great wine without great fruit. For the first time this year, we are proud to list the viticulturist for many estates. As with the winemaker, we acknowledge that in many instances the viticulturist heads a team, and while we honour everyone, we regret that space constraints preclude the opportunity to name them all.

Est. 1985

Keep in mind that some makers consider the year in which they purchased the land to be the year of establishment, others the year in which they first planted grapes, others the year they first made wine, and so on. There may also be minor complications where there has been a change of ownership or break in production.

Dozens 8500

This figure (representing the number of 9-litre/12-bottle cases produced each year) is merely an indication of the size of the operation. Some winery entries do not feature a production figure, this is typically because the winery (principally, but not exclusively, the large companies) regards this information as confidential.

Vyds 18ha

The hectares of vineyard/s owned by the winery.

Pooley Wines is a glowing exemplar of a boutique Tasmanian family estate. Three generations of the family have been involved in its development, with the little hands of the fourth generation now starting to get involved. (...) (TS)

Winery summaries have been written by members of the tasting panel, as denoted by their initials.

Tasting notes

ΨΨΨΨΨ **Jack Denis Pooley Pinot Noir 2020, Tasmania** This 33% whole-bunch pinot has depth beyond that of its siblings. It's full-on forest floor, full-on savoury spices, with tannins made to measure, but all bow down to the primacy of the dark berry fruit of the impossibly long finish. World class. Screw cap. 13.1% alc. RATING 99 DRINK 2022-2037 $140 JH ✪ ♥

The inadequacies of reducing the complexities of a wine to a number are patently apparent, but nonetheless we persist with the international 100-point system because it is universally understood. Space constraints dictate that only the top wines for each winery are printed in full in this book, with points, drinking windows and prices included for other wines. Tasting notes for wines that are 95 points and over are printed in red. Tasting notes for all wines receiving 84 points or above appear on www.winecompanion.com.au.

97–99	**GOLD**	ΨΨΨΨΨ	**Exceptional** Wines of major trophy standard in important wine shows.
95–96		ΨΨΨΨΨ	**Outstanding** Wines of gold medal standard, usually with a great pedigree.
94	**SILVER**	ΨΨΨΨΨ	Wines on the cusp of gold medal status.
90–93		ΨΨΨΨ⦿	**Highly recommended** Wines of silver medal standard, demonstrating great quality, style and character, and worthy of a place in any cellar.
89	**BRONZE**	ΨΨΨΨ	**Recommended** Wines on the cusp of silver medal standard.
86–88		ΨΨΨΨ	Wines of bronze medal standard; well-produced, flavoursome wines, usually not requiring cellaring.
84–85		ΨΨΨ⦿	**Acceptable** Wines of good commercial quality, free from significant fault.
80–83		ΨΨΨ	**Over to you** Everyday wines, without much character, and/or somewhat faulty.
75–79		ΨΨ⦿	**Not recommended** Wines with one or more significant winemaking faults.

✪   **Special value** Wines considered to offer special value for money within the context of their glass symbol status. This can apply at any price point, and for consistency a basic algorithm is applied to take into account the price of a wine and the points it is awarded. A value rosette is given, for instance, to $11 wines scoring 85 or more points, $21 wines scoring 90 or more, $35 wines of 95 or more and $200 wines with 98 or more.

♥   **Shortlisted for 2023 Awards** Nominated by the tasting panel as the best example of this variety/style in its region.

Jack Denis Pooley Pinot Noir 2020, Tasmania This 33% whole-bunch pinot has depth beyond that of its siblings. (...)
Screw cap. 13.1% alc. RATING 99 DRINK 2022–2037 $140 JH ✪ ♥

This year, we have again included viticultural and winemaking background of wines, where available. In most cases, constraints do not permit these to be included in book, but you can find the full details at the start of the note at www.winecompanion.com.au.

This tasting note will usually have been made within the 12 months prior to publication. Even that is a long time, and during the life of this book the wine will almost certainly change. More than this, remember that tasting is a highly subjective and imperfect art.

The initials DB, EL, JF, JH, JP, NG, PR and TS appearing at the end of the note signify that Dave Brookes, Erin Larkin, Jane Faulkner, James Halliday, Jeni Port, Ned Goodwin MW, Philip Rich or Tyson Stelzer tasted the wine and provided the tasting note and rating. Biographies for each member of the tasting team and their regional focuses can be found on pages 4–7.

Screw cap

The closures in use for the wines tasted are (in descending order): screw cap 90.7% (last year 86.8%), one-piece natural cork 4.1% (last year 6%), Diam 3.9% (last year 5.6%) and crown seal 0.7%. The remaining 0.6% (in order of importance) are Vinolok, agglomerate, Zork, synthetic and can. It seems the rise and rise of screw caps knows no end, with a continued move away from natural cork and Diam.

13.1% alc.

This piece of information is in one sense self-explanatory. What is less obvious is the increasing concern of many Australian winemakers about the rise in levels of alcohol, and much research and practical experimentation (for example picking earlier, or higher fermentation temperatures in open fermenters) is occurring. Reverse osmosis and yeast selection are two of the options available to decrease higher-than-desirable alcohol levels. Recent changes to domestic and export labelling mean the stated alcohol will be within a maximum of 0.5% difference to that obtained by analysis.

DRINK 2022–2037

The optimal time to drink a wine is of course subjective; some of us love young wines and others old. This is as personal to the taster as their review and their score. We have proposed dates according to when we would most love to drink this wine, and we commend these to you as a reference for managing your cellar and when to drink each bottle. We have long published drink-to dates, and for the first time this year, we are proud to introduce drink-from dates.

$140

Prices are provided by the winery, and should be regarded as a guide, particularly if purchased retail.

Winery of the Year

Pooley Wines Tasmania

When Denis and Margaret Pooley planted seven rows of pinot noir and 10 rows of riesling in the Coal River Valley as a retirement plan in 1985 – described by their family today as 'nothing more than a distraction for them' – they cannot have had an inkling of just how far their little farm would ascend in Tasmanian wine. Now, Pooley Wines is the Wine Companion 2023 Winery of the Year.

Tucked into a bend of the Coal River, there is a deep spirit about their quaint Cooinda Vale vineyard, the source of Pooley's finest wines. To their granddaughter, winemaker Anna Pooley, sense of place is everything: 'This is where the heart and soul of wine exists.' Their wines eloquently articulate the native Tasmanian spirit and the ruggedly beautiful landscapes of their Cooinda Vale and Butcher's Hill vineyards. Pooley Wines produces the pinnacle of Australian pinot noir, chardonnay and riesling.

Anna Pooley and her husband Justin Bubb returned to Tasmania to establish the winemaking arm of the family estate in 2012. The ascension of their wines since has been nothing short of breathtaking, with quality rising emphatically with every season, all the while doubling production. The fourth generation of the family now offers them avid assistance in the running of the winery.

Their wines are intricately engineered to heighten a sense of place. Crafted with intuition and talent, every tool of winemaking is applied purposefully, sensitively and yet courageously; be it barrel fermentation, wild yeast, skin contact, residual sugar, selective malolactic or whole-bunch fermentation. The results speak for themselves: their Margaret Pooley Riesling was our Riesling of the Year last year, my top Tasmanian riesling again this year, and Jack Denis Pooley Pinot Noir 2020 was James' highest-pointed pinot noir this year.

With biological farming and organics now weaving into the tapestry of this fabled family story, even greater things are yet in store for what was once but a distraction – and is now Winery of the Year. (TS)

Runners-up

Giant Steps Yarra Valley

Across two reviewers (JF & PR), Giant Steps received a staggeringly impressive 95–98 points for 21 of the 26 wines they submitted to this year's guide. Giant Steps already has a reputation for producing award-winning single-vineyard pinot noirs, and it's fair to say that the single-vineyard chardonnays are now equally compelling. In 2020, the American-based Jackson Family Wines purchased Giant Steps. Steve Flamsteed, who left before the 2022 vintage but still consults to Giant Steps, made a massive contribution to the brand's well-earned reputation. With his successor Melanie Chester as chief winemaker, and a new winery that will sit atop the Sexton vineyard, the future could not be more exciting for one of the Yarra and Australia's most exciting producers. (PR)

Grosset Clare Valley

Grosset has become synonymous with Polish Hill Riesling, widely regarded as one of Australia's greatest rieslings. Jeff Grosset steers his ship in a measured and precise way, producing wines of exceptional quality, year upon year. The excellence at Grosset is not limited to the rieslings (although it is a significant part of the story); the wines as a whole show their terroir and age-worthiness, and number among Australia's most collected. (EL)

Bannockburn Vineyards Geelong

The vision that Geelong businessman Stuart Hooper had in the early 70s, of planting a vineyard to classic French varieties that would excel, has been delivered through a series of strong-minded, creative winemakers. Early Geelong pioneering winemaker, Gary Farr (very much attuned to a Burgundian way of doing things), laid the groundwork and it has been improved upon by subsequent makers, including the thoughtful anarchist Michael Glover. Since 2015, the steady hand of winemaker Matt Holmes has been on the till. Long-time viticulturist Lucas Grigsby remains as ever a rock, producing organic fruit across 21ha of vines. Bannockburn has been celebrated for its Burgundian varieties and the degree of complexity and depth achieved in both chardonnay and pinot noir. With five pinots produced, the producer has style and diversity of the grape well covered. However, this is not to dismiss the quality of its lively, spice-fuelled shiraz, something of an unsung hero. (JP)

Serrat Yarra Valley

Serrat, the love child of Tom and Nadège Carson, submitted all six wines they made to this year's guide. Five of them received 96 points or more. Equally important, this was achieved with what is, for the Yarra Valley, a diverse and exciting range of wines. As you'd expect from Tom Carson, whose reputation for chardonnay, pinot noir and shiraz viognier is well recognized, these wines have all excelled in the excellent 2021 vintage. More surprising for some is the sheer quality of the grenache, a variety not usually associated with the Yarra – and which more than held its own in the line-up for Grenache of the Year at this year's *Halliday Wine Companion* Awards – and the Fourre-Tout barbera, blended with nebbiolo and a little grenache and pinot noir. That they are well-priced is a bonus. (PR)

McHenry Hohnen Vintners Margaret River

McHenry Hohnen is tucked away off the Bussell Highway to the south of Margaret River. The wines have bound from strength to strength, a comment never truer than under the stewardship of winemaker Jacopo 'Japo' Dalli Cani. Under his leadership, the wines have been catapulted into a new realm of quality. The chardonnays particularly exemplify that hard-to-achieve balance of pleasurable on release, and capable of graceful ageing. The move towards organics and sustainable farming have had a positive impact on the quality of the wines, and it is a delight to witness so much diversity in the vineyards – from experimental clones and new plantings, to sheep, chickens, olives and vegetables. McHenry Hohen is an estate on the move – divert your eyes at your peril. (EL)

Yangarra Estate Vineyard **McLaren Vale**

This address has won plenty before. And it will again. Deservedly so. The quality of wines from the straight varietal expressions to the top of the totem are not merely outstanding in an Australian context, but are truly world-class. And I use this term with scant trepidation. Biodynamic accreditation, a nursery system that propagates the right material for the right sites (with an emphasis on Rhône over robotic) and a culture that believes in grenache as the harbinger of a better future, equipped with the sort of viticulture and winemaking prowess that delivers. What else? The Ovitelli white is an additional bow in the quiver worth getting excited about. Very excited! (NG)

Stargazer Wine **Tasmania**

It seems impossible that someone could achieve so much before establishing Stargazer Wine in 2012. New Zealander Sam (Samantha) Connew completed postgraduate courses in viticulture and winemaking at Lincoln University in Christchurch, followed by vintages in Australia, Italy, Spain and Oregon on the Northern/Southern rollercoaster. She drew breath for 10 years as chief winemaker at Wirra Wirra, followed by several vintage stints in the Hunter Valley, before rising to become Chair of Judges at the Sydney Royal Wine Show. Numerous board, advisory and academic positions followed. In 2012 she finally stepped off the roundabout by acquiring an 11ha vineyard (now called Palisander) in Tasmania's Coal River district. Riesling, pinot noir, chardonnay and an aromatic white blend all rating between 95–97 points this year put Stargazer in the running for Winery of the Year. (JH)

Previous Winery of the Year recipients were Paringa Estate (2007), Balnaves of Coonawarra (2008), Brookland Valley (2009), Tyrrell's (2010), Larry Cherubino Wines (2011), Port Phillip Estate/Kooyong (2012), Kilikanoon (2013), Penfolds (2014), Hentley Farm Wines (2015), Tahbilk (2016), Mount Pleasant (2017), Mount Mary (2018), Seville Estate (2019), Jim Barry Wines (2020), Henschke (2021) and Yarra Yering (2022).

Winemaker of the Year

Winemaker of the Year is awarded to the individual whose wines in the *Companion* this year most exemplify best winemaking practice. It is acknowledged that, even in the smallest winery, credit is never due only to one individual but to a team. In listing each nomination we also recognise and applaud the teams around them.

Again this year we are proud to announce the runners-up for Winemaker of the Year. Each of the eight members of the tasting team put forward one nomination. The shortlist was discussed rigorously while tasting at least one of each nominee's wines together during our Awards judging. Our final decision was multifaceted, taking into account all of the wines submitted for this edition, with a glance to the full history of wines submitted in the past, and our personal knowledge of each of the individuals and their winemaking talents. Narrowing down one winner was again a very difficult process, and each nominee is deserving in his or her own right. All are every bit worthy. And one, as it turns out, especially so.

Glenn Goodall, Xanadu Margaret River

Glenn was nominated for this award last year, and if success was not achieved this year, guess who would have been nominated next year? Glenn started at Xanadu in 1999, and took on the role of chief winemaker in 2006. Since then, the quality of the wines has gone from strength to consistent strength. His belief that the vineyard is central to the success of the wine has steered his winemaking decisions towards prefacing terroir in all wines, from the DJL to the Reserve range. Due to his leadership, focus and attention to detail, the wines exude excellence at every pricepoint. However, his award-winning wines are not the whole story. It is not enough in life to be good at your job – in Glenn's case, he has given his time and knowledge generously and freely over many years to the Australian wine show system. He speaks at seminars and contributes to expert panels and supports his local and interstate peers. His ready smile and open nature are just 'the sauce on the pie at Mossy's' (ask him). All of this should tell you that Glenn is not only an exceptionally talented winemaker, but a widely loved and respected member of this industry. This award has been a long time coming, and there is nobody more deserving. Congratulations. (EL)

Runners-up

Tom Carson, Serrat Yarra Valley

Tom Carson's reputation for making world-class, award-winning wines now spans a quarter century – from when he started at Yering Station in 1997, to being the first winemaker awarded a Jimmy Watson trophy for pinot noir when Yabby Lake Block 1 Pinot Noir 2012 triumphed at the 2013 Melbourne Royal Wine Awards. Tom is still the winemaker and general manager at Yabby Lake and in 2001, he and his wife Nadège planted the first 1ha of their Serrat vineyard in the Yarra Valley. It's on the back of Serrat's 2021 wines (five received 96–98 points), including the expected chardonnay, pinot noir and shiraz viognier (the 2014 was James Halliday's Wine of the Year) as well as a stunning grenache and a gorgeous and well-priced red blend, that Tom has been nominated as Winemaker of the Year. (PR)

Greg Follett, Lake Breeze Wines Langhorne Creek

The Follet family have been farmers since 1880, grape growers since the 1930s, and leading winemakers in Langhorne Creek since 1987. The 20 000 dozen annual production doesn't require all the grapes, the surplus sold. Winner of our Best Value Winery last year, value for money is absolutely exceptional. This year, 14 wines – comprised of no fewer than eight varieties – picked up six scores between 95 and 97 points, with grenache, shiraz, cabernet sauvignon and a cabernet blend ranking in our Top Rated by Variety. A grand track record of national show success spanning decades reflects the pedigree of this estate, and Greg Follett's deep knowledge of the terroir behind his wines. (JH)

Ian Hongell, Torbreck Vintners Barossa Valley

Torbreck winemaker Ian Hongell has taken the label's wines to a new level since joining their team in the western Barossa in 2016 after many years as winemaker at Peter Lehmann wines. Working closely with viticulturist Nigel Blieschke, Ian has upped the ante at this renowned wine estate with his intricate knowledge of Barossa terroir and considered approach to winemaking. Torbreck has always had access to great ancient vineyards and has produced much-loved wines, albeit with a distinct house style. During Ian's tenure, that potent house style has evolved somewhat; it's still distinctly Torbreckian, but the site sings with a clearer voice within the wine's shape, providing added detail and insight into the individual vineyards in the Torbreck quiver. And this is a very good thing indeed. (DB)

Adam Wadewitz, Shaw + Smith Adelaide Hills

As he reaches 10 years at Shaw + Smith, chief winemaker Adam Wadewitz can reflect on a decade in which he has gone from strength to strength, capitalising on a celebrated earlier residency at Best's Wines. It's no surprise that his past experience producing top-quality riesling and shiraz has been employed at Shaw + Smith and been rewarded with some stunning releases, showing the huge potential for both grapes in the Adelaide Hills. And, all the while, we have seen him deliver a sensitive rendering of pinot noir, near perfection in the M3 Chardonnay and continued purity in sauvignon blanc releases, the grape that first put Shaw + Smith on the wine map. But there's more. Always open to new experiences and avenues, he explores winemaking in Tasmania (Tolpuddle), matchmaking regions and varieties to well-priced offerings (The Other Wine Co.) and making a more personal range of wines with friends under his own label (Elderslie). Now chief winemaker and co-CEO at Shaw + Smith, we can only imagine the possibilities for the maker during the next 10 years. (JP)

Natalie Fryar, Bellebonne Tasmania

The sensitivity, insight and tenacity required to craft truly great sparkling wine of elegance and endurance must rank as a winemaker's highest calling. Nobody in Tasmania embodies this more emphatically than Natalie Fryar. After 14 years building an intimate knowledge of the vines and the growers of Tasmania as sparkling winemaker for Jansz, in 2015 she poured her heart and soul (and house, car and life savings) into her finest creation, Bellebonne (Best New Winery nominee 2022). Nat's superpower is to heighten the inimitable delicacy and expression of Pipers River through courageous barrel fermentation, all the while building a suppleness and texture all of her own. Her talents do not stop with her own wines, and (on and off the record) she continues to have a hand in defining the greatness of many of the finest sparklings on the island. Her transformational touch is unmistakable. (TS)

Rob Mack, Aphelion Wine McLaren Vale

Mack is an interesting character. Standoffish, but jittery. Wise, but eager to learn. Sort of humble, but in your face. An accountant by trade, Mack is soon to embark on the master of wine program. He has worked about the place, most importantly abroad. He has gleaned an understanding of attenuated tannins and natural acidity, the firmament of savouriness, freshness and poise in a place like McLaren Vale where teeming fruit is the challenge rather than the virtue, as many may claim. Mack's Aphelion wines have been very good for a while, nudging the regional pantheon without quite opening the door. His new quiver of single-site grenache, however, has kicked it in. A mandala of diaphanous tannins, briny acidity and haunting red fruits crushed with Indian spices, these are the sort of wines that transcend the banner of 'exceptional regional wine' by virtue of their inimitability on an international scale. They are, it must be said, world-class. (NG)

Bryan Martin, Ravensworth Canberra District

Innovative and experimental. Respectful yet always curious. Unencumbered and super-smart. There are many ways to describe one of the country's most exciting winemakers, yet Bryan Martin's wines are the proof. Beautiful riesling and elegant shiraz viognier are mainstays of the region, yet there's an ethereal Ravensworth quality too. Texture is key, which is why he works with ambient yeasts, adopting a range of vessels from ceramic eggs to oak foudres, clay amphorae to concrete pyramids. A love of Italian varieties means Bryan grows sangiovese yet looks to Hilltops to source nebbiolo and barbera. The Ravensworth range is distinct and four-pronged, comprising the Estate, Regional, Esoteric and The Long Way Round. All have a story and all reveal Bryan's tenacity and talent. (JF)

Previous Winemaker of the Year recipients were Robert Diletti (2015), Peter Fraser (2016), Sarah Crowe (2017), Paul Hotker (2018), Julian Langworthy (2019), Vanya Cullen (2020), Brett Grocke (2021) and Michael Dhillon (2022).

Viticulturist of the Year

We were greatly encouraged by the enthusiasm with which our introduction of Viticulturist of the Year was received last year, and we are delighted to continue to highlight these unsung heroes of Australian wine. This award goes to the individual whose wines in this year's *Companion* most fully exemplify best practice in the vineyard. For the first time this year, we are proud to highlight the viticulturist for individual estates throughout the book and website. As for Winemaker of the Year, we recognise that credit is never due only to one individual and in naming each nomination we recognise and applaud also the teams who support them.

The process or nomination and selection of Viticulturist of the Year follows that of Winemaker of the Year. It is indicative of the calibre of our winner that he was the only nominee this year to be shortlisted as a finalist not only for Winemaker of the Year and Viticulturist of the Year but also Winery of the Year.

Tom Carson, Serrat Yarra Valley

In 2001, Tom and Nadège Carson planted 1ha of pinot noir, chardonnay, viognier and a handful of grenache vines on the Yarra Valley floor, 3km from Yarra Glen. Tom describes the site as ideal, 'In the central part of the valley and a lovely little amphitheatre of north- and east-facing slopes.' Inspired by the great vineyards of Europe, vines were planted at a density of 8800 vines/ha, more than 4 times the Australian average, yielding just one bottle per vine. Today they have 3.63ha planted, with 1.2ha of pinot noir, 0.85ha of shiraz, 0.6ha of chardonnay, 0.4ha of grenache, 0.28ha of nebbiolo and 0.3ha in total of barbera, grenache blanc and malbec. They planted varieties for which the Valley is noted, but also took a punt on what might work well for the future. The decision to plant grenache, based partly on Nadège's family's long history with the variety in Banyuls and the warm site's suitability for the variety, has been fortuitous. The 2021 is a superb wine, that while more elegant and different in style to McLaren Vale, is equally good. (PR)

Runners-up

Hannah McKay, Pooley Wines Tasmania

After overseeing the rise and rise of Vasse Felix to organic viticulture, Hannah McKay took up her post in the vineyards of Pooley Wines shortly before harvest 2020. Her nomination as Viticulturist of the Year is awarded not only for the wines harvested under her tenure – responsible for Pooley's ranking as Winery of the Year, no less – but for the work that she has initiated in securing the sustainable future of this family estate. Progress to toward organic certification is well underway across new and existing plantings, biological farming has been put in place, biodiversity zones and insectariums established, and green waste has been upcycled as vineyard nourishment. Watch this space. (TS)

Michael Lane, Yangarra Estate Vineyard McLaren Vale

Compared to Europeans, we Australians talk a lot about winemakers and their arts, be they of the light or dark side. Even Americans have long spoken of site and viticulture far more than us. After all, without quality fruit we have lousy wine. Once we begin to speak more about viticulture we will be responsible for far more world-class wine. After all, when under the guise of somebody like Michael Lane, viticulture is a conduit of superlative wine and the moments that define it. Yangarra's biodynamic weave of freshness, tannic refinement and incorrigible depth across the range would simply not exist were it not for Lane's deft touch. A touch that somehow meets the lenticular sweet spot of involvement without intervention. (NG)

Chris Davies, Windows Estate Margaret River

Windows Estate is responsible for wines of precise identity and superlative quality. It is 100% owned and operated by husband-and-wife team Jo and Chris Davies; Jo runs sales and front of house, while Chris is responsible for the dirt, the vines and the winemaking. He has taken the vineyards through organic certification and tends them with care and attention to detail. The wines are beautiful, graceful things of balance and life, which show the vineyard in the glass in the most eloquent of ways. The chardonnays are a kaleidoscopic blend of clones and characters, exemplifying what is possible from a small site in a great region. Not only is Chris doing a magnificent job in his own corner of the world, but he is also representative of many of the high-quality, family-run vineyards in Australia that have the potential to go under the radar due to their boutique size. Yet here they are, here Windows is: unearthed for you. (EL)

Adrian Hoffmann, Dimchurch Vineyards Barossa Valley

Adrian Hoffmann is a Barossa boy through and through. A fifth-generation grapegrower, tireless promoter of the region and current custodian of the stellar Hoffmann property and Dimchurch Vineyards in the famous northern Barossa subregion of Ebenezer. The first 20ha Dallwitz block with its gnarled old shiraz vines, planted 1888–1912, is the jewel in the Hoffmann crown. He's a big unit, with a big, bushy beard, exactly what you'd expect an ace northern Barossa grapegrower should look like – and an ace he is. His highly sought-after grapes have made their way into some of the most famous and prized wines of the region including John Duval, Two Hands, Glaetzer, Sami-Odi, First Drop and the stellar Chris Ringland Hoffmann Shiraz. With a strong Barossa lineage, great farming, leadership within the wine community and an impeccable vineyard, Adrian continues to strengthen the Hoffmann family legacy in the Barossa and beyond. (DB)

Bruce Chalmers, Chalmers Murray Darling

In a changing climate, Australian winemakers are benefiting mightily from the work performed by the Chalmers family. Chalmers is a significant importer and supplier of 'alternative' grape varieties, primarily Mediterranean, that hold their acidity in hot, dry conditions. In winemaking terms, they push boundaries, explore new flavours and textures in a range of wines produced at Merbein (under the viticultural direction of Bruce Chalmers) and Heathcote (under Troy McInnes). Just try pecorino, vermentino, negroamaro and aglianico – among many others – and try not to get excited. (JP)

Best Value Winery

Best Value Winery of the Year is closely tied to the awarding of rosettes for wines offering special value for money at their price point (see page 15). With more than 1300 rosettes awarded this year, the number of value wineries featured throughout these pages is again considerable. In narrowing down a top 10, I prioritised not only the highest number of rosettes and the highest strike rate but also inclusion of at least two value wines under $30, and in the case of our top three finalists, a good number under $20, too! While great value can occur at any price point, an everyday quaffing price holds a special place for us all.

When it comes to value, Western Australia leads the country, with three of our nine top contenders, including one very worthy winner!

Deep Woods Estate Margaret River

Deep Woods has been nudging this award for a number of years now, and it is the consistently high quality of wine, spread over a broad range of prices, that eventually got them over the line. The team, led by previous Winemaker of the Year Julian Langworthy, has shown a thrilling (some may say flagrant) disregard for accepted pricepoint quality; their entry-level wines present compelling drinking propositions, and their Reserve range (among the cheapest of the best in Margaret River) frequently blitz the competition in the quality–value stakes. Of 16 wines submitted this year, Deep Woods topped the ranks in both strike rate and number of special value rosettes (14), including five wines under $20. Immune to hyperbole, this is an estate to watch (and buy, and drink). Hearty congratulations are due. (EL)

Runners-up

Xanadu Wines Margaret River

It's high stakes in Margaret River for Best Value Winery. The region is widely reputed for its high-quality wines which command a higher-than-average bottom-line price. However, in the hands of Glenn Goodall, Brendan Carr and the team at Xanadu, this is not an issue. The wines are made to an exceptional standard at every pricepoint, showcasing their deep understanding of both the art of winemaking and the terroir of the region. While the Reserve and Stevens Road wines are undoubtedly the jewel in the Xanadu crown, the Black Label (the 2016 Cabernet Sauvignon was the 2018 Jimmy Watson winner) has time and again proven its quality and ageability, an astounding feat for a wine of circa $40; not to mention the brilliant wines in the DJL range. Roll on Xanadu – the future is bright indeed. (EL)

Hoddles Creek Estate Yarra Valley

This great vineyard has been created by the D'Anna family with minimal assistance from outsiders. The property was purchased in 1960, the vines planted in 1997. In the interim, father Tony D'Anna had driven up most weekends from Melbourne to tend the veggie patch, using water from the creek that permanently flowed. Son Franco enrolled in CSU's viticulture course in 1998, as planting vines had started the previous year. As the vines grew, Franco's knowledge of the challenges – and the answers – accumulated. The winery was built in 2003, and in 2018 the family purchased the adjacent Gembrook Road property, planting it with pinot noir on grafted rootstock. Says Franco, 'Phylloxera will come. We want to be ahead of the curve.' The value for money represented across this portfolio is unparalleled, with 10 of 14 wines submitted this year receiving special value rosettes, including eight under $30. (JH)

Bondar Wines McLaren Vale

A husband-and-wife team that has done everything right from the outset of Bondar Wines in 2009. The Rayner Vineyard, with vine plantings dating back to the 1950s, straddles a ridge that has Blewitt Springs sand on the eastern side and Seaview with its heavier clay loam over limestone on the western side. Shiraz is its key, with grenache flourishing on the Blewitt Springs side. Of eight wines submitted this year, six were awarded special value rosettes, including three under $30. (JH)

Bleasdale Vineyards Langhorne Creek

Bleasdale Vineyards breathes history, with direct descendants of the Potts family still actively involved with the running of the business. The climate is almost identical to that of Coonawarra, and the heat spikes of (say) the Barossa seldom challenge the otherwise calm, cool growing season. Malbec is its ace in the hole, ever reliable, and superb cabernet sauvignons should be no surprise given Langhorne Creek's climate. Then there's Paul Hotker, 2018 *Companion* Winemaker of the Year. Recognising that Bleasdale's larder of malbec, cabernet sauvignon and shiraz needed some balance, he went to the Adelaide Hills and purchased riesling and pinot gris, with both the wines receiving value rosettes – as did almost every wine in the portfolio. (JH)

Garagiste Mornington Peninsula

The talented Barnaby Flanders focuses on Mornington Peninsula's leading varieties of chardonnay and pinot noir, turning them into exceptional wines. It's all about small batches from single sites leading the premium range at a reasonable $45, but there's also Le Stagiaire, the entry-level wines at $30. Le Stagiaire wines are unequivocally the best value wines on the Peninsula, matched to excellence, of course. Both the chardonnay and pinot noir are stonkingly good but there's also a terrific pinot gris, another variety that excels in this region. (JF)

Nick O'Leary Wines Canberra District

Nick O'Leary has earned a reputation for making top-notch riesling sourced from the Canberra District, including the family vineyard, Heywood, plus another distinguished site called Westering, one of the oldest vineyards in the Canberra District, planted 50 years ago. The White Rocks Riesling produced from the Westering vineyard is excellent value at $38, the Heywood Riesling at $34, and his regional offering crafted from several vineyards comes in at $25. No matter your choice, there's a guarantee of an excellent drink. The reds are equally impressive, from savoury tempranillo to cool and spicy shiraz. If anything, Nick O'Leary represents quality and deliciousness in equal measure. (JF)

Duke's Vineyard **Porongurup**

If you've ever been down to Porongurup, you'll understand precisely this pristine, picturesque little spot, tucked away in the eastern reaches of the Great Southern. Duke's Magpie Hill vineyard is planted at the base of the Porongurup Range, and this site produces wines that are an ode to high-quality, cool-climate elegance, punching far above their weight for price and quality. The vineyard is only so big, the production can only be so much; this heartbreaking limitation on quantity only adds to the excitement and the chase – if Duke's is not already on your radar, you are missing out. (EL)

Riposte **Adelaide Hills**

To know the man behind Riposte, Tim Knappstein, is to know that during his long winemaking history – he recently celebrated his 60th vintage – he has embraced and produced wines that everyday Australians can afford and enjoy. First at the Stanley Wine Company in Clare, then out on his own at Knappstein, also in Clare, Tim Knappstein fashioned beautifully clean, smart, precise wines, that were well priced to boot. He and his son, Nick, continue apace at Riposte in the Adelaide Hills with little fanfare or fuss, sharing a similar philosophy. Be amazed at the quality of a host of Hills-sourced wines – from pinot gris, sauvignon blanc and chardonnay to pinot noir priced at just $24. (JP)

Previous Best Value Winery recipients were Hoddles Creek Estate (2015), West Cape Howe (2016), Larry Cherubino Wines (2017), Grosset (2018), Provenance (2019), Domaine Naturaliste (2020), Best's (2021) and Lake Breeze Wines (2022).

Best New Winery

The Best New Winery of the Year is the finest winery submitting to the *Companion* for the first time. This year we are proud to introduce the 10 top wineries swinging into our line-up for the first time. Our winner was confirmed by one 96-point score, two 95s, and all five of its remaining submissions between 91 and 94 points.

Living Roots Adelaide Hills

As they themselves say, 'Living Roots is an urban winery in the Finger Lakes region of New York and a not-so-urban winery in the Adelaide Hills.' It was founded by husband-and-wife team Sebastian (an Adelaide native and sixth-generation winemaker) and Colleen (a New York native and marketer) Hardy. There's more skin in the game than 400 dozen production of eight wines. The range of the Australian wines includes some very smart offerings, all scoring between 91 and 96 points this year, and all priced under $40. (JH)

Runners-up

Arila Gardens Barossa Valley

With 8ha of prime viticultural real estate in the northern Barossa parish of Moppa, Arila Gardens produce a range of outstanding wines with a focus on shiraz and grenache. It's a family-run affair with winemaker Adam Clay and his wife Marie, joined by Adam's parents David and Cheryl, farming the property according to holistic and sustainable viticultural practices. Their vineyards are split into 'gardens' according to soil type – sand, quartz and ironstone, each imparting particular characters in the wines. The vine age runs back to the early 1900s for the grenache plantings and 1940s for the shiraz. These are deep, soulful wines with a sense of place that is true to their regional roots and represents an exciting addition to the Barossa winescape. (DB)

Montague Estate Margaret River

Montague Estate has burst onto the scene with a range of wines in the first two vintages that show brilliant quality and great expression of terroir. Sourcing fruit from Margaret River (the home vineyard) and Frankland River, the wines speak volumes: we have only seen the beginning of Montague Estate. (EL)

Chance Encounter McLaren Vale

Expressions of indelible regional clarity without extraneous clutter, Chance Encounter avails the drinker with a potpourri of McLaren Vale spice aside the fecund richness of Barossa and the altitudinal freshness of the Adelaide Hills. Accessibility to South Australia's holy triumvirate at a fair price. What's not to love? (NG)

Trait Wines Margaret River

A winery doesn't need to be large scale to be eligible for this award, and Trait wines is the perfect example of that. Husband and wife Theo Truyts and Clare Trythall's quest to revive a vineyard in Margaret River (planted in 1988) has led to beautiful things in their wines. They are working on regenerating and restoring the land in order to produce elegant and expressive wines of variety and place. We've barely even begun to scratch the surface of potential of this winery. (EL)

Clarnette Grampians

Leigh Clarnette is well known in Victoria, he is one half of the Grampians wine duo, Clarnette & Ludvigsen. This year, Leigh decided it was time for a new chapter. Since the death of his dear friend and mentor, Kym Ludvigsen, in 2013, he had been resolute in keeping the Ludvigsen name on the label. This year, no more. Clarnette is born. So, it's a new name and a new start, but the quality of Clarnette's winemaking craft and attention to detail in the winery remains. And that's a good thing. (JP)

Usher Tinkler Wines Hunter Valley

Tinkler is a maverick. In a region that boasts long-lived, savoury reds and tensile whites, Tinkler respects tradition while dabbling far and wide. His Nose to Tail line serves up value, while the Reserve Chardonnay and Shiraz are modern in the best sense. His play in the minimal arena, too, is loads of fun: 'Death by Semillon' is an ironic turn of phrase as much as handling, shifting the traditional obsession with retaining fruit on its head, with extended skin maceration and brief oak maturation. (NG)

Solum Wines Mornington Peninsula

It's exciting to include fledgling Solum Wines in this auspicious line-up, the brainchild of 31-year-old Ryan Horaczko. While immersed in all things vinous from a young age, Ryan only enrolled in viticulture and winemaking studies in 2017; he also works part-time with Darrin Gaffy at Principia on the Peninsula. That in part gave Ryan the confidence to make his inaugural Solum Wines from vintage 2020, just two – a gentle yet impressive pinot noir from fruit grown in Red Hill and a savoury Pyrenees syrah. A Peninsula chardonnay will be the next addition. I can't wait. (JF)

MBK South Australia

MBK is derived from the names of the three founders: Mario and Ben Barletta and Kim Falster. Brothers Ben and Mario came from a retail background (Walkerville Cellars, Adelaide). The company started in 2014, but its genesis was back in 1993, making 'house wine' to sell in the store. They have never missed a vintage, but wines were sold exclusively to a private customer base, until now. Splashing into the Companion for the first time this year, it's in the running for Best New Winery. (EL)

Ossa Wines Tasmania

Ossa Wines is emblematic of the ever-increasing size of the Tasmanian wine industry, fuelled by investment on a grand scale by the Fogarty Wine Group and Rod and Cecile Roberts (joint owners of Tasmanian Vintners, the largest contract winemaker in the state), who own the real estate on which the 20-hectare Ossa vineyard is situated. It is run off-grid (solar), as part of a sustainable platform eradicating noxious plant species and fencing wildlife zones. The multi-award winning wine was made by Liam McElhinney. Watch this space. (JH)

Previous Best New Winery recipients were Rob Dolan Wines (2014), Flowstone (2015), Bicknell fc (2016), Bondar Wines (2017), Dappled (2018), Mewstone (2019), Shy Susan (2020), Varney Wines (2021) and Place of Changing Winds (2022).

Halliday Wine Club

Introducing Halliday Wine Club, a monthly subscription of top-rated wines.

Our purpose at Halliday is to ensure our members never drink a bad bottle of wine again. Now, Halliday Wine Club takes that one step further by delivering some of Australia's best wines directly to your door.

Gold medal wines only (95+ points)

Australia's leading authority on wine

Curated wine selections from over 9000 wines tasted

Delivering the stories behind the wine

Continue your wine journey with us.

Find out more at **winecompanion.com.au/wineclub** or scan the QR code.

Dark Horses

Dark Horses are wineries that are not new to the *Companion* but who have received a 5-star rating for the first time this year.

L.A.S Vino Margaret River

Nic Peterkin was born with pedigree winemaking blood in his veins, but it is his own ingenuity and hard work that have got him to where L.A.S. Vino is today. Nic has consistently produced wines that push boundaries and show a penchant for his calculated, out-of-the-box style of thinking. Whether it is alternate fermentation vessels, wildly extended time on skins (one nebbiolo once spent something like 400+ days on skins), experimental processes (fermenting grapes in sea water, or using the yeast of native flora, for example), Nic throws himself at wine with a freshness, vivacity and curiosity that are catching. To say that the wines are expressive and individual is true, but it doesn't quite tell the whole story. These wines have a tendency to extract unexpected descriptors, flavours and experiences from the writer, and the drinker, all the while portraying a classicism and accuracy of site that make them so brilliant. (EL)

Runners-up

Zilzie Wines Murray Darling

One of the stars of the Murray Darling wine region, Zilzie Wines consistently brings a range of well-made, affordable wines to the drinker's attention. Its depth and breadth of labels covers everything from the $9 Bulloak range of wines and the excellent value-for-money $20 Regional Collection, which showcases wine from the Adelaide Hills and McLaren Vale, right through to the premium Platinum Edition range at $45. Few producers cover such broad wine ground. Members of the Forbes family have worked their land for more than 100 years and bring a deep understanding of the challenges that lie ahead. As part of a sustainable future, they have committed to reducing carbon emissions and introducing 100% renewable energy by 2025. They plan to be around for another 100 years. (JP)

Kimbolton Wines Langhorne Creek

Kimbolton Wines is a relative newcomer to Langhorne Creek, established in 1998. It originally formed part of the Potts Bleasdale estate, and in 1946 it was acquired by Henry and Thelma Case, grandparents of current owners, brother-and-sister team Nicole Clark and Brad Case. The 55-hectare vineyard of high-quality cabernet and shiraz is far, far more than the production requires for its 2500 dozen bottles both for wines and sale of grapes. But it has an unusual support role of fiano, montepulciano and carignan, which brings customers to the cellar door that opened in December 2018. This has a repurposed shipping container with a rooftop view of the surrounding dead-flat vinescape. (JH)

Aylesbury Estate Geographe

It's sort of fitting that a winery in the Geographe would be nominated for a Dark Horse wine, for there is no more 'Dark Horse' region in WA than this. It seems to be overlooked, or driven by, as people head to Margaret River, but the truth is, here, many vignerons, drinkers and winemakers understand the attraction of the Geographe. Aylesbury Estate typifies the versatility and quality of which the region is capable. With a range of varieties as diverse as arneis, tempranillo, chardonnay, cabernet sauvignon and gamay, there is plenty to experience here, and all the better if you do it in person; the natural beauty of the Ferguson Valley cannot be overstated. (EL)

Pt. Leo Estate Mornington Peninsula

Pt. Leo Estate is perhaps best known for its 16ha sculpture park dotted through the extensive landscaped garden, and a diverse range of dining experiences. However, the wines tasted for this edition have stepped up a gear, securing five stars for Pt. Leo Estate for the first time this year. (JF)

Yarradindi Wines Upper Goulburn

Where to start with the long and varied career of Hugh Cuthbertson, the driver behind Yarradindi Wines? He ran the Talavera wine company in Melbourne, which started his love affair with fortified wines, before moving to Mildara Blass as a marketing manager. All the while he worked with his parents at their Murrindindi Vineyards property in the Yea Valley and helped with winemaking. This became his focus when he left the corporate world and created Cheviot Bridge, which sourced fruit from a number of vineyards in the Valley. Which brings us to Yarradindi Wines and the Mr Hugh label. The crown in this range of well-made wines are the magnificent old fortified soleras, a cache that Cuthbertson acquired that once belonged to Melbourne's great wine merchant, WJ Seabrook. (JP)

Wine of the Year

Anointing just one Wine of the Year from more than 8000 wines tasted for this edition was no trivial task. The complexity of the challenge was again compounded this year by bringing the full tasting panel in on the final decision. Every standout wine of every style from every taster was on the table to be assessed blind, rigorously discussed and voted upon. The winner of each category was then in the running for Wine of the Year. Lining up 18 winners in one taste-off to single out one winner would have proven insurmountable, so again we first voted on our Sparkling Wine of the Year, White Wine of the Year and Red Wine of the Year. The three were then tasted off, and the panel cast its votes for Wine of the Year. It was ultimately between the white and the red, and the result could not have been closer, with only one vote between them. Like last year, it was again decided that the Fortified Wine of the Year would not be judged for Wine of the Year. The age and rarity of Seppeltsfield 100 Year Old Para Vintage Tawny 1922 put it in a class of its own.

Best's Wines Foudre Ferment Riesling 2021, Great Western

A wine style that started a minor revolution in Australia when it was first made, with extended skin contact, wild fermentation and maturation on lees in foudre. Each vintage tingles and impresses, and in a good year like 2021, it excels. Jasmine florals, bergamot, lime cordial, lemon curd and peach-skin aromas. A wine of some complexity and nuance, featuring bright, vibrant fruits and soft, mealy texture, with a hint of savouriness. Seamless and sustained. (JP)

Previous Wine of the Year recipients were Bass Phillip Reserve Pinot Noir 2010 (2014), Xanadu Stevens Road Cabernet Sauvignon 2011 (2015), Serrat Shiraz Viognier 2014 (2016), Best's Thomson Family Shiraz 2014 (2017), Henschke Hill of Grace 2012 (2018), Duke's Vineyard Magpie Hill Reserve Riesling 2017 (2019), Yangarra Estate Vineyard High Sands McLaren Vale Grenache 2016 (2020), Brokenwood Graveyard Vineyard Hunter Valley Shiraz 2018 (2021) and Yarra Yering Dry Red No 1 2019 (2022).

Sparkling Wine of the Year

Gilbert Family Wines Blanc de Blancs Chardonnay 2016, Orange

Clearly a great deal of work has gone into the sparkling wine programme here. The wines are stellar. Intentionally tensile and bone dry, with zero dosage. Given that natural acidity in Australia is never Champagne's equal, it's a savvy move. The partial oak fermentation endows breadth and grip across the mid palate, while toning the fervent drive of quince, bitter almond and citrus zest. Toast, too, after 50 months on lees. Long and of such exactitude that it pulls the saliva from the mouth in readiness for the next glass. And the next. A great fizz. (NG)

Runners-up

Pipers Brook Vineyard Kreglinger Brut Rosé 2017, Tasmania
Teusner MC Sparkling Shiraz 2017, Barossa Valley

White Wine of the Year

Best's Wines Foudre Ferment Riesling 2021, Great Western

Runners-up

Henschke Julius Riesling 2021, Eden Valley
Stella Bella Wines Luminosa Chardonnay 2020, Margaret River
Brokenwood Sunshine Vineyard Semillon 2014, Hunter Valley
Briar Ridge Vineyard Albariño 2021, Hunter Valley
Flowstone Wines Queen of the Earth Sauvignon Blanc 2020, Margaret River
Spinifex Luxe 2021, Barossa

Red Wine of the Year

Mount Mary Quintet 2020, Yarra Valley

A blend of 44/30/18/4/4% cabernet sauvignon/merlot/cabernet franc/malbec/petit verdot. From a cool year, with the poor flowering reducing the crop of the Quintet varieties by around 50%, this is an essay in elegance and understatement. A medium, bright and translucent ruby red, this is beautifully perfumed with aromas of just-ripened blackcurrants, red cherries, rose petals and gentle cedar notes from the oak. The palate is exceptionally pure-fruited and gently textured. The wine finishes with these incredibly silky, long tannins that are in perfect harmony with the fruit and acid. This majestic wine is gorgeous to drink even now, but those that still have some in their cellar in 10–15 years (if not longer) will be grateful. (PR)

Runners-up

Lowestoft La Maison Pinot Noir 2020, Tasmania
Chalk Hill Alpha Crucis Old Vine Grenache 2020, McLaren Vale
Battles Wine Granitis Shiraz 2020, Perth Hills
Hickinbotham Clarendon Vineyard The Peake Cabernet Shiraz 2020, McLaren Vale
Bleasdale Vineyards The Iron Duke Cabernet Sauvignon 2020, Langhorne Creek
Koomilya Cabernet Touriga 2018, McLaren Vale

Top Rated by Variety

The following lists represents the 446 top-scoring wines in this edition. Your quick reference guide to the most exciting wines of the year, of every style, irrespective of price!

As always, the number of wines in each category is limited by a rating cut-off that reflects the strength of its class. Again this year, shiraz stands tall as Australia's top-scoring variety, with more high-rating wines than any other. Cabernet sauvignon and its family of blends takes up second place, closely followed by chardonnay. Pinot noir and riesling trail a little further behind.

The winner of each category was determined collaboratively by the full tasting panel again this year. Page 11 explains the tasting team's judging process to determine the wine of the year in each class. The winner is the favourite of the whole team, which is why it does not always appear as the highest scoring entry in its category. Wines nominated by the tasting panel for judging are marked with ♥ at the end of their tasting notes. All nominated wines can be found at www.winecompanion.com.au.

Scores are individual to each taster, and to highlight this we have introduced the initials of each taster in our lists for the first time. Just as our reviews carry our own unique voices, so too we all score slightly differently, and this diversity is something that we celebrate.

As outlined in the introduction, for the first time this year we judged the Award winners blind. There are advantages in assessing a wine in the context of all the detail of its full identity. There is also great benefit in assessing nothing but the wine in the glass. Which is best? One result in particular confirms the validity of both. In our final taste-off for Chardonnay of the Year – one of the finest and largest classes – successive vintages of Penfolds Yattarna and Oakridge 864 came forward as two of the top three wines last year (revealed) and this year (blind). We are again delighted with all of the wines that have come forward, and it's encouraging to see great wines ultimately triumph, irrespective of process.

Some wine names have been shortened, but still allow the exact wine to be identified. Full tasting notes for each can, of course, be found in the body of the book.

Sparkling White

Australian sparkling is increasingly coming of age, finding ever greater refinement and distinction. The sparkling epicentre of Tasmania again occupies almost 40% to take a strong lead in our shortlist. Orange has leapt forward into second place this year, with five inclusions, pipping Tasmania and greater Victoria at the post for the top gong. There was but one vote between Chandon Australia Vintage Blanc de Blancs 2016 and Bellebonne Blanc de Blancs 2015 on first vote from the panel. Gilbert Family Wines Blanc de Blancs Chardonnay 2016 was a close third place, and shot to the lead when the three were put to the revote. The cool mainland zones of the Adelaide Hills, Yarra Valley and King Valley each mounted a noble challenge. The diversity of the balance of our list is exciting, with Pemberton, Margaret River and Pyrenees all joining the ranks. Even prosecco has twice fought its way to the top this year.

Sparkling White of the Year: Gilbert Family Wines Blanc de Blancs 2016, Orange

Rating & Taster	Wine	Region
96 (TS)	House of Arras EJ Carr Late Disgorged 2005	Tasmania
96 (TS)	House of Arras EJ Carr Late Disgorged 2006	Tasmania
96 (JH)	TarraWarra Estate Late Disgorged Reserve Blanc de Blanc 2010	Yarra Valley
96 (NG)	Printhie Wines Swift Blanc de Blancs 2011	Orange
96 (TS)	Bellebonne Blanc de Blancs 2015	Tasmania
96 (JH)	Gembrook Hill Blanc de Blancs 2015	Yarra Valley
96 (PR)	Chandon Australia Vintage Blanc de Blancs 2016	Victoria
96 (JH)	Petaluma Croser Pinot Noir Chardonnay 2017	Piccadilly Valley
96 (JP)	Mitchell Harris Wines Sabre 2018	Victoria
95 (NG)	Printhie Wines Swift Cuvée Brut NV	Orange
95 (PR)	Chandon Australia Non Vintage Blanc de Blancs NV	Victoria
95 (TS)	House of Arras Grand Vintage 2008	Tasmania
95 (EL)	Sittella Wines Grand Prestige Late Disgorged 2009	Pemberton
95 (TS)	Clover Hill Cuvée Prestige Late Disgorged Blanc de Blancs 2010	Tasmania
95 (JP)	Grampians Estate Kelly's Welcome Cuvée 2011	Western Victoria
95 (TS)	House of Arras Grand Vintage 2013	Tasmania
95 (JP)	Deviation Road Beltana Blanc de Blancs 2015	Adelaide Hills
95 (EL)	Wills Domain Cuvée D'Elevage Chardonnay Pinot Noir 2015	Margaret River
95 (NG)	Colmar Estate Chardonnay Pinot Noir 2015	Orange
95 (JH)	Chandon Australia Winemaker Explorations Cuvée 205 2015	Yarra Valley
95 (JP)	Brown Brothers Patricia Pinot Noir Chardonnay Brut 2015	King Valley
95 (TS)	Lowestoft Grand Reserve Méthode Traditionnelle 2016	Tasmania
95 (JH)	Chandon Australia Vintage Brut 2016	Victoria
95 (EL)	Sittella Wines Marie Christien Lugten Grand Vintage 2016	Pemberton
95 (NG)	Gilbert Family Wines Chardonnay Pinot Noir Pinot Meunier 2016	Orange
95 (TS)	Bellebonne Blanc de Blancs 2016	Tasmania
95 (JP)	Blue Pyrenees Estate Midnight Cuvée 2017	Pyrenees
95 (TS)	Bellebonne Natalie Fryar Vintage Cuvée 2017	Tasmania
95 (JH)	Pirie Traditional Method 2017	Tasmania
95 (TS)	Apogee Deluxe Brut 2017	Tasmania
95 (JP)	Petaluma Croser Pinot Noir Chardonnay 2018	Piccadilly Valley
95 (TS)	Bellebonne Natalie Fryar Vintage Cuvée 2018	Tasmania
95 (JP)	Dal Zotto Wines Pucino VP Prosecco 2021	King Valley
95 (JP)	Risky Business Wines Prosecco NV	King Valley

Sparkling Rosé

Sparkling rosé is now firmly established as a serious category in Australian wine in its own right. Tasmania continues to lead the way, representing almost two-thirds of the list this year, with the Adelaide Hills and Yarra Valley its only contenders. Having won our inaugural Sparkling Rosé of the Year 2022 with her Bellebonne Vintage Rosé 2017, this year Australia's Sparkling Rosé Queen Natalie Fryar is responsible for half of our finalists (two under Bellebonne and three under Pipers Brook and Lowestoft, to whom she consults). It was Pipers Brook versus Deviation Road in the final panel vote, with Pipers Brook the convincing winner.

Sparkling Rosé of the Year: Pipers Brook Vineyard Kreglinger Brut Rosé 2017, Tasmania

Rating & Taster	Wine	Region
96 (TS)	Bellebonne Natalie Fryar Vintage Rosé 2019	Tasmania
96 (JP)	Deviation Road Altair Brut Rosé NV	Adelaide Hills
95 (TS)	Pipers Brook Vineyard Kreglinger Brut Rosé NV	Tasmania
95 (JH)	Dominique Portet Brut Rosé LD NV	Yarra Valley
95 (JH)	Yarrabank Brut Rosé 2013	Yarra Valley
95 (TS)	Lowestoft Rosé Méthode Traditionnelle Sparkling 2017	Tasmania
94 (TS)	Bellebonne Bis Rosé NV	Tasmania
94 (JP)	Sidewood Estate Late Disgorged Isabella Rosé 2015	Adelaide Hills
94 (TS)	Apogee Deluxe Sparkling Rosé 2018	Tasmania

Sparkling Red

Shiraz again dominates Australia's best sparkling reds (with the single exception of a cabernet shiraz blend from David Franz), with South Australia and Victoria sharing almost equal representation in our short list. In the final taste-off between Billy Button and Teusner, it was the Barossa for the win.

Sparkling Red of the Year: Teusner MC Sparkling Shiraz 2017, Barossa Valley

Rating & Taster	Wine	Region
95 (JP)	Billy Button Wines The Cherished Sparkling Shiraz 2017	Alpine Valleys
95 (JP)	Grampians Estate Rutherford Sparkling Shiraz 2019	Grampians
94 (DB)	David Franz Nicole Sparkling NV	Barossa Valley
92 (NG)	Mr Riggs Wine Company Battle Axe Sparkling Shiraz NV	McLaren Vale
92 (NG)	Samuel's Gorge Comet Tail Sparkling Shiraz 2018	McLaren Vale
92 (JP)	Cofield Wines Sparkling Shiraz 2018	Rutherglen

Riesling

The diversity of regions claiming a coveted position in our riesling shortlist this year is testimony largely to the strength of the 2021 vintage across South Eastern Australia. Fifteen regions spanning five states have risen to the top, confidently led by the Clare Valley, followed by Eden Valley and closely by Tasmania. So strong was this class that we could not separate our two winners on first tasting or on a revote. Diversity is celebrated in method, too, contrasting the laser precision of Henschke Julius with the body and texture of Best's Foudre Ferment. It is a grand statement indeed that a foudre ferment style should not only win this category, but go on to White Wine of the Year and all the way to Wine of the Year. On sheer numbers, riesling again ranks behind only shiraz, chardonnay, cabernet and pinot noir as the strongest category in the country – just in case we needed another reminder that we all ought to be drinking more of this magnificent and affordable variety!

Joint Rieslings of the Year:
Best's Wines Foudre Ferment Riesling 2021, Great Western
Henschke Julius Riesling 2021, Eden Valley

Rating & Taster	Wine	Region
98 (EL)	Grosset G110 Riesling 2021	Clare Valley
98 (JH)	Henschke Julius Riesling 2021	Eden Valley
97 (JH)	Crawford River Wines Reserve Riesling 2015	Henty
97 (TS)	Moorilla Estate Muse Riesling 2018	Tasmania
97 (EL)	Jim Barry Wines Loosen Barry Wolta Wolta Dry Riesling 2019	Clare Valley
97 (JH)	Stargazer Wine Palisander Vineyard Riesling 2020	Tasmania
97 (JH)	Mount Horrocks Watervale Riesling 2021	Clare Valley
97 (EL)	Frankland Estate Isolation Ridge Riesling 2021	Frankland River
97 (EL)	Frankland Estate Smith Cullam Riesling 2021	Frankland River
97 (EL)	Grosset Polish Hill Riesling 2021	Clare Valley
97 (EL)	Duke's Vineyard Magpie Hill Reserve Riesling 2021	Porongurup
97 (PR)	Oakridge Wines Horst Riesling 2021	Yarra Valley
97 (JH)	Stargazer Wine Coal River Valley Riesling 2021	Tasmania
97 (DB)	Leo Buring Leonay DWY17 Riesling 2021	Eden Valley
97 (JH)	Henschke Peggy's Hill Riesling 2021	Eden Valley
97 (EL)	Jim Barry Wines The Florita Riesling 2021	Clare Valley
96 (EL)	Jim Barry Wines Cellar Release The Florita Riesling 2015	Clare Valley
96 (JP)	ATR Wines Hard Hill Road Writer's Block Riesling 2020	Great Western
96 (JH)	Best's Wines Riesling 2021	Great Western
96 (EL)	Rieslingfreak No. 2 Polish Hill River Riesling 2021	Clare Valley
96 (TS)	Penfolds Bin 51 Riesling 2021	Eden Valley
96 (EL)	Forest Hill Vineyard Block 2 Riesling 2021	Mount Barker
96 (EL)	Taylors St Andrews Riesling 2021	Clare Valley
96 (EL)	Forest Hill Vineyard Block 1 Riesling 2021	Mount Barker
96 (NG)	Bloodwood Riesling 2021	Orange
96 (NG)	Coates Wines The Riesling 2021	Adelaide Hills
96 (JF)	Granite Hills Knight 1971 Block Riesling 2021	Macedon Ranges
96 (EL)	Cherubino Riesling 2021	Porongurup
96 (EL)	Skillogalee Trevarrick Single Contour Riesling 2021	Clare Valley
96 (JH)	3 Drops Riesling 2021	Great Southern
96 (JF)	Nick O'Leary Wines White Rocks Riesling 2021	Canberra District
96 (JF)	Clonakilla Riesling 2021	Canberra District
96 (DB)	Orlando Steingarten Riesling 2021	Eden Valley
96 (JP)	Crawford River Wines Riesling 2021	Henty
96 (EL)	Grosset Springvale Riesling 2021	Clare Valley
96 (JF)	Helm Premium Riesling 2021	Canberra District
96 (JH)	Shaw + Smith Riesling 2021	Adelaide Hills
96 (EL)	Grosset Alea Riesling 2021	Clare Valley
96 (JH)	Forest Hill Vineyard Riesling 2021	Mount Barker

96 (JP)	Seppelt Drumborg Vineyard Riesling 2021	Henty
96 (NG)	Colmar Estate Block 5 Riesling 2021	Orange
96 (JP)	ATR Wines Chockstone Riesling 2021	Great Western
96 (TS)	Pooley Wines Margaret Pooley Tribute Riesling 2021	Tasmania

Chardonnay

On top scores, chardonnay ranks a very close third behind shiraz and cabernet for the strongest category in Australian wine today. Margaret River again towers above all others, alone putting forth a tremendous showing of more than half of this year's standouts. Of the balance, the Yarra Valley stands tall, responsible for almost two-thirds. No surprise that, just like last year, the two regions went head-to-head with Yattarna in the final taste-off. And just to prove that lightening can strike in the same place twice, Oakridge 864 was also again a contender for top three. To have two of the same three wines come forward in one of the finest and largest classes in successive years, one judged revealed and the other blind, proves that great wines ultimately triumph, regardless of method. On first vote all three scored equally, and on revote, there was just one vote between them, with Stella Bella Luminosa a stunning winner. All three are deserving – don't miss them.

Chardonnay of the Year: Stella Bella Wines Luminosa Chardonnay 2020, Margaret River

Rating & Taster	Wine	Region
98 (EL)	Pierro Chardonnay VR 2018	Margaret River
98 (JH)	Bannockburn Vineyards S.R.H. 2019	Geelong
98 (TS)	Penfolds Yattarna Bin 144 Chardonnay 2019	South Eastern Australia
98 (EL)	Leeuwin Estate Art Series Chardonnay 2019	Margaret River
98 (PR)	Oakridge Wines 864 Funder & Diamond Vineyard Chardonnay 2020	Yarra Valley
98 (EL)	Cullen Wines Kevin John 2020	Margaret River
98 (TS)	Penfolds Reserve Bin A Chardonnay 2020	Adelaide Hills
97 (JH)	TarraWarra Estate Cellar Release Reserve Chardonnay 2012	Yarra Valley
97 (EL)	Windows Estate La Fenêtre Chardonnay 2018	Margaret River
97 (JP)	Giaconda Estate Vineyard Chardonnay 2019	Beechworth
97 (JH)	Fighting Gully Road Smith's Vineyard Chardonnay 2019	Beechworth
97 (EL)	Paul Nelson Wines Karriview Vineyard Chardonnay 2019	Denmark
97 (JH)	Hoddles Creek Estate 1er Chardonnay 2020	Yarra Valley
97 (EL)	L.A.S. Vino Wildberry Springs Chardonnay 2020	Margaret River
97 (EL)	Driftwood Estate Single Site Chardonnay 2020	Margaret River
97 (EL)	McHenry Hohnen Vintners Brook Vineyard Chardonnay 2020	Margaret River
97 (EL)	Vasse Felix Heytesbury Chardonnay 2020	Margaret River
97 (JH)	Deep Woods Estate Reserve Chardonnay 2020	Margaret River
97 (PR)	Oakridge Wines Vineyard Series Henk Chardonnay 2020	Yarra Valley
97 (EL)	Nocturne Wines Tassell Park Vineyard Chardonnay 2020	Margaret River
97 (EL)	Cherubino Chardonnay 2020	Margaret River
97 (EL)	Xanadu Wines Stevens Road Chardonnay 2020	Margaret River

97 (EL)	Fraser Gallop Estate Palladian Chardonnay 2020	Margaret River
97 (JH)	Credaro Family Estate 1000 Crowns Chardonnay 2020	Margaret River
97 (EL)	Moss Wood Chardonnay 2020	Margaret River
97 (JH)	Mount Mary Chardonnay 2020	Yarra Valley
97 (EL)	McHenry Hohnen Vintners Hazel's Vineyard Chardonnay 2020	Margaret River
97 (EL)	Xanadu Wines Reserve Chardonnay 2020	Margaret River
97 (JH)	Mandoon Estate Reserve Chardonnay 2020	Margaret River
97 (PR)	Giant Steps Sexton Vineyard Chardonnay 2021	Yarra Valley
97 (PR)	Medhurst Estate Vineyard Chardonnay 2021	Yarra Valley
97 (PR)	Seville Estate Reserve Chardonnay 2021	Yarra Valley
97 (PR)	Gundog Estate D'Aloisio's Vineyard Chardonnay 2021	Yarra Valley

Semillon

It's a foregone conclusion that the Hunter again corners the category of dry semillon, but to do so with standouts from no fewer than nine vintages is grand testimony to its global uniqueness. Our Semillon of the Year was a convincing winner for the panel.

Semillon of the Year: Brokenwood Sunshine Vineyard Semillon 2014, Hunter Valley

Rating & Taster	Wine	Region
97 (NG)	RidgeView Wines Impressions Semillon 2010	Hunter Valley
97 (NG)	Leogate Estate Wines Museum Release Reserve Semillon 2011	Hunter Valley
97 (NG)	Tyrrell's Wines Vat 1 Semillon 2017	Hunter Valley
97 (NG)	Tyrrell's Wines Single Vineyard Belford Semillon 2017	Hunter Valley
97 (NG)	Briar Ridge Vineyard Dairy Hill Single Vineyard Semillon 2021	Hunter Valley
96 (NG)	Pepper Tree Wines Single Vineyard Alluvius Semillon 2011	Hunter Valley
96 (NG)	Pooles Rock Single Vineyard Semillon 2011	Hunter Valley
96 (NG)	Mount Pleasant Lovedale Semillon 2014	Hunter Valley
96 (NG)	Thomas Wines Braemore Cellar Reserve Semillon 2016	Hunter Valley
96 (NG)	Brokenwood Oakey Creek Vineyard Semillon 2016	Hunter Valley
96 (NG)	Tyrrell's Wines Single Vineyard HVD Semillon 2017	Hunter Valley
96 (NG)	Brokenwood Oakey Creek Vineyard Semillon 2017	Hunter Valley
96 (NG)	Brokenwood Oakey Creek Vineyard Semillon 2019	Hunter Valley
96 (NG)	Pepper Tree Wines Single Vineyard Alluvius Semillon 2021	Hunter Valley
96 (NG)	Audrey Wilkinson Marsh Vineyard Semillon 2021	Hunter Valley
96 (JH)	De Iuliis Single Vineyard Semillon 2021	Hunter Valley
96 (JH)	Thomas Wines Braemore Individual Vineyard Semillon 2021	Hunter Valley
96 (NG)	Drayton's Family Wines Susanne Semillon 2021	Hunter Valley
95 (NG)	Leogate Estate Brokenback Vineyard Semillon 2011	Hunter Valley
95 (NG)	Carillion Wines Aged Release Tallavera Grove Semillon 2014	Hunter Valley
95 (NG)	Peter Drayton Wines TJD Reserve Semillon 2014	Hunter Valley
95 (NG)	Keith Tulloch Wine Museum Release Semillon 2015	Hunter Valley
95 (NG)	De Iuliis Aged Release Semillon 2016	Hunter Valley

95 (NG)	Vinden Wines Aged Release Reserve Semillon 2016	Hunter Valley
95 (EL)	Alkoomi Wandoo 2016	Frankland River
95 (NG)	Tyrrell's Wines Single Vineyard Stevens Semillon 2017	Hunter Valley
95 (NG)	Leogate Estate Brokenback Vineyard Semillon 2017	Hunter Valley
95 (NG)	Leogate Estate Creek Bed Reserve Semillon 2017	Hunter Valley
95 (NG)	Two Rivers Museum Release Stone's Throw Semillon 2018	Hunter Valley
95 (DB)	David Franz Long Gully Road Ancient Vine Semillon 2020	Barossa Valley
95 (JH)	Meerea Park XYZ Semillon 2021	Hunter Valley
95 (EL)	Moss Wood Semillon 2021	Margaret River
95 (JH)	Tyrrell's Wines Johnno's Semillon 2021	Hunter Valley
95 (NG)	Audrey Wilkinson The Ridge Reserve Semillon 2021	Hunter Valley
95 (NG)	Margan Wines White Label Fordwich Hill Semillon 2021	Hunter Valley
95 (NG)	Sweetwater Wines Single Estate Semillon 2021	Hunter Valley
95 (NG)	De Iuliis The Garden Vineyard Semillon 2021	Hunter Valley
95 (NG)	Keith Tulloch Wine Latara Vineyard Semillon 2021	Hunter Valley
95 (NG)	Whispering Brook Semillon 2021	Hunter Valley
95 (NG)	Brokenwood Tallawanta Vineyard Semillon 2021	Hunter Valley
95 (NG)	Gundog Estate The Chase Semillon 2021	Hunter Valley

Sauvignon Blanc

It seems the dominant region in our sauvignon blanc shortlist oscillates between Margaret River and the Adelaide Hills according to which was blessed with the finest vintage. The Adelaide Hills takes the honours from Margaret River this year (just!), thanks exclusively to the stunning 2021 season. Notable, too, that while back vintages dominated the line-up last year, this year's great season put forward almost two-thirds of the list. Wrattonbully is not to be underestimated, and last year's winner of Terre à Terre Crayeres again stepped forward and went head-to-head with Margaret River's Flowstone. There was but one vote between them on first count, and the same result on revoting, with Flowstone ahead on both counts.

Sauvignon Blanc of the Year: Flowstone Wines Queen of the Earth Sauvignon Blanc 2020, Margaret River

Rating & Taster	Wine	Region
97 (EL)	Terre à Terre Crayeres Vineyard Sauvignon Blanc 2021	Wrattonbully
96 (JH)	Bannockburn Vineyards Sauvignon Blanc 2018	Geelong
96 (JH)	Domaine Naturaliste Sauvage Sauvignon Blanc 2020	Margaret River
96 (JP)	Shaw + Smith Sauvignon Blanc 2021	Adelaide Hills
95 (TS)	Domaine A Lady A Sauvignon Blanc 2018	Tasmania
95 (EL)	Flowstone Wines Sauvignon Blanc 2020	Margaret River
95 (JH)	Moss Wood Ribbon Vale Elsa 2020	Margaret River
95 (PR)	Oakridge Wines Vineyard Series Willowlake Sauvignon 2020	Yarra Valley
95 (PR)	Gembrook Hill Sauvignon Blanc 2020	Yarra Valley
95 (JP)	Vintage Longbottom H Sauvignon Blanc 2021	Adelaide Hills
95 (JH)	Deep Woods Estate Sauvignon Blanc 2021	Margaret River
95 (EL)	Fermoy Estate Coldfire Fumé Blanc 2021	Margaret River
95 (JP)	Deviation Road Sauvignon Blanc 2021	Adelaide Hills

95 (JF)	Hanging Rock Winery Jim Jim Sauvignon Blanc 2021	Macedon Ranges
95 (EL)	Terre à Terre Down to Earth Sauvignon Blanc 2021	Wrattonbully
95 (JF)	Port Phillip Estate Sauvignon 2021	Mornington Peninsula
95 (JP)	Riposte The Foil Sauvignon Blanc 2021	Adelaide Hills
95 (JP)	Geoff Weaver Single Vineyard Sauvignon Blanc 2021	Adelaide Hills
95 (JP)	Longview Vineyard Whippet Sauvignon Blanc 2021	Adelaide Hills
95 (EL)	Howard Park Sauvignon Blanc 2021	Western Australia
95 (JP)	Sidewood Estate Sauvignon Blanc 2021	Adelaide Hills

Other Whites and Blends

The depth and breadth of the top end of other white varieties in Australia is exemplified in a final role call of no fewer than 12 different varieties and blends hailing from eight regions. Our final judging exemplified this diversity, with a Hunter Valley albariño, Yarra Valley marsanne, Mornington Peninsula savagnin and a Tasmanian pinot gris rising to the top. Indicative of the importance in this category of building texture and complexity in the winery, our winner enjoyed wild fermentation, skin contact, partial barrel fermentation and lees age.

Other White of the Year: Briar Ridge Vineyard Albariño 2021, Hunter Valley

Rating & Taster	Wine	Region
97 (JF)	Crittenden Estate Cri de Coeur Sous Voile Savagnin 2017	Mornington Peninsula
97 (DB)	Yalumba The Virgilius Viognier 2019	Eden Valley
97 (NG)	Brash Higgins R/SM Field Blend Riesling Semillon 2020	McLaren Vale
97 (NG)	Yangarra Estate Vineyard Roux Beaute Roussanne 2020	McLaren Vale
97 (NG)	Thistledown Our Fathers Just Like Heaven Roussanne 2021	McLaren Vale
96 (NG)	Lillypilly Estate Angela Muscat NV	Riverina
96 (EL)	Clairault Streicker Ironstone Block Chenin Blanc 2019	Margaret River
96 (NG)	Yangarra Estate Vineyard Ovitelli Blanc 2020	McLaren Vale
96 (EL)	Windows Estate Petit Lot Chenin Blanc 2020	Margaret River
96 (EL)	L.A.S. Vino CBDB Chenin Blanc Dynamic Blend 2020	Margaret River
96 (JH)	Hahndorf Hill Winery GRU Grüner Veltliner 2021	Adelaide Hills
96 (JP)	Weathercraft Wine Amphora Blanco 2021	Beechworth
96 (JP)	Chrismont Pinot Gris 2021	King Valley
96 (JH)	Primo Estate Pecorino 2021	Adelaide Hills

Rosé

Testimony to rosé's coming of age in Australia, our 22 standouts this year represent an incredible 19 different varieties and blends spanning 11 regions. It's this diversity that makes this category so refreshing and exhilarating. This was the theme of our judging, too, with five wines from five different regions and five different blends each awarded first place votes by one or more judges. Our winner confidently stepped forward with three first place votes.

Rosé of the Year: **Spinifex Luxe 2021, Barossa**

Rating & Taster	Wine	Region
97 (JH)	Giant Steps Rosé 2021	Yarra Valley
96 (JF)	Cobaw Ridge Il Pinko Rosé 2020	Macedon Ranges
96 (JH)	Bondar Wines Grenache Rosé 2021	McLaren Vale
96 (JF)	Bindi Wines Dhillon Col Mountain Vineyard Rosé 2021	Heathcote
95 (EL)	L.A.S. Vino Albino PNO Rosé 2020	Margaret River
95 (NG)	Samson Tall Mataro Cinsault Rosé 2021	McLaren Vale
95 (JP)	Sutton Grange Winery Fairbank Rosé 2021	Central Victoria
95 (JP)	La Prova Nebbiolo Rosato 2021	Adelaide Hills
95 (JH)	Head Wines Rosé 2021	Barossa
95 (JP)	Tahbilk Grenache Mourvèdre Rosé 2021	Nagambie Lakes
95 (JP)	Bellarine Estate First Blush Rosé 2021	Geelong
95 (EL)	Cherubino Willows Vineyard Rosé 2021	Margaret River
95 (JF)	Scorpo Wines Rosé 2021	Mornington Peninsula
95 (JP)	La Linea Tempranillo Rosé 2021	Adelaide Hills
95 (JH)	Victory Point Wines Rosé 2021	Margaret River
95 (JF)	Port Phillip Estate Salasso Rosé 2021	Mornington Peninsula
95 (PR)	Dominique Portet Single Vineyard Rosé 2021	Yarra Valley
95 (NG)	mazi wines Mataro Cinsault Grenache Rosé 2021	McLaren Vale
95 (JF)	Foxeys Hangout Rosé 2021	Mornington Peninsula
95 (JF)	Handpicked Wines Regional Selections Rosé 2021	Yarra Valley
95 (JH)	Medhurst Estate Vineyard Rosé 2021	Yarra Valley
95 (JF)	Yabby Lake Single Vineyard Pinot Noir Rosé 2021	Mornington Peninsula

Pinot Noir

More than 50 pinot noirs rating 96 or more points is a grand statement in itself. That these hail from just 10 regions is a reflection of the narrow specificity of this variety. Most profound of all, almost three-quarters come from just three regions (half of these from the Yarra Valley, the balance Tasmania, followed by the Mornington Peninsula). The final judging came down to a two-horse race, between Pooley Jack Denis Pooley and relative newcomer, Lowestoft La Maison. Lowestoft's win is a credit both to this historic vineyard in the Derwent Valley and to the new injection of life it has received from the Fogarty Group.

Pinot Noir of the Year: **Lowestoft La Maison Pinot Noir 2020, Tasmania**

Rating & Taster	Wine	Region
99 (JH)	Pooley Wines Jack Denis Pooley Pinot Noir 2020	Tasmania
98 (JH)	Ossa Wines Pinot Noir 2020	Tasmania
98 (PR)	Giant Steps Applejack Vineyard Pinot Noir 2021	Yarra Valley
97 (JP)	Savaterre Pinot Noir 2018	Beechworth
97 (JH)	Bannockburn Vineyards De La Terre 2019	Geelong
97 (JP)	Bannockburn Vineyards Serré 2019	Geelong
97 (JH)	Helen's Hill Estate The Smuggler Single Clone Pinot Noir 2019	Yarra Valley
97 (JH)	Pooley Wines Butcher's Hill Pinot Noir 2020	Tasmania

97 (PR)	Oakridge Wines Vineyard Series Willowlake Pinot Noir 2020	Yarra Valley
97 (JH)	Castle Rock Estate Pinot Noir 2020	Porongurup
97 (JH)	Pooley Wines Cooinda Vale Pinot Noir 2020	Tasmania
97 (PR)	Seville Estate Dr McMahon Pinot Noir 2020	Yarra Valley
97 (PR)	Coldstream Hills Reserve Pinot Noir 2020	Yarra Valley
97 (JH)	Chatto Isle Black Label Pinot Noir 2020	Tasmania
97 (JH)	Seppelt Drumborg Vineyard Pinot Noir 2020	Henty
97 (JF)	Bass Phillip Premium Old Vines Pinot Noir 2020	Gippsland
97 (JH)	Stargazer Wine Palisander Vineyard Pinot Noir 2020	Tasmania
97 (JH)	Montalto Single Vineyard Merricks Block Pinot Noir 2020	Mornington Peninsula
97 (JH)	Mount Mary Pinot Noir 2020	Yarra Valley
97 (PR)	Giant Steps Primavera Vineyard Pinot Noir 2021	Yarra Valley
97 (JF)	Stonier Wines W-WB Pinot Noir 2021	Mornington Peninsula
97 (PR)	Seville Estate Old Vine Reserve Pinot Noir 2021	Yarra Valley
97 (PR)	Serrat Yarra Valley Pinot Noir 2021	Yarra Valley
96 (EL)	Moss Wood Pinot Noir 2019	Margaret River
96 (JF)	Garagiste Terre de Feu Pinot Noir 2019	Mornington Peninsula
96 (JH)	Strelley Farm Estate Pinot Noir 2019	Tasmania
96 (EL)	Paul Nelson Wines Karriview Vineyard Pinot Noir 2019	Denmark
96 (TL)	Sidewood Estate Abel Pinot Noir 2019	Adelaide Hills
96 (PR)	Punch Lance's Vineyard Close Planted Pinot Noir 2019	Yarra Valley
96 (JH)	Montalto Single Vineyard Tuerong Pinot Noir 2020	Mornington Peninsula
96 (JH)	Montalto North One Pinot Noir 2020	Mornington Peninsula
96 (JH)	Hoddles Creek Estate DML Pinot Noir 2020	Yarra Valley
96 (JH)	Scotchmans Hill Bellarine Peninsula Pinot Noir 2020	Geelong
96 (JF)	Giant Steps Applejack Vineyard Pinot Noir 2020	Yarra Valley
96 (JH)	Chatto Intrigue Black Label Pinot Noir 2020	Tasmania
96 (PR)	Yarra Yering Carrodus Pinot Noir 2020	Yarra Valley
96 (JF)	Bindi Wines Block 5 Pinot Noir 2020	Macedon Ranges
96 (JF)	Bass Phillip Estate Pinot Noir 2020	Gippsland
96 (JH)	Montalto Single Vineyard Main Ridge Block Pinot Noir 2020	Mornington Peninsula
96 (JP)	Michael Hall Wines Pinot Noir Lenswood 2020	Piccadilly Valley
96 (JF)	Curly Flat Western Pinot Noir 2020	Macedon Ranges
96 (PR)	Oakridge Wines Vineyard Series Hazeldene Pinot Noir 2020	Yarra Valley
96 (PR)	Giant Steps Fatal Shore Pinot Noir 2021	Southern Tasmania
96 (PR)	Gundog Estate Syme on Yarra Vineyard Pinot Noir 2021	Yarra Valley
96 (PR)	Giant Steps Pinot Noir 2021	Yarra Valley
96 (PR)	Mayer Dr Mayer Pinot Noir 2021	Yarra Valley
96 (PR)	De Bortoli PHI Single Vineyard Pinot Noir 2021	Yarra Valley
96 (PR)	Giant Steps Sexton Vineyard Pinot Noir 2021	Yarra Valley
96 (JP)	Ashton Hills Vineyard Reserve Pinot Noir 2021	Piccadilly Valley
96 (PR)	Coombe Yarra Valley Tribute Series Lady Celia Pinot Noir 2021	Yarra Valley
96 (JF)	Stonier Wines KBS Vineyard Pinot Noir 2021	Mornington Peninsula
96 (JF)	Stonier Wines Reserve Pinot Noir 2021	Mornington Peninsula
96 (JF)	Stonier Wines Georgica Vineyard Pinot Noir 2021	Mornington Peninsula

Grenache and Grenache Blends

The old-vine grenache resources of McLaren Vale and the Barossa are a national treasure, and in usual form, McLaren Vale has put forward more than half of our list of heroes and the Barossa almost one-third. The rise of cooler regions like Frankland River and the Yarra Valley is a trend to watch closely, but the old guard has this territory secured (for now). Again this year, 90-year-old Blewitt Springs bush vines convincingly declared their mettle, winning first place votes from four of the tasting team and securing another win for McLaren Vale.

Grenache of the Year: Chalk Hill Alpha Crucis Old Vine Grenache 2020, McLaren Vale

Rating & Taster	Wine	Region
97 (JH)	Ministry of Clouds Kintsugi 2018	McLaren Vale
97 (NG)	Yangarra Estate Vineyard High Sands Grenache 2019	McLaren Vale
97 (NG)	Yangarra Estate Vineyard Ovitelli Grenache 2020	McLaren Vale
97 (NG)	Bekkers Grenache 2020	McLaren Vale
97 (EL)	bakkheia The Wonderful Miss Gerry Grenache 2020	Geographe
97 (NG)	Thistledown Sands of Time Grenache 2021	McLaren Vale
97 (PR)	Serrat Yarra Valley Grenache Noir 2021	Yarra Valley
97 (DB)	Brothers at War Peace Keeper Grenache 2021	Barossa Valley
96 (NG)	Varney Wines GSM 2019	McLaren Vale
96 (DB)	Torbreck Vintners Les Amis Grenache 2019	Barossa Valley
96 (JH)	Purple Hands Wines Grenache 2020	Barossa Valley
96 (DB)	Head Wines Ancestor Vine Springton 2020	Eden Valley
96 (NG)	Thistledown Sands of Time Grenache 2020	McLaren Vale
96 (JH)	Living Roots Grenache 2020	McLaren Vale
96 (DB)	Yalumba Vine Vale Grenache 2020	Barossa Valley
96 (NG)	Chapel Hill 1948 Vines Grenache 2020	McLaren Vale
96 (JH)	Ministry of Clouds Grenache 2020	McLaren Vale
96 (DB)	Spinifex Single Vineyard Moppa Grenache 2020	Barossa Valley
96 (JH)	Bondar Wines Junto GSM 2020	McLaren Vale
96 (NG)	Vanguardist Wines Grenache 2020	McLaren Vale
96 (EL)	Swinney Farvie Grenache 2020	Frankland River
96 (JH)	Patritti Wines Marion Vineyard Grenache Shiraz 2020	Adelaide
96 (NG)	Aphelion Wine Brini Single Vineyard Grenache 2021	McLaren Vale
96 (NG)	Aphelion Wine Rapture Grenache 2021	McLaren Vale
96 (JH)	Z Wine Roman Old Vine GSM 2021	Barossa Valley
96 (NG)	Bondar Wines Rayner Vineyard Grenache 2021	McLaren Vale
96 (NG)	Thistledown She's Electric Old Vine Grenache 2021	McLaren Vale
96 (DB)	Utopos Grenache 2021	Barossa Valley
96 (DB)	Sons of Eden Notus Grenache 2021	Barossa Valley
96 (JH)	Lake Breeze Wines Old Vine Grenache 2021	Langhorne Creek
96 (DB)	St Hugo Grenache Shiraz Mataro 2021	Barossa Valley

Shiraz

On sheer weight of top-scoring wines, shiraz again surpasses all others as Australia's leading variety. But for its prolific plantings across every region in the country, it is telling that our 40 highlights hail from just 16 regions. Of 13 hopefuls in our final Awards judging, the top six places contrasted the might of the Barossa, McLaren Vale and Eden Valley with the restraint of the cool reaches of Canberra, Beechworth and Perth Hills, testimony to the vast diversity of this chameleon variety. It's exciting to see Perth Hills ascend among the greats to top this coveted list.

Shiraz of the Year: Battles Wine Granitis Shiraz 2020, Perth Hills

Rating & Taster	Wine	Region
99 (DB)	Henschke Hill of Grace 2017	Eden Valley
98 (TS)	Penfolds G5 NV	South Australia
98 (DB)	Torbreck Vintners The Laird 2017	Barossa Valley
98 (JH)	O'Leary Walker Wines The Sleeper Reserve Shiraz 2018	Barossa Valley
98 (JH)	Scotchmans Hill Bellarine Peninsula Shiraz 2019	Geelong
98 (PR)	Serrat Yarra Valley Shiraz Viognier 2021	Yarra Valley
97 (NG)	Pepper Tree Wines Tallawanta Single Vineyard Shiraz 2011	Hunter Valley
97 (DB)	Chris Ringland Hoffmann Vineyard Shiraz 2013	Barossa Valley
97 (DB)	Sons of Eden Autumnus Shiraz 2016	Eden Valley
97 (TS)	Penfolds Grange Bin 95 2017	South Australia
97 (DB)	Henschke Hill of Roses 2017	Eden Valley
97 (DB)	Henschke Mount Edelstone 2017	Eden Valley
97 (JH)	St Hallett Old Block Shiraz 2017	Barossa
97 (JH)	Tyrrell's Wines Single Vineyard Stevens Shiraz 2018	Hunter Valley
97 (JH)	Wolf Blass Platinum Label Medlands Vineyard Shiraz 2018	Barossa Valley
97 (JP)	Tahbilk 1860 Vines Shiraz 2018	Nagambie Lakes
97 (TS)	Penfolds St Henri Shiraz 2018	South Australia
97 (EL)	Wynns Coonawarra Estate Michael Shiraz 2019	Coonawarra
97 (DB)	Greenock Creek Wines Fifteen Claims Shiraz 2019	Barossa Valley
97 (JH)	Hayes Family Wines Redman Vineyard Shiraz 2019	Coonawarra
97 (JH)	The Story Wines Syrah 2019	Grampians
97 (JH)	Paul Osicka Shiraz 2019	Heathcote
97 (JH)	Sons of Eden Zephyrus Shiraz 2019	Barossa
97 (NG)	Mount Pleasant Maurice O'Shea Shiraz 2019	Hunter Valley
97 (EL)	Katnook Prodigy Shiraz 2019	Coonawarra
97 (DB)	Maverick Wines Ahrens' Creek Ancestor Vine Shiraz 2019	Barossa Valley
97 (DB)	Head Wines Wilton Hill Barossa Ranges Shiraz 2019	Eden Valley
97 (EL)	Kilikanoon Wines Attunga 1865 Shiraz 2019	Clare Valley
97 (EL)	Jim Barry Wines The Armagh Shiraz 2019	Clare Valley
97 (JH)	Spinifex Single Vineyard Moppa Shiraz 2019	Barossa Valley
97 (JP)	Eldorado Road Perseverance Old Vine Shiraz 2019	Beechworth
97 (EL)	Frankland Estate Smith Cullam Syrah 2020	Frankland River
97 (EL)	Swinney Farvie Syrah 2020	Frankland River
97 (JH)	Lake Breeze Wines Section 54 Shiraz 2020	Langhorne Creek
97 (JH)	Windows Estate Petit Lot Basket Pressed Syrah 2018	Margaret River

97 (PR)	Yarra Yering Underhill 2020	Yarra Valley
97 (JH)	Bondar Wines Midnight Hour Shiraz 2020	McLaren Vale
97 (JH)	Bondar Wines Violet Hour Shiraz 2020	McLaren Vale
97 (PR)	Seville Estate Old Vine Reserve Shiraz 2020	Yarra Valley
97 (PR)	Mayer Syrah 2021	Yarra Valley

Cabernet Shiraz Blends

Cabernet shiraz blends are the pride and glory of South Australia and have defined its red winemaking history for some 140 years. The state still confidently dominates the top end of this category, and it is the warmer regions of McLaren Vale, the Barossa and Langhorne Creek that have excelled this year.

Cabernet Shiraz of the Year: Hickinbotham Clarendon Vineyard The Peake Cabernet Shiraz 2020, McLaren Vale

Rating & Taster	Wine	Region
98 (JH)	Lake Breeze Wines The Drake 2016	Langhorne Creek
98 (TS)	Penfolds Superblend 802.B Cabernet Shiraz 2018	South Australia
98 (TS)	Penfolds Superblend 802.A Cabernet Shiraz 2018	South Australia
97 (JH)	Bremerton Wines B.O.V. 2018	Langhorne Creek
97 (DB)	John Duval Wines Integro 2018	Barossa
97 (DB)	Maverick Wines The Maverick 2019	Barossa

Cabernet Sauvignon

The distinguished cabernet sauvignon and its blends rank second only to shiraz as Australia's top-performing variety this year. Flying solo, the dominance of Margaret River is complete, claiming more than half of the coveted positions in our best-of line-up. Second and third places rightly go to Coonawarra and Yarra Valley respectively, albeit both well behind Margaret River in sheer numbers. It was therefore an unexpected and refreshing outcome that the three contenders to come forward in our final judging would hail from Langhorne Creek, Pyrenees and the Yarra Valley. Even more surprising that the single Langhorne Creek listing in our top 28 should rise all the way to the top. No surprise at all for anyone who's avidly following the rise and rise of 2018 Winemaker of the Year Paul Hotker at Bleasdale Vineyards.

Cabernet Sauvignon of the Year: Bleasdale Vineyards The Iron Duke Cabernet Sauvignon 2020, Langhorne Creek

Rating & Taster	Wine	Region
98 (EL)	Woodlands Xavier Cabernet Sauvignon 2018	Margaret River
98 (PR)	Yarra Yering Carrodus Cabernet Sauvignon 2020	Yarra Valley
97 (JH)	Bloodwood Maurice 2016	Orange
97 (JH)	Mandoon Reserve Research Station Cabernet Sauvignon 2017	Margaret River
97 (DB)	Yalumba The Menzies Cabernet Sauvignon 2017	Coonawarra
97 (EL)	Parker Coonawarra Estate First Growth 2018	Coonawarra
97 (EL)	Voyager Estate MJW Cabernet Sauvignon 2018	Margaret River
97 (JH)	Thompson Estate The Specialist Cabernet Sauvignon 2018	Margaret River

97 (JH)	Domaine Naturaliste Morus Cabernet Sauvignon 2018	Margaret River
97 (EL)	Leeuwin Estate Art Series Cabernet Sauvignon 2018	Margaret River
97 (JH)	Domaine Naturaliste Rebus Cabernet Sauvignon 2018	Margaret River
97 (JP)	Blue Pyrenees Richardson Reserve Cabernet Sauvignon 2018	Pyrenees
97 (EL)	McHenry Hohnen Hazel's Vineyard Cabernet Sauvignon 2019	Margaret River
97 (EL)	Wynns Coonawarra Estate Davis Cabernet Sauvignon 2019	Coonawarra
97 (EL)	Wynns Coonawarra Estate John Riddoch Cabernet Sauvignon 2019	Coonawarra
97 (TS)	Penfolds Bin 707 Cabernet Sauvignon 2019	South Australia
97 (EL)	Stella Bella Wines Luminosa Cabernet Sauvignon 2019	Margaret River
97 (EL)	Xanadu Wines Reserve Cabernet Sauvignon 2019	Margaret River
97 (JH)	Deep Woods Estate Reserve Cabernet Sauvignon 2019	Margaret River
97 (JH)	Houghton Jack Mann Cabernet Sauvignon 2019	Frankland River
97 (EL)	Xanadu Wines Stevens Road Cabernet Sauvignon 2019	Margaret River
97 (EL)	Moss Wood Cabernet Sauvignon 2019	Margaret River
97 (PR)	Medhurst Reserve Cabernet 2019	Yarra Valley
97 (PR)	Oakridge Wines 864 Oakridge Vineyard Cabernet Sauvignon 2019	Yarra Valley
97 (EL)	Nocturne Wines Sheoak Vineyard Cabernet Sauvignon 2020	Margaret River
97 (EL)	Penley Estate Helios Cabernet Sauvignon 2020	Coonawarra
97 (EL)	Deep Woods Estate G5 Cabernet Sauvignon 2020	Margaret River

Cabernet and Family

Cabernet and family embraces cabernet-dominant blends as well as other bordeaux varieties and their blends. Again this year, Margaret River is all over this class, putting forward almost as many highlights as every other region put together. In our Awards Judging, Cullen Diana Madeline and Mount Mary Quintet sprinted into a strong lead, with very little between them. Mount Mary took the prize on a count of first place votes.

Cabernet and Family of the Year: Mount Mary Quintet 2020, Yarra Valley

Rating & Taster	Wine	Region
99 (EL)	Vasse Felix Tom Cullity Cabernet Sauvignon Malbec 2018	Margaret River
98 (JH)	Cullen Wines Diana Madeline 2020	Margaret River
97 (EL)	McHenry Hohnen Vintners Rolling Stone 2018	Margaret River
97 (JH)	Lake Breeze Arthur's Reserve Cabernet Sauvignon Malbec 2019	Langhorne Creek
97 (EL)	Grosset Gaia 2019	Clare Valley
97 (PR)	Yarra Yering Dry Red No. 1 2020	Yarra Valley
97 (PR)	Yeringberg Yeringberg 2020	Yarra Valley
96 (NG)	Patina Jezza 2003	Orange
96 (JH)	The Islander Estate Vineyards The Independence Malbec 2016	Kangaroo Island
96 (EL)	Woodlands Margaret 2018	Margaret River

96 (EL)	Pierro Cabernet Sauvignon Merlot L.T.Cf. 2018	Margaret River
96 (JH)	Stefano Lubiana Chicane Malbec 2018	Tasmania
96 (EL)	Pierro Reserve Cabernet Sauvignon Merlot 2018	Margaret River
96 (EL)	Frankland Estate Olmo's Reward 2019	Margaret River
96 (JH)	Houghton C.W. Ferguson Cabernet Malbec 2019	Frankland River
96 (EL)	Aravina Estate Wildwood Ridge Reserve Stella BDX 2019	Margaret River
96 (JP)	Tahbilk BDX Blend Old Block Vines 2019	Nagambie Lakes
96 (EL)	Wills Domain Paladin Hill Matrix 2020	Margaret River
96 (EL)	Deep Woods Estate Single Vineyard Cabernet Malbec 2020	Margaret River
96 (JH)	Bleasdale Vineyards Generations Malbec 2020	Langhorne Creek

Other Reds and Blends

No other class spreads its wings as far or as wide as other reds, and our top 20 comprises a smorgasbord of no fewer than 17 different varieties and blends from 13 regions. Trends? Cool-climate nebbiolo. Cool-climate regions in general. But just to prove that well-established varieties from traditional regions still have clout in this hipster category, our final taste-off saw Swinney Mourvèdre Syrah Grenache up against Koomilya Cabernet Touriga, with this magnificent site in McLaren Vale proving its superiority.

Other Red of the Year: Koomilya Cabernet Touriga 2018, McLaren Vale

Rating & Taster	Wine	Region
97 (PR)	De Bortoli PHI Gamay Noir 2021	Yarra Valley
96 (JH)	Carillion Wines Stonefields Arbitrage Cabernet Merlot Shiraz 2013	Wrattonbully
96 (JP)	Pizzini Coronamento Nebbiolo 2016	King Valley
96 (JP)	Dal Zotto Wines L'Immigrante Nebbiolo 2016	King Valley
96 (JP)	Campbells The Barkly Durif 2017	Rutherglen
96 (JH)	Giaconda Nebbiolo 2017	Beechworth
96 (JH)	Hewitson Old Garden Vineyard Mourvèdre 2018	Barossa Valley
96 (JP)	Eldorado Road Onyx Durif 2019	North East Victoria
96 (PR)	Denton Nebbiolo 2019	Yarra Valley
96 (JF)	Cobaw Ridge Lagrein 2019	Macedon Ranges
96 (EL)	Cherubino Riversdale Vineyard Shiraz Mataro 2020	Frankland River
96 (NG)	Brash Higgins NDV Amphora Project Nero d'Avola 2020	McLaren Vale
96 (EL)	Swinney Mourvèdre Syrah Grenache 2020	Frankland River
96 (PR)	Yarra Yering Dry Red No. 2 2020	Yarra Valley
96 (NG)	SC Pannell Aglianico 2020	McLaren Vale
96 (PR)	Yarra Yering Dry Red No. 3 2020	Yarra Valley
96 (PR)	Serrat Fourre-Tout 2021	Yarra Valley
96 (JF)	Nick O'Leary Wines Heywood Tempranillo 2021	Canberra District
96 (JP)	Best's Wines Old Vine Pinot Meunier 2021	Great Western
96 (EL)	Nikola Estate Gallery Range: The Surrealist 2021	Geographe Swan Valley

Sweet

Great sweet wines are sadly scarce in Australia, so much so that this category suffered a brief hiatus last year. We're proud to reinstate it this year, with six highlights that exemplify a wide diversity of styles, from late-harvest riesling, to dried trebbiano, even flor maturation. Sweetness can play a vital role in white wines, especially in cool, acid-driven vintages like 2021. Riesling rightfully dominates this class and takes top honours in Brown Brothers' luscious and decadent Noble Riesling.

Sweet Wine of the Year: Brown Brothers Patricia Noble Riesling 2019, Victoria

Rating & Taster	Wine	Region
96 (TS)	Pressing Matters R139 Riesling 2021	Tasmania
95 (NG)	Kangarilla Road The Veil 2018	McLaren Vale
95 (JP)	Pizzini Per gli Angeli 2012	King Valley
95 (TS)	Craigow Dessert Riesling 2021	Tasmania
95 (DB)	Heggies Vineyard Botrytis Riesling 2021	Eden Valley

Fortified

Again this year, Rutherglen muscat and muscadelle (Topaque) rightfully dominate our best-of line-up, declaring an extraordinary age, status and distinction that rank them as truly unique in the world. But when it comes to one fortified to rule them all and in the darkness bind them, Seppeltsfield 100 Year Old conquered All Saints Estate Museum Muscat in our final show-down. It has no contender anywhere on earth.

Fortified of the Year: Seppeltsfield 100 Year Old Para Vintage Tawny 1922, Barossa Valley

Rating & Taster	Wine	Region
100 (JP)	All Saints Estate Museum Muscat NV	Rutherglen
100 (JP)	All Saints Estate Museum Muscadelle NV	Rutherglen
99 (JP)	Campbells Merchant Prince Rare Muscat NV	Rutherglen
98 (JP)	Chambers Rosewood Rare Muscadelle NV	Rutherglen
98 (JP)	Morris Old Premium Rare Topaque NV	Rutherglen

Best wineries by region

This is the full roll call of 5-star wineries of the year arranged by region. This encompasses a three-tier classification (fully explained on page 13). The winery names printed in red denote the best of the best with a long track record of excellence, typically upholding a 5-star rating for ten years. Five red stars are awarded to wineries who have typically upheld 5-star ratings for at least four years. Wineries with 5 black stars have achieved excellence this year (and sometimes longer). With 393 wineries qualifying this year, this heroic list is your quick reference guide to the finest estates in the country.

ADELAIDE HLLS

Ashton Hills Vineyard ★★★★★
Charlotte Dalton Wines ★★★★★
Coates Wines ★★★★★
CRFT Wines ★★★★★
Deviation Road ★★★★★
Geoff Weaver ★★★★★
Hahndorf Hill Winery ★★★★★
Karrawatta ★★★★★
La Linea ★★★★★
La Prova ★★★★★
Living Roots ★★★★★
Longview Vineyard ★★★★★
Murdoch Hill ★★★★★
Petaluma ★★★★★
Pike & Joyce ★★★★★
Riposte ★★★★★
Shaw + Smith ★★★★★
Sidewood Estate ★★★★★
The Lane Vineyard ★★★★★
Wicks Estate Wines ★★★★★

ADELAIDE

Heirloom Vineyards ★★★★★

ALPINE VALLEYS

Billy Button Wines ★★★★★
Pipan Steel ★★★★★

BALLARAT

Tomboy Hill ★★★★★

BAROSSA VALLEY

Arila Gardens ★★★★★
Brothers at War ★★★★★
Chris Ringland ★★★★★
Dorrien Estate ★★★★★
Dutschke Wines ★★★★★
Elderton ★★★★★
Eperosa ★★★★★
Glaetzer Wines ★★★★★
Grant Burge ★★★★★
Greenock Creek Wines ★★★★★
Groom ★★★★★
Hayes Family Wines ★★★★★
Head Wines ★★★★★
Hentley Farm Wines ★★★★★
John Duval Wines ★★★★★
Langmeil Winery ★★★★★
Laughing Jack ★★★★★
Liebich Wein ★★★★★
Massena Vineyards ★★★★★
Maverick Wines ★★★★★
Orlando ★★★★★
Penfolds ★★★★★
Peter Lehmann ★★★★★
Purple Hands Wines ★★★★★
Schubert Estate ★★★★★
Schwarz Wine Company ★★★★★
Seppeltsfield ★★★★★
Sons of Eden ★★★★★
Soul Growers ★★★★★
Spinifex ★★★★★

St Hallett ★★★★★
St Hugo ★★★★★
Teusner ★★★★★
Thorn-Clarke Wines ★★★★★
Torbreck Vintners ★★★★★
Turkey Flat ★★★★★
Two Hands Wines ★★★★★
Utopos ★★★★★
Vanguardist Wines ★★★★★
Wolf Blass ★★★★★
Z Wine ★★★★★

BEECHWORTH

A.Rodda Wines ★★★★★
Eldorado Road ★★★★★
Fighting Gully Road ★★★★★
Giaconda ★★★★★
Savaterre ★★★★★
Serengale Vineyard ★★★★★
Vignerons Schmölzer & Brown ★★★★★

BENDIGO

Sutton Grange Winery ★★★★★

CANBERRA DISTRICT

Clonakilla ★★★★★
Collector Wines ★★★★★
Helm ★★★★★
Lark Hill ★★★★★
Lerida Estate ★★★★★
Mount Majura Vineyard ★★★★★
Nick O'Leary Wines ★★★★★
Ravensworth ★★★★★

CENTRAL RANGES

Gilbert Family Wines ★★★★★
Mount Terrible ★★★★★

CLARE VALLEY

Gaelic Cemetery Vineyard ★★★★★
Grosset ★★★★★
Jim Barry Wines ★★★★★
Kilikanoon Wines ★★★★★
Knappstein ★★★★★
Mount Horrocks ★★★★★
Naked Run Wines ★★★★★
O'Leary Walker Wines ★★★★★
Pikes ★★★★★

Rieslingfreak ★★★★★
Taylors ★★★★★

COONAWARRA

Balnaves of Coonawarra ★★★★★
Bellwether ★★★★★
Katnook ★★★★★
Leconfield ★★★★★
Lindeman's (Coonawarra) ★★★★★
Majella ★★★★★
Parker Coonawarra Estate ★★★★★
Penley Estate ★★★★★
Wynns Coonawarra Estate ★★★★★

DENMARK

Harewood Estate ★★★★★

EDEN VALLEY

Flaxman Wines ★★★★★
Henschke ★★★★★
Pewsey Vale ★★★★★
Poonawatta ★★★★★
Yalumba ★★★★★

FRANKLAND RIVER

Alkoomi ★★★★★
Frankland Estate ★★★★★
Swinney ★★★★★

GEELONG

Austin's Wines ★★★★★
Banks Road ★★★★★
Bannockburn Vineyards ★★★★★
Clyde Park Vineyard ★★★★★
Lethbridge Wines ★★★★★
Mulline ★★★★★
Oakdene ★★★★★
Provenance Wines ★★★★★
Robin Brockett Wines ★★★★★
Scotchmans Hill ★★★★★

GEOGRAPHE

Aylesbury Estate ★★★★★
bakkheia ★★★★★
Capel Vale ★★★★★
Ironcloud Wines ★★★★★
Willow Bridge Estate ★★★★★

GIPPSLAND

Bass Phillip ★★★★★
Blue Gables ★★★★★
Narkoojee ★★★★★
Patrick Sullivan Wines ★★★★★

GLENROWAN

Baileys of Glenrowan ★★★★★

GRAMPIANS

Fallen Giants ★★★★★
Grampians Estate ★★★★★
Mount Langi Ghiran Vineyards ★★★★★
The Story Wines ★★★★★

GREAT SOUTHERN

Castelli Estate ★★★★★
Forest Hill Vineyard ★★★★★
Paul Nelson Wines ★★★★★
Singlefile Wines ★★★★★

GREAT WESTERN

ATR Wines ★★★★★
Best's Wines ★★★★★
Seppelt ★★★★★

HEATHCOTE

Chalmers ★★★★★
Heathcote Estate ★★★★★
Jasper Hill ★★★★★
Paul Osicka ★★★★★
Sanguine Estate ★★★★★
Syrahmi ★★★★★
Tellurian ★★★★★

HENTY

Crawford River Wines ★★★★★

HUNTER VALLEY

Audrey Wilkinson ★★★★★
Briar Ridge Vineyard ★★★★★
Brokenwood ★★★★★
Carillion Wines ★★★★★
De Iuliis ★★★★★
Glandore Estate ★★★★★
Gundog Estate ★★★★★
Keith Tulloch Wine ★★★★★
Lake's Folly ★★★★★

Leogate Estate Wines ★★★★★
Margan Wines ★★★★★
McLeish Estate Wines ★★★★★
Meerea Park ★★★★★
Mount Pleasant ★★★★★
Pepper Tree Wines ★★★★★
RidgeView Wines ★★★★★
Sweetwater Wines ★★★★★
Thomas Wines ★★★★★
Tyrrell's Wines ★★★★★
Vinden Wines ★★★★★

KANGAROO ISLAND

The Islander Estate Vineyards ★★★★★

KING VALLEY

Brown Brothers ★★★★★
Dal Zotto Wines ★★★★★
Pizzini ★★★★★

LANGHORNE CREEK

Ben Potts Wines ★★★★★
Bleasdale Vineyards ★★★★★
Bremerton Wines ★★★★★
Kimbolton Wines ★★★★★
Lake Breeze Wines ★★★★★

LENSWOOD

Mt Lofty Ranges Vineyard ★★★★★

MACEDON RANGES

Bindi Wines ★★★★★
Cobaw Ridge ★★★★★
Curly Flat ★★★★★
Granite Hills ★★★★★
Hanging Rock Winery ★★★★★
Passing Clouds ★★★★★

MARGARET RIVER

Amelia Park Wines ★★★★★
Aravina Estate ★★★★★
Brookland Valley ★★★★★
Brown Hill Estate ★★★★★
Cape Mentelle ★★★★★
Cape Naturaliste Vineyard ★★★★★
Clairault Streicker Wines ★★★★★
Credaro Family Estate ★★★★★
Cullen Wines ★★★★★

Deep Woods Estate ★★★★★
Devil's Lair ★★★★★
Domaine Naturaliste ★★★★★
Driftwood Estate ★★★★★
Evans & Tate ★★★★★
Evoi Wines ★★★★★
Fermoy Estate ★★★★★
Flametree ★★★★★
Flowstone Wines ★★★★★
Fraser Gallop Estate ★★★★★
Hay Shed Hill Wines ★★★★★
Howard Park ★★★★★
Jilyara ★★★★★
Juniper ★★★★★
L.A.S.Vino ★★★★★
Leeuwin Estate ★★★★★
McHenry Hohnen Vintners ★★★★★
Montague Estate ★★★★★
Moss Wood ★★★★★
Mr Barval Fine Wines ★★★★★
Nocturne Wines ★★★★★
Peccavi Wines ★★★★★
Pierro ★★★★★
Snake + Herring ★★★★★
Stella Bella Wines ★★★★★
Thompson Estate ★★★★★
tripe.Iscariot ★★★★★
Vasse Felix ★★★★★
Victory Point Wines ★★★★★
Voyager Estate ★★★★★
Wills Domain ★★★★★
Windows Estate ★★★★★
Wise Wine ★★★★★
Woodlands ★★★★★
Xanadu Wines ★★★★★

MCLAREN VALE

Angove Family Winemakers ★★★★★
Aphelion Wine ★★★★★
Bekkers ★★★★★
Bondar Wines ★★★★★
Brash Higgins ★★★★★
Chalk Hill ★★★★★
Chapel Hill ★★★★★
Clarendon Hills ★★★★★
Coriole ★★★★★
Dodgy Brothers ★★★★★
Dune Wine ★★★★★

Gemtree Wines ★★★★★
Grounded Cru ★★★★★
Hardys ★★★★★
Haselgrove Wines ★★★★★
Hickinbotham Clarendon Vineyard
    ★★★★★
Hugh Hamilton Wines ★★★★★
Inkwell ★★★★★
Kay Brothers ★★★★★
Koomilya ★★★★★
Ministry of Clouds ★★★★★
Mr Riggs Wine Company ★★★★★
Oliver's Taranga Vineyards ★★★★★
Paralian Wines ★★★★★
Primo Estate ★★★★★
SC Pannell ★★★★★
Serafino Wines ★★★★★
Smidge Wines ★★★★★
Varney Wines ★★★★★
Vigena Wines ★★★★★
Wirra Wirra Vineyards ★★★★★
Yangarra Estate Vineyard ★★★★★

MORNINGTON PENINSULA

Crittenden Estate ★★★★★
Dexter Wines ★★★★★
Eldridge Estate of Red Hill ★★★★★
Foxeys Hangout ★★★★★
Garagiste ★★★★★
Hurley Vineyard ★★★★★
Kerri Greens ★★★★★
Kooyong ★★★★★
Main Ridge Estate ★★★★★
Merricks Estate ★★★★★
Montalto ★★★★★
Moorooduc Estate ★★★★★
Paringa Estate ★★★★★
Port Phillip Estate ★★★★★
Principia ★★★★★
Pt. Leo Estate ★★★★★
Quealy Winemakers ★★★★★
Scorpo Wines ★★★★★
Stonier Wines ★★★★★
Trofeo Estate ★★★★★
Willow Creek Vineyard ★★★★★
Yabby Lake Vineyard ★★★★★

MOUNT BARKER

3 Drops ★★★★★
Plantagenet ★★★★★
Poacher's Ridge Vineyard ★★★★★
West Cape Howe Wines ★★★★★

MOUNT LOFTY RANGES

Michael Hall Wines ★★★★★

MUDGEE

Robert Oatley Vineyards ★★★★★

MURRAY DARLING

Zilzie Wines ★★★★★

NAGAMBIE LAKES

Mitchelton ★★★★★
Tahbilk ★★★★★
Tar & Roses ★★★★★

ORANGE

Bloodwood ★★★★★
Colmar Estate ★★★★★
Patina ★★★★★
Printhie Wines ★★★★★
Ross Hill Wines ★★★★★

PERTH HILLS

Millbrook Winery ★★★★★

PICCADILLY VALLEY

Tapanappa ★★★★★
Terre à Terre ★★★★★

PORONGURUP

Castle Rock Estate ★★★★★
Duke's Vineyard ★★★★★

PORT PHILLIP

Shadowfax Winery ★★★★★

PYRENEES

Blue Pyrenees Estate ★★★★★
Dalwhinnie ★★★★★
DogRock Winery ★★★★★
Mitchell Harris Wines ★★★★★
Taltarni ★★★★★

RIVERINA

Lillypilly Estate ★★★★★
McWilliam's ★★★★★

RUTHERGLEN

All Saints Estate ★★★★★
Buller Wines ★★★★★
Campbells ★★★★★
Chambers Rosewood ★★★★★
Jones Winery & Vineyard ★★★★★
Morris ★★★★★
Mount Ophir Estate ★★★★★
Pfeiffer Wines ★★★★★
Stanton & Killeen Wines ★★★★★

SOUTH AUSTRALIA

Byrne Vineyards ★★★★★
Dandelion Vineyards ★★★★★
Thistledown Wines ★★★★★

SOUTHERN FLEURIEU

Salomon Estate ★★★★★

SOUTHERN HIGHLANDS

Centennial Vineyards ★★★★★

SOUTH WEST AUSTRALIA

Kerrigan + Berry ★★★★★

STRATHBOGIE RANGES

Fowles Wines ★★★★★

SUNBURY

Craiglee ★★★★★

SWAN DISTRICT

Mandoon Estate ★★★★★

SWAN VALLEY

Corymbia ★★★★★
Faber Vineyard ★★★★★
Houghton ★★★★★
Nikola Estate ★★★★★
Sandalford ★★★★★
Sittella Wines ★★★★★

TASMANIA

Apogee ★★★★★
Bay of Fires ★★★★★
Bellebonne ★★★★★
Chatto ★★★★★
Craigow ★★★★★
Domaine A ★★★★★
Freycinet ★★★★★
House of Arras ★★★★★
Jansz Tasmania ★★★★★
Josef Chromy Wines ★★★★★
Lowestoft ★★★★★
Lost Farm Wines ★★★★★
Mewstone Wines ★★★★★
Pipers Brook Vineyard ★★★★★
Pooley Wines ★★★★★
Pressing Matters ★★★★★
Riversdale Estate ★★★★★
Stargazer Wine ★★★★★
Stefano Lubiana ★★★★★
Stoney Rise ★★★★★
Tamar Ridge ★★★★★
Tolpuddle Vineyard ★★★★★

UPPER GOULBURN

Yarradindi Wines ★★★★★

VARIOUS

Handpicked Wines ★★★★★

WESTERN AUSTRALIA

Battles Wine ★★★★★
Byron & Harold ★★★★★
Cherubino ★★★★★

YARRA VALLEY

Bicknell fc ★★★★★
Bird on a Wire Wines ★★★★★
Chandon Australia ★★★★★
Coldstream Hills ★★★★★
Coombe Yarra Valley ★★★★★
Dappled Wines ★★★★★
De Bortoli ★★★★★
Denton ★★★★★
Dominique Portet ★★★★★
Fetherston Vintners ★★★★★

Gembrook Hill ★★★★★
Giant Steps ★★★★★
Helen's Hill Estate ★★★★★
Hoddles Creek Estate ★★★★★
Mac Forbes ★★★★★
Mayer ★★★★★
Medhurst ★★★★★
Mount Mary ★★★★★
Oakridge Wines ★★★★★
Pimpernel Vineyards ★★★★★
Punch ★★★★★
Punt Road ★★★★★
Rochford Wines ★★★★★
Salo Wines ★★★★★
Serrat ★★★★★
Seville Estate ★★★★★
TarraWarra Estate ★★★★★
Yarra Yering ★★★★★
Yering Station ★★★★★
Yeringberg ★★★★★

Australian vintage charts

Each number represents a mark out of 10 for the quality of vintages in each region. As always, these ratings are volunteered by key winemakers in each region. Of course, every variety and vineyard is unique, so these numbers should thus be regarded as indicative rather than prescriptive, and bear relative reference only to that region (and not to cross-regional comparisons). We have introduced East Coast Tasmania for the first time this year – timely as the 2022 harvest exemplified just how much East Coast weather patterns can contrast Tasmania's north and south!

Red wine   White wine   Fortified

Region	2017	2018	2019	2020	2021
NSW					
Hunter Valley					
	8	9	8	–	7
	9	8	9	–	8
Mudgee					
	7	9	7	–	8
	6	8	7	–	7
Orange					
	7	9	8	–	7
	8	8	9	–	8
Canberra District					
	9	9	9	–	8
	8	8	9	–	9
Hilltops					
	9	9	9	–	8
	7	8	8	–	8
Southern Highlands					
	6	8	7	–	7
	6	8	8	–	7
Tumbarumba					
	9	9	8	–	7
	8	9	8	–	8
Riverina/Griffith					
	8	8	8	7	8
	8	8	8	7	8
Shoalhaven					
	7	8	7	–	7
	8	8	8	–	7
SA					
Barossa Valley					
	7	9	9	8	9
	8	7	7	7	8
Eden Valley					
	7	9	9	7	9
	10	9	9	8	10
Clare Valley					
	8	7	8	6	8
	9	7	9	8	9
Adelaide Hills					
	8	8	9	8	8
	9	7	8	9	8
McLaren Vale					
	9	8	8	8	9
	8	7	7	9	8
Southern Fleurieu					
	9	10	8	9	9
	8	8	7	9	9
Langhorne Creek					
	8	9	9	8	10
	7	7	7	7	6
Kangaroo Island					
	8	9	8	–	9
	9	9	9	–	9
Adelaide Plains					
	8	–	–	9	9
	8	–	–	9	9
Coonawarra					
	7	9	10	8	9
	9	8	8	8	8
Wrattonbully					
	9	9	10	10	10
	9	9	10	10	10
Padthaway					
	8	–	10	10	9
	8	–	9	9	10
Mount Benson & Robe					
	7	9	8	8	9
	9	9	9	9	9
Riverland					
	7	8	8	7	9
	8	8	8	8	9
VIC					
Yarra Valley					
	8	7	9	8	10
	8	7	8	8	10

Mornington Peninsula

2017	2018	2019	2020	2021
8	9	8	7	10
9	8	9	8	9

Geelong

2017	2018	2019	2020	2021
8	8	10	5	7
7	7	8	7	8

Macedon Ranges

2017	2018	2019	2020	2021
7	9	8	8	8
8	7	7	10	9

Sunbury

2017	2018	2019	2020	2021
–	–	7	7	8
–	–	8	8	8

Gippsland

2017	2018	2019	2020	2021
9	9	9	9	10
9	9	9	10	10

Bendigo

2017	2018	2019	2020	2021
8	8	9	9	10
7	8	8	8	9

Heathcote

2017	2018	2019	2020	2021
7	8	9	9	8
7	7	6	7	7

Grampians

2017	2018	2019	2020	2021
9	8	9	8	7
8	8	9	7	7

Pyrenees

2017	2018	2019	2020	2021
8	10	8	8	8
8	8	8	7	8

Henty

2017	2018	2019	2020	2021
5	10	9	6	9
8	10	8	8	9

Beechworth

2017	2018	2019	2020	2021
7	8	8	–	9
7	8	9	–	9

Nagambie Lakes

2017	2018	2019	2020	2021
8	9	9	8	8
7	7	7	7	8

Upper Goulburn

2017	2018	2019	2020	2021
7	9	8	8	9
9	8	9	8	9

Strathbogie Ranges

2017	2018	2019	2020	2021
7	9	8	8	–
7	9	8	7	–

King Valley

2017	2018	2019	2020	2021
8	9	9	–	7
10	9	7	–	9

Alpine Valleys

2017	2018	2019	2020	2021
9	9	7	–	9
10	10	9	–	10

Glenrowan

2017	2018	2019	2020	2021
7	8	9	–	8
7	7	7	–	7

Rutherglen

2017	2018	2019	2020	2021
6	9	8	–	8
6	9	8	–	7

Murray Darling

2017	2018	2019	2020	2021
7	7	8	8	–
8	8	8	8	–

WA

Margaret River

2017	2018	2019	2020	2021
8	9	8	9	8
8	9	9	9	8

Great Southern

2017	2018	2019	2020	2021
7	10	8	8	–
9	9	8	8	–

Manjimup

2017	2018	2019	2020	2021
7	8	7	8	7
8	9	8	8	8

Pemberton

2017	2018	2019	2020	2021
7	9	10	9	9
9	9	9	8	9

Geographe

2017	2018	2019	2020	2021
8	8	8	9	8
8	8	8	8	7

Perth Hills

2017	2018	2019	2020	2021
9	8	8	9	8
9	9	7	7	8

Swan Valley

2017	2018	2019	2020	2021
6	9	8	9	8
7	8	10	8	10

QLD

Granite Belt

2017	2018	2019	2020	2021
6	10	8	–	7
9	9	8	–	8

South Burnett

2017	2018	2019	2020	2021
8	9	9	7	8
8	9	8	9	10

TAS

Northern Tasmania

2017	2018	2019	2020	2021
8	8	9	7	9
7	8	9	6	9

Southern Tasmania

2017	2018	2019	2020	2021
9	8	9	8	8
9	9	8	9	9

East Coast Tasmania

2017	2018	2019	2020	2021
–	–	–	–	8
–	–	–	–	9

Australian vintage 2022: a snapshot

Australia lived up to its reputation as a land of climatic extremes across the entire season of harvest 2022. Some regions on the east coast experienced their wettest season on record, while others in the west were inflicted with their hottest and driest in history. Desperate prayers for rain following the debilitating droughts of 2019 and 2020 opened the floodgates to unleash the full deluge of La Niña in 2021, and 2022 delivered the same fate all the way from southeast Queensland to the east coast of Tasmania, and as far inland as the eastern rim of Central Victoria. This was a grower's vintage in which vigilant attention to disease management made the vintage for many sites. Between the extremes of the east and west coasts, South Australia and most of Victoria and Tasmania heaved a sigh of relief when the La Niña drenching forecast for summer never eventuated, making way for another stunning season of below-average temperatures. A long and glorious ripening period harked back to those wonderfully cool and classic seasons of the 1980s and 1990s. In almost every region, yields were heavily impacted by dismal weather, particularly around flowering and budburst. This perhaps proved to be a blessing in disguise for some wineries, after the bumper 2021 harvest and Chinese market crash left inventories at their fullest levels in 15 years. As always, publishing timelines dictated that this vintage snapshot had to be written during harvest, and in this particularly late season, some varieties are yet to be picked in some regions. No 2022 wines have yet been completed, so these accumulated opinions of the vintage are the initial impressions of key winemakers in each region.

New South Wales

The **Hunter Valley** is well adept at handling cool and wet vintages, and 2022 put these skills to the test, with more rainfall prior to the ripening period than even the sodden 2008 and 2012 vintages, though slightly less than both proved to be a blessing over harvest itself. Higher than expected crop levels meant that some whites didn't achieve ripeness, though unlike 2008 and 2012, lower-cropped reds were relatively unscathed. Good viticultural management proved to be the key to a season of great fruit flavour and impressive natural acid retention. 'As always, the Hunter defied the odds!' grinned a relieved Iain Riggs (Mistress Block Vineyard). **Mudgee** was less fortunate, inflicted not only with 900mm of rainfall, but with hail in some sites. Crop loads were consequently low, which proved fortuitous for early flavour development in this cool season. A late harvest yielded small volumes of high-quality wines with high natural acidity. **Orange** likewise suffered from low yields, and high disease pressure kept viticulturists on their toes, but for those who got it right there was minimal input required from winemakers. Drew Tuckwell (Printhie) described this cool season as 'old-school Orange weather, quite possibly the greatest vintage in my 15 years in Orange!' It was the wettest season on record in the **Canberra District** and very cool, with hailstorms in January reducing yields by 60% and in some vineyards destroying the crop altogether. Harvest conditions were perfectly dry and cool, and those who maintained diligent disease control reported above average quality in riesling, chardonnay and gewürztraminer, with reds still to be harvested at the time of writing. It was likewise a cool and wet vintage that rewarded attentive growers in **Hilltops**, with a harvest three weeks later than usual, presenting exceptional whites and reds of impressive depth of colour and flavour. The vintage was a disaster in the **Southern Highlands**, with cool temperatures and excessive rainfall precluding the ambition of ripeness. One of the most important vignerons in the region described it as the worst season he has ever seen, after harvesting just one tonne out of a possible 100. **Tumbarumba** suffered from disease pressure throughout the growing season, but the blessing of drier conditions and cool temperatures at the end of the ripening period produced excellent flavour development. The wettest November on record in the **Shoalhaven Coast** wiped out some vineyards' crops altogether. What survived faced 725mm of rain in March (more than double the March 2021 record of 320mm). Only the white varieties that ripened earlier stood a chance. These showed predictably high natural acid levels. A late harvest in the **Riverina** called for diligence in both disease mitigation and careful fruit selection. Cool, wet seasons such as this are ideal for botrytis, with good spread across all vineyards and a relatively early pick. **Murray Darling** basked in the cooler weather and benefited from some timely rain events, with a late harvest yielding promising quality.

South Australia

In recent decades, a cool ripening season is a blessing in the **Barossa Valley** and 2022 delivered below-average temperatures and bright, sunny days from February through to a harvest two weeks later than average. Good winter and spring rainfall set the vines up for reasonable yields, though they were impacted heavily and sporadically, first by inclement conditions during fruit set, then by spring frost, then by severe hailstorms in late October in central Barossa and late February in the north. Vineyards not impacted were optimistic about elegant and structured wines with depth and length of flavour. **Eden Valley** played out a similar story, where the October hailstorm was the worst in living memory. February–April made the vintage, with a lingering Indian summer of mild yet dry days of below-average temperatures and cold nights ripening low but intense crops of bountiful flavour and natural acidity. In Stephen Henschke's words, 'A later vintage suiting both riesling and shiraz perfectly.' After three lean years, the **Clare Valley** enjoyed a vintage of both quality and quantity. Moderate crops of all varieties basked in mild, sunny days with no rain or humidity. Jeffrey Grosset summed it up as 'a beautiful, idyllic vintage of uninterrupted, stunningly beautiful weather, more typical of the better vintages of the 1980s and 1990s!' In **McLaren Vale**, inconsistent set reduced yields by about 15% compared with the large crops of 2021. Mild conditions of warm days, cool nights, minimal rain and no heat spikes lingered from February through April, producing what Chester Osborn (d'Arenberg) described as 'the best reds I have seen in years.' Expect vibrant wines of supple tannins and bright natural acidity. The **Adelaide Hills** experienced a very cool season and the latest harvest since 2011. Variable conditions during flowering impacted yields, particularly in pinot noir and chardonnay, on a site-by-site basis. A cool, relatively dry autumn furnished long ripening, upholding very good natural acidity while building flavoursome whites and deep, rich reds. Harvest was likewise late in the **Adelaide Plains**, with warm days and cool nights making for great flavour development and retention of natural acidity. A cool season in **Coonawarra** saw good yields enjoy extended ripening through mild autumn days and cool nights. On the day of harvest of John Riddoch Cabernet Sauvignon, Sue Hodder informed me that she has never seen such a steady and varietally-separated vintage in her 30 years at Wynns. The region is excited about wines of varietal definition, with whites of great natural acidity and reds of deep colour, and cabernet sauvignon is the predictable standout. **Wrattonbully** experienced a classic vintage with a delayed start to the season and mild ripening conditions produced superb sauvignon blanc and reds of excellent flavour and acidity. **Padthaway** produced slightly below-average yields under mild and dry conditions with sauvignon blanc, chardonnay, shiraz and cabernet sauvignon the highlights. **Mount Benson** and **Robe** experienced an exceptional vintage that one prominent grower described as 'the best of cool-climate viticulture, with colour, flavour and natural acidity in spades!' In **Langhorne Creek**, cool conditions and below-average rainfall from February facilitated full flavour ripeness and good colour at moderate alcohol levels, producing excellent wines across the board, in particular malbec, cabernet, shiraz, grenache and petit verdot. Paul Hotker (Bleasdale) waxed, 'It is difficult for me to believe that this year could be better than 2021, but this vintage I think is the best I have experienced in Langhorne Creek.' Windy, cold and wet conditions led to poor set and reduced yields in the **Southern Fleurieu** and **Kangaroo Island**, while a much cooler than average summer resulted in delayed harvests and fantastic wines. In the **Riverland**, yields were knocked around by localised spring frosts and severe hail and wind storms. Mild and dry conditions in summer and autumn facilitated excellent flavour development.

Victoria

It was a story of quality over quantity in the **Yarra Valley**, with miserable flowering conditions and spring rains knocking yields to 30–40% below average. Cool and dry conditions led up to a late harvest of outstanding chardonnay of high natural acidity, set to go down among the top four vintages of the past decade. Aromatic whites were particularly fragrant, pinot noir perfumed, bright and charming, and cabernet sauvignon especially outstanding. On the **Mornington Peninsula**, a severe storm with 100km/h winds during flowering obliterated yields by up to 60% in some sites and 30% in others. Fears of accelerated ripening of such small crops were mitigated by mild and dry conditions in March, producing extraordinary quality. Whites showed excellent natural acidity and flavour, while pinots exhibited great colour, balance and poise. Yields in **Geelong** likewise suffered from extreme conditions during flowering, and also from early season frost and disease pressure through summer. The result was concentrated and powerful fruit of but half the usual crop levels. In **Gippsland**, one of the coolest and wettest seasons was reminiscent of vintages of the 20th century. Warm and dry conditions favoured the pinot noir and chardonnay harvest, with later harvest reds still in question at the time of writing. A wet spring in the **King Valley** made disease mitigation paramount, making way for idyllic, cool and dry ripening conditions through February and March. Similar conditions in the **Alpine Valleys** produced sensational quality from well-managed vineyards. **Beechworth** experienced one of its latest harvests ever, in spite of fairly early budburst. A cool season produced chardonnay that Rick Kinzbrunner (Giaconda) described as 'at the highest end of the scale'. A few bursts of heavy rainfall between veraison and picking kept viticulturists on their toes in **Upper Goulburn**, though a warm, extended ripening period ensured good fruit development before a compressed harvest. In **Henty**, yields were down around 25% as a result of variable flowering and set. A dry, warm autumn encouraged even progression of ripeness and good flavour development, particularly in riesling, chardonnay and pinot noir. In the **Macedon Ranges**, Michael Dhillon listed 2022 among the seven toughest seasons since his family planted their Bindi vineyard in 1988. Wet, humid and cool from start to finish, yields were a little down in pinot noir and more so in chardonnay. Flavour was achieved at low baumes in chardonnay of depth and intensity, and pinot noir of brightness, purity, depth and length. A wet year made vigilance in disease control vital in **Sunbury**. Cool conditions caused slow ripening even for modest yields of shiraz and cabernet. In **Nagambie Lakes**, summer was mild and largely dry, though picking had to work around some late summer and early autumn rain. A late burst of warmth through most of April got the later-ripening varieties across the line. Cold and windy conditions during flowering knocked yields around in **Bendigo**. Moderate conditions facilitated slow ripening, particularly favourable in warmer sites, though heavy and untimely rain events proved a challenge at both ends of harvest. A lovely, mild season in **Heathcote** produced very close to average yields of very high-quality fruit. In the **Grampians**, frost and hail impacted yields. The ripening season was largely mild and dry, with no significant heat waves, making significant late summer rain events the key challenge of the vintage. Similarly cool conditions in **Pyrenees** made for extended ripening, great varietal expression and exceptional natural acid balance across all varieties. In **Rutherglen**, rain affected yields during flowering and a large rain event toward the end of January preceded a harvest of relatively cool temperatures. In **Glenrowan**, these cool conditions from budburst until harvest enabled all red varieties to fully ripen, with durif the standout.

Western Australia

In **Margaret River**, wet and windy weather around fruit set impacted yields, particularly in chardonnay, though a bumper year for Marri tree blossoming kept the birds at bay. Summer arrived early and was fine and warm, with a few very hot periods, though classic Margaret River weather of crisp, clear days and cold nights prevailed through mid–late April to end the harvest. Whites ripened later and reds earlier than usual, the latter harvest punctuated by some minor rain events. Glenn Goodall (Xanadu) describes this year's vintage as 'a cracker' and Tim Lovett (Leeuwin) as 'an epic vintage!' **Great Southern** saw extremes in all directions this season. In the north, **Frankland River** experienced one of the driest growing seasons on record, with a hot January. A cooler February gave whites and especially reds a chance to gain flavour, with shiraz a particular highlight. In the south, **Albany** experienced a challenging season, with the latest budburst ever, amidst the driest and warmest summer on record, exceeding 44 degrees on one day in February. Pinot noir and chardonnay were the highlights, with later-ripening reds variable. By contrast, **Denmark** enjoyed a mild ripening season of healthy yields, leading to a late harvest of good flavours at low sugar levels. Bushfire smoke gave the region a scare in early February, but to date no smoke taint has been reported. **Mount Barker** likewise experienced a late harvest in spite of brutal summer heatwaves, moderated by significant rainfall and a dramatic drop in temperature in April. Whites, and riesling in particular, consequently upheld great acidity. Reds are too early to call at the time of writing, though are showing promising depth of colour at low sugar levels. In **Manjimup**, a hot summer saw white harvest kick off in late February with good flavour and acid levels. A dramatic drop in temperature and sunlight around mid March slowed the red harvest, furnishing promising pinot noir and elegantly styled cabernet sauvignon and shiraz of low alcohol. Vintage was unusually late in **Pemberton**, even after a hot and dry January and February. Whites showed flavour, texture and balance, and in his 52nd year of winemaking, Bill Pannell (Picardy) suggested the pinots looked 'as good or perhaps better than we have made to date.' In **Geographe**, a long and warm summer allowed all varieties to achieve ripeness in the absence of disease or bird pressure, though yields were low in chardonnay and shiraz. Summer was extremely hot and dry in the **Swan Valley**, so much so that vines shut down and suspended grape ripening in the mid-January heat. Smart growers harvested at lower-than-normal baumes rather than leaving fruit to hang out and dehydrate, though this proved to be a challenge with picking crews in short supply. Whites were full and bold, early harvested reds were lighter bodied than usual, and fortifieds were the highlight of the season. **Perth Hills** was subject to similarly severe extremes, with relentlessly scorching conditions from the start of December until late February, including 17 days over 40 degrees.

Tasmania

East Coast Tasmania experienced its coolest and wettest season in many years, with an unusually wet October, January and March proving particularly challenging for viticulturists. 'I almost felt like a Hunter Valley winemaker!' exclaimed Claudio Radenti (Freycinet). One of the coolest and wettest Octobers in history hampered flowering, reducing yields by 30–40%, while the cool ripening period produced wines of low alcohol, slightly higher acidity and greater elegance. By contrast, **Southern Tasmania** enjoyed dry conditions during harvest, with Hobart experiencing its driest February in 64 years. Record October rain impacted flowering, fruit set and consequently moderated yields, with wet conditions lingering on until January. Flavour ripeness came at lower baumes, and plenty of natural Tasmanian acidity was retained. **Northern Tasmania** likewise dodged the forecast harvest deluge, with only two major rain events between veraison and picking. A cool spring moderated yields, while a long spell of warm, sunny weather after Christmas furnished fantastic ripening conditions. 'One of the warmest and most consistent periods I've experienced in Tasmania,' reported Tom Wallace (Tamar Ridge). Early reports are of stunning wines of all styles.

Queensland

The multiple flood events of southeast Queensland and northern New South Wales of summer and autumn 2022 will long be remembered, and the **Granite Belt** was caught right in between. Very cool and wet conditions resulted in below-average fruit set and moderated yields, and ultimately in grapes harvested at lower than usual sugar levels. Incessant disease pressure required particular vigilance on the part of viticulturists. Symphony Hill picked shiraz in May for the first time, at just 13 baume. **South Burnett** likewise suffered moderated yields, with the white harvest beginning as early as late December, in an attempt to take advantage of a narrow window of dry weather. 'After that it was pretty tragic,' reported Sarah Boyce (Nuova Scuola), 'with tonnes of rain and floods.' Many didn't harvest reds at all.

Australian wineries
and wines

A. Rodda Wines

PO Box 589, Beechworth, Vic 3747 **Region** Beechworth
T 0400 350 135 www.aroddawines.com.au **Winemaker** Adrian Rodda **Est.** 2010
Dozens 800 **Vyds** 2ha

Adrian Rodda has been winemaking since '98. Originally working with David Bicknell at Oakridge, he was involved in the development of the superb Oakridge 864 Chardonnay, his final contribution to 864 coming in '09. At the start of '10 he and wife Christie, a doctor, moved to Beechworth and co-leased Smiths Vineyard with Mark Walpole of Fighting Gully Road. Smiths Vineyard, planted to chardonnay in '78, is a veritable jewel. He makes 2 additional single-vineyard chardonnays: Willowlake, with fruit sourced from the Yarra Valley vineyard of the same name; and Baxendale from a site in Whitlands at 560-620m elevation. (JH)

Ⴑ Ⴑ Ⴑ Ⴑ Ⴑ **Tête de Cuvée Cabernets 2019, Beechworth** 69/29/2% cabernet
sauvignon/merlot/petit verdot. Deeply coloured and concentrated in the glass and boasting a classic cabernet-led bouquet of cassis, mulberry, bramble, herbs, leaves, chocolate and vanilla. Stands up straight, firm in structure in nicely measured tannins with concentrated fruit which has yet to fully reveal. It's asking for more time in bottle. Give it some. Screw cap. 14% alc. RATING 95 DRINK 2022-2035 $85 JP
Triangle Block Smith's Vineyard Chardonnay 2019, Beechworth Sadly, due to bushfires, Adrian Rodda did not make a '20 chardonnay, but fortunately we get to enjoy this stunning '19 for some time. A wine of grace and quiet power. Aromas of citrus blossom, wild flowers, white nectarine and mandarin skin are lifted and perfumed. Beechworth citrusy acidity drives the wine against a background of crushed almond meal, cashew, vanilla and gentle spice. Finishes with a grapefruit pithiness that is brisk and clean. A long life awaits. Screw cap. 13% alc. RATING 95 DRINK 2022-2031 $85 JP
Aquila Audax Vineyard Tempranillo 2019, Beechworth It's a lively wine, with a full roster of cherries from red, black, dried, glacé, pickled ... take your choice, and finish with a sprinkle of spices. Screw cap. 14% alc. RATING 94 DRINK 2021-2029 $38 JH

Ⴑ Ⴑ Ⴑ Ⴑ Ⴑ **Willow Lake Vineyard Chardonnay 2020, Yarra Valley** RATING 92
DRINK 2021-2030 $45 JH
Cuvée de Chais Cabernets 2019, Beechworth RATING 92
DRINK 2022-2027 $38 JP

Abbey Vale

1071 Wildwood Road, Yallingup Hills, WA 6282 **Region** Margaret River
T (08) 9755 2121 www.abbeyvalewines.com.au **Open** Wed–Sun 10–5 **Winemaker** Ben Roodhouse, Julian Langworthy **Est.** 2016 **Dozens** 2000 **Vyds** 17ha

Situated in the north of the Margaret River region, the Abbey Vale vineyards were established in '85 by the McKay family. The highest quality fruit comes from the original plantings of chardonnay, shiraz and cabernet sauvignon. The picturesque cellar door offers a range of local produce and artisan cheeses to accompany the wines, and overlooks a large dam that provides visitors with one of the most sublime views in the region. (JH)

Ⴑ Ⴑ Ⴑ Ⴑ Ⴑ **Premium RSV Chenin Blanc 2021, Margaret River** I've seen this wine a number of times and the acidity is truly a standout highlight – pithy and titillating. The fruit around it is purely apricots, apples, honeydew melon, spring blossoms and brine. Generally all-round delicious. Highly recommended. Yum. Screw cap. 12.5% alc. RATING 94 DRINK 2021-2031 $25 EL ☉

Ⴑ Ⴑ Ⴑ Ⴑ Ⴑ **Premium RSV Semillon Sauvignon Blanc 2021, Margaret River**
RATING 93 DRINK 2022-2024 $25 EL ☉
Premium RSV Chardonnay 2021, Margaret River RATING 91
DRINK 2022-2026 $25 EL
Premium RSV Rosé 2021, Margaret River RATING 90 DRINK 2021-2023 $25 EL

Acres Wilde

1185 Glenrowan–Boweya Road, Taminick, Vic 3675 **Region** North East Victoria
T 0427 701 017 **www.**acreswilde.com.au **Winemaker** Chris Beach **Est.** 2011
Dozens 260

Chris Beach made his way into the wine industry after working in various farming pursuits; beef, dairy, orchards and tractor driving. Along the way there was also overseas travel and stints at snow resorts and in the building industry. However, the past 15 years have been spent in the vineyards and wineries of North East Victoria. He is currently working as a cellar hand at a Glenrowan winery, making his own wine under his own label in his down time. Grapes are bought in and all winemaking processes are performed by him. At first, his 'winery' was a brick garage, but he is now happy to report that he has moved up in the world and is utilising a large tin shed. Grapes are fermented in half-tonne picking bins, hand plunged, basket pressed, and he says he prefers to follow a minimal approach as much as possible. (JP)

Classic Muscat NV, Rutherglen Fantastic to see a Rutherglen producer interested in pursuing this great Australian fortified tradition which firmly placed Rutherglen on the international wine map. It may not be the most complex Classic Muscat, but it certainly boasts strong luscious and delicious factors – very important! – in dried fruits, nougat, fig and fruitcake. Clean and fresh, spirit-wise. Excellent inaugural release. 500ml. Screw cap. 17.3% alc. RATING 89 DRINK 2022-2022 $15 JP ✪

Riesling 2019, King Valley A complex riesling revealing bottled-aged jasmine, honeysuckle, toast, lemon curd, apricot and kerosene notes. At the top of its game and drinking well now, thanks to bright, lemony acidity. Screw cap. 12.4% alc. RATING 88 DRINK 2022-2024 $20 JP

Ruby #1 NV, North East Victoria A blend of 3 vintages and regions – 2013 Glenrowan, 2014 King Valley, 2015 Rutherglen. Attractive floral aromatics mix with dark berries, anise, licorice and spice. Nicely matched spirit at play here, elevating the fruit. Amaro bitters on the finish. 500ml. Screw cap. 16.9% alc. RATING 88 DRINK 2022-2022 $15 JP ✪

After Hours Wine

455 North Jindong Road, Carbunup, WA 6285 **Region** Margaret River
T 0438 737 587 **www.**afterhourswine.com.au **Open** Fri–Mon 10–4 or by appt
Winemaker Phil Potter **Est.** 2006 **Dozens** 3000 **Vyds** 8.6ha

Warwick and Cherylyn Mathews acquired the long-established Hopelands Vineyard in '05, planted to cabernet sauvignon (2.6ha), shiraz (1.6ha), merlot, semillon, sauvignon blanc and chardonnay (1.1ha each). The first wine was made in '06, after which they decided to completely rework the vineyard. The vines were retrained, with a consequent reduction in yield. (JH)

P.J. Cabernet Sauvignon 2018, Margaret River Blood plum, raspberry, cloves and oak. The wine is plush and very ripe, making it perfect drinking in the short-medium term. Plenty of pleasure here. Screw cap. 14.5% alc. RATING 91 DRINK 2021-2031 $32 EL

Alkimi Wines

PO Box 661, Healesville, Vic 3777 **Region** Yarra Valley
T 0410 234 688 **www.**alkimiwines.com **Winemaker** Stuart Dudine **Est.** 2014
Dozens 700 **Vyds** 0.5ha

The name is taken from the phonetic spelling of alchemy, the medieval concept of transmuting base metals into gold and similar works of magic. It's appropriate for owner and winemaker Stuart Dudine, because there are unexplained gaps in his wine journey. He worked in Europe with the gifted winemaker Emmerich Knoll in Austria, and with Stéphane Ogier at Château Mont-Redon in France. His love of the Rhône Valley sprang from his time at Henschke, working with syrah, grenache and mourvèdre. Based in the Yarra Valley since '12, he has worked for Yarra Yering, Oakridge and Mac Forbes and currently makes the wines for

Kellybrook. His overall raison d'être is to find vineyard parcels that perform exceptionally well in their patch of soil, year in and year out, across the seasons. Exports to Singapore. (JH)

ŸŸŸŸŸ Chardonnay 2020, Yarra Valley A bright green gold. Complex aromas of white peach and nectarines, together with grilled cashews and just a touch of spice from the well-handled older oak. Rich and full flavoured, this is also nicely balanced, with the acidity flowing evenly and gently through the wine. Screw cap. 12.8% alc. RATING 91 DRINK 2021-2023 $40 PR

Marsanne 2020, Yarra Valley Medium gold with green tinges. Honeyed, with some apricot, quince and a little almond meal. There's some honeysuckle nuance on the palate, finishing with a refreshing, quinine-like crisp finish. Screw cap. 13.1% alc. RATING 90 DRINK 2022-2025 $35 PR

Syrah 2017, Yarra Valley A light–medium hue and still quite bright ruby red. Some reduction along with cranberries, raspberries and light spice. A touch light, it's nevertheless showing bright fruit, crunchy acidity and fine dusty tannins. Delicious in its own way. Screw cap. 13.4% alc. RATING 90 DRINK 2021-2023 $33 PR

ŸŸŸŸ Mistral Series Syrah Rosé 2021, Yarra Valley RATING 89 DRINK 2021-2023 $30 PR

Grenache 2020, Heathcote RATING 89 DRINK 2022-2025 $35 JP

Pinot Noir 2020, Yarra Valley RATING 88 DRINK 2021-2025 $40 PR

Alkina   ★★★★

41 Victor Road, Greenock, SA 5360 **Region** Barossa Valley
T (08) 8562 8246 **www.**alkinawine.com **Open** Fri–Mon 11–5 **Winemaker** Amelia Nolan, Alberto Antonini **Viticulturist** Johnny Schuster **Est.** 2015 **Dozens** 3500 **Vyds** 43ha

Alkina was born in 2015 when Alejandro Bulgheroni purchased his Greenock property with its 1950s-planted vineyard. The front 40ha of the farm has been NASAA certified organic and biodynamic since 2018. The organically farmed back block, formerly the Owens vineyard, was added in 2017. In '17, the addition of terroir expert, Pedro Parra, to the team led to the Polygon mapping project; a deep dive into what makes the unique terroir of the property tick; cellar techniques are tweaked to enhance soil-to-glass transparency. Think traditional western Barossa grape varieties with wild yeasts, some with a little skin contact, whole-bunch ferments, concrete eggs and fermenters, Italian clay amphorae, Georgian Qvevri and older large-format oak and you're on the right track. Exports to the UK, the US, Singapore and Hong Kong.

ŸŸŸŸŸ Kin Rosé 2021, Barossa Valley The palest of pinks in the glass with shades of blood orange, watermelon and white peach fruit with a splash of citrus, hints of soft spice, blossom and a whiff of amaro herbs and stone. Crisp and savoury with tangy acid drive and an awful lot of pourmeanotherglassness. Screw cap. 13.2% alc. RATING 93 DRINK 2022-2025 $35 DB

Kin Semillon 2021, Barossa Valley Whole-berry wild ferment in Georgian qvevri and stainless-steel tank, 6 months of skin contact. Straw in hue with notes of Meyer lemon, almond blossom, apples, souk-like spice, ginger and stone. Super-slinky texture, a light shading of rose petal and dried herbs, with a gorgeous stony savouriness and crystalline mineral clarity. Screw cap. 13.2% alc. RATING 93 DRINK 2022-2026 $35 DB

Kin Shiraz 2021, Barossa Valley Juicy, wild and vinous with pronounced bunchy tones. Pure plum and black fruits, exotic spice, amaro herbs, purple flowers and earth with grippy, sinewy tannin sway and a slurpy, wild-eyed feel on the finish. Screw cap. 13.9% alc. RATING 93 DRINK 2022-2027 $35 DB

Night Sky GSM 2020, Barossa Valley Musky-edged deep dark plum and blackberry with hints of dried cranberry, exotic spice, amaro herbs, licorice, violets and leather. A light wash of bunchy complexity on the palate, juicy dark berry fruits, flexing sandy tannins and bright minerally drive. Delicious! Screw cap. 13% alc. RATING 93 DRINK 2022-2032 $48 DB

Kin Grenache 2021, Barossa Valley Fragrant, airy grenache, with perfumed red cherry, raspberry and red plum notes cut through with exotic spice, rose petals, gingerbread and plenty of whole-bunchy (100%) Turkish delight and amaro tones. The palate is perfumed and exotic, the tannins are perhaps a little terse for some, but I dig them. I love the rosewater and red-fruit fan on the exit. Sinewy and exotic. Screw cap. 14.6% alc. RATING 92 DRINK 2022–2028 $35 DB

Red Semillon 2021, Barossa Valley Coppery straw in the glass showing notes of poached pear, apples, pressed flowers, stone, soft spice and preserved lemon. There is a loose-knit, oxidative feel to its palate shape with minerally acid drive and excellent clarity Lovely drinking. Screw cap. 12.2% alc. RATING 92 DRINK 2022–2028 $40 DB

Alkoomi

1411 Wingebellup Road, Frankland River, WA 6396 **Region** Frankland River
T (08) 9855 2229 **www**.alkoomiwines.com.au **Open** 7 days 10–4.30 Frankland River
Mon–Sat 11–5 Albany **Winemaker** Andrew Cherry **Viticulturist** Tim Penniment
Est. 1971 **Dozens** 80 000 **Vyds** 164ha
Established in 1971 by Merv and Judy Lange, Alkoomi has grown from 1ha to one of WA's largest family-owned and -operated wineries. Now owned by daughter Sandy Hallett and her husband Rod, Alkoomi is continuing the tradition of producing high-quality wines which showcase the Frankland River region. Alkoomi is actively reducing its environmental footprint; future plans will see the introduction of new varietals. A second cellar door is located in Albany. Exports to all major markets. (JH)

Alkoomi Collection Shiraz 2020, Frankland River Co-fermented with 'a bit' of viognier. Silky, floral, velvety, robust, dusty, ripe and spiced. All very good things here, and unbelievably wrapped up in $28 and smart packaging. The Alkoomi Collection range is a bit of a marvel. Blood plum, mulberry, blackberry and raspberry with lashings of salted licorice, ferrous and lavender. Another ripping wine here – bravo team Cherry. Screw cap. 14.5% alc. RATING 95 DRINK 2021–2031 $28 EL ✪

Melaleuca 2018, Frankland River The extremely complex bouquet of this riesling sends the nasal receptors scurrying in all directions: juice, pith, zest and spice; the palate rolling all these up into a profoundly satisfying bundle of lemon and lime flavours. Screw cap. 12.5% alc. RATING 95 DRINK 2021–2033 $35 JH ✪

Wandoo 2016, Frankland River At 5 years old, this is a revelation in terms of its freshness, liveliness and intensity. Check, check and check. On the nose: lemongrass, preserved lemons, honey, hay and beeswax. The palate is where this really has the opportunity to project: apples, salted citrus, walnuts, cheesecloth and white pepper. Texturally, it is expansive and cushioned. Brilliant. Years left in the tank. Screw cap. 11.5% alc. RATING 95 DRINK 2021–2031 $35 EL ✪ ♥

Alkoomi Collection Cabernet Sauvignon 2020, Frankland River RATING 93 DRINK 2021–2031 $28 EL

Grazing Collection Riesling 2021, Frankland River RATING 92 DRINK 2022–2029 $18 JH ✪

Alkoomi Collection Riesling 2021, Frankland River RATING 92 DRINK 2023–2033 $28 EL

Grazing Collection Shiraz 2020, Frankland River RATING 92 DRINK 2021–2028 $18 EL ✪

Grazing Collection Cabernet Merlot 2020, Frankland River RATING 91 DRINK 2021–2027 $18 EL ✪

Alkoomi Collection Chardonnay 2021, Frankland River RATING 90 DRINK 2021–2027 $28 EL

All Saints Estate

205 All Saints Road, Wahgunyah, Vic 3687 **Region** Rutherglen
T 1800 021 621 **www.**allsaintswine.com.au **Open** 7 days 10–5 & public hols 11–5
Winemaker Nick Brown **Est.** 1864 **Dozens** 22 000 **Vyds** 47.9ha
The winery rating reflects the fortified wines, including the unique releases of Museum Muscat and Muscadelle, each with an average age of more than 100 years (and table wines). The 1-hat Terrace Restaurant makes this a must-stop for any visitor to North East Victoria, as does the National Trust–listed property with its towering castle centrepiece. All Saints and St Leonards are owned and managed by fourth-generation Brown family members Eliza, Angela and Nick. Eliza is an energetic and highly intelligent leader, wise beyond her years, and highly regarded by the wine industry. Exports to the US, the Philippines, and Hong Kong. (JH)

99999 **Museum Muscadelle NV, Rutherglen** A once-in-a-lifetime treat, this fortified has an average age of 100+ years. Few makers can release a museum fortified, All Saints Estate does it with ease such is its library (solera) of old vintages laid down year after year. This is vinous history and it shows, in its deep, olive green hues and level of absolute intensity and concentration. But it also comes with a fineness and a freshness. Flavours are remarkably precise and not at all overly sweet, full of rancio with nuts, dried fruits, toffee, orange peel and so much more that saturates the palate. Remarkable. Miniatures also available for $160. Screw cap. 18% alc. RATING 100 $1200 JP

Museum Muscat NV, Rutherglen It's hard to divide your emotions from your analytical need to describe and separate the perfume (heaven) from the taste (super-concentrated) and the lasting impression that just goes and goes. The senses go into overdrive. The intense flavours of treacle, honey, fig, balsamic and roasted nuts are lifted by rose oil and aromatics. Above all, it's the gentle and oh, so careful blending of younger material and spirit that really reveals the quality of winemaking and the wine. Quite an amazing, once-in-a-lifetime experience. Miniatures also available at $160. Screw cap. 18% alc. RATING 100 $1200 JP ♥

Grand Muscat NV, Rutherglen The average age for the Grand Muscat classification is 25 years. All Saints Estate has a fineness of touch across all of its fortifieds, a real elegance which is here in spades. An intense tasting experience awaits, wrapped in bright neutral spirit, rich and layered in treacle, chocolate-covered coffee beans, fruitcake, fig and golden walnuts. Smooth, clean, delicious and moreish. 375ml. Vinolok. 18% alc. RATING 97 $75 JP ✪

Rare Muscat NV, Rutherglen The official Rare Muscat classification is for fortifieds with an average 30+ years. All Saints' Rare averages 45 years, testament to the astonishing breadth and depth of stocks in its possession. How those stocks are managed, how neutral spirit is used to brighten and freshen them is the secret to a great muscat. It's here in a luscious core of dried fruit, fruitcake, soused raisins, honey and treacle-drenched walnut. Then comes the clean, driving spirit elevating everything into sheer decadence. 375ml. Vinolok. 18% alc. RATING 97 $120 JP ✪

99999 **Pierre 2019, Rutherglen** 48/48/4% cabernet sauvignon/merlot/cabernet franc. A wine to honour the memory of Peter Brown, who loved a good bordeaux. The aroma, as always, is lifted and aromatic, thanks to merlot in large part, in violet, rose petal, musk and spicy black and red fruits. So smooth, so seamless on the palate and elegant. Excellent balance for one still so young, auguring well for a long life, which it will definitely enjoy. Screw cap. 13.9% alc. RATING 95 DRINK 2022-2031 $45 JP

Classic Muscat NV, Rutherglen Fabulous concentration here, as per the house style, while also establishing real elegance and spirit freshness. It's a fine balance to achieve and it's quite effortless in nougat, orange peel, raisin freshness with dark chocolate and creamy caramels. Long, unwavering finish. Vinolok. 18% alc. RATING 95 $45 JP

Grand Muscadelle NV, Rutherglen All Saints Estate prefers to use the variety muscadelle rather than the term Topaque to name this fortified, which boasts an average age of 25 years. The colour is walnut brown, the scent is one of innate, intoxicating beauty rich in raisin, prune, plum pudding, chocolate and malty toffee.

A fortified of some authority in its complete comprehensive complexity. 375ml. Vinolok. 18% alc. RATING 95 $75 JP

Grand Tawny NV, Rutherglen We need these aged beauties to remind ourselves of the absolute fabulous-ness of this fortified wine style. This is a great Aussie fortified by any measure, bringing complex aromas rich in nutty rancio, dried fruits, toffee and walnut with an enduring fresh vanillin thread. Unctuous, concentrated, melts in the mouth. Yum! 375ml. Vinolok. 18% alc. RATING 95 $75 JP

Rare Muscadelle NV, Rutherglen A fortified to celebrate on a number of levels: average age (minimum of 30 years), intensity, complexity and, above all, a world-class fortified from a master blender. The blender's art is on display here, combining a range of aged wines while maintaining a freshness that is not only inviting but calls for another sip – and another. Where to start? Caramel, raisin, fruitcake, malt biscuits, honeyed gingerbread, toffee, orange peel … you get the idea. Opulence in a glass. 375ml. Vinolok. 18% alc. RATING 95 $120 JP

Durif 2019, Rutherglen The winemaker understands durif better than most, seeking out its elegant, polished side. This is the result. Blueberry, plums, dark chocolate and lively spice inhabit the glass. The grape's noteworthy (aka formidable) tannins are putty in the maker's hands, tamed and put to good use as the elegant backdrop for a flavoursome wine aided by sweet spicy oak. Signature Rutherglen style. Screw cap. 14% alc. RATING 94 DRINK 2021-2031 $35 JP

Family Cellar Durif 2018, Rutherglen A serious adaptation of Rutherglen durif, one that embraces the grape's natural dominance of tannin and fruit power while making it more than approachable now. A tricky winemaking performance if ever there was one. Dark, dense in colour and mood, highlighting the grape's black fruits, plum pudding spices, pepper and earthy side, with a light savouriness. Generous but delivered with sapid, fine tannin elegance. A keeper. Screw cap. 14.2% alc. RATING 94 DRINK 2021-2032 $80 JP

Allegiance Wines

3446 Jingellic Road, Tumbarumba, NSW 2653 **Region** Various
T 0434 561 718 **www.**allegiancewines.com.au **Open** By appt **Winemaker** Contract
Est. 2009 **Dozens** 40 000 **Vyds** 8ha

When Tim Cox established Allegiance Wines in '09 he had the decided advantage of having worked in the Australian wine industry across many facets for almost 30 years. He worked on both the sales and marketing side, and also on the supplier side with Southcorp. He started Cox Wine Merchants to act as distributor for Moppity Vineyards, with whom he successfully partnered for over 5 years. Having started out as a virtual wine business, Allegiance has recently purchased its own vineyards and now has 8ha under vine in Tumbarumba, planted to 5.5ha pinot gris, 2ha chardonnay and 0.5ha shiraz. It also purchases fruit from the Barossa, Coonawarra, Margaret River, Hilltops and Tumbarumba. Exports to NZ. (JH)

The Artisan Reserve Shiraz 2020, Barossa Valley Aromas of dark and black summer-berry fruits are cut through with notes of licorice, dark chocolate, earth and oak spice. Bright and textural with lovely ripe fruit and fine willowy tannins, finishing elegant, balanced and long. Screw cap. 15% alc. RATING 92 DRINK 2021-2031 $60 DB

Single Vineyard Graciano 2020, McLaren Vale This drinks akin to a more mid-weighted, frisky red, with Mediterranean herb-crusted edges, gently angular and astringent. White pepper, clove, raspberry, lavender and thyme. The oak is far better integrated here than in the other reds in the tier. Screw cap. 14% alc. RATING 91 DRINK 2022-2027 $30 NG

Alumni Riesling 2021, Eden Valley Pale straw in the glass. It's fairly tightly bound on first sniff, but a bit of swishing reveals fruit notes of lime, lemon and crunchy green apple cut through with notes of marzipan, light blossom and crushed stone. Expansive and grapefruity on the palate, finishing with pleasing focus and a little squeak of phenolic grip, before fading off dry and appley. Screw cap. 11% alc. RATING 90 DRINK 2021-2028 $25 DB

Local Legend Mataro 2021, McLaren Vale Good drinking. The oak, a little less heavy handed than the higher tier. All hand picked and extracted with aplomb. Szechuan red pepper, clove, licorice root and darker-fruit aspersions, lifted by violet florals. The finish, spicy and edgy. The acidity, as with the range, a bit too tangy. But satisfying, by virtue of its savouriness and intelligent makeup of varieties. Screw cap. 14.5% alc. RATING 90 DRINK 2022-2027 $25 NG

Single Vineyard Grenache 2019, McLaren Vale Hand picked and clearly extracted with the sort of aplomb that glimpses the tensile, more red-fruited and herb-infused contemporary expressions that the region does so well. Bravo! In used French wood for 18 months. The green tannins that these barrels impart detract from the potential quality. The finish, menthol and a bit hard. Loads of promise. Screw cap. 14% alc. RATING 90 DRINK 2022-2028 $30 NG

💯💯💯💯 **Emily Jane Pinot Grigio 2021, Tumbarumba** RATING 88 DRINK 2021-2023 $25 JF
Fullylove Chardonnay 2021, Tumbarumba RATING 88 DRINK 2022-2024 $25 JF
Pinot Grigio 2021, Tumbarumba RATING 88 DRINK 2021-2023 $30 JF
The Artisan Mataro 2020, McLaren Vale RATING 88 DRINK 2022-2032 $40 NG
Single Vineyard Mataro 2019, McLaren Vale RATING 88 DRINK 2022-2027 $30 NG

Allinda ★★★☆

119 Lorimers Lane, Dixons Creek, Vic 3775 **Region** Yarra Valley
T 0432 346 540 **www**.allindawinery.com.au **Winemaker** Al Fencaros, Jeff Bashford
Est. 1991 **Dozens** 7000 **Vyds** 3.5ha
Winemaker Al Fencaros has a Bachelor of Wine Science from CSU and was formerly employed by De Bortoli in the Yarra Valley. Al's grandparents made wine in Hungary and Serbia, and Al's father continued to make wine after migrating to Australia in the early '60s. The vineyard is now over 30 years old, and is managed without the use of chemical fertilisers, herbicides or pesticides. The Allinda wines are produced onsite; all except the Shiraz from Heathcote are estate-grown. Limited retail distribution in Melbourne and Sydney. (JH)

💯💯💯💯💯 **Pinot Noir 2019, Yarra Valley** A very bright, youthful, crimson red and an equally youthful nose, redolent of bright red and black fruits along with a some whole-bunch-derived herbal notes. A little reduction. Juicy and fresh in the mouth, this is gently loose knit and while ready to drink now, there's enough stuffing and fine-grained tannins to ensure this will still be looking good 3–5 years from now. Screw cap. 13.5% alc. RATING 90 DRINK 2021-2026 $35 PR

Altus Rise ★★★★

10 North Street, Mount Lawley, WA 6050 (postal) **Region** Margaret River
T 0400 532 805 **www**.altusrise.com.au **Winemaker** Laura Bowler **Est.** 2019 **Vyds** 0ha
Altus Rise was founded by friends Chris Credaro, Kim O'Hara and Jan Skrapac. All have abundant experience of the wine industry. Chris is a highly experienced viticulturist and member of the Credaro family and its extensive vineyard holdings. Kim O'Hara has 20 years of wine sales and marketing experience, while Jan Skrapac has a wealth of financial and management expertise. (JH)

💯💯💯💯💯 **Ascension Shiraz 2020, Margaret River** Margaret River shiraz from the '20 vintage is, on the whole, effortless, concentrated and sweet. They're wonderful wines. Perhaps it's the best shiraz vintage for Margaret River yet. This wine displays all of that concentration and sweet fruit – its luscious poise and layers of berries are testament to the sunshine and easy ripening. Screw cap. 14.5% alc. RATING 94 DRINK 2021-2028 $35 EL

💯💯💯💯💯 **Ascension Cabernet Sauvignon 2020, Margaret River** RATING 92 DRINK 2022-2029 $35 EL

Amadio Wines

461 Payneham Road, Felixstow, SA 5070 **Region** Adelaide
T (08) 8365 5988 **www**.amadiowines.com **Open** Mon–Fri 10–5:30
Winemaker Danniel Amadio **Viticulturist** Danniel Amadio, Caj Amadio **Est.** 2004
Dozens 50 000 **Vyds** 126.5ha

Danniel Amadio says he has followed in the footsteps of his Italian grandfather, selling wine from his cellar (cantina) direct to the consumer. Amadio Wines has substantial vineyards, primarily in the Adelaide Hills and Barossa Valley. They also source contract-grown grapes from Clare Valley, McLaren Vale and Langhorne Creek, with a strong suite of Italian varieties. The Kangaroo Island Trading Company wines are produced with fifth-generation islanders Michael and Rosie Florance from their Cygnet River vineyard; there is a second cellar door in the main street of Kingscote on Kangaroo Island. Exports to Asia, the US, Canada and Sweden. (JH)

Trading Company Cabernet Sauvignon 2015, Kangaroo Island Cellar release. The wine was last tasted by Steven Creber in July '17, given 92 points and finishing with 'just a little patience is required.' He was totally correct; it has aged very impressively, opening up finely detailed blackcurrant varietal fruit, with a savoury backdrop to the medium-bodied palate. The length is excellent, as are the balance and line, taking you back to the colour, a vivid purple crimson. Cork. 14.5% alc. RATING 95 DRINK 2022-2030 $39 JH

Aglianico 2019, Adelaide Hills RATING 90 DRINK 2022-2029 $40 JP
Sebastien's Cabernet Sauvignon 2014, Adelaide Hills RATING 90 DRINK 2022-2028 $60 JP

Amelia Park Wines

3857 Caves Road, Wilyabrup, WA 6280 **Region** Margaret River
T (08) 9755 6747 **www**.ameliaparkwines.com.au **Open** 7 days 10–5 **Winemaker** Jeremy Gordon **Est.** 2009 **Dozens** 25 000 **Vyds** 9.6ha

Jeremy Gordon's winemaking career started with Evans & Tate, and Houghton thereafter, before moving to the eastern states to broaden his experience. He eventually returned to Margaret River, and after several years founded Amelia Park Wines with his wife Daniela Gordon and business partner Peter Walsh. Amelia Park initially relied on contract-grown grapes, but in '13 purchased the Moss Brothers site in Wilyabrup, allowing the construction of a new winery and cellar door. Exports to Singapore, Indonesia, Taiwan, South Korea, Myanmar, Philippines, Thailand, India and Vietnam. (JH)

Semillon Sauvignon Blanc 2021, Margaret River A 60/40% blend. Citrus, lemon blossom and cut-grass aromas set the scene for the complex palate, with both texture and structure achieved without the use of oak. Impressive at any price, let alone this. Screw cap. 12.5% alc. RATING 95 DRINK 2021-2025 $23 JH ♥
Shiraz 2020, Frankland River Vivid crimson purple. Vibrant black cherry, cracked pepper, multiple spice aromas and a tightly focused palate, with acidity driving its freshness. Oak and tannins are very much the junior partners. Screw cap. 14.5% alc. RATING 95 DRINK 2023-2035 $33 JH ♥
Bush Vine Tempranillo 2020, Frankland River When you see 'bush vine' and 'Frankland River', you must assume the fruit is from the Swinney vineyard, as this is. The 2020 vintage was excellent and the wines on the whole have been quite tannic on release – no bad thing, but a defining character of the vintage. In this case, the tannins are certainly present, but they are filigreed into the fruit in such a way that they are chewy and embedded. This is far more elegant than expected, with a layer of complexity that lies behind the wall of fruit and structure. Really, really smart. Screw cap. 14.5% alc. RATING 95 DRINK 2022-2032 $50 EL
Reserve Shiraz 2019, Frankland River The ferrous-ironstone character that underpins the muscular but succulent fruit is key to the region's success, adding an extra dimension of complexity to the shiraz grown here. So it goes, for this wine. Graphite tannins encase the mulberry, blackberry and roasted pomegranate fruit,

while the undertow of regionality carries the wine across the tongue. Screw cap.
14.5% alc. RATING 95 DRINK 2022-2032 $70 EL

Reserve Cabernet Sauvignon 2020, Margaret River The nose here is leafy
and concentrated: freshly turned earth, blackberry bramble, saltbush and licorice. In
the mouth the wine is structured and savoury, yet plump – the fruit is layered with
oodles of cassis, mulberry and hints of raspberry, but the main chords are tobacco
leaf, licorice root and clove. This wine will really blossom in 5 years; decant it in
the short term. Screw cap. 14.5% alc. RATING 94 DRINK 2022-2035 $70 EL

Cabernet Merlot 2020, Margaret River Such a gorgeous nose here: licorice,
bramble, cassis, cigar and freshly turned earth. In the mouth the wine performs
as promised. The tannins are firm but fine – they will melt into the fruit with
some time in a decanter. There's something old-school about this, in a really
great way. Perhaps classical is a better word. Screw cap. 14.5% alc. RATING 94
DRINK 2021-2031 $35 EL

Malbec 2020, Margaret River Fresh and bright: layers of garden herbs,
bubblegum, graphite, brine and red apples, on both note and palate. Gorgeous
really … an ethereal rendition of malbec from Margaret River, reinforcing the
regional DNA of power without weight. A fine smudge of tannins wipe across
the finish, which fade into memory like the brush of a stick of charcoal on card.
A beautiful thing. Screw cap. 14.5% alc. RATING 94 DRINK 2021-2031 $50 EL

Cabernet Merlot 2019, Margaret River Includes small amounts of malbec
and petit verdot. A perfumed array of red- and blackcurrant fruits opens
proceedings, followed by a supple and juicy palate in the Amelia Park style,
engendered by the prolonged post-fermentation maceration in tank. Screw cap.
14.5% alc. RATING 94 DRINK 2023-2033 $33 JH

ΨΨΨΨΨ **Chardonnay 2020, Margaret River** RATING 90 DRINK 2021-2026 $33 JH

Amherst Winery

285 Avoca Road, Amherst, Vic 3371 **Region** Pyrenees
T 0400 380 382 **www.**amherstwinery.com **Open** By appt **Winemaker** Luke Jones
Viticulturist Norman Jones **Est.** 1989 **Dozens** 1500 **Vyds** 2.5ha
In '89 Norman and Elizabeth Jones planted vines on a property with an extraordinarily rich
history, commemorated by the name Dunn's Paddock. Samuel Knowles was a convict who
arrived in Van Diemen's Land in 1838. He endured continuous punishment until he fled to
SA in 1846. He changed his name to Dunn and in 1851 married 18yo Mary Taaffe. They
walked to Amherst, pushing a wheelbarrow carrying their belongings. The original lease title
is in his name. In Jan 2013 Norman and Elizabeth's son Luke and his wife Rachel acquired
the Amherst Winery business; Luke has a wine marketing diploma and a diploma in wine
technology. (JH)

ΨΨΨΨΨ **North-South Shiraz 2019, Pyrenees** A well-built shiraz displaying typical
Pyrenees generosity in black fruits and spice with a spray of local bay leaf,
eucalyptus (just so you know where it hails from!). Smooth and supple across the
palate with an array of dark cherries, ripe plum, sweet chocolate, earth and spice.
Good to go now. Screw cap. 14% alc. RATING 90 DRINK 2022-2025 $28 JP

ΨΨΨΨ **Lachlan's Chardonnay 2020, Pyrenees** RATING 88 DRINK 2022-2024 $25 JP

Anderson

1619 Chiltern Road, Rutherglen, Vic 3685 **Region** Rutherglen
T (02) 6032 8111 **www.**andersonwinery.com.au **Open** Mon–Sat 10–4
Winemaker Howard and Christobelle Anderson **Est.** 1992 **Dozens** 2000 **Vyds** 8.8ha
Having notched up a winemaking career spanning over 55 years, including a stint at Seppelt
(Great Western), Howard Anderson and family started their own winery, initially with a
particular focus on sparkling wine but now extending across all table wine styles. Daughter
Christobelle graduated from the University of Adelaide in '03 with first class honours, and has
worked in Alsace, Champagne and Burgundy either side of joining her father full-time in '05.

The original estate plantings of shiraz, durif and petit verdot (6ha) have been expanded with tempranillo, saperavi, brown muscat, chenin blanc and viognier. (JH)

🍷🍷🍷🍷🍷 **Cellar Block Durif 2016, Rutherglen** A classic and slightly formidable Rutherglen durif that combines power with a full-on, sweet-hearted and aromatic varietal display. Leaves quite a lasting impression. Dense aromas of cassis, blackberry, bramble, berry, licorice, dark cacao and earth. A complex gathering of flavours awaits, inky and intense, led by prominent savoury tannins but there, in the centre, lies an aromatic oasis of sweet violets, anise and spice. A charming chameleon. Assured of a long, long life. Trophy, Rutherglen Wine Show '19. Screw cap. 14.9% alc. RATING 95 DRINK 2022-2036 $45 JP

🍷🍷🍷🍷🍷 **Storyteller Basket Press Durif 2016, Rutherglen** RATING 93 DRINK 2021-2032 $35 JP
Cellar Block Saperavi 2016, Rutherglen RATING 91 DRINK 2022-2030 $45 JP

Anderson & Marsh

6815 Great Alpine Road, Porepunkah, Vic 3740 **Region** Alpine Valleys
T 0419 984 982 **Open** By appt **Winemaker** Eleana Anderson, Jo Marsh **Est.** 2014
Dozens 60
A joint project between Alpine Valleys winemakers Eleana Anderson (of Mayford Wines) and Jo Marsh (of Billy Button). The first vintage of Catani Blanc de Blanc was made in '14 and was joined by Parell Albariño in '18 and Parell Tempranillo in '19 (Parell is Spanish for pair). Close friends and neighbours, they set out to produce the style of sparkling wines they love to drink – crisp and tight – from the town where they both live, Porepunkah. A local parcel of albariño became available in '18 which they were both very interested in, so they decided to make it together under their new label. Tempranillo was an obvious choice to partner with the albariño. (JH)

🍷🍷🍷🍷🍷 **Parell Albariño 2021, Alpine Valleys** With each release, these 2 talented winemakers work hard to unravel the Spanish grape's great mystery, not to mention suitability to our soils. They come mighty close in 2021, delivering a complex and aromatic wine of some beauty. Honeysuckle, lemon, pithy grapefruit, honeydew melon and a touch of preserved lemon savouriness join a fleshy, mealy texture and spiced palate. Utterly attention grabbing, not to mention, delicious. Screw cap. 13% alc. RATING 95 DRINK 2022-2025 $35 JP ❂

Anderson Hill

407 Croft Road, Lenswood, SA 5240 **Region** Lenswood
T 0407 070 295 **www.**andersonhill.com.au **Open** Wed–Sun 11–5 **Winemaker** Ben Anderson **Viticulturist** Ben Anderson **Est.** 1994 **Dozens** 4000 **Vyds** 9ha
Ben and Clare Anderson planted their vineyard in Lenswood, in the Adelaide Hills, in '94. A substantial part of the grape production is sold (Hardys and Penfolds have been top-end purchasers of the chardonnay), but enough is retained to produce their wines. The cellar door has panoramic views, making the venue popular for functions. Exports to Norway. (JH)

🍷🍷🍷🍷🍷 **Single Vineyard Reserve Pinot Noir 2020, Lenswood** The best, 'most expressive' barrels of the vintage were selected for this reserve pinot. Brooding comes to mind as a descriptor here, also wild and autumnal: you get the drift. An abundance of black cherries, forest floor, baking spices, dried herbs and tilled earth combine with a degree of unsuspecting intensity and concentration. Tightly wrapped in vanillin oak and fine tannins, it waits quietly in bottle. Built to last. Cork. 13.5% alc. RATING 95 DRINK 2022-2028 $80 JP
O Series Shiraz 2020, Adelaide Hills Bright, vibrant and fresh – and just look at that intense purple colour! Catches the eye and the senses, with a lifted fragrance of dark sweet red fruits, earth, oak spice and tapenade. Lively across the

palate, everything brought together by a fine mesh of tannins. The complete Hills
shiraz package. Screw cap. 14.7% alc. RATING 94 DRINK 2022–2030 $50 JP

ŸŸŸŸŸ O Series Pinot Noir 2020, Lenswood RATING 93 DRINK 2022–2028 $40 JP
Maggie's Perch Shiraz 2020, Adelaide Hills RATING 90 DRINK 2021–2024
$30 JP
Single Vineyard Reserve Shiraz 2020, Adelaide Hills RATING 90
DRINK 2022–2027 $95 JP

Andrew Peace Wines   ★★★★

Murray Valley Highway, Piangil, Vic 3597 **Region** Swan Hill
T (03) 5030 5291 **www.apwines.com Open** Mon–Fri 9–5, Sat 12–4
Winemaker Andrew Peace, David King **Est.** 1995 **Dozens** 180 000 **Vyds** 270ha
The Peace family has been a major Swan Hill grapegrower since '80, moving into winemaking
with the opening of a $3 million winery in '96. Varieties planted include chardonnay,
colombard, grenache, malbec, mataro, merlot, pinot gris, riesling, sangiovese, sauvignon blanc,
semillon, tempranillo and viognier. The planting of sagrantino is the largest of only a few such
plantings in Australia. Exports to all major markets. (JH)

ŸŸŸŸŸ Full Moon Durif 2020, Swan Hill Combines all the things we love about
durif – power and beauty, all within a medium-bodied frame. Deep, inky purple-
black cherry hues. Aromatic of blueberry, black cherry, dark chocolate and
smokey lapsang souchong tea. For all its abundant complex fruit, it remains finely
edged in sapid, fine tannins. Great value here. Screw cap. 13.5% alc. RATING 91
DRINK 2022–2027 $22 JP ✪
Australia Felix Premium Barrel Reserve Cabernet Shiraz 2019,
Wrattonbully Good concentration and drive here, courtesy of Wrattonbully fruit,
from mulberry and plum through to boysenberry and blackberry. Fruit quality
is aided by some restrained oak influence – 6–8 months in French oak – which
brings light spice and fine but firm tannins. This kind of tight structure will reward
cellaring. Screw cap. 14% alc. RATING 90 DRINK 2022–2029 $30 JP
Australia Felix Sagrantino 2019, Swan Hill The 2021 vintage experienced
some very high temperatures which helps explain the rather high-ish alcohol and
ripeness apparent in this wine. That said, sagrantino – a bold wine in general –
handles it well. Dark and dense garnet in the glass with cassis, black cherry, licorice,
earth and savoury leather aromas. Coated in sturdy tannins, it proceeds to deliver
full-bodied flavour intensity through to the finish, finishing with a flourish of
dryness. Light the barbecue, bring out the steaks and enjoy. Screw cap. 14.5% alc.
RATING 90 DRINK 2022–2032 $33 JP

ŸŸŸŸ Masterpeace Chardonnay 2021, Victoria RATING 89 DRINK 2022–2025
$15 JP ✪
Masterpeace Pinot Grigio 2021, Victoria RATING 89 DRINK 2022–2025
$15 JP ✪
Winemakers Choice Chardonnay 2021, Barossa RATING 89
DRINK 2022–2024 $23 JP
Masterpeace Rosé 2021, Victoria RATING 88 DRINK 2022–2024 $15 JP ✪
Masterpeace Shiraz 2021, Victoria RATING 88 DRINK 2022–2025 $15 JP ✪
Full Moon Boothy's Choice Chardonnay 2021, Victoria RATING 88
DRINK 2022–2025 $22 JP
Chenin Blanc 2020, Swan Hill RATING 88 DRINK 2022–2024 $23 JP

Angas & Bremer   ★★★★

8 The Parade West, Kent Town, SA 5067 **Region** Langhorne Creek
T (08) 8537 0600 **www.angasandbremer.com.au Winemaker** Peter Pollard **Est.** 2017
Dozens 7500
Langhorne Creek's climate is profoundly driven by the Southern Ocean and its average
altitude of 20m, lower than that of any other region on the mainland. You might expect ample

rainfall, but its growing season total of just 161mm (barely beaten by that of Kangaroo Island's 156mm) makes irrigation essential. The net outcome is a climate that proffers generous yields with a lower-than-average need for sprays, reducing soil compaction by tractors and the overall cost per tonne of grapes. Thus most growers have organic accreditation, Angas & Bremer included. It has a registered compost area for vintage waste, and sprays winery waste water on a native eucalyptus woodlot. Exports to most major markets. (JH)

ŸŸŸŸŸ **Touriga Nacional 2020, Langhorne Creek** By some distance the best of these releases, the bright crimson-purple colour setting the pace. It's only just into medium-bodied territory, the flavours of red and blue fruits cosseted by gentle spicy, earthy tannins. Ready now, but will hold for a few years. Value plus. Screw cap. 14% alc. RATING 91 DRINK 2021-2025 $20 JH ○
The Creek 2019, Langhorne Creek A 44/28/21/5/2% blend of grenache, touriga, malbec, graciano and shiraz; a master blend, though it's the first 3 parts that run the show. The wine will please almost all who know the price, and others who don't even know that. It's got some jujube/glacé cherry fruit flavours, and isn't necessarily dry, but it will stand up for all those home-delivered pizzas and such like. Screw cap. 14.5% alc. RATING 90 DRINK 2022-2023 $20 JH ○

Angas Plains Estate

317 Angas Plains Road, Langhorne Creek, SA 5255 **Region** Langhorne Creek
T (08) 8537 3159 **www**.angasplainswines.com.au **Open** Mon–Fri 11–5, Sat 12–4
Winemaker Peter Douglas, Phillip Cross **Viticulturist** Phillip Cross **Est.** 1994
Dozens 3000 **Vyds** 15.2ha
In '94 Phillip and Judy Cross began the Angas Plains Estate plantings, first with cabernet sauvignon, followed by shiraz, and then a small block of chardonnay predominantly used as a sparkling base. The location on ancient Angas River flood plains, together with cooling evening breezes from the local Lake Alexandrina, proved ideally suited to the red varieties. Skilled contract winemaking has resulted in some excellent wines from the estate-grown shiraz and cabernet sauvignon. Exports to Singapore and Hong Kong. (JH)

ŸŸŸŸŸ **PJs Cabernet Sauvignon 2019, Langhorne Creek** Bright crimson-purple hue. Here the oak is more obvious than that of its shiraz sibling, but the depth of the blackcurrant and black-olive fruit handles the competition with panache. Value plus. Screw cap. 14.5% alc. RATING 94 DRINK 2022-2027 $25 JH ○

ŸŸŸŸŸ **PJs Shiraz 2019, Langhorne Creek** RATING 90 DRINK 2022-2032 $25 JH

Angove Family Winemakers

Bookmark Avenue, Renmark, SA 5341 **Region** McLaren Vale
T (08) 8580 3100 **www**.angove.com.au **Open** Mon–Fri 10–5, Sat 10–4, Sun & public hols 10–3 **Winemaker** Tony Ingle, Paul Kernich, Ben Horley, Amelia Anspach
Viticulturist Nick Bakkum **Est.** 1886 **Dozens** 500 **Vyds** 300ha
Founded in 1886, Angove Family Winemakers is one of Australia's most successful wine businesses – a fifth-generation family company with a tradition of excellence and an eye for the future. Angove wines includes The Medhyk, Warboys Vineyard, Family Crest, Organics, and Long Row brands. The McLaren Vale cellar door is nestled in the family's certified organic and biodynamic Warboys Vineyard on Chalk Hill Road, the Renmark cellar door in Bookmark Avenue. In early '19 Angove acquired the celebrated 12.7ha Angel Gully Vineyard in Clarendon from Primo Estate, and renamed the vineyard Angels Rise. Angove is committed to remaining privately owned and believes remaining in family hands enables the company to be master of its own destiny. Exports to all major markets. (JH)

ŸŸŸŸŸ **Warboys Vineyard Grenache 2019, McLaren Vale** The perfumed, flowery bouquet of red berries and spices heralds a vibrant, glistening palate, the texture and structure are tannin-free zones (yet neither fined nor filtered). Screw cap. 14.5% alc. RATING 98 DRINK 2022-2029 $75 JH ○

🍷🍷🍷🍷🍷 **Family Crest Shiraz 2019, McLaren Vale** You'd never guess Angove is a recent arrival in McLaren Vale. This is a near-perfect illustration of varietal character with eiderdown tannins underlaying a Magimix blend of dark chocolate and blood plum fruit. Generosity is its calling card, and it won't die any time soon. A multipurpose player with food. Screw cap. 14.5% alc. RATING 95 DRINK 2023–2039 $25 JH ✪

Single Vineyard Blewitt Springs Shiraz 2019, McLaren Vale It is an enthralling experience to taste across these iterations of shiraz from this estate. This cooler '19 vintage, among the best. Not the densest, perhaps, but ethereal and pliant. Planted in the '40s. Suave, juicy and fresh. Blue fruits and suede. Reminds me of a '90s rock song. A whiff of promise, a skittle of youthful vibrancy, some sandy tannic authority and a spurt of maritime salinity, suggesting a longish future. Good vibes. Screw cap. 14.5% alc. RATING 95 DRINK 2021–2029 $44 NG

The Medhyk Shiraz 2018, McLaren Vale This is good, defined by a splay of ripe grape tannins melding effortlessly with a band of oak, gentle bottle age and the reductive stamp of the house, imparting tension and, in this instance, not too much of the iodine note. Old-vine punch. Mottled blue and black berries, Seville orange, some spice and soaring Blewitt Springs violets. Plush, but taut. Measured, but generous. Very good warm-climate shiraz, as far as warm-climate shiraz goes. Screw cap. 14% alc. RATING 95 DRINK 2021–2033 $65 NG

Angus the Bull   ★★★☆

2/14 Sydney Road, Manly, NSW 2095 (postal) **Region** Central Victoria
T (02) 8966 9020 **www**.angusthebull.com **Winemaker** Hamish MacGowan **Est.** 2002
Dozens 20 000
Hamish MacGowan took the virtual winery idea to its ultimate conclusion, with a single wine (Angus the Bull Cabernet Sauvignon) designed to be drunk with a perfectly cooked steak. Each year parcels of grapes are selected from a number of sites across Central Victoria, the flexibility of this multiregional blending approach designed to minimise vintage variation. Recently the range has been extended to include the Wee Angus Merlot and a limited Single Vineyard Heathcote wine called Black Angus. Exports to NZ, the UK, Ireland, Sweden, Denmark, Canada, Japan, South Korea, Hong Kong, Singapore, Thailand, Vietnam, Philippines, Indonesia, Fiji, Papua New Guinea and Vanuatu. (JH)

🍷🍷🍷🍷🍷 **Cabernet Sauvignon 2019, Central Victoria** With 8/2% merlot/petit verdot. Brings both energy and elegance to a glass of cabernet that is quite captivating. Superb scent of cassis, plum, some roasting herbs, spice and violet florals. That 2% of petite verdot brings added tannic backbone to the wine. Ripe and fresh on the palate, it holds its flavour before finishing long and firm. Screw cap. 14% alc. RATING 90 DRINK 2021–2025 $23 JP

🍷🍷🍷🍷 **Wee Angus Merlot 2020, Central Victoria** RATING 89 DRINK 2021–2027 $19 JP ✪
Cabernet Sauvignon 2020, Central Victoria RATING 89 DRINK 2022–2027 $23 JP

Anvers   ★★★★

633 Razorback Road, Kangarilla, SA 5157 **Region** Adelaide Hills
T (08) 7079 8691 **www**.anvers.com.au **Open** Sun 11–5 **Winemaker** Kym Milne MW
Est. 1998 **Dozens** 10 000 **Vyds** 24.5ha
Myriam and Wayne Keoghan's principal vineyard is in the Adelaide Hills at Kangarilla. The vineyard is 17ha of sauvignon blanc, chardonnay, shiraz, barbera and gamay. Winemaker Kym Milne has experience gained across many of the wine-producing countries in both northern and southern hemispheres. Exports to the UK and other major markets. (JH)

🍷🍷🍷🍷🍷 **Shiraz Rosé 2021, Adelaide Hills** So juicy! So pretty, too, in shades of subtle, dusty pink. Shiraz brings a wealth of red fruits, lifted florals and sweet, enticing fragrance. Textural and smooth with a dusty cherry earthiness. The effect on the palate is one of restraint, allowing the juiciness and acid crunch to prevail. Very smart. Screw cap. 13% alc. RATING 91 DRINK 2021-2024 $25 JP

ŶŶŶŶ **Razorback Road Sauvignon Blanc 2021, Adelaide Hills** RATING 89 DRINK 2021-2024 $25 JP

Aphelion Wine ★★★★★

18 St Andrews Terrace, Willunga, SA 5172 **Region** McLaren Vale
T 0404 390 840 **www**.aphelionwine.com.au **Open** By appt **Winemaker** Rob Mack
Est. 2014 **Dozens** 2500

Aphelion Wine is akin to a miniature painting done with single-hair paintbrushes. When you consider the credentials of winemaker Rob Mack and co-founder Louise Rhodes Mack, great oaks come to mind. Rob has accumulated 2 degrees in accounting and management in '07, and wine science from CSU in '16. He scaled the heights of direct marketing as wine buyer and planner for Laithwaites Wine People, and spent the next 18 months as production manager for Direct Wines in McLaren Vale. He has worked with 5 wineries, 4 in McLaren Vale. Rob was voted Young Gun of Wine '18 and Aphelion won Best Small Producer at the McLaren Vale Wine Show in '19. Exports to the UK, the US, Canada and Hong Kong. (JH)

ŶŶŶŶŶ **Brini Single Vineyard Grenache 2021, McLaren Vale** An exploration of Blewitt Springs, likely the finest subregion for the finest grape in the country – grenache. A single site in the northeast corner on sandy loams. Very pinot-like. Sandalwood, bergamot, camphor, sapid sour cherry, lapsang and Asian spiced-plum notes drive across a patina of herb-flecked tannins, all skeletal and fibrous. This is very fine. The plumpest of these single-site expressions, yet the most complete. Screw cap. 14.5% alc. RATING 96 DRINK 2022-2028 $70 NG ✪

Rapture Grenache 2021, McLaren Vale Sourced from 2 lauded sites in Blewittt Springs, one owned by the Brini and the other, by the Wait families (see the single-vineyard explorations). Pithy and firm, yet exotic, free flowing and generous, stained with blood orange, mescal, white pepper, pink grapefruit and fecund strawberry. Very long. Well amid the pantheon of regional greats. Screw cap. 13.8% alc. RATING 96 DRINK 2022-2030 $100 NG

Wait Single Vineyard Grenache 2021, McLaren Vale Arguably the most filigreed and complex of these single-vineyard iterations by virtue of its brood and carnal complexities: blood orange seeped with kirsch, woodsmoke and clove. Like the finest Sicilian-accented negroni. Straddles pinosity and nebbiolo-inspired boniness all at once, while laying the structural lattice to define a long, thrilling ride to the finish. Yet there is the mescal and dill-pickle note suggesting a bit more ripeness may be not such a bad idea. Screw cap. 14.1% alc. RATING 95 DRINK 2022-2030 $70 NG

Pir Blewitt Springs Chenin Blanc 2021, McLaren Vale This is excellent. While I had yet to taste any chenin from Australia that I thought world class (sorry, Erin!), this may be it. Once picked too early on acidity, this is now dutifully ripe. A wine of textural mettle. Composed across a scale of varying weights, beginning with natural acidity, saline and maritime. Filling out with lees work, all lanolin, oatmeal and cheesecloth. And finishing with an oaky lattice, embellishing the experience as much as cushioning it. Thoroughly impressive. A fine chenin. Screw cap. 13.2% alc. RATING 94 DRINK 2021-2026 $38 NG

Trenerry Single Vineyard Grenache 2021, McLaren Vale The lightest and most ethereal of the single-vineyard explorations. Orange macerated with cinnamon. Pink grapefruit. Clove. Dill pickle. Orangina. Cranberry. The tannins, diaphanous and frisky, etching the gums while eking out the long finish. This is more nebbiolo of feel than pinot, grenache's stylistic brethren. I would argue that while fascinating, it could use some mid-palate stuffing and a smidge more physiological ripeness in its strive towards completion. Delicious all the same. Screw cap. 13.3% alc. RATING 94 DRINK 2022-2028 $70 NG

ŸŸŸŸŸ **Welkin Nero d'Avola 2021, McLaren Vale** RATING 93 DRINK 2021-2023
$28 NG
Callow Grenache Blanc 2021, McLaren Vale RATING 93 DRINK 2021-2025
$38 NG
The Confluence Grenache 2021, McLaren Vale RATING 93
DRINK 2021-2024 $38 NG
Welkin Grenache 2021, McLaren Vale RATING 92 DRINK 2021-2023
$28 NG
Welkin Rosé 2021, McLaren Vale RATING 92 DRINK 2021-2022 $28 NG
Welkin Clairette 2021, McLaren Vale RATING 91 DRINK 2021-2023 $28 NG
Welkin Sparkling Chenin Blanc 2021, Adelaide Hills RATING 90 $28 NG

Apogee ★★★★★

1083 Golconda Road, Lebrina, Tas 7254 **Region** Northern Tasmania
T (02) 6395 6358 **www**.apogeetasmania.com **Open** By appt **Winemaker** Dr Andrew
Pirie **Viticulturist** Andrew Pirie **Est.** 2007 **Dozens** 1000 **Vyds** 2ha
Andrew Pirie (or Dr Andrew Pirie AM) has stood tall among those viticulturists and
winemakers who have sought to understand and exploit Tasmania's terroir and climate over
the past 40 years. He is as far removed from soap-box oratory as it is possible to be, quietly
spoken and humble. His vision almost 50 years ago – longer still on some measures – saw
the establishment of Pipers Brook Vineyard in 1974, using the detailed studies of Tasmania's
regional climates in '72. In '77 he became the first (and last) person to complete study for
his doctorate in viticulture from the University of Sydney. While making some of the best
table wines to come from Tasmania in the last quarter of the 20th century, his focus shifted
to sparkling wine in '99. In 2007 he acquired a 2ha site near Lebrina in the Pipers River
district, planting pinot noir (62%), chardonnay (16%) and a little pinot meunier (2%) for
sparkling wine, as well as pinot gris (20%) for table wine. Apogee's historic farm cottage is
now an intimate cellar door where (by appointment) visitors can observe a hand disgorging
demonstration. Pinot gris and pinot noir are also made under the Alto label. Exports to
Germany and the US. (JH)

ŸŸŸŸŸ **Deluxe Brut 2017, Tasmania** Andrew Pirie has captured the crystalline tension
of 2017 with impressive clarity. Pinot noir leads out, the rose petal and Turkish
delight signature of the region present, if a little subdued by oxidative handling,
bringing out more of a spicy red apple mood. Chardonnay draws out a high-
strung finish of impressive drive and crunchy grapefruit brightness, promising
grand endurance. Subtle brioche and ginger nut are the blessing of 47 months lees
age, integrated with subtle dosage. Diam. 12.5% alc. RATING 95 $70 TS
Alto Pinot Gris 2021, Tasmania Pinot gris doesn't come much better than this,
pitting pear and white peach against crisp and steely acidity on an ultra-long finish.
Screw cap. 14% alc. RATING 95 DRINK 2022-2031 $45 JH ♥
Deluxe Sparkling Rosé 2018, Tasmania 79/16/5% pinot noir/chardonnay/
meunier. Aged 23 months on lees. Disgorged 25 Jan 2021. 8.5g/L dosage. A pretty,
medium salmon-copper hue heralds rich aromas and flavours of blood orange,
fruit-mince spice and berry compote. There is a plush succulence to its juicy
wild strawberry mood, countered by the grip of fine-grained, well-executed skin
tannins and the racy line of cool Pipers River acidity. Its pedigree is defined in the
manner in which it effortlessly unites these contrasting extremes, and in a finish
that holds its magnitude and integrity with confidence. A main-course-ready
Apogee vintage to drink now. Diam. 12.9% alc. RATING 94 $75 TS

Apricus Hill ★★★★

550 McLeod Road, Denmark, WA 6333 **Region** Denmark
T 0427 409 078 **www**.apricushill.com.au **Open** Fri–Mon 11 & school hols
Winemaker James Kellie **Est.** 1995 **Dozens** 800 **Vyds** 8ha
When the then owners of Somerset Hill Vineyard, Graham and Lee Upson, placed the
vineyard on the market, James and Careena Kellie of Harewood Estate purchased it

with 2 purposes: first, to secure a critical fruit source for Harewood, and second, to make and market a small range of single-vineyard, single-varietal wines for sale exclusively through the spectacular cellar door, with its sweeping vista. Thus Somerset Hill became Apricus Hill. Exports to Japan. (JH)

ŸŸŸŸ̦ **Single Vineyard Pinot Noir 2020, Denmark** Morello cherries, raspberry bush (the bramble, the sweet fruit, the lot), finely crushed black pepper and bright acidity. This is a lovely, structural wine – another impressive release. The chalky tannins are a highlight. Screw cap. 14% alc. RATING 93 DRINK 2021-2028 $35 EL

ŸŸŸŸ **Single Vineyard Chardonnay 2020, Denmark** RATING 89 DRINK 2021-2026 $35 EL

Aramis Vineyards

411 Henley Beach Road, Brooklyn Park, SA 5032 **Region** McLaren Vale
T (08) 8352 2900 **www**.aramisvineyards.com **Winemaker** Renae Hirsch (red), Peter Leske (white) **Viticulturist** Daniel Lavrencic **Est.** 1998 **Dozens** 12 000 **Vyds** 26ha
Aramis Vineyards was founded in '98 by Lee Flourentzou. Located barely 2km from the Gulf of St Vincent, it is one of the coolest sites in McLaren Vale, planted to shiraz (18ha) and cabernet sauvignon (8ha), the 2 varieties best suited to the site. This philosophy leads Aramis to source grapes from other regions that best represent each variety, including sauvignon blanc and chardonnay from Adelaide Hills and riesling from Eden Valley. The city-based cellar door also features wines from other boutique producers. Exports to the US, Japan, Hong Kong, Singapore and NZ. (JH)

ŸŸŸŸ̦ **Morpheus Shiraz Viognier 2018, McLaren Vale** Sweet and sappy. Blue fruits, kirsch, anise, cedar and almost molten black volcanic accents, delineated by firm, impeccably extracted tannins, almost pulpy. The finish, hot. The bottle, as with all these wines, better served as a dumb bell. Yet this impactful wine is good, boasting considerable power and refinement. Cork. 14.2% alc. RATING 93 DRINK 2021-2029 $85 NG

Nemesis Cabernet Sauvignon 2018, McLaren Vale These wines ply power, considerable heat and impressive extraction with a focus on whole berries in the ferment. The result, a burn across the finish as much as admiration for the pulpy, detailed quilt of tannin. Saline. Cassis, kirsch, black olive tapenade and bay leaf. The finish long, forceful and expansive, ploughing across the palate with a sweetness and stamp of bouquet garni. Cork. 14.4% alc. RATING 93 DRINK 2021-2031 $85 NG

White Label Sauvignon Blanc 2021, Adelaide Hills Boasting the kind of exuberant Hills' sauvignon grapefruit, citrus, green apple intensity we have come to love. It bounces with energy in the glass! Tight in zippy acidity, there is a flourish of snow pea and spice which gets the mouth-watering and, suddenly, you're thinking of Asian dishes for dinner. Screw cap. 11.5% alc. RATING 92 DRINK 2021-2025 $22 JP ✪

Governor Syrah 2015, McLaren Vale Made in a reductive style to implement aromas of blueberry and dried nori. The barrel-fermented element and nature of the new oak (30%) imparts a smoked-barbecue characteristic. The finish, hot. The acidity, a bit shrill. But don't get me wrong, this is a slick package that many will enjoy if they can lift the bottle to the corkscrew. Cork. 14.5% alc. RATING 92 DRINK 2021-2025 $300 NG

The Bastion Shiraz 2018, McLaren Vale A few more dollars spent delivers a more ambitious oak regime and higher-quality fruit. Blue and black berries, damson plum, pine resin oak and a core of oak-derived smoked meats and barbecue aromas. This is full-bodied, warm-climate shiraz 101. A crowd pleaser, to be sure. Screw cap. 14.5% alc. RATING 90 DRINK 2021-2028 $35 NG

ŸŸŸŸ **White Label Pinot Grigio 2021, Adelaide Hills** RATING 89 DRINK 2021-2025 $22 JP

Single Vineyard Cabernet Sauvignon 2019, McLaren Vale RATING 89
DRINK 2021-2026 $35 NG
White Label Cabernet Sauvignon 2019, McLaren Vale RATING 88
DRINK 2021-2025 $22 NG

Aravina Estate ★★★★★

61 Thornton Road, Yallingup, WA 6282 **Region** Margaret River
T (08) 9750 1111 **www**.aravinaestate.com **Open** 7 days 11–5 **Winemaker** Ryan Aggiss
Est. 2010 **Dozens** 10 000 **Vyds** 28ha
In 2010 Steve Tobin and family acquired the winery and vineyard of Amberley Estate from
Accolade, but not the Amberley brand. Steve has turned the property into a multifaceted
business with a host of attractions including a sports car collection, restaurant and wedding
venue. (JH)

🍷🍷🍷🍷🍷 **Wildwood Ridge Reserve Stella BDX 2019, Margaret River**
53/24/13/10% cabernet sauvignon/merlot/malbec/cabernet franc. 2019 was a
cooler year in Margaret River and the cabernet (and cabernet blends) from the
region were characterised by their lifted perfume, lighter weight and earlier-
drinking prowess. This has all of these attributes; the aromas are defined by salted
cassis, redcurrant, licorice and star anise, while the palate is supple and lithe. The
tannins, while being very fine knit, assert themselves at the front of the palate,
suggesting that in a year or 2, they will soften and lean back into the fruit, opening
that window for optimal consumption in a years' time. What a gorgeous thing.
Screw cap. 14% alc. RATING 96 DRINK 2023-2037 $120 EL
Wildwood Ridge Reserve Chardonnay 2021, Margaret River Worked
and savoury, with salted yellow peach, brine, red apple skins and a hint of curry
leaf. Balanced, spicy and quite beautiful. Very smart, from an 'at times' challenging
vintage. Screw cap. 12.5% alc. RATING 95 DRINK 2022-2030 $55 EL

🍷🍷🍷🍷🍷 **Wildwood Ridge Reserve Cabernet Sauvignon 2020, Margaret River**
RATING 93 DRINK 2022-2032 $65 EL
Single Vineyard Block 4 Chenin Blanc 2021, Margaret River RATING 92
DRINK 2022-2028 $35 EL
Wildwood Ridge Reserve Malbec 2020, Margaret River RATING 92
DRINK 2022-2029 $55 EL
The A Collection Rosé Grenache 2021, Margaret River RATING 91
DRINK 2022-2023 $25 EL
The A Collection Sauvignon Blanc Semillon 2021, Margaret River
RATING 90 DRINK 2022-2024 $25 EL
Limited Release Tempranillo 2021, Margaret River RATING 90
DRINK 2022-2028 $35 EL
Limited Release Classic Muscat NV, Margaret River RATING 90 $35 EL

Arila Gardens ★★★★★

103 Moppa Rd, Nuriootpa, SA 5355 **Region** Barossa Valley
T 0411 244 429 **www**.arilagardens.com **Open** By appt **Winemaker** Adam Clay
Viticulturist Adam Clay **Est.** 2018 **Dozens** 1000 **Vyds** 7ha
Adam and Marie Clay purchased the 8ha in Moppa in 2018, after overseas harvests and a
decade as a winemaker at Penfolds in the Barossa. Adam's parents, Dave and Cheryl also work
in the vineyard and office. Arila, an indigenous word for 'sand, land and earth', is split into
3 distinct terroirs; Sand Garden, Quartz Garden and Ironstone Garden, with grenache vines
planted in 1900 and shiraz in the 40s. The Gardens of Moppa wines are regional expressions,
blended across the estate vineyards. The Garden Selection wines are crafted from the best
individual rows and sections of each terroir, exploring the nuance of site. Arila make wines
from Barossa grape varieties that sing clearly of their subregional soils, have snappy packaging
and a very bright future. (DB)

🍷🍷🍷🍷🍷 **Quartz & Ironstone Gardens 2020, Barossa Valley** Intense purple red in the glass with abundant floral-flecked dark plum and black fruits, with hints of licorice, brown spices, earth, coal dust, pressed flowers and dark chocolate. Wonderful fruit density, balance and flow, with tight tannin support, bright acidity and a finish that trails off nicely with memories of cassis, kirsch and spice. Screw cap. 14.5% alc. RATING 96 DRINK 2022–2038 $85 DB

Sand & Quartz Gardens Shiraz 2019, Barossa Valley An impressively proportioned shiraz showing impeccable balance, fruit purity and flow. Deep black plum and black cherry fruits, cut through with violets, bitter dark chocolate, earth, roasting meats, deep spice, licorice and a waft of mint chocolate, musk and espresso. Contemporary yet slightly broody with a sense of latent power, fine, compact tannin heft and a dry, dark finish that leaves you contemplating extended cellaring. Impressive stuff. Screw cap. 14.5% alc. RATING 95 DRINK 2024–2034 $85 DB

Gardens of Moppa Shiraz 2020, Barossa Valley Deep satsuma plum and black cherry notes are underscored by hints of dark spice, roasting meats, earth, dark chocolate and black licorice. Support comes in the way of assertive cocoa-like tannins and there is a broody side to its black-fruited finish. Screw cap. 14.5% alc. RATING 94 DRINK 2022–2032 $40 DB

🍷🍷🍷🍷🍷 **Sand Garden Grenache 2020, Barossa Valley** RATING 93 DRINK 2022–2030 $85 DB

Sand Garden Grenache 2019, Barossa Valley RATING 93 DRINK 2022–2032 $85 DB

Gardens of Moppa Grenache Shiraz Mataro 2020, Barossa Valley RATING 92 DRINK 2022–2028 $40 DB

Arlewood Estate ★★★★

679 Calgardup Road West, Forest Grove, WA 6286 **Region** Margaret River
T (08) 9757 6676 **www**.arlewood.com.au **Open** Fri–Sun 11–5 or by appt
Winemaker Cath Oates **Viticulturist** Colin Bell **Est.** 1988 **Dozens** 3000 **Vyds** 6.08ha
The antecedents of today's Arlewood shifted several times; they might interest a PhD researcher, but – with one exception – have no relevance to today's business. That exception was the '99 planting of the vineyard by the then Xanadu winemaker Jurg Muggli. Garry Gossatti purchased the run-down, close-planted vineyard in '08, and lived in the onsite house from '08–12. His involvement in the resurrection of the vineyard was hands-on, and the cool site in the south of Margaret River was, and remains, his obsession. Garry's sons Jordan and Adrian now work in the vineyard and Garry drives down every weekend from Perth, clearly believing that the owner's footsteps make the best fertiliser. Exports to the UK and Hong Kong. (JH)

🍷🍷🍷🍷🍷 **Chardonnay 2020, Margaret River** What a wine! powerful, concentrated, complex and long, with a spike of spice and texture through the centre of the palate. Plenty to like here. The phenolic structure creates a tunnel through which the fruit can pour, straight into the long finish. Very impressive. Margaret River and chardonnay are just meant to be together. Screw cap. 13.5% alc. RATING 94 DRINK 2021–2025 $40 EL

🍷🍷🍷🍷🍷 **Chardonnay 2019, Margaret River** RATING 93 DRINK 2020–2028 $40 EL
Cabernet Sauvignon 2019, Margaret River RATING 92 DRINK 2021–2028 $40 EL
Cabernet Merlot 2020, Margaret River RATING 91 DRINK 2021–2031 $25 EL

 # Arli Wine ★★★☆

2/540 Goulburn Valley Highway, Shepparton North, Vic 3531 **Region** Goulburn Valley
T 0427 529 183 **www**.arliwine.com.au **Winemaker** John Kremor **Est.** 2021
Dozens 300

Raised on his parents' vineyard in Merbein, John Kremor was destined for a life in wine. His first job was at BRL Hardy in Buronga, working his way up from the laboratory and cellar into the role of assistant winemaker. During his time there, he and his partner, Leanna, also redeveloped a local dried-fruit property with cabernet sauvignon and chardonnay, selling the fruit to a local winery. A work opportunity outside of wine took him to the Goulburn Valley in the late '90s. In '21 John returned to his first love, sourcing and making small parcels of wine from the Goulburn Valley region. His label is named after the couple's beloved Italian Water Dog, Arli. (JP)

🍷🍷🍷🍷🍷 **Dookie Hills Riesling 2021, Central Victoria** A smart price for an attractive, citrus-focused riesling. Whereas the floral, citrus and apple aromas are quite delicate, the palate is altogether different: firm and dry with an emerging textural quality. Lemon pith, lime and grapefruit are carried well along a lively acid line. Screw cap. 12.3% alc. RATING 90 DRINK 2021-2027 $15 JP ✪

Armstead Estate

366 Moorabbee Road, Knowsley, Vic 3523 **Region** Heathcote
T (03) 5439 1363 **www**.armsteadestate.com.au **Open** First w'end of month 11–5 or by appt **Winemaker** Rob Ellis **Est.** 2003 **Dozens** 1100 **Vyds** 0.6ha
Armstead Estate vineyard is centrally located within the Heathcote region on the banks of Lake Eppalock. Founder Peter Armstead planted the first shiraz vines in '03 on an east-facing slope just metres from the lake. Tom and Emily Kinsman purchased the estate in July '17. They are growing and sourcing fruit from a number of well-known vineyards across the Heathcote region, making quality wines with the assistance of Rob Ellis. (JH)

🍷🍷🍷🍷🍷 **The Matilda Reserve Shiraz 2019, Heathcote** In keeping with its origins, a vibrant and deeply coloured shiraz from Heathcote, bursting in sweet, ripe black fruits and a distinctive mineral earthiness on the bouquet. Maintains a fine balance in fruit and oak, power and elegance throughout. Palate is based around a core of fine, sturdy tannins carrying plum, blackberries, anise, chocolate and a touch of savoury tapenade, all dressed in discreet oak. Cork. 14.4% alc. RATING 95 DRINK 2022-2031 $55 JP

🍷🍷🍷🍷🍷 **hECK Home Blend NV, Victoria** RATING 90 DRINK 2022-2026 $45 JP

Artwine

72 Bird in Hand Road, Woodside, SA 5244 **Region** Mount Lofty Ranges
T 0411 422 450 **www**.artwine.com.au **Open** 7 days 11–5 **Winemaker** Contract
Est. 1997 **Dozens** 10 **Vyds** 21ha
Owned by Judy and Glen Kelly, Artwine has 3 vineyards. Two are in Clare Valley: one on Springfarm Road, Clare; the other on Sawmill Road, Sevenhill. The third vineyard is in the Adelaide Hills at Woodside, which houses their cellar door. Artwine currently has 15 varieties planted. The Clare Valley vineyards have tempranillo, shiraz, riesling, pinot gris, cabernet sauvignon, fiano, graciano, grenache, montepulciano, viognier and cabernet franc. The Adelaide Hills vineyard has prosecco, pinot noir, merlot and albariño. (JH)

🍷🍷🍷🍷🍷 **Wicked Stepmother Fiano 2021, Clare Valley** Granny Smith apples, honey, nashi pears and green grapes at the height of summer (the table kind, not the crushing kind). This is juicy, concentrated and quite delicious. Don't let the name/ label put you off, the wine inside the bottle is gorgeous. Has a fine sliver of star anise and white pepper that really elevates it out of the park. Screw cap. 12.5% alc. RATING 93 DRINK 2022-2025 $35 EL
Grumpy Old Man Grenache 2020, Clare Valley Hung deli meat, cold jasmine tea, raspberry and rhubarb humbugs, heirloom tomatoes and exotic spice. This is a savoury – almost meaty – grenache, which maintains an air of sweetness and clarity among the salted prosciutto/pastrami characters. Trophy Best Grenache at the Australian Single Vineyard Wine Show '21, gold medal Clare Valley Wine Show '21. Screw cap. 14.5% alc. RATING 93 DRINK 2022-2032 $40 EL

The Real Thing Albariño 2021, Adelaide Hills Haven't seen too many albariños from the Hills but if this is what the grape is capable of, then bring it on. The young wine is positively shining, putting its best lemon, grapefruit and melon feet forward with some zesty, bright fruit on display. Meanwhile, there is an underlying savouriness emerging on the palate of wet gravel and beeswax, together with an enduring mouthfeel. Screw cap. 12.5% alc. RATING 92 DRINK 2021-2026 $35 JP

Pack Leader Cabernet Franc 2020, Clare Valley Cabernet franc is so like cabernet sauvignon (both in structure and flavour), yet so different. Crunchy, leafy and a bit herbal, this franc is seen through the lens of a warm year in Clare Valley. Both elements lend it a depth, breadth and fullness of texture. This is a satisfying, uncomplicated iteration of the variety, which will likely please many. Screw cap. 14.5% alc. RATING 91 DRINK 2022-2028 $40 EL

ŸŸŸŸ **Prosecco Rosa Prosecco 2021, Adelaide Hills** RATING 89 $27 JP
Ti Amo Arneis 2021, Adelaide Hills RATING 89 DRINK 2021-2025 $35 JP
In the Groove 2021, Adelaide Hills RATING 88 DRINK 2021-2025 $35 JP
The Grace Graciano 2020, Clare Valley RATING 88 DRINK 2021-2027 $35 EL

Ashbrook Estate   ★★★★☆

379 Tom Cullity Drive, Wilyabrup, WA 6280 **Region** Margaret River
T (08) 9755 6262 **www**.ashbrookwines.com.au **Open** 7 days 10–5
Winemaker Catherine Edwards, Brian Devitt **Viticulturist** Richard Devitt, Brian Devitt
Est. 1975 **Dozens** 12 500 **Vyds** 17.4ha
This fastidious producer of consistently excellent estate-grown table wines shuns publicity and is less known than is deserved, selling much of its wine through the cellar door and to a loyal mailing list clientele. It is very much a family affair: Brian Devitt is at the helm, winemaking is by his daughter Catherine, and viticulture by son Richard who is also a qualified winemaker. Exports to Singapore, Indonesia, Japan, Denmark, Germany, the UK and the US. (JH)

ŸŸŸŸŸ **Reserve Chardonnay 2018, Margaret River** Crushed salted pistachios and walnuts on the nose. This is creamy, satisfying, saline and layered with orchard fruit. In the mouth, the wine is complex, plump and deeply satisfying. Classically structured and totally beautiful. This is not a wine driven by trend or style, rather, it has faithfully followed the same path, year in, year out, in the Ashbrook house style, and here it has met the perfect vintage match. The collision of the 2 is surely the most fortuitous intersect possible, producing one of the greatest Ashbrook Reserve chardonnay in years. Screw cap. 13.5% alc. RATING 96 DRINK 2022-2037 $65 EL ✪

Chardonnay 2020, Margaret River This is creamy, opulent and layered with abundant stone fruit. The flavour in the mouth is stitched together with fine threads of saline acidity, culminating in a long finish. The '20 vintage brings an effortlessness to the wine, the length of flavour the final indicator of quality. Brilliant value for money. Screw cap. 13.5% alc. RATING 94 DRINK 2021-2031 $35 EL

Shiraz 2019, Margaret River Very perfumed and decidedly pretty. The oak is currently presenting as one of the key players here, however it brings with it a swag of dark chocolate, licorice and aniseed. This is really classy. The fruit is pure and consistent and dark in the mouth, paving a way across the tongue and lingering for an age. Screw cap. 14% alc. RATING 94 DRINK 2021-2031 $32 EL

ŸŸŸŸŸ **Riesling 2021, Margaret River** RATING 93 DRINK 2022-2029 $27 EL ✪
Sauvignon Blanc 2021, Margaret River RATING 92 DRINK 2021-2024 $27 EL
Cabernet Sauvignon 2019, Margaret River RATING 92 DRINK 2021-2031 $35 EL
Chardonnay 2019, Margaret River RATING 92 DRINK 2020-2028 $35 EL
Rosé 2020, Margaret River RATING 90 DRINK 2020-2021 $27 EL

Ashton Hills Vineyard

126 Tregarthen Road, Ashton, SA 5137 **Region** Adelaide Hills
T (08) 8390 1243 **www.**ashtonhills.com.au **Open** Fri–Mon 11–5 **Winemaker** Liam Van
Pelt **Viticulturist** Anton Groffen **Est.** 1982 **Dozens** 3000 **Vyds** 3ha
Stephen George made Ashton Hills one of the great producers of pinot noir in Australia,
and by some distance the best in the Adelaide Hills. With no family succession in place,
he sold the business to Wirra Wirra in Apr '15. It had been rumoured for some time that he
was considering such a move, so when it was announced, there was a sigh of relief that it
should pass to a business such as Wirra Wirra, with undoubted commitment to retaining the
extraordinary quality of the wines. Stephen continues to live in the house on the property
and provides ongoing consulting advice. Exports to the US, Hong Kong, Denmark and the
Netherlands. (JH)

🍷🍷🍷🍷🍷 **Reserve Chardonnay 2021, Piccadilly Valley** A blend from 2 vineyards;
wild-yeast fermented in barrel; matured in seasoned French oak. This is a serious
chardonnay, displaying impeccable balance and poise. Struck flint, grapefruit, white
peach, green apple with hints of charry vanillin oak and honeysuckle. There's a
tightness, too, at play and a savoury wildness. So intricate. Give it time to unwind.
Screw cap. 12% alc. RATING 96 DRINK 2022-2031 $85 JP
Reserve Pinot Noir 2021, Piccadilly Valley This offers a walk on the
wild side with its earth and forest floor, hummus and prune in concert with
black-hearted fruits. Makes quite an entrance and then keeps you entranced
as you subconsciously pick out flavours and sensations across its fine tannin-
led palate. And still so much more to give. Screw cap. 13.5% alc. RATING 96
DRINK 2022-2031 $85 JP
Estate Pinot Noir 2021, Piccadilly Valley The '21 vintage was widely
considered to be an excellent vintage in Piccadilly Valley. Pinot was a standout.
Here, it delivers an exotic edge to an impressively vibrant red-garnet hue, with a
mix of black cherry, cranberry and red berries, forest notes, a hint of musk here,
bitter wild herbs there. All dressed up in fine tannins and ready to go. Screw cap.
13.5% alc. RATING 95 DRINK 2022-2029 $60 JP
Pinot Noir 2021, Piccadilly Valley In the dark and brooding class of pinot,
with undergrowth, autumnal leaves, dark berries, woodsy spices and sage. The
amount of whole bunches has been decreased from '20, a good sign, bringing an
element of added complexity rather than sharpness. A strong, firm, exciting young
pinot. Screw cap. 13.5% alc. RATING 94 DRINK 2022-2028 $40 JP

🍷🍷🍷🍷🍷 **Pinot Noir Vintage Rosé 2018, Piccadilly Valley** RATING 93 $40 JP
Chardonnay 2021, Piccadilly Valley RATING 93 DRINK 2023-2028 $40 JP
Estate Riesling 2021, Piccadilly Valley RATING 93 DRINK 2022-2028 $40 JP

Atlas Wines

PO Box 458, Clare, SA 5453 **Region** Clare Valley
T 0419 847 491 **www.**atlaswines.com **Winemaker** Adam Barton **Est.** 2008
Dozens 8000 **Vyds** 24ha
Before establishing Atlas Wines, owner and winemaker Adam Barton had an extensive
winemaking career: in McLaren Vale, the Barossa Valley, Coonawarra, the iconic Bonny Doon
Vineyard in California and at Reillys Wines in the Clare Valley. He has 6ha of shiraz and 2ha
of cabernet sauvignon grown on a stony ridge on the eastern slopes of the region, and sources
small batches from other distinguished sites in the Clare and Barossa valleys. The quality of the
wines is extraordinarily good and consistent. Exports to the UK and the US. (JH)

🍷🍷🍷🍷🍷 **The Spaniard 2020, Clare Valley** Blend of 60/25/15% tempranillo/grenache/
mataro. This is a damn fine blend. It offers lots of joy without any complication.
A burst of juicy red and black fruits interspersed with baking spices, cola
and jamon, a touch of meaty reduction and the right amount of savouriness.
Lipsmacking. Screw cap. 14.5% alc. RATING 93 DRINK 2021-2027 $28 JF

Pinot Noir 2020, Adelaide Hills The inaugural release and it's a very pretty wine. A pale ruby hue with delicate aromatics of red cherries and woodsy spices, Campari and a waft of what smells like whole-bunch aromatics. It also has that distinct Adelaide Hills spearmint note, working well as a seasoning. The palate is lighter framed, with fine tannins and a juiciness throughout. This is the type of pinot that is well-suited to warmer weather, so don't be afraid to give it a slight chill. A lovely drink. Screw cap. 13% alc. RATING 92 DRINK 2021-2026 $35 JF

ATR Wines ★★★★★

103 Hard Hill Road, Armstrong, Vic 3377 **Region** Great Western
T 0457 922 400 **www.**atrwines.com.au **Open** Thurs–Sun & public hols 1–5
Winemaker Adam Richardson **Est.** 2005 **Dozens** 4000 **Vyds** 7.6ha
Perth-born Adam Richardson began his winemaking career in '95, working for Normans, d'Arenberg and Oakridge along the way. He has held senior winemaking roles, ultimately with TWE America before moving back to Australia with his wife Eva and children in late '15. In '05 he had put down roots in the Grampians region, establishing a vineyard with old shiraz clones from the 19th century and riesling, extending the plantings with tannat, nebbiolo, durif and viognier. The wines are exceptionally good, no surprise given his experience and the quality of the vineyard. He also runs a wine consultancy business, drawing on experience that is matched by few consultants in Australia. Exports to Europe. (JH)

⦿⦿⦿⦿⦿ **Chockstone Riesling 2021, Grampians** Riesling is the winemaker's great strength and passion. It shows clearly each vintage. You could drown in the aromatic beauty of the scent: white flowers, lime, green apple, lemon zest, spice and musk. Dry and stylish acidity (it's the only word to describe the combination of bright and soft acidity) caress the palate, mouth-wateringly so. A touch of barely there sugar helps amplify the depth of fruit. A delight. Screw cap. 12% alc. RATING 96 DRINK 2022-2033 $24 JP ✪ ♥
Hard Hill Road Writer's Block Riesling 2020, Great Western A different, more subdued and complex interpretation of riesling from this maker. Excitingly fragrant in jasmine florals, citrus, baked apple, bergamot and orange peel. Builds and builds in the mouth, creamy and bright, the intensity of flavour assisted by hints of pear and almond. A wine of some depth, and it's only just revealing the tip of the iceberg. Screw cap. 12% alc. RATING 96 DRINK 2022-2033 $38 JP ✪
Hard Hill Road Writer's Block Riesling 2021, Great Western A treat to see how the high natural acidity (9g/L) has been managed, cajoled into expressing itself while allowing the fruit an equally big say. Pristine, pure apple blossom, lemon, grapefruit pith, lime zest and green apple. The small amount of sugar (2g/L) is barely noticeable but brings a sherbet lift and fruit-tingle quality that just brings the fruit alive. Screw cap. 12% alc. RATING 95 DRINK 2022-2033 $38 JP
Chockstone Shiraz 2020, Grampians The wildness of the Grampians just seems to effortlessly bring a high level of attractive herbals and spice to its shiraz. This is one example, where the scent alone offers a walk through country: acacia, bracken, anise, pepper and sage. Well supported by blackberries and dark chocolate, with woodsy oak tannins. Another Chockstone shiraz to enjoy now or cellar and forget. Screw cap. 14.5% alc. RATING 95 DRINK 2022-2045 $28 JP ✪
Hard Hill Road The Field 2020, Great Western 52/22/10/9/5/2% shiraz/riesling/nebbiolo/durif/tannat/viognier. Love the imaginative freedom that this wine gives the winemaker, a free-wheeling, anything-goes kind of blend that works so very well. Each grape contributes a strength: the aromatics of viognier and riesling are there on the bouquet together with gentle, fragrant rose petal and violet, spice and blackberries. It's generous and deep in flavour, with well-managed woodsy tannins and soft acidity. Bravo. Screw cap. 14.5% alc. RATING 95 DRINK 2022-2031 $45 JP
Hard Hill Road Great Western Petite Sirah 2019, Grampians Inky, midnight purple-black hue. Retains the grape's easy ability to be bold and full bodied, but also brings a degree of elegance – not quite so easy to achieve – in

rosemary, black pepper, black cherry and blueberry, dressed easily in black tea tannins. Screw cap. 14.5% alc. RATING 95 DRINK 2022-2034 $50 JP

Chockstone Rosé 2021, Grampians The winemaker deliberately selected each of these strange vinous bedfellows – nebbiolo, durif, shiraz, tannat and a 'touch' of riesling – for this rosé. It's a standout in the glass in ruddy pink. Nebbiolo brings some attractive florals to add to the aroma of red berries and musk. Concentrated and creamy on the palate with a whisper of sweetness. Screw cap. 13.5% alc. RATING 94 DRINK 2022-2025 $22 JP ✪

Hard Hill Road Close Planted Shiraz 2020, Great Western Always a super-spicy young red, which is, to a large part, what Grampians shiraz is all about. It's all here too, the mix of black berries, licorice and chocolate, then a blast of herbs and spice, black pepper, fennel seeds, sage, gum leaves and bay leaves. It's tied together with a big ribbon of tight, firm tannins. Screw cap. 14.5% alc. RATING 94 DRINK 2022-2035 $45 JP

ΨΨΨΨΩ **Chockstone Pinot Gris 2021, Grampians** RATING 93 DRINK 2022-2025 $24 JP ✪
Hard Hill Road Petite Sirah 2020, Great Western RATING 93 DRINK 2023-2035 $50 JP
Tannat 2019, Great Western RATING 93 DRINK 2022-2027 $45 JP
Hard Hill Road Mule Variation 2020, Great Western RATING 92 DRINK 2022-2036 $45 JP
Hard Hill Road Tannat 2020, Great Western RATING 92 DRINK 2022-2033 $45 JP
Hard Hill Road Close Planted Shiraz 2019, Great Western RATING 91 DRINK 2022-2036 $45 JP

Atze's Corner Wines ★★★★

451 Research Road, Nuriootpa, SA 5355 **Region** Barossa Valley
T 0407 621 989 **www.**atzes.com **Open** Fri–Sat 1–sunset, Sun & public hols 12–5.30
Winemaker Andrew Kalleske **Est.** 2005 **Dozens** 2500 **Vyds** 30ha
The seemingly numerous members of the Kalleske family have widespread involvement in grapegrowing and winemaking in the Barossa Valley. This venture is that of Andrew Kalleske, son of John and Barb. In '75 they purchased the Atze Vineyard, which included a small block of shiraz planted in '12, but with additional plantings along the way, including more shiraz in '51. Andrew purchases some grapes from the family vineyard. It has 20ha of shiraz, with small amounts of mataro, petit verdot, grenache, cabernet, tempranillo, viognier, petite sirah, graciano, montepulciano, vermentino and aglianico. The wines are all estate-grown and made onsite. The cellar door is designed to enjoy the sunset over the 100+yo vineyard. Exports to South Korea and Hong Kong. (JH)

ΨΨΨΨΨ **Eddies Old Vine Shiraz 2018, Barossa Valley** A deeply coloured and wonderfully aromatic wine, bursting with super-ripe damson plum, summer berry fruit and mulberry characters. Weighty with excellent fruit purity, flow and presence on the palate, finishing long, opulent and delicious. Cork. 15% alc. RATING 94 DRINK 2021-2038 $60 DB

Forgotten Hero Shiraz 2018, Barossa Valley Deeply coloured and very perfumed, with aromas of ripe damson plums and summer berry fruits, underscored with sweet oak spice, licorice, pressed flowers, vanilla bean and espresso. Oak initially dominates the palate, but then the rich fruit rolls in, the fine tannin cascades down and the wine trails off opulently in a wash of fruit and spice. Cork. 15.5% alc. RATING 94 DRINK 2021-2038 $110 DB

ΨΨΨΨΩ **The Giant Durif 2020, Barossa Valley** RATING 92 DRINK 2022-2032 $35 DB
The Giant Durif 2019, Barossa Valley RATING 92 DRINK 2021-2030 $35 DB
Bachelor Shiraz 2020, Barossa Valley RATING 91 DRINK 2022-2030 $35 DB
John & Barb's Old Vine Grenache 2019, Barossa Valley RATING 91 DRINK 2021-2032 $60 DB

The Mob Montepulciano 2018, Barossa Valley RATING 91
DRINK 2021-2026 $30 DB
Opulent 2020, Barossa Valley RATING 90 DRINK 2022-2029 $25 DB
The Mob Montepulciano 2019, Barossa Valley RATING 90
DRINK 2020-2028 $35 DB

Audrey Wilkinson   ★★★★★

750 De Beyers Road, Pokolbin, NSW 2320 **Region** Hunter Valley
T (02) 4998 1866 **www**.audreywilkinson.com.au **Open** 7 days 10–5
Winemaker Xanthe Hatcher **Est.** 1866 **Vyds** 47ha
Audrey Wilkinson is one of the most historic and beautiful properties in the Hunter Valley,
known for its stunning views and pristine vineyards. It was the first vineyard planted in
Pokolbin, in 1866. The property was acquired in '04 by the late Brian Agnew and has been
owned and operated by his family since. The wines, made predominantly from estate-grown
grapes, are released in 3 tiers: Audrey Wilkinson Series, Winemakers Selection and Reserve,
the latter only available from the cellar door. Exports to the US, Canada, UK, Finland and
Czech Republic. (JH)

🍷🍷🍷🍷🍷 **Marsh Vineyard Semillon 2021, Hunter Valley** Fine boned. Playing a card of
greater austerity and classicism than its Ridge sibling. Real tension here, with the
fruit tucked beneath a veneer of mineral, talc, juicy acidity and a verdant rub of
fennel, greengage and lemongrass. This will age stupendously well, as long as one
has the patience. Screw cap. 11.5% alc. RATING 96 DRINK 2021-2034 $40 NG ✪
Marsh Vineyard Chardonnay 2021, Hunter Valley A mid-weighted, fully
flavoured expression that manages to stuff a lot into a framework of match-struck
mineral, praline and toasted-hazelnut-cum-phenolic grippiness. The most Euro-
styled of the suite. Peach, creamed cashew and nougat. Fine length. This will
please those seeking ample flavour and freshness in the same glass, with a plenitude
of textural detail. Very good for the region. Screw cap. 12.5% alc. RATING 95
DRINK 2022-2030 $40 NG
The Ridge Reserve Semillon 2021, Hunter Valley A pale–mid yellow
with green glints, this is riper than most, facilitating delicious drinking right off
the bat. Lemon balm, tonic, orange pastille and quince. An expansive mid palate,
unravelling across a beam of acidity, juicy and effusive, serving to tow the wine to
impressive length. Delicious. Screw cap. 12% alc. RATING 95 DRINK 2021-2032
$45 NG
The Oakdale Chardonnay 2015, Hunter Valley Impressive, capturing
tension by virtue of avoiding malo. Best is the nutty complexity: praline, toasted
hazelnut and the waft of curd and apricot, ginger and white peach that follows.
Reminiscent of Meursault without quite the chew or depth. Scintillating length in
a regional context. Screw cap. 12.5% alc. RATING 95 DRINK 2022-2028 $75 NG
The Oakdale Chardonnay 2021, Hunter Valley This sits pretty, between
the textural elements of the Marsh and the limber, impeccably poised and fresh
Winemakers Selection (their lack of apostrophe). Flint. Stone fruits glimpsed, but
far from overt. Lovely oak, tucking in the seams. A gentle creaminess, but nothing
obtuse. For Hunter chardonnay this plays a discreet, tightly held deck. Flavour, to
be sure. But loads tucked away to reward mid-term cellaring. Screw cap. 12.5% alc.
RATING 94 DRINK 2022-2030 $45 NG

🍷🍷🍷🍷🍷 **Winemakers Selection Semillon 2021, Hunter Valley** RATING 93
DRINK 2021-2027 $30 NG
Semillon 2021, Hunter Valley RATING 92 DRINK 2021-2029 $23 NG ✪
Winemakers Selection Chardonnay 2021, Hunter Valley RATING 92
DRINK 2022-2027 $35 NG
Tempranillo 2021, Hunter Valley RATING 91 DRINK 2022-2027 $40 NG
Winemakers Selection Shiraz 2021, Hunter Valley RATING 91
DRINK 2022-2027 $40 NG

Austin's Wines

870 Steiglitz Road, Sutherlands Creek, Vic 3331 **Region** Geelong
T (03) 5281 1799 **www**.austinswines.com.au **Open** By appt **Winemaker** Dwayne
Cunningham **Viticulturist** Craig Blake **Est.** 1982 **Dozens** 25 000 **Vyds** 61.5ha
Pamela and Richard Austin have quietly built their business from a tiny base, and it has
flourished. The vineyard has been progressively extended to just over 60ha. Son Scott and his
partner Belinda, both with a varied but successful career outside the wine industry, took over
management and ownership in '08. The quality of the wines is admirable. In early '22 they
opened a new cellar door in a converted shearing shed. (JH)

🍷🍷🍷🍷🍷 **Curated Shiraz 2021, Geelong** Some new winemaking territory visited here,
exploring the role of whole bunches, concrete eggs and Croatian oak, among
other things, and the result is an intriguing mix of the savoury and the sweet-
fruited, the textural and the earthy dry. Dark cherry, cherry liqueur, cassis, dried
herbs, smokey charcuterie and leathery, spicy oak broaden our interpretation
and appreciation of Geelong shiraz in an exciting way. Screw cap. 13.8% alc.
RATING 95 DRINK 2022-2031 $65 JP
Moorabool Valley Pinot Noir 2020, Geelong A tightly layered and complex
wine, that speaks of the wilder side of the grape: the briar, undergrowth, tilled
earth and black fruits. Taut on the palate with smooth tannins and plenty of dark
cherry, plum and dark chocolate. That layer of spice caps it off beautifully. Screw
cap. 13.6% alc. RATING 95 DRINK 2021-2030 $45 JP
Moorabool Valley Riesling 2020, Geelong Highly fragrant in lemon citrus,
lime blossom, talc and spiced apple. Holds impressive concentration and length
with a leesy nougat mealiness running along a gentle, textural palate. Complex,
with an intriguing almost-rosewater spice. Screw cap. 12.5% alc. RATING 94
DRINK 2021-2027 $45 JP

🍷🍷🍷🍷🍷 **Curated Off Dry Riesling 2021, Geelong** RATING 92 DRINK 2022-2026
$40 JP
6Ft6 Prosecco NV, King Valley RATING 90 $25 JP
6Ft6 Pinot Gris 2021, King Valley Geelong RATING 90 DRINK 2021-2026
$25 JP
Moorabool Valley Chardonnay 2020, Geelong RATING 90
DRINK 2021-2027 $45 JP

Aylesbury Estate

★★★★★

72 Ratcliffe Road, Ferguson, WA 6236 **Region** Geographe
T 0427 922 755 **www**.aylesburyestate.com.au **Winemaker** Luke Eckersley, Damian
Hutton **Viticulturist** Ryan Gibbs **Est.** 2015 **Dozens** 6500 **Vyds** 9ha
Ryan and Narelle Gibbs are the 6th generation of the pioneering Gibbs family in the Ferguson
Valley. When the family first arrived in 1883, they named the farm Aylesbury, after the town
in England whence they came. For generations the family ran cattle on the 200ha property,
but in 1998 they decided to plant 4.2ha of cabernet sauvignon to diversify the business.
Merlot (2.5ha) followed in '01, and sauvignon blanc (1.6ha) in '04. In '08 Ryan and Narelle
took over the business from Ryan's father, selling the grapes until '15, when they made the
first Aylesbury Estate wines. Three years later, they purchased the nearby 52 Stones vineyard,
adding cooler-climate varieties chardonnay, arneis and gamay to the Aylesbury range. (JH)

🍷🍷🍷🍷🍷 **Q05 Ferguson Valley Tempranillo 2020, Geographe** Beautiful wine, here.
Salted black licorice, mulberries, raspberries, lashings of blackberry and a waft of
violets through the finish. I want to say pretty, but it has bigger muscles and more
density than that – although elements of it are undoubtedly pretty. Very smart
wine. Screw cap. 14.5% alc. RATING 95 DRINK 2021-2028 $35 EL ✪
The Pater Series Ferguson Valley Cabernet Sauvignon 2019,
Geographe Gorgeous cabernet, here. Cassis, bramble, exotic spice, raspberry,
bitter cocoa and licorice straps. The acidity is briny and moreish. A really lovely

rendition of cabernet sauvignon, from an extraordinarily pretty part of WA, the Ferguson Valley. Screw cap. 14.5% alc. RATING 95 DRINK 2021-2036 $50 EL

The Pater Series Ferguson Valley Chardonnay 2020, Geographe A real seaside vibe here – the palate is extremely salty, layered with kelp/nori, brine, salted yellow peach, malt biscuit, curry leaf and crushed oyster shell through the finish. Very long in the mouth, it lingers long after it has gone. This is a brilliant wine, certainly well made, but the savoury, salty palate will polarise the crowd. Screw cap. 13.8% alc. RATING 94 DRINK 2021-2031 $50 EL

Q05 Ferguson Valley Arneis 2021, Geographe RATING 92 DRINK 2021-2025 $35 EL

B Minor

100 Long Gully Road, Healesville, Vic 3777 **Region** Victoria
T 0433 591 617 **www.**bminor.com.au **Winemaker** Various **Est.** 2019 **Dozens** 5000
B Minor was originally a small artisan wine brand created in '10 focusing on producing fresh, creative wines specifically targeting on-premise and specialty retail venues in the US and Australia. Its original philosophy was to create an international brand. In '20, Qiqi Fu bought out a partner in B Minor and runs the business, enlisting Best's Wines and others as contract winemakers. Qiqi Fu now principally sells B Minor wines through the B Minor website in addition to Melbourne retailers and restaurants. (JP)

Shiraz 2020, Grampians Qiqi Fu is back with another vibrant, youthful Grampians shiraz that captures the region and its no. 1 red grape so well. Fruit is sourced from a renowned local producer and is fragrant and complex, offering dark spice, licorice, ripe plum and spiced oak. Fine, supple tannins make it highly appealing now, but you just know there is plenty left in reserve. Screw cap. 14% alc. RATING 94 DRINK 2021-2032 $39 JP

Syrah 2021, Yarra Valley RATING 93 DRINK 2022-2028 $32 PR
Riesling 2021, Nagambie Lakes RATING 92 DRINK 2021-2028 $18 JP ❂
Pinot Noir 2021, Yarra Valley RATING 91 DRINK 2022-2026 $23 PR ❂

Baddaginnie Run

PO Box 579, North Melbourne, Vic 3051 **Region** Strathbogie Ranges
T (03) 9348 9310 **www.**baddaginnierun.net.au **Winemaker** Sam Plunkett **Est.** 1996
Dozens 2500 **Vyds** 24ha
Winsome McCaughey and Professor Snow Barlow (Professor of Horticulture and Viticulture at the University of Melbourne) spend part of their week in the Strathbogie Ranges, and part in Melbourne. The business name, Seven Sisters Vineyard, reflects the seven generations of the McCaughey family associated with the land since 1870; Baddaginnie is the nearby township. Exports to the US. (JH)

Shiraz 2019, Strathbogie Ranges Brilliant black cherry red-purple hue, very attractive. What a sparky introduction, all Damson plum, cherry, black berries, aniseed and spice. The sweet, plummy theme is ongoing throughout this wine, which is more a drink-now than drink-later style. Fresh, clean and generously fruity, it highlights the mineral-edged Bogies style beautifully. Screw cap. 14.9% alc. RATING 92 DRINK 2021-2024 $21 JP ❂

Merlot 2019, Strathbogie Ranges RATING 89 DRINK 2021-2024 $21 JP
Rosé 2020, Central Victoria RATING 88 DRINK 2021-2021 $17 JP ❂

Bailey Wine Co

PO Box 368, Penola, SA 5277 **Region** Coonawarra
T 0417 818 539 **www.**baileywineco.com **Winemaker** Tim Bailey **Est.** 2015
Dozens 750

After 2 decades living and working in Coonawarra, Tim Bailey decided to take a busman's holiday by establishing his own small wine business. Tim worked at Leconfield for 21 years, and has also worked in the Sonoma Valley of California, travelling through the Napa Valley as well as France. Tim has a simple philosophy: 'Find great growers in the regions and let the vineyard shine through in the bottle.' Thus he sources Clare Valley riesling, Grampians shiraz, Adelaide Hills chardonnay and Coonawarra cabernet sauvignon. (JH)

🍷🍷🍷🍷🍷 **Hyde Park Vineyard Shiraz 2019, Grampians** Hyde Park Vineyard is 5km southwest of Great Western and shares the subregion's lively shiraz spice. It's very much evident in this wine, with its winding layers of cassia bark, bush mint and aniseed. Brings a natural buoyancy and energy to the grape against a background of blueberry, black fruits, savoury oak and fine, velvety tannins. The best of both worlds with good drinking now or later. Screw cap. 14% alc. RATING 95 DRINK 2021-2033 $30 JP ✪

Baileys of Glenrowan ★★★★★

779 Taminick Gap Road, Glenrowan, Vic 3675 **Region** Glenrowan
T (03) 5766 1600 **www**.baileysofglenrowan.com.au **Open** 7 days 10–5 **Winemaker** Paul Dahlenburg, Elizabeth Kooij **Est.** 1870 **Dozens** 15 000 **Vyds** 144ha
Since 1998 the utterly committed Paul Dahlenburg has been in charge of Baileys and has overseen an expansion in the vineyard and the construction of a 2000t capacity winery. The cellar door has a heritage museum, winery viewing deck, contemporary art gallery and landscaped grounds preserving much of the heritage value. Baileys has also picked up the pace with its muscat and Topaque, reintroducing the Winemakers Selection at the top of the tree, while continuing the larger volume Founder series. Casella Family brands purchased the brand and the Glenrowan property from TWE in December 2017. The vineyards and winery have been steadily undergoing conversion to organic since 2011, producing the first full range of certified organic table wines from the 2019 vintage. Baileys had plenty to celebrate for its 150th anniversary in 2020. (JH)

🍷🍷🍷🍷🍷 **Winemakers Selection Rare Old Muscat NV, Glenrowan** The late, great Harry Tinson helped lay some of the foundations for a fine fortified library at Baileys that today's winemaker, Paul Dahlenburg, now draws upon. This is a taste of that history, of walnut and plum pudding, honey and raisin, dried fruits and treacle, chocolate and grilled and so much more, wrapped in fresh, clean spirit. A wine to get lost in. 375ml bottle. Vinolok. 17.5% alc. RATING 95 $75 JP
Winemakers Selection Rare Old Topaque NV, Glenrowan Topaque at the top of its game, exquisitely crafted, bringing a number of elements together – age, luscious intensity and concentration, sympathetic spirit – that remains quintessentially hedonistic. That's the thing with the Rare classification, it indulges emotionally. Mahogany walnut in colour, it brings aromatic florals in concert with dried fruits, chocolate, butterscotch, fruitcake, burnt butter and more. Lives long in the mouth and the memory. 375ml bottle. Vinolok. 17.5% alc. RATING 95 $75 JP

🍷🍷🍷🍷 **Organic Small Batch Series Nero d'Avola 2021, Glenrowan** RATING 89 DRINK 2022-2024 $20 JP
Organic Small Batch Series Fiano 2021, Glenrowan RATING 88 DRINK 2022-2024 $20 JP
Organic Small Batch Series Rosé 2021, Glenrowan RATING 88 DRINK 2022-2024 $20 JP

bakkheia ★★★★★

2718 Ferguson Road, Lowden, WA 6240 **Region** Geographe
T (08) 9732 1394 **www**.bakkheia.com.au **Open** By appt **Winemaker** Michael Edwards
Est. 2006 **Dozens** 1000 **Vyds** 3ha
This is the retirement venture of Michael and Ilonka Edwards. Michael had a career in the navy and marine industry while Ilonka enjoyed a career in the fashion and lifestyle industry. They moved to the Preston Valley in WA in '05 and purchased a property that had a patch

of cabernet sauvignon planted in '99. They now have 3ha of grenache, mourvèdre, graciano, tempranillo, cabernet sauvignon, shiraz and malbec; purchasing chardonnay and sauvignon blanc from a neighbour. They have an unusual approach to marketing, starting with the winery name linked to the Roman words for Bacchus and bacchanalian frenzies induced by wine, lots of wine. Rather than selling through liquor stores, they set up a membership system. Exports to Singapore. (JH)

ŸŸŸŸŸ The Wonderful Miss Gerry Preston Valley Grenache 2020, Geographe This has incredible intensity of flavour. There is blood and plum (distinct from blood plums), graphite and rocks. Star anise, licorice and aniseed, with bacon fat, maple and raspberry humbugs. A touch of stewed rhubarb, red apples and black tea. There's nori and black sesame in there too. It's all there. The concentration is a marvel, actually. The first thing I said when I put this in my mouth was 'wow'. Screw cap. 15.1% alc. RATING 97 DRINK 2022-2032 $21 EL ✪ ♥

ŸŸŸŸŸ Command Cabernet Sauvignon 2019, Geographe This is really earthy, laden with tobacco, damp leaves, blackberry compote, cigar box, black tea, red currants and licorice. The tannins are super-smooth, but firm, and shaping the fruit in the mouth and through the finish. It is here that they leave a chew, and a thought in the trail of flavour that lingers after the wine has gone. Really smart. A compelling cabernet from Geographe. Screw cap. 14.4% alc. RATING 95 DRINK 2022-2040 $75 EL

Monsieur Lapena Merlot 2016, Geographe Wears its age well. It is savoury and natural (unpretentious), with mulberry, tobacco, coffee grounds and salted licorice. A string of rhubarb tart acidity slowly curls its way through the fruit. Leather strap and granular tannins are a highlight. It is long and precise and medium weighted at best. An intriguing wine of layers and earth. Screw cap. 14.5% alc. RATING 95 DRINK 2022-2032 $35 EL ✪

United & Undaunted Preston Valley Mourvèdre 2020, Geographe Mulberry compote, red licorice, pink peppercorn and red capsicum. In the mouth the wine is supple and pliable with creamy tannins – a feature of the 2020 reds, I am finding. This is plush and almost lush, working within a medium-bodied framework. The tannins are spot on: chewy, back palate and flavoursome. Another smart release from Mick Edwards. Screw cap. 14.2% alc. RATING 94 DRINK 2022-2029 $32 EL

The Groszman Graciano 2020, Geographe This is a brilliant graciano. It perfectly harnesses the black gritty tannins and the midnight licorice fruit the variety is so capable of, and whips them hard down the track. Go faster. A stream of toasted exotic spice, black tea and a profusion of blackberries in their wake. Very good indeed. Screw cap. 14.2% alc. RATING 94 DRINK 2022-2029 $35 EL

The Matelot Malbec 2020, Geographe A surprisingly minty nose initially, but after 30 mins in the glass this has finally settled down. Alpine mountain herbs, black fruit and graphite tannins form the business at the front, however it is in the finish that the fun happens … this is slightly chewy, slightly herbal and really quite succulent – all of it adding up to a black cherry kirsch vibe through the tail. It's engaging and inviting drinking, and although it will likely age gracefully over the next 7 years or so, the vibrancy and cherry kick is happening now. Only a lucky few will be able to score these wines; it's worth considering the mailing list. Screw cap. 13.4% alc. RATING 94 DRINK 2022-2029 $35 EL

Balgownie Estate   ★★★★☆

Hermitage Road, Maiden Gully, Vic 3551 **Region** Bendigo
T (03) 5449 6222 **www.**balgownieestatewines.com.au **Open** 7 days 11–5
Winemaker Tony Winspear **Est.** 1969 **Dozens** 10 000 **Vyds** 35.28ha
Balgownie Estate is the senior citizen of Bendigo, its original vineyard plantings now 50 years old. The estate also has a cellar door at 1309 Melba Hwy in the Yarra Valley (Yarra Glen), where operations fit in neatly with the Bendigo wines. Balgownie has the largest vineyard-based resort in the Yarra Valley, with over 65 rooms and a limited number of spa suites.

In Apr '16 a Chinese investment company purchased the Balgownie Bendigo and Yarra Valley operations for $29 million. Exports to the UK, the US, Canada, Fiji, Hong Kong, Singapore and NZ. (JH)

🍷🍷🍷🍷🍷 **Centre Block Shiraz 2019, Bendigo** A beguiling shiraz that highlights what Balgownie founder, Stuart Anderson, originally saw in the site and the potential of the grape. Deep and intense in colour, the aromas sitting in the dark plum, black cherry, chocolate and spice spectrum, warm and inviting. A touch of bay leaf helps lift the palate, carried by supple tannins and toasty, woodsy oak. Screw cap. 14% alc. RATING 95 DRINK 2022–2031 $65 JP

Pinot Noir 2019, Yarra Valley There's a lot to like here. Combines the grape's earthy herbal side with a rush of cherry-red berry plushness. Generous scent of cherry, plum, briar and lemon thyme. Succulent across the palate finishing with a cranberry tartness that gives the tastebuds a right shake. Clean and vibrant. Screw cap. 13.2% alc. RATING 94 DRINK 2021–2026 $45 JP

🍷🍷🍷🍷🍷 **Pinot Noir Chardonnay 2018, Macedon Ranges** RATING 93 $50 JP
Viognier 2020, Bendigo RATING 93 DRINK 2021–2026 $35 JP
Shiraz 2019, Bendigo RATING 93 DRINK 2022–2028 $48 JP
Cabernet Sauvignon 2019, Bendigo RATING 93 DRINK 2022–2029 $48 JP
Chardonnay 2020, Bendigo RATING 92 DRINK 2022–2025 $40 JP
Chardonnay 2019, Macedon Ranges RATING 92 DRINK 2021–2027 $50 JP
Nouveau Rosé Shiraz 2021, Bendigo RATING 90 DRINK 2022–2024 $28 JP

Ballandean Estate Wines   ★★★☆

354 Sundown Road, Ballandean, Qld 4382 **Region** Granite Belt
T (07) 4684 1226 **www**.ballandeanestate.com **Open** 7 days 9–5 **Winemaker** Dylan Rhymer, Angelo Puglisi **Est.** 1932 **Dozens** 12 000 **Vyds** 34.2ha
A rock of ages in the Granite Belt, owned by the ever-cheerful and charming Angelo and Mary Puglisi. Ballandean Estate's cool climate, high altitude and granitic terroir deliver national and international award-winning wines. Mary introduced a gourmet food gallery at the cellar door, featuring foods produced by local food artisans as well as Greedy Me gourmet products made by Mary herself. Ballandean Estate can't always escape the unpredictable climate of the Granite Belt. (JH)

🍷🍷🍷🍷🍷 **Red Liqueur Muscat NV, Granite Belt** Aged 10+ years in 100yo 5000L oak foudres, topping up via the solera system. Luscious and rich, brimming with apricots, marmalade, raisins, dried figs and a hint of musk. Sweet and powerful, it brims with caramel and fruitcake, concluding both sweet and spirity, with spirit poking out. Impressive length. Screw cap. 19.5% alc. RATING 91 $65 TS

Ballycroft Vineyard & Cellars   ★★★★

1 Adelaide Road, Greenock, SA 5360 **Region** Barossa Valley
T 0488 638 488 **www**.ballycroft.com **Open** 7 days 11–4 by appt **Winemaker** Joseph Evans **Viticulturist** Joseph Evans **Est.** 2005 **Dozens** 600 **Vyds** 4ha
This micro-business is owned by Joseph and Sue Evans. Joe's life on the land started in 1984; he later obtained a viticulture degree from Roseworthy. Between '92 and '99 he worked in various capacities at Rockford Wines, and then at Greenock Creek Wines. Joe and Sue are a 2-person band, so would-be visitors to the cellar door would be wise to make an appointment for a personal tasting with one of them. Groups of up to 8 are welcome. (JH)

🍷🍷🍷🍷🍷 **Small Berry Cabernet Sauvignon 2019, Langhorne Creek** Medium red in hue with aromas of blackcurrant, blackberry and red cherry, along with hints of berry danish, spice box, red licorice, purple flowers and cedar. Smooth fruit attack with gentle, powdery tannins and a saline edge to the acid profile. Screw cap. 14.8% alc. RATING 91 DRINK 2021–2030 $40 DB

Small Berry American Oak Greenock Shiraz 2019, Barossa Valley Red and dark plum fruits with some red-cherry lift, along with notes of baking spice,

red licorice, earth and pressed flowers. The fruit is savoury, pure and true. The oak kicks in a little more on the palate, with a coconut sheen before finishing stony and calm. Screw cap. 15.1% alc. RATING 91 DRINK 2021-2030 $50 DB
Small Berry French Oak Greenock Shiraz 2019, Barossa Valley Saturated red in the glass, with aromas of plush blackberry and black plum, cut through with hints of blackstrap licorice, kirsch, cedar and oak spice. Concentrated black fruits on the palate, with a fair lick of cedary oak, powdery tannin and a saline flick to its tail, finishing dense and chewy. Screw cap. 15.5% alc. RATING 91 DRINK 2021-2030 $50 DB

ΨΨΨΨ **Small Berry Montepulciano 2021, Langhorne Creek** RATING 89 DRINK 2021-2025 $25 DB
Small Berry Mataro 2019, Barossa Valley RATING 88 DRINK 2021-2030 $36 DB

Balnaves of Coonawarra

15517 Riddoch Highway, Coonawarra, SA 5263 **Region** Coonawarra
T (08) 8737 2946 **www**.balnaves.com.au **Open** Mon–Fri 9–5, w'ends 11.30–4.30
Winemaker Jacinta Jenkins, Pete Bissell **Viticulturist** Pete Balnaves **Est.** 1975
Dozens 10000 **Vyds** 74.33ha
Grapegrower, viticultural consultant and vigneron, Doug Balnaves has over 70ha of high-quality estate vineyards. The wines are invariably excellent, often outstanding; notable for their supple mouthfeel, varietal integrity, balance and length – the tannins are always fine and ripe, the oak subtle and perfectly integrated. Coonawarra at its best. Exports to the UK, the US, Canada, Indonesia and South Korea. (JH)

ΨΨΨΨΨ **The Tally Reserve Cabernet Sauvignon 2019, Coonawarra** Released as a 5yo wine, the Tally has built a reputation over the years as a Coonawarra icon. Concentrated, brooding and dense, this is firmly on the midnight spectrum: by that, I mean blackberries, licorice, mulberries, aniseed, cigar box and graphite. The tannins that shape the affair are fine and omnipresent, and they come with that extra flex of chewy salted licorice. There is so much to masticate on here as the wine lingers through the finish. It is glorious. ProCork. 14.5% alc. RATING 96 DRINK 2024-2044 $90 EL
Cabernet Sauvignon 2019, Coonawarra The indefatigable fruit here is a solid match for the oak – at no point does it wither beneath the weight of it. This is a classically styled, almost old-school cabernet, but it has been handled with class. That fruit, as mentioned, is glorious. A beautiful wine which will no doubt age gracefully. Screw cap. 14.5% alc. RATING 95 DRINK 2022-2037 $45 EL

ΨΨΨΨΩ **The Blend 2019, Coonawarra** RATING 93 DRINK 2021-2029 $20 EL ✪
Chardonnay 2020, Coonawarra RATING 92 DRINK 2022-2029 $30 EL

Banca Ridge

22 McGlew Street, Stanthorpe, Qld 4380 **Region** Granite Belt
T (07) 4685 5050 **www**.qcwt.edu.au **Open** 7 days 10–4 **Winemaker** Peter Orr
Est. 2001 **Dozens** 1500 **Vyds** 1.2ha
Banca Ridge was an initiative of the Stanthorpe State High School, which has established the first commercial school winery in Qld. It has 0.5ha each of marsanne and merlot, and students are involved in all stages of the grape growing and winemaking process under the direction of Peter Orr. More recently the business has become part of the Queensland College of Wine Tourism, designed to train students in the wine, hospitality and tourism industry, and the wines produced are a credit to the school and the program. (JH)

ΨΨΨΨΩ **Petit Verdot 2019, Granite Belt** The endurance and confidence of petit verdot stands up to 24 months in new and old oak barrels so very much better than its counterparts here. With signature depth of colour and a compact core of impressive blackcurrant, blackberry and cassis fruit, it's destined to age, thanks equally to finely coiled tannins and bright acid line. While too many Queensland wines are overpriced, there's great value here from Queensland College of Wine Tourism. Screw cap. 14% alc. RATING 90 DRINK 2026-2031 $25 TS

Bangor Vineyard

20 Blackman Bay Road, Dunalley, Tas 7177 **Region** Southern Tasmania
T 0418 594 362 **www.**bangorshed.com.au **Open** 7 days 11–5 **Winemaker** Tasmanian Vintners **Viticulturist** Matt Dunbabin **Est.** 2010 **Dozens** 2000 **Vyds** 4ha
Bangor Vineyard's story starts in 1830 and has seen 5 generations of farming. Today it is a 6200ha property on the Forestier Peninsula in Tasmania, with 5100ha of native forest, grasslands and wetlands, and 35km of coastline. Both Matt and Vanessa Dunbabin have PhDs in plant ecology and plant nutrition, putting beyond question their ability to protect this wonderful property – until 2000ha were burnt in the '13 bushfires that devastated their local town of Dunalley and surrounding areas. They established a cellar door in partnership with Tom and Alice Gray from Fulham Aquaculture, also badly affected by the fires, and the Bangor Vineyard Shed was born. The vineyard is planted to 1.5ha each of pinot noir and pinot gris, and 1ha of chardonnay. (JH)

Jimmy's Hill Barrel Aged Gris 2020, Tasmania This site produces gris with the structure and body to handle wild fermentation and 10 months' maturation on lees in large-format French oak barrels. This builds a creamy texture that sits neatly in the presence of cool-season acidity and fine, toned phenolic structure. The spice and vanilla cream of French oak are well matched to the signature ripe pear flavours of gris, and only ask for a little longer in bottle to unite. Screw cap. 14% alc. RATING 93 DRINK 2023-2024 $49 TS
Jimmy's Hill Pinot Gris 2021, Tasmania Fleshy, spicy, ripe pears and almost-ripe apricots define an accurate and generous gris. The bright acidity of a cool season in a cool site keeps things energised, nicely supported by well-gauged phenolic bite. Screw cap. 14% alc. RATING 92 DRINK 2022-2022 $34 TS

Lagoon Bay Riesling 2021, Tasmania RATING 89 DRINK 2022-2022 $36 TS
Reserve Chardonnay 2019, Tasmania RATING 89 DRINK 2026-2032 $75 TS
Maria Pinot Rosé 2021, Tasmania RATING 88 DRINK 2022-2022 $38 TS

Banks Road

600 Banks Road, Marcus Hill, Vic 3222 **Region** Geelong
T 0455 594 391 **www.**banksroad.com.au **Open** Fri–Sun 11–5 **Winemaker** William Derham **Est.** 2001 **Dozens** 2000 **Vyds** 6ha
Banks Road is a family-owned and operated winery on the Bellarine Peninsula. The estate vineyard is adopting biodynamic principles, eliminating the use of insecticides and moving to eliminate the use of all chemicals on the land. The winery not only processes the Banks Road grapes, but also makes wine for other small producers in the area. All in all, an impressive business. (JH)

Soho Road Vineyard Bellarine Peninsula Pinot Noir 2019, Geelong
Speaks of its cool maritime home with its fine features, linear line and drive, not to mention a light saline, rock–pool quality. Lots of red and black cherry, wild plum notes surrounded by a forest of briar, undergrowth and bracken. Palate is taut with sinewy tannins and cherry, dark chocolate, pepper and vanilla. Spicy kick to close. Screw cap. 12.8% alc. RATING 95 DRINK 2021-2027 $44 JP
Soho Road Vineyard Barrique Eight Bellarine Peninsula Pinot Noir 2019, Geelong A walk into the forest. Smell the undergrowth, the earth, the autumnal leaves wrapped around black cherry, dark chocolate and pepper. That pepperiness brings real spark to the palate, helping to raise the profile and energy of the wine. Well-managed oak is totally integrated. This has so much to give. Screw cap. 13.3% alc. RATING 95 DRINK 2021-2029 $75 JP
CS Wine Co Shiraz 2019, Heathcote Sourced from the Greenstone Vineyard and arrives in typical Heathcote deep purple hues. There's an elegance here, real

poise with a touch of whole-bunch-driven lifted aromas of dried herbs and violet mingling with black fruits, anise and cassia bark. The palate is fully integrated, framed in background vanillin oak. Finishes clean, long. A stunner for the price. Screw cap. 13.5% alc. RATING 94 DRINK 2021-2032 $28 JP ✪

Will's Selection Bellarine Peninsula Chardonnay 2018, Geelong Nicely delivered complex chardonnay, with some bottle age, that allows the full expression to be revealed. White nectarine, melon, pithy grapefruit and barrel-fermented nutty, nougat savouriness. Smooth and even textural ride on the palate, with a long finish. A study in concentration. Screw cap. 12.8% alc. RATING 94 DRINK 2021-2027 $60 JP

♥♥♥♥♀ **Bellarine Pinot Noir 2019, Geelong** RATING 92 DRINK 2021-2025 $38 JP
Will's Selection Bellarine Peninsula Pinot Noir 2019, Geelong RATING 92 DRINK 2021-2027 $60 JP
Bellarine Pinot Gris 2021, Geelong RATING 90 DRINK 2021-2025 $32 JP
Bellarine Chardonnay 2018, Geelong RATING 90 DRINK 2021-2026 $38 JP

Bannockburn Vineyards ★★★★★

92 Kelly Lane, Bannockburn, Vic 3331 **Region** Geelong
T (03) 5281 1363 **www.**bannockburnvineyards.com **Open** By appt
Winemaker Matthew Holmes **Viticulturist** Lucas Grigsby **Est.** 1974 **Dozens** 6000
Vyds 21.2ha
The late Stuart Hooper had a deep love for the wines of Burgundy, and was able to drink the best. When he established Bannockburn, it was inevitable that pinot noir and chardonnay would form the major part of the plantings, with lesser amounts of riesling, sauvignon blanc, cabernet sauvignon, shiraz and merlot. Bannockburn is still owned by members of the Hooper family, who continue to respect Stuart's strong belief in making wines that reflect the flavours of the certified organic vineyard. Exports to Canada, Hong Kong, Japan, Singapore and the UK. (JH)

♥♥♥♥♥ **S.R.H. 2019, Geelong** A superbly balanced wine, the fruit foremost, effortlessly holding its graceful line and length, and perfect to drink tonight or in a decade. Screw cap. 13.8% alc. RATING 98 DRINK 2022-2034 $77 JH ✪

De La Terre 2019, Geelong Typically powerful and complex, with dark fruits that have made light work of the oak, but haven't moved out of primary mode. Will cruise along the next 15–20 years, as the savoury, forest floor and spice notes develop in a leisurely fashion. Screw cap. 13.3% alc. RATING 97 DRINK 2022-2034 $67 JH ✪

Serré 2019, Geelong Serré is French for 'tightly packed' and refers to the close-planted block of pinot noir, planted in '84 and certified organic. Love the delicacy on display here, the slow creep of florals, red berries, leaf, sage and spice that work their way deep into the senses. And so smooth. Textbook tannin integration and a long, floating finish caps off this most complete wine. Screw cap. 12.9% alc. RATING 97 DRINK 2021-2029 $95 JP ✪ ♥

♥♥♥♥♥ **S.R.H. 2021, Geelong** Superlative Geelong chardonnay! The long, cool '21 season has brought something extra to S.R.H., a multitude of layers of flavour and depth – more than usual – that so impresses. Keeps trim while exploring nectarine, peach, mango skin, baked apple, citrus, honeysuckle with lemon butter and nougat. Good, honest energy throughout. And the taste stays with you a long, long time. Screw cap. 13.5% alc. RATING 96 DRINK 2022-2033 $89 JP

Sauvignon Blanc 2018, Geelong Made in 3 batches of equal size: the first fermented on skins, the second in French oak, the last fermented in tank. Unsurprisingly providing a wine of power and length. Grapefruit hits a high note on the finish and aftertaste, the texture is also very important. Screw cap. 13% alc. RATING 96 DRINK 2021-2028 $30 JH ✪

Pinot Noir 2021, Geelong A wine of real gravitas and presence, the '21 reflects a most impressive year. Abundant, enticing aromas in pristine red fruits, maritime herbs, humus and dusty beets. The palate fairly bristles in fruit freshness and energy, the tannins pricking the tastebuds and laying the foundation for a long life. Oak? Yes, it's evident in the texture and the binding but totally integrated. Screw cap. 13.5% alc. RATING 95 DRINK 2022-2033 $69 JP

Chardonnay 2021, Geelong True to the Bannockburn style, which offers both power and finesse. The former is set in structure and solid in body. The latter is all about a world of marvellous fruit and oak flavours: mandarin skin, nectarine, white peach, buttered toast, almond bread, quince paste. It's dense, lifted by a citrusy acidity that is just so cleansing, so right. Screw cap. 13.4% alc. RATING 95 DRINK 2022-2031 $69 JP

Grigsby Chardonnay 2021, Geelong Named in honour of veteran viticulturist Lucas Grigsby, this is the first release from Bannockburn's close-planted chardonnay block. Well composed and compact, Grisgby combines a creamy textural mouthfeel with a world of intense citrus, nectarine and almond skin, with a clean cut of tart quince to finish. Works the tastebuds in all directions before closing in tight and long. Screw cap. 13% alc. RATING 95 DRINK 2022-2031 $79 JP

Pinot Noir 2019, Geelong The fruit powers through, led by black cherry and red plum with violets, dried flowers and herbs. All combine beautifully on the palate, woven tight by fine tannins. This is a solid youngster with the kind of force of fruit intensity that we normally associate with the maker. Screw cap. 13.5% alc. RATING 95 DRINK 2021-2029 $67 JP

Shiraz 2018, Geelong A powerful wine that needs more time in bottle, and will richly repay patience. Screw cap. 14.2% alc. RATING 94 DRINK 2022-2035 $46 JH

S.R.H. 2018, Geelong Arrives fully formed, with a budding complexity that will only engage the drinker more with age. Brings Geelong's chardonnay strengths to the bouquet with a depth of stone fruits, citrus and a light herbal interlude. Warm, textural and toasty in the mouth with melon, nectarine and baked bread. The presence of acidity is noted, but never obvious. Screw cap. 13.1% alc. RATING 94 DRINK 2021-2030 $77 JP

Douglas 2017, Geelong An 82/11/7% blend of cabernet sauvignon/ shiraz/merlot. Reflects the cool vintage, fresh and lively, and has the balance for prolonged cellaring. How it will be assessed isn't easy to predict, it's very savoury but not green or unripe. Screw cap. 13.7% alc. RATING 94 DRINK 2022-2037 $35 JH

Barmah Park Wines   ★★★☆

945 Moorooduc Road, Moorooduc, Vic 3933 **Region** Mornington Peninsula
T (03) 5978 8049 **www.**barmahparkwines.com.au **Open** Wed–Sun 11–5
Winemaker Richard McIntyre, Jeremy Magyar, Han Tao Lau **Est.** 2000 **Dozens** 5000
Vyds 2.75ha
Barmah Park has plantings of pinot gris and pinot noir (using clones MV6 and G5V15), producing wines under the Arthurs Seat, Lighthouse and Vintage labels. The restaurant overlooks the vines and offers breakfast and lunch, as well as dinner on weekends. Exports to Asia. (JH)

🍷🍷🍷🍷🍷 **The Vintage Year Shiraz 2017, Barossa Valley** Inky black plum and blackberry fruit aromas with hints of licorice, spice box, dark chocolate, dill, bay leaf, espresso and oak spice. Impressive fruit-weight on display and the oak ratchets up a little on the palate, finishing flush with black fruits, baking spice and cedary nuance. Concentrated and impressive. Screw cap. 16.1% alc. RATING 93 DRINK 2021-2032 $118 DB

🍷🍷🍷🍷 **The Vintage Year Pinot Noir 2018, Mornington Peninsula** RATING 88 DRINK 2021-2025 $85 JF

Barossa Boy Wines

Underground Barossa, 161 Murray Street, Tanunda, SA 5382 **Region** Barossa Valley
T (08) 8563 7550 **www.**barossaboywines.com.au **Open** Mon–Fri 10–4, Sat 10–1
Winemaker Trent Burge **Est.** 2016 **Dozens** 3500

Sixth-generation Barossan, Trent Burge is the son of Grant and Helen Burge, and a self-styled country boy who liked nothing better than exploring the family's 356ha of vineyards spread across the Barossa. In '06 he joined the Grant Burge business, learning every facet of winemaking and marketing. In Feb '16, Accolade acquired the Grant Burge business, making it inevitable that Trent would strike out on his own. The slick website, the high-quality labelling and packaging of his Barossa Boy Wines bear witness to his marketing experience. His grapes come from vineyards in special sites across the Barossa and Eden valleys, and it's a fair bet the family vineyards play a large role in that. Exports to the UK, Canada, Singapore and South Korea. (JH)

♀♀♀♀♀ Cheeky Tilly Riesling 2021, Eden Valley Crisp, refreshing drinking from the uniformly excellent 2021 Eden Valley vintage. Aromas of freshly squeezed lime, lemon and grapefruit juice with hints of wet stone, almond paste, orange blossom and citrus zest. These characters transpose neatly onto the palate, which shows excellent clarity and drive with a distinct mineral-like pulse. Screw cap. 12% alc. RATING 90 DRINK 2021–2028 $30 DB

Young Wisdom Mataro 2019, Barossa Subdued plummy fruit notes with hints of spice, earth, blueberry pie, licorice and French oak. These characters transpose neatly onto the palate, which is flush with spicy plum and earthy notes. Tannins are fine and sandy and there's a nice savoury shape to the finish. Diam. 15.5% alc. RATING 90 DRINK 2021–2028 $50 DB

Double Trouble Shiraz Cabernet Sauvignon 2018, Barossa 55/45% shiraz/cabernet. Fruit characters of satsuma plum, raspberry and red cherry with hints of cocoa powder, cedar, licorice and tobacco leaf. There's a nice savoury elegance on the palate, tight powdery tannins and a dark- and red-fruited spice trail on the exit. Screw cap. 14.5% alc. RATING 90 DRINK 2021–2028 $30 DB

Barr-Eden Estate

PO Box 117, Nuriootpa, SA 5355 **Region** Barossa Valley
T 0437 091 277 **www.**loveovergold.com.au **Winemaker** Contract **Est.** 2014
Dozens 400 **Vyds** 6.25ha

Loved by all who knew him, the late Bob McLean stood large over many parts of the SA wine industry and in '97 he purchased a block of shiraz in the Eden Valley. He was a friend of Joel Matschoss, who looked after the vineyard in the last years of Bob's life. In '14 Joel showed the fruit to Pierre-Henri Morel, newly arrived from the Northern Rhône Valley, where he had been Michel Chapoutier's right-hand man. Pierre-Henri was so impressed, he and Joel purchased the fruit, vinified it and the Love Over Gold label was born. A joint venture followed between Joel, Pierre-Henri, Michael Twelftree and Tim Hower to acquire the property with plans to grow. Exports to the UK, the US, Canada, France, South Korea and Singapore. (JH)

♀♀♀♀♀ Avenue to Gold Mengler's Hill Shiraz 2018, Eden Valley Wonderfully high-toned and detailed aromatics with tight dark and red plum and cherry fruit encased in spice and stone. There's a sense of space to the palate; fine yet plush, powdery tannins and bright high-country acidity pulsing through the wine, finishing savoury and pure. Diam. 13.8% alc. RATING 94 DRINK 2021–2031 $70 DB

Barrgowan Vineyard

30 Pax Parade, Curlewis, Vic 3222 **Region** Geelong
T (03) 5250 3861 **www.**barrgowanvineyard.com.au **Open** By appt **Winemaker** Dick Simonsen **Est.** 1998 **Dozens** 150 **Vyds** 0.2ha

Dick and Dib (Elizabeth) Simonsen began planting their shiraz (with 5 clones) in 1994, intending to make wine for their own consumption. With all clones in full production, the Simonsens make a maximum of 200 dozen and accordingly release small quantities of Shiraz, which sell out quickly. The vines are hand pruned, the grapes hand picked, the must basket pressed, and all wine movements are by gravity. (JH)

🍷🍷🍷🍷🍷 **Simonsens Bellarine Peninsula Shiraz 2020, Geelong** Registers immediately as cool-climate shiraz. That scent of blackberries and blue fruits; and the light dusting of aniseed, black pepper and dried herbs gives it away. Concentrated, complex fruit shines on the palate, the work of 27yo vines. That pepperiness first noted on the nose builds, making a distinctive and attractive feature on the palate, too, in tandem with grainy tannins and a background of woodsy spice and warm oak. Diam. 13.4% alc. RATING 91 DRINK 2021–2027 $35 JP

Barringwood

60 Gillams Road, Lower Barrington, Tas 7306 **Region** Northern Tasmania
T 0416 017 475 **www.**barringwood.com.au **Winemaker** Josef Chromy Wines
(Jeremy Dineen) **Est.** 1993 **Dozens** 3000 **Vyds** 5ha
Barringwood has been producing elegant wines from the ultra-cool climate of northwest Tasmania for over 20 years, the vines planted in 1993. The vineyard is perched on a steep north-facing slope (overlooking the Don valley across to Bass Strait), with one of the longest growing seasons in Tasmania allowing the grapes time to develop complexity while retaining acidity. Vanessa and Neil Bagot were captivated by the property and purchased Barringwood in 2012. They have developed 2 new vineyards at Cranbrook and Evandale, with further plantings planned. (JH)

🍷🍷🍷🍷🍷 **Mill Block Pinot Noir 2020, Tasmania** There's a cool elegance and restraint to Tasmania's northwest that is beautifully articulated here. By contrast to the Estate Pinot, more vine age is well met by more whole bunches and more new oak, yet both are played with classic Jeremy Dineen discernment, leaving the stage to beautifully tangy, bright, elegant red fruits that carry with impressive persistence, silky structure and effortless harmony. Screw cap. 12.1% alc. RATING 93 DRINK 2025–2032 $60 TS

Schönburger 2021, Tasmania Impressively varietal and characterful, this is a flamboyant schönburger, brimming with signature musk and rosewater. The palate is eminently fleshy and fruity, with fruit sweetness nicely countered by just the right edge of phenolic bite. Lovers of gewürztraminer, give this a whirl with Asian fusion. Screw cap. 13.5% alc. RATING 91 DRINK 2021–2021 $30 TS

Estate Pinot Noir 2020, Tasmania A full 2.7% lower in alcohol than the '19, and all the finer for it; an elegant, pale, lunchtime pinot of pretty strawberry and red cherry fruit. Fine fruit and oak tannins are well played to bring structure to a short finish. Restrained winemaking makes no attempt to push above the weight of the fruit – bravo. Value. Screw cap. 12% alc. RATING 91 DRINK 2021–2024 $38 TS

Pinot Gris 2021, Tasmania By stark contrast to the grigio-esque elegance of its predecessor, this is a true gris: ripe, rich, oily, powerful and loaded with signature, spicy pear. Phenolics rise to the occasion, bringing both control and bite to a long finish. No lack of character, though at the expense of grace and harmony. Screw cap. 13.5% alc. RATING 90 DRINK 2021–2021 $36 TS

Grazier's Pinot Noir 2020, Tasmania Whole bunches (18%) and oak have been carefully played to leave the main game to tangy, spicy berry fruits. Bright acidity and fine, firm tannins promise potential. $60 is a lot to pay for the fruit of 4yo vines, and this lacks the persistence and seamlessness that come with vine maturity, but nonetheless it's well executed and inherently balanced. Screw cap. 12% alc. RATING 90 DRINK 2024–2030 $60 TS

🍷🍷🍷🍷 **Méthode Traditionelle Cuvée NV, Tasmania** RATING 89 $35 TS
Riesling 2021, Tasmania RATING 89 DRINK 2021–2024 $34 TS

Barristers Block Premium Wines

141 Onkaparinga Valley Road, Woodside, SA 5244 **Region** Adelaide Hills
T (08) 8389 7706 **www.**barristersblock.com.au **Open** 7 days 10.30–5
Winemaker Lodestone Winery **Viticulturist** Lachlan Allen **Est.** 2002 **Dozens** 12 000
Vyds 40ha
Owner Jan Siemelink-Allen has over 20 years in the industry, first as a grapegrower of 10ha
of cabernet sauvignon and shiraz in Wrattonbully, then as a wine producer from that region.
In '06 she and her family purchased a 8ha vineyard planted to sauvignon blanc and pinot noir
near Woodside in the Adelaide Hills. Exports to Japan and Malaysia. (JH)

Limited Release The Bully Shiraz 2019, Wrattonbully Wrattonbully enjoys
similar tannin profiles to neighbouring Coonawarra, and they are on show here,
bringing firm structure in support of some flavoursome black fruits, plums and
spicy oak. A tight package. Screw cap. 14.6% alc. RATING 92 DRINK 2022-2028
$42 JP
JP Shiraz 2019, Wrattonbully A very tidy wine. Not a step out of place as
it delivers a very strong argument for the excitement factor that is Wrattonbully
shiraz. Bramble, bracken, blackberry, blueberry, licorice, chocolate and a hint
of peppermint. Touches on the odd savoury note as it travels across the palate.
Integrated oak joins with supple tannins to close. Darn good! Diam. 14.5% alc.
RATING 92 DRINK 2022-2033 $99 JP
Cabernet Sauvignon 2019, Wrattonbully A deep, dark coloured cabernet
with what we might call brooding (aka contemplative) qualities, especially over
a medium-rare steak, such is the pronounced tannin focus. Loamy earth, leather,
cassis, plums and sweetly spiced oak all play their part, too. Screw cap. 14.5% alc.
RATING 91 DRINK 2022-2029 $36 JP
Limited Release Aston Fiano 2021, Langhorne Creek Frisky, fresh and
citrus zesty, you don't see a lot of fiano from this part of the world but it works
very well. Citrus, wild herb notes and spiced apple provide lift. The palate is crisp,
even and juicy, with developing mealy texture and citrus zing to finish. Screw cap.
12.8% alc. RATING 90 DRINK 2021-2024 $32 JP
**Poetic Justice Tempranillo Shiraz Cabernet Sauvignon 2020, South
Australia** A brash young red with tempranillo the interloper on the great Aussie
red blend. Nevertheless, the 3 grapes hit it off, bringing black fruits, blueberries,
spice, anise and all the good bits in their personalities to bear, while cabernet
brings the tannic grunt. A great success with pizza, I'm sure. Screw cap. 14% alc.
RATING 90 DRINK 2022-2025 $26 JP
Limited Release Chardonnay 2020, Adelaide Hills The Barristers Block
vineyard was burnt out during the disastrous Dec '19 Cudlee Creek bushfire. A
major donation of fruit from Mark Joyce is how this wine came about, and it is
dedicated to him. Fresh, bright chardonnay driven by ripe fruit, with plenty of
peach, pear, nectarine and lemon curd. A light flintiness lifts the palate, contributing
to an emerging complexity. Sensitive oak handling with creamy nougat works the
palate through to the finish. Screw cap. 13.8% alc. RATING 90 DRINK 2021-2025
$32 JP

Poetic Justice Blush Sparkling Pinot Noir 2021, Adelaide Hills RATING 89
$26 JP
Legally Red Limited Release Sparkling Shiraz 2019, Wrattonbully
RATING 89 $26 JP
Poetic Justice Charlize Rosé 2021, Adelaide Hills RATING 89
DRINK 2021-2024 $26 JP
Poetic Justice Pinot Gris 2021, Adelaide Hills RATING 89
DRINK 2021-2024 $26 JP
Poetic Justice Sauvignon Blanc 2021, Adelaide Hills RATING 89
DRINK 2021-2025 $26 JP
The JP Cabernet Sauvignon 2019, Wrattonbully RATING 89
DRINK 2023-2032 $99 JP

Limited Release Riesling 2021, Adelaide Hills RATING 88 DRINK 2022-2025 $32 JP
Limited Release Tempranillo 2019, Adelaide Hills RATING 88 DRINK 2022-2025 $36 JP

Barwon Ridge Wines ★★★★

50 McMullans Road, Barrabool, Vic 3221 **Region** Geelong
T 0418 324 632 **www.**barwonridge.com.au **Open** w'ends, public hols & by appt
Winemaker Jack Rabbit Vineyard (Nyall Condon) **Est.** 1999 **Dozens** 900 **Vyds** 3.6ha
In 1999 Geoff and Joan Anson planted chardonnay, shiraz and marsanne at Barwon Ridge, the vines growing slowly in the limestone soil. The vineyard nestles in the Barrabool Hills, just to the west of Geelong. Geoff and Joan focus on producing premium fruit; the vineyard is now planted to pinot noir, pinot meunier, shiraz, cabernet sauvignon, marsanne and chardonnay. The wines are made at Leura Park. The vineyard is part of the re-emergence of winemaking in the Barrabool Hills, after the area's first boom from the 1840s to the '80s. The well-written website contains a wealth of information about the history of the region. (JH)

ŸŸŸŸŸ Marsanne 2013, Geelong Cellar release. Hitting its straps and looking good, marsanne with bottle age can be exciting and complex. Vivid honeysuckle, peach, apricot and toast aromas. Luxuriant to taste, just flows effortlessly, a meld of still juicy natural acidity and warm-hearted, spiced fruit through to a long, gentle finish. Quite delicious. Screw cap. 12.8% alc. RATING 93 DRINK 2021-2025 $40 JP
Cabernet Shiraz 2018, Geelong Hand-picked 50/50% cabernet sauvignon/shiraz, wild fermented in French oak then matured a further 6 months. You don't see a lot of cabernet shiraz blends from Geelong. This gives food for thought, with its blackcurrant, sage, mint and well-managed oak. Keeps to a tidy, medium-bodied frame, but it shows plenty of energy in ripe fruit and spice as it works its way across the palate. A very satisfying combo. Screw cap. 14.3% alc. RATING 90 DRINK 2021-2026 $40 JP

ŸŸŸŸ Pinot Noir 2018, Geelong RATING 89 DRINK 2021-2025 $40 JP
Joan's Sparkling Rosé Chardonnay Pinot Noir Pinot Meunier NV, Geelong RATING 88 $40 JP

Bass Phillip ★★★★★

16 Hunts Road, Leongatha South, Vic 3953 **Region** Gippsland
T (03) 5664 3366 **www.**bassphillip.com **Open** By appt **Winemaker** Jean-Marie Fourrier, John Durham **Est.** 1979 **Dozens** 1500 **Vyds** 11ha
Phillip Jones handcrafted tiny quantities of superlative pinot noir which, at its best, had no equal in Australia. Painstaking site selection, ultra-close vine spacing and the very cool climate of South Gippsland are the keys to the magic of Bass Phillip and its eerily Burgundian pinots. One of Australia's greatest small producers, they are heading down a new path after Jones sold the assets (winery, stock and 14ha of vineyards) in May 2020 to a syndicate led by Burgundian winemaker Jean-Marie Fourrier (who has known Jones for 14 years) and 2 Singaporeans who already have lucrative wine businesses. (JH)

ŸŸŸŸŸ Premium Old Vines Pinot Noir 2020, Gippsland A best-barrel selection. It's a sterling wine. Incredibly savoury with charcuterie, dried herbs and wafts of earth and autumn leaves with the oak both etched into and bolstering the palate. Fuller bodied but not weighty. This feels quite effortless, as the plush tannins and refreshing acidity work towards a lingering, very long finish. Quite a beauty. Cork. 14.2% alc. RATING 97 DRINK 2022-2040 $250 JF ❤

ŸŸŸŸŸ Estate Chardonnay 2020, Gippsland Such incredible depth and drive as it shows off its flinty sulphides, smoky oak and leesy flavours with aplomb. There's also stone fruit and Meyer lemon, ginger spice and more. The acidity keeps this buoyant and lively. Great definition across the palate, savoury and moreish. An excellent Estate Chardonnay. Screw cap. 13% alc. RATING 96 DRINK 2022-2030 $82 JF

Estate Pinot Noir 2020, Gippsland Striking aromatics set the scene: a heady mix of florals, forest floor, blood orange and spiced cherries. The palate unfurls with a core of sweet-savoury flavours from fruit and oak, fine tannins and everything superbly integrated and aligned. There's complexity, detail and definition all in one. Screw cap. 14.2% alc. RATING 96 DRINK 2022-2036 $98 JF

Premium Old Vines Chardonnay 2020, Gippsland While the Estate has a tighter profile and is mouth-watering, this has more complexity and richness. A touch of flinty, moreish sulphides is infused into the stone-fruit and citrus accents, with nougat. Layers of flavour, with the spicy oak beautifully integrated and adding to its profile and structure. Full bodied yet contained, with fresh acidity throughout. Screw cap. 13.4% alc. RATING 96 DRINK 2022-2030 $106 JF

Bass River Winery ★★★★

1835 Dalyston Glen Forbes Road, Glen Forbes, Vic 3990 **Region** Gippsland
T (03) 5678 8252 **www.**bassriverwinery.com **Open** Thurs–Tues 10–5 **Winemaker** Frank Butera **Viticulturist** Pasquale Butera, Frank Butera **Est.** 1998 **Dozens** 1500 **Vyds** 6ha
The Butera family's 44ha property supports grass-fed beef and olive groves as well as viticulture. Pinot noir, chardonnay, riesling, merlot and cabernet were first planted here in 1998. Both the winemaking and viticulture are handled by father-and-son team Pasquale and Frank. The small production is principally sold through the cellar door, with some retailers and restaurants in the South Gippsland area. Exports to Japan and the UK. (JH)

🍷🍷🍷🍷🍷 **1835 Vintage Brut Chardonnay Pinot Noir 2017, Gippsland** A 50/50 split between the varieties and disgorged Feb '21. A well-balanced, delicious outcome with an appley and citrus freshness matched to the richer, more complex flavours of bottle age from buttered toast and creamed honey. A good food fizz, rather than an aperitif. Diam. 12.5% alc. RATING 93 $45 JF

Single Vineyard Rosé 2020, Gippsland An equal blend of pinots noir, meunier and gris with the latter barrel fermented. The result is a delightfully refreshing, tangy and dry drink. Flavours of watermelon and pink cherries with cranberry tartness and a dusting of spice seal the deal. Screw cap. 12% alc. RATING 90 DRINK 2021-2022 $25 JF

1835 Pinot Noir 2020, Gippsland A paler hue and lighter structure this vintage yet it offers immediate appeal and drinkability. Hints of strawberries and musk, cranberries and warm spices that lead onto the palate. Supple tannins and refreshing acidity make this good drinking in the short term. Screw cap. 13% alc. RATING 90 DRINK 2021-2025 $50 JF

🍷🍷🍷🍷 **1835 Chardonnay 2020, Gippsland** RATING 88 DRINK 2021-2026 $40 JF

Battle of Bosworth ★★★★

92 Gaffney Road, Willunga, SA 5172 **Region** McLaren Vale
T (08) 8556 2441 **www.**battleofbosworth.com.au **Open** 7 days 11–5 **Winemaker** Joch Bosworth **Est.** 1996 **Dozens** 15 000 **Vyds** 80ha
Owned and run by Joch Bosworth (viticulture and winemaking) and partner Louise Hemsley-Smith (sales and marketing), this winery takes its name from the battle that ended the War of the Roses, fought on Bosworth Field in 1485. The vineyards were established in the early '70s in the foothills of the Mount Lofty Ranges. The vines are fully certified A-grade organic. The label depicts the yellow soursob (Oxalis pes-caprae), whose growth habits make it an ideal weapon for battling weeds in organic viticulture. Shiraz, cabernet sauvignon and chardonnay account for 75% of the plantings. The Spring Seed Wine Co wines are made from estate vineyards. Exports to the UK, the US, Canada, Sweden, Norway, Belgium, Hong Kong and Japan. (JH)

🍷🍷🍷🍷🍷 **Puritan Shiraz 2021, McLaren Vale** While these sort of pulpy, whole-berry, gently extracted wines are now ubiquitous here, this address was one of the first to craft them well. Violet. Iodine parlayed as dried nori. Blueberry. Pepper and clove and star anise. The finish long, while crackling across the palate with a contagious energy. Juicy and beautifully articulated. This vintage, this stellar effort, is the prototype for zero-preservative shiraz. Screw cap. 14.5% alc. RATING 93 DRINK 2021-2023 $22 NG ✪

Heretic 2020, McLaren Vale Touriga, graciano, shiraz. An example of why one blends touriga, despite its velocity, aromatic presence and spicy verve. Lovely drinking. White peppercorn, violet, blue and red fruits and pastrami. The tannins, gritty, savoury and nicely shaped. The finish long and pointed, in search of food. Screw cap. 13.5% alc. RATING 93 DRINK 2021-2027 $28 NG

White Boar 2018, McLaren Vale A much fresher and more intuitive range of wines than in the past, here. This full-weighted expression, no exception. Malty oak. Darker fruit, with no jamminess or excess. Pepper grind, clove and a spurt of tangy acidity across the finish. Vinosity and fine intensity across the mid palate. Sits somewhere between a richer old-school wine and a more exuberant contemporary expression, without the aromatic electricity. A bit stolid. Screw cap. 14.5% alc. RATING 93 DRINK 2021-2028 $45 NG

Chardonnay 2021, McLaren Vale Good drinking. Plays a flinty mineral chord, offsetting the Vale's inclination towards riper fruit, from canned peach to dried mango. The oak, nestled nicely. Mid weighted and juicy across the mid palate. The finish boasts tension and flare, as much as an ease of approachability. A foil for those who seek ample flavour, as much a vehicle for those pinning for freshness and linearity. Well done. Screw cap. 13% alc. RATING 92 DRINK 2021-2026 $25 NG ✪

Best of Vintage 2019, McLaren Vale 70/30% petit verdot/shiraz. Opaque. Presumably the intent is to impart some ferrous mettle to the warm-climate fleshiness of shiraz. Idiosyncratic. Bitter chocolate/vanilla/cedar oak dominates the nose. A slick of licorice strap, boysenberry, Cherry Ripe and spice. This is a rich wine. Top-heavy oak and fruit. Rustic, in a way. It packs a punch with plenty of flavour, but the second glass is not easy. Screw cap. 14% alc. RATING 92 DRINK 2021-2032 $50 NG

Shiraz 2020, McLaren Vale This address services a reliable style, sitting somewhere between a contemporary predilection for lifted aromas, a lighter touch and reductive tension; and a denser palate of dried fruits, macerated cherry and kirsch. Rich and mouth-filling, if not lacking a bit of precision. This is, however, picking straws. Screw cap. 14% alc. RATING 91 DRINK 2021-2027 $28 NG

Touriga Nacional 2020, McLaren Vale There is a reason why touriga is largely a blending agent in Portugal. There is little mid palate. Lilac, sure. Blue-fruit allusions and white pepper, yes. But otherwise? This is a delicious wine, don't get me wrong. Vibrant and very digestible. Yet it is altogether simple and best slugged with a slight chill. All said, in a zeitgeist of lighter, fresher and simpler – or at least a transition from the clunky warm-climate slugfest of excessively worked rich wines – perhaps this is the point. And a good one it is. Screw cap. 13.5% alc. RATING 91 DRINK 2021-2023 $28 NG

Battles Wine ★★★★★

77 Aitken Drive, Winthrop, WA 6150 (postal) **Region** Western Australia
T 0434 399 964 **www.**battleswine.com.au **Winemaker** Lance Parkin **Est.** 2018
Dozens 850

Battles Wine was started by friends Lance Parkin (winemaker) and Kris Ambrozkiewicz (sommelier, sales) in 2019. Parkin was a winemaker at Houghton in the Swan Valley before the sale to the Yukich family in '19, at which point the Swan Valley-based component of the Houghton team disbanded and formed their own ventures. Battles focuses on a small collection of tiny-quantity wines from a variety of regions (at this stage, Margaret River, the Great Southern and Geographe) made with great attention to detail, and vineyard provenance top of mind. Ambrozkiewicz (aka Ambro) has a longstanding and intense love of wine, paired with an impressively honed bank of wine knowledge and years of sales experience. (EL)

🍷🍷🍷🍷🍷 **Chardonnay 2021, Margaret River** This is pure and viscous. The flavour is palate staining, yet delicate – a feat in itself. Yellow peach, saline acidity, red apple skins, preserved lemons and white nectarine are packaged in a glassy, polished and crystalline casing of phenolics; the fruit and oak so seamlessly entwined as to be one. Superb. Screw cap. 13.3% alc. RATING 96 DRINK 2021-2036 $45 EL ✪

Granitis Shiraz 2020, Perth Hills The power of suggestion is strong – this is granitic, mineral, shaley and cooling. The fruit is pungently inky and intense, speaking of mulberries, raspberries, blood plums and vanilla pod. The tannins are like fine-grit sandpaper, they shape and impact the voluminous fruit and keep it all hemmed in. This is bloody and raw, like a mainline into the dirt. It's wild … but it's also compact, controlled, restrained, flowing and sleek. A svelte wine of circumstance and presence. Screw cap. 13.8% alc. RATING 96 DRINK 2021-2036 $40 EL ✪ ❤

Blendaberg 2021, Great Southern Riesling from Swinney and Whispering Hill vineyards, gewürz and pinot grigio from Swinney. With the lean citrus backbone of riesling, the lychee, rose petals and Turkish delight from the gewürz and the abundance of pears and apples from the grigio, you can guess what this may taste like. The blend is expertly judged: each variety has a voice. Plump, super-pretty, bright, textural and delicious. All good things, no? Screw cap. 12.5% alc. RATING 94 DRINK 2021-2031 $32 EL

Pinot Grigio 2021, Frankland River Fruit from the Swinney vineyard. Normally I wouldn't be so turned on by pinot grigio, but having seen this wine a few times, it is absolutely dead-centre, plum pinot grigio. Nashi pear, green apple, brine and citrus zest on the nose translates perfectly in the mouth. This is crunchy, fresh, flowery and gorgeous. It is literally like biting into a ripe pear in summer. Totally beautiful. 90 dozens only. Screw cap. 12.5% alc. RATING 94 DRINK 2021-2026 $32 EL

♟♟♟♟♟ **Riesling 2021, Great Southern** RATING 91 DRINK 2021-2031 $32 EL

Bay of Fires   ★★★★★

40 Baxters Road, Pipers River, Tas 7252 **Region** Northern Tasmania
T (03) 6382 7622 **www.**bayoffireswines.com.au **Open** Thurs–Mon 10–5 by appt
Winemaker Penny Jones **Est.** 2001

Hardys purchased its first grapes from Tasmania in '94, with the aim of further developing and refining its sparkling wines, a process that quickly gave birth to House of Arras. The next stage was the inclusion of various parcels of chardonnay from Tasmania in the '98 Eileen Hardy, then the development in '01 of the Bay of Fires brand. Under the umbrella of Accolade Wines today, Bay of Fires is home to non-vintage sparkling white and rosé, alongside impressive riesling, sauvignon blanc, pinot gris, chardonnay and pinot noir. Sourcing is with a particular focus on the Tamar, Coal and Derwent Valleys and East Coast. It shares its cellar door in Pipers River with House of Arras and Eddystone Point, offering visitors some of the most extensive masterclasses and experiences in the state. Exports to the US, Asia and NZ.

♟♟♟♟♟ **Riesling 2021, Tasmania** Long ripening in this cool season produced higher-than-average sugar levels, delivering impressive concentration and presence. This is perfectly countered with a spine of cool Tasmanian acidity that draws out a grand finish of lingering preserved lemon, Golden Delicious apple and wild honey. Body and flesh contrast the bite of ripe phenolic grip. Exemplary line and length confirm an impressive riesling with a long life before it. Screw cap. 12.9% alc. RATING 94 DRINK 2026-2031 $46 TS

♟♟♟♟♟ **Pinot Gris 2021, Tasmania** RATING 93 DRINK 2022-2022 $46 TS
Chardonnay 2020, Tasmania RATING 93 DRINK 2025-2035 $60 JH
Pinot Noir 2020, Tasmania RATING 92 DRINK 2025-2035 $61 TS
Sauvignon Blanc 2021, Tasmania RATING 91 DRINK 2022-2022 $46 TS

Bay of Shoals Wines   ★★★★☆

49 Cordes Road, Kingscote, Kangaroo Island, SA 5223 **Region** Kangaroo Island
T (08) 8553 0289 **www.**bayofshoalswines.com.au **Open** 7 days 11–5 **Winemaker** Kelvin Budarick **Est.** 1994 **Dozens** 5000 **Vyds** 15ha

John Willoughby's vineyard overlooks the Bay of Shoals, which is the northern boundary of Kingscote, Kangaroo Island's main town. Planting of the vineyard began in 1994 and it now comprises riesling, sauvignon blanc, savagnin, pinot gris, pinot noir, cabernet sauvignon and shiraz. In addition, 460 olive trees have been planted to produce table olives. (JH)

ŸŸŸŸŸ **Albariño 2021, Kangaroo Island** Don't bother searching for perfumes first up on the bouquet, for they aren't there. The palate is another matter, packed with intense flavours ranging through Granny Smith apple, blood orange and grapefruit, causing a traffic jam as each elbows their siblings, which only serves to sharpen their defences. Will stand up to every type of Asian dish. The '21 vintage magic is not to be gainsaid. Screw cap. 12% alc. RATING 95 DRINK 2021–2028 $30 JH ✪

ŸŸŸŸŸ **Shiraz 2017, Kangaroo Island** RATING 93 DRINK 2022–2033 $25 JH ✪
Sparkling Shiraz 2018, Kangaroo Island RATING 90 $38 JH

Bekkers ★★★★★

212-220 Seaview Road, McLaren Vale, SA 5171 **Region** McLaren Vale
T 0408 807 568 **www.**bekkerswine.com **Open** Thurs–Sat 10–4 or by appt
Winemaker Emmanuelle Bekkers **Viticulturist** Toby Bekkers **Est.** 2010 **Dozens** 1500
Vyds 18ha
Bekkers brings together 2 high-performing, highly experienced and highly credentialled business and life partners. Toby Bekkers graduated with an honours degree in applied science in agriculture from the University of Adelaide, and over the ensuing years has had broad-ranging responsibilities as general manager of Paxton Wines in McLaren Vale, and as a leading exponent of organic and biodynamic viticulture. Emmanuelle was born in Bandol in the south of France, and obtained 2 university degrees, in biochemistry and oenology, before working for the Hardys in the south of France, which led her to Australia and a wide-ranging career, including Chalk Hill. Exports to the UK, the US and France. (JH)

ŸŸŸŸŸ **Grenache 2020, McLaren Vale** If anybody believes that other varieties in this country can match the world-class persuasions of McLaren Vale grenache they are sorely mistaken. Here, thorough evidence. A rich wine, harnessing the riper tendencies of the vintage while promoting fragrance, a diaphanous levity to the tannic latticework and that uncanny pinosity that makes grenache like this so compelling. Svelte, dense and yet so fresh. Molten raspberry, crushed black rock, Berger spice and orange peel. A faint whiff of mescal and clove derived from the whole-bunch inclusion (20%) imbues additional savouriness. This is very fine. Screw cap. 14.5% alc. RATING 97 DRINK 2022–2030 $90 NG ✪

ŸŸŸŸŸ **Syrah 2020, McLaren Vale** As with all wines here, this is a wine of consummate class and refinement. While the grenache is the leading light, this sits comfortably in second place. Carnal spice, pepper grind, salami and blue to darker fruits are strung across a bow of saline tannic tension, rolled into a firm gristly knot. Superlative grape tannins, mind you, extracted with a confident aplomb. The oak, a mere echo. This glimpses the finest crus of the northern Rhône through the lens of the Vale. Exciting. Exceptional. Rewarding. Screw cap. 14.2% alc. RATING 96 DRINK 2022–2030 $120 NG
Syrah Grenache 2020, McLaren Vale As with all of these cuvées, the tannins maketh the wine, so tautly drawn and sanguine are they across a chest of pulpy blue fruits, bergamot, violet and clove. A trail of peppery freshness drives long. Screw cap. 14% alc. RATING 95 DRINK 2022–2029 $90 NG

Beklyn Wines ★★★

PO Box 802, Goolwa, SA 5214 **Region** Currency Creek
T 0405 189 363 **www.**beklynwines.com **Winemaker** Mark and Rebekah Shaw
Est. 2016 **Dozens** 600 **Vyds** 20ha
Mark and Rebekah Shaw's wine journey began while working in vineyards in McLaren Vale in '94. In '02 they built their first home in Currency Creek on the Fleurieu Peninsula. They

planted 10ha of shiraz, and have recently planted another 10ha. Their first wine ('16) was from purchased grapes from 3 vineyards in McLaren Vale, but in the future grapes from their estate plantings will be used. The pattern of grape growing and selling part of the production and using the remainder to make their own wines is a sensible approach. 'Beklyn' means 'pretty brook', derived from the passage of water flowing through the estate. (JH)

🍷🍷🍷🍷 **Single Vineyard Shiraz 2020, Currency Creek** Still very youthful, but has a juicy, fresh palate with a spice, plum, blackberry and licorice blend reflecting 12 months maturation in French and American oak. Should repay short cellaring. Screw cap. 14.5% alc. RATING 89 DRINK 2022-2029 $45 JH

Bellarine Estate

2270 Portarlington Road, Bellarine, Vic 3222 **Region** Geelong
T (03) 5259 3310 **www**.bellarineestate.com.au **Open** Saturday 11–4 **Winemaker** Julian Kenny **Viticulturist** Julian Kenny **Est.** 1995 **Dozens** 1500 **Vyds** 10.5ha
Established in 1996 by Peter and Lizette Kenny, Bellarine Estate is family run from the ground up. Every stage of the winemaking process, all the way to the final bottling, occurs on-site. This business runs parallel with the Bellarine Brewing Company, also situated in the winery, and the extended operating hours of Julian's Restaurant. It is a popular meeting place. The vineyard is planted to chardonnay, pinot noir, shiraz, merlot, viognier and sauvignon blanc. Exports to the US. (JH)

🍷🍷🍷🍷🍷 **First Blush Rosé 2021, Geelong** 70/20/7/3% merlot/pinot noir/ shiraz/ viognier. A co-ferment with ageing in French oak (5% new) brings a rich dimension to this coral-hued rosé. Expressive summer berry scents mix with musk and woodsy spice. Opens warmly with a strong textural bent and keeps on going. Can imagine this excellent rosé with fresh-caught prawns on the beach. Screw cap. 12% alc. RATING 95 DRINK 2022-2026 $28 JP ✪

🍷🍷🍷🍷🍷 **Two Wives Shiraz 2020, Geelong** RATING 93 DRINK 2021-2031 $38 JP
James' Paddock Chardonnay 2021, Geelong RATING 92 DRINK 2022-2026 $35 JP
Phil's Pinot Noir 2021, Geelong RATING 91 DRINK 2022-2026 $40 JP
Portarlington Ridge Chardonnay 2021, Geelong RATING 90 DRINK 2022-2026 $25 JP
James' Paddock Chardonnay 2020, Geelong RATING 90 DRINK 2021-2026 $35 JP

Bellarmine Wines

1 Balyan Retreat, Pemberton, WA 6260 **Region** Pemberton
T 0409 687 772 **www**.bellarmine.com.au **Open** By appt **Winemaker** Dr Diane Miller **Est.** 2000 **Dozens** 5000 **Vyds** 20.2ha
This vineyard is owned by German residents Dr Willi and Gudrun Schumacher. Long-term wine lovers, the Schumachers decided to establish a vineyard and winery of their own, choosing Australia partly because of its stable political climate. The vineyard is planted to riesling, pinot noir, chardonnay, shiraz, sauvignon blanc and petit verdot. The flagship wines are 3 styles of riesling – dry, off-dry and sweet. Exports to the UK, the US and Germany. (JH)

🍷🍷🍷🍷🍷 **Dry Riesling 2021, Pemberton** Super-floral, minerally nose; graphite and white pepper colour the edges of orange blossoms, fennel flower and green apple skins. On the palate the ever-present briny acidity encases the fruit and ushers it through the long, pithy finish. More powerful than it initially appears – the acidity really is the engine room in this cool vintage. Screw cap. 11.5% alc. RATING 93 DRINK 2021-2031 $27 EL ✪
Select Riesling 2021, Pemberton Orange blossom, lime flesh, white currants and spice form the beginning, middle and end of this lovely story. Drink it on a hot day or with spicy food – or both. Gorgeous. Screw cap. 8% alc. RATING 91 DRINK 2021-2031 $27 EL

Half-Dry Riesling 2021, Pemberton This is so pretty. Delicate, floral and superfine; so fine that it needs some space in order to express itself eloquently in the glass. Screw cap. 9.5% alc. RATING 90 DRINK 2021-2027 $27 EL

Bellebonne

3 Balfour Place, Launceston, Tas 7250 (postal) **Region** Northern Tasmania
T 0412 818 348 **www**.bellebonne.wine **Winemaker** Natalie Fryar **Est.** 2015
Dozens 600
Bellebonne Natalie Fryar's passion project. She spent 14 years as sparkling winemaker for Jansz, establishing herself as one of Australia's top sparkling winemakers and winning the title of 'rosé queen', while gaining an intimate knowledge of Tasmania's top sparkling sites. She crafts her elegant and sublime Bellebonne cuvées in miniscule quantities from tiny pockets of growers' vines in Tasmania's sparkling epicentre of Pipers River. To finance her first vintage flying solo, she sold a house, worked waitressing shifts and 'bought my cleaner's Ford Festiva and drove it to Tassie with my red Kelpie on the front seat.' She maintains a consulting hand in a number of Northern Tasmania's best sparklings and lends her blending skills to creating her outstanding Abel Gin. Exports to Hong Kong. (TS)

ΨΨΨΨΨ **Natalie Fryar Vintage Rosé 2019, Tasmania** Aged 2 years on lees; 7.5g/L dosage. There's a dashing elegance and coiled restraint that set '19 in a more contemplative and seductive mood than its predecessors. It's refined, toning the usual fragrant lift of Pipers' pinot back to its core of strawberry hull and red apple, opening and elevating to gorgeous red cherries in time. Barrel fermentation supports like only Nat Fryar can orchestrate, building creaminess and drawing out the finish without for a moment disrupting its elegant flow of purity. Another triumph. Diam. 12% alc. RATING 96 $83 TS

Blanc de Blancs 2015, Tasmania If there were ever an inaugural sparkling worthy of being lobbed into the market at a 3-digit price tag, this is it. It's taken more than 6 years for Natalie Fryar's first flagship to see the light of day, such is the long game of sparkling wine. A radiant, medium straw-yellow hue, it abounds in generous pineapple, Golden Delicious apple, fresh fig and preserved lemon. Six years has blessed it with brushstrokes of brioche, vanilla custard and even a hint of nutmeg. Texturally it is a marvel, at once creamy and silky, yet taut, determined and enduring. Acidity, phenolics and lees texture entwine in a complete and singular trajectory and a mesmerising finish. Enticing now, it has places to go over the coming decade, too. With this wine, Natalie transcends the moniker of 'rosé queen' to become Australia's 'sparkling queen'. Diam. 12% alc. RATING 96 $110 TS ♥

Natalie Fryar Vintage Cuvée 2018, Tasmania A luminous, pale straw hue signals elegance and tension in a cuvée that embodies incredible texture and presence. The white fruit and lemon-zest cut of chardonnay leads out, meshed with the strawberry hull and red apple of pinot; the union polished by the creamy, spicy flow of old barrels. Intricately assembled, with every detail of acidity, phenolics and dosage uniting in a seamless, enduring finish. Diam. 12% alc. RATING 95 $75 TS

Natalie Fryar Vintage Cuvée 2017, Tasmania 60/40% chardonnay/pinot noir. Spice-laden, textural, silky and refined, this is a vintage that showcases Nat Fryar's wizardry in crafting mouthfeel and finesse. Texture is the game here, delivering both creaminess and tension; toning the drive of Pipers River acidity, embracing the control of superfine phenolic grip and tactically achieving both. Apple, Beurre Bosc pear, preserved lemon and the charcuterie nuances of barrel fermentation seem more the outcome than the imperative here. Everything is held in unerring, unrelenting line and length. Bravo. Screw cap. 12% alc. RATING 95 $73 TS

Blanc de Blancs 2016, Tasmania Pineapple, fig and grapefruit meet the subtle beginnings of brioche and vanilla nougat. There's an inherent phenolic grip to this season, well embraced here by silky texture on a lingering finish. Diam. 12% alc. RATING 95 $110 TS

Bis Rosé NV, Tasmania 82/18% pinot noir/chardonnay. Wow! I loved the inaugural Bis last year and its successor is even brighter in its gorgeous, medium salmon hue, fresher in its red berry fruit allure, more lifted in its rose petal fragrance and more tangy on its energetic finish. It's at once a deeply serious, pitch-perfect snapshot of the essence of Pipers River, and at the same time effortlessly appealing and party-ready. This should be everybody's house rosé – if only there were more to go around! Just 400 dozen made. Diam. 12% alc. RATING 94 $43 TS

Bellwether

14183 Riddoch Highway, Coonawarra, SA 5263 **Region** Coonawarra
T 0417 080 945 **www**.bellwetherwines.com.au **Open** 7 days 12–4 **Winemaker** Sue Bell **Viticulturist** Mike Wetherall, Peter Bird, Nick and Heather Laycock, Ashley Ratcliff, Rob Bennett, the Chalmers family, Brett Proud **Est.** 2008 **Dozens** 2500
Underpinning Sue Bell's winemaking philosophy is the impact of climate change and the need for future classic varieties to be grown in the right regions. She works with a community of growers to showcase a diverse range including shiraz, malbec, barbera, tempranillo, riesling, chardonnay, montepulciano and nero d'Avola. In '08, Sue and business partner, Andrew Rennie, bought the historic Glen Roy shearing shed, built around 1868 and sitting on 6h of classic Aussie bush. It is now a winery and cellar door with space to host food, wine and music events. There's an extensive produce garden, a camping area and glamping, too. It's all part of her thoughtful plan to reconnect with the land sustainably and with purpose. A must visit for wine lovers. Exports to the UK and Singapore. (JF)

♥♥♥♥♥ Chardonnay 2017, Tasmania A sun-kissed hue entices, as do the florals and stone-fruit aromatics, with a waft of ginger spice. This is complex, detailed and impressive. The palate is key with its tight acid line cutting through the richness of flavours resulting in a moreish and savoury wine. Screw cap. 12.6% alc. RATING 96 DRINK 2021-2027 $70 JF ✪
Cabernet Sauvignon 2016, Coonawarra The flagship red in the range is released with bottle age and always reveals an elegance. A neat fusion of cassis and potpourri, curry leaf, ironstone and earth with a sprinkling of woodsy spices. Medium bodied as it unfurls with fine, powdery tannins and great persistence. A contemplative wine in a way, yet equally lovely to drink. Screw cap. 14% alc. RATING 96 DRINK 2021-2031 $70 JF ✪
Ant Series Malbec 2019, Wrattonbully This savoury, juicy wine impresses and entices from the very start with its noir-red hue, followed by bold aromas and flavours. It's earthy, gravelly and ferrous, yet the full-bodied palate is smooth as velvet thanks to those plush tannins. This is a sophisticated malbec. Bravo. Screw cap. 13.3% alc. RATING 95 DRINK 2022-2032 $35 JF ✪
Shiraz 2019, Wrattonbully No matter which way you look at it, this is a classy, cool-climate shiraz. The whole bunches, about 50%, accentuate its earthiness, savouriness and of course, the beautiful fruit. Licorice and baking spices plus well-integrated oak, comprising 30% new French puncheons, all add to its complexity. Fuller bodied, with ripe tannins, lively acidity and layers of detail. Screw cap. 13.1% alc. RATING 95 DRINK 2021-2032 $70 JF
Cabernet Sauvignon 2015, Coonawarra There's a purity and refinement to this vintage, with cooler characters at play, yet this is totally ripe. A core of excellent fruit, with a light infusion of twigs, bitter herbs and warming spices. It's not showy or big, which is the raison d'être of this premium wine. Instead, it has a composed, light- to medium-bodied palate with raw silk tannins, plus a vibrancy throughout. Screw cap. 13% alc. RATING 95 DRINK 2021-2030 $70 JF

♥♥♥♥♡ Ant Series Tempranillo 2020, Wrattonbully RATING 93 DRINK 2021-2028 $35 JF
Ant Series Riesling 2019, Tasmania RATING 92 DRINK 2021-2027 $35 JF
Ant Series Barbera 2020, Wrattonbully RATING 91 DRINK 2021-2026 $35 JF

Ant Series Cabernet 2018, Coonawarra RATING 91 DRINK 2023-2033
$35 JF
Ant Series Montepulciano 2020, Riverland RATING 90 DRINK 2021-2023
$35 JF
Ant Series Vermentino 2018, Heathcote RATING 90 DRINK 2021-2022
$35 JF

Ben Haines Wine

342 Rae Street, Fitzroy North, Vic 3068 (postal) **Region** Yarra Valley
T 0417 083 645 **www.**benhaineswine.com.au **Winemaker** Ben Haines **Est.** 2010
Dozens 4000
Ben Haines graduated from the University of Adelaide in 1999 with a degree in viticulture,
waiting a couple of years (immersing himself in music) before focusing on his wine career.
An early interest in terroir led to a deliberate choice of gaining experience in diverse regions
including the Yarra Valley, McLaren Vale, Adelaide Hills, Langhorne Creek, Tasmania and
Central Victoria, as well as time in the US and France. His services as a contract winemaker
are in high demand, and his name pops up all over the place. Exports to the US and Asia. (JH)

ŸŸŸŸŸ Syrah 2021, Great Western A gorgeous, bright, medium crimson-purple hue.
A wine on the 'natural' spectrum that excites from the first with its aromas of
satsuma plums, bright red cherries and white and black pepper. Even better on the
palate, this has excellent depth while remaining light on its feet at the same time.
Well-shaped and structured, this tapers into a long and satisfying finish. Note that
as a low-sulphur wine, this really needs to be opened and consumed on the same
day. Diam. 13% alc. RATING 95 DRINK 2021-2026 $40 PR

ŸŸŸŸŸ Gruyere + Tarrawarra Chardonnay 2021, Yarra Valley RATING 93
DRINK 2021-2025 $40 PR

Ben Potts Wines

The Winehouse,1509 Langhorne Creek Road, Langhorne Creek, SA 5255
Region Langhorne Creek
T (08) 8537 3029 **www.**benpottswines.com.au **Open** 7 days 10–5 **Winemaker** Ben
Potts **Est.** 2002
Ben Potts is the 6th generation to be involved in grapegrowing and winemaking in
Langhorne Creek, the first being Frank Potts, founder of Bleasdale Vineyards. Ben completed
the oenology degree at CSU, and ventured into winemaking on a commercial scale in
2002 (aged 25). Fiddle's Block Shiraz is named after great-grandfather Fiddle; Lenny's Block
Cabernet Sauvignon Malbec after grandfather Len; and Bill's Block Malbec after father Bill.
Exports to Switzerland and Singapore. (JH)

ŸŸŸŸŸ Fiddle's Block Shiraz 2019, Langhorne Creek Delicious shiraz showing
the sense of place to perfection; small red and black berry fruits on a medium-
bodied framework of spicy, savoury fruit and oak tannins; lip-smacking finish and
aftertaste. Trophy Best Shiraz at Langhorne Creek Wine Show '21. Screw cap.
14.8% alc. RATING 96 DRINK 2022-2042 $40 JH ✿
Lenny's Block Cabernet Sauvignon 2019, Langhorne Creek Bright
crimson-purple hue, promised and delivered fragrant spicy cassis flavours supported
by superfine tannins. Trophy Best Cabernet Sauvignon Langhorne Creek Wine
Show '21. Screw cap. 14.5% alc. RATING 95 DRINK 2022-2035 $40 JH

Bendbrook Wines

Section 19 Pound Road, Macclesfield, SA 5153 **Region** Adelaide Hills
T (08) 8388 9773 **www.**bendbrookwines.com.au **Open** By appt **Winemaker** Leigh
Ratzmer **Viticulturist** John Struik **Est.** 1998 **Dozens** 2500 **Vyds** 5.5ha
John and Margaret Struik have established their vineyard on either side of a significant bend
in the Angas River that runs through the property, with cabernet sauvignon on one side

and shiraz on the other. The name comes from the bend in question, which is indirectly responsible for the flood that occurs every 4–5 years. Exports to Hong Kong. (JH)

♥♥♥♥♀ SL Cabernet Sauvignon 2019, Adelaide Hills First, that name! The vineyard slope is home to a large sliding log (hence SL) which invariably heads downhill during rain events. Cool cabernet vibes aplenty here, with the scent of wild herbs a real drawcard on the bouquet: blackcurrant, plum, earth and pepper. Has the feel of the bush and eucalyptus in the glass, supported by black fruits, spice and firm grainy tannins. Linear and firm to close. Screw cap. 13.5% alc. RATING 92 DRINK 2021-2027 $28 JP

♥♥♥♥ Goat Track Shiraz 2018, Adelaide Hills RATING 88 DRINK 2021-2027 $39 JP

Bended Knee Vineyard

PO Box 334, Buninyong, Vic 3357 **Region** Ballarat
T (03) 5341 8437 **www.**bendedknee.com.au **Winemaker** Peter Roche **Viticulturist** Peter Roche, Molly Wheatland **Est.** 1999 **Dozens** 250 **Vyds** 1.5ha
Peter and Pauline Roche have 0.5ha each of chardonnay and pinot noir planted at moderately high density, and 0.25ha of ultra-close-planted pinot noir at the equivalent of 9000 vines/ha. Here 4 clones have been used: 114, 115, G5V15 and 777. The Roches say, 'We are committed to sustainable viticulture and aim to leave the planet in better shape than we found it'. Ducks, guinea fowl and chooks are vineyard custodians, and all vine canopy management is done by hand, including pruning and picking. Although production is tiny, Bended Knee wines can be found at some of Melbourne's best restaurants. (JH)

♥♥♥♥♀ Pinot Noir 2019, Western Victoria A fine follow-up to the '18, with the same lilting herbal, undergrowth attraction that is very much of its cool-climate origins. Finely balanced with redcurrant, pomegranate and cherry-musk aromas and sinewy and deceptively strong palate, with a firm anchor of tannins. Screw cap. 13.5% alc. RATING 92 DRINK 2021-2027 $40 JP

Beresford Wines

252 Blewitt Springs Road, McLaren Flat, SA 5171 **Region** McLaren Vale
T (08) 8383 0362 **www.**beresfordwines.com.au **Open** 7 days 10–5 **Winemaker** Chris Dix **Est.** 1985 **Dozens** 9000 **Vyds** 28ha
This is a sister company to Step Rd Winery in Langhorne Creek, owned and run by VOK Beverages. The estate plantings are shiraz (13ha), cabernet sauvignon (9.3ha), grenache (3ha) and chardonnay (2.7ha), but they account for only a part of the production. Some of the wines offer excellent value. Exports to the UK, Germany, Denmark, Poland, Singapore and Hong Kong. (JH)

♥♥♥♥♥ Limited Release Cabernet Sauvignon 2019, McLaren Vale Classy wine. The sort of rich expression of cabernet that the Vale does so well. Chiefly because there is no jamminess or excess, just a strident level of extract with telltale notes of dried sage, bouquet garni, tapenade and currant. Plenty of scrub, too. To be churlish, the acidity is a little shrill and the tannins, a tad aggressive. But I have faith that time in the bottle will mollify them. Screw cap. 13.8% alc. RATING 95 DRINK 2022-2035 $80 NG
Estate Cabernet Sauvignon 2019, McLaren Vale A supple, detailed, savoury and highly regional mid-weighted cab. I am surprised to read that the 14–16 months' maturation was in both French and American oak, such is the plough of pure fruits and its herbal undercarriage, from black and red currants, green olive, sage and tomato leaf. Oak-derived maltiness, too. The finish is long and toothsome. An easy segue to the second, third and fourth glass. Lovely drinking. Screw cap. 13.5% alc. RATING 94 DRINK 2022-2030 $50 NG

♥♥♥♥♀ Barrel Select G.S.M 2020, McLaren Vale RATING 92 DRINK 2022-2026 $30 NG

Classic Cabernet Sauvignon 2019, McLaren Vale RATING 92
DRINK 2022-2030 $30 NG
Estate Shiraz 2019, McLaren Vale RATING 92 DRINK 2022-2030 $50 NG

Berton Vineyard

55 Mirrool Avenue, Yenda, NSW 2681 **Region** Riverina
T (02) 6968 1600 **www.**bertonvineyards.com.au **Open** Mon–Fri 10–4, Sat
11–4 **Winemaker** James Ceccato, Bill Gumbleton, Glen Snaidero **Est.** 2004
Dozens 1.2 million **Vyds** 104ha
The Berton Vineyards partners – Bob and Cherie Berton, James Ceccato and Jamie Bennett –
have almost 100 years' combined experience in winemaking, viticulture, finance, production
and marketing. The 30ha property in the Eden Valley was acquired in '96 and the vines
planted. Wines are released under various labels: Berton Vineyards (Reserve, Winemakers
Reserve, Metal Label), Foundstone, Outback Jack and Head Over Heels. Exports to the UK,
the US, Sweden, Norway and Japan. (JH)

Bonsai Shiraz 2018, High Eden Another classically styled red that pulls few
surprises but delivers on all fronts: elevated Eden Valley violets, purple fruits, anise
and Asian five-spice. Full, plush, creamy, gently pulpy and nicely pliant, as it winds
its way along some malty oak to a long, seamless finish. Screw cap. 14.5% alc.
RATING 92 DRINK 2021-2033 $40 NG
Reserve Botrytis 2019, Riverina If seeking a high-quality sticky at an
affordable price, look no further. This is good. Dried mango, pineapple chunks,
tangerine, ginger and candied-orange zest, doused in honey, stream along febrile
acid rails. The finish, attractively bitter with a sweetness that lingers without being
cloying. Screw cap. 11% alc. RATING 92 DRINK 2021-2030 $20 NG ☻

Best's Wines

111 Best's Road, Great Western, Vic 3377 **Region** Great Western
T (03) 5356 2250 **www.**bestswines.com **Open** Mon–Sat 10–5, Sun 11–4
Winemaker Justin Purser, Jacob Parton **Viticulturist** Ben Thomson **Est.** 1866
Dozens 25 000 **Vyds** 147ha
Best's winery and vineyards date back to 1866. One of the vines planted in the Nursery Block
has defied identification and is thought to exist nowhere else in the world. The Thomson
family has owned the property since 1920. Best's consistently produces elegant, supple wines;
the Bin No. 0 is a classic, the Thomson Family Shiraz is magnificent. Very occasionally a unique
pinot meunier (with 15% pinot noir) is made solely from 1868 plantings of those 2 varieties.
Best's were awarded Wine of the Year '17 and Best Value Winery '21; in '23 they win Wine of
the Year once more. Exports to the US, Canada, Singapore, Japan and Sweden. (JH)

Riesling 2021, Great Western As ever, a very distinguished riesling, its fluid
power and the insistence of the palate results in exceptional length, crackling
minerally acidity married with lemon and lime fruit. Bargain. Screw cap. 11% alc.
RATING 96 DRINK 2021-2036 $25 JH ☻
Foudre Ferment Riesling 2021, Great Western A wine style that started
a minor revolution in Australia when it was first made, with extended skin
contact, wild fermentation and maturation on lees in foudre. Each vintage
it tingles and impresses and in a good year like '21, it excels. Jasmine florals,
bergamot, lime cordial, lemon curd and peach-skin aromas. A wine of some
complexity and nuance, featuring bright, vibrant fruits, soft mealy texture with
a hint of savouriness. Seamless and sustained. Screw cap. 11.5% alc. RATING 96
DRINK 2022-2030 $35 JP ☻ ♥
Old Vine Pinot Meunier 2021, Great Western Prepare yourself for an
exquisite beauty of a wine. It enjoys an effortless purity of fruit; from aroma to
palate there's a delicacy of concentrated red berries, pomegranate, violet, dusty
earth, underbrush and dried herbs. Superfine across the palate, almost sinewy at this
early stage, but supported by firm, focused tannins for a lot more time in bottle.
A lot more. Screw cap. 12% alc. RATING 96 DRINK 2022-2037 $125 JP ♥

Bin No. 0 Shiraz 2020, Great Western Best's celebrates old vines. Bin O is a case in point, with vines dating back to 1868 employed here to produce a stunning and elegant beauty. Bin O's signature black fruits, woody spice and violets are concentrated and deep, followed by velvety tannins that effortlessly glide over the tongue. Quite a powerful combination. Screw cap. 14% alc. RATING 96 DRINK 2022–2041 $85 JP

Young Vine Pinot Meunier 2021, Great Western Young is always a relative term at Best's – these 'young vines' were planted in '71. An English garden of arresting aromatic scents, of violets, cranberry, cherry, plum, anise and sage. As always, quietly complex and fleshy, finishing firm in the embrace of fine tannins. Welcomes more time in bottle, as long as you might have. Screw cap. 12% alc. RATING 95 DRINK 2022–2033 $35 JP ✪

LSV Shiraz Viognier 2020, Great Western A co-ferment with a small amount of viognier brings forth a complex and fragrant wine. Viognier helps lift the bouquet in violet, anise, pepper and briar with black fruits and blueberry. The palate stretches out across the palate in fine, lithe tannins. Fabulous flavour concentration and deliciousness for the price. Screw cap. 14% alc. RATING 95 DRINK 2022–2033 $35 JP ✪

Cabernet Sauvignon 2020, Great Western Delivers a nuanced interpretation of the grape, proving once again that cabernet is right at home in the Grampians. Briar, bush mint, bay leaf, bracken and earth here, a dollop of vanillin oak and concentrated black fruits there, with taut tannins laying the groundwork for a long, brilliant future. Screw cap. 14% alc. RATING 95 DRINK 2022–2035 $25 JP ✪

Cabernet Franc 2020, Great Western Light–medium bodied, but a perfumed bouquet and lissom palate with a light-fingered hand just touching the keys of the piano's tune of admirable length and finish. A rare cabernet franc; like many other growers in Victoria in '82, these vines were sold to Best's as merlot. Screw cap. 13.5% alc. RATING 95 DRINK 2021–2031 $45 JH

Thomson Family Shiraz 2020, Great Western Oozes class and elegance. Destined for a long and fruitful life, Thomson Family Shiraz embraces blackcurrant, blood plum, bramble, briar, earth and spice. Fine in features, it can be deceiving because there is a strength here, built on old vines and the gentlest of oak which allows the fruit to sing. Screw cap. 14% alc. RATING 95 DRINK 2022–2043 $250 JP

White Gravels Hill Shiraz 2020, Great Western Firm in structure, fine in detail, White Gravels Hill is bright and pristine in cherry, plum, baking spice, chocolate and earth. Almost bounces in the glass, such is the tightly focused energy. Screw cap. 13% alc. RATING 94 DRINK 2022–2033 $45 JP

Hamill Single Vineyard Shiraz 2020, Great Western A most convincing young wine with both density and concentration of ripe fruit, well managed, enhanced, by plenty of toasty oak and spice. Firm in structure, generous in ripe, cherry pip tannins, it has plenty of time on its side. Screw cap. 14% alc. RATING 94 DRINK 2022–2035 $60 JP

🍷🍷🍷🍷🍷 **Nursery Block Dry Red 2021, Great Western** RATING 93 DRINK 2022–2028 $45 JP

Pinot Noir 2021, Great Western RATING 92 DRINK 2022–2027 $25 JP ✪

Rosé 2021, Great Western RATING 92 DRINK 2022–2026 $25 JP ✪

Bin No. 1 Shiraz 2020, Great Western RATING 92 DRINK 2022–2033 $25 JP ✪

Bethany Wines   ★★★★☆

378 Bethany Road, Tanunda, SA 5352 **Region** Barossa Valley
T (08) 8563 2086 **www.**bethany.com.au **Open** Mon–Sat 10–5, Sun 1–5
Winemaker Alex MacClelland **Est.** 1981 **Dozens** 18 000 **Vyds** 38ha
The Schrapel family has been growing grapes in the Barossa Valley for over 140 years, their winery nestled high on a hillside on the site of an old bluestone quarry. Geoff and Rob Schrapel produce a range of consistently well made and attractively packaged wines. Bethany has vineyards in the Barossa and Eden Valleys. Exports to all major markets. (JH)

🍷🍷🍷🍷🍷 **East Grounds Shiraz 2019, Barossa Valley** The wines of the foothills have a 'pretty' aspect to their aromatic profiles. There is a blossomy sheen to the red and dark cherry and plum fruits here; cut with spice, fresh acid line, fine grippy tannin and a sapid, plummy plume on the finish, which trails off admirably with a pure, yet savoury palate shape. Lovely drinking and very approachable now. Screw cap. 14.5% alc. RATING 95 DRINK 2021–2035 $55 DB

GR Reserve Shiraz 2019, Barossa Valley The GR is always a step up in both fruit weight and oak influence compared to the high-toned, flighty expressions that characterise the Bethany portfolio. There is plenty of muscle and sinew on display, with rich plum and summer berry fruit, cedar oak heft, spice box and pencil-case notes, licorice and dark chocolate. Rich and pure, with just a hint of heat poking through, it's a wonderful, structured display of foothills elegance. Screw cap. 14.5% alc. RATING 94 DRINK 2021–2035 $125 DB

🍷🍷🍷🍷🍷 **Blue Quarry Single Vineyard Riesling 2021, Eden Valley** RATING 93 DRINK 2021–2028 $40 DB

Blue Quarry Barrel Select Cabernet Sauvignon 2019, Barossa Valley RATING 93 DRINK 2021–2032 $45 DB

LE Shiraz 2019, Barossa RATING 93 DRINK 2021–2031 $75 DB

First Village Rosé 2021, Barossa Valley RATING 92 DRINK 2021–2024 $25 DB ✪

Blue Quarry Barrel Select Shiraz 2019, Barossa Valley RATING 92 DRINK 2021–2032 $45 DB

First Village Grenache 2020, Barossa Valley RATING 91 DRINK 2021–2028 $32 DB

Blue Quarry Single Vineyard Chardonnay 2021, Eden Valley RATING 90 DRINK 2021–2025 $40 DB

Bicknell fc   ★★★★★

41 St Margarets Road, Healesville, Vic 3777 **Region** Yarra Valley
T 0488 678 427 **www**.bicknellfc.com **Winemaker** David Bicknell **Est.** 2011
Dozens 7600 **Vyds** 2.5ha
This is the busman's holiday for Oakridge chief winemaker David Bicknell and viticulturist Nicky Harris. It is focused purely on chardonnay and pinot noir, with no present intention of broadening the range nor the volume of production. The fruit comes from Val Stewart's close-planted vineyard at Gladysdale, planted in '88. The wines are labelled Applecross, the name of the highest mountain pass in Scotland, a place that David Bicknell's father was very fond of. (JH)

🍷🍷🍷🍷🍷 **Applecross Chardonnay 2020, Yarra Valley** A bright green gold, this opens with green apple, lemon curd, some Japanese pickled ginger and a touch of freshly picked spearmint, while the fresh, nicely complex and compact, finely tuned palate finishes gently vanillin and long. Screw cap. 13% alc. RATING 95 DRINK 2022–2026 $50 PR

Applecross Pinot Noir 2020, Yarra Valley A light, bright, cherry red. Red apple and cherry skins, pomegranate and a light incense stick spice. A lighter and moreish expression of Yarra pinot that finishes with chalky tannins and a mouth-watering cherry-pip acidity. Screw cap. 12.5% alc. RATING 94 DRINK 2022–2027 $50 PR

Big Easy Radio   ★★★★

11 Stonehouse Lane, Aldinga, SA 5773 **Region** McLaren Vale
T 0437 159 858 **www**.bigeasyradio.com **Winemaker** Matt Head **Est.** 2017
Dozens 4000 **Vyds** 4ha
Matt Head has ventured far and wide to bring challenging blends (varietal and regional) together in triumph. Moreover, these (most attractive, if left field) wines are all very competitively priced. Exports to Denmark and Japan. (JH)

♟♟♟♟♟ **Free Love Rollin' On Fiano Vermentino 2021, Langhorne Creek** 80/20% fiano/vermentino co-fermented. Some lees handling has imparted breadth and notes of almond tuile to a finely textured palate, saline, crunchy and effortless. Quince, preserved lemon, orange pastille and pistachio riffs teem long. Delicious drinking, demonstrating the effortless synergy between region and this wave of righteously placed Mediterranean varieties. Screw cap. 12.5% alc. RATING 93 DRINK 2021-2024 $30 NG

Looking Forward to Yesterday Merlot 2021, McLaren Vale This is delicious. While merlot isn't the first variety that springs to mind when dreaming of the Vale, the wine is plump, full weighted, juicy and impeccably proportioned. Dark plum and tomato leaf notes, slightly pulpy of feel, are bridged to the mellifluous finish by svelte tannins, dusty, pliant and refined. Lovely drinking. Screw cap. 13.9% alc. RATING 93 DRINK 2021-2024 $30 NG

Perpetual Holidaze Grenache 2021, McLaren Vale Pickled cherry, ume, kirsch and white pepper, splayed across the finish by the frisky tannins and bright, saline freshness. The 30% whole bunches adds to the complexity and tannic framework. I'd like a little more volume and mid-palate oomph, but the finesse, freshness and poise cannot be denied. Very good drinking. Screw cap. 13.5% alc. RATING 92 DRINK 2021-2025 $40 NG

Funtime Fountain The Montepulciano & The Sangiovese 2020, McLaren Vale Maturation in 500L older puncheons to liberate Sangiovese's frisky tannins, while imbuing breadth and detail. Done well. A peripatetic year marked by extreme heat and diurnal swings. A bit stewed, with a raisiny element to damson plum compote, sandalwood and a ferrous billow of darker fruit elements. The finish, a bit edgy and hard. Yet this is nothing an aggressive decant and a slab of protein can't fix. Screw cap. 14% alc. RATING 92 DRINK 2021-2025 $40 NG

Forget Babylon Malbec 2020, McLaren Vale This is often my favourite wine of the range. On this occasion, though, it is a bit heavy and hot across the finish. A warm vintage, to be sure. Dark plum, boysenberry, violet and plenty of mocha oak. The finish, long and expansive, if not a bit too sweet. Screw cap. 14.5% alc. RATING 91 DRINK 2021-2026 $40 NG

♟♟♟♟ **Drink the Sun Rosé 2021, McLaren Vale** RATING 88 DRINK 2021-2022 $30 NG

Billy Button Wines ★★★★★

11 Camp Street, Bright, Vic 3741 and 61 Myrtle St, Myrtleford, Vic 3737
Region Alpine Valleys
T (03) 5755 1569 **www.**billybuttonwines.com.au **Open** 7 days 12–6 **Winemaker** Jo Marsh, Glenn James **Est.** 2014 **Dozens** 6000
Jo Marsh makes light of the numerous awards she won during her studies for her degree in agricultural science (oenology) at the University of Adelaide. She then won a contested position in Southcorp's Graduate Recruitment Program; she was appointed assistant winemaker at Seppelt Great Western in '03. By '08 she had been promoted to acting senior winemaker, responsible for all wines made onsite. After Seppelt, she became winemaker at Feathertop, and after 2 happy years decided to step out on her own in '14. She has set up a grower network in the Alpine Valleys and makes a string of excellent wines. Billy Button also shares a cellar door with Bush Track Wines in the heart of Myrtleford. (JH)

♟♟♟♟♟ **The Cherished Sparkling Shiraz 2017, Alpine Valleys** Jo Marsh has a long history with sparkling shiraz, having worked at Seppelt, the traditional home of the style. Hence, the name of this wine. The Cherished showcases all that we love about the style, the dark fruits, the depth of spice, the hint of sweetness and the slow build of savouriness that brings with it so many options when it comes to food matching. And, all the while, it's fresh and delicious. Crown. 14.5% alc. RATING 95 $40 JP ♥

The Affable Barbera 2021, Alpine Valleys A little ripper of a wine, full of life. You can feel the energy. Lifted perfume in sour cherry, blackberry, licorice and lavender. Masses of fruit flavour fills the mouth with a good, firm cut of acidity bringing home a clean finish. Impressive and approachable, as always. Screw cap. 14% alc. RATING 95 DRINK 2022-2027 $32 JP ✪

The Alluring Tempranillo 2021, Alpine Valleys The use of Flexcube, i.e. no oak, ensures some powerfully persuasive fruit is elevated and totally engaging in this utterly delicious wine. Captures the grape and its perfect suitability to the Alpine Valleys in a fine display of juicy, dark fruits and lively spice, red licorice and supple tannins. Screw cap. 14.5% alc. RATING 95 DRINK 2022-2029 $32 JP ✪

The Groovy Grüner Veltliner 2021, Alpine Valleys Grüner loves a cool climate and responds accordingly. Crisp, elegant and oh, so delicate in aromas of apple blossom, green apple, lime and white peach. Maintains an even demeanour, lightly textural, with nectarine, peach, spiced apple and impressive length of flavour. So good. Screw cap. 13% alc. RATING 95 DRINK 2021-2026 $27 JP ✪

The Clandestine Schioppettino 2021, Alpine Valleys This northern Italian variety has to be considered a future star variety of the Alpine Valleys if the last few releases are anything to go by. It's a meal-in-itself kind of wine, a rolling, fragrant mix of bramble, black pepper, wild berries, anise, chocolate, briar and earthiness in one. Finely etched acid and tannin shape the palate ripe in fruit and with real presence in the glass. Screw cap. 14% alc. RATING 95 DRINK 2022-2027 $32 JP ✪ ♥

The Beloved Shiraz 2020, Bendigo Fruit sourced from Bendigo due to smoke taint in the Alpine Valleys. Well, this is an eye opener! Jo Marsh dives right in and delivers a stunning wine. Vibrant purple hues. Upbeat, fragrant aromas of red fruits, blackberry, plum, sweet vanillin oak and a fleck of signature Bendigo eucalyptus. Energy to burn on the palate, nicely promoted by supple tannins and balanced oak. An easy-to-love shiraz right here. Screw cap. 14.5% alc. RATING 95 DRINK 2021-2032 $32 JP ✪

Ancestrale Prosecco 2021, King Valley Méthode ancestrale. This is one lively, traditional style of prosecco, lemon butter in hue with a rousing array of apple, ginger, preserved lemon and spice aromas. Fruit complexity meets energy in this delightfully expressive sparkling. Savoury intrigue runs loose through the palate with fruit peel, almond and glacé fruits. Dry with enlivening acidity, not to mention bubble. Crown. 10.5% alc. RATING 94 $32 JP

Rosso 2021, Alpine Valleys King Valley A blend of 5 Mediterranean red grapes, 37/23/18/13/9% barbera/tempranillo/dolcetto/refosco/sangiovese. Demonstrates why blends matter, and even more so why Mediterranean grape varieties are so well suited to this part of the world. Vivid, deep purple hues. Red cherry, wild raspberry, fennel seed, earth and spice aromas are welcoming, fresh and vital. The palate is supple and even with a brisk acid crunch. So good, so more-ish. Terrific value. Screw cap. 13.5% alc. RATING 94 DRINK 2021-2025 $22 JP ✪

The Classic Chardonnay 2021, Alpine Valleys Fruit sourced from 3 vineyards for this attractive, well-rounded chardonnay that fills the mouth with bursts of citrus, melon, white peach, grilled nuts and nougat. Very tasty and tangy, too, as it sweeps across the mouth with a touch of cedary oak to finish. Screw cap. 12% alc. RATING 94 DRINK 2022-2029 $32 JP

🍷🍷🍷🍷🍷 **The Socialite Prosecco 2021, Alpine Valleys** RATING 93 $32 JP
The Honest Fiano 2021, Alpine Valleys RATING 93
DRINK 2021-2025 $32 JP
The Renegade Refosco 2021, Alpine Valleys RATING 93
DRINK 2022-2026 $32 JP
The Feisty Friulano 2021, King Valley RATING 93
DRINK 2021-2026 $27 JP ✪
The Happy Gewürztraminer 2021, Alpine Valleys King Valley RATING 92
DRINK 2021-2026 $27 JP
The Rustic Sangiovese 2021, Alpine Valleys RATING 92
DRINK 2022-2026 $32 JP

Zero Dosage Prosecco 2021, Alpine Valleys RATING 91 $32 JP
The Versatile Vermentino 2021, Alpine Valleys RATING 91
DRINK 2021-2026 $27 JP
The Little Rascal Arneis 2021, Alpine Valleys RATING 91
DRINK 2021-2025 $27 JP
The Dapper Durif 2019, Alpine Valleys RATING 91 DRINK 2022-2028 $32 JP
Wildflower Prosecco NV, King Valley RATING 90 $22 JP
Rosato 2021, Alpine Valleys King Valley RATING 90
DRINK 2021-2024 $20 JP ✪
The Delinquent erduzzo 2021, Alpine Valleys RATING 90
DRINK 2021-2027 $27 JP
The Demure Pinot Blanc 2021, Alpine Valleys RATING 90
DRINK 2021-2024 $27 JP
The Mysterious Malvasia 2021, Alpine Valleys RATING 90
DRINK 2021-2025 $27 JP

Bimbadgen

790 McDonalds Road, Pokolbin, NSW 2320 **Region** Hunter Valley
T (02) 4998 4600 **www.**bimbadgen.com.au **Open** 7 days a week, 10–4
Winemaker Richard Done **Viticulturist** Liz Riley **Est.** 1968 **Dozens** 30 000 **Vyds** 26ha
Bimbadgen's Palmers Lane vineyard was planted in 1968 and the McDonalds Road
vineyard shortly thereafter. Both sites provide old-vine semillon, shiraz and chardonnay, with
tempranillo a more recent addition. Since assuming ownership in '97, the Lee family has
applied the same level of care and attention to cultivating Bimbadgen as they have to other
properties in their portfolio. The small but impressive production is consumed largely by the
owner's luxury hotel assets, with limited quantities available in the Sydney market. Exports to
the UK, Switzerland, Germany, the Netherlands, Japan and Taiwan. (JH)

🍷🍷🍷🍷🍷 **Single Vineyard McDonalds Road Semillon 2021**, Hunter Valley If the
Palmer's Lane is the more nervous and jittery of texture, this is the more ample
and reassured, belying its light weight. While the Signature may age the longest,
this is delicious drinking already and will only grow in stature. Barley water, lemon
balm, dried hay and icy pole riffs. Really juicy across the mid palate, with nothing
brittle, hard or unwanted. Delicious drinking. Screw cap. 10.2% alc. RATING 93
DRINK 2022-2032 $40 NG
Signature Semillon 2021, Hunter Valley A reticent traditionalist. The body
is light and the alcohol low, even for a category that dwells in these zones. Scents
of lemon sherbet, citrus balm, lemongrass and tonic. A bit shins and elbows at this
nascent stage. To be expected. I have faith, given past experience and the quality of
this cooler year, that this will develop beautifully. Time – and lots of it – needed.
My score, on the lower end of possibilities. Screw cap. 10% alc. RATING 93
DRINK 2023-2042 $65 NG
Signature Shiraz 2017, Hunter Valley An aged release. A rich synthesis of
quintessential Hunter scents of varnish, sweet loamy earth and terracotta, along
with black- and blue-fruit allusions, root spice, salami, anise and an intriguing core
of dried porcini and umami. The throes of age, casting complexities. The oak,
mocha and bitter chocolate. The finish, long and persuasive, if not a bit hot. Good
drinking with lots of life left. Screw cap. 14.3% alc. RATING 93 DRINK 2021-2032
$110 NG
Signature Palmers Lane Semillon 2021, Hunter Valley The semillons
here are on the lower end of what is already a low-alcohol spectrum. I like this.
The sort of balletic tightrope walker that straddles an imminent drinkability with
enough structural mettle for age-worthiness. Nettle, greengage, lemongrass and
tonic. Pithy citrus notes, too. Energetic, crunchy and long. Finely poised. Good
drinking. Screw cap. 10.2% alc. RATING 92 DRINK 2022-2033 $65 NG
Sparkling Blanc de Blancs 2019, Hunter Valley A creamy fizz, showcasing
honeydew melon, ripe golden apple and citrus notes. Little autolytic complexity,
but sits nicely in the mouth. Plenty frothy, mitigating the soft acidity. Finishes

with a trickle of easygoing sweetness across the finish. Cork. 12% alc. RATING 90
$50 NG

♥♥♥♥   **Chardonnay 2019, Hunter Valley** RATING 88 DRINK 2021–2024 $25 NG

Bindi Wines

343 Melton Road, Gisborne, Vic 3437 (postal) **Region** Macedon Ranges
T (03) 5428 2564 **www.**bindiwines.com.au **Winemaker** Michael Dhillon, Stuart
Anderson (Consultant) **Est.** 1988 **Dozens** 2000 **Vyds** 6ha
One of the icons of Macedon. The chardonnay is top-shelf, the pinot noir as remarkable
(albeit in a very different idiom) as Bass Phillip, Giaconda or any of the other tiny-production,
icon wines. The addition of Heathcote-sourced shiraz under the Pyrette label confirms Bindi
as one of the greatest small producers in Australia. Michael Dhillon was the Companion's
inaugural Winemaker of the Year in 2022. Exports to the UK, the US and other major
markets. (JH)

♥♥♥♥♥   **Dhillon Col Mountain Vineyard Rosé Grenache 2021, Heathcote** I adore
everything about this rosé, from its pastel pink-bronze hue, its cherry blossom and
rose aroma to its flavour profile – watermelon, alpine strawberries and cinnamon.
It has texture, length and is delightfully dry and crisp. Screw cap. 13% alc.
RATING 96 DRINK 2022–2024 $32 JF ✪
Kostas Rind Chardonnay 2020, Macedon Ranges While Quartz gets the
bow for its complexity and depth, Kostas Rind is no slouch. A lovely balance of
citrus, white stone fruit, ginger spice and a touch of nutty lees that are more like
seasoning, same with the oak influence. There's a lightness and purity with some
complex sulphides and ultra-refreshing acidity. Very satisfying. Utterly enticing.
Screw cap. 13% alc. RATING 96 DRINK 2022–2032 $65 JF ✪
Quartz Chardonnay 2020, Macedon Ranges The depth of flavour
emanating from Quartz leaves me in awe. It's layered and rich, yet not heavy.
Fuller bodied, with lemon, poached fruit and spiced with ginger flower and
powder. Long and pure, with the oak flavoursome and knitted well into the body
of the wine. It is complete and approachable now, but will garner even more
complexity in time. Screw cap. 13% alc. RATING 96 DRINK 2022–2033 $100 JF
Block 5 Pinot Noir 2020, Macedon Ranges Colour is not an attribute
in '20 – it's a much lighter hue – but Block 5 has the most of the 3 pinots on
offer at this time. It's also the most elegant, defined and poised. A balance of
flavours from sweet and tangy cherries, rhubarb compote, Campari and a waft of
autumn leaves. The palate is superfine and long, extended by filigree tannins in
sync with the refreshing acidity. Diam. 12.5% alc. RATING 96 DRINK 2022–2035
$135 JF ♥
Dixon Pinot Noir 2020, Macedon Ranges A gentle and supple Dixon
offering charm as it opens up to red roses and rosehips, a whisper of spiced
cherries and blood orange. Plenty of sweet fruit, bitter herbs and chinotto
mingling on the just mid-weighted palate, with bright acidity and furry, if fine,
tannins in tow. It doesn't have power, but it has detail. It'll also garner more
complexity in time. Diam. 12.5% alc. RATING 95 DRINK 2022–2030 $65 JF
Original Vineyard Pinot Noir 2020, Macedon Ranges While there's a
lightness of touch here – and such a different shape across the palate this vintage –
Original is a delight. Heady aromas, cherries and poached rhubarb, light herbal
tones, earthy and almost thirst quenching. Mid weighted, with acidity the driver
rather than tannin structure, which are nonetheless savoury and fine. Diam.
12.5% alc. RATING 95 DRINK 2022–2034 $85 JF
Dhillon Col Mountain Vineyard Shiraz 2015, Heathcote Released with
5 years' bottle age and looks so youthful, a red hue with a purple tinge. Complex
aromas and flavours of Chinese five-spice, menthol, pink peppercorns with some
savoury meaty reduction, alongside a core of dark fruit. Full bodied, rich yet well
balanced, with persuasive tannins tending to a slight green-walnut bitterness on
the finish. Spot on now, but more time ahead of it. Diam. 14% alc. RATING 95
DRINK 2022–2030 $75 JF

Pyrette Shiraz 2020, Heathcote An exuberant purple red, with wafts of charry smoky oak, cured meats and the darkest fruit spiked with spices. Full bodied, yet a gloss throughout and while the tannins still feel somewhat raw, that points more to the fact the wines is youthful and still coming together. Simply a matter of time. Diam. 14% alc. RATING 94 DRINK 2023-2035 $40 JF

🍷🍷🍷🍷🍷 **Kaye Pinot Noir 2018, Macedon Ranges** RATING 93 DRINK 2022-2030 $100 JF

Bird on a Wire Wines   ★★★★★

51 Symons Street, Healesville, Vic 3777 (postal) **Region** Yarra Valley
T 0439 045 000 **www.**birdonawirewines.com.au **Winemaker** Caroline Mooney
Est. 2008 **Dozens** 850
This is the full-time business of winemaker Caroline Mooney. She grew up in the Yarra Valley and has had other full-time winemaking jobs in the valley for over 10 years. The focus is on small, single-vineyard sites owned by growers committed to producing outstanding grapes. Having worked at the legendary Domaine Jean-Louis Chave in the '06 vintage, she has a special interest in shiraz and marsanne, both grown from distinct sites on a single vineyard in the Yarra Glen area. Exports to the UK. (JH)

🍷🍷🍷🍷🍷 **Chardonnay 2018, Yarra Valley** Quite a deep but bright green gold. White nectarines, a little struck match, lemon curd and toasted hazelnuts can all be found on the nose of this very well-constructed wine. Quite rich by the standards of some Yarra chardonnay, this is textured and flavourful, but it's also fine and very well balanced. Finishes subtle and long and is drinking superbly now. Screw cap. 13.1% alc. RATING 96 DRINK 2021-2025 $50 PR

Syrah 2017, Yarra Valley A medium and still bright cherry red. On the nose there is some black olive tapenade, fresh coffee grounds and a little cacao to go with the concentrated black plums. The medium-bodied and persistent palate reveals dark cherries and savoury notes. The wine culminates in a long, satisfying finish with supple, still quite persistent tannins. Good now, this will continue to improve for some time yet. Screw cap. 14% alc. RATING 95 DRINK 2021-2027 $50 PR

🍷🍷🍷🍷🍷 **Marsanne 2017, Yarra Valley** RATING 91 DRINK 2021-2023 $45 PR

Bittern Estate   ★★★

8 Bittern-Dromana Road, Bittern, Vic 3918 **Region** Mornington Peninsula
T 0417 556 529 **www.**bitternestate.com.au **Open** Fri–Mon 11–5 **Winemaker** Carl Tiesdell-Smith **Viticulturist** Garry Zerbe **Est.** 2013 **Dozens** 4500 **Vyds** 7ha
The Zerbe family has been involved in horticulture for many generations since arriving from Prussia in 1854, planting fruit trees in what is now suburban Melbourne. Generations later, in 1959, the family planted an apple and pear orchard called Tathravale. In '96, Garry and Karen Zerbe began planting the Bittern Vineyard on this property, the extended family providing the third generation of grapegrowers. In that year the family produced its first full array of wine styles under the Bittern Estate label. There was an involvement with Box Stallion, but following land sales by third parties, that venture terminated. Continuity is provided by the winemaking team of Alex White and Carl Tiesdell-Smith. (JH)

🍷🍷🍷🍷 **Pinot Noir 2019, Mornington Peninsula** Already advanced colour on the rim towards a pale ruby centre. Full of florals, sweet dark cherries and pips, cedary oak, menthol and baking spices galore. Fleshy and ripe across the fuller-bodied palate and savoury in outlook, with raspy, grippy tannins, charred radicchio bitterness and a dry finish. Best now and even better with rich fare. Screw cap. 14.4% alc. RATING 88 DRINK 2022-2024 $30 JF

BK Wines

Knotts Hill, Basket Range, SA 5138 **Region** Adelaide Hills
T 0410 124 674 **www.**bkwines.com.au **Open** By appt **Winemaker** Brendon Keys
Est. 2007 **Dozens** 4000

BK Wines is owned by NZ-born Brendon and Kirsty Keys. Brendon has packed a great deal into the past decade. He bounced between Australia and NZ before working in California with the well-known Paul Hobbs; he then helped Paul set up a winery in Argentina. Brendon's tag-line is 'Wines made with love, not money', and he has not hesitated to confound the normal rules of engagement in winemaking. If he isn't remembered for this, the labels for his wines should do the trick. Exports to Canada, Norway, Italy, France, Cambodia, South Korea, NZ, Japan, Singapore and Hong Kong. (JH)

ŢŢŢŢŢ **Archer Beau Single Barrel Chardonnay 2019, Piccadilly Valley** This is the best barrel sourced from the 2019 Swaby vineyard. A slow burn, Archer Beau builds and builds, layer upon layer in the mouth as it moves into a complex, interesting whole. Yellow peach, nectarine, mango skin, spice, dusty lemon and almond-meal aromas. Juicy, filigree-fine acidity pulls the drawstring on a deep, richly textured wine with a savoury, buttery fig flourish as it moves towards the long finish. Screw cap. 12.8% alc. RATING 92 DRINK 2021-2026 $110 JP
Carbonic Pinot Noir 2021, Lenswood A wild-fermented pinot noir that has undergone carbonic maceration and the result is a soft, morello cherry-fruited, herbal-strewn young red that is quite individual in taste. Give it a swish and watch it unfurl. Cork. 12.5% alc. RATING 90 DRINK 2022-2024 $34 JP

ŢŢŢŢ **Remy Single Barrel Pinot Noir 2019, Lenswood** RATING 88 DRINK 2022-2026 $110 JP

Black & Ginger

★★★★☆

563 Sugarloaf Road, Rhymney, Vic 3374 **Region** Great Western
T 0409 964 855 **www.**blackandginger.com.au **Winemaker** Hadyn Black **Est.** 2015
Dozens 500

This is the venture of 2 friends who met in '02 after attending the same high school. Hadyn Black is cellar hand and winemaker, working in the Great Western region. Darcy Naunton (Ginger) is an entrepreneur in Melbourne. Their common interest in wine saw them take a great leap in '15 and buy 1t of shiraz from the renowned Malakoff Vineyard in the Pyrenees, with further vintages following. Hadyn and partner Lucy Joyce purchased a rundown vineyard in Great Western in late '16, naming the wine Lily's Block after Hadyn's mother, who did much of the pruning and picking but unfortunately passed away before tasting the wine. (JH)

ŢŢŢŢŢ **Cinco Rojas 2020, Great Western** A blend of garnacha, graciano, tinta roriz, tinta cão and touriga nacional. Five Iberian red varieties in 1 field blend, picked and fermented together and looking pretty smart in the finished product. Combines red-hearted intensity of summer berries, pepper, wild herbs and bitter chocolate with a rousing savouriness and taut Iberian-style tannins that makes this a truly memorable wine. Australian wine producers take note, this style is the future in a changing climate. Screw cap. 12.9% alc. RATING 95 DRINK 2021-2026 $39 JP
Miss Piggy Muscat & Riesling 2021, Great Western 70/30% orange muscat/riesling. Ok, a readjustment is needed here. Set those muscat expectations aside, this is definitely not sweet, spicy or grapey. This is quietly elegant, textural and dry, with impressive apple blossom, white peach, citrus and pear notes. The riesling is strong in this relationship and orange muscat is a willing, attentive partner, never overpowering. Screw cap. 13% alc. RATING 94 DRINK 2021-2025 $18 JP ✪

ŢŢŢŢŢ **Lorelei Gewürztraminer 2021, Henty** RATING 93 DRINK 2021-2025 $18 JP ✪
Arrawatta Vineyard Grenache Nouveau 2021, Great Western RATING 90 DRINK 2021-2023 $39 JP

BlackJack Vineyards ★★★★☆

3379 Harmony Way, Harcourt, Vic 3453 **Region** Bendigo
T (03) 5474 2355 **www.**blackjackwines.com.au **Open** W'ends & some public hols 11–5
Winemaker Ian McKenzie, Ken Pollock **Est.** 1987 **Dozens** 3000 **Vyds** 6ha
Established by the McKenzie and Pollock families on the site of an old apple and pear orchard
in the Harcourt Valley, BlackJack is best known for very good shiraz. Despite some tough
vintage conditions, BlackJack has managed to produce supremely honest, full-flavoured and
powerful wines, all with an edge of elegance. (JH)

🍷🍷🍷🍷🍷 **Mr Ramoy 2019, Bendigo** Cabernet and shiraz. A heady introduction in
plum, blackberry, vanilla and dried herbs shows the great Aussie grape duo in full,
delicious flight. Built for the cellar, the French oak is not shy, but it does fit well, an
amply suitable partner for the generosity of fruit and tannin. Screw cap. 14.5% alc.
RATING 95 DRINK 2021–2033 $75 JP

🍷🍷🍷🍷🍷 **Rosa 2020, Bendigo** RATING 91 DRINK 2021–2024 $25 JP
Block 6 Shiraz 2019, Bendigo RATING 91 DRINK 2021–2032 $40 JP
Cabernet Merlot 2019, Bendigo RATING 90 DRINK 2021–2027 $30 JP

Bleasdale Vineyards ★★★★★

1640 Langhorne Creek Road, Langhorne Creek, SA 5255 **Region** Langhorne Creek
T (08) 8537 4000 **www.**bleasdale.com.au **Open** 7 days 10–5 **Winemaker** Paul Hotker,
Matt Laube **Viticulturist** Sarah Keough **Est.** 1850 **Vyds** 45ha
One of the most historic wineries in Australia; in '20 it celebrated 170 years of continuous
winemaking by the direct descendants of the founding Potts family. Not so long before the
start of the 21st century, its vineyards were flooded every winter by diversion of the Bremer
River, which provided moisture throughout the dry, cool, growing season. In the new
millennium, every drop of water is counted. The vineyards have been significantly upgraded
and refocused: shiraz accounts for 45% of plantings, supported by 7 other proven varieties;
sauvignon blanc, pinot gris and chardonnay are sourced from the Adelaide Hills. Exports to
all major markets. (JH)

🍷🍷🍷🍷🍷 **The Iron Duke Cabernet Sauvignon 2020, Langhorne Creek** A best-of-
the-best barrel selection. The bright colour is as it should be, the bouquet rimmed
with the violets that are often talked about (not by me, until, that is, you come
across a wine such as this). Notes of cedar and cassis are not far behind in their
appeal. Then the glory of this magnificent wine's palate takes total control of all
the senses, the sheer intensity of the fruit making the finely tempered tannins and
French oak applaud from the wings of the stage. Screw cap. 14% alc. RATING 98
DRINK 2025–2050 $79 JH ♥ ❤

🍷🍷🍷🍷🍷 **Generations Malbec 2020, Langhorne Creek** Typical intense malbec colour.
Winemaker Paul Hotker has this wine on a string, dancing to his every command.
This has the gravitas of a great red wine that just happens to be made from
malbec; its mouth-watering intensity of forest blackberries, cloves and black olive
drawn out on the finish by ripe tannins. Trophy and top gold Royal Adelaide Wine
Show '21, gold Perth Royal Wine Awards '21. Screw cap. 14% alc. RATING 96
DRINK 2022–2035 $35 JH ♥ ❤
Chardonnay 2021, Adelaide Hills Wild ferment and mlf in French puncheons
(25% new), matured for 9 months. White peach and grapefruit flavours jostle for
primacy, neither achieving it. Nor does the mlf or oak – this is a wine of and for
all. Screw cap. 12.5% alc. RATING 95 DRINK 2022–2032 $30 JH ♥
Second Innings Malbec 2020, Langhorne Creek Bright colour. A highly
aromatic bouquet with the particular spice – half pepper, half clove – of Bleasdale
Vineyards. The palate is a broad church of plum, blackberry and red cherry – and
a hint of clove on the finish. Outstanding value. Screw cap. 14% alc. RATING 95
DRINK 2022–2032 $22 JH ♥

Wellington Road Shiraz Cabernet 2020, Langhorne Creek A 50/50%
blend, the cabernet crushed, the shiraz destemmed; open fermented and
8–12 days on skins. Pressed to French puncheons (25% new) for 12 months'
maturation. Clever winemaking has optimised the high-quality grapes in a full-
bodied framework that will underwrite long-term cellaring. Screw cap. 14% alc.
RATING 95 DRINK 2025-2035 $32 JH ✪

Frank Potts 2020, Langhorne Creek A 76/15/7/2% blend of cabernet
sauvignon, malbec, petit verdot and merlot. Bright, near vivid, crimson; an elegant
cabernet-driven wine, with notes of cedar, cigar box and cassis on the bouquet and
palate alike. It's medium bodied and lithe, an English gentleman's claret. Screw cap.
14% alc. RATING 95 DRINK 2023-2030 $35 JH ✪

Generations Shiraz 2020, Langhorne Creek Opens with a bright crimson-
red hue. It has the inherent pliable mouthfeel of Langhorne Creek that offers the
widest window of opportunity to drink half and cellar half. It has varietal plum,
blackberry, licorice and spice flavours held within a silken web of fine tannins.
Drink any place at any time. Screw cap. 14% alc. RATING 95 DRINK 2025-2035
$35 JH ✪

Pinot Gris 2021, Adelaide Hills This will come as a surprise for those
expecting another ho-hum white wine. There is both flavour and texture
complexity, largely nashi pear and citrus, plus tropical and spice slants. Screw cap.
12.5% alc. RATING 94 DRINK 2021-2025 $22 JH ✪

Riesling 2021, Adelaide Hills Cool fermented with some solids to build
texture. Neatly balances 8.4g/L TA and 5.5g/L RS. The perfumed apple- and
citrus-blossom bouquet introduces a dangerously enjoyable wine, with freshness
its calling card. Screw cap. 11% alc. RATING 94 DRINK 2022-2031 $30 JH ✪

Bloodwood   ★★★★★

231 Griffin Road, Orange, NSW 2800 **Region** Orange
T (02) 6362 5631 **www**.bloodwood.biz **Open** By appt **Winemaker** Stephen Doyle
Est. 1983 **Dozens** 4000 **Vyds** 8.43ha

Rhonda and Stephen Doyle are 2 of the pioneers of the Orange district; 2024 will mark
Bloodwood's 40th anniversary. The estate vineyards (chardonnay, riesling, merlot, cabernet
sauvignon, shiraz, cabernet franc and malbec) are planted at an elevation of 810–860m, which
provides a reliably cool climate. The wines are sold mainly through the cellar door and by an
energetic, humorous and informatively run mailing list. Bloodwood has an impressive track
record across the full gamut of wine styles, especially riesling; all of the wines have a particular
elegance and grace. Very much part of the high-quality reputation of Orange. (JH)

🍷🍷🍷🍷🍷 **Maurice 2016, Orange** Painstakingly lengthy bench-top blending sessions
using the best wines in barrel worked to perfection: 90% cabernet sauvignon,
10% pressings of cabernet franc, merlot and malbec. Superb colour deep through
to the crimson rim. This is positively luscious, redolent of cassis, black olive and
cedar adding a dimension of flavour and texture. Seriously good wine. Screw cap.
14% alc. RATING 97 DRINK 2026-2041 $42 JH ✪

🍷🍷🍷🍷🍷 **Riesling 2021, Orange** Such a generous and mellifluous departure from the
more brittle South Australian expressions: lithe, long limbed, dry, juicy and yet
driven by an effortless undercarriage of vibrant mineral force more reminiscent of
great Germanic gear. Glazed quince, apricot pith, preserved lemon, fennel, white
pepper and tonic. The finish, a sublime confluence of natural acidity and gentle
phenolic rails pulsing very long. A steal! Better, a fine wine indeed. Screw cap.
13.5% alc. RATING 96 DRINK 2022-2032 $30 NG ✪ ♥

Maurice 2018, Orange A cabernet-dominated barrel cull, with a dollop
of malbec, cabernet franc and merlot. It is a pleasure to taste this release.
More curvaceous than the straight-laced cab. More resinous and layered, too.
Graphite, cassis, a sluice of menthol, bay leaf and assorted herbs, but best are the
blazing florals that lift the wine. The oak, massaged into the fray. The length,
exceptional. Lovely drinking. Screw cap. 13.1% alc. RATING 96 DRINK 2021-2032
$40 NG ✪ ♥

Schubert Chardonnay 2021, Orange Among the finest iterations of this consistently excellent wine in recent memory. A cool attenuated year, befitting. Classy oak emits nougat, cedar, vanilla pod and toasted nuts. Wild-yeast-inflected dashi, too. A stream of stone fruits too, flecked with citrus accents, flows long. Quinine bitterness marks the finish. Shins and elbows in its nascency, this will age beautifully. Screw cap. 13.5% alc. RATING 95 DRINK 2022-2030 $36 NG

Cabernet Sauvignon 2018, Orange This is in a nice place, although the oak bridling will meld with a little more age. Finely tuned scents of mulch, Cuban cigar, graphite, currant and a whisper of menthol. Mid weighted, immensely savoury and sleek, but for the bristle of oak around the seams. Shapely tannins make this. Finishes with a waft of sage and green olive. Sophisticated cool-climate cabernet, here. Excellent drinking now and onwards for close to a decade. Screw cap. 13.5% alc. RATING 95 DRINK 2021-2030 $35 NG ✪

Cabernet Sauvignon 2017, Orange Has the presence and detail of cool-grown cabernet that has achieved phenolic ripeness and appropriate structure. Blackcurrant, bay leaf and cigar-box oak are fused with fine tannins on the long palate. Screw cap. 13.9% alc. RATING 95 DRINK 2022-2037 $34 JH ✪

Merlot Noir 2017, Orange An elegant, medium-bodied wine that has abundant personality and varietal expression. It offers a lacy texture to the red and blue berries and cedary oak, the tannins superfine yet persistent. Screw cap. 13.7% alc. RATING 94 DRINK 2022-2037 $34 JH

Blue Gables   ★★★★★

100 Lanigan Road, Maffra West Upper, Vic 3859 **Region** Gippsland
T (03) 5148 0372 **www.**bluegables.com.au **Open** W'ends 10–5 by appt
Winemaker Alastair Butt, Mal Stewart (sparkling) **Est.** 2004 **Dozens** 1800 **Vyds** 3.7ha
Blue Gables is the culmination of a long-held dream for chemical engineer Alistair and journalist wife Catherine Hicks. They purchased 8ha of a north-facing hillside slope from Catherine's father's dairy farm and built a two-storey gabled roof farmhouse, hence the name. This small vineyard, nestled high above the Macalister Irrigation District in East Gippsland, was established in 2004 with the planting of the first vines, and continued in '05 with 0.8ha each of sauvignon blanc, pinot gris and shiraz and 0.4ha of chardonnay. Sangiovese and pinot noir were added in 2017. (JH)

🍷🍷🍷🍷🍷 **Pinot Noir 2020, Gippsland** A light yet striking garnet hue, matched to brighter and more buoyant red fruits within. Think cherries and poached rhubarb dusted with spices, sweet at the core, yet savoury on the finish. It just hits medium bodied, with lithe tannins and refreshing acidity to close. There's a certain elegance to this and its vitality makes it better suited to drinking in its youth. Screw cap. 13% alc. RATING 95 DRINK 2021-2026 $48 JF

Keith Thomas Reserve Shiraz 2019, Gippsland This flagship red spends a year in a single new French oak barrel and the fruit has taken that all in its stride. An impressive, structured wine but not unwieldy, with the sweet dark plum and cherry accents all spiced up with menthol, licorice, cinnamon quills and cedar. While it will continue to unfurl with more bottle age, tensile tannins and its freshness will probably see a lot of early drinking. Fair enough, too. Screw cap. 14% alc. RATING 95 DRINK 2022-2029 $70 JF

🍷🍷🍷🍷🍷 **Rosé 2021, Gippsland** RATING 93 DRINK 2021-2022 $30 JF
Hanratty Hill Shiraz 2021, Gippsland RATING 92 DRINK 2023-2030 $35 JF
Pinot Gris 2020, Gippsland RATING 92 DRINK 2021-2023 $30 JF
Pinot Noir 2021, Gippsland RATING 90 DRINK 2022-2026 $48 JF
Jesse Chardonnay 2019, Gippsland RATING 90 DRINK 2021-2025 $35 JF

Blue Pyrenees Estate ★★★★★

656 Vinoca Road, Avoca, Vic 3467 **Region** Pyrenees
T (03) 5465 1111 **www**.bluepyrenees.com.au **Open** 7 days 11–5 **Winemaker** Carmel
Keenan, Mel Newman **Viticulturist** Sean Howe **Est.** 1963 **Dozens** 60000 **Vyds** 149ha
Remy Cointreau established Blue Pyrenees Estate (then known as Château Remy) in 1963,
growing ugni blanc for brandy. Forty years later, the business was sold to a small group of
Sydney businessmen. The core of the business is the very large estate plantings of shiraz and
cabernet, most decades old, but with newer arrivals, including viognier. In 2019 Blue Pyrenees
Estate was purchased by Glenlofty Wines, forming the largest producer in the Pyrenees.
Exports to the US, Canada, UK, Japan and Germany. (JH)

🍷🍷🍷🍷🍷 **Richardson Reserve Cabernet Sauvignon 2018, Pyrenees** The first among
equals, the '18 Richardson Reserve Cabernet just pips its Reserve Shiraz sibling
with its incredible level of concentration and total integration. It's a seamless,
impressive performance. Ripe, yet well composed in blackberries, briar, a sweet
dry leafy thread and spice, notably dressed in vanillin oak. Layers of fine cabernet
tannins roam the palate, elegant in shape and bringing with them a long, smooth,
fresh finish. The late Colin Richardson would have been proud. Screw cap.
14% alc. RATING 97 DRINK 2022–2034 $160 JP ♥

🍷🍷🍷🍷🍷 **Midnight Cuvée 2017, Pyrenees** Traditional method. Finely beaded in the
glass, it carries a complex floral and citrus bouquet with layers of delicate yeasty,
nutty autolysis. A stylish sparkling, delicate and textural in citrus, crisp apple
flavours and nougatine. Finishes clean, fresh with zip. Cork. 12.5% alc. RATING 95
$37 JP
Richardson Cabernet Sauvignon 2018, Pyrenees A serious wine in
memory of a seriously lovely wine man, the late Colin Richardson. Colin loved
a rousing and evocative red, something to get your teeth into and also be awed
by. The cabernets made in his honour follow that principle. The '18, while still
in building mode, is ready for its close-up right now, bursting in sweet blackberry
fruits, almost riotous spice, rich in clove and aniseed, with a signature Pyrenees
menthol, leafy edge. Ripe tannins keep the structure keen, something for the
journey ahead. Screw cap. 14.5% alc. RATING 95 DRINK 2020–2035 $72 JP
Richardson Reserve Shiraz 2018, Pyrenees With 4% viognier. Bring a
decanter to this wine when it is released. It's tight and focused at this early stage,
with so much promise just brimming below the surface. Signature Pyrenees
menthol notes are pervasive, but nicely countered by dense, ripe blackberries,
raspberries, plums, licorice, chocolate and earth. Tannins are muscular. They'll be
needed for the journey ahead. Diam. 13.5% alc. RATING 95 DRINK 2022–2033
$160 JP

Blueberry Hill Vineyard ★★★★

Cnr McDonalds Road/Coulson Road, Pokolbin, NSW 2320 **Region** Hunter Valley
T (02) 4998 7295 **www**.blueberryhill.com.au **Open** 7 days 10–5 **Winemaker** First
Creek Winemaking Services **Est.** 1973 **Dozens** 2000 **Vyds** 4.25ha
Blueberry Hill Vineyard is part of the old McPherson Estate, with fully mature plantings of
shiraz, chardonnay, pinot noir, sauvignon blanc, merlot and cabernet sauvignon. Part of the grape
production is sold to other winemakers, part used for the extensive Blueberry Hill range. (JH)

🍷🍷🍷🍷🍷 **Connoisseur Shiraz 2019, Hunter Valley** A big step up from the entry-level
range and well worth the hike in price. Again, savoury. A mid-weight luncheon
wine. Dusty. Japanese ume plums, red cherry, sassafras, orange zest and violet.
The oak, in perfect proportion, facilitating a long, effortless flow. Fine intensity
from entry to finish. Screw cap. 13% alc. RATING 94 DRINK 2021–2035 $50 NG

🍷🍷🍷🍷🍷 **Vineyard Shiraz 2019, Hilltops** RATING 92 DRINK 2021–2032 $40 NG
Connoisseur Cabernet Sauvignon 2019, Hunter Valley RATING 91
DRINK 2021–2029 $40 NG

Bondar Wines

148 McMurtrie Road, McLaren Vale, SA 5171 **Region** McLaren Vale
T 0460 898 158 **www.**bondarwines.com.au **Open** Fri–Sun 11–5 **Winemaker** Andre
Bondar **Viticulturist** Ben Lacey **Est.** 2013 **Dozens** 3000 **Vyds** 13.5ha
Husband and wife Andre Bondar and Selina Kelly began a deliberately unhurried journey in
2009, which culminated in the purchase of the celebrated Rayner Vineyard post-vintage '13.
Andre had been a winemaker at Nepenthe wines for 7 years, and Selina had recently
completed a law degree. They changed focus and began to look for a vineyard capable of
producing great shiraz. The Rayner Vineyard had all the answers: a ridge bisecting the land,
Blewitt Springs sand on the eastern side; and the Seaview, heavier clay loam soils over limestone
on the western side. The vineyard has been substantially reworked and includes 10ha of shiraz,
with smaller amounts of grenache, mataro, touriga, carignan, cinsault and counoise. Exports to
Hong Kong, the UK and the US. (JH)

ΨΨΨΨΨ Violet Hour Shiraz 2020, McLaren Vale A beautiful wine in every
dimension – its crimson colour, haunting perfumed bouquet, caressing the mouth
with its perfectly ripened fruit, superfine tannins, and subtle but relevant oak. One
of the great bargains. Screw cap. 14% alc. RATING 97 DRINK 2022-2035 $30 JH ✪
Midnight Hour Shiraz 2020, McLaren Vale 100% whole-bunch fermentation
has produced an exotic array of foresty flowers, intense but finely balanced juicy,
small berry fruits and sheer, silky tannins somewhere in the mix, oak ditto. Has the
stamp of authority of a great wine. 60 dozen made. Screw cap. 14% alc. RATING 97
DRINK 2026-2041 $40 JH ✪

ΨΨΨΨΨ Grenache Rosé 2021, McLaren Vale Pale salmon pink; full-on perfume of
rose petals and bath powder, but it's the intensity of the brilliantly juicy palate that
makes this so special. Screw cap. 13% alc. RATING 96 DRINK 2021-2025 $27 JH ✪
Rayner Vineyard Grenache 2021, McLaren Vale From the cool,
attenuated '21 vintage, this is a showcase of persimmon, Seville orange and the
pithiest pucker from a sour cherry I am yet to experience. Raspberry bon-bon
shifts to the domineering flavour with air. The tannins, white pepper-clad and
moreish. Sandy, saline and gritty. Very fine. A protean expression, shifting endlessly
with air to a succulent vibrato. Entrenched in the pantheon of the Vale. Screw cap.
13.8% alc. RATING 96 DRINK 2021-2027 $40 NG ✪
Junto GSM 2020, McLaren Vale 68/10/9/7/5/1% grenache/shiraz/mataro/
carignan/cinsaut/counoise. Bright, clear crimson; a perfumed, red-fruited, spiced
bouquet lights the way, the palate making off with this opening by adding high-
quality tannins. Whether or not a shotgun marriage, it comes together in glistening
unison. RATING 96 DRINK 2021-2031 $28 JH ✪
Chardonnay 2020, Adelaide Hills Early pickup of green-gold colour; no
surprise that it should be fragrant, layered and complex, with roasted almond
through to white-fleshed stone fruit and grapefruit. Screw cap. 13% alc. RATING 95
DRINK 2022-2030 $35 JH ✪
Rayner Vineyard Shiraz 2020, McLaren Vale As far as warm-climate
Australian shiraz goes, this has to be at the pinnacle of the totem, at least if one
seeks detail, freshness and the sort of aromatics reminiscent of syrah rather than
'jam juice' (as a critic I once worked closely with called the then SA norm). Violet,
white pepper, tapenade, pastrami and boysenberry. A little cocoa oak, nicely placed.
But better, the lithe and slinky tannins, taut and stylish, serving as a pixelated
matrix to the long flow of fruit. Screw cap. 14% alc. RATING 95 DRINK 2021-2032
$45 NG

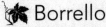 # Borrello

Unit 3/8 Owen Tucker Lane, Margaret River, WA 2685 **Region** Margaret River
T (08) 9758 7074 **www.**borrellovineyards.com.au **Winemaker** Paul Atwood
Viticulturist Aaron Paganoni **Est.** 2019 **Dozens** 1550 **Vyds** 6.7ha

Borrello is a new winery on the scene in Margaret River, owned by Carl and Carla Borrello. Carl is a third-generation Borrello local (his grandfather Nicola (aka Nick) emigrated to the Perth Hills from Italy in 1927, where Carl's father Ted later worked in the vineyards) and moved down to Margaret River to establish the Down To Earth grape growing and viticulture. Borrello was borne of a desire to work with some of the better parcels themselves, instead of selling them, with winemaker Paul Atwood (ex-Leeuwin fame) at the helm. The range of wines are made from fruit sourced from around WA, including Margaret River, Swan Valley and Frankland River. (EL)

ㅗㅗㅗㅗㅗ **Chardonnay 2020, Margaret River** Crushed nuts, ripe yellow peaches and even summer mangoes on the nose. In the mouth the wine is fine, creamy and very pretty. The fruit expression here is quite clear, unfettered as it is by any overt impact of oak. It is there, but it serves the fruit, rather than defines the wine. Brilliant, classy value for money. Screw cap. 12.5% alc. RATING 93 DRINK 2021–2028 $28 EL
Cabernet Sauvignon 2020, Margaret River This is ripe, plump and saturated with cassis and raspberry fruit. The tannins through the finish are a little metallic, but the fruit that precedes them is wonderful. Perhaps a vigorous decant will sort this out. Screw cap. 13.5% alc. RATING 90 DRINK 2021–2028 $30 EL
Shiraz 2018, Frankland River Blood plum, licorice and already showing some development in the mouth in the form of rhubarb, aniseed, poached plum and mulberry. The tannins are firmly entrenched in the fruit, but they present as fine ridges of shape, rather than marbled throughout. It is engaging and medium+ bodied. Screw cap. 14.5% alc. RATING 90 DRINK 2021–2027 $28 EL

ㅗㅗㅗㅗ **Grenache 2020, Swan Valley** RATING 89 DRINK 2022–2027 $22 EL
Trebbiano 2021, Swan Valley RATING 88 DRINK 2022–2024 $20 EL
Sauvignon Blanc 2020, Margaret River RATING 88 DRINK 2022–2024 $22 EL

Bowen Estate ★★★★

15459 Riddoch Highway, Coonawarra, SA 5263 **Region** Coonawarra
T (08) 8737 2229 **www.**bowenestate.com.au **Open** Mon–Fri 10–5, w'ends 10–4
Winemaker Emma Bowen **Viticulturist** Doug Bowen **Est.** 1972 **Dozens** 12000
Vyds 33ha
Bowen Estate is a family-run business, not far off its 50th vintage. Regional veteran Doug Bowen presides over one of Coonawarra's landmarks, but he has handed over full winemaking responsibility to daughter Emma, 'retiring' to the position of viticulturist. Exports to the UK, the Maldives, Sri Lanka, Singapore, Japan and NZ. (JH)

ㅗㅗㅗㅗㅗ **Cabernet Sauvignon 2020, Coonawarra** Concentrated and minty, this is lush with bay leaf and sage, cassis and licorice. The focused tannins and length of flavour suggest this will age very well indeed. Screw cap. 14.5% alc. RATING 94 DRINK 2022–2036 $32 EL

ㅗㅗㅗㅗ **Shiraz 2020, Coonawarra** RATING 91 DRINK 2022–3032 $32 EL

Bowman's Run ★★★☆

1305 Beechworth-Wodonga Road, Wooragee, Vic 3747 **Region** Beechworth
T 0417 383 209 **Open** By appt **Winemaker** Daniel Balzer **Est.** 1989 **Dozens** 200
Vyds 1ha
Struan and Fran Robertson have cabernet sauvignon, riesling and small plots of shiraz and traminer dating back to 1989. The tiny winery is part of a larger general agricultural holding. (JH)

ㅗㅗㅗㅗ **Granite Rise Cabernet Sauvignon 2017, Beechworth** Looking perky and fresh as a 4yo with sweet aromas of plums and cassis, dark spices and cacao powder. Earthy and dark-fruited, with a touch of herbal savouriness lifting the palate. Fine tannins are holding firm. All up, everything is coming together very nicely indeed.

Capable of further ageing with confidence. Screw cap. 13.7% alc. RATING 90
DRINK 2021-2025 $30 JP

🍷🍷🍷🍷 **Creek Flat Shiraz 2017, Beechworth** RATING 89 DRINK 2021-2025 $35 JP

Box Grove Vineyard ★★★★

955 Avenel-Nagambie Road, Tabilk, Vic 3607 **Region** Nagambie Lakes
T 0409 210 015 **www**.boxgrovevineyard.com.au **Open** By appt **Winemaker** Sarah
Gough **Est.** 1995 **Dozens** 2500 **Vyds** 28.25ha
This is the venture of the Gough family, with industry veteran (and daughter) Sarah Gough
managing the vineyard, winemaking and marketing. Having started with 10ha each of shiraz
and cabernet sauvignon under contract to Brown Brothers, Sarah decided to switch the focus
of the business to what could loosely be called 'Mediterranean varieties'. These days shiraz
and prosecco (glera) are the main varieties, with smaller plantings of pinot gris, primitivo,
vermentino, roussanne, sousão, grenache, nebbiolo, negroamaro, mourvèdre and viognier.
Osteria (an Italian word meaning a place that serves wine and food) hosts tastings and meals
prepared by visiting Melbourne chefs, by appointment. Exports to the UK. (JH)

🍷🍷🍷🍷🍷 **Prosecco 2021, Nagambie Lakes** Brings a savoury layer to prosecco, striking
a different chord, bringing preserved lemon, grapefruit pith, nashi pear and apple.
Crunchy, enlivening acidity. A prosecco that fits both aperitif style and will match
nicely with food. Screw cap. 11.7% alc. RATING 94 $25 JP

🍷🍷🍷🍷🍷 **Mourvèdre 2021, Nagambie Lakes** RATING 90 DRINK 2021-2025 $28 JP

Brand & Sons – Coonawarra ★★★☆

11 Mary Street, Coonawarra, SA 5263 **Region** Coonawarra
T 0488 771 046 **www**.brandandsons.com.au **Winemaker** Sam Brand
Viticulturist Trent Brand **Est.** 2000 **Dozens** 5000 **Vyds** 95ha
The Brand family story starts with the arrival of Eric Brand in Coonawarra in 1950. He
married Nancy Redman and purchased a 24ha block from the Redman family, relinquishing
his job as a baker and becoming a grapegrower. It was not until '66 that the first Brand's Laira
wine was made. The family sold the Brand's Laira winery to McWilliam's Wines in 1994, with
Eric's son Jim Brand staying on as chief winemaker until he passed away in 2005. Today the
business is run by Sam Brand, the fourth generation of this family, which has played a major
role in Coonawarra for over 70 years. (JH)

🍷🍷🍷🍷🍷 **Sanctuary Cabernet Sauvignon 2015, Coonawarra** This is a huge wine;
the fruit is an avalanche of flavour, cascading blackberries, bramble, cocoa dust and
licorice. In the mouth the wine is precisely thus, although it does take some time
to open up, such as the fortress of oak and tannin that encases it. If you choose to
drink this in the next couple of years, the (firm) advice is to decant it, to give the
fruit and spice nuance a fighting chance to reveal themselves fully. This is sturdy,
traditional and densely packed with flavour. Screw cap. 14.3% alc. RATING 92
DRINK 2022-2042 $130 EL

Brand's Laira Coonawarra ★★★★☆

14860 Riddoch Highway, Coonawarra, SA 5263 **Region** Coonawarra
T (08) 8736 3260 **www**.brandslaira.com **Open** Mon–Fri 9–4.30, w'ends & public hols
11–4 **Winemaker** Peter Weinberg, Amy Blackburn **Est.** 1966 **Vyds** 278ha
Three days before Christmas 2015, Casella Family Brands received an early present when it
purchased Brand's Laira from McWilliam's. Over the years McWilliam's had moved from 50%
to 100% ownership of Brand's and thereafter it purchased an additional 100ha of vineyards
(taking Brand's to its present 278ha) and had expanded both the size, and the quality, of the
winery. Exports to select markets. (JH)

🍷🍷🍷🍷🍷 **Stentiford's Old Vines Shiraz 2018, Coonawarra** Concentrated, black and
dense, with finely knit tannins and a framework of oak that has all but sunk into

the fruit. The alcohol leaves a real licorice trail through the finish, threatening to rear up and make itself known, but backs down at the last. A wine of longevity, breadth and detail. Deliciously old-school. Very good. Screw cap. 14.7% alc. RATING 95 DRINK 2022–2037 $80 EL

ȚȚȚȚȚ Blockers Shiraz 2019, Coonawarra RATING 90 DRINK 2021–2029 $25 EL

Brangayne of Orange ★★★★

837 Pinnacle Road, Orange, NSW 2800 **Region** Orange
T (02) 6365 3229 **www.**brangayne.com **Open** Sun–Fri 11–4, Sat 11–5
Winemaker Simon Gilbert, Will Gilbert **Viticulturist** David Hoskins **Est.** 1994
Dozens 3500 **Vyds** 25.7ha
The Hoskins family (formerly orchardists) moved into grapegrowing in 1994 and have progressively established high-quality vineyards. Brangayne produces good wines across all mainstream varieties ranging, remarkably, from pinot noir to cabernet sauvignon. It sells a substantial part of its crop to other winemakers. (JH)

ȚȚȚȚȚ **Merlot 2019, Orange** Despite the alcohol noted, this drinks like a mid-weighted leafy wine, with fringes of red plum, tomato bush and spearmint. The tannins, lithe and well-shaped. Prosaic, in the best sense. Screw cap. 14.4% alc. RATING 91 DRINK 2021–2024 $40 NG
Pinot Grigio 2021, Orange The best white wine here. Made in a grigio style, meaning lighter of weight, crunchy and a bit thinner across the mid palate. Still, a good spurt of Asian pear, spiced apple and white pepper strung across a gently chewy, talcy finish. Screw cap. 12.5% alc. RATING 90 DRINK 2021–2023 $25 NG

ȚȚȚȚ **Riesling 2021, Orange** RATING 89 DRINK 2021–2026 $30 NG

Brash Higgins ★★★★★

California Road, McLaren Vale, SA 5171 **Region** McLaren Vale
T (08) 8556 4237 **www.**brashhiggins.com **Open** By appt **Winemaker** Brad Hickey
Est. 2010 **Dozens** 1000 **Vyds** 7ha
American Brad Hickey arrived in Australia to work vintage '07 in McLaren Vale, where he met his now partner Nicole Thorpe. Together they established Brash Higgins in 2010. Brad has a varied background, including 10 years as head sommelier at some of the best New York restaurants, then a further 10 years of baking, brewing and travelling to the best-known wine regions of the world. Nicole's 7ha Omensetter Vineyard looks over the Willunga Escarpment and was planted to shiraz and cabernet sauvignon in 1997. Drought prompted them to graft their first 0.5ha of shiraz to nero d'Avola in 2009; they have since grown plantings to 3ha. Both the estate vineyard and the winery are certified organic. Exports to the UK, the US and Canada. (JH)

ȚȚȚȚȚ **R/SM Field Blend Riesling Semillon 2020, McLaren Vale** It took me a while to get my head around these bedfellows, planted – serendipitously as it turns out – alongside each other. I can only conclude that this wine is venerable. Stunning, even. Perhaps I was falling into the dull trap of seeking varietal personality when, in fact, this is all about place and a courageous textural interplay, from grainy truffled lees traits, to candied quince, rooibos and lemon-peel skinsy chutney, a staining degree of briny salinity and Blewitt Springs sandiness. The breadth of well-positioned oak, too. This drinks and feels like a top expression from the Loire, with an ersatz manzanilla-meets-maritime veil. Formidably long, moreish and extremely impressive. Wow! Screw cap. 13.5% alc. RATING 97 DRINK 2022–2026 $39 NG ♻ ♥

ȚȚȚȚȚ **NDV Amphora Project Nero d'Avola 2020, McLaren Vale** Dark, spiced cherry scents meld with bitters, bergamot, anise, clove, sassafras and cardamom. The tannins, a gristly bristle, corral the teeming fruit and confer a welcome savouriness. This is a serious nero d'Avola of impact, immaculate detail and a textural precision that unravels with each sip. Far from the pulpy, vapid expressions that too often define the domestic norm. Excellent wine here. The mandala of moreish tannins, its opus. Screw cap. 14.5% alc. RATING 96 DRINK 2022-2030 $45 NG ✪

CHN Willamba Hill Vineyard Chenin Blanc 2020, McLaren Vale A consistently delicious and highly versatile wine. Fermented wild in barriques. Medium weight, succulent and intense. Riffs on cactus pear, celery salt, dried hay, apple tarte tatin and lemon curd are reeled across a carapace of saline acidity and a gentle phenolic rail. Texture, an opus. Ripeness, perfect. Better the day after opening, so compact is the framework. Screw cap. 11.5% alc. RATING 95 DRINK 2021-2026 $39 NG

Bloom 2015, McLaren Vale RATING 95 DRINK 2022-2050 $145 NG

MATO Lennon Vineyard Mataro 2017, McLaren Vale Great drinking. All the better because this full-weighted red has been held back in order to beam complexity and a welcome suppleness upon release, no matter the ferrous varietal personality. Add white pepper, hung game, green olive and suede. The finish is spicy, long, mescal-bunchy (50%) around the fringes, but nourishing and immensely satisfying. This thrums after a day open. Perhaps the score could be higher? My sort of wine. Screw cap. 13.7% alc. RATING 94 DRINK 2022-2028 $39 NG

Brash Road Vineyard   ★★★★☆

PO Box 455, Yallingup, WA 6282 **Region** Margaret River
T 0448 448 840 **www.**brashvineyard.com.au **Winemaker** Bruce Dukes (Contract)
Est. 2000 **Dozens** 1500 **Vyds** 18ha

Brash Road Vineyard was established in 1998 as Woodside Valley Estate. While most of the grapes were sold to other Margaret River producers, cabernet sauvignon, shiraz, chardonnay and merlot were made, and in '09 the cabernet sauvignon and the shiraz earned the winery a 5-star rating. It is now owned by Chris and Anne Carter (managing partners, who live and work onsite), Brian and Anne McGuinness, and Rik and Jenny Nitert. The vineyard is now mature and produces high-quality fruit. (JH)

🍷🍷🍷🍷🍷 Single Vineyard Syrah 2019, Margaret River This is redolent of ripe red and black berries of every kind; the luscious fruit on the palate transcends the shackles of oak that bind it and ascends into an almost hedonistic space. Very pretty. Spicy. Quite slinky. The gritty tannins are a highlight – they balance the supple fruit. Screw cap. 14.4% alc. RATING 95 DRINK 2021-2028 $40 EL

Single Vineyard Chardonnay 2020, Margaret River The Brash Road Vineyard has long been responsible for wines of concentration and this is no different. Seen here through the lens of the ripe, fast and graceful '20 vintage, the wine is powerful and structured. The oak is firmly countersunk into the fruit, providing a backbone and shape, but at no point hindering the fruit from expressing itself. Screw cap. 14.5% alc. RATING 94 DRINK 2021-2031 $40 EL

Single Vineyard Cabernet Sauvignon 2019, Margaret River Fruit from the Yallingup Hills area, in the north. Ripe, pure and structural, this is a cabernet with supple, red fruit at its core, powered by freshness and life and shaped by firm tannins. These characters are all we need to see for the confidence to cellar the wine, however, if you value energy and vivacity in your cabernet, it drinks beautifully right now. Screw cap. 14.2% alc. RATING 94 DRINK 2021-2036 $50 EL

🍷🍷🍷🍷🍸 Single Vineyard Sauvignon Blanc 2021, Margaret River RATING 93 DRINK 2021-2024 $28 EL

Brave Souls Wine

12 Clevedon Street, Botany, NSW, 2019 (postal) **Region** Barossa Valley
T 0420 968 473 **www.**bravesoulswine.com.au **Winemaker** Corey Ryan, Simon Cowham, David Fesq **Viticulturist** Simon Cowham **Est.** 2017 **Dozens** 3500

The story of Brave Souls and its co-founder Julia Weirich has a strong Australian can-do air about it, albeit with German beginnings. Julia obtained her degree in industrial engineering and decided to travel to Australia, where in '13 she became marketing coordinator at Fesq & Co. She later took off for winemaking experience at Bass Phillip, NZ, Burgundy, southern and central Italy and South Africa, eventually returning to Australia (where she really wanted to make wine) to Fesq to take the new role of European Wine Manager, and to Sons of Eden making Brave Souls Wine. In 2020, Julia returned overseas and the winemaking is now undertaken by Corey Ryan and Simon Cowham of Sons of Eden, alongside David Fesq. The wines are named for three men who risked their lives to rescue passengers of the SS *Admella* when it was shipwrecked off the South Australian coast in 1859.

The Able Seaman 2020, Barossa Valley A blend of 59/27/14% grenache/shiraz/mourvèdre. Plump and juicy aromatics bound forth – plum jam along with red cherry and mulberry lift. Packed firmly with spice and earthen notes, a little purple floral note flitting around above. Great density, flow and plush fruit presence. Lovely drinking. Screw cap. 14.5% alc. RATING 95 DRINK 2021–2029 $29 DB ✪

The Whaler Shiraz 2020, Barossa RATING 92 DRINK 2021–2028 $29 DB

Bream Creek

Marion Bay Road, Bream Creek, Tas 7175 **Region** Southern Tasmania
T 0419 363 714 **www.**breamcreekvineyard.com.au **Winemaker** Liam McElhinney
Viticulturist Fred Peacock **Est.** 1990 **Dozens** 6500 **Vyds** 7.6ha
Until 1990 the Bream Creek fruit was sold to Moorilla Estate, but since then the winery has been independently owned and managed by Fred Peacock, legendary for the care he bestows on the vines under his direction. (JH)

Riesling 2021, Tasmania A gorgeous, pristine take on the magnificent and cool 2021 season in a cool site, juxtaposed with the presence and confidence of one of Tasmania's oldest commercial riesling plantings. I love the contrast of gorgeous rose petal, musk and guava aromatics with succulent palate concentration, fine phenolic bite, and just the right nudge of RS to tone racy Tasman Sea acidity. Screw cap. 12.5% alc. RATING 94 DRINK 2021–2027 $33 TS
Reserve Chardonnay 2021, Tasmania In the right hands, the gracefulness of Tasmania's cooler seasons is alluring indeed. A barrel selection of just 100 dozen, this is an altogether more toned, introverted and serious chardonnay than Bream Creek's estate chardonnay. To its great credit, it's less flippant and tropical, with a resolute focus on grapefruit tension and white peach flavour. A touch more new oak (not too much) builds structure and tone, while leaving the main act to impressive persistence of spicy white fruits. Best yet. Screw cap. 13.4% alc. RATING 94 DRINK 2023–2031 $50 TS

Blanc de Blanc 2015, Tasmania RATING 93 $60 TS
Sauvignon Blanc 2021, Tasmania RATING 92 DRINK 2021–2022 $33 TS
Chardonnay 2021, Tasmania RATING 92 DRINK 2022–2024 $38 TS
Pinot Noir 2020, Tasmania RATING 92 DRINK 2025–2028 $45 TS
Cuvée Traditionelle 2015, Tasmania RATING 91 $48 TS
Reserve Pinot Noir 2019, Tasmania RATING 91 DRINK 2021–2024 $70 TS
Late Disgorged 2007, Tasmania RATING 90 $75 TS

Bremerton Wines

15 Kent Town Road, Langhorne Creek, SA 5255 **Region** Langhorne Creek
T (08) 8537 3093 **www.**bremerton.com.au **Open** 7 days 10–5 **Winemaker** Rebecca Willson **Est.** 1988 **Dozens** 30 000 **Vyds** 120ha
Bremerton has been producing wines since 1988. Rebecca Willson (chief winemaker) and Lucy Willson (marketing manager) were the first sisters in Australia to manage and run a winery. With 120ha of premium vineyards (80% of which goes into their own labels), they grow cabernet sauvignon, shiraz, verdelho, chardonnay, sauvignon blanc, malbec, merlot, fiano, graciano and petit verdot. Exports to most major markets. (JH)

🍷🍷🍷🍷🍷 **B.O.V. 2018, Langhorne Creek** A 'best of vintage' barrel blend of 76/24% shiraz/cabernet sauvignon. Vivid crimson-purple colour. This transcends the normal face of Langhorne Creek thanks to the pure intensity of a remarkable wine that has the ability to cruise through 30+ years. Blackberry and blackcurrant wrap around each other on a juicy, supple palate. Diam. 14.5% alc. RATING 97 DRINK 2025–2055 $85 JH ✪

🍷🍷🍷🍷🍷 **Old Adam Shiraz 2019, Langhorne Creek** One of Bremerton's 3 red wine flagbearers, its style is as consistent as possible, courtesy of 20 months' maturation in French and American oak, and long-standing estate blocks in a region that imparts its special softness. It delivers a superbly balanced wine, with luscious dark berry fruits at its core, marrying this with quality oak that partners just-so tannins. A wine that will add yet more to its elegance over the decades to come. Diam. 14.5% alc. RATING 96 DRINK 2024–2044 $56 JH ✪

Special Release Fiano 2021, Langhorne Creek This has a striking bouquet, ranging from honeysuckle through to the fresh-squeezed lemon that carries it into the multidimensional, mouth-watering crystalline acidity. This is such a great variety, requiring nothing from the winemaker other than making the right decision on the harvest date. Screw cap. 12% alc. RATING 95 DRINK 2022–2027 $24 JH ✪

Special Release Grenache 2021, Langhorne Creek Bright clear colour. Adventurous vinification also used by some highly regarded pinot noir makers. One-third whole-bunch carbonic maceration within some ferments, then crushed and destemmed for completion of fermentation and 8 months in stainless steel and aged barriques. A mix of wild strawberry, and a film of spicy, earthy tannins on the mouth-watering finish. Screw cap. 14.5% alc. RATING 94 DRINK 2022–2025 $24 JH ✪

Briar Ridge Vineyard   ★★★★★

593 Mount View Road, Mount View, NSW 2325 **Region** Hunter Valley
T (02) 4990 3670 **www.**briarridge.com.au **Open** 7 days 10–5 **Winemaker** Alex Beckett (Winemaker), Gwyn Olsen (Consultant Winemaker) **Viticulturist** Belinda Kelly **Est.** 1972 **Dozens** 9500 **Vyds** 39ha

Semillon and shiraz have been the most consistent performers in the Hunter Valley. Underlying the suitability of these varieties to the region, Briar Ridge has been a model of stability, and has the comfort of substantial estate vineyards from which it is able to select the best grapes. It also has not hesitated to venture into other regions, notably Orange. Alex Beckett took over winemaking duties from Gwyn Olsen in 2017 (Gwyn remains as a consultant) and in '20 he embarked on the master of wine program. Exports to the UK, Europe and Canada. (JH)

🍷🍷🍷🍷🍷 **Dairy Hill Single Vineyard Semillon 2021, Hunter Valley** Wild-yeast fermented, warmer than the regional standard, and left on lees for 4 months post-ferment. I adore the sentiment behind this, but the textural build has been pushed radically. Watch the neighbours! But, I love this. A sign of the future rather than the past. A bright one! Scents of tatami, porcini, lanolin, citrus peel, glazed quince and gin and tonic. White pepper, again. Delicious. Rich for the idiom. Palate-staining finish. Thoroughly impressive. Screw cap. 11.8% alc. RATING 97 DRINK 2021–2033 $45 NG ✪

🍷🍷🍷🍷🍷 **Albariño 2021, Hunter Valley** Maker Alex Beckett has a good handle on this, as he does with fiano, a wine whose evolution I am following with great anticipation. Everything done right: hand picked, fermented spontaneously, with a small portion (15%) in older barriques and a brief period on skins in the press and on lees, post-fermentation. All texture-building exercises. Yet albariño's pithy stone, frangipani, saline oyster shell to white pepper riffs are not subsumed, but accentuated. Fine textural detail, energetic trajectory and succulent length, the whirl of acidity whetting the palate for the next glass. This is exceptional. Kudos! Screw cap. 13.1% alc. RATING 95 DRINK 2021–2024 $30 NG ✪ ♥

Stockhausen Shiraz 2017, Hunter Valley A museum release, presumably before Alex Beckett really kicked things into a different gear. Yet his fingerprint seems to be on the lithe tannic refinement and understated subtle nature of the wine. The Cherry Ripe, clove, anise and leather polish, are cushioned by a latticework of well-appointed oak and just enough freshness. Nice drinking. I'd hold this even a bit longer. Screw cap. 14% alc. RATING 95 DRINK 2021–2032 $40 NG

Briar Hill Single Vineyard Chardonnay 2017, Hunter Valley An aged release with a bit of bottle age imparting considerable complexity. A wisp of vanillin oak melds with a core of leesy nourishment, conferring breadth and notes of oatmeal and creamed cashew. Stone-fruit accents aplenty. The finish, long limbed and effortless, with a crackle of mineral and an expanding sweetness. Exceptional Hunter chardonnay, light years from the austere contemporary norm. A wine for those seeking both refinement and flavour. Screw cap. 13% alc. RATING 95 DRINK 2021–2025 $45 NG

Museum Release Dairy Hill Single Vineyard Semillon 2014, Hunter Valley While things may be done differently now – more abstemious selection, ambient-yeast fermentation and a greater textural tapestry – this is very good. Mandarin, tangerine, pickled ginger and lemon zest. A balletic straddle of oxidative complexity and the rapier-like firing line of semillon harvested early à la Hunter. Excellent length of tonic, lime and bitters. Screw cap. 12% alc. RATING 94 DRINK 2021–2027 $63 NG

H.R.B Shiraz Pinot Noir 2013, Hunter Valley An aged release. Homage to the great pioneering styles of 'Hunter River Burgundy'. A fine nose of carnal decadence, from rusty nail, sarsaparilla and sweet, fecund strawberry. The tannins, lithe and long limbed. The acidity, dutiful but not pushed. Delicious drinking, with an immediacy about it. All in the here and now. Screw cap. 13% alc. RATING 94 DRINK 2021–2024 $65 NG

Brinktop Vineyard ★★★☆

66 Brinktop Road, Penna, Tas 7171 **Region** Southern Tasmania
T 0407 224 543 **www.**brinktop.com.au **Winemaker** Todd Goebel **Est.** 2017
Dozens 600 **Vyds** 8ha

Todd Goebel and Gillian Christian have been growing grapes and producing wine in the Coal River Valley since '99, Brinktop their recently established new business. It began with the purchase of a house that had a 1ha vineyard, and that led to a permanent change in their lives. In Sept '17 they moved across the valley to Brinktop, taking with them some select barrels of pinot noir and tempranillo made by Todd from the '17 vintage. They adopted the name Brinktop Killara for one of the wines, Killara being the name of the property when they purchased it. It's a 65ha property, and they have established 8ha of vines, chiefly selected clones of pinot noir, then chardonnay, shiraz and a little tempranillo. Their first vintage was 2018. (JH)

ϘϘϘϘϘ Chardonnay 2021, Tasmania Fruit from 3yo vines rarely has the confidence to uphold 40% new French oak, the result here clearly reflecting both high-class barrels and sensitive execution. Refreshing and youthful, it's cut with tense Coal River Valley acidity that traces a crystalline tail. Give it a few years to come together. Screw cap. 13.8% alc. RATING 92 DRINK 2025–2028 $38 TS

Brokenwood ★★★★★

401-427 McDonalds Road, Pokolbin, NSW 2321 **Region** Hunter Valley
T (02) 4998 7559 **www.**brokenwood.com.au **Open** Mon–Fri 11–5, Sat–Sun 10–5
Winemaker Stuart Hordern, Kate Sturgess **Viticulturist** Kat Barry **Est.** 1970
Dozens 100 000 **Vyds** 64ha

Brokenwood's big-selling Hunter Semillon provides the volume to balance the limited quantities of the flagships ILR Semillon and Graveyard Shiraz. Brokenwood purchased the Graveyard Vineyard from Hungerford Hill in '78 and has fully rehabilitated the vineyard.

There is also a range of wines coming from regions including Beechworth, Orange, Central Ranges, McLaren Vale, Cowra and elsewhere. In '17 Iain Riggs celebrated his 35th vintage at the helm of Brokenwood, offering a unique mix of winemaking skills, management and a diverse business. He also contributed a great deal to various wine industry organisations. Iain retired in '20, but remains on the board of directors and consults on any issue where his experience will assist. Exports to all major markets. (JH)

🍷🍷🍷🍷🍷 **Sunshine Vineyard Semillon 2014, Hunter Valley** The wine's magic has nothing to do with the winemaking and everything to do with the site and 7 years in bottle. The perfumed bouquet of lemon zest, frangipani and toast leads into a mouth-watering citrus- and honey-accented palate. The length, finish and aftertaste sing in perfect harmony. Screw cap. 11.5% alc. RATING 97 DRINK 2022-2030 $66 JH ✪ ❤

🍷🍷🍷🍷🍷 **Lillydale Vineyard Chardonnay 2021, Yarra Valley** A wine with a marrow reminiscent of a Japanese childhood: tatami straw, dried shiitake and umami. I have segued here after tasting Hunter wines and the savoury, understated reflective state of this, impressive. Thrust of extract, parry of energy and ebb of savoury oak, nutty and fine. A bit youthful and jangly-tangy, perhaps, but this will come good. Very. Screw cap. 13% alc. RATING 96 DRINK 2022-2030 $66 NG ✪

Lillydale Vineyard Chardonnay 2020, Yarra Valley An elegant chardonnay in best Yarra style, white peach and pink grapefruit the drivers through the long palate and lingering aftertaste, its best years still to come. Screw cap. 12.5% alc. RATING 96 DRINK 2021-2030 $66 JH ✪

Oakey Creek Vineyard Semillon 2019, Hunter Valley A warm year that spins palate-staining extract, yet this remains precise and intense, but so deft on its feet as to be spellbinding. Freshly cut grass, honeydew melon and lemongrass to rosemary-soused gin and tonic. Strident length. Impressive tension. Age-worthy, to be sure. Its current state, but a glimpse of its future. Screw cap. 10.7% alc. RATING 96 DRINK 2022-2032 $66 NG ✪

Rayner Vineyard Shiraz 2019, McLaren Vale Deep colour. The bouquet and palate use different mediums to convey an eerily similar blend of plum, vanilla bean and dark chocolate, framed by cedary oak. Screw cap. 14.5% alc. RATING 96 DRINK 2022-2034 $100 JH

Oakey Creek Vineyard Semillon 2017, Hunter Valley A brilliant wine! Nascent of feel. Coiled taut, despite bottle age. Already delicious, yet the potential energy a reflection of a very fine year. Buttered toast just evident. Lime splice, orange pastille, lemon curd and pink grapefruit pulp. The acidity, juicy rather than brittle. The trail across the palate, long, a little chalky and refined. Exquisite. Loads in store. Screw cap. 11.5% alc. RATING 96 DRINK 2022-2032 $66 NG ✪

Oakey Creek Vineyard Semillon 2016, Hunter Valley A lovely green glint to the straw-yellow hue. Exceptional aromas attesting to how good '17 is, particularly for whites. Dried tatami mat. Lemongrass, orange pastille, lemon balm and citrus verbena. Immensely long, tactile and juicy, with plenty in store. Screw cap. 11.1% alc. RATING 96 DRINK 2021-2032 $66 NG ✪

Maxwell Vineyard Chardonnay 2021, Hunter Valley Home turf. Top of the tree. Or very close to it. There is almost a grating intensity to the fruit of so many '21s in the Hunter. Here, an exercise in how to soothe, calm and placate it, with an optimal picking window and the assiduous use of oak and lees, following an ambient fermentation. A clay site, embellishing flavour and texture. Very impressive. Age for a few years and tuck in. Screw cap. 12.5% alc. RATING 95 DRINK 2022-2030 $66 NG

Tallawanta Vineyard Semillon 2021, Hunter Valley This is force of structure, but an incipient glimpse of what lies in store. The greatest wines reveal little in their youth, serving but a platitude of textures and poise that allows us to think ahead. With this in mind, this augurs very well. Precise, compact and dense. Intense of lemongrass thrust and delicate of balmy, lanolin linger. All good signs. Screw cap. 12.7% alc. RATING 95 DRINK 2021-2033 $66 NG

Indigo Vineyard Chardonnay 2021, Beechworth The most balletic wine among this stellar suite of chardonnays, each spanning one of Australia's premium regions. A pirouette of pumice and a mineral twirl. Granitic of feel. Good terroir-to-glass transfer. A whiff of nectarine, white peach, fig and toasted almond. Yet lightweight, despite the paradoxical intensity of flavour and streamlined length. This will age well. Screw cap. 12.5% alc. RATING 95 DRINK 2021-2031 $75 NG

Wade Block 2 Vineyard Shiraz 2020, McLaren Vale In this hot and dry year, the elevated sands of Blewitt Springs, home to Wade Block, have offered a superior expression: fresher, more detailed and digestible. The stamp of reduction, apparent in notes of iodine and violet. But boysenberry, kirsch and Cherry Ripe packed in too. A skein of peppery freshness tows this long to a beguiling finish. Screw cap. 14% alc. RATING 95 DRINK 2021-2030 $75 NG

Rayner Vineyard Shiraz 2020, McLaren Vale Vinous, powerful and pliant. A whiff of reduction serves to impart tension to teeming notes of dried nori, sea spray and blue fruits, swabbed with black-olive tapenade. The finish, nicely defined for such a warm year, pushing long. This has a stellar track record and I see no reason why this won't adhere to it. Screw cap. 14% alc. RATING 95 DRINK 2021-2032 $110 NG

Indigo Vineyard Shiraz 2019, Beechworth The colour is an arresting and clear royal purple, the bouquet with spice firing the lively, fresh, medium-bodied palate, red and black cherry fruit the mainstream flavours. Screw cap. 13.5% alc. RATING 95 DRINK 2022-2029 $75 JH

7 Acre Shiraz 2019, Hunter Valley While the lighter Hunter mould is evocative of pinot to a certain degree, as well as persuasive, easier-drinking styles, there is something compelling about a mid-weighted wine with just a bit more tannic mettle. Here it is. Still savoury. Still light on its feet. But with an earthy beef-bouillon scent muddled with Hunter terracotta, spiced cherry, mint and classy oak. Very good drinking now. Better in several years. Screw cap. 13.5% alc. RATING 95 DRINK 2022-2033 $110 NG

Tallawanta Vineyard Shiraz 2019, Hunter Valley Almost a continuum of Graveyard, on a similarly exposed east-facing slope. A warm year, accentuating the burly tannins of the block. Violet, sarsaparilla, the fecund, sweet earth of the Hunter and a flood of dark cherry and licorice strap across the long, firm finish. A powerful brood to this. Will age exceptionally well. Screw cap. 13.5% alc. RATING 95 DRINK 2022-2035 $150 NG

Maragle Vineyard Chardonnay 2021, Tumbarumba Delicate and powdery of texture, with an altitudinal thrust of sour stone fruits. Pithy and nicely edgy. The finish, long and pliant. A gently creamy nougat note. The least intricate of this fine suite, perhaps, but no less poised, intense or impressive. Screw cap. 13% alc. RATING 94 DRINK 2021-2028 $66 NG

Brookland Valley ★★★★★

4070 Caves Road, Wilyabrup, WA 6280 **Region** Margaret River
T (08) 9755 6042 **www**.brooklandvalley.com.au **Open** 7 days 11–5
Winemaker Courtney Treacher **Est.** 1984
Brookland Valley has an idyllic setting, its restaurant, Flutes, overlooking the waters of Wilyabrup Brook. The vineyard is located on the edge of Leeuwin's Naturaliste Ridge and is planted predominately to cabernet sauvignon and chardonnay. Winemaker Courtney Treacher completed her degree in viticulture and oenology in '02, gaining experience in the Swan Valley, Perth Hills, Margaret River and the Hunter Valley along the way. She joined Houghton Wines as a cellarhand in '04, working her way up to her current role as senior winemaker for both Houghton and Brookland Valley Wines, both owned by Accolade. The quality, value for money and consistency of the wines are exemplary. (JH)

🍷🍷🍷🍷🍷 **Limited Release Reserve Chardonnay 2020, Margaret River** If you wanted to pinpoint a classic, typical, Margaret River chardonnay nose, this would be it. Pink grapefruit, salted yellow peaches, red apple skins, fresh curry leaves and brine – lots of it. The power of the Gingin clone in this part of the world is absolute, driving power and explosive flavour at once. This is still frisky (being so young), but there's a certain attractiveness and appeal about that. However, it will morph into a more complete version of itself in 3–5 years from now. Screw cap. 13.5% alc. RATING 96 DRINK 2022-2035 $77 EL

ŸŸŸŸŸ Estate Chardonnay 2020, Margaret River RATING 91 DRINK 2021-2027 $52 JH

Brothers at War ★★★★★

58 Murray Street, Tanunda, SA 5252 **Region** Barossa Valley
T 0405 631 889 **www.**brothersatwar.com.au **Open** 7 days 11–5 **Winemaker** Angus Wardlaw **Viticulturist** Chris Alderton **Est.** 2013 **Dozens** 5000 **Vyds** 15ha
Brothers Angus and Sam Wardlaw are the men behind this exciting addition to the contemporary Barossa wine scene and, as the name suggests, they could have possibly had the odd rumble as they were growing up under the watch of their father, Barossa winemaker, David Wardlaw. Established in 2013 with a small intake of shiraz, the brothers gathered pace over the ensuing years, adding vigneron Chris Alderton to the mix and today the formidable trio craft a superb range of pure-fruited, vibrant wines from across the Barossa and Eden Valleys. They riff on the classic grape Barossa varieties in a modern, elegant style that speaks clearly of their regional roots. Brothers at War is a young winery with a very bright future indeed. (DB)

ŸŸŸŸŸ Peace Keeper Grenache 2021, Barossa Valley A red-purple hue, with great clarity and detail, the pure plummy fruits underscored with floral flourishes along with ginger spice and a calm, airy sense of space on the palate. The Peace Keeper is a wonderfully composed and balanced wine with nary a hair out of place. Superb drinking and astonishing value for money. Screw cap. 13.5% alc. RATING 97 DRINK 2021-2031 $38 DB ✪ ♥

ŸŸŸŸŸ Single Vineyard Old Vine Shiraz 2019, Barossa Valley Pristine and pure plum and black-fruit characters on display here, showing great concentration, cut with whole-bunch spice, earthy bass notes and a light floral lift. For all its impressive fruit intensity, there is clarity and detail to the wine's flow across the palate, excellent balance and an enduring finish of great purity. Impressive stuff. Cork. 14% alc. RATING 96 DRINK 2021-2035 $110 DB
Single Vineyard Syrah 2019, Eden Valley A purely fruited wine showing ripe satsuma plum and macerated berry fruits with abundant spice, dark chocolate and earth. There's some sinew to the tannin structure which matches the fruit profile perfectly, a touch of amaro herbal interest on the finish and a quartz-like acidity that provides a vivid driving pulse, finishing savoury and meaty. Cork. 15% alc. RATING 95 DRINK 2021-2035 $80 DB

Brothers in Arms ★★★★☆

Lake Plains Road, Langhorne Creek, SA 5255 **Region** Langhorne Creek
T (08) 8537 3182 **www.**brothersinarms.com.au **Open** By appt **Winemaker** Jim Urlwin
Viticulturist Guy Adams **Est.** 1998 **Dozens** 25 000 **Vyds** 85ha
The Adams family has been growing grapes at Langhorne Creek since 1891, when the vines at the famed Metala vineyards were planted. Guy Adams is the fifth generation of the family to own and work the vineyard, and has both improved the viticulture and expanded the plantings. In 1998 they decided to hold back a small proportion of the production for the Brothers in Arms label; now they dedicate 85ha to it (40ha each of shiraz and cabernet sauvignon and 2.5ha each of malbec and petit verdot). Exports to the UK, the US, Canada, Sweden, Denmark, Singapore, South Korea, Malaysia, and Hong Kong. (JH)

ŸŸŸŸŸ Shiraz 2019, Langhorne Creek A full-bodied mouthful of powerful dark berry, spice and plum fruit coupled with positive oak and firm, racy fruit. While it needs time in bottle, it has the balance to guarantee success. Screw cap. 14.5% alc. RATING 95 DRINK 2025-2035 $45 JH

Shiraz 2020, Langhorne Creek RATING 93 DRINK 2023–2032 $45 JH
Cabernet Sauvignon 2019, Langhorne Creek RATING 92 DRINK 2024–2034
$45 JH

Brown Brothers ★★★★★

239 Milawa–Bobinawarrah Road, Milawa, Vic 3678 **Region** King Valley
T (03) 5720 5500 **www.**brownbrothers.com.au **Open** 7 days 9–5 **Winemaker** Joel
Tilbrook, Cate Looney, Geoff Alexander, Katherine Brown, Tom Canning, Simon
McMillan **Viticulturist** Brett McClen, Sean Dean **Est.** 1889 **Dozens** 1 million
Vyds 570ha

Brown Brothers draws upon a considerable number of vineyards spread throughout a range of
site climates – from very warm to very cool. An expansion into Heathcote added significantly
to its armoury. In '10 Brown Brothers acquired Tasmania's Tamar Ridge. In May '16 it
acquired Innocent Bystander, and with it a physical presence in the Yarra Valley. Known for
the diversity of varieties with which it works, Brown Brothers produces good value wines. Its
cellar door in Milawa receives the greatest number of visitors in Australia. A founding member
of Australia's First Families of Wine. Exports to all major markets. (JH)

Patricia Cabernet Sauvignon 2017, King Valley Always a strength in the
Patricia range, this cabernet style is effortless and all class. Quality of fruit is the
star, with oak bringing a layer of nuance and complexity to a solid core of cassis
and plum fruits with bracken, earth, violets, cassia bark and a dusting of powdery
cocoa. Brings both cabernet leafiness and spiced-filled liveliness to the finish. A joy
to drink. Screw cap. 14.5% alc. RATING 96 DRINK 2022–2030 $62 JP ✪ ♥
Patricia Pinot Noir Chardonnay Brut 2015, King Valley 77/23% pinot
noir/chardonnay. Taste the complexity that comes with 6 years on lees, it's
thrilling. Citrus and stone-fruit aromas mix with yeasty brioche, roasted nuts,
lemon butter and shortbread. The palate is superbly textured with fine acid crunch
and a mouth-watering lemon pithiness. Cork. 12.5% alc. RATING 95 $48 JP
Patricia Chardonnay 2020, East Coast Tasmania Another assured and
beautifully refined example of chardonnay from Patricia's new home on the east
coast of Tasmania. The fruit shines in delicious stone fruits and members of the
citrus family, together with a bright splash of beachy rock-pool notes. Flavour
runs deep and long, intensified on the palate through the delivery of cool-climate
zippy acidity. Smart use of oak here with an attractive almond-nougat intervention
through the middle palate. Another top Patricia to honour the late family
matriarch. Screw cap. 12.5% alc. RATING 95 DRINK 2022–2030 $48 JP
Patricia Noble Riesling 2019, Victoria Year after year, this wine is incredibly
consistent in style and quality. Deep golden hues with the scent of dried apricot,
orange marmalade, cumquat, orange peel and dried fig. The palate is dense and
sticky, beautifully balanced and textural and deliciously layered in concentrated
citrus. Stunning! 375ml. Screw cap. 10.8% alc. RATING 95 DRINK 2022–2025
$36 JP ♥

Pinot Noir Chardonnay Meunier NV, South Eastern Australia RATING 93
$25 JP ✪
Premium Brut Prosecco NV, King Valley RATING 93 $27 JP ✪
Limited Release Single Vineyard Montepulciano 2019, Heathcote
RATING 91 DRINK 2021–2025 $25 JP
Sparkling Moscato 2021, Victoria RATING 91 DRINK 2022–2024 $17 JP ✪
Origins Series Chardonnay 2021, King Valley RATING 90 DRINK 2022–2024
$18 JP ✪
Sparkling Moscato Rosé 2021, Victoria RATING 90 DRINK 2022–2024
$17 JP ✪

Brown Hill Estate

925 Rosa Brook Road, Rosa Brook, WA 6285 **Region** Margaret River
T (08) 9757 4003 **www.**brownhillestate.com.au **Open** 7 days 10–5 **Winemaker** Nathan
Bailey, Angus Pattullo **Viticulturist** Nathan Bailey **Est.** 1995 **Dozens** 3000 **Vyds** 22ha
The Bailey family is involved in all stages of wine production, with minimum outside help.
Their stated aim is to produce top quality wines at affordable prices, via uncompromising
viticultural practices emphasising low yields. They have shiraz and cabernet sauvignon
(8ha each), semillon, sauvignon blanc and merlot (2ha each). The quality of the best wines in
the portfolio is very good. (JH)

▼▼▼▼▼ **Golden Horseshoe Reserve Chardonnay 2020, Margaret River** Scores
with its elegance and balance; fruit, not oak, is dominant. The fruit flavours sit
midway between grapefruit and white peach, acidity neatly tying a neat bow
around the fruit. Screw cap. 13.5% alc. RATING 95 DRINK 2021-2030 $50 JH
Fimiston Reserve Shiraz 2019, Margaret River Excellent colour; an
expressive and fresh bouquet sends all the right messages of a juicy blend of red
and black fruits, latent spice and fine-spun tannins on the long fresh finish. Screw
cap. 14% alc. RATING 95 DRINK 2024-2034 $50 JH
Bill Bailey Shiraz Cabernet 2019, Margaret River Shiraz and cabernet is
co-planted, harvested together and co-fermented before 18 months in French
and American oak. Co-fermentation brings a very early seamlessness to wine,
and it is an exciting concept when executed correctly. This wine is silky, medium
bodied and perfumed, with no discernible boundary between cabernet and shiraz,
although both component parts are present. The oak too is invisible, serving only
to cradle the fruit and usher it through the finish. Very smart. Screw cap. 14.5% alc.
RATING 94 DRINK 2022-2035 $90 EL

▼▼▼▼▽ **Perseverance Signature Range Cabernet Merlot 2019, Margaret River**
RATING 92 DRINK 2022-2032 $80 EL
Ivanhoe Reserve Cabernet Sauvignon 2019, Margaret River RATING 90
DRINK 2023-2033 $50 EL

Brown Magpie Wines ★★★★

125 Larcombes Road, Modewarre, Vic 3240 **Region** Geelong
T (03) 5266 2147 **www.**brownmagpiewines.com **Open** 7 days 11–4 Jan, w'ends 11–4
Nov–Apr **Winemaker** Shane Breheny, Daniel Greene **Viticulturist** Loretta Breheny
Est. 2000 **Dozens** 5000 **Vyds** 9ha
Shane and Loretta Breheny's 20ha property is situated predominantly on a gentle, north-facing
slope, with cypress trees on the western and southern borders providing protection against the
wind. Vines were planted over 2001–02, with pinot noir (4ha) taking the lion's share, followed
by pinot gris and shiraz (2.4ha each) and 0.1ha each of chardonnay and sauvignon blanc.
Viticulture is Loretta's love; winemaking (and wine) is Shane's. (JH)

▼▼▼▼▽ **Modewarre Mud Reserve Single Vineyard Shiraz 2018, Geelong** A
sinewy, coiled, youthful reserve wine that calls upon the drinker for some patience.
Medium bodied and finely voiced, it offers a study in cool-climate shiraz, with red
fruits, blueberry, herbal, almost pinot-esque in delicacy and fine tannins. It remains
a wine in building mode, a little arms and legs still, especially when it comes to
cedary oak on the back palate. Give it time. Screw cap. 13.5% alc. RATING 93
DRINK 2022-2028 $60 JP
Single Vineyard Shiraz 2019, Geelong A tantalising mix of lightly savoury
and deeply spicy, it feeds the need of shiraz lovers who want a little complexity
while also experiencing the grape's dark-berried heart. The bouquet is loaded
with black cherry, wild blackberries, licorice, spice, briar and wet earth. They
gather on the palate, running in layers through to a long, taut finish. The
earthy savoury thread really elevates the wine. Screw cap. 13.2% alc. RATING 92
DRINK 2021-2029 $45 JP

Modewarre Mud Reserve Single Vineyard Shiraz 2019, Geelong
A young single-vineyard shiraz with plenty in the way of dark purple colour, delivering a shiraz that needs further ageing to reveal its true personality. A solid core of blackcurrant fruit is key here; it's the driver, the chord that brings the wine together in intensity and concentration, makes it sing. It's joined by cool-climate plums, spice, chocolate, pepper, toasty vanillin oak and dense tannins. In other words, there's a lot happening here and it revolves around good fruit. Give it time. Screw cap. 13.5% alc. RATING 91 DRINK 2022-2027 $60 JP

Single Vineyard Pinot Noir 2019, Geelong Cool-climate finesse here with Geelong's signature brightness of red cherry fruit, minty/herbal/garrigue and floral aromatics. Sports an almost Mediterranean pungency, with energy and life, with a sinewy tannic dryness. Finishes a tad short. Screw cap. 12.8% alc. RATING 90 DRINK 2021-2025 $48 JP

🍷🍷🍷🍷 **Single Vineyard Chardonnay 2021, Geelong** RATING 89 DRINK 2021-2027 $35 JP
Single Vineyard Pinot Gris 2021, Geelong RATING 88 DRINK 2021-2024 $30 JP

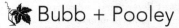

Bubb + Pooley ★★★★

1092 Cambridge Road, Cambridge, Tas, 7170 **Region** Tasmania
www.bubbandpooley.com.au **Winemaker** Anna Pooley, Justin Bubb **Est.** 2021 **Vyds** 3ha
Justin Bubb and Anna Pooley each have more than 20 years' experience making benchmark wines. Justin oversees winery operations and management while Anna takes care of vineyard liaisons and harvest. In '21 they established their own brand, with an aspiration to make wines that are 'raw, expressive and speak of place'. Their inaugural release comprised fruit purchased from friends: riesling from Pressing Matters, pinot noir and chardonnay from Brinktop and syrah from Milton Vineyard. Fermentation and maturation are largely in hand-crafted concrete vessels of different shapes, chosen to enhance the texture of each variety. In late '22, they purchased an established vineyard at Campania in the Coal River Valley, with 8000 vines of pinot noir and 2500 each of chardonnay and cabernet planted in '00, with plans to plant more in '23. (TS)

🍷🍷🍷🍷🍷 **Riesling 2021, Tasmania** The essence of cool-season riesling, charged with tremendous stamina and endurance. Great concentration of pure kaffir lime and Granny Smith apple reach long across the palate and through a strong finish. Fruit and acid are the theme here, and oak, phenolics and residual have been tactically deployed to build body, structure and presence with no impact on purity. A dramatic debut, and clearly going places. Screw cap. 13.2% alc. RATING 94 DRINK 2023-2031 $45 TS

🍷🍷🍷🍷🍷 **Pinot Noir 2021, Tasmania** RATING 93 DRINK 2026-2031 $65 TS
Chardonnay 2021, Tasmania RATING 92 DRINK 2022-2028 $55 TS

Bull Lane Wine Company

PO Box 77, Heathcote, Vic 3523 **Region** Heathcote
T 0427 970 041 **www**.bulllane.com.au **Winemaker** Simon Osicka **Viticulturist** Alison Phillips **Est.** 2013 **Dozens** 500
After a successful career as a winemaker with what is now TWE, Simon Osicka, together with viticulturist partner Alison Phillips, returned to the eponymous family winery just within the eastern boundary of the Heathcote region in '10. Spurred on by a decade of drought impacting on the 60yo dry-grown vineyard, and a desire to create another style of shiraz, Simon and Alison spent considerable time visiting Heathcote vineyards with access to water in the lead-up to the '10 vintage. After the weather gods gave up their tricks of '11, Bull Lane was in business. Exports to Denmark. (JH)

🍷🍷🍷🍷🍷 **Marsanne 2021, Heathcote** The maker was inspired by the textural and food-friendly marsannes he made when working at Domaine Jean Louis Chave in the Rhône Valley in '10. He captures the grape's warmth and complexity easily in a good year like '21. An array of ripe scents and flavours in citrus, peach, spiced apple, mandarin skin, apricot kernel, with honeysuckle and jasmine florals. Skin contact has contributed to the wine's gentle creaminess and almond-nougat light savouriness. Delicious. Screw cap. 13.5% alc. RATING 95 DRINK 2022-2027 $30 JP ✪

ŸŸŸŸŸ Shiraz 2020, Heathcote RATING 93 DRINK 2022-2027 $30 JP

Buller Wines

2804 Federation Way, Rutherglen, Vic 3685 **Region** Rutherglen
T (02) 6032 9660 **www.**bullerwines.com.au **Open** 7 days 10–5 **Winemaker** Dave Whyte **Est.** 1921 **Dozens** 10000 **Vyds** 32ha
In '13, after 92 years of ownership and management by the Buller family, the business was purchased by Gerald and Mary Judd, a well-known local couple and family with extensive roots in the North East. They are hands-on in the business and have overseen major investment in the cellar, storage, operations and, importantly, vineyards. White and sparkling wines from the King Valley have been added to the range and there is a new restaurant and refurbished cellar door. Buller celebrated 100 years in '21. Exports to the UK, Belgium, Taiwan, the US, Japan and NZ. (JH)

ŸŸŸŸŸ **Calliope Rare Topaque NV, Rutherglen** The base for this wine comes from the '40s. A joy to behold and enjoy. Immense concentration here and yet it maintains a degree of elegance and aromatic floral lift. It is not as dense as some in this classification; it makes its mark with dried fruits, malt toffee, honey gingerbread and golden raisins. Flows like honey with a burst of toasted walnuts and almond across the palate. Freshness of spirit is the key here, it gives lift and life to this great iconic style. Screw cap. 18% alc. RATING 96 $120 JP
Calliope Grand Muscat NV, Rutherglen Once you enter the Grand Muscat classification, you are in another world where degrees of lusciousness and pleasure become almost superfluous. This offers a deep-seated flavour intensity in toffee-covered figs, chocolate, coffee bean and pan forte. Aged muscat material is used generously, to be nicely countered by fresh, neutral spirit. More please! 500ml. Screw cap. 18% alc. RATING 96 $150 JP
Calliope Rare Muscat NV, Rutherglen By its very name, not every producer can fulfil the requirements of the Rare Muscat classification, that is, an average of 50+ years ageing. Thanks to the Buller family who set this original solera in place, we have gems like this to enjoy. Age doesn't tire, it brings forth layers of immense complexity countered by a dash of fresh, neutral spirit. 500ml. Screw cap. 18% alc. RATING 96 $250 JP
Calliope Grand Topaque NV, Rutherglen The step up in price and complexity for the Grand fortified level is obvious in this wine. Colour is now deep amber-walnut brown. Aromas bring forth equally colourful imagery of malt toffee biscuits, walnuts, plum pudding and caramel drenched coffee cake. Gets the tastebuds working, as does the lusciousness and warmth of spice and fruit and sweet deliciousness to be enjoyed on the palate. 500ml. Screw cap. 18% alc. RATING 95 $150 JP

ŸŸŸŸŸ **Calliope Rare Frontignac NV, Rutherglen** RATING 93 $250 JP
The 1928 Block Shiraz 2018, Rutherglen RATING 92 DRINK 2022-2033 $70 JP
Balladeer Durif 2019, Rutherglen RATING 91 DRINK 2021-2030 $29 JP
Fine Old Tawny NV, Rutherglen RATING 91 $28 JP
The Nook Prosecco NV, King Valley RATING 90 $23 JP
Calliope Shiraz 2017, Rutherglen RATING 90 DRINK 2021-2030 $45 JP
Fine Old Muscat NV, Rutherglen RATING 90 $28 JP

Bunkers Margaret River Wines

1142 Kaloorup Road, Kaloorup, WA 6280 **Region** Margaret River
T (08) 9368 4555 **www.bunkerswines.com.au Winemaker** Severine Logan
Viticulturist Murray Edmonds **Est.** 2010 **Dozens** 5500 **Vyds** 34ha
Over the past 20+ years, Mike Calneggia had his fingers in innumerable Margaret River
viticultural pies. While Bunkers Wines, owned by Mike and Sally Calneggia, is only a small
part of his viticultural undertakings, it has been carefully targeted from the word go. It has
6 mainstream varieties (cabernet, semillon, merlot, chardonnay, sauvignon blanc and shiraz)
joined by rising star, tempranillo, in the northern part of the Margaret River. Severine Logan
is winemaker and Murray Edmonds the viticulturist. Mike and daughter Amy are responsible
for sales and marketing. They say, 'The world of wine is full of serious people making serious
wines for an ever-decreasing serious market … Bunkers wines have been created to put the
'F' word back into wine, 'FUN', that is.' Exports to Japan. (JH)

ŶŶŶŶ   **Windmills Shiraz Tempranillo Rosé 2021, Western Australia** Juicy, bright,
plump and slightly sweet, with a vein of tart acidity that courses through it. All
things will come together in the fridge: this is lovely, uncomplicated summer
drinking. Screw cap. 13% alc. RATING 89 DRINK 2022-2023 $20 EL
Bears Cabernet Merlot 2020, Margaret River Broody and black nose,
littered with Chinese five-spice, aniseed and blackberries. In the mouth the wine
has fine tannins, kind of chalky and shapely, which assist in ushering the fruit
through the finish. Drink it in the short term to catch that vibrancy and energy.
Screw cap. 14.4% alc. RATING 89 DRINK 2021-2027 $20 EL
Guillotines Shiraz 2020, Margaret River When you pick up a bottle for $20,
I believe you want it to be like this: juicy, satisfying, flavoursome, uncomplicated
and fresh. This is all of that; the shiraz fruit framed by the ripe, powerful and glossy
vintage of 2020. Screw cap. 14.5% alc. RATING 89 DRINK 2021-2027 $20 EL

Bunnamagoo Estate

603 Henry Lawson Drive, Mudgee, NSW 2850 **Region** Mudgee
T 1300 304 707 **www.bunnamagoowines.com.au Open** 7 days 10–4
Winemaker Robert Black **Est.** 1995 **Dozens** 100 000 **Vyds** 108ha
Bunnamagoo Estate stands on one of the first land grants in the region and is situated near
the historic town of Rockley. A 6ha vineyard planted to chardonnay, merlot and cabernet
sauvignon was established by Paspaley Pearls. The winery and cellar door are located at
the much larger and warmer Eurunderee Vineyard (102ha) at Mudgee. Exports to the UK,
Singapore, Fiji, Papua New Guinea, Indonesia and Hong Kong. (JH)

ŶŶŶŶŶ   **Blanc de Blancs 2016, Central Ranges** A non-malo style, buffered with very
low dosage (3g/L) and an impressive 5 years on lees, this works exceptionally well.
Baked apple, cinnamon and a waft of aldehydic complexity reminiscent of the
sourdough signature of fine grower champagne. Lightweight, febrile of energy and
brimming with flavour, towed to good length by a thrumming undercurrent of
acidity. Screw cap. 12.5% alc. RATING 94 $50 NG

ŶŶŶŶŶ   **Dry Style Riesling 2021, Mudgee** RATING 90 DRINK 2021-2029 $25 NG
Tempranillo 2021, Mudgee RATING 90 DRINK 2021-2028 $25 NG

Burke & Wills Winery

3155 Burke & Wills Track, Mia Mia, Vic 3444 **Region** Heathcote
T (03) 5425 5400 **www.wineandmusic.net Open** By appt **Winemaker** Andrew Pattison,
Robert Ellis **Est.** 2003 **Dozens** 1200 **Vyds** 1.6ha
After 18 years at Lancefield Winery in the Macedon Ranges, Andrew Pattison moved his
operation a few kilometres north to set up Burke & Wills Winery at the southern edge of
the Heathcote region. The vineyards at Mia Mia comprise 0.6ha of shiraz, 0.6ha of bordeaux
varieties (cabernet sauvignon, petit verdot, merlot and malbec) and 0.4ha of gewürztraminer.
He still sources a small amount of Macedon Ranges fruit from his former vineyard; additional

grapes are contract-grown in Heathcote. In '17 the winery won the inaugural Premier's Award for Best Victorian Wine with the '15 Vat 1 Shiraz. (JH)

🍷🍷🍷🍷🍷 **The Aristocrat 2019, Heathcote** 50/21/17/12% Petit verdot/merlot/malbec/ cabernet sauvignon, co-fermented bar the later-ripening petit verdot. Made with serious intent and ageing in mind. But first a decant, which allows the violets, dark chocolate, dark cherries, cassis and woody spices full rein. It's well structured, with a vibrant core of flavour, gravel and earth. Tannins are firm and tightly buttoned up. A wine that will benefit from time in bottle. Screw cap. 13.5% alc. RATING 91 DRINK 2021-2029 $45 JP

Mia Mia Gewürztraminer 2021, Heathcote You don't see a lot of gewürztraimer from Heathcote, but it does seem quite at home when you do. Sports sound varietal flavour and concentration, with pretty aromas of blossom and rose petal, lime and spice on display. Palate is svelte and dry, with added hints of ginger and lychee. Finishes ripe and clean. Screw cap. 13.5% alc. RATING 90 DRINK 2021-2025 $28 JP

🍷🍷🍷🍷 **Mr. Burke's Favourite Big Red Shiraz 2019, Heathcote** RATING 89 DRINK 2021-2031 $20 JP

Pattison Family Reserve Malbec 2015, Macedon Ranges Heathcote RATING 89 DRINK 2021-2024 $32 JP

Vat 1 French Oak Shiraz 2017, Heathcote RATING 88 DRINK 2021-2027 $36 JP

Bush Track Wines ★★★★

161 Myrtle Street, Myrtleford, Vic 3737 **Region** Alpine Valleys
T 0409 572 712 **www**.bushtrackwines.com.au **Open** 7 days 12–6 **Winemaker** Jo Marsh, Eleana Anderson **Est.** 1987 **Dozens** 550 **Vyds** 8.8ha
Bob and Helen McNamara established the vineyard in 1987, planting 11 different clones of shiraz with smaller quantities of chardonnay, cabernet sauvignon and sangiovese. They have made small volumes of wines since '06, improving vineyard practices along the way and hiring local winemakers Jo Marsh (Billy Button Wines) and Eleana Anderson (Mayford Wines). Bush Track Wines shares a cheery cellar door with Billy Button in Myrtleford. (JH)

🍷🍷🍷🍷🍷 **Conmara Ovens Valley Shiraz 2018, Alpine Valleys** A solid, tarry, oak-framed wine that brings a savoury edge to the usual spiced-fuelled Ovens Valley shiraz we know. While mocha-chocolate oak is noted, it is in keeping and combines well with the richness of blackberry fruit and generous spice with a thread of bush mint. Wood tannins run deep. Screw cap. 14% alc. RATING 90 DRINK 2021-2028 $50 JP

🍷🍷🍷🍷 **Sangiovese Cabernet 2019, Alpine Valleys** RATING 89 DRINK 2021-2025 $30 JP

Blanc de Blancs Chardonnay 2021, Alpine Valleys RATING 88 $30 JP

Ovens Valley Rosé 2021, Alpine Valleys RATING 88 DRINK 2021-2024 $20 JP

Cabernet Sauvignon 2019, Alpine Valleys RATING 88 DRINK 2022-2023 $30 JP

Buttermans Track ★★★★

75 Yow Yow Creek Road, St Andrews, Vic 3761 **Region** Yarra Valley
T 0433 649 640 **www**.buttermanstrack.com.au **Open** w'ends 11–5 **Winemaker** Joel and Gary Trist **Est.** 1991 **Dozens** 600 **Vyds** 2.13ha
I became intimately acquainted with Buttermans Track in the latter part of the '80s when Coldstream Hills purchased grapes from the Roberts family's Rising Vineyard. I had to coax a 3t truck with almost no brakes and almost no engine to tackle the hills and valleys of the unsealed Buttermans Track. Louise and Gary Trist began planting a small vineyard in '91 on a small side road just off the Buttermans Track. They established 0.86ha of pinot noir, 0.74ha of

shiraz and 0.53ha of sangiovese. The Trist family sold the grapes to Yarra Valley wineries. From '08 onwards a small parcel of sangiovese was retained for the Buttermans Track label, which now includes other varieties, son Joel joining Gary in the winery. (JH)

ŸŸŸŸŸ Sangiovese 2019, Yarra Valley A deep ruby red. Good varietal definition with its core of black fruits, lifted, savoury herbs and a little tobacco. Medium bodied, ripe and energetic, this finishes with succulent yet firm tannins that will work perfectly with food and ensure that this will just get even better over the next 6–8 years. Screw cap. 12.2% alc. RATING 94 DRINK 2023-2029 $32 PR

ŸŸŸŸŸ Riesling 2021, Upper Goulburn RATING 93 DRINK 2022-2028 $27 PR ✪
Sangiovese Rosé 2021, Yarra Valley RATING 92 DRINK 2022-2024 $27 PR
Syrah 2018, Yarra Valley RATING 92 DRINK 2022-2027 $32 PR
Pinot Noir 2018, Yarra Valley RATING 92 DRINK 2022-2027 $40 PR

Byrne Vineyards ★★★★★

PO Box 15, Kent Town BC, SA 5071 **Region** South Australia
T (08) 8132 0022 **www**.byrnevineyards.com.au **Winemaker** Mark Robinson, Phil Reedman MW **Est.** 1963 **Dozens** 120000 **Vyds** 200ha
The Byrne family has been involved in the SA wine industry for 3 generations, with vineyards in the Clare Valley and Riverland. Wine styles include vine-dried, field blends, vegan-friendly wines and regional wines. Exports to the UK, the US, Canada, Germany, Denmark, Sweden, Norway, the Netherlands, Poland, NZ and Japan. (JH)

ŸŸŸŸŸ Calcannia Grenache 2021, Clare Valley Jubey, spicy and mineral on the nose, with layers of raspberry humbug, red licorice, anise and even a hint of ginger. In the mouth, the exactitude of the '21 vintage comes to the fore. This is precise and restrained, almost lean, with rivulets of flavour that flow across the tongue. Really sensational. The oak is largely imperceptible, save for a spicy, supporting role, which gives the fruit ample room to shine with its own light. Marvellous. Screw cap. 15% alc. RATING 95 DRINK 2022-2030 $28 EL ✪
Calcannia Sangiovese 2021, Clare Valley Concentrated, black and brooding, with dense, silky tannins and poignant purple fruit. There is buoyancy in the fruit, despite the river of texture that flows through the mouth. The back palate is really moreish. A lot going on and it's all good. Screw cap. 15% alc. RATING 95 DRINK 2022-2029 $28 EL ✪

Byron & Harold ★★★★★

57 River Way, Walter Point, WA 6152 (postal) **Region** Western Australia
T 0402 010 352 **www**.byronandharold.com.au **Winemaker** Kate Morgan **Est.** 2011 **Dozens** 36000 **Vyds** 34ha
The owners of Byron & Harold make a formidable partnership, covering every aspect of winemaking, sales, marketing, business management and administration. Paul Byron and Ralph (Harold) Dunning together have more than 65 years of experience in the Australian wine trade, working at top levels for some of the most admired wineries and wine distribution companies. Andrew Lane worked for 20 years in the tourism industry, including in a senior role with Tourism Australia, leading to the formation of the Wine Tourism Export Council. More recently he developed the family vineyard (Wandering Lane). Exports to the UK, Canada and NZ. (JH)

ŸŸŸŸŸ The Companions Cabernet Sauvignon 2020, Great Southern Margaret River Super-concentrated and dark, with rivulets of cassis, mulberry, blackberry and licorice. The Great Southern component lends an earthy, dark and bloody base upon which the supple red-fruited Margaret River component can play. Good companions. Screw cap. 14.5% alc. RATING 95 DRINK 2022-2039 $45 EL
The Partners Shiraz 2020, Great Southern This is a big wine and it's very good. It's layered with blackberry, raspberry, licorice and clove, backed by spicy French oak that is secured to every stud of flavour – totally seamless in its

dovetailing. Elegant, for the brawn and density that it conveys. The velvety tannins are a major highlight. Screw cap. 14.8% alc. RATING 95 DRINK 2021-2031 $60 EL

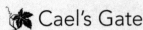 The Protocol Cabernet Sauvignon 2020, Margaret River RATING 93 DRINK 2022-2036 $55 EL
The Partners Riesling 2021, Great Southern RATING 91 DRINK 2021-2028 $40 EL
Rose & Thorns Cabernet Sauvignon 2019, Great Southern RATING 90 DRINK 2021-2029 $28 EL

Cael's Gate

697 Wollombi Road, Broke, NSW 2330 **Region** Hunter Valley
T 0424 152 037 **www.**caelsgate.com.au **Winemaker** Chris Chew **Viticulturist** Trevor Tolson **Est. Dozens** 250

Cael's Gate is a family-owned operation sourcing grapes from Mudgee, the Hunter and the Riverina, with the flexibility to prioritise depending on the nature of the vintage and quality of material. There is currently a shiraz and cabernet from the Riverina, a region that was not afflicted with the recent smoke issues of other districts. The Riverina may well be better known for sweet botrytised styles and large-volume expressions of a simple, fruit-forward persuasion, yet Cael's Gate defies the status quo with aplomb. All the fruit is hand picked. Extraction is judicious. Pretty good French oak is employed too. The result is a duo of high-quality reds that may well come to be known as 'Super Riverinas', so divergent from regional styles to date. (NG)

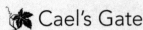 Handpicked Cabernet Sauvignon 2020, Riverina Hand-picked fruit, small-batch fermented and matured in decent French oak. Restrained and earthen of aroma. Mercifully, no jammy or monochromatic notes. Warm, avuncular, honest and real. What a find! Earthen aromas of terracotta and loam. Ample blackcurrant, hedgerow, bramble and mocha. The tannins, gently astringent, a little rustic, but nicely al dente. The oak, a bit pokey, but it drinks well. Almost Euro of feel. A stellar achievement. A Super Riverina! Screw cap. 14.5% alc. RATING 92 DRINK 2021-2027 $48 NG
Handpicked Shiraz 2020, Riverina A richly endowed wine that straddles a warm-climate strut of dark-fruit aspersions, with a cooler air of lilac, mace, iodine, pepper, tapenade and clove. Plenty of fruit, but tension too. A whiff of beef jerky marks a long, thrumming finish, punctuated with an accent of clunky mocha oak, the sole caveat. Screw cap. 14.5% alc. RATING 91 DRINK 2021-2026 $48 NG

Calabria Family Wines

1283 Brayne Road, Griffith, NSW 2680 **Region** Riverina
T (02) 6969 0800 **www.**calabriawines.com.au **Open** 7 days 10–4 **Winemaker** Bill Calabria, Emma Norbiato, Tony Steffania, Jeremy Nascimben **Est.** 1945 **Vyds** 100ha

Calabria Family Wines was born in the Riverina, but has since cast its net wide over the Barossa Valley, too, starting with the purchase of the 100+-year-old William vineyard in 2015. Its 3 Bridges range is anchored on Riverina estate vineyards, and the Saint Petri, Elizabetta, Alternato and other labels on the Barossa. The family has increased its plantings of durif and has added aglianico, nero d'Avola, montepulciano, pinot bianco and St Macaire (once grown in Bordeaux, and now on the verge of extinction, this 2ha is the largest planting in the world). There is a second, family-friendly cellar door at 284 Magnolia Road in Vine Vale in the Barossa Valley, open 11–5 daily. Exports to the UK, the US, Canada, Japan, Fiji, Denmark and Finland. (JH)

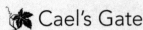 Saint Petri GSM 2020, Barossa Valley A bright red purple in the glass with notes of red cherry, cranberry and red plum combined with hints of Asian spice, red licorice and whiffs of jasmine, tea, kalamata olives and sage. There's a lovely fruit weight, very composed, spicy red fruits flowing in, gypsum-like tannin and great tension on the finish. Screw cap. 14.4% alc. RATING 94 DRINK 2022-2032 $90 DB

♥♥♥♥♡ Elisabetta Durif 2020, Barossa Valley RATING 93 DRINK 2022-2032 $50 DB
Elisabetta Shiraz 2020, Barossa Valley RATING 93 DRINK 2022-2036
$50 DB
75th Anniversary Release Durif 2019, Riverina Barossa Valley RATING 93
DRINK 2021-2028 $75 NG
3 Bridges Golden Mist Botrytis 2006, Riverina RATING 93
DRINK 2021-2026 $40 NG
Alternato Red Blend 2020, Barossa Valley RATING 92 DRINK 2022-2027
$45 DB
Alternato Malbec 2020, Barossa Valley RATING 91 DRINK 2022-2028
$45 DB
3 Bridges Durif 2020, Riverina RATING 91 DRINK 2021-2026 $25 NG
3 Bridges Botrytis Semillon 2018, Riverina RATING 91 DRINK 2021-2025
$25 NG
Museum Release Botrytis Semillon 2000, Riverina RATING 91
DRINK 2021-2025 $60 NG
Alternato Sangiovese 2020, Barossa Valley RATING 90 DRINK 2022-2027
$45 DB
3 Bridges Chardonnay 2019, Tumbarumba RATING 90 DRINK 2021-2024
$25 NG

Calneggia Family Vineyards Estate

1142 Kaloorup Road, Kaloorup, WA 6280 **Region** Margaret River
T (08) 9368 4555 **www**.cfvwine.com.au **Winemaker** Severine Logan
Viticulturist Murray Edmonds **Est.** 2010 **Dozens** 1500 **Vyds** 34ha
The Calneggia family has owned vineyards and been involved in wine in the Margaret River
region for over 30 years. The family owns several premium vineyards and labels across the
region including Rosabrook, Bunkers and Bramble Lane and now their first Calneggia Family
Vineyards Estate wines. (JH)

♥♥♥♥ Rosé 2021, Margaret River Watermelon pip, cherries and raspberries on the
nose. In the mouth the wine is pretty and generous, with a tart edge of apple skins
and spice. Screw cap. 13% alc. RATING 88 DRINK 2021-2023 $26 EL
Rosé 2020, Margaret River All things in place here in this pretty rosé –
flavours span the full spectrum of red berries, bolstered by gentle sprinkles of
spice and bright acidity. Despite the 13% alcohol, there is a trace of heat through
the finish. Decent summertime drinking to be had, and a super-smart new label.
Screw cap. 13% alc. RATING 88 DRINK 2021-2021 $25 EL

Campbells

4603 Murray Valley Highway, Rutherglen, Vic 3685 **Region** Rutherglen
T (02) 6033 6000 **www**.campbellswines.com.au **Open** 7 days 10–5 **Winemaker** Julie
Campbell **Est.** 1870 **Dozens** 36000 **Vyds** 72ha
Campbells has a long and rich history, with 5 generations of wine making. There were difficult
times: phylloxera's arrival in the Bobbie Burns Vineyard in 1898; the Depression of the 1930s;
and premature deaths. But the Scottish blood of founder John Campbell has ensured that
the business flourished. There have been spectacular successes in unexpected quarters (white
table wines, especially riesling) and expected success with muscat and topaque. Following the
death of Colin Campbell in '19, daughters Jane and Julie Campbell are now at the helm, as
managing director and head winemaker respectively. A founding member of Australia's First
Families of Wine. Exports to the UK, the US and other major markets. (JH)

♥♥♥♥♥ Merchant Prince Rare Muscat NV, Rutherglen The oldest base wine is
more than 70 years old. Definitely a once-in-a-lifetime experience (or more,
if possible!) that displays the fortified winemaker's great art so beautifully, with
enviable refinement and elegance. It is both luscious and multi-faceted in flavours.
The house style brings deep pockets of the most delicious spice to enliven plum

pudding, burnt fig, salted caramel, nougat with a chocolate-covered almond nuttiness. Infinite charm. 375ml. Screw cap. 17.5% alc. RATING 99 $126 JP ✪

Isabella Rare Topaque NV, Rutherglen Oh my, takes your breath away! One look and you know you are in Rare territory: dark walnut brown with olive tinge. Moves slowly in the glass and asks the drinker to pause and contemplate its astounding richness and concentration of aromas and flavours gathered over decades. Boiled fruitcake, malt biscuits, soused raisins, caramel, treacle and chocolate aromas gather pace on the palate. A wine to get lost in, with its layers of complexity, dense and deep. Count the minutes the taste remains alive in the mouth. 375ml. Screw cap. 17.5% alc. RATING 97 $140 JP ✪

🍷🍷🍷🍷🍷 **The Barkly Durif 2017, Rutherglen** First impression? This is one serious, structured red wine. And the second? Make mine a medium-rare steak. The Barkly affords durif the status it deserves, celebrating its bold ways and its much underrated elegant herbal/floral detail and savoury tannins. A masterful winemaking performance. Screw cap. 14.5% alc. RATING 96 DRINK 2022-2033 $70 JP ✪

Grand Muscat NV, Rutherglen Grand is a step up in average age in the classification and everything else follows. There is seamless beauty here. Deep walnut hue. Complexity rises dramatically with dark chocolate, licorice, treacle, raisin, plum pudding and baking spice. Intense. Runs smoothly across the palate, so naturally warm and sweet and fresh. Memorable. 375ml. Screw cap. 17.5% alc. RATING 96 $70 JP ✪

Grand Topaque NV, Rutherglen Topaque is about elegance and poise. Here it is multiplied by age and winemaker skill to reveal both delicacy and concentration. It's a fine tightrope walked and mastered here, with its lifted aromatics, freshness and utter deliciousness in dark malt biscuit, dried dates, fruit cake, butterscotch and nutty rancio qualities. And so, so smooth. Very special. 375ml. Screw cap. 17.5% alc. RATING 96 $70 JP ✪

Bobbie Burns Shiraz 2019, Rutherglen This release celebrates 50 vintages of Bobbie Burns. The wine is symbolic of the generosity and enduring style of Rutherglen shiraz, not to mention an upfront, honest approach to winemaking that lets the fruit sing. Incredibly consistent performer in ripe, spicy black fruits, dusty cocoa powder, earth and spice. Strong yet measured on the palate with fine, lithe tannins guaranteeing longevity. Brilliant wine for the price. Screw cap. 14.8% alc. RATING 95 DRINK 2022-2030 $25 JP ✪

Classic Muscat NV, Rutherglen Yes, it's a rich and powerful expression of what Classic represents, according to the classification, but there is so much more to explore. The house style is a fine elegance wedded to spirit freshness, that brings life to an incredible complexity of flavours: of rose oil, vanilla, walnut and treacle and a gorgeous array of dried fruits. 500ml. Screw cap. 17.5% alc. RATING 95 $40 JP

Classic Topaque NV, Rutherglen An alluring Classic Topaque, appearing darker, more concentrated and drier than its muscat equivalent and, I might add, slightly more mysterious with an additional intriguing leatherwood honeyed, nutty spice in play in concert with the rich fruitcake, malt biscuity, butterscotch sweetness. A wine of contemplation and a great deal of sensory enjoyment. 500ml. Screw cap. 17.5% alc. RATING 95 $40 JP

 # Camwell Wines

526 Colville Rd, Willunga South, SA 5172 **Region** McLaren Vale
T 0431 323 891 **www**.Camwellwines.com **Open** By appt **Winemaker** Kendra White Cameron, Bradley White Cameron **Viticulturist** Derek Cameron, Bradley White Cameron **Est.** 2013 **Dozens** 500

Camwell joins the small legion of sustainably minded wineries in McLaren Vale. The winery is 100% solar powered, while the use of machinery in the vineyard is kept to a bare minimum. Owners Brad Cameron and Kendra White Cameron may be young, but Kendra's international background (an American educated at the University of Edinburgh) means she sees the region through a different lens, while Brad's local nous and care of his family's long grape-growing lineage is invaluable. Exports to Singapore. (NG)

ΨΨΨΨΨ **Teli Skin Contact Viognier 2021, McLaren Vale** The nourishment of flavour and textural intrigue gleaned from skins adds a dimension that may surprise newcomers to the style. The secret is to get the chewy phenolics to the point where they add structure and immense versatility at the table without impinging excessively on the flow of flavour. In this case, ginger chutney, apricot, bitter almond, orange amaro and quinine. The finish, salty and long, defined by chewy detail of uncanny precision and moreishness. Lovely gear. Agglomerate. 12.9% alc. RATING 93 DRINK 2022-2025 $29 NG

Cabernet Sauvignon 2019, McLaren Vale Despite the alcoholic warmth to this, the sheath of sage, tomatillo, olive and mulberry leaf-clad tannins, a forcefield of restraint and savouriness, cannot be denied. Sure, there is a morass of SA sweetness amid the fray, yet the effect of structure pushing against the tannin is contagious, drawing me in for the second and third glass. Lovely stuff. Screw cap. 14.9% alc. RATING 93 DRINK 2022-2032 $35 NG

Fumé Blanc Sauvignon Blanc 2021, McLaren Vale Sauvignon blanc lends itself so well to this skin-inflected style. It shapeshifts from a grape that largely delivers dull and overtly fruity styles on these shores, to something of riveting texture and aromatic persuasion, down-gearing away from tangy tropical accents to something more grounded. Lanolin, waxy quince skin, lemon dew and tatami mat. The finish long, bitter, salty and skinsy of texture. Nourishing and absolutely delicious. Agglomerate. 12% alc. RATING 92 DRINK 2022-2025 $29 NG

Nero d'Avola 2021, McLaren Vale Nero is a breeder of succulent, pithy and gulpable mid to full-weighted wines that are so punchy and fresh that they become an addiction. Clearly, very well suited to the maritime clime of the Vale. Dark cherry smeared across a roll of black olive tapenade, thyme, rosemary and lilac. The aldehydes, stuffed within the fray, imparting a carnal Italianesque element to the wine that detracts from typical regional sweetness, while imbuing poise and effortless drinkability. Lovely. Screw cap. 13.6% alc. RATING 92 DRINK 2022-2025 $35 NG

Cape Bernier Vineyard   ★★★

230 Bream Creek Road, Bream Creek, Tas 7175 **Region** Southern Tasmania
T (03) 6253 5443 **www**.capebernier.com.au **Open** Fri–Mon 12–5
Winemaker Frogmore Creek (Alain Rousseau) **Est.** 1999 **Dozens** 1800 **Vyds** 4ha
Andrew and Jenny Sinclair took over from founder Alastair Christie in '14. The vineyard plantings consist of 2ha of pinot noir (including 3 Dijon clones), 1.4ha of chardonnay and 0.6ha of pinot gris on a north-facing slope with spectacular views of Marion Bay. The property is one of several in the region that have transitioned from dairy and beef cattle to wine production and tourism. Exports to Singapore. (JH)

ΨΨΨΨ **Chardonnay Pinot Noir Cuvée Brut 2016, Tasmania** Led by chardonnay, this is an elegant take on East Coast sparkling. Medium straw hue. Citrus, stone fruits and baked apple are infused with the subtle spicy, biscuity complexity of 5 years lees age. A little oxidative baked apple development marks the finish, making this a style to drink now. Diam. 12% alc. RATING 89 $50 TS

Cape Grace Wines

281 Fifty One Road, Cowaramup, WA 6284 **Region** Margaret River
T (08) 9755 5669 **www**.capegracewines.com.au **Open** 7 days 10–5 **Winemaker** Dylan Arvidson, Mark Messenger (Consultant) **Viticulturist** Robert Karri-Davies **Est.** 1996
Dozens 2000 **Vyds** 6.25ha
Cape Grace can trace its history back to 1875, when timber baron MC Davies settled at Karridale, building the Leeuwin lighthouse and founding the township of Margaret River; 120 years later, Robert and Karen Karri-Davies planted their vineyard to chardonnay, shiraz

and cabernet sauvignon, with smaller amounts of cabernet franc, malbec and chenin blanc. Robert is a self-taught viticulturist; Karen has over 15 years of international sales and marketing experience in the hospitality industry. Winemaking is carried out on the property; consultant Mark Messenger is a veteran of the Margaret River region. Exports to Singapore. (JH)

🍷🍷🍷🍷🍷 **Chardonnay 2020, Margaret River** The '20 vintage in Margaret River was wonderful – warm and short, but the wines carry grace and effortlessness, despite the heat. This wine is perfect testament to that: salted yellow peach, briny acidity and layers of citrus blossom, zest and curry leaf spice. The oak is there but it is concealed within the numerous folds of ripe fruit. A beautiful wine. Screw cap. 13.9% alc. RATING 95 DRINK 2021-2031 $38 EL

Basket Pressed Cabernet Sauvignon 2019, Margaret River An interesting mix of Szechuan peppercorn and raspberry on the nose, the characters testament to both the growing area and the time in oak. In the mouth the wine is silken and pliable, with a swipe of graphite tannins through the cool mineral finish. Very smart. Screw cap. 14.4% alc. RATING 94 DRINK 2022-2036 $55 EL

🍷🍷🍷🍷🍷 **Reserve Chardonnay 2019, Margaret River** RATING 91 DRINK 2021-2028 $68 EL

Cab Mac Shiraz 2021, Margaret River RATING 90 DRINK 2021-2025 $28 EL

Cape Jaffa Wines ★★★★

459 Limestone Coast Road, Mount Benson via Robe, SA 5276 **Region** Mount Benson **T** (08) 8768 5053 www.capejaffawines.com.au **Open** 7 days 11–4 **Winemaker** Anna and Derek Hooper **Est.** 1993 **Dozens** 10 000 **Vyds** 22.86ha
Cape Jaffa was the first of the Mount Benson wineries. Cape Jaffa's fully certified biodynamic vineyard provides 50% of production, with additional fruit sourced from a certified biodynamic grower in Wrattonbully. Having received the Advantage SA Regional Award in '09, '10 and '11 for its sustainable initiatives in the Limestone Coast, Cape Jaffa is a Hall of Fame inductee. Exports to the UK, Canada, Thailand, the Philippines, Hong Kong and Singapore. (JH)

🍷🍷🍷🍷🍷 **Sauvignon Blanc 2021, Mount Benson** Lemongrass, crushed shell, jalapeño and juniper, mingle with green apple, pear and white pepper. The acidity is erring towards tart, but otherwise this is nice – the spice component elevates the experience. Screw cap. 12.4% alc. RATING 91 DRINK 2021-2023 $20 EL ❂

Cape Landing ★★★★☆

1098 Calgardup Road, Forest Grove, WA 6286 **Region** Margaret River **T** 0488 006 169 www.capelanding.com.au **Winemaker** Bruce Dukes, Remi Guise **Viticulturist** James Harris **Est.** 1998 **Dozens** 2500 **Vyds** 14ha
The current owner, Mark Lewis, purchased the property in '16 from Cheryl and Larry de Jong, who had established the vineyard in the late '90s. For many years the vineyard supplied most of its grapes to other wineries in the area. The vineyard is planted to chardonnay, sauvignon blanc, shiraz and cabernet sauvignon. Cellar door is currently in the planning. Exports to the Cayman Islands. (EL)

🍷🍷🍷🍷🍷 **Blackwood Chardonnay 2020, Margaret River** Restrained, sophisticated, and with a line of saline acid that streaks down the side of the fruit (like a black striped minnow). This is long and sophisticated, with great flavour concentration. It feels effortless, and that is in line with what we have come to expect from the 2020 vintage in the context of Margaret River whites. Screw cap. 13.2% alc. RATING 95 DRINK 2022-2032 $65 EL

🍷🍷🍷🍷🍷 **Blackwood Syrah 2020, Margaret River** RATING 92 DRINK 2022-2029 $60 EL

Reserve Chardonnay 2020, Margaret River RATING 91 DRINK 2022-2029 $35 EL

Reserve Syrah 2020, Margaret River RATING 90 DRINK 2022-2027 $30 EL

Cape Mentelle ★★★★★

331 Wallcliffe Road, Margaret River, WA 6285 **Region** Margaret River
T (08) 9757 0888 **www**.capementelle.com.au **Open** 7 days 10–5 **Winemaker** Coralie
Lewis **Est.** 1970 **Dozens** 80000 **Vyds** 145ha

Part of the LVMH (Louis Vuitton Möet Hennessy) group. Cape Mentelle is firing on all
cylinders, with the winemaking team fully capitalising on the extensive and largely mature
vineyards, which obviate the need for contract-grown fruit. It is hard to say which of the
wines is best; the ranking, such as it is, varies from year to year. That said, sauvignon blanc
semillon, chardonnay, shiraz and cabernet sauvignon lead the portfolio. Exports to all major
markets. (JH)

♀♀♀♀♀ **Shiraz 2017, Margaret River** With 3/2% grenache/viognier. Sophisticated and
detailed vinification has paid big dividends, from bunch thinning and hand picking
through to the finished wine. Medium bodied, but richly textured, black and blue
fruits, the oak positive but integrated, the tannins likewise. Margaret River shiraz
has come of age. Screw cap. 14.5% alc. RATING 96 DRINK 2022-2037 $49 JH ✪
Wallcliffe Sauvignon Blanc Semillon 2020, Margaret River This is typically
heavy on oak on release, almost too much for immediate enjoyment, however,
having had the pleasure of some older bottles, the oak is justified in time. The
question is … how long do we wait? Here: the harmony of a ripe, powerful
vintage and the significant impact of oak means that the wine achieves a certain
loud balance, even at this young, boisterous age. Buy it and save it for a couple of
years at least, you'll be glad you did. Concentrated, intense and even pure. Very
impressive. Screw cap. 14% alc. RATING 95 DRINK 2022-2037 $49 EL
Cabernet Sauvignon 2017, Margaret River 90/5/5% cabernet sauvignon/
merlot/petit verdot. Although cool and wet, '17 is responsible here for a wine
that is ripe and rich. The red fruit on the palate has both density and power, yet
is nuanced by a soft leafy, floral character. The palate is plush and bolstered by oak
which is making a significant impact right now, but the tannins remain fine. Clove
bud and aniseed lace together through the finish. The length of flavour is the
ultimate testament to quality here. Cork. 14.5% alc. RATING 95 DRINK 2021-2035
$110 EL

♀♀♀♀♀ **Chardonnay 2020, Margaret River** RATING 93 DRINK 2022-2029 $55 EL
Cabernet Sauvignon 2018, Margaret River RATING 93 DRINK 2022-2042
$110 EL
Sauvignon Blanc 2021, Margaret River RATING 91 DRINK 2022-2024
$30 EL

Cape Naturaliste Vineyard ★★★★★

1 Coley Road (off Caves Road), Yallingup, WA 6282 **Region** Margaret River
T (08) 9755 2538 **www**.capenaturalistevineyard.com.au **Open** 7 days 10.30–5
Winemaker Mark Messenger, Craig Brent-White, David Moss, Rick Hoyle-Mills
Est. 1997 **Dozens** 5400 **Vyds** 10.7ha

Cape Naturaliste Vineyard has a long and varied history going back 150 years, when it was
a coaching inn for travellers journeying between Perth and Margaret River. Later it became a
dairy farm and in '70 a mining company purchased it, intending to extract nearby mineral
sands. The government stepped in and declared the area a national park, whereafter in '80
Craig Brent-White purchased the property. The vineyard is planted to cabernet sauvignon,
shiraz, merlot, semillon and sauvignon blanc, and is run on an organic and biodynamic basis
with little or no irrigation. Exports to the UK, the US, and Canada. (JH)

♀♀♀♀♀ **Torpedo Rocks Single Vineyard Cabernet Sauvignon 2018, Margaret
River** Cassis, blackcurrant and firm graphite tannins are the order of the day
here. Elegant and supple. Saltbush and bay leaf colour the edges of the fruit,
while saline acidity (a hallmark of Margaret River) threads it all together. The
power of the 2018 vintage is on display through the finish, with staying power

and concentration for days. Screw cap. 13.8% alc. RATING 95 DRINK 2022-2032 $50 EL

Torpedo Rocks Reserve Shiraz Cabernet Merlot 2017, Margaret River This is really elegant. The tannins are fine and supple, and the fruit is in perfect concert with the oak and the acidity. 1700 bottles. Screw cap. 13.8% alc. RATING 95 DRINK 2022-2032 $75 EL

Torpedo Rocks Reserve Cabernet Malbec Merlot 2019, Margaret River 70/15/15% cabernet sauvignon/malbec/merlot. Cabernet and merlot were the original bedfellows in Margaret River, but over the years, malbec has surreptitiously crept under the covers. The blend is brighter, shinier and more lush than before, owing not only to the compatibility of the varieties, but also to the suitability of malbec to Margaret River. All 3 varieties are evident: the cabernet brings the assertive tannin, the palate shape and the black fruit, the malbec brings the frisky top notes, the pepper and the plushness through the finish, and the merlot brings a soft cushion to the middle palate. Decanting is recommended – after 30 mins in the glass, this has opened up significantly. Screw cap. 14.7% alc. RATING 94 DRINK 2022-2035 $50 EL

ΨΨΨΨΩ **Torpedo Rocks Reserve Single Vineyard Shiraz 2017, Margaret River** RATING 90 DRINK 2022-2027 $60 EL

Capel Vale   ★★★★★

118 Mallokup Road, Capel, WA 6271 **Region** Geographe
T (08) 9727 1986 **www**.capelvale.com.au **Open** Thurs–Mon 10–4.30
Winemaker Daniel Hetherington **Est.** 1974 **Dozens** 21 000 **Vyds** 52ha
Established in '74 by Perth-based medical practitioner Dr Peter Pratten and Elizabeth Pratten. The first vineyard adjacent to the winery was planted on the banks of the quiet waters of Capel River. The viticultural empire has since expanded, spreading across Geographe (9ha), Mount Barker (15ha) and Margaret River (28ha). There are 4 tiers in the Capel Vale portfolio: Debut (varietals), Regional Series, Black Label Margaret River Chardonnay and Cabernet Sauvignon and, at the top, the Single Vineyard Wines. Exports to all major markets. (JH)

ΨΨΨΨΨ **Single Vineyard Series Whispering Hill Riesling 2021, Mount Barker** A general lack of winemaking input (oak, bâtonnage, mlf, etc) allows the grape to speak of the environment it was raised in. The wine is pure, layered with graphite and minerals, lemon zest and apple skins. The acidity is seamlessly inlaid into the fruit; at no point does it veer off course. It is zesty and pert, leaving little deposits of salt and brine on the tongue as it makes its way through to memory. A wonderful wine. Screw cap. 12% alc. RATING 95 DRINK 2021-2036 $40 EL

Single Vineyard Series The Scholar Cabernet Sauvignon 2020, Margaret River The '20 vintage will be fondly remembered by winemakers and viticulturists in Margaret River for its timely nature and high quality (grapes were off the vine and in the shed before Easter, mostly). As is often the way, sadly the yields were small. This wine is pure and bright, the acidity is still a bit frisky at this early stage, but the fruit density and tannin shape show that the wine will age gracefully through this stage and emerge a swan at the other end. Screw cap. 14% alc. RATING 94 DRINK 2022-2036 $90 EL

ΨΨΨΨΩ **Regional Series Riesling 2021, Mount Barker** RATING 93 DRINK 2021-2031 $27 EL ✿

Black Label Chardonnay 2021, Margaret River RATING 93 DRINK 2022-2030 $50 EL

Regional Series Cabernet Sauvignon 2020, Margaret River RATING 92 DRINK 2021-2028 $27 EL

Capercaillie Wines

4 Londons Road, Lovedale, NSW 2325 **Region** Hunter Valley
T (02) 4990 2904 **www.**capercailliewines.com.au **Open** 7 days 10–4.30
Winemaker Lance Mikisch **Viticulturist** Lance Mikisch **Est.** 1995 **Dozens** 5000
Vyds 5ha

A successful winery in terms of the quality of its wines, as well as their reach outwards from the Hunter Valley. The Capercaillie wines have generous flavour. Its fruit sources are spread across South Eastern Australia, although the portfolio includes wines that are 100% Hunter Valley. (JH)

The Creel 2014, Hunter Valley A museum release from a fine vintage, showing extremely well. The orb of aged semillon's buttered toast, citrus marmalade, lanolin, spiced quince and lemon drop is in full affect. The acidity, towing fine length. Precise. Lightweight yet very intense of flavour, this is a wine that showcases the paradoxes of complexity. Screw cap. 11.5% alc. RATING 95 DRINK 2022-2030 NG

The Sonse Method Traditional Chardonnay 2014, Hunter Valley RATING 91 $35 NG

Capital Wines

13 Gladstone Street, Hall, ACT 2618 **Region** Canberra District
T (02) 6230 2022 **www.**capitalwines.com.au **Open** By appt **Winemaker** Alex McKay, Greg Gallagher **Est.** 1986 **Dozens** 3500 **Vyds** 5ha

In early '20, Bill Mason, Colin and Kay Andrews of Jirra at Jeir Station acquired Capital Wines from Andrew and Marion McEwin. The cellar door in Hall, less than 15 minutes from the heart of the national capital, features the Capital Wines range, Kosciuszko wines from Tumbarumba (owned by Bill Mason and family) and the Jirra at Jeir Station wines from Murrumbateman. Jeir Station, halfway between Hall and Murrumbateman, supplies much of the fruit for the Capital wines. (JH)

The Whip Riesling 2021, Canberra District Smelling of a spring garden with its honeysuckle and lemon-blossom aromas, it's also really spicy, full of cinnamon and powdered ginger. The delicate palate is all lime-juice freshness with tangy acidity, yet feels soft across the palate. Screw cap. 12.2% alc. RATING 92 DRINK 2021-2028 $32 JF

The Abstainer Rosé 2021, Canberra District A glass or 2 of this on a warm day or night would be lovely, as it's refreshing. It's tangy and juicy, made from sangiovese, so there's good acidity. Plenty of watermelon and strawberry flavours, with a touch of sweetness on the finish. Screw cap. 12.2% alc. RATING 90 DRINK 2021-2022 $28 JF

The Ambassador Tempranillo 2021, Riverina Made in a joven style, so it's full of upfront juicy red fruits, especially plums and cherries, laced with licorice and cola plus a savoury edge from some meaty reduction. Tangy, spritely acidity, textural tannins and no excuse needed other than to pour it immediately. Screw cap. 12.6% alc. RATING 90 DRINK 2021-2024 $32 JF

Carillion Wines

749 Mount View Road, Mount View, NSW 2325 **Region** Hunter Valley
T (02) 4990 7535 **www.**carillionwines.com.au **Open** Thurs–Mon 10–5
Winemaker Andrew Ling **Viticulturist** Liz Riley, Tim Esson, Pete Balnaves **Est.** 2000
Dozens 5000 **Vyds** 148ha

In '00 the Davis family decided to select certain parcels of fruit from their 28ha Davis Family Vineyard in the Hunter Valley, along with the family's other vineyards in Orange (the 30ha Carillion Vineyard) and Wrattonbully (the 90ha Stonefields Vineyard), to make wines that are a true expression of their location. To best reflect this strong emphasis on terroir, the resulting wines were categorised into 3 labels, named after their respective vineyards. In recent years Tim Davis has taken over the reins from his father John, and brought these wines under the Carillion banner. He also launched the Lovable Rogue range of wines, which highlight his keen interest in alternative grape varieties (particularly Italian), as well as exploring innovative and experimental winemaking methods. (JH)

🍷🍷🍷🍷🍷 **Aged Release Stonefields Arbitrage Cabernet Merlot Shiraz 2013, Wrattonbully** Extraordinarily youthful crimson-purple hue. Cedar, cigar box and spice aromas surround a well of black fruits, tannins beating the drum on the finish. This is still evolving. Screw cap. 14.5% alc. RATING 96 DRINK 2025-2033 $40 JH ✪
Aged Release Tallavera Grove Semillon 2014, Hunter Valley Verging on an optimal point of drinking, this is a window into just how glorious regional semillon can be with age. Middle age, perhaps. Still time left in the wine's bones, but I'd be drinking up. Waxy. Scents of orange blossom, lanolin, butter and lemon curd, like a dairy's pasture during the spring. The finish, long and juicy. The wine of a weightier feel than its low alcohol suggests. A paradox of complexity. Screw cap. 12% alc. RATING 95 DRINK 2021-2025 $40 NG
GM198 Clone Riesling 2021, Orange Fine, expressive and succulent riesling, verging into the stone-fruit spectrum of the greatest Germanics. Gently nudging mid weight. Apricot pith, rosewater, musk and spa salts. The finish, talcy, long and brimming with Rose's lime juice. Almost pumice-like of texture. Impressive. Screw cap. 12% alc. RATING 94 DRINK 2021-2028 $30 NG ✪

🍷🍷🍷🍷🍷 **Origins Old Grafts Semillon 2021, Hunter Valley** RATING 93 DRINK 2021-2033 $30 NG
Six Clones Pinot Noir 2021, Orange RATING 93 DRINK 2022-2027 $35 NG
Lovable Rogue Skin Contact Vermentino 2021, Hunter Valley RATING 91 DRINK 2021-2024 $30 NG
The Volcanics Cabernet Sauvignon 2019, Orange RATING 90 DRINK 2021-2026 $50 NG

Carlei Estate | Carlei Green Vineyards ★★★★☆

1 Alber Road, Upper Beaconsfield, Vic 3808 **Region** Victoria
T (03) 5944 4599 **www.carlei.com.au Open** W'ends 12–5 **Winemaker** Sergio Carlei, David Carlei, David Papadimitriou **Est.** 1994 **Dozens** 10 000 **Vyds** 2.25ha
Sergio Carlei has come a long way, graduating from home winemaking in a suburban garage to his own (commercial) winery in Upper Beaconsfield. Along the way Carlei acquired a bachelor of wine science from CSU, and established a vineyard with organic and biodynamic accreditation adjacent to the Upper Beaconsfield winery, plus 7ha in Heathcote. Contract winemaking services are now a major part of the business. Exports to the US and Singapore. (JH)

🍷🍷🍷🍷🍷 **Nord Fruit Day Shiraz 2020, Heathcote** Fruit Day is part of the biodynamic lunar calendar indicating a good day for harvesting grapes and tasting wine (among other positives). A more highly lifted and aromatic wine compared to its Root Day sibling, that really seduces in perfumed violet, florals, black fruits, pomegranate and fine-grained spices. Strikes an attractive balance between ripe fruits, depth of flavour and freshness, aided by firm, bright tannins. Screw cap. 14% alc. RATING 95 DRINK 2020-2030 $59 JP
Carlei Estate Nord Shiraz 2020, Heathcote Enticing, warm-hearted shiraz from the northern end of Heathcote. Offers a complex and elegant set of flavours including licorice, anise, chocolate and lively black fruits laid out long and deep across the palate. Concentrated fruit meets dense tannins. Will enjoy time in the cellar. Screw cap. 14.5% alc. RATING 94 DRINK 2022-2027 $59 JP
Carlei Estate Sud Shiraz 2020, Heathcote Everything is sitting pretty with this wine – in the sweet spot, you might say – whether it's the plush fruits that sweep across the palate enlivened by spice, licorice and warm, toasty oak, or the

loose-knit tannins that invite another sip. Overall, a wine that can be enjoyed now or later. Screw cap. 14% alc. RATING 94 DRINK 2022-2027 $59 JP

♟♟♟♟♟ **Nord Root Day Shiraz 2020, Heathcote** RATING 92 DRINK 2022-2028 $59 JP

Casa Freschi   ★★★★

159 Ridge Rd Ashton SA 5137 **Region** Adelaide Hills
T 0409 364 569 **www.**casafreschi.com.au **Open** Fri–Sun, 12–5 or by appt
Winemaker David Freschi **Viticulturist** David Freschi **Est.** 1998 **Dozens** 2000
Vyds 7.55ha
David Freschi is a quality-obsessed vigneron, currently producing single-vineyard wines from 2 vineyards (in the Adelaide Hills and in Langhorne Creek). David Freschi's parents, Attilio and Rosa, planted 2.5ha of cabernet sauvignon, shiraz and malbec in '72 in Langhorne Creek. David expanded the plantings with 2ha of close-planted nebbiolo in '99. The pursuit of white wines eventually led David to the Adelaide Hills, where he purchased a 3.2ha site at 580m in Ashton and planted chardonnay, pinot gris, riesling and gewürztraminer at 8000 vines/ha, all grown using organic principles. The wines are made at the gravity-fed micro-winery. Exports to the UK, Singapore, Philippines and Japan. (JH)

♟♟♟♟♟ **Chardonnay 2019, Adelaide Hills** A complex, convincing Hills chardonnay showing a composed set of citrus, peachy stone fruits, almond, nougat and barrel-derived flavours. Juicy on the palate headlining assertive acidity, more peach and grilled-nuts intensity with a crunchy, bright resolve. Screw cap. 13% alc. RATING 94 DRINK 2022-2029 $55 JP

♟♟♟♟♟ **Ragazzi Chardonnay 2020, Adelaide Hills** RATING 93 DRINK 2022-2026 $30 JP
Profondo Old Vines 2018, Langhorne Creek RATING 92 DRINK 2022-2030 $70 JP
Ragazzi Pinot Grigio 2020, Adelaide Hills RATING 90 DRINK 2022-2024 $30 JP

Casella Family Brands   ★★★★

Wakely Road, Yenda, NSW 2681 **Region** Riverina
T (02) 6961 3000 **www.**casellafamilybrands.com **Winemaker** John Casella **Est.** 1969
Dozens 12.5 million **Vyds** 5000ha
Casella established Yellow Tail as a world brand overnight by Southcorp withdrawing the distribution of (inter alia) its bestselling Lindemans Bin 65 Chardonnay in the US. Casella has built a portfolio of premium and ultra-premium wines through its acquisition of Peter Lehmann in '14; and then Brand's Laira winery, cellar door and the use of the brand name from McWilliam's in '15. In Dec '17 Casella purchased Baileys of Glenrowan. Casella now has over 5000ha of vineyards spread across Australia. It is second only to Treasury Wine Estates in export sales (by value), followed by Pernod Ricard and Accolade. Casella celebrated its 50th anniversary in '19. Exports to all major markets. (JH)

♟♟♟♟♟ **Limited Release Cabernet Sauvignon 2019, Barossa Valley** It is intriguing how much more character cabernet often shows than shiraz in hot climates. Its thrum of currant, darker fruits, tapenade and dried herb is immutable, in the best sense. Lifted cabernet aromas. American oak-charred mocha-bourbon-laden tannins. A creamy core. A delicious, older-school full-bodied expression. Screw cap. 14.5% alc. RATING 93 DRINK 2022-2033 $45 NG
Limited Release Shiraz 2019, Barossa Valley This is an archetypal, full-bodied old-school wine that is built to please. Fermented at warmer temperatures to maximise extraction. Matured 24 months in American oak and bottle, setting the tone. Kirsch, fruitcake spice and dried fruits, violet and a finish analogous to a liquid version of blueberries and cream. The oak, sweet and grippy, lays the tracks for a long, pushy finish. Plenty to like. Screw cap. 14.5% alc. RATING 92 DRINK 2022-2031 $45 NG

Castelli Estate

380 Mount Shadforth Road, Denmark, WA 6333 **Region** Great Southern
T (08) 9364 0400 **www.**castelliestate.com.au **Open** By appt **Winemaker** Mike Garland
Est. 2007 **Dozens** 20 000

Castelli Estate will cause many small winery owners to go green with envy. When Sam Castelli purchased the property in late '04, he was intending simply to use it as a family holiday destination. But because there was a partly constructed winery he decided to complete the building work and simply lock the doors. However, wine was in his blood courtesy of his father, who owned a small vineyard in Italy's south. The temptation was too much and in '07 the winery was commissioned. Fruit is sourced from some of the best sites in WA: Frankland River, Mount Barker, Pemberton and Porongurup. Exports to the US, South Korea, Singapore and Japan. (JH)

🍷🍷🍷🍷🍷 **Silver Series Shiraz Malbec 2019, Frankland River** Super-swish new packaging for a wine that routinely outdoes itself in the value-for-money stakes. 51/49% shiraz/malbec. Inky, intense and concentrated with brilliantly dense tannins on the palate. Frankland does the ferrous/ironstone/rust/blood/dirt characters so well – and they are all here in spades. If you like saturated fruit flavours and robust shape then this is unequivocally for you. Delish. Screw cap. 14.5% alc. RATING 94 DRINK 2021-2028 $25 EL ✪

Shiraz 2019, Frankland River This wine is routinely impressive, and this cool-year iteration is no exception. 2019 has imbued it with a medium-weight body, as opposed to the usually muscular and savoury countenance that we have become used to. Yet, it is concentrated and silky, with layers of mulberries, raspberries, licorice and spice through the finish. Screw cap. 14.6% alc. RATING 94 DRINK 2021-2028 $34 EL

Cabernet Sauvignon 2019, Frankland River Good lord, this is good. Initially, the nose opens with graphite and steel shavings, but the fruit beneath it rises up and absorbs almost everything in its savoury, red embrace. This will show best another year from now, when everything has come together even more. Routinely an impressive wine. This vintage no exception. Screw cap. 14.6% alc. RATING 94 DRINK 2021-2036 $38 EL

🍷🍷🍷🍷🍷 **Silver Series Cabernet Merlot 2019, Frankland River Margaret River** RATING 93 DRINK 2021-2028 $25 EL ✪

Fiore Del Campo 2021, Frankland River Pemberton Mount Barker RATING 91 DRINK 2021-2027 $29 EL

Empirica Pinot Gris 2021, Pemberton RATING 90 DRINK 2021-2026 $29 EL

Castle Rock Estate

2660 Porongurup Road, Porongurup, WA 6324 **Region** Porongurup
T (08) 9853 1035 **www.**castlerockestate.com.au **Open** 7 days 10–4.30
Winemaker Robert Diletti **Est.** 1983 **Dozens** 4500 **Vyds** 11.2ha

An exceptionally beautifully sited vineyard (riesling, pinot noir, chardonnay, sauvignon blanc, cabernet sauvignon and merlot), winery and cellar door on a 55ha property with sweeping vistas of the Porongurup Range, operated by the Diletti family. The standard of viticulture is very high, and the vineyard itself is ideally situated. The 2-level winery, set on a natural slope, maximises gravity flow. The rieslings have always been elegant and have handsomely repaid time in bottle; the pinot noir is the most consistent performer in the region; the shiraz is a great cool-climate example; and chardonnay has joined a thoroughly impressive quartet, elegance the common link. Rob Diletti's excellent palate and sensitive winemaking mark Castle Rock as one of the superstars of WA. (JH)

🍷🍷🍷🍷🍷 **Pinot Noir 2020, Porongurup** Perfect colour; a great pinot at the dawn of its life; plum and cherry riddled with spice, char, violets and forest floor. Sophisticated and confident. Screw cap. 13.5% alc. RATING 97 DRINK 2022-2035 $38 JH ✪

TTTTT Shiraz 2019, Great Southern The grapes come from Mount Barker. The 28 April harvest underlines the very cool climate and resultant vibrantly fresh and elegant array of red, blue and black fruits, resting on a bed of fine tannins. Screw cap. 13.5% alc. RATING 96 DRINK 2022–2035 $34 JH ✪

A&W Riesling 2021, Porongurup The pinnacle of rieslings made at Castle Rock, and a scintillatingly true, pristine expression of Porongurup. Green apples, white spring florals (jasmine, stephanotis, honeysuckle), crushed chalk and hints of juniper. Fine saline acidity is the thread that pulls it all together. It is delicate, but it is so long; the flavour enduring, dragging out the finish. You must be prepared for a quiet wine here, however once you are attuned to the tone it is possible to hear the reverberations long after the wine is gone. Screw cap. 11.5% alc. RATING 95 DRINK 2021–2036 $39 EL

Shiraz 2020, Porongurup Aromas of cool-climate shiraz fruit on show, paraded across the top of the wine in a procession of blackcurrant pastille, blue fruits, anise, fennel flower and graphite. In the mouth the wine is precisely as expected: detailed, super-pretty, elegant, chalky and supple. The endlessly attractive mineral tannins are a highlight. What a gloriously fine wine for the price. Screw cap. 13.8% alc. RATING 95 DRINK 2021–2031 $34 EL ✪

Sauvignon Blanc 2021, Porongurup The Porongurup Range is a place of great beauty. If you haven't been, you really must add it to the list. Castle Rock Estate is a great place to start: not only are the wines sensational, but the positioning of the vineyard on top of the hill … well that's pretty impressive, too. As for this wine; cool, elegant, and clearly made by a riesling maker, such is its purity and finesse. '21 was responsible for delicate wines and this is a wonderful example. Screw cap. 12.8% alc. RATING 94 DRINK 2021–2024 $23 EL ✪

Riesling 2021, Porongurup Just like '20, this is a sensational wine. Typified by quietly searing flavour intensity that really creeps up on you. Salty, pithy and fine, this has an understated volume that emerges mid palate onwards. Super-restrained, minerally and very pretty. Screw cap. 11% alc. RATING 94 DRINK 2021–2031 $26 EL ✪

Catlin Wines   ★★★★☆

39B Sydney Road, Nairne, SA 5252 **Region** Adelaide Hills
T 0411 326 384 **www.**catlinwines.com.au **Winemaker** Darryl Catlin **Est.** 2013
Dozens 2000
Darryl Catlin grew up in the Barossa Valley with vineyards as his playground, picking bush-vine grenache for pocket money as a youngster. Stints with Saltram, the Australian Bottling Company and Vintner Imports followed in his 20s, before he moved on to gain retail experience at Adelaide's Royal Oak Cellar, London's Oddbins and McKay's Macquarie Cellars. Next, he studied for a winemaking degree while working at Adelaide's East End Cellars. Then followed a number of years at Shaw + Smith, rising from cellar hand to winemaker, finishing in '12 and establishing his own business the following year. Exports to the UK. (JH)

TTTTT Nitschke Riesling 2021, Adelaide Hills The winemaker typically makes Clare riesling but here takes a stab at Adelaide Hills riesling. The result shows the potential of the grape in the region. Riesling brightness is turned down, the spice and charm factor turned up and the result is rather special. Spring wildflowers, lavender, apple, lime and spice scents are transformed on to the palate with depth and concentration. Not to mention, generous mouthfeel and persistence. A stunning wine. Screw cap. 11.5% alc. RATING 95 DRINK 2021–2025 $32 JP ✪

GB's Montepulciano Rosé 2021, Adelaide Hills Now, this is different. Montepulciano as a rosé brings its plums, cherries and Italian herbals to the party and it's quite a tasty, lightly savoury treat. Confection-pink hues translate into a lifted aromatic fragrance but it is the bright flavours and textural mouthfeel that will suddenly arrest the tastebuds. A perfect versatile food-match rosé right here. Screw cap. 12.5% alc. RATING 94 DRINK 2021–2025 $22 JP ✪

ΨΨΨΨႳ **Pudding and Pie 2021, Adelaide Hills** RATING 93 DRINK 2021–2027 $32 JP
The Gellert Single Vineyard Gamay 2021, Adelaide Hills RATING 93
DRINK 2021–2026 $32 JP
The Astria Blanc de Blancs 2021, Adelaide Hills RATING 91 $32 JP
Cheese and Kisses Single Vineyard Fumé Blanc 2021, Adelaide Hills
RATING 91 DRINK 2021–2026 $32 JP
The Molly Mae Riesling 2021, Clare Valley RATING 90 DRINK 2021–2031
$22 JP

Cavalry Wines   ★★★
PO Box 193, Nagambie, Vic 3608 **Region** Heathcote
T 0411 114 958 **www.**cavalrywines.com **Open** By appt **Winemaker** Adam Foster
Est. 2016 **Dozens** 700 **Vyds** 9.6ha
The vineyard was planted in the '60s with 5.8ha of shiraz, 2.7ha of cabernet sauvignon
and a field blend of chardonnay, verdelho and riesling. The first owner made a little wine
for his personal use, but most of the grape production was used to make excellent grappa.
More recently the grapes were sold to other wineries, and a major part continues to be sold.
The current owners are Peter Nash, previously an insurance underwriter, and Josephine
Hands, a former teacher. Ardent wine lovers with a history of small investments in wine,
their next step in retirement was to become vignerons – and to put the property in trust
for their grandchildren. The winery shares 3 boundaries with the Australian Army whence
its name. (JH)

ΨΨΨΨ **Marian Shiraz 2019, Heathcote** A fairly traditional Aussie shiraz, showing
plenty of ripe fruit and sweetly spiced oak supported by plums, dried herbs and
cassia bark. Palate is supple and medium weighted, with a touch of leathery
sandalwood oak to close. Screw cap. 13% alc. RATING 89 DRINK 2021–2026
$28 JP
Christine Cabernet Shiraz 2019, Heathcote Harks of the Aussie bush,
bracken with a marked eucalyptus twang set among blackberries, licorice and
dark roasted spices. Firm on the palate, with sturdy tannins drawn tight. Screw cap.
13.5% alc. RATING 89 DRINK 2021–2026 $35 JP
Rosaria Premium Shiraz 2019, Heathcote Lacking the elegance of the '18,
Rosaria presents a more angular, dark-fruited wine resting on a savoury bed of
sturdy tannins and charred wood. The mid palate is plush in licorice, plum, dark
cherry and chocolate before finishing with a dry astringency. Screw cap. 13.5% alc.
RATING 88 DRINK 2021–2028 $51 JP

Centare   ★★★★
160 Healesville Kooweerup Road, Healesville, Vic 3777 **Region** Yarra Valley
T 0407 386 314 **www.**centarevineyard.com **Winemaker** Nicole Esdaile **Est.** 2018
Dozens 2000 **Vyds** 5ha
A vineyard originally planted in 1998 on Healesville Kooweerup Road and acquired by
Simon Li in '18. Nicole Esdaile from Wine Network Consulting is the winemaker/ project
manager and Ray Guerin is the consulting viticulturalist, with the wines being made at the
Sunshine Creek facility. New plantings at extremely high density began in Nov '20 with
aspirations to produce a cabernet blend of the highest quality. (JH)

ΨΨΨΨႳ **Old Block Shiraz 2020, Yarra Valley** A vibrant crimson purple. A nicely put
together and polished wine with red and black fruits, a little white pepper and
some charcuterie notes. The oak is slick but well handled. Medium bodied and
even better on the palate, which is redolent of red fruits and spice. Ripe, fine
tannins round out a wine that can be enjoyed now and over the next 5–10 years.
Screw cap. 13.9% alc. RATING 91 DRINK 2022–2028 $65 PR
Old Block Chardonnay 2020, Yarra Valley A bright green gold. Nectarine
and guava fruit aromas together with biscuity oak and a little cashew. Textured,
layered and gently saline, this should continue to develop and become

more complex over the next 3–5 years. Screw cap. 13% alc. RATING 90
DRINK 2021-2026 $50 PR

Old Block Cabernet Sauvignon 2020, Yarra Valley With 3.5/3.5% merlot/
malbec. A medium cherry-crimson colour. Aromas of subtle red fruits and a little
blackberry bush. Medium bodied and elegant with fine tannins, this well-framed
wine is approachable now but will continue to improve over the medium term.
Screw cap. 13.2% alc. RATING 90 DRINK 2022-2028 $65 PR

Centennial Vineyards   ★★★★★

'Woodside', 252 Centennial Road, Bowral, NSW 2576 **Region** Southern Highlands
T (02) 4861 8722 **www**.centennial.net.au **Open** 7 days 10–5 **Winemaker** Tony Cosgriff
Est. 2002 **Dozens** 10 000 **Vyds** 28.65ha
Centennial Vineyards, jointly owned by wine professional John Large and investor Mark
Dowling, covers 133ha of beautiful grazing land, with the vineyard planted to pinot noir
(7.13ha), chardonnay (6.76ha), pinot gris (4.06ha) and smaller amounts of riesling, pinot
meunier, albariño, tempranillo, grüner veltliner and gewürztraminer. Centennial purchased the
8.2ha Bridge Creek Vineyard in Orange to meet the challenge of the Southern Highlands'
capricious weather. (JH)

Reserve Pinot Noir Rosé 2021, Southern Highlands A gentle coral
with onion-skin edges. A small portion fermented in barrel. While pinot is
not a favoured variety for rosé, at least for me, this is exceptional for the idiom.
Fine boned, thirst slaking, intense of delicate rose, powdered musk and red
berry accents and best, supremely long. Fine. Screw cap. 12.7% alc. RATING 93
DRINK 2021-2022 $33 NG

Reserve Corvina Rondinella Rosé 2021, Orange An iconoclastic blend,
based on the great wines of the Veneto: Valpolicella, Amarone and Bardolino. This
takes me there! Partially wild fermented and here, a greater barrel component
(20%) than the other rosés in the quiver. Onion skin with a mottled pink. Loads of
personality. Tangerine, cumquat, mandarin, loganberry and tamarind. Like sucking
on an exotic smoothie of equal parts hippy quotient and tangy red berries. Dry,
yet nicely burnished with flavour from the mid palate to the long finish. Screw
cap. 12.8% alc. RATING 92 DRINK 2021-2022 $28 NG

Reserve Cabernet Sauvignon Rosé 2021, Orange Another exceptional rosé
amid a fine arsenal. 5% barrel ferment, on this occasion. Australians seldom expect
this stiff-upper-lipped variety to be used for rosé and yet Clairet, that savoury,
deep-coloured rosé of Bordeaux, is defined by it. A thrust of intense redcurrant,
tomato bush and root spice, toned by a parry of vibrant cool-climate acidity and a
waft of phenolics. Great table wine across virtually any dish imaginable. Screw cap.
13.2% alc. RATING 92 DRINK 2021-2022 $33 NG

Bong Bong Quattro Bianco 2021, Southern Highlands Tumbarumba
A slinky, spunky blend of a delicious knockabout, the quality akin to the good,
savoury, everyday whites of Europe. The apposite blend, perfect material for these
cool-climate growing zones; 65% gris, with chardonnay, albariño and gewürz.
Pistachio, lemon balm, grape spice and a pithy stone-fruit element. Unbeatable for
a white at this price, at least in this expensive land. Chill, slug and smile. You have
won the lottery! Screw cap. 12.5% alc. RATING 91 DRINK 2021-2023 $20 NG ✪

Reserve Bridge Creek Merlot 2019, Orange Hand harvested, cold
macerated and fermented on skins for 10 days. Matured 13 months in French
wood (15% new). Just about right for the material on hand. Redcurrant, damson
plum, tomato leaf, sage, dried tobacco and assorted garden herbs. A verdant
expressions, straddling the better side of ripeness. The finish, long and detailed
and savoury and frankly, impressive. Particularly for the price. Screw cap. 14% alc.
RATING 91 DRINK 2021-2025 $28 NG

Bridge Creek Mencia 2019, Orange Good. A shame, really, that due to
the fires there is no '20. This would have tasted even better, 6 months ago in its
effusive glory. Pepper grind, clove and menthol across the finish. Mid weighted

of feel despite a clasp of heat marking the finish. I'd drink this up. Screw cap.
13.9% alc. RATING 91 DRINK 2021-2023 $30 NG

Finale Nouveau Autumn Semillon 2021, Riverina Bottled a mere 3 months
after harvest, thus the Nouveau moniker. Fresh and dainty, despite the expansive
sweetness across the lightweight frame. Orange blossom, pineapple, dried mango
and canned peach. A spurt of acidity mitigates any cloying effect. Screw cap.
11.5% alc. RATING 91 DRINK 2021-2025 $29 NG

Reserve Single Vineyard Tempranillo 2019, Central Ranges Red-fruit
aromas sluiced with clove, pepper, bergamot and rosehip. Juicy, detailed enough
and mellifluous drinking. A bit tangy. A relatively simple wine in the very best
sense: its capacity to pair with a slew of options at the table. Screw cap. 14.3% alc.
RATING 90 DRINK 2021-2024 $35 NG

ΨΨΨΨ **Rosé 2021, Orange** RATING 89 DRINK 2021-2022 $25 NG
Shiraz 2019, Hilltops RATING 89 DRINK 2021-2025 $29 NG

Chain of Ponds ★★★★

8 The Parade West, Kent Town, SA 5067 (postal) **Region** South Australia
T (08) 7324 3031 **www**.chainofponds.com.au **Winemaker** Greg Clack **Est.** 1985
Dozens 20 000
It is years since the Chain of Ponds brand was separated from its then 200ha of estate vineyards,
which were among the largest in the Adelaide Hills. It does, however, have long-term contracts
with major growers. Prior to the '15 vintage, Greg Clack came onboard as full-time chief
winemaker. In May '16 Chain of Ponds closed its cellar door and moved to Project Wine's
small-batch processing facility at Langhorne Creek. The Single Vineyard series and estate wine
are all sourced from the Adelaide Hills; the budget Novello range from further afield. Exports
to the UK, the US, Canada, Singapore, Hong Kong, the Philippines and Japan. (JH)

ΨΨΨΨΨ **Grave's Gate Shiraz 2020, Adelaide Hills** It hits well above its pricepoint –
outstanding value here – to deliver a joyous Hills shiraz experience in deep spicy
aromas and fruits with black cherry, plum, violet and an earthy nuance. A fine
line of supple tannins brings length and balance. Screw cap. 14.5% alc. RATING 94
DRINK 2021-2026 $20 JP

ΨΨΨΨΨ **Morning Star Single Vineyard Pinot Noir 2020, Adelaide Hills** RATING 93
DRINK 2021-2026 $35 JP
Novello Rosé 2021, Adelaide RATING 90 DRINK 2021-2024 $16 JP ✪
Stopover Single Vineyard Barbera 2021, Adelaide Hills RATING 90
DRINK 2021-2026 $35 JP

Chalk Hill ★★★★★

56 Field Street, McLaren Vale **Region** McLaren Vale
T (08) 8323 6400 **www**.chalkhillwines.com.au **Open** 7 days 11–6 **Winemaker** Renae
Hirsch **Viticulturist** Jock Harvey **Est.** 1973 **Dozens** 20 000 **Vyds** 89ha
The growth of Chalk Hill has accelerated after passing from parents John and Diana Harvey
to grapegrowing sons Jock and Tom. Both are heavily involved in wine industry affairs.
Further acquisitions mean the vineyards now span each district of McLaren Vale, planted to
both the exotic (savagnin, barbera and sangiovese) and mainstream (shiraz, cabernet sauvignon,
grenache, chardonnay and cabernet franc). The Alpha Crucis series is especially praiseworthy.
Exports to most markets; exports to the US under the Alpha Crucis label, to Canada under
the Wits End label. (JH)

ΨΨΨΨΨ **Alpha Crucis Old Vine Grenache 2020, McLaren Vale** The bouquet is
expressive and enticing, as is the gorgeous, juicy and mouth-watering medium-
bodied palate. Moving the wine back and forth in the mouth unlocks rivulets of
earthy spices, running through the pomegranate and red forest fruits. Precision and
purity. Screw cap. 14% alc. RATING 98 DRINK 2022-2030 $55 JH ♥

ŢŢŢŢŢ **Alpha Crucis Clarendon Syrah 2020, McLaren Vale** The best of the
3 subregional expressions. An effortless flow from the attack to the finish, as echoes
of the northern Rhône mesh with a warmer Australian idiom: red and blue fruits,
bergamot, nori, sassafras, clove, turmeric, sandalwood and souk spice. This is really
exceptional as far as syrah/shiraz goes in these parts. Mid-weighted feel. So easy to
drink. A long, intricate glide. Gorgeous grape tannins. The oak, a mere addendum.
Exceptional drinking. Screw cap. 14% alc. RATING 96 DRINK 2021-2030
$55 NG ✪ ♥

Alpha Crucis Syrah 2020, McLaren Vale A cull of the best barrels across
the 3 subregions. Damn! South Australian syrah is almost an oxymoron, yet I
enjoy having preconceptions destroyed. This achieves that. A miracle! The tannins,
a quilt with an exotic weave. The acidity, palpably natural. The length, endless.
This is statuesque and absolutely gorgeous. Screw cap. 14.5% alc. RATING 96
DRINK 2021-2032 $85 NG

Alpha Crucis Chardonnay 2021, Adelaide Hills Chewy, nourishing and
tightly furled. Embryonic, with little but the intensity of the palate, the medium
weight and the flurry to the finish suggestive of what is to come. Apricot pith,
white peach, grilled hazelnuts and vanilla pod emerge with a solid workout in
the glass. A long stream of textural incantations of oak, acidity and phenolics.
Fine bones and tension to this. Time will tell. Screw cap. 13% alc. RATING 94
DRINK 2022-2030 $55 NG

Alpha Crucis Blewitt Springs Syrah 2020, McLaren Vale The most
reductive of these 3 subregional syrahs. Very floral and lifted, to be sure.
Boysenberry, white pepper, seaweed and charcuterie. Less ethereal beauty than
the Clarendon. Less rugged firmness than the Seaview. Decant aggressively
or wait for a few years. It is very good. Potentially, fine. Screw cap. 14% alc.
RATING 94 DRINK 2022-2030 $55 NG

Alpha Crucis Seaview Syrah 2020, McLaren Vale As much as grenache is
the motherlode of the region, this is good. Blue-fruit aspersions, pepper, ample
florals and a glimpse of something darker and warmer at its core. The texture,
controlled reductive tension and a firm backbone of chiselled oak tannins, doused
in anise, making for savouriness, while evincing a welcome authority light years
from the plush regional norm. Caveat: a bit hot. Screw cap. 14% alc. RATING 94
DRINK 2021-2030 $55 NG

Chalmers   ★★★★★

118 Third Street, Merbein, Vic 3505 **Region** Murray Darling
T 0400 261 932 **www.**chalmers.com.au **Winemaker** Bart van Olphen, Tennille and
Kim Chalmers **Viticulturist** Bruce Chalmers, Troy McInnes **Est.** 1989 **Dozens** 10 000
Vyds 27ha

The Australian wine industry owes a debt of gratitude to the Chalmers family. For more
than a decade, the family, led by Bruce and Jenni Chalmers, have led the way in importing
new, 'alternative' grape varieties to this country through their Merbein nursery and vineyard.
They were prescient in seeing the need for varieties that are suited to Australian conditions
and a changing climate. The Chalmers family have been pioneers of Mediterranean varieties,
most recently falanghina, pecorino and ribolla gialla. With vineyards in the Murray Darling
(established in the 1980s) and Heathcote regions (2011), and under the second generation
Kim and Tennille Chalmers, the family produces cutting-edge wines. From the Chalmers
Project (experimental, micro-fermentation wines), the Montevecchio label (approachable
blends), La Sorelle (a celebration of Heathcote and Murray Darling fruit), Dott. (a tribute to
viticulturist Dr Rod Bonfiglioli) and Chalmers label (single-vineyard wines) and more, the
family excels as both growers and producers, never content with the status quo. (JP)

ŢŢŢŢŢ **Pecorino 2021, Heathcote** Pecorino offers a glimpse into the future, where
climate change will encourage the planting of more Mediterranean grape varieties
in Australia. It shows its class here with the lifted scent of honeysuckle, citrus and
baked apple. Rich and textural, it fills the mouth with delicious flavour that goes
and goes, replete in peach, nectarine and dried herbs wrapped in a light blanket of

honey. Acidity balances everything very nicely. Screw cap. 13.5% alc. RATING 95
DRINK 2022-2027 $31 JP ✪

Bush Vine Negroamaro 2020, Murray Darling What was once a 'project'
wine to test the limits of dry growing, makes it to the big time, both literally
and figuratively. It makes an immediately impressive impact on the palate and in
its dense colour and generosity. With ripeness turned up, it goes on the excite
in vibrant plum, blackberry pastille, prune and licorice. Tannins remain firm
while the palate runs long in black fruits, exotic spice with an upfront, earthy
honesty. The grape of Puglia makes a big quality statement in Australia. Screw cap.
14.5% alc. RATING 95 DRINK 2022-2027 $55 JP

Aglianico 2019, Heathcote The classic southern Italian red grape is incredibly
well suited to the climate and soils of Heathcote. Each vintage re-affirms that. A
complex, fleshy expression of the grape is wrapped in black cherry, white pepper,
allspice, dark chocolate, licorice and a gentle savouriness. A lovely depth of flavour
with hints of almond nuttiness is just developing on the palate. It's going to age
into a beauty. Screw cap. 13% alc. RATING 95 DRINK 2022-2027 $43 JP

ΨΨΨΨΩ **Felicitas 2018, Heathcote** RATING 93 $43 JP
Vermentino 2021, Heathcote RATING 93 DRINK 2022-2027 $27 JP ✪
Falanghina 2021, Heathcote RATING 93 DRINK 2022-2026 $31 JP
Col Fondo Aglianico 2021, Heathcote RATING 92 $35 JP
Greco 2021, Heathcote RATING 92 DRINK 2022-2028 $31 JP
Nero d'Avola 2021, Heathcote RATING 92 DRINK 2022-2026 $27 JP
Rosato 2021, Heathcote RATING 91 DRINK 2022-2025 $27 JP
Bush Vine Inzolia 2021, Murray Darling RATING 91 DRINK 2022-2026
$55 JP
Dott. Ribolla Gialla 2021, Heathcote RATING 90 DRINK 2022-2027 $35 JP
Montevecchio Rosso Field Blend 2020, Heathcote RATING 90
DRINK 2022-2026 $25 JP

🌿 ChaLou Wines ★★★★

569 Emu Swamp Road, Emu Swamp, NSW 2800 **Region** Orange
T 0459 689 696 **www**.chalouwines.com.au **Open** Sat–Sun 11–4 **Winemaker** Nadja
Wallington, Steve Mobbs **Viticulturist** Steve Mobbs **Est.** 2020 **Dozens** 1500 **Vyds** 6ha
ChaLou is a collaborative project between winemakers Steve Mobbs and Nadja Wallington.
They met at university before taking different forks in the road, gleaning ample experience
in different parts of the globe. Serendipitously, they reunited in Orange in 2014 with a
genuine love of farming and each other. This is palpable when tasting the wines. The
proprietary vineyard is in Orange, sited at circa 900m elevation. Varieties planted there include
riesling, chardonnay, pinot noir, pinot gris, shiraz, viognier, sauvignon blanc and arneis, with
warmer-climate varieties grenache, mourvèdre, petit verdot and a bit more viognier sourced
from a Canowindra site at 400m, certified organic. The estate range is complemented by
a less expensive Dreaded Friend line. These are sassy, fresh and eminently approachable
expressions. (NG)

ΨΨΨΨΨ **Riesling 2021, Orange** Plenty of character, if not ideal refinement. Yet! The
style augurs well for a bright future. Orange peel, pink grapefruit, camphor, ginger
and tarte tatin. Prodigious length. Will age very well. Texturally, reminds me of
Hochkirch (if they made an off-dry wine), Australia's most Alsatian of riesling and
a personal fave. Screw cap. 11% alc. RATING 94 DRINK 2021-2030 $35 NG

ΨΨΨΨΩ **Dreaded Friend Rosé 2021, Orange** RATING 92 DRINK 2021-2023 $28 NG
Chardonnay 2021, Orange RATING 92 DRINK 2021-2028 $35 NG
Dreaded Friend Cabernet Franc 2021, Central Ranges RATING 92
DRINK 2021-2024 $35 NG
Dreaded Friend Grenache 2021, Central Ranges RATING 90
DRINK 2021-2023 $35 NG

Chambers Rosewood

Barkly Street, Rutherglen, Vic 3685 **Region** Rutherglen
T (02) 6032 8641 **www.**chambersrosewood.com.au **Open** 7 days 10–4
Winemaker Stephen Chambers **Est.** 1858 **Dozens** 5000 **Vyds** 50ha
Chambers' Rare Muscat and Rare Muscadelle (previously Topaque or Tokay) are the greatest
of all in the Rutherglen firmament and should be treated as national treasures; the other wines
in the hierarchy also magnificent. Stephen Chambers (6th generation) is winemaker, but father
Bill is seldom far away. Exports to the UK, the US, Canada, Belgium, Denmark and NZ. (JH)

ɪɪɪɪɪ **Rare Muscadelle NV, Rutherglen** It is believed that Rosewood's third-
generation winemaker, Will Chambers, started this solera in the 1890s. Hence,
the drinker is paying for a taste of history. It's a divine encounter with immense
concentration, intensity of flavour and an expert eye on freshness, too. Devour the
dense, baroque-like sweetness of caramel butterscotch, chocolate-covered citrus
peel, Saunders malt extract, raisin and toasted-almond rancio flavours that never
end. Magical! 375ml. Screw cap. 18% alc. RATING 98 $250 JP

ɪɪɪɪɪ **Grand Muscat NV, Rutherglen** The solera for this fortified was started in the
1930s. You read that correctly, 1930s! Winemaker Stephen Chambers looks to a
higher level of wood-derived flavour and greater lusciousness in his Grand Muscat,
which comes, in big part, from the depth of his astonishing solera system. This
will be the start of a great fortified love affair for many, such is its sweet abandon
into rich raisiny Christmas cake, dried fruit, butterscotch, roasted coffee and
alluring rancio nuttiness. And so fresh. Bravo! 375ml bottle. Screw cap. 18.5% alc.
RATING 96 $60 JP ✪
Classic Tawny NV, Rutherglen A fortified blend of shiraz, grenache, touriga
nacional, grand noir and graciano. A glorious tawny that is both fresh and divinely
rich in rancio nuttiness, walnuts drenched in toffee and dried fruits. 750ml. Screw
cap. 18% alc. RATING 95 $25 JP ✪
Old Vine Muscat NV, Rutherglen Equivalent to the Classic Muscat
classification. A beauty of a fortified, displaying all of the seductive allure of the
grape in honeyed fruitcake, dried figs and chocolate raisins, fuelled by lingering
rose oil aromatics. And so fresh. An intriguing wine to start a fortified obsession.
375ml. Screw cap. 18% alc. RATING 95 $30 JP ✪

🍂 Chance Encounter

38 Close Street, Birkenhead, SA 5015 (postal) **Region** McLaren Vale
T 0411 276 244 **www.**chanceencounterwines.com.au **Winemaker** Jason Barrette
Viticulturist Adam Brown **Est.** 2018 **Dozens** 434
Chance Encounter is a compilation of Adelaide Hills chardonnay from Woodside, alongside
shiraz and cabernet from Marananga in the Barossa Valley, and iterations of the same grapes
from the Delabole district of McLaren Vale. The red wines are fully flavoured and densely
packed, yet avoid straying into excess. No wonder, given that winemaker Jason Barette served
under Peter Gago at Penfolds. There is a brazen confidence manifest in the meld of French and
less fashionable American oak that is used to craft the reds. Yet it is not without justification;
the quality is stellar. The tannin management sublime, serving to corral the dark-fruit accents
while imbuing the wines with a pliant sweetness, well suited to their powerful makeup. The
wines are sold online. (NG)

ɪɪɪɪɪ **Single Vineyard Cabernet Sauvignon 2020, McLaren Vale** This is very
food friendly. Maritime, saline and impressively long. Despite a makeup that bodes
heaviness, the wine is fresh, buoyant with aromas of red and black currant, effusive
of length and refined of impressionable tannins. As cabernet should be! The oak,
even the American component, is apposite. Saltbush, sage, green olive, bitter
chocolate and tomato leaf. Yet the thrum of the curranty core, the wine's marrow.
2,000 bottles. Screw cap. 14% alc. RATING 95 DRINK 2022-2033 $55 NG

ɪɪɪɪɪ **Single Vineyard Shiraz 2020, McLaren Vale** RATING 93 DRINK 2022-2030
$55 NG

Chandon Australia

727 Maroondah Highway, Coldstream, Vic 3770 **Region** Yarra Valley
T (03) 9738 9200 **www**.chandon.com.au **Open** 7 days 10.30–4.30 **Winemaker** Dan
Buckle, Glenn Thompson, Adam Keath **Est.** 1986 **Vyds** 184ha
Established by Möet & Chandon, this is one of the 2 most important wine facilities in the
Yarra Valley; the tasting room has a national and international reputation, having won a
number of major tourism awards in recent years. The sparkling wine product range evolved
with the '94 acquisition of a substantial vineyard in the cool Strathbogie Ranges and the '14
purchase of the high-altitude vineyard established by Brown Brothers, supplementing the large
intake from the Yarra Valley at various altitudes. Under the leadership of chief winemaker Dan
Buckle the high-quality standards have been maintained. Exports to Japan, Thailand, Indonesia,
Singapore, South Korea, Malaysia, Vietnam, Philippines, Taiwan and Hong Kong. (JH)

ŸŸŸŸŸ **Blanc de Blancs 2016, Victoria** All estate-grown fruit from Whitlands,
Strathbogie and Greenpoint in the Yarra. Disgorged after 4 and a half years on lees,
dosage 5g/L. Bright gold with green tinges. Honeyed with grilled hazelnuts, white
peaches, a hint of orange oil and aromas of freshly baked gougères. Both vinous
and fine boned, this accomplished and complex wine finishes dry and long. A
great New World sparkling. Diam. 12.5% alc. RATING 96 $39 PR ✪ ❤
Méthode Traditionelle Brut 2016, Victoria Fruit from the Strathbogie
Ranges and King Valley. Not shown on the new, bold labels that the wine was
disgorged in June '21, the only label claim is traditional method. The fine mousse
is very active in the mouth, and the dosage has been kept to a low level ex the
long time the wine was on tirage. Diam. 12.5% alc. RATING 95 $39 JH
Winemaker Explorations Cuvée 205 2015, Yarra Valley Upper Yarra Valley;
fermented in traditional 205L oak barrels, hence its name. The colour is bright and
fresh, the bouquet complex (remembering this is only the first brief fermentation),
and given that this disgorgement took place in Nov '19, the flavour development
in bottle has been a success. The one question is the dosage – a tad drier might
have been a major success. Diam. 12.5% alc. RATING 95 $42 JH
Blanc de Blancs NV, Victoria 90% from '17 vintage, 24 months on lees, 6g/L
dosage. A bright, green gold. Aromas of struck match, toast, freshly fried crêpes as
well as white stone fruits. The mousse is fine and delicate. An elegant, persistent
and very well-put together wine and a ridiculously good Australian sparkling at
this price. Diam. 12.5% alc. RATING 95 $25 PR ✪

ŸŸŸŸŸ **Méthode Traditionelle Brut NV, Victoria** RATING 93 $25 PR ✪
Winemakers Exploration Ancestral Rosé 2018, King Valley RATING 92
$42 JF
Brut Rosé NV, King Valley Strathbogie Ranges Yarra Valley RATING 92
$25 PR ✪

Chapel Hill ★★★★★

1 Chapel Hill Road, McLaren Vale, SA 5171 **Region** McLaren Vale
T (08) 8323 8429 **www**.chapelhillwine.com.au **Open** 7 days 11–5 **Winemaker** Michael
Fragos, Bryn Richards **Viticulturist** Rachel Steer **Est.** 1971 **Dozens** 70000 **Vyds** 44ha
A leading medium-sized winery in McLaren Vale. In late 2019 the business was purchased
from the Swiss Thomas Schmidheiny group – which owns the respected Cuvaison winery
in California and vineyards in Switzerland and Argentina – by Endeavour Drinks (part of the
Woolworths group). Wine quality is unfailingly excellent. The production comes from estate
plantings of shiraz, cabernet sauvignon, chardonnay, verdelho, savagnin, sangiovese and merlot,
plus contract-grown grapes. The red wines are not filtered or fined, and there are no tannin or
enzyme additions, just SO$_2$ – natural red wines. Exports to all major markets. (JH)

ŸŸŸŸŸ **1948 Vines Grenache 2020, McLaren Vale** This is an incredibly exciting
wine. Known for reliable wines, this address has suddenly come to play ball
with the artisans! There is nothing heavy or clumsy about this, as with so much
grenache from bigger companies. Just old-vine sap cleaved by finely tuned

extraction, sound choice of oak and some bunches in the mix. A sandy, gently gritty tannic frame contains kirsch, Asian plum, sandalwood and bergamot notes. The effect is svelte, fresh and lively. Pinosity a-go-go. The weight and intensity, effortless of feel. Thoroughly impressive, boding so well for the future of this great variety. Screw cap. 14.5% alc. RATING 96 DRINK 2021–2028 $65 NG ✪

Gorge Block Cabernet Sauvignon 2016, McLaren Vale One of 3 bottle-aged releases from this venerated site to commemorate 50 years of existence. The finest, I suppose, as much as I cherish the '12. Finer because of its detail, the refined weave of its tannins, unwinding across notes of cassis, bouquet garni, green olive, sage and licorice. Finer, because of the suave intensity, the build across the palate, the thrust of fruit and parry of structure. Finer, because I keep going back. Screw cap. 14.5% alc. RATING 96 DRINK 2022–2038 $75 NG ✪

Gorge Block Cabernet Sauvignon 2020, McLaren Vale I've said it before, but the Vale is the finest warm-climate source of cabernet in the country. Saline. Sea spray, a smear of black olive, saltbush, dried sage and blackcurrant. Distinctly maritime. Matured largely in tight-grained older oak for 20 months. A firmament of intelligently gleaned tannins, oak and grape, serve as the savoury marrow. Long and refined. Excellent drinking. This will age very well. Screw cap. 14.5% alc. RATING 95 DRINK 2022–2033 $65 NG

The Vicar Shiraz 2020, McLaren Vale This is very good. Extracted as a metallurgist shifts diamonds from the rough. A wine that behaves far more persuasively than most hot-climate shiraz: fresh, palpably natural of structural lattice and somehow refined. Sure, there is weight and power, but far more intriguing is a sublime undercarriage of bracken, clove, star anise, charcuterie and tapenade. There is a bit of fruit, too, but writing about it undersells this. A wine of character. Majestic tannins, the opus. Screw cap. 14.5% alc. RATING 95 DRINK 2022–2035 $75 NG

The Chosen Gorge Block Cabernet Sauvignon 2012, McLaren Vale Barely at late adolescence, with a long way to go in its evolution. Currant, sage, cigar box and violet. There is an intriguing lilt across the finish of mocha oak melded with olive paste, dried tobacco and pencil lead. The sweetness expands. As forceful as it is, it feels immaculately poised. A long meander rather than a bludgeon. Lovely warm-climate cab. Screw cap. 14.5% alc. RATING 95 DRINK 2021–2027 $75 NG

🍷🍷🍷🍷🍷 **Small Batch #01 Shiraz Mourvèdre 2020, McLaren Vale** RATING 93 DRINK 2021–2026 $28 NG

The MV Cabernet Sauvignon 2020, McLaren Vale RATING 93 DRINK 2021–2029 $33 NG

Road Block Shiraz 2020, McLaren Vale RATING 93 DRINK 2021–2029 $65 NG

Cabernet Shiraz 2019, McLaren Vale RATING 93 DRINK 2021–2028 $28 NG

Small Batch #01 GSM 2020, McLaren Vale RATING 92 DRINK 2021–2024 $28 NG

Zinfandel 2020, McLaren Vale RATING 92 DRINK 2021–2024 $28 NG

The MV Mourvèdre 2020, McLaren Vale RATING 92 DRINK 2021–2026 $33 NG

The MV Shiraz 2020, McLaren Vale RATING 92 DRINK 2021–2026 $33 NG

Small Batch #03 Home Grown Shiraz 2020, McLaren Vale RATING 91 DRINK 2022–2025 $28 NG

Mr. Vinecombe Cabernet Sauvignon Shiraz Merlot 2020, McLaren Vale RATING 90 DRINK 2021–2026 $20 NG ✪

The Vinedresser Cabernet Sauvignon 2020, McLaren Vale RATING 90 DRINK 2021–2026 $26 NG

Charlotte Dalton Wines   ★★★★★

Factory 9, 89–91 Hill Street, Port Elliot, SA 5212 **Region** Adelaide Hills
T 0466 541 361 **www.charlottedaltonwines.com.au Open** Fri–Mon 11–3 (7 days 26 Dec–26 Jan) **Winemaker** Charlotte Hardy **Est.** 2015 **Dozens** 1200

Charlotte Hardy has been making wines for 20 years, with a star-studded career at Craggy Range (NZ), Château Giscours (Bordeaux) and David Abreu (California), but has called SA home since 2007. Her winery is part of her Basket Range house, which has been through many incarnations since starting life as a pig farm in 1858. Much later it housed the Basket Range store, and at different times in the past 2 decades it has been the winery to Basket Range Wines, The Deanery Wines and now Charlotte Dalton Wines. Exports to the UK, US, Canada and Sweden. (JH)

ŸŸŸŸŸ **Love Me Love You Shiraz 2020, Adelaide Hills** A smaller production of this wine, due to local bushfires and drought, but it stands up well with a cast of fresh red fruits, including raspberry, bringing a singular juiciness. New oak (35%) is present but well integrated, a background note to all of the lively fruit, spice and pepper happening upfront. Screw cap. 14.5% alc. RATING 94 DRINK 2022-2026 $37 JP

Love You Love Me Semillon 2019, Adelaide Hills You don't see a lot of Hills semillon, but maybe this smart, intelligently made wine heralds a change. A very confident, expressive semillon with 3 years under its belt and showing jasmine, apple blossom and white flower aromas, spiced apple, lemongrass, spice. Rich in flavour, creamy in texture but delivered with a tangy juiciness that makes you have to have another sip. Screw cap. 12% alc. RATING 94 DRINK 2022-2025 $30 JP ✿

ŸŸŸŸŸ **Fred Fiano 2021, Langhorne Creek** RATING 93 DRINK 2022-2024 $35 JP
A Change Is Coming Pinot Noir 2021, Adelaide Hills RATING 92 DRINK 2022-2026 $42 JP
Mr Lincoln Rosé 2021, Adelaide Hills Langhorne Creek RATING 91 DRINK 2022-2024 $30 JP
Ærkeengel Semillon 2019, Adelaide Hills RATING 91 DRINK 2022-2025 $42 JP
Beyond the Horizon Shiraz 2019, Adelaide Hills RATING 90 DRINK 2021-2028 $47 JP

Charteris Wines   ★★★★

1946 Broke Road, Pokolbin, NSW 2320 **Region** Hunter Valley
T 0412 121 319 **www**.charteriswines.com **Open** 7 days 10–5 **Winemaker** PJ Charteris
Viticulturist PJ Charteris **Est.** 2008 **Dozens** 2000 **Vyds** 1.7ha
Owners Peter James (PJ) Charteris and partner Christina Pattison met at Brokenwood in the Hunter Valley in 1999. PJ was the chief executive winemaker at Brokenwood, and Christina was the marketing manager. Together they have over 3 decades of winemaking and wine marketing experience. For NZ-born PJ, finding a top pinot noir site in Central Otago was a spiritual homecoming (they claim to have searched both Australia and NZ for the right combination of site and variety). They also have a vineyard with the gold-plated address of Felton Road, Bannockburn, planted to clones 115 777 and Abel. PJ carries on a consultancy business in Australia, with some, though not all, of his focus being the Hunter Valley. (JH)

ŸŸŸŸŸ **Semillon 2021, Hunter Valley** An intriguing wine, clearly embellished with ample lees handling to impart breadth and textural nourishment. Light of alcohol, but mid-weight of feel. Lemon squash, fennel, raw almond and a creamy, savoury oatmeal element to the broad mid palate. A bitter quinine twist to the gently chewy finish. I like this. A different regional stroke. It will age well. Screw cap. 11.5% alc. RATING 93 DRINK 2021-2029 $35 NG

Chardonnay 2021, Hunter Valley Saline, gently mid-weighted, brisk and intense of flavour, marked by nectarine and white peach. The oak, a well-positioned signpost directing the fray to good length while imparting riffs on cashew and curd. I'd be drinking this on the earlier side. Screw cap. 12.8% alc. RATING 93 DRINK 2021-2027 $40 NG

Shiraz 2019, Hunter Valley This is very good, impressively honest regional shiraz. Old-vine vinosity. A striking fidelity to the region across riffs of sweet loam and terracotta. Mocha oak, sits nicely. Dark cherry, sarsaparilla, clove, thyme and lavender. The finish, long and dutifully savoury. Screw cap. 13.5% alc. RATING 93 DRINK 2021-2030 $45 NG

Le Fauve Pinot Gris 2021, Orange Picked on acidity, this is a lightweight wine of aromatic intensity, albeit, a bit of a shrill finish. Muddled orange, cinnamon and Asian pear skins. A fine tactile feel marking the mid palate. The finish, long and energetic. This needs foods. Rather impressive. Screw cap. 12% alc. RATING 92 DRINK 2021-2024 $30 NG

Le Fauve Rouge 2021, Orange Hilltops A blend of Orange pinot noir and Hilltops tempranillo. It works well. A lightness of being, bound to a firm tannic twine and darker brood. Clove, cigar, dark cherry, mulch, mint and leather varnish. Dry and firm, with a certain obduracy to the finish that cries out for food. Fun drinking. Screw cap. 13% alc. RATING 92 DRINK 2021-2028 $35 NG

Le Fauve Rosé 2021, Hilltops Very good rosé. The lightness of hue belies the intensity of red currant, wild strawberry, rosehip and musk flavours that stream long across the plate. Crunchy. Thirst slaking. A pin-pointed endeavour to whet the palate, draw the saliva and make one reach for another glass. Screw cap. 13% alc. RATING 90 DRINK 2021-2022 $30 NG

Chateau June-Jerome

1667 Graphite Road, Glenoran, WA 6258 **Region** Manjimup
T 0408 626 569 www.chateaujune-jerome.com **Open** By appt **Winemaker** Clint Robertson, Mark Aitken **Viticulturist** Clint Robertson **Est.** 2015 **Dozens** 250 **Vyds** 4ha
Clint and Melissa Robertson made the actual (and existential) move from 'mines to vines' in 2015 with the purchase of what is now the Chateau June-Jerome vineyard, and launched their first wine (a chardonnay) in '17 under this label. The now 25yo vineyard is situated in the Southern Forest region of Manjimup. The 4ha vineyard is currently planted to chardonnay and cabernet sauvignon, with hand-picked fruit selected from the local region, including riesling, pinot noir, merlot and syrah. While not yet certified organic, the property is managed with minimal chemical intervention using organic principles. Available in WA only. (EL)

Syrah 2019, Manjimup A super-spicy nose ... licorice, garden mint, mulberry and raspberry compote with lashings of black cherry. On the palate it is cooling and laden with graphite tannins, jasmine tea, black pepper and anise, dusted with a eucalypt, bush-smoke character through the finish. This is medium bodied at best, an elegant and exciting wine. Screw cap. 13.5% alc. RATING 92 DRINK 2022-2026 $36 EL

Rosé 2021, Manjimup RATING 89 DRINK 2021-2022 $30 EL

Château Tanunda

9 Basedow Road, Tanunda, SA 5352 **Region** Barossa Valley
T (08) 8563 3888 www.chateautanunda.com **Open** 7 days 10–5 **Winemaker** Neville Rowe **Est.** 1890 **Dozens** 150 000 **Vyds** 100ha
This is one of the most historically significant winery buildings in the Barossa Valley, built from bluestone quarried in the late 1880s. It has been restored by the Geber family. Château Tanunda owns almost 100ha of vineyards in Bethany, Eden Valley, Tanunda and Vine Vale, with additional fruit sourced from a group of 30 growers covering the panoply of Barossa districts. The wines are made from hand-picked grapes, basket pressed and neither fined nor filtered. There is an emphasis on single-vineyard and single-district wines under the Terroirs of the Barossa label. The impressive building houses the cellar door, the Grand Cellar and the Barossa Small Winemakers Centre, offering wines from boutique winemakers. Daughter Michelle joined as managing director in 2018; Château Tanunda celebrated its 130th anniversary in '20. Exports to all major markets. (JH)

Terroirs of the Barossa Greenock Shiraz 2019, Barossa Valley Château Tanunda have captured the subregional nuance nicely here. Deep, rich blackberry and satsuma plum notes are underscored by dark spice, ironstone, espresso, cedar, blackstrap licorice and earth. Impressive fruit depth and smoothly textured flow, tight talcy tannins providing the scaffolding, bright acidity the drive, as the wine drifts into the distance, opulent, black-fruited and pure. Cork. 14.5% alc. RATING 94 DRINK 2022-2038 $60 DB

ŸŸŸŸŸ Heritage Release Old Vine Shiraz 2019, Barossa RATING 93 DRINK 2020-2035 $40 DB
Terroirs of the Barossa Marananga Shiraz 2019, Barossa Valley RATING 93 DRINK 2021-2035 $60 DB
The Everest Shiraz 2018, Barossa RATING 93 DRINK 2022-2035 $350 DB
Grand Cabernet Sauvignon 2020, Barossa RATING 92 DRINK 2020-2030 $25 DB ✪
Grand GSM 2021, Barossa RATING 91 DRINK 2022-2028 $25 DB
Grand Shiraz 2020, Barossa RATING 91 DRINK 2022-2028 $25 DB
The Chateau Single Vineyard Cabernet Sauvignon 2019, Barossa RATING 91 DRINK 2021-2028 $38 DB
The Whole Dam Family 2019, Barossa Valley RATING 91 DRINK 2022-2026 $40 DB
50 Year Old Vines Barossa Cabernet Sauvignon 2019, Barossa Valley RATING 91 DRINK 2022-2032 $80 DB

Chatto

68 Dillons Hill Road, Glaziers Bay, Tas 7109 **Region** Southern Tasmania
T (03) 6114 2050 **www.**chattowines.com **Winemaker** Jim Chatto **Viticulturist** Paul Lipscombe **Est.** 2000 **Dozens** 1000 **Vyds** 1.5ha

Jim Chatto is recognised as having one of the very best palates in Australia, and has proved to be an outstanding winemaker. He and wife Daisy long wanted to get a small Tasmanian pinot business up and running but, having moved to the Hunter Valley in '00, it took 6 years to find a site that satisfied all of the criteria they consider ideal. It is a warm, well-drained site in one of the coolest parts of Tasmania, looking out over Glaziers Bay. They have planted 8 clones of pinot noir, with a spacing of 5000 vines/ha. The '19 crop was lost to bushfire smoke taint, but the many Tasmanian vigneron friends of the Chatto family came to the rescue. (JH)

ŸŸŸŸŸ Isle Black Label Pinot Noir 2020, Tasmania A very arresting and complex bouquet of dark berries and forest floor, the palate with an infusion of savoury spices, the texture and structure perfect. Screw cap. 13.5% alc. RATING 97 DRINK 2024-2035 $90 JH ✪

ŸŸŸŸŸ Intrigue Black Label Pinot Noir 2020, Tasmania A stunning bouquet, with outright perfume sure to emerge in a year or 2; the palate already with spices alongside pure red and black cherry fruit. Screw cap. 13% alc. RATING 96 DRINK 2023-2033 $70 JH ✪
Bird Pinot Noir 2020, Tasmania Jim Chatto has sensitively gauged that the elegant fruit of Pipers River calls for neither whole bunches nor new oak in the cool '20 season, thus upholding the purity and innocence of rose petal, red cherries and strawberries. Velvet-fine tannins embrace the bright acidity of the region and carry a long and refined finish. Screw cap. 12.5% alc. RATING 94 DRINK 2022-2030 $65 TS
Seven Inch Pinot Noir 2020, Tasmania Chatto's '20s are a fascinating insight into the distinct zones of Tasmanian pinot, and his neighbour in the Huon Valley delivers his most exotic and characterful rendition. Spicy dark-berry compote meets sarsaparilla, mixed spice and black-cherry liqueur. It's at once fleshy and toned, tangy and fine boned, with exemplary tannin detail played out on a medium-length finish. Screw cap. 13.5% alc. RATING 94 DRINK 2022-2028 $65 TS

Cherry Tree Hill

12324 Hume Highway, Sutton Forest, NSW 2577 **Region** Southern Highlands
T (02) 8217 1409 **www.**cherrytreehill.com.au **Open** 7 days 10–5 **Winemaker** Anton
Balog, Mark Balog **Viticulturist** Ian Evans **Est.** 2000 **Dozens** 3500 **Vyds** 13.5ha
Gabi Lorentz began the establishment of the Cherry Tree Hill vineyard in '00 with the
planting of cabernet sauvignon and riesling, soon followed by merlot, sauvignon blanc and
chardonnay. Since then, 5.5ha of the merlot and cabernet have been re-grafted to pinot
noir, destined for both still and sparkling wine. Gabi's inspiration was childhood trips on a
horse and cart through his grandfather's vineyard in Hungary. Gabi's son David is now the
owner and manager of the business. (JH)

🍷🍷🍷🍷🍷 **Hayden Reserve Pinot Noir 2019, Southern Highlands** A combination
of clones, with MV6 (35%) and 777 (30%) leading the way. Arguably the most
complete wine of this intriguing suite, although I don't necessarily prefer it to
the solid MV6. More red fruit, orange peel and expansive sweetness across the
mid palate here, sluiced with a fine skein of oak and grape tannins. The length,
too, impressive. A mid-weighted wine of considerable finesse and class. Screw cap.
13.5% alc. RATING 93 DRINK 2021-2029 $50 NG
MV6 Pinot Noir 2019, Southern Highlands A curb of vanillin oak frames
sour cherry, damson plum, root spice and a carnal underbelly of forestry and
mulch. Fine, pointed aromas. The palate boasts mid-weighted sap, tension and a
welcome reticence, auguring well for several years in bottle. An intriguing wine, in
the very best sense. A benchmark of the region. Screw cap. 13.5% alc. RATING 93
DRINK 2023-2028 $50 NG
Chardonnay 2019, Yarra Valley A well-crafted, medium-bodied, loosely knit
expression, in the best sense. Plying a mineral pungency with a striving for real
flavour, there is plenty on offer. Stone-fruit accents, honeydew melon, roasted
almonds and praline. The oak, like a blowhole that stems the flow while liberating
it when necessary, allowing the flavours to ebb and flow long. Lovely drinking.
Screw cap. 13% alc. RATING 92 DRINK 2021-2025 $25 NG ❂
114/115 Pinot Noir 2019, Southern Highlands A different oak regime to
the pace-setting MV6, this meld of earlier-ripening clones is altogether more lifted,
red-fruited and ethereal. Mid weighted, but strongly in the chiffon-like camp.
Think sour cherry, spiced rhubarb and ume. The tannins, lithe and gentle. The
finish, sweet and easy. A charming wine that is a tad prosaic, but very delicious.
Screw cap. 13% alc. RATING 92 DRINK 2021-2025 $50 NG
777 Pinot Noir 2019, Southern Highlands A bit more thrust of fruit and
parry of structure (particularly the toasty François Frères oak) than the 114/115,
without the meaty, ferrous undertones and intensity of the MV6. Plenty of flavour:
sassafras, mulch and strawberry. Screw cap. 13% alc. RATING 92 DRINK 2021-2027
$50 NG
Halle Reserve Merlot 2019, Southern Highlands The considered effort to
make quality wine here is palpable and largely successful. Classy aromas of fresh
mint, damson plum, tomato bush and red cherry. The tannins, lithe and sinewy,
service impressive herbal length. Savoury. Medium bodied. Ready to go. I would
not age this further. The fruit will dry out. Screw cap. 13.8% alc. RATING 92
DRINK 2021-2023 $50 NG
Sauvignon Blanc 2021, Southern Highlands A medium-bodied sauvignon
with real verve, playing a card of guava, hedgerow, Thai herb and greengage
without the sweet-sour acidity that is the bane of so many. The feel is waxy and
savoury, rather than tangy and shrill. One of poise and mellifluous drinkability.
Screw cap. 12.5% alc. RATING 90 DRINK 2021-2022 $25 NG

🍷🍷🍷🍷 **Pinot Rosé Pinot Noir 2021, Yarra Valley** RATING 89 DRINK 2021-2022
$25 NG
Riesling 2021, Clare Valley RATING 89 DRINK 2021-2029 $35 NG
Reserve The Wedding Cabernet Sauvignon 2019, Southern Highlands
RATING 89 DRINK 2021-2023 $50 NG

Cherubino

3462 Caves Road, Wilyabrup, WA 6280 **Region** Western Australia
T (08) 9382 2379 **www.**larrycherubino.com **Open** 7 days 10–5 **Winemaker** Larry
Cherubino, Andrew Siddell, Matt Buchan **Est.** 2005 **Dozens** 8000 **Vyds** 120ha

Larry Cherubino has had a particularly distinguished winemaking career, first at Hardys
Tintara, then Houghton and thereafter as consultant and Flying Winemaker in Australia, NZ,
South Africa, the US and Italy. He has developed numerous ranges, including Cherubino,
single-vineyard range The Yard, and the single-region Ad Hoc label. The range and quality
of his wines is extraordinary, the prices irresistible. The runaway success of the business has
seen the accumulation of 120ha of vineyards, the appointment of additional winemakers and
Larry's own appointment as director of winemaking for Robert Oatley Vineyards. Exports
to the UK, the US, Canada, Ireland, Switzerland, Hong Kong, South Korea, Singapore and
NZ. (JH)

♀♀♀♀♀ Cherubino Chardonnay 2020, Margaret River This wine amassed 8 trophies
at shows in '21 and was made in such tiny quantities that sales are now limited
to a bottle a customer. If you can still get it. Distinctive for its custard powder
nose, this is an opulent, luxurious chardonnay of voluminous depth and power.
Salted peach, kiwi-fruit acidity and long, undulating layers of flavour. Immediately,
and obviously, a gold-pointed wine in the chardonnay class I judged at Margaret
River Wine Show '21. One for the ages. Screw cap. 13.5% alc. RATING 97
DRINK 2022-2037 $95 EL ✪

♀♀♀♀♀ Cherubino Riesling 2021, Porongurup The delicacy inherent in Porongurup
rieslings can be deceiving – you see spring florals and you see chalk, and you come
to a 'delicate' conclusion. But 'delicate' doesn't cover the extension of flavour and
intensity through the finish, which seems to come so effortlessly to the producers
in the area. This has jasmine, green apples, lemon zest and limestone on the nose
and palate. Poised and super-pretty, this has all the length to indicate that the fruit
has the horsepower required for ageing, but as with all Porongurup rieslings, it is
beautiful to drink in its youth, too. Choose your weapon. Screw cap. 11.5% alc.
RATING 96 DRINK 2021-2036 $45 EL ✪

The Yard Acacia Shiraz 2020, Frankland River This wine is sensational.
Oh my goodness. It's saturated, earthy and polished, laden with ferrous, blood,
raspberries and licorice. The tannins are firm, fine and yet pliable. The whole affair
is just, well, sensational. What a wine. Frankland River is here and this is what it
does best. Eat your heart out. Screw cap. 14.5% alc. RATING 96 DRINK 2021-2031
$35 EL ✪

Cherubino Gingin Wilyabrup Chardonnay 2020, Margaret River
Expansive flavours of yellow peach, nectarine, red apple skins and brine are
tumbled together to create a voluminous experience – the fruit billows in the
mouth and spills out over a long finish. Lush and evocative. The acid is high
(7.47g/L), but it is countersunk into the fruit so it is structuring, rather than
intrusive. Not to be missed. Screw cap. 13.1% alc. RATING 96 DRINK 2022-2037
$55 EL ✪

Cherubino Chardonnay 2020, Pemberton Pemberton has an uncanny knack
for concentrated flavour in white wines particularly, and the Dijon clones express
so beautifully here. It tastes like malo has been blocked (although no mention),
which makes for mouth-puckering drinking right now. Having said that, the
fruit is so intense that there is a strange balance achieved here. Saline, fine, taut
and pure … a classy wine to the very end. Screw cap. 13.9% alc. RATING 96
DRINK 2022-2037 $65 EL ✪ ♥

Cherubino Riversdale Vineyard Shiraz Mataro 2020, Frankland River
The nose here has everything you could both want and expect from a blend
of these 2 varieties: the shiraz brings the blackberries, the licorice and the spice,
while the mataro is responsible for the purple berries, earth and cocoa dust. In the
mouth the wine is dense and concentrated, shaped by velvet tannins and populated
by explosive fruit power. There is deli meat, with salted plums alongside. The

inimitable Frankland River DNA of red earth, ferrous ironstone and blood is laced through the finish … A very (very) smart wine. Screw cap. 14.9% alc. RATING 96 DRINK 2022-2032 $65 EL ✪

Cherubino Caves Road Vineyard Chardonnay 2020, Margaret River The selection of parcels linked by Caves Road, from the (comparative) warmth of Wilyabrup, then south through Wallcliffe, thence to the (comparative) cool of Karridale, has pre-ordained the magic of the generosity of the white stone-fruit mid palate and the precision of the citrusy acidity on the finish. No less magical is the way the wine has made light work of its fermentation and 10 months' maturation in new and 1yo French oak. While it's a truly lovely chardonnay now, it will gain more complexity and richness through to the end of the decade. Screw cap. 13.5% alc. RATING 96 DRINK 2022-2029 $75 JH ✪

Uovo Grenache 2021, Frankland River The colour! Beautiful to look at. Magenta. This is chalky, textural, supple and pretty. The clarity of raspberry and rhubarb fruit in the mouth is impressive. The tannins finish cooling and fine. This is lovely. A breath of fresh air. Screw cap. 15% alc. RATING 95 DRINK 2022-2027 $70 EL

Riesling 2021, Mount Barker A delicate and fine expression of riesling from Mount Barker, a region that typically produces a big muscly, brawny style. This speaks of green apples and brine, fine white spice, nashi pears and preserved lemons. The key here is the lingering length of flavour; its tingly, pop-rocky acidity is an entertaining aftermath of the wine. It beckons for another sip. Screw cap. 12.1% alc. RATING 95 DRINK 2021-2031 $45 EL

Cherubino Willows Vineyard Rosé 2021, Margaret River This is a seriously delicious rosé. Flavoursome, balanced, long and satisfying. Grenache produces a different vibe when used for rosé – it's not savoury and earthy like mataro, or spicy and lifted like sangiovese; it's sweet, plush and generous. The muscly varietal characters are seen on their softer side. Hard to go past this wine. Screw cap. 13% alc. RATING 95 DRINK 2021-2025 $39 EL

Laissez Faire Chardonnay 2020, Porongurup From the cool climes of the Porongurup Range comes this lithe, creamy and delicate chardonnay. All good things are spooling out of this glass right now: salted lemons, white peach, crushed nuts, red apples and a few fresh curry leaves. It's beautiful. Screw cap. 13% alc. RATING 95 DRINK 2021-2031 $44 EL

The Yard Riversdale Shiraz 2020, Frankland River This is seriously good. It is earthy and textured, slightly more grounded than the Acacia shiraz from '20 (which I also loved, it's just different to this), and loaded with red berries, earthy spice and shaped by oak. The tannins are a real highlight, they're slightly gravelly, slightly chewy, and add an extra dimension of pleasure to the wine. A standout. Screw cap. 14.5% alc. RATING 95 DRINK 2021-2031 $35 EL ✪

Dijon Wychwood Vineyard Karridale Chardonnay 2020, Margaret River Taut and pure. A little (10%) mlf goes a long way. It forms a luscious bedrock of texture in the mouth, on which the fruit seemingly floats. The acidity is far less of an issue than expected; the high-acid clones, in addition to the cool growing area, has the potential to lead to very high – sometimes austere – acid. But, courtesy of the warm and glorious '20 vintage, all is in balance. A silky, seamless and very fine wine. Screw cap. 13% alc. RATING 95 DRINK 2022-2035 $55 EL

Elevation Chardonnay 2020, Margaret River The Cherubino chardonnays are starting to shine so brightly it's a wonder they make anything else. This is powerful, spicy, creamy, rich and super-elegant. The spool of flavour through the finish captures peaches, nectarines, apples, pears, white pepper and brine. The length gives us so much opportunity to assess all of these characters that more emerge, given time. What a superstar. Screw cap. 13.5% alc. RATING 95 DRINK 2021-2031 $55 EL

Cherubino Shiraz 2020, Frankland River Impossibly vibrant aromatically, and inchoate in the glass too, for that matter. The youth is almost obscuring the regional DNA of ferrous ironstone and dirt that Frankland achieves so effortlessly … but it is here, emerging nearly an hour after it was poured. This is littered with licorice, black cherries and Szechuan pepper, but to see the wonders that this wine will no doubt produce in the future, patience will be key. It is as tight as tight can be right now, however the shape and length of the tannins and flavour, coupled with the vineyards' history, tell us what we need to know. Screw cap. 14% alc. RATING 95 DRINK 2022-2034 $65 EL

Riversdale Block 7 Shiraz 2020, Frankland River Inchoate as this wine is at this stage, the fruit carries all of the expected DNA from the vineyard and the region: blood, blood plums, ferrous ironstone and red dirt. To add to that, there is some essence of cherry kirsch, overlaid with hung deli meat and red licorice that colours in the edges of the experience. The texture, the intensity and the balance all say this will be sensational, but it is far too early to tell – the wine has barely left infancy. Don't. Touch. It. Screw cap. 14.9% alc. RATING 95 DRINK 2024-2039 $65 EL

The Yard Justin Shiraz 2020, Frankland River Another utterly sensational wine here. It shares many similarities with The Yard Acacia Shiraz 2020, yet this seems the more structured, the firmer of the 2. They both carry the regional DNA of ferrous, ironstone, red dirt, blood and raspberry, however this is framed by more pronounced tannins and slightly lighter/more delicate fruit weight. A wildly impressive wine. Frankland River is an absolute marvel. Screw cap. 14.5% alc. RATING 95 DRINK 2021-2031 $35 EL ✪

Pedestal Semillon Sauvignon Blanc 2021, Margaret River Juniper, jalapeño, lime cordial, green apples and green table grapes. Bright and lithe and endowed with a slippery texture in the mouth, no doubt aided by the short time spent in oak. Balanced and supple – a joyous wine of poise and grace. Screw cap. 12.4% alc. RATING 94 DRINK 2021-2031 $27 EL ✪

The Yard Riversdale Riesling 2021, Frankland River The vines are grown in red dirt, and the rocky soils are responsible for the region's DNA. This is a plum expression: salted preserved lemons, apples, citrus zest, graphite, tightly coiled acidity and spring. Screw cap. 12.6% alc. RATING 94 DRINK 2021-2031 $29 EL ✪

Laissez Faire IV 2021, Frankland River 44/33/15/8% counoise/mataro/shiraz/grenache. The most vibrant of magentas in the glass, superseded only by the vibrancy of aroma: pomegranate essence, raspberry, plum skin, pink lady apples, damsons and more. In the mouth the wine is crunchy, bright and totally delicious. A wonderful wine if you're on the hunt for something different. Screw cap. 14.5% alc. RATING 94 DRINK 2021-2031 $34 EL

Chris Ringland ★★★★★

Franklin House, 6–8 Washington Street, Angaston, SA 5353 **Region** Barossa Valley **T** (08) 8564 3233 **www**.chrisringland.com **Open** By appt **Winemaker** Chris Ringland **Est.** 1989 **Dozens** 120 **Vyds** 2.05ha

The wines made by Chris Ringland for his eponymous brand were at the very forefront of the surge of rich, old-vine Barossa shiraz wines discovered by Robert Parker in the '80s. As a consequence of very limited production, and high-quality (albeit polarising) wine, it assumed immediate icon status. The production of 120 dozen does not include a small number of magnums, double magnums and imperials that are sold each year. The addition of 0.5ha of shiraz planted in '99, joined by 1.5ha planted in '10, has had little practical impact on availability. Exports to the UK, the US, France, Germany, Spain, South Korea, Japan and Hong Kong. (JH)

🍷🍷🍷🍷🍷 **Hoffmann Vineyard Shiraz 2013, Barossa Valley** Adrian Hoffmann's epic patch of ancient vines in Ebenezer is renowned among Barossa-philes. Winemaker Chris Ringland has a long-standing relationship with Adrian and his land. Pop your nose in the glass and you quickly double-take, trying to take in the sheer concentration and monolithic quality of the fruit. Über-intense blackberry, black cherry and cassis notes jump out of the glass with hints of cherry clafoutis, clove and baking spice, blackstrap licorice, bay leaf, earth, dark soy, smoked meats and dried herbs. The fruit weight and density is peaking the meters, the tannin long and sandy fine. That hefty 16.5% alcohol is perfectly in balance, with fine acidity providing drive and frame. It's a beast, and I mean that in the best way possible. Give it an extended decant and enjoy. Cork. 16.5% alc. RATING 97 DRINK 2021-2038 $550 DB

🍷🍷🍷🍷🍷 Dimchurch Barossa Shiraz 2015, Barossa Valley A Chris Ringland barrel selection from Adrian Hoffmann's epic Ebenezer shiraz holdings. It's another showcase of fruit power, concentration and density, with compacted blackberry, black cherry and cassis fruit in spades undercut with spice box, licorice, maraschino cherry, dates, fruitcake and a fair shunt of cedary, vanillin oak. The aromas all transpose neatly onto the palate; the cedar and pencil-case aromas ratchet up a notch, the long-chain, grippy yet willowy tannins kick in and the wine rumbles on to an incredibly concentrated finish with just a little alcohol heat. Monolithic, cellar worthy and, again, give it an extended decant. Cork. 17% alc. RATING 95 DRINK 2021-2038 $175 DB

Chrismont

251 Upper King River Road, Cheshunt, Vic 3678 **Region** King Valley
T (03) 5729 8220 **www.**chrismont.com.au **Open** 7 days 10–5 **Winemaker** Warren Proft, Prasad Patil **Viticulturist** Arnie Pizzini, Warren Proft **Est.** 1980 **Dozens** 25 000 **Vyds** 100ha
Arnie and Jo Pizzini's substantial vineyards in the Cheshunt and Whitfield areas of the upper King Valley have been planted to riesling, chardonnay, pinot gris, merlot, barbera, sagrantino, marzemino, arneis, prosecco, fiano, petit manseng, tempranillo, sangiovese and nebbiolo. The La Zona range ties in the Italian heritage of the Pizzinis and is part of the intense interest in all things Italian. In Jan '16 the Chrismont cellar door, restaurant and larder was opened. A feature is the 'floating' deck over the vineyard, which can seat up to 150 people and has floor-to-ceiling glass looking out over the Black Ranges and King Valley landscape. Exports to the Philippines, Malaysia and Singapore. (JH)

🍷🍷🍷🍷🍷 Pinot Gris 2021, King Valley The winemaker aims for a luscious style and delivers a little treasure. The grape is in its happy place here, with a striking, fully ripened, complex wine with a touch of the exotic. Talc, musk, citrus, spiced apple and peach aromas unfurl. While luscious with supple texture, it keeps its freshness all the while as you discover layer after layer of quince, citrus, apple, grilled nuts and the most captivating spice. Screw cap. 13.5% alc. RATING 96 DRINK 2021-2026 $26 JP ✪

🍷🍷🍷🍷🍷 La Zona Prosecco NV, King Valley RATING 93 $22 JP ✪
La Zona Arneis 2019, King Valley RATING 91 DRINK 2021-2026 $22 JP ✪
Riesling 2021, King Valley RATING 90 DRINK 2021-2025 $19 JP ✪
Petit Manseng 2021, King Valley RATING 90 DRINK 2022-2026 $26 JP

Churchview Estate

8 Gale Road, Metricup, WA 6280 **Region** Margaret River
T (08) 9755 7200 **www.**churchview.com.au **Open** Mon–Sat 10–5 **Winemaker** Dave Longden **Est.** 1998 **Dozens** 25 **Vyds** 56ha
The Fokkema family, headed by Spike Fokkema, emigrated from the Netherlands in the '50s. Business success in the following decades led to the acquisition of the 100ha Churchview Estate (named for the heritage-listed church that can be seen from the cellar door) in '97, and to the progressive establishment of substantial vineyards (planted to 16 varieties), certified organic since 2014. Exports to all major markets. (JH)

🍷🍷🍷🍷🍷 The Bartondale Cabernet Sauvignon 2020, Margaret River Plush and ripe. The moderately high alcohol is concealed within the folds of fruit, the time in oak has already yielded a wine of power and shape. While young, this is very good now, excellent in fact. A testament to the unique year that birthed it. If you can get some before your children finish school, I would advise it. Screw cap. 15% alc. RATING 94 DRINK 2022–2032 $55 EL

¶¶¶¶♀ St Johns Limited Release Cabernet Malbec Petit Verdot Merlot 2020, Margaret River RATING 92 DRINK 2024–2032 $35 EL
St Johns Limited Release Malbec 2019, Margaret River RATING 92 DRINK 2021–2031 $40 EL
St Johns Limited Release Shiraz Viognier 2020, Margaret River RATING 90 DRINK 2021–2031 $35 EL
St Johns Limited Release Wild Fermented Chenin Blanc 2020, Margaret River RATING 90 DRINK 2023–2033 $30 EL

¶¶¶¶ St Johns Limited Release Petit Verdot 2020, Margaret River RATING 89 DRINK 2022–2028 $35 EL

Cimicky Wines

100 Hermann Thumm Drive, Lyndoch, SA 5351 **Region** Barossa Valley
T (08) 8524 4025 **www**.cimickywines.com.au **Open** By appt **Winemaker** Sam Kurtz, Charles Cimicky, Andrew Aldridge **Viticulturist** Sam Kurtz **Est.** 1972 **Dozens** 15 000 **Vyds** 14.42ha

The Cimicky property was originally settled in Lyndoch in 1842 by early German pioneers. Karl Cimicky purchased the property in 1970, expanding the vineyards and building the imposing Tuscan-style winery, which he named Karlsburg. When Karl retired in the '80s, his son Charles Cimicky took over the business. The winery was completely refitted and, despite historically keeping an ultra-low profile, they produced a range of highly acclaimed red wines. In '18 Charles and Jennie sold the business to the Hermann Thumm Drive Property Partnership. Exports to the US, Canada, Switzerland, Germany, Malaysia and Hong Kong. (JH)

¶¶¶¶¶ Blackmoor Shiraz 2018, Barossa Valley Rich and opulent aromas of blackberry, dark plum and black cherry fruits, layered with fruitcake spice, black licorice, Old Jamaica chocolate, blackforest cake and a fair lick of cedary oak. Weighty, cedary and concentrated, with a deep fruit resonance, compact tannins and cassis-rich finish. Screw cap. 14.5% alc. RATING 94 DRINK 2022–2035 $100 DB
Icon Basket Pressed Shiraz 2016, Barossa Valley Magnum cellar release. Ripe blackberry, blood plum and black cherry fruits are underscored by notes of baking spice, roasting meats, tobacco leaf, cedar, licorice, mocha and dark Old Jamaica chocolate. Some light leathery nuance floats in on the full-bodied palate which is beginning to show the light complex sheen of age. Some tight tannin support and red fruit notes come in on the extended finish. Lovely drinking. Diam. 14.8% alc. RATING 94 DRINK 2022–2032 $350 DB

¶¶¶¶♀ Hidden Gem Shiraz Cabernet 2019, Barossa Valley RATING 91 DRINK 2022–2030 $35 DB

Circe Wines

PO Box 22, Red Hill, Vic 3937 **Region** Mornington Peninsula
T 0417 328 142 **www**.circewines.com.au **Winemaker** Dan Buckle **Est.** 2010
Dozens 800 **Vyds** 2.9ha

Circe was a seductress and minor goddess of intoxicants in Homer's Odyssey. Circe Wines is the partnership of winemaker Dan Buckle and marketer Aaron Drummond, very much a weekend and holiday venture, inspired by their mutual love of pinot noir. They have a long-term lease of a vineyard in Hillcrest Road, not far from Paringa Estate. Dan says, 'It is not far from the Buckle Vineyard my dad planted in the 1980s'. Circe has 1.2ha of vines, half chardonnay and half MV6 pinot noir. They have also planted 1.7ha of pinot noir (MV6, Abel, 777, D2V5 and Bests' Old Clone) at a vineyard in William Road, Red Hill. Dan Buckle's real job is chief winemaker at Chandon Australia. Exports to the UK. (JH)

¶¶¶¶¶ Hillcrest Road Vineyard Chardonnay 2020, Mornington Peninsula Dan Buckle says there's often a peach-like character to Mornington Peninsula chardonnay, which is why he prefers a bit of tension for Circe. Well, this is a tightrope and lean as they come, yet exhilaratingly refreshing. All grapefruit and lemon, pith and juice, flinty and some nutty, creamy lees, ever so lightly bolstering the palate. There's no new oak to hinder the purity of fruit and powdery texture. The razor-sharp acidity will ensure this lasts some distance and with more time in bottle, add some weight to this fine-boned wine. Screw cap. 12.5% alc. RATING 94 DRINK 2023–2030 $70 JF

Hillcrest Road Vineyard Pinot Noir 2020, Mornington Peninsula The 50% whole bunches in the ferment (no new oak) has given this a deep ruby hue and an added layer of complexity and flavour. It is an austere style, deceptively light, as cherries and pips, blood orange, stems and radicchio start to appear. Sinewy tannins are in the background as the acidity takes the lead, rending this refreshing and the finish long. Screw cap. 13% alc. RATING 94 DRINK 2023–2030 $70 JF

ҮҮҮҮ **Pinot Noir 2020, Mornington Peninsula** RATING 92 DRINK 2022–2028 $40 JF

Clairault Streicker Wines   ★★★★★

3277 Caves Road, Wilyabrup, WA 6280 **Region** Margaret River
T (08) 9755 6225 **www.**clairaultstreicker.com.au **Open** Wed–Sun 10–5
Winemaker Bruce Dukes **Viticulturist** Christopher Gillmore **Est.** 1976 **Dozens** 12 000 **Vyds** 113ha

This multifaceted business is owned by New York resident John Streicker. It began in '02 when he purchased the Yallingup Protea Farm and vineyards. This was followed by the purchase of the Ironstone Vineyard in '03 and then the Bridgeland Vineyard. The Ironstone Vineyard is one of the oldest vineyards in Wilyabrup. In Apr '12, Streicker acquired Clairault, bringing a further 40ha of estate vines, including 12ha now over 40 years old. The 2 brands are effectively run as one venture. A large part of the grape production is sold to winemakers in the region. Exports to the US, Canada, Norway, Dubai, Malaysia, Singapore and Hong Kong. (JH)

ҮҮҮҮҮ **Streicker Ironstone Block Chenin Blanc 2019, Margaret River** Green mango, apple skins, brine, lanolin and apricots. All classic chenin things. There is also capgun, flint, garden mint and elderflower. On the palate the phenolics really create a plump, pillowy shape in the mouth. This is moving towards Saumur in style, I would be hard pressed to pick it as an Aussie. The phenolics are absolutely countersunk into the fruit in a very sleek way, the spices are flinty and savoury, but in no way cloud the purity of the fruit. A wonderful, nuanced wine. Very long. Screw cap. 12.5% alc. RATING 96 DRINK 2021–2036 $28 EL ✪

Clairault Estate Chardonnay 2020, Margaret River Pure, taut, tense acidity courses through this wine. The 2020 vintage conditions have lent an effortlessness to the fruit; it casually sways from salted peach, nectarine, red apples, cashews, pawpaw and back to peach. A beautiful, poised wine. Ready now. Screw cap. 13% alc. RATING 95 DRINK 2023–2036 $50 EL

Clairault Estate Cabernet Sauvignon 2018, Margaret River Despite the extended stint in oak, the immutably plump fruit of the 2018 vintage shines through it all. Cassis, raspberry, licorice and powder-fine tannins are the order of the day. Immediate pleasure today, and in the future, too. Screw cap. 15% alc. RATING 94 DRINK 2022–2037 $60 EL

Streicker Bridgeland Block Syrah 2017, Margaret River This is a restrained and spicy iteration of Margaret River shiraz; blackberry, mulberry, cassis, za'atar, clove, aniseed and brine. The tannins in the mouth are pliable, shapely and so gorgeous … chalky, fine and flexible. A supremely elegant wine. Lingering. Screw cap. 14% alc. RATING 94 DRINK 2022–2030 $45 EL

Streicker Ironstone Block Old Vine Cabernet Sauvignon 2017, Margaret River Bitter cocoa on the nose, paired with mulberry, kelp, black pepper, aniseed, clove and cassis. The fruit is quiet, as can be expected from such a cool vintage.

The overlay of winemaking shapes the wine in the mouth. Elegant and restrained, a spicy, savoury style of cabernet. Persistent flavour through the finish. Screw cap. 13% alc. RATING 94 DRINK 2023-2037 $50 EL

Clairault Chardonnay 2020, Margaret River RATING 91 DRINK 2023-2028 $28 EL
St Johns Limited Release Shiraz Viognier 2020, Margaret River RATING 90 DRINK 2021–2031 $35 EL
Clairault Sauvignon Blanc Semillon 2021, Margaret River RATING 90 DRINK 2021-2023 $22 EL
Streicker Bridgeland Block Fumé Blanc 2020, Margaret River RATING 90 DRINK 2022-2032 $30 EL

Clandestine

PO Box 501 Mount Lawley, WA 6050 **Region** Various
T 0427 482 903 **www.**clandestinevineyards.com.au **Winemaker** Andrew Vessey (WA), Ben Riggs and Daniel Zuzolo **Est.** 2020 **Dozens** 2000
Owners Nick and Trudy Stacy source fruit and winemaking in the key regions of Margaret River, Mount Barker, Adelaide Hills and McLaren Vale. The new range of Clandestine wines are vegan-friendly and use minimal sulphites and/or preservatives. Exports to the UK, the US and Singapore. (EL)

Shiraz 2020, Mount Barker Brawn and muscle define the fruit here – the palate is propped by firm tannins and propelled by pert acidity. If the fruit were not so concentrated and intense, it would have a hard time carrying the other components, however as it stands, it is an impressive rendition of shiraz from Mount Barker, especially for the price. Screw cap. 14.5% alc. RATING 94 DRINK 2021-2028 $30 EL ✪

Malbec 2020, Margaret River RATING 93 DRINK 2021-2028 $30 EL
Cabernet Sauvignon 2020, Mount Barker RATING 92 DRINK 2022-2032 $30 EL
Pinot Noir 2021, Adelaide Hills RATING 91 DRINK 2022-2026 $30 JP
Hearts & Minds Grenache 2021, McLaren Vale RATING 91 DRINK 2021-2025 $60 NG
Pinot Grigio 2021, Adelaide Hills RATING 90 DRINK 2022-2024 $25 JP
Tempranillo Rosé 2021, Geographe RATING 90 DRINK 2021-2023 $25 EL
Chardonnay 2021, Margaret River RATING 90 DRINK 2021-2026 $30 EL

Clare Wine Co

PO Box 852, Nuriootpa, SA 5355 **Region** Clare Valley
T (08) 8562 4488 **www.**clarewineco.com.au **Winemaker** Reid Bosward, Stephen Dew **Est.** 2008 **Dozens** 5000 **Vyds** 36ha
An affiliate of Kaesler Wines, its primary focus is on exports. The Polish Hill and Watervale vines are primarily planted to shiraz, cabernet and riesling, but a little semillon, malbec, chardonnay and touriga are grown, too. Exports to Malaysia, Singapore and Hong Kong. (JH)

Watervale Riesling 2021, Clare Valley This is plump, generous and round, with a thin seam of mineral acid that courses through the palate. There is a distinct Bickford's lime character that is woven throughout this wine. Overall, bright and pretty, and in the context of '21, showing admirable restraint in the volume of flavour. Uncomplicated drinking. Screw cap. 13% alc. RATING 89 DRINK 2021-2028 $25 EL

Clarence House Wines

193 Pass Road, Cambridge, Tas 7170 (postal) **Region** Southern Tasmania
T (03) 6247 7345 **www.**chwine.com.au **Open** By appt **Winemaker** Anna Pooley, Justine Pooley **Est.** 1998 **Dozens** 3500 **Vyds** 15ha

Clarence House was built in 1830 at Clarence Vale, Mount Rumney. The house has been kept in great condition, and in 1998 present owner, David Kilpatrick, began planting vines on a northeast-sloping block opposite the house. While pinot noir and chardonnay account for over 8ha of the plantings, the remainder includes pinot blanc and tempranillo. (JH)

TTTT **Block 1 Pinot Noir 2020, Tasmania** Fruit and oak tannins and tangy, cool season acidity lay the framework for great potential. Spicy, floral whole bunch influence sets off crunchy morello cherry and strawberry fruit that carries the line and length of well-established and happy vines. Screw cap. 13.6% alc. RATING 94 DRINK 2027-2035 $50 TS

TTTT **Reserve Pinot Noir 2021, Tasmania** RATING 93 DRINK 2026-2036 $45 TS

Clarendon Hills

363 The Parade, Kensington Park, 5068, SA **Region** McLaren Vale
www.clarendonhills.com.au **Winemaker** Roman Bratasiuk **Viticulturist** Roman Bratasiuk **Est.** 1990 **Dozens** 10000 **Vyds** 33ha

Age and experience, it would seem, have mellowed Roman Bratasiuk – and the style of his wines. Once formidable and often rustic, they are now far more sculpted and smooth. Roman purchased a 160ha property high in the hill country of Clarendon at an altitude close to that of the Adelaide Hills. Here he established a vineyard with single-stake trellising similar to that used on the steep slopes of Germany and Austria; it produces the Domaine Clarendon Syrah. He makes up to 20 different wines each year, all consistently very good, a tribute to the old vines. Sons Adam and Alex have joined their father in the business – Adam in the winery, Alex managing the future direction of Clarendon Hills. Exports to the US, Europe and Asia. (JH)

TTTT **Sandown Cabernet Sauvignon 2018, McLaren Vale** We ignore cabernet and cohorts from the Vale at our peril. This maritime iteration, lifted by elevation and fine geologies, is very fine. A smoother sheath than its BDX sibling. Yet a rattle of gritty mineral precision is similarly defining its core. Full weighted, yet almost ethereal, so deft is the extraction. The oak, all class. Blackcurrant, mulberry, mulch, pencil shavings and porcini dashi laden with umami. Thickens as it opens, ladling kirsch, black olive and sage across the super finish. Settle in and nuzzle. Screw cap. 14.6% alc. RATING 96 DRINK 2022-2038 $100 NG

Onkaparinga Syrah 2018, McLaren Vale Perhaps my favourite of all renditions of syrah here, at least for now. Not the wine to bide time over. In fact, I'd be drinking this up. Like drinking the richest, most nourishing miso soup, so laden is it with iodine and umami. Boysenberry, clove, barbecued meats and Asian five-spice. The tannins, thick but more svelte than the other cuvées. This drives long and relatively fresh. Screw cap. 14.6% alc. RATING 95 DRINK 2021-2028 $120 NG

Onkaparinga Grenache 2020, McLaren Vale Here, the signature of power is met by a bridle of impeccably hewn tannins, oak and grape. The flavours, despite their force, latent and reticent. This needs a bit of time, but is the most elegant iteration of the suite. Dark cherry, clove, anise, mint, leather polish, tamarind and a souk of herb and spice drifting across the senses. The sole caveat, the hot finish. Screw cap. 14% alc. RATING 94 DRINK 2021-2029 $90 NG

Domaine Clarendon BDX 2018, McLaren Vale As the acronym suggests, a bordeaux-inspired blend. A fine nose. Some black molten rock, almost schistous, reminiscent of Priorat's llicorella. Primary and mineral, with blackcurrant, Cuban cigar, graphite, mint, a swab of tapenade and beautifully detailed, yet forceful tannins, serving as an orb of tension, saline restraint and imperious structure. The varietal coda, never in doubt. Classy oak, too. Palate-staining, finding its way into every crevice. Immensely savoury, prodigiously long and very rewarding. Delicious drinking from a fine year. Screw cap. 14.6% alc. RATING 94 DRINK 2022-2030 $40 NG

Astralis 2018, McLaren Vale In the clutch, where oak tannins jitter portentously around a core of savoury fruit, already exhibiting Japanese miso, boysenberry, iodine, white pepper, licorice straps, clove and turmeric. Incredibly complex, with the oak carriage still a tad hard. Make no mistake, this will deliver once in the zone. Screw cap. 14.7% alc. RATING 94 DRINK 2022-2028 $450 NG

ŸŸŸŸŸ Old Vines Grenache 2020, McLaren Vale RATING 93 DRINK 2021-2025
$30 NG
Blewitt Springs Grenache 2020, McLaren Vale RATING 93
DRINK 2021-2027 $60 NG
Blewitt Springs Grenache 2018, McLaren Vale RATING 93
DRINK 2021-2026 $70 NG
Romas Grenache 2018, McLaren Vale RATING 93 DRINK 2021-2026
$110 NG
Sandown Blewitt Springs Syrah 2018, McLaren Vale RATING 93
DRINK 2021-2030 $120 NG
Romas Grenache 2020, McLaren Vale RATING 92 DRINK 2021-2026
$110 NG
Domaine Clarendon Syrah 2018, McLaren Vale RATING 92
DRINK 2021-2024 $40 NG
Old Vines Grenache 2018, McLaren Vale RATING 91 DRINK 2021-2024
$40 NG

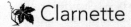 Clarnette

★★★★☆

270 Westgate Road, Armstrong, Vic 3377 **Region** Grampians
T 0409 083 833 **www.**clarnette-ludvigsen.com.au **Open** By appt **Winemaker** Leigh
Clarnette **Viticulturist** Andrew Toomey **Est.** 2022 **Dozens** 400 **Vyds** 15.5ha
With the death of his great friend, viticulturist and business partner, Kym Ludvigsen, in 2013, winemaker Leigh Clarnette has taken the plunge and retired their long-running wine business, Clarnette & Ludvigsen. He will now operate under Clarnette. Riesling, chardonnay, shiraz and tempranillo will continue to be sourced from the Ludvigsen family's 14ha vineyard in the heart of the Grampians. Under the new Clarnette brand, Leigh has also begun sourcing from other vineyards in the region, including the Portuguese clone of tempranillo (tinta roriz). In '21, he added pinot noir from the Pyrenees and is also keen to source grapes closer to his home in Ballarat. He says 'I feel Kym on my shoulder every day. It's reality, though, and to excite current and emerging customers I must re-shape to survive and thrive.' (JP)

ŸŸŸŸŸ Riesling 2021, Grampians Always a star performer and once again, it shines. Riesling lovers will rejoice in the fineness of detail, the subtle beauty of apple-blossom scents mixing with lemon sorbet, grapefruit and talc. Brisk acidity provides admirable line and length but it is the absolute zing, the sherbety brightness that so engages. That's a wow and still so young. Can only get better. Screw cap. 11% alc. RATING 95 DRINK 2021-2030 $28 JP ✪

ŸŸŸŸŸ C&L Rosé 2021, Grampians Blend of 40/25/17/11/7% shiraz/sangiovese/grenache/riesling/viognier. Winemaker Leigh Clarnette pursues texture and body in rosé. Here, he delivers. Rose gold meets ruddy pink in hue, it presents a subtle picture of dried herbs, acacia, cranberry, spice and florals. When you consider that 5 grapes contributed to this rosé, that's a lot of personality. It runs smooth, long and super-fresh. Screw cap. 12.5% alc. RATING 92 DRINK 2021-2024 $25 JP ✪
Le Grampian Chardonnay 2020, Grampians There's a lot happening here; a budding complexity in early building mode. Already has a sound groundwork in place with the scent of nougat, cashew, peach and buttered baked bread. Launches into ripe summer stone fruits on the palate, with an accompanying smoked almond mealiness, running deep and long. All it needs is a plate of something delicious. Screw cap. 14% alc. RATING 92 DRINK 2021-2026 $35 JP

ŸŸŸŸŸ Ludvigsen Chardonnay 2020, Grampians RATING 92 DRINK 2022-2026
$33 JP
Ludvigsen Shiraz 2020, Grampians RATING 92 DRINK 2022-2028 $55 JP
Tempranillo 2021, Grampians RATING 90 DRINK 2022-2025 $27 JP

Claymore Wines

7145 Horrocks Way, Leasingham, SA 5452 **Region** Clare Valley
T (08) 8843 0200 **www.**claymorewines.com.au **Open** Mon–Sat 11–5, Sun & public hols
11–4 **Winemaker** Rebekah Richardson **Est.** 1998 **Dozens** 35 000 **Vyds** 50ha
Claymore Wines is the venture of Anura Nitchingham, a medical professional who imagined
this would lead the way to early retirement (which, of course, it did not). In '96 a 16ha block
at Penwortham was purchased and planted to shiraz, merlot and grenache; the first wines
were made in '97. Since then their portfolio has expanded to approximately 57ha, including
5 additional sites dotted from Auburn to Watervale, with vine ages ranging from 30–80+ years.
The wine labels are inspired by music that moves them: U2, Pink Floyd, Prince and more.
Exports to most major markets including the UK, the US, Canada and the EU. (JH)

🍷🍷🍷🍷🍷 **Joshua Tree Riesling 2021, Clare Valley** The 2021 vintage was a godsend for
almost all regions in South Australia, and the rieslings from this vintage are typified
by balance and restraint across the board. In many cases, the wines produced this
year are among the finest in decades – no small feat. This wine is generous and
plump in the mouth, littered with green apples, ripe limes, nashi pears and juniper
berries, punctuated by pockets of juicy, salty acidity. The wine is glorious now,
but it will age gracefully too. Screw cap. 12% alc. RATING 95 DRINK 2021–2031
$22 EL ✪
Dark Side of the Moon Shiraz 2020, Clare Valley Blood plum, red licorice,
blackberries, mulberries, raspberries and spice. This is a satisfying, dense and a
compelling drink, especially at the price. Few places on the planet can achieve
concentration in shiraz like South Australia can. It's very impressive. Screw cap.
14.8% alc. RATING 94 DRINK 2021–2031 $25 EL ✪

🍷🍷🍷🍷🍷 **Nirvana Reserve Shiraz 2020, Clare Valley** RATING 93 DRINK 2021–2027
$50 EL

Clonakilla

3 Crisps Lane, Murrumbateman, NSW 2582 **Region** Canberra District
T (02) 6227 5877 **www.**clonakilla.com.au **Open** Mon–Fri 11–4, w'ends 10–5
Winemaker Tim Kirk, Chris Bruno **Viticulturist** Greg Mader **Est.** 1971 **Dozens** 20 000
Vyds 16ha
The indefatigable Tim Kirk, with an inexhaustible thirst for knowledge, is the winemaker and
manager of this family winery founded by his father, scientist Dr John Kirk. It is not at all
surprising that the quality of the wines is exceptional, especially the Shiraz Viognier, which
has paved the way for numerous others but remains the icon. Demand for the wines outstrips
supply, even with the '98 acquisition of an adjoining 20ha property by Tim and wife Lara Kirk,
planted to shiraz and viognier. In '07 the Kirk family purchased another adjoining property,
planting another 1.8ha of shiraz, plus 0.4ha of grenache, mourvèdre and cinsault. Exports to
all major markets. (JH)

🍷🍷🍷🍷🍷 **Riesling 2021, Canberra District** As pure as a spring day and smelling of a
citrus orchard in bloom. A heady mix of lime and lemon sprinkled with ginger
powder are just teasers, as this is complex and beguiling. The palate is long and
defined by acidity as much as the power of the fruit. It has texture, succulence
and a slickness rendering it assured and impressive. Screw cap. 12% alc. RATING 96
DRINK 2021–2035 $35 JF ✪
T&L Vineyard Block Two Shiraz Viognier 2019, Canberra District A
stunning wine. Pepper, baking spices, a smidge of eucalyptus and a savoury umami-
seaweed note infuse the intense dark fruits, while a touch of smoky reduction
adds an extra layer of complexity. Full bodied, deep and rich with beautiful
tannin structure. This is a refined, classy red. Screw cap. 14% alc. RATING 96
DRINK 2021–2034 $120 JF ❤
Viognier 2021, Canberra District A tight, almost racy, style for a return to
Canberra District fruit, following bushfires that halted vintage '20. Lots of white
blossom, spice and freshness to the aromas, yet more citrus in outlook. Some white

stone fruit, apricot kernel and a tickle of tannin, while the palate is poised with very good acidity and a hint of the complexity of barrel-ferment and oak-aged flavours. Screw cap. 13.5% alc. RATING 95 DRINK 2022-2028 $50 JF

T&L Vineyard Block One Shiraz Viognier 2019, Canberra District It is fascinating to taste Block One alongside its sibling Block Two, each a superb cool-climate shiraz co-fermented with 6% viognier. While there's a DNA thread through them, they are certainly unique. This feels more structured, full bodied and rich; layered with dark fruits, woodsy spices and a hint of eucalyptus. But oh, so polished and detailed with compact, grainy tannins and terrific length. A very good wine with its best days ahead of it. Screw cap. 14% alc. RATING 95 DRINK 2022-2034 $120 JF

Chardonnay 2021, Tumbarumba RATING 93 DRINK 2022-2031 $50 JF
Shiraz 2020, Eden Valley RATING 93 DRINK 2022-2030 $40 JF
Ceoltoiri 2021, Canberra District RATING 92 DRINK 2022-2028 $50 JF
Murrumbateman Pinot Noir 2021, Canberra District RATING 92 DRINK 2023-2030 $50 JF
Shiraz 2021, Hilltops RATING 91 DRINK 2022-2030 $35 JF

Clos Clare   ★★★★☆

45 Old Road, Watervale, SA 5452 **Region** Clare Valley
T (08) 8843 0161 **www.closclare.com.au Open** W'ends 11–5 **Winemaker** Sam and Tom Barry **Est.** 1993 **Dozens** 1600 **Vyds** 2ha
Clos Clare was acquired by the Barry family in '07. Riesling continues to be made from the 2ha unirrigated section of the original Florita Vineyard (the major part of that vineyard was already in Barry ownership). Its red wines come from a vineyard beside the Armagh site. Exports to the UK. (JH)

Watervale Riesling 2021, Clare Valley This is very smart. It is mineral, tightly coiled, powerful and sleek, all at once. The fruit is embedded in the acid; the acid likewise is wrapped in a sheath of talcy phenolics. Very fine … I love the spool of flavour through the finish. Pristine. Stonking value for money. Screw cap. 12% alc. RATING 95 DRINK 2022-2031 $32 EL

Cemetery Block Shiraz 2018, Clare Valley There's loads of spicy blackberries, blood plum and deli meat in here, with a fine, whippy splay of tannins that create pliable shape in the mouth. Mid weight. Smart. Delicious. Classy. Screw cap. 14% alc. RATING 94 DRINK 2022-2028 $28 EL

The Hayes Boy Grenache 2020, Clare Valley RATING 92 DRINK 2022-2027 $28 EL

Clover Hill   ★★★★☆

60 Clover Hill Road, Lebrina, Tas 7254 **Region** Northern Tasmania
T (03) 5459 7900 **www.cloverhillwines.com.au Open** 7 days 10–4.30
Winemaker Robert Heywood, Peter Warr **Est.** 1986 **Dozens** 12000 **Vyds** 23.9ha
Clover Hill was established by Taltarni in 1986 with the sole purpose of making a premium sparkling wine. It has 23.9ha of vineyards (chardonnay, pinot noir and pinot meunier) and its sparkling wine is excellent, combining finesse with power and length. The American owner and founder of Clos du Val (Napa Valley), Taltarni and Clover Hill has brought these businesses and Domaine de Nizas (Languedoc) under the one management roof, the group known as Goelet Wine Estates. Exports to the UK, the US and other major markets. (JH)

Cuvée Prestige Late Disgorged Blanc de Blancs 2010, Tasmania Traditional method; disgorged Dec '21; RS 5g/L. A full yellow hue with a golden tint declares that this has finally achieved its glorious prime. Delightfully complex and complete, brimming with preserved lemons, exotic spice, vanilla bean, brioche and saffron. Zesty stamina and creamy, silky allure rarely unite with such effortless confidence. And, best of all, it won't begin to fade any time soon. Diam. 12.5% alc. RATING 95 $150 TS

ＹＹＹＹＹ **Vintage Release 2017, Tasmania** RATING 93 $50 TS
Cuvée Exceptionnelle Blanc de Blancs 2016, Tasmania RATING 93 $70 TS
Vintage Release 2016, Tasmania RATING 92 $50 TS
Tasmanian Cuvée Rosé NV, Tasmania RATING 91 $36 TS

Clyde Park Vineyard   ★★★★★

2490 Midland Highway, Bannockburn, Vic 3331 **Region** Geelong
T (03) 5281 7274 **www**.clydepark.com.au **Open** 7 days 11–5 **Winemaker** Terry
Jongebloed **Est.** 1979 **Dozens** 6000 **Vyds** 10.1ha
Clyde Park Vineyard, established by Gary Farr but sold by him many years ago, has passed
through several changes of ownership. Now owned by Terry Jongebloed and Sue Jongebloed-
Dixon, it has significant mature plantings of pinot noir (3.4ha), chardonnay (3.1ha), sauvignon
blanc (1.5ha), shiraz (1.2ha) and pinot gris (0.9ha), and the quality of its wines is consistently
exemplary. Exports to the UK and Hong Kong. (JH)

ＹＹＹＹＹ **Single Block B3 Bannockburn Chardonnay 2021, Geelong** So much here
to enjoy and applaud, first for its deep complexity which runs in tandem with an
utter deliciousness. Boasts all the things drinkers love about B3: its aromatic florals
and honeysuckle, citrus intensity and layers of nougat, almond meal and vanillin
toasty oak. Fills the mouth and then keeps going. Screw cap. 12.5% alc. RATING 96
DRINK 2022-2034 $85 JP
C Block Chardonnay 2021, Geelong Powerfully expressive of the variety
and the Bannockburn subregion with a wealth of generous stone fruits, baked
apple, citrus, almond meal and spice. Lanolin smooth texture flows in tandem with
well-integrated oak and a chalky minerality, finishing luxuriously long. Screw cap.
12.5% alc. RATING 95 DRINK 2022-2031 $48 JP
Pinot Noir 2021, Geelong By any reckoning an excellent pinot noir, expressing
its region's suitability to the variety. Offers up complex, mellow, woody spices (a
feature of Clyde Park reds) across beautifully ripe dark berries, dried herbs, briar
and bay leaf with some brambly, herbal edges. Flows effortlessly through to the
finish dispensing spice, fruit, fine tannins and a lasting splash of warm vanillin oak.
Screw cap. 12.5% alc. RATING 95 DRINK 2022-2033 $48 JP
Single Block E Shiraz 2021, Geelong A nicely realised expression of
concentrated spice and pepper on offer – there's a lot! – with Dutch licorice,
plum, blackberry and chocolate. So lively! And there's more to explore across this
multi-layered wine with stemmy savouriness and roasted coffee oak amid a firm
tannin presence. Screw cap. 13% alc. RATING 95 DRINK 2022-2031 $85 JP
Pinot Gris 2021, Geelong The maker understands the grape so well,
exploring its silky, textural side as well as its complex, spice-laden, honeyed side.
White flowers, spiced pears, Gala apples and a striking perfumed rose scent are
inviting. Flavours build through the textural palate with a touch of honey and
glacé pineapple, nicely cut with crisp acidity. Screw cap. 12.5% alc. RATING 94
DRINK 2022-2025 $40 JP

ＹＹＹＹＹ **Rosé 2021, Geelong** RATING 93 DRINK 2022-2025 $35 JP
Single Block F College Bannockburn Pinot Noir 2021, Geelong
RATING 93 DRINK 2022-2031 $85 JP
Fumé Blanc 2021, Geelong RATING 92 DRINK 2022-2025 $40 JP
Shiraz 2021, Geelong RATING 92 DRINK 2022-2030 $48 JP

Coates Wines   ★★★★★

185 Tynan Road, Kuitpo, SA 5172 **Region** Adelaide Hills
T 0417 882 557 **www**.coates-wines.com **Open** W'ends & public hols 11–5
Winemaker Duane Coates **Est.** 2003 **Dozens** 2500
Duane Coates has a bachelor of science, a master of business administration and a master
of oenology from the University of Adelaide; for good measure he completed the theory
component of the MW program in 2005. Having made wine in various parts of the world,

and in SA, he is more than qualified to make and market Coates wines. Nonetheless, his original intention was to simply make a single barrel of wine employing various philosophies and practices outside the mainstream; there was no plan to move to commercial production. The key is organically grown grapes. Exports to the UK and the US. (JH)

🍷🍷🍷🍷🍷 **The Riesling 2021, Adelaide Hills** Among the finest rieslings in the land, by virtue of the intelligence behind its craftsmanship, as much as the deliciousness of the results: kaffir lime, talc and blossom. Few surprises there. Yet the fleck of oak and further latticework derived from natural yeast, lees and grape skins, spiels an intriguing narrative more Germanic of feel and texturally compelling than the domestic norm. Very impressive. Screw cap. 12% alc. RATING 96 DRINK 2022-2030 $35 NG ✪ ♥

The Reserve Chardonnay 2020, Adelaide Hills Very high-quality chardonnay here. A warm year, not without its challenges. But in these hands, stone-fruit accents stream long, corralled by classy vanilla-pod oak and crunchy acidity. Plenty of dried porcini, toasted hazelnut and nougatine at its core. A wine that feels latent; reticent even, despite its power, persistence and length. This will age well. Screw cap. 13% alc. RATING 96 DRINK 2022-2030 $35 NG ✪ ♥

The Semillon Sauvignon Blanc 2021, Adelaide Hills Oak is the orb around which this classic bordeaux blend should gravitate. Without it, the meld is zesty, fruity and too often, ordinary. With it, the stars align. Here, optimally ripe parcels mesh with fresher portions. All fermented spontaneously in used French wood. The result, giddy. Guava, hedgerow and sugar snap peas find effortless confluence with tatami hay, spearmint and lemon balm. This will age beautifully over the short–medium term. Screw cap. 13% alc. RATING 95 DRINK 2021-2026 $30 NG ✪

The Chardonnay 2021, Adelaide Hills A fine, long-focused lens on classy domestic chardonnay. The meld of nougat lees, vanillin oak and pithy glazed stone fruits, finely tuned. Praline, quinine, orange verbena and toasted cashew, too. The finish, precise, measured and extremely long. This stands to go the distance. Screw cap. 13% alc. RATING 95 DRINK 2022-2030 $35 NG ✪

The Mourvèdre 2021, McLaren Vale Fermented wild. Unfined and unfiltered. The sort of wine, unfettered and pure of intent, that could be considerably more expensive. Blueberry and florals. A twine of ferrous tannic persuasion, dried tobacco and a verdant smattering of herb. The finish, long and persuasive. Screw cap. 14% alc. RATING 95 DRINK 2022-2031 $35 NG ✪

The Cabernet Shiraz 2017, Langhorne Creek McLaren Vale A gracious, full-bodied wine that is brimming with umami salty warmth and showcasing the virtues of ageing this producer's wines. In this case, as a later release. Classic Australiana with real tannins and quality oak. Tapenade, terracotta, mint, cigar box, pencil shavings and graphite. Mocha oak, a background hum. Sumptuous length and effortless complexity, unravelling beautifully across the long finish. This is a wine of immaculate poise that is already approachable, but stands to deliver even more. Drinks like a warm-vintage petit châteaux. Screw cap. 14% alc. RATING 95 DRINK 2022-2032 $40 NG

The Cabernet Sauvignon 2020, Langhorne Creek A burly year defined by Duane Coates' precise – and much needed – tannin management. Taut, juicy and alloyed, the tannins serve to anchor a splay of cassis, mint, dried tobacco, sage and graphite into a savoury whole. The oak, the pulley. Maritime salinity defines the finish. Screw cap. 13.5% alc. RATING 94 DRINK 2021-2030 $35 NG

🍷🍷🍷🍷 **The Sauvignon Blanc 2021, Adelaide Hills** RATING 93 DRINK 2021-2025 $30 NG

La Petite Cuvée NV, McLaren Vale Adelaide Hills RATING 90 $26 NG

Cobaw Ridge

31 Perc Boyers Lane, Pastoria, Vic 3444 **Region** Macedon Ranges
T (03) 5423 5227 **www**.cobawridge.com.au **Open** W'ends 12–5 **Winemaker** Nelly
Cooper, Alan Cooper **Viticulturist** Alan Cooper **Est.** 1985 **Dozens** 1000 **Vyds** 5ha
When the Coopers started planting in the early '80s there was scant knowledge of the best
varieties for the region, let alone the Cobaw Ridge site. They have now settled on chardonnay
and syrah; lagrein and close-planted, multi-clonal pinot noir are more recent arrivals to
thrive. Cobaw Ridge is fully certified biodynamic, and all winery operations are carried out
according to the biodynamic calendar. Exports to the UK, Poland, Hong Kong, Singapore
and Taiwan. (JH)

🍷🍷🍷🍷🍷 **Il Pinko Rosé 2020, Macedon Ranges** Could there be a more perfect rosé?
A classy, savoury wine with a seamless balance of aromas and flavours – think
Angostura bitters, potpourri, blood orange and its peel. But what sets this
apart from so many other examples is its texture, akin to raw silk and talc-like,
giving the wine more shape. Superfine acidity guides and glides to a long finish.
Stunning. My favourite rosé from vintage '20. Diam. 13.1% alc. RATING 96
DRINK 2021-2025 $42 JF ✪ ♥

Syrah 2019, Macedon Ranges A wine that's so alive it pulses with energy and
vitality. It comes up all savoury and spicy at first, with a damp-forest fragrance, red
roses, licorice root, mint chocolate and cedary oak. The fruit within is excellent.
It's elegant across its more mid-weighted palate, the tannins superfine and the
finish long. Totally seductive syrah. Diam. 13.8% alc. RATING 96 DRINK 2022-2034
$65 JF ✪ ♥

Lagrein 2019, Macedon Ranges A variety where the colour – an exuberant
and compelling deep purple – kickstarts the joy. It's cooling, with alpine herbs,
ironstone, freshly rolled tobacco and pepper but really, it's a symphony of cherries
from black, spiced, macerated to morello. The lithe acidity and shapely tannins
are hand-in-hand. It's refreshing and ready now, with a pleasing if astringent
finish, but it will garner more complexity in time. Diam. 12.7% alc. RATING 96
DRINK 2021-2029 $85 JF

Syrah 2018, Macedon Ranges Sit back, relax and take in the beauty of this
wine. It politely introduces itself with a heady fragrance of florals, wood smoke,
autumn leaves and alpine herbs. Then it reveals its true savoury personality across
the supple palate with fine, textural tannins, quality oak, umami, vegemite and
dark chocolate infusing the core of perfect fruit. Diam. 13.7% alc. RATING 96
DRINK 2021-2033 $62 JF ✪

Chardonnay 2020, Macedon Ranges The test of any site – and by association
the winemaker – is what happens in difficult vintages. The '20 vintage turned
into a challenge, with all manner of wild climatic conditions. Still, here is a most
delicious, savoury, funky and satisfying drink. An amalgam of lemon and lime,
baked quince, grilled nuts and cedary oak spice with moreish, flinty smoky
sulphides. It has a power across the palate, yet everything is reined-in by fine
acidity. The only downside, a small crop equals not enough wine to go around the
fan base. Diam. 13.4% alc. RATING 95 DRINK 2021-2028 $62 JF

🍷🍷🍷🍷🍷 **Pinot Noir 2020, Macedon Ranges** RATING 93 DRINK 2021-2027 $62 JF

Cobb's Hill

Oakwood Road, Oakbank, SA 5243 **Region** Adelaide Hills
T (08) 8388 4054 **www**.cobbshillestate.com.au **Open** 7 days 11–5 **Winemaker** Shaw
Smith **Est.** 1997 **Dozens** 400
Sally and Roger Cook have a 140ha property in the Adelaide Hills that takes its name from
Cobb Co, which used it as a staging post and resting place for 1000 horses. The Cooks
now use the property to raise Angus cattle, grow cherries and, more recently, grapes. Three
different sites on the property, amounting to just over 10 ha, were planted to selected clones
of sauvignon blanc, chardonnay, semillon, riesling and merlot. Part of the production is sold

to Shaw + Smith, who vinify the remainder for Cobb's Hill. The Sauvignon Blanc has been most successful. (JH)

🍷🍷🍷🍷♀ **Goldrush Riesling 2021, Adelaide Hills** Good concentration here in fragrant lime, apple, white peach, citrus blossom, spices and wisps of straw. A nice linear, long palate smoothly struck and crisp in citrus-bright acidity. With 3g/L RS, you get a well-rounded wine with just a hint of sweetness. Screw cap. 13% alc. RATING 90 DRINK 2022–2026 $34 JP

Shotgun Shiraz Pinot Noir 2021, Adelaide Hills Get used to seeing more of this traditional blend, a speciality in the Hunter Valley, and now gaining wider acceptance. It works a treat here, employing the sweet, dark fruits of shiraz with the cherry and raspberry of pinot, arriving soft and plummy on the palate. Fills the mouth with great flavour while also securing a firm, linear tannin base. So versatile at the table. Screw cap. 13% alc. RATING 90 DRINK 2022–2026 $34 JP

🍷🍷🍷🍷 **Mail Run Rosé Shiraz 2021, Adelaide Hills** RATING 89 DRINK 2022–2024 $28 JP

Pinot Gris 2021, Adelaide Hills RATING 88 DRINK 2022–2024 $28 JP

Sidesaddle Sauvignon Blanc 2021, Adelaide Hills RATING 88 DRINK 2022–2024 $28 JP

Shooting Star Sparkling Rosé 2021, Adelaide Hills RATING 88 DRINK 2022–2022 $30 JP

Cockfighter's Ghost ★★★☆

576 De Beyers Road, Pokolbin, NSW 2320 **Region** Hunter Valley
T (02) 4993 3688 **Open** 7 days 10–5 **Winemaker** Xanthe Hatcher **Est.** 1988 **Vyds** 16ha
Once the less-expensive sibling of Pooles Rock, Cockfighter's Ghost is now an autonomous suite of slick, conventionally made wines. While there are few surprises across a range that delivers regional staples, the elevated Single Vineyard line is sourced from the Adelaide Hills and McLaren Vale, rather than the perceived home turf of the Hunter. A Reserve range delivers a fortified from the Hunter and a cabernet from Coonawarra, making it open season on interregional hunting. The Black Label suite, however, brings the brand back to the hearth, with Hunter Valley fruit comprising all but the shiraz which is sourced from nearby Gundagai. The wines can be tasted at the Poole Rock cellar door, along with other wines across the Agnew Family holdings. (NG)

🍷🍷🍷🍷♀ **Single Vineyard Cabernet Sauvignon 2020, McLaren Vale** Meets the pricepoint and then some, nicely capturing the Vale's generous ways and easygoing attitude. Brings a solid varietal context to the aroma with its lifted leafiness, blackberry, plum, undergrowth and herbal notes. Fills the mouth with a warm embrace of fruit, tobacco leaf and licorice, all the while against a firm tannin presence. Top wine for the price. Screw cap. 14.5% alc. RATING 90 DRINK 2022–2025 $25 JP

🍷🍷🍷🍷 **Single Vineyard Sauvignon Blanc 2021, Adelaide Hills** RATING 89 DRINK 2022–2025 $25 JP

Single Vineyard Sangiovese 2020, McLaren Vale RATING 89 DRINK 2022–2025 $25 JP

Single Vineyard Pinot Gris 2021, Adelaide Hills RATING 88 DRINK 2022–2025 $25 JP

Single Vineyard Shiraz 2020, McLaren Vale RATING 88 DRINK 2022–2025 $25 JP

Cofield Wines ★★★★☆

Distillery Road, Wahgunyah, Vic 3687 **Region** Rutherglen
T (02) 6033 3798 **www.cofieldwines.com.au** **Open** Mon–Sat 9–5, Sun 10–5
Winemaker Damien Cofield, Peter Berks **Est.** 1990 **Dozens** 13 000 **Vyds** 15.4ha

Sons Damien (winery) and Andrew (vineyard) took over responsibility for the business from parents Max and Karen Cofield in '07. Collectively, they have developed an impressively broad-based product range with a strong cellar-door sales base. A 20ha property at Rutherglen, purchased in '07, is planted to shiraz, durif and sangiovese. Peter Berks joined the winemaker team in '20. (JH)

🍷🍷🍷🍷🍷 **Provincial Netherby Shiraz 2018, Rutherglen** Seamless integration on display here with fruit, oak and tannins acting as one. Complex and fragrant, the wine moves with poise, carrying dark berries, dark chocolate, plum and spice, finely layered and sporting long, ripe tannins. Quite a medium-bodied shiraz wonder. Screw cap. 14.5% alc. RATING 95 DRINK 2021–2033 $45 JP

🍷🍷🍷🍷🍷 **Sparkling Shiraz 2018, Rutherglen** RATING 92 $30 JP
Quartz Vein Durif 2018, Rutherglen RATING 92 DRINK 2022–2034 $45 JP
Sauvignon Blanc 2021, King Valley RATING 90 DRINK 2021–2024 $22 JP

Colab and Bloom

1436 Brookman Road, Willunga, SA 5172 **Region** South Australia
T 0428 581 177 **www**.fielddaywineco.com **Winemaker** Daniel Zuzolo **Est.** 2014
Formed in '17, Colab and Bloom is a collaboration between wine marketer, Nick Whiteway, and winemakers and winegrowers throughout South Australia. The emphasis is on fun and fresh wines from emerging varieties. Grapes are sourced from the Adelaide Hills, Southern Fleurieu and Riverland; nero d'Avola and sangiovese are grown at Vasarelli's in Currency Creek, the tempranillo by David Blows in Macclesfield. Grapes are processed across a number of winery locations, including Project Wines in Langhorne Creek, DiFabio in McLaren Flat and Haselgrove in McLaren Vale. Future releases include a Currency Creek prosecco and fiano. The company, together with Monterra, sits under the general wine umbrella of Field Day Wine Co. Exports to the US, Canada and Hong Kong. (JP)

🍷🍷🍷🍷🍷 **Tempranillo 2021, Adelaide Hills** This is one fresh, bright young tempranillo. There's a good sense of ripeness, of black cherries, plums, baking spices and baked earth on the bouquet. Vibrant on the palate, the flavours become more expansive taking in red licorice, blackberries, blue and red fruits, chocolate and sweet spices. Supple and juicy. Drink early. Screw cap. 14% alc. RATING 90 DRINK 2022–2026 $22 JP

🍷🍷🍷🍷 **Sangiovese 2021, Adelaide Hills** RATING 88 DRINK 2022–2025 $22 JP
Pinot Gris 2021, South Australia RATING 88 DRINK 2021–2024 $28 JP

Coldstream Hills

★★★★★

29–31 Maddens Lane, Coldstream, Vic 3770 **Region** Yarra Valley
T (03) 5960 7000 **www**.coldstreamhills.com.au **Open** Fri–Mon 10–5
Winemaker Andrew Fleming, Greg Jarratt, James Halliday AM (Consultant) **Est.** 1985
Vyds 100ha
Founded by James Halliday AM, Coldstream Hills has 100ha of estate vineyards as its base, 3 in the Lower Yarra Valley and 2 in the Upper Yarra Valley. Chardonnay and pinot noir continue to be the principal focus; merlot and cabernet sauvignon came on stream in '97, sauvignon blanc around the same time, Reserve Shiraz later still. Vintage conditions permitting, Chardonnay and Pinot Noir are made in Reserve, Single Vineyard and varietal forms. In addition, Amphitheatre Pinot Noir was made in tiny quantities in '06 and '13. A winery was erected in '10 with a capacity of 1500t. There is a plaque in the fermentation area commemorating the official opening on 12 Oct '10 and naming the facility the 'James Halliday Cellar'. Exports to Singapore and Japan. (JH)

🍷🍷🍷🍷🍷 **Reserve Pinot Noir 2020, Yarra Valley** A medium, deep, crimson purple. Crushed strawberries, Asian spices, coriander seeds, rose petals and a gentle char can all be found in this superb pinot. Sappy and silky, with good flow and persistent, structured, but satiny tannins. The balance here is spot-on and while you can enjoy this now, it will only become more complex over the next ten years. Screw cap. 13% alc. RATING 97 DRINK 2021-2031 $85 PR ❂

🍷🍷🍷🍷🍷 **Rising Vineyard Chardonnay 2020, Yarra Valley** A bright green gold. A wine of excellent concentration from a cooler year. Complex with grapefruit, rock melon, orange blossom, a little vanilla bean and some matchstick reduction which has been handled perfectly. A richer style that will appeal to those who find some Yarra chardonnays too lean. This is also finely tuned, beautifully balanced and remains light on its feet at the same time. Screw cap. 13% alc. RATING 95 DRINK 2021-2028 $45 PR

The Dr's Block Pinot Noir 2020, Yarra Valley A bright, lively crimson red. This has terrific purity, with freshly picked cherries, raspberries, coriander seeds and just a little spice and reduction. The palate is fresh and crunchy, with cherry and cranberry fruit. The wine finishes long, with mouth-watering acidity and a Campari-like twist on the finish. Only the second time this has been made, and well worth hunting down! Screw cap. 12.5% alc. RATING 95 DRINK 2021-2030 $50 PR

Reserve Chardonnay 2020, Yarra Valley This is a concentrated, powerful Coldstream Hills Reserve. Aromas of ripe stone fruits, cumquat, mandarin peel, ginger and grilled nuts lead onto the palate, which has real drive and density. Nutty and gently honed, the acidity is already perfectly integrated into the wine. It can be enjoyed now, but the wine's track record is such that this will still be looking good in 7-10 years. Screw cap. 13% alc. RATING 95 DRINK 2021-2028 $60 PR

Collector Wines   ★★★★★

7 Murray Street, Collector, NSW 2581 **Region** Canberra District
T (02) 6116 8722 **www.collectorwines.com.au** **Open** Thurs–Mon 10–4
Winemaker Alex McKay **Est.** 2007 **Dozens** 6000 **Vyds** 6ha
Owner and winemaker Alex McKay makes exquisitely detailed wines, bending to the dictates of inclement weather on his doorstep, heading elsewhere if need be. He was part of a talented team at Hardys' Kamberra Winery and, when it was closed down by Hardys' then new owner CHAMP, decided to stay in the district. He is known to not speak much, and when he does, his voice is very quiet. So you have to remain alert to appreciate his unparalleled sense of humour. No such attention is needed for his wines, which are consistently excellent, their elegance appropriate for their maker. A new cellar door will open in October 2022. Exports to Thailand and Japan. (JH)

🍷🍷🍷🍷🍷 **Tiger Tiger Chardonnay 2019, Tumbarumba** One of the finest Tumbarumba chardonnays around. A perfect balance of stone fruit, grapefruit, mouth-watering smoky flinty sulphides with just the right amount of palate-buffering creamy lees to offset the electrifying acidity. Superb drink. Screw cap. 12.9% alc. RATING 96 DRINK 2022-2029 $38 JF ❂

Lantern 2019, Hilltops Spanish amigos, as in 54/41% tempranillo/touriga, with a splash of grenache to great effect. This has a core of excellent bright red-berried fruit and black cherries, but is savoury through and through. Lots of warm spices, freshly rolled tobacco with grainy savoury tannins working across the medium-bodied palate, with plenty of fresh acidity to close. Screw cap. 13.2% alc. RATING 95 DRINK 2022-2028 $30 JF ❂

Landfall Pinot Meunier 2021, Tumbarumba While it's a fresh and vibrant wine, there's no shortage of flavour and punch. Sweet strawberries and berries punctuate the smoky, meaty reduction, woodsy spices and pepper. The lighter-framed palate is savoury and spicy, with poppy acidity and the right amount of tannins to lead out the finish. Compelling. Screw cap. 12.9% alc. RATING 94 DRINK 2022-2026 $34 JF

Marked Tree Red Shiraz 2019, Canberra District An excellent dark red befitting a structured wine, but this is not weighty. Full of dark cherries, licorice, fennel plus cedary oak, yet it sits right in the savoury camp, with ripe tannins and a flourish across the medium-bodied palate to a lightly dry finish. Screw cap. 13% alc. RATING 94 DRINK 2022-2030 $30 JF ✪

ΨΨΨΨΨ **Night Watch Grenache 2021, Hilltops** RATING 92 DRINK 2022-2028 $34 JF

Colmar Estate   ★★★★★

790 Pinnacle Road, Orange, NSW 2800 **Region** Orange
T 0419 977 270 **www.**colmarestate.com.au **Open** 7 days 11–4 **Winemaker** Will Rikard-Bell **Viticulturist** Ian 'Pearcy' Pearce **Est.** 2013 **Dozens** 2000 **Vyds** 5.9ha
The inspiration behind the name is clear when you find that owners Bill and Jane Shrapnel have long loved the wines of Alsace: Colmar is the main town in that region. The Shrapnels realised a long-held ambition when they purchased an established, high-altitude (980m) vineyard in May '13. Everything they have done has turned to gold: notably grafting cabernet sauvignon to pinot noir, merlot to chardonnay, and shiraz to pinot gris. The plantings are now 1.51ha of pinot noir (clones 777, 115 and MV6), 1.25ha of chardonnay (clones 95, 96 and P58), 1.24ha of riesling and lesser quantities of sauvignon blanc, pinot gris and gewürztraminer. (JH)

ΨΨΨΨΨ **Block 5 Riesling 2021, Orange** This producer is becoming a tour de force of fizz and riesling. A pure, intensely flavoured expression of such filigreed structure, a testimony. It makes me want to eat schnitzel or any array of washed cheeses, so fresh and juicy is the acidity, impeccably placated with a gentle sweet wash. A kernel of lime, jasmine and quince paste skitters across the energetic finish. Impressive length and driving persistence. Very fine. Screw cap. 12% alc. RATING 96 DRINK 2021-2028 $35 NG ✪
Chardonnay Pinot Noir 2015, Orange Very fine. The penultimate disgorgement, with a whopping 66 months on lees. Fresh and yet toasty, rich and serious, such is the autolytic depth. These dichotomies define classy fizz. A whiff of sourdough straight out of the oven, apple pie, jasmine and peat, as the magic of yeast and its umami ways take over. Impressively long and palate staining. Still primary of tone. Will age very well. Screw cap. 12% alc. RATING 95 $60 NG
Le Moche Pinot Gris Traminer Riesling 2021, Orange An Edelzwicker sort of quasi field blend that is so delicious, it feels as it were merely delivered from the vineyard – a righteous meld of variety, clonal material, handling and geology – rather than made. A little more phenolics might be nice. 980m elevation. Basalt. Courage, oak and Germanic varieties. A match made in heaven. One of only 2 great blends of this mix here (the other, Tasmania's Stargazer). Rosewater, orange verbena, grape spice, lychee and tarte tatin, but pear rather than apple. A trail of cinnamon and star anise, fuelled by natural acidity, a sweep of RS (barely detectable) and moxie, lingering long. Fine. Screw cap. 12.5% alc. RATING 95 DRINK 2021-2026 $32 NG ✪
Block 6 Riesling 2021, Orange A single site pitched at 980m elevation. A warmer slope than the Block 5 brethren, facing southwest. Made a bit drier, as a consequence. Lime blossom, Granny Smith apple, spa salts and frangipani riffs careen along a zingy acid neck that, despite the cool year, feels dutifully poised, natural and perfect for the style. Not quite the immaculate patina of the Block 5, but a wine with a striking cadence all the same. Screw cap. 12% alc. RATING 94 DRINK 2021-2028 $35 NG

ΨΨΨΨΨ **Pinot Gris 2021, Orange** RATING 93 DRINK 2021-2025 $32 NG
Block 1 Pinot Noir 2021, Orange RATING 93 DRINK 2021-2027 $65 NG
Pinot Shiraz 2021, Orange RATING 92 DRINK 2021-2026 $45 NG
Pinot Noir 2021, Orange RATING 91 DRINK 2021-2025 $50 NG

Colvin Wines

19 Boyle Street, Mosman, NSW 2088 (postal) **Region** Hunter Valley
T (02) 9908 7886 **www**.colvinwines.com.au **Winemaker** Andrew Spinaze, Mark
Richardson **Est.** 1999 **Dozens** 500 **Vyds** 5.2ha

In '90 Sydney lawyer John Colvin and wife Robyn purchased the De Beyers Vineyard, which
has a history going back to the second half of the 19th century. By '67, when a syndicate
bought 35ha of the original vineyard site, no vines remained. The syndicate planted semillon
on the alluvial soil of the creek flats and shiraz on the red clay hillsides. Up to '98 all the
grapes were sold to Tyrrell's, but since '99 quantities have been made for the Colvin Wines
label. These include Sangiovese, from a little over 1ha of vines planted by John in '96 because
of his love of the wines of Tuscany. (JH)

De Beyers Vineyard Semillon 2019, Hunter Valley Archetypal: lightweight,
balletic of precision and nudging the equivalent of a teenage phase, edgy and
reticent, delivering talc, lanolin, lemongrass and curd without touching on the
glories that come with patience and further cellaring. A warm year, handled with
care. Fine length, poise and the ease of drinkability that comes with these precepts.
Screw cap. 10.5% alc. RATING 93 DRINK 2021-2032 $25 NG ✪

De Beyers Vineyard Sangiovese 2018, Hunter Valley RATING 88
DRINK 2021-2024 $33 NG

Comyns & Co

Shop 6, 1946 Broke Road, Pokolbin, NSW 2320 **Region** Hunter Valley
T 0400 888 966 **www**.comynsandco.com.au **Open** 7 days 10–4.30 **Winemaker** Scott
Comyns **Est.** 2015 **Dozens** 2000

The stars came into alignment for Scott Comyns in '18. Having left Pepper Tree Wines in
a state of glory at the end of '15, he went out on his own, establishing Comyns & Co with
nothing other than his experience as a winemaker for 17 vintages in the Hunter Valley to
sustain him. Then Andrew Thomas founded Thomas Wines in the region and Scott joined
him as a full-time winemaker, leaving Comyns & Co as a side activity. That has now all
changed, as Missy and Scott have opened a 7-days-a-week cellar door in the Peppers Creek
Village, Scott having quit his winemaking role at Thomas Wines. (JH)

Cabernet Sauvignon Shiraz 2021, Hunter Valley I like this. It has a bit more
concentration than the other reds in this suite. Not that concentration makes
for good wine, necessarily. It doesn't. However, there is something warming and
avuncular about it. Fuller bodied and brimming with scents of campfire, dark
cherry, well-worn leather, terracotta, licorice, rhubarb and bracken. After the sassier
suite, this is something to get the teeth into. Mouth-filling, savoury, highly regional
and impressively persistent. Screw cap. 13.5% alc. RATING 94 DRINK 2021-2026
$35 NG

Single Vineyard Casuarina Semillon 2021, Hunter Valley RATING 93
DRINK 2021-2029 $28 NG
Single Vineyard Pokolbin Estate Riesling 2021, Hunter Valley RATING 93
DRINK 2021-2026 $30 NG
Mrs White Blend 2021, Hunter Valley RATING 92 DRINK 2021-2024
$28 NG
Popsy Sparkling Grüner Veltliner 2021, Hunter Valley RATING 91 $35 NG
Shiraz Viognier 2021, Hunter Valley RATING 91 DRINK 2021-2024 $35 NG
Shiraz 2021, Hunter Valley RATING 91 DRINK 2021-2024 $35 NG
Reserve Chardonnay 2021, Hunter Valley RATING 91 DRINK 2021-2025
$35 NG
Pinot Noir Shiraz 2021, Hunter Valley RATING 90 DRINK 2021-2023
$35 NG

Condie Estate

480 Heathcote-Redesdale Road, Heathcote, Vic 3523 **Region** Heathcote
T 0404 480 422 **www**.condie.com.au **Open** W'ends & public hols 11–5
Winemaker Richie Condie **Est.** 2001 **Dozens** 1500 **Vyds** 6.8ha
Richie Condie worked as a corporate risk manager for a multinational company off the back
of a bachelor of commerce degree, but after establishing Condie Estate, completed several
viticulture and winemaking courses, including a diploma of winemaking at Dookie. Having
first established 2.4ha of shiraz, Richie and wife Rosanne followed with 2ha of sangiovese and
0.8ha of viognier. In '10 they purchased a 1.6ha vineyard that had been planted in '90, where
they established a winery and cellar door. (JH)

🍷🍷🍷🍷🍷 **The Max Shiraz 2018, Heathcote** The Max is a superb endorsement of the
many strengths of Heathcote shiraz: deep, penetrating purple colour, concentrated
and lively black fruits and spice, not to mention generosity. The palate is dense
yet has a degree of elegance with a swathe of fruit, licorice, earth and florals. The
length is quite striking. Gold medal, Australian Small Winemakers Show. Screw cap.
14.5% alc. RATING 94 DRINK 2021–2028 $50 JP

🍷🍷🍷🍷🍷 **The Gwen Shiraz 2018, Heathcote** RATING 91 DRINK 2021–2028 $30 JP
Paisani Nero d'Avola 2020, Heathcote RATING 90 DRINK 2021–2025 $30 JP

Cooke Brothers Wines

Shed 8, 89-91 Hill Street, Port Elliot, SA 5212 **Region** South Australia
T 0409 170 684 **www**.cookebrotherswines.com.au **Open** Fri–Sun 12–5
Winemaker Ben Cooke **Est.** 2016 **Dozens** 800
The 3 brothers (eldest to youngest) are: Simon, Jason and Ben. While the elder brothers are not
actively involved in the business, Ben is the partner of Charlotte Hardy, winemaker/owner of
Charlotte Dalton Wines. Ben has had a long career in wine: 7 years' retail for Booze Brothers
while at university the first time around; 2 vintages at Langhorne Creek 2000–01; and full-
time cellar hand/assistant winemaker at Shaw + Smith '03–12 while undertaking 2 degrees
externally (wine science and viticulture) at CSU from '04–11. If this were not enough, he
had 3 northern Californian vintages at the iconic Williams Selyem winery in '08, '12 and '13.
He is now a full-time viticulturist with a vineyard management contracting company that he
founded in '12. Exports to Canada. (JH)

🍷🍷🍷🍷🍷 **Deanery Vineyard Chardonnay 2020, Adelaide Hills** A well-composed
wine, nicely coiled, releasing flinty grapefruit, lemon curd, white peach, nectarine
and hazelnut oak. Creamy in texture, complex in delivery with juicy, chalky acidity.
Screw cap. 13% alc. RATING 95 DRINK 2022–2026 $45 JP

🍷🍷🍷🍷🍷 **Mataro Rosé 2021, McLaren Vale** RATING 91 DRINK 2022–2024 $30 JP

Cooks Lot

Ferment, 87 Hill Street, Orange, NSW 2800 **Region** Orange
T (02) 9550 3228 **www**.cookslot.com.au **Open** Tues–Sat 11–5 **Winemaker** Duncan
Cook **Est.** 2002 **Dozens** 4000
Duncan Cook began making wines for his eponymous brand in '02, while undertaking his
oenology degree at CSU. He completed his degree in '10 and now works with a number
of small growers. Orange is unique in the sense that it has regions at various altitudes; fruit
is sourced from vineyards at altitudes that are best suited for the varietal and wine style. (JH)

🍷🍷🍷🍷🍷 **Allotment No. 5 Arneis 2021, Orange** A huge step up from the other whites
in the suite. Detailed. Succulent and intense. The degree of ripeness, beguiling.
And yet there is nothing heavy about this. Rather, a flow of Granny Smith apple
and pear tarte tatin notes, etched by juicy acidity pulling it long. As good as arneis
gets on these shores. Screw cap. 13% alc. RATING 93 DRINK 2021–2024 $45 NG
Allotment No. 8 Handpicked Shiraz 2019, Orange A brilliant mid ruby,
segueing to anise, clove, pepper grind, salumi and menthol on the nose. The palate

expands across a spectrum of blue fruits, vanilla-pod oak and a brace of star anise, mescal and more white pepper, melding with tangy acidity and streaming long. Intense of flavour. My only minor gripe, the feel of the acidity. Otherwise, high quality. Screw cap. 13.5% alc. RATING 93 DRINK 2021-2030 $35 NG

Iconique Barrique Cabernet Sauvignon 2016, Orange Hilltops A modicum of bottle age has served this well. It is just beginning to surface after what was surely a period tucked beneath a stern tannic bow. A fine nose: graphite, mulch, currant. The finish, sumptuous, detailed and morphing into a polymerised phalanx of graphite, lead, tapenade and bouquet garni. The finish, long, forceful and brushed with sage. A bit hot, but a minor gripe. Screw cap. 14.5% alc. RATING 93 DRINK 2021-2032 $50 NG

Coola Road

Private Mail Bag 14, Mount Gambier, SA 5291 **Region** Mount Gambier
T 0487 700 422 **www.**coolaroad.com **Winemaker** John Innes **Est.** 2013 **Dozens** 1000 **Vyds** 103.5ha
Thomas and Sally Ellis are the current generation of the Ellis family, who have owned the Coola grazing property on which the vineyard is now established for over 160 years. They began planting the vineyard in the late '90s with pinot noir, and have since extended the range to include sauvignon blanc, chardonnay, riesling and pinot gris. As the largest vineyard owner in the region, they decided they should have some of the grapes vinified to bring further recognition to the area. (JH)

Single Vineyard Riesling 2021, Mount Gambier Tight, bright and light, this is diaphanous and quite gorgeous. Its highlight, and main attribute, is its delicacy, showing a fine array of sea spray, green apple, kiwi skin, jasmine tea and citrus blossom. Very pretty. Screw cap. 11% alc. RATING 90 DRINK 2022-2028 $20 EL ✪

Single Vineyard Pinot Gris 2021, Mount Gambier RATING 89 DRINK 2022-2024 $20 EL

Coombe Yarra Valley

673-675 Maroondah Highway, Coldstream, Vic 3770 **Region** Yarra Valley
T (03) 9739 0173 **www.**coombeyarravalley.com.au **Open** Mon, Wed–Sun 10–5
Winemaker Travis Bush **Viticulturist** Xavier Mende **Est.** 1999 **Dozens** 10000 **Vyds** 60ha
Coombe Yarra Valley is one of the largest and oldest family estates in the Yarra Valley. Once home to world famous opera singer Dame Nellie Melba, it continues to be owned and operated by her descendants, the Vestey family. Coombe's wines come from 60ha of vineyards planted in '98 on the site of some of the original vineyards planted in the 1850s. The renovated motor house and stable block now contain the cellar door, providore, gallery and restaurant which overlook the gardens. Exports to the UK and Japan. (JH)

Tribute Series Lady Celia Pinot Noir 2021, Yarra Valley A medium, very bright crimson. Fragrant, with lifted, freshly picked red cherries, raspberries, some floral notes and a little cinnamon and nutmeg spice. Medium bodied, this is very composed and I really like the balance between the fruit, the use of whole bunches, oak and tannins, which are superfine and long. Lovely wine. Screw cap. 12.5% alc. RATING 96 DRINK 2023-2028 $65 PR ✪

Tribute Series Lady Pamela Chardonnay 2021, Yarra Valley A bright green gold. A pure core of white peach and nectarine fruit, with the oak sitting very discreetly in the background. A touch of spice and gently honeyed, too. I like the wine's gently creamy mouthfeel, which is nicely balanced by the wine's fine vein of acidity. Finishes long and even. Screw cap. 12.5% alc. RATING 95 DRINK 2022-2027 $65 PR

Tribute Series Mr. Mark Shiraz 2021, Yarra Valley A gorgeous crimson purple. Compact and needing time to unfurl, a good swirl reveals aromas of sweet cherries, blackberries, exotic spices and some floral notes. Medium bodied, with excellent depth of fruit and lovely, persistent yet fine tannins, this very well-put-together wine can be enjoyed now or cellared for up to 10 years. Screw cap. 13.5% alc. RATING 95 DRINK 2022-2031 $65 PR

♥♥♥♥♡ **Tribute Series Nellie Melba Blanc de Blancs 2018, Yarra Valley** RATING 93 $65 PR
Chardonnay 2021, Yarra Valley RATING 93 DRINK 2022-2027 $37 PR
Pinot Noir 2021, Yarra Valley RATING 93 DRINK 2022-2027 $37 PR
Shiraz 2021, Yarra Valley RATING 93 DRINK 2022-2026 $37 PR
Pinot Gris 2021, Yarra Valley RATING 93 DRINK 2022-2025 $30 PR
Chardonnay 2019, Yarra Valley RATING 92 DRINK 2021-2024 $37 PR
Rosé 2021, Yarra Valley RATING 91 DRINK 2022-2024 $30 PR
Shiraz 2020, Yarra Valley RATING 91 DRINK 2022-2026 $37 PR
Tribute Series Pinot Noir 2020, Yarra Valley RATING 90 DRINK 2022-2027 $65 PR

Cooter & Cooter

82 Almond Grove Road, Whites Valley, SA 5172 **Region** McLaren Vale
T 0438 766 178 **www.**cooter.com.au **Winemaker** James Cooter, Kimberly Cooter
Est. 2012 **Dozens** 800 **Vyds** 23ha
The cursive script on the Cooter & Cooter wine labels was that of various Cooter family businesses operating in SA since 1847. James comes from a family with more than 20 years in the wine industry. Kimberley is also a hands-on winemaker; her father is Walter Clappis, a veteran McLaren Vale winemaker. Their vineyard, on the southern slopes of Whites Valley, has 18ha of shiraz and 3ha of cabernet sauvignon planted in '96, and 2ha of old-vine grenache planted in the '50s. They also buy Clare Valley grapes to make riesling. (JH)

♥♥♥♥♡ **Watervale Riesling 2021, Clare Valley** An exceptional, cool and attenuated vintage in the Clare. Dry grown, hand picked, fermented cool with plenty of solids to impart a bit more breadth and generosity than the steely archetype. Still, plenty tensile. Lime blossom, tangerine and lemon zest are catapulted across a dry and austere mid-weighted palate by a battery of talcy acidity. Screw cap. 12% alc. RATING 91 DRINK 2021-2029 $23 NG ✪

Corang Estate

533 Oallen Road, Nerriga, NSW 2622 **Region** Southern New South Wales
T 0400 102 781 **www.**corangestate.com.au **Open** By appt **Winemaker** Michael Bynon, Alex McKay **Viticulturist** Michael Bynon, Liz Riley **Est.** 2018 **Dozens** 1500 **Vyds** 1ha
Corang Estate is the business of Michael and Jill Bynon. Michael has been in the wine industry for 30 years, attending Roseworthy Agricultural College and moving from a marketing career to join the senior corporate ranks. He passed the master of wine tasting examination. Jill is a linguist and marketing professional, fluent in French, having spent much time in France before moving to Australia from her native Scotland in '03. It was here that she met Michael, and having bought a bush block and erected a small house, they planted 0.5ha each of shiraz and tempranillo in '18. They also purchase grapes from high-altitude vineyards comparable to that of their own, which is at 600m. (JH)

♥♥♥♥♡ **Tempranillo 2021, Hilltops** An enticing deep purple red and very much a joven style, as it's a juicy, youthful wine – even a touch raw at this stage. Expect a raft of bright, sweet and tangy cherries of all colours, some meaty reduction, layers of woodsy spices, sarsaparilla and fresh herbs. Sandy tannins work across a lighter-framed palate and while the acidity is a touch shrill, partner with food to temper it and don't be afraid to chill this down on a warm day. Screw cap. 13% alc. RATING 90 DRINK 2021-2025 $25 JF

♥♥♥♥ **Cabernet Sauvignon 2021, Hilltops** RATING 89 DRINK 2023-2028 $25 JF
Sauvignon Blanc 2021, Tumbarumba RATING 88 DRINK 2021-2022 $25 JF

Corduroy ★★★★

226 Mosquito Hill Road, Mosquito Hill, SA 5214 **Region** Adelaide Hills
T 0405 123 272 **www**.corduroywines.com.au **Winemaker** Phillip LeMessurier
Viticulturist Mark Vella, Ben Lacey **Est.** 2009 **Dozens** 320
Phillip and Eliza LeMessurier moved to the Adelaide Hills, continuing the model they originally created in the Hunter under the tutelage of Andrew Thomas at Thomas Wines. In the Hills, they are matching place and variety to good effect. (JH)

♼♼♼♼♼ **Pedro's Pinot Noir 2020, Adelaide Hills** Quite a delicate rendition of Hills' pinot noir from a challenging vintage. Has some real strengths, in particular its medium-bodied, finely balanced focus on layers of deep fruit concentration. Red berries, undergrowth, cinnamon, dried flowers and musk are elevated by bright acidity and even-handed tannins. Dances on the tongue. Screw cap. 12.8% alc. RATING 92 DRINK 2021-2028 $45 JP
The Wale Shiraz 2018, Adelaide Hills Sourced from the Anvers Vineyard in Echunga, which grew some particularly peppery shiraz in '18. A generous year, too, bringing forth a stream of blackberry, plum fruits, briar, aniseed and aforementioned peppery notes. Fleshy and ripe, texture is very much a key to the appeal of this elegant wine. Screw cap. 14% alc. RATING 90 DRINK 2021-2026 $45 JP

♼♼♼♼ **Chardonnay 2020, Adelaide Hills** RATING 89 DRINK 2021-2026 $30 JP
Mansfield Chardonnay 2020, Adelaide Hills RATING 89 DRINK 2021-2028 $45 JP
Pinot Noir 2020, Adelaide Hills RATING 88 DRINK 2021-2025 $30 JP

Coriole ★★★★★

Chaffeys Road, McLaren Vale, SA 5171 **Region** McLaren Vale
T (08) 8323 8305 **www**.coriole.com **Open** 7 days 11–5 **Winemaker** Duncan Lloyd
Est. 1967 **Dozens** 30 000 **Vyds** 48.5ha
While Coriole was established in 1967, the cellar door and gardens date back to 1860, when the original farm houses that now constitute the cellar door were built. The oldest shiraz forming part of the estate plantings was planted in 1917, and since '85, Coriole has been an Australian pioneer of sangiovese and the Italian white variety fiano. More recently, it has planted picpoul, adding to grenache blanc, negro amaro, sagrantino, montepulciano and prosecco. Coriole celebrated its 50th anniversary in '19, presumably counting from the year of its first commercial wine release. Exports to all major markets. (JH)

♼♼♼♼♼ **Rubato Reserve Fiano 2021, McLaren Vale** The stupendous '20 was quite possibly the most exciting wine I tasted last year. This, borne of a cooler and more attenuated growing season. Perhaps a warmer year suits this skin-inflected, barrel-fermented style. The jury is out. Either way, this is intoxicating. Brilliant! The flavours expand, persist and unravel across a vibrato of saline freshness, a leesy breadth, a whiff of oak and the ginger-chutney skinsiness that segues to quince, apricot and jasmine. A flying finish. A truly world-class wine. Screw cap. 13% alc. RATING 95 DRINK 2022-2028 $50 NG
Laneway Sangiovese 2020, McLaren Vale This is the closest to good chianti yet, from grapes grown on these shores. I am not advocating emulation necessarily, but the semblance is striking. Red fruits. A pinosity and lightness of being, before the thirst-slaking flirt of sangiovese's tannins, frisk and edge, kick in. Long limbed, strident and impeccably extracted. Acid, bright, too. Sour cherry, mint (in a good way), thyme, rosemary and wild red berries serve to convey an understated and confident versatility. Fine. Screw cap. 13.7% alc. RATING 95 DRINK 2021-2028 $60 NG
Willunga 1920 Single Vineyard Shiraz 2020, McLaren Vale Dense. Mocha oak. Black fruits. Volcanic powdered rocks. Power and plenty of heat packed across the throaty finish. Yet there is a beguiling latency to this. I feel that what I am tasting will transmogrify into something truly compelling such are the florals,

vinosity and creamy yet tightly furled core of compressed, succulent, glorious tannins. Screw cap. 14.5% alc. RATING 95 DRINK 2023-2040 $110 NG

Lloyd Reserve Shiraz 2019, McLaren Vale A nice vintage. Dense. Palate staining, but nothing jammy or obtuse. The oak, unresolved. A big wine, to be sure. Clove, licorice strap, mace and a core of gruntish black and blue-fruit aspersions, tightly furled within the structural carapace. This, too, needs time. Will blossom for those inclined. Screw cap. 14.5% alc. RATING 95 DRINK 2023-2033 $120 NG

Fiano 2021, McLaren Vale Long a pioneer of this outstanding variety, recent critical acclaim and gradual acceptance by the punter is iterated as greater confidence in the vineyard and winery. More concentration, detail and a certain fealty to the better example of Campania, fiano's spiritual home, the result. Glazed quince, bitter almond, pistachio, apricot and wild fennel. A sluice of welcome phenolics defies the long finish as much as the saline acidity. Very good. Great vintage, to boot. Screw cap. 13% alc. RATING 94 DRINK 2021-2025 $28 NG ✪

Sangiovese 2020, McLaren Vale Has all the attributes expected of sangiovese, most obviously the play between all the cherries of the rainbow; from fresh, to sour, to poached, backed by superfine tannins. It's a wine I would drink now or over time. Screw cap. 14.1% alc. RATING 94 DRINK 2021-2029 $28 JH ✪

Galaxidia Single Vineyard Shiraz 2020, McLaren Vale Winning on the brilliant vineyard name alone, this is a throaty, highly floral full-bodied shiraz. While it has spent 18 months in oak (20% new), the oak is nestled nicely, serving as a signpost to sapid flavours of Cherry Ripe, anise, molten raspberry liqueur and peppery freshness. Sure there are oak-derived vanilla and cedar elements but they tone, corral and suppress the fruit in the best sense, adjoining the grape tannins in a union of tension. Liberation will come with time and patience. Screw cap. 14% alc. RATING 94 DRINK 2022-2035 $60 NG

The Riesling Block Single Vineyard Shiraz 2020, McLaren Vale It is fascinating to vacillate between this and its single-vineyard sibling Galaxidia. While the latter is pulpier, lifted, reductive and floral, this is a drive across the palate, tactile and pliant. The long mesh of tannins, grape and oak, serving as the engine room. More savoury. Restrained, perhaps. Red cherry, clove, licorice and a finish of white pepper-soused freshness. The sweetness expands subtly. This is an exercise in finely boned structure. Screw cap. 14% alc. RATING 94 DRINK 2022-2035 $60 NG

Mary Kathleen Reserve Cabernet Sauvignon 2019, McLaren Vale Cabernet excels in these parts. The volume is simply turned up: extract and application of tannins – grape and oak – needed to corral the fruit. Yet this sort of Mediterranean expression remains true to varietal personality when executed well. And here it is: cassis, mulch, sage, bay leaf, tapenade and ample oak, positioned as chamois tannins. Brusque, but all high quality. Needs time. Screw cap. 14.4% alc. RATING 94 DRINK 2022-2038 $65 NG

ƔƔƔƔƔ **Negroamaro 2021, McLaren Vale** RATING 92 DRINK 2022-2025 $28 NG
Piquepoul 2021, McLaren Vale RATING 92 DRINK 2021-2024 $28 NG
Estate Shiraz 2020, McLaren Vale RATING 91 DRINK 2022-2030 $32 NG
Nero 2021, McLaren Vale RATING 90 DRINK 2021-2024 $28 NG

Corryton Burge   ★★★★☆

161 Murray Street, Tanunda, SA 5352 **Region** Barossa Valley
T (08) 563 7575 **www.**corrytonburge.com **Open** Mon–Fri 10–4, Sat 12–5
Winemaker Trent Burge, Andrew Cockram and Matthew Pellew **Est.** 2020
Dozens 4000

A new-ish label with a long history. Siblings Trent (winemaker) and Amelia (marketing) Burge are 6th-generation Barossans. Trent has spent almost 2 decades working in the family vineyards and winery, creating his Barossa Boy Wines brand; Amelia returned to the business in '19, also launching her own Amelia Burge Sparkling Wine range. Their shared enterprise takes its name from the family's grand 1845 Corryton Park Homestead in Eden Valley. Sourcing is from the Burge family's 300ha of vines in southern and central Barossa and Adelaide Hills, and a network of 20 growers as far flung as the Coal River Valley in Tasmania.

Their father Grant Burge plays a mentoring role, and the winemaking team at the family's Illaparra winery is also acknowledged. (TS)

⚐⚐⚐⚐⚐ **Grenache 2021, Barossa Valley** Perfumed and fragrant with jasmine-fringed plum and blueberry characters supported by ginger spice, red licorice, cola and softly spoken oak. Spacious and pretty in the mouth too, with billowy tannins and a gentle tide of ripe plum and spice on the finish. Screw cap. 15.5% alc. RATING 91 DRINK 2021-2028 $28 DB

Cornelian Bay Pinot Noir 2020, Southern Tasmania Aromas of dark cherry fruits with raspberry edges and hints of violets, soft spice and earth, with lighter shades of roasting game, herbs and forest floor. Delicate cherry fruits with a meaty facet and oak spice appearing on the palate, backed by loose, earthy tannins and floral flecks. Screw cap. 13.5% alc. RATING 91 DRINK 2021-2026 $45 DB ❤

Shiraz 2019, Barossa Fruit notes of plum and dark-fruit compote underscored by baking spice, licorice, dark chocolate, espresso and earth. Lovely fruit weight, purity and flow on the palate, tight sandy tannins and a medium-length finish. Screw cap. 14.5% alc. RATING 91 DRINK 2021-2030 $28 DB

Pinot Gris 2021, Adelaide Hills Inviting aromas of white peach and nashi pear are underscored by hints of almond paste, crème fraîche and white flowers. The mouthfeel is textural and slinky, with ripe pear fruit, clotted cream, soft spice and light herbs. The finish is clean, dry and moreish. Screw cap. 12.5% alc. RATING 90 DRINK 2021-2024 $28 DB

Riesling 2021, Eden Valley It's a tightly wound little thing at the moment, all steely lime juice, grapefruit and crisp Granny Smith fruit with a little Christmas lily and marzipan further in the background. Very linear and driven on the palate, with pure citrus fruits and a vivid, dry finish. Screw cap. 12.5% alc. RATING 90 DRINK 2021-2028 $28 DB

⚐⚐⚐⚐ **The Patroness Chardonnay 2021, Adelaide Hills** RATING 89 DRINK 2021-2025 $28 DB

Corymbia ★★★★★

7046 Caves Road, Redgate WA 6286 **Region** Swan Valley
T 0439 973 195 **www.**corymbiawine.com.au **Open** By appt **Winemaker** Robert Mann, Genevieve Mann **Viticulturist** Robert Mann, Genevieve Mann **Est.** 2013 **Dozens** 900 **Vyds** 3.5ha

Rob Mann is a 6th-generation winemaker from the second-oldest wine region in Australia. He was chief winemaker at Cape Mentelle in Margaret River, where he and wife Genevieve lived. Rob's father had established a family vineyard in the Swan Valley more than 25 years ago, where they both worked together in Rob's early years as a winemaker. Genevieve worked as a winemaker in her native South Africa, as well as France, California and South Australia before meeting Rob and moving to Margaret River in '07 to be winemaker for Howard Park. They now have 3.5ha in Margaret River and the Swan Valley, planted to 1.6ha chenin blanc, 0.4ha tempranillo, 0.2ha malbec and 1.3ha cabernet sauvignon. Exports to Singapore. (JH)

⚐⚐⚐⚐⚐ **Chenin Blanc 2021, Swan Valley** Delicate, as usual, with a flood of green apple, white flowers, Turkish apricots, cheesecloth and beeswax. This has Australian bush, and wide open summer air, and saltbush, too. The phenolics have a bitter little kick in them through the finish … but that's ok, I was waiting for it. The waxy, lanolin character is exactly en pointe for the variety. Screw cap. 12.7% alc. RATING 95 DRINK 2022-2030 $32 EL ✪

Chenin Blanc 2020, Swan Valley Despite all the international chaos, '20 was a great vintage in WA. Warm, low yielding and with plenty of structure and power. That shows in the intensity of white summer apricot, green apple skin, lanolin and crushed cashew that spools out over the very long, neat finish. Saline acid laces all of these characters together. Another brilliant release. Screw cap. 12.5% alc. RATING 95 DRINK 2021-2036 $32 EL ✪

Cabernet Sauvignon 2020, Margaret River The aromas are finely layered with cassis, exotic spice, saltbush, dried bay leaf … there's also a faint backdrop of bacon fat, reminiscent of the Rhône. The tannins on the palate are a standout; superfine and laid out like a web over the fruit. Very classy. This '20 has more obvious fruit and structure than the '19, but we expect that from the vintage. Drink this while you wait for the '19. Screw cap. 13.5% alc. RATING 95 DRINK 2021–2031 $64 EL

ŸŸŸŸŸ **Rocket's Vineyard Tempranillo Malbec 2020, Swan Valley** RATING 93 DRINK 2021–2031 $42 EL

Coughlan Estate ★★★★

39 Upper Capel Road, Donnybrook, WA 6239 **Region** Geographe
T 0409 831 926 **www**.coughlanestate.com.au **Open** Thurs–Mon 11–4
Winemaker Bruce Dukes, Remi Guise **Viticulturist** Ryan Gibbs **Est.** 1978
Dozens 2000 **Vyds** 3ha
Coughlan Estate (formerly Barton Jones) has 3ha of semillon, chenin blanc, shiraz and cabernet sauvignon from 1978 – the vines are some of the oldest in the region. The vineyard and cellar door are on gentle north-facing slopes, with extensive views over the Donnybrook area. (JH)

ŸŸŸŸŸ **Chenin Blanc 2020, Geographe** Barrel fermentation has imbued this wine with texture and spice, the fruit is a tapestry of apples, apricots, pears and citrus, embroidered with threads of saline acidity and spice. Texturally this is slippery and fluid, like the surface of a calm lake. Very smart indeed. Drink it now or give it time – it'll go the distance and then some. Screw cap. 13.3% alc. RATING 93 DRINK 2021–2036 $32 EL
Cabernet Sauvignon 2020, Geographe Fruit from Donnybrook. As expected from the region, variety and vintage: plush, plump, layered with chocolate and mulberries and imminently drinkable. Not complex, but modern, bouncy and shapely. All good things. Delicious. Screw cap. 13.9% alc. RATING 90 DRINK 2021–2031 $33 EL

ŸŸŸŸ **Semillon Sauvignon Blanc 2021, Geographe** RATING 89 DRINK 2021–2023 $26 EL
Shiraz 2020, Geographe RATING 89 DRINK 2021–2028 $35 EL
Semillon 2020, Geographe RATING 88 DRINK 2022–2027 $26 EL

Coulter Wines ★★★★

6 Third Avenue, Tanunda, SA 5352 (postal) **Region** Adelaide Hills
T 0448 741 773 **www**.coulterwines.com **Winemaker** Chris Coulter **Est.** 2015
Dozens 800
Chris Coulter fell in love with wine in the early '90s. In '07 he undertook a winemaking degree and secured work with Australian Vintage Limited, gaining large-volume winemaking experience first in Mildura and then at (the then) Château Yaldara in the Barossa Valley, remaining there through '14 under Australian Vintage Limited, and thereafter as part of the 1847 winemaking team after its acquisition of the Yaldara site. Coulter Wines was born in the '15 vintage as a side project, making wines from another universe – nothing other than SO_2 is added, movements are by gravity and the wine is unfiltered where practicable. He purchases and hand picks grapes from vineyards mainly in the Adelaide Hills. Exports to Singapore. (JH)

ŸŸŸŸŸ **C1 Chardonnay 2021, Adelaide Hills** A wine still in evolution but with a bright future ahead, the intensity of the high altitude (450m) and cool-climate fruit flavour, taut and firm. Fresh, sherbet-like acidity kick starts the chardonnay off into high-powered lemon zest, lime, grapefruit and mandarin aromas and flavours. Oak remains a background note, a textural ally throughout. Screw cap. 12.5% alc. RATING 94 DRINK 2021–2027 $32 JP

🍷🍷🍷🍷🍷 C2 Sangiovese 2021, Adelaide Hills RATING 92 DRINK 2021-2026 $29 JP
C4 Experimental Tempranillo 2021, Adelaide Hills RATING 92
DRINK 2021-2026 $29 JP
C5 Barbera 2021, Adelaide Hills RATING 91 DRINK 2021-2026 $32 JP
C6 Gamay 2021, Adelaide Hills RATING 90 DRINK 2021-2025 $35 JP

Crabtree Watervale Wines   ★★★★

North Terrace, Watervale SA 5452 **Region** Clare Valley
T (08) 8843 0069 **www**.crabtreewines.com.au **Open** 7 days 10.30–4.30
Winemaker Kerri Thompson **Est.** 1984 **Dozens** 5500 **Vyds** 12.1ha
Crabtree is situated in the heart of the historic and iconic Watervale district, the tasting
room and courtyard (set in the produce cellar of the original 1850s homestead) looking out
over the estate vineyard. The winery was founded in 1984 by Robert Crabtree, who built a
considerable reputation for medal-winning riesling, shiraz and cabernet sauvignon. In '07 it
was purchased by an independent group of wine enthusiasts, and the winery firmly continues
in the tradition of estate-grown premium wines. Robert remains a shareholder. (JH)

🍷🍷🍷🍷🍷 **Watervale Riesling 2021, Clare Valley** Tingly and bright, this has a
savoury seam of phenolics that course through the wine. The acidity is
salty and enlivening. All things pert and lifted here, with a wonderful linger
of flavour through the finish. Very smart. Screw cap. 12.5% alc. RATING 92
DRINK 2021-2031 $32 EL
Watervale Rosé 2021, Clare Valley Shiraz, grenache. A deep magenta in
the glass, this is no blushing rosé. It's full bodied and luscious, but not too sweet.
There's watermelon, raspberry and loads of red berries. Lots to love, and one for
the non-Provence rosé drinkers playing at home. Screw cap. 13.5% alc. RATING 90
DRINK 2022-2023 $28 EL
Watervale Shiraz 2018, Clare Valley Elegant and spicy, rather than plumply
fruited (in fact, it could do with some concentration in this regard), this has
licorice root, pepperberries, finely ground Szechuan, cocoa and blackcurrant
pastille. The wine has good length of flavour through the finish, giving further
time for assessment. Lovely. Screw cap. 14% alc. RATING 90 DRINK 2021-2027
$32 EL

Craiglee   ★★★★★

785 Sunbury Road, Sunbury, Vic 3429 **Region** Sunbury
T (03) 9744 4489 **www**.craigleevineyard.com **Open** first Sun each month
Winemaker Patrick Carmody **Est.** 1976 **Dozens** 2000 **Vyds** 9.5ha
A winery with a proud 19th-century record, Craiglee recommenced winemaking in '76 after
a prolonged hiatus. Produces one of the finest cool-climate shiraz wines in Australia, redolent
of cherry, licorice and spice in the better (warmer) vintages; lighter bodied in the cooler ones.
Mature vines and improved viticulture have made the wines more consistent over the past
10 years or so. (JH)

🍷🍷🍷🍷🍷 **Shiraz 2018, Sunbury** There are some wines that are special and unique because
they not dictated to by fashion or shareholders and more importantly, they have
a strong sense of place. That's Craiglee. Expect a taste of dark plums, cedary oak,
pepper and spice, licorice and gum leaf. The palate is full bodied, with ripe, silky
tannins hugging all the way through to a resounding finish. Stamped with Craiglee
DNA. Screw cap. 14% alc. RATING 96 DRINK 2022-2038 $60 JF ✪
Reserve Shiraz 2018, Sunbury An opulent, rich wine dripping with dark fruit,
loads of spices, wafts of eucalyptus, meaty reduction, toasty/cedary oak and so
much more. It's full bodied with velvety tannins, a bit of oomph from the vintage
but not excessive. It's built for the long haul, if you can wait. Screw cap. 14% alc.
RATING 96 DRINK 2023-2040 $135 JF
Reserve Shiraz 2017, Sunbury The best 3 barrels of the vintage make the
Reserve. This is all gloss and glorious. Full bodied, with dark fruits and spiced

to the max with a grind of black pepper and cedary oak doing its bit, both structurally and flavour-wise. Tannins are supple and fine. There's no shortage of flavour, yet this retains a certain elegance. Screw cap. 13.5% alc. RATING 96 DRINK 2023-2040 $135 JF

JADV Shiraz 2018, Sunbury How large the JADV – 'just a dash of viognier' – is not known. Doesn't matter. This is terrific. Ripe plums, baking spices, licorice, cedary oak and it's luscious across the full-bodied palate. The tannins are ripe and plump, there's a savouriness throughout and a lot of pleasure within. Screw cap. 14% alc. RATING 95 DRINK 2022-2033 $45 JF

ΨΨΨΨΩ **Cabernet Sauvignon 2018, Sunbury** RATING 93 DRINK 2022-2030 $35 JF
Chardonnay 2020, Sunbury RATING 92 DRINK 2022-2027 $40 JF

Craigow   ★★★★★

528 Richmond Road, Cambridge, Tas 7170 **Region** Southern Tasmania
T 0418 126 027 **www**.craigow.com.au **Open** By appt **Winemaker** Frogmore Creek (Alain Rousseau), Tasmanian Vintners **Est.** 1989 **Dozens** 800 **Vyds** 8.75ha

Barry and Cathy Edwards have moved from being grapegrowers with only one wine to a portfolio of impressive wines – with long-lived Riesling of particular quality, closely attended by Pinot Noir – while continuing to sell most of their grapes. Craigow's wines express the unique character of the Coal River region. Varieties are selected to suit the area's growing conditions—they're the same cool-climate European varieties that thrive in Burgundy, Alsace and the Loire Valley. (JH)

ΨΨΨΨΨ **Pinot Noir 2020, Tasmania** An enduring and confident style, more deeply rooted in a Côte de Beaune-esque structural framework and savoury mood than Côte de Nuits fruitiness. Powder-fine tannins, bright acidity and lingering morello cherry tang unite in a spectacular finish, filled with grand promise. Screw cap. 12.5% alc. RATING 95 DRINK 2030-2040 $50 TS

Dessert Riesling 2021, Tasmania An exuberant exoticism of fig, orange and honey is set off by toasty, spicy nuances of fermentation in old oak puncheons. Perfect ripeness delivers wonderful body and richness, with sweetness well judged to ensure that the vibrant acidity of the cool '21 vintage remains the hero of a long and enduring finish. Delightful. 375mL. Screw cap. 8.8% alc. RATING 95 DRINK 2022-2046 $39 TS

Riesling 2021, Tasmania Wonderfully poised. A pale straw-green hue gives no hint of the depth of complexity contained within, wonderfully fragrant and rich with orange blossom, apricot and peach. A core of pure lemon and lime is the blessing of a cool year of excellent natural acid retention, perfectly balanced with 9g/L RS. Delightful from the outset, with the magnificent promise to build spicy, honeyed allure over the coming decades. Screw cap. 12.3% alc. RATING 94 DRINK 2022-2041 $33 TS

Crawford River Wines   ★★★★★

741 Hotspur Upper Road, Condah, Vic 3303 **Region** Henty
T (03) 5578 2267 **www**.crawfordriverwines.com **Open** By appt **Winemaker** Belinda Thomson **Viticulturist** Belinda Thomson **Est.** 1975 **Dozens** 3000 **Vyds** 11ha

Once a tiny outpost in a little-known wine region, Crawford River is now a foremost producer of riesling (and other excellent wines), originally thanks to the unremitting attention to detail and skill of its founder and winemaker, John Thomson. His elder daughter Belinda has worked alongside her father part-time from '04–11 (full-time between June '05–08) and has been chief winemaker since '12. She obtained her viticulture and oenology degree in '02 and has experience in Marlborough, Bordeaux, Tuscany and the Nahe. Between '08 and '16 she was a senior winemaker and technical director of a winery in Rueda, Spain. Younger daughter Fiona is in charge of sales and marketing. Exports to the UK and Japan. (JH)

⚼⚼⚼⚼⚼ **Reserve Riesling 2015, Henty** Still incredibly youthful and fine, with little or no colour development. The delicately scented bouquet is matched with a tightly furled palate, with grapefruit zest and acidity made to precise measure. Deserves a cheer for bravery in pricing. Screw cap. 13.5% alc. RATING 97 DRINK 2021–2040 $120 JH ✪

⚼⚼⚼⚼⚼ **Riesling 2021, Henty** A marvel! So fully formed in its youth and delivering outstanding deliciousness. The maker balances ripe riesling fruit – white nectarine, grapefruit, Delicious apple, lime – with racy, cool-climate acidity to deliver a wine complex in flavour, warm in texture and lively in personality. It's quite a feat. Screw cap. 13.5% alc. RATING 96 DRINK 2022–2031 $50 JP ✪

Young Vines Riesling 2021, Henty Don't let the term Young Vines distract from the beauty of this wine. It's a ripper. The flavours are resoundingly fresh, vital and alive. Apple-blossom scents lead you into a world of lemon, lime, spiced apple with a bright edge of lime and mandarin zest. Silky smooth texture is a real feature, highlighting the winemaker's resolve to move this wine into serious riesling territory. She succeeds. Screw cap. 13.5% alc. RATING 95 DRINK 2022–2033 $36 JP

Cabernets 2019, Henty A blend of 75/25% cabernets sauvignon/franc. The first rule of Cabernets is to decant. The second is to put it into context as a super-cool-climate, linear example of the breed. In 2019, it is fine-edged and elegant with aromas of dark fruits, violets and leaf, and heavy in exotic spices: anise, fennel seed and nutmeg. Oak is integrated, tannins are staunch and enduring, more than enough for the long life ahead. Screw cap. 13.5% alc. RATING 94 DRINK 2022–2030 $36 JP

Credaro Family Estate   ★★★★★

2175 Caves Road, Yallingup, WA 6282 **Region** Margaret River
T (08) 9756 6520 **www.credarowines.com.au Open** 7 days 10.30–5 **Winemaker** Trent Kelly, Paul Callaghan **Viticulturist** Chris Credaro **Est.** 1988 **Dozens** 25 000 **Vyds** 110ha
The Credaro family first settled in Margaret River in 1922, migrating from northern Italy. Initially a few small plots of vines were planted to provide the family with wine in the European tradition. The most recent vineyard acquisition was a 40ha property, with 18ha of vineyard, in Wilyabrup (now called the Summus Vineyard) and the winery has been expanded to 1200t with 300 000L of additional tank space. Credaro now has 7 separate vineyards (150ha in production), spread throughout Margaret River; Credaro either owns or leases each property and grows and manages the vines with its own viticulture team. Exports to the US, Singapore and Taiwan. (JH)

⚼⚼⚼⚼⚼ **1000 Crowns Chardonnay 2020, Margaret River** Elegance takes the pulpit from the word go, and doesn't relinquish it. The fruit aromas are grapefruit, nectarine and white peach, braced by zesty acidity that drives the wine into the longest finish I've encountered for some time. Oak is merely a vehicle. Screw cap. 12.5% alc. RATING 97 DRINK 2022–2038 $75 JH ✪

⚼⚼⚼⚼⚼ **Kinship Chardonnay 2021, Margaret River** RATING 93 DRINK 2022–2030 $40 EL

Kinship Cabernet Sauvignon 2020, Margaret River RATING 93 DRINK 2022–2030 $40 EL

1000 Crowns Shiraz 2020, Margaret River RATING 93 DRINK 2022–2029 $75 EL

Five Tales Cabernet Sauvignon 2020, Margaret River RATING 92 DRINK 2021–2031 $24 EL ✪

1000 Crowns Cabernet Sauvignon 2019, Margaret River RATING 92 DRINK 2022–2032 $100 EL

Kinship 2020, Margaret River RATING 90 DRINK 2021–2024 $40 EL

Kinship Shiraz 2020, Margaret River RATING 90 DRINK 2025–2035 $40 JH

CRFT Wines

45 Rangeview Drive, Carey Gully, SA 5144 **Region** Adelaide Hills
T 0413 475 485 **www.crftwines.com.au Open** Fri–Sun 12–5 **Winemaker** Candice
Helbig, Frewin Ries **Viticulturist** Candice Helbig, Frewin Ries **Est.** 2012 **Dozens** 1000
Vyds 1.9ha

Life and business partners NZ-born Frewin Ries and Barossa-born Candice Helbig crammed
multiple wine lives into a relatively short period, before giving up secure jobs and establishing
CRFT in '13. Frewin's CV includes Cloudy Bay and the iconic Sonoma pinot noir
producer Williams Selyem, among others. Candice is a 6th-generation Barossan. She trained
as a laboratory technician before moving to winemaking at Hardys, gaining her degree in
oenology and viticulture from CSU and on to Boar's Rock and Mollydooker. The core focus
is on small-batch single-vineyard Adelaide Hills pinot noir, chardonnay and grüner veltliner.
The Arranmore vineyard was purchased in '16, gaining NASAA organic certification in '19,
and wines are made with a minimal-intervention approach. Exports to Luxembourg and
Singapore. (JH)

🍷🍷🍷🍷🍷 **Arranmore Vineyard Grüner Veltliner 2021, Piccadilly Valley** Vegan
friendly. Of the 3 grüners produced at CRFT, Arranmore is the floral and spiced
beauty, fine-boned and linear. Lifted aromas of apple blossom, white peach, lemon
thyme and citrus. A wave of summer fruits, citrus and spice envelops the tastebuds
nicely, tempered by a firm line of crisp, bright acidity. Screw cap. 13.5% alc.
RATING 95 DRINK 2021-2025 $31 JP ❂

The Blefari Vineyard Chardonnay 2021, Piccadilly Valley Quite a
compelling single-vineyard wine; a juicy celebration of chardonnay with
impressive complexity. Nougat, apple, nectarine and honeysuckle aromas invite
further inspection. Once in, be prepared to be seduced with a fine line of racy
acidity tied to concentrated, lively fruit. Quite mouth-watering. Screw cap.
13% alc. RATING 95 DRINK 2022-2030 $45 JP

Longview Vineyard Grüner Veltliner 2021, Adelaide Hills Vegan friendly.
Adelaide Hills grüner veltliner deserves our attention. This is a case in point, a
crisp, dry, super-fresh wine bursting in pear, apple and citrus with a touch of saline.
Places the tastebuds on alert before easing into a soft, textural warmth. More
please! Screw cap. 13.5% alc. RATING 94 DRINK 2021-2026 $31 JP

🍷🍷🍷🍷🍷 **K1 Vineyard Kuitpo Grüner Veltliner 2021, Adelaide Hills** RATING 93
DRINK 2021-2027 $31 JP

The Schmidt Vineyard Mencia 2021, Barossa Valley RATING 93
DRINK 2022-2028 $31 JP

The Arranmore Vineyard Pinot Noir 2021, Piccadilly Valley RATING 93
DRINK 2022-2029 $43 JP

The Arranmore Vineyard Chardonnay 2021, Piccadilly Valley RATING 92
DRINK 2022-2028 $55 JP

The Whisson Lake Vineyard Pinot Noir 2021, Adelaide Hills RATING 91
DRINK 2022-2029 $43 JP

The Rohrlach Vineyard Shiraz 2021, Barossa Valley RATING 91
DRINK 2022-2028 $45 JP

The Scanlon Vineyard Pinot Noir 2021, Adelaide Hills RATING 90
DRINK 2022-2026 $43 JP

The Arranmore Vineyard White Pinot Noir 2021, Piccadilly Valley
RATING 90 DRINK 2022-2028 $45 JP

Crittenden Estate

25 Harrisons Road, Dromana, Vic 3936 **Region** Mornington Peninsula
T (03) 5981 8322 **www.crittendenwines.com.au Open** 7 days 10.30–4.30
Winemaker Rollo Crittenden, Matt Campbell **Est.** 1984 **Dozens** 10 000 **Vyds** 4.8ha
Garry Crittenden was a pioneer on the Mornington Peninsula, establishing the family
vineyard over almost 40 years and introducing a number of avant-garde pruning and

canopy management techniques. Much has changed – and continues to change – in cool-climate vineyard management. Crittenden has abandoned the use of synthetic fertilisers in the vineyard, focusing on biological soil health using natural tools such as compost and cover crops. Pinot noir and chardonnay remain the principal focus at the top tier, but they also produce some remarkable savagnin made under flor in the Jura style. In 2015, winemaking returned to the family vineyard on the Mornington Peninsula in a newly built facility, with son Rollo in charge of the winemaking and general management and daughter Zoe overseeing marketing. Exports to the UK. (JH)

ΨΨΨΨΨ **Cri de Coeur Sous Voile Savagnin 2017, Mornington Peninsula** Bearing witness to a wine's creation – as in tasting all since its inception in '11 and understanding the story behind sous voile – allows a picture to form. Winemaker Matt Campbell is credited with kickstarting the revolution à la Jura at Crittenden Estate and all I can say is, thank you. Oh and '17, the finest to date. Spending nearly 4 years under flor and matched to an excellent vintage has created a complex, savoury and utterly compelling wine. Expect a harmony of grilled almonds, toffee praline, salted lemons, poached quince with mouth-watering, heady aldehydes. The palate is incredibly silky and long, yet has lots of tangy acidity too; it's elegant and importantly, ultra-fresh and alive. What a wine. Alas, just 800 bottles made. Diam. 14.5% alc. RATING 97 DRINK 2022-2030 $85 JF ✪ ♥

ΨΨΨΨΨ **Macvin #3 Savagnin NV, Mornington Peninsula** The third rendition is created with a blend of 50% flor-aged savagnin from the excellent '17 vintage and savagnin grape juice from '21, fortified with grape spirit then left in the barrel for 10 months. An enticing amber hue with dried pears, toast and honey, then pear juice and toasted pain d'épice flavours tantalise. The palate is luscious and sweet yet balanced with acidity; there's a fine if slippery texture across the palate. Hard to put the glass down. Diam. 17% alc. RATING 96 $90 JF

Pinot Gris 2021, Mornington Peninsula It's always a go-to gris, because aside from the varietal inputs, it's a terrific drink. Honeysuckle, ginger spice, nashi pear and lemon-cream tart. Luscious across the palate, yet finishes with a gentle acid freshness. Screw cap. 13% alc. RATING 95 DRINK 2022-2025 $34 JF ✪

Oggi 2021, Mornington Peninsula 62/38% pinot grigio/white muscat. A coppery orange colour and so fragrant (via the muscat) with honeysuckle, musk, lychee and a burst of spices. The palate has plenty of grip, a sway of phenolics adding texture and intrigue, plus flavours of blood orange and Angostura bitters. It's super-dry. A fabulous aperitif style. Bravo. Screw cap. 12% alc. RATING 95 DRINK 2022-2024 $35 JF ✪

Cri de Coeur Chardonnay 2020, Mornington Peninsula Wild ferment, 80% mlf, and 11 months in French oak (60% new). I can only imagine how tight and linear this would be without the mlf and new oak, as it's still taut and bristling with nervous energy. It needs more time to add some flesh to its fine shape. A hint of grilled nuts and creamy lees bind to the lemon and white nectarine flavours. Racy across the palate thanks to the acidity, which keeps this bright and the finish long. Diam. 12.5% alc. RATING 95 DRINK 2023-2030 $85 JF

Cullen Wines   ★★★★★

4323 Caves Road, Wilyabrup, WA 6280 **Region** Margaret River
T (08) 9755 5277 **www**.cullenwines.com.au **Open** 7 days 10–4.30 **Winemaker** Vanya Cullen, Andy Barrett-Lennard **Viticulturist** Vanya Cullen **Est.** 1971 **Dozens** 20 000 **Vyds** 49ha

A pioneer of Margaret River, Cullen Wines has always produced long-lived wines of highly individual style from the mature estate vineyard. The vineyard has progressed beyond organic to biodynamic certification and, subsequently, has become the first vineyard and winery in Australia to be certified carbon positive. Winemaking is in the hands of Vanya Cullen, daughter of founders Kevin and Diana Cullen; she is possessed of an extraordinarily good palate and generosity to the cause of fine wine. Vanya is also a pioneer of biodynamic viticulture in Australia and was awarded the Companion's inaugural Viticulturist of the Year in 2022, Cullen's 50th anniversary year. Exports to all major markets. (JH)

ＴＴＴＴＴ **Diana Madeline 2020, Margaret River** The perfumed bouquet has already soaked up the 13 months in 50% new oak, the purity of the fruit in a cassis-redcurrant-blueberry spectrum. The small berries of a quasi-drought summer might have imposed awkward tannins, but the medium-bodied palate is so perfectly balanced it has a drinking span of 30 years and counting. Screw cap. 13% alc. RATING 98 DRINK 2025-2055 $150 JH ✪ ♥

Kevin John 2020, Margaret River 2020 was a fast and short vintage with heartbreakingly low yields in Margaret River, yet it produced wines of effortless grace and poise. This is most certainly one of those. Like a rhythmic pulse of flavour in the mouth … steady, like a heartbeat. All elements are in harmony: fruit, acid, phenolics; they gently seesaw between each other, spooling out a seemingly never-ending trail of flavour. Breathtakingly beautiful, again. Screw cap. 13.9% alc. RATING 98 DRINK 2021-2035 $150 EL ✪ ♥

ＴＴＴＴＴ **Mangan East Block Wilyabrup 2020, Margaret River** Malbec with 18% petit verdot. Inky midnight colour in the glass. The wine is restrained and savoury on the nose: Szechuan peppercorn, saffron, salted licorice, black tea, mulberries at the height of summer, and blackberries. In the mouth, the tannins are supremely elegant and create a mouth-coating experience. Lighter than it feels, and brighter than it looks. Beautiful, frisky, energetic wine. Screw cap. 13.5% alc. RATING 95 DRINK 2021-2031 $55 EL

Grace Madeline 2018, Margaret River A blend of 60/40% sauvignon blanc/semillon. Intense, powerful and concentrated, this has layers of spice and shape which show themselves across the long finish. The phenolics and oak will take the fruit through graceful (no pun intended) decades in the cellar – this vineyard has proven its ability to do that. Energy and vivacity make this wine a standout. Screw cap. 13% alc. RATING 95 DRINK 2021-2036 $39 EL

Mangan Vineyard Sauvignon Blanc Semillon 2021, Margaret River A blend of 59/35/6% sauvignon blanc/semillon/verdelho. The verdelho provides distinct chalky structure on the palate and through the finish, adding to the complexity of the wine. An interesting observation and lesson in the significance of the blend. This, like all the others, is very good. Screw cap. 12.5% alc. RATING 94 DRINK 2021-2031 $29 EL ✪

Wilyabrup Cabernet Sauvignon Merlot 2020, Margaret River This is super-restrained; the length allows the delicate fruit to unfurl and unfold over the palate. Mulberry, salted blood plum, dusted cassis and bramble overlaid with saltbush, licorice, fennel flower and cigar. A gorgeous wine. Effortless. Screw cap. 13% alc. RATING 94 DRINK 2021-2031 $45 EL

Cumulus Vineyards   ★★★★

1705 Euchareena Road, Molong, NSW 2866 **Region** Orange
T 1300 449 860 **www**.cumulusvineyards.com.au **Winemaker** Debbie Lauritz **Est.** 1995
Dozens 193 000 **Vyds** 508ha
At 600m above sea level, the 508ha Cumulus vineyard is one of the largest single estates in NSW. The wines are made at the Robert Oatley winery in Mudgee and are released under the Cumulus, Soaring, Climbing, Rolling, Luna Rosa, Block 50, Head in the Clouds, Alte and Inkberry labels. Exports to most major markets. (JH)

ＴＴＴＴＴ **Euchareena Road Block 14 Chardonnay 2019, Orange** Smart chardonnay for the price. The oak, an artful combo of new and used, works well, although still a bit shins and elbows. Disjointed. Almond paste, dried mango and stone-fruit allusions. Some creamed cashew at its core. Medium of feel. Good length. Would be better with full malo, but a good drink all the same. Screw cap. 13% alc. RATING 91 DRINK 2021-2024 $25 NG

Euchareena Road Block 15 Chardonnay 2021, Orange Given the higher alcohol, presumably picked later than Block 14. The better for it. More flavour: stone-fruit inflections meld with dried mango and tropical hints. The oak embellishment, attractive, reeling off scents of vanilla pod. Some almond meal and toasted nuts at its core. Sophisticated drinking for the price, if not a tad hot at the finish. Screw cap. 14.3% alc. RATING 90 DRINK 2021–2027 $25 NG

ΨΨΨΨ **Euchareena Road Block 14 Chardonnay 2021, Orange** RATING 88 DRINK 2021–2027 $25 NG
Euchareena Road Block 14 Chardonnay 2020, Orange RATING 88 DRINK 2022–2027 $25 NG
Alte Shiraz 2018, Orange RATING 88 DRINK 2021–2025 $20 NG
Euchareena Road Shiraz 2018, Orange RATING 88 DRINK 2021–2025 $25 NG

Cupitt's Estate

58 Washburton Road, Ulladulla, NSW 2539 **Region** Shoalhaven Coast
T (02) 4455 7888 **www**.cupittsestate.com.au **Open** 7 days 11–5 by appt
Winemaker Wally Cupitt **Est.** 2007 **Dozens** 9000 **Vyds** 3ha
Griff and Rosie Cupitt run a combined winery and restaurant complex, taking full advantage of their location on the south coast of NSW. Rosie studied oenology at CSU and has more than a decade of vintage experience, taking in France and Italy; she also happens to be the Shoalhaven representative for Slow Food International. The Cupitts have 3ha of vines centred on sauvignon blanc and semillon, and also source fruit from Hilltops, Canberra District, Tumbarumba and Orange. Sons Wally and Tom have now joined the business. (JH)

ΨΨΨΨΨ **Shiraz 2020, Heathcote** Fine aromas of blueberry, dark cherry, iodine, violet, mace and barrel-fermented barbecue tones. This is a good wine. It could be very good. It needs more tannic extension and freshness. The latter may not be achievable in a place like Heathcote, but the former surely is. Screw cap. 14% alc. RATING 92 DRINK 2022–2027 $38 NG
Viognier 2021, Hilltops This achieves what the gewürztraminer doesn't quite manage: textural amplitude and aroma. This is viognier's wont, rather than acidity per se. Spiced apricot, glazed quince, honeysuckle and orange verbena. A lees-derived almond-meal accent defines the full-weighted mid palate. The finish, long on personality. More phenolic chew would be welcome, but a very solid wine. Screw cap. 14% alc. RATING 91 DRINK 2022–2026 $32 NG

ΨΨΨΨ **Alphonse Sauvignon 2021, Shoalhaven Coast** RATING 89 DRINK 2022–2025 $34 NG
Ruby's Cabernet Sauvignon 2021, Hilltops RATING 88 DRINK 2021–2022 $30 NG
Gewürtzraminer 2021, Tumbarumba RATING 88 DRINK 2022–2025 $32 NG

Curator Wine Company

28 Jenke Road, Marananga, SA 5355 **Region** Barossa Valley
T 0411 861 604 **www**.curatorwineco.com.au **Open** By appt **Winemaker** Tom White
Est. 2015 **Dozens** 5000 **Vyds** 8ha
This business is owned by Tom and Bridget White, who have made a number of changes in direction over previous years and have now decided to focus on shiraz and cabernet sauvignon from the Barossa Valley, a decision that has been rewarded. The vineyard at Marananga is planted on ancient red soils rich in ironstone and quartzite, and the wines are naturally fermented. (JH)

ΨΨΨΨΨ **Single Barrel Grenache 2020, Barossa Valley** Super-pure satsuma plum fruits with high tones of raspberry coulis, studded with exotic spice, red licorice, gingerbread, earth and light amaro tones. Serious grenache here, composed, laden with spice, fine in tannin with a savoury, almost meaty edge to the exit. Agglomerate. 14.5% alc. RATING 94 DRINK 2022-2032 $125 DB

ŶŶŶŶŶ Shiraz 2020, Barossa Valley RATING 92 DRINK 2022-2028 $35 DB
Marananga Cabernet Sauvignon 2020, Barossa Valley RATING 92 DRINK 2022-2032 $35 DB
Rosé Montepulciano 2021, Barossa Valley RATING 90 DRINK 2021-2024 $25 DB
Hamlets Shiraz 2019, Barossa Valley RATING 90 DRINK 2021-2028 $30 DB

Curlewis Winery ★★★★

55 Navarre Road, Curlewis, Vic 3222 **Region** Geelong
T (03) 5250 4567 **www**.curlewiswinery.com.au **Open** Sat 11–4 **Winemaker** Stefano Marasco, Rainer Breit (Consultant) **Viticulturist** Stefano Marasco **Est.** 1998
Dozens 1000 **Vyds** 2.8ha
Curlewis was established by self-taught winemaker Rainer Breit and Wendy Oliver, who extended the original pinot noir vineyard (now 35yo) with more pinot noir (Pommard clone) and small amounts of chardonnay and arneis. They retired in '11, selling the business to Stefano Marasco and Leesa Freyer. Stefano continues to make the wines using Old World techniques including wild yeast, hot fermentation, post-ferment maceration, prolonged lees contact, neither fining nor filtering the wine. Rainer and Wendy remain part of the Curlewis team as consultants and great friends. Exports to Canada, Sweden, Maldives, Malaysia, Singapore and Hong Kong. (JH)

ŶŶŶŶŶ Reserve Pinot Noir 2019, Geelong Definitely in reserved mode: tightly contained and concentrated in both structure and presence. There's a lot happening in this wine, from the dark and brooding colour to the perfumed bouquet, boasting both autumnal, earthy notes and black berries, sweet cherry pie fruits. Densely sheeted tannins hold everything tight, lending a focus for both fruit and oak. A wine you may wish to age just a little longer. Screw cap. 13% alc. RATING 95 DRINK 2022-2029 $85 JP

ŶŶŶŶŶ Estate Pinot Noir 2019, Geelong RATING 93 DRINK 2022-2029 $45 JP

Curly Flat ★★★★★

263 Collivers Road, Lancefield, Vic 3435 **Region** Macedon Ranges
T (03) 5429 1956 **www**.curlyflat.com **Open** Fri–Sun 12–5 **Winemaker** Matt Harrop, Ben Kimmorley **Est.** 1991 **Dozens** 6000 **Vyds** 13ha
Founded by Phillip Moraghan and Jenifer Kolkka in '91, Jenifer has been the sole owner of Curly Flat since '17. The focus has always been on the vineyard, a dedicated team ensuring quality is never compromised. Matt Harrop is now overseeing production. Exports to the UK, Japan and Hong Kong. (JH)

ŶŶŶŶŶ Western Pinot Noir 2020, Macedon Ranges My pick of the 3 Curly Flat '20 pinots, for its completeness and balance. This is composed, moreish and fabulous now, with its heady aromas of florals, forest floor and earthiness, to flavours of red cherries enmeshed in a light mix of baking spices. There's a brightness within and while there's plenty of tannin, this is more medium weighted, with a long persistent finish. Screw cap. 13.2% alc. RATING 96 DRINK 2021-2033 $57 JF ✪
Pinot Gris 2021, Macedon Ranges This is a beauty. Flavoursome with nashi pear, lemon drops, a decent smattering of ginger spice and a creaminess throughout. Texture abounds but not at all weighty, as it feels effortless. Screw cap. 13.6% alc. RATING 95 DRINK 2021-2025 $30 JF ✪
White Pinot 2021, Macedon Ranges Gosh this is good: complex, savoury yet equally refreshing. Tantalising pinot characters of cherries and wild strawberries, warm earth and forest-floor aromas. The palate comes alive with a richness, a plumpness of fruit, yet finishes dry and oh, so satisfying. Screw cap. 14% alc. RATING 95 DRINK 2021-2024 $30 JF ✪

Chardonnay 2020, Macedon Ranges A svelte and charming drink with a core of good fruit, all citrus and white nectarine, bound by a savoury overlay. Flinty sulphides, a smidge of creamy nuttiness and a succulence across the palate as the livewire acidity drives this to a long finish. Screw cap. 13% alc. RATING 95 DRINK 2021-2028 $48 JF

Pinot Noir 2020, Macedon Ranges There's an intensity and depth to Curly Flat's pinots of late and as with this, never going overboard. It's deep, complex and earthy with damp undergrowth alongside cherries, blood orange and Angostura bitters, plus savoury oak spice. Lots of tannin, but well placed across its more medium-bodied palate and with spritely acidity, it feels effortless to the end. Screw cap. 13% alc. RATING 95 DRINK 2021-2030 $57 JF

ŸŸŸŸŸ **Central Pinot Noir 2020, Macedon Ranges** RATING 92 DRINK 2022-2033 $57 JF

Curtis Family Vineyards ★★★★☆

514 Victor Harbor Road, McLaren Vale, SA 5171 **Region** McLaren Vale
T 0439 800 484 **www.**curtisfamilyvineyards.com **Winemaker** Mark Curtis **Est.** 1973
Dozens 10 000
The Curtis family traces its history back to 1499 when Paolo Curtis was appointed by Cardinal de Medici to administer Papal lands in the area around Cervaro. (The name Curtis is believed to derive from Curtius, a noble and wealthy Roman Empire family.) The family has been growing grapes and making wine in McLaren Vale since '73, having come to Australia some years previously. Exports to the US, Canada and Thailand. (JH)

ŸŸŸŸŸ **Ancestor Shiraz 2018, McLaren Vale** While not to my taste necessarily, this address' better wines are those made to an older-school creed: old-vine sourcing, hand picked, longish fermentations (14 days), finished in a combination of French and American oak. Good quality if this is your thing. Creamy texture. Venerable poise. Red and darker fruits. Best, though, the vinosity and length, refraining from excess with each step across the palate. Screw cap. 14% alc. RATING 95 DRINK 2021-2032 $180 NG

ŸŸŸŸŸ **Pasha MV Shiraz 2018, McLaren Vale** RATING 93 DRINK 2021-2028 $100 NG

Small Batch Durif 2021, South Australia RATING 92 DRINK 2021-2028 $60 NG

Heritage Grenache 2021, McLaren Vale RATING 91 DRINK 2022-2025 $35 NG

d'Arenberg ★★★★☆

58 Osborn Road, McLaren Vale, SA 5171 **Region** McLaren Vale
T (08) 8329 4888 **www.**darenberg.com.au **Open** 7 days 10.30–4.30
Winemaker Chester Osborn, Jack Walton **Viticulturist** Giulio Dimasi **Est.** 1912
Dozens 220 **Vyds** 197.2ha
Nothing, they say, succeeds like success. Few operations in Australia fit this dictum better than d'Arenberg, which has kept its 100+yo heritage while moving into the 21st century with flair and élan. At last count the d'Arenberg vineyards, at various locations, have 37 varieties planted, as well as more than 50 growers in McLaren Vale. Its considerable portfolio of richly robed red wines, shiraz, cabernet sauvignon and grenache are the cornerstones. The ultra-modern and iconic 5-level Cube cellar door offers a range of wine experiences including a wine sensory room and a virtual fermenter; art exhibitions are a regular feature, too. A founding member of Australia's First Families of Wine. Exports to all major markets. (JH)

ŸŸŸŸŸ **The Sardanapalian Shiraz 2015, McLaren Vale** Opaque. A capacious wine, but the level of extraction and fitting oak tannins serve it well. Perhaps the most articulate of this single-vineyard range, its vocabulary less constrained by winemaking stuff: graphite, plum, dark cherry, anise, clove and something pungently mineral verging on volcanic. Firm but detailed, and not without flow or charm. Pliant and long. The moreish and almost Italianate tannins, its opus. Screw cap. 14% alc. RATING 94 DRINK 2021-2035 $105 NG

🍷🍷🍷🍷♀ **The Bamboo Scrub Single Vineyard Shiraz 2015, McLaren Vale**
RATING 93 DRINK 2021-2026 $105 NG
The Blind Tiger Shiraz 2015, McLaren Vale RATING 93 DRINK 2021-2027 $105 NG
Pollyanna Polly Chardonnay Pinot Noir Pinot Meunier NV, Adelaide Hills RATING 92 $36 NG
The Anthropocene Epoch Mencia 2020, McLaren Vale RATING 92 DRINK 2021-2025 $30 NG
The Dead Arm Shiraz 2018, McLaren Vale RATING 92 DRINK 2021-2038 $75 NG
J.R.O Afflatus Shiraz 2015, McLaren Vale RATING 92 DRINK 2021-2025 $105 NG
The Amaranthine Single Vineyard Shiraz 2015, McLaren Vale RATING 92 DRINK 2021-2026 $105 NG
The Eight Iron Shiraz 2015, McLaren Vale RATING 92 DRINK 2021-2035 $105 NG
The Piceous Lodestar Shiraz 2015, McLaren Vale RATING 92 DRINK 2021-2030 $105 NG
The Sisypheanic Euphoria Single Vineyard Shiraz 2015, McLaren Vale RATING 92 DRINK 2021-2033 $105 NG
The Beautiful View Grenache 2014, McLaren Vale RATING 92 DRINK 2021-2026 $105 NG
The McLaren Sand Hills Grenache 2014, McLaren Vale RATING 92 DRINK 2021-2025 $105 NG
The Money Spider Roussanne 2021, McLaren Vale RATING 91 DRINK 2021-2024 $21 NG○
The Sensorial Surfer Fiano 2021, McLaren Vale RATING 91 DRINK 2021-2024 $25 NG
The Witches Berry Chardonnay 2021, McLaren Vale RATING 91 DRINK 2021-2026 $26 NG
The Noble Mud Pie Viognier Semillon Riesling 2021, Adelaide Hills RATING 91 DRINK 2022-2028 $12 NG○

Dal Zotto Wines   ★★★★★

Main Road, Whitfield, Vic 3733 **Region** King Valley
T (03) 5729 8321 **www**.dalzotto.com.au **Open** 7 days 10–5 **Winemaker** Michael Dal Zotto, Daniel Bettio **Est.** 1987 **Dozens** 60 000 **Vyds** 46ha
The Dal Zotto family is a King Valley institution; ex-tobacco growers, then contract grapegrowers, they are now 100% focused on their Dal Zotto wine range. Founded by Otto and Elena, ownership has now passed to sons Michael and Christian and their partners Lynne and Simone, who handle winemaking, sales and marketing respectively. Dal Zotto is producing increasing amounts of Italian varieties of consistent quality from its substantial estate vineyard. The cellar door is in the centre of Whitfield, and is also home to their Trattoria (open Wed–Sun). Exports to the UK, UAE, the Philippines and Singapore. (JH)

🍷🍷🍷🍷🍷 **L'Immigrante Nebbiolo 2016, King Valley** With each vintage, nebbiolo takes
big strides in the King Valley. Here, we see the coming together of both captivating beauty and the kind of depth and power we look for in the grape. Aromatic and perfumed in rose, forest berries, black cherry and anise. The palate is charged and alive in red berries, forest undergrowth, cola, earth and leather. Those naturally high tannins are nicely controlled, coiled, waiting. Approach now, but also with the thought of further ageing. Screw cap. 14.1% alc. RATING 96 DRINK 2022-2039 $82 JP

Pucino VP Prosecco 2021, King Valley A different look for the popular Pucino, with a vintage release that brings added complexity and introduces a touch of savouriness. Aromas embrace a core of citrus and apple and then explore baked quince, white peach, orange peel and acacia. The '21 vintage was a ripper in the King Valley, and there's good natural balance and texture here, together with a concentrated flavour that finishes with a thread of intriguing preserved lemon. Crown. 10.5% alc. RATING 95 $27 JP ❂

L'Immigrante Contro Shiraz 2017, King Valley Released as a 5yo, it takes confidence to enter this kind of winemaking territory. Bottle age brings developed characters, but here it also brings a degree of freshness and potential for further ageing. Tricky stuff. Complex, yes. Takes the shiraz grape and gives it a savoury jolt, with leather and smoked meats meets bramble, blackberry and licorice, with a just a hint of espresso. Svelte in tannins, textural and running deep in flavour, it's quite the seducer. Screw cap. 13.6% alc. RATING 95 DRINK 2022-2035 $74 JP

Fiano 2021, King Valley The fiano grape continues its takeover of our hearts and minds, with another strong performance. Pear skin, stone fruits, quince jelly and spice offer an attractive introduction to a wine that retains a strong presence in the glass, while at the same time appearing deliciously easy to get to know. Look to the texture, the spice and the downright ease with which it bewitches. Screw cap. 13.8% alc. RATING 94 DRINK 2022-2026 $27 JP ❂

ΨΨΨΨΨ Pucino Prosecco NV, King Valley RATING 93 $21 JP ❂
Pinot Grigio 2021, King Valley RATING 93 DRINK 2022-2025 $27 JP ❂
Pinot Bianco 2021, King Valley RATING 92 DRINK 2022-2026 $29 JP
V S NV, King Valley RATING 92 DRINK 2022-2022 $89 JP
Rosato 2021, King Valley RATING 91 DRINK 2022-2024 $21 JP ❂
Nebbiolo 2019, King Valley RATING 91 DRINK 2022-2029 $46 JP
Arneis 2021, King Valley RATING 90 DRINK 2022-2025 $28 JP
Sangiovese 2021, King Valley RATING 90 DRINK 2022-2025 $28 JP

Dalfarras ★★★★

PO Box 123, Nagambie, Vic 3608 **Region** Nagambie Lakes
T (03) 5794 2637 **www**.dalfarras.com.au **Open** Mon–Sat 9–5, Sun 11–5
Winemaker Alister Purbrick **Est.** 1991 **Dozens** 8750 **Vyds** 20.97ha
The project of Alister Purbrick and artist wife Rosa (née Dalfarra), whose paintings adorn the labels of the wines. Alister is best known as winemaker at Tahbilk (see separate entry), the family winery and home, but this range of wines is intended to (in Alister's words) 'Allow me to expand my winemaking horizons and mould wines in styles different from Tahbilk'. Wines are available for tasting at Tahbilk. (JH)

ΨΨΨΨΨ Prosecco 2021, Victoria An engaging young prosecco, with a touch of herbal interplay among the lemony citrus and apply varietal notes. Bright and tangy, it introduces a textural quality on the palate with some bready notes. Chalky dry on the finish. Cork. 11% alc. RATING 90 $20 JP ❂

Nero d'Avola 2019, Nagambie Lakes Voluptuous and soft, fragrant and juicy, there is a lot to be said for this little charmer, employing the new Italian kid on the block, nero d'Avola. Dried herb, dark cherry, leaf and cinnamon with woody oak nicely integrated. Bright as a button and ready to go. Screw cap. 13% alc. RATING 90 DRINK 2021-2024 $20 JP ❂

ΨΨΨΨ Pinot Grigio 2021, Nagambie Lakes RATING 89 DRINK 2021-2024 $20 JP
Sangiovese Rosé 2021, Central Victoria RATING 88 DRINK 2021-2024 $20 JP

Dalrymple Vineyards ★★★★☆

1337 Pipers Brook Road, Pipers Brook, Tas 7254 **Region** Northern Tasmania
T (03) 6382 7229 **www**.dalrymplevineyards.com.au **Open** By appt **Winemaker** Peter Caldwell **Est.** 1987 **Dozens** 4000 **Vyds** 17ha

Dalrymple was established many years ago by the Mitchell and Sundstrup families; the vineyard and brand were acquired by Hill-Smith Family Vineyards in late '07. Peter Caldwell has been responsible for the vineyard, viticulture and winemaking since '10. He brought with him 10 years' experience at Te Kairanga Wines (NZ) and 2 years with Josef Chromy Wines. His knowledge of pinot noir and chardonnay is comprehensive. In Dec '12 Hill-Smith Family Vineyards acquired the 120ha property on which the original Frogmore Creek Vineyard was established; 10ha of that property is pinot noir specifically for Dalrymple. (JH)

ΨΨΨΨΨ Single Site Coal River Valley Pinot Noir 2020, Tasmania There's a beautiful fragrance to this wine, somewhere between roses and violets, holding from the first moment of its captivating bouquet to the last trace of its enduring finish. Pitch-perfect red cherries run in tandem, intricately upheld by fine, mineral tannins. A triumph. Screw cap. 14% alc. RATING 95 DRINK 2022-2032 $64 TS

ΨΨΨΨΨ Single Site Swansea Pinot Noir 2020, Tasmania RATING 93 DRINK 2025-2032 $64 TS
Estate Pinot Noir 2020, Tasmania RATING 92 DRINK 2022-2027 $38 TS
Cave Block Pipers River Chardonnay 2019, Tasmania RATING 90 DRINK 2022-2022 $38 TS

Dalwhinnie   ★★★★★
448 Taltarni Road, Moonambel, Vic 3478 **Region** Pyrenees
T (03) 5467 2388 **www**.dalwhinnie.wine **Open** 7 days 10–4.30 **Winemaker** Julian Langworthy **Viticulturist** John Fogarty **Est.** 1976 **Dozens** 3500 **Vyds** 23ha
Dalwhinnie wines have tremendous depth of flavour, reflecting the relatively low-yielding but well-maintained vineyards. The vineyards are dry-grown and managed organically, hence the low yield, but the quality more than compensates. A 50t high-tech winery allows the wines to be made onsite. It was good to see that Dalwhinnie was acquired by the Fogarty Wine Group in '20. Exports to the UK and the US. (JH)

ΨΨΨΨΨ Moonambel Chardonnay 2020, Pyrenees Julian Langworthy, knows a thing or 2 about chardonnay. Here, he delivers a complex and elegant interpretation, bringing flinty minerals, pristine sherbety lemon and grapefruit with pear, peach skin and almond flavours into a restrained, harmonious whole. Lithe, juicy and delicious now, with some way to go. Screw cap. 13% alc. RATING 95 DRINK 2022-2030 $50 JP
Moonambel Shiraz 2019, Pyrenees Captures the intense fruit power of Pyrenees shiraz beautifully, perfectly. Ripe, dark plums, cassis, aniseed and nutmeg aromas present lifted and fresh, before settling into the palate with gusto. Generous in flavour, but also well measured and smooth, not to mention lingering. A gentle thread of menthol throughout lets you know you are in the Pyrenees. Screw cap. 14% alc. RATING 95 DRINK 2022-2033 $70 JP
The Eagle Shiraz 2019, Pyrenees Deep and inky purple hues introduce a wine of obvious class, with further ageing on its mind. One for the cellar, but should you open now expect a warm, enveloping opulence filling the mouth with sweet blackberries, cassis, chocolate, spice and a deep-grained earthiness. Time in oak brings woodsy spice and a rich texture which is seamless, bringing width and length to the flavour profile. Screw cap. 14% alc. RATING 95 DRINK 2022-2033 $185 JP
Three Valleys Pinot Noir 2020, Tasmania The Fogarty Group's foray into Tasmania has facilitated a stunning new pinot for Dalwhinnie. A seamless union of its 3 valleys, this is a beautiful rendition of the elegance of '20, delivering accurate, graceful black and red cherry fruits, set off with silky tannins. It's delightful from the outset and will only blossom in the cellar. Screw cap. 13.5% alc. RATING 94 DRINK 2025-2030 $70 TS
Moonambel Cabernet 2019, Pyrenees A wine of some poise, enhanced by the fragrant addition of a little cabernet franc and merlot, releasing the prettiest aromas of violet, lilac, sweet dark spices, briar and ripe black cherries. The palate drizzles dark berry flavours across beautifully textured, taut tannins, finishing long and with good grip. Screw cap. 13.5% alc. RATING 94 DRINK 2022-2030 $70 JP

Dalwood

700 Dalwood Road, Dalwood, NSW 2335 **Region** Hunter Valley
T (02) 4998 7666 **www**.dalwoodestate.com.au **Open** Long weekends **Winemaker** Bryan
Currie **Est.** 1828 **Vyds** 23ha

The chain of events making the oldest winery the youngest isn't far removed from the white
rabbit appearing out of the magician's hat. George Wyndham arrived in Australia in 1823
and promptly set about assembling vast agricultural holdings stretching from Inverell to the
Liverpool Plains. He berated the Sydney Agricultural Show for holding the Wine Show
in Feb, and for awarding gold medals that weren't in fact 24-carat gold. In 1904, Penfolds
purchased Wyndham Estate and renamed it Dalwood. In '67 Penfolds sold the winery and
vineyard to Perc McGuigan, leaving McGuigan free to rename it Wyndham Estate. In Dec '17
TWE (aka Penfolds) sold the Dalwood brand to Sam and Christie Arnaout and Sweetwater
Wines. The synergy of this assemblage is obvious. (JH)

ᛜᛜᛜᛜᛜ **Chardonnay 2021, Hunter Valley** This is very good, combining Hunter
ripeness and intensity with a contemporary underbelly of pungent mineral and
classy oak. Nectarine, apricot and canned peach. A white-pepper-doused finish,
energetic and crunchy, lingers long and savoury. An intriguing wine to think about
and revisit. A regional benchmark in the making, comparable to top expressions
around the country. Screw cap. 12.5% alc. RATING 95 DRINK 2021–2028 $40 NG

ᛜᛜᛜᛜᛜ **Estate Grown Tempranillo Touriga 2021, Hunter Valley** RATING 93
DRINK 2022–2027 $45 NG
Estate Grown Tempranillo Touriga 2020, Hunter Valley RATING 92
DRINK 2021–2025 $45 NG
Estate Shiraz 2020, Hunter Valley RATING 90 DRINK 2021–2024 $45 NG

Dandelion Vineyards

PO Box 138, McLaren Vale, SA 5171 **Region** South Australia
T (08) 8323 8979 **www**.dandelionvineyards.com.au **Winemaker** Elena Brooks **Est.** 2007
Vyds 124.2ha

Elena Brooks crafts full-bodied wines across South Australia's premium regions: Adelaide
Hills, Eden Valley, Langhorne Creek, McLaren Vale, Barossa Valley and Fleurieu Peninsula.
She endeavours to draw upon vineyards untempered by over-management, as much as she
strives for a softer impact in the winery. As a result, Dandelion wines are increasingly bright,
transparent and stamped by a more sensitive oak regime than in the past. Grenache, a strong
suit. Exports to all major markets. (NG)

ᛜᛜᛜᛜᛜ **Red Queen of the Shiraz 2019, Eden Valley** From Colin Kroehn's vineyard
planted in 1912, that he has looked after for over 65 years. Dense opaque colour;
paints the glass. Crammed to the gills with black and purple fruits of every
persuasion, this full-bodied red wine also has a castle of tannins and oak. Screw
cap. 14.5% alc. RATING 96 DRINK 2025–2055 $250 JH
Wonderland of the Riesling 2021, Eden Valley From Colin Kroehn's
vineyard. Best appreciated in 10 years, by which time the presently closed bouquet
will have gained presence, and the palate built to balance the effervescent acidity;
the points for then, not now. Screw cap. 10.9% alc. RATING 95 DRINK 2030–2040
$60 JH
Faraway Tree Grenache 2020, McLaren Vale By any measure, a wine of
class that showcases the intrigue and appeal of grenache. Explores the grape's
floral confection and perfumed attributes, while also delving deep into a world
of Middle Eastern spice, pepper, wild berries and game. Moves with real energy
across the palate, aided and abetted by fine, woodsy oak tannins. Screw cap.
14.5% alc. RATING 95 DRINK 2021–2030 $120 JP
Moonrise Kingdom 2020, McLaren Vale This is good. A savvy blend,
serving a confluence of pulpy aromatics; firm, sandy-feeling tannins and a skein of
freshness that works with the morass of fruit, extract and perfume going on around
it. Matured 18 months in new and used French wood, imparting vanilla and a

waft of mocha. Nothing over the top. The finish, a long beam of pixelated tannins, chewy and savoury and akin to biting into the ripest grape skins imaginable. A smart wine in this vintage. Screw cap. 14.5% alc. RATING 95 DRINK 2021-2030 $120 NG

Pride of the Cabernet Sauvignon 2020, Fleurieu A medium- to full-bodied exercise with cabernet, the tannins neatly controlled, but still able to proclaim its patrician upbringing, blackcurrant and bramble fruits to the fore. Screw cap. 14.5% alc. RATING 94 DRINK 2025-2035 $30 JH ✪

Lion's Tooth of Shiraz Riesling 2020, McLaren Vale What may seem incongruous makes sense: blending high-acid riesling (5%) with shiraz, a variety prone to overripeness in a climate this warm. Plenty of whole-bunch nourishment imparts a souk of spice, hints of mescal and an echo of clove, while embellishing the tannic arsenal. This works very well. The extraction, just right. The oak, well nestled amid blueberry, anise and iodine. Fine succulent length, defined as much by the gritty tannins as the balanced saline freshness. Screw cap. 14% alc. RATING 94 DRINK 2021-2028 $40 NG

ɦɦɦɦɧ **Treasure Trove of Grenache 2019, McLaren Vale** RATING 93 DRINK 2021-2026 $40 NG

Damsel of the Barossa Merlot 2020, Barossa Valley RATING 92 DRINK 2021-2030 $30 JP

Lionheart of the Barossa Shiraz 2020, Barossa Valley RATING 92 DRINK 2021-2030 $30 DB

March Hare of the Barossa Mataro 2020, Barossa Valley RATING 92 DRINK 2021-2028 $60 DB

Midnight Rainbow of Petite Sirah 2019, McLaren Vale RATING 92 DRINK 2021-2030 $120 NG

Enchanted Garden of the Riesling 2021, Eden Valley RATING 91 DRINK 2022-2030 $28 JP

Twilight of the Chardonnay 2021, Adelaide Hills RATING 90 DRINK 2022-2028 $28 JP

Wishing Clock of the Sauvignon Blanc 2021, Adelaide Hills RATING 90 DRINK 2021-2024 $28 JP

Menagerie of the Barossa GSM 2020, Barossa Valley RATING 90 DRINK 2021-2028 $30 DB

Dappled Wines   ★★★★★

1 Sewell Road, Steels Creek, Vic 3775 **Region** Yarra Valley
T 0407 675 994 **www.**dappledwines.com.au **Open** By appt **Winemaker** Shaun Crinion **Est.** 2009 **Dozens** 800

Owner and winemaker Shaun Crinion was introduced to wine in '99, working for his winemaker uncle at Laetitia Winery & Vineyards on the central coast of California. His career since then has been so impressive I (James) can't cut it short: 2000 Devil's Lair, Margaret River and Corbett Canyon Vineyard, California; '02 Houghton, Middle Swan; '03 De Bortoli, Hunter Valley; '04-06 Pipers Brook, Tasmania; '06 Bay of Fires, Tasmania; '06-07 Williams Selyem, California; '08 Domaine Chandon, Yarra Valley; '10 Domaine de Montille, Burgundy; '09- present Dappled Wines (plus part-time for Rob Dolan). His longer-term ambition is to buy or establish his own vineyard. (JH)

ɦɦɦɦɦ **Champs de Cerises Single Vineyard Chardonnay 2020, Yarra Valley** A high-quality wine, making its mark from the first whiff with fragrant pink grapefruit, white peach and nectarine to the fore, toasted almonds and a whisper of French oak, all playing the same song on the palate through to the finish. Screw cap. 13% alc. RATING 96 DRINK 2022-2035 $45 JH ✪

Limited Release Tradition Cabernets 2019, Yarra Valley An 84/16% blend of cabernet sauvignon and cabernet franc. The wine is, as one expects from owner and winemaker Shaun Crinion, all about elegance, finesse and attention to detail, with fruit, tannins and oak all on duty. Gentle cassis is the heartbeat of the

cabernet sauvignon, a leafy, cedary whisper from the cabernet franc, and structure from the tannins. Diam. 13% alc. RATING 95 DRINK 2022-2035 $35 JH ✪
Appellation Chardonnay 2020, Yarra Valley Right in the heart of the mainstream of quality Yarra Valley chardonnay with stone fruit and citrus flavours, and a lingering finish. Screw cap. 13% alc. RATING 94 DRINK 2022-2028 $35 JH

🍷🍷🍷🍷🍷 **Appellation Upper Pinot Noir 2020, Yarra Valley** RATING 93 DRINK 2022-2027 $35 JH
Champs de Cerises Single Vineyard Upper Pinot Noir 2020, Yarra Valley RATING 92 DRINK 2021-2027 $45 JH

David Franz

94 Stelzer Road, Stone Well, SA 5352 **Region** Barossa Valley
T 0417 454 556 **www**.david-franz.com **Open** 7 days 11–5 **Winemaker** David Franz Lehmann **Viticulturist** David Franz Lehmann **Est.** 1998 **Dozens** 6600 **Vyds** 33.92ha
David Franz (Lehmann) is one of Margaret and Peter Lehmann's sons. He took a very circuitous path around the world before establishing his eponymous winery. His wife Nicki accompanied him on his odyssey and, together with their 3 children, 2 dogs, a mess of chickens and a surly shed cat, all live happily together in their house and winery. The utterly unique labels stem from (incomplete) university studies in graphic design. Exports to the UK, the US, Japan and Hong Kong. (JH)

🍷🍷🍷🍷🍷 **Long Gully Road Ancient Vine Semillon 2020, Barossa Valley** Pale straw in the glass, with aromas of Meyer lemon, apple, dried grass, soft spice, marzipan, white flowers, stone fruit and stone. Great detail, clarity and tension with a brisk acid cadence, a light squeak of phenolics, dots of clotted cream cutting in on the palate and a dry, pure stony finish. Great drinking. Screw cap. 12.8% alc. RATING 95 DRINK 2022-2035 $50 DB ♥
Nicole Sparkling NV, Barossa Valley 75/25% cabernet sauvignon/shiraz. Sparkling red alchemy with some 14 years on yeast lees, hand disgorged and freshened with a slurp of '20 cabernet. Boisterous red bubbles with notes of blackberry, cassis, blackforest cake, leather, polished mahogany, fruitcake spice and dark chocolate. Fizzy, rich, comforting and very long of finish, it's a beauty. Screw cap. 14.5% alc. RATING 94 $80 DB
Gewürztraminer 2021, Eden Valley A head-spinningly perfumed gewürztraminer. Aromas of citrus fruits infused with characters of Turkish delight, rosewater, lychees, bath salts, white flowers and crushed stone. The aromas transpose neatly over to the palate, yet it is bone dry, savoury and sapid; nary a note of the variety's sometimes gloopy lack of detail. This is a wonderful rendition of the grape. Screw cap. 12.6% alc. RATING 94 DRINK 2022-2032 $27 DB ✪
Plane Turning Right 2017, Barossa Valley 43/40/14/3% merlot/petit verdot/malbec/cabernet sauvignon. Aged in seasoned oak hogsheads for 24 months on full lees. A complex and captivating blend with juicy plummy fruits underscored by complex notes of black and red currants, exotic spice, sage, spearmint, olive tapenade, washed-rind cheese and dried citrus rind. Sleek and savoury with a meaty edge. Screw cap. 13.5% alc. RATING 94 DRINK 2022-2028 $27 DB ✪
Marg's Blood Semillon 2011, Barossa Valley Cellar release, from 137yo semillon vines. Mid pale straw in colour with fruit notes of Meyer lemon, green apple and citrus fruits with hints of dried hay, preserved lemon, stone, white flowers, lemon butter, nougat and pastry. Incredibly long, sustained finish with creamy, citrus notes and a hints of dried herbs and spice. Superb drinking from a challenging year. Screw cap. 12.3% alc. RATING 94 DRINK 2022-2032 $75 DB

🍷🍷🍷🍷🍷 **Riesling 2020, Eden Valley** RATING 93 DRINK 2022-2032 $27 DB ✪
Madiera Clone Semillon 2020, Barossa Valley RATING 93 DRINK 2022-2035 $27 DB ✪
1923 Survivor Vines Grenache Noir 2018, Barossa Valley RATING 93 DRINK 2022-2027 $27 DB ✪

Eden Edge Riesling Semillon 2020, Eden Valley RATING 92
DRINK 2022–2026 $27 DB
Brother's Ilk Moskos' Birdwood Vineyard Chardonnay 2018, Adelaide
Hills RATING 92 DRINK 2022–2028 $50 DB
Alexander's Reward Cabernet Sauvignon Shiraz 2016, Barossa Valley
RATING 92 DRINK 2022–2030 $50 DB
Benjamin's Promise Shiraz 2016, Barossa Valley RATING 92
DRINK 2022–2030 $50 DB
Larrikin VIII NV, Barossa Valley RATING 92 DRINK 2022–2028 $50 DB
Late Harvest Sauvignon Blanc 2018, Adelaide Hills RATING 92
DRINK 2022–2030 $27 DB
Cellar Release Riesling 2011, Eden Valley RATING 91 DRINK 2022–2026
$50 DB
Georgie's Walk Cabernet Sauvignon 2016, Barossa Valley RATING 90
DRINK 2022–2030 $50 DB
Georgie's Walk Cellar Release Cabernet Sauvignon 2011, Barossa
Valley RATING 90 DRINK 2022–2026 $100 DB
Nicki's Symphony No.2 NV, Barossa Valley RATING 90 DRINK 2022–2026
$27 DB

David Hook Wines   ★★★☆

Pothana Winery, 62 Pothana Lane, Belford, NSW 2335 **Region** Hunter Valley
T (02) 6574 7164 **www**.davidhookwines.com.au **Open** Sat 10.30–3.30 by appt
Winemaker David Hook **Est.** 1984 **Dozens** 10000 **Vyds** 8ha
David Hook had over 25 years' experience as a winemaker for Tyrrell's and Lake's Folly, also
doing the full Flying Winemaker bit with jobs in Bordeaux, the Rhône Valley, Spain, the US
and Georgia. The Pothana Vineyard has been in production for almost 40 years and the wines
made from it are given the 'Old Vines' banner. This vineyard is planted on the Belford Dome,
an ancient geological formation that provides red clay soils over limestone on the slopes, and
sandy loams along the creek flats; the former for red wines, the latter for white. (JH)

 Pinot Grigio 2021, Hunter Valley Pinot grigio needs a cool climate – not a
hot one – to show its best. No vinification issues. Screw cap. 12% alc. RATING 88
DRINK 2021–2022 $19 JH

DCB Wine   ★★★★

505 Gembrook Road, Hoddles Creek, Vic 3139 **Region** Yarra Valley
T 0419 545 544 **www**.dcbwine.com.au **Winemaker** Chris Bendle **Est.** 2013
Dozens 1300
DCB is a busman's holiday for Chris Bendle, currently a winemaker at Hoddles Creek Estate,
where he has been since 2010. He previously made wine in Tasmania, NZ and Oregon, so
he is the right person to provide wines that are elegant, affordable and reward the pleasure of
drinking (Chris's aim); the wines also offer excellent value. Exports to the UK and Japan. (JH)

 Chardonnay 2021, Yarra Valley A bright green gold. Stone fruits intermingle
with more savoury, charcuterie notes and a little grilled cashew. Taut, with good
persistence, this very well-priced modern Yarra chardonnay should fill out nicely
over next 6–12 months. Screw cap. 13.1% alc. RATING 92 DRINK 2022–2025
$25 PR●
Pinot Noir 2021, Yarra Valley A light bright crimson. With its aromas of
cherries and brown spice, this bright, light-to medium-bodied and savoury wine
flows nicely across the palate. Fine, powdery tannins round out wine that will
provide both value and enjoyment in the short–medium term. Screw cap. 13% alc.
RATING 92 DRINK 2022–2026 $25 PR●

De Beaurepaire Wines

182 Cudgegong Road, Rylstone, NSW 2849 **Region** Central Ranges
T 0429 787 705 **www.**debeaurepairewines.com **Open** Wed–Sun 11–5
Winemaker Richard de Beaurepaire, Will de Beaurepaire, Jacob Stein (Contract),
Lisa Bray (Contract), Alex Cassegrain (Contract) **Viticulturist** Richard de Beaurepaire
Est. 1998 **Dozens** 12000 **Vyds** 55ha

The large De Beaurepaire vineyard was planted by Janet and Richard de Beaurepaire in
'98 and is situated on one of the oldest properties west of the Blue Mountains, in Rylstone,
at an altitude of 570–600m. The altitude, coupled with limestone soils and frontage to the
Cudgegong River, provides grapes (and hence wines) very different from the Mudgee norm
(hence they prefer to use the broader Central Ranges GI). The vineyard is planted to merlot,
shiraz, cabernet sauvignon, pinot noir, petit verdot, viognier, chardonnay, semillon and pinot
gris. Exports to Singapore, the Philippines, Fiji, Japan, Thailand, Cambodia and France. (JH)

♙♙♙♙♙ **Leopold Rylstone Shiraz Viognier 2017, Central Ranges** While Côte
Rôtie is clearly the aspirational model, this is far weightier. But very good. Sweet
loamy scents meld with riffs on dark cherry, sassafras and kirsch. The tannins,
pixelated and doused with pepper and clove. Dutch licorice, too. The finish, long
and forceful; yet composed and elegant. A chiaroscuro of complexities. Screw cap.
14.5% alc. RATING 95 DRINK 2022-2032 $60 NG

La Comtesse Rylstone Chardonnay 2018, Central Ranges Sophisticated,
finely tuned and benefitting from some bottle age. This reminds me of a
contemporary expression from the Mâconnais. Plump but tensile, all at once.
White peach, nectarine, vanilla pod, nougat and toasted hazelnuts. Long and
streamlined. Exceptional drinking now and across a short to early mid-term
window. Screw cap. 12.7% alc. RATING 94 DRINK 2021-2025 $35 NG

Victor Rylstone Cabernet Sauvignon 2017, Central Ranges This is
coming into its own nicely. A cool, attenuated season. And it shows. Hedgerow,
mint, red and black currant. This feels far more savoury, fresh and delicate than
the alcohol on the label suggests. Medium bodied of feel. Long and lithe. A little
prickly, but the drinkability is such that the structural elements melt into the
confluence of parts. Screw cap. 14.5% alc. RATING 94 DRINK 2021-2027 $60 NG

♙♙♙♙♙ **Jeannette Reserve Rylstone Chardonnay 2018, Central Ranges**
RATING 93 DRINK 2022-2030 $60 NG

Billet Doux Rylstone Semillon Sauvignon Blanc 2018, Central Ranges
RATING 92 DRINK 2021-2023 $30 NG

De Bortoli

Pinnacle Lane, Dixons Creek, Vic 3775 **Region** Yarra Valley
T (03) 5965 2271 **www.**debortoli.com.au **Open** 7 days 10–5 **Winemaker** Stephen
Webber, Sarah Fagan, Andrew Bretherton **Viticulturist** Rob Sutherland, Andrew Ray,
Brian Dwyer **Est.** 1987 **Dozens** 350000 **Vyds** 520ha

Arguably the most successful of all Yarra Valley wineries, not only in terms of the sheer volume
of production but also the quality of its wines. It is run by the husband-and-wife team of
Leanne De Bortoli and Steve Webber, but owned by the De Bortoli family. The wines are
released in 3 quality (and price) groups: at the top Single Vineyard, then Estate Grown and in
third place Villages. Small-volume labels increase the offer with Riorret Single Vineyard Pinot
Noir, Melba, La Bohème, an aromatic range of Yarra Valley wines and Vinoque, enabling trials
(at the commercial level) of new varieties and interesting blends in the Yarra. The Bella Riva
Italian varietal wines are sourced from the King Valley, and Windy Peak from Victorian regions
including the Yarra, King Valley and Heathcote. The PHI wines are made from the 7.5ha
Lusatia Park Vineyard established by the Shelmerdine family in the Yarra Valley, purchased in
November '15, and from Heathcote. Rutherglen Estates was added to the De Bortoli portfolio
in 2019. Exports to all major markets. (JH)

♙♙♙♙♙ **PHI Gamay Noir 2021, Yarra Valley** Vibrant crimson. Reminiscent of
cru Beaujolais with its aromas of dark cherries, satsuma plums, violets and

spice. Medium bodied and very nicely weighted, this has excellent depth while remaining light on its feet at the same time. Finishes long with crunchy, perfectly judged chalky tannins. A joy to drink. Screw cap.,13.3% alc. RATING 97 DRINK 2022-2028 $35 PR ✪ ♥

✿✿✿✿✿ **PHI Single Vineyard Pinot Noir 2021, Yarra Valley** A light, very bright crimson. Perfumed and bright as a button with its aromas of pomegranate, cranberries and strawberries along with a dusting of Asian spices. Equally bright on the palate, it's not a big wine, but it's got good depth. It finishes with crisp acidity and fine, supple tannins, giving this lovely wine structure and focus. Screw cap. 13.5% alc. RATING 96 DRINK 2022-2028 $33 PR ✪

Lusatia Chardonnay 2019, Yarra Valley A very bright and fresh green gold. Aromas of ruby grapefruit, lemon butter on charred toast, with some lightly grilled cashews. Fleshy on entry, the palate is well balanced with good weight. A fine line of acidity runs through the wine culminating in an impressive, wet-stone finish. Screw cap. 12.5% alc. RATING 96 DRINK 2022-2028 $80 PR

Melba Vineyard Cabernet Sauvignon 2019, Yarra Valley Only released in good years. A medium-deep cherry red. Aromas of cassis, black plum, olive tapenade and cigar box are present, developing complexity the longer it sits in the glass. Medium bodied, richly fruited and structured, this impressive wine was built for the long haul. It will reward those with both the wallet and patience to cellar it. Screw cap. 13% alc. RATING 96 DRINK 2024-2034 $150 PR

PHI Grenache Amphora 2021, Heathcote A fascinating winemaking – and tasting – experience. The use of a terracotta amphora delivers a primary, pure flavour and intensity in cherry, plum, anise and baked earth. There's an easy balance and minerality here – thank the ancient Cambrian soils – which combines with a developing textural intrigue to deliver a wine of poise and grace. Screw cap. 14% alc. RATING 95 DRINK 2022-2031 $44 JP

Riorret Lusatia Park Pinot Noir 2020, Yarra Valley A medium ruby crimson. Bright, with briary red fruits, orange peel and a little allspice. Good depth and crunch on the palate, this relies as much on the wine's fresh acidity for its structure as it does on its fine, silky tannins. A lovely wine from this great site in the Yarra. Screw cap. 13.5% alc. RATING 95 DRINK 2022-2029 $45 PR

Section A8 Syrah 2020, Yarra Valley A vibrant crimson purple. Ultra-perfumed and lifted with red and black fruits and whole-bunch-inspired pink peppercorns. Medium bodied and firmly structured, this savoury and compact wine will need at least another 6–12 months to open up and become even more seductive. Screw cap. 14.2% alc. RATING 95 DRINK 2022-2029 $55 PR

Estate Grown Cabernet Sauvignon 2019, Yarra Valley An impressive deep crimson purple. Textbook Yarra cabernet, redolent of perfectly ripened blackberry and cranberry fruits intermingled with gentle cedary oak and a touch of blackberry leaf. Medium bodied, with excellent concentration and structure, this extremely well priced wine is delicious now but, equally, will still be looking good 10 years from now. Screw cap. 13% alc. RATING 95 DRINK 2023-2030 $28 PR ✪

Lusatia Pinot Noir 2019, Yarra Valley A very deep ruby red. Densely packed with dark plums, Christmas cake spices and a complex cured meat/umami character. A rich mouthful of dark plummy fruit, with powdery and persistent tannins rounding out a wine that will need another 2–3 years before it really hits its straps. Screw cap. 13.7% alc. RATING 94 DRINK 2023-2030 $100 PR

De Bortoli (Riverina)   ★★★★☆

De Bortoli Road, Bilbul, NSW 2680 **Region** Riverina
T (02) 6966 0100 **www.**debortoli.com.au **Open** Mon–Sat 9–5, Sun 9–4
Winemaker Darren De Bortoli, Julie Mortlock, John Coughlan **Viticulturist** Kevin De Bortoli **Est.** 1928 **Vyds** 367ha

Famous among the cognoscenti for its superb Noble One, which in fact accounts for only a tiny part of its total production, this winery turns out low-priced varietal wines that are invariably competently made. They come from estate vineyards, but also from contract-grown grapes. In June '12 De Bortoli received a $4.8 million grant from the Federal Government's Clean Technology Food and Foundries Investment Program. This grant supported an additional investment of $11 million by the De Bortoli family in their 'Re-engineering Our Future for a Carbon Economy' project. De Bortoli is a founding member of Australia's First Families of Wine. Exports to all major markets. (JH)

ΨΨΨΨΨ **Black Noble NV, Riverina** A blend of select barrels of Noble One, fortified and aged on average 10 years. Spiritous and heady, with a waft of volatility servicing punch and a lilt of freshness across notes of spiced dates, cinnamon, char, walnut, polished floor boards, tamarind and clove. Extremely exotic, unctuous and resinous. Morocco revisited in liquid form. The complexity, a given. The finish, endless. Screw cap. 17.5% alc. RATING 96 $52 NG ✪
Old Boys 21 Years Old Tawny NV Fine aromas brimming with the aged complexity of a mediaeval souk: mahogany, date, walnut, cedar, tamarind, sandalwood and bitter orange. A volatile rancio riff services lift and freshness. This is a compelling wine on many levels. I wish the acidity was not so shrill, but there is plenty of nourishing warmth to placate it. Screw cap. 19% alc. RATING 94 $64 NG

ΨΨΨΨΨ **8 Years Old Fine Tawny NV** RATING 93 $34 NG
Show Liqueur 8 Years Old Muscat NV, Riverina RATING 93 $36 NG
Noble One Botrytis Semillon 2019, Riverina RATING 93 DRINK 2022-2040 $94 NG
Deen De Bortoli Vat 5 Botrytis Semillon 2018, Riverina RATING 91 DRINK 2022-2032 $17 NG ✪

de Capel Wines ★★★★

101 Majors Lane, Lovedale, NSW 2320 **Region** Hunter Valley
T 0419 994 299 www.decapelwines.com.au **Open** By appt **Winemaker** Daniel Binet **Viticulturist** Jenny Bright **Est.** 2008 **Dozens** 400 **Vyds** 2ha
Owners David and Elisabeth Capel's love of wine and a rural life led them to the purchase of their 11ha property in '01 at which time the land (previously used for livestock) was mainly cleared, with small patches of remnant vegetation. It wasn't until '08 that they undertook major soil improvements, installed all of the vineyard infrastructure and personally planted 2.2ha of vines under the direction of viticulturist Jenny Bright. They say, 'We are very fortunate to have the support (and muscle) of our close friends and family who put in an amazing effort every vintage and help us to hand-pick every single grape that we grow'. It precisely follows the early years (1971–77) of Brokenwood. (JH)

ΨΨΨΨΨ **Josephine Semillon 2021, Hunter Valley** Cool-fermented. Strong typicity of region and varietal representation. Lemon drop, tatami hay, lemongrass, raw almond and icy pole. Crunchy, fresh and long, with a welcome rail of phenolic pucker adding additional detail. Screw cap. 10.5% alc. RATING 92 DRINK 2021-2033 $25 NG ✪
Henry Chardonnay 2021, Hunter Valley A fine, cool, attenuate vintage. Unusual in the best sense. This, as with the range, offers good drinking: balanced, uncluttered and extremely versatile. Cantaloupe, white peach and cashew flavours are contained within a deftly applied rim of gentle vanilla-pod oak. Screw cap. 13% alc. RATING 91 DRINK 2021-2025 $25 NG

De Iuliis ★★★★★

1616 Broke Road, Pokolbin, NSW 2320 **Region** Hunter Valley
T (02) 4993 8000 www.dewine.com.au **Open** 7 days 10–5 **Winemaker** Michael De Iuliis **Est.** 1990 **Dozens** 15 000 **Vyds** 30ha
The Iuliis family acquired a property at Lovedale in '86 and planted 18ha of vines in '90, selling the grapes from the first few vintages to Tyrrell's but retaining increasing amounts for release under the De Iuliis label. In '99 the land on Broke Road was purchased and a winery and cellar door were built prior to the '00 vintage. In '11 De Iuliis purchased 12ha of

the long-established Steven Vineyard in Pokolbin. Winemaker Michael De Iuliis completed postgraduate studies in oenology at the Roseworthy campus of the University of Adelaide and was a Len Evans Tutorial scholar. He has lifted the quality of the wines into the highest echelon. Exports to the US, Belgium, Italy and Singapore. (JH)

🍷🍷🍷🍷🍷 **Single Vineyard Semillon 2021, Hunter Valley** The Garden vineyard is planted on the sandy flats of central Pokolbin, the grapes hand picked on Jan '22, and whole-bunch pressed to tank for a slow cool ferment. It's a glorious semillon, unusually expressive for its age, both opulently rich and fruit-complex with Tahitian lime and Meyer lemon, backed by touches of nectarine. Screw cap. 10.5% alc. RATING 96 DRINK 2022-2036 $35 JH ✪

The Garden Vineyard Semillon 2021, Hunter Valley This has the makings of a real keeper. Austere. Demure. Yet the skein of extract that runs toe to toe with the fine line of acidity, is impressive. It makes one wonder what lies behind it all. Only time will tell. Raw ginger, spa salts, jasmine and gin and tonic, the current notes. Await the crescendo! Screw cap. 10.5% alc. RATING 95 DRINK 2021-2033 $45 NG

Limited Release Shiraz 2019, Hunter Valley A sumptuous interpretation of a warm year. Lots of extract, complemented by oak that, while still unresolved, should find its place in time. Blue and black fruits. A core of raspberry liqueur. Spice, sassafras and Hunter earth, driving long. Bury this and believe. Screw cap. 14.4% alc. RATING 95 DRINK 2022-2033 $80 NG

Aged Release Semillon 2016, Hunter Valley This address' aged releases are always impressive. This, no exception. Candied barley and ginger. Lanolin, lemon drop and quince. Brioche, too. The finish is not one marked by the precision and effortless flow of top years. Yet I like the mesh of phenolic texture and moderate freshness, perhaps as much. This makes for excellent versatility at the table. Delicious wine. Screw cap. 11% alc. RATING 95 DRINK 2021-2026 $45 NG

Special Release Pecorino 2021, Hunter Valley A variety from the Marche and Abruzzo regions of central Italy, the first such planted in the Hunter Valley. The dried herb and citrus-skin aromas are striking, and carry onto the palate without missing a beat. It has a similar in-your-face power to fiano, in each case increasing their textural allure – and shouting for food matches. Screw cap. 12% alc. RATING 94 DRINK 2021-2026 $25 JH ✪

🍷🍷🍷🍷🍷 **LDR Vineyard Shiraz 2020, Hunter Valley** RATING 93 DRINK 2021-2026 $40 NG

Semillon 2021, Hunter Valley RATING 92 DRINK 2021-2026 $25 NG ✪
LDR Vineyard Shiraz Touriga 2020, Hunter Valley RATING 92 DRINK 2021-2023 $40 NG
Steven Vineyard Shiraz 2020, Hunter Valley RATING 92 DRINK 2021-2025 $40 NG
Chardonnay 2021, Hunter Valley RATING 91 DRINK 2021-2024 $25 NG
Special Release Montepulciano 2021, Hunter Valley RATING 91 DRINK 2021-2022 $35 NG
Shiraz 2020, Hunter Valley RATING 90 DRINK 2025-2035 $25 JH

Deep Woods Estate ★★★★★

889 Commonage Road, Yallingup, WA 6282 **Region** Margaret River
T (08) 9756 6066 **www.**deepwoods.wine **Open** Mon, Wed–Sun – 10–5
Winemaker Julian Langworthy, Emma Gillespie, Andrew Bretherton **Viticulturist** John Fogarty **Est.** 1987 **Dozens** 50000 **Vyds** 14ha
Deep Woods Estate is a key part of the dynamic wine business of Peter Fogarty that includes Millbrook in the Perth Hills, Evans & Tate, Margaret River Vintners and extensive vineyard holdings in Wilyabrup and elsewhere in Margaret River, plus in Smithbrook in Pemberton. The Fogarty business is the largest producer in WA with 600000 dozen. There is a similar multifaceted stream in Tasmania, with Tasmanian Vintners (a 50/50% deal between Peter and Tasmanian businessman Rod Roberts), the acquisition of the outstanding Lowestoft Vineyard

planted in the '80s with pinot noir in high-density configuration and a 120ha vineyard site at Forcett. Lake's Folly in the Hunter Valley was the first move, Dalwhinnie in the Pyrenees the most recent acquisition. Exports to Germany, Malaysia, Singapore and Japan. Deep Woods is the Wine Companion 2023 Best Value Winery. (JH)

ΨΨΨΨΨ **Single Vineyard G5 Cabernet Sauvignon 2020, Margaret River** Rose petals, raspberry leaf tea, red snakes, Szechuan and pink peppercorns and red apple skins. This is gorgeous. Utterly, utterly beautiful. The fruit is ripe and rippling, the tannins poised and totally in cahoots, working together to spiral across the palate and fly through the finish. Arm in arm, they spool out flavour as they go, all of it caught in the web of fine, saline acidity. Screw cap. 14% alc. RATING 97 DRINK 2022-2037 $50 EL ✪

Reserve Chardonnay 2020, Margaret River To say the wine is elegant does it no justice. It's way more than that; line, length and balance likewise. This is a barrel-by-barrel selection from a large number, ex a specific vineyard source. White peach and pink grapefruit play off against each other, oak a means to an end. Screw cap. 13% alc. RATING 97 DRINK 2022-2042 $65 JH ✪

Reserve Cabernet Sauvignon 2019, Margaret River Deep, vivid crimson purple. Fascinating bouquet that has the bay leaf I often find on the back palate/ finish of quality cabernet sauvignon; also cassis (no surprise) wrapped in a fine gauze of oak and pliable tannins. Line, length and balance are all attributes of a classic Margaret River cabernet. Screw cap. 14% alc. RATING 97 DRINK 2024-2049 $85 JH ✪

ΨΨΨΨΨ **Single Vineyard Cabernet Malbec 2020, Margaret River** This is a sensational wine, impossibly intense and saturated with flavour, and the volume is boosted in 2020. Decant it, because the frisky malbec needs the oxygen to calm it down. It'll live an age, though. Screw cap. 14% alc. RATING 96 DRINK 2022-2037 $50 EL ✪

Reserve Shiraz 2020, Margaret River This is as powerful as any of its breed, with the blackest of black fruits and tannins normally the confines of cabernet sauvignon, French oak lost in the wash. Screw cap. 14% alc. RATING 96 DRINK 2030-2045 $65 JH ✪

Sauvignon Blanc 2021, Margaret River Much richer – and more complex – than the vast majority, with the precision brought by the cool Karridale district in the far south of Margaret River, the busts of passionfruit and snow peas, and the smoky notes ex barrel ferment that all play hide and seek on the bouquet and palate alike. Impossible to beat the value offered here. Screw cap. 13% alc. RATING 95 DRINK 2021-2023 $20 JH ✪

Single Vineyard Chardonnay 2021, Margaret River A cool vintage, coupled with the southern growing area of Karridale, has imbued this wine with laser acidity and precise drive in the mouth. With citrus, red apples, white peach, creamy cashews and loads of brine (with some apricot squares through the finish) this provides a startlingly clear view of the 'other' style of chardonnay that Margaret River does so well. Harnessed volume is converted into superfine layers of taut fruit. It's concentrated, but it's also glass-like, with shards of acidity and chalky phenolics. Very cool. Screw cap. 13% alc. RATING 95 DRINK 2022-2032 $50 EL

Rosé 2021, Margaret River Expansive, full of flavour and textural, this is yet another exciting release of the estate rosé. Red apples, raspberry, lemony acidity and oodles of exotic market spices. Finer and more precise than the '20 release, in line with the cool year that birthed it. Screw cap. 13% alc. RATING 94 DRINK 2021-2024 $35 EL

Hillside Cabernet Sauvignon 2020, Margaret River Just $25, and you know it's going to be good. Fine, shapely, powdery tannins (slightly chewy, too) back up the concentrated ripe red and black berry fruit. With a sprinkling of ground star anise, peppercorns and laced together with briny acidity, this is a cracking little wine. Super-smart. Screw cap. 14% alc. RATING 94 DRINK 2021-2031 $25 EL ✪

Cabernet Sauvignon Merlot 2020, Margaret River '20 was a glorious vintage and it's here for all to see. Structural, dense, concentrated and broody, the length of flavour tails out through the long finish – in fact, far longer than any $35 wine has any business being. Screw cap. 14% alc. RATING 94 DRINK 2021–2035 $35 EL

Shiraz et al 2020, Margaret River Vivid colour. $20 beggars belief. It's the real deal – a wine with layer upon layer of red and black fruits and serious tannins, and then given that time in French oak. Screw cap. 14.5% alc. RATING 94 DRINK 2023–2033 $20 JH ✪

Delamere Vineyards   ★★★★

Bridport Road, Pipers Brook, Tas 7254 **Region** Northern Tasmania
T (03) 6382 7190 **www**.delamerevineyards.com.au **Open** Fri–Mon 10.30–4.30, or by appt **Winemaker** Shane Holloway, Fran Austin **Est.** 1982 **Dozens** 5000 **Vyds** 12ha
Delamere was one of the first vineyards planted in the Pipers Brook area. It was purchased by Shane Holloway and Fran Austin and their families in '07. Shane and Fran are in charge of viticulture and winemaking. The vineyard has since been expanded, doubling the area under vine to 12ha, planted exclusively to pinot noir and chardonnay. (JH)

🍷🍷🍷🍷🍷 **Rosé NV, Tasmania** 100% pinot noir. This is hands down their finest non-vintage rendition yet. It brims with the inimitable, glorious rosewater and Turkish delight perfume that signs Pipers River pinot, carrying a vibrant palate of exact wild strawberry and red-cherry precision. Sporting a pretty, pale salmon hue, it delivers impressive fruit presence and freshness, energised by perfectly ripe and wonderfully energetic acidity. Diam. 13.1% alc. RATING 93 $40 TS

Cuvée 2016, Tasmania aged 4 years on lees; 3g/L dosage. The '16 vintage has delivered a rich and solid vintage cuvée, well handled by Delamere to yield a cuvée of integrity and attraction. The ripeness of pineapple, Golden Delicious apple and bruised pear is heightened by the accentuated wild honey, fruit-mince spice and toast of 5 years age. Well-deployed phenolic grip brings control to succulent generosity, holding the finish with confidence and appeal. Diam. 12.5% alc. RATING 92 $55 TS

Late Disgorged Blanc de Blancs 2010, Tasmania Still projecting a bright, medium straw hue at 11 years of age, this is a notably ripe and powerful take on Pipers River chardonnay. It's got it all going on: bruised pear, Golden Delicious apple, grilled pineapple, glacé fig, honey, fruit mince spice, even suggestions of vegemite and pan juices. Time has brought creaminess to its texture, concluding with spicy, honeyed, sweet generosity. Screw cap. 13% alc. RATING 92 $150 TS

🍷🍷🍷🍷 **Cuvée NV, Tasmania** RATING 88 $40 TS

Delatite   ★★★★☆

390 Pollards Road, Mansfield, Vic 3722 **Region** Upper Goulburn
T (03) 5775 2922 **www**.delatitewinery.com.au **Open** 7 days 10–5 **Winemaker** Andy Browning **Viticulturist** David Ritchie **Est.** 1982 **Dozens** 16000 **Vyds** 28ha
With its sweeping views across to the snow-clad alps, this is uncompromising cool-climate viticulture. Increasing vine age (the earlier plantings were between 1968–82, others between '84–2011) and the adoption of organic (and partial biodynamic) viticulture, have also played a role in providing the red wines with more depth and texture. The white wines are all wild-yeast fermented and are as good as ever. Exports to the UK and Japan. (JH)

🍷🍷🍷🍷🍷 **Pinot Gris 2021, Upper Goulburn** An ultra-cool-climate vineyard meets its match in this young, complex, texturally exciting pinot gris. They were made for each other. A light blush colour indicates some skin contact, a good sign, before aromas burst in lively aromatics: citrus blossom, honeysuckle, green apple and spice. Glides across the tongue in spiced apple, pear and nougat with just a hint of sweetness. Plenty of flavour with terrific balance. Screw cap. 13% alc. RATING 95 DRINK 2022–2028 $30 JP ✪

♟♟♟♟♀ Pet Nat Riesling Gewürztraminer 2021, Upper Goulburn RATING 93
DRINK 2022–2022 $39 JP
Robert's Block Reserve Syrah 2019, Upper Goulburn RATING 93
DRINK 2021–2028 $110 JP
Tempranillo Rosé 2021, Upper Goulburn RATING 91 DRINK 2021–2025
$30 JP
Tempranillo 2020, Upper Goulburn RATING 91 DRINK 2021–2025 $38 JP
Mansfield Red 2019, Upper Goulburn RATING 90 DRINK 2021–2031 $38 JP
Donald's Block Reserve Cabernet Merlot 2018, Upper Goulburn
RATING 90 DRINK 2021–2030 $110 JP

Della Fay Wines

3276 Caves Road, Yallingup, WA 6284 **Region** Margaret River
T (08) 9755 2747 **www.**kellysvineyard.com.au **Open** By appt **Winemaker** Michael
Kelly **Viticulturist** Michael Kelly **Est.** 1999 **Dozens** 3000 **Vyds** 6.4ha
This is the venture of the Kelly family, headed by district veteran Michael Kelly. He gained his
degree in wine science from CSU before working at Seville Estate and Mount Mary in the
Yarra Valley and Domaine Louis Chapuis in Burgundy, then returning to WA and working for
Leeuwin Estate and Sandalford. Michael became the long-term winemaker at Fermoy Estate,
while he and his family laid the groundwork for their own brand, buying prime viticultural
land in Caves Road, Yallingup, in 1999. They planted cabernet sauvignon, sauvignon blanc,
vermentino, nebbiolo, chardonnay, merlot, malbec and petit verdot; they also make Shiraz
from Geographe. 'Della Fay' honours the eponymous Kelly family matriarch. Exports to the
Netherlands, South Korea, Singapore and Hong Kong. (JH)

♟♟♟♟♀ **Reserve Shiraz 2018, Geographe** Geographe is a really strong region for
shiraz in WA, but often overlooked in favour of some of the bigger names. It's like
the Little Engine That Could … This is concentrated and intense, layered with
fine shavings of deli meat, exotic market spice, blackberry, raspberry, fennel seeds
and clove through the finish. Screw cap. 14.5% alc. RATING 92 DRINK 2021–2028
$30 EL

Denton

Viewhill Vineyard, 160 Old Healesville Road, Yarra Glen, Vic 3775 **Region** Yarra Valley
T 0402 346 686 **www.**dentonwine.com **Open** By appt **Winemaker** Luke Lambert
Viticulturist Julian Parrott **Est.** 1997 **Dozens** 2500 **Vyds** 31.3ha
Leading Melbourne architect John Denton and son Simon began the establishment of
the vineyard with a first stage planting in '97, completing the plantings in '04. The name
Viewhill derives from the fact that a granite plug 'was created 370 million years ago, sitting
above the surrounding softer sandstones and silt of the valley'. This granite base is most
unusual in the Yarra Valley, and, together with the natural amphitheatre that the plug created,
has consistently produced exceptional grapes. The principal varieties planted are pinot noir,
chardonnay and nebbiolo. Exports to Japan and Hong Kong. (JH)

♟♟♟♟♟ **Nebbiolo 2019, Yarra Valley** A bright, medium, ruby red. There's lots going on
here. Aromas of dark cherries, cherry and sandalwood, dried roses, orange peel and
botanicals such as quinine and juniper. The palate is ripe and beautifully brought
back into focus by the wine's refreshing acidity and grippy yet fine tannins.
Finishes ferrous and long. Screw cap. 14% alc. RATING 96 DRINK 2023–2029
$70 PR ✪
Shed Nebbiolo 2020, Yarra Valley An impressive, deep, ruby crimson.
Highly aromatic with aromas of dark, morello cherries, chinotto, licorice root and
botanicals such as juniper and bergamot. Super-fresh on the palate, this is both
plush and sweetly-fruited, yet has plenty of drive and those signature, structured
nebbiolo tannins. A beautifully put together and well-priced wine by a winery
and winemaker who have really hit their stride with this difficult to nail variety.
Screw cap. 13.5% alc. RATING 95 DRINK 2022–2027 $44 PR

ettty Rosé Nebbiolo 2021, Yarra Valley RATING 93 DRINK 2022-2024 $40 PR
Shed Chardonnay 2021, Yarra Valley RATING 92 DRINK 2022-2025 $30 PR
Shed Pinot Noir 2021, Yarra Valley RATING 91 DRINK 2021-2026 $30 PR

Derwent Estate ★★★★

329 Lyell Highway, Granton, Tas 7070 **Region** Southern Tasmania
T (03) 6263 5802 **www**.derwentestate.com.au **Open** 7 days 10–5 **Winemaker** John
Schuts **Viticulturist** Andrew Hanigan **Est.** 1992 **Dozens** 10000 **Vyds** 10.75ha
Three generations of the Hanigan family are involved in the management of their historic
Mt Nassau property, owned by the family since 1913. Given that over the last 100 years the
property has at various times been involved with sheep, cattle, vegetable production, quarrying
and the production of lime, the addition of viticulture in '92 was not surprising. The vineyard
has grown in stages, some of the grapes bound for Bay of Fires and Penfolds Yattarna. The
grapes retained by Derwent Estate have produced consistently exceptional wines. Exports to
Japan. (JH)

etttt Chardonnay 2019, Tasmania From a cool site that supplied the legendary
Penfolds Yattarna for 10 years straight, this is a chardonnay of impressive freshness
and drive at a full 3 years of age. Accurate, bright lemon, white peach and
grapefruit are eloquently supported by the texture and cashew nut influence of
partial wild fermentation in 25% new French oak barrels. Impressive line and
lingering, crystalline acidity promise great things in the cellar. Screw cap. 13.2% alc.
RATING 94 DRINK 2024-2032 $50 TS

ettty Calcaire Chardonnay 2018, Tasmania RATING 93 DRINK 2028-2038 $89 TS

Deviation Road ★★★★★

207 Scott Creek Road, Longwood, SA 5153 **Region** Adelaide Hills
T (08) 8339 2633 **www**.deviationroad.com **Open** 7 days 10–5 **Winemaker** Kate Laurie
Est. 1999 **Dozens** 8000 **Vyds** 11.05ha
Continuing a 5-generation family winemaking tradition, Hamish and Kate Laurie created
their first wine from the 30yo Laurie family-owned vineyard on Deviation Road in '02. In '04
Hamish and Kate purchased their property at Longwood, which is the current home to 4ha of
shiraz and pinot noir, the winery and tasting room. Disgorging equipment from Kate's family's
Manjimup winery, originally imported from Champagne, was shipped to the Adelaide Hills in
'08 enabling the first Deviation Road traditional method sparkling wine release. Hamish and
Kate consistently produce wines that represent the cool-climate terroir of the Adelaide Hills.
Exports to the UK, the US and Hong Kong. (JH)

etttt Altair Brut Rosé NV, Adelaide Hills 55/45% pinot noir/chardonnay. Base
vintage '18; 40 months on lees. Disgorged Oct '21. 8g/L dosage. A finely beaded,
salmon-pink sparkling that rates among Australia's best. Confidently presented
with complexity and poise, Altair wears a delicate sheen of savoury autolysis with
almonds, baked pastry, poached pear, bright red berries aromas. Layer upon layer
of delicate flavour, texture and depth. Runs fine, long and so impressive. All class.
Cork. 12.5% alc. RATING 96 $38 JP ✪ ❤
Beltana Blanc de Blancs 2015, Adelaide Hills 74 months on lees. Disgorged
Sept '21. 6g/L dosage. So enticing in aromas of white peach, citrus and apple with
oyster shell and sea spray. Fresh as yesterday with outstanding, mouth-watering
lemony acidity, and then the deep complexity of flavours comes into full view and
wow. Super-elegant. Cork. 12.5% alc. RATING 95 $105 JP
Sauvignon Blanc 2021, Adelaide Hills Typically pure and super-expressive
for a Hills sauvignon, dressed in Tahitian lime, green mango, gooseberry and citrus.
Feel the depth of fruit and intensity of flavour on the palate: so, so impressive.
Clean, tangy and supple, with a snow-pea-shoot green finish. Screw cap. 12.5% alc.
RATING 95 DRINK 2021-2025 $30 JP ✪

🍷🍷🍷🍷♀ Loftia Vintage Brut 2018, Adelaide Hills RATING 93 $48 JP
Chardonnay 2021, Adelaide Hills RATING 93 DRINK 2022-2030 $48 JP
Pinot Noir 2021, Adelaide Hills RATING 93 DRINK 2022-2027 $55 JP
Mary's Reserve Shiraz 2020, Adelaide Hills RATING 93 DRINK 2022-2030 $65 JP
Pinot Gris 2021, Adelaide Hills RATING 92 DRINK 2021-2026 $30 JP
Southcote Blanc de Noirs 2019, Adelaide Hills RATING 92 DRINK 2022 $50 JP

Devil's Corner

The Hazards Vineyard, Sherbourne Road, Apslawn, Tas 7190 **Region** East Coast Tasmania
T (03) 6257 8881 **www**.devilscorner.com.au **Open** 7 days 10–5 **Winemaker** Tom
Wallace, Anthony de Amicis **Est.** 1999 **Dozens** 70 000 **Vyds** 175ha
Long the affordable little sibling of Tamar Ridge and Pirie within the Brown Family Wine
Group, Devil's Corner has increasingly grown up into a premium wine identity in its own
right. Its home is the spectacular and picturesque Hazards Vineyard on Tasmania's East Coast,
still the largest vineyard in the state, though the company's Kayena Vineyard (see Tamar Ridge)
is also a substantial source for many of its blends. Riesling, sauvignon blanc, chardonnay,
pinot gris, pinot noir and sparkling are all prominent in its range, with a premium pinot noir
syrah blend recently introduced, and a straight syrah in the pipeline. The cellar door offers
sensational views across the Hazards Vineyard to the Freycinet peninsula and The Hazards
range itself. Exports to all major markets. (JH)

🍷🍷🍷🍷🍷 Mt Dove Pinot Syrah 2020, Tasmania The pinot/syrah blend is seeing a
quiet renaissance among top producers across Australia's cooler zones, and is an
exciting new direction for Devil's Corner. The fine-ground pepper and powder-
fine tannins of Derwent Valley syrah mesh seamlessly with a red cherry core of
Hazards Vineyard pinot noir. Whole bunches and oak have been fine-tuned to let
vibrant acidity and those crafted tannins draw out a long finish. Patience. Screw
cap. 13.2% alc. RATING 94 DRINK 2025-2030 $65 TS
Resolution Chardonnay 2019, Tasmania Resolution represents fantastic value,
and a big step up from the entry-level Devil's Corner repertoire. Tamar and East
Coast Tasmania unite here with impressive precision of grapefruit and white peach,
nicely contrasting with the cashew of French oak. It will appreciate a year or 2 to
find its feet. Tasmanian acidity lays out a bright, long, mineral finish that promises
medium-term endurance. Screw cap. 12.5% alc. RATING 94 DRINK 2023-2029
$34 TS

🍷🍷🍷🍷♀ Pinot Noir Rosé 2021, Tasmania RATING 93 DRINK 2021-2022 $25 TS ✪
Pinot Grigio 2021, Tasmania RATING 91 DRINK 2021-2022 $22 TS ✪
Resolution Pinot Noir 2019, Tasmania RATING 90 DRINK 2027-2034 $34 TS

Devil's Lair

Rocky Road, Forest Grove via Margaret River, WA 6286 **Region** Margaret River
T (08) 9759 2000 **www**.devils-lair.com **Winemaker** Ben Miller, Matt Godfrey **Est.** 1990
Having rapidly carved out a high reputation for itself through a combination of clever
packaging and impressive wine quality, Devil's Lair was acquired by Southcorp in '96. The
estate vineyards have been substantially increased since, now with sauvignon blanc, semillon,
chardonnay, cabernet sauvignon, merlot, shiraz, cabernet franc and petit verdot, supplemented
by grapes purchased from contract growers. Production has increased from 40 000 dozen to
many times greater, largely due to its Fifth Leg and Dance with the Devil wines. The top-tier
9th Chamber wines are only made in exceptional vintages. Exports to the UK, the US and
other major markets. (JH)

🍷🍷🍷🍷🍷 Cabernet Sauvignon 2020, Margaret River Silky, supple and so typically
Margaret River cabernet here. The fruit is both red and black, shimmering and
dappled in its own way. The tannins are more assertive here than in previous
vintages, but that's no surprise coming from the powerfully ripe '20 vintage. The

fruit is more than up to the task, the length of flavour ultimately indicating its quality and future potential. Screw cap. 14% alc. RATING 95 DRINK 2021-2036 $50 EL

🍷🍷🍷🍷🍷 **Chardonnay 2020, Margaret River** RATING 93 DRINK 2021-2030 $50 JH
Dance with the Devil Chardonnay 2020, Margaret River RATING 92 DRINK 2021-2025 $15 JH ✪
Dance with the Devil Cabernet Sauvignon 2020, Margaret River RATING 92 DRINK 2021-2028 $25 EL ✪
The Hidden Cave Cabernet Shiraz 2020, Margaret River RATING 91 DRINK 2021-2027 $25 EL

Dexter Wines   ★★★★★

210 Foxeys Road, Tuerong, Vic 3915 (postal) **Region** Mornington Peninsula
T (03) 5989 7007 **www.**dexterwines.com.au **Winemaker** Tod Dexter **Viticulturist** Tod Dexter **Est.** 2006 **Dozens** 1800 **Vyds** 7.1ha
Tod Dexter travelled to the US with the intention of enjoying some skiing; having done that, he became an apprentice winemaker at Cakebread Cellars, a well-known Napa Valley establishment. After 7 years he returned to the Mornington Peninsula, and began the establishment of his vineyard in '87; planted to pinot noir (4ha) and chardonnay (3.1ha). To keep the wolves from the door he became winemaker at Stonier and leased his vineyard to them. Having left Stonier to become the Yabby Lake winemaker, and spurred on by turning 50 in '06 (and at the urging of friends), he and wife Debbie established the Dexter label. The quality of his wines has been impeccable, the Pinot Noir especially so. Exports to the UAE and Japan. (JH)

🍷🍷🍷🍷🍷 **Chardonnay 2021, Mornington Peninsula** There's good drive and energy in the glass, thanks to the refreshing acidity. Of course there's more than that. There's a citrus party going on, with juice, zest, lemon balm and curd. The palate is tight yet a mille-feuille of creamy lees adds to the enjoyment; the finish is long and intense. Screw cap. 13.5% alc. RATING 95 DRINK 2022-2031 $45 JF
Pinot Noir 2021, Mornington Peninsula A lovely pinot that sits comfortably in its light- to mid-weighted palate, filled with juicy cherries, a squeeze of blood orange plus a pleasing savoury overlay. Lots of heady spices and a hint of eucalyptus and native mint. The oak is tucked in nicely, with supple tannins. There's nothing else to do but to pour it. Now. Screw cap. 13.5% alc. RATING 95 DRINK 2022-2031 $60 JF

🍷🍷🍷🍷🍷 **Pinot Noir 2020, Mornington Peninsula** RATING 92 DRINK 2021-2027 $60 JF

DiGiorgio Family Wines   ★★★★

14918 Riddoch Highway, Coonawarra, SA 5263 **Region** Coonawarra
T (08) 8736 3222 **www.**digiorgio.com.au **Open** 7 days 10–5 **Winemaker** Peter Douglas, Bryan Tonkin **Est.** 1998 **Dozens** 25000 **Vyds** 353.53ha
Stefano DiGiorgio emigrated from Abruzzo, Italy, in 1952. Over the years, he and his family gradually expanded their holdings at Lucindale to 126ha. In '89 he began planting cabernet sauvignon, chardonnay, merlot, shiraz and pinot noir. In '02 the family purchased the historic Rouge Homme winery and its surrounding 13.5ha of vines from Southcorp. The plantings have since been increased to over 350ha, the lion's share to cabernet sauvignon. The enterprise offers full winemaking services to vignerons on the Limestone Coast. Exports to all major markets. (JH)

🍷🍷🍷🍷🍷 **Sparkling Merlot 2020, Coonawarra** No oak. It's soft (both texturally, and with regards to the mousse), plush and littered with black and purple berries and red licorice. The sweetness through the finish balances any tannins that are hanging around. Lush. Screw cap. 13% alc. RATING 90 $29 EL

Kongorong Riesling 2021, Mount Gambier Spring florals and lime zest on the nose. In the mouth it gathers momentum, with green apples and pithy acidity, talcy texture the stars. Smart, mineral and very fine. The '21 vintage is a sensational lens through which to view this wine. Screw cap. 11.9% alc. RATING 90 DRINK 2022-2028 $20 EL ✪

Lucindale Shiraz 2020, Limestone Coast Really good intensity here, with savoury tannins shaping black forest fruits, and all of it wrapped in a slick, sweet oak box. Nicely done. Great value for money. Screw cap. 14% alc. RATING 90 DRINK 2022-2027 $20 EL ✪

Montepulciano 2020, Limestone Coast Very bright and juicy, with lashings of field strawberries and blood, deli meat, cherries and licorice. There's an attractive rusticity about this that elevates it (could be the tannins) and is very appealing. Screw cap. 13.5% alc. RATING 90 DRINK 2022-2025 $25 EL

Cabernet Sauvignon 2019, Coonawarra Satisfying intensity of fruit here – there's a hint of leaf, but it refrains from being herbal ... think more along the lines of brambly cassis and blackberry. The oak makes a firm but otherwise well-integrated impact on the wine . It's an old-school vibe, but it's well handled. Screw cap. 13.5% alc. RATING 90 DRINK 2022-2029 $29 EL

Emporio Merlot Cabernet Sauvignon Cabernet Franc 2019, Coonawarra Soft and plush, this is layered with blackberry, cocoa, cassis and red earth. It is leafy and gentle, with a smattering of exotic spice through the finish (star anise, licorice root and blood plum). Classical. Screw cap. 13.5% alc. RATING 90 DRINK 2022-2029 $29 EL

♟♟♟♟ **Lucindale Cabernet Sauvignon 2019, Limestone Coast** RATING 89 DRINK 2022-2026 $20 EL

Cabernet Franc 2021, Coonawarra RATING 88 DRINK 2022-2025 $25 EL

Dinny Goonan ★★★★☆

880 Winchelsea-Deans Marsh Road, Bambra, Vic 3241 **Region** Port Phillip
T 0438 408 420 **www.**dinnygoonan.com.au **Open** 7 days Jan, w'ends & public hols Nov–Jun **Winemaker** Dinny Goonan, Angus Goonan **Est.** 1990 **Dozens** 1500 **Vyds** 5.5ha

The genesis of Dinny Goonan dates back to 1988, when Dinny bought a 20ha property near Bambra, in the hinterland of the Otway Coast. Dinny had recently completed a viticulture diploma at CSU and initially a wide range of varieties was planted in what is now known as the Nursery Block, to establish those best suited to the area. As these came into production Dinny headed back to CSU, where he completed a wine science degree. Production is focused on shiraz and riesling, with more extensive plantings of these varieties. (JH)

♟♟♟♟♟ **Single Vineyard Riesling 2021, Port Phillip** Another winning riesling from the maker sourcing single-vineyard fruit from the Otway Hinterland, giving ever-increasing credence to the grape in this part of the world. So enticingly fragrant in white flowers, citrus blossom, lime, lemon drop and orange peel. Clean, with a delicious purity of fruit, well supported by brisk acidity. Screw cap. 13% alc. RATING 95 DRINK 2021-2032 $30 JP ✪

♟♟♟♟ **Chardonnay 2021, Port Philip** RATING 92 DRINK 2022-2028 $35 JP
Outlier Riesling 2021, Port Philip RATING 92 DRINK 2022-2029 $49 JP
Single Vineyard Shiraz 2020, Port Phillip RATING 92 DRINK 2021-2030 $32 JP
Blanc de Bambra 2016, Port Phillip RATING 91 DRINK 2021-2021 $40 JP
Otway Hinterland Rosé 2021, Port Phillip RATING 90 DRINK 2021-2025 $25 JP
Pinot Noir 2021, Port Philip RATING 90 DRINK 2022-2027 $35 JP

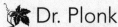 ## Dr. Plonk

PO Box 772, McLaren Vale 5172 **Region** McLaren Vale
T 0409 533 332 **www**.drplonk.wine **Winemaker** Matt Brown **Viticulturist** Richard
Leask **Est.** 2004 **Dozens** 800 **Vyds** 12.5ha

Dr. Plonk encompasses a few tiers: the more experimental Fu Manchu, the denser and more
pliant The Good Doctor and the everyday swigging Château Dateau. There is substance to
the styles and considerable thought to what is grown and how it is farmed. It is no wonder
that Dr. Plonk's conceptual embryo was borne of maker Matt Brown's experience at Alpha
Box & Dice. This experience led to the inaugural bottling of Good Doctor's Tonic in '04.
Subsequently, foresight deemed tannat and the late-ripening mourvèdre to be righteous
replacements for sauvignon blanc, ripped out in '09 when the 16ha site in the Willunga
Foothills became Brown's home base. Later, under the guidance of viticulturalist Richard
Leaske, montepulciano and carignan were also planted. Exports to the UK, Canada and
Denmark. (NG)

🍷🍷🍷🍷🍷 The Good Doctor's Cure Mataro Shiraz 2018, McLaren Vale An
extremely characterful wine of power and a riveting exactitude of tannic burr.
Meaty, carnal, ferrous. Sanguine. Gorgeous tannins of thorough persuasiveness.
I would like a little mid-palate plushness, possibly deliverable care of grenache in
the future. Very good, in any case, to see shiraz play its rightful back-burner role
across a swashbuckling expression of strident confidence and wonderful tannins.
Screw cap. 14.5% alc. RATING 94 DRINK 2022-2028 $32 NG

🍷🍷🍷🍷🍷 Fu Manchu Mourvèdre Rosé 2021, McLaren Vale RATING 93
DRINK 2022-2024 $28 NG
Fu Manchu Cabernet Sauvignon 2020, McLaren Vale RATING 91
DRINK 2022-2026 $40 NG
Fu Manchu Montepulciano 2021, McLaren Vale RATING 90
DRINK 2022-2025 $28 NG

Dodgy Brothers

PO Box 655, McLaren Vale, SA 5171 **Region** McLaren Vale
T 0450 000 373 **www**.dodgybrotherswines.com **Winemaker** Wes Pearson **Est.** 2010
Dozens 2000

This is a partnership between Canadian-born Flying Winemaker Wes Pearson, viticulturist
Peter Bolte and grapegrower Peter Sommerville. Wes graduated from the University of
British Columbia's biochemistry program in '08, along the way working at wineries including
Château Léoville-Las Cases in Bordeaux. Also in '08 he and his family moved to McLaren
Vale, and after working at several wineries, he joined the Australian Wine Research Institute as
a sensory analyst. Peter Bolte has over 35 vintages in McLaren Vale under his belt and was the
original Dodgy Brother. Peter Sommerville's vineyard provides cabernet sauvignon, cabernet
franc and petit verdot for the Dodgy Brothers Bordeaux blend. Exports to Canada. (JH)

🍷🍷🍷🍷🍷 Juxtaposed Old Vine Sandy Corner Block Wait Vineyard Blewitt
Springs Shiraz 2020, McLaren Vale A site planted in 1943, this is the marrow
of Blewitt Springs: lilac, energy and a sandy skein of tannins melded to crunchy,
saline, peppery freshness. Medium rather than heavy of feel. Destemming, crushing
and maturation in old Hungarian hogsheads serve as a platform for a beatific shiraz
that already drinks beautifully. Even if twice as expensive, it would still represent
good value. Screw cap. 14% alc. RATING 95 DRINK 2021-2030 $37 NG

🍷🍷🍷🍷🍷 Juxtaposed Fiano 2021, McLaren Vale RATING 93 DRINK 2021-2024
$29 NG
Juxtaposed Old Vine Grenache 2020, McLaren Vale RATING 93
DRINK 2021-2026 $39 NG

DogRidge Wine Company ★★★★

129 Bagshaws Road, McLaren Flat, SA 5171 **Region** McLaren Vale
T (08) 8383 0140 **www.**dogridge.com.au **Open** Mon–Fri 11–5, w'ends 12–4
Winemaker Fred Howard **Viticulturist** Dave Wright **Est.** 1991 **Dozens** 18 000
Vyds 56ha

Dave and Jen Wright (co-owners with Fred and Sarah Howard) had a combined background of dentistry, art and a CSU viticultural degree when they moved from Adelaide to McLaren Flat to become vignerons. They inherited shiraz and grenache vines planted in the early '40s as a source for Château Reynella fortified wines, and their vineyards now include some of the oldest vines in the immediate district. Quality at one end, value-packed at the other. Exports to Canada, Singapore and Japan. (JH)

TTTTT **Old Mates Grenache Shiraz 2018, McLaren Vale Barossa** Ripe and heady, but far from jammy or overly strung up by excessive additions or clumsy oak. Plush, with accents of raspberry bon-bon, cranberry, clove, white pepper and tangerine. A detailed, easygoing finish. Few surprises, but plenty of pleasure. Screw cap. 15% alc. RATING 92 DRINK 2021–2026 $30 NG

Butterfingers Barrel Aged Bâtonnage 2020, McLaren Vale As the name suggests, this is a no-holds-barred, buttery chardonnay in a style of yore. Given the intention, it achieves its goal with rich, torrefied aplomb: nougat, popcorn, brûlée and oodles of stone- to tropical-fruit allusions, stuffed between a wafer of vanillin oak. Screw cap. 14% alc. RATING 90 DRINK 2021–2025 $25 NG

Square Cut Cabernet 2017, McLaren Vale This address has crafted some exceptional cabernet-derived wines in the past. This is rich. A bit trop, but not without some charm in an old-school Australian way: green olive, sage, menthol and scrub, with bay leaf-doused tannins and an aftermath of mulch, currant and heat. Screw cap. 15% alc. RATING 90 DRINK 2021–2028 $30 NG

TTTT **Il Cucciolo Pinot Grigio 2021, Adelaide** RATING 89 DRINK 2021–2023 $20 NG

Running Free Grenache Rosé 2021, McLaren Vale RATING 88 DRINK 2021–2022 $25 NG

DogRock Winery ★★★★★

114 Degraves Road, Crowlands, Vic 3377 **Region** Pyrenees
T 0409 280 317 **www.**dogrock.com.au **Open** By appt **Winemaker** Allen Hart
Viticulturist Andrea Hart **Est.** 1998 **Dozens** 1000 **Vyds** 6.2ha

This is the venture of Allen (now full-time winemaker) and Andrea (viticulturist) Hart. Having purchased the property in '98, the planting of shiraz, riesling, tempranillo, grenache, chardonnay and marsanne began in '00 (0.2ha of touriga nacional added in '16 and arinto and azal in '20). Given Allen's former post as research scientist and winemaker with Foster's, the attitude taken to winemaking is unexpected. The estate-grown wines are made in a low-tech fashion, without gas cover or filtration; the Harts say, 'All wine will be sealed with a screw cap and no DogRock wine will ever be released under natural cork bark'. DogRock installed the first solar-powered irrigation system in Australia, capable of supplying water 365 days a year, even at night or in cloudy conditions. (JH)

TTTTT **Shiraz 2020, Pyrenees** Great value here with another excellent display of just how good Pyrenees shiraz can be at this pricepoint. Over-delivers in lifted, fragrant aromas and flavours that fill the mouth with intense black cherry, blueberry, bramble, baking spice, earth and bitter chocolate. Attractive freshness throughout, juicy, vibrant tannins to close. Screw cap. 14% alc. RATING 95 DRINK 2022–2030 $30 JP ✪

Degraves Road Single Vineyard Shiraz 2020, Pyrenees Sourced from a vineyard now 20 years old, there is a lot to enjoy about this Reserve Shiraz, not least the fine, linear and focused nature of the wine. Vibrant and juicy in its youthful black fruits, plums and spice with a gentle thread of vanillin oak, it remains beautifully integrated and fine edged on the palate. Love the drive, the

focused line and length through to the finish. Screw cap. 14% alc. RATING 95
DRINK 2022-2032 $38 JP

Degraves Road Single Vineyard Arinto 2021, Pyrenees Arinto is a
Portuguese variety from north of Lisbon, known for its retention of acidity.
It otherwise has similarities to Hunter Valley semillon, with lemony fruit and
cleansing acidity. Its length and aftertaste, coupled with fresh but not sharp
acidity, suggest it will cellar well. One to watch. Screw cap. 11.5% alc. RATING 94
DRINK 2021-2031 $30 JH ✪

ŶŶŶŶŶ **Degraves Road Single Vineyard Riesling 2021, Pyrenees** RATING 92
DRINK 2025-2035 $28 JH

Degraves Road Single Vineyard Chardonnay 2020, Pyrenees RATING 92
DRINK 2021-2025 $28 JH

Degraves Road Blanc de Blancs Chardonnay 2017, Pyrenees RATING 90
$38 JP

Domaine A   ★★★★★

105 Tea Tree Road, Campania, Tas 7026 **Region** Southern Tasmania
T (03) 6260 4174 **www.domaine-a.com.au Open** Sat–Sun 11–5 **Winemaker** Conor
van der Reest **Est.** 1973 **Dozens** 5000 **Vyds** 11ha

In '18 ownership of Domaine A passed from Peter Althaus, its long-term custodian, to
Moorilla Estate. There were no changes to existing employees, with Conor van de Reest
continuing as winemaker. The inclusion of Domaine A's stock in the sale would have been of
particular relevance with the opening of Mona's 172-room hotel on the Moorilla property in
'22. Mona is Australia's largest private museum showing ancient, modern and contemporary
art, founded by philanthropist and collector David Walsh. Exports to Singapore, Japan and
Hong Kong. (JH)

ŶŶŶŶŶ **Lady A Sauvignon Blanc 2018, Tasmania** 87/13% sauvignon blanc/semillon,
some new oak. Wonderfully opulent, succulent, alluring and uncharacteristically
yet delightfully approachable in its youth, brimming with all the gooseberry pie,
lantana and custard apple to be expected. Big, bold and downright gorgeous.
Screw cap. 14% alc. RATING 95 DRINK 2021-2028 $66 TS ♥

Pinot Noir 2014, Tasmania Exotic allure beckons from the glass in tones of
star anise, licorice, berry compote, black cherry liqueur, fruit-mince spice and
lavender. Harmony and tannin finesse are at the pinnacle of what this estate can
deliver, presenting a long finish of exacting line, drawn out by beautifully resolved,
velvety tannins. Benchmark Domaine A, ready to turn heads and win hearts. Cork.
13.7% alc. RATING 95 DRINK 2021-2026 $75 TS

Stoney Vineyard Cabernet Sauvignon 2018, Tasmania With 9.5/3/0.5%
merlot/cabernet franc/petit verdot. At less than a third of the price of its big
brother, baby Domaine A has long been one of the bargains of Tasmanian reds.
This is textbook cabernet of magnificent stature and grand longevity. All the
usual suspects are here in full measure: pure blackcurrant, cigar box and the
subtle perfume of the lavender row that borders this fabled vineyard. Tannins
are superfine-ground and mineral, energising a very long finish and bringing
tingling anticipation for what the future will invariably hold. Screw cap. 13.7% alc.
RATING 94 DRINK 2033-2043 $35 TS

Cabernet Sauvignon 2011, Tasmania Inimitable Domaine A. The dynamic
edge of cabernet in the cool '11 season infuses incredible energy, yet still
achieves impeccable ripeness and balance. The fragrant lavender notes and wild
garrigue that set this site apart are on display, as a decade of age rallies gamey,
meaty complexity. It holds its own on the finish, with reflections of blackcurrant
fruit still holding. Beginning to show some dryness and development amid a
fanfare of tannins that promise another decade still – but will the fruit hold
out? I'd err on the side of caution and drink soon. Cork. 13.8% alc. RATING 94
DRINK 2022-2026 $110 TS

♀♀♀♀♀ Merlot 2015, Tasmania RATING 93 DRINK 2021-2022 $75 TS
Pinot Noir 2015, Tasmania RATING 93 DRINK 2021-2023 $75 TS
Cabernet Sauvignon 2012, Tasmania RATING 93 DRINK 2027-2032 $110 TS
Petit a 2014, Tasmania RATING 91 DRINK 2021-2024 $40 TS

Domaine Asmara ★★★★

Gibb Road, Toolleen, Vic 3551 **Region** Heathcote
T (03) 5433 6133 www.domaineasmara.com **Open** 7 days 9–6.30 **Winemaker** Sanguine
Estate **Est.** 2008 **Dozens** 3000 **Vyds** 12ha
Chemical engineer Andreas Greiving had a lifelong dream to own and operate a vineyard, and
the opportunity came along with the global financial crisis. He was able to purchase a vineyard
planted to shiraz, cabernet sauvignon, cabernet franc, durif and viognier, and have the wines
contract-made. The venture is co-managed by his partner Hennijati who works as a dentist.
The red wines are made from controlled yields of 1–1.5t/acre, hence their concentration.
Exports to the UK, Vietnam, Malaysia, and Hong Kong. (JH)

♀♀♀♀♀ **Reserve Cabernet Sauvignon 2020, Heathcote** A solid, well-built cabernet
that carries considerable dark-fruited ripeness on the aroma in tandem with sweet,
toasty oak. It's very early days for this wine, but it's laying down a good base for
the future in plum, cassis, dark spices, juniper and earth, with an assertive ripe
tannin clip. Cork. 15% alc. RATING 93 DRINK 2022-2030 $35 JP
Infinity Shiraz 2020, Heathcote Infinity maintains its super-ripe, super-oak
tradition in '20. The maker doesn't do shy and retiring. Deep, dark, intense cassis,
blackberry, licorice, earthy and coffee mocha oak aromas. A touch of eucalyptus
brings a touch of local terroir. Dense tannins are wound tight. Cork. 15.5% alc.
RATING 93 DRINK 2021-2030 $88 JP
Private Reserve Shiraz 2020, Heathcote Explores the richer side of
Heathcote shiraz while harnessing its generosity to deliver a full-flavoured wine
with medium- long-term cellaring on its side. There's a good range of aromas
from vanilla-mocha scented oak, blood plum and blackberry to toasted spice. High
alcohol is noted as part of the richness of the palate, but it's not intrusive. Ripe
tannins complete the picture. Screw cap. 15.2% alc. RATING 90 DRINK 2022-2028
$49 JP
Infinity Durif 2020, Heathcote Co-fermented with 2% viognier. It's hard to
see where 2% viognier ended up in this resolutely old-school version of durif
which is deep, dense, darkly-fruited and all-round hearty stuff. Ripe plum, black
berry, cedary oak, dark chocolate, vanilla and baking spices aplenty. Sturdy in
build and thick in tannin, Infinity will relish time in the cellar. Cork. 14.8% alc.
RATING 90 DRINK 2022-2038 $88 JP

Domaine Naturaliste ★★★★★

160 Johnson Road, Wilyabrup, WA 6280 **Region** Margaret River
T (08) 9755 6776 www.domainenaturaliste.com.au **Open** 7 days 10–5
Winemaker Bruce Dukes **Est.** 2012 **Dozens** 12 000 **Vyds** 21ha
Before I tell you that Bruce Dukes' career has spanned over 3 decades and that he's had
years of experience both locally and abroad, it's likely a good idea to start at the finish:
Bruce Dukes is wholly talented, and while he makes high-quality acclaimed wines for his
own estate – Domaine Naturaliste – he also does this for a raft of other, smaller producers
in Margaret River and Geographe. His winemaking style is one of fresh, pure fruit over
obvious or intrusive winemaking artifact, and the wines routinely possess a polish and eminent
drinkability. Bruce holds both a degree in agronomy from the University of WA and a master's
degree in viticulture and agronomy from the University of California (Davis) and has been in
Margaret River since 2000. Exports to the UK, the US and Canada. (EL)

♀♀♀♀♀ **Rebus Cabernet Sauvignon 2018, Margaret River** The bouquet is a
fragrant mix of cassis, cedar, cigar box and bay leaf, the intense palate with a
tapestry of flavours. Yet it has the lightest of tannin touches encouraging a quick
return to the glass. Screw cap. 14% alc. RATING 97 DRINK 2023-2038 $36 JH ❂

Morus Cabernet Sauvignon 2018, Margaret River This swings into action from the first whiff, with a cavalcade of dark berry fruits of all persuasions, the precisely delineated palate that follows with cassis, redcurrant, a sombre edge of earth and dried olive, joining mouth-watering tannins. Cork. 14% alc. RATING 97 DRINK 2023-2043 $89 JH ❂

♟♟♟♟♟ **Sauvage Sauvignon Blanc 2020, Margaret River** A great white wine vintage. Bright straw green, barrel fermented in French puncheons (33% new), but that is not the only winemaking input, some enriching use of solids also in play. It's complex, with a lineage that will ensure the wine has a very healthy life ahead. Screw cap. 13% alc. RATING 96 DRINK 2022-2025 $33 JH ❂ ♥

Purus Chardonnay 2020, Margaret River Distinctly mineral with crushed granite, quartz and sand littered throughout the bounty of white peach, nashi pear, red apple skins and little flecks of flint. An extremely elegant and nuanced wine – supremely beautiful. Knife-edge stuff. Screw cap. 12.5% alc. RATING 95 DRINK 2021-2031 $53 EL

Discovery Syrah 2020, Margaret River Pink berries and raspberry dust adorn the nose and palate. Typically spicy and plump, this is a cracking wine for the price, delivering both reliable satisfaction and something simply sexy. The fruit has a distinct Beaujolais character. Gorgeous. Screw cap. 14% alc. RATING 94 DRINK 2021-2027 $25 EL ❂

Artus Chardonnay 2020, Margaret River Total fruit horsepower here – rumbling undercurrents of ripe yellow peach littered with crushed and toasted cashew and pepper. The acidity that threads its way through it all is briny and fresh, roping in the voluptuous fruit and creating balance in the mouth. Where the Purus is mineral and lean, this is complex, nutty and intense. Choose your weapon. Screw cap. 13.5% alc. RATING 94 DRINK 2021-2031 $53 EL

Le Naturaliste Cabernet Franc 2019, Margaret River Margaret River is a home for all the bordeaux varieties, particularly so in the case of cabernet franc, with its fragrant cherry-accented fruit and supple medium-bodied palate. Elsewhere in Australia, it is often found wanting. Cork. 14% alc. RATING 94 DRINK 2021-2030 $89 JH

Dominique Portet   ★★★★★

870 Maroondah Highway, Coldstream, Vic 3770 **Region** Yarra Valley
T (03) 5962 5760 **www**.dominiqueportet.com **Open** 7 days 10–5 **Winemaker** Ben Portet, Tim Dexter **Est.** 2000 **Dozens** 15 000 **Vyds** 9ha
Dominique Portet spent his early years at Château Lafite and was one of the first Flying Winemakers, commuting to Clos du Val in the Napa Valley where his brother was also a winemaker. He then spent over 20 years as managing director of Taltarni and Clover Hill. He then moved to the Yarra Valley where in '00 built his winery and cellar door, planting a quixotic mix of cabernet sauvignon, sauvignon blanc, merlot, malbec, cabernet franc and petit verdot. Son Ben is now executive winemaker, Dominique consultant and brand marketer. Ben himself has a winemaking CV of awesome scope, covering all parts of France, South Africa, California and 4 vintages at Petaluma. Exports to Canada, India, Dubai, Hong Kong, Singapore, Malaysia and Japan. (JH)

♟♟♟♟♟ **Cabernet Sauvignon 2019, Yarra Valley** With 2/1% merlot/petit verdot. A gorgeous, bright, medium crimson-purple hue. A supremely fragrant wine, with aromas of blackcurrant, currant leaf, chocolate powder and a hint of cedar and spice. On the palate, this thoughtfully put-together wine marries intensity and elegance in equal measure, with focused cassis fruit and superfine tannins that make this a wine to be enjoyed now and over the next 10 or so years. Cork. 13.5% alc. RATING 96 DRINK 2022-2032 $70 PR ❂

Brut Rosé LD NV, Yarra Valley Traditional method, 24+ months on lees (disgorged on demand), 6g/L dosage. Pale salmon. Yarra Valley sparkling wine is increasingly sourced – as this is – from the Upper Yarra Valley. Vivid aromas build on the 60/40% pinot noir and chardonnay base wine, take in red cherry and

wild strawberry (the pinot), brioche and toast (the chardonnay). Diam. 13% alc.
RATING 95 $36 JH
Single Vineyard Rosé 2021, Yarra Valley A blend of 50/40/10% cabernet/
merlot/malbec. A perfect pale salmon. Subtle and complex, with aromas of wild
strawberry, redcurrants, a gentle leafiness and even a hint of Vietnamese mint.
The textbook palate is dry and savoury, with light redcurrant fruit and this finishes
bone dry, with just the right amount of grip and refreshing acidity. Screw cap.
13% alc. RATING 95 DRINK 2021–2025 $42 PR ♥
Single Vineyard Chardonnay 2020, Yarra Valley A complex bouquet
with white stone fruit, fig, cashew and nougat that doesn't falter in the mouth,
the citrus-edged acidity clearing and cleansing the finish. Screw cap. 13% alc.
RATING 95 DRINK 2021–2029 $38 JH

ŸŸŸŸŸ **Fontaine Cabernet Sauvignon 2020, Yarra Valley** RATING 93
DRINK 2021–2026 $24 PR ✪
Fontaine Rosé 2021, Yarra Valley RATING 92 DRINK 2021–2023 $24 PR ✪

Dorrien Estate

Cnr Barossa Valley Way/Siegersdorf Road, Tanunda, SA 5352 **Region** Barossa Valley
T (08) 8561 2235 **www.**dorrienestate.com.au **Winemaker** Nick Badrice **Est.** 1982
Dozens 1 million **Vyds** 109.6ha
Dorrien Estate is the physical base of the vast Cellarmasters network – the largest direct
sales outlet in Australia. It also makes wine for many producers across Australia at its modern
winery, which has a capacity of 14.5 million litres in tank and barrel; however, a typical make
of each wine will be little more than 1000 dozen. Most of the wines made for others are
exclusively distributed by Cellarmasters. Acquired by Woolworths in May '11. (JH)

ŸŸŸŸŸ **Mockingbird Hill Dr J.W.D. Bain Riesling 2021, Clare Valley** Like walking
through an apple orchard: blossoms, apples and the occasional grassy interlude. This
typifies the capacity for the beauty that '21 is so frequently leaving in its wake.
Chalky, talcy, minerally and fine, with a plume of flavour through the finish. A big
yes. Screw cap. 12% alc. RATING 95 DRINK 2022–2032 $30 EL ✪
Dorrien Estate Icon Shiraz 2019, Barossa Dorrien Estate's 'big gun' under
the famous Krondorf label. With a slated May '24 release, we could be accused
of infanticide here, but I think it's worth penning some thoughts even at this
stage of its evolution. It's impressive, showing heady fruit purity and depth yet
retaining freshness and a sense of space and clarity of detail that bodes well
for its future release. Certainly one to jot down and keep an eye on when it
finally comes roaring onto the fine wine market. Diam. 14.5% alc. RATING 95
DRINK 2024–2038 $300 DB
Bin 79 Tribute Cabernet Sauvignon 2019, Barossa Valley A deeply
resonant cabernet sauvignon from the famous Krondorf label that sticks to the
truism regarding the variety in the Barossa. Gone are the herbaceous capsicum
notes and in their place, a solid slab of blackberry and cassis fruit, singing with
baking spice, dark chocolate, cedary oak and earth. It's fresh-faced with a cascade
of ripe tannin and support for the rich black fruit. Long and very appealing.
Agglomerate. 14.5% alc. RATING 94 DRINK 2021–2035 $160 DB

ŸŸŸŸŸ **Krondorf Stone Altar Old Vine Grenache 2020, Barossa Valley**
RATING 93 DRINK 2021–2028 $60 DB
Krondorf Single Site Moculta Shiraz 2019, Eden Valley RATING 93
DRINK 2021–2031 $40 DB
**Riddoch The Representative Cabernet Sauvignon Merlot 2019,
Coonawarra** RATING 93 DRINK 2022–2037 $45 EL
**Bloodbrother Republic McLaren Flat Cabernet Sauvignon 2020,
McLaren Vale** RATING 92 DRINK 2021–2026 $25 NG ✪
Blood Brother Republic Single Vineyard Shiraz 2020, McLaren Vale
RATING 92 DRINK 2021–2028 $36 NG

Blood Brother Republic Single Vineyard Cabernet Sauvignon 2020,
McLaren Vale RATING 92 DRINK 2021-2030 $36 NG
Krondorf Single Site Marananga Shiraz 2019, Barossa Valley RATING 92
DRINK 2021-2035 $40 DB
Cellar Release Cat Amongst the Pigeons Fat Cat Shiraz 2015, Barossa
Valley RATING 92 DRINK 2022-2027 $33 EL
Blood Brother Republic Flat Shiraz 2020, McLaren Vale RATING 91
DRINK 2021-2025 $25 NG
Krondorf Founder's View Grenache 2020, Barossa Valley RATING 91
DRINK 2021-2025 $26 DB
Krondorf Old Salem Shiraz 2019, Barossa RATING 91 DRINK 2021-2030
$42 DB
Riddoch Elgin's Crossing Sparkling Shiraz NV, Coonawarra RATING 90
$25 EL
Mockingbird Hill Dr J.W.D. Bain Shiraz 2020, Clare Valley RATING 90
DRINK 2022-2027 $30 EL
William Light Shiraz 2020, Clare Valley RATING 90 DRINK 2022-2027
$40 EL
Riddoch The Pastoralist Cabernet Sauvignon 2019, Coonawarra
RATING 90 DRINK 2021-2036 $45 EL

DOWIE DOOLE

695 California Road, McLaren Vale, SA 5171 **Region** McLaren Vale
T 0459 101 372 **www.**dowiedoole.com **Open** 7 days 10–5 **Winemaker** Chris Thomas
Est. 1995 **Dozens** 25 000 **Vyds** 90ha
DOWIE DOOLE was founded in 1995 by Drew Dowie and Norm Doole. They had been
connected to the McLaren Vale community for many years as grapegrowers in the region.
Vineyard management is now led by champions of sustainable viticulture practices Dave
Gartelmann and Drew Dowie. In May '16, with winemaker and managing director Chris
Thomas leading a group of like-minded investors, DOWIE DOOLE acquired 35ha of vines
of the 53ha Conte Tatachilla Vineyard, book-ended by 50yo bush-vine grenache and grafted
vermentino, aglianico and lagrein. In October '18, DOWIE DOOLE purchased Possum
Vineyard, including its vineyards in Blewitt Springs and 500t winery. Exports to all major
markets. (JH)

ŶŶŶŶŶ DD Cabernet Sauvignon 2019, McLaren Vale This is good. Despite cab's
forceful tannic kit, the feel is one of poise, floral lift and relatively effortless
drinking in the context of this lineup. Almost pulpy of feel, so vivacious is it.
Blackcurrant, dried sage, lilac, graphite and green olive. The finish drives long, with
a dash of heat and some oak tannins which, on this occasion, are positioned well.
Screw cap. 14.4% alc. RATING 93 DRINK 2022-2027 $30 NG
Doole Vineyard Shiraz 2020, McLaren Vale A large-framed, older-school
expression. Molten raspberry, dark cherry, anise and mocha-chocolate oak. There
is so much intensity of fruit scrummaged between the frames of vanillin oak, that
can't be denied by virtue of its sheer force of personality. Plenty of fans, to be sure.
Screw cap. 14.5% alc. RATING 92 DRINK 2022-2032 $60 NG
DD Grenache 2019, McLaren Vale Matured 22 months in 80/20% French/
American wood, marking this with an older-school aura that glimpses a tauter,
more contemporary style. Sarsaparilla, black cherry, licorice strap and Asian
spice, harnessed by the coconut chip and vanilla-pod frame of the wood. The
winemaking at this address seems to suit a warmer year such as this. Screw cap.
14.5% alc. RATING 91 DRINK 2021-2026 $30 NG

ŶŶŶŶ Rosé 2021, McLaren Vale RATING 88 DRINK 2021-2022 $25 NG
DD Sauvignon Blanc 2018, McLaren Vale RATING 88 DRINK 2021-2022
$25 NG
CT Shiraz 2018, McLaren Vale RATING 88 DRINK 2021-2025 $35 NG

Drayton's Family Wines

555 Oakey Creek Road, Pokolbin, NSW 2321 **Region** Hunter Valley
T (02) 4998 7513 **www**.draytonswines.com.au **Open** Mon–Fri 8–5, w'ends & public
hols 10–5 **Winemaker** Mark Smith **Est.** 1853 **Dozens** 40 **Vyds** 72ha

Six generations of the Drayton family have successively run the family business; it is now in
the hands of Max Drayton, and sons John and Greg. The family has suffered more than its
fair share of misfortune over the years, but has risen to the challenge. The wines come in part
from blocks on the estate vineyards that are over 120 years old and in prime Hunter Valley
locations. Mark Smith took over as winemaker from Edgar Vales in time for the '21 vintage.
Exports to Ireland, Bulgaria, Turkey, Vietnam, Malaysia, Indonesia, Singapore and Taiwan. (JH)

Susanne Semillon 2021, Hunter Valley This is very good. The harsh acidity
that marks these wines at times is, here, a natural-feeling salve. An effortless two-
step with a fine, cool vintage and restrained fruit: gooseberry, lemon squash, pink
grapefruit and talc. This is rapier-like of intensity and bolshy of length. Will age
very well. Screw cap. 11.2% alc. RATING 96 DRINK 2022-2033 $60 NG ✪

Susanne Semillon 2017, Hunter Valley RATING 93 DRINK 2021-2026
$60 NG
William Shiraz 2017, Hunter Valley RATING 93 DRINK 2022-2030 $60 NG
Joseph Shiraz 2014, Hunter Valley RATING 92 DRINK 2021-2026 $60 NG

Driftwood Estate

3314 Caves Road, Wilyabrup, WA 6282 **Region** Margaret River
T (08) 9755 6323 **www**.driftwoodwines.com.au **Open** 7 days 11–4 **Winemaker** Kane
Grove **Est.** 1989 **Dozens** 18 000 **Vyds** 22ha

Driftwood Estate is a well-established landmark on the Margaret River scene. Quite apart
from offering a casual dining restaurant capable of seating 200 people (open 7 days for lunch
and dinner) and a mock Greek open-air theatre, its wines feature striking and stylish packaging
and opulent flavours. Its wines are released in 4 ranges: Single Site, Artifacts, The Collection
and Oceania. Exports to the UK, Canada, and Singapore. (JH)

Single Site Chardonnay 2020, Margaret River I have seen this wine, blind,
3 times in '21, and it is so firmly imprinted on my memory that I hardly needed
to taste it again today, save but for the context it could bring to the surrounding
wines. It is pure, fine, lingering and spicy. The fruit is woven into the very fabric
of the wine, threaded in place by fine strands of briny acidity that is pronounced,
but sings, rather than intrudes. The spicy, toasty oak holds it together and is
perfectly matched to the fruit. Succulent and streamlined. Several previous
vintages have been as impressive. Get on board. Screw cap. 13% alc. RATING 97
DRINK 2022-2037 $70 EL ✪

Artifacts Meritage 2020, Margaret River 41/36/20/3% petit verdot/malbec/
cabernet sauvignon/other. Delicious, in a word. There is plentiful tannin – fine,
soft and shapely – and loads of fresh fruit: blackberries, raspberries, pomegranate,
blood plums and red apples; with spice and additional flavours galore (dark
chocolate, nutmeg, star anise, a strap or 2 of red licorice, fresh tobacco leaves and
fennel). This is very good. Screw cap. 14% alc. RATING 95 DRINK 2022-2032
$35 EL ✪
Single Site Cabernet Sauvignon 2019, Margaret River Shaved hung deli
meat, blackberry pie, salted black licorice and the sweet gummy character you get
off blackcurrant pastilles. The tannins are soft and pliable; they coat the tongue
and cheeks and blanket the fruit in a velvet sheath. Quite different to the wines
from its neighbours; for that individuality, quite beautiful. Screw cap. 14.3% alc.
RATING 95 DRINK 2022-2037 $70 EL
Artifacts Petit Verdot 2019, Margaret River Super-aromatic: raspberry
compote, black snakes, cocoa, lavender and brine. The flavours on the palate
obediently follows suit. This is vibrant, glossy, detailed and quite delicious. The

tannins are reigned in, harnessed: they shape the fruit and curve the wine in the mouth, but at no point do they intrude on the flavour. Lovely, lovely. Screw cap. 14% alc. RATING 94 DRINK 2021-2028 $34 EL

Artifacts Cabernet Sauvignon 2019, Margaret River Really brilliant. This has cassis, raspberry, salted licorice, hints of saltbush and bay leaf, fine crushed black pepper, briny acidity and plump yet fine mouthfeel. It is shapely. This is another producer on the rise in Margaret River, and this is a wonderful wine. Seek it out. Screw cap. 14% alc. RATING 94 DRINK 2021-2031 $35 EL

Duke's Vineyard ★★★★★

Porongurup Road, Porongurup, WA 6324 **Region** Porongurup
T (08) 9853 1107 **www**.dukesvineyard.com **Open** 7 days 10–4.30 **Winemaker** Robert Diletti **Est.** 1998 **Dozens** 3500 **Vyds** 10ha

When Hilde and Ian (Duke) Ranson sold their clothing manufacturing business in '98, they were able to fulfil a long-held dream of establishing a vineyard in the Porongurup subregion of Great Southern with the acquisition of a 65ha farm at the foot of the Porongurup Range. They planted shiraz and cabernet sauvignon (3ha each) and riesling (4ha). Hilde, a successful artist, designed the beautiful, scalloped, glass-walled cellar door sales area, with its mountain blue cladding. Great wines at great prices. (JH)

🍷🍷🍷🍷🍷 **Magpie Hill Reserve Riesling 2021, Porongurup** A super-floral nose leads into a tense and citrus-driven palate. The acidity is saline and omnipresent, curling and flicking around the fruit, shaping it all through the long finish. This has already developed and grown so much in the bottle between this glass and the last (a couple of months ago, that it surely has a very long road ahead of it. White pepper, lime flesh and laser-like precision through the finish. Layered and dappled – gorgeous. Screw cap. 11.8% alc. RATING 97 DRINK 2021-2041 $42 EL ✪

🍷🍷🍷🍷🍷 **Magpie Hill Reserve Shiraz 2020, Porongurup** Another startlingly impressive cuvée from this vineyard. Silky texture in the mouth, plump, concentrated black fruit and layers of sweet spice. It's a marvel. Love the plum through the finish … Screw cap. 14.1% alc. RATING 96 DRINK 2021-2031 $42 EL ✪

Magpie Hill Reserve Cabernet Sauvignon 2020, Porongurup Classic pure cassis fruit on the mid palate, cloistered by fine dusty tannins and a sprinkling of exotic spice. Aniseed, white pepper, blood plum and raspberry form the core of this wine; a sumptuous, fine-boned and satisfying cabernet. Screw cap. 13.7% alc. RATING 95 DRINK 2021-2031 $42 EL

The First Cab 2020, Porongurup As with last year, this is intensely flavoured with lashings of redcurrants, pomegranate, raspberry and cassis. The fruit is framed by a chorus of exotic spices that pick and lift the fruit throughout the evolution of the wine across the palate. The tannins are very fine and chalky, providing grip and shape and power through the finish. Supple, cool-climate cabernet … super-gorgeous. Screw cap. 13.5% alc. RATING 95 DRINK 2021-2033 $60 EL

Single Vineyard Riesling 2021, Porongurup Pristine, pure and precise. Laser-like acidity coils around and around on the palate, creating a vortex of energy and life in which the fruit can float. Long and saline; what a beautiful wine. The thing about Porongurup riesling is the floral aromatics coupled with austere acidity; the best have both in spades, one sometimes disguising the other, but never stepping out alone. Screw cap. 11.5% alc. RATING 94 DRINK 2021-2031 $26 EL ✪

Dune Wine ★★★★★

PO Box 9, McLaren Vale, SA 5171 **Region** McLaren Vale
T 0403 584 845 **www**.dunewine.com **Winemaker** Duncan and Peter Lloyd **Est.** 2017 **Dozens** 1700 **Vyds** 8ha

This is the project of Duncan and Peter Lloyd (of Coriole fame) using fruit sourced from a single vineyard in Blewitt Springs. The brothers grew up immersed in a world of wine, olive oil, illegal goat's cheese and great food. Both worked in kitchens from the age of 13 and continued to develop a love of good food and wine. Duncan studied winemaking before leaving McLaren Vale to work in Tasmania and Margaret River, and then in Chianti and the Rhône Valley. He returned to McLaren Vale as he couldn't understand why you would want to live anywhere else. Peter also left the area after university, with eclectic occupations in France and England. He shares Duncan's views on McLaren Vale, though for now he lives in Melbourne. Exports to Sweden and Taiwan. (JH)

ŸŸŸŸŸ **The Empty Quarter 2020, McLaren Vale** A co-fermented blend of shiraz, grenache and mourvèdre, plus a little negroamaro. Notes of plum and glacé cherry on the bouquet are outgunned by the black and red fruits and firm tannins of the medium- to full-bodied palate, with an unexpected juicy finish. Intriguing wine. Screw cap. 14.3% alc. RATING 95 DRINK 2022-2027 $28 JH ✪
Desert Sands Shiraz 2019, McLaren Vale The lowest-yielding cuvée, such is the density, savouriness and pliancy of the tannins, al dente as they stream across the gums to ensure the fruit, no matter how ripe, maintains a sense of decorum. Chiselled. Blue-fruit aspersions, creamy-ish oak (10% new) and loads of star anise, cocoa powder and tapenade. Serious texture, without being too cerebral. Screw cap. 14.4% alc. RATING 95 DRINK 2021-2029 $32 NG ✪
Pyla 2021, McLaren Vale Nero, carignan, mourvèdre and negroamaro, with dollops of montepulciano and grenache. Portentous blend. Great varieties all, obfuscated to date by the country's effete fascination with French stuff. No cultural cringe here! Blueberry, rosemary, thyme, anise, clove, raspberry, lilac and a ferruginous burr across the back end. Alive. Fresh. Lovely tannins for this imminently drinkable style! Nothing soupy or insipid. Delicious! Screw cap. 13.5% alc. RATING 94 DRINK 2021-2026 $32 NG
Blewitt Springs Shiraz 2020, McLaren Vale A harmonious array of red and black cherries whipped together with hints of nutmeg and cinnamon, all of which linger on the finish and aftertaste. Screw cap. 14.2% alc. RATING 94 DRINK 2021-2035 $28 JH ✪

ŸŸŸŸŸ **El Beyda 2021, McLaren Vale** RATING 93 DRINK 2021-2025 $28 NG
Paliomera Shiraz 2021, McLaren Vale RATING 93 DRINK 2021-2027 $32 NG
Athabasca Chenin Blanc 2021, McLaren Vale RATING 92 DRINK 2021-2026 $28 NG
Tirari 2020, McLaren Vale RATING 92 DRINK 2021-2024 $26 NG
Bonaire Rosé 2021, McLaren Vale RATING 91 DRINK 2021-2023 $26 NG
Cactus Canyon 2021, McLaren Vale RATING 90 DRINK 2021-2024 $28 NG

Dutschke Wines ★★★★★

Lot 1 Gods Hill Road, Lyndoch, SA 5351 **Region** Barossa Valley
T (08) 8524 5485 **www.dutschkewines.com Open** By appt **Winemaker** Wayne Dutschke **Est.** 1998 **Dozens** 5000 **Vyds** 15ha
Winemaker and owner Wayne Dutschke set up business with uncle (and grapegrower) Ken Semmler in '90 to produce wine. Since then, Dutschke Wines has built its own small winery around the corner from Ken's vineyard and the portfolio has increased. While Wayne has now been making small-batch wines for over 30 years, his use of whole-berry ferments, open fermenters, basket presses and a quality oak regime have all remained the same. He was crowned Barossa Winemaker of the Year in '10, inducted into the Barons of Barossa in '13 and is the author of a children's book about growing up in a winery, called My Dad has Purple Hands. Exports to the US, Canada, Denmark, Germany, the Netherlands and Taiwan. (JH)

ŸŸŸŸŸ **Single Barrel Max's Vineyard Shiraz 2008, Barossa Valley** Wayne Dutschke has an intuitive ability to coax the best out of southern Barossa fruit with incredible fruit density and concentration, while retaining perfume and detail. Case in point here. Pure satsuma plum and summer berry fruits with notes of black cherry, licorice, espresso and dark chocolatey oak. For all the fruit weight, there is a sense of freshness to the wine's gait. The tannins are sandy, fine and super-ripe and the finish trails off in a vapour trail of black cherry, plum, and dreamy oak spice. Lovely stuff. Screw cap. 15% alc. RATING 96 DRINK 2021-2031 $175 DB

Single Barrel St Jakobi Vineyard 75 Block #1 Shiraz 2008, Barossa Valley A single-barrel release. The fruit concentration and intensity is peaking the meters, with hints of baking spice, licorice, Old Jamaica chocolate and oak-derived notes of espresso, cedar and pipe tobacco. Beautifully composed on the palate, the rich fruit rolls through with a sense of latent power behind its concentrated yet graceful presence. Spice and cedary oak sweep onto the mid palate. The tannins are sandy and superfine and the wine trails off impressively. A classically composed, southern Barossa beauty. Screw cap. 15.5% alc. RATING 96 DRINK 2021-2031 $175 DB

Single Barrel Staker Vineyard Shiraz 2008, Barossa Valley Deep blackberry and black cherry fruits cut through with baking spice, kirsch, dark chocolate, espresso and earth. Concentration and detail are a recurring theme with these single-barrel wines and again the balance is spot on. The wines retain freshness at heady levels of fruit intensity and the pure drinking enjoyment is writ large. Screw cap. 15% alc. RATING 95 DRINK 2021-2031 $175 DB

 GHR Neighbours Shiraz 2020, Barossa Valley RATING 93 DRINK 2031-2035 $35 DB

St Jakobi Single Vineyard Lyndoch Shiraz 2020, Barossa Valley RATING 93 DRINK 2021-2035 $48 DB

Eden Road Wines

3182 Barton Highway, Murrumbateman, NSW 2582 **Region** Canberra District
T 0466 226 808 **www.**edenroadwines.com.au **Open** Wed–Fri 11–4.30, Sat–Sun 10–4.30
Winemaker Celine Rousseau **Est.** 2006 **Dozens** 14000 **Vyds** 5.34ha
The name of this business reflects an earlier time when it also had a property in the Eden Valley. Now based in the Canberra District, having purchased one of Canberra's oldest vineyards (est. 1972) and wineries at Dookuna. Syrah, sauvignon blanc and riesling are sourced from the estate vineyards in Canberra, with chardonnay and pinot noir coming from Tumbarumba. In '21, the estate vineyards were converted to organic. Exports to the UK and the US. (JH)

 Riesling 2021, Canberra District A monastic riesling with its razor-sharp acidity first up, Rose's lime juice second, and ultimately gaining control. Good to see young rieslings bringing prices such as this. Screw cap. 12% alc. RATING 95 DRINK 2025-2040 $50 JH

Edinger Estate ★★★★

796 Rosa Glen Road Margaret River, WA 6285 **Region** Margaret River
T 0417 942 695 **Winemaker** Cliff Royle, Julian Scott **Viticulturist** Beau O'Loughlin
Est. 1998 **Dozens** 1000 **Vyds** 120ha
Edinger Estate is the reincarnation of Chalice Bridge vineyard in Margaret River (the Chalice Bridge Estate brand was purchased by Moppity Vineyards in 2013, the large vineyard retained by Rob Edinger). Later renamed as Edinger Estate, the wines are made from 100% estate-owned fruit from the vineyard in Rosa Glen. The estate was sold in 2022. (EL)

The Rebecca Chardonnay 2020, Margaret River The effortlessness of the '20 fruit is on show here: very pretty and expertly balanced, this is all about stone fruit, saline acidity (the acid is fluid; it doesn't have the coarse briny crunch that some do) and fresh curry leaves. In the mouth the wine doesn't waver, as it makes its way across the palate and through into the finish. The oak starts the creep in at the end, however at this young stage we will forgive that, it will pipe down. Screw cap. 13.5% alc. RATING 93 DRINK 2021-2031 $40 EL

The Rebecca Chardonnay 2019, Margaret River The cooler '19 season has produced a wine far nuttier and creamier than the follow-up 2020. This is subdued, languid and calm, the oak playing a more dominant role through the finish. While this may offer more immediate drinking pleasure for some, it may pay to hang onto it for a few more years yet, to allow that oak to recede into the concentrated fruit. It is lovely now, though. Screw cap. 13.5% alc. RATING 92 DRINK 2022-2029 $40 EL

Shiraz 2018, Margaret River Crushed ants, mulberry, salted licorice, fig on the tree, clove, dark chocolate and ironstone. In the mouth the wine is exactly that. Brooding, dense and ripe, layered with stewed plums and Christmas cake spice. Screw cap. 14.5% alc. RATING 90 DRINK 2021-2028 $30 EL

1837 Barossa

119-131 Yaldara Drive, Lyndoch, SA 5351 **Region** Barossa Valley
T (08) 7200 1070 **www.**1837barossa.com.au/ **Open** Mon–Sun 11–5 **Winemaker** Guido Auchli, Peter Gajewski, Ben Cooke **Viticulturist** Michael Heinrich **Est.** 1999 **Vyds** 25ha
The ambition of the Swiss tech entrepreneurial Auchli family, 1837 Barossa commemorates the date on which Colonel William Light named the Barossa. Red wines hail exclusively from the estate near Lyndoch, while whites are sourced from Eden Valley growers. Viticulture is overseen by fifth-generation grower Michael Heinrich, with a philosophy of minimal chemical input. The spectacular estate offers accommodation in its recently refurbished Barossa Manor, including a restaurant, cellar door and seminar centre. Exports to Europe. (TS)

PPPP **Summer Breeze Pinot Rosé 2021, Eden Valley** A pale, pale pink rosé produced from pinot noir and pinot grigio, showing characters of redcurrant, raspberry and ruby red grapefruit along with hints of stone, jasmine, almond paste and green apple. A little phenolic swirl adds texture and mouthfeel and the wine finishes crisp, clean and dry with a red-fruited flourish. Screw cap. 12% alc. RATING 90 DRINK 2022-2025 $20 DB ✪

Barossa Legend Rare Single Block Shiraz 2019, Barossa Valley Deep red purple in the glass, showing characters of rich blackberry, blood plum and black cherry, with hints of baking spice, licorice, espresso, cedar and blackberry jam. Weighty with cedary oak influence flowing in on the palate, tight, feathery tannin and a cassis-rich finish. A traditional style. Cork. 14.5% alc. RATING 90 DRINK 2022-2030 $74 DB

PPPP **Fond Memories Single Block Pinot Gris 2021, Eden Valley** RATING 89 DRINK 2022-2025 $30 DB

President's Reserve Estate Shiraz Cabernet Sauvignon 2019, Barossa Valley RATING 89 DRINK 2022-2030 $44 DB

Stormy Romance Pinot Grigio 2021, Eden Valley RATING 88 DRINK 2022-2025 $20 DB

1847 | Chateau Yaldara

Chateau Yaldara, Hermann Thumm Drive, Lyndoch, SA 5351 **Region** Barossa Valley
T (08) 8524 0200 **www.**1847wines.com **Open** 7 days 10–5 **Winemaker** Chris Coulter **Est.** 1947 **Dozens** 50000 **Vyds** 100ha
1847 Wines is wholly owned by Chinese group Treasure Valley Wines. The year is when Barossa pioneer Johann Gramp planted his first vines in the region. There is in fact no other connection between Gramp and the business he established and that of 1847 Wines, other than the fact that the 80ha estate is in the general vicinity of Gramp's original plantings. A 1000t winery was built in 2014, handling the core production together with new varieties and blends. This was underpinned by the acquisition of Château Yaldara in '14, providing a major retail outlet and massively enhanced production facilities. Exports to the US, Canada, Germany, Morocco, Sri Lanka, Vietnam, Singapore, Taiwan and Hong Kong. (JH)

PPPPP **Paradigm Shiraz Cabernet Sauvignon 2017, Barossa Valley** Ripe blood-plum notes meld with rich blackberry and blackcurrant fruits, black licorice, dark spice, cedar, earth and espresso. Full bodied, with an initial blast of sappy, cedary

oak before settling down in rich black-fruited, traditionally framed comfort;
tight of tannin and long of finish. Old-school style. Cork. 14.6% alc. RATING 91
DRINK 2022-2032 $59 DB

ŸŸŸŸ Salute Cabernet Sauvignon 2018, Barossa Valley RATING 89
DRINK 2021-2028 $29 DB
Salute Shiraz 2018, Barossa Valley RATING 88 DRINK 2021-2028 $29 DB

Ekhidna

67 Branson Road, McLaren Vale, SA 5171 **Region** McLaren Vale
T 0499 002 633 **www.**ekhidnawines.com.au **Open** Fri–Sun 11–5 **Winemaker** Matthew
Rechner **Est.** 2001 **Dozens** 2000
Matt Rechner entered the wine industry in '88, spending most of the years since at Tatachilla
in McLaren Vale, starting as laboratory technician and finishing as operations manager.
Frustrated by the constraints of large winery practice, he decided to strike out on his own in
'01. The quality of the wines has been such that he has been able to build a winery and cellar
door, the winery facilitating the use of various cutting-edge techniques. (JH)

ŸŸŸŸŸ Barrel Ferment Grenache 2019, McLaren Vale Translucent. Crystalline.
A bold step forward. Succulent, pinot-esque grenache. Small red berries pop
through the mouth. Seville orange, thyme and lavender, too. This is glimpsing
the style of the top-drawer regional producers. Not quite there. Almost. Fine,
auguring for exciting releases into the future. Screw cap. 14.5% alc. RATING 92
DRINK 2022-2027 $45 NG
Whole Bunch Grenache 2019, McLaren Vale This is the qualitative
barometer for the range. The rest falls in line. Pressed to older French wood for
16 months. A little less time in better and larger oak, will help moving forward.
Fecund strawberry notes and an underbelly of woodsmoke, sandalwood and
bergamot. The tannins, diaphanous, fibrous, juicy and nicely firm. The oak, mocha
and a bit clunky. A superb site with almost a superb wine to match. Screw cap.
14.5% alc. RATING 92 DRINK 2022-2028 $45 NG
King's Hill Shiraz 2019, McLaren Vale Rich, but compact and considerably
refined. This should shape up well with patience. Palate-staining glycerol, riffs
on violet, iodine. blueberry and tapenade, corralled by a gritty, saline lattice
of tannin. Long and crunchy. Good wine. Screw cap. 14.5% alc. RATING 92
DRINK 2022-2033 $80 NG
Rechner Shiraz 2017, McLaren Vale Clearly glorious material servicing a juicy
mid palate of blue, red and darker fruits. Anise, clove, lilac, menthol and biltong,
supporting. The finish is layered, long and juicy. Among the more impressive wines
of the stable. Screw cap. 14.5% alc. RATING 92 DRINK 2022-2030 $95 NG
She Viper Shiraz 2019, McLaren Vale An archetypal powerful shiraz, in an
old-school regional mould. Plenty of fans, to be sure. Best, this is not as servile
to the oak tannins, as with some of the more expensive wines in the range.
Subsequently, oodles of blue and black fruits, Sangria, baking spice, licorice, clove
and dried citrus accents teem long. The oak, a bit rustic, but not out of place with
the style. Good drinking on the earlier side, before the tannins dry out the fruit.
Screw cap. 14.5% alc. RATING 91 DRINK 2022-2030 $30 NG
Cabernet 2018, McLaren Vale There is a great deal to like here. Firstly, the
celebration of cabernet's quality in the Vale, an almost furtive call to arms. Secondly,
the vinosity, crunch and impeccable saddle of easy-riding tannins melded to
pristine varietal character: cassis, pencil lead, graphite, sage and bayleaf, swabbed
with green olive tapenade. There is pulp, sass and vibrancy here that is missing
elsewhere (with the exception of the bunchy grenache). Lovely drinking. Screw
cap. 14.5% alc. RATING 91 DRINK 2022-2026 $30 NG
Single Row 14 Shiraz 2018, McLaren Vale A lighter touch here, without any
forfeit of the rich, older-school signature of this address. Florals. More energy and
bounce to the fruit. Plenty of mocha vanilla, but iodine, scents of barbecued meats,
anise and blueberry, too. Creamy across the mid palate, with a burst of freshness

and some sinewy, woodsy oak tannins directing it to satisfying length. Screw cap.
14.5% alc. RATING 91 DRINK 2021-2030 $65 NG

35 Degrees The Shiraz 2016, McLaren Vale The zenith of the shiraz cuvées,
serving up a confluence of older vines and better sites, articulated as the finest,
most abstemiously selected barrels. Aged extensively in barrel and bottle, before
release. Oak-dominant aromas of vanilla, coconut and cedar. A melody of blue and
black fruits. Prodigious concentration. Palate staining. Licorice, clove and camphor.
The caveat of minty, menthol-soaked oak tannins, drying the finish. Screw cap.
14.5% alc. RATING 91 DRINK 2022-2028 $130 NG

ΨΨΨΨ Echidna Grenache Shiraz 2020, McLaren Vale RATING 88
DRINK 2022-2026 $30 NG

Elderslie ★★★★

PO Box 93, Charleston, SA 5244 **Region** Adelaide Hills
T 0404 943 743 **www**.eldersliewines.com.au **Winemaker** Adam Wadewitz **Est.** 2015
Dozens 600 **Vyds** 8ha

Winemaker Adam Wadewitz and wine marketer Nicole Roberts bring a wealth of experience
gained in many parts of the wine world. They each have their partners (Nikki Wadewitz and
Mark Roberts) onboard and also have real-life jobs. In '16 Nicole accepted the position of
executive officer of the Adelaide Hills Wine Region, having had brand development roles
with 3 of the Hills' leading winemakers. She also heads up marketing and sales at Bird In
Hand. Adam carved out a career at the highest imaginable level, aided by becoming joint dux
of the Len Evans Tutorial in '09. He was senior winemaker at Best's, where he made the '12
Jimmy Watson winner; and is now senior winemaker for Shaw + Smith and their associated
Tolpuddle Vineyard in Tasmania. (JH)

ΨΨΨΨΨ Hills Blend #2 Gamay 2020, Adelaide Hills A sophisticated gamay, eerily
reminiscent of a top-flight Hills pinot noir. Striking colour, a deep hue in the glass,
with a wealth of red cherry fruit, plum, dusty cacao, cassia bark and lavender. Dives
deep into an intense, spice-fuelled palate, supple and even, with a light smokiness
and complexity. Superb gamay. You may not look at the grape in the same way
ever again. Screw cap. 13% alc. RATING 95 DRINK 2021-2026 $42 JP

Elderton ★★★★★

3-5 Tanunda Road, Nuriootpa, SA 5355 **Region** Barossa Valley
T (08) 8568 7878 **www**.eldertonwines.com.au **Open** Mon–Fri 10–5, w'ends, hols 11–4
Winemaker Julie Ashmead, Brock Harrison **Viticulturist** Peter Wild, Conrad Pohlinger
Est. 1982 **Dozens** 45 000 **Vyds** 65ha

The founding Ashmead family, with mother Lorraine supported by sons Allister and Cameron,
continues to impress with their wines. Julie Ashmead (married to Cameron), fifth-generation
winemaker at Campbells in Rutherglen, is head of production, overseeing viticulture and
winemaking. Elderton has 3 vineyards. Two are in the Barossa Valley – Nuriootpa (Elderton's
original estate vineyard, with plantings dating back to 1894, with shiraz, cabernet sauvignon
and merlot) and Greenock (originally planted by the Helbig family in 1915, purchased in
2010, consisting of shiraz, grenache, carignan, mourvèdre, cabernet sauvignon, chardonnay and
semillon). The third is the Craneford Vineyard in the Eden Valley (planted to shiraz, cabernet
sauvignon, riesling and chardonnay). Energetic promotion and marketing in Australia and
overseas are paying dividends. Elegance and balance are the keys to these wines. Exports to
all major markets. (JH)

ΨΨΨΨΨ Command Barossa Shiraz 2019, Barossa Valley Estate-grown shiraz planted
circa 1894, aged for 24 months in new French and American oak puncheons.
Rich and commanding as always, with intense dark plum, blackberry and black
cherry fruits, fruitcake spice, black strap licorice, high-cocoa dark chocolate,
cedar and roasting meats. Full bodied and pure with superb fruit depth, superfine
gypsum-like tannins and a concentrated and balanced finish that lingers admirably.
Screw cap. 14.9% alc. RATING 96 DRINK 2022-2038 $160 DB

Ashmead Barossa Cabernet Sauvignon 2020, Barossa Valley Very tightly coiled aromatic profile showing blackberry, cassis and blackcurrant fruits sheathed in fruitcake spice, briar, espresso, pressed flowers, earth and dried herbs. Fruit pure with a graceful line across the palate, chocolaty oak, fine tannin and an elegant cassis-laden exit. Screw cap. 14.2% alc. RATING 95 DRINK 2022-2038 $130 DB
Helbig 1915 Shiraz 2020, Barossa Valley An impressively proportioned wine with considerable fruit density and power. Broody and concentrated blackberry and dark plum fruits with hints of cassis, clove, coal dust, sour cherry, salted licorice, dark chocolate, turned earth and dried herbs. It's no wallflower with a thick-shouldered, lumbering gait across the palate, super concentrated black fruits, tight assertive tannins the provide savoury support and a hint of alcohol on the intense finish. One for the power hounds. Cork. 15.2% alc. RATING 95 DRINK 2022-2038 $350 DB

ŢŢŢŢŢ **Neil Ashmead Grand Tourer Shiraz 2020, Barossa Valley** RATING 93 DRINK 2021-2035 $65 DB
Ode to Lorraine Cabernet Shiraz Merlot 2019, Barossa Valley RATING 92 DRINK 2021-2036 $65 DB
Shiraz 2019, Barossa RATING 90 DRINK 2022-2028 $38 DB

Eldorado Road   ★★★★★

46-48 Ford Street, Beechworth, Vic 3747 **Region** Beechworth
T (03) 5725 1698 **www**.eldoradoroad.com.au **Open** Fri–Sat 11–6, Sun–Mon 11–4
Winemaker Paul Dahlenburg, Ben Dahlenburg, Laurie Schulz **Est.** 2010 **Dozens** 1500
Vyds 4ha
Paul Dahlenburg (nicknamed Bear), Lauretta Schulz (Laurie) and their children leased a 2ha block of shiraz planted in the 1890s with rootlings supplied from France (doubtless grafted) in the wake of phylloxera's devastation of the Glenrowan and Rutherglen plantings. Bear and Laurie knew about the origins of the vineyard, which was in a state of serious decline after years of neglect. The owners of the vineyard were aware of its historic importance and were more than happy to lease it. Years of tireless work reconstructing the old vines has resulted in tiny amounts of exceptionally good shiraz; they have also planted a small area of nero d'Avola and durif. (JH)

ŢŢŢŢŢ **Perseverance Old Vine Shiraz 2019, Beechworth** The concentration of fruit is truly extraordinary. Seductive in deep purple, gloriously complex and in total harmony, Perseverance is a wonderful celebration of old vines. Dark violet aromas meet a groundswell of black fruits, plum, anise, sage and tilled earth. Unfolds gently, seamlessly, elegantly and so long. Only 118 dozen produced. Screw cap. 14.6% alc. RATING 97 DRINK 2022-2033 $85 JP

ŢŢŢŢŢ **Onyx Durif 2019, North East Victoria** Durif re-imagined, courtesy of cool-climate elegance (Beechworth) mixed with a dose of generosity (Rutherglen) that needs to be tasted by every drinker who was ever scared witless by the grape. This is not scary, rather it's brilliantly delivered as a serious wine of some beauty: aromatic, blueberry, plum, dark chocolate and spice all lifted, fresh and plush. Bravo. Screw cap. 14.3% alc. RATING 96 DRINK 2022-2034 $37 JP ❂ ♥
Quasimodo Nero d'Avola Durif Shiraz 2019, Beechworth From one of the state's more thoughtful winemakers comes a complex blend of fruit sourcing and winemaking. Each grape was treated separately to make this beaut wine. The price belies the work and the wow factor achieved. Vibrant blueberry, black cherry, plum, anise, earth and spice take the lead, to be enhanced by sweet, vanillin oak. Finishes long and supple with an ongoing thread of rosemary. Screw cap. 13.5% alc. RATING 95 DRINK 2022-2027 $29 JP ❂

Eldridge Estate of Red Hill

120 Arthurs Seat Road, Red Hill, Vic 3937 **Region** Mornington Peninsula
T 0414 758 960 **www**.eldridge-estate.com.au **Open** Fri–Mon 11–5 **Winemaker** David
Lloyd **Est.** 1985 **Dozens** 1000 **Vyds** 3ha

Wine has been a constant throughout David Lloyd's life and career. His father, a church
minister, baptised and married many members of the Hardy winemaking clan. While studying
for a BSc at Monash Uni, David joined the wine club and 'fell in love with the mix of science
and art that is winemaking.' With his wife, Wendy, he bought a vineyard on the Mornington
Peninsula in '95 and planted chardonnay, pinot noir and gamay. Later, friends in Oregon
alerted him to the qualities of 20 different clones of pinot noir, setting him off on a complex
clonal journey that earned him the moniker 'the clone ranger'. A visit to Burgundy in '08
inspired him to create a passetoutgrains, the Burgundian blend of pinot noir and gamay; thus
PTG, one of Eldridge's biggest sellers, was born. In '12, Wendy was diagnosed with stage
4 cancer and sadly died 2 years later; David has fought and won his own cancer battles since.
In early '22, he placed Eldridge Estate on the market. Exports to the US. (JP)

🍷🍷🍷🍷🍷 **PTG 2021, Mornington Peninsula** Such a cheery wine, with enchanting
aromas of violets, baking spices and red fruit. The mid-weighted palate leads
with tangy, ultra-refreshing acidity, a pop of cherries and raspberries, finishing
with a gentle radicchio bitterness and fine, sandy tannins. 100% refreshment,
100% enjoyment guaranteed. Screw cap. 14% alc. RATING 95 DRINK 2022-2026
$35 JF ✪

Single Vineyard Chardonnay 2020, Mornington Peninsula A well-
composed and finely tuned outcome, with more citrus tones of grapefruit and
lemon, ginger powder and spicy cedary oak, plus a whiff of woodsmoke. A tight
palate, yet not lean, as there's some nutty-creamy lees. The refreshing acidity guides
this to a resounding finish. Screw cap. 13% alc. RATING 95 DRINK 2022-2028
$70 JF

Wendy Chardonnay 2020, Mornington Peninsula There's a restraint
with the chardonnays this vintage. Not lacking flavour though, just a seemingly
tighter palate. Grapefruit and white nectarines, spicy and savoury, long and pure.
Everything tucked in neatly, including the oak. The acidity is lively and allows
the finish to unfurl and linger. Screw cap. 13% alc. RATING 95 DRINK 2022-2029
$80 JF

Single Vineyard Fumé Blanc 2021, Mornington Peninsula Guava, fresh
basil and lemongrass with a squirt of lemon juice all link to the varietal spectrum.
But it's talc-like texture, woodsy spices and a level of complexity link it to the
fumé style. No harsh edges at all with bright acidity to close. Screw cap. 13% alc.
RATING 94 DRINK 2022-2025 $35 JF

🍷🍷🍷🍷🍸 **Single Vineyard Gamay 2020, Mornington Peninsula** RATING 93
DRINK 2022-2026 $60 JF

Burkitt Blend Pinot Noir 2020, Mornington Peninsula RATING 93
DRINK 2021-2026 $70 JF

Ellis Wines

52 Garsed Street, Bendigo Victoria 3550 **Region** Heathcote
T 0401 290 315 **www**.elliswines.com.au **Open** Mon–Fri 11–4 **Winemaker** Guy
Rathjen, Nina Stocker **Viticulturist** Bryan Ellis **Est.** 1999 **Dozens** 3000 **Vyds** 54.18ha

Bryan and Joy Ellis own this family business, daughter Raylene Flanagan is the sales manager,
and all its vineyard blocks are named after family members. For the first 10 years the Ellises
were content to sell the grapes to a range of distinguished producers. However, since then a
growing portion of the crop has been vinified. Exports to Hong Kong. (JH)

🍷🍷🍷🍷🍷 **Premium Shiraz 2018, Heathcote** Made with longevity in mind, this
premium edition of Heathcote shiraz is all about control. It's biding its time, taut
as a drum, but so good. Aged 14 months in new and aged French oak, it offers
an intensity of tightly focused vanillin oak with well-composed damson plums,

cassis, licorice, tapenade and bitter chocolate. Dark and ripe, long and fine in sturdy tannins, it's bound for further time in the cellar. Screw cap. 14.8% alc. RATING 95 DRINK 2022–2030 $70 JP

Signature Label Shiraz 2019, Heathcote A rich, oak-influenced style in keeping with the producer's style of red-wine making which demands further bottle ageing. Tight and focused, it delivers a complex array of scents and flavours, of clove, cardamom spice, violet with a thread of herbal complexity before settling into a solid core of plums, blueberries and cassis. The overarching influence of oak resonates in tandem with burly tannins. Screw cap. 14.8% alc. RATING 94 DRINK 2022–2031 $40 JP

🍷🍷🍷🍷🍷 **Signature Label Moscato Muscat 2021, Heathcote** RATING 92 $22 JP ✪

Signature Label Viognier 2021, Heathcote RATING 91 DRINK 2022–2026 $27 JP

Eperosa ★★★★★

Lot 552 Krondorf Road, Tanunda, SA 5352 **Region** Barossa Valley
T 0428 111 121 **www**.eperosa.com.au **Open** Fri–Sat 11–5 **Winemaker** Brett Grocke
Est. 2005 **Dozens** 1000 **Vyds** 8.75ha

Eperosa owner and Wine Companion 2021 Winemaker of the Year Brett Grocke qualified as a viticulturist in '01 and, through Grocke Viticulture, consults and provides technical services to over 200ha of vineyards spread across the Barossa Valley, Eden Valley, Adelaide Hills, Riverland, Langhorne Creek and Hindmarsh Valley. He is ideally placed to secure small parcels of organically managed grapes, hand-picked, whole-bunch fermented and foot-stomped, and neither filtered nor fined. The wines are of impeccable quality – the use of high-quality, perfectly inserted, corks will allow the wines to reach their full maturity decades hence. Exports to the UK, the US and Canada. (JH)

🍷🍷🍷🍷🍷 **L.R.C. Shiraz 2020, Barossa Valley** With 2% riesling to give it some added spark. Deep damson plum and blackberry fruit, packed with exotic spice, roasting meats, violets and savoury nuance. Gorgeous texture and flow in the mouth. Meaty-edged plummy fruits and abundant spice, gravelly tannin and a bright, savoury flick to its tail. Cork. 13.9% alc. RATING 96 DRINK 2021–2035 $60 DB ✪

Stonegarden 1858 Grenache 2020, Eden Valley Bright red purple in the glass with perfumed characters of red cherry, satsuma plum and dried cranberry. Hints of purple flowers, exotic spice, ginger cake, charcuterie, light amaro herbs and earth. Airy and spacious with a delightful floral plume in the mouth, pure fruit profile and fine, billowing tannins. Cork. 14% alc. RATING 95 DRINK 2022–2030 $60 DB

Krondorf 1903 Grenache 2020, Barossa Valley Displaying a pale, pinot-esque hue in the glass and the most gorgeous, gossamer aromatic profile with notes of red cherry and plum, raspberry and redcurrant with hints of exotic spice, jasmine, gingerbread, struck flint, red licorice and earth. Light in body with a diaphanous air, complex meaty notes flitting in and out, gypsum-like tannin in support. Rayas-like in its flow. Cork. 11.7% alc. RATING 94 DRINK 2022–2028 $35 DB

🍷🍷🍷🍷🍷 **Magnolia 1965 Shiraz 2020, Barossa Valley** RATING 93 DRINK 2020–2030 $60 DB

Grenache Mataro 2020, Barossa Valley RATING 92 DRINK 2022–2025 $30 DB

Magnolia Vine Vale Shiraz 2020, Barossa Valley RATING 92 DRINK 2022–2028 $30 DB

Magnolia 1941 Semillon 2020, Barossa Valley RATING 92 DRINK 2022–2028 $35 DB

Magnolia 1950 Grenache 2020, Barossa Valley RATING 92 DRINK 2022–2027 $35 DB

Magnolia 1896 Shiraz 2020, Barossa Valley RATING 92 DRINK 2022-2030 $80 DB
Magnolia Blanc #2 Semillon NV, Barossa Valley RATING 92
DRINK 2022-2027 $30 DB

Ernest Hill Wines

307 Wine Country Drive, Nulkaba, NSW 2325 **Region** Hunter Valley
T (02) 4991 4418 **www.ernesthillwines.com.au Open** 7 days 10–5 **Winemaker** Mark
Woods **Est.** 1999 **Dozens** 6000 **Vyds** 12ha
This is part of a vineyard originally planted in the early '70s by Harry Tulloch for Seppelt
Wines; it was later renamed Pokolbin Creek Vineyard, and later still (in '99) the Wilson
family purchased the upper (hill) part of the vineyard, and renamed it Ernest Hill. It is now
planted to semillon, shiraz, chardonnay, verdelho, traminer, merlot and tempranillo. Exports
to Singapore. (JH)

🍷🍷🍷🍷🍷 **Shareholders Shiraz 2019, Hunter Valley** A warm year, defined by exuberant
sweet cherry fruit and weight. Tamarind, pomegranate and candied orange zest, to
boot. A bit sweet, I suppose, but there is such inherent value, a nostalgic classicism
and yet, a contemporary freshness about these wines that is winning. It will, to be
sure, age well. Very. Screw cap. 14% alc. RATING 94 DRINK 2021-2032 $30 NG ❁

🍷🍷🍷🍷🍷 **Shareholders Shiraz 2010, Hunter Valley** RATING 93 DRINK 2021-2024 $30
NG
Cyril Premium Hunter Semillon 2021, Hunter Valley RATING 92
DRINK 2021-2026 $26 NG
Andrew Watson Reserve Premium Tempranillo 2017, Hunter Valley
RATING 92 DRINK 2021-2024 $35 NG

Evans & Tate

Cnr Metricup Road/Caves Road, Wilyabrup, WA 6280 **Region** Margaret River
T (08) 9755 6244 **www.evansandtate.wine Open** By appt **Winemaker** Matthew Byrne,
Feleasha Prendergast **Est.** 1970 **Vyds** 12.3ha
The history of Evans & Tate has a distinct wild-west feel to its ownership changes since 1970,
when it started life as a small 2-family-owned business centred on the Swan District. Suffice
it to say, it was part of a corporate chess game between McWilliam's Wines and the Fogarty
Wine Group. It is now 100% owned by Fogarty, who previously held 70%. This doubles
Fogarty's production to 600000 dozen, cementing its place as the largest producer of WA
wine. Exports to all major markets. (JH)

🍷🍷🍷🍷🍷 **Redbrook Reserve Cabernet Sauvignon 2018, Margaret River** Potently
intense fruit here – the wine enters the mouth with fanfare and pomp; the fruit
that gathers there is riddled with cassis, raspberry leaf, black tea, pepper, exotic
spice and more. Classical cabernet from Margaret River, from a great vintage.
Exactly what we have come to expect from the Redbrook Reserve range. Screw
cap. 14.5% alc. RATING 96 DRINK 2022-2037 $65 EL ❁
Redbrook Estate Chardonnay 2019, Margaret River A reliably brilliant
wine, this year is no exception. Classy fruit collides with toasty oak, all of it
punctuated by bright acidity and fine texture. Super-smart+. Screw cap. 13% alc.
RATING 95 DRINK 2021-2031 $40 EL
Redbrook Reserve Chardonnay 2019, Margaret River Fresh and powerful,
with a distinct linearity, thanks to the cool '19 vintage. This is so taut and coiled
right now as to be almost closed. It won't remain that way forever, but in the
meantime, a decant is advised. Screw cap. 13% alc. RATING 95 DRINK 2022-2032
$65 EL
Single Vineyard Chardonnay 2019, Margaret River Scintillating acidity
and ripe fruit are the hallmarks of good Margaret River chardonnay, and both are
here in spades. Classy oak frames the picture. The length of flavour shows us the

final piece of the puzzle. Smart beyond its price. Screw cap. 13.5% alc. RATING 94
DRINK 2021–2031 $35 EL

Redbrook Estate Cabernet Merlot 2019, Margaret River This is routinely
a very smart wine and this year is no exception. Savoury overtones colour
the nose with layers of peppercorn, hung deli meat and ironstone and ferrous
notes, while the juicy undercurrent of red and black fruits courses beneath it all.
Compelling drinking. Screw cap. 14.5% alc. RATING 94 DRINK 2021–2031 $40 EL

Redbrook Estate Shiraz 2019, Margaret River Hand picked, 90% whole
bunches, wild ferment, matured for 9 months in old, large-format French oak.
This kind of vinification should be more widespread in Margaret River, where
the shiraz fruit doesn't respond as well to heavy doses of oak as it does in South
Australia. It's a different beast here, responding to a soft hand, and this wine is
testament to the goods that such an attitude can yield. Spicy, silky and plump: this
is an elegant wine and it has been treated as such. Screw cap. 14.5% alc. RATING 94
DRINK 2021–2028 $40 EL

🍷🍷🍷🍷♀ **Single Vineyard Malbec 2020, Margaret River** RATING 93 DRINK 2022–2032
$35 EL

Broadway Chardonnay 2020, Margaret River RATING 92 DRINK 2021–2028
$29 EL

Single Vineyard Shiraz Cabernet 2020, Margaret River RATING 90
DRINK 2021–2031 $35 EL

Evoi Wines

529 Osmington Road, Bramley, WA 6285 **Region** Margaret River
T 0437 905 100 **www**.evoiwines.com **Open** 7 days 10–5 **Winemaker** Nigel Ludlow
Est. 2006 **Dozens** 10 000

NZ-born Nigel Ludlow has a graduate diploma in oenology and viticulture from Lincoln
University, NZ. Time at Selaks was a stepping stone to Flying Winemaking stints in Hungary,
Spain and South Africa, before a return as senior winemaker at Nobilo. He thereafter moved
to Victoria, and finally to Margaret River. It took time for Evoi to take shape, the first vintage
of chardonnay being made in the lounge room of Nigel's house. By 2010 the barrels had been
evicted to more conventional storage and since '14 the wines have been made in leased space
at a commercial winery. Quality has been exceptional. Exports to the UK, the Caribbean,
Norway and Hong Kong. (JH)

🍷🍷🍷🍷🍷 **Chardonnay 2019, Margaret River** Trying to unpick the characters in this
wine is no simple thing. The concentration of flavour is impressive; this tells a
story of curry leaf, white peach, brine, hazelnuts and exotic white spice. The palate
has all of these, with the addition of dragon fruit, pink grapefruit, sourdough and
crushed-shell minerality woven through the very (very) long finish. Astounding
wine for the money. Ridiculous, in fact. Screw cap. 13.5% alc. RATING 95
DRINK 2020–2035 $32 EL ✪

Reserve Chardonnay 2020, Margaret River Somehow, this has more seamless
integration of oak and fruit compared to the estate wine of the same vintage, with
similar vinification. Pure and taut, this is concentrated in all ways – the flavour
notch is dialled up to high. A touch of boot polish on the nose, which shows
again through the finish as orange zest and turmeric. A big and powerful wine
from a vintage that will be remembered as being the same. Screw cap. 13.5% alc.
RATING 94 DRINK 2021–2031 $75 EL

🍷🍷🍷🍷♀ **The Satyr Reserve 2018, Margaret River** RATING 93 DRINK 2022–2036
$80 EL

Cabernet Sauvignon 2019, Margaret River RATING 92 DRINK 2021–2028
$38 EL

Sauvignon Blanc Semillon 2020, Margaret River RATING 91
DRINK 2021–2025 $24 EL

Chardonnay 2020, Margaret River RATING 90 DRINK 2021–2028 $35 EL

Faber Vineyard

233 Haddrill Road, Baskerville, WA 6056 **Region** Swan Valley
T (08) 9296 0209 **www.**fabervineyard.com.au **Open** Fri–Sun 11–4 **Winemaker** John
Griffiths **Est.** 1997 **Dozens** 4000 **Vyds** 4.5ha

John Griffiths, former Houghton winemaker, teamed with wife Jane Micallef to found Faber
Vineyard. They have established shiraz, verdelho (1.5ha each), brown muscat, chardonnay
and petit verdot (0.5ha each). John says, 'It may be somewhat quixotic, but I'm a great fan of
traditional warm-area Australian wine styles, wines made in a relatively simple manner that
reflect the concentrated ripe flavours one expects in these regions. And when one searches,
some of these gems can be found from the Swan Valley.' Exports to Hong Kong. (JH)

Liqueur Muscat NV, Swan Valley This is sensational. It is both fresh and aged;
vibrant and brooding. It is like liquid velvet in the mouth and has silken toffee,
jersey caramels, fresh honeycomb, morning coffee, dark fruitcake, summer figs, date,
and a plethora of other flavours in the same vein. Pure, complex and astounding.
500ml. Screw cap. 18% alc. RATING 97 $60 EL ♣ ♥

CBP Chenin Blanc 2021, Swan Valley 12.5% is remarkable alcohol for such
a sun-drenched place as the Swan – and this wine is remarkable. Really obvious
barrel-ferment characters (toast, spice, nutmeg, curry leaf etc.) swarm around the
chenin fruit (green apples, apricots, bush flowers, cheesecloth and lanolin). The
estate chenin is a gloriously pure, unfettered expression of Swan Valley chenin; this
CBP is a more complex, worked and substantial flex of the same variety. There's
no right or wrong, you choose – both are sensational. Screw cap. 12.5% alc.
RATING 95 DRINK 2021-2036 $36 EL
Grenache 2021, Swan Valley Swan Valley grenache – what joy. It's more
rugged and fierce than the grenache found in other parts of the state, but with
that comes a robustness of flavour and density, which is most welcome. Black
pepper, raspberry, mulberry, clove and pomegranate dust. It's salty and savoury,
but that fruit has such a sweet, sweet core. The sun shines brightly on the Swan,
and it is evident here in the glass, in a very positive way. Really recommend a
short decant – the fruit has already blossomed in the time it has spent in the glass.
Screw cap. 14% alc. RATING 94 DRINK 2021-2028 $34 EL
Petit Verdot 2020, Swan Valley As one of Australia's oldest wine regions, the
Swan Valley (est. 1829) doesn't get the attention it deserves. For such a gloriously
sun-drenched place, it is capable of producing wines of detail and finesse, as this
is. Super-concentrated! Black cats, blackberry, lavender, aniseed and peppercorns.
There's so much to like about this. It's floral and glossy and full bodied. A
wonderful wine. Screw cap. 14.5% alc. RATING 94 DRINK 2021-2031 $35 EL

Fallen Giants

4113 Ararat-Halls Gap Road, Halls Gap, Vic 3381 **Region** Grampians
T (03) 5356 4252 **www.**fallengiants.com.au **Open** By appt **Winemaker** Justin Purser
Viticulturist Rebecca Drummond **Est.** 1969 **Dozens** 3000 **Vyds** 10.5ha

The first time some drinkers may have heard of Fallen Giants was in 2021 when the Fallen
Giants Shiraz 2019 took home the Jimmy Watson Memorial Trophy at the Melbourne Royal
Wine Awards. It took out Best Victorian Shiraz and the well-regarded Trevor Mast Trophy for
Best Shiraz. For those with long memories, this did not come as such a big surprise. Originally
planted in 1969, the (now) Fallen Giants vineyard had once been part of the Grampians' well-
regarded Mount Langi Ghiran, before being bought by the late Trevor Mast. Following his
death, it was purchased by siblings Aaron and Rebecca Drummond and renamed Fallen Giants
in '13. The name takes its meaning from the local Djab Wurrung and Jardiwadjali people and
references the creation of Halls Gap. The Drummonds grew up on the Mornington Peninsula;
Aaron went on to work for the Rathbone Wine Group, while Rebecca headed into global
financial market trading. Together, they work at making some of the better wines of the
Grampians wine region. (JP)

TTTTT **Cabernet Sauvignon 2020, Grampians** A striking wine from the get-go, so fragrant in regional Aussie bush characters. A lovely gentle complexity awaits the drinker with concentrated black fruits, cassis, licorice, spice, a splash of mocha oak and layers of dense tannins. Screw cap. 14.5% alc. RATING 95 DRINK 2021-2031 $35 JP ✪

Shiraz 2020, Grampians The follow-up vintage to the '19 winner of the Jimmy Watson Trophy at the '21 Melbourne Royal Wine Awards. The '20 is similarly blessed with great elegance and poise. A sheer, fragrant lift to the perfume in peppery red fruits, baking spices and plum with convincing, concentrated flavours. Tannins run fine through to the finish with a gentle grip. Screw cap. 14.5% alc. RATING 95 DRINK 2021-2033 $35 JP ✪

Block 3 Shiraz 2020, Grampians The beauty of Grampians shiraz is celebrated here. It starts and ends with great balance in every aspect, from grape to wine, coming alive in the process. Supple blackberries, cassia, licorice, cassia bark and tilled earth wrapped firmly in fine, lithe tannins. Great definition with time to burn. Screw cap. 13.5% alc. RATING 95 DRINK 2021-2030 $60 JP

Riesling 2021, Grampians Sweet herbal notes and lifted florals introduce a steely, lemon, lime-cordial and white-nectarine-perfumed riesling that shows the full appeal of the Grampians' most underrated white grape. Great focus and drive, not to mention longevity, thanks to brisk acidity. Screw cap. 12.5% alc. RATING 94 DRINK 2021-2028 $30 JP ✪

TTTTꟼ **Rosé 2021, Grampians** RATING 90 DRINK 2021-2024 $25 JP

False Cape Wines   ★★★★

1054 Willson River Road, Dudley East, SA 5222 **Region** Kangaroo Island **T** 0447 808 838 **www.**falsecapewines.com.au **Open** 7 days 11–5 **Winemaker** Greg Follett, Nick Walker **Viticulturist** Jamie Helyar **Est.** 1999 **Dozens** 6000 **Vyds** 30ha Julie and Jamie Helyar's False Cape Vineyards links third-generation Kangaroo Island farming with third-generation Langhorne Creek grape growers. It is the largest vineyard on Kangaroo Island with 30ha of vines (shiraz and sauvignon blanc with 10ha each, 6ha of cabernet sauvignon and lesser amounts of chardonnay, riesling, pinot gris, merlot and pinot noir). Wines are made by Julie's brother, Greg Follett, of Lake Breeze in Langhorne Creek; Nick Walker of O'Leary Walker makes the Riesling. False Cape is entirely off-grid, completely relying on solar power; the red grape varieties are dry-grown, free-range turkeys providing pest control management and sheep are used for weed management during winter. The wines are consistently well made and low priced. Exports to Switzerland and Hong Kong. (JH)

TTTTT **Willson River Riesling 2021, Kangaroo Island** Lovely riesling, with an even flow from the first sip to the finish. Lime, Meyer lemon and grapefruit float on crisp, natural acidity. Screw cap. 12% alc. RATING 94 DRINK 2022-2032 $22 JH ✪

Unknown Sailor Cabernet Merlot 2019, Kangaroo Island The colour is excellent, crimson through to the rim. The mouthfeel of this medium-bodied blend is compelling, fruit, tannins and oak coalesce, blackcurrant at its centre. Screw cap. 14% alc. RATING 94 DRINK 2023-2030 $27 JH ✪

The Captain Cabernet Sauvignon 2019, Kangaroo Island The only question about this richly flavoured, blackcurrant-fruited wine is the impact of the oak, particularly obvious on the finish. Nonetheless, it's integrated into the mainframe of perfectly ripened cabernet sauvignon and will steadily diminish with bottle age. Screw cap. 14% alc. RATING 94 DRINK 2023-2034 $41 JH

TTTTꟼ **Lady Ann Rosé 2021, Kangaroo Island** RATING 92 DRINK 2022-2023 $22 JH ✪

Silver Mermaid Sauvignon Blanc 2021, Kangaroo Island RATING 91 DRINK 2021-2023 $22 JH ✪

Ship's Graveyard Shiraz 2020, Kangaroo Island RATING 91 DRINK 2025-2035 $27 JH

Montebello Pinot Gris 2021, Kangaroo Island RATING 90 DRINK 2022-2023 $22 JH

Farmer & The Scientist

Jeffreys Road, Corop, Vic 3559 **Region** Heathcote
T 0400 141 985 **www.**farmerandthescientist.com **Winemaker** Glenn James, Jo Marsh,
Jess Dwyer **Viticulturist** Brian Dwyer **Est.** 2013 **Dozens** 1000 **Vyds** 8ha
The Farmer is Brian Dwyer; the Scientist, wife Jess. Brian is a viticulturist who learnt his
craft with Southcorp, Jess has a degree in science amplified by teaching. She became doubly
qualified by working in wineries and vineyards from a young age. (JH)

🍷🍷🍷🍷🍷 **Fiano 2021, Heathcote** This fiano is gently complex in quince, pear and cut
apple, opening on to a smooth textured palate. A saline tang lifts the middle palate.
Acidity is keen. You have to say the grape has a bright future in the Heathcote
region. Screw cap. 13.1% alc. RATING 90 DRINK 2021–2025 $25 JP

🍷🍷🍷🍷 **Single Vineyard Tempranillo 2021, Heathcote** RATING 88
DRINK 2022–2025 $28 JP
Single Vineyard Shiraz 2021, Heathcote RATING 88 DRINK 2022–2025 $28 JP

Farmer's Leap Wines

41 Hodgson Road, Padthaway, SA 5271 **Region** Padthaway
T (08) 8765 5155 **www.**farmersleap.com **Open** 7 days 10–4 **Winemaker** Renae Hirsch
Est. 2004 **Dozens** 12000 **Vyds** 357ha
Scott Longbottom and Cheryl Merrett are third-generation farmers in Padthaway. They
commenced planting the vineyard in '93 on the family property and now there are shiraz,
cabernet sauvignon, chardonnay and merlot. Initially the majority of the grapes were sold, but
increasing quantities held for the Farmer's Leap label have seen production rise. Exports to
Canada, Singapore, South Korea, Japan, Taiwan and Hong Kong. (JH)

🍷🍷🍷🍷🍷 **The Brave Shiraz 2019, Padthaway** Concentrated and intense, this is a
mouthful of billowing flavour; mulberries, blueberry compote, raspberry and
licorice are a small nod to the cavalcade of fruit that is contained therein. The long
finish is admirable, offering further opportunity to assess and pick out new flavours.
Very smart indeed. Screw cap. 14.5% alc. RATING 93 DRINK 2022–2032 $40 EL
Shiraz 2019, Padthaway Inky, concentrated and a little bit bloody, this is riddled
with salted plum, red apple skins, boysenberry and mulberry by the bucketload.
The ferrous character on the palate offsets all of these flavours and elevates the
wine out of sight. Screw cap. 14.5% alc. RATING 91 DRINK 2022–2027 $25 EL
Cabernet Sauvignon 2019, Padthaway Vibrant, structured and moving to
firm, this is a flavoursome, concentrated cabernet that hits all the marks. Ripe,
balanced, powerful, fresh. All good things. Screw cap. 14.5% alc. RATING 90
DRINK 2022–2028 $25 EL

Fermoy Estate

838 Metricup Road, Wilyabrup, WA 6280 **Region** Margaret River
T (08) 9755 6285 **www.**fermoy.com.au **Open** 7 days 11–5 **Winemaker** Jeremy
Hodgson **Viticulturist** Andrew Keig **Est.** 1985 **Dozens** 25000 **Vyds** 27.28ha
A long-established winery with plantings of semillon, sauvignon blanc, chardonnay, cabernet
sauvignon, merlot and shiraz. The Young family acquired Fermoy Estate in '10 and built a
larger cellar door which opened in '13, signalling the drive to increase domestic sales. They
are happy to keep a relatively low profile, however difficult that may be given the quality
of the wines. Jeremy Hodgson brings with him a first-class honours degree in oenology
and viticulture, and a CV encompassing winemaking roles with Wise Wines, Cherubino
Consultancy and, earlier, Plantagenet, Houghton and Goundrey Wines. (JH)

🍷🍷🍷🍷🍷 **Reserve Chardonnay 2020, Margaret River** Of all the Fermoy wines, the
Reserve Chardonnay was the wine I was holding out to see. My memory of
previous vintages is of acidity so finely woven into the fruit that the affair becomes
succulent and juicy … chewy and satisfying. It brings a smile to the face. As
this does. Concentrated, classical, a little bit creamy, a little bit nutty, definitely

spicy and voluminous in its powerful fruit explosion in the mouth. It won't always be just $65, though we can hope it will. Screw cap. 13.5% alc. RATING 96 DRINK 2022–2037 $65 EL ✪

Reserve Cabernet Sauvignon 2019, Margaret River 100% Houghton clone + Wilyabrup = a great match. Somehow the dirt and sky here combine with the clone to produce a decidedly red, supple, succulent style of cabernet. Also, it must be said here, Fermoy is on the up: watch this star rise. This is precisely as we hope: bright, spicy, layered with raspberry, pomegranate, red licorice and pink peppercorn. In the mouth it is exactly thus, with the added bonus of spring flowers, crushed graphite and Pink Lady Apples. Gold medal Royal Adelaide Wine Show 2021. Screw cap. 14% alc. RATING 96 DRINK 2022–2042 $95 EL

Coldfire Fumé Blanc 2021, Margaret River The 50% skin-contact component is really clear here and it is glorious. There is orange zest, soft orange blossom, nougat, cardamom, cumin, brine, white peach, turmeric, toasty oak and poached apples and rhubarb. 'Clementine, lavender, kernel' says the back of the bottle: apt. This is ethereal and fully integrated … totally awesome. Brilliant. Screw cap. 13% alc. RATING 95 DRINK 2022–2028 $30 EL ✪

Cabernet Sauvignon 2019, Margaret River 100% Houghton clone. You know when you spot Houghton clone from Wilyabrup that you're in for a succulent, red-fruited time. It's a combination of the clone and the dirt, and it's good. While the oak is initially prominent now, the fruit behind it is precisely as expected – singing. This may need a little more time for the oak to recede, however the fruit is bang-on, and the tannins are a highlight. Gorgeous. Screw cap. 14% alc. RATING 95 DRINK 2021–2036 $45 EL

Cabernet Sauvignon Merlot 2019, Margaret River If Fermoy isn't edging onto your radar, you need to perk up. The wines have refreshed packaging, which reiterates the value found inside the bottles. This is very smart. Succulent, pure fruit is shaped by fine, chalky tannins that help the flavour sail over the palate and off into the distance. Really impressive for the price, it looks the part too. Screw cap. 14.5% alc. RATING 94 DRINK 2021–2031 $27 EL ✪

Blackwater Cabernet Shiraz 2019, Margaret River Spicy black fruit and very fine tannins are the calling cards here. It is supple and medium weight, savoury and cooling somehow … mineral. A very modern expression of cabernet shiraz – I really like it. Fermoy: on the boil. Screw cap. 14% alc. RATING 94 DRINK 2022–2030 $40 EL

♟♟♟♟♟ **Vintage Brut Rosé 2020, Margaret River** RATING 93 $45 EL
Chardonnay 2020, Margaret River RATING 92 DRINK 2021–2027 $35 EL
Merlot 2019, Margaret River RATING 92 DRINK 2022–2029 $30 EL
Vintage Brut Premier 2017, Margaret River RATING 91 $45 EL

Fernfield Wines ★★★☆

112 Rushlea Road, Eden Valley, SA 5235 **Region** Eden Valley
T 0402 788 526 **www**.fernfieldwines.com.au **Open** Fri–Mon 11–4
Winemaker Rebecca Barr, Scott Barr **Viticulturist** Rebecca Barr, Scott Barr, Mark Bartholomaeus **Est.** 2002 **Dozens** 1500 **Vyds** 1ha
The establishment date of 2002 might, with a little poetic licence, be shown as 1864. Bryce Lillecrapp is the fifth generation of the Lillecrapp family; his great-great-great-grandfather bought land in the Eden Valley in 1864, subdividing it in 1866, establishing the township of Eden Valley and building the first house, Rushlea Homestead. Bryce restored this building and opened it in 1998 as a bicentennial project; it now serves as Fernfield Wines' cellar door. Ownership passed to Rebecca Barr and husband Scott in 2013. (JH)

♟♟♟♟♟ **Gold Leaf Reserve Shiraz 2015, Eden Valley** Aromas of red and dark summer berry fruits, plum and red cherry with hints of baking spice, pressed flowers, tobacco and red licorice. Bright and red-fruited palate, with a lively acid line, fine, gravelly tannin and a wash of red cherry, plum and oak-derived spice on the finish. Screw cap. 14.5% alc. RATING 90 DRINK 2021–2028 $64 DB

Ferngrove

276 Ferngrove Road, Frankland River, WA 6396 **Region** Frankland River
T (08) 9363 1300 **www**.ferngrove.com.au **Winemaker** Craig Grafton, Adrian Foot
Viticulturist Chris Zur **Est.** 1998 **Vyds** 220ha

For over 20 years, Ferngrove has been producing consistent examples of cool-climate wines across multiple price brackets. The Ferngrove stable includes the flagship Orchid wines, Black Label, White Label and Independence ranges. Ferngrove Vineyards Pty Ltd enjoys the benefits of majority international ownership. Exports to all major markets. (JH)

🍷🍷🍷🍷🍷 **Independence Shiraz 2020, Great Southern** 95/5% shiraz/viognier, co-fermented. Red fruits and flowers on the nose; 5% viognier is a noticeable hit, but it's well judged in this case. Potent midnight fruits mingle with the daytime vibes of raspberries and pink peppercorn. Lots to like, and all the while retaining the thing that makes it great: that Frankland River DNA of ferrous, ironstone, red dirt and blood plum. Distinctive, delicious and shapely. Unbelievable value for money. Screw cap. 14% alc. RATING 94 DRINK 2021–2028 $26 EL ✪
Orchid Range Dragon Syrah 2019, Frankland River Fine boned, delicate and long, tempered by sinewy tannins and supple, pliable red and black fruits. The wine lingers in the mouth, leaving behind it a trail of ironstone, raspberries, pink peppercorns, hung deli meat, roasted beetroot and aniseed. The tannins are a highlight; firm and very finely knit. Screw cap. 13.5% alc. RATING 94 DRINK 2021–2031 $40 EL

🍷🍷🍷🍷🍷 **Estate Shiraz 2020, Frankland River** RATING 93 DRINK 2022–2032 $40 EL
Black Label Shiraz 2020, Frankland River RATING 92 DRINK 2021–2028 $22 EL ✪
Orchid Range Diamond Chardonnay 2020, Frankland River RATING 92 DRINK 2021–2028 $32 EL
Orchid Range Dragon Shiraz 2020, Western Australia RATING 92 DRINK 2022–2032 $70 EL
Orchid Range King Malbec 2020, Frankland River RATING 92 DRINK 2021–2028 $40 EL
Black Label Chardonnay 2020, Frankland River RATING 90 DRINK 2021–2027 $22 EL
Malbec 2020, Frankland River RATING 90 DRINK 2022–2028 $22 EL

Fetherston Vintners

1/99a Maroondah Highway, Healesville, Vic 3777 **Region** Yarra Valley
T 0417 431 700 **www**.fetherstonwine.com.au **Winemaker** Chris Lawrence **Est.** 2015
Dozens 1500

Chris Lawrence and Camille Koll established Fetherston Vintners in '15. Chris enrolled in the oenology degree with the University of Southern Queensland, graduating in '14. During his time at Yering Station ('10–14) he worked his way up from junior cellar hand to assistant winemaker. A vintage at Domaine Serene in Oregon's Willamette Valley in '12 gave him further insight into the study of great chardonnay and pinot noir. In '14 he took on the role of winemaker at Sunshine Creek in the Yarra Valley. Camille is Yarra born and bred, growing up in Hoddles Creek. After finishing school, she began a 7-year stint at Domaine Chandon, giving her invaluable insight into professional branding, marketing and customer service. Chris's late grandfather was Tony Fetherston. (JH)

🍷🍷🍷🍷🍷 **Chardonnay 2020, Yarra Valley** A really bright green gold. Opening with some reduction and matchstick, there are some lovely just-ripened nectarine and green-apple aromas too. Tightly wound and with good energy, this just needs another 6 months or so to really hit its straps. Screw cap. 12.3% alc. RATING 93 DRINK 2022–2026 $38 PR
Peony Nebbiolo Rosé 2021, Pyrenees Light bright salmon pink. Raspberries and wild strawberries along with a little spice and grilled herbs. Savoury and

textured, this finishes dry with crunchy acidity. Screw cap. 12% alc. RATING 92 DRINK 2021-2023 $28 PR

Shiraz 2019, Yarra Valley An attractive and medium deep purple. Aromas of black cherries and well-handled savoury and floral notes from the whole bunches. Medium bodied, with an attractive combination of gentle, sweet fruit and savoury black olives, coffee and soft velvety tannins. A very nice effort. Screw cap. 13.7% alc. RATING 92 DRINK 2021-2026 $38 PR

Lily Sparkling 2021, Yarra Valley Early picked sauvignon blanc, from the Upper Yarra. Fermented and matured in neutral barriques before undergoing a secondary fermentation in bottle. Not disgorged. A natural, cloudy, yet bright green gold. There are stone fruits, kiwi, a little passionfruit along with some fresh croissant dough. Clean, crisp, dry and flavoursome, this has summer and warm nights written all over it! Screw cap. 11.5% alc. RATING 91 DRINK 2022-2024 $28 PR

Camellia Cabernet Sauvignon 2021, Yarra Valley Lively crimson purple in colour. An interesting and successful attempt to make a fruit-forward, supple, drink-now cabernet. Ripe with blackberry and blackcurrant fruits, the palate is equally ripe and juicy-fruited. Finishes moderately long with fine, powdery tannins which would disappear completely, I'm guessing, when had with food. Screw cap. 13.2% alc. RATING 90 DRINK 2021-2025 $28 PR

ŢŢŢŢ **Fungi Pinot Noir 2021, Yarra Valley** RATING 89 DRINK 2021-2024 $28 PR
Iris Chardonnay 2021, Yarra Valley RATING 89 DRINK 2021-2023 $28 PR
Pinot Noir 2020, Yarra Valley RATING 89 DRINK 2021-2024 $38 PR

Fighting Gully Road   ★★★★★

Kurrajong Way, Mayday Hill, Beechworth, Vic 3747 **Region** Beechworth
T 0407 261 373 www.fightinggullyroadwines.com.au **Open** By appt **Winemaker** Mark Walpole **Viticulturist** Mark Walpole **Est.** 1997 **Dozens** 3500 **Vyds** 10.5ha
Mark Walpole and his partner Carolyn De Poi found their elevated north-facing site south of Beechworth in '95. They commenced planting the Aquila Audax Vineyard in '97 with cabernet sauvignon and pinot noir, subsequently expanding with significant areas of sangiovese, tempranillo, shiraz, petit manseng and chardonnay. In '09 they were fortunate to lease the oldest vineyard in the region, planted by the Smith family in 1978 to chardonnay and cabernet sauvignon – in fact, Mark shares the lease with long-time friend Adrian Rodda (see A. Rodda Wines). Mark says, 'We are now making wine in a building in the old and historic Mayday Hills Lunatic Asylum – a place that should be full of winemakers!' Exports to Hong Kong. (JH)

ŢŢŢŢŢ **Black Label Smith's Vineyard Chardonnay 2019, Beechworth** The Smith's Vineyard's chardonnay vines were planted in 1978, the fruit of very high quality. The light touch of winemaker Mark Walpole results in a wine which is at once delicate and precise, yet complex and harmonious, akin to a top-quality chablis. Age shall not weary it. Screw cap. 13.5% alc. RATING 97 DRINK 2024-2040 $85 JH ✪

ŢŢŢŢŢ **Black Label Syrah 2018, Beechworth** No overt winemaking inputs here, a feat only performed when there is complete confidence in fruit quality. Seamless entry into a dark world of black fruits, blackstrap licorice, earth, anise and bush mint. Once in, you're hooked. Screw cap. 14% alc. RATING 95 DRINK 2022-2030 $70 JP

Black Label Aglianico 2018, Alpine Valleys A fascinating grape brought to life and, importantly, managed beautifully, massaging its notoriously high tannin and acidity and bringing forth a veritable cavalcade of exotic, savoury aromas and flavours in bramble, black cherry, cracked pepper and allspice. Focused, firm tannins run long, presenting a good argument for further ageing. Screw cap. 14% alc. RATING 94 DRINK 2022-2028 $45 JP

Fire Gully

4051 Caves Road, Wilyabrup, WA 6280 **Region** Margaret River
T (08) 9755 6220 **www.**firegully.com.au **Open** 7 days 10–5 **Winemaker** Dr Michael
Peterkin **Est.** 1988 **Dozens** 5000 **Vyds** 13.4ha
A 6ha lake created in a gully ravaged by bushfires gave the name. In '98, Mike Peterkin, of
nearby Pierro, purchased the vineyard; he manages it in conjunction with former owners Ellis
and Margaret Butcher. He regards the Fire Gully wines as entirely separate from those of
Pierro. The vineyard, adjacent to Moss Wood, is planted to cabernet sauvignon, merlot, shiraz,
semillon, sauvignon blanc and chardonnay. Wines are available for tasting at the Pierro cellar
door. Exports to all major markets. (JH)

ΥΥΥΥΥ **Shiraz 2018, Margaret River** The '18 vintage was seriously sensational in
Margaret River, and it's a sure thing in the glass, in '21. Spicy, rich and long with
oomph and 'go', without the brawny arm-wrestle that can come from 'bigger'
vintages, although there is some warmth on the finish. Good times lay ahead.
Screw cap. 15% alc. RATING 93 DRINK 2021–2028 $50 EL
Semillon 2020, Margaret River Grassy and bright with nashi pears, Granny
Smith apples and salted citrus. Wall to wall with flavour, punctuated by pert, juicy
acidity that keeps everything fresh and alive. Screw cap. 12.5% alc. RATING 92
DRINK 2021–2031 $37 EL
**E. + M. Butcher Pioneer Reserve Cabernet Sauvignon 2018, Margaret
River** Layers of chocolate and nori adorn the nose, while cassis, blackberry and
intensely piquant notes of rhubarb and raspberry colour the boundaries of the
palate. The oak has made a serious impact on this wine, particularly through the
finish, suggesting that further time may be needed to pull it all together. Screw cap.
14.5% alc. RATING 91 DRINK 2022–2032 $70 EL
Chardonnay 2020, Margaret River Bitter walnuts, green pineapple, crushed
cashew and yellow peach. It's a bit 'knees and elbows' at this stage, but the fruit
is plump, creamy and satisfying. It will come together in a year or 2. Screw cap.
14% alc. RATING 90 DRINK 2021–2031 $40 EL

ΥΥΥΥ **Rosé 2021, Margaret River** RATING 88 DRINK 2021–2023 $37 EL

Fireblock

28 Kiewa Place, Coomba Park, NSW 2428 (postal) **Region** Clare Valley
T (02) 6554 2193 **Winemaker** O'Leary Walker **Est.** 1926 **Dozens** 2500 **Vyds** 6ha
Fireblock (formerly Old Station Vineyard) is owned by Bill and Noel Ireland, who purchased
the then almost-70-year-old Watervale vineyard in '96. The vines, planted in '96 (3ha of shiraz
and 2ha of grenache), are dry-grown; the riesling (1ha) was replanted to the Geisenheim clone
in '08 when town water became available. The wines are skilfully contract-made, winning
trophies and gold medals at capital city wine shows. Exports to Sweden and Malaysia. (JH)

ΥΥΥΥ **Geisenheim Clone Watervale Riesling 2020, Clare Valley** A medium gold
hue with a flicker of olive. Lovely aromatics, a mix of florals, ginger spice and
lemon barley water. The usual citrus flavours come to the fore alongside talc-like
texture and spritely acidity, with some grip on the finish. Screw cap. 11.5% alc.
RATING 88 DRINK 2021–2027 $22 JF

Firetail

21 Bessell Road, Rosa Glen, WA 6285 **Region** Margaret River
T (08) 9757 5156 **www.**firetail.com.au **Open** 7 days 11–5 **Winemaker** Bruce Dukes,
Peter Stanlake **Est.** 2002 **Dozens** 1000 **Vyds** 4.2ha
Named for the Red-eared Firetail, a bird found only in the southwest corner of WA. Jessica
Worrall and Rob Glass are fugitives from the oil and gas industry. In 2002 they purchased a
historic vineyard in Margaret River that had been planted between 1979 and '81 to sauvignon
blanc, semillon and cabernet sauvignon; they have also planted chardonnay and malbec. (JH)

�␣ᵧᵧᵧᵧ Sauvignon Blanc 2021, Margaret River This has admirable intensity of
flavour, with plenty of guava, gooseberry, green apple, salted pineapple and fine
white spice. Screw cap. 12.5% alc. RATING 90 DRINK 2022-2025 $25 EL

ᵧᵧᵧᵧ Cabernet Malbec 2021, Margaret River RATING 88 DRINK 2021-2026
$25 EL

First Drop Wines ★★★★

38 Barossa Valley Way, Nuriootpa, SA 5355 **Region** Barossa Valley
T 0488 299 233 **www**.firstdropwines.com **Open** Wed–Sat 10–4, Sun 11–4
Winemaker John Retsas, Kurt Northam **Est.** 2004 **Dozens** 30000
First Drop Wines HQ is in the striking 'Home of the Brave' building on the southern edge
of Nuriootpa in the Provenance Barossa precinct. John Retsas is the man behind the dynamic
brand, with its striking wine labels and delicious wines sourced from vineyards across the
Barossa, Adelaide Hills and McLaren Vale. There is a heavy emphasis on the 'alternative'
(appropriate) varieties with Italian and Portuguese grape varieties making their savoury and
delicious presence felt; of course, shiraz, grenache, cabernet sauvignon and mataro also play
a role, with a contemporary slant. Exports to the US, Canada, the UK, Sweden, Belgium,
Poland, Germany, Denmark, Ukraine, Singapore, Hong Kong, Greece, Norway, South Korea
and Japan. (DB)

ᵧᵧᵧᵧᵧ Mother's Milk Barossa Shiraz 2020, Barossa Valley A wonderful, plushly-
fruited Barossa shiraz packed full of vibrant satsuma plum and juicy blueberry
characters, underscored by hints of maraschino cherry, Asian spice, violets,
turned earth, roasting meats and a nuance of softly spoken oak. There's depth of
fruit and intensity here, but also a sense of sapid juiciness with ripe, fine, sandy
chocolatey tannins adding ample support. The wine fans out with a plume of
spiced plum fruits on the finish. Wonderful value. Screw cap. 14.5% alc. RATING 94
DRINK 2021-2030 $28 DB ❂

ᵧᵧᵧᵧ␣ Disciples Willunga Cabernet Sauvignon 2015, McLaren Vale RATING 93
DRINK 2021-2031 $100 DB
Disciples Cabernet Sauvignon 2014, McLaren Vale RATING 93
DRINK 2021-2028 $100 DB
Disciples Seppeltsfield Shiraz 2010, Barossa Valley RATING 93
DRINK 2021-2028 $120 DB
Moderno 2021, Adelaide Hills RATING 92 DRINK 2021-2026 $28 DB
The Matador Garnacha 2020, Barossa Valley RATING 92 DRINK 2021-2027
$25 DB ❂
Touriga Nacional 2020, McLaren Vale RATING 92 DRINK 2021-2027 $25
DB ❂
Minchia Montepulciano 2018, Adelaide Hills RATING 91 DRINK 2021-2026
$45 DB
Disciples Monastrell 2012, Barossa Valley RATING 91 DRINK 2021-2028
$60 DB

First Foot Forward ★★★★

6 Maddens Lane, Coldstream, Vic 3770 **Region** Yarra Valley
T 0402 575 818 **www**.firstfootforward.com.au **Open** By appt **Winemaker** Martin
Siebert **Viticulturist** Robin Wood **Est.** 2013 **Dozens** 800
With an impressive CV that includes Yarra Yering and Coldstream Hills in the Yarra as well
as Benjamin Leroux (Burgundy) and Pegasus Bay (NZ), Martin Siebert landed at Tokar
Estate as chief winemaker in time for the cracking 2012 vintage, starting his own First Foot
Forward (or F3 as he refers to it!) a year later. Mainly sourcing fruit from the marginal Patch
vineyard from '13–'17, Siebert has since sourced fruit for F3 from the Lone Star vineyard at
Gladysdale. He likens himself to a classically trained musician dabbling in punk music, using
terracotta amphorae and eggs as well as some skin contact on the whites. That these well-
crafted expressions from cooler sites in the Upper Yarra are also well priced is a bonus. (PR)

�♥♥♥♥♀ Amphora Ferment Single Vineyard Sauvignon Blanc 2021, Yarra Valley
Fermentation began on skins before being pressed to 800L amphorae. The result
is a slightly different and excellent take on sauvignon blanc. Bright green gold, this
leaps out of the glass with its aromas of fresh guava, passionfruit, kiwi and snow
pea tendrils. The flavour-packed palate is bright, gently textured and balanced and
the finish is crisp and long. Screw cap. 13% alc. RATING 93 DRINK 2022-2025
$25 PR ❂

Upper Chardonnay 2021, Yarra Valley Bright green gold in colour and
offering aromas of white nectarines, orange blossom, grilled nuts and a little fresh
gunflint. The palate is saline, moreish and long on this well-priced and well-
made single-vineyard Yarra Valley chardonnay. Screw cap. 13% alc. RATING 93
DRINK 2022-2025 $30 PR

Upper Pinot Noir 2021, Yarra Valley A light, bright crimson, this has red
berry fruits, lifted floral aromatics and a little savoury spice. The well-weighted
palate has good depth, while remaining light on its feet at the same time. It's still
a pup and I can see this blossoming and opening up over the next few months.
Screw cap. 13.5% alc. RATING 93 DRINK 2022-2027 $30 PR

Naturally Petulant Pet Nat 2021, Yarra Valley Shiraz, sauvignon blanc and
chardonnay, co-fermented. A cloudy pale apricot hue, with aromas of freshly cut
passionfruit and papaya. Sweet-fruited on entry, this well-made example finishes
bubbly and dry. Screw cap. 12.5% alc. RATING 90 $30 PR

Fishbone Wines   ★★★★☆

422 Harmans Mill Road, Wilyabrup, WA 6285 **Region** Margaret River
T (08) 9755 6726 **www**.fishbonewines.com.au **Open** Thurs–Mon 10–4.30
Winemaker Stuart Pierce **Est.** 2009 **Dozens** 15 **Vyds** 9.1ha
Fishbone Wines' 9.1ha vineyard includes chardonnay, tempranillo and cabernet sauvignon;
and 1ha of newer plantings of malbec, vermentino and pinot noir. The Fishbone wines are
created with minimal intervention. The range includes the 'accessible' Blue Label range,
single vineyard Black Label range and the 'icon' Joseph River wines. The restaurant features a
Japanese-inspired menu with a terrace overlooking the property. Exports to the US, Canada,
Dubai, Singapore and Taiwan. (JH)

♥♥♥♥♥ Black Label Shiraz 2020, Margaret River This is very smart, but also very
young – it has that exuberance and friskiness that you just know will settle down
in a year or so. But it's good. Layers of licorice, exotic market spice, clove, raspberry
and red snakes mingle amicably, the soiree guided by the firm hand of tannins off
to the side. Very well handled. Screw cap. 14.2% alc. RATING 95 DRINK 2021-2028
$45 EL

Joseph River Estate Reserve Chardonnay 2020, Margaret River This is
intense. The oak, the fruit and the acid are all dialled up, yet they are in balance.
The ripe fruit, courtesy of the '20 vintage, speaks of yellow peaches, cashews,
nougat, Turkish apricots, red apples and nectarines. The acidity that courses
through the wine is salty and bright, further punctuating the satisfying fruit
concentration. Screw cap. 13.8% alc. RATING 94 DRINK 2021-2031 $55 EL

♥♥♥♥♀ Black Label Cabernet Sauvignon Merlot 2019, Margaret River
RATING 90 DRINK 2021-2033 $45 EL

Flametree   ★★★★★

Cnr Caves Road/Chain Avenue, Dunsborough, WA 6281 **Region** Margaret River
T (08) 9756 8577 **www**.flametreewines.com **Open** 7 days 10–5 **Winemaker** Cliff
Royle, Julian Scott **Est.** 2007 **Dozens** 20
Flametree, owned by the Towner family (John, Liz, Rob and Annie), has had extraordinary
success since its first vintage in 2007. The usual practice of planting a vineyard and then
finding someone to make the wine was turned on its head: a state-of-the-art winery was
built, and grape purchase agreements signed with growers in the region. Show success was
topped by the winning of the Jimmy Watson Trophy with its '07 Cabernet Merlot. If all this

were not enough, Flametree has secured the services of winemaker Cliff Royle. Exports to the UK, Canada, Indonesia, Malaysia, Singapore, Papua New Guinea, Fiji and Hong Kong. (JH)

ŸŸŸŸŸ S.R.S. Wallcliffe Chardonnay 2020, Margaret River As usual, this is an absolute mouthful of saline acid, powerful peachy fruit and a whole lot of oak/ spice and funk. Delish. The '20 vintage was big (in terms of flavour, not yields) and this is clearly evident in the glass; marzipan, crushed nuts and a little bit of nougat in the background. The vintage suits the style, making this an exceptional iteration of S.R.S. Chardonnay. It will keep – the acid and the fruit say so – but it is so delicious now, the question is, why would you wait? Screw cap. 13.3% alc. RATING 96 DRINK 2021-2031 $65 EL ☺

Flaxman Wines ★★★★★

662 Flaxmans Valley Road, Flaxmans Valley, SA 5253 **Region** Eden Valley
T 0411 668 949 www.flaxmanwines.com.au **Open** Thurs–Fri, Sun 11–4, Sat 11–5
Winemaker Colin Sheppard **Est.** 2005 **Dozens** 1200 **Vyds** 2ha
After visiting the Barossa Valley for over a decade, Melbourne residents Colin and Fi Sheppard decided on a tree change and in '04 found a small, old vineyard overlooking Flaxmans Valley, consisting of 90yo riesling, 90yo shiraz and 70yo semillon. The vines are dry grown, hand pruned, hand picked and treated – say the Sheppards – as their garden. Yields are restricted to under 4t/ha and exceptional parcels of locally grown grapes are also purchased. Colin has worked at various Barossa wineries and his attention to detail (and understanding of the process) is reflected in the consistent high quality of the wines. (JH)

ŸŸŸŸŸ Estate Shiraz 2018, Eden Valley Col and Fi Sheppard don't make much of this wine (a mere 90 dozen) and what has always impressed me is the sense of space, detail and freshness they coax from these old vines with their gorgeous plum and summer-berry fruit profile and stoney, savoury line. Chewy tannin and bright acidity provide the framework. The wine has a lovely sense of being calm and comfortable in its own skin. It's lovely. Screw cap. 13.5% alc. RATING 95 DRINK 2021-2035 $120 DB
Riesling 2021, Eden Valley A beautiful perfumed nose with fragrant Christmas lily and citrus blossom notes coming to the fore, along with fresh lime juice and stone. The wine displays excellent fruit purity and texture on the palate, the crystalline acidity reining everything in nicely and driving it forward to a pure Bickford's Lime crescendo. Screw cap. 12.5% alc. RATING 94 DRINK 2021-2030 $30 DB ☺

ŸŸŸŸŸ Shhh Cabernet Sauvignon 2018, Eden Valley RATING 93 DRINK 2021-2030 $50 DB
The Stranger 2018, Barossa Valley Eden Valley RATING 92 DRINK 2021-2031 $40 DB

Flowstone Wines ★★★★★

11298 Bussell Highway, Forest Grove, WA 6286 **Region** Margaret River
T 0487 010 275 www.flowstonewines.com **Open** By appt **Winemaker** Stuart Pym
Viticulturist Stuart Pym **Est.** 2013 **Dozens** 1500 **Vyds** 3ha
Veteran Margaret River winemaker Stuart Pym's career constituted long-term successive roles: beginning with Voyager Estate in '91, thereafter with Devil's Lair, and finishing with Stella Bella in '13, the year he and Perth-based wine tragic Phil Giglia established Flowstone Wines. In '03 Stuart purchased a small property on the edge of the Margaret River Plateau in the beautiful Forest Grove area, progressively planting chardonnay, cabernet sauvignon, gewürztraminer and touriga. From '17, Flowstone leased a vineyard at Karridale, planted to long-established sauvignon blanc and chardonnay. The lease puts the vineyard on par with the estate plantings; the best fruit is retained, the balance sold. Thus Queen of the Earth Sauvignon Blanc appeared for the first time in '17. Exports to the UK and Japan. (JH)

♚♚♚♚♚ **Queen of the Earth Sauvignon Blanc 2020, Margaret River** Intense, sweaty, concentrated ... this is a rippling pool of flavour. The oak impact is significant (as usual), meaning it is built to last. Margaret River excels at concentrated sauvignon blanc and this big, oaky style is becoming more and more prevalent, led by a cohort of brilliant, skilled producers – one of whom is Flowstone's Pym. So: here we have quenching wine, stuffed to the gills with salted pineapple, crunchy, ripe Granny Smith apples, saline acidity ... and lots of other good green things. Delicious. Screw cap. 12.8% alc. RATING 96 DRINK 2022-2037 $55 EL ✪ ♥

Moonmilk Shiraz Grenache 2020, Margaret River With 3% viognier. A delicious fresh and juicy blend of red cherry and raspberry fruit on the bouquet, the palate adding feathery tannins on the lingering finish. Screw cap. 14% alc. RATING 95 DRINK 2021-2028 $25 JH ✪

Sauvignon Blanc 2020, Margaret River The '20 vintage will be remembered for wines of grace, power and effortlessness. Stuart Pym at Flowstone makes sauvignon blanc of concentration, liquidity (the silky, mellifluous mouthfeel of the wines), poise and intensity. This is all of that and more. Made in tiny quantities, and sold for far less than they should be. Don't tell Pym we said that. Screw cap. 13% alc. RATING 95 DRINK 2021-2030 $32 EL ✪

Queen of the Earth Cabernet Sauvignon 2018, Margaret River The QOTE wines have developed a cult following, and like all good cult products, they each have a few polarising things about them that really appeal. In the case of this cabernet, that's 3 years in oak. It certainly makes an impact, however, apply to that what we already know about the endurance, power and intensity of the '18 fruit in Margaret River and you may come close to the answer. It will be excellent and it will live an age, perhaps the longest in the region ... but it's best to exercise restraint in the short term. Screw cap. 14.5% alc. RATING 95 DRINK 2022-2042 $74 EL

Moonmilk White 2021, Margaret River Viognier, pinot gris, gewürztraminer, sauvignon blanc. Turkish dried apricots, crushed pistachios, rose petals, red apple skins and lashings of fine white spice. This is saline, silky and succulent verging on opulent; all the while, desperately interesting. Another sensational Moonmilk release, although at $22, one wonders how Stuart Pym can afford to feed his dogs. Screw cap. 12% alc. RATING 94 DRINK 2022-2026 $22 EL ✪

Chardonnay 2019, Margaret River Released after 30 months in bottle. Concentrated, plump, textural, savoury – a total mouthful of flavour. Crushed quartz, oyster shell, jasmine tea tannins, ripe (juicy, dripping and salted) yellow peach flesh, juniper and elderflower. Very long in the mouth, it really lingers. Seamless. Screw cap. 13% alc. RATING 94 DRINK 2021-2029 $36 EL

Queen of the Earth Chardonnay 2019, Margaret River Fermented in French oak (50% new) and matured 18 months in barrel with occasional bâtonnage. Oak is a big part of the story here, however the fruit quietly endures. It's kind of like burying your feet in the sand at the beach as the waves rush in – there's both a grounded quality, and a moving ebb-and-flow quality about this wine. Briny, minerally and layered with salted stone fruit and summer figs. Another impressive Queen of the Earth. It is a style completely unto itself. Screw cap. 13.1% alc. RATING 94 DRINK 2022-2037 $55 EL

♚♚♚♚♛ **Cabernet Sauvignon Touriga 2017, Margaret River** RATING 93 DRINK 2021-2036 $36 EL

Flying Fish Cove   ★★★★☆

3763 Caves Road, Wilyabrup, WA 6280 **Region** Margaret River
T (08) 9755 6600 **www.**flyingfishcove.com **Open** By appt **Winemaker** Simon Ding, Damon Easthaugh **Est.** 2000 **Vyds** 25ha
Flying Fish Cove has 2 strings to its bow: contract winemaking for others and the development of its own brand. Long-serving winemaker Simon Ding had a circuitous journey before falling prey to the lure of wine. He finished an apprenticeship in metalwork in '93. In '96 he obtained

a bachelor of wine science, then joined the Flying Fish Cove team in '08. Exports to the UK, the US, Canada and Malaysia. (JH)

♟♟♟♟♟ **The Wildberry Reserve Chardonnay 2021, Margaret River** Creamy, citrusy and pert, with a line of fine saline acidity that bifurcates the wine in the mouth: on one side, the orchard fruit, on the other, the oak. Screw cap. 12.4% alc. RATING 91 DRINK 2022–2027 $50 EL

Chardonnay 2021, Margaret River The high-solids ferment is evident in the glass, by way of the curry-leaf and brine characters that eddy about. There is a pronounced creaminess, and nuttiness here suggesting mlf, and if so, it is well played. It imbues the wine with an extra dimension of textural complexity, and softens the apparent acidity (which, given the overt green apple and nashi pear characters, may have been hard given the cool season). All in all, a handy little wine. Screw cap. 12.8% alc. RATING 90 DRINK 2022–2028 $29 EL

Forest Hill Vineyard   ★★★★★

Cnr South Coast Highway/Myers Road, Denmark, WA 6333 **Region** Great Southern **T** (08) 9848 2399 **www.**foresthillwines.com.au **Open** 7 days 10.30–5 **Winemaker** Liam Carmody, Guy Lyons **Viticulturist** Ross Pike **Est.** 1965 **Dozens** 12 000 **Vyds** 36ha
This family-owned business is one of the oldest 'new' winemaking operations in WA and was the site of the first grape plantings in Great Southern in 1965. The Forest Hill brand became well known, aided by the fact that a '75 Riesling made by Sandalford from Forest Hill grapes won 9 trophies. The quality of the wines made from the oldest vines (dry-grown) on the property is awesome (released under the numbered vineyard block labels). Exports to the UK, the US and Finland. (JH)

♟♟♟♟♟ **Riesling 2021, Mount Barker** An entrancing riesling with a perfumed bouquet of white flowers, lime blossom and more, the palate a ringmaster playing off the pure lime and passionfruit flavours with a rivulet of acidity that dances through to the aftertaste. Screw cap. 12.5% alc. RATING 96 DRINK 2021–2036 $29 JH ✪

Block 2 Riesling 2021, Mount Barker Fermented in a combination of stainless steel and oak (one seasoned Austrian demi-muid). Kept on lees until bottling in Oct. 3g/L RS. Textural, dense and super-long; even without the prior knowledge of RS, it is evident in a little glycerol slick through the finish, perfectly in sync with the plump fruit that precedes it. Similarly, the oak component is invisible, save for the texture in the mouth. This is the complete package – it's a burster. Not only is it awesome now, but this is going to age with interest and grace. Stock up. Screw cap. 12.5% alc. RATING 96 DRINK 2021–2036 $38 EL ✪

Block 1 Riesling 2021, Mount Barker 1.4g/L RS. This is long, with palate-staining intensity of flavour. The lack of oak or bâtonnage means this is pure fruit horsepower. The drive and composition of this wine illustrates both the brawn of Mount Barker and the grace of the old vines of Block 1. The cool '21 season delivers a finer expression of this wine. Screw cap. 12.5% alc. RATING 96 DRINK 2021–2036 $55 EL ✪

Block 9 Shiraz 2020, Mount Barker Savoury, spicy, and laden with intrigue, this wine carries across the palate and through to the extraordinarily long finish with grace and ease. Hung deli meat, black and red fruits and sprinklings of Chinese five-spice and licorice root. Very smart. Very long. Powerful. The tannins shape the wine in the mouth and cup the fruit as it makes its journey through time. Lovely. Screw cap. 14% alc. RATING 96 DRINK 2021–2031 $60 EL ✪

Block 5 Cabernet Sauvignon 2020, Mount Barker Svelte, concentrated and muscular in the most wonderful of ways. Mount Barker can give that salivating, bloody character of ferrous and red dirt (like Frankland River can) and it fills me with satisfaction to taste wine laced in this way. Inchoate as this wine is, all of the hallmarks required for ageing are here in spades. Just 840 bottles made. Screw cap. 14% alc. RATING 96 DRINK 2022–2039 $65 EL ✪

Gewürztraminer 2021, Mount Barker I routinely love this wine. It combines the power, might and muscle that comes so easily in Mount Barker, with the floral, exotic, lifted, gypsy vibes of the gewürtztraminer to stunning effect. Caravans of rose petals, crushed pistachios and granite, combined with nashi pears, lychee, star anise, jasmine tea and Granny Smith apples roll across the palate. A distinct quartz-like minerality flows through it, all of it laced together within a fine and glassy structure. It's light as a feather, and cleansing and mineral through the finish. Stunning. Screw cap. 13% alc. RATING 95 DRINK 2022-2027 $30 EL ✪

Block 8 Chardonnay 2021, Mount Barker This is routinely a – if not the – greatest chardonnay in the Great Southern region. It is sensational. The high acid is folded into layers of voluminous citrus and stone fruit, and the crushed curry-leaf character is pleasingly pervasive throughout all the Forest Hill chardonnays. It manages lean and taut, concentrated and savoury, although it may need a year or 2 for the acid to settle into the fruit succinctly. Superb. Screw cap. 13% alc. RATING 95 DRINK 2022-2032 $50 EL

Shiraz 2020, Mount Barker An attractive bouquet, and a purple-crimson hue. Warm spices and a modicum of oak quickly gain traction on a medium-bodied palate, riding high on juicy red and black cherries, licorice and perfectly pitched tannins. There's freshness, too, on the finish. Screw cap. 14% alc. RATING 95 DRINK 2023-2039 $30 JH ✪

Highbury Fields Riesling 2021, Great Southern Progressively unfolds its charms, the lime and apple blossom bouquet pleasing, the well-balanced palate bringing ripe, tangy citrus flavours to the table. Screw cap. 12.5% alc. RATING 94 DRINK 2021-2036 $24 JH ✪

🍷🍷🍷🍷🍷 **Chardonnay 2021, Mount Barker** RATING 93 DRINK 2022-2032 $32 EL
Highbury Fields Shiraz 2020, Great Southern RATING 93 DRINK 2021-2027 $24 EL ✪
Cabernet Sauvignon 2020, Mount Barker RATING 93 DRINK 2021-2031 $32 EL
Highbury Fields Cabernet Sauvignon 2020, Great Southern RATING 91 DRINK 2021-2031 $24 EL
Highbury Fields Chardonnay 2021, Great Southern RATING 90 DRINK 2022-2027 $24 EL

Forester Estate ★★★★

1064 Wildwood Road, Yallingup, WA 6282 **Region** Margaret River
T (08) 9755 2000 **www**.foresterestate.com.au **Open** By appt **Winemaker** Kevin McKay, Todd Payne **Est.** 2001 **Dozens** 52 000 **Vyds** 33.5ha

Forester Estate is owned by Kevin and Jenny McKay. Winemaker Todd Payne has had a distinguished career, starting in the Great Southern, thereafter the Napa Valley, back to Plantagenet, then Esk Valley in Hawke's Bay, plus 2 vintages in the Northern Rhône Valley, one with esteemed producer Yves Cuilleron in '08. His move back to WA completed the circle. The estate vineyards are planted to sauvignon blanc, semillon, chardonnay, cabernet sauvignon, shiraz, merlot, petit verdot, malbec and fer. The tasting room is housed in a French Renaissance-style castle, built in 2007. Exports to Switzerland and Japan. (JH)

🍷🍷🍷🍷🍷 **Lifestyle Cabernet Sauvignon 2020, Margaret River** Another beautiful, approachable and ready-now release from the Lifestyle range. Plump, supple and moving to floral, with fine structure and decent length. There's a little hint of crushed ant and gravel/ferrous on the nose that elevates the drinking experience here. Unmissable at the price. Screw cap. 13.5% alc. RATING 93 DRINK 2021-2028 $25 EL ✪

Chardonnay 2020, Margaret River An interestingly green nose, given the warmer year, with aromas of jalapeño, lemongrass, nashi pear and green apple. Even hints of coriander and green capsicum. In the mouth the oak serves to frame the fruit and give it a toasty, spicy character. It is green, but it's no bad thing, and it doesn't taste like an indication of underripeness – the fruit has been handled well and it's an engaging drink. Screw cap. 13.5% alc. RATING 93 DRINK 2021-2031 $35 EL

Lifestyle Shiraz 2019, Margaret River Vibrant, spicy, juicy and delicious. Uncomplicated drinking here, all things kept in check, the fruit riding out in front. Screw cap. 13.7% alc. RATING 93 DRINK 2021–2031 $25 EL ✪

Home Block Shiraz 2019, Margaret River With a serious slew of accolades to its name already, this is a valuable wine for the relatively little money spent. The tannins are a highlight here; finely threaded into every aspect of the fruit and acting as a web in which the flavour of the wine is caught. Blood plum, pastille, mulberry and cassis through the finish, accompanying ironstone, ferrous and aniseed character. All good things. Screw cap. 13.2% alc. RATING 93 DRINK 2021–2028 $35 EL

Cabernet Sauvignon 2019, Margaret River Leafy, earthy and layered, with crushed rocks and spice on the nose. In the mouth, all of these characters come to the fore, bolstered by blackforest fruit, five-spice and aniseed. Mid weight at best, this is elegant and brambly and very nice. Screw cap. 13.9% alc. RATING 93 DRINK 2021–2031 $35 EL

Sauvignon Blanc 2021, Margaret River Concentrated and tight; layers of apple, citrus, brine and pear. Super-refreshing and pert – everything one could want from sauvignon blanc! The juicy acid is a highlight. Screw cap. 12.6% alc. RATING 92 DRINK 2021–2023 $27 EL

Lifestyle Cabernet Merlot 2019, Margaret River A super-pretty, plump, floral, uncomplicated cabernet with a fine smudge of chalky tannins through the finish. Very, very lovely. Screw cap. 13.4% alc. RATING 92 DRINK 2021–2027 $25 EL ✪

Yelverton Reserve Chardonnay 2019, Margaret River Crushed cashews, white peaches and layers of juicy, salty acidity. The impact of oak through the finish clamps down on the fruit somewhat, however this would most likely be alleviated with either a decant or some further time in bottle. Dense and powerful, perhaps even moving towards blocky. Screw cap. 13% alc. RATING 91 DRINK 2022–2032 $80 EL

Lifestyle Sauvignon Blanc 2021, Margaret River Gooseberry, green apples and lemon zest on both the nose and palate. A little hint of complexing funk contributes another layer of interest. This is pert, fresh and flavoursome. Screw cap. 12.4% alc. RATING 90 DRINK 2021–2023 $25 EL

Rosé 2021, Margaret River Juicy, bouncy, bright rosé. It should look just like this. Perfect summer drinking. Screw cap. 12.5% alc. RATING 90 DRINK 2021–2023 $25 EL

🍷🍷🍷🍷 **Lifestyle Semillon Sauvignon Blanc 2021, Margaret River** RATING 89 DRINK 2022–2024 $25 EL

Fourth Wave Wine ★★★★

Suite 1, Level 3, The Forum, 240-244 Pacific Highway, Charlestown NSW 2290
Region Various
T 1300 778 047 **www.**fourthwavewine.com.au **Winemaker** Various **Est.** 2009
Based in the suburbs of Newcastle, Fourth Wave Wine was founded in 2009 by Nicholas and Frances Crampton, boasting wine industry nous; finance and IT skills respectively. Assisted by winemaker and consultant, Corey Ryan, Fourth Wave makes wine in 6 countries with a total production of 300,000 dozen bottles packaged under a panoply of brands. A modern-day global negoçiant, if you will. Domestically, brands include Elephant in the Room, Little Giant, Burns and Fuller and Take it to the Grave. While savvy marketing is key to their success, the intrinsic qualities of many of the wines cannot be denied. Exports to Canada, South Korea, Malaysia, Singapore, Europe and NZ. (NG)

🍷🍷🍷🍷🍷 **Little Giant Little Batch Nebbiolo 2020, Adelaide Hills** A deceptive wine colour with some orange in the hue; the bouquet of savoury, spicy, sour cherry and Middle Eastern spices; the finish and aftertaste lasting for an eternity. Call in the psychiatrist. Screw cap. 14.5% alc. RATING 92 DRINK 2021–2024 $27 JH

Little Giant Cabernet Sauvignon 2020, Coonawarra Atypical packaging signals the atypical experience in the glass. Bright, spicy and super-vibrant, this casts off the density of Coonawarra tannin of old, and brings a sumptuous, lip-smacking array of flavours to the fore. For all the talk of breaking barriers, this retains the classic Coonawarra mint, cassis and bramble, albeit in a very fine, slick way. Brilliant value here. Screw cap. 14.5% alc. RATING 90 DRINK 2022-2028 $22 EL

ᵀᵀᵀᵀ   **Tread Softly Pinot Noir 2021, Yarra Valley** RATING 89 DRINK 2021-2023 $22 PR
Wild Folk Natural Shiraz 2021, Barossa RATING 89 DRINK 2022-2024 $27 JH
Farm Hand One of a Kind Sangiovese 2021, McLaren Vale RATING 88 DRINK 2021-2022 $22 JH
Little Giant Shiraz 2019, Barossa RATING 88 DRINK 2022-2027 $22 DB

Fowles Wine

1175 Lambing Gully Road, Avenel, VIC 3664 **Region** Strathbogie Ranges
T (03) 5796 2150 **www**.fowleswine.com **Open** 7 days, 9–5 **Winemaker** Lindsay Brown, Sam Atherton **Viticulturist** Glenn Chisholm **Est.** 1968 **Dozens** 80 000 **Vyds** 145ha
This family-owned winery is led by Matt Fowles, with chief winemaker Lindsay Brown heading the winemaking team. The large vineyard is primarily focused on riesling, chardonnay, shiraz and cabernet sauvignon, but also includes arneis, vermentino, pinot gris, sauvignon blanc, pinot noir, mourvèdre, sangiovese and merlot. Marketing is energetic, with the well-known Ladies who Shoot their Lunch label also available, presented in a 6-bottle gun case. Exports to the UK, the US and Canada. (JH)

ᵀᵀᵀᵀᵀ   **Ladies who Shoot their Lunch Wild Ferment Shiraz 2019, Strathbogie Ranges** On the more generous side, this vintage, but still there is tremendous vitality and complexity to the wine. Fragrant red fruits, plum, anise, spice and violet aromas. Fresh and even to taste, with firm tannins the launch pad for dark cherry, plum, red licorice, dried herbs and a long, pepper-dusted finish. Screw cap. 14.9% alc. RATING 95 DRINK 2021-2030 $35 JP ✪
The Exception Madame Shiraz 2018, Strathbogie Ranges You could do weightlifting with the heavy bottles for The Exception wines. The use of French oak – hence the name, Madame, according to the maker – fits the shiraz like a glove. A complex, enticing set of black fruits, dark plum fruits, spice and chocolate. Tannins are plentiful and warm, toasty oak is nicely enmeshed. Terrific balance on display. Diam. 14.6% alc. RATING 95 DRINK 2022-2035 $80 JP
The Exception Cowboy Shiraz 2018, Strathbogie Ranges From a top year comes a rich, ripe, flavoursome red that delivers quite a compelling wine. The use of American oak does not go unnoticed, but it inveigles its way into the heart of a dense collection of black fruits, spice, earth, chocolate and wild herbs, carrying sweet toasty oak and happy tannins. It's early days yet. One for the cellar. Diam. 14.6% alc. RATING 94 DRINK 2022-2033 $80 JP

ᵀᵀᵀᵀ♀   **Stone Dwellers Single Vineyard Riesling 2021, Strathbogie Ranges** RATING 93 DRINK 2022-2032 $30 JP
Stone Dwellers Single Vineyard Mourvèdre 2020, Strathbogie Ranges RATING 93 DRINK 2021-2030 $30 JP
Ladies who Shoot their Lunch Wild Ferment Chardonnay 2020, Victoria RATING 92 DRINK 2021-2027 $35 JP
Stone Dwellers Single Vineyard Vermentino 2020, Strathbogie Ranges RATING 91 DRINK 2021-2025 $30 JP
Ladies who Shoot their Lunch Wild Ferment Pinot Noir 2020, Strathbogie Ranges RATING 91 DRINK 2021-2026 $35 JP
Stone Dwellers Limited Release Riesling 2016, Strathbogie Ranges RATING 91 DRINK 2021-2024 $30 JP

Foxeys Hangout

795 White Hill Road, Red Hill, Vic 3937 **Region** Mornington Peninsula
T (03) 5989 2022 **www.**foxeys-hangout.com.au **Open** 7 days 11–5 **Winemaker** Tony
and Michael Lee **Est.** 1997 **Dozens** 14000 **Vyds** 3.4ha

After 20 successful years in hospitality operating several cafes and restaurants (including one
of Melbourne's first gastropubs in the early '90s), brothers Michael and Tony Lee planted
their first vineyard in '97 at Merricks North. The venture takes its name from the tale of
2 fox hunters in the '30s hanging the results of their day's shooting in opposite branches of an
ancient eucalypt, using the tree as their scorecard. Michael and Tony also manage the former
Massoni Vineyard at Red Hill established by Ian Home, planting more chardonnay and pinot
noir and opening their cellar door. Michael makes the sparkling wines, Tony (a qualified chef)
makes the table wines and also cooks for the cellar door kitchen. (JH)

ŸŸŸŸŸ **Rosé 2021, Mornington Peninsula** A 3-way blend of pinot noir, pinot gris
and shiraz and a delicious, delightful and refreshing drink. A stream of spices comes
sluicing through the watermelon, Packham pear and raspberry flavours, making it
all juicy and tangy across the palate. It has texture though, as it's not a one-trick
pony. Refreshing acidity and a twist of blood orange on the finish make it all the
more appealing. Screw cap. 13% alc. RATING 95 DRINK 2022–2024 $28 JF ✪
Pinot Noir 2021, Mornington Peninsula No doubt Mornington Peninsula
producers were relieved to say adieu to '20: the wines were a mixed bunch.
Then there's this vintage. It's very good. Incredible fruit weight and intensity in
this pinot, without being heavy. A fine blend of macerated red cherries, woodsy
spices and fresh herbs, with a touch of autumnal earthiness. Fuller bodied, with a
succulence across the palate buoyed by velvety tannins and tangy acidity. The finish
lingers long enough to think, 'I'll have another glass, thanks'. Screw cap. 13.5% alc.
RATING 95 DRINK 2022–2031 $40 JF
Morning Sun Vineyard Pinot Noir 2021, Mornington Peninsula What's
intriguing about this wine, is it appears to be a lightweight – it's subtle and
gentle. But the flavours build, the shapely, lithe tannins kick in, bolstering the
mid-weighted palate. The acidity keeps everything tucked in. It's savoury and
moreish, the core of fruit just top notch. A delightful drink. Screw cap. 13.5% alc.
RATING 95 DRINK 2022–2029 $45 JF
White Gates Pinot Gris 2021, Mornington Peninsula A restrained style,
with the complexity coming in whispers and layers. Honeysuckle, pears, white
nectarine, ginger-spiced lemon curd and a touch of creamy lees set the scene.
There's more: lovely texture, smooth and light yet with just enough dainty
phenolics to add shape and pull across the palate. Terrific wine. Screw cap.
13.5% alc. RATING 95 DRINK 2022–2025 $45 JF

ŸŸŸŸŸ **Morning Sun Vineyard Chardonnay 2021, Mornington Peninsula**
RATING 93 DRINK 2022–2028 $45 JF
Pinot Gris 2021, Mornington Peninsula RATING 92 DRINK 2022–2023 $32 JF
Field Blend White Single Vineyard 2021, Mornington Peninsula
RATING 91 DRINK 2022–2024 $40 JF
The Red Fox Pinot Noir 2020, Mornington Peninsula RATING 91
DRINK 2022–2025 $32 JF
Shiraz 2020, Mornington Peninsula RATING 90 DRINK 2024–2030 $45 JF
Chardonnay 2020, Mornington Peninsula RATING 90 DRINK 2022–2025
$90 JF

Frankland Estate

Frankland Road, Frankland, WA 6396 **Region** Frankland River
T (08) 9855 1544 **www.**franklandestate.com.au **Open** Mon–Fri 10–4, public hols
& w'ends by appt **Winemaker** Hunter Smith, Brian Kent **Est.** 1988 **Dozens** 20000
Vyds 34.5ha

A significant operation, situated on a large sheep property owned by Barrie Smith and Judi Cullam. The vineyard has been established progressively since 1988. The introduction of an array of single-vineyard rieslings has been a highlight, driven by Judi's conviction that terroir is of utmost importance, and the soils are indeed different; the Isolation Ridge Vineyard is organically grown. Frankland Estate has held important International Riesling tastings and seminars for more than a decade. Exports to all major markets. (JH)

ΨΨΨΨΨ **Isolation Ridge Riesling 2021, Frankland River** Sandalwood, preserved citrus, black tea leaves and jasmine seamlessly merge into the more expected Frankland River riesling characters of lemon zest, green apple skins and chalk. In the mouth, the acidity is like a coiled spring, cushioned by voluminous fruit padding on all sides. This is svelte and streamlined, but it has presence and viscosity, too. There is subtle structural integrity and a spool of lingering flavour through the finish … what a superb wine. This is generous, but it's tense and taut too … disguised austerity. Slatey. Screw cap. 13.5% alc. RATING 97 DRINK 2022-2042 $52 EL ✪ ♥

Smith Cullam Riesling 2021, Frankland River Supreme balance. This wine is silky and lush (thanks to the RS, as this is the off-dry style for the house), but it is carried on linear tracks of steel-like acidity … they crest the horizon, which seems never-ending. Such is the length of flavour and zen focus of this wine. White flowers, black tea, nashi pear skin, mandarin pith, lemon zest, nutmeg, even oud … tea tree … it's a seriously good wine. And if you've had the pleasure of an older bottle, this wonderful melange of characters makes even more sense. Spectacular. In terms of vintage context, this cool (and sometimes wet!) year has imbued this with detail and poise. Screw cap. 11.5% alc. RATING 97 DRINK 2022-2042 $75 EL ✪

Smith Cullam Syrah 2020, Frankland River The nose is so fragrant that it takes some time to unpick it all. Winter mandarin, pink peppercorn, citrus blossom, blackberry, plum, licorice, clove, star anise, lavender and fennel flower. In the mouth, the graphite and black-tea tannins are a masterclass in svelte. They weave and thread through all aspects of the experience, becoming briefly savoury, before trailing out over a long finish. It is the tannins that reveal to us how inchoate this wine truly is. It needs time. It will be superlative. For now, it is tightly wound, coiled even and needs time to unfurl and show its potential. What a profound wine. Wow. Owns the Syrah moniker. Screw cap. 14.5% alc. RATING 97 DRINK 2022-2037 $120 EL ✪ ♥

ΨΨΨΨΨ **Olmo's Reward 2019, Frankland River** Cabernet franc, malbec and cabernet sauvignon. This is concentrated and supple to start, but the flow of tannins doesn't tread the same path of, say, a Margaret River cabernet blend (nor should it). Here, the tannins are gravelly and leaning towards rustic, speaking of ferrous and ironstone. They lend a graphite quality and are the key to this wine. The fruit is abundant within the framework of the phenolics; a snow dome of cassis, blackberry, nori, iodine, blood plum and licorice. It's a beautiful wine with longevity and patience in equal measure. Screw cap. 14.5% alc. RATING 96 DRINK 2022-2038 $85 EL

Riesling 2021, Frankland River Takes only a millisecond, once you taste the wine, for the mouth to flood with juicy lime flavours plus splashes of tropical fruits. Totally delicious now, but has the structure to develop well into the next decade. Screw cap. 12.5% alc. RATING 95 DRINK 2021-2035 $30 JH ✪

Isolation Ridge Syrah 2020, Frankland River This is very grownup. It has the slick and gloss of beautifully ripe fruit, but it also has the blood, gravel and rust that underpins all reds grown in Frankland River. While this has resolutely earned its 'syrah' moniker, it has enough savoury grunt and brooding chutzpah to accurately reflect the region, too. Bravo. Screw cap. 14% alc. RATING 95 DRINK 2022-2037 $52 EL

Shiraz 2018, Frankland River The crimson-rimmed deep purple sets the scene for a powerful yet fragrant wine, with poached spiced plum fruit, ripe tannins and French oak beating a delicate tattoo on the finish. Screw cap. 12.5% alc. RATING 95 DRINK 2022-2033 $32 JH ✪

Cabernet Sauvignon 2020, Frankland River Really epic intensity here. This is fresh, pert, bloody, concentrated and savoury, all at once. The tannins are superfine and plentiful, creating a malleable and supple structure from which the fruit suspends. Very cool wine. Screw cap. 14% alc. RATING 94 DRINK 2022-2035 $32 EL

Fraser Gallop Estate

493 Metricup Road, Wilyabrup, WA 6280 **Region** Margaret River
T (08) 9755 7553 **www.frasergallopestate.com.au Open** 7 days 11–4 **Winemaker** Clive Otto, Ellin Tritt **Viticulturist** Mike Bolas **Est.** 1999 **Dozens** 10000 **Vyds** 20ha
Nigel Gallop began the development of the vineyard in 1999, planting what is now just over 20ha of cabernet sauvignon and chardonnay (6.8ha each) as well as semillon, petit verdot, cabernet franc, malbec, merlot and sauvignon blanc. The wines have been made by Clive Otto since '07, and in that time have amassed an impressive array of domestic and international acclaim. The house style is very much on the precise, pure end of the spectrum, with the flagship white (the Palladian Chardonnay) routinely coming in at lower alcohol than many. The Parterre range offers consistent, indelible, compelling value for money. Exports to the UK, Czech Republic, Sweden, Hong Kong, Thailand, Indonesia and Singapore. (EL)

🍷🍷🍷🍷🍷 **Palladian Chardonnay 2020, Margaret River** We must all follow different houses for their different styles. Here, Fraser Gallop's chardonnay style is on show: lower alcohol, pristine, crystalline fruit, shaped by fine saline acid and curving in a quartz-like, delicate manner through the finish. This '20 Palladian is the best, finest, most magical, most alluring Palladian release I have ever tried. It is off the charts. Screw cap. 12.5% alc. RATING 97 DRINK 2022-2037 $140 EL ✪

🍷🍷🍷🍷🍷 **Parterre Cabernet Sauvignon 2019, Margaret River** Houghton clone in Wilyabrup expresses itself as supple, succulent, red fruited and powerful; it imbues the wines with grace and ease. So too, this release. This has all these attributes, layers of pomegranate, raspberry, red licorice, saltbush, cassis and peppercorn. A beautiful wine, with a proven track record for graceful ageing. This vintage will be no exception. Screw cap. 14% alc. RATING 96 DRINK 2021-2036 $50 EL ✪
Palladian Cabernet Sauvignon 2018, Margaret River Up from $110 in the last vintage, but if there was ever a vintage to jump – '18 c'est ça. The length of flavour is astoundingly long: enduring and persistent, it allows the fruit to promenade across the tongue, showing every feather and facet. Restrained and powerful, this surely needs a decant at this inchoate stage. The tannins present as firm yet fine. A wonderful wine. Screw cap. 14% alc. RATING 96 DRINK 2021-2041 $140 EL
Parterre Chardonnay 2020, Margaret River Yeah wow: this is textural, rich and creamy, but it has sublime balance and poise. It is an incredibly elegant wine, showing restraint and line. The length of flavour lingers long after the wine has gone – salted white peach, red apple skins, fig and summer nectarine. Partial mlf brings almond meal and crushed macadamia, more obvious in the texture than in flavour. Glorious wine. Screw cap. 12% alc. RATING 95 DRINK 2021-2031 $50 EL
Parterre Chardonnay 2019, Margaret River The acidity is the most striking element here: it feels very much countersunk into the abundant white stone fruit, and it has a distinct saltiness about it. This drags the substantial fruit characters over the palate and through into the long finish. Quite something. Screw cap. 12.5% alc. RATING 95 DRINK 2020-2028 $43 EL

Freeman Vineyards

101 Prunevale Road, Prunevale, NSW 2587 **Region** Hilltops
T 0429 310 309 **www.freemanvineyards.com.au Open** By appt **Winemaker** Dr Brian Freeman, Xanthe Freeman **Est.** 1999 **Dozens** 5000 **Vyds** 175ha
Dr Brian Freeman spent much of his life in research and education, in the latter with a role as head of CSU's viticulture and oenology campus. In '04 he purchased the 30yo Demondrille

Vineyard and acquired the neighbouring vineyard. A decade later he acquired a number of other vineyards within a 10km radius. In all he has 22 varieties that range from staples such as shiraz, cabernet sauvignon, semillon and riesling through to more exotic varieties such as háslevelü and Italian varieties prosecco (glera), sangiovese, nebbiolo, rondinella and corvina. (JH)

ŸŸŸŸŸ **Aged Release Rondinella Corvina Secco 2009, Hilltops** While it's moving into tertiary territory, this still has fruit; mostly dark plums with kirsch, plus Middle Eastern spices, especially sumac. It's earthy with some wood char. Medium bodied with velvety textural tannins. Drinking superbly now. Screw cap. 14.5% alc. RATING 92 DRINK 2021–2025 $100 JF
Secco Rondinella Corvina 2016, Hilltops A style that uses fresh and dehydrated grapes. It tastes very ripe this vintage, yet overall balanced. Full bodied, rich and concentrated, with loads of tannin to the fore. Expect prune, savoury spices, old wood and charred radicchio. Give it lots of air to loosen up and probably best drunk in the short term. Screw cap. 14.8% alc. RATING 91 DRINK 2022–2027 $40 JF
Prosecco 2021, Hilltops A super-vibrant fizz with its lemon and lime flavours infused with fennel seed and fresh bitter herbs. The dry finish lingers and it's refreshing to the last drop. Crown. 11.5% alc. RATING 90 $25 JF

ŸŸŸŸ **Bianco Pinot Grigio 2021, Hilltops** RATING 88 DRINK 2022–2023 $20 JF
Nebbiolo 2018, Hilltops RATING 88 DRINK 2021–2024 $40 JF

Freycinet ★★★★★

15919 Tasman Highway via Bicheno, Tas 7215 **Region** East Coast Tasmania
T (03) 6257 8574 **www**.freycinetvineyard.com.au **Open** 7 days 10–5
Winemaker Claudio Radenti, Lindy Bull, Keira O'Brian **Est.** 1979 **Dozens** 9000
Vyds 15.9ha
The Freycinet vineyards are situated on the sloping hillsides of a small valley. The soils are brown dermosol on top of Jurassic dolerite; and the combination of aspect, slope, soil and heat summation produces red grapes with unusual depth of colour and ripe flavours. One of the foremost producers of pinot noir, with an enviable track record of consistency – rare in such a temperamental variety. The Radenti (sparkling), Riesling and Chardonnay are also wines of the highest quality. In '12 Freycinet acquired part of the neighbouring Coombend property from Brown Brothers. The 42ha property extends to the Tasman Highway and includes a 5.75ha mature vineyard and a 4.2ha olive grove. Exports to the UK and Singapore. (JH)

ŸŸŸŸŸ **Riesling 2021, Tasmania** A riesling of many personalities, spicy, rich and complex, succulent yet crisp, layered with baked apple, grapefruit and lime. A cool-season 'fines herbes' overlay lends enticing contrast to the mid-palate succulence of perfectly ripe fruit. A spine of acidity delivers endurance to a long finish. Screw cap. 13% alc. RATING 94 DRINK 2022–2031 $35 TS
Wineglass Bay Sauvignon Blanc 2020, Tasmania Serious sauvignon of flesh and texture. A portion of French oak-barrel fermentation brings a compelling depth, richness, body and spicy overlay. Stone fruits, grapefruit and custard apple propagate long and full, impeccably freshened by the cool air of Freycinet. Screw cap. 14% alc. RATING 94 DRINK 2022–2023 $28 TS ❂
Chardonnay 2020, Tasmania Tasted a full year before its release, this is a chardonnay in its complete yet embryonic glory, the contrast between a warm site (by Tasmanian standards) and the purity and energy of a cool season. Pitch-perfect ripeness highlights bursts of grapefruit, white peach and fig, perfectly encased in classy cashew-nut French oak, already seamlessly integrated. It holds impressive persistence and line. Screw cap. 13.5% alc. RATING 94 DRINK 2023–2027 $45 TS

ŸŸŸŸŸ **Louis Chardonnay 2019, Tasmania** RATING 90 DRINK 2022–2023 $28 TS
Louis Pinot Noir 2019, Tasmania RATING 90 DRINK 2022–2024 $40 TS

Frogmore Creek

699 Richmond Road, Cambridge, Tas 7170 **Region** Southern Tasmania
T (03) 6274 5844 **www.**frogmorecreek.com.au **Open** Thurs–Mon 10–5
Winemaker Alain Rousseau, John Bown **Est.** 1997 **Dozens** 40 000 **Vyds** 55ha
Frogmore Creek is a Pacific Rim joint venture, the owners being Tony Scherer of Tasmania and Jack Kidwiler of California. The business has grown substantially, first establishing its own organically managed vineyard, and thereafter by a series of acquisitions. First was the purchase of the Hood/Wellington Wines business; next was the purchase of the large Roslyn Vineyard near Campania; and finally (in Oct '10) the acquisition of Meadowbank Estate, where the cellar door is now located. In Dec '12 the original Frogmore Creek vineyard was sold to Hill-Smith Family Vineyards. Exports to the US, Japan and NZ. (JH)

Cuvée 2018, Tasmania 73/25/2% pinot noir/meunier/chardonnay; 2g/L RS. A blanc de noirs of tension and endurance that belies a season characterised by a very warm Jan. Medium, bright straw hue. Impressive depth of red apples, strawberries and red cherries, energised by grapefruit-like acidity. Lees age brings the subtle beginnings of biscuity complexity. Bright, lively and impeccably balanced. Diam. 11.5% alc. RATING 93 $49 TS

Riesling 2021, Tasmania Aged on lees 8 weeks; 4g/L RS. A vintage of crisp acidity brings tension to a generous riesling of rich, spicy, fleshy fruit presence. It confidently straddles the full fruit spectrum, from lemon and lime to white peach and nectarine, pear, even fig and star fruit. Firm phenolic grip brings control to a long finish as much as a cut of energetic acidity. Food-pairing versatility at its finest. Screw cap. 13% alc. RATING 93 DRINK 2022-2028 $34 TS

FGR Riesling 2019, Tasmania Aged on lees 8 weeks; 40g/L RS. Medium-sweet riesling sits proud in Tasmania and FGR has long been a benchmark. It's surprising more haven't followed. A touch of reductive complexity quickly vaporises to reveal impressive purity of Granny Smith apple and lime fruit. Bright acid line is the hero of a long finish, and residual sits comfortably within a hint of the phenolic texture of a warm, dry season. Screw cap. 9.9% alc. RATING 93 DRINK 2022-2027 $34 TS

Chardonnay 2021, Tasmania A chardonnay of contrasts, fragrant and tropical with exotic allusions of orange-coloured fruits, pawpaw, persimmon and loquat. Yet tense and straight, the malic acidity of this cool season upheld in full soprano voice to lay out a crystalline finish of impressive drive and energy. In spite of its dual personality, it's perfectly ripe. Serve it as you might a top-shelf riesling with a touch of bottle age. Screw cap. 13.5% alc. RATING 92 DRINK 2022-2026 $38 TS

Single Block Series Pinot Noir Cortaillod Clone 2019, Tasmania The child of a warm and dry summer, this is a pinot of exuberant, spicy and juicy berry fruits of all kinds. A long spell in French oak barrels infuses firm, fine tannins, contrasting the bright acidity of the Coal River Valley and calling for further time to integrate. It possesses the integrity and persistence to go the distance. Screw cap. 13.8% alc. RATING 91 DRINK 2024-2031 $48 TS

Single Block Series Barbera 2018, Tasmania RATING 88 DRINK 2022-2022 $48 TS

Gaelic Cemetery Vineyard

Gaelic Cemetery Road, Stanley Flat, SA 5453 **Region** Clare Valley
T (02) 8006 6987 **www.**gaeliccemeteryvineyard.com **Open** By appt **Winemaker** Adam Clay **Viticulturist** Tony Marshall **Est.** 2005 **Dozens** 2000 **Vyds** 16.8ha
Gaelic Cemetery Vineyard was planted in 1996, adjacent to the historic cemetery of the region's Scottish pioneers. Situated in a secluded valley of the Clare hills, the low-cropping vineyard, said the founders, 'is always one of the earliest ripening shiraz vineyards in the region and mystifyingly produces fruit with both natural pH and acid analyses that can only be described as beautiful numbers'. The result is hands-off winemaking. Previously owned by the Pike family, Gaelic Cemetery was purchased by the Pirathon in 2019. Exports to the UK, the US, Canada, Germany, Singapore, Taiwan and Hong Kong. (JH)

ΨΨΨΨΨ **White Hut Riesling 2021, Clare Valley** This has layers of squishy, ripe citrus fruit (think the sweet fleshy limes in midsummer) on the mid palate and volumes of flavour that undulate through the long finish. Restrained, long and very impressive – you gotta love vintages like '21: even, classical, cool, beautiful. As is this wine. Screw cap. 11.5% alc. RATING 95 DRINK 2021-2036 $36 EL
McAskill Riesling 2021, Clare Valley This consists of layers of mouth-filling, palate-staining fruit concentration, testament to the wonderful '21 vintage. Green apples, lime, lemon pith, some citrus florals and damp-chalk phenolics. As an outfit, the White Hut riesling offers more immediate drinking pleasure, but the spiny acidity and phenolic structure in this wine speak to the long life ahead of it. Very smart, classy and exciting. Screw cap. 11.5% alc. RATING 95 DRINK 2021-2038 $55 EL
McAskill Cabernet Malbec 2020, Clare Valley The more cabernet malbec blends I see, the more convinced I become of their combined power and synchronicity; they are truly meant to be together, each filling in the gaps of the other. The complete picture, as is in my glass right now, is one of undulating power, concentrated fruit, pliable tannins and enduring length of flavour. There is a precision to the engineering of this wine. Drink it from the end of '22, better yet – '24. Glorious. Screw cap. 14.5% alc. RATING 95 DRINK 2022-2038 $55 EL
McAskill Shiraz 2020, Clare Valley Fascinating core of scintillatingly pure purple fruit. The oak that ensconces it is dusty, toasty and laden with spice. For all the concentration in the mouth – and this is concentrated – the wine exhibits gorgeous balance and restraint. There's a deeply attractive ferrous aroma through the finish which tops it all off. Screw cap. 14.5% alc. RATING 95 DRINK 2021-2035 $55 EL
White Hut Shiraz 2020, Clare Valley Licorice, cloves, blackberries and Christmas spice. This is silken and concentrated, moving towards dense; the oak should be more obvious than it is. Instead, it serves to cradle the fruit and usher it through the long finish. Very smart wine, here. Screw cap. 14.5% alc. RATING 94 DRINK 2021-2031 $36 EL

ΨΨΨΨΨ **Celtic Farm Shiraz Cabernet 2020, Clare Valley** RATING 93 DRINK 2021-2028 $28 EL
Celtic Farm Riesling 2021, Clare Valley RATING 91 DRINK 2021-2031 $28 EL

Gala Estate ★★★★

14891 Tasman Highway, Cranbrook, Tas 7190 **Region** East Coast Tasmania
T 0408 681 014 **www**.galaestate.com.au **Open** 7 days 10–4 by appt **Winemaker** Pat Colombo, Keira O'Brien **Est.** 2009 **Dozens** 5000 **Vyds** 11ha
This vineyard is situated on a 4000ha sheep station, with the 6th, 7th and 8th generations – headed by Robert and Patricia (nee Amos) Greenhill. The 11ha vineyard is heavily skewed to pinot noir (7ha), the remainder planted (in descending order of area) to chardonnay, pinot gris, riesling, shiraz and sauvignon blanc. The main risk is spring frost, and overhead spray irrigation serves 2 purposes: it provides adequate moisture for early season growth and frost protection at the end of the growing season. (JH)

ΨΨΨΨΨ **1821 Pinot Noir 2020, Tasmania** The best parcels of the estate vineyard present greater depth and persistence of black and red berry fruits, nuanced with black pepper and spice, backed with a little more new oak to better resolve a backdrop of finely structured tannin. Well poised and harmonious, it promises to uncoil impressively over the coming decade. Screw cap. 13.5% alc. RATING 94 DRINK 2025-2030 $65 TS
Black Label Emerald Syrah 2020, Tasmania The potential for syrah on Tasmania's east coast is tremendous, and even in this cooler season I love the contrast here between black fruit depth, black-pepper personality and perfectly polished, fine-woven tannins. Everything holds with impressive line, length, confidence and endurance. Who would have guessed that Gala's finest

release this year would be shiraz? Best yet. Screw cap. 13.5% alc. RATING 94
DRINK 2025-2040 $65 TS

ᵀᵀᵀᵀᵀ White Label Pinot Rosé 2021, Tasmania RATING 93 DRINK 2021-2022
$32 TS
White Label Pinot Noir 2020, Tasmania RATING 93 DRINK 2021-2022
$32 TS
Black Label Pinot Noir 2018, Tasmania RATING 93 DRINK 2027-2032
$65 TS
White Label Pinot Gris 2021, Tasmania RATING 91 DRINK 2021-2022
$32 TS
Black Label Pinot Gris 2020, Tasmania RATING 91 DRINK 2022-2022 $65 TS
Black Label Pinot Noir 2019, Tasmania RATING 91 DRINK 2029-2034
$65 TS
White Label Sauvignon Blanc 2021, Tasmania RATING 90
DRINK 2022-2022 $32 TS

Galafrey

Quangellup Road, Mount Barker, WA 6324 **Region** Mount Barker
T (08) 9851 2022 **www**.galafreywines.com.au **Open** 7 days 10–5 **Winemaker** Kim Tyrer
Est. 1977 **Dozens** 3500 **Vyds** 12ha
The Galafrey story began when Ian and Linda Tyrer gave up high-profile jobs and arrived in
Mount Barker to start growing grapes and making wine, the vine-change partially prompted
by their desire to bring up their children to be in a country environment. The dry-grown
vineyard they planted continues to be the turning point, the first winery established in an
ex-whaling building (long since replaced by a purpose-built winery). The premature death of
Ian at a time when the industry was buckling at the knees increased the already considerable
difficulties the family had to deal with, but deal with it they did. Daughter Kim Tyrer is now
CEO of the business, with Linda in charge of the day-to-day management of Galafrey. Exports
to Canada and Singapore. (JH)

ᵀᵀᵀᵀᵀ Dry Grown Reserve Riesling 2021, Mount Barker This is an austere and
staunch riesling, a clear expression of the Mount Barker muscle and heft. Tight,
long and pure, this wine will age gracefully, but will drink more pleasurably in
a few years once some aged characters have begun to creep into it. Right now;
salted preserved lemon, lime zest, whispers of mango on the nose and plenty of
briny acidity in the mouth. Screw cap. 12% alc. RATING 93 DRINK 2023-2033
$28 EL
Dry Grown Vineyard Shiraz 2018, Mount Barker Intensely concentrated
nose, with layers of Christmas-cake spice, plum, fig, blackberry, mulberry and
clove, all of it backed by spicy, resinous oak. On the palate, the wine performs
as expected; saturating the mouth in flavour. Impressive. Screw cap. 14% alc.
RATING 93 DRINK 2021-2028 $35 EL
The Jovial 2018, Mount Barker 'Last made in '04, after the passing of Dad'
says winemaker, Kim Tyrer. Made for Ian Tyrer, founder of Galafrey wines, this is
a blend of cabernet sauvignon, merlot and cabernet franc, from the brilliant '18
vintage. Savoury, dense and packed with dark chocolate, new leather and cigar
spice, this is a powerful wine. Traditionally styled, firm and savoury. Will likely look
more complete when it is a bit older – one to collect and put away. Screw cap.
14% alc. RATING 92 DRINK 2022-2036 $45 EL

Gapsted Wines

3897 Great Alpine Road, Gapsted, Vic 3737 **Region** Alpine Valleys
T (03) 5751 9100 **www**.gapstedwines.com.au **Open** Thurs–Mon 10–5
Winemaker Andrew Santarossa, Michael Cope-Williams, Toni Pla Bou, Greg Bennet
Est. 1997 **Dozens** 250 000 **Vyds** 256.1ha

Gapsted is the major brand of the Victorian Alps Winery, which started life (and continues) as a large-scale contract winemaking facility. The quality of the wines made for its own brand has led to the expansion of production not only under that label, but also under a raft of subsidiary labels. As well as the substantial estate plantings, Gapsted sources traditional and alternative grape varieties from the King and Alpine valleys. Exports to Canada, Germany, Norway, Sweden, UAE, India, Thailand, South Korea, Malaysia, Singapore, Vietnam, Cambodia, Hong Kong and Japan. (JH)

🍷🍷🍷🍷🍷 **Limited Release Fiano 2021, King Valley** There's a lot of drinking joy to be had with this wine, celebrating ripe tropical fruits, pear skin, citrus and spiced apple, all smoothly rolled out across the palate. A soft, textural landing brings with it plenty of scope for food matching. Screw cap. 14% alc. RATING 92 DRINK 2022-2024 $25 JP ✪

Ballerina Canopy Cabernet Sauvignon 2019, King Valley Certainly on the riper, plush side of the cabernet coin, but that's not such a bad thing. This is definitely approachable upon release in full black-fruited flight mode, but there's also some lovely leafy definition and regional mountain herbs seeing the wine through to the finish. Screw cap. 14.5% alc. RATING 91 DRINK 2022-2032 $31 JP

🍷🍷🍷🍷 **Limited Release Sparkling Saperavi NV, Alpine Valleys** RATING 89 $37 JP
Limited Release Single Vineyard Riesling 2021, King Valley RATING 89 DRINK 2021-2024 $25 JP
Limited Release Sparkling Pinot Grigio Rosé NV, King Valley RATING 88 $25 JP
High Country Chardonnay 2021, King Valley RATING 88 DRINK 2022-2024 $20 JP
High Country Pinot Gris 2021, King Valley RATING 88 DRINK 2022-2024 $20 JP
High Country Shiraz 2019, King Valley RATING 88 DRINK 2021-2024 $20 JP
Ballerina Canopy Shiraz 2019, Heathcote RATING 88 DRINK 2022-2030 $31 JP
Limited Release Sangiovese 2019, Heathcote RATING 88 DRINK 2021-2025 $31 JP

Garagiste   ★★★★★

72 Blaxland Ave, Frankston South, Vic 3199 **Region** Mornington Peninsula
T 0439 370 530 **www**.garagiste.com.au **Winemaker** Barnaby Flanders **Est.** 2006
Dozens 2200 **Vyds** 6ha

Barnaby Flanders was a co-founder of Allies Wines in 2003, with some of the wines made under the Garagiste label. Allies has since gone its own way and Barnaby has a controlling interest in the Garagiste brand. The focus is on the Mornington Peninsula. The grapes are hand-sorted in the vineyard and again in the winery. Chardonnay is whole-bunch pressed, barrel-fermented with wild yeast in new and used French oak, mlf variably used, 8–9 months on lees. Seldom fined or filtered. Exports to the UK, Canada, Norway, Singapore, Japan and Hong Kong. (JH)

🍷🍷🍷🍷🍷 **Le Stagiaire Chardonnay 2021, Mornington Peninsula** This has to be the best value chardonnay from the peninsula matched to quality but also, this vintage has delivered the finest to date. It's superbly balanced with pristine fruit, the right amount of flinty sulphides, savouriness, texture and definition. There's some tension on the palate, a purity to the acidity and excellent length. What a wine. Screw cap. 13% alc. RATING 96 DRINK 2022-2030 $30 JF ✪

Merricks Chardonnay 2021, Mornington Peninsula Made the same as its Tuerong sibling, so site trumps everything. This is sublime. Flinty, spicy, citrusy and intense, in a good and satisfying way. The palate glides with such precision thanks to minerally fresh acidity. Mornington Peninsula chardonnay, but perhaps not as you know it. Bravo. Screw cap. 13% alc. RATING 96 DRINK 2022-2031 $45 JF ✪

Tuerong Chardonnay 2021, Mornington Peninsula Plenty of flavour and succulence across the palate, yet it remains taut thanks to its acidity. Grapefruit, dried fig, oak spice, lemon curd and creamy lees come together on the flavour spectrum. A cracking wine. Screw cap. 13% alc. RATING 96 DRINK 2022–2028 $45 JF ✪ ♥

Terre de Feu Pinot Noir 2019, Mornington Peninsula There's attention to detail with all the Garagiste wines, none more so than Terre de Feu. Beautifully harnessed flavours of cherry and pips, Middle Eastern spices, wood smoke, twigs and a grind of pepper. Furry tannins shapely across the fuller-bodied palate and mouth-watering acidity to close. Stamped with savouriness and serious intent. Screw cap. 13.5% alc. RATING 96 DRINK 2022–2034 $75 JF ✪

Le Stagiaire Pinot Gris 2021, Mornington Peninsula While this offers restrained PG flavours – pears, apple pie, spiced up with ginger and musk – 7 months in barrel on lees has added more complexity and depth. The citrussy acidity lights up the finish and extends the length. Screw cap. 13% alc. RATING 95 DRINK 2022–2026 $30 JF ✪

Tuerong Aligoté 2021, Mornington Peninsula Barnaby Flanders can only source a small amount of aligoté, but he weaves magic with the fruit anyway. Layers of flavour and depth: lemon, tart apple and stone fruit dance along with savoury, smoky notes. A whisper of sulphides and a smidge of nutty lees is teasing out the otherwise tight palate, led by a line of excellent acidity. Screw cap. 13% alc. RATING 95 DRINK 2022–2028 $35 JF ✪

Balnarring Pinot Noir 2021, Mornington Peninsula A savoury stamp this vintage, that decompresses the slight sweet-cherry accent into a minor component. Chinese five-spice, chinotto, wood smoke and a smatter of dried herbs form the core of flavours. But texture is key. Fine sandpaper tannins and the mouth-watering acidity leads everything to a decisive, slightly dry finish. An austere, compelling style. Screw cap. 13.4% alc. RATING 95 DRINK 2022–2030 $45 JF

Merricks Pinot Noir 2021, Mornington Peninsula Of the 2 single-vineyard wines (the other Balnarring), Merricks is making a statement in '21 – look at me. It's not big, but it packs a punch. The 50% whole bunches in the ferment have imparted Italian flavours of chinotto, amaro and Mediterranean herbs with a distinct ferrous-stony note. Pop and crunch to the acidity and raw-silk tannins in harmony across the even palate. A stylish and super-savoury drink. Screw cap. 13.5% alc. RATING 95 DRINK 2023–2031 $45 JF

Le Stagiaire Pinot Noir 2021, Mornington Peninsula While there's a flutter of cherries and spice with plum fruit sweetness across the palate, this is a much more savoury offering than usual. Lighter framed, with peach-fuzz tannins, raspberry-sorbet acidity and freshness throughout. Good to pour now. Screw cap. 13.5% alc. RATING 94 DRINK 2022–2028 $30 JF ✪

♀♀♀♀♀ **Cuvée de Coeur Pinot Noir 2018, Mornington Peninsula** RATING 91 $50 JF

Gartelmann Wines   ★★★★

701 Lovedale Road, Lovedale, NSW 2321 **Region** Hunter Valley
T (02) 4930 7113 **www.**gartelmann.com.au **Open** Mon–Sat 9–5, Sun 10–4
Winemaker Liz Silkman, Rauri Donkin **Est.** 1996 **Dozens** 7700
In '96 Jan and Jorg Gartelmann purchased what was previously the George Hunter Estate – 16ha of mature vineyards, most established by Oliver Shaul in '70. In a change of emphasis, the vineyard was sold and Gartelmann now sources its grapes from the Hunter Valley and other NSW regions, including the cool Rylstone area in Mudgee. Almost 25 years later, in Dec '20, the business was purchased by local chef Matt Dillow who was already running The Deck cafe based at Gartelmann. (JH)

♀♀♀♀♀ **Benjamin Semillon 2021, Hunter Valley** This will put on weight with time, but for now a tensile line of lightweight riffs on lemon grass, tonic, pimento

and citrus. Plenty of promise. Faith and patience needed. Screw cap. 10.5% alc.
RATING 92 DRINK 2023-2033 $27 NG

🍷🍷🍷🍷 **Wilhelm Shiraz 2018, Hunter Valley** RATING 88 DRINK 2021-2024 $30 NG

Gatt Wines

417 Boehms Springs Road, Flaxman Valley, SA 5235 **Region** Eden Valley
T (08) 8564 1166 **www.gattwines.com Winemaker** David Norman **Viticulturist** Gil
Rogers **Est.** 1972 **Dozens** 8000 **Vyds** 56.24ha
When you read the hyperbole that sometimes accompanies the acquisition of an existing wine
business, about transforming it into a world-class operation, it is easy to sigh and move on.
When Ray Gatt acquired Eden Springs, he proceeded to translate words into deeds. As well
as the 19.15ha Eden Springs Vineyard, he also acquired the historic Siegersdorf Vineyard (now
21.79ha) on the Barossa floor and the neighbouring Graue Vineyard (15.3ha). The change
of name from Eden Springs to Gatt Wines in '11 was sensible. Exports to Canada, Denmark,
Finland, France, Germany, Hong Kong, Italy, Japan, South Korea, Macau, Sweden, the US, the
UK and Canada. (JH)

🍷🍷🍷🍷🍷 **Old Vine Shiraz 2019, Barossa Valley** Deep plum, blackberry and black
cherry underscored with baking spice, licorice, chocolate, violets, roasting meats
and earth. Classic in structure with a wash of black fruits on the palate, bright
acidity and tight, sandy tannin. Medium bodied and awash with kirsch and spice
on the exit. Screw cap. 14.5% alc. RATING 93 DRINK 2032-2035 $100 DB
Cabernet Sauvignon 2019, Barossa Valley Varietally precise blackberry,
blackcurrant and cassis notes combine with clove, cinnamon, licorice, briar,
chocolate and espresso. Fine gypsum-like tannin grip, lovely fruit density and
detail and a leafy cassis-rich finish that trails away nicely. Screw cap. 14.5% alc.
RATING 92 DRINK 2022-2032 $60 DB
Cabernet Sauvignon 2018, High Eden Bright and fragrant with crunchy
blackberry and blackcurrant notes, edged with briar and dried herbs along with
hints of dark spice, cedar, mocha coffee and licorice. Bright acidity drives things
along nicely, powdery tannin adds support and the finish trails with crème de
cassis, spice and herbs. Screw cap. 14.5% alc. RATING 92 DRINK 2022-2032
$60 DB
Shiraz 2019, Barossa Valley Ripe satsuma plum and blackberry fruit comes
laden with spice and floral facets. Beneath lies a dark chocolate and licorice base
with a meaty edge and light cedar tones. There's superfine tannin and a morello
cherry burst that lingers on the finish nicely. Screw cap. 14.5% alc. RATING 91
DRINK 2022-2032 $60 DB
Riesling 2020, High Eden Pale straw with notes of Bickford's lime cordial,
grapefruit, tangerine, almond paste, orange blossom and stone. Pure and endearing,
there's an almost stone-fruit richness to the palate shape, along with a nervy acidity
that drives the wine forward. Screw cap. 12.5% alc. RATING 90 DRINK 2022-2028
$20 DB ❂
Shiraz 2019, High Eden Notes of blood plum, black cherries and mulberry
combine with hints of roasting meats, dark chocolate exotic spice, salumi, bay leaf,
licorice and sage. Meaty and loose-knit on the palate with a bright acid pulse,
some macerated strawberry tones and a finish that is rich in plum and spice. Screw
cap. 13.5% alc. RATING 90 DRINK 2022-2032 $60 DB

🍷🍷🍷🍷 **Eden Springs Cabernet Sauvignon 2021, High Eden** RATING 89
DRINK 2021-2028 $40 DB
Eden Springs Shiraz 2018, High Eden RATING 89 DRINK 2021-2028
$40 DB

Gembrook Hill

Launching Place Road, Gembrook, Vic 3783 **Region** Yarra Valley
T (03) 5968 1622 **www.**gembrookhill.com.au **Open** By appt **Winemaker** Andrew
Marks **Est.** 1983 **Dozens** 1500 **Vyds** 5ha

Ian and June Marks established Gembrook Hill, one of the oldest vineyards in the
southernmost part of the Upper Yarra Valley. The northeast-facing vineyard is in a natural
amphitheatre; the low-yielding sauvignon blanc, chardonnay and pinot noir are not irrigated.
The minimal approach to winemaking produces wines of a consistent style with finesse and
elegance. The unexpected death of Ian in Mar '17, and the decision of former winemaker
Timo Mayer to concentrate on his own label, left son Andrew Marks in charge of winemaking
at Gembrook Hill (and his own label, The Wanderer). Exports to the UK, the US, Denmark,
Japan and Malaysia. (JH)

ŸŸŸŸŸ **Blanc de Blancs 2015, Yarra Valley** Traditional method, on tirage 6 years,
5.5g/L dosage – brave, but I'm ok with it; disgorged May '21. Well made,
doubtless whole-bunch pressed, no pressings. Diam. 11.5% alc. RATING 96 $58
JH ✪
Sauvignon Blanc 2020, Yarra Valley A pale, bright green gold. Consistently
good, this restrained sauvignon blanc has aromas of green apple, lemongrass and
just a hint of fresh peas. Gently textured, fresh, clean and crisp with a long lemon-
curd finish. A serious wine in an oversaturated sauvignon blanc market. Screw cap.
12% alc. RATING 95 DRINK 2021–2025 $32 PR ✪ ♥
Chardonnay 2020, Yarra Valley A medium green gold. Complex with aromas
of yellow peach, grapefruit pith and spices. A powerful and creamy textured wine,
this will provide enjoyment now and over next 5 or so years. Diam. 12.5% alc.
RATING 94 DRINK 2021–2027 $40 PR

ŸŸŸŸŸ **Pinot Noir 2020, Yarra Valley** RATING 93 DRINK 2021–2026 $55 PR

Gemtree Wines

167 Elliot Road, McLaren Flat, SA 5171 **Region** McLaren Vale
T (08) 8323 0802 **www.**gemtreewines.com **Open** 7 days 11–5 **Winemaker** Mike Brown,
Joshua Waechter **Viticulturist** Melissa Brown **Est.** 1998 **Dozens** 90 000 **Vyds** 123ha

Gemtree Wines is owned and operated by husband-and-wife team Melissa and Mike Brown.
Mike (winemaker) and Melissa (viticulturist) firmly believe it is their responsibility to improve
the land for future generations, and the vineyards are farmed organically and biodynamically.
Exports to the UK, US, Canada, Sweden, Denmark, Norway, Finland, Japan and NZ. (JH)

ŸŸŸŸŸ **Cinnabar GSM 2021, McLaren Vale** A fine nose reminiscent of Asian plum,
pumice, kirsch, thyme and rosemary of the Southern Rhône. Nothing is heavy,
desiccated, too sweet or out of sorts. A swathe of chalky, pungent tannins corral,
direct, impart tension and make me salivate for the next glass. Exceptional GSM.
Screw cap. 14% alc. RATING 95 DRINK 2022–2028 $26 NG ✪

ŸŸŸŸŸ **Luna de Fresa Tempranillo Grenache Rosé 2021, McLaren Vale**
RATING 93 DRINK 2021–2022 $26 NG ✪
Small Batch SBE Grenache 2021, McLaren Vale RATING 93
DRINK 2022–2029 $50 NG
Small Batch SBO Grenache 2021, McLaren Vale RATING 93
DRINK 2022–2029 $50 NG
Uncut Shiraz 2020, McLaren Vale RATING 93 DRINK 2021–2026 $26 NG ✪
Luna Crescente Fiano 2021, McLaren Vale RATING 92 DRINK 2021–2024
$26 NG
Small Batch Fiano 2021, McLaren Vale RATING 92 DRINK 2021–2024
$35 NG
Small Batch Pet Nat Grenache 2021, McLaren Vale RATING 91 $35 NG
Luna Temprana Tempranillo 2021, McLaren Vale RATING 91
DRINK 2021–2023 $26 NG

 # Genista Wines

PO Box 969, Williamstown, SA 5351 (postal) **Region** Barossa Valley
www.genistawines.com **Winemaker** Lloyd Broom **Viticulturist** Lloyd Broom **Est.** 2017
Dozens 100 **Vyds** 3.2ha

Lloyd Broom and Sarah Gregory made the move from Melbourne to the Barossa Valley after purchasing their vineyard in Cockatoo Valley, between the villages of Lyndoch and Williamstown. The vineyards are split into two blocks: Home block with 1.6ha of shiraz and Gipson block with 1.2ha of shiraz and 0.4ha of grenache. The wines from this young estate reflect their plantings and ring true to their southern Barossan roots, with rich dark fruits and bright earthy lines. A portion of the proceeds from sales of the grenache go to Barossa Wildlife Rescue and the label features 3 feathered and furred friends adopted by the winery. (DB)

🍷🍷🍷🍷🍷 **Taking The Mickie Shiraz 2020, Barossa Valley** Bright red/purple in the glass with primary, plum and dark berry aromas, baking spice, licorice, dark chocolate and floral top notes. There is a little more fruit density with this release: it's still medium bodied, but it carries a bit more fruit heft and fine, sandy tannin sway. Compact, a little broody at this stage of its evolution but delicious nevertheless. Screw cap. 14.5% alc. RATING 90 DRINK 2021–2028 $30 DB
Taking The Mickie Shiraz 2018, Barossa Valley There is a pleasing sense of space and detail to the '18 edition of this wine; a little less oak too. The fruit profile is plummy and ripe with plenty of spice along with a flicker of violets and earth. Ripe sandy tannins and fine, acidity provide the architecture and the finish is full of savoury detail. Screw cap. 14.5% alc. RATING 90 DRINK 2021–2028 $30 DB

🍷🍷🍷🍷 **Duck, Duck, Cat Grenache 2020, Barossa Valley** RATING 89
DRINK 2021–2028 $30 DB
Taking The Mickie Shiraz 2017, Barossa Valley RATING 89
DRINK 2021–2028 $30 DB

Geoff Merrill Wines

291 Pimpala Road, Woodcroft, SA 5162 **Region** McLaren Vale
T (08) 8381 6877 **www**.geoffmerrillwines.com.au **Open** Mon–Fri 10–4.30, Sat 12–4.30
Winemaker Geoff Merrill, Scott Heidrich **Est.** 1980 **Dozens** 55 000 **Vyds** 45ha

If Geoff Merrill ever loses his impish sense of humour or his zest for life, high and not-so-high, we shall all be the poorer. The product range consists of 3 tiers: premium (varietal); Reserve, being the older wines, reflecting the desire for elegance and subtlety of this otherwise exuberant winemaker; and, at the top, Henley Shiraz. Exports to all major markets. (JH)

🍷🍷🍷🍷🍷 **Pimpala Vineyard Cabernet Merlot 2006, McLaren Vale** An aged museum release, this is showing well. Drinking this toned heavyweight is akin to snuggling into a worn leather chair and reminiscing. Riffs on hoisin, dried walnut, porcini and polished mahogany. The tannins, abstinent signposts well appointed. The acidity, a bit harsh, but given the nourishment of Father Time and the complexities imparted, it is a small price to pay to revisit a fine vintage from a different era. Screw cap. 14% alc. RATING 92 DRINK 2021–2026 $70 NG

🍷🍷🍷🍷 **Henley Shiraz 2003, McLaren Vale** RATING 89 DRINK 2021–2024 $215 NG
Henley Shiraz 2000, McLaren Vale RATING 88 DRINK 2021–2024 $265 NG

Geoff Weaver

2 Gilpin Lane, Mitcham, SA 5062 (postal) **Region** Adelaide Hills
T (08) 8272 2105 **www**.geoffweaver.com.au **Winemaker** Geoff Weaver **Est.** 1982
Dozens 3000 **Vyds** 12.3ha

This is the business of one-time Hardys chief winemaker Geoff Weaver. The Lenswood vineyard was established between 1982 and '88, and invariably produces immaculate riesling and sauvignon blanc and long-lived chardonnays. The beauty of the labels ranks supreme. Exports to the UK, Hong Kong and Singapore. (JH)

🍷🍷🍷🍷🍷 **Single Vineyard Sauvignon Blanc 2021, Adelaide Hills** This is an excellent example of a sauvignon that is super-tasty now, but with so much potential still to explore. So versatile. Well composed, crisp and balanced in lime, citrus, apple, green mango and spice. It softens through to the finish, maintaining a chalky clean texture. Screw cap. 13.5% alc. RATING 95 DRINK 2021–2026 $30 JP ❂

🍷🍷🍷🍷🍷 **Riesling 2021, Adelaide Hills** RATING 92 DRINK 2021–2026 $30 JP

Ghost Rock Vineyard ★★★★

1055 Port Sorrell Road, Northdown, Tas 7307 **Region** Northern Tasmania
T (03) 6428 4005 **www**.ghostrock.com.au **Open** 7 days 11–5 **Winemaker** Justin Arnold
Viticulturist Izaak Perkins, Marty Smith **Est.** 2001 **Dozens** 12 000 **Vyds** 30ha
In '01, Cate and Colin Arnold purchased the former Patrick Creek Vineyard planted exclusively to pinot noir in 1989. The vineyards, situated among the patchwork fields of Sassafras to the south and the white sands of the Port Sorell Peninsula to the north, now total 30ha: pinot noir (14 clones) remains the bedrock of the plantings, with other varieties including chardonnay, pinot gris, riesling and sauvignon blanc. Ownership has passed to son Justin and his wife Alicia (who runs the cooking school and cellar door). Justin's experience in the Yarra Valley (Coldstream Hills), Margaret River (Devil's Lair) and Napa Valley (Etude) has paid dividends – the business is going from strength to strength, and the capacity of the 100t winery has been tripled. Exports to Japan, Hong Kong and the UK. (JH)

🍷🍷🍷🍷🍷 **Catherine Cuvée Exceptionelle 2016, Tasmania** Aged 3 years on lees. There is a power, a presence and an immediacy to the '16 harvest in Northern Tasmania, confidently projected here in a rich and strong blend. Grilled pineapple, fig and even a suggestion of prune show considerable toasty, spicy development at just 5 years of age, beginning to show some dryness on the finish. Drink up. Diam. 12.5% alc. RATING 90 $49 TS

Giaconda ★★★★★

30 McClay Road, Beechworth, Vic 3747 **Region** Beechworth
T (03) 5727 0246 **www**.giaconda.com.au **Open** By appt **Winemaker** Rick
Kinzbrunner, Nathan Kinzbrunner **Viticulturist** Casey White **Est.** 1982 **Dozens** 2500
Vyds 4ha
These wines have a super-cult status and, given the small production, are extremely difficult to find; they are sold chiefly through restaurants and via their website. All have a cosmopolitan edge befitting Rick Kinzbrunner's international winemaking experience. The Chardonnay is one of Australia's greatest and is made and matured in the underground wine cellar hewn out of granite. This permits gravity flow and a year-round temperature range of 14–15°C, promising even more for the future. Exports to the UK, UAE, the US, Canada, Singapore, Sweden, Norway, Germany and NZ. (JH)

🍷🍷🍷🍷🍷 **Estate Vineyard Chardonnay 2019, Beechworth** The secret – if there is one – to Giaconda chardonnay is the depth of complexity achieved. It is a thing of wonder to get lost in, as you wander through layer upon layer of stone fruits, citrus and grilled nuts, almond cream, spice and then gently embedded oak. Luscious. Intriguing. Stylish. Screw cap. 13.5% alc. RATING 97 DRINK 2022–2036 $129 JP ❂ ♥

🍷🍷🍷🍷🍷 **Warner Vineyard Shiraz 2019, Beechworth** Seriously good any way you look at it: stylish presence in the glass, the meshing of fruit and oak, tannin management or the sheer enjoyment it brings. A world of black- and blue-berried fruit awaits; intertwined with an autumnal, earthy, undergrowth character, deep spice and a touch of savouriness. Glides with the aid of supple tannins to a firm, lingering close. Screw cap. 13.8% alc. RATING 96 DRINK 2021–2045 $105 JP
Nebbiolo 2017, Beechworth A must-have for nebbiolo lovers. Its colour is, as expected, light and bright, the bouquet with spices spilling everywhere, but with varietal fruit that comes into play, loud and clear, on the finely crafted blend of

sour cherries and cigar box on the long palate. The tannins provide background music, and could have succeeded without them. Cork. 14% alc. RATING 96 DRINK 2025-2035 $115 JH

Estate Vineyard Pinot Noir 2019, Beechworth Decant or apply some air to this tightly coiled youngster, or approach it a day after opening. The reward is a fully expressive wine that reaches some impressive heights. Makes it look easy. Fresh thyme, orange rind, violet and dark red-berried scents mingle with more earthy notes. Presents an inner strength, a solid core of deep, dark fruits, exotic spice and a lingering line of herbal notes as it works its way into your senses. Sapid, fine tannins aplenty. A study in power and concentration. Screw cap. 13.8% alc. RATING 95 DRINK 2021-2035 $99 JP

Estate Vineyard Shiraz 2019, Beechworth Quite the charmer, blessed with a natural beauty and restraint, a feature of the vineyard year in, year out. Begins with a heady aroma of blueberries, black fruits, dried herbs, Asian five-spice and anise. The use of whole bunches brings the palate into focus: taut, sappy and leafy amid the fruit, spice and vanillin oak, with some assertive tannins striding the middle palate. Quite beguiling but, if you can, afford this wine more time. Cork. 13.8% alc. RATING 95 DRINK 2022-2037 $99 JP

Giant Steps   ★★★★★

314 Maroondah Highway, Healesville, Vic 3777 **Region** Yarra Valley
T (03) 5962 6111 **www**.giantstepswine.com.au **Open** 7 days 11–4 **Winemaker** Melanie Chester, Steve Flamsteed, Jess Clark **Viticulturist** Ashley Wood **Est.** 1997 **Dozens** 30 000 **Vyds** 60ha

Since the sale of Innocent Bystander in '16, the focus has been on the high-quality, single-vineyard, single-variety wines in what is demonstrably a very distinguished portfolio. Its vineyard resources comprise the Sexton Vineyard (32ha) in the Lower Yarra and Applejack Vineyard (13ha) in the Upper Yarra; there is also the Primavera Vineyard in the Upper Yarra under long-term supervised contract and Tarraford Vineyard in the Lower Yarra under long-term lease. Giant Steps was purchased by Jackson Family Wines in Aug '20. Exports to the UK, the US, Canada, Sweden, Hong Kong, Singapore and NZ. (JH)

ŸŸŸŸŸ Applejack Vineyard Pinot Noir 2021, Yarra Valley I've long considered the Applejack vineyard to be one of the greatest sites for pinot in Australia and I'm not sure I've seen a better version than the '21. A deep, bright, crimson purple. Maraschino cherry into plum, there's an exotic and riotous amalgam of Asian five-spice and a gentle savoury, umami character. What elevates this vintage is the concentration, along with Applejack's trademark perfume and spice. Just so vibrant and fresh on the palate, the tannins are both silky and plentiful. You will have no problems opening and enjoying this now, but the wine's track record suggests you'll thank me if you still have some to drink 7–10 years from now, if not longer. Screw cap. 13.5% alc. RATING 98 DRINK 2022-2032 $70 PR ✪ ♥

Rosé 2021, Yarra Valley 100% pinot noir, hand picked specifically for this rosé, wild-yeast fermented. Vibrantly fresh aromas and flavours; rose petals, violets and delicate spices on the bouquet, wild strawberries and raspberries on the mouth-watering palate. Great wine, not just great rosé. And it will repay cellaring. Screw cap. 12% alc. RATING 97 DRINK 2021-2025 $30 JH ✪ ♥

Sexton Vineyard Chardonnay 2021, Yarra Valley Smells tightly wound and concentrated with aromas of ripe peach and nectarine, together with just a hint of lanolin and apple custard. Equally powerful and punchy on the palate. This has more of everything, including sprightly acid and some phenolic grip on the very long, stone-fruit pithy finish. Today, this is my pick of the 4 single-vineyard '21 chardonnays, but who knows what will come out on top in 5 or even 10 years from now! Screw cap. 13% alc. RATING 97 DRINK 2022-2028 $65 PR ✪

Primavera Vineyard Pinot Noir 2021, Yarra Valley A very bright crimson purple. So pure and perfumed with briary cherries, ripe redcurrants and freshly cut roses. Poised, juicy and energetic, the wine has so much tang and crunch, you barely notice that this is also structured finishing with long, gently puckering tannins. A wine with immediate appeal, but also one that will reward at least another 7–10 years in the cellar. Screw cap. 13% alc. RATING 97 DRINK 2022-2031 $70 PR ✪

TTTTT **Pinot Noir 2021, Yarra Valley** A very bright, light–medium crimson red. A gentle waft of fresh raspberries and cranberries, with just the right amount of spice-rack spices. Delicious right out of the gate, this medium-bodied and refreshing wine will age well too. The perfect introduction to modern Yarra pinot. Screw cap. 13.5% alc. RATING 96 DRINK 2021-2026 $38 PR ✪

Applejack Vineyard Chardonnay 2021, Yarra Valley A very bright green gold. Very bright and pure fruited, with its aromas of freshly poached apples, just-picked white peach and a little spice. The oak is already perfectly integrated. The flow and texture on the palate is seamless and I love that bit of 'chew' on the finish. Screw cap. 12.5% alc. RATING 96 DRINK 2022-2028 $65 PR ✪

Sexton Vineyard Pinot Noir 2021, Yarra Valley A dark, deep crimson. A more robust Yarra Valley pinot with its aromas of dark cherries, black plum and a dried-earth character that makes it quite different to the other Giant Step single-vineyard pinots. Sweetly fruited, concentrated and structured on the palate, what this impressive wine doesn't have in finesse, it makes up for in power and grunt. This should still be looking good 10, if not 15, years from now. Screw cap. 13.5% alc. RATING 96 DRINK 2023-2032 $70 PR ✪

Fatal Shore Pinot Noir 2021, Southern Tasmania A gorgeous, bright, crimson. Perfumed and seductive, this leaps out of the glass with an array of aromas including red and black fruits, peony, Asian spices, orange peel and a hint of fresh vanilla bean. More sweet fruited and textured on the mid palate compared to the more fine-boned and linear Yarra single-vineyard pinots. Concentrated but not heavy, with ripe, gently chewy and persistent tannins rounding out an impressive and still quite tightly wound wine that will need another year or 2 to relax and really hit its straps. Screw cap. 13.5% alc. RATING 96 DRINK 2023-2029 $75 PR ✪

Clay Ferment Ocarina Chardonnay 2020, Yarra Valley It's quite astonishing how these vessels shape the feel and taste of the final blend. This chardonnay is tight, linear and superfine with its acid profile. Yet it has plenty of flavour with hints of citrus, lemon salts and a smidge of creamed honey. It's refreshing and pulsating with energy. A super drink. Screw cap. 12.5% alc. RATING 96 DRINK 2021-2030 $60 JF ✪

Wombat Creek Vineyard Chardonnay 2020, Yarra Valley Giant Steps' higher-elevation sites, as in this and Applejack Vineyard, have turned out racy, long and superfine wines – it's the moreish, mouth-watering acidity. Of course, there's more: the complex flavours and heady aromas. Smoky, slinky and talc-like texture to the acidity, with a dab of creamed honey and citrus on the palate. There's a lot of precision and it's a pure wine in a way that evolves superbly in the glass. Screw cap. 13% alc. RATING 96 DRINK 2021-2029 $60 JF ✪

Applejack Vineyard Pinot Noir 2020, Yarra Valley Pinot purity right here, folks. There's a certain precision and definition, too. A delightful combo of joy and complexity: rhubarb and freshly grated beetroot, sweet red cherries, florals and warm spices, with the oak neatly tucked in. Superfine tannins, laser-like acidity and terrific length seal the deal. Screw cap. 13.5% alc. RATING 96 DRINK 2021-2031 $65 JF ✪

Chardonnay 2021, Yarra Valley A super-bright green gold. Vibrant aromas with perfectly ripened stone fruits, grapefruit pith and an attractive touch of lemongrass and ginger. Gently textured, balanced and satisfying. A class act from beginning to end. Screw cap. 12.5% alc. RATING 95 DRINK 2021-2025 $38 PR

Wombat Creek Vineyard Pinot Noir 2021, Yarra Valley A light bright crimson. Perfumed and lifted with some wild strawberry, musk sticks and dried rose petals. Silky textured, the stems are already pretty well integrated into the wine and there's a long, sappy and gently sinewy finish. This has all the components to improve and become more complex in bottle over the next 10 years. Screw cap. 13.5% alc. RATING 95 DRINK 2022-2032 $65 PR

Tarraford Vineyard Chardonnay 2021, Yarra Valley A fuller, bright, green gold. Quite restrained, with aromas of stone fruits, oatmeal and a little wet rock. I like both the intensity and restraint on the palate and this may, paradoxically, need the longest of the 4 single-vineyard '21 chardonnays to open up. Screw cap. 13.5% alc. RATING 95 DRINK 2022-2028 $65 PR

Fatal Shore Pinot Noir 2020, Tasmania Fruit from the Coal River Valley in Tassie, but made in the Yarra via the gentle way that defines Giant Steps. Yet the density and power of the place, the fruit intensity, comes through strongly. Dark cherries abound but so too savoury, umami flavours of soy sauce and dried porcini with meaty reduction and spicy oak adding another layer. Full bodied with shapely tannins and a persuasive finish. A neat counterpoint to the Yarra Valley single-vineyard wines. Screw cap. 13.5% alc. RATING 95 DRINK 2022-2034 $75 JF

Applejack Vineyard Chardonnay 2020, Yarra Valley Gosh this is so good. It kicks off with a whiff of enticing sulphides, hinting at celery salt, fennel and lemon balm. It's super-tight and linear with the lively, zesty acidity driving through convincingly to the long finish. However, there's a smidge of nutty creamy lees adding texture and a savoury overlay – it's definitely not a fruit-driven wine. It needs time to unfurl and will continue to do so. Screw cap. 13% alc. RATING 95 DRINK 2021-2029 $60 JF

Sexton Vineyard Chardonnay 2020, Yarra Valley Perhaps the most approachable of the single-vineyard chardonnays, as it's flavoursome and rich without being over-the-top. Expect beeswax, white florals and some ginger spice, plus lots of texture and concentrated flavours across the full palate. Importantly, everything is in balance. There's a neat acid line too and this is just right for drinking now, rather than cellaring. Screw cap. 13% alc. RATING 95 DRINK 2021-2026 $60 JF

Primavera Vineyard Pinot Noir 2020, Yarra Valley The north-facing Primavera site in Woori Yallock sits at 230m elevation and has morphed into the prettiest of the single-vineyard pinots this vintage. While it has a delicacy, there's plenty of definition too. Wonderful aromas and very spicy, with beautifully balanced flavours of red fruits, umami and truffle. Then lacy tannins take hold, while the partial whole-bunch fermentation has given the wine a sapidity and vivacity. A lovely wine. Screw cap. 13.5% alc. RATING 95 DRINK 2021-2030 $65 JF

Sexton Vineyard Pinot Noir 2020, Yarra Valley This is superbly composed, and for a young pinot, it's drinking beautifully now. Heady with florals, dark cherries and lots of earthy characters. Fuller bodied, with supple and shapely tannins, while the juicy acidity keeps this rather buoyant. Of course, if you can wait, this will also reward with extra cellar time. Screw cap. 13.5% alc. RATING 95 DRINK 2021-2031 $65 JF

Harry's Monster 2019, Yarra Valley 59/40/1% merlot/cabernet sauvignon/ petit verdot. Don't be fooled by its approachability. This is a classy, medium-bodied rendition that will unfurl given more time and garner more complexity. Today, it's almost pretty with its array of red and blue fruits, finely chiselled tannins and the smooth texture across the palate. Screw cap. 14% alc. RATING 95 DRINK 2022-2034 $55 JF

Syrah Carignan Grenache 2019, Yarra Valley An 85/11/4% varietal split and made into an early-drinking style that's taking the Valley by storm. Giant Steps make an LDR – light dry red – but this has an altogether different take with its flavour profile. Super-bright and juicy fruit, a mix of dark plums and red berries, sarsaparilla with a light dusting of spice. The palate is actually quite refined, with svelte tannins and refreshing acidity. Given the style brief, this is pitch perfect. It's hard to put this down. So I didn't. Screw cap. 13.5% alc. RATING 95 DRINK 2021-2027 $38 JF

Harry's Monster 2020, Yarra Valley 55/40/5% merlot/cabernet/petit verdot. A medium deep, bright, plummy red. A good effort from this cooler year, this smells of dark cherry, damson plums, cedar and a dusting of fine, good-quality dark cacao powder. Good depth on the medium-bodied palate, too. The tannins are fine and persistent with good grip on the finish and while approachable now, with food, this will continue to improve in the bottle for at least the next 5–6 years, if not longer. Screw cap. 13.5% alc. RATING 94 DRINK 2023-2028 $65 PR

Gibson ★★★★☆

190 Willows Road, Light Pass, SA 5355 **Region** Barossa Valley
T (08) 8562 4224 **www**.gibsonwines.com.au **Open** 7 days 11–5 **Winemaker** Rob Gibson **Est.** 1996 **Dozens** 11 000 **Vyds** 12.4ha
Rob Gibson spent much of his working life as a senior viticulturist for Penfolds, involved in research tracing the characters that particular parcels of grapes give to a wine, which left him with a passion for identifying and protecting what is left of the original vineyard plantings in Australia. He has a vineyard (merlot) in the Barossa Valley at Light Pass, and one in the Eden Valley (shiraz and riesling) and also purchases grapes from McLaren Vale and the Adelaide Hills. Exports to Germany and Taiwan. (JH)

🍷🍷🍷🍷🍷 **Australian Old Vine Collection Shiraz 2018, Eden Valley** A wonderfully composed Eden Valley shiraz from the folks at Gibson. Satsuma plum, red cherry and blackberry fruits of impressive grace and ripeness are cut with fruitcake spice, licorice, sage, dark chocolate, violets and earth. Smooth and velvety on the palate with great flow and presence, melt-in-the-mouth tannins and a finish that shows bright acidity and lingers persistently with pure black fruits, spice and cedar. Cork. 14.5% alc. RATING 95 DRINK 2022-2035 $135 DB

🍷🍷🍷🍷🍷 **Burkes Hill Riesling 2021, Eden Valley** RATING 92 DRINK 2022-2030 $35 DB
Reserve Shiraz 2019, Barossa RATING 92 DRINK 2022-2030 $55 DB
Isabelle Cabernet Merlot 2019, Barossa RATING 91 DRINK 2022-2028 $30 DB

Gilbert Family Wines ★★★★★

137 Ulan Road, Mudgee, NSW 2850 **Region** Central Ranges
T (02) 6373 1325 **www**.gilbertfamilywines.com.au **Open** Mon 10–2, Thurs 10–4, Fri–Sat 10–5, Sun 10–4 **Winemaker** Simon Gilbert, Will Gilbert **Est.** 2004 **Dozens** 18 000 **Vyds** 25.81ha
The Gilbert Family Wine Company was established in 2004 by fifth-generation winemaker Simon Gilbert; 6th-generation Will Gilbert took over the reins in '14. Will draws on extensive Old and New World winemaking experience to push boundaries with different techniques and ideas to make the Gilbert Family wines from Orange and Mudgee. Gilbert + Gilbert wines from the Eden Valley draw from the family history – Joseph Gilbert of Pewsey Vale was the first to plant grapes in the Eden Valley in 1847. Exports to the UK, the US, Canada, Norway, Denmark, Japan, Taiwan and Hong Kong. (JH)

🍷🍷🍷🍷🍷 **Blanc de Blancs 2016, Orange** Clearly a great deal of work has gone into the sparkling wine programme here. The wines are stellar. Intentionally tensile and bone dry, with zero dosage. Given that natural acidity in Australia is never Champagne's equal, a savvy move. The partial oak fermentation, too, endowing breadth and grip across the mid palate, while toning the fervent drive of quince, bitter almond and citrus zest. Toast, too, after 50 months on lees. Long and of such exactitude that it pulls the saliva from the mouth in readiness for the next glass. And the next. A great fizz. Screw cap. 12.2% alc. RATING 97 $66 NG ✪ ❤

🍷🍷🍷🍷🍷 **Méthode Traditionelle Chardonnay Pinot Noir Pinot Meunier 2016, Orange** A zero-dosage expression of febrile mineral energy. Partially fermented in neutral wood before an impressive 50 months on lees, this is aperitif material par excellence. Subtle is the echo of the red grapes: strawberry and redcurrant. Bright is chardonnay's pungent acid mettle. Long and steely is the finish, verging on a masochistic austerity. A subtle whiff of toast. Wine to whet the palate and prime the hunger. Homage to Champagne's growers. Very good. Cork. 12.6% alc. RATING 95 $66 NG gilbert RS11 Riesling 2021, Orange Green apple, pine-lime splice, tonic, ginger and lemon zest. Lightweight, yet boasting a torque of febrile intensity to drive the fray long. Drinking like a local Spätlese without quite the natural acidity. This may build with time. A good wine. Possibly very good. Screw cap. 11.5% alc. RATING 94 DRINK 2021-2030 $36 NG

Gilberts ★★★★☆

30138 Albany Highway, Kendenup via Mount Barker, WA 6323 **Region** Mount Barker **T** 1800 708 110 **www**.gilbertwines.com.au **Open** Thurs–Mon 10–5 **Winemaker** West Cape Howe **Est.** 1985 **Dozens** 3000 **Vyds** 9ha
Once a part-time occupation for third-generation sheep and beef farmers Jim and Beverly Gilbert, but now a full-time job and a very successful one. In 2014 the fourth generation, sons Clinton and Matthew, joined the management of the business. The mature vineyard (shiraz, chardonnay, riesling and cabernet sauvignon) coupled with contract winemaking at West Cape Howe, has long produced high-class wines. Exports to Canada. (JH)

🍷🍷🍷🍷🍷 Reserve Shiraz 2019, Mount Barker This is lovely! Super-elegant, dark fruit in the mouth offers a cascade of flavour, caught within the confines of the restraint and finesse on offer here. Mount Barker can often yield muscular wines, and here the wine is attractively toned rather than tanked, a wonderful thing. Licorice, blackberries, mulberries and aniseed, with no small measure of bramble and pie. The acidity through the finish is refreshing and bright. Screw cap. 14.5% alc. RATING 95 DRINK 2021-2031 $40 EL

🍷🍷🍷🍷🍷 JMG Riesling 2021, Mount Barker RATING 93 DRINK 2021-2031 $25 EL ✪
Riesling 2021, Mount Barker RATING 93 DRINK 2021-2031 $28 EL
3 Devils Shiraz 2020, Mount Barker RATING 92 DRINK 2021-2027 $25 EL ✪

Gioiello Estate ★★★★

350 Molesworth-Dropmore Road, Molesworth, Vic 3718 **Region** Upper Goulburn **T** 0419 375 422 **www**.gioiello.com.au **Winemaker** Scott McCarthy (Contract) **Est.** 1987 **Dozens** 3000 **Vyds** 8.97ha
The Gioiello Estate vineyard was established by a Japanese company and originally known as Daiwa Nar Darak. Planted between 1987 and '96, it accounts for just under 9ha of a 400ha property of rolling hills, pastures, bushland, river flats, natural water springs and billabongs. Now owned by the Schiavello family, the vineyard continues to produce high-quality wines. (JH)

🍷🍷🍷🍷🍷 Merlot 2019, Upper Goulburn A charming and serious merlot that moves – no, glides – across the palate in the pursuit of savouriness. It's ripe in blackberry, mulberry, stewed plums, violet and a leafiness that brings an attractive herbal edge. Surrounded in toasty oak and leather, it calls out for a food accompaniment. Screw cap. 14.4% alc. RATING 92 DRINK 2022-2026 $27 JP
Mt Concord Syrah 2019, Upper Goulburn A different wine to the previous release, one that appears noticeably riper and ultra-savoury. Black fruits and a complex meat fragrance. Densely packed in leather, tar and sturdy tannins. A good decant before enjoying is recommended. Screw cap. 14.1% alc. RATING 92 DRINK 2022-2026 $45 JP
Old House Merlot 2019, Upper Goulburn Allows the fruit the open stage to perform in ripe blue berries, plum, leaf and baking spices. Fairly glides across the tongue building in woody spice, chocolate and fine, easy tannins. Screw cap. 14.4% alc. RATING 92 DRINK 2022-2026 $45 JP
Old Hill Chardonnay 2020, Upper Goulburn An engaging chardonnay boasting a flinty edge on the bouquet, with peach, nectarine and citrus. Flavours run thick and even across the palate, enhanced by oak-derived mealy texture. Screw cap. 12.7% alc. RATING 90 DRINK 2022-2024 $35 JP

🍷🍷🍷🍷 Syrah 2019, Upper Goulburn RATING 89 DRINK 2022-2026 $27 JP

Gippsland Wine Company

6835 South Gippsland Hwy, Loch, VIC 3945 **Region** Gippsland
T 0477 555 235 **www**.gippslandwinecompany.com **Open** Fri–Sun 11–5
Winemaker Marcus Satchell **Est.** 2010 **Dozens** 1500 **Vyds** 5ha
Mark Heath has worked in some big-name wine companies, mainly in sales and marketing.
In '11, he and his wife, Jane Taylor, bought a run-down site in Loch Village. The appeal of
Gippsland was the charm of a region full of owner-operators rather than large-scale businesses.
With some hard work, it didn't take long for the north-facing 1.2ha vineyard planted around
1999 to cabernet sauvignon, sangiovese and chardonnay to come back to life. From day one,
he secured local winemaker Marcus Satchell (Dirty Three Wines) to make the wines. Today,
Gippsland Wine Company leases 4 other vineyards within a 20km radius from Loch Village,
planted to several varieties including riesling, pinot noir, sauvignon blanc and shiraz. (JF)

ΨΨΨΨΩ **Loch Village Chardonnay 2020, Gippsland** A very good wine, sharp and
controlled. A pared-back style with grapefruit and lemon, flinty, super-zesty
with laser-fine acidity. Tight across the palate with some grilled nuts and creamy
lees – not much, just enough to give it shape. Screw cap. 13% alc. RATING 93
DRINK 2022-2027 $40 JF
Moyarra Vineyard Fumé Blanc 2020, Gippsland Loads of pine-lime Splice
and fresh West Indian lime juice flavours infuse the tight palate, even if there's
texture. It's light on its feet, refreshing with tangy acidity right through. Screw cap.
12% alc. RATING 90 DRINK 2022-2025 $35 JF

Gipsie Jack Wine Co

The Winehouse, 1509 Langhorne Creek Road, Langhorne Creek, SA 5255
Region Langhorne Creek
T (08) 8537 3029 **www**.gipsiejack.com.au **Open** 7 days 10–5 **Winemaker** John
Glaetzer, Ben Potts **Est.** 2004
The partners of Gipsie Jack are John Glaetzer and Ben Potts, named after John Glaetzer's Jack
Russell dog Gipsie. Glaetzer and Potts say, 'We want to make this label fun, like in the 'old
days'. No pretentiousness, no arrogance, not even a back label. A great wine at a great price,
with no discounting.' Exports to Switzerland and Singapore. (JH)

ΨΨΨΨΨ **Dolcetto 2019, Langhorne Creek** Light ruby-red hue; the aromas, flavours
and light- to medium-bodied palate are all encapsulated by the colour. It's red-fruit
dominant, the mouthfeel beguiling, with silky tannins and a fresh finish. Truly
delicious, great value. Trophy and gold medal Best Alternative Variety (White
or Red) Langhorne Creek Wine Show '21. Screw cap. 14.5% alc. RATING 95
DRINK 2022-2029 $22 JH ✪
Malbec 2019, Langhorne Creek Good crimson-purple colour, the bouquet
and palate reaffirming the unique symbiotic bond between Langhorne Creek and
malbec, with exotic spiced plum and earth flavours, and a moderately firm, mouth-
watering finish. Screw cap. 14.8% alc. RATING 94 DRINK 2022-2032 $22 JH ✪

ΨΨΨΨΩ **Shiraz 2019, Langhorne Creek** RATING 90 DRINK 2025-2030 $19 JH ✪

Glaetzer Wines

PO Box 824 Tanunda, SA 5352 **Region** Barossa Valley
T (08) 8563 0947 **www**.glaetzer.com **Winemaker** Ben Glaetzer **Est.** 1996
Dozens 15 000 **Vyds** 20ha
With a family history in the Barossa Valley dating back to 1888, Glaetzer Wines was established
by Colin Glaetzer after 30 years of winemaking experience. Son Ben worked in the Hunter
Valley and as a Flying Winemaker in many of the world's wine regions before returning to
Glaetzer Wines and assuming the winemaking role. The wines are made with great skill and
abundant personality. Exports to all major markets. (JH)

🍷🍷🍷🍷🍷 **Amon-Ra Unfiltered Shiraz 2020, Barossa Valley** Always a picture of pure fruit density and latent power, the latest release of Ben Glaetzer's Amon Ra continues that theme of Barossa concentration. Glossy blackberry, black cherry and satsuma plum fruit flow readily, that compact Ebenezer power on full display. Hints of baking spice, earth, licorice and dark chocolate come into play, along with tightly packed, gypsum-like tannins for support, impressive acid cadence and a persistent and enduring exit. Always impressive. Screw cap. 14.5% alc. RATING 96 DRINK 2021-2035 $100 DB

Anaperenna 2020, Barossa Valley A polished, glossy rendition of the great Australian shiraz cabernet blend from Ben Glaetzer. Wonderfully pure blackberry and plum fruits with a touch of blueberry lift, melding with deep spice, licorice, Old Jamaica chocolate and earth. Cedary oak flows in on the palate before retreating back into the fruit which shines brightly throughout. Tannins are gravelly and long and there is a sense of freshness to its form. Self-assured and wonderfully pure drinking. Cork. 14.5% alc. RATING 95 DRINK 2021-2035 $52 DB

🍷🍷🍷🍷🍷 **Bishop Shiraz 2019, Barossa Valley** RATING 93 DRINK 2021-2035 $33 DB
Wallace Shiraz Grenache 2019, Barossa Valley RATING 91 DRINK 2021-2031 $23 DB ✪

Glaetzer-Dixon Family Winemakers

93 Brooker Avenue, Hobart, Tas 7000 **Region** Southern Tasmania
T 0417 852 287 **www**.gdfwinemakers.com **Open** By appt **Winemaker** Nick Glaetzer
Est. 2008 **Dozens** 2500 **Vyds** 12ha
History does not relate what Nick Glaetzer's high-profile Barossa Valley winemaker relatives thought of his decision to move to Tasmania in '05 to make cutting-edge cool-climate styles. While his winemaking career began in the Barossa Valley, he reached into scattered parts of the New World and Old World alike, working successively in Languedoc, the Pfalz, Margaret River, Riverland, Sunraysia, the Hunter Valley and Burgundy. To date, fruit has all been sourced from growers; '22 will be the first harvest from Nick's new 12ha estate vineyard. The urban winery and cellar door is based in an old ice factory on the outskirts of Hobart. Exports to the US, Canada, the Netherlands and Singapore. (JH)

🍷🍷🍷🍷 **Rêveur Pinot Noir 2017, Tasmania** Sweet, juicy wild strawberry fruit contrasts firm, fine tannin structure and lifted musk stick and exotic spice character, concluding with drying oak tannins. Screw cap. 13.7% alc. RATING 89 DRINK 2022-2027 $56 TS

Überblanc Riesling 2019, Tasmania Boasting an exuberant golden yellow hue, this is a succulent, spicy and savoury riesling that relies equally on acidity and long lees age for texture structure. Flavours of custard apple and golden kiwifruit make for a generous style, with a touch of phenolic bitterness on the close. Screw cap. 12.5% alc. RATING 88 DRINK 2021-2023 $26 TS

La Judith Pinot Noir 2016, Tasmania Powerful pinot noir, released with all the complexity and promise of 5 years of age. Spicy black fruits of impressive depth and carry float on firm rails of finely textured tannins. Oxidative dryness makes the finish look a little tired already. Even at this age, oak is assertive; and an older barrel might well have given this impressive fruit a more confident voice. Cork. 13.9% alc. RATING 88 DRINK 2022-2022 $220 TS

Glandore Estate

1595 Broke Road, Pokolbin, NSW 2320 **Region** Hunter Valley
T (02) 4998 7140 **www**.glandorewines.com **Open** 7 days 10–5 **Winemaker** Duane Roy, Nick Flanagan **Est.** 2004 **Dozens** 9000 **Vyds** 8ha
Glandore Estate is the reincarnation of the Brokenback Vineyard established as part of The Rothbury Estate in the early '70s, but it had an even longer history. It was purchased by legendary grapegrowers Mick and Jack Phillips in the '30s, and given the Glandore name.

Owners David Madson, John Cambridge and Peter McBeath, who acquired the property in '04 (with existing chardonnay vines), extended the plantings with savagnin, semillon and viognier. Tempranillo, sangiovese, nebbiolo and pinot grigio have been added more recently. (JH)

🍷🍷🍷🍷🍷 **Cellarhands Maluna Vineyard Shiraz 2019, Hunter Valley** Among the finest young Hunter shiraz tasted in recent memory. Despite the warmth of the vintage, this is mid weighted, savoury and dangerously digestible, even young. Sarsaparilla, sweet earth, red cherry, a garni of lavender, thyme and lilac edge across a balancing beam of impeccably wrought tannins, taut and long limbed. A beautiful wine for the ages. Cork. 13.5% alc. RATING 96 DRINK 2021-2033 $120 NG
Hamish Shiraz 2019, Hunter Valley This is worth the step up in price, exponential as it is to the quality. The tannins, a kit of impressive tension, driving across the palate while bridging blueberry, Bing cherry, seaweed salt, violet and charcuterie notes. The oak, classy. Best, the Hunter's sweet loam and terracotta accent, marking the sumptuous finish. Make no mistake, as modern as this may feel, it is firmly of place. Screw cap. 14.5% alc. RATING 95 DRINK 2021-2031 $75 NG

🍷🍷🍷🍷🍷 **Chloe R.D. Blanc de Blancs Chardonnay 2019, Hunter Valley** RATING 93 $60 NG
Regional Series Nebbiolo 2021, Hilltops RATING 93 DRINK 2021-2026 $38 NG
Ginger Rose Shiraz Viognier 2019, Hunter Valley RATING 93 DRINK 2021-2028 $55 NG
TPR Reserve Tempranillo 2018, Hunter Valley RATING 93 DRINK 2021-2027 $55 NG
Cellarhands Brokenback Chardonnay 2019, Hunter Valley RATING 92 DRINK 2021-2027 $100 NG

Glenguin Estate ★★★★☆

Milbrodale Road, Broke, NSW 2330 **Region** Hunter Valley
T (02) 6579 1009 **www**.glenguinestate.com.au **Winemaker** Robin Tedder MW, Rhys Eather **Viticulturist** Dave Grosser, Andrew Tedder **Est.** 1993 **Dozens** 2000 **Vyds** 5ha
Glenguin Estate was established by the Tedder family, headed by Robin Tedder MW. It is close to Broke and adjacent to Wollombi Brook. The backbone of the production comes from almost 30yo plantings of Busby clone semillon and shiraz. Vineyard manager Andrew Tedder, who has considerable experience with organics and biodynamics, is overseeing the ongoing development of Glenguin's organic program. (JH)

🍷🍷🍷🍷🍷 **Cellar Aged Glenguin Vineyard Semillon 2013, Hunter Valley** Elemental winemaking serves to preserve the pristine nature of fruit and style. Bottle age and a superlative vintage in '13, does the rest. Archetypal aromas of barley sugar, lanolin, lemon balm and buttered toast. Dried tatami straw and ginger, too. A bit short, if I am churlish. Strongly of place and delicious all the same. Screw cap. 11% alc. RATING 93 DRINK 2021-2024 $30 NG
Glenguin Vineyard Shiraz 2019, Hunter Valley A delicious wine, demonstrating what the Hunter does like nowhere else: mid-weighted shiraz of a red-fruited persuasion, toned by a dusty swathe of savoury tannins. In this case, gentle ones. Digestible. Versatile. Imminently drinkable. Luncheon claret made from shiraz! Bing cherry, red licorice and a whiff of thyme and mint delivered by a dollop of whole bunches (10%). Filigreed. Drink cool. Lovely wine. Screw cap. 13.5% alc. RATING 92 DRINK 2021-2026 $27 NG

Glenlofty Estate

123 Glenlofty-Warrenmang Road, Glenlofty, Vic 3469 **Region** Pyrenees
T (03) 5354 8228 **www**.glenloftywines.com.au **Open** By appt **Winemaker** Carmel Keenan, Scott Gerrard. **Est.** 1993 **Dozens** 25 000 **Vyds** 136ha

The vineyard was established by Southcorp after exhaustive soil and climate research to supply grapes for Seppelt and Penfolds wines. In Aug '10 Treasury Wine Estates sold the vineyard to Canadian-based Roger Richmond-Smith and winemaking moved to Blue Pyrenees Estate. Glenlofty Wines subsequently purchased the nearby 30ha Decameron Station, bringing the total vineyard holdings to over 130ha. In April '19 Glenlofty Wines also purchased Blue Pyrenees Estate, making it the largest producer in the Pyrenees. Exports to the US, Canada, Singapore, New Zealand. (JH)

The Ridge Block Shiraz 2019, Pyrenees A big, lovable red from a region that brings a cuddly generosity to its shiraz. It's all here: dark plums, blackberries, anise, chocolate, leather and sweet mocha-choc oak. Brings panforte, earth, leather and oak complexity with a touch of alcohol warmth to the palate. Finely honed tannins bring it to a close. One for the cellar for a while. Cork. 13.5% alc. RATING 92 DRINK 2022-2032 $50 JP

The Decameron Block Cabernet Sauvignon 2019, Pyrenees RATING 89 DRINK 2022-2034 $50 JP
Estate Cabernet Sauvignon 2019, Pyrenees RATING 88 DRINK 2022-2026 $32 JP
Estate Shiraz 2019, Pyrenees RATING 88 DRINK 2022-2032 $32 JP

Glenwillow Wines ★★★★

Bendigo Pottery, 146 Midland Highway, Epsom, Vic 3551 **Region** Bendigo
T 0428 461 076 **www**.glenwillow.com.au **Open** Thurs–Mon & public hols 10.30–5
Winemaker Adam Marks **Est.** 1999 **Dozens** 750 **Vyds** 2.8ha
Peter and Cherryl Fyffe began their vineyard at Yandoit Creek, 10km south of Newstead, in '99. They planted 1.8ha of shiraz and 0.3ha of cabernet sauvignon, later branching out with 0.6ha of nebbiolo and 0.1ha of barbera. Planted on a mixture of rich volcanic and clay loam interspersed with quartz and buckshot gravel, the vineyard has an elevated north-facing aspect, which minimises the risk of frost. (JH)

Reserve Shiraz 2016, Bendigo A well-matured set of aromas coming through here, one of earth, leather, spice and black fruits. A dense wine indeed. The palate is inhabited by dark chocolate, licorice, woodsy spice and earthy savoury notes against a sweet core of dark fruits. Plenty of sturdy tannins to see it through the decade. Screw cap. 14.4% alc. RATING 93 DRINK 2021-2028 $60 JP
Shiraz 2018, Bendigo A strong follow-up to the '17 with pronounced ripe and juicy fruit nicely assuaged by French oak. Bendigo's natural promotion of eucalyptus and menthol is controlled, a minor note among the celebration of blackberry, plum, spice and choc-mocha. Tannins are firm but fair. Dances across the palate. Screw cap. 14% alc. RATING 91 DRINK 2021-2026 $28 JP

Sparkling Shiraz 2018, Bendigo RATING 88 $38 JP
Rosé 2021, Bendigo RATING 88 DRINK 2021-2023 $25 JP

Golding Wines

52 Western Branch Road, Lobethal, SA 5241 **Region** Adelaide Hills
T (08) 8189 4500 **www**.goldingwines.com.au **Open** By appt **Winemaker** Darren Golding, Natasha Mooney **Est.** 2002 **Dozens** 5000 **Vyds** 26.12ha
The Golding family story began in the Adelaide Hills 3 generations ago through market gardening and horticulture. Viticulture became part of the picture in '95 when their Western Branch Road Vineyard was planted. Darren and Lucy Golding took the helm in '02, launching the Golding Wines brand. Viticultural holdings have increased recently with the purchase of more vineyard and new plantings of gamay and dornfelder added to the existing pinot noir, shiraz, chardonnay, savagnin, pinot gris and sauvignon blanc. The cellar door is in their rustic sandstone barn. Exports to the UK, the US, Canada, Hong Kong, the Philippines, Malaysia and Singapore. (JH)

🍷🍷🍷🍷🍷 **Rosie May Chardonnay 2021, Adelaide Hills** Complex mealy notes sit across nectarine, peach, preserved lemon and oak spice. Thoroughly whets the appetite with just one whiff. Impressive clarity and fruit concentration. The palate rolls through in creamy, harmonious style with a solid background in bright acidity. Will age well. Screw cap. 12.5% alc. RATING 95 DRINK 2022–2030 $45 JP

🍷🍷🍷🍷🍷 **Marjorie Chardonnay 2015, Adelaide Hills** RATING 93 $55 JP
Ombre Gamay 2021, Adelaide Hills RATING 91 DRINK 2021–2026 $40 JP
Portrait Series Rosie May Chardonnay 2019, Adelaide Hills RATING 90 DRINK 2021–2027 $45 JP

Gomersal Wines ★★★★

203 Lyndoch Road, Gomersal, SA 5352 **Region** Barossa Valley
T (08) 8563 3611 **www**.gomersalwines.com.au **Open** Thurs–Sun 10–4
Winemaker Barry White **Viticulturist** Barry White **Est.** 1887 **Dozens** 10 200
Vyds 20.2ha
The 1887 establishment date has a degree of poetic licence. In 1887 Friedrich W Fromm planted the Wonganella Vineyards, following that with a winery on the edge of the Gomersal Creek in '91; it remained in operation for 90 years, finally closing in 1983. In 2000 a group of friends 'with strong credentials in both the making and consumption ends of the wine industry' bought the winery and re-established the vineyard, planting 17ha of shiraz, 2.2ha of mourvèdre and 1ha of grenache. Exports to Switzerland, Iceland, South Korea, Singapore and NZ. (JH)

🍷🍷🍷🍷🍷 **Shiraz 2018, Barossa Valley** The black, cracking soils of Gomersal Plain can be responsible for wine of substantial heft and fruit intensity; muscular and deep with a sense of latent power. Case in point here. Classically composed, weighty black fruits at its core with a deep earthy resonance, finely packed tannins providing ample support and rich, black fruit finish. Screw cap. 15% alc. RATING 92 DRINK 2021–2031 $60 DB
GSM 2019, Barossa Valley Mid red-purple hues with aromas of red plum, red cherry and cranberry along with gingery spice, violets, red licorice, earth and mocha. At the lighter end of medium bodied, with fine tannin, bright acidity and a spicy fan of red and dark fruits on the finish. Excellent value here. Screw cap. 14.8% alc. RATING 91 DRINK 2022–2028 $20 DB ✪
Lyndoch Road Shiraz Mataro 2018, Barossa Valley Spicy blood plum and summer-berry compote notes mesh with hints of purple florals, roasting meats, licorice, dark chocolate and light tobacco and oak spice. Oak flow increases on the palate, fine, tight tannins too, with a touch of amaro herbs on the finish. Screw cap. 15% alc. RATING 91 DRINK 2022–2028 $30 DB
Lyndoch Road Shiraz Cabernet 2018, Barossa Valley Pure aromas of blackcurrant and blackberry wash from the glass along with hints of satsuma plum, baking spice, cedar, pipe tobacco and earth. The cedary oak comes charging in on the palate before retreating into the fruit, supported by powdery tannin and a cassis- and graphite-like finish. Screw cap. 14.8% alc. RATING 91 DRINK 2021–2031 $30 DB
Riesling 2021, Clare Valley Clare Valley riesling is loved for a reason; it is lush, generous and laden with citrus, while the acidity is like a coiled spring within. There's an aspect of tartness to this – like green apple skin, but is counterbalanced by fine pithy acid. This is all that, and through the lens of the cool, restrained and even '21 vintage, it is all the better. Screw cap. 12.5% alc. RATING 90 DRINK 2022–2029 $20 EL ✪

🍷🍷🍷🍷 **Reserve Shiraz 2018, Barossa Valley** RATING 89 DRINK 2022–2032 $35 DB

Grace Farm

741 Cowaramup Bay Road, Gracetown, WA 6285 **Region** Margaret River
T (08) 9384 4995 **www.gracefarm.com.au Open** Wed–Sun 11–5 **Winemaker** Jonathan
Mettam **Viticulturist** Tim Quinlan **Est.** 2006 **Dozens** 3000 **Vyds** 8.19ha
Situated in the Wilyabrup district, Grace Farm is the small, family-owned vineyard of
Elizabeth and John Mair. It takes its name from the nearby coastal hamlet of Gracetown.
Situated beside picturesque natural forest, the vineyard is planted to cabernet sauvignon,
chardonnay, sauvignon blanc and semillon with smaller amounts of cabernet franc, petit verdot
and malbec. Viticulturist Tim Quinlan conducts tastings (by appointment), explaining Grace
Farm's sustainable viticultural practices. (JH)

ΨΨΨΨΨ **Reserve Chardonnay 2020, Margaret River** Crushed nuts, white peach;
creamy, taut and saline. The nose has characters of pea tendril, lemongrass and
saltbush, while the palate is a silky, acid driven affair that spools out flavours over a
long finish. Screw cap. 13.5% alc. RATING 93 DRINK 2022-2032 $70 EL
Reserve Cabernet Sauvignon 2017, Margaret River Released as a
4yo wine. The '17 vintage was cool in Margaret River, and it has imparted upon
this wine a sense of green peppercorns, flat-leaf parsley and tobacco leaf. In the
mouth the tannins are a highlight – they are savoury and slightly chewy (a very
good thing, in my mind), and provide a sense of place for the fruit. This is a soft,
pared-back-claret style of cabernet, with medium body and fine tannins which
display overall delicacy. Screw cap. 13.3% alc. RATING 91 DRINK 2022-2032
$70 EL
Chardonnay 2020, Margaret River The concentrated yellow peach and red
apple fruit here is shaped on all sides by oak. The oak is tasty, and the cooper/
toast is well matched to the fruit, but it is prominent at this stage. The acidity
that flows through the wine like life blood is salty and fine, a balancing character
to the rest. Very smart. Give it another year. Screw cap. 13.5% alc. RATING 90
DRINK 2022-2029 $35 EL

Grampians Estate

1477 Western Highway, Great Western, Vic 3377 **Region** Grampians
T (03) 5354 6245 **www.grampiansestate.com.au Open** 7 days 10–5 **Winemaker** Andrew
Davey, Tom Guthrie **Est.** 1989 **Dozens** 2000 **Vyds** 8ha
Graziers Sarah and Tom Guthrie began their diversification into wine in 1989, but their core
business continues to be fat lamb and wool production. They have acquired the Garden Gully
winery at Great Western, giving them a cellar door and a vineyard with 140+yo shiraz and
100+yo riesling. Grampians Estate followed its success of being Champion Small Winery
of Show at the Australian Small Winemakers Show for the second year running in '18 by
winning the Premier's Trophy for Champion Wine of Victoria in '19. These successes led to a
major expansion of the cellar door, with a new cafe and outdoor area. (JH)

ΨΨΨΨΨ **Rutherford Sparkling Shiraz 2019, Grampians** 24 months on lees, disgorged
Oct '21. Intense purple colour, with a lively mousse. Lifted, fragrant and quite
delicate on the bouquet, this is a good example of the modern take on sparkling
shiraz: less in-your-face; woody and savoury and more in tune with the fruit.
Blackberries, plum, violets and a spice thread that includes pepper, runs long and
creamy. Crown. 14% alc. RATING 95 $40 JP
Kelly's Welcome Cuvée 2011, Western Victoria 36/35/29% Henty
pinot noir/Mafeking chardonnay/Henty pinot meunier. Another sparkling that
winemaker, Tom Guthrie, 'forgot' and hence saw 9.5 years on lees. Dosage 10g/L.
A complex floral and citrus nose with additional yeasty complexity, grilled nuts
and toasted bread. Belies its age with an assertive, crisp freshness and concentrated
grapefruit, citrus, quince and orange rind flavours. Crown. 11.5% alc. RATING 95
$50 JP
St Ethel's Shiraz 2020, Great Western Encapsulates the perfect fit of grape
and region that is shiraz – a big percentage of old vines in this instance – and the

Grampians. Boasts an intense wild herb, Aussie bush character, generous black fruits and spice that places you immediately in the locale, braced by earth and savoury leather notes. Altogether a seamless wine of class. Screw cap. 14% alc. RATING 95 DRINK 2022–2033 $50 JP

Streeton Reserve Shiraz 2019, Grampians Shows impressive poise from the get go, with ripe, sweet black fruits accompanied by a strong savoury, earthy, meaty thread. Medium weight, rich in wood spice and dark chocolate, finishing in fine, commanding tannins. A cellaring specialist. Screw cap. 13.5% alc. RATING 95 DRINK 2022–2033 $80 JP

ΨΨΨΨ **Muirhead Sparkling Rosé 2013, Henty** RATING 88 $50 JP
Drovers' Rosé 2021, Grampians RATING 88 DRINK 2022–2025 $25 JP
Woolclasser's GST 2020, Grampians RATING 88 DRINK 2022–2025 $28 JP

Granite Hills

1481 Burke and Wills Track, Baynton, Vic 3444 **Region** Macedon Ranges
T (03) 5423 7273 **www**.granitehills.com.au **Open** By appt **Winemaker** Llew Knight, Rowen Anstis **Viticulturist** Andrew Conforti **Est.** 1970 **Dozens** 5000 **Vyds** 11.5ha
Granite Hills is one of the enduring classics, having pioneered the successful growing of riesling and shiraz in an uncompromisingly cool climate. The vineyard includes riesling, chardonnay, shiraz, cabernet sauvignon, cabernet franc, merlot and pinot noir (the last also used in its sparkling wine). The Rieslings age superbly, and the Shiraz was the forerunner of the cool-climate school in Australia. Exports to Japan. (JH)

ΨΨΨΨΨ **Knight 1971 Block Riesling 2021, Macedon Ranges** OK. This is another few levels up from the Estate riesling. It's meant to be significantly different and more complex, as the fruit comes off the 1971 plantings. It's special with such precision, clarity and length. A burst of lime and lemon freshness and a flutter of spice to follow as it builds across the tightly held palate. A hint of ginger cream, lemon verbena and while the acidity is perky, there's just a softness on the finish. A lovely, lovely wine. Screw cap. 13% alc. RATING 96 DRINK 2022–2035 $38 JF ✪
Knight Riesling 2021, Macedon Ranges Granite Hills has long held the riesling mantle in this region. It's an ever-reliable drink thanks to its vitality, crunchy acidity, length plus all the citrus, tangy and juicy flavours. It's also stylish and pure. Screw cap. 13% alc. RATING 95 DRINK 2022–2033 $28 JF ✪
Knight Riesling 2013, Macedon Ranges Aged release. A slight green-straw hue and a very good colour for its age. It's showing no signs of slowing down soon, thanks to the acidity across the fine palate. There are still lively lime juice and zest flavours dallying with the tertiary elements – a hint of toastiness and lime marmalade. Screw cap. 12.5% alc. RATING 95 DRINK 2022–2028 $40 JF

ΨΨΨΨΩ **TOR Riesling 2019, Macedon Ranges** RATING 93 DRINK 2022–2028 $50 JF
Knight Grüner Veltliner 2021, Macedon Ranges RATING 92 DRINK 2022–2025 $28 JF
The Gordon 2016, Macedon Ranges RATING 91 DRINK 2022–2026 $30 JF

Grant Burge

279 Krondorf Road, Barossa Valley, SA 5352 **Region** Barossa Valley
T (08) 8563 7675 **www**.grantburgewines.com.au **Open** 7 days 10–5 **Winemaker** Craig Stansborough **Viticulturist** Rodney Birchmore **Est.** 1988 **Dozens** 400 000
Grant and Helen Burge established the eponymous Grant Burge business in 1988. It grew into one of the largest family-owned wine businesses in the valley. In February '15, Accolade Wines announced it had acquired the Grant Burge brand and the historic Krondorf Winery. The 356ha of vineyards remain in family ownership and continue to supply premium grapes to the Accolade-owned business. Exports to all major markets. (JH)

ΨΨΨΨΨ **Corryton Park Cabernet Sauvignon 2019, Barossa** Plenty of aromatic detail and crunch on display here, with high-toned blackcurrant and blackberry fruits along with cassis and kirsch notes, with hints of briar, wild herbs, chocolate, cedar, tobacco leaf and earth. There is freshness and crunch on the palate too, along with a lovely swell of ripe cabernet fruit, fine, powdery tannins and a finish that swells gracefully with blackcurrant and cedary flair. Screw cap. 14.3% alc. RATING 95 DRINK 2021-2035 $48 DB

The Holy Trinity GSM 2019, Barossa A delicious, mid-weighted wine for those that seek the holy trinity of red blends. There's depth of both fruit and spice here, but not at the expense of detail and space, with the wine retaining an airy palate shape, lovely ripe fruit, sandy tannins and a savoury trail of berry, plum and spice. Screw cap. 14.2% alc. RATING 94 DRINK 2021-2031 $48 DB

ΨΨΨΨΩ **Thorn Riesling 2021, Eden Valley** RATING 92 DRINK 2021-2030 $27 DB
Balthasar Shiraz 2019, Eden Valley RATING 92 DRINK 2021-2031 $48 DB
Filsell Old Vine Shiraz 2019, Barossa RATING 92 DRINK 2021-2032 $48 DB

Green Door Wines

1112 Henty Road, Henty, WA 6236 **Region** Geographe
T 0439 511 652 **www**.greendoorwines.com.au **Open** Thurs–Sun 11–4.30
Winemaker Ashley Keeffe, Vanessa Carson **Est.** 2007 **Dozens** 1200 **Vyds** 4ha
Ashley and Kathryn Keeffe purchased what was then a rundown vineyard in '06. With a combination of new and pre-existing vines, the vineyard includes fiano, mourvèdre, grenache, verdelho, tempranillo and shiraz. The wines are made in a small onsite winery using a range of winemaking methods, including the use of amphora pots. (JH)

ΨΨΨΨΨ **Amphora Garnacha 2021, Geographe** A touch of bacon fat and black pepper, with Szechuan pepper and licorice. This is tannic (in a chewy, malleable, thick kind of way) and spicy, while the acidity courses through the gauntlet of fruit (blackberries, mulberries and raspberry compote). All of this culminates in one really engaging package. Smart and well handled. Screw cap. 14% alc. RATING 94 DRINK 2022-2029 $45 EL

ΨΨΨΨΩ **Amphora Tempranillo 2020, Geographe** RATING 91 DRINK 2022-2028 $40 EL
Amphora Reserva Tempranillo 2020, Geographe RATING 91 DRINK 2022-2028 $50 EL
Fiano 2021, Geographe RATING 90 DRINK 2021-2026 $28 EL

Greenock Creek Wines

450 Seppeltsfield Road, Marananga SA 5355 **Region** Barossa Valley
T (08) 8563 2898 **www**.greenockcreekwines.com.au **Open** 7 days 11–5
Winemaker Alex Peel, Peter Atyeo **Viticulturist** Peter Atyeo **Est.** 1984 **Dozens** 4000
Vyds 22ha
Founders Michael and Annabelle Waugh deliberately accumulated a series of old dryland, low-yielding Barossa vineyards back in the '70s, aiming to produce wines of unusual depth of flavour and character. They succeeded handsomely in this aim, achieving icon status and stratospheric prices in the US, making the opinions of Australian scribes irrelevant. The Waughs retired in '18 and the business was purchased by a group headed by Sydney-based Jimmy Chen. Peter Atyeo stayed on as assistant winemaker and manager, with Alex Peel (formerly Ross Estate and Yaldara) stepping in as winemaker. Older vineyards were remediated, new sites brought into the fold, and winemaking facilities updated. Exports to Asia and the EU. (JH)

ΨΨΨΨΨ **Fifteen Claims Shiraz 2019, Barossa Valley** Intense and concentrated blackberry, black plum and black cherry fruit notes with plenty of cedary oak nuance and hint of deep, dark spice, formic acid, salted black licorice, Old Jamaica chocolate, fig jam and earth. Weighty, full bodied and super-concentrated, with ripe, sandy tannins retreating back into the fruit and intense blackberry jam and a cedary plume on the long finish. Cork. 15% alc. RATING 97 DRINK 2022-2042 $150 DB ✪

ŸŸŸŸŸ Third Estate Shiraz 2020, Barossa Valley Deep, impenetrable red purple with aromas of cedar-infused black fruits, blood plum and crème de cassis notes. Dredged with deep spice, licorice, dark bitter chocolate and earth. Pitch-perfect tannin support, incredible fruit density and balance despite heady alcohol levels. Super-impressive. Screw cap 16% alc. RATING 96 DRINK 2022-2035 $80 DB

Alices Shiraz 2020, Barossa Valley If you are after a full-bodied, impressively concentrated shiraz, this might be right up your alley. It's no wallflower, weighing in at 16% alcohol, but the balance is there and the fruit, cascading layers of ripe satsuma plum and blackberries, is a thing of wonder. There's some assertive fine-ground tannin, dark-chocolate-dipped raspberries, plenty of spice and licorice, and it's a wonderful, voluptuous sashay of fruit across your palate. Screw cap. 16% alc. RATING 95 DRINK 2022-2038 $40 DB

Cabernet Sauvignon 2020, Barossa Valley Deep, impenetrable red-purple colour with a wash of concentrated red and black berry fruits, cedary oak, some prune, deep spice and earthen tones in the mix also. Incredibly concentrated and dense, which is a Greenock Creek trademark, an impressive trademark at that. A ripper. Screw cap. 15.5% alc. RATING 95 DRINK 2020-2035 $50 DB

Greenock Estate

12 Basedow Road, Tanunda, SA 5352 **Region** Barossa Valley
T (08) 8563 2898 **www**.greenockestate.com **Open** By appt **Winemaker** Jo Irvine, Frederick Law, Steve Kurtz **Viticulturist** Steve Kurtz **Est.** 1948 **Dozens** 6000
Vyds 30ha
The establishment date is that of the Kurtz Family vineyards, which supply Greenock Estate with its grapes. The first Greenock Estate wine was made in '02, and the first wines reached Asia in '09. Exports to the US, Malaysia and Hong Kong. (JH)

ŸŸŸŸŸ High Ride Cabernet Sauvignon 2020, Barossa Valley Deep red in the glass with characters of ultra-ripe blackberry and blackcurrant fruits dredged with baking spice, fig, dried currants, cedar, earth and licorice. Some red fruits swoop in on the silky and elegant palate, with a curtain of ripe tannin and bright acid drive. Screw cap. 15.5% alc. RATING 91 DRINK 2022-2032 $45 DB

Greenstone Vineyards

179 Glenview Road, Yarra Glen, Vic 3775 **Region** Yarra Valley
T (03) 9730 1022 **www**.greenstonevineyards.com.au **Open** Thurs–Mon 10–5
Winemaker Han Tao Lau, Sam Atherton, David Li **Est.** 2003 **Dozens** 20 000
Vyds 39.2ha
In Jan '15, the former Sticks Winery (originally Yarra Ridge, established in 1982) was purchased by a group of investors, along with the Greenstone brand and vineyard in Heathcote. The Greenstone vineyard, just north of the Heathcote township at Colbinabbin at the base of the Camel Range, derives its names from the soils on which the 20ha of vines are planted (the lion's share to 17ha of shiraz). The Yarra Valley vineyard is planted mainly to chardonnay (11.7ha) and also includes 4.1ha of pinot noir and smaller plantings of sauvignon blanc, viognier, cabernet sauvignon and petit verdot. (JH)

ŸŸŸŸŸ Estate Series Cabernets 2019, Yarra Valley Mainly cabernet with a little petit verdot. A deep, crimson purple. A positive nose with aromas of blackberries and other dark fruits, well-handled cedary oak and a touch of violets. Big, chewy and dense on the palate, this is a wine built for the long haul. Screw cap. 13.5% alc. RATING 92 DRINK 2023-2033 $45 PR

Estate Series Chardonnay 2021, Yarra Valley Made from vines planted near Yarra Glen in the '80s. Barrel fermented and matured in French oak puncheons (37% new) before going into stainless steel for 2 months before bottling. A bright, green gold, this leaps out of the glass with its aromas of ripe, yellow peach and nectarine fruit, honeydew melon and fresh vanilla bean from the oak. Still very youthful, all components need another 3–6 months to come together. Screw cap. 13% alc. RATING 90 DRINK 2022-2026 $45 PR

Estate Series Shiraz 2019, Heathcote This is a ripe, plush shiraz with plenty of concentration. While mid-term ageing is on its mind, it's also more than ready to be dipped into now. Fragrant black berry and blue fruits, briar, dark toasted spices and licorice build through the palate finishing with a firm resolve. Screw cap. 14.5% alc. RATING 90 DRINK 2021–2027 $45 JP

♟♟♟♟ **Gusto Sangiovese 2021, Heathcote** RATING 89 DRINK 2021–2025 $30 JP
Gusto Pinot Grigio Pinot Grigio 2021, Mornington Peninsula RATING 88 DRINK 2021–2023 $30 PR
Estate Series Sauvignon Blanc 2021, Yarra Valley RATING 88 DRINK 2021–2024 $35 PR

Groom ★★★★★

28 Langmeil Road, Tanunda, SA 5352 (postal) **Region** Barossa Valley
T (08) 8563 1101 **www**.groomwines.com **Winemaker** Daryl Groom, Lisa Groom, Jeanette Marschall **Est.** 1997 **Dozens** 2000 **Vyds** 27.8ha
The full name of the business is Marschall Groom Cellars, a venture established by David and Jeanette Marschall and their 6 children, and Daryl and Lisa Groom and their 4 children. Daryl was a highly regarded winemaker at Penfolds before he moved to Geyser Peak in California. Years of discussion between the families resulted in the purchase of a 35ha block of bare land adjacent to Penfolds' 130yo Kalimna Vineyard. Shiraz was planted in 1997, giving its first vintage in '99. The next acquisition was an 8ha vineyard at Lenswood in the Adelaide Hills, planted to sauvignon blanc. In '00, 3.2ha of zinfandel was planted on the Kalimna Bush Block. Exports to the US. (JH)

♟♟♟♟♟ **Shiraz 2020, Barossa Valley** Deeply coloured with aromas of satsuma plum and blueberry compote. Lovely fruit weight and spice-laden mid palate, with pitch-perfect flow and balance, fine pillowy tannins for support and an extended spicy finish. Great drinking now but will cellar well, too. Cork. 14.7% alc. RATING 96 DRINK 2021–2038 $50 DB ✪
Bush Block Zinfandel 2020, Barossa Valley Impressively pure blackberry and black cherry-fruit characters, dredged deeply with fruitcake spice with hints of mince pies, Old Jamaica chocolate, earth and well-judged vanillin oak. Great flow, balance and pure, savoury-edged appeal. Go zinfandel! Cork. 14.9% alc. RATING 95 DRINK 2028–2035 $30 DB ✪

♟♟♟♟ **Sauvignon Blanc 2021, Adelaide Hills** RATING 89 DRINK 2021–2023 $24 DB

Grosset ★★★★★

King Street, Auburn, SA 5451 **Region** Clare Valley
T 1800 088 223 **www**.grosset.com.au **Open** 10–5 Wed–Sun (Spring) **Winemaker** Jeffrey Grosset, Brent Treloar **Viticulturist** Matthew O'Rourke **Est.** 1981 **Dozens** 11 000
Vyds 21ha
Jeffrey Grosset wears the unchallenged mantle of Australia's foremost riesling maker. Grosset's pre-eminence is recognised both domestically and internationally; however, he merits equal recognition for the other wines in his portfolio: Semillon Sauvignon Blanc from Clare Valley and Adelaide Hills, Chardonnay and Pinot Noir from the Adelaide Hills and Gaia, a bordeaux blend from the Clare Valley; these are all benchmarks. Jeffrey's quietly spoken manner conceals a steely will. Four estate-owned vineyards in the Clare Valley are certified organic and biodynamic. Best Value Winery in the Wine Companion 2018. Exports to all major markets. (JH)

♟♟♟♟♟ **G110 Riesling 2021, Clare Valley** Streamlined, long, lingering rivulets of spicy, almost austere riesling. It has integrity, shape and line, punctuated by detailed nuance and poise. It is spicy – even tense in its disposition – layered with nutmeg, spring flowers, brine, green apple skins, crushed limestone, mineral slate, snow pea tendril and even lemongrass. It is a kaleidoscope of flavour and texture, the puzzle pieces so small that it's hard to put them all together – describing it is a challenge (which is a good sign for the wine). It is enigmatic, statuesque and epic in every way. But it's also quiet, so do not underestimate it – make sure you tune in to its frequency. Screw cap. 12.8% alc. RATING 98 DRINK 2022-2042 $123 EL ✪ ♥

Polish Hill Riesling 2021, Clare Valley Grosset Polish Hill is always a supremely elegant, powerful wine with a proven track record of graceful ageing in the cellar, and a release such as this is the foundation upon which that reputation is built. This is concentrated, structured and long, with jasmine tea, saffron, lemon pith, aniseed, fennel flower, green apple skins and white pepper – all of which colour in the background for the lime flesh and Clare volume of flavour. Brilliant. Drink it now or cellar it as you normally would – it is sensational. Screw cap. 12.9% alc. RATING 97 DRINK 2021-2041 $72 EL ✪

Gaia 2019, Clare Valley Cabernet sauvignon and cabernet franc. 5000 bottles made. Elegant. This has grunt and low-down power, but the engine is built into a chassis of fine fruit and supple tannins. The acidity acts as the titanium bolt that holds it together, creating a strengthening framework of life and finesse. Blackberries, cassis, licorice, mulberry and raw cocoa, with nori, pink peppercorns and pastrami, blood plum, kelp and brine. Marvellous. Screw cap. 13.7% alc. RATING 97 DRINK 2022-2042 $89 EL ✪ ♥

ΨΨΨΨΨ **Alea Riesling 2021, Clare Valley** Alea … the pretty, sweet thing in the family. Behind the incredibly attractive facade lies a complex, layered and wonderful wine that consists of exotic spice, citrus fruits and saline acidity, all shaped by fine, chalky structure. This '21 iteration is a precise and restrained version of itself, showing length, elegance and, most importantly, supreme deliciousness. Screw cap. 12.3% alc. RATING 96 DRINK 2021-2036 $44 EL ✪

Springvale Riesling 2021, Clare Valley Where the Polish Hill is the powerful, muscular one of the family, the Springvale is the often underestimated little sibling. Similarly powerfully structured, but leaning towards the spicy end of the spectrum rather than plum in the middle of fleshy fruit power. This is structured and saline, with layers of cut lime, red apple skins, saffron, turmeric and citrus pith. All of it encased in briny acidity and stretched out over an interminably long finish. Generous and structured at once. Super-smart. Screw cap. 12.9% alc. RATING 96 DRINK 2021-2041 $50 EL ✪

Apiana Fiano 2021, Clare Valley This is a cool wine; a super-spicy nose, peppered with salted pear, smoked almonds, green apple skins, white currants and loads of cumin and roasted macadamias. The palate is saline, long and concentrated, hanging around long after the last sip. Citrus blossom, preserved limes and fine, chalky phenolics. Way more to think about here than the usual fiano. Screw cap. 12.9% alc. RATING 95 DRINK 2021-2025 $50 EL

Grounded Cru   ★★★★★

49 Ingoldby Road, McLaren Flat, SA 5052 **Region** McLaren Vale
T 0438 897 738 **www.**groundedcru.com.au **Open** By appt **Winemaker** Geoff Thompson, Matt Jackman **Viticulturist** Geoff Thompson, Matt Jackman **Est.** 2015
Dozens 18 000
Established as a brand in 2015 with an inaugural release of wines in '17, Grounded Cru draws fruit from high-quality vineyards in McLaren Vale, Langhorne Creek and the Adelaide Hills, regions that maker Geoff Thompson believes 'talk to each other' due to a complementary patina of mesoclimates, soil types, rainfall, altitude and varying degrees of maritime influence. Thompson was formerly chief winemaker at McPherson Wines in Nagambie. Conversely, his approach at Grounded Cru is one that seeks textural intrigue over obvious fruit, with European styling melded to Australian generosity. The Mediterranean varieties on offer are superlative, boasting poise and savoury tannins laden with briar. Exports to the UK. (NG)

ΨΨΨΨΨ **Cru GSM 2020, McLaren Vale** 66/28/6% grenache/shiraz/mourvèdre. A fine nose of cardamom, white pepper and clove. Refined, as much as it is jubilant. Raspberry bon-bon, licorice strap, salumi and violet. Best, though, the chiffon screen of tannins that direct the wine long. Lovely drinking. Screw cap. 14.5% alc. RATING 95 DRINK 2021-2026 $30 NG ✪

Inc Cabernet Sauvignon 2019, McLaren Vale A producer that turned my head last vintage and continues to rise to the crème of the Vale. Everything delicious! As good as warm-climate maritime cab gets. A benchmark cabernet for the region. Sumptuous, without being heavy. Ripe, without being sweet. Savoury, sans greenery. A long cylinder of tannins, alloyed, finely mettled and impeccably extracted. With courage. Blackcurrant, sage, saltbush, green olive and a creamy mocha core, in the best sense. Lovely drinking. Beautifully crafted. Screw cap. 14.5% alc. RATING 95 DRINK 2022-2032 $55 NG

ΨΨΨΨΨ Cru Rosé Grenache 2021, McLaren Vale RATING 93 DRINK 2021-2022 $26 NG ✪
Cru Grenache 2020, McLaren Vale RATING 93 DRINK 2021-2024 $30 NG
Inc Shiraz 2019, McLaren Vale RATING 93 DRINK 2021-2030 $55 NG
Cru Shiraz 2020, McLaren Vale RATING 92 DRINK 2021-2025 $30 NG
Cru Pinot Gris 2021, Adelaide Hills RATING 90 DRINK 2021-2025 $26 JP
Pinot Noir 2021, Adelaide Hills RATING 90 DRINK 2021-2025 $30 JP

Grove Estate Wines   ★★★★

4100 Murringo Road, Young, NSW 2594 **Region** Hilltops
T (02) 6382 6999 **www**.groveestate.com.au **Open** 7 days 9.00–4.30 **Winemaker** Brian Mullany, Tim Kirk, Bryan Martin **Est.** 1989 **Dozens** 4000 **Vyds** 100ha
Grove Estate Vineyard was re-established in 1989 by Brian and Suellen Mullany on the site where grapes were first planted in Lambing Flat (Young) in 1861 by Croatian settlers who brought vine cuttings with them from Dalmatia. One of the original pickers' huts has been refurbished as the cellar door. Further plantings in '98 were made on their Bit O' Heaven Vineyard, the 2 sites with vastly different soils. The wines are made at Clonakilla by Tim Kirk and Bryan Martin. (JH)

ΨΨΨΨΨ The Italian 2021, Hilltops A blend of 45/30/15/10% sangiovese/barbera/ sagrantino/nebbiolo. Bright, juicy and tangy, with all sorts of cherry flavours, aniseed and twigs plus an uplifting herbal character. A terrific lighter-framed red for warmer weather and everything in between. Screw cap. 13.5% alc. RATING 93 DRINK 2022-2024 $28 JF
Shiraz Viognier 2021, Hilltops An alluring dark purple; a lot of charm to this, even if it lacks complexity. Sweet, ripe – to a touch overripe – fruit aromas, with a dash of pepper and woodsy spices, violets and a herbal, pine-needle freshness. Fuller bodied, plump tannins and overall, a very good wine matched to its price. Screw cap. 14% alc. RATING 91 DRINK 2022-2027 $30 JF
Shiraz 2020, Hilltops An outrageous vibrant purple hue, so it starts off right. A solid mix of plums, squishy currants, lots of woodsy spices and extract but overall, it's juicy and appealing. There's fruit-oak sweetness across the full-bodied palate yet halted by vice-like tannins and a bitter finish. It is also somewhat raw, perhaps indicative of its youth. Time should help out. Good wine and great value too. Screw cap. 14.5% alc. RATING 91 DRINK 2022-2029 $22 JF ✪
Reserve Cabernet Sauvignon 2018, Hilltops Not clear why this is a Reserve. It is youthful, lively and still feels as if it is coming together, with a sensation of raw wood tannins. And yet, lots of blackberries and bramble berries, mint and cedary spice. Fuller bodied, with the sweet fruit ambling along and finishes well. Screw cap. 14.5% alc. RATING 91 DRINK 2023-2028 $30 JF
Barbera 2021, Hilltops A dark magenta colour entices as it takes off with Mediterranean herbs and a strong native mint aroma and flavour, which might be too much for some. Still, there's plenty of juicy tangy fruit, spice and amaro while the palate is plush, rich and a little exotic. Screw cap. 13.5% alc. RATING 90 DRINK 2022-2025 $25 JF

ΨΨΨΨ The Partners Cabernet Sauvignon 2021, Hilltops RATING 88 DRINK 2023-2028 $25 JF
The Garibaldi Nebbiolo Shiraz 2020, Hilltops RATING 88 DRINK 2021-2027 $25 JF

Gundog Estate

101 McDonalds Road, Pokolbin, NSW 2320 **Region** Hunter Valley
T (02) 4998 6873 **www**.gundogestate.com.au **Open** 7 days 10–5 **Winemaker** Matthew
Burton **Est.** 2006 **Dozens** 7000 **Vyds** 5ha

Matt Burton makes 4 different Hunter Semillons, and Shiraz from the Hunter Valley,
Murrumbateman and Hilltops. The cellar door is located in the historic Pokolbin schoolhouse,
next to the old Rosemount and Hungerford Hill building on McDonalds Road. The Burton
McMahon wines are a collaboration between Matt Burton and Dylan McMahon of Seville
Estate, and focus on the Yarra Valley. In '16, Gundog opened a second cellar door at 42 Cork
Street, Gundaroo. Exports to the UK. (JH)

Burton McMahon D'Aloisio's Vineyard Chardonnay 2021, Yarra Valley
A clear, bright green gold. A superb single-vineyard wine from the moment you
put your nose in the glass, there's aromas of mandarin, white stone fruits, fresh-cut
camelias and a hint of white clover honey. Even better on the palate, this is both
powerful and restrained. Finishes saline and long and I gotta admit, it was too good
to spit! Screw cap. 13% alc. RATING 97 DRINK 2022–2027 $40 PR ✪

Burton McMahon Syme on Yarra Vineyard Pinot Noir 2021, Yarra Valley
A bright, medium crimson. Poised with aromas of pomegranate, freshly picked
strawberries and raspberries, as well as hints of cardamon and sandalwood. Equally
good on the palate, which is nuanced, even and beautifully balanced. Subtle but
with plenty of stuffing, this gorgeous and well-crafted wine finishes with fine,
gentle but firm tannins. Screw cap. 13.6% alc. RATING 96 DRINK 2022–2027
$40 PR ✪

Burton McMahon George's Vineyard Pinot Noir 2021, Yarra Valley
A pale, bright crimson. There's a delicacy here, with its aromas of red fruits, subtle
white flowers and a gentle cardamon spice. On the palate this has a red apple
skin crunch and the wine finishes fine, subtle and long. Screw cap. 13.6% alc.
RATING 95 DRINK 2022–2027 $40 PR

The Chase Semillon 2021, Hunter Valley This is very good, reflecting
an outstanding vintage marked by a confluence of fleshy fruit and lightweight
precision. Riffs on lemon squash, icy pole, Granny Smith apple and aniseed,
verging on pastis. The acidity, juicy rather than brittle. The finish long and
effortless. Delicious wine. Screw cap. 11.3% alc. RATING 95 DRINK 2022–2035
$40 NG

Burton McMahon George's Vineyard Chardonnay 2021, Yarra Valley
A pale but bright green gold. With its aromas of mandarin, orange peel, freshly cut
pear, grilled nuts and a little matchstick, this is all about restraint. Tightly wound on
the palate, this has terrific line and length (think of Glen McGrath at his prime)
and finishes with a pithy, subtle, lemon oil nuance. This is built for the cellar and
I can see this very good wine opening up and becoming even more complex in
another year or 2. Screw cap. 13% alc. RATING 94 DRINK 2023–2028 $40 PR

Wild Semillon 2021, Hunter Valley A contemporary take on a traditional
and largely austere style, rendering it softer, more textural and immediate of
appeal. This is achieved with a meld of solids, skin contact and varying degrees
of sugar and dryness before blending. Aromas of lemongrass, citrus balm, fennel
and grapefruit. Succulent, fresh and juicy. Good drinking. Screw cap. 11.5% alc.
RATING 94 DRINK 2021–2030 $40 NG

M Burton Shiraz 1 Shiraz NV, Canberra District Blend of vintages '18 and
'19. Akin to the mid-weighted, dry red table wines that I tasted from my father's
glass as a kid. Gently musty while smelling of tilled earth, loamy and moist.
Savoury. The tannins, long limbed, lithe and spellbinding, as they commune with
sappy red fruits, star anise, iodine, nori and blueberry accents, ultimately becoming
more reminiscent of a contemporary cooler-climate style. Could use just a
bit more pop. Cork. 14.1% alc. RATING 94 DRINK 2021–2030 $150 NG

Guthrie Wines

★★★★

661 Torrens Valley Road, Gumeracha, SA 5253 **Region** Adelaide Hills
T 0413 332 083 **www**.guthriewines.com.au **Open** By appt **Winemaker** Hugh Guthrie
Est. 2012 **Dozens** 1500

Growing up on his family's farm in the Adelaide Hills, Hugh Guthrie developed an early interest in the wines and vineyards of the region, completing a master of oenology at the University of Adelaide before working in wineries around Australia and abroad. Most recently he was a winemaker at The Lane Vineyard, winner of many awards for its wines. His partner Sarah looks after the business side of Guthrie, in addition to her day job as an anaesthetist. In '14 Hugh held his breath, jumped, quit his day job, and became full-time winemaker at Guthrie Wines. (JH)

🍷🍷🍷🍷 **Clones Pinot Noir 2021, Adelaide Hills** Another dip into the wonderful world of clones with 777, 114, 145 and MV6 being celebrated. They're a complex bunch, contributing plush fruits, firm tannins and a healthy structure for further ageing. Moves from cherry cola and red fruits to light spice and the odd, earthy, savoury moment in between, not forgetting the vanillin oak and smooth tannins. It's a busy clonal treat. Screw cap. 13% alc. RATING 92 DRINK 2022-2026 $27 JP

Wild Grüner 2021, Adelaide Hills Guthrie certainly brings a liveliness and super-freshness to its wines, lead by a wildly energetic wild-ferment grüner (love the label, by the way!). Jumps in red apple, creamy apple sauce, nashi pear and plenty of spice and vanilla as it careens across the tongue. Drink early. Screw cap. 12.5% alc. RATING 90 DRINK 2022-2024 $25 JP

Clones Chardonnay 2021, Adelaide Hills Multi-clonal chardonnay, fermented wild in French oak (30% new) and matured 8 months on lees. And what of the clones? There are 3: B76, B95 and Entav. Hope that helps, but really it's the taste that counts and it's fresh in stone-fruit juiciness, papaya, citrus and mandarin skin, dressed in some classy nougat-almond oak. Early and easy drinking assured. Screw cap. 13% alc. RATING 90 DRINK 2022-2025 $27 JP

🍷🍷🍷🍷 **The Mondo Sauvignon Blanc 2021, Adelaide Hills** RATING 88 DRINK 2022-2024 $22 JP

Sleepless Nights Pinot Rosé 2021, Adelaide Hills RATING 88 DRINK 2022-2024 $24 JP

Hackersley

★★★★

1133 Ferguson Road, Dardanup, WA 6236 **Region** Geographe
T (08) 9381 6247 **www**.hackersley.com.au **Open** Thurs–Sun 10–4 **Winemaker** Kim Horton **Viticulturist** AHA Viticulture **Est.** 1997 **Dozens** 1000 **Vyds** 12ha

Hackersley was founded by the Ovens, Stacey and Hewitt families, friends since their university days, and with (so they say) the misguided belief that growing and making their own wine would be cheaper than buying it (now owned solely by Jeff and Kerry Ovens). They found a 'little piece of paradise in the Ferguson Valley just south of Dardanup', and in 1998 they planted just under 8 ha of the mainstream varieties; interestingly, they turned their back on chardonnay. Plantings have been extended to include tempranillo, petit verdot and mondeuse, with vermentino planned. Most of the crop is sold to Houghton, but a small quantity is made for the Hackersley label. The Ovens family recently sold the business but remain involved in the winery and cellar door. (JH)

🍷🍷🍷🍷 **Petit Verdot 2019, Geographe** Blueberries, violets and lavender on the nose. In the mouth the wine is intense and dark, just as we expect from PV. The fruit is layered with aniseed and licorice; blue fruits and black. Spicy. Rich. Screw cap. 13.5% alc. RATING 92 DRINK 2021-2029 $35 EL

Mondeuse 2019, Geographe Fruit from Hackersley Estate vineyard in the Ferguson Valley (another place to add to the travel list …). Matured in oak for 18 months (20% new). Mondeuse is a long way from its home in Savoie, France. However, it might just belong here. This is floral, pretty, rustic, red-fruited, vibrant and chalky – all good things. A littering of mountain flowers and summer berry fruits keep the party going. Screw cap. 13.5% alc. RATING 91 DRINK 2021-2026 $35 EL

Ferguson Valley Merlot 2019, Geographe Very fine, soft and quite pure, although the fruit is lacking any real oomph or drive. It has been constructed in a way that highlights the fruit purity, but comes at the expense of any real complexity. A lovely wine, well handled, with blood plums, mulberry and heirloom tomato. Screw cap. 14.5% alc. RATING 90 DRINK 2022-2027 $30 EL

Ferguson Valley Cabernet Merlot 2013, Geographe 60/40% cabernet sauvignon/merlot. Matured in French oak for 18 months (20% new). This has certainly matured into middle+ age, and is now a soft, graceful, silky wine. Dried tobacco, blood plum, fig and poached raspberry make up the core of fruit, while the star anise and fennel-seed characters compose the spice. There's still some life left in the old girl yet, but consider drinking prior to '26. Screw cap. 13.5% alc. RATING 90 DRINK 2022-2026 $35 EL

ɪɪɪɪ **Ferguson Valley Shiraz 2019, Geographe** RATING 89 DRINK 2021-2027 $30 EL

Hahndorf Hill Winery ★★★★★

38 Pain Road, Hahndorf, SA 5245 **Region** Adelaide Hills
T (08) 8388 7512 **www**.hahndorfhillwinery.com.au **Open** Mon–Sat 10.30–4
Winemaker Larry Jacobs **Est.** 2002 **Dozens** 6000 **Vyds** 6.5ha

Larry Jacobs and Marc Dobson purchased Hahndorf Hill Winery in 2002. Larry and Marc established the near-iconic Mulderbosch Wines in '88. It was purchased at the end of '96 and the pair eventually found their way to Australia and Hahndorf Hill. In '06, their investment in the winery and cellar door was rewarded by induction into the South Australian Tourism Hall of Fame. Now a specialist in Austrian varieties, they have imported 6 clones of grüner veltliner and 2 clones of St Laurent into Australia and also produce blaufränkisch and zweigelt. In '16 the winery was awarded Best Producer Under 100t at the Adelaide Hills Wine Show, and their wines too have had trophy and medal success. Exports to the UK, Singapore and Japan. (JH)

ɪɪɪɪɪ **GRU Grüner Veltliner 2021, Adelaide Hills** Has more weight and gravitas than its siblings, but the same balance and length: it's a crying shame that I don't methodically lay down the Hahndorf Hill grüners for a decade or so to watch their development, giving the same reward as fine rieslings. Screw cap. 13% alc. RATING 96 DRINK 2021-2030 $30 JH ✪

ɪɪɪɪɪ **Rosé 2021, Adelaide Hills** RATING 93 DRINK 2021-2023 $24 JP ✪
Shiraz 2019, Adelaide Hills RATING 93 DRINK 2021-2028 $45 JP
Blueblood Blaufränkisch 2019, Adelaide Hills RATING 93 DRINK 2021-2028 $45 JP
White Mischief Grüner Veltliner 2021, Adelaide Hills RATING 90 DRINK 2021-2023 $25 JP
Zsa Zsa Zweigelt 2019, Adelaide Hills RATING 90 DRINK 2021-2024 $45 JP

Hamelin Bay ★★★★

McDonald Road, Karridale, WA 6288 **Region** Margaret River
T 0417 954168 **www**.hbwines.com.au **Open** 7 days 10.30–4.30 **Winemaker** Richard Drake-Brockman **Est.** 1992 **Dozens** 5000 **Vyds** 23.5ha

The Hamelin Bay vineyard was established by the Drake-Brockman family, pioneers of the region. Richard Drake-Brockman's great-grandmother, Grace Bussell, was famous for her courage when, in 1876, aged 16, she rescued survivors of a shipwreck not far from the mouth of the Margaret River. Richard's great-grandfather Frederick, known for his exploration of the Kimberley, read about the feat in Perth's press and rode 300km on horseback to meet her – they married in 1882. Hamelin Bay's vineyard and winery is located within a few kilometres of Karridale, at the intersection of the Brockman and Bussell Highways, which were named in honour of these pioneering families. Exports to the UK, Canada, Malaysia and Singapore. (JH)

ŸŸŸŸŸ **Five Ashes Vineyard Sauvignon Blanc 2021, Margaret River** Sandalwood, saffron curls, hints of lychee, nashi pear and jasmine florals. Pretty, bright and fresh, with saline acidity that whirls through the mouth. Lovely, delicate, oyster shell wine. Persistent, lingering finish. A beautiful wine. Classy. Screw cap. 12.5% alc. RATING 94 DRINK 2021–2023 $26 EL ✿

ŸŸŸŸŸ **Five Ashes Vineyard Cabernet Sauvignon 2020, Margaret River** RATING 93 DRINK 2021–2030 $33 EL
Five Ashes Vineyard Chardonnay 2020, Margaret River RATING 93 DRINK 2021–2030 $33 EL
Five Ashes Vineyard Shiraz 2020, Margaret River RATING 92 DRINK 2022–2030 $33 EL
Five Ashes Reserve Shiraz 2020, Margaret River RATING 92 DRINK 2021–2030 $55 EL
Rampant Red 2020, Margaret River RATING 90 DRINK 2021–2025 $22 EL

Handpicked Wines   ★★★★★

50 Kensington Street, Chippendale, NSW 2008 **Region** Various
T (03) 5983 0039 **www.**handpickedwines.com.au **Open** Mon–Fri 11–10, w'ends 10–10
Winemaker Peter Dillon, Rohan Smith **Est.** 2001 **Dozens** 100 000 **Vyds** 83ha
Handpicked Wines is a multi-regional business with a flagship vineyard and winery on the Mornington Peninsula and vineyards in the Yarra Valley, Barossa Valley and Tasmania. They also make wines from many of Australia's leading fine wine regions. Five of Handpicked's vineyards focus on high-quality pinot noir and chardonnay – 2 in Tasmania's Tamar Valley, Capella Vineyard in the Mornington Peninsula and 2 in the Yarra Valley, including Wombat Creek in the Upper Yarra, the highest elevation vineyard in the valley. Director of winemaking Peter Dillon travels extensively to oversee quality throughout the regions; he and assistant winemaker Rohan Smith work closely with a team of viticulturists who manage the vineyards. Exports to the US, Canada, the Philippines, South Korea, Cambodia, Malaysia, Singapore, Japan and Taiwan. (JH)

ŸŸŸŸŸ **Regional Selections Pinot Gris 2021, Mornington Peninsula** A fairly tight style with unusually racy acidity, so I'm assuming the fruit had been picked early. Oh and it's totally delicious. Light flavours of nashi pear and lemon, ginger blossom flower and fennel seeds. Finely tuned across the palate, with a mouth-watering finish. Screw cap. 12.9% alc. RATING 95 DRINK 2022–2025 $29 JF ✿
Trial Batch Riesling 2021, Tasmania There's a lot to enjoy here, starting with its heady aroma of lemon blossom, mandarin peel, grapefruit and ginger powder. The palate is finely tuned with tangy lemon-and-lime juice, a sherbet-powder feel to the lively acidity with a lick of sweetness on the finish, giving this some depth. It has a touch of raw-silk texture via phenolics, too. All in all, a lovely wine. Screw cap. 11.2% alc. RATING 95 DRINK 2022–2028 $29 JF ✿
Regional Selections Rosé 2021, Yarra Valley Sangiovese and nebbiolo come together to form this ultra-pale copper-hued rosé. It's delicious. Lightly aromatic, a squirt of red berries, a sprinkle of fresh basil and lemon balm with lemony freshness guaranteed. A juiciness across the palate, a mere hint of tannins to add some shape but ultimately, this is crisp, racy and seemingly thirst quenching. Screw cap. 12.2% alc. RATING 95 DRINK 2022–2023 $29 JF ✿
Trial Batch Nebbiolo 2020, Pyrenees Seductive aromas of cherries and pips, tar and roses, damp earth and potpourri. The palate is far from weighty, almost lighter framed for nebbiolo, but the tannins have some give and grip on the finish, with plenty of acidity keeping it buoyant. It's neatly pitched. There's enough complexity matched to the refreshment factor to drink this now or leave for a few years. Screw cap. 13.8% alc. RATING 95 DRINK 2022–2028 $29 JF ✿
Regional Selections Shiraz 2020, McLaren Vale Excellent colour, deep but bright. Clever winemaking has resulted in a wine that makes space for regional expression and varietal purity. It results in a calm, unhurried palate unfolding black fruits, notes of Asian spice and tannins that sneak up on the finish. Its overall

freshness and balance are hallmarks of a very smart wine. Screw cap. 14.4% alc. RATING 95 DRINK 2022-2030 $29 JH ✪

Collection Shiraz 2020, Heathcote An excellent dark red with a purple tinge; dark plums, bay leaves, sweet cedary oak, baking spices and an earthy ferrous note set the regional and varietal flavours. It's deep, rich and concentrated, with plush savoury tannins sashaying across the full-bodied palate, yet this doesn't feel weighty. It's complex, detailed and refreshing in its own way. Screw cap. 14.8% alc. RATING 95 DRINK 2022-2030 $70 JF

Wombat Creek Vineyard Chardonnay 2020, Yarra Valley An intense and electrifying wine thanks to its overt acidity, yet the power of fruit can hold its own. It's also flinty, smoky, loaded with grapefruit and lemon juice plus zest, with toasty oak that's well integrated. It's youthful and still in its high-energy phase, a bit more time in bottle will allow some mellowing. Of course, plenty will go for the style immediately as it's super-refreshing. Screw cap. 12.2% alc. RATING 95 DRINK 2023-2030 $70 JF

Trial Batch Skin-Contact Riesling 2021, Mornington Peninsula This comes up a treat. A cloudy straw hue; ginger flower, lemon barley water, fennel and sherbet-like acidity. A burst of fruit sweetness on the palate but in essence, a savoury drink with its chewy, textural tannins. Given the unsuitability of riesling on the Peninsula, this is an excellent way to transmogrify it. More please. Screw cap. 12.1% alc. RATING 94 DRINK 2022-2025 $29 JF ✪

🍷🍷🍷🍷 **Highbow Hill Vineyard Chardonnay 2020, Yarra Valley** RATING 93 DRINK 2023-2030 $70 JF

Collection Cabernet Sauvignon 2019, Margaret River RATING 93 DRINK 2023-2034 $70 JF

Collection Chardonnay 2020, Mornington Peninsula RATING 92 DRINK 2022-2027 $50 JF

Trial Batch Riesling 2020, Tasmania RATING 91 DRINK 2021-2026 $29 JH

Hanging Rock Winery ★★★★★

88 Jim Road, Newham, Vic 3442 **Region** Macedon Ranges
T (03) 5427 0542 **www.**hangingrock.com.au **Open** 7 days 10–5 **Winemaker** Robert Ellis **Est.** 1983 **Dozens** 20000 **Vyds** 14.5ha
The Macedon area has proved marginal in spots and the Hanging Rock vineyards, with their lovely vista towards the rock, are no exception. John Ellis thus elected to source additional grapes from various parts of Victoria to produce an interesting and diverse range of varietals at different pricepoints. In '11 John's children Ruth and Robert returned to the fold: Robert has an oenology degree from the University of Adelaide, after that working as a Flying Winemaker in Champagne, Burgundy, Oregon and Stellenbosch. Ruth has a degree in wine marketing from the University of Adelaide. Exports to Japan and other major markets. (JH)

🍷🍷🍷🍷🍷 **Jim Jim Sauvignon Blanc 2021, Macedon Ranges** An altogether refreshing and satisfying wine, delivering some varietal punch with a bit more complexity across the palate. Succulent and juicy citrus aromas and flavours alongside fresh basil, just-mown grass and pea shoots with a dash of passionfruit juice and pith. It also is finely tuned, finishes long and you'll be pouring another glass quick smart. Screw cap. 13% alc. RATING 95 DRINK 2022-2023 $35 JF ✪

JSE Members Reserve Shiraz 2019, Heathcote With 14% cabernet sauvignon. Always a strong performer, JSE is immediately friendly, generous and delicious. Delivers impressive concentration and drive. Chocolate, licorice, berries, cherries and dried herbs move into a vanillin oak smoothness that sits so well in the wine. The palate is sapid, juicy, youthful and taut. Screw cap. 14.5% alc. RATING 95 DRINK 2021-2034 $45 JP

Shiraz 2019, Heathcote It's early days for this wine – consider some cellar time, if you can. Tight as a drum, prominent in dark fruits, inky tannins and generous in oak. The stage is set for a rich, textured, inky, intense shiraz. Screw cap. 14.3% alc. RATING 94 DRINK 2022-2033 $80 JP

🍷🍷🍷🍷🍷 The Jim Jim Three 2021, Macedon Ranges RATING 93 DRINK 2022-2024
$35 JF
Reserve Shiraz 2009, Heathcote RATING 93 DRINK 2022-2034 $120 JP
Tarzali Riesling 2021, Strathbogie Ranges RATING 92 DRINK 2022-2028
$25 JP ✪
Jim Jim Chardonnay 2020, Macedon Ranges RATING 91 DRINK 2022-2027
$50 JF
Jim Jim Pinot Noir 2019, Macedon Ranges RATING 90 DRINK 2022-2029
$60 JF

Happs ★★★★

575 Commonage Road, Dunsborough, WA 6281 **Region** Margaret River
T (08) 9755 3300 **www.**happs.com.au **Open** 7 days 10–5 **Winemaker** Erl Happ, Mark
Warren **Est.** 1978 **Dozens** 15 000 **Vyds** 35.2ha
One-time schoolteacher, potter and winemaker Erl Happ is the patriarch of a 3-generation
family. More than anything, Erl has been a creator and experimenter: building the self-
designed winery from mudbrick, concrete form and timber; and making the first crusher. In
'94 he planted a new 30ha vineyard at Karridale to no less than 28 varieties, including some
of the earliest plantings of tempranillo in Australia. The Three Hills label is made from varieties
grown at this vineyard. Erl passed on his love of pottery to his son Myles, and Happs Pottery
now has 4 potters, including Myles. Exports to the US, Denmark, the Netherlands, Malaysia,
the Philippines, Vietnam, Hong Kong and Japan. (JH)

🍷🍷🍷🍷🍷 Sauvignon Blanc Semillon 2020, Margaret River Super-pretty talcy fruit laid
out on a smorgasbord of cassis, red apples, juniper, musk sticks, lemon flesh, lime
zest and slices of pink grapefruit. Loads of flavour. Spot on texturally, too. Very
smart. Screw cap. 13.4% alc. RATING 94 DRINK 2021-2025 $24 EL ✪
Three Hills Chardonnay 2020, Margaret River Textural, complex and super-
classy. This wine is worked and savoury, but the undercurrent of ripe, undulating
fruit carries all the (winemaker) hand and shape through a long finish. Very smart
indeed. Screw cap. 13.4% alc. RATING 94 DRINK 2021-2031 $45 EL

🍷🍷🍷🍷🍷 Welcome Home Shiraz 2020, Margaret River RATING 93 DRINK 2021-2027
$30 EL
Bone Dry Rosé 2021, Margaret River RATING 91 DRINK 2021-2023 $22
EL ✪
Merlot 2020, Margaret River RATING 91 DRINK 2022-2029 $24 EL
Three Hills Eva Marie 2020, Margaret River RATING 91 DRINK 2021-2028
$30 EL
Three Hills Petit Verdot 2020, Margaret River RATING 91
DRINK 2022-2029 $38 EL
Three Hills Merlot 2020, Margaret River RATING 90 DRINK 2022-2029
$24 EL
Fields of Gold Chardonnay 2020, Margaret River RATING 90
DRINK 2021-2027 $30 EL
Three Hills Sangiovese 2020, Margaret River RATING 90 DRINK 2022-2026
$38 EL

Harcourt Valley Vineyards ★★★★

3339 Calder Highway, Harcourt, Vic 3453 **Region** Bendigo
T (03) 5474 2223 **www.**harcourtvalley.com.au **Open** Sun 12–4 **Winemaker** Quinn
Livingstone **Est.** 1975 **Dozens** 2500 **Vyds** 4ha
Harcourt Valley Vineyards was planted in 1975. It has the oldest planting of vines in the
Harcourt Valley. Using 100% estate-grown fruit, Quinn Livingstone (second-generation
winemaker) is making a number of small-batch wines. Minimal fruit handling is used in the
winemaking process. The tasting area overlooks the vines, with a large window that allows
visitors to see the activity in the winery. (JH)

ΨΨΨΨΨ **Single Vineyard Old Vine Shiraz 2019, Bendigo** Deep, dense inky colour is no problem here. Neither is the generous amount of black fruits, plums, toasted spices and nutty oak that fills out every inch of this ripe and curvy shiraz. The palate is smoothly shaped, warm and earthy with a hint of savouriness. Presents as a hearty wine, but with some decanting loosens up nicely. Screw cap. 14% alc. RATING 94 DRINK 2021–2030 $60 JP

ΨΨΨΨΨ **Barbara's Shiraz 2019, Bendigo** RATING 92 DRINK 2021–2029 $25 JP ❂
Barbara's Shiraz 2020, Bendigo RATING 91 DRINK 2021–2029 $25 JP
Rosé 2021, Heathcote RATING 90 DRINK 2021–2023 $20 JP ❂

Hardys   ★★★★★
202 Main Road, McLaren Vale, SA 5171 **Region** McLaren Vale
T (08) 8329 4124 **www**.hardyswines.com **Open** Sun–Fri 11–4, Sat 10–4
Winemaker Nic Bowen **Viticulturist** Adam Steer **Est.** 1853
The Thomas Hardy and the Berri Renmano group merged in 1992 and prospered over the next 10 years. This led to another merger in '03, with Constellation Wines of the US and BRL Hardy, creating the largest wine group in the world (the Australian arm was known as Constellation Wines Australia or CWA); but it is now part of the Accolade Wines group. The various Hardys wine brands are Eileen Hardy and Thomas Hardy wines. Exports to all major markets. (JH)

ΨΨΨΨΨ **HRB Riesling 2021, Tasmania Clare Valley Eden Valley** A highly sophisticated riesling with a dry Germanic twang, more pronounced than the typical Australian. By this I mean the meld of bath-salt freshness and phenolics; lime cordial, quince, lemon balm, fennel and stone-fruit inflections; juicy acidity, rather than the brittle norm. A glimpse of yonder, while still firmly entrenched in the culture of home. Lightweight and energetic. Intense of flavour and beautifully tactile. This evinces class and authority. Very good. Screw cap. 12.4% alc. RATING 95 DRINK 2021–2031 $35 NG ❂
Eileen Hardy Shiraz 2019, McLaren Vale Powerful and heady, yet taut, spicy and introverted. White pepper and clove serve up first impressions. Blueberry, violet and a ferrous meatiness unravel with a work-out in the glass. The finish is exceptionally long and detailed, if not drying and in need of time. This should come together very well. Screw cap. 14.6% alc. RATING 95 DRINK 2023–2035 $100 NG
Eileen Hardy Chardonnay 2019, Yarra Valley This wine is still identifying the pieces of the jigsaw puzzle, making the future all the more interesting. Right now it's not easy to call. Screw cap. 14% alc. RATING 95 DRINK 2023–2030 $125 JH
Reynella Basket Pressed Cabernet Sauvignon 2017, McLaren Vale With 11/2/1% merlot/shiraz/malbec. Greater than the sum of its parts, each a mere tool in a drive towards weight, complexity and detail, driven by the black olive / saline notes of this maritime zone. Warm and rich, sure. But fresh, layered, impeccably balanced and immensely savoury. The swab of sage-brushed tannins across the attenuated finish, a mark of class. Screw cap. 14.2% alc. RATING 95 DRINK 2021–2029 $73 NG
HRB Chardonnay 2020, Yarra Valley Pemberton Margaret River Very good, embellishing a mid-weighted and tensile framework with spiced apple, nashi pear, apricot and cantaloupe accents. The oak is used impeccably, serving as a bridge across a mid palate of nougatine and toasted nuts, to the long, streamlined finish. Classy wine. Screw cap. 13.1% alc. RATING 94 DRINK 2021–2030 $35 NG

ΨΨΨΨΨ **HRB Chardonnay 2019, Yarra Valley Pemberton Margaret River** RATING 93 DRINK 2021–2028 $35 NG
HRB Shiraz 2019, McLaren Vale Frankland River Pyrenees RATING 93 DRINK 2022–2030 $35 NG
Reynella Basket Pressed Shiraz 2017, McLaren Vale RATING 93 DRINK 2021–2031 $70 DB

Reynella Basket Pressed Cabernet Sauvignon 2016, McLaren Vale
RATING 93 DRINK 2021-2026 $73 NG
HRB Pinot Noir 2020, Tasmania Yarra Valley Western Australia
RATING 92 DRINK 2022-2028 $35 NG
HRB Cabernet Sauvignon 2019, Margaret River Coonawarra Frankland
River RATING 92 DRINK 2022-2031 $35 NG
Tintara T Series Fiano 2021, McLaren Vale RATING 91 DRINK 2021-2024
$30 NG

Hare's Chase

56 Neldner Road, Marananga, SA 5355 **Region** Barossa Valley
T 0434 160 148 **www.**hareschase.com **Winemaker** Matt Reynolds **Est.** 1998
Dozens 5000 **Vyds** 16.8ha
Hare's Chase was created by 2 families, headed respectively by (ex Penfolds) Peter Taylor as then winemaker, with over 30 vintages' experience, and Mike de la Haye as general manager. Together they purchased a 100+yo vineyard in the Marananga Valley area of the Barossa Valley, in 1997. The vineyard has some of the best red soil available for dry-grown viticulture. Extensive replanting means that three-quarters of the vineyard is planted to now 20+yo shiraz vines, with some mourvèdre, cabernet sauvignon and tempranillo. Exports to the US, Canada, Switzerland, Singapore, Hong Kong and Malaysia. (JH)

ΨΨΨΨ **Ironscraper Shiraz 2019, Barossa Valley** Deep, opulent dark and black summer-berry fruits with plentiful spice, earth, licorice and dark chocolate notes. Concentrated and chewy with sandy tannin providing support and a bright acid line. Screw cap. 15.5% alc. RATING 88 DRINK 2021-2028 $35 DB

Harewood Estate

1570 Scotsdale Road, Denmark, WA 6333 **Region** Denmark
T (08) 9840 9078 **www.**harewood.com.au **Open** Fri–Mon 11–5 (school hols 7 days)
Winemaker James Kellie **Est.** 1988 **Dozens** 15 000 **Vyds** 19.2ha
In 2003 James and Careena Kellie, responsible for the contract making of Harewood's wines since '98, purchased the Harewood Estate. They constructed a 300t winery, offering both contract winemaking services and the ability to expand the Harewood range to include subregional wines from across the Great Southern region. Exports to the UK, the US, Denmark, Sweden, Switzerland, Indonesia, Hong Kong, Malaysia, Macau, Singapore and Japan. (JH)

ΨΨΨΨΨ **Riesling 2021, Denmark** There is a character here that is not present in the Tunney or Porongurup riesling – like toasted saffron or turmeric, cashew. The fruit strays to the sugar snap pea end of the spectrum. It's a lovely, textural and layered wine with faceted fruit and spice characters. Screw cap. 12% alc. RATING 94 DRINK 2021-2036 $30 EL ✪

ΨΨΨΨΨ **Riesling 2021, Porongurup** RATING 93 DRINK 2021-2036 $30 EL
Tunney Riesling 2021, Great Southern RATING 93 DRINK 2021-2036 $30 EL
Riesling 2021, Mount Barker RATING 92 DRINK 2021-2036 $30 EL
Flux-V Pinot Noir 2020, Denmark RATING 92 DRINK 2021-2028 $30 EL
Flux-VI Riesling 2018, Great Southern RATING 92 DRINK 2021-2031 $30 EL
Reserve Chardonnay 2020, Great Southern RATING 91 DRINK 2021-2028 $34 EL
Pinot Noir 2021, Denmark RATING 90 DRINK 2023-2028 $20 JH ✪
Sauvignon Blanc Semillon 2021, Denmark RATING 90 DRINK 2021-2024 $21 EL ✪

Harkham Winery

266 De Beyers Road, Pokolbin, NSW 2321 **Region** Hunter Valley
T (02) 4998 7648 **www**.harkhamwine.com **Open** Fri 12–5, Sat 10–5, Sun 10–4
Winemaker Richard Harkham **Est.** 1985 **Dozens** 1500 **Vyds** 3ha
In 2005, Terry Efrem and Richard Harkham acquired Windarra Estate from the founding
Andresen family. They manage the vineyard organically, and practise minimal intervention
in the winery, reaching its zenith with the preservative-free Aziza's Shiraz and Chardonnay,
and the Old Vines Shiraz. Exports to the US, France and Hong Kong. (JH)

Aziza's Preservative Free Chardonnay 2021, Hunter Valley An outlier
amid the largely conventional Hunter winescape. A fine vintage, attenuated and
cool. No adds, yet plenty of flavour. Creamed cashew, toasted hazelnuts and
praline. Stone-fruit accents buried within, yet this is all about texture, chew and a
saline drift to a long, creamy finish. Diam. 13% alc. RATING 93 DRINK 2022-2026
$40 NG

Hark Angel Shiraz 2021, Hunter Valley Lithe, succulent, mid weighted,
savoury and ready. All proceeds to a Myanmar charity. Dark cherry, licorice,
bergamot, lilac and a weave of supple, spicy tannins across a nourishing finish. This
is delicious. Arguably the best red of the suite in this vintage. Screw cap. 13% alc.
RATING 92 DRINK 2022-2027 $40 NG

Old Vines Shiraz 2020, Hunter Valley Despite the drying, charred tannins,
the craftsmanship uses them to the rich wine's stylistic advantage. Volcanic
rock, desiccated plum, boysenberry, smoked meat and violet. Almost Amarone-
like of density, verging on carnal. Yet there is a levity and honesty about the
wine. The finish, hot. But the package is an honest reflection of a year that was
and offers an uncanny versatility with meat, meat and more meat! Screw cap.
15.2% alc. RATING 92 DRINK 2022-2025 $150 NG

Shibuya Meltdown Semillon 2021, Hunter Valley An incantation of balletic
weight, skinsy detail, an airy feel of zero adds and a salty, quinine-doused finish
layered with pickled ginger. Sudsy across the mid palate with riffs on lemon
drop, freshly lain tatami mat and almond meal. This pushes and pulls the regional
envelope of convention. In the best sense. Screw cap. 10.5% alc. RATING 91
DRINK 2022-2028 $40 NG

Aziza's Preservative Free Shiraz 2021, Hunter Valley A consistently
delicious expression of energetic, minimally messed with local shiraz. The sweet
rolled earth of the region, ably captured. Yet the sapidity and pithy, poached riffs
on damson plum, Asian spice and dried nori, as attractive as any conventional
expression. It is the resolute imminency about it all that appeals most of all. Diam.
13% alc. RATING 91 DRINK 2022-2027 $50 NG

Alchimie Rosé 2021, Cowra RATING 89 DRINK 2021-2022 $35 NG

Harris Organic

179 Memorial Avenue, Baskerville, WA 6065 **Region** Swan Valley
T (08) 9296 0216 **www**.harrisorganicwine.com.au **Open** Thurs–Mon 11–4.30
Winemaker Duncan Harris **Viticulturist** Duncan Harris **Est.** 1998 **Dozens** 500
Vyds 1.8ha
Owner and winemaker Duncan Harris says Harris is the only organic winery (certified in
September 2006) in the Swan Valley. The wines are made from estate vineyards (muscadelle,
chenin blanc, chardonnay, pedro ximénez, verdelho, shiraz, malbec and muscat à petit grains
blanc and rouge), producing both still and fortified wines. Exports to Canada and Japan. (JH)

Shiraz 2020, Swan Valley Sour black cherries, red snakes and pomegranate
in the mouth. The tannins provide very little in the way of structure or shape,
however this does lead to slippery, slurpy, soft, easy drinking. This is very fresh
and vibrant, for sure the highlight. Diam. 13% alc. RATING 88 DRINK 2022-2027
$45 EL

Hart of the Barossa

Cnr Vine Vale Road/Light Pass Road, Tanunda, SA 5352 **Region** Barossa Valley
T 0412 586 006 **www**.hartofthebarossa.com.au **Open** Fri–Sat 11–4 or by appt
Winemaker Michael Hart, Alisa Hart, Rebekah Richardson **Est.** 2007 **Dozens** 2000
Vyds 6.5ha
The ancestors of Michael and Alisa Hart arrived in SA in 1845, their first address (with
7 children) a hollow tree on the banks of the North Para River. Michael and Alisa personally
tend the vineyard, which is the oldest certified organic vineyard in the Barossa Valley and
includes a patch of 120yo shiraz. The quality of the wines coming from these vines is
exceptional; unfortunately, there is only enough to fill 2 hogsheads a year (66 dozen bottles).
The other wines made are also impressive, particularly given their prices. Exports to Germany
and Hong Kong. (JH)

🍷🍷🍷🍷🍷 **Ye Faithful Limited Release Old Vine Shiraz 2017, Barossa Valley** Aromas
of dark plum and blackberry fruits are cut with hints of dark spice, turned earth,
roasting meats, vanilla bean, tobacco, dark chocolate and macerated berry fruits.
Weighty and pure on the palate, with considerable fruit power, sweetly spiced
oak and fine, compact tannin, finishing flush with lovely dark and black fruits and
a toothsome, 'classical' flair. Screw cap. 15.5% alc. RATING 95 DRINK 2021–2035
$115 DB

🍷🍷🍷🍷🍷 **The Blesing Cabernet Sauvignon 2019, Barossa Valley** RATING 92
DRINK 2021–2030 $50 DB
Ye Brave Limited Release Shiraz 2018, Barossa Valley RATING 92
DRINK 2021–2030 $35 DB
Soul Mate Limited Release Rosé 2021, Barossa Valley RATING 91
DRINK 2021–2024 $25 DB

Harvey River Estate

Third Street, Harvey, WA 6220 **Region** Geographe
T (08) 9729 2085 **www**.harveyriverestate.com.au **Open** Wed–Sat 10–4, Sun 10–2
Winemaker Stuart Pierce **Est.** 1999 **Dozens** 20000 **Vyds** 18.5ha
Harvey River Estate has a long and significant tradition of winemaking in WA's southwest.
The Sorgiovanni family have been farming and making wine on the original property
since Guiseppe (Joe) arrived from Italy in 1928. Orchards evolved into a standalone business
and Harvey Fresh went on to become one of WA's largest milk and juice processors. The
Harvey River Estate label was established in '99, the range of popular varietals designed to be
enjoyed in the short–medium term including sauvignon blanc, chardonnay, sauvignon blanc
semillon, rosé, merlot, shiraz, cabernet sauvignon. The fruit for these wines is predominantly
from the family-owned vineyards in Geographe. Exports to the US, Canada, Taiwan and
Singapore. (JH)

🍷🍷🍷🍷🍷 **Barbera 2021, Geographe** 87/13% barbera/dolcetto. Alpine herbs, blackberry,
blood plum(skin), aniseed, fennel flower, raspberry and red apples. Gorgeous,
vibrant, joyful drinking in the short term, if you seek to to capture the slinky,
frisky vibes this thing has going on. Delicious. Screw cap. 14.8% alc. RATING 93
DRINK 2022-2024 $30 EL
Montepulciano 2021, Geographe A combination of dense, dark and broody,
with brightness, vivacity and electric life. The texture is smooth and just a little
bit rustic (just enough for charm), and the fruit is alive. Popping. Yum. Screw cap.
15% alc. RATING 92 DRINK 2021-2026 $30 EL

Haselgrove Wines

187 Sand Road, McLaren Vale, SA 5171 **Region** McLaren Vale
T (08) 8323 8706 **www**.haselgrove.com.au **Open** 7 days 9.30–5.30 **Winemaker** Alex
Sherrah **Est.** 1981 **Dozens** 45000 **Vyds** 9.7ha

Italian-Australian industry veterans Don Totino, Don Luca, Tony Carrocci and Steve Maglieri decided to purchase Haselgrove 'over a game of cards and couple of hearty reds' in '08. The modern small-batch winery produces the Legend Series (Ambassador, Col Cross, The Lear and The Cruth), the Origin Series, the Alternative Series, First Cut and the 'H' by Haselgrove Series. Exports to Canada, Germany, Malaysia, South Korea, Hong Kong, Vietnam, Taiwan, Singapore, Denmark and NZ. (JH)

ΨΨΨΨΨ **The Ambassador Single Vineyard Shiraz 2020, McLaren Vale** This is perhaps the juiciest, most succulent and contemporary of these top-tier iterations, and yet it is the most drinkable, detailed and restrained. Powerful and pulpy, sure. But there is a corset of necessary tannins without overt reduction. I'd like even more, but the mace and clove and tapenade soothe the long finish. The Col Cross is spicier and arguably firmer. Yet it feels reductive and forced. This is very good if shiraz is your go-to. Diam. 14.5% alc. RATING 95 DRINK 2022-2032 $90 NG
The Cruth Shiraz 2020, McLaren Vale A blend of subregional vineyards in Blewitt Springs and the proprietary site in McLaren Flat. And yet … the tannins are a beautifully knitted weave, expanding across the cheeks while enveloping the senses. This is sweet, sure. Shiraz just is. Bumptious, too. But it is hot-climate shiraz à l'Australienne. If this is what we do well, then this is pretty good. Screw cap. 14.5% alc. RATING 95 DRINK 2022-2036 $150 NG

ΨΨΨΨΨ **Col Cross Single Vineyard Shiraz 2020, McLaren Vale** RATING 93 DRINK 2022-2032 $90 NG
The Lear Shiraz 2020, McLaren Vale RATING 93 DRINK 2022-2030 $90 NG
Catkin Shiraz 2019, McLaren Vale RATING 92 DRINK 2021-2028 $40 NG
First Cut Cabernet Sauvignon 2019, McLaren Vale RATING 91 DRINK 2021-2027 $23 NG ✪

Hay Shed Hill Wines   ★★★★★

511 Harmans Mill Road, Wilyabrup, WA 6280 **Region** Margaret River
T (08) 9755 6046 **www.**hayshedhill.com.au **Open** 7 days 10–5 **Winemaker** Michael Kerrigan **Est.** 1987 **Dozens** 24000 **Vyds** 18.55ha
Mike Kerrigan, former winemaker at Howard Park, acquired Hay Shed Hill in late 2006 (with co-ownership by the West Cape Howe syndicate) and is now the full-time winemaker. He had every confidence that he could dramatically lift the quality of the wines and has done precisely that. The estate-grown wines are made under the Vineyard and Block series. The Block series showcases the ultimate site-specific wines, made from separate blocks within the vineyard. The Pitchfork wines are made from contract-grown grapes in the region and the KP Wines label is a collaboration between Michael and his daughter Katie Priscilla Kerrigan. Exports to the UK, the US, Denmark, Singapore, Japan and Hong Kong. (JH)

ΨΨΨΨΨ **Tempranillo 2020, Margaret River** Dr John Gladstones long ago – before much was grown in Australia – placed tempranillo alongside pinot noir as an early ripening variety. Deep crimson purple, it is only medium bodied but has exceptional texture and structure, its red (cherry) and blue fruits coalescing with a fine tannin mesh. Screw cap. 14% alc. RATING 95 DRINK 2022-2037 $30 JH ✪
Block 2 Cabernet Sauvignon 2019, Margaret River '19 was cool in Margaret River, and the wines are aromatic, nuanced and accessible right now. This is silky and fine, the fruit prioritised at every stage in the mouth. The tannins have been obliterated into the fruit; smashed to smithereens so fine as to be at one with the berries. Lovely, sumptuous, sleek cabernet. Screw cap. 14% alc. RATING 95 DRINK 2022-2036 $60 EL
Block 1 Semillon Sauvignon Blanc 2020, Margaret River From some of the oldest semillon and sauvignon blanc vines in the Margaret River, and involves some barrel ferment that increases complexity, depth and length. Moves it into a place all of its own. Screw cap. 12% alc. RATING 94 DRINK 2022-2026 $30 JH ✪
Block 6 Chardonnay 2020, Margaret River Concentrated and intense, this – like the other chardonnays from this estate – shows a vein of minerality sewn

into the line of the fruit on the palate. Red apple skins, white peach, finely grated nutmeg and brine through the finish. Class act. Screw cap. 12.5% alc. RATING 94 DRINK 2021–2028 $40 EL

Block 8 Cabernet Franc 2020, Margaret River Supple, leafy fruit in this glass – loaded with pleasure. Concentrated and somehow effortless (thank you '20), this has firm yet flexible tannic structure that shapes the wine through the tail. Very smart, and apparently, very limited quantities as well. Screw cap. 14% alc. RATING 94 DRINK 2021–2036 $40 EL

Block 6 Chardonnay 2019, Margaret River Complex, layered and toasty, exhibiting a combination of honeysuckle, hazelnut, white peach and red apple skin. There is a core of exotic spice on the palate, making this a heck of a ride. The intensity of flavour is a marvel that carries long through the finish – like a javelin. Screw cap. 12.5% alc. RATING 94 DRINK 2020–2035 $40 EL

ϼϼϼϼϼ **KP Naturally Chenin Blanc 2021, Margaret River** RATING 92 DRINK 2021–2031 $30 EL

Block 10 Petit Verdot 2020, Margaret River RATING 92 DRINK 2021–2031 $40 EL

Morrison's Gift 2019, Margaret River RATING 92 DRINK 2021–2031 $28 EL

G40 Riesling 2021, Mount Barker RATING 91 DRINK 2021–2028 $25 EL

Pinot Gris 2021, Margaret River RATING 91 DRINK 2022–2024 $25 JH

Vermentino 2021, Mount Barker RATING 91 DRINK 2022–2024 $25 JH

KP Naturally Grenache 2021, Margaret River RATING 91 DRINK 2021–2025 $30 EL

Morrison's Gift Chardonnay 2020, Margaret River RATING 91 DRINK 2021–2027 $28 EL

Cabernet Sauvignon 2019, Margaret River RATING 91 DRINK 2021–2031 $28 EL

Malbec 2019, Margaret River RATING 91 DRINK 2021–2028 $30 EL

KP Naturally Rosé, Geographe RATING 90 DRINK 2021–2023 $35 EL

Grenache 2020, Margaret River RATING 90 DRINK 2022–2028 $30 EL

Shiraz Tempranillo 2019, Margaret River RATING 90 DRINK 2021–2026 $22 EL

Hayes Family Wines ★★★★★

102 Mattiske Road, Stone Well, SA 5352 **Region** Barossa Valley
T 0499 096 812 **www.**hayesfamilywines.com **Open** Sat 11–4.30 or by appt
Winemaker Andrew Seppelt **Est.** 2014 **Dozens** 1000 **Vyds** 5ha
Hayes Family Wines is a small family-owned wine producer nestled among organically farmed vineyards in Stone Well on the western ridge of the Barossa Valley. The Hayes family has decades of agriculture and business experience. Shiraz, grenache, mataro and semillon are produced from the old vineyard in Stone Well, and also from Ebenezer and Koonunga in the northern Barossa. (JH)

ϼϼϼϼϼ **Redman Vineyard Shiraz 2019, Coonawarra** From an outstanding vintage that has produced wines with a superb texture and structure to the medium to full-bodied palate. While the tannins are plentiful, they are ripe and bend to the array of blackberry and blueberry flavours. Screw cap. 13.6% alc. RATING 97 DRINK 2029–2059 $60 JH ✪

ϼϼϼϼϼ **Fromm Vineyard Grenache 2021, Barossa Valley** Bright red-purple hue. Pure and endearing, with gorgeous red cherry, satsuma plum and cranberry fruit notes, Asian five-spice, red licorice, gingerbread and purple floral high tones. Savoury and moreish with a lovely fruit weight and flow, tannins just right, acidity providing the cadence and a spicy, plummy finish of some length. Screw cap. 14.5% alc. RATING 95 DRINK 2022–2032 $40 DB

Estate Stone Well Block 9 Shiraz 2019, Barossa Valley Very good depth and hue. An expressive bouquet of licorice, polished leather and wild blackberries, the full-bodied palate mimicking the bouquet and adding a fistful of tannins. While not ready to drink now, it is well balanced. Screw cap. 14.5% alc. RATING 95 DRINK 2030-2040 $60 JH

Blanc de Noirs 2019, Adelaide Hills 100% pinot noir, méthode traditionnelle, disgorged Oct '21. An impressive sparkling wine. Pale straw in the glass with enthusiastic fine bubbles racing to the surface. Aromas of crisp apple and citrus fruits with some redcurrant notes in the distance. Hints of soft spice, white flowers, brioche, clotted cream, Monte Carlo biscuits and crushed quartz. These characters neatly transpose to the palate, which is vibrant and vivid with excellent tension, drive and stony pizzaz. Diam. 12% alc. RATING 94 $45 DB ♥

Vineyard Series Koonunga Creek Block Grenache 2021, Barossa Valley Deep red purple in the glass with lifted aromas of blood plum, mulberry, black cherry and blueberry fruits cut with exotic spice, jasmine, ginger cake, earth and a hint of musk and licorice. Deep, resonant fruit profile, earth and pure with fine-ground tannin and ample acid drive on the rich, plummy finish. Lovely. Screw cap. 14.7% alc. RATING 94 DRINK 2022-2032 $40 DB

Reserve Shiraz 2019, Barossa Valley Pretty fruit aromas of blackberry and satsuma plum are lifted by hints of violets, oak spice, dark chocolate, boysenberry pastries, earth and a whiff of oats. There's a lovely fruit flow to the wine, drawn into line by fine, ripe tannin and bright acidity, finishing long, elegant and pure of fruit. Screw cap. 14.6% alc. RATING 94 DRINK 2021-2031 $100 DB

Reserve Cabernet Sauvignon 2019, Coonawarra Classic aromas of blackberry, cassis and blackcurrant with classy, cedary oak, dark spice, some lovely floral high tones and an understorey of light briar and herbal notes. Medium bodied, with a taut canvas of ripe black fruits, tight, robust tannins and impressive persistence, it seems set for excellent cellaring potential. Screw cap. 14.5% alc. RATING 94 DRINK 2021-2035 $100 DB

Head Wines ★★★★★

PO Box 58, Tanunda, SA 5352 **Region** Barossa Valley
T 0413 114 233 **www**.headwines.com.au **Open** By appt Feb–Apr **Winemaker** Alex Head **Est.** 2006 **Dozens** 6000

Head Wines is the venture of Alex Head. In 1997, he finished a degree in biochemistry from Sydney University. Experience in fine wine stores, importers and an auction house was followed by vintage work at wineries he admired: Tyrrell's, Torbreck, Laughing Jack and Cirillo Estate. The names of the wines reflect his fascination with Côte-Rôtie in the Northern Rhône Valley. The 2 aspects in Côte-Rôtie are known as Côte Blonde and Côte Brune. Head's Blonde comes from an east-facing slope in the Stone Well area, while The Brunette comes from a very low-yielding vineyard in the Moppa area. In each case, open fermentation (with whole bunches) and basket pressing precedes maturation in French oak. Exports to the UK, Denmark, the Netherlands, Russia, South Korea and NZ. (JH)

🍷🍷🍷🍷🍷 **Wilton Hill Barossa Ranges Shiraz 2019, Eden Valley** The colour is a saturated red purple, giving a hint of the intensity to come. Dark and black fruit of impressive density abound, cut deeply with spice and earth. It's a wonderfully expressive wine, both of latent fruit power and of site. The balance is pitch perfect, with ample tannin and mineral-like acid support. Very impressive. Diam. 14.8% alc. RATING 97 DRINK 2021-2041 $149 DB ✪

🍷🍷🍷🍷🍷 **The Contrarian Shiraz 2020, Barossa** An expressive, fragrant bouquet 100% in tune with red cherry fruits, freshness and vitality foremost from start to finish. The urge to have a second glass will be omnipresent. Screw cap. 13.5% alc. RATING 96 DRINK 2022-2035 $39 JH ✪

Ancestor Vine Springton Grenache 2020, Eden Valley Experiencing a wine made from these ancestor vines is an exercise in texture, restraint and grace. Vivid plum and red fruits cut with exotic spice, fennel tops, ginger cake, cola and purple flowers. Just beautiful drinking: a wine that is very composed and comfortable in its own skin. Savoury and fine. Screw cap. 14.5% alc. RATING 96 DRINK 2021-2035 $109 DB

Rosé 2021, Barossa 50/45/5% grenache/mataro/viognier. A heady bouquet and ultra-complex palate has made the investment of time and money worthwhile. Screw cap. 13.5% alc. RATING 95 DRINK 2021-2025 $27 JH ✪

Head Red GSM 2020, Barossa The rich bouquet, hinting at luscious fruits, doesn't deceive. A vibrant, supple trifecta of cherry, plum and raspberry. Screw cap. 14.5% alc. RATING 95 DRINK 2021-2031 $27 JH ✪

Heart & Home Dry Red 2020, Barossa 79/21% cabernet sauvignon and shiraz. This is all about cabernet sauvignon kicking up its heels in the Barossa Valley and making no apologies for doing so. There is an edge of authority to its expression provided by the firm tannins, shiraz ending any suggestion of excess force. Bargain on a grand scale. Screw cap. 14.5% alc. RATING 94 DRINK 2021-2031 $23 JH ✪

Head Red Shiraz 2020, Barossa A medium-bodied blend of cherry, plum and blackberry fruits, complexed by ripe though savoury tannins. Excellent balance. Screw cap 14.5% alc. RATING 94 DRINK 2022-2041 $27 JH ✪

The Blonde Barossa Shiraz 2020, Barossa Valley Aromas of dark and black plum and berry fruits, cut through with spice, pepper, roasting meats and earth. Impressive fruit density in the mouth, with wonderful flow and presence, tightly packed tannin and a savoury, meaty plume of plummy fruit on the finish. Screw cap. 14.5% alc. RATING 94 DRINK 2021-2031 $54 DB

Heartland Wines   ★★★★☆

The Winehouse, Wellington Road, Langhorne Creek, SA 5255 **Region** Langhorne Creek **T** (08) 8333 1363 **www.**heartlandwines.com.au **Open** Mon–Fri 9–5 **Winemaker** Ben Glaetzer **Est.** 2001 **Dozens** 50000 **Vyds** 200ha
Heartland is a joint venture of veteran winemakers Ben Glaetzer and Scott Collett. It focuses on cabernet sauvignon and shiraz from Langhorne Creek, with John Glaetzer (Ben's uncle and head winemaker at Wolf Blass for over 30 years) liaising with his network of growers and vineyards. Ben makes the wines at Barossa Vintners. Exports to all major markets. (JH)

♟♟♟♟♟ **Directors' Cut Shiraz 2019, Langhorne Creek** Excellent hue and depth, an early harbinger of a very good vintage, the bouquet and palate living up to the promise. It is a broad-shouldered, luscious and rich wine, borrowing some dark chocolate from McLaren Vale, adding licorice and plum fruit flavours. Screw cap. 14.5% alc. RATING 95 DRINK 2022-2039 $37 JH

♟♟♟♟♟ **Shiraz 2019, Langhorne Creek** RATING 92 DRINK 2023-2033 $22 JH ✪
Spice Trader Shiraz 2017, Langhorne Creek RATING 91 DRINK 2022-2027 $19 JH ✪
Cabernet Sauvignon 2018, Langhorne Creek RATING 90 DRINK 2022-2027 $22 JH

Heathcote Estate   ★★★★★

Drummonds Lane, Heathcote, Vic 3523 (postal) **Region** Heathcote **T** (03) 5974 3729 **www.**yabbylake.com **Open** 7 days 10–4 **Winemaker** Tom Carson, Chris Forge, Luke Lomax **Est.** 1999 **Dozens** 5000 **Vyds** 34ha
Heathcote Estate and Yabby Lake Vineyard are owned by the Kirby family of Village Roadshow Ltd. They purchased a prime piece of Heathcote red Cambrian soil in 1999, planting shiraz (30ha) and grenache (4ha). The wines are matured exclusively in French oak. The arrival of the hugely talented Tom Carson as group winemaker in 2008 has added lustre to the winery and its wines. Exports to the US, the UK, Canada, Sweden, Singapore and Hong Kong. (JH)

♟♟♟♟♟ **Single Vineyard Shiraz 2020, Heathcote** Superlative wine showing great elegance. Concentrated ripe dark plum, blackberries, dried herbs, earthy sweetness, violet and more. The palate is laid out long in soft, ripe tannins, mouth-filling with an impressive regional and varietal declaration. Screw cap. 13.5% alc. RATING 96 DRINK 2022-2030 $50 JP ✪

20th Anniversary Single Vineyard Shiraz 2019, Heathcote A worthy anniversary wine of elegance and appropriate gravitas, dressed in fine detail of perfect, fragrant, blackberry, cassis fruits and spice. Arrives fully formed and seamlessly structured, fuelled by energised fine tannins. Screw cap. 13% alc. RATING 96 DRINK 2022–2036 $200 JP

♥♥♥♥♀ **Single Block Release Block C Shiraz 2020, Heathcote** RATING 90 DRINK 2022–2030 $60 JP

Heathcote Winery

185 High Street, Heathcote, Vic 3523 **Region** Heathcote
T (03) 5433 2595 **www**.heathcotewinery.com.au **Open** 7 days 11–5 **Winemaker** Rachel Gore **Est.** 1978 **Dozens** 8000 **Vyds** 11ha
The cellar door of Heathcote Winery is situated in the main street of Heathcote, housed in a restored miner's cottage built by Thomas Craven in 1854 to cater for the huge influx of gold miners. The winery is immediately behind the cellar door. The first vintage was processed in 1983, following the planting of the vineyards in '78. Shiraz and shiraz viognier account for 90% of the production. (JH)

♥♥♥♥♥ **The Wilkins Shiraz 2018, Heathcote** Only made in exceptional years. This is the fifth Wilkins release, named after owner, Stephen Wilkins. Deep and dense in toasty mocha-scented oak, ripe plums, dark berries and earthy notes, all combining to produce a brooding, concentrated whole. A svelte palate, fine in tannin, looks set for good drinking now as well as with age. Screw cap. 14.5% alc. RATING 95 DRINK 2022–2032 $120 JP

♥♥♥♥♀ **Mail Coach Shiraz 2019, Heathcote** RATING 92 DRINK 2022–2028 $35 JP
Slaughterhouse Paddock Single Vineyard Shiraz 2019, Heathcote RATING 92 DRINK 2022–2030 $55 JP

Hedonist Wines

Rifle Range Road, McLaren Vale, SA 5171 **Region** McLaren Vale
T (08) 8323 8818 **www**.hedonistwines.com.au **Winemaker** Walter Clappis, Kimberly Cooter, James Cooter **Est.** 1982 **Dozens** 18 000 **Vyds** 35ha
Walter Clappis has been making wine in McLaren Vale for 40 years, and over that time has won innumerable trophies and gold medals, including the prestigious George Mackey Memorial Trophy with his '09 The Hedonist Shiraz, chosen as the best wine exported from Australia that year. Daughter Kimberly and son-in-law James Cooter (both with impressive CVs) support him on the winery floor. The NASAA-certified organic and biodynamic estate plantings of shiraz, cabernet sauvignon, tempranillo and grenache are the cornerstones of the business. Exports include the UK, the US, Canada, Singapore and Thailand. (JH)

♥♥♥♥♀ **The Hedonist Shiraz 2020, McLaren Vale** Nicely done. Richly flavoured, suave of feel and long limbed of tannins. A bit of heat, but easily ignored amid a cornucopia of palate-staining dark fruits, pepper grind, charcuterie and an exotic spice kitchen that alludes to the northern Rhône rather than traditional sweetness of the Vale. A steal, glimpsing a great deal more sophistication than the price tag suggests. Screw cap. 14% alc. RATING 93 DRINK 2022–2030 $25 NG **✪**
The Hedonist Sangiovese 2021, McLaren Vale Fine aromas suggestive of spiced cherry, sandalwood, licorice and menthol. Medium bodied with just enough tannic framework, grape and vanillin oak, to keep the fruit sweetness from slipping into excess. Solid drinking for the everyday table. Screw cap. 13.5% alc. RATING 90 DRINK 2022–2026 $27 NG

Heggies Vineyard

Heggies Range Road, Eden Valley, SA 5235 **Region** Eden Valley
T (08) 8561 3200 **www**.heggiesvineyard.com **Open** By appt **Winemaker** Marc van
Halderen **Est.** 1972 **Dozens** 15 000 **Vyds** 62ha
Heggies was the second of the high-altitude (570m) vineyards established by the Hill-Smith
family. Plantings on the 120ha former grazing property began in 1973; the principal varieties
are riesling, chardonnay, viognier and merlot. There are also 2 special plantings: a 1.1ha reserve
chardonnay block and 27ha of various clonal trials. Exports to all major markets. (JH)

ŸŸŸŸŸ **Botrytis Riesling 2021, Eden Valley** The tightrope walk and tension between
fruit sweetness and acidity is delicious and fascinating in equal measure here, with
characters of lime-edged apricot drops, lemon barley, dried honey, gingerbread and
a dusting of soft spice and jasmine. Floral and head-spinningly pure on the palate,
with nary a hint of cloying. A clean, precise bolt of pure botrytis fruit and spice on
the finish lingers beautifully. Screw cap. 10.5% alc. RATING 95 DRINK 2021-2028
$28 DB ✪ ♥
Estate Riesling 2021, Eden Valley A cracking lime-pure '21 riesling, with it's
gorgeous blossomy perfume, quartz-like minerality and swift, sherbety cadence
across the tongue. It's a great Heggies release. Screw cap. 11.5% alc. RATING 94
DRINK 2021-2031 $26 DB ✪

ŸŸŸŸŸ **Cloudline Chardonnay 2021, Eden Valley** RATING 91 DRINK 2022-2027
$24 DB
Estate Chardonnay 2019, Eden Valley RATING 90 DRINK 2021-2027
$31 DB

Heirloom Vineyards

PO Box 39, McLaren Vale, SA 5171 **Region** Adelaide
T (08) 8323 8979 **www**.heirloomvineyards.com.au **Winemaker** Elena Brooks **Est.** 2004
Another venture for winemaker Elena Brooks and her husband Zar. They met during the
2000 vintage and one thing led to another, as they say. Dandelion Vineyards and Zonte's
Footstep came along first, and continue, but other partners are involved in those ventures. The
lofty aims of Heirloom are 'to preserve the best of tradition, the unique old vineyards of SA,
and to champion the best clones of each variety, embracing organic and biodynamic farming'.
The quality of the wines has been consistently very good. Exports to all major markets. (JH)

ŸŸŸŸŸ **Shiraz 2020, McLaren Vale** The deep – verging on opaque – colour rings
a bell warning of the arrival of an exotic full-bodied shiraz, arguing the toss on
varietal expression (unctuous blackberry and licorice) and sense of place (dark
chocolate) with ripe, gently chewy tannins and a benison of oak. Screw cap.
14.5% alc. RATING 96 DRINK 2022-2040 $40 JH ✪
Assen's Fortalice Chardonnay 2021, Adelaide Hills Quite a mouthful of
a name, but in the mouth it delivers a supreme elegance, no edges, just a finely
controlled cool-climate poise. Crunchy lemon, lime, nashi pear, quince and a touch
of savoury almond skin and biscuit rise from the glass. They gather on the palate,
integrated and complex, given life and energy by brisk acidity. Could enjoy now but
there's more to come. Screw cap. 12.5% alc. RATING 95 DRINK 2022-2031 $60 JP
Alcala Grenache 2021, McLaren Vale Everything is done right here. The
oak, too, to make a change. It nestles amid a spine of edgy whole-bunch tannins,
appositely extracted grape skin ones and salty maritime acidity. This echoes the
transparent wines of Spain's Gredos, arguably the most exciting newcomer to the
grenache patrimony. Kirsch, thyme, mescal and pine, as if this is positioned in a
higher site than it is. Thirst-slaking, layered, fresh and riveting. Great gear! Screw
cap. 14.5% alc. RATING 95 DRINK 2021-2028 $80 NG
Alcazar Castle Pinot Noir 2021, Adelaide Hills Just starting out on a long
journey, there is a solid foundation here for a wonderfully complex wine that
will shine with more time in the bottle. The elements are all here. Structure is
deceptively firm in tannin but also elegant with no hard edges. Fruit is equally

hard to categorise, both bold in dark berries and forest floor and bracken, but with delicate threads of spice and amaro-like bitters. A fascinating wine. Screw cap. 13.3% alc. RATING 95 DRINK 2022-2031 $80 JP

Alcalá Grenache 2020, McLaren Vale McLaren Vale grenache is never short on flavour, but here it shines with complexity and finesse. Marries the grape's floral beauty with mulberry, cherry cola, red licorice and juniper. At once both bright and contemplative, it has time on its hands, aided by subtle tannins and well-managed oak. Screw cap. 14.5% alc. RATING 95 DRINK 2021-2030 $80 JP

Anevo Fortress Grenache Touriga Tempranillo 2020, McLaren Vale So much potential with this trio. Juicy, succulent and mouth-coating, GTT offers a fragrant welcome mixed with warm, sweet spices – paprika, cardamom – and jubey, black fruits. Touriga's bold tannins are resident on the palate, bringing structural integrity across a swathe of ripe, generous fruit, chocolate, licorice and spicy oak flavours. Finishes dry and powdery, tannic fine. Screw cap. 14.2% alc. RATING 94 DRINK 2021-2030 $80 JP

A'Lambra Shiraz 2020, Barossa Valley Vivid crimson purple stains the glass as it is swirled. As yet it is a black hole in space, sucking all into its vortex, even the tannins that are surely there along with the black fruits. Needs a stray decade or 2. Screw cap. 14.6% alc. RATING 94 DRINK 2030-2050 $150 JH

ŸŸŸŸŸ **Touriga 2021, McLaren Vale** RATING 92 DRINK 2021-2025 $40 NG
Alcala Grenache 2020, McLaren Vale RATING 92 DRINK 2021-2022 $80 JH
Pinot Noir 2021, Adelaide Hills RATING 91 DRINK 2022-2028 $40 JP
Cabernet Sauvignon 2020, Coonawarra RATING 91 DRINK 2022-2032 $40 EL

Helen's Hill Estate   ★★★★★

16 Ingram Road, Lilydale, Vic 3140 **Region** Yarra Valley
T (03) 9739 1573 **www.**helenshill.com.au **Open** Thurs–Mon 10–5 **Winemaker** Scott McCarthy **Est.** 1984 **Dozens** 15 000 **Vyds** 53ha

Helen's Hill Estate is named after the previous owner of the property, Helen Fraser. Venture partners Andrew and Robyn McIntosh and Roma and Allan Nalder combined childhood farming experience with more recent careers in medicine and finance to establish and manage the day-to-day operations of the estate. It produces 2 labels: Helen's Hill Estate and Ingram Road, both made onsite. Scott McCarthy started his career early by working vintages during school holidays before gaining diverse and extensive experience in the Barossa and Yarra valleys, Napa Valley, Languedoc, the Loire Valley and Marlborough. The winery, cellar door complex and elegant 140-seat restaurant command some of the best views in the valley. Exports to the Maldives and Hong Kong. (JH)

ŸŸŸŸŸ **The Smuggler Single Clone Pinot Noir 2019, Yarra Valley** This is a striking and delicious wine, with fluid drive and line to its mix of dark cherries, spices and pomegranate. The balance between fruit, oak and tannin is perfect, as is its length. Diam. 12.8% alc. RATING 97 DRINK 2023-2035 $60 JH ✪

ŸŸŸŸŸ **Breachley Block Single Vineyard Chardonnay 2020, Yarra Valley** A striking, high-quality chardonnay that is as intense as it is long, with a layered palate of grapefruit and white stone fruit, stiletto acidity lingering on the back palate and aftertaste. Screw cap. 13.3% alc. RATING 96 DRINK 2022-2032 $35 JH

Hill Top Single Vineyard Syrah 2020, Yarra Valley A high-toned, intensely focused shiraz, the syrah soubriquet spot on. Black and blue berry fruits are moulded together with a splash of spice and peremptory tannins. Screw cap. 14.8% alc. RATING 95 DRINK 2025-2040 $35 JH ✪

Range View Single Clone Pinot Noir 2019, Yarra Valley A whirl of power and complexity takes hold the moment the wine is first tasted, seated on a fortress of texture, the flavours savoury, giving the illusion of whole bunch, the tannins in line with the overall power of the wine. Diam. 12.8% alc. RATING 95 DRINK 2024-2034 $60 JH

Long Walk Single Vineyard Pinot Noir 2020, Yarra Valley You would never guess the alcohol is as low as it is; the colour is deep, the fruit expression ripe. Black cherry, plum and a hint of choc mint drive the palate through to a lingering finish and persistent aftertaste. Screw cap. 11.7% alc. RATING 94 DRINK 2022–2035 $35 JH

Helm ★★★★★

19 Butts Road, Murrumbateman, NSW 2582 **Region** Canberra District
T (02) 6227 5953 **www.**helmwines.com.au **Open** Fri–Mon 10–4 **Winemaker** Ken Helm **Viticulturist** Ben Osbourne **Est.** 1973 **Dozens** 5000 **Vyds** 11ha
Ken Helm celebrated his 44th vintage in '20. Riesling has been an all-consuming interest, ultimately rewarded with rieslings of consistently high quality. He has also given much to the broader wine community, extending from the narrow focus of the Canberra District to the broad canvas of the international world of riesling: in '00 he established the Canberra International Riesling Challenge. In '14 his youngest child Stephanie (and husband Ben Osborne, Helm's vineyard manager) purchased Yass Valley Wines, rebranding it as The Vintner's Daughter (for which no wines were tasted this year). In '17 Helm completed construction of a separate 40 000L insulated winery with a double-refrigeration system dedicated to the production of riesling, the old winery now producing cabernet sauvignon. (JH)

♀♀♀♀♀ **Premium Riesling 2021, Canberra District** Such a composed and classy wine. Yes, it has lemon blossom, ginger spice and citrus flavours – and tantalisingly so – but there's a depth that rightly puts this into premium territory. Best of all, texture is its hallmark, with talc-like acidity and a sheen across the palate as it glides towards a long finish. Screw cap. 11.5% alc. RATING 96 DRINK 2021–2035 $60 JF ❂
Classic Dry Riesling 2021, Canberra District While lemony acidity is the driver, this is full of lime cordial and zest, barely ripe red apples and loads of spice. Expect a juiciness and vibrancy, but a smidge of texture leaning towards its dry, ultra-fresh finish. Screw cap. 11.5% alc. RATING 95 DRINK 2021–2031 $38 JF
Classic Cabernet Sauvignon 2019, Canberra District A spot-on Classic with its wave of cassis and currants, baking spices and pepper, tobacco and gum leaf. The medium-bodied palate is defined by cocoa tannins and fresh acidity to close. Looks smart now and will offer more savouriness in time. Screw cap. 13% alc. RATING 95 DRINK 2022–2028 $50 JF
Premium Cabernet Sauvignon 2019, Canberra District Drink the Classic and age the Premium. That would be one way to approach Helm's cabernets, although this is remarkably open and ready. More concentrated but not too much, with blueberries, boysenberries and a whorl of spices and savoury tones. Fuller bodied, with the oak adding to its shape and tannins, which are textural, defined and neatly etched into the body of the wine. Screw cap. 13% alc. RATING 95 DRINK 2022–2034 $90 JF

♀♀♀♀♀ **Half Dry Riesling 2021, Canberra District** RATING 93 DRINK 2021–2028 $30 JF
Riesling 2021, Tumbarumba RATING 93 DRINK 2021–2033 $35 JF

Hemera Estate ★★★★

1516 Barossa Valley Way, Lyndoch, SA 5351 **Region** Barossa Valley
T (08) 8524 4033 **www.**hemeraestate.com.au **Open** 7 days 10–5 **Winemaker** Jason Barrette **Est.** 1999 **Dozens** 15 000 **Vyds** 22ha
Hemera Estate was originally founded by Darius and Pauline Ross in 1999 as Ross Estate Wines. The name change came about in '12 after the business was sold to Winston Wine. This purchase also saw renewed investment in the winery, vineyard and tasting room, and a focus on consistently producing high-quality wines. Running very much on an estate basis, the winery and tasting room are located on the 22ha vineyard in the southern Barossa Valley; it's primarily planted to shiraz, followed by cabernet sauvignon and 1912 planted grenache,

with smaller plantings of cabernet franc, mataro and tempranillo. Exports to Japan, Thailand and Singapore. (JH)

ŶŶŶŶŶ **Limited Release Home Block Shiraz 2019, Barossa Valley** Cedar-edged, ripe blackberry and dark plum fruits are underscored by hints of baking spice, licorice and dark chocolate. Dense and berry-packed on the palate, some date and deep spice notes showing through, with fine chocolatey tannins and plenty of pure, pleasing fruit weight and latent power on display. Screw cap. 14.5% alc. RATING 95 DRINK 2021-2031 $60 DB

ŶŶŶŶŶ **Single Vineyard GSM 2020, Barossa Valley** RATING 93 DRINK 2021-2028 $60 DB

Henschke ★★★★★
1428 Keyneton Road, Keyneton, SA 5353 **Region** Eden Valley
T (08) 8564 8223 **www**.henschke.com.au **Open** Mon–Sat 9–4.30 & public hols 10–3
Winemaker Stephen Henschke **Viticulturist** Prue Henschke **Est.** 1868 **Dozens** 30 000
Vyds 100ha
Henschke is the foremost medium-sized wine producer in Australia. Stephen and Prue Henschke have taken a crown jewel and polished it to an even greater brilliance. Year on year they have quietly added labels for single vineyards, single varieties or blends. The wines hail from the Eden Valley (the majority), the Barossa Valley or the Adelaide Hills. There's a compelling logic and focus – no excursions to McLaren Vale, Coonawarra, etc. There are now 4 wines from the Hill of Grace Vineyard: the icon itself, Hill of Roses (also shiraz), Hill of Peace (semillon) and Hill of Faith (mataro); the last 2 are only made in exceptional years. Recognition as Winery of the Year in the '21 Companion was arguably long overdue. Exports to all major markets. (JH)

ŶŶŶŶŶ **Hill of Grace 2017, Eden Valley** Grace by name, grace by nature; it's a perfectly framed, elegant snapshot of pristine fruit, site and season. Precisely ripened berry fruits are underscored with notes of Asian five-spice, sage, jasmine, licorice, mocha, blackberry pastille, charcuterie, wild flowers and cherry clafoutis. Pitch-perfect and elegant on the palate, the tannin/acid architecture tuned and sympatico with the pristine ancestor-vine fruit and a very long, silken finish that resonates with style and place. My goodness it's lovely. Screw cap. 14.5% alc. RATING 99 DRINK 2022-2065 $900 DB ♥

Julius Riesling 2021, Eden Valley Citrus and passionfruit blossom soar as you swirl the glass, and the palate achieves the seemingly impossible with the volume of turbo-charged fruit. It reaches every receptor in the mouth and there's no hint of added acidity, the balance and length faultless. Screw cap. 11.5% alc. RATING 98 DRINK 2021-2034 $47 JH ✪ ♥

Peggy's Hill Riesling 2021, Eden Valley The blossom-filled bouquet surges instantly from the glass, citrus leading, apple tucked in close behind, the palate every bit as expressive. The crisp acidity provides the framework to carry the long finish and aftertaste; world class for a song. Screw cap. 12% alc. RATING 97 DRINK 2021-2031 $25 JH ✪

Mount Edelstone 2017, Eden Valley Bright, intense blackberry and blackcurrant fruits mesh with hints of Asian spice, tar, turned earth, rosehip, sage and high-cocoa dark chocolate. Displaying a beautiful pure dark fruit flow, it's a wonderfully complex wine with ripe long-grain tannins and sprightly mineral acid drive, finishing very long and graceful with a core of cassis and spice. Will cellar magnificently. Screw cap. 14.5% alc. RATING 97 DRINK 2022-2052 $235 DB

Hill of Roses 2017, Eden Valley From vines in the Hill of Grace vineyard that are too young for inclusion in the stellar Hill of Grace. Aromas of prime blackberry and dark plum fruits mesh with hints of pressed flowers, red cherry and mulberry high notes, spice, sage, cassis and licorice. Medium bodied, composed and displaying a wonderful sense of grace and calm with detailed, red and dark fruits, powdery tannin, impeccable balance and a pitch-perfect savoury flow on the enduring finish. Vinolok. 14.5% alc. RATING 97 DRINK 2021-2040 $430 DB

🍷🍷🍷🍷🍷 **The Wheelwright Vineyard 2017, Eden Valley** Shiraz. Notes of mulberry, blueberry and redcurrant flit above the bass tones of dark and black berry fruits, cut with spice, licorice, dark chocolate, sage and a scattering of brambly, briar-like notes. Graceful red fruits and spice feature on the palate, which, like all Henschke wines, shows detail and elegance with perhaps a little more red fruit coming through, with a balance and clarity of form that impresses greatly. Vinolok 14% alc. RATING 96 DRINK 2021-2036 $140 DB

Keyneton Euphonium Barossa 2018, Barossa 65/23/9/3% shiraz/cabernet sauvignon/cabernet franc/merlot. Detail is a wonderful thing. If you stick your nose in the glass and close your eyes, perhaps tilt your head just so, you can pick out the individual components of this wine, yet they mesh together perfectly. Juicy berry and plum fruits, abundant spice, fine-grind tannin grip, a fine lacy acid line and an elegant, perfectly poised, slow fade out of pure fruit. Screw cap. 14.5% alc. RATING 95 DRINK 2022-2038 $65 DB

Apple Tree Bench 2018, Barossa A blend of 55/45% shiraz/cabernet sauvignon that melds depth and purity of fruit with famed Henschke elegance and detail, into one perfumed and enticing vinous offering. There's a perfectly ripe flow of blackberry, blackcurrant and plum fruit, with blue-fruited lift and hints of licorice, bay leaf, cardamom and chocolate. There's a velvety fruit-flow on the palate, bright acid drive and an exquisitely balanced finish that trails off in a cloud of black fruits and spice. A wonderfully composed Great Australian Blend. Screw cap. 14% alc. RATING 95 DRINK 2021-2036 $70 DB

Johann's Garden 2020, Barossa Valley A wonderfully composed 80/20% grenache/mataro blend showing fragrant fruit notes of ripe satsuma plum, blueberry and cranberry with hints of Asian spice, redcurrant jelly, gingerbread, earth and a light whiff of orange blossom. Medium bodied, with the trademark Henschke detail and clarity of fruit; everything in its place, nothing clashing, with bright, lacy acidity, gentle fine sandy tannin grip and pure easy-drinking, savoury-edged flow. Screw cap. 14.5% alc. RATING 94 DRINK 2022-2032 $63 DB

Johann's Garden 2019, Barossa Valley 78/19/3% grenache/mataro/shiraz. A beautifully fine Barossan red blend where the spicy purity of grenache steals the limelight. Aromas of ripe red and dark plum fruit, with flashes of cranberry and hints of ginger cake, red cherry clafoutis, spice and a liminal swish of something floral and pretty ... orange blossom perhaps? In the mouth the wine shows lovely balance and cadence, as the fruit rides precisely across the palate. Excellent presence and flow with light, lacy tannin support and an effortless air of drinkability. Screw cap. 14.5% alc. RATING 94 DRINK 2021-2030 $63 DB

Marble Angel Vineyard Cabernet Sauvignon 2019, Barossa Valley Bright red-purple hue, with aromas of plump, ripe summer berry fruits, baking spice, licorice and lighter wafts of eucalyptus, fruitcake and softly spoken French oak. There is a lovely flow to the 2019 Marble Angel's palate, with ripe, blackberry and dark plum fruits lifted by redcurrant high tones along with hints of cassis, dark chocolate and pencil shavings. The fruit weight is impressive, the oak use judicious and the tannins provide a fine, powdery framework for the rich fruit. Screw cap. 14.5% alc. RATING 94 DRINK 2021-2035 $75 DB

Abbotts Prayer Vineyard 2019, Adelaide Hills 58/42% merlot/cabernet sauvignon. A lifted beauty on the bouquet, resplendent in rose petal, violet, cassis, raspberry, bush mint and anise. Firm and focused on the palate, with an undercurrent of undergrowth, earth and graphite. Screw cap. 14.5% alc. RATING 94 DRINK 2021-2032 $110 JP

Tappa Pass Vineyard Selection Shiraz 2019, Barossa This edition of the Tappa Pass shows wonderful fruit weight and palate presence. Blackberry, black cherry and satsuma plum fruit combine with spice, earth and a delightful floral flicker. Cascading ripe tannin and bright mineral-like framework steers the pure fruit nicely and the finish is long and enduring. Screw cap. 14.5% alc. RATING 94 DRINK 2021-2035 $120 DB

Hentley Farm Wines

Cnr Jenke Road/Gerald Roberts Road, Seppeltsfield, SA 5355 **Region** Barossa Valley
T (08) 8562 8427 **www**.hentleyfarm.com.au **Open** 7 days 10–4 **Winemaker** Andrew
Quin **Est.** 1997 **Dozens** 20000 **Vyds** 44.7ha

Keith and Alison Hentschke purchased Hentley Farm in 1997, as a mixed farming property
with an old vineyard. Keith studied agricultural science at Roseworthy, later adding an MBA.
During the '90s he had a senior production role with Orlando, before moving on to manage
Fabal, one of Australia's largest vineyard management companies. Establishing a great vineyard
like Hentley Farm required all of his knowledge. A total of 38.2ha were planted between '99
and '05. In '04 an adjoining 6.5ha vineyard, christened Clos Otto, was acquired. Shiraz
dominates the plantings, with 32.5ha. Situated on the banks of Greenock Creek, the vineyard
has red clay loam soils overlaying shattered limestone, lightly rocked slopes and little topsoil.
Exports to the US and other major markets. (JH)

🍷🍷🍷🍷🍷 **Riesling 2021, Eden Valley** Bright straw-green; a vibrant bouquet and
palate puts lime and a wisp of passionfruit in a setting of dry, minerally acidity.
Crisp and crunchy, but ultimately fruit-driven. Screw cap. 11% alc. RATING 95
DRINK 2021–2031 $25 JH ✪

MC Riesling 2021, Barossa Valley There's a wonderful aromatic profile here; a
steely, almost Germanic peachiness among the crisp, focused lime and citrus fruits
cut with frangipani and almond blossom. Great velocity and texture with pitch-
perfect tension between fruit and acidity and a vivid, crisp, refreshing line. Screw
cap. 11% alc. RATING 95 DRINK 2021–2035 $35 DB ✪

OD Riesling 2021, Barossa Valley Pale straw with beautifully composed,
freshly squeezed lime, grapefruit and juicy white peach, along with hints of
orange blossom, almond paste and stone. Pure and just lovely to drink, the wine
sits at 21g/L RS but the bright acidity tends to rein that sugar in. The wine
finishes off-dry, clean and absolutely delicious. Screw cap. 9% alc. RATING 95
DRINK 2021–2035 $35 DB ✪

The Stray Grenache Shiraz 2020, Barossa Valley The final blend completed
with the addition of zinfandel. A bright, breezy and juicy red wine demanding to
be enjoyed without delay, ablaze with red fruits, but calm in extract and alcohol.
Minimal oak all the better. Screw cap. 14.5% alc. RATING 95 DRINK 2021–2029
$32 JH ✪

Shiraz 2020, Barossa Valley Bright, deep, crimson-purple colour. A complex
bouquet of juicy plum and blackberry fruit, licorice and dark chocolate is replayed
on the full-bodied palate, replete with full-on ripe tannins. Pretty smart entry
point. Screw cap. 14.8% alc. RATING 94 DRINK 2025–2040 $32 JH

🍷🍷🍷🍷🍷 **Zinfandel 2019, Barossa Valley** RATING 93 DRINK 2021–2026 $40 DB
Viognier 2021, Barossa Valley RATING 91 DRINK 2021–2026 $43 DB

Henty Estate

657 Hensley Park Road, Hamilton, Vic 3300 (postal) **Region** Henty
T 0458 055 860 **www**.henty-estate.com.au **Winemaker** Michael Hilsdon **Est.** 1991
Dozens 1400 **Vyds** 7ha

Peter and Glenys Dixon hastened slowly with Henty Estate. In 1991 they began the planting
of 4.5ha of shiraz, 1ha each of cabernet sauvignon and chardonnay, and 0.5ha of riesling.
In their words, 'we avoided the temptation to make wine until the vineyard was mature',
establishing the winery in 2003. Encouraged by neighbour John Thomson, they limited the
yield to 3–4t per ha on the VSP-trained, dry-grown vineyard. Michael Hilsdon and Matilda
McGoon purchased Henty Estate in 2018, their first vintage in '19. (JH)

🍷🍷🍷🍷🍷 **The Quintessential Shiraz Cabernet 2019, Barossa Valley** Vivid and
vibrant red purple in the glass with aromas of super-ripe, juicy dark plum and
blackberry fruits underscored with baking spice, jasmine, licorice and earth.
Stunning fruit purity on the palate, juicy and vital with fine, gypsum-like tannins
providing support and a plush, bright finish that carries admirably. Super drinking.
Screw cap. 14.8% alc. RATING 93 DRINK 2021–2031 $62 DB

Hentyfarm Wines

250 Wattletree Road, Holgate, NSW 2250 **Region** Henty
T 0423 029 200 **www**.hentyfarm.com.au **Open** By appt **Winemaker** Ray Nadeson,
Jono Mogg **Est.** 2009 **Dozens** 800

Dr John Gladstones names the Henty GI the coolest climate in Australia, cooler than Tasmania
and the Macedon Ranges. This is both bane and blessing, for when it's cold, it's bitterly so. The
other fact of life it has to contend with is its remoteness, lurking just inside the South Australia,
Victorian border. The rest is all good news, for this region is capable of producing riesling,
chardonnay and pinot noir of the highest quality. Seppelt's Drumborg Vineyard focuses on
riesling, pinot noir and chardonnay; Crawford River on riesling. In '09, Jonathan Mogg and
partner Belinda Low made several weekend trips in the company of (then) Best's winemaker,
Adam Wadewitz, and his partner, Nikki. They were able to buy grapes from Alastair Taylor
and the first vintage of Chardonnay was made in '09. (JH)

♀♀♀♀♀ **Pinot Meunier 2019, Henty** Fabulous to see more pinot meunier from this
part of the world. A cloudy, light ruddy-red colour with a strong pinot-led nose
of red berries, redcurrant, plums and spice with a lick of oak. This is a gently spicy
wine, the palate flowing sinewy and fine with neat tannins. Screw cap. 12.5% alc.
RATING 92 DRINK 2021-2026 $35 JP

♀♀♀♀ **Riesling 2021, Henty** RATING 89 DRINK 2021-2025 $25 JP
Pinot Gris 2021, Henty RATING 88 DRINK 2021-2024 $25 JP
The Farm Shiraz 2017, Barossa Valley RATING 88 DRINK 2021-2028 $30 JP

Heritage Wines

399 Seppeltsfield Road, Marananga, SA 5355 **Region** Barossa Valley
T (08) 8562 2880 **www**.heritagewinery.com.au **Open** Mon–Fri 10–5, w'ends 11–5
Winemaker Stephen Hoff **Est.** 1984 **Dozens** 3000 **Vyds** 8.3ha

A little-known winery that deserves a wider audience, for veteran owner and winemaker
Stephen Hoff is apt to produce some startlingly good wines. At various times the riesling
(from old Clare Valley vines), cabernet sauvignon and shiraz (now the flag-bearer) have all
excelled. The vineyard is planted to shiraz (5.5ha), cabernet sauvignon (2.5ha) and malbec
(0.3ha). Exports to the UK, Thailand, Hong Kong, Malaysia and Singapore. (JH)

♀♀♀♀♀ **E+P VP 2020, Barossa Valley** A Portuguese-style VP. Deep impenetrable red
in colour with saturated plum, black cherry and cassis fruit characters interwoven
with spice, fruitcake, brandy snaps, dates, fig pastry and a hint of malt extract.
Weighty and sweetly comforting, with fine tannin cascading through the wine
and a bright line. It's quite delicate and very approachable, even at this stage of its
evolution, but will repay extended cellaring. Cork. 18.5% alc. RATING 94 $37 DB

Hesketh Wine Company

28 The Parade, Norwood, SA 5067 **Region** South Australia
T (08) 8362 8622 **www**.heskethwinecompany.com.au **Open** Mon–Thurs 10–4, Fri–Sat
10–10, Sun 10–6 **Winemaker** James Lienert, Keeda Zilm, Andrew Hardy **Est.** 2006
Dozens 40 000

Headed by Jonathon Hesketh, this is part of WD Wines Pty Ltd, which also owns Parker
Coonawarra Estate (see separate entry), St John's Road and Vickery Wines. Jonathon spent
7 years as the global sales and marketing manager of Wirra Wirra, and 2.5 years as general
manager of Distinguished Vineyards in NZ. He is also the son of Robert Hesketh, one of the
key players in the development of many facets of the SA wine industry. Jonathon says, 'After
realising long ago that working for the man (Greg Trott) was never going to feed 2 dogs,
4 children, 2 cats, 4 chickens and an ever-so-patient wife, the family returned to Adelaide in
early '06 to establish Hesketh Wine Company'. A new cellar door opened in 2022. Exports
to all major markets. (JH)

ŸŸŸŸ♀ **Regional Selections Riesling 2021, Eden Valley** Classic aromas of freshly squeezed lime juice and grapefruit with hints of Bickford's lime cordial, Christmas lily, almond paste, kaffir lime and crushed stone. Tight and focused throughout its length, driving along with limey precision, just a touch of textural interest and a sapid, saline to its porcelain-like framework of acidity. Great value from a wonderful Eden Valley vintage. Screw cap. 11% alc. RATING 92 DRINK 2021-2031 $24 DB ✪

Regional Selections Nebbiolo Bianco 2021, Adelaide Hills A rare bird this one – nebbiolo bianco (arneis). A tempestuous grape variety that seems to feel at home in the cool climes of the Adelaide Hills. It's a crisp, slinky, medium-bodied kind of style. Flashes of citrus and crunchy pear, some light tropical tones and hints of marzipan, white flowers and stone. Textural on the palate, with a scattering of mountain herbs, bright acidity and plenty of drinking interest and enjoyment. Screw cap. 12.5% alc. RATING 91 DRINK 2021-2024 $24 DB

Fumé Blanc 2021, Mount Gambier Woo-wee! There's a lot going on here. Gooseberry, yellow plum and tropical fruits meld with notes of soft spice, clotted cream, lemon curd, vanillin, tomato leaf and dried herbs. Complex, textural and creamy with a cleansing, stark acid line. A really interesting style. One for the adventurous sauv blanc drinkers. Screw cap. 12% alc. RATING 91 DRINK 2021-2024 $34 DB

Regional Selections Fiano 2021, Clare Valley A slinky textural take on this popular grape variety. Fruit characters of nashi pear and custard apple are joined by hints of almond paste, white flowers, pine nuts and crushed stone. Some leesy clotted cream notes on the palate, which fills out nicely, showing lovely texture before that bright acidity propels the wine to a crisp and savoury exit. Great drinking. Screw cap. 11.5% alc. RATING 90 DRINK 2021-2024 $24 DB

Hewitson   ★★★★☆

66 Seppeltsfield Road, Nuriootpa, SA 5355 **Region** Adelaide
T (08) 8212 6233 www.hewitson.com.au **Open** Mon, Tues, Thurs–Sat 11–4.30
Winemaker Dean Hewitson **Viticulturist** Dean Hewitson **Est.** 1996 **Dozens** 25 000
Vyds 12ha
Dean Hewitson was a winemaker at Petaluma for 10 years, during which time he managed to do 3 vintages in France and one in Oregon, as well as undertaking his master's at the University of California, Davis. It is hardly surprising that the wines are immaculately made from a technical viewpoint. Dean sources old-vine mourvèdre from Friedrich Koch's Old Garden vineyard, planted in 1853 at Rowland Flat, as well as shiraz and grenache from 60+yo vines in Tanunda and 30+yo riesling from the Eden Valley. Grenache, carignan, cinsault, cabernet sauvignon and muscat are sourced from the Barossa, sauvignon blanc and chardonnay from the Adelaide Hills. Exports to Europe, Asia and the US. (JH)

ŸŸŸŸŸ **Old Garden Vineyard Mourvèdre 2018, Barossa Valley** Every vine is part of Friedrich Koch's bush-pruned 1853 planting, the oldest in the world. A positively juicy wine, with exotic spices woven through the collage of red fruits, large and small, and its superfine tannins. Oak also makes a contribution. Diam. 14% alc. RATING 96 DRINK 2023-2038 $88 JH

Belle Ville Rosé 2021, Barossa Valley A blend of mourvèdre and cinsault. At once complex and juicy, sweetness engendered by the fruit, not RS. High quality. Screw cap. 12.5% alc. RATING 94 DRINK 2021-2022 $26 JH ✪

Gun Metal Riesling 2021, Eden Valley This wastes no time in imparting its message of Rose's lime juice and a squeeze of Meyer lemon and of grapefruit. The acidity is there of course, but it's essentially gentle. All of which makes this ready now (and later, if you wish). Screw cap. 12.5% alc. RATING 94 DRINK 2021-2029 $28 JH ✪

ŸŸŸŸ♀ **Miss Harry Grenache Shiraz Mourvèdre 2020, Barossa Valley** RATING 93 DRINK 2021-2030 $28 DB

The Mad Hatter Shiraz 2019, Barossa Valley RATING 93 DRINK 2021-2030 $50 DB

Ned & Henry's Shiraz 2020, Barossa Valley RATING 92 DRINK 2021-2030 $30 DB

Baby Bush Mourvèdre 2020, Barossa Valley RATING 91 DRINK 2021-2030 $28 DB

LuLu Shiraz 2019, Barossa Valley RATING 91 DRINK 2021-2030 $26 DB

Hickinbotham Clarendon Vineyard ★★★★★

92 Brooks Road, Clarendon, SA 5157 **Region** McLaren Vale
T (08) 8383 7504 **www**.hickinbothamwines.com.au **Open** By appt **Winemaker** Chris Carpenter, Peter Fraser **Viticulturist** Michael Lane **Est.** 2012 **Dozens** 4800 **Vyds** 87ha
Alan Hickinbotham established the vineyard bearing his name in 1971 when he planted dry-grown cabernet sauvignon and shiraz in contoured rows on the sloping site. He was a very successful builder; this is his first venture into wine but his father, Alan Robb Hickinbotham, had a long and distinguished career, which included co-founding the oenology diploma at Roseworthy in '36. In 2012, Clarendon and the stately sandstone house on the property were purchased by Jackson Family Wines; it is run as a separate business from Yangarra Estate Vineyard, with different winemaking teams and wines. The vineyards are undergoing biodynamic conversion. Exports to all major markets. (JH)

🍷🍷🍷🍷🍷 **The Peake Cabernet Shiraz 2020, McLaren Vale** A nose tingling with a visceral energy, such is the mineral-clad spine to this wine. Rich and powerful, to be sure, as the sweetness of shiraz and its blue-fruit aspersions meander across cabernet's bones of finely tuned tannins, dried herb and cedar-oak cladding. Yet the overall effect is one of umami warmth, savoury depth and immense potential. This is an iconic wine and deservedly so. Screw cap. 14% alc. RATING 97 DRINK 2022-2038 $200 NG ❤

🍷🍷🍷🍷🍷 **Trueman Cabernet Sauvignon 2020, McLaren Vale** As always, an immensely classy and richly flavoured wine, shaped as much by a curl of juicy, precise and beautifully alloyed tannins, as it is by the sheath of blueberry, currant, sage, graphite and dried herbs. The frame of cedar oak, all class. The finish is tenacious, ferrous and densely packed with a nascent energy auguring for much more to come. Bury this. Screw cap. 14.5% alc. RATING 96 DRINK 2022-2035 $80 NG ❤

Brooks Road Shiraz 2020, McLaren Vale A sumptuous wine that manages to hold its cards of spice and flamboyant fruits close to a chest of riches. This sits on a diplomatic cushion between the Rhône-inflected contemporary styles that splay pepper, clove and blue fruits about the mouth, and a richer, more lustrous regional note. The tannins etch the cheeks and wind down the side of the tongue, keeping to the path of righteousness. Fine indeed. Screw cap. 14% alc. RATING 95 DRINK 2022-2035 $80 NG

The Nest Cabernet Franc 2020, McLaren Vale This is softer and easier, perhaps, than in the recent past. Lilac, chilli, blueberry and a sapid thrust of red fruit, vanilla-pod oak and cedar oak, applied impeccably. Beautifully done. Polished, plush and certainly not devoid of personality. Australia meets Napa. Milk-chocolate layering. Bury this and believe. Screw cap. 14.5% alc. RATING 95 DRINK 2022-2035 $80 NG

Hidden Creek ★★★★

Eukey Road, Ballandean, Qld 4382 **Region** Granite Belt
T (07) 4684 1383 **www**.hiddencreek.com.au **Open** w'ends 10-4 **Winemaker** Andy Williams **Est.** 1997 **Dozens** 1000 **Vyds** 2ha
A beautifully located vineyard and winery at 1000m on a ridge overlooking the Ballandean township and the Severn River Valley. The granite boulder–strewn hills mean that the 70ha property only provides 2ha of vineyard, in turn divided into 3 different blocks planted to shiraz and merlot. Other varieties are sourced from local growers. The business is owned

by a group of Brisbane wine enthusiasts. Queensland Winery of the Year, Queensland Wine Awards '18. (JH)

ŸŸŸŸŸ **Viognier 2021, Granite Belt** Well-crafted viognier, projecting accurate varietal hallmarks of almost ripe apricot, lemonade and ginger. Barrel fermentation lends creamy texture, toning the vibrant acidity of almost 1000m elevation. Good length and longevity. Screw cap. 13.3% alc. RATING 92 DRINK 2023-2027 $45 TS
Verdelho 2021, Granite Belt Fleshy stone fruits and tropicals contrast the crunch and freshness of almost 1000m of elevation. There's a lovely slippery feel to the palate, upholding a focus on lingering nashi pear and star fruit. Acidity is well integrated and phenolics appropriately downplayed. Screw cap. 13.1% alc. RATING 90 DRINK 2022-2022 $35 TS

Highbank ★★★★
Riddoch Highway, Coonawarra, SA 5263 **Region** Coonawarra
T (08) 8736 3311 **www.**highbank.com.au **Open** By appt **Winemaker** Dennis Vice
Est. 1985 **Dozens** 2000 **Vyds** 4ha
Mount Gambier lecturer in viticulture Dennis Vice makes small quantities of single-vineyard chardonnay, merlot, sauvignon and Coonawarra cabernet. The wines are sold through local restaurants and the cellar door, with limited Melbourne distribution. The major part of the grape production is sold. Exports to Japan. (JH)

ŸŸŸŸŸ **Single Vineyard Cabernet Sauvignon Merlot Cabernet Franc 2015, Coonawarra** The nose here is just gorgeous – it's got that earthy, cassis-laden, tobacco-leaf, cigar-box character that classically styled cabernet can do so well. Alluring. In the mouth this is brambly and expansive in its display of forest fruits and secondary spice (think along the lines of dried bay leaf, oregano, black peppercorns, jasmine tea and a dusting of cocoa), while being suggestive of fresh leather and resinous oak. Certainly drinking well now, but at 7 years of age, it is approaching its peak window of pleasure. Screw cap. 14.5% alc. RATING 94 DRINK 2022-2029 $59 EL

ŸŸŸŸŸ **Family Reserve Single Vineyard Cabernet Sauvignon 2017, Coonawarra** RATING 93 DRINK 2022-2035 $89 EL

Higher Plane ★★★★☆
98 Tom Cullity Drive, Cowaramup, WA 6284 **Region** Margaret River
T (08) 9755 9000 **www.**higherplanewines.com.au **Open** At Juniper Estate, 7 days 10–5 **Winemaker** Mark Messenger, Luc Fitzgerald **Viticulturist** Ianto Ward **Est.** 1996 **Dozens** 3000 **Vyds** 14.52ha
Higher Plane was purchased by Roger Hill and Gillian Anderson, owners of Juniper Estate, in 2006. The brand was retained with the intention of maintaining the unique and special aspects of the site in the south of Margaret River distinct from those of Wilyabrup in the north. The close-planted vineyard is sustainably farmed using organic principles. Sons Nick and Tom (with winemaking experience in the Yarra Valley) run the business. Chardonnay, sauvignon blanc and cabernet sauvignon are the major plantings, with smaller amounts of merlot, shiraz, malbec, petit verdot and verdejo. Exports to Singapore. (JH)

ŸŸŸŸŸ **Cabernet Malbec 2020, Margaret River** The '20 vintage was beautiful: ripe and graceful, glossy and polished. This wine is perfectly that; the combination of cabernet and malbec is the way of the future, surely. Both pure and structured – beautiful. There is enough licorice, ferrous, kelp, raspberry and cassis to balance the seesaw ... the fulcrum, brine. It's really good. Screw cap. 14% alc. RATING 95 DRINK 2021-2031 $28 EL ✪
Fiano 2021, Margaret River Comes through strongly with that illusion of oak on the bouquet, then a super-fresh palate with great energy and drive in a citrus skin, zest and juice theme. Screw cap. 13.5% alc. RATING 94 DRINK 2022-2026 $28 JH ✪

ŦŦŦŦŲ Malbec 2021, Margaret River RATING 92 DRINK 2021-2024 $28 JH
Reserve Cabernet Sauvignon 2016, Margaret River RATING 92
DRINK 2022-2032 $40 EL
Fumé Blanc 2021, Margaret River RATING 91 DRINK 2022-2028 $28 EL
Syrah 2020, Margaret River RATING 91 DRINK 2021-2027 $28 EL

Hill-Smith Estate ★★★☆

40 Eden Valley Road, Anagaston, SA 5353 **Region** Eden Valley
T (08) 8561 3200 **www**.hillsmithestate.com **Winemaker** Louisa Rose **Est.** 1979
Dozens 5000 **Vyds** 12ha
The Eden Valley vineyard sits at an altitude of 510m, providing a cool climate that extends
the growing season; rocky, acidic soil coupled with winter rainfall and dry summers, results in
modest crops. The Parish Vineyard in the Coal River Valley of Tasmania was purchased from
Frogmore Creek in 2012. (JH)

ŦŦŦŦŲ Chardonnay 2021, Eden Valley The excellent '21 vintage and great
winemaking have worked wonders here. Crunchy, bright and detailed white
peach and nectarine fruit with hints of soft spice, marzipan, blossom and stone.
Tangy and crisp with a nice creamy texture, complexity and a sprightly, nervy
line. Screw cap. 12.5% alc. RATING 91 DRINK 2022-2027 $24 DB

Hirsch Hill Estate ★★★☆

2088 Melba Highway, Dixons Creek, Vic 3775 **Region** Yarra Valley
T 1300 877 781 **www**.hirschhill.com **Winemaker** Rob Dolan **Viticulturist** Stephen
Sadlier **Est.** 1998 **Dozens** 1700 **Vyds** 13ha
The Hirsch family planted their vineyard to pinot noir (predominantly), cabernet sauvignon,
chardonnay, merlot and cabernet franc. (New plantings of 2.5ha of sauvignon blanc, shiraz and
viognier were lost in the Black Saturday bushfires.) The vineyard is part of a larger racehorse
stud, situated in a mini-valley at the northern end of the Yarra Valley. (JH)

ŦŦŦŦŲ Chardonnay 2020, Yarra Valley A bright green gold signals a wine of freshness
and vibrancy. Stone fruits intermingle with nicely judged gun-flint sulphides
and the generously flavoured palate is kept in focus by a line of acidity that runs
through the wine. Screw cap. 13.2% alc. RATING 92 DRINK 2022-2025 $27 PR

Hither & Yon ★★★★

17 High Street, Willunga, SA 5172 **Region** McLaren Vale
T (08) 8556 2082 **www**.hitherandyon.com.au **Open** 7 days 11–4 **Winemaker** Richard
Leask **Viticulturist** Richard Leask **Est.** 2012 **Dozens** 10 000 **Vyds** 73ha
Brothers Richard and Malcolm Leask started Hither & Yon in 2012, the Old Jarvie label added
in '16. The grapes are sourced from 78ha of family vineyards at 7 sites scattered around McLaren
Vale. Currently there are 20 varieties, with more to come. Richard manages the vineyards
while Malcolm runs the business. The historic, tiny cellar door in Willunga has a vintage feel
with a cafe and music events. The Hither & Yon labels feature the brand's ampersand, with a
different artist creating the artwork for each wine. Old Jarvie (www.oldjarvie.com.au) focuses
on blends. Exports to the US, Japan, Taiwan, Malaysia, Singapore and Canada. (JH)

ŦŦŦŦŲ Nero d'Avola 2020, McLaren Vale A very warm year, this mid-weighted
wine still manages verve, nero's dusty pliancy and easy drinkability. Raspberry, lilac,
bergamot, blue-fruit aspersions, anise and thyme. A succulent swigger, best served
cool. Screw cap. 13.5% alc. RATING 93 DRINK 2021-2023 $33 NG
Rosé 2021, McLaren Vale This is good rosé, hewn of a majestic variety, hand
picked and fermented wild. There is a ferrous chew as much as a sluice of red
berries, a smattering of dried herb, tobacco and plenty of saline freshness. The
wine expands, unwinding across its textural latticework while billowing intensity
and impressive length. Screw cap. 12.9% alc. RATING 92 DRINK 2021-2022
$26 NG

Carignan 2021, McLaren Vale Grapes like this excite me. They are torrid and equipped with natural astringency and bright acidity. The wines have tension, detail and the savoury sort of lattice between fruit and finish that is required for a second glass. This is handled orchestrally. Red fruits, thyme, rosemary and scrub. A deft approach to gentle extraction that renders character without carignan's facility for hardness. Simple. Perhaps. But a tattoo of crushable drinkability reads 'thrills with a chill'. Screw cap. 14% alc. RATING 92 DRINK 2021-2023 $33 NG

Touriga Tempranillo 2021, McLaren Vale This is delicious drinking, attesting to the future of the Vale as makers become more proficient with better-suited varieties. Touriga services the floral perfume and vibrancy, while tempranillo fills the mid palate with dark cherry, thyme, mint and sage, pushing the flavours long across a twine of dusty chamois tannins. Mid weighted of feel, immensely versatile and nicely savoury. Agglomerate. 14% alc. RATING 92 DRINK 2021-2025 $33 NG

Pinot Noir 2021, Adelaide Hills Straight-shooting Hills pinot with telltale notes of sandalwood, dark cherry, bergamot, rhubarb and sarsaparilla. These can get too sweet at times but here, handled with aplomb. Mid weighted, lithe and expansive. Quality drinking at a fair price. Agglomerate. 13.5% alc. RATING 92 DRINK 2021-2026 $36 NG

Syrah 2021, Adelaide Hills This is good. Lifted, fresh and transparent, as a veil of blueberry, sapid red cherry and nori is given flutter by white pepper-doused acidity and a clench of reductive tension, perhaps a bit too heavily handled. Nothing, though, that an aggressive decant won't resolve. Agglomerate. 14% alc. RATING 92 DRINK 2021-2026 $45 NG

Petit Blanc 2021, McLaren Vale While it is not on the label, this is straight-up muscat à petits grains, lightweight, beautifully aromatic and palpably dry, this is the sort of wine served as an apero while staring at the Mediterranean, from the Languedoc to the Côte d'Azur. Honey blossom, jasmine, musk, grape spice, dill and a rub of citrus unwind across a talcy palate. Delicious drinking. Screw cap. 12% alc. RATING 91 DRINK 2021-2023 $26 NG

Old Jarvie The Enforcer 2021, McLaren Vale A combo of crushed shiraz and mataro, together with whole-berry grenache. The juiciest wine of the everyday reds. But even then, there is something underwhelming about it, suggesting vineyard management and yields are out of kilter. The tannins, underripe. Raspberry, anise, clove and tar. Screw cap. 14.5% alc. RATING 91 DRINK 2021-2025 $30 NG

Old Jarvie The Saviour 2021, McLaren Vale 44/30/26% mazuelo/garnacha/monastrell. Attractive. Mid weighted. Red fruits, rhubarb, menthol and a savoury twine of rosemary and thyme-doused tannins. Some lower-yielding concentration would be welcome. Screw cap. 14.5% alc. RATING 91 DRINK 2021-2025 $30 NG

Cabernet Sauvignon 2020, McLaren Vale Good-drinking cabernet. Jubey, relatively soft and easygoing, without being anodyne. The extraction of 16 days seems deft in lieu of the bright attack, tannic detail and lithe, crunchy finish. Red-fruit aspersions, some garden herb and green-olive notes round out the package. Screw cap. 13.5% alc. RATING 91 DRINK 2021-2026 $29 NG

Grenache 2020, McLaren Vale Old vines, dating from the '40s. Whole-berry aromatics of kirsch, rosewater and mulled wine. A swathe of menthol-laced tannins define the mid palate, while drying the finish. There is a lightness of being. A welcome pliancy, too. Just too minty. Screw cap. 14.5% alc. RATING 91 DRINK 2021-2026 $100 NG

Tempranillo 2021, McLaren Vale An everyday quaff, suggesting that handling of this early ripening variety is getting better. Bing cherry, iodine, lilac and lavender. The tension is serviced by reduction as much as a verdant lilt and vanillin streak of gentle tannins. Screw cap. 14% alc. RATING 90 DRINK 2021-2024 $29 NG

Grenache Touriga 2021, McLaren Vale Nice drinking. Grenache's pinosity playing rhythm to touriga's aromatic and peppery vibrato. The wine just needs a juicier chord across the mid palate. Rose petal, lilac, smattered Mediterranean herb and cherry soda. Energetic and effusive of flavour. A prosaic, eminently drinkable wine destined for the fridge. Screw cap. 14.5% alc. RATING 90 DRINK 2021-2024 $33 NG

Hobbs Barossa Ranges

Artisans of the Barossa, 24 Vine Vale Road, Tanunda, SA 5352 **Region** Barossa Valley
T (08) 8563 3935 **www**.hobbsvintners.com.au **Open** 7 days 11–5 **Winemaker** Pete Schell, Chris Ringland (Consultant), Allison and Greg Hobbs **Est.** 1998 **Dozens** 1500 **Vyds** 6.2ha
Hobbs Barossa Ranges is the venture of Greg and Allison Hobbs. The estate vineyards revolve around 1ha of shiraz planted in 1905, 1ha planted in '88, 1ha planted in '97 and 1.82ha planted in 2004. The viticultural portfolio is completed with 0.6ha of semillon planted in the 1960s and an inspired 0.4ha of viognier ('88). Gregor Shiraz, an Amarone-style shiraz in full-blooded table-wine mode, and a quartet of dessert wines are produced by cane cutting, followed by further desiccation on racks. The Grenache comes from a Barossa floor vineyard; the Semillon, Viognier and White Frontignac from estate-grown grapes. The Tin Lids wines are made with 'the kids', Sean, Bridget and Jessica. Exports to the UK, the US, Germany, Singapore and Taiwan. (JH)

🍷🍷🍷🍷🍷 **1905 Shiraz 2019, Eden Valley** The Hobbs wines have always been big burly brawlers. Solid slabs of incredibly concentrated fruit with voluptuous textures. Anachronistic? Maybe. Impressive for the heft and purity? Always! Pure, heady satsuma plum, cassis and blueberry pie characters mesh with brown spice, fig jam, espresso, dark chocolate, violets and cedar. The cedary notes ratchet up on the palate which shows a rolling swell of black fruits and spice, backed by fine, powdery tannins and an unctuous mouthfeel. Strap in! Cork. 15.2% alc. RATING 95 DRINK 2021-2032 $170 DB
Gregor Shiraz 2019, Eden Valley Produced Amarone-style. Phew-wee! It's a big, concentrated wine. There is a little bit of alcohol peeking through, but it's rich, black-fruited and impressive in both fruit purity and texture. Full-blooded, heady drinking. Screw cap. 15.5% alc. RATING 94 DRINK 2021-2030 $150 DB

🍷🍷🍷🍷🍷 **Tango Shiraz Viognier 2019, Eden Valley** RATING 92 DRINK 2021-2020 $120 DB
Behr Creek 2020, Eden Valley RATING 90 DRINK 2021-2030 $50 DB
Tin Lids Aria Secca Shiraz 2020, Eden Valley RATING 90 DRINK 2021-2030 $50 DB

Hoddles Creek Estate

505 Gembrook Road, Hoddles Creek, Vic 3139 **Region** Yarra Valley
T (03) 5967 4692 **www**.hoddlescreekestate.com.au **Open** By appt **Winemaker** Franco D'Anna, Chris Bendle **Viticulturist** Franco D'Anna **Est.** 1997 **Dozens** 30 000 **Vyds** 33.3ha
The D'Anna family established their vineyard on a property that had been in the family since 1960. The vines are hand pruned and hand harvested. A 300t, split-level winery was built in 2003. Son Franco is the viticulturist and inspired winemaker; he graduated to chief wine buyer by the time he was 21. He completed a bachelor of commerce before studying viticulture at CSU. A vintage at Coldstream Hills, then 2 years' vintage experience with Peter Dredge at Witchmount and, with Mario Marson (ex-Mount Mary) as mentor in '03, has put an old head on young shoulders. The Wickhams Road label uses grapes from an estate vineyard in Gippsland as well as purchased grapes from the Yarra Valley and Mornington Peninsula. Exports to the UK, Denmark, Brazil, Dubai and Japan. (JH)

🍷🍷🍷🍷🍷 **1er Chardonnay 2020, Yarra Valley** Draws you in within a split second of the first sniff of the bouquet; wild ferment in French oak and lees contact create a wine that is very complex, on the edge of funk, but not letting it dominate the white peach, melon and grapefruit flavours. Gentle acidity carrys the very long finish and lingering aftertaste. Screw cap. 13.2% alc. RATING 97 DRINK 2022-2032 $55 JH ✪

Wickhams Road Chardonnay 2021, Yarra Valley It sidles up to you, and it's only on the second taste that its sheer intensity and class drops its guard. The price of the wine should be doubled, to reflect this perfect rendition of the varietal array of pink grapefruit and blood orange. There's great mouthfeel and precise balance. Screw cap. 13% alc. RATING 96 DRINK 2022-2036 $19 JH ✪

DML Pinot Noir 2020, Yarra Valley More bright red-hued than its 1er Pinot sibling, a sign of a wine built around the beautifully delineated fruit aromas and flavours. Cherry, strawberry and plum all in the game, spontaneously giving it pleasure; long and refined. Screw cap. 13% alc. RATING 96 DRINK 2022-2032 $60 JH ✪

Wickhams Road Pinot Noir 2021, Gippsland The ravishingly fragrant bouquet of flowers and red and purple fruits, morphing into fruits of the forest. Spice and dried berries share 50% of the palate, rose petals et al. the other half. The fruit attack on the tip of the tongue is of surgical precision. Screw cap. 13.5% alc. RATING 95 DRINK 2022-2031 $20 JH ✪

Wickhams Road Pinot Noir 2021, Yarra Valley Like its siblings, a light but brilliantly clear colour. A highly perfumed bouquet of strawberries leads into a palate with the precision and clarity of a Dutch painter 300 or so years ago. There's no other producer in the Yarra Valley to even come close to the value offered by this wine. Screw cap. 13% alc. RATING 95 DRINK 2022-2036 $20 JH ✪

Skins Pinot Gris 2021, Yarra Valley A bright, medium-deep amber terracotta. Complex with pear skin, red currants, savoury fennel-seed notes and a little Turkish delight. Equally good on the palate, this delicious non-binary wine is textured and saline and the digestif-like grippy tannins are begging for a plate of charcuterie to accompany it. 500ml bottle. Screw cap. 12.5% alc. RATING 95 DRINK 2021-2024 $25 PR ✪

Pinot Noir 2020, Yarra Valley Don't be alarmed by the pale ruby colour – this is not at all wimpy. Instead, it's a refined and lighter-framed rendition with layers of flavour. It has an almost whole-bunch character, but winemaker Franco d'Anna destems the fruit. Still, expect flavours of earthy rhubarb and grated raw beetroot with a sappy freshness. Tangy, spritely acidity and fine tannins add to the pleasure of drinking. Screw cap. 13.2% alc. RATING 95 DRINK 2023-2030 $25 JF ✪

Pinot Gris 2020, Yarra Valley A pale copper hue, with wafts of almond meal, pears in puff pastry and poached quinces lightly spiced with ginger. The palate is surprisingly delicate and laden with citrus. Refreshing, lively and the acidity more pronounced than usual. It has texture, with some phenolic grip and decent length, too. An excellent drink. Screw cap. 12% alc. RATING 95 DRINK 2021-2024 $22 JF ✪

1er Pinot Noir 2020, Yarra Valley Crystal clear. The scented, gently spicy bouquet leads with cherries and forest fruits, plum tucked in behind, progressively gathering impact with repeated visits to the glass. The palate likewise unfolds its savoury, spicy array of small forest-floor wild strawberry fruits. Screw cap. 13.2% alc. RATING 95 DRINK 2022-2030 $60 JH

1er Pinot Noir 2019, Yarra Valley At first, this seems richly fruited with soused cherries and plums. Be patient. The savoury elements kick in and take over the lead: smoky reduction, Angostura bitters, charry oak and textural, tooth-coating tannins, yet there's detail within. Plenty of layers to this, making it a complex and compelling wine. Screw cap. 13.2% alc. RATING 95 DRINK 2021-2032 $55 JF

Syberia Chardonnay 2019, Yarra Valley A superfine Yarra Valley chardonnay. Finesse, purity and the certainty of a long and prosperous life in bottle are its calling cards. Screw cap. 12.8% alc. RATING 95 DRINK 2022-2034 $60 JH

Chardonnay 2020, Yarra Valley Another terrific well-priced chardy that consistently punches above its weight. A balance of flavours from stone fruit and lemon zest to savoury spices and neat phenolics. It has texture, even a plumpness, but the wine is well contained, thanks to mouth-watering acidity. It's moreish and lingers long. Smart now, and will unfurl in the next few years. Screw cap. 13.2% alc. RATING 94 DRINK 2022-2029 $22 JF ◐

Hollick Estates ★★★★☆

11 Racecourse Road, Penola, SA 5277 **Region** Coonawarra
T (08) 8737 2318 **www.**hollick.com **Open** 7 days 11–5, public holidays 11–4
Winemaker Trent Nankivell **Est.** 1983 **Dozens** 40000 **Vyds** 87ha
Established in 1983 by the Hollick family, Hollick Estates' vineyard, winery, restaurant and cellar door overlooks Coonawarra. The estate-grown wines come from 3 vineyards, 2 in Coonawarra and 1 in nearby Wrattonbully, reflecting the characteristics of each site. The classic Coonawarra varieties of cabernet sauvignon, shiraz and chardonnay are made, along with The Nectar (botrytis riesling), barbera and tempranillo. Exports to most major markets. (JH)

🍷🍷🍷🍷🍷 **Ravenswood Cabernet Sauvignon 2019, Coonawarra** Cassis, blackberries and mint fondant on the nose. In the mouth the wine is structured and concentrated, the tannins providing a barrier to pleasure at this stage. However, as it is still 18 months from release, presumably this will sort itself out in time. The fruit in this glass is such a wonderful thing: it is vibrant, crackling with life and energy, and ready for a long life in front of it. Screw cap. 14.9% alc. RATING 95 DRINK 2023-2043 $89 EL

🍷🍷🍷🍷🍷 **Old Vines Cabernet Sauvignon 2019, Coonawarra** RATING 92 DRINK 2022-2032 $36 EL
Wilgha Shiraz 2019, Coonawarra RATING 92 DRINK 2022-2032 $69 EL
Shiraz 2020, Coonawarra RATING 91 DRINK 2021-2027 $27 EL

Holm Oak ★★★★

11 West Bay Road, Rowella, Tas 7270 **Region** Northern Tasmania
T (03) 6394 7577 **www.**holmoakvineyards.com.au **Open** Thurs–Sun 11–5
Winemaker Rebecca Duffy **Viticulturist** Tim Duffy **Est.** 1983 **Dozens** 15000
Vyds 15ha
Holm Oak takes its name from its grove of oak trees, planted around the beginning of the 20th century and originally intended for the making of tennis racquets. A boutique family affair, winemaker Rebecca Duffy has extensive winemaking experience in Australia and California; and husband Tim, a viticultural agronomist, manages the vineyard (pinot noir, pinot gris, cabernet sauvignon, chardonnay, riesling and small amounts of merlot, arneis, shiraz and cabernet franc). Cellar door, winery, family home (and a pet pig named Pinot) all co-exist on the vineyard site. Exports to the UK, the US and Japan. (JH)

🍷🍷🍷🍷🍷 **Pinot Noir 2020, Tasmania** Wonderful, crystal-clear crimson; the floral, red-fruit assemblage on the bouquet moves seamlessly into a complex palate in terms of the forest strawberry and cherry fruit, but a pure and tightly focused palate flowing effortlessly through to a long, fresh finish and lingering aftertaste. Screw cap. 13% alc. RATING 95 DRINK 2023-2033 $35 JH ◐

🍷🍷🍷🍷 **Arneis 2021, Tasmania** RATING 89 DRINK 2022-2022 $28 TS
The Perfectionist Shiraz Pinot Noir 2021, Tasmania RATING 89 DRINK 2024-2026 $45 TS
Sparkling Rosé NV, Tasmania RATING 88 $40 TS
The Protégé Pinot Noir 2021, Tasmania RATING 88 DRINK 2021-2023 $25 TS
Cabernet Franc 2021, Tasmania RATING 88 DRINK 2027-2031 $35 TS
Chardonnay 2020, Tasmania RATING 88 DRINK 2025-2028 $35 TS

Home Hill

38 Nairn Road, Ranelagh, Tas 7109 **Region** Southern Tasmania
T (03) 6264 1200 **www.**homehillwines.com.au **Open** 7 days 10–5 **Winemaker** Catalina
Collado **Viticulturist** Sean Bennett **Est.** 1993 **Dozens** 3500 **Vyds** 10.2ha
Terry and Rosemary Bennett planted their first 0.5ha of vines in 1994 on gentle slopes in the
beautiful Huon Valley. The plantings have gradually been increased to 10.2ha, including pinot
noir, chardonnay, pinot gris and sylvaner. Home Hill has had great success with its exemplary
pinot noirs, consistent multi-trophy and gold medal winners in the ultra-competitive
Tasmanian Wine Show. Impressive enough but pales into insignificance in the wake of
winning the Jimmy Watson Trophy at the Melbourne Wine Awards '15. (JH)

🍷🍷🍷🍷🍷 Kelly's Reserve Pinot Noir 2020, Tasmania A worthy leader of Home Hill's
impressive trilogy of '20 pinots, this is a wine that exemplifies a judicious and
even hand in both the vines and the wines. Wonderful and accurate red-fruit
purity sings with the integrity and drive of mature vines. It's impeccably and
gently supported by the fragrance of a touch of whole bunches and just the right
harmonising presence of oak. Benchmark Huon. Screw cap. 13.6% alc. RATING 95
DRINK 2023–2030 $79 TS

🍷🍷🍷🍷🍷 Estate Pinot Noir 2020, Tasmania RATING 93 DRINK 2023–2030 $50 TS

HOOSEGG

45 Caldwell Lane, Orange NSW 2800 **Region** Orange
T 0448 983 033 **www.**hoosegg.com **Open** By appt **Winemaker** Philip Shaw
Viticulturist Philip Shaw **Est.** 2016
This seems certain to be the last oenological resting place of Philip Shaw, the genius who
made the Rosemount Estate empire possible. It was none of his fault that increasing its
production from 700 000 dozen bottles in '00 to more than 2 million dozen in '02 was not
even close to being sustainable, nor that (figuratively) the sky should fall down on its new
owner (Southcorp) and Rosemount's brand value. Shaw was several jumps in front of the field;
he had put in train the purchase of the Koomooloo Vineyard, and the following year excised
47ha from Koomooloo for Philip Shaw Wines. In '15 he passed ownership of Philip Shaw
Wines to his sons and built a 50t winery for his business HOOSEGG. (JH)

🍷🍷🍷🍷🍷 Double Happy Cabernet Sauvignon 2018, Orange By far the best of the
suite. Statuesque, yet light on its feet. A mid-weighted wine that feigns power,
unafraid to reveal the greenery of cabernet's DNA amid the foil of blackcurrant,
olive, mocha and bay leaf, sage and bouquet garni notes. Long, refined and
exciting. Screw cap. 13.5% alc. RATING 95 DRINK 2021–2032 $140 NG
Everything is Going According to Plan Chardonnay 2018, Orange A fine
nose, alluding to tension and refinement: white peach, cashew and nougatine.
The oak, impeccably slotted. The tail, long, vibrant and detailed, inflected with
porcini, orange blossom and almond meal. Lovely drinking. Screw cap. 13.1% alc.
RATING 94 DRINK 2021–2028 $58 NG
Mountain Dragon Merlot 2018, Orange Make no mistake, the qualitative
barometer is set to aspirational. The pricing and monikers, reflective. Very good
merlot. Plummy, with a subtle underbelly of tomato leaf and scattered garden
herb. The mocha-cedar oak, a welcome addendum. A smooth operator with a
salubrious sheen. Cork. 13.4% alc. RATING 94 DRINK 2021–2028 $118 NG
Seven Heaven Chardonnay 2018, Orange Stone-fruit allusions, creamed
cashew and almond-powder lees notes. Toasted hazelnuts and truffle. A great
aromatic spectrum. The finish, slippery and classy all the same. Screw cap.
12.5% alc. RATING 94 DRINK 2021–2027 $118 NG

🍷🍷🍷🍷🍷 Self Made-Up Man Cabernet Shiraz Merlot Cabernet Franc 2018,
Orange RATING 93 DRINK 2021–2028 $58 NG
Jade Moon Cabernet Franc 2018, Orange RATING 93 DRINK 2021–2027
$118 NG
Magic Monkey Shiraz 2018, Orange RATING 92 DRINK 2021–2028 $118 NG

Houghton

4070 Caves Road, Wilyabrup, WA 6280 **Region** Swan Valley
T (08) 9755 6042 **www**.houghton-wines.com.au **Open** 7 days 11–5
Winemaker Courtney Treacher **Viticulturist** Stephen Kirby **Est.** 1836 **Dozens** 43 000
Houghton's reputation was once largely dependent on its (then) White Burgundy. Its portfolio now changed to a kaleidoscopic range of high-quality wines from the Margaret River, Frankland River, Great Southern and Pemberton regions to the fore. The Jack Mann and Gladstones red wines stand at the forefront, but to borrow a saying of the late Jack Mann, 'There are no bad wines here'. In Nov '19 the Houghton property was sold to the Yukich family, who had acquired part of the property in '90 and established Oakover Wines. The reunited vineyard was relaunched as Nikola Estate (see separate entry), in honour of Nikola Yukich, who emigrated from Croatia and planted vines in the Swan Valley over 90 years ago. The Houghton brand was retained by Accolade. Exports to the UK and Asia. (JH)

ΨΨΨΨΨ **Jack Mann Single Vineyard Cabernet Sauvignon 2019, Frankland River**
This is pure cabernet sauvignon, from a deep well of blackcurrant and black olive fruit, and tannins to make sure the wine outlives you. Screw cap. 14% alc.
RATING 97 DRINK 2024–2064 $175 JH

ΨΨΨΨΨ **C.W. Ferguson Cabernet Malbec 2019, Frankland River** Bright crimson rim; a brooding yet luscious blend filled with blackcurrant and plum fruit, and leaving just enough room in the mouth for tannins to make a furtive dash for it. The aftertaste is particularly appealing, as is the length of that aftertaste. Screw cap. 14% alc. RATING 96 DRINK 2022–2039 $78 JH
Gladstones Cabernet Sauvignon 2019, Margaret River Seemingly picked earlier than most, the colour not deep, à la the Englishman's claret of bygone days. On the plus side, it has excellent balance, no sign of green fruit, and can be enjoyed now as much as in 5 years. Screw cap. 13.5% alc. RATING 95 DRINK 2022–2030 $100 JH
Wisdom Pinot Noir 2020, Pemberton This is routinely delicious, never more so than in this ripe vintage. Supple red cherries are overlaid by the classic Pemberton olive-tapenade character, all of it wrapped in a sheath of fine, malleable, almost chewy tannins. This has curve, charm and life. A lovely wine. Screw cap. 13.5% alc. RATING 94 DRINK 2022–2029 $45 EL

House of Arras

Bay of Fires, 40 Baxters Road, Pipers River, Tas 7252 **Region** Northern Tasmania
T (03) 6362 7622 **www**.houseofarras.com.au **Open** Thurs–Mon 10–5 by appt
Winemaker Ed Carr **Est.** 1995
The rise and rise of the fortunes of the House of Arras has been due to 2 things: the exceptional skills of winemaker Ed Carr, and its access to high-quality Tasmanian chardonnay and pinot noir. While there have been distinguished sparkling wines made in Tasmania for many years, none has so consistently scaled the heights as that of Arras. The complexity, texture and structure of the wines are akin to that of Bollinger RD and Krug; the connection stems from the 7–15+ years the wines spend on lees prior to disgorgement. Exports to the UK, the US and Asia. (JH)

ΨΨΨΨΨ **EJ Carr Late Disgorged 2006, Tasmania** 67/33% chardonnay/pinot noir. Disgorged March '21 after 14 years on lees; 2.6g/L dosage. The glories of long lees age are expounded to full effect here in a panorama of texture and secondary and tertiary complexity. Notes of glacé pear and grilled pineapple, backed with the fig and spice of pinot noir. All the toasty, spicy, honeyed and dried-fruit personality expected of EJ Carr is here in full measure, upheld with lemon zest energy and tension. Dynamic Tasmanian acidity and pinpoint phenolic grip are perfectly played, and the lightest touch of dosage is all it calls for. With monumental length and grand integrity, it has another glorious decade before it yet. Cork. 12.5% alc. RATING 96 $256 TS

EJ Carr Late Disgorged 2005, **Tasmania** Museum re-release en magnum, on lees for 15 years; disgorged April '21. EJ Carr 2005 has held its form resolutely in magnum since its April '21 release in bottle, a mythical conjunction between primary, secondary and tertiary that centres it in a delightful place in its breathtaking trajectory. White fruits of all kinds are preserved amid glorious layers of patisserie, spice and the beginnings of sweet pipe smoke. The dry phenolic grip of the house assumes a rightful place amid its rich folds of complexity, upholding tension on a grand finish that promises confidence for many years yet. Cork. 12.5% alc. RATING 96 $400 TS

Grand Vintage 2013, **Tasmania** 62/38% chardonnay/pinot noir. 2.7g/L dosage. This cuvée leads out with the crunch of Tasmanian chardonnay that characterises Arras. Seven years on lees, in concert with a touch of new French oak, has amassed considerable depth of roast almonds, toast, vanilla custard and biscuity personality, with a hint of sautéed mushrooms. Wonderful drive of lemon, grapefruit, dried pear and a touch of ginger project through a finish of magnificent line and length. Dried-extract phenolic grip is prominent, yet well matched to its fruit presence and secondary allure, promising grand endurance. Cork. 12.5% alc. RATING 95 $119 TS

Grand Vintage 2008, **Tasmania** Museum re-release en magnum. Aged 12 years on lees; 5.4g/L dosage. A bright, radiant straw hue at 13 years of age proclaims the energy and endurance of this great season in Tasmania, and in magnum it is still embarking on its extraordinary life. Grapefruit, Beurre Bosc pear and lemon define a crunchy style of generous yet very fine phenolic grip and well-toned acidity. All the layers of toasty, biscuity, spicy complexity that we love of Arras are here in full measure, yet with a dynamic vibrancy that demands many more years of patience yet. Cork. 12.5% alc. RATING 95 $250 TS

ＴＴＴＴＴ Blanc de Blancs 2013, **Tasmania** RATING 93 $130 TS
A by Arras Premium Cuvée Rosé NV, **Tasmania** RATING 90 $32 TS

House of Cards   ★★★★☆

17/3220 Caves Road, Yallingup, WA 6282 **Region** Margaret River
T (08) 9755 2583 **www**.houseofcardswine.com.au **Open** 7 days 10–5 **Winemaker** Travis Wray **Viticulturist** Travis Wray **Est.** 2011 **Dozens** 5000 **Vyds** 12ha
House of Cards is owned and operated by Elizabeth and Travis Wray; Travis managing the vineyard and making the wines, Elizabeth managing sales and marketing. The name of the winery is a reflection of the gamble that all viticulturists and winemakers face every vintage: 'You have to play the hand you are dealt by Mother Nature'. They only use certified organic estate-grown grapes, open-top fermentation, hand plunging and manual basket pressing. It's certainly doing it the hard way, but it must seem all worthwhile when they produce wines of such quality. (JH)

ＴＴＴＴＴ Ace of Spades 2020, **Margaret River** 90/10% cabernet/malbec. Cassis, blackberry bush (the whole thing: berries, leaves and bramble), tobacco leaf, Szechuan peppercorns, red and green apples, licorice and pomegranate. In the mouth the wine is intense and primary, giving away its '20 origins (a stellar vintage: short, ripe and responsible for largely sensational wines). Jasmine tea tannins shape the affair and guide it through the finish. While everything is in its place already, it will certainly benefit from another year in its bottle, allowing it to settle and really start to stride. Screw cap. 14.2% alc. RATING 94 DRINK 2021–2036 $65 EL

ＴＴＴＴＴ Three Card Monte Single Vineyard Sauvignon Blanc 2021, **Margaret River** RATING 93 DRINK 2022–2025 $28 EL
Black Jack Single Vineyard Malbec 2020, **Margaret River** RATING 93 DRINK 2021–2028 $48 EL
Queen of Diamonds Blanc de Blancs 2015, **Margaret River** RATING 92 $52 EL
The Royals Single Vineyard Chardonnay 2021, **Margaret River** RATING 90 DRINK 2022–2028 $52 EL

Howard Park

Miamup Road, Cowaramup, WA 6284 **Region** Margaret River
T (08) 9756 5200 **www**.burchfamilywines.com.au **Open** 7 days 10–5 **Winemaker** Nic
Bowen, Mark Bailey **Viticulturist** David Botting, Steve Kirby **Est.** 1986 **Vyds** 183ha
Over the last 30 years, the Burch family has slowly acquired vineyards in Margaret River and
Great Southern. The Margaret River vineyards range from Leston in Wilyabrup to Allingham
in southern Karridale; Great Southern includes Mount Barrow and Abercrombie, with
Houghton cabernet clones, planted in 1975, all in Mount Barker. At the top of the portfolio
are the Howard Park Abercrombie Cabernet Sauvignon and the Allingham Chardonnay,
followed by the rieslings, chardonnay and sauvignon blanc; next come pairs of shiraz and
cabernet sauvignon under the Leston and Scotsdale labels. The Miamup and the Flint Rock
regional ranges were established in 2012. The feng shui–designed cellar door is a must-see. A
founding member of Australian First Families of Wines. Exports to all major markets. (JH)

🍷🍷🍷🍷🍷 **Allingham Chardonnay 2020, Margaret River** Creamy, saline, nutty … this
is a powerful, yet effortless rendition of Allingham, with spooling briny acidity and
enduring stone fruit through the finish. A lovely wine. Perhaps the best Allingham
yet. Screw cap. 13% alc. RATING 96 DRINK 2022-2037 $89 EL
Sauvignon Blanc 2021, Western Australia Complex, concentrated and
utterly delicious. This is balanced and poised and so wonderful. The acidity is
plump and juicy – like ripe lemons, or lime flesh. All things in place, backed
by texture that can only come from a bit of barrel ferment, drawing out
over a long finish. My word – what a wine. Screw cap. 12.5% alc. RATING 95
DRINK 2021-2031 $31 EL ✪
Chardonnay 2020, Margaret River A complete-package chardonnay: rich
and opulent, restrained by briny acidity and structured by toasty oak. All things
in balance with great length of flavour. '20 was such a glorious vintage for
chardonnay (and others) in the area. Effortless grace. Screw cap. 13% alc.
RATING 95 DRINK 2021-2031 $58 EL
Howard Park Leston Cabernet Sauvignon 2018, Margaret River
Raspberry, red dirt, pomegranate, gravel, purple flowers, graphite, salted plum,
red licorice and ferrous notes, too. This is very elegant. The fruit has wonderful
intensity and concentration. It remains a very restrained, medium-bodied style of
cabernet – this wine rarely pushes the richter for volume – and through the lens
of the ripe and powerful '18 vintage, it has a boost of the very best kind. Screw
cap. 14.5% alc. RATING 95 DRINK 2021-2036 $50 EL
Museum Release Riesling 2013, Great Southern At 8 years of age, this
wine is re-released to the public, and it shows precisely why patience is a virtue.
Beeswax and honeycomb aromatics swirl in and out of the citrus blossom, pink
grapefruit, apple skins and crushed chalk. This is floral, long and layered, with
a maintained core of austere acid that punches through the diaphanous fruit
and spice. A graceful wine of poise and line. Screw cap. 12% alc. RATING 95
DRINK 2021-2036 $41 EL
Museum Release Riesling 2014, Mount Barker My note on release
(Sep '14) was 'The potent bouquet borders on spicy, with flowers behind; the
palate has excellent structure and depth, the flavours centred on a rich vein of
citrus, bolstered by firm acidity.' Balanced in its youth, and retains that today.
Screw cap. 12% alc. RATING 94 DRINK 2021-2029 $41 JH

🍷🍷🍷🍷 **Howard Park Leston Cabernet Sauvignon 2019, Margaret River**
RATING 93 DRINK 2022-2036 $50 EL
Howard Park Scotsdale Cabernet Sauvignon 2019, Great Southern
RATING 93 DRINK 2022-2032 $50 EL
Howard Park Leston Shiraz 2018, Margaret River RATING 93
DRINK 2021-2028 $50 EL
Jeté Grand Vintage 2017, Mount Barker RATING 92 $54 EL
Howard Park Leston Shiraz 2019, Margaret River RATING 92
DRINK 2021-2028 $50 EL

Arboretum Chardonnay 2019, Margaret River RATING 92
DRINK 2021-2028 $35 EL
Howard Park Scotsdale Cabernet Sauvignon 2018, Great Southern
RATING 92 DRINK 2021-2031 $50 EL
Howard Park Miamup Sauvignon Blanc Semillon 2021, Margaret River
RATING 91 DRINK 2022-2024 $28 EL
Flint Rock Chardonnay 2020, Great Southern RATING 91
DRINK 2021-2027 $28 EL
Arboretum Grenache Shiraz 2020, Swan Valley Great Southern
RATING 91 DRINK 2021-2027 $30 EL
Jeté Brut NV, Great Southern RATING 90 $38 JH
Flint Rock Riesling 2021, Great Southern RATING 90 DRINK 2022-2028
$28 EL
Howard Park Miamup Chardonnay 2021, Margaret River RATING 90
DRINK 2022-2027 $29 EL
Arboretum Pinot Gris 2020, Mount Barker RATING 90 DRINK 2022-2024
$30 EL

Howard Vineyard ★★★★

53 Bald Hills Road, Nairne, SA 5252 **Region** Adelaide Hills
T (08) 8188 0203 **www.**howardvineyard.com **Open** 7 days by appt **Winemaker** Tom
Northcott **Viticulturist** Tom Northcott **Est.** 1998 **Dozens** 6000 **Vyds** 70ha
Howard Vineyard is a family-owned Adelaide Hills winery set among towering gum trees,
and terraced lawns. Pinot noir, chardonnay, pinot gris and sauvignon blanc are sourced from
the 470m altitude Schoenthal 'Beautiful Valley' Vineyard, near Lobethal; Howard's Nairne
Vineyard in the warmer Mount Barker district is home to shiraz, cabernet sauvignon and
cabernet franc. All the wines are estate-grown. Winemaker Tom Northcott has a bachelor
degree in viticulture and oenology from Adelaide University, and has worked vintages in the
South of France, Barossa Valley, Western Australia and Tasmania. (JH)

ioioio **Pinot Noir 2021, Adelaide Hills** Beautifully composed. Exhibits all of the
qualities we love in Hills pinot, notably the cool elegance it achieves almost
effortlessly. It might seem quite delicate, with florals and red fruits interspersed
with woody spices and herbs, but there is an underlying solid presence of fine-
grained tannins steering and contributing to a harmonious whole. Screw cap.
13% alc. RATING 92 DRINK 2021-2030 $40 JP
Pinot Noir 2020, Adelaide Hills A most impressive youngster in terms of
flavour development, structure, texture and just general deliciousness. Launches
into a highly perfumed scent of strawberry, sour cherry, well-measured spice and a
touch of sweet florals. Dances across the tongue, lively and free-flowing, with flecks
of undergrowth. Finishes long. Screw cap. 12% alc. RATING 92 DRINK 2021-2025
$35 JP
Cabernet Franc Rosé 2021, Adelaide Hills Of the 2 rosés released by
Howard Vineyard, this is the serious one, the drier and more statuesque. Works a
savoury line, too, in between the soft aromatics, the cherry nougat flavours and the
developing textural appeal. Juicy and super-tasty. Screw cap. 13% alc. RATING 91
DRINK 2021-2025 $35 JP
Rosé 2021, Adelaide Hills Cabernet Sauvignon/merlot/cabernet franc. A tasty,
pale rosé for the price, brimming with cherries, strawberries and a dusting of light
spice. Works the mouth with juicy acidity and a pleasurable amount of texture.
Screw cap. 12.5% alc. RATING 90 DRINK 2021-2024 $20 JP ✪

ioio **Blanc de Blanc 2021, Adelaide Hills** RATING 89 $35 JP
Shiraz Cabernet 2021, Adelaide Hills RATING 89 DRINK 2021-2026 $35 JP
Pinot Gris 2021, Adelaide Hills RATING 89 DRINK 2021-2024 $25 JP
Sangiovese 2021, Adelaide Hills RATING 89 DRINK 2021-2023 $35 JP
Amos Chardonnay 2020, Adelaide Hills RATING 89 DRINK 2021-2027
$50 JP

Pinot Noir Chardonnay 2021, Adelaide Hills RATING 88 $30 JP
Block Q Sauvignon Blanc 2021, Adelaide Hills RATING 88
DRINK 2021-2023 $25 JP

Hugh Hamilton Wines ★★★★★

94 McMurtrie Road, McLaren Vale, SA 5171 **Region** McLaren Vale
T (08) 8323 8689 **www.hughhamiltonwines.com.au Open** 7 days 11–5 **Winemaker** Nic
Bourke **Est.** 1991 **Dozens** 18 500 **Vyds** 21.4ha
In 2014, fifth-generation family member Hugh Hamilton handed over the reins to daughter
Mary. She developed the irreverent black sheep packaging. The business embraces both
mainstream and alternative varieties, its 85+yo shiraz and 65+yo cabernet sauvignon at its
Blewitt Springs vineyard providing the ability to develop the Black label. There have been
changes: in the way the vines are trellised, picking and fermenting in small open fermenters,
using gravity for wine movements and maturation in high-quality French oak. The
Tonnellerie trio of wines, made from the same shiraz fruit, are raised in oak from different
French cooperages: Ermitage, Vicard and François Frères. The cellar door is lined with
the original jarrah from Vat 15 of the historic Hamilton's Ewell winery, the largest wooden
vat ever built in the Southern Hemisphere. Exports to the UK, the US, Canada, Denmark,
Germany, Switzerland, Finland, South Korea, Singapore and Japan. (JH)

ΨΨΨΨΨ **Tonnellerie Ermitage Single Barrel Cellar Vineyard Shiraz 2019,
McLaren Vale** Possibly the best suited oak to the wine, at least if one is to
winnow down to a single cooperage for this particular vintage. Better to use
portions of all 3, perhaps. Smoked baby-back ribs, charcuterie and violet. Hoisin
and Asian spice, too. The oak, embedded amid the extract, almost adding to the
poise and force of the material, while corralling it. Despite the alcohol, this feels
fresh, coiled and uncannily restrained, if not a bit monochromatic. Good drinking.
Screw cap. 14.8% alc. RATING 95 DRINK 2021-2028 $50 NG
Tonnellerie Vicard Shiraz 2019, McLaren Vale This is the intermediary.
Far better suited than François Frères to hot-climate shiraz's sweet forcefulness,
but arguably less suited than the Ermitage oak's promotion of smokiness, spiced
exotica and tension. The sort of happy intermediary, servicing a greater herbal and
slightly sweeter spectrum, resplendent with finer-boned oak tannins that I prefer.
Acidity, shrill. At least now. If the wine were a meld of this and Ermitage, it would
score higher. Screw cap. 14.8% alc. RATING 95 DRINK 2021-2028 $50 NG
Black Blood III Shiraz 2020, McLaren Vale The finest of this premium
triumvirate. The same conventional approach applied. The French oak 'neutral',
but palpable across milk-chocolate seams. These tie jubilant florals, red- and blue-
fruited allusions, anise and again, some menthol accents together. Altogether more
energetic and engaging. Despite its heavy weight, there is a nice tactile mouthfeel
and a sense – only just – of greater lightness. Screw cap. 14.8% alc. RATING 94
DRINK 2021-2030 $79 NG

ΨΨΨΨΦ **The Mongrel Sangiovese 2021, McLaren Vale** RATING 93
DRINK 2021-2024 $27 NG ✪
Black Blood II Shiraz 2020, McLaren Vale RATING 93 DRINK 2021-2032
$79 NG
Tonnellerie Francois Freres Shiraz 2019, McLaren Vale RATING 93
DRINK 2021-2026 $50 NG
Jekyll & Hyde Shiraz Viognier 2019, McLaren Vale RATING 93
DRINK 2021-2026 $33 NG
The Nimble King Cabernet Sauvignon 2020, McLaren Vale RATING 92
DRINK 2021-2028 $50 NG
Three Bags Full GSM 2020, McLaren Vale RATING 92 DRINK 2021-2024
$33 NG
Black Ops Shiraz 2020, McLaren Vale RATING 92 DRINK 2021-2026
$35 NG
The Oddball Saperavi 2019, McLaren Vale RATING 92 DRINK 2022-2028
$70 NG

The Ruffian Liqueur Muscat NV, Rutherglen RATING 92 $30 NG
The Villain Cabernet Sauvignon 2020, McLaren Vale RATING 91
DRINK 2021-2025 $29 NG
Black Blood I Shiraz 2020, McLaren Vale RATING 91 DRINK 2021-2030
$79 NG
Ancient Earth Shiraz 2019, McLaren Vale RATING 91 DRINK 2021-2029
$50 NG
Oddball the Great Saperavi 2018, McLaren Vale RATING 91
DRINK 2021-2032 $150 NG
The Floozie Rosé 2021, McLaren Vale RATING 90 DRINK 2021-2022
$24 NG
Cinderella Chardonnay 2021, Adelaide Hills RATING 90 DRINK 2021-2025
$32 NG
The Moocher Mourvèdre 2020, McLaren Vale RATING 90
DRINK 2021-2025 $29 NG
The Rascal Shiraz 2019, McLaren Vale RATING 90 DRINK 2021-2026
$29 NG

Hugo Wines ★★★★

246 Elliott Road, McLaren Flat, SA 5171 **Region** McLaren Vale
T (08) 8383 0098 **www**.hugowines.com.au **Open** 7 days 11–4 **Winemaker** Renae
Hirsch **Viticulturist** Will Hugo **Est.** 1982 **Dozens** 7000 **Vyds** 20ha
Hugo came into prominence in the late '80s with some lovely ripe, sweet reds, which, while
strongly American oak–influenced, were outstanding. It picked up the pace again after a dull
period in the mid-'90s and has made the most of the recent run of good vintages. The estate
plantings include shiraz, cabernet sauvignon, chardonnay, grenache and sauvignon blanc, with
part of the grape production sold. Exports to Canada.(JH)

ΨΨΨΨ **Grenache Shiraz 2019, McLaren Vale** An old-school behemoth. Bitter
chocolate, vanilla-mocha-bourbon oak. American oak, too, surely. Twiggy and
sweet. Dark fruit. Anise, clove and black olive. Large framed. The finish, gentler and
less acerbic than what I recall. Screw cap. 14.5% alc. RATING 88 DRINK 2021-2028
$26 NG

Humis Vineyard ★★★★

3730 Heathcote-Rochester Road, Corop, Vic 3559 **Region** Heathcote
T 0419 588 044 **www**.humisvineyard.com **Open** By appt **Winemaker** Cathy Branson
Est. 2011 **Dozens** 800 **Vyds** 13.5ha
Both the wine labels and the letter from Hugh Jones to me giving the background to his and
wife Michelle's venture share a battered, old-fashioned typeface. The letter was as interesting
for what it didn't say as for what it did, although there was a connection in an improbable way
because my mother Muriel's house name was Missy, also Michelle's nickname. The snapshot
approach of the website's 'About Us' explains that in 2010, with the wine industry on its knees
and a drought in full swing in Heathcote, Hugh saw a dusty paddock running down to a dry
Lake Cooper with a 'for sale' sign. The decision was obvious: buy. The ace in the hole was the
irrigation water available to the property. (JH)

ΨΨΨΨΨ **Marsanne 2021, Heathcote** Jasmine, apple blossom, lemon, grapefruit rind and
nectarine scents introduce a wine that quietly goes about its business of providing
not only a good drink but a textural, complex wine that can easily having you
want more. Screw cap. 13.5% alc. RATING 92 DRINK 2022-2026 $29 JP
Grenache 2021, Heathcote An honest and easygoing grenache tasted before
release, that celebrates the fruit in all of its youthful exuberance. Deep cherry
red-purple hue. Balanced and ripe in flavours in the glass with macerated black
cherries, plum, red licorice, musk and pastille confection, it's given life and length
through fine, firm tannins. Screw cap. 13.8% alc. RATING 91 DRINK 2022-2027
$25 JP

Hungerford Hill

2450 Broke Road, Pokolbin, NSW 2320 **Region** Hunter Valley
T (02) 4998 7666 **www.**hungerfordhill.com.au **Open** 7 days 10–5 **Winemaker** Bryan
Currie **Est.** 1967 **Dozens** 22 000 **Vyds** 5ha
Sam and Christie Arnaout purchased Hungerford Hill in Dec '16, planning to refocus the
50yo label on its Hunter Valley origin, also adding significant new Lower Hunter vineyards
at Sweetwater and Dalwood – the oldest continuously operating vineyard in Australia (see
separate entries). Hungerford Hill uses these vineyards to bolster its Hunter Valley wines while
continuing its 20+-year association with the cool-climate Tumbarumba and Hilltops regions.
Exports to all major markets. (JH)

Block 8 Dalwood Vineyard Chardonnay 2021, Hunter Valley As a general
statement, '21 has served up a suite of regional chardonnay that, at the zenith,
boasts an intensity of fruit and expansive sweetness seldom seen. This, an example.
Hand picked, fermented wild and embellished with just the right amount of
oak and lees, assuaging, appeasing, augmenting and corralling the beam of stone
fruits, nougat and toasted nuts. Exceptional craftsmanship behind this. Screw cap.
12.5% alc. RATING 94 DRINK 2021–2028 $40 NG
Chardonnay 2021, Tumbarumba As exciting as contemporary domestic
chardonnay can be, it can be a little 'paint by numbers'. This differentiates itself
by virtue of its texture: a rail of moreish phenolics, as if the grapes have been
crushed in a Burgundian vein as opposed to the safe whole-bunch pressing that
remains the norm here. Full mlf, too. How good! Praline, toasted hazelnut, almond
meal and tangerine. Flecks of nectarine, too, around the edges. This drives long,
chewy and rich of flavour and density. Packed. Screw cap. 13% alc. RATING 94
DRINK 2022–2030 $40 NG

Fiano 2021, Hilltops RATING 93 DRINK 2021–2024 $27 NG ✪
Fumé Blanc 2021, Tumbarumba RATING 93 DRINK 2021–2025 $27 NG ✪
Pinot Gris 2021, Tumbarumba RATING 93 DRINK 2021–2025 $27 NG ✪
Shiraz 2021, Hilltops RATING 93 DRINK 2022–2028 $45 NG
Epic Shiraz 2018, Hunter Valley RATING 93 DRINK 2022–2030 $150 NG
Pinot Grigio 2021, Hilltops RATING 92 DRINK 2021–2023 $27 NG
Semillon 2021, Hunter Valley RATING 92 DRINK 2021–2033 $27 NG
Preservative Free Shiraz 2021, Hunter Valley RATING 92 DRINK 2021–2024
$35 NG
Tempranillo Graciano 2021, Hilltops RATING 92 DRINK 2022–2025 $45 NG
Pinot Meunier 2021, Tumbarumba RATING 92 DRINK 2021–2025 $40 NG
Block 8 Dalwood Vineyard Chardonnay 2020, Hunter Valley RATING 92
DRINK 2021–2025 $40 NG
Sauvignon Blanc 2021, Tumbarumba RATING 91 DRINK 2021–2023 $27 NG
Tempranillo 2021, Hilltops RATING 91 DRINK 2021–2026 $45 NG
Vermentino 2020, Hunter Valley RATING 91 DRINK 2021–2024 $27 NG
Dalliance Chardonnay Pinot Noir Meunier 2018, Tumbarumba
RATING 90 $45 NG
Sangiovese 2021, Hilltops RATING 90 DRINK 2022–2026 $45 NG
Shiraz 2020, Hunter Valley RATING 90 DRINK 2021–2026 $45 NG

Hunter-Gatherer Vintners

362 Pipers Creek-Pastoria Road, Pipers Creek, Vic 3444 **Region** Macedon Ranges
T 0407 821 049 **www.**hgwines.com.au **Open** Sat–Sun 12–5 **Winemaker** Brian Martin
Est. 2015 **Dozens** 1000 **Vyds** 5ha
In late 2015 winemaker Brian Martin purchased a vineyard which had passed through a
number of ownerships since its establishment in 1999. It was first known as Loxley Vineyard,
and later Harmony Row. It has a long-established cellar door, and offers Shiraz, Pinot Noir,
Riesling and Chardonnay (and a couple of sparkling wines) under the Hunter-Gatherer label.
Alternative varieties are marketed under the Marvio label. (JH)

ΨΨΨΨ **Macedon Pinot Noir 2020, Macedon Ranges** This spends 16 months in French oak, 30% new, yet the wine feels lightweight, both in its structure and flavour profile. A delicate mix of barely ripe cherries, a sprinkle of baking spices and herbs with a blood orange lift. Fine tannins and some juicy acidity come together to offer refreshment. Screw cap. 13.5% alc. RATING 89 DRINK 2022-2026 $40 JF

Sangiovese 2020, Heathcote It's juicy and bright, keying in a range of cherry flavours with warm spices including pepper and fresh herbs. The palate is tight yet light, focusing on tangy acidity. Enjoyable for its immediate appeal. Screw cap. 13.5% alc. RATING 88 DRINK 2022-2024 $35 JF

Hurley Vineyard ★★★★★

101 Balnarring Road, Balnarring, Vic 3926 **Region** Mornington Peninsula
T (03) 5931 3000 **www.**hurleyvineyard.com.au **Winemaker** Kevin Bell **Est.** 1998
Dozens 1100 **Vyds** 3.5ha

It's never as easy as it seems. Despite leading busy city lives, Kevin Bell and wife Tricia Byrnes have done most of the hard work in establishing Hurley Vineyard themselves, with some help from family and friends. Kevin completed the applied science (wine science) degree at CSU, drawing on a wide circle of fellow pinot noir makers in Australia and Burgundy. He has not allowed a significant heart issue to prevent him continuing with his first love. (JH)

ΨΨΨΨΨ **Lodestone Balnarring Pinot Noir 2020, Mornington Peninsula** In cooler vintages, Lodestone appears to step up a notch. The lightest hue of the 3 single-site pinots. While the fruit is destemmed, there's an attractive herbal, almost stemmy, character and it's a finer rendition overall. Light cherry accents – both sweet and tart – red roses, ferrous and earthy. It's often a powerful, rich wine but not here, it feels lighter framed, with grainy tannins, lots of tangy acidity and plenty of refreshment. Diam. 13.1% alc. RATING 95 DRINK 2022-2027 $77 JF

Garamond Balnarring Pinot Noir 2020, Mornington Peninsula If you're expecting a structured and powerful Garamond, which is usually part of its makeup, '20 didn't deliver such a wine. Instead, this is an elegant, finer rendition, led by tangy acidity rather than its tannins, which are grainy yet defined. Lots of perfume from native mint, eucalyptus, baking spices and pepper, to flavours of blood orange, chinotto, black cherries and Campari. Diam. 13.1% alc. RATING 95 DRINK 2022-2028 $92 JF

ΨΨΨΨΨ **Hommage Balnarring Pinot Noir 2020, Mornington Peninsula** RATING 93 DRINK 2023-2028 $77 JF

Hutton Vale Farm ★★★★☆

65 Stone Jar Road, Angaston, SA 5353 **Region** Eden Valley
T (08) 8564 8270 **www.**huttonvale.com **Open** By appt **Winemaker** Kym Teusner
Est. 1960 **Dozens** 1500 **Vyds** 27.1ha

John Howard Angas arrived in SA in 1843 and inter alia gave his name to Angaston, purchasing and developing significant farming property close to the still embryonic town. He named part of this Hutton Vale and it is this property that is now owned and occupied by his great-great-grandson John and wife Jan Angas. Since 2012, the Angases grow the grapes and Kym Teusner is responsible for the winemaking, sales and marketing of Hutton Vale wines. The vineyards were badly affected by a grass fire in Aug '14. While much of the vineyard has regenerated, some of the oldest grenache vines were completely destroyed. Small quantities of its wines are exported to the UK. (JH)

ΨΨΨΨΨ **Shiraz 2018, Eden Valley** A special vineyard that routinely expresses blueberries laced with graphite, sheets of hung deli meat, raspberry, ground white pepper, fresh nutmeg and littered with crushed pink peppercorns. No matter how it is made, or by whom, the fruit shines in a way that evokes memories of the nearby landscape … towering gum trees, exposed granite boulders in places, and fresh,

open air. This is spicy, layered and nuanced. It's really good. Screw cap. 14.4% alc.
RATING 96 DRINK 2022-2039 $75 EL ✪
Grenache Mataro 2018, Eden Valley 85/15% grenache/mataro. The mataro is
so pronounced here – it gives off an earthy, almost minty aroma of mulberries and
licorice root. The palate is where the grenache shines, it is redolent of raspberry
and dustings of raw cocoa. Not as complex as I was hoping for, but certainly there
is a lot of pleasure here. Screw cap. 15% alc. RATING 94 DRINK 2022-2032 $65 EL
Cabernet Sauvignon 2018, Eden Valley Concentrated and intense, this
is saturated – positively dripping – with flavour. Blueberries, fresh soft licorice,
poached raspberries and fennel flower compose the core, while exotic spice and
resinous oak frame the picture. The carriage of flavour across the palate hints at the
quality of fruit that goes into it. The memory of it lingers long after the wine is
gone. Screw cap. 14.5% alc. RATING 94 DRINK 2022-2037 $70 EL

Idavue Estate

470 Northern Highway, Heathcote, Vic 3523 **Region** Heathcote
T 0429 617 287 **www.**idavueestate.com **Open** W'ends 10.30–5 **Winemaker** Andrew
Whytcross, Sandra Whytcross **Est.** 2000 **Dozens** 600 **Vyds** 5.7ha
Owners and winemakers Andrew and Sandra Whytcross produce award-winning wines; the
vineyard managed by Andy, the winery run using normal small-batch winemaking techniques.
Shiraz is the flagship wine, with cabernet sauvignon, chardonnay and semillon also grown
and made on the estate. The Barrelhouse cellar door is adorned with music paraphernalia and
guitars, and regularly holds blues music events. (JH)

ㅇㅇㅇㅇㅇ **Shiraz 2019, Heathcote** The alcohol reading might look on the high side but
read the wine, it's surprisingly light on its feet, to the point of elegance. Plenty of
toasty oak, spice and blackberry aromas with hints of dusty cacao. Smooth and
svelte on the palate, with ripe black and plum flavours, fine tannins and a hint
of eucalyptus. It's long – very long – on the finish. Good value here. Screw cap.
15% alc. RATING 94 DRINK 2021-2031 $30 JP ✪

ㅇㅇㅇㅇㅇ **Shiraz Cabernet 2018, Heathcote** RATING 91 DRINK 2021-2034 $30 JP
Shiraz 2018, Heathcote RATING 90 DRINK 2021-2030 $30 JP

❧ Idée Fixe

Vasse Felix, Caves Road, Cowaramup, WA, 6284 **Region** Margaret River
T 08 9756 5000 **www.**ideefixe.com.au **Open** 7 days 10–5 **Winemaker** Michael
Langridge **Viticulturist** Bart Molony, Tristan Moore **Est.** 2018 **Vyds** 29ha
The first vintage of Idée Fixe (meaning 'fixation') was released in '20. Paul Holmes a Court
(owner of Vasse Felix) purchased a 35ha plot of land in Karridale in '10, planting an array of
chardonnay clones suited to sparkling base, alongside a small plot of pinot noir. In '12, Vasse
Felix released a cellar door-only Blanc de Blanc, the genesis of Idée Fixe. Between '16–19 the
Watershed vineyards were purchased for Vasse Felix, and the buildings and winery for Idée
Fixe. A state-of-the-art overhaul of all aspects of the property is underway – the vineyards have
been largely regrafted and the winery equipment replaced with new high-spec facilities for
sparkling winemaking. Until a cellar door is built, wines can be tasted at Vasse Felix. Exports
to UK, Hong Kong, NZ and Singapore. (EL)

ㅇㅇㅇㅇㅇ **Brut Premier 2019, Margaret River** Textural, creamy and lithe, the phenolics
through the finish cast a savoury tail of flavour – cheesecloth and lanolin. The
texture of the palate is a highlight, creamy and silky smooth. There is power
here, and density too, but it's contained, and when viewed through the lens
of this cool vintage, it is imbued with a glassy character. Screw cap. 12% alc.
RATING 92 $52 EL

Il Cattivo

65 Bay View Road, Port Elliot, SA 5212 **Region** Currency Creek
T (08) 7079 1033 www.ilcattivo.com.au **Winemaker** Anthony Catinari, Richard Bate
Viticulturist Anthony Catinari **Est.** 2017 **Dozens** 1550 **Vyds** 1ha
A new winery venture by property developer Anthony Catinari, whose 2017-planted estate vineyard overlooks Fisherman's Bay at the seaside tourist township of Port Elliot, on the south coast of the Fleurieu Peninsula. The 1ha vineyard is planted to fiano and montepulciano, channeling Anthony's family roots in Italy's Abruzzo region. Additional fruit is sourced from McLaren Vale and the Adelaide Hills, and more plantings of Italian and Spanish varieties, as well as Georgian variety saperavi, are planned. The winemaking is carried out onsite, Anthony has sought training and seeks consultant advice when needed. (TL)

Arneis 2021, Southern Fleurieu The faintly funky bouquet raises questions on the fermentation regime, but the power and layered intensity of the palate overrides those questions with its savoury mix of citrus, herb and mineral flavours running through to the lingering finish. Screw cap. 13.2% alc. RATING 90 DRINK 2022-2023 $24 JH

In Dreams

3/436 Johnston Street, Abbotsford, Vic 3067 **Region** Yarra Valley
T (03) 8413 8310 www.indreams.com.au **Winemaker** Anthony Fikkers **Est.** 2013
Dozens 1200
'Hand-crafted wines begin with a dream, the dream of what might be as the first vine is planted.' So said Nina Stocker, the first winemaker for In Dreams. Anthony Fikkers took over winemaking in 2019. Pinot noir and chardonnay are sourced from 3 low-yielding vineyards in the cool Upper Yarra Valley. The cooler microclimate of the area lends itself to traditional winemaking techniques, such as small-batch fermentation and delicate use of French oak, which allow the fruit to express itself. Exports to the UK, Europe and Asia. (JH)

Chardonnay 2020, Yarra Valley A vibrant green gold. Nectarines and citrus aromas intermingled with some matchstick and almonds. A savoury wine with good freshness and crunch. Screw cap. 12% alc. RATING 89 DRINK 2021-2023 $26 PR
Pinot Noir 2020, Yarra Valley A light brick red. Cranberries and red fruits together with dried strawberries and a gentle sage-like herbal fragrance. A lighter-framed wine with bright, crunchy acidity and fine tannins. Screw cap. 13% alc. RATING 88 DRINK 2021-2023 $30 PR

In Praise of Shadows

212 Seaview Road, McLaren Vale, SA 5171 **Region** McLaren Vale
T www.inpraiseofshadows.com.au **Open** By appt **Winemaker** Rob Mack, Brett Trewartha **Est.** 2017 **Dozens** 2000
Inspired by the eponymous essay on Japanese aesthetics by Jun'ichirō Tanizaki, In Praise of Shadows wines are about an immediacy, pleasure and the embrace of what lies in front of our eyes, rather than that which has fallen to the wayside of the past. In essence, Ikigai, or our reason for being. The wines, fine-boned, energetic and floral, are Mediterranean-accented, befitting McLaren Vale and the elevated reaches of Blewitt Springs and Clarendon, from whence much of the fruit is sourced. An emphasis is placed on organic material and a less-is-more approach, without it being a mantra. Grenache and shiraz are the motherlode, while creative Iberian blends allude to ample intrigue in store. (NG)

Grenache 2021, McLaren Vale A partial carbonic fermentation. Pressed to older wood, of formats both large and small. This approach delivers a fragrant delicacy redolent of lilac, rosewater, nori, raspberry, Seville orange and white pepper. The tannins, suave and juicy, with just enough gritty assertiveness to corral the sweet fruit. This is delicious drinking. And the price, a veritable steal. Best with a chill. Screw cap. 13.2% alc. RATING 93 DRINK 2021-2025 $30 NG

L'Ombre Grenache Mataro Shiraz 2021, McLaren Vale Nothing overt. Just jubey, Mediterranean flavours of tapenade, brine, clove, lavender and steaming bitumen amid the garrigue. The tannins, very soft. But they build with air nicely, cleaving a savouriness from the initial sweet fruit and directing that salty seaside feel long. Drink with a brisk chill. So good! Screw cap. 13.4% alc. RATING 93 DRINK 2021-2024 $30 NG

Mankai Touriga Nacional 2020, McLaren Vale 39/39/22% touriga/graciano/ grenache. Floral. Violet. Rosewater and raspberry bon-bon scents. Some clove, white pepper, tobacco leaf and mace, too. Expansive across the mid palate, a gentle tannic twine unravels to a sappy succulence and juicy spurt of ongoing sweet fruit. Delicious drinking. Screw cap. 13.8% alc. RATING 93 DRINK 2021-2024 $28 NG

Grenache 2020, McLaren Vale This is grenache iterated with a delicious immediacy. Not to age, but to guzzle. A beauty expressed as clove, sassafras, white pepper, mescal and that intoxicating meld of porcini growing on a wet forest floor, smattered with fecund wild berries and bracken. Screw cap. 14.5% alc. RATING 92 DRINK 2021-2025 $30 NG

Shiraz 2019, McLaren Vale Pulpy, effusive of energy and aromatic. Blood plum, pepper grind, salumi, dried nori, porcini dashi and the tequila whiff of the stems in the ferment, bound to a twine of herbal tannins that corral the fruit as much as define the lithe, gently astringent and easygoing finish. Screw cap. 14.2% alc. RATING 92 DRINK 2021-2025 $30 NG

L'Ombre Grenache Mataro Shiraz 2019, McLaren Vale My initial take was that this is a little underdone. A meld, perhaps, of fruit picked earlier and later. While that may well be the case, it grows in stature with air. Mid weighted of feel, immensely savoury and compressed nicely by a lithe tannic lattice crusted in spice, this is good, brisk drinking. As is the wont at this address. Screw cap. 14.2% alc. RATING 91 DRINK 2021-2024 $30 NG

ꡂ꡷꡷ **Vox Pop Pinot Noir 2021, Adelaide Hills** RATING 88 $30 NG
Sakura Rosé 2021, McLaren Vale RATING 88 DRINK 2021-2022 $28 NG

Indigo Vineyard

1221 Beechworth-Wangaratta Road, Everton Upper, Vic 3678 **Region** Beechworth **T** (03) 5727 0233 www.indigovineyard.com.au **Open** 7 days 11–4 **Winemaker** Marc Scalzo, Stuart Hordern **Viticulturist** Daniel Abotomey **Est.** 1999 **Dozens** 6000 **Vyds** 46.15ha

Indigo Vineyard has a little over 46ha of vineyards planted to 11 varieties, including the top French and Italian grapes. The business sells about half of its fruit to Brokenwood, where Indigo wines are made by Marc Scalzo and and Stuart Hordern. Exports to Singapore. (JH)

ꡂꡂꡂꡂꡂ **Secret Village Chardonnay 2021, Beechworth** A fair dose of Beechworth class to this chardonnay, with signature purity of fruit and great concentration. Presents a restrained, steely backbone embracing grapefruit, lemon, lime zest and white peach, with alluring hints of flint and spice. An emerging complexity is apparent together with a hazelnut-almond savouriness. Altogether, it's got age on its side. Screw cap. 12.5% alc. RATING 95 DRINK 2022-2031 $60 JP

ꡂꡂꡂꡂ꡷ **Pinot Noir 2021, Beechworth** RATING 93 DRINK 2022-2029 $40 JP
Small Batch Chardonnnay 2021, Beechworth RATING 93 DRINK 2022-2026 $45 JP
Secret Village Pinot Noir 2021, Beechworth RATING 93 DRINK 2022-2028 $65 JP

Inkwell

PO Box 33, Sellicks Beach, SA 5174 **Region** McLaren Vale **T** 0430 050 115 www.inkwellwines.com **Open** By appt **Winemaker** Dudley Brown **Est.** 2003 **Dozens** 800 **Vyds** 12ha

Inkwell was born in 2003 when Dudley Brown returned to Australia from California and bought a rundown vineyard on the serendipitously named California Road. He inherited 5ha of neglected shiraz, and planted an additional 7ha to viognier (2.5ha), zinfandel (2.5ha) and heritage shiraz clones (2ha). The 5-year restoration of the old vines and establishment of the new reads like the ultimate handbook for aspiring vignerons, particularly those who are prepared to work non-stop. The reward has been rich. Dudley is adamant that the production will be capped at 1000 dozen; almost all the grapes are sold. Exports to the US and Canada. (JH)

ŢŢŢŢŢ **Black and Blue Late Harvest Fortified Zinfandel 2018, McLaren Vale**
A very fine expression, far more about elegance, detail and composure, than sheer heft. Roasted chestnut, sassafras, maraschino cherry and amaro-like herbal lift. Long and gorgeous. A plume of freshness, belying the spiritous core. Cork. 16.4% alc.
RATING 96 $40 NG ✪
Black and Blue Late Harvest Fortified Zinfandel 2017, McLaren Vale
Sticky date, turmeric, cardamom, sandalwood, cinnamon, candied orange zest and an ineffable spice trail that draws me to journeys in Morocco and visits to many a souk. Real pile-driving walnut rancio complexity. Sanguine, wood smoky and very fine. Cork. 16.8% alc. RATING 96 $40 NG ✪
Pressure Drop Cabernet Sauvignon 2019, McLaren Vale Maritime, mid-weighted cabernet that retains a lilt of hedgerow, mint, paprika and bouquet garni, herbal and nourishing, against a backdrop of blackcurrant and pastille. A strong glimpse of the Médoc. Savoury and finely detailed. The French oak serving as fine cladding, corralling and directing the melee long. Cork. 13.7% alc. RATING 95
DRINK 2021-2030 $40 NG
Infidels Primitivo 2019, McLaren Vale This is delicious. Always idiosyncratic, the wines here are woven with plentiful stories to tell. And surely, that is the point of good wine. Organically farmed. No adds aside from a psychologically reassuring dollop of SO_2. Well-appointed French and sweeter American oak, lubricating a spool of tamarind, sangria and blood plum, all spreading across an interface of dusty, pliant tannins and saline freshness. Cork. 14.1% alc. RATING 94
DRINK 2021-2026 $30 NG ✪
Sweet Thing Fortified Viognier 2019, McLaren Vale Tastes akin to a mistelle, as if the ferment was muted very, very early. Spiced apricot, ginger and cardamom. Like an Indian-inspired rice pudding. Sweet, but more savoury than sticky, so to speak. Spiritous, but not hot. This is delicious. Not particularly complex, but makes for a delicious apero with an ice cube. Straight up! Cork. 17.4% alc. RATING 94 $40 NG

ŢŢŢŢŢ **Road to Joy Shiraz Primitivo 2019, McLaren Vale** RATING 93
DRINK 2021-2027 $26 NG ✪
Perfect Day Shiraz 2019, McLaren Vale RATING 93 DRINK 2022-2028
$40 NG
Dark Star Late Harvest Fortified Zinfandel NV, McLaren Vale RATING 93
$50 NG
Tangerine Dub Style Arinto 2021, South Australia RATING 92
DRINK 2021-2024 $26 NG
High Violet Grenache Mataro 2021, McLaren Vale RATING 92
DRINK 2021-2024 $30 NG
Infidels Primitivo 2020, McLaren Vale RATING 92 DRINK 2021-2027
$30 NG
Blonde on Blonde Viognier 2019, McLaren Vale RATING 92
DRINK 2021-2023 $30 NG
Tangerine Viogner 2021, McLaren Vale RATING 91 DRINK 2021-2024
$30 NG
Piece of my Heart Grenache 2018, McLaren Vale RATING 91
DRINK 2021-2023 $30 NG
Deeper Well Shiraz 2014, McLaren Vale RATING 91 DRINK 2022-2024
$80 NG

Pink Cashmere Nouveau Mataro 2021, McLaren Vale RATING 90
DRINK 2021-2023 $30 NG
Dub Style No 15 Re-Mix 2018, McLaren Vale RATING 90 DRINK 2021-2024
$26 NG

Innocent Bystander

316 Maroondah Highway, Healesville, Vic 3777 **Region** Yarra Valley
T (03) 5999 9222 **www**.innocentbystander.com.au **Open** Mon–Tues 12–5, Fri–Sun
12–10 **Winemaker** Joel Tilbrook, Cate Looney, Geoff Alexander, Katherine Brown, Tom
Canning **Est.** 1997 **Dozens** 49 000 **Vyds** 45ha
In Apr '16, Brown Brothers and Giant Steps announced that the Innocent Bystander brand
(including Mea Culpa) and stock had been sold to Brown Brothers. As part of the acquisition,
Brown Brothers purchased the White Rabbit Brewery site adjacent to Giant Steps and this has
become the cellar door home of Innocent Bystander. Its business is in 2 completely different
wine categories, both fitting neatly together. On one hand is the big volume (confidential) of
vintage moscato, the grapes coming from the King Valley; and non vintage prosecco, similarly
sourced. The other side of the business is the premium, high-quality Yarra Valley single varietal
wines with substantial brand value. Exports to the UK, the US and other major markets. (JH)

🍷🍷🍷🍷🍷 **Mea Culpa Pinot Noir 2020, Yarra Valley** Light, clear reddish crimson; there's
a wholly admirable delicacy of touch by the winemaking team. Hand picked,
hand plunged, and matured 9 months in French oak. Red cherry and a hint of
rhubarb are painted on a fine mosaic of tannins. Screw cap. 12.5% alc. RATING 95
DRINK 2025-2030 $49 JH

🍷🍷🍷🍷🍷 **Rosé 2021, Yarra Valley** RATING 92 DRINK 2021-2023 $20 JH ❂
Pinot Gris 2021, King Valley Yarra Valley RATING 90 DRINK 2021-2025 $20
JH ❂

Iron Gate Estate

Cnr Oakey Creek Road/Ingles Lane, Pokolbin, NSW 2320 **Region** Hunter Valley
T (02) 4998 6570 **www**.irongateestate.com **Open** 7 days 10–4 **Winemaker** Geoff
Broadfield, Jade Hafey **Est.** 1996 **Dozens** 4500 **Vyds** 8.7ha
Iron Gate Estate would not be out of place in the Napa Valley, which favours bold architectural
statements made without regard to cost; no expense was spared in equipping the winery or
on the lavish cellar door facilities. The winery and its equipment have been upgraded since
the arrival in 2018 of veteran winemaker Geoff Broadfield, who has reshaped the business
plan. The Classic range comes exclusively from estate fruit, while the Primera range includes
wines that are the best expression of a given variety from the estate and NSW regions. (JH)

🍷🍷🍷🍷🍷 **Fenix Cabernet Shiraz 2019, Mudgee** 60/40% cabernet/shiraz. Another
high-impact wine, albeit, with the virtues of cabernet's verdant foliage and
spearmint ebb, suffusing lift and energy as a counterpoint to sheer weight. Much
better than the straight shiraz because of it. Redcurrant, anise, mint and bouquet
garni. Savoury and refined. Detailed and fresh in the context of the range. Lovely
wine. Screw cap. 14.5% alc. RATING 95 DRINK 2021-2029 $75 NG

🍷🍷🍷🍷🍷 **Verdelho 2021, Hunter Valley** RATING 92 DRINK 2021-2025 $25 NG ❂
Primera Chardonnay 2021, Hunter Valley RATING 92 DRINK 2021-2025
$35 NG
Reserve Shiraz 2019, Mudgee RATING 92 DRINK 2022-2032 $58 NG

Ironcloud Wines

Suite 16, 18 Stirling Highway, Nedlands, WA 6009 (postal) **Region** Geographe
T 0401 860 891 **www**.ironcloudwines.com.au **Winemaker** Michael Ng **Est.** 1999
Dozens 2500 **Vyds** 11ha

In 2003 owners Warwick Lavis and Geoff and Karyn Cross purchased the then-named Pepperilly Estate, which had been planted in 1999 on red gravelly loam soils. Peppermint trees line the Henty Brook, the natural water source for the vineyard. In 2017 Michael Ng, formerly chief winemaker for Rockcliffe, succeeded Coby Ladwig. (JH)

ϘϘϘϘϘ **Rock of Solitude Ferguson Valley Touriga 2020, Geographe** As has become habit for this wine, Ironcloud has nailed the balance of savoury spice and pure fruit here, all of it teetering on a fulcrum of tannin. Campfire, blackberry, licorice, a kick of red dirt, sandalwood and black tea … it floats on the tongue, while the tannins are chewy and textural. Tangible. It's awesome. Another touriga triumph. Screw cap. 14.5% alc. RATING 95 DRINK 2022–2029 $35 EL ✪

The Alliance Ferguson Valley Chardonnay 2020, Geographe Toasty, creamy, languid and long, this is an opulent and pure expression of chardonnay from the picturesque Ferguson Valley. Screw cap. 13.5% alc. RATING 95 DRINK 2021–2031 $50 EL

Rock of Solitude Ferguson Valley Cabernet Malbec 2020, Geographe Gosh, this is good. Super-supple fruit that achieves both plushness of tannins and a velvety mouthfeel. Cabernet from Geographe has a really generous chocolate character that is woven through the blackcurrant and cassis fruit. It makes for pleasurable drinking. Add to that a whack of malbec and the resulting wine is floral, satisfying, elegant and delicious. Great effort. Screw cap. 14% alc. RATING 94 DRINK 2021–2031 $32 EL

Rock of Solitude Single Vineyard Ferguson Valley Purple Patch GSM 2020, Geographe The riper profile of this wine is evident in the mouth, prompting a quick check of the alcohol. However as grenache has the propensity to run with the sun and lean towards muscly tannins and a raspberry-lolly character in the mouth, all is well with the wine. It is beautiful in fact: plush, floral, sweet and shapely. The tannins are woven through the fruit, structuring the wine and driving it through the finish. Screw cap. 14.7% alc. RATING 94 DRINK 2021–2028 $32 EL

ϘϘϘϘϘ **Pepperilly Ferguson Valley Cabernet Shiraz 2020, Geographe** RATING 93 DRINK 2021–2027 $25 EL ✪

Rock of Solitude Ferguson Valley Chardonnay 2021, Geographe RATING 92 DRINK 2021–2028 $35 EL

Irvine   ★★★★

63 Valley Road, Angaston, SA 5353 **Region** Eden Valley
T (08) 8564 1110 **www**.irvinewines.com.au **Open** By appt **Winemaker** Lachlan Duncan **Viticulturist** Peter Miles **Est.** 1983 **Dozens** 20 000 **Vyds** 140ha

When James (Jim) Irvine established his eponymous winery, he chose to produce merlot from the Eden Valley. He was a much-in-demand consultant, bobbing up in all sorts of places. Yet when he decided to sell the business in 2014, its potential was greatly increased with the dowry provided by the purchasing Wade and Miles families. In 1867 Henry Winter Miles planted 0.8ha of shiraz. Successive generations of the Miles family had added to the vineyard portfolio from 1967, both acquiring existing vineyards and planting others. Henry's great-grandson Peter Miles and partner John Wade collectively own 160ha spread through the Barossa and Eden valleys, although only 140ha fall within the new Irvine partnership. Exports to the UK, Switzerland, UAE, Singapore, Malaysia, Japan, Taiwan and Hong Kong. (JH)

ϘϘϘϘϘ **Icon Series Old Vine Shiraz 2019, Barossa Valley** Vibrant primary fruit notes of damson plum, blackberry and red cherry underscored by hints of fruitcake spice, purple flowers, tobacco leaf, licorice, earth and a healthy dose of choc-mint. Full bodied, with cedary blackberry jam notes on the palate, fine, tight tannin and a mint-speckled creme-de-cassis finish. Cork. 14.5% alc. RATING 93 DRINK 2022–2036 $75 DB

Spring Hill Riesling 2021, Eden Valley Pale straw in the glass with aromas of crisp green apple and lime juice with hints of crushed stone, orange blossom and fennel. Dry and savoury with light clotted cream. Textural elements and bright acidity drive things along. Screw cap. 11.5% alc. RATING 90 DRINK 2021–2028 $25 DB

The Estate Shiraz 2020, Eden Valley Deep dark and black plum fruits supported by blackberry and mulberry, dredged with baking spice and earth along with notes of jasmine, licorice, sage and dark chocolate. Medium bodied, with a lovely savoury fruit flow, enchanting floral facets and supple, pliable tannins for support. Screw cap. 14.7% alc. RATING 90 DRINK 2021–2028 $35 DB

ΨΨΨΨ **Spring Hill Shiraz 2020, Barossa** RATING 88 DRINK 2021–2025 $25 DB
The Estate Merlot 2020, Eden Valley RATING 88 DRINK 2021–2027 $35 DB

Jack Rabbit Vineyard ★★★★

85 McAdams Lane, Bellarine, Vic 3221 **Region** Geelong
T (03) 5251 2223 **www.**jackrabbitvineyard.com.au **Open** 7 days 10–5 **Winemaker** Nyall Condon **Viticulturist** David Sharp **Est.** 2010 **Dozens** 5000 **Vyds** 20ha
Nestled onsite next to the acclaimed Jack Rabbit Restaurant is 1.5ha of pinot noir. Jack Rabbit Vineyard also owns another 18.5ha of vineyards across The Bellarine, planted on sandy loam, clay and volcanic-influenced soils, all going in to their range of estate-grown wines. (JH)

ΨΨΨΨΩ **The Bellarine Shiraz 2020, Geelong** Love the blueberries and spice that bring so much freshness and a separate layer of complex flavour to this shiraz. They join plums, blackberry, cinnamon, blackstrap licorice, earth and a sweet core of smoky oak to deliver a smart, tasty wine. Screw cap. 13.3% alc. RATING 92 DRINK 2022–2028 $45 JP

The Bellarine Rosé 2021, Geelong Hits the rosé spot first up with its bright tea-rose and orange hues and lively scents of watermelon ice, summer berry and rose petal. Keeps the structure tight and focused on the palate with fruit gently unfurling. An excellent dry rosé with class. Screw cap. 12% alc. RATING 90 DRINK 2021–2024 $35 JP

ΨΨΨΨ **Bellarine Pinot Grigio 2021, Geelong** RATING 89 DRINK 2022–2024 $35 JP
The Bellarine Chardonnay 2020, Geelong RATING 89 DRINK 2022–2024 $38 JP
The Bellarine Pinot Noir 2020, Geelong RATING 89 DRINK 2022–2030 $45 JP
Bellarine Peninsula Riesling 2021, Geelong RATING 88 DRINK 2022–2024 $35 JP

Jackson Brooke ★★★★

126 Beaconsfield Parade, Northcote, Vic 3070 (postal) **Region** Henty
T 0466 652 485 **www.**jacksonbrookewine.com.au **Winemaker** Jackson Brooke
Est. 2013 **Dozens** 500
Jackson Brooke graduated from the University of Melbourne in 2004 with a science degree and, having spent a summer working at Tarrington Vineyards, went on to study oenology at Lincoln University in NZ. A vintage at Wedgetail Estate in the Yarra Valley was followed by stints in Japan, Southern California and then 3 years as assistant winemaker to Ben Portet. With his accumulated knowledge of boutique winemaking, he has abandoned any idea of building a winery for the foreseeable future, currently renting space at Witchmount Estate. (JH)

ΨΨΨΨΨ **Chardonnay 2020, Henty** A strong follow-up to the '19 vintage with similarly fine features and precise cool-climate detail. Citrus-drenched aromas and flavours join in unison with white peach, Pink Lady apple, pear and just-baked bread. Bright quince-like acidity runs away with the wine. All's right for a rewarding future. Screw cap. 12.5% alc. RATING 94 DRINK 2021–2028 $28 JP ❂

ΨΨΨΨΩ **G.D. Syrah 2020, Henty** RATING 93 DRINK 2022–2028 $48 JP
Doeven Vineyard Riesling 2021, Henty RATING 92 DRINK 2021–2028 $28 JP

Westgate Vineyard Shiraz 2020, Grampians RATING 92 DRINK 2021–2028 $28 JP
Pinot Meunier 2020, Henty RATING 90 DRINK 2021–2024 $28 JP
Pinot Noir 2020, Henty RATING 90 DRINK 2021–2024 $28 JP

Jackson's Hill Vineyard ★★★★

Mount View Road, Mount View, NSW 2321 **Region** Hunter Valley
T 1300 720 098 **Open** By appt **Winemaker** Greg Walls **Est.** 1983 **Dozens** 10 000
Vyds 10ha
One of the low-profile operations on the spectacularly scenic Mount View Road, making small quantities of estate-grown wine. Sold through the cellar door and Australian Wine Selectors. (JH)

♟♟♟♟♟ **Panoramic Cabernet Franc 2020, Hunter Valley** Thoroughly impressive, given the challenging vintage. This has been extracted with considerable aplomb, from fruit relatively unscathed. The finish, slightly bitter, but not unattractive. Otherwise, redcurrant, spearmint, lilac, chilli and a brush of thyme across an effortless finish. Mid weighted, characterful and altogether, a remarkable effort. Screw cap. 13.5% alc. RATING 92 DRINK 2021–2024 $28 NG
Panoramic Sauvignon Blanc 2021, Orange Solid drinking, glimpsing the more savoury and herbal style of the Loire as much as it beams the talc, guava and spa salts of more typically New World styles. Mid weighted, pert and crunchy. Nicely coiled, without being hard, while unravelling to good length. Screw cap. 12.5% alc. RATING 91 DRINK 2021–2023 $26 NG
Panoramic Cabernet Sauvignon 2019, Langhorne Creek Light, bright crimson. A fresh, fragrant and crisp style, with red cherry and purple fruits on both bouquet and palate, but needing a touch of regional chocolate. Screw cap. 14.3% alc. RATING 90 DRINK 2022–2026 $28 JH

♟♟♟♟ **Panoramic Chardonnay 2020, Mount Barker** RATING 89 DRINK 2021–2026 $26 EL

Jacob's Creek ★★★★☆

2129 Barossa Valley Way, Rowland Flat, SA 5352 **Region** Barossa Valley
T (08) 8521 3000 **www**.jacobscreek.com **Open** 7 days 10–4.30 **Winemaker** Dan Swincer **Est.** 1973 **Dozens** 5 700 000 **Vyds** 740ha
Jacob's Creek (owned by Pernod Ricard) is one of the largest-selling brands in the world, and the global success of the base range has had the perverse effect of prejudicing many critics and wine writers who sometimes fail to objectively look behind the label and taste what is in fact in the glass. Exports include the UK, the US, Canada and other major markets. (JH)

♟♟♟♟♟ **Limited Release Estate Riesling 2021, Barossa Valley** A riesling of sizzling focus and purity, pale straw in the glass and showing characters of Granny Smith apple, lime and grapefruit with hints of marzipan, almond blossom, crushed stone and white flowers. Tightly coiled and running on rails with a brisk acid cadence and some yellow plum notes floating in on the palate. Lovely. Screw cap. 12% alc. RATING 94 DRINK 2022–2035 $50 DB

♟♟♟♟♟ **Organic Shiraz 2018, McLaren Vale** RATING 93 DRINK 2022–2030 $60 NG
Survivor Vine Shiraz 2018, Barossa RATING 93 DRINK 2023–2033 $65 DB
Limited Release Field Blend 2021, Barossa Valley RATING 91 DRINK 2021–2028 $30 DB

Jaeschke's Hill River Clare Estate ★★★★☆

406 Quarry Road, Clare, SA 5453 **Region** Clare Valley
T (08) 8843 4100 **www**.hillriverclareestate.com.au **Open** 7 days 10–4
Winemaker Angela Meaney, Steve Braglia **Viticulturist** James Meyer **Est.** 1980
Dozens 1750 **Vyds** 180ha

The Jaeschke family has been broadacre farming in the Hill River district for over 50 years. In May 2010 they purchased the neighbouring 180ha vineyard established by Penfolds in '80. It is planted to 17 varieties, including 21.2ha of riesling, the success of which has led to a stream of trophies and gold medals since '13, the first entry in wine shows. The venture began as the idea of daughter Michelle, with the expectation of a medal or 2. That success, together with a cellar-door grant from PIRSA, led to the introduction of a cellar door, deck and lawn area for picnics, with barbeque facilities provided too. (JH)

ŶŶŶŶŶ **Single Vineyard Rosé 2021, Clare Valley** We live in a world where the pursuit of achieving the 'right' Provençal colour often comes at the cost of flavour. And might I remind everyone now: we do not drink colour. This rosé has more colour than most, and brings with it plenty of fleshy flavour – raspberry, pomegranate, cherries, lashings of spice, sprinkling of rose petals and a gently sweet little lick of RS (less than 2g/L) through the finish. A lot of uncomplicated pleasure here. Screw cap. 12.6% alc. RATING 91 DRINK 2021-2023 $20 EL ✪

ŶŶŶŶ **Single Vineyard Polish Hill River Valley Riesling 2021, Clare Valley** RATING 89 DRINK 2021-2028 $20 EL
Limited Release The Ruby 2020, Clare Valley RATING 89 DRINK 2021-2025 $28 EL
Single Vineyard Polish Hill River Valley Shiraz 2018, Clare Valley RATING 88 DRINK 2021-2027 $20 EL
Limited Release Cabernet Sauvignon 2018, Clare Valley RATING 88 DRINK 2021-2027 $25 EL

James & Co Wines ★★★★

136 Main Street, Rutherglen, Vic 3685 **Region** Beechworth
T 0447 341 373 **www.**jamesandcowines.com.au **Open** Thurs–Mon 10–6
Winemaker Ricky James **Est.** 2011 **Dozens** 750
Ricky and Georgie James intended to buy land in Beechworth and establish a vineyard planted primarily to sangiovese. They say, 'Serendipity led us to Mark Walpole, and we were given the chance to purchase fruit from his Fighting Gully Road Vineyard'. They have set up their home and cellar door in Rutherglen and intend to float between the 2 regions. (JH)

ŶŶŶŶŶ **Sangiovese Rosé 2021, Alpine Valleys** One of the strengths of the James & Co. portfolio, the rosé comes in pretty tea-rose hues. Fragrant aromas of red cherry, wild raspberry fruits and dusty florals, fresh and clean. The palate is supple with musky strawberry, cherry flavours and fresh- as-the-alpine-air acidity. Screw cap. 13% alc. RATING 90 DRINK 2021-2025 $28 JP
Shiraz 2021, Beechworth A joyous, energetic young shiraz that is just itching to be drunk and enjoyed early. Brilliant purple hues, lifted black pepper, spice and black cherry fruits jump from the glass. A medium-bodied, plummy, sweet-fruited wine that simply loves life. Screw cap. 14% alc. RATING 90 DRINK 2022-2025 $55 JP

ŶŶŶŶ **Pinot Grigio 2021, Alpine Valleys** RATING 89 DRINK 2021-2024 $28 JP
Sparkling Rosé 2021, Beechworth RATING 88 $40 JP

James Estate ★★★★

1142-1210 Hermitage Road, Pokolbin, NSW 2320 **Region** Hunter Valley
T (02) 6547 5168 **www.**jamesestatewines.com.au **Open** Fri–Sun 10–4
Winemaker Giacomo Soldani **Est.** 1997 **Dozens** 10 000 **Vyds** 86ha
James Estate has had an unsettled corporate existence at various times since 1997, but has now straightened the ship under the ownership of Sydney-based businessman Sam Fayad. The vineyard is planted to shiraz, cabernet sauvignon, merlot, petit verdot, cabernet franc, semillon, chardonnay and verdelho. (JH)

ŶŶŶŶŶ **Reserve Baerami Vineyard Shiraz Pinot 2021, Hunter Valley** Among the better expressions of this classic Hunter blend from the vintage. A skein of white pepper freshness finds confluence with a gentle astringency, serving to suppress the fruit into a ball of tension and freshness, without overwhelming it in the name of structure alone. Sappy notes of root spice, lilac, black and red cherry, licorice strap and chinotto unravel effortlessly. I'd drink this as I would a beaujolais, young and with a good chill. Screw cap. 13.5% alc. RATING 93 DRINK 2021-2025 $40 NG

Upper Shiraz 2021, Hunter Valley This has been crafted in an easy-drinking fashion. Mid weighted and lithe, with florals, Turkish delight and purple pastille accents suggesting the use of ample whole berries in the ferment and gentle extraction. Solid. Screw cap. 13.5% alc. RATING 90 DRINK 2021-2026 $40 NG

Jansz Tasmania   ★★★★★

1216b Pipers Brook Road, Pipers Brook, Tas 7254 **Region** Northern Tasmania
T (03) 6382 7066 **www**.jansz.com.au **Open** 7 days 11–4 **Winemaker** Jennifer Doyle
Viticulturist Jennifer Doyle **Est.** 1985 **Dozens** 38 000 **Vyds** 30ha
Jansz is part of Hill-Smith Family Vineyards and was one of the early sparkling wine labels in Tasmania, stemming from a short-lived relationship between Heemskerk and Louis Roederer. Its 15ha of chardonnay, 12ha of pinot noir and 3ha of pinot meunier correspond almost exactly to the blend composition of the Jansz wines. Part of the former Frogmore Creek Vineyard purchased by Hill-Smith Family Vineyards in Dec 2012 is dedicated to the needs of Jansz Tasmania. Exports to all major markets. (JH)

ᵽᵽᵽᵽᵽ **Pontos Hills Vintage Cuvée 2017, Tasmania** Debut release. A field blend of chardonnay, pinot noir and meunier. Aged 33 months on lees. 5.5g/L dosage. This a powerful vintage sparkling that delivers considerable depth of spicy figs, baked apple, fruit mince spice and Beurre Bosc pear. Age has brought a creamy texture and layers of brioche and vanilla nougat. A grapefruit-pith sensation lends tension, freshness and bite to the finish. An impressive and unique new expression of Jansz, with medium-term promise. Diam. 12% alc. RATING 92 $50 TS

Late Disgorged Vintage Cuvée 2013, Tasmania Disgorged May '21; 4g/L dosage. There's a tension and endurance on display here, infused by a very mild season of above-average yields. More than 7 years on lees have delivered bountiful layers of toast, mixed spice, honey and roasted hazelnuts, heightening the creamy texture of partial barrel fermentation. It holds impressive persistence and line, with a little phenolic bitterness on the end. Diam. 12.5% alc. RATING 92 $56 TS

Premium Cuvée NV, Tasmania Arguably Tasmania's most important wine, this is consistently one of the best-value sparklings on the shelves. It boasts all the tension and freshness to be expected from a core of Tassie chardonnay, blessed with more spicy complexity than ever. It's advertised to have at least 18 months on lees, but it's currently much more, blended from vintages '17 and right back to '13. The result is more creamy and toasty than ever. Impressive. Diam. 12% alc. RATING 91 $30 TS

ᵽᵽᵽᵽ **Vintage Cuvée 2017, Tasmania** RATING 89 $47 TS
Single Vineyard Vintage Chardonnay 2016, Tasmania RATING 89
DRINK 2026-2030 $65 TS
Non Vintage Premium Rosé NV, Tasmania RATING 89 DRINK 2022-2022
$30 TS
Vintage Rosé 2018, Tasmania RATING 88 DRINK 2022-2022 $53 TS

Jasper Hill   ★★★★★

88 Drummonds Lane, Heathcote, Vic 3523 **Region** Heathcote
T (03) 5433 2528 **www**.jasperhill.com.au **Open** By appt **Winemaker** Ron Laughton,
Emily McNally **Est.** 1979 **Dozens** 2000 **Vyds** 26.5ha
The red wines of Jasper Hill, crafted by father-daughter team Ron Laughton and Emily McNally, are highly regarded and much sought after. The low-yielding dry-grown vineyards are managed organically and tended by hand. As long as vintage conditions allow, these are wonderfully rich and full-flavoured wines. Emily also purchases fruit from Heathcote for her 2 side projects, creating Lo Stesso Fiano and Shiraz with friend Georgia Roberts, as well as

Occam's Razor Shiraz. The family celebrated their 40th vintage in '21. Exports to the UK, the US, Singapore, Japan, Belgium, France and Denmark. (JH)

🍷🍷🍷🍷🍷 **Lo Stesso Fiano 2021, Heathcote** Ah, fiano, looks like you have found a welcoming home in Heathcote. Another stunning interpretation of the Italian grape by Emily McNally, delving deep into its repertoire of forthright pear and apple and finds additional layers of dried fruits, guava, mango skin, nougat and spice. Rolled in texture and topped by delicious acidity. Screw cap. 12.5% alc. RATING 95 DRINK 2022-2026 $30 JP ⊙
Lo Stesso Shiraz 2020, Heathcote A fascinating, complex styling of the grape. Seriously dark red garnet in hue, serious intent on the aroma, too, in black licorice, cassis, mountain herbs, bush mint, earth and undergrowth. A touch of savoury nuance and sturdy tannins connects the latticework of flavour that runs deep and long. A most thoughtful wine. Cork. 14.5% alc. RATING 95 DRINK 2022-2028 $46 JP

🍷🍷🍷🍷🍷 **Georgia & Friends Shiraz 2020, Heathcote** RATING 93 DRINK 2022-2033 $82 JP

jb Wines

PO Box 530, Tanunda, SA 5352 **Region** Barossa Valley
T 0408 794 389 **www**.jbwines.com **Open** By appt **Winemaker** Joe Barritt **Est.** 2005
Dozens 500 **Vyds** 18ha
The Barritt family has been growing grapes in the Barossa since the 1850s. This particular venture was established in 2005 by Lenore, Joe and Greg Barritt. It is based on shiraz, cabernet sauvignon and chardonnay (with tiny amounts of zinfandel, pinot blanc and clairette) planted between 1972 and 2003. Greg runs the vineyard operations; Joe, with a Bachelor of Agricultural Science from the University of Adelaide, followed by 10 years of winemaking in Australia, France and the US, is now the winemaker. Exports to Denmark. (JH)

🍷🍷🍷🍷 **Heart Sparkling Chardonnay Pinot Meunier 2016, Barossa Valley** 90/10% chardonnay/pinot meunier, disgorged July '21. Pale straw in the glass with fine bubbles and aromas of green apple and lemon with hints of brioche, proving dough, soft spice and stone. The aromas transpose over to the crisp yet expansive palate, with notes of yellow fruits on the finish. Diam. 12.5% alc. RATING 88 $30 DB

Jeanneret Wines

22 Jeanneret Road, Sevenhill, SA 5453 **Region** Clare Valley
T (08) 8843 4308 **www**.jeanneretwines.com **Open** Mon–Sat 10–5 & public hols,
Sun 12–5 **Winemaker** Ben Jeanneret, Harry Dickinson **Est.** 1992 **Dozens** 18000
Vyds 36.5ha
Ben Jeanneret has progressively built the range and quantity of wines he makes at the onsite winery. In addition to the estate vineyards, Jeanneret has grape purchase contracts with owners of an additional 20ha of hand-pruned, hand-picked, dry-grown vines spread throughout the Clare Valley. The Rieslings are very good indeed. Exports to Canada, Belgium, Sweden, South Korea and Japan. (JH)

🍷🍷🍷🍷🍷 **Big Fine Girl Riesling 2020, Clare Valley** Cheesecloth, pie crust, lemon zest, apples and brine. This is plump and delicious – the textural palate really enhances the broadcast of fruit flavours, the juicy acid drags the wine across the palate and through into the long finish. This is a cool wine … interesting, engaging, delicious, different. Like it. Screw cap. 12.5% alc. RATING 94 DRINK 2021-2031 $27 EL ⊙

🍷🍷🍷🍷🍷 **Minerva Cabernet Sauvignon 2018, Clare Valley** RATING 93 DRINK 2022-2042 $55 EL
Single Vineyard Sevenhill Riesling 2019, Clare Valley RATING 92 DRINK 2021-2031 $35 EL

Single Vineyard Watervale Riesling 2019, Clare Valley RATING 92 DRINK 2021–2028 $35 EL
Cabernet Malbec 2018, Clare Valley RATING 91 DRINK 2022–2032 $28 EL
Rosé Gastronomique 2021, Clare Valley RATING 90 DRINK 2022–2024 $35 EL
Malbec 2019, Clare Valley RATING 90 DRINK 2021–2027 $27 EL
Stand and Deliver Shiraz 2018, Clare Valley RATING 90 DRINK 2021–2031 $55 EL
Denis Reserve Shiraz 2018, Clare Valley RATING 90 DRINK 2022–2037 $110 EL

Jericho Wines ★★★★☆

211 Kays Road, McLaren Vale, SA 5171 **Region** Adelaide Hills/McLaren Vale
T 0410 519 945 **www**.jerichowines.com.au **Open** By appt **Winemaker** Neil and Andrew Jericho **Est.** 2012 **Dozens** 5000

The family winemaking team consists of father and son, Neil and Andrew Jericho. Neil has over 45 years of winemaking experience in Rutherglen, King Valley and the Clare Valley; and Andrew over 15 years in McLaren Vale working as senior winemaker for Maxwell Wines and Mollydooker. Andrew obtained his bachelor of oenology from the University of Adelaide and obtained experience at Grace Vineyard in the Shanxi Province of China. His partner Kaye is an experienced vintage widow, their eldest daughter Sally worked for Wine Australia for a decade and has degrees in marketing and accounting. Youngest son Kim was torn between oenology, hospitality and graphic design; he opted for the latter, hence designing the highly standout label and Jericho branding. Exports to Singapore. (JH)

🍷🍷🍷🍷🍷 **Limited Release Average 24 Years Age Tawny NV** Greater age has only imbued further grace. Depth, implacable richness and yet, an uncanny lightness of being. Few fortifieds achieve this magical dichotomy, with a cloying sweetness the bane of many. Spiced dates, mahogany, walnut, salted almonds, turmeric, tamarind, clove and the spice bazaars of the Middle East are all tucked into the seams of a magic carpet ride. Screw cap. 19.8% alc. RATING 96 $80 NG

🍷🍷🍷🍷 **Selected Vineyards Fiano 2021, Adelaide Hills** RATING 93 DRINK 2021–2024 $26 NG ✪
Selected Vineyards Grenache 2021, McLaren Vale RATING 93 DRINK 2021–2023 $26 NG ✪
Selected Vineyards Pinot Grigio 2021, Adelaide Hills RATING 93 DRINK 2021–2023 $26 NG ✪
Selected Vineyards Fumé Blanc 2021, Adelaide Hills RATING 93 DRINK 2021–2024 $27 NG ✪
Corydon Vineyard Adelaide Hills Syrah 2019, McLaren Vale RATING 93 DRINK 2022–2027 $42 NG
The Chase Shiraz 2019, McLaren Vale RATING 93 DRINK 2021–2025 $42 NG
Selected Vineyards GSM 2020, McLaren Vale RATING 92 DRINK 2021–2024 $26 NG
Selected Vineyards S3 Shiraz 2019, McLaren Vale RATING 92 DRINK 2021–2026 $26 NG
Selected Vineyards Rosé 2021, Adelaide Hills RATING 91 DRINK 2021–2022 $26 NG

Jilyara ★★★★★

2 Heath Road, Wilyabrup, WA 6280 **Region** Margaret River
T (08) 9755 6575 **www**.jilyara.com.au **Open** By appt **Winemaker** Kate Morgan, Laura Bowler **Viticulturist** Craig Cotterell **Est.** 2017 **Dozens** 4000 **Vyds** 10ha

Craig Cotterell and Maria Bergstrom planted the 9.7ha Jilyara Vineyard in '95. Until '17 the crop was sold to other producers in the region, but the game changed that year. They have 6.4ha of cabernet sauvignon, 0.9ha each of malbec and sauvignon blanc, 0.8ha of chardonnay, 0.4ha of merlot and 0.3ha of petit verdot. There are 3 tiers: at the top The Williams' Block duo of Chardonnay and Cabernet Sauvignon (incorporating small amounts of malbec and petit verdot); next comes the Heath Road banner with Chardonnay, Malbec and Cabernet Sauvignon; the last group is Honeycomb Corner with a Sauvignon Blanc and Cabernet Sauvignon. The packaging is very smart, a design-house dream, visually bringing together the local Noongar word of 'Djilyaro' for bee (there is a beehive at each corner of the block). Exports to NZ. (JH)

🍷🍷🍷🍷🍷 **The Williams' Block Cabernet Sauvignon 2020, Margaret River** The '20 vintage was warm and short, producing red wines of lush fruit and firm tannins. Here, the fruit is almost spilling from the glass, such is the opulence and concentration of characters: red currants, pomegranates, blackberries and raspberries. The oak has a sweet biscuity flavour – Malt-O-Milk, or oatmeal or something similar – and the tannins are supremely awesome: chewy, dense, pliable, like cocoa and almost whippy. Epic wine. Really smart. Screw cap. 14.5% alc. RATING 96 DRINK 2022-2042 $75 EL ✪

Heath Road Chardonnay 2021, Margaret River This is surprisingly nutty, in a really great way. It's cashews, it's pine nuts, it's toasty sweet vanillin oak … This is saline and slinky; the fruit, although present, is very much secondary to the work and it drinks beautifully for it. Creamy and sophisticated. Screw cap. 12% alc. RATING 95 DRINK 2022-2032 $35 EL ✪

Heath Road Cabernet Sauvignon 2020, Margaret River Tasted next to the Honeycomb Corner cabernet ($22), and this is immediately plusher, softer and more dense, with better concentration and more harmonious interplay between tannin and fruit. The cassis and blackberry are cushioned by bay and saltbush, the saline acidity bringing everything together. Very smart. Will age. Screw cap. 14.5% alc. RATING 94 DRINK 2022-2038 $35 EL

The Williams' Block Chardonnay 2020, Margaret River Far more restrained and effortless than the '19, but perhaps that is what comes with a warmer, riper year – the fruit presumably came in off the vine in a glorious fashion, requiring less work in the sheds to extract flavour. A very fine wine. Screw cap. 12.5% alc. RATING 94 DRINK 2022-2032 $75 EL

🍷🍷🍷🍷🍷 **Heath Road Malbec 2020, Margaret River** RATING 93 DRINK 2022-2029 $35 EL

Honeycomb Corner Cabernet Sauvignon 2020, Margaret River RATING 90 DRINK 2022-2029 $22 EL

Jim Barry Wines ★★★★★

33 Craig Hill Road, Clare, SA 5453 **Region** Clare Valley
T (08) 8842 2261 **www.**jimbarry.com **Open** Mon–Sat 10–4 **Winemaker** Tom Barry, Ben Marx, Topsi Wallace **Viticulturist** Derrick Quinton **Est.** 1959 **Dozens** 80 000 **Vyds** 380ha

Jim Barry's wine business is led by Peter Barry; the third generation represented by Peter and Sue Barry's children, Tom, Sam and Olivia. Tom's wife is also called Olivia, and she (Olivia Hoffmann) has set a whirlwind pace, graduating with a bachelor of commerce from the University of Adelaide, then a master of wine business. Peter purchased the famed Florita Vineyard with his brothers in '86 (one of the oldest vineyards in the Clare Valley, planted in 1962). The second generation also purchased Clos Clare in '08 with its high-quality vineyards (see separate entry). Jim Barry Wines is able to draw upon 345ha of mature Clare Valley vineyards, plus 35ha in Coonawarra. In Nov '16, Jim Barry Wines released the first commercial assyrtiko grown and made in Australia. A founding member of Australia's First Families of Wine. Exports to all major markets. (JH)

🍷🍷🍷🍷🍷 **The Florita Riesling 2021, Clare Valley** Tasted alongside the Florita Cellar Release ('15) and the Wolta Wolta ('19), and never was there a more achingly beautiful trio of wines. This ranks slightly higher than the Cellar Release due to its startling clarity, and scintillating, persuasive power. It will live forever and a day, and I bet at Cellar Release time in '27, when we see this wine again, you will be thanking your lucky stars you stocked up now, in '22. Astounding. Screw cap. 12% alc. RATING 97 DRINK 2022-2042 $55 EL ✪

Loosen Barry Wolta Wolta Dry Riesling 2019, Clare Valley This is full on – intensely concentrated, penetrating flavour and acidity that is so seamlessly countersunk into all aspects of the experience that you barely notice any one aspect of it. And yet, as time slows in a moment of emergency, so too does this – it veritably suspends time. The flavour lives on interminably. I'm quivering in anticipation for the '21 release … in the meantime, drinking this experiential wine. Screw cap. 12.3% alc. RATING 97 DRINK 2022-2042 $120 EL ✪

The Armagh Shiraz 2019, Clare Valley This is a big, savoury, meaty shiraz with layers and layers of concentrated purple fruits, hung deli meat, salted licorice, heirloom tomatoes, amaro herbs, freshly grated nutmeg, bay leaf and clove. The magical thing about this wine is actually not the flavours themselves (although impressive), but the way they spool out over the palate and through the extremely long, seemingly interminable finish. It is unfailingly consistent, the tannins fine and omnipresent. The whole package densely and patiently unfurls in the mouth. The wine is a masterpiece. Forever awaits. Screw cap. 14.1% alc. RATING 97 DRINK 2022-2049 $400 EL ❤

♟♟♟♟♟ **The McRae Wood Shiraz 2019, Clare Valley** Savoury, spicy and intense shiraz here, with emphasis on the savoury. This has layers of shaved hung deli meat, amaro herbs, a hint of bacon fat, mulberries, blood plums, salted licorice and tapenade, too. The tannins are firm, promising a long life in front of it, although everything is already so nicely integrated, you could drink it tonight. You could, but you shouldn't – it'll evolve so nicely over the years to come. Screw cap. 14% alc. RATING 96 DRINK 2022-2039 $60 EL ✪

Cellar Release The Florita Riesling 2015, Clare Valley Released after 6 years in bottle, and when you drink it you'll agree this was a wise move. This is gloriously toasty: yellow flowers (there's a buttercup vibe through the finish), hinoki, Golden Delicious apples, preserved lemons, yellow peach, pulverised quartz, saline acidity and a creamy undercurrent of crushed nuts. This is verging on sublime. Or perhaps it just is. Screw cap. 12.3% alc. RATING 96 DRINK 2022-2035 $65 EL ✪

First Eleven Cabernet Sauvignon 2019, Coonawarra As a Test tragic, I've got to tell you, it's a pleasure to be faced with so many cricketing references. Fruit from the Penola Cricket Ground vineyard. There is a highly attractive, pure core of fruit on the mid palate (cassis, blackberry and blood plum swirl in a vortex of flavour here), cloistered by savoury, exotically spiced tannins. The length of flavour too, is admirable, providing ample opportunity for more flavours to emerge. The fine tannins that shape this elegant wine are a highlight; chalky, shapely and a little bit chewy (good). Screw cap. 14% alc. RATING 95 DRINK 2022-2037 $60 EL

Assyrtiko 2021, Clare Valley Assyrtiko is perfectly poised for our climate and food, giving an array of nashi pears, green apples, briny acidity and a pleasant, sun-drenched hay vibe that most of us can only imagine. Delicious and uncomplicated. Drink it in the short term for maximum freshness. Screw cap. 12.% alc. RATING 94 DRINK 2021-2024 $35 EL

Crimson Gold Shiraz 2018, Clare Valley Good thing that Jim Barry was into wine as well as horses, because this wine is more streamlined, sleek and impressive here than it sounds like its namesake ever was on the track. Gorgeous. Plenty of exotic spice, blood, hung deli meat, leather strap, raw cocoa and purple berries to capture and hold interest. Brilliant value. Screw cap. 14% alc. RATING 94 DRINK 2022-2029 $30 EL ✪

John Duval Wines

Artisans of the Barossa, 24 Vine Vale Road, Tanunda, SA 5352 **Region** Barossa Valley
T (08) 8562 2266 **www**.johnduvalwines.com **Open** 7 days, 11–5 **Winemaker** John
Duval **Est.** 2003 **Dozens** 8000

John Duval is an internationally recognised winemaker, having been the custodian of
Penfolds Grange during his role as chief red winemaker from 1986–2002. He established his
eponymous brand in '03 after almost 30 years with Penfolds and provides consultancy services
to clients all over the world. While his main focus is on old-vine shiraz, he has extended his
portfolio with other Rhône varieties. John was joined in the winery by son Tim in '16. Wines
can be tasted at Artisans of the Barossa. Exports to all major markets. (JH)

🍷🍷🍷🍷 **Integro 2018, Barossa** 90/10% cabernet/shiraz. Stunning fruit purity and detail
on display here, with cascades of blackberry and blackcurrant along with cassis,
kirsch, spice, cedar and licorice. The fruit is the star though. Achingly pure and
beautifully integrated with all the components of the wine. Lovely tannin and
oak management too, with an opulent yet graceful flow through to the enduring
finish. Screw cap. 14% alc. RATING 97 DRINK 2021-2041 $220 DB

🍷🍷🍷🍷 **Eligo 2019, Barossa** The Eligio has always been a study of concentration of
fruit and detail and nothing has changed with this release. Powerful blackberry
and plum fruits, graphite-cored and studded with spice, earth and dark chocolate.
Substantial granitic tannin plunges through the heady fruit providing ample
support and the finish trails off admirably. Screw cap. 14.5% alc. RATING 95
DRINK 2021-2038 $130 DB
Annexus Grenache 2020, Barossa There's an airy sense of space to this wine.
Medium-weight ripe plummy fruit, dotted with spice and gingerbread notes and a
touch of cola, fine feathery tannins and lively Eden valley cadence. A mere 1 barrel
produced, due to low yields. Screw cap. 14% alc. RATING 94 DRINK 2021-2030
$70 DB

John Kosovich Wines

180 Memorial Avenue, Baskerville, WA 6056 **Region** Swan Valley
T (08) 9296 4356 **www**.johnkosovichwines.com.au **Open** Wed–Mon 10.30–4.30
Winemaker Anthony Kosovich **Viticulturist** Ray Kosovich **Est.** 1922 **Dozens** 2000
Vyds 10.9ha

Jack Kosovich and his brothers immigrated from Croatia shortly before the outbreak of
WWI. Jack purchased the property in 1922. A 7m white gum beam cut from a tree felled by
Jack in the nearby hills became the supporting structure for the cellar roof. John took over
winemaking aged 15, making fortified wines and rough red wines. In the '60s, John changed
the vineyard to produce white wines. Riesling was the first variety planted, chenin blanc,
chardonnay and verdelho followed. In '89 John established a 3.5ha vineyard in Pemberton,
changing the face of the business forever, albeit continuing with the magnificent Rare Muscat.
In '95 John became a member of the Order of Australia for his long contribution to the wine
industry. Son Anthony (Arch) has since taken over the winemaking and this year the family
business celebrates 100 years. (JH)

🍷🍷🍷🍷 **Chenin Blanc 2021, Swan Valley** This is a younger-release chenin and
shows all of the fresh precision and nuance that comes at this inchoate stage. It is
decidedly savoury and spicy actually; cloves, star anise, pickle juice and brine, along
with the more expected characters of apples, apricots, lanolin, cheesecloth and wax.
We know how well these wines age, and now we can experience their youth, too.
A shift in head space from the usually toasty Kosovich chenins, but a good one.
Screw cap. 13% alc. RATING 93 DRINK 2022-2029 $40 EL

John's Blend

Bridge Road, Langhorne Creek, SA 5255 **Region** Langhorne Creek
T (08) 8537 3029 **www**.johnsblend.com.au **Open** At The Winehouse, Langhorne Creek
Winemaker John Glaetzer **Est.** 1974 **Dozens** 2000 **Vyds** 23ha
John Glaetzer was Wolf Blass's right-hand man almost from the word go; the power behind
the throne of the 3 Jimmy Watson trophies awarded to their wines ('74, '75, '76) and the small
matter of 11 Montgomery trophies for Best Red Wine at the Adelaide Wine Show. This has
always been a personal venture on the side, as it were, of John and wife Margarete, officially
sanctioned, of course, and needing little marketing effort. Exports to Canada, Switzerland,
Indonesia and Singapore. (JH)

Margarete's Shiraz 2019, Langhorne Creek Youthful crimson colour; the
vines 30–80 years old. Cruises along the creek with enough juicy fruit to keep
followers of this brand happy. Cork. 14.5% alc. RATING 91 DRINK 2024-2034
$35 JH

Individual Selection Cabernet Sauvignon 2018, Langhorne Creek The
label details 43 months in oak, and while the mouthfeel and fruit flavour are good,
the oak is oppressive. Cork. 14.5% alc. RATING 90 DRINK 2025-2035 $35 JH

Jones Road

2 Godings Road, Moorooduc, Vic 3933 **Region** Mornington Peninsula
T (03) 5978 8080 **www**.jonesroad.com.au **Open** W'ends 11–4 **Winemaker** Travis Bush
Est. 1998 **Dozens** 6000 **Vyds** 26.5ha
After establishing a very large and very successful herb-producing business in the UK, Rob
Frewer and family migrated to Australia in '97. By a circuitous route they ended up with a
property on the Mornington Peninsula, planting pinot noir and chardonnay, then pinot gris,
sauvignon blanc and merlot. They have since leased another vineyard at Mount Eliza and
purchased Ermes Estate in '07. (JH)

Pinot Noir 2020, Mornington Peninsula A lean style, yet a pretty wine in a
way, with its pale ruby hue followed by aromas of cherries, forest floor, aniseed and
cedary spice. Lighter framed, with sinewy tannins and lemony acidity to close. Best
in its youth. Screw cap. 12.2% alc. RATING 88 DRINK 2022-2026 $42 JF

Jones Winery & Vineyard

61 Jones Road, Rutherglen, Vic 3685 **Region** Rutherglen
T (02) 6032 8496 **www**.joneswinery.com **Open** By appt **Winemaker** Mandy Jones
Viticulturist Arthur Jones **Est.** 1860 **Dozens** 3000 **Vyds** 10ha
Jones Winery & Vineyard was established in 1860 and stands as testament to a rich
winemaking tradition. Since 1927, the winery has been owned and operated by the Jones
family. Two blocks of old vines have been preserved (including 1.69ha of shiraz), supported
by further blocks progressively planted between '75 and the present day. Today, Jones Winery
& Vineyard is jointly operated by winemaker Mandy Jones, who brought years of experience
working in Bordeaux, and her brother Arthur Jones. Together they produce a small range of
boutique wines. Exports to France. (JH)

LJ 2019, Rutherglen 95/5% shiraz/grenache. L.J. is the opposite of over-
thinking your winemaking. This is a down to earth wine, honest and solid. Some
years the oak seems a little forward, this year it hums gently in the background
letting the 114yo vineyard take centre stage with some incredible concentrated
fruit quality and intensity. The palate is supple, ripe and glossy with an earthy,
savoury Rutherglen finale. Screw cap. 14.1% alc. RATING 95 DRINK 2022-2032
$80 JP

Rare Muscat NV, Rutherglen Mandy Jones has a delicate touch with fortifieds,
bringing depth – as you would expect of the Rare classification – with an
intriguing aromatic freshness. Fig, raisin, toffee and malt with marzipan, orange
peel and rose petal, so lasting on the tongue, mixed with a chocolate panforte

nuttiness. Fills the mouth and the senses. 500ml bottle. Vinolok. 18.5% alc.
RATING 95 $160 JP

ρρρρ૨ Shiraz 2019, Rutherglen RATING 93 DRINK 2022-2029 $35 JP
Classic Muscat NV, Rutherglen RATING 93 $40 JP
Marsanne Roussanne 2021, Rutherglen RATING 91 DRINK 2022-2027
$25 JP
Fiano 2021, Rutherglen RATING 91 DRINK 2022-2025 $30 JP
Durif 2019, Rutherglen RATING 91 DRINK 2022-2033 $40 JP
Sparkling Shiraz NV, Rutherglen RATING 90 $42 JP

Josef Chromy Wines   ★★★★★

370 Relbia Road, Relbia, Tas 7258 **Region** Northern Tasmania
T (03) 6335 8700 **www**.josefchromy.com.au **Open** 7 days 10–5 **Winemaker** Jeremy
Dineen, Ockie Myburgh **Viticulturist** Luciano Caravia **Est.** 2004 **Dozens** 40 000
Vyds 60ha
Josef Chromy escaped from Czechoslovakia in 1950, arriving in Tasmania 'with nothing but
hope and ambition'. He went on to own or develop such well-known Tasmanian wine brands
as Rochecombe (now Bay of Fires), Jansz, Heemskerk and Tamar Ridge. In '07, aged 76, Josef
launched Josef Chromy wines. The foundation of the business is the Old Stornoway Vineyard,
with 60ha of mature vines; the lion's share is planted to pinot noir and chardonnay, with a little
pinot gris, riesling and sauvignon blanc, too. Josef has won a string of awards for his services
to the Tasmanian wine industry and his wines earn similar respect. Talented and hard-working
winemaker Jeremy Dineen handed over the reins to his capable offsider Ockie Myburgh in
January '21. Exports to all major markets. (JH)

ρρρρρ Rosé 2021, Tasmania Pinot has always been the star at Chromy – sparkling, still,
white, red or pink – and never has it looked as sophisticated in rosé guise as this.
Pale, bright salmon pink. Erupting with rose petals, morello cherries, strawberry
hull and guava. Elegant yet concentrated. Grand line and length. Refreshing,
enveloping Relbia acidity seals the deal. Already a strong contender for the rosé of
the vintage! Screw cap. 13.5% alc. RATING 95 DRINK 2021-2023 $32 TS ✪ ♥
Pinot Noir 2020, Tasmania There is an ever more pronounced stamp of terroir
on Tasmania's increasingly demarcated subregions, and wines like this declare it
with authority. The definition of Relbia pinot, at once deeply set in black cherry,
black plum, anise and licorice, at the same time soaring with violet fragrance
and all the energy of Tasmanian acidity and finely textured tannins. Is Relbia the
Gevrey of the Tamar and is Chromy its Chambertin? This wine says, 'yes, and yes!'
Screw cap. 13% alc. RATING 95 DRINK 2025-2035 $43 TS
Pinot Gris 2021, Tasmania I love the contrast of gris' generosity and the
tension of Northern Tasmania, eloquently captured by the mild '21 season. It
upholds the mood of gris in its texture, spice and pear and stone-fruit flesh, yet
tactically surfs the line of grigio in its elegant allure and lemon tang. Old oak has
been skilfully deployed to build mouthfeel without in any way diminishing purity
or tension. Best yet. Screw cap. 14% alc. RATING 94 DRINK 2021-2026 $30 TS ✪

ρρρρ૨ Riesling 2021, Tasmania RATING 92 DRINK 2028-2036 $32 TS
Chardonnay 2020, Tasmania RATING 92 DRINK 2024-2030 $39 TS
Zweigelt 2020, Tasmania RATING 92 DRINK 2022-2026 $50 TS
PEPIK Pinot Noir 2020, Tasmania RATING 91 DRINK 2022-2023 $26 TS

JS Wine   ★★★★

42 Lake Canobolas Road, Nashdale, Orange, NSW 2800 **Region** Orange
T 0433 042 576 **www**.jswine.com.au **Open** Thurs–Sun 11–5 **Winemaker** Philip Shaw
Est. 2016 **Dozens** 2700 **Vyds** 26ha
I (James) simply can't resist quoting the opening to the background information provided:
'Located on the west side of Australia's agricultural province of New South Wales. JS Wines'
estate is about 8km from the centre of Orange, 3 hours' drive from Sydney'. The vineyard

and the quality of the wines brings together 3 winemakers who have long-term firsthand knowledge of the Orange region. The estate's natural basalt volcanic soil is afforded ample sunshine by day and the benefit of cooler night temperatures to create the ideal environment for producing quality local wine. (JH)

ΨΨΨΨ̦ **Reserve The Sunflower Chardonnay 2019, Orange** A stylish, mid-weighted expression in the contemporary mould. Extended time on lees to impart a bow of tension and a whiff of smokiness. Stone-fruit allusions and quality French oak, serving to imbue a nuttiness and creamy finish of nougatine. The poise, impeccable. The length, impressive. Screw cap. 13.5% alc. RATING 93 DRINK 2021-2026 $108 NG

ΨΨΨΨ **The Night Sky Cabernet Franc 2019, Orange** RATING 88 DRINK 2021-2024 $80 NG
Reserve Pinot Noir 2019, Orange RATING 88 DRINK 2021-2024 $96 NG

Juniper   ★★★★★

98 Tom Cullity Drive, Cowaramup, WA 6284 **Region** Margaret River
T (08) 9755 9000 **www**.juniperestate.com.au **Open** 7 days 10–5 **Winemaker** Mark Messenger, Luc Fitzgerald **Viticulturist** Ianto Ward **Est.** 1973 **Dozens** 12 000 **Vyds** 19.5ha

Roger Hill and Gillian Anderson purchased the Wrights' Wilyabrup property in 1998, driven by the 25yo vineyard with dry-grown cabernet as the jewel in the crown. They also purchased complementary vineyards in Forest Grove (Higher Plane) and Wilyabrup; the vineyards are sustainably farmed using organic principles. Sons Nick and Tom (formerly a winemaker in the Yarra Valley) are now running the business. The Juniper Crossing and Small Batch wines are sourced from the 3 vineyards, while the Single Vineyard releases are made only from the original vineyard on Tom Cullity Drive. Exports to the UK, the US, Canada, Singapore and Hong Kong. (JH)

ΨΨΨΨ̦ **Cornerstone Karridale Chardonnay 2021, Margaret River** No mlf; an interesting move to block mlf with a such a high proportion of Clone 95, and certainly the acidity feels very high in the mouth (stinging; like pure lemon juice). The fruit beyond is succulent and glossy: yellow peaches, apples and nashi pears are the order fo the day. By the time this is released (Dec '22), it will have likely grown into the swan it was always destined to be. Screw cap. 12.5% alc. RATING 93 DRINK 2022-2029 $60 EL
Three Fields Cabernet Sauvignon 2020, Margaret River Bright crimson. Man alive, this packs a punch, with alternating layers of cassis and tannins that go on and on. Each part is so clearly articulated, the requisite balance will allow this to cruise through the 10+ years it needs. Screw cap. 14% alc. RATING 93 DRINK 2030-2050 $35 JH
Cornerstone Karridale Chardonnay 2020, Margaret River Karridale is in the cool south of Margaret River, giving a pea tendril, lemongrass character on the nose here. In the mouth the wine is silky and slinky, the oak however, interjects through the finish and interrupts the flow of fruit. Otherwise seamless, with juicy salty acidity. Screw cap. 13% alc. RATING 93 DRINK 2022-2032 $70 EL
Cornerstone Karridale Cabernet Sauvignon 2019, Margaret River Fresh garden mint, bay leaf, soft licorice, hints of curry leaf, snapped green twig and jasmine tea. In the mouth the wine is littered with white pepper, fennel flower and aniseed; it is restrained and tense, the tannins still enmeshed in the fruit. Like an un-pickable lock, this needs the only key that will open it: time. Screw cap. 13.5% alc. RATING 93 DRINK 2022-2032 $70 EL
Canvas Nouveau 2021, Margaret River 77/23% shiraz. This is incredibly aromatic: red snakes, licorice, violets, green peppercorn and Szechuan pepper. On the palate it is sweet, jolly, bouncy and bright. A lot to like. On the simple side perhaps, but begging to be chilled and consumed this summer. Joyful. Screw cap. 13% alc. RATING 91 DRINK 2021-2023 $29 EL

Three Fields Shiraz 2020, Margaret River Juicy, vibrant and alive, with a spine of firm tannin that runs like a ridge through the velvety fruit. Kind of luscious in its own nouveau-ish way. Spicy, brambly, tart and a little bit crunchy, with an attractive bloody character that makes it interesting and cool. Screw cap. 14% alc. RATING 91 DRINK 2022-2027 $29 EL

Canvas Malbec 2021, Margaret River Very pretty. The fruit here has a distinct red-snake vibe to it. The tannins curl around on the palate and caress the fruit as it trundles through into the finish. A procession of red and black berries, bound together by juicy acidity. Quite a joyous little number. Screw cap. 14% alc. RATING 90 DRINK 2021-2027 $32 EL

Crossing Original Red 2020, Margaret River 80/10/4/3/3% cabernet sauvignon/merlot/cabernet franc/malbec/petit verdot. For a little cheapie – this packs a punch. Perfectly Margaret River, uncomplicated in its expression, and coloured by a bevy of bright fruits. Compelling! Screw cap. 14% alc. RATING 90 DRINK 2021-2026 $18 EL ✪

♟♟♟♟ **Canvas Tempranillo 2020, Margaret River** RATING 89 DRINK 2022-2027 $29 EL
Canvas Fiano 2021, Margaret River RATING 88 DRINK 2021-2023 $29 EL
Three Fields Chardonnay 2021, Margaret River RATING 88 DRINK 2022-2027 $32 EL
Three Fields Sauvignon Blanc Semillon 2020, Margaret River RATING 88 DRINK 2022-2025 $29 EL

Kaesler Wines

Barossa Valley Way, Nuriootpa, SA 5355 **Region** Barossa Valley
T (08) 8562 4488 **www.**kaesler.com.au **Open** 7 days 11–5 by appt **Winemaker** Reid Bosward, Stephen Dew **Est.** 1990 **Dozens** 20 000 **Vyds** 36ha
The first members of the Kaesler family settled in the Barossa Valley in 1845. The vineyards date back to 1893, but the Kaesler family ownership ended in 1968. Kaesler Wines was eventually acquired by a small group of investment bankers (who have since purchased Yarra Yering), in conjunction with former Flying Winemakers Reid and Bindy Bosward. Reid's experience shows through in the wines, which come from estate vineyards adjacent to the winery, and from 10ha in the Marananga area that includes shiraz planted in 1899. The Small Valley Vineyard wines, made by Stephen Dew, are produced from 49ha in the Adelaide Hills. Exports to all major markets. (JH)

♟♟♟♟♟ **Old Bastard Shiraz 2019, Barossa Valley** Muscular, big-boned shiraz. Everything is at volume. Fruit concentration and density, toothsome tannin and oak profile, alcohol and power. When done well, that is just mighty fine and that is the case here. Strap in. Cork. 15% alc. RATING 95 DRINK 2021-2031 $260 DB

Old Vine Semillon 2021, Barossa Valley A tautly stretched and precise Barossa semillon with pristine fruit characters of lemon and crunchy green apple along with hints of almond meal, lanolin, soft spice, dried herbs and white flowers. There's a dot of clotted cream on the palate which is finely formed and possesses a wonderfully pure, stony, citrus-flecked finish. Drink gleefully or cellar. Screw cap. 11.5% alc. RATING 94 DRINK 2021-2035 $25 DB ✪

The Fave Grenache 2020, Barossa Valley There's a lovely purple floral edge to this wine's ripe red plum, red cherry and cranberry fruit notes. Exotic and spicy too with hints of gingerbread, watermelon and warm earth. Spacious and airy with a substantial tweak of powdery tannin and zippy acidity. Just a touch of heat on the finish but great drinking. Screw cap. 14% alc. RATING 94 DRINK 2021-2027 $45 DB

Old Vine Shiraz 2019, Barossa Valley There's an impressive display of fruit density and concentration in the '19 Old Vine Shiraz. Concentrated black plum, cherry and blackberry fruits pack considerable punch, layered as they are with deep dark spice notes, licorice, Old Jamaica chocolate and oak nuance. Toothsome, compact tannins plunge through the fruit and the finish echos with blackberry

compote and earthy spices. Screw cap. 15% alc. RATING 94 DRINK 2021-2028
$90 DB

Reach For The Sky Shiraz 2018, Barossa Valley Quite a different style of
shiraz when compared with some of the other powerful styles in their portfolio.
There a wild, vinous edge to the wine; succulent … juicy even, with densely
packed spice laying under ripe black cherry and satsuma plum characters in
sedimentary-like layers. Savoury with chewy tannin grip and a swell of lovely ripe
spicy black fruits on the finish. Cork. 14.5% alc. RATING 94 DRINK 2021-2028
$45 DB

ΨΨΨΨΩ **The Bogan Shiraz 2020, Barossa Valley** RATING 93 DRINK 2021-2029
$55 DB

Stonehorse Shiraz 2019, Clare Valley RATING 93 DRINK 2021-2031 $25
EL ✪

Avignon 2018, Barossa Valley RATING 92 DRINK 2023-2029 $35 JH

Love Child Viognier 2020, Barossa Valley RATING 91 DRINK 2021-2026
$35 DB

Kalleske

6 Murray Street, Greenock, SA 5360 **Region** Barossa Valley
T (08) 8563 4000 **www.**kalleske.com **Open** 7 days 10–5 **Winemaker** Troy Kalleske
Viticulturist Kym Kalleske **Est.** 1999 **Dozens** 10000 **Vyds** 50ha

The Kalleske family has been growing and selling grapes on a mixed farming property at
Greenock for over 140 years. Sixth-generation Troy Kalleske, with brother Tony, established
the winery and created the Kalleske label in '99. The vineyard is planted mainly to shiraz
(31ha) and grenache (7ha), with smaller amounts of chenin blanc, semillon, viognier, cabernet
sauvignon, mataro, durif, petit verdot, tempranillo and zinfandel. The vines vary in age,
with the oldest dating back to 1875. All are grown biodynamically. Exports to all major
markets. (JH)

ΨΨΨΨΩ **Eduard Old Vine Shiraz 2019, Barossa Valley** An impressive, saturated red
purple in the glass, with aromas of ripe satsuma plum, summer berry fruits, cedar,
Asian spice, earth and dark chocolate. Impressive fruit intensity and concentration
with super-ripe berry fruits, spice, plenty of oak heft and an intense, ripe finish
that retains freshness and appeal. Impressive structure. Screw cap. 15% alc.
RATING 93 DRINK 2021-2035 $90 DB

Rosina Rosé 2021, Barossa Valley 92/8% grenache/shiraz. Such a pretty-
smelling wine, with aromas of redcurrant, raspberry and strawberries, brushed with
jasmine and soft spice. Fragrant in the mouth too, with a wash of bright red fruit,
crushed stone and floral flourish. It finishes dry and savoury. Screw cap. 12.5% alc.
RATING 92 DRINK 2021-2023 $22 DB ✪

Clarry's GSM 2021, Barossa Valley For me, Clarry's GSM has always been
a wine that emphasises the fruit density that is on display from Moppa and
Greenock. Fruit-pure with a sense of latent power, minimal interruption from oak
and both impressive fruit density and enjoyment. Screw cap. 14.5% alc. RATING 92
DRINK 2021-2028 $23 DB ✪

Parallax Grenache 2021, Barossa Valley It's grenache Jim, but not as we
know it. Before us, is Kalleske's distinctly lo-fi take on the much-loved variety.
It cuts a decidedly funky, pinot-esque line across the tongue with Campari-
like amaro and herbal nuances, souk-like spice and crunchy red-fruited verve.
Wild-eyed and sapidly beguiling drinking. Screw cap. 12% alc. RATING 92
DRINK 2021-2025 $29 DB

Moppa Shiraz 2020, Barossa Valley A wonderfully perfumed shiraz. There's a
wee bit of petit verdot (8%) which accounts for those deep black fruit bass notes,
while a smidgen of viognier (3%) explains the jasmine and frangipani high-tones
to the deep plum and blackberry fruit below. There's a lot to like here; first the
price, then that plush spicy fruit, washed with fragrance and inherent drinkability.
Very nice. Screw cap. 14.5% alc. RATING 92 DRINK 2021-2028 $30 DB

Greenock Single Vineyard Shiraz 2020, Barossa Valley That characteristic Kalleske perfumed lift is present here with jasmine-draped satsuma plum fruit of impressive ripeness, dredged in spice, earth and dark chocolate. Like the Greenock Hotel, it's welcoming on the palate with oodles of plush fruit, fine powdery tannins and an effortless Barossan appeal. Screw cap. 14.5% alc. RATING 92 DRINK 2021-2030 $45 DB

JMK Shiraz VP 2021, Barossa Valley A luscious shiraz-based VP. Heady plum and blackberry jam characters along with hints of cassis, brandy snaps, figs, chocolate cake, baking spice and kirsch. Intense and heady with a sweetly unctuous palate, chewy tannin backbone and rich, fruitcake finish. Screw cap. 18.5% alc. RATING 92 $25 DB ✪

Florentine Single Vineyard Chenin Blanc 2021, Barossa Valley Pale strawy in the glass with aromas of crunchy pear, melon and yellow plum with hints of almond paste, white flowers and stone. Crunchy pear fruit again on the palate, with bright acidity, plentiful drive and a gentle phenolic tweak on the dry finish. Screw cap. 12% alc. RATING 91 DRINK 2021-2024 $22 DB ✪

Zeitgeist Shiraz 2021, Barossa Valley Wild-fermented, aged in stainless steel and bottled without sulphur dioxide, it's a wild-eyed, pure and raw rendering of a much-loved grape variety. Primal, dense, sapid and vivid. Wild stuff. Screw cap. 14.5% alc. RATING 90 DRINK 2021-2025 $29 DB

Old Vine Single Vineyard Grenache 2020, Barossa Valley There's a red-fruited aromatic presence here, red and yellow plums, a splash of raspberry coulis, plenty of ginger spice and an almost musky, pressed-flower aspect. That floral component leaps forth again on the palate with ripe macerated raspberry notes, gingerbread and plenty of spice, finishing savoury with just a touch of heat. Screw cap. 15% alc. RATING 90 DRINK 2021-2028 $50 DB

Kangarilla Road ★★★★☆

44 Hamilton Road, McLaren Flat, SA 5171 **Region** McLaren Vale
T (08) 8383 0533 **www**.kangarillaroad.com.au **Open** Mon–Fri 9–4.30, w'ends 11–4
Winemaker Kevin O'Brien **Viticulturist** Kevin O'Brien **Est.** 1997 **Dozens** 30000
Vyds 5ha
In January 2013, Kangarilla Road founders Kevin and Helen O'Brien succeeded in breaking the mould for a winery sale, crafting a remarkable win-win outcome. They sold their winery and surrounding vineyard to Gemtree Wines, which has had its wine made at Kangarilla Road since '01 under the watchful eye of Kevin. The O'Briens have retained their adjacent JOBS vineyard and the Kangarilla Road wines continue to be made by Kevin at the winery. Luck of the Irish, perhaps. Exports to the UK, Ireland, the US, Switzerland, the Netherlands, Denmark, Japan, South Korea and Taiwan. (JH)

♥♥♥♥♥ **The Veil 2018, McLaren Vale** Seeded with flor and left in older oak for 3 years. Delicious. Chamomile, saltbush, preserved Moroccan lemon and some lees-derived almond biscuit. The finish, nicely firm and bitter. Wonderfully savoury. Prodigiously versatile. Drink this with hard cheese, Thai salads … or, as my imagination goes into over-drive, just be creative. Screw cap. 13.5% alc. RATING 95 DRINK 2021-2027 $35 NG ✪

Black St Peters Zinfandel 2020, McLaren Vale This is a high-octane wine that nevertheless delivers remarkable poise and fidelity to the variety: brambly black fruits, candied orange peel and the sweet-sour spiciness endemic to a variety that ripens peripatetically within its bunches. The oak is applied beautifully, serving as the harness to a long, sweeping flow of flavour. Screw cap. 15.5% alc. RATING 94 DRINK 2022-2030 $50 NG

Q Shiraz 2020, McLaren Vale A dense, corpulent wine that never strays into jammy caricature. The blue-fruit riffs are pulpy, pithy and of an impeccably extracted wiry tension. The oak sits at the edges, nestled nicely while serving its purpose to impart savoury tones while harnessing the sweetness. This bristles with intent, such is the insular feel. Clove, iodine, lilac, mocha and pepper revel within. When this opens, it will be an explosion. In the very best sense, so refined are the

tannins and impeccably ripe the fruit. Give this a few years. Screw cap. 14.5% alc.
RATING 94 DRINK 2022-2035 $70 NG

ŸŸŸŸŸ Sixmo Chardonnay 2021, Adelaide Hills RATING 93 DRINK 2022-2027
$60 JP
The Devil's Whiskers Shiraz 2020, McLaren Vale RATING 93
DRINK 2022-2030 $45 NG
Primitivo 2019, McLaren Vale RATING 93 DRINK 2021-2025 $30 NG
Cabernet Sauvignon 2021, McLaren Vale RATING 92 DRINK 2021-2027
$30 NG
Shiraz 2019, McLaren Vale RATING 90 DRINK 2022-2028 $30 NG

Karrawatta ★★★★★

164 Greenhills Road, Meadows, SA 5201 **Region** Adelaide Hills
T (08) 8537 0511 **www**.karrawatta.com.au **Open** 7 days 11–4 **Winemaker** Mark
Gilbert **Viticulturist** Mark Gilbert **Est.** 2013 **Dozens** 5000 **Vyds** 59.25ha
Mark Gilbert is the great-great-great-grandson of Joseph Gilbert, who established the Pewsey
Vale vineyard and winery in 1847. Joseph Gilbert had named the property Karrawatta, but
adopted Pewsey Vale after losing the toss of a coin with his neighbour. The Karrawatta of
today has 12.43ha of vines in the Adelaide Hills, 38.07ha in Langhorne Creek and 8.75ha
in McLaren Vale. The vineyards are all hand pruned, the small-batch wines fashioned with
minimum intervention. Exports to the US, Canada and Hong Kong. (JH)

ŸŸŸŸŸ Tutelina Shiraz 2019, McLaren Vale Langhorne Creek Adelaide Hills
Despite the highish alcohol, there is an air of elegance and deceptive beauty to this
wine. And it changes in the glass, which adds that extra degree of intrigue. Plum,
olive, cassis, earth and leather, cocoa powder and charcuterie vie for your attention,
folding and layering over and over across the palate. And, above it all, lifted herbal
and floral aromatics, too, of violet, star anise and sage. Quite the individual taste
experience. Cork. 15% alc. RATING 96 DRINK 2022-2032 $275 JP
Christo's Paddock Cabernet Sauvignon 2019, Langhorne Creek A
cabernet with great elegance and depth of flavour but the X factor here is the
range and spread of aromatic spice. It's a captivating feature. Drenched in black
fruits, blueberry, clove, nutmeg, bush mint and leafy cabernet aromas. Maintains
an even, supple flow of flavour, tannins and oak, running long and true. A delight!
Screw cap. 14.5% alc. RATING 95 DRINK 2022-2029 $62 JP
Spartacus Cabernet Sauvignon Malbec Shiraz 2019, Langhorne Creek
While it can't be denied that Spartacus is every bit as heroic in size as its namesake,
the cabernet blend retains real charm and finesse. Ripe plum, black fruits, toasted
spices, violet, acacia and earth are just a tip of the aroma iceberg. Smoothly layered
across the palate in waves of supple tannin, fruit, integrated oak and a hint of
savouriness. Spartacus shines. Cork. 14.5% alc. RATING 95 DRINK 2022-2033
$92 JP

ŸŸŸŸŸ Popsie Blanc de Blancs Chardonnay 2018, Adelaide Hills RATING 93
$62 JP
Anth's Garden Chardonnay 2020, Adelaide Hills RATING 91
DRINK 2021-2026 $46 JP
Ace of Trumps Chapel Hill Road 2020, McLaren Vale RATING 91
DRINK 2022-2030 $92 JP
Anna's Sauvignon Blanc 2021, Adelaide Hills RATING 90 DRINK 2021-2025
$34 JP
Dairy Block Shiraz 2020, Adelaide Hills RATING 90 DRINK 2022-2028
$42 JP
Bush Vine Grenache 2020, McLaren Vale RATING 90 DRINK 2021-2028
$46 JP
Joseph Shiraz 2020, Langhorne Creek RATING 90 DRINK 2021-2034 $62 JP

Kate Hill Wines

21 Dowlings Road, Huonville, Tas 7109 **Region** Southern Tasmania
T 0448 842 696 **www**.katehillwines.com.au **Open** Wed–Sun 11–4 **Winemaker** Kate
Hill **Est.** 2008 **Dozens** 2000 **Vyds** 4ha

When Kate Hill and her husband Charles came to Tasmania in 2006, Kate had worked as a
winemaker in Australia and overseas for 10 years. Kate has always sourced fruit from vineyards
across southern Tasmania; in '16 she also planted 4ha of her own pinot noir, chardonnay and
shiraz. A cellar door followed in '17. The aim is to produce approachable, delicate wines.
Exports to Singapore. (JH)

Shiraz 2018, Tasmania The warm ripening season of '18 has given birth to a
Coal River Valley shiraz of character and balance. Ripe blackberry and plum fruit
is well backed by black pepper and salumi. Fine tannins carry a finish of accurate
line and length. Ready now, with a few year's potential. Screw cap. 13.8% alc.
RATING 92 DRINK 2022-2025 $50 TS

Huon Valley Pinot Noir 2016, Tasmania Medium crimson with some
bricking beginning. A mature pinot noir of forest-floor complexity and reflections
of tangy berry fruits. The cool acidity of the Huon defines a tangy finish, well
supported by fine, integrated tannins and a little bitterness. Ready now. Screw cap.
13.2% alc. RATING 90 DRINK 2022-2022 $55 TS

Pinot Noir 2017, Tasmania RATING 88 DRINK 2022-2022 $38 TS

Katnook ★★★★★

Riddoch Highway, Coonawarra, SA 5263 **Region** Coonawarra
T (08) 8737 0300 **www**.katnookestate.com.au **Open** Mon–Fri 10–5, w'ends 12–5
Winemaker Dan McNicol **Est.** 1979 **Dozens** 90 000 **Vyds** 198ha

Katnook has taken significant strides since acquisition by Freixenet, the Spanish cava producer.
The historic stone woolshed in which the second vintage in Coonawarra (1896) was made,
and which has served Katnook since 1980, has been restored. Likewise, the former office of
John Riddoch has been restored and is now the cellar door. Well over half of the total estate
plantings are cabernet sauvignon and shiraz; the Odyssey Cabernet Sauvignon and Prodigy
Shiraz are the duo at the top of a multi-tiered production. In Mar '18 Freixenet announced
that Henkell, the Oetker Group's sparkling wine branch, had acquired 50.67% of Freixenet's
shares, creating the world's leading sparkling wine group. The brand was sold to Accolade in
Aug '20. Exports to all major markets. (JH)

Prodigy Shiraz 2019, Coonawarra Did someone say bacon fat? This is
supremely aromatic and hedonistic – there is fresh maple, forest-fruit compote,
salted licorice, raw cocoa, blood plum and mulberries. In the mouth the wine
follows suit, the trump card – nay, the bower – is the web of savoury tannin that
extends to all reaches of the mouth. This is chewy and good. A beautiful wine.
Screw cap. 14.2% alc. RATING 97 DRINK 2022-2042 $129 EL ✪

Odyssey Cabernet Sauvignon 2019, Coonawarra Polished antique cedar,
blackberry and blueberry. The texture in the mouth is dense and concentrated,
a tour de force of tense structure and perfectly ordered fruit. All things in
place, and of the traditional school. Classy. Screw cap. 14.3% alc. RATING 95
DRINK 2022-2042 $92 EL

Kay Brothers ★★★★★

57 Kays Road, McLaren Vale, SA 5171 **Region** McLaren Vale
T (08) 8323 8211 **www**.kaybrothers.com.au **Open** 7 days 11–4 **Winemaker** Duncan
Kennedy **Viticulturist** Duncan Kennedy **Est.** 1890 **Dozens** 10 500 **Vyds** 22ha

A traditional winery with a rich history and just over 20ha of priceless old vines. The red
and fortified wines can be very good. Of particular interest is Block 6 Shiraz, made from
125yo vines. Both vines and wines are going from strength to strength. Celebrated its 130th

anniversary in '20. Exports to the US, Canada, Hong Kong, Singapore, Thailand, South Korea, the UK, Germany and Switzerland. (JH)

ŸŸŸŸŸ **Basket Pressed Mataro 2020, McLaren Vale** This address has turned a corner over the last few years. For the better. Fidelity to this great variety is embedded in leather, tapenade, pastrami, licorice strap and hung-game riffs. Plenty of blue and black fruits, too, expanding nicely across the persistent finish. Savouriness, the tattoo. Screw cap. 14.5% alc. RATING 95 DRINK 2022–2030 $29 NG ✪

Block 6 Shiraz 2019, McLaren Vale The lowest yields on record for this regional icon, drenched, as always, in personality. Dark cherry, boysenberry, licorice straps and the usual melee but best, the gritty carapace of nourishing grape tannins, corralling and directing the flavours long. This is a wine of largesse and restraint. Old-school, but good. Screw cap. 14.3% alc. RATING 95 DRINK 2022–2039 $125 NG

Griffon's Key Reserve Grenache 2020, McLaren Vale Blood plum, tamarind, turmeric, raspberry and raw ginger. The nose, as exotic as it is grounded and compelling; the degree of maceration and tannic implements, impeccable. This has weight, yet a dichotomous sense of ethereal lightness that defines all very good wines. This is a cuvée on the up. Screw cap. 14% alc. RATING 94 DRINK 2022–2030 $49 NG

ŸŸŸŸŸ **Basket Pressed Shiraz 2020, McLaren Vale** RATING 93 DRINK 2022–2035 $30 NG

Cuthbert Cabernet Sauvignon 2018, McLaren Vale RATING 93 DRINK 2022–2030 $49 NG

Basket Pressed Grenache 2020, McLaren Vale RATING 92 DRINK 2022–2028 $29 NG

Hillside Shiraz 2019, McLaren Vale RATING 92 DRINK 2022–2032 $49 NG

Grenache Rosé 2021, McLaren Vale RATING 91 DRINK 2022–2023 $25 NG

Ironmonger 2019, McLaren Vale RATING 91 DRINK 2022–2028 $35 NG

Keith Tulloch Wine ★★★★★

989 Hermitage Road, Pokolbin, NSW 2320 **Region** Hunter Valley
T (02) 4998 7500 **www**.keithtullochwine.com.au **Open** By appt Thurs–Sat 11–4,
Sun 10–3 **Winemaker** Keith Tulloch, Brendan Kaczorowski, Alisdair Tulloch
Viticulturist Brent Hutton **Est.** 1997 **Dozens** 10 000 **Vyds** 12.7ha
Keith Tulloch is, of course, a member of the Tulloch family, which has played a leading role in the Hunter Valley for over a century. Formerly a winemaker at Lindemans and Rothbury Estate, he developed his own label in '97. There is the same almost obsessive attention to detail, the same almost ascetic intellectual approach, the same refusal to accept anything but the best as that of Jeffrey Grosset. In Apr '19 the winery became the first Hunter Valley winery to become certified carbon neutral under the National Carbon Offset Standard (NCOS). Exports to the UK. (JH)

ŸŸŸŸŸ **The Doctor Shiraz 2018, Hunter Valley** The evolution of winemaking is palpable from the '14 to this. The former vintage praised, yet there is far greater freshness, poise and detail here. A beautiful drink that will age prodigiously. Stewed red plum, pickled cherry tamarind and a souk of spice. Immaculate tannins, a veil of freshness and nothing out of place. Very fine. Screw cap. 14.5% alc. RATING 96 DRINK 2022–2032 $150 NG

Latara Vineyard Semillon 2021, Hunter Valley Broader and waxier of feel, belying the tensile nature of the cool year. Hewn of dark volcanic clays, imparting a warmth and amplitude. Rivets of talcy acidity, phenolic chew and pungent mineral weld a streamlined wine of a beguiling generosity, focus and force. Lemon squash, guava, jasmine, fennel and raw pistachio ricochet to a long finish. This will age exceptionally well. Screw cap. 10.5% alc. RATING 95 DRINK 2021–2034 $35 NG ✪

Eagles Rest Vineyard Chardonnay 2021, Hunter Valley Euro sensibility. Mid weighted, fresh and of searing intensity, such is the nature of the cooler attenuated '21 growing season. Vanilla pod, creamed cashew, nougatine and nectarine. This wine sits beautifully in the mouth. Poised, strident and confident. Immaculate. Screw cap. 13% alc. RATING 95 DRINK 2021–2030 $40 NG

Ewen Vineyard Chardonnay 2021, Hunter Valley A tensile, reductively handled sibling to the broader Eagle's Rest. Stirred in high-class oak, to embellish texture. Lime curd and struck-match notes, reminiscent of Chassagne Montrachet's great Nöel Ramonet. Idiosyncratic, in the best sense. Pummelling riffs on nectarine and white peach drive across a long, pungent, affably creamy finish. A fine counterpoint to the range that melds flavour, power and precision. Screw cap. 13% alc. RATING 95 DRINK 2021–2030 $45 NG

Field of Mars Shiraz 2019, Hunter Valley A warm year, embellished by an exceptional site and superlative craftsmanship. The oak, the frame to clove, lilac, sweet cherry and tamarind. An underbelly of Hunter loam and Asian spice. A powerful wine, with the bones to facilitate age and the detailed cogs to promote freshness. Screw cap. 14.5% alc. RATING 95 DRINK 2023–2033 $95 NG

Field of Mars Block 4 Chardonnay 2019, Hunter Valley Exceptional chardonnay, drawing on the ripeness and extract of the year with aplomb. The oak, perfectly nestled, casting notes of dried hazelnut, porcini and tatami straw, freshly lain. The finish, impressive. A scintillating contemporary Hunter chardonnay. Screw cap. 13% alc. RATING 95 DRINK 2021–2028 $65 NG

Museum Release Semillon 2015, Hunter Valley Already delicious, splaying chords of buttered toast, brioche, lemon oil and glazed quince across a long finish. Yet there is a feel to this wine, lightweight, taut and of great intensity, that there is more to come. Latent, with its current state a mere glimpse of a grand future, perhaps. The parry of extract and thrust of structure, auguring well. Screw cap. 10.5% alc. RATING 95 DRINK 2021–2028 $65 NG

Barrel Aged Fortified Viognier 2016, Hunter Valley While I have never come across fortified viognier in the Rhône, I've come across a few here. A whiff of apricot, orange blossom and tamarind, before toasted walnuts, date and dried fig evidence the ripe nature of the fruit and extended barrel ageing. The depth of rancio complexity facilitates something to ponder life's ebbs and flows. Delicious wine. Screw cap. 18% alc. RATING 95 $65 NG

Field of Mars Block 2 Semillon 2019, Hunter Valley A warm year endowing a rich feel and generous extract, iterated as riffs on barley sugar, lemon candy, cantaloupe and ginger. Impressively, the wine is driven to a long, impactful finish by virtue of phenolics and force of personality, rather than any brittle acidity. A tenacious, rather than elegant, expression. Screw cap. 10.5% alc. RATING 94 DRINK 2021–2026 $55 NG

ΨΨΨΨΨ **Field of Mars Block 1 Viognier 2021, Hunter Valley** RATING 93 DRINK 2021–2025 $55 NG

McKelvey Vineyard Shiraz 2020, Hunter Valley RATING 93 DRINK 2021–2025 $48 NG

Museum Release The Kester Shiraz 2014, Hunter Valley RATING 93 DRINK 2022–2030 $120 NG

Chardonnay 2021, Hunter Valley RATING 92 DRINK 2021–2025 $35 NG

Semillon 2021, Hunter Valley RATING 91 DRINK 2021–2027 $30 NG

Shiraz Viognier 2020, Hunter Valley RATING 91 DRINK 2022–2024 $38 NG

Kellybrook   ★★★★☆

Fulford Road, Wonga Park, Vic 3115 **Region** Yarra Valley
T (03) 9722 1304 **www**.kellybrookwinery.com.au **Open** Fri–Sun 11–5
Winemaker Stuart Dudine **Est.** 1962 **Dozens** 3000 **Vyds** 8.4ha
The vineyard is at Wonga Park, one of the gateways to the Yarra Valley. A very competent producer of beer, cider and apple brandy (in Calvados style) as well as table wine. When it

received its winery licence in 1970, it became the first winery in the Yarra Valley to open its doors in the 20th century, a distinction often ignored or forgotten. (JH)

ΨΨΨΨ♀ **Blanc de Blancs 2018, Yarra Valley** Second disgorgement. Three years on lees, disgorged winter '21. Dosage of 6g/L. A light yellow gold with green tinges. Subtle with ripe, yellow apple, discreet dried apricot and a gentle waft of fresh dough. Youthful and nicely balanced with green apple, white peach and a hint of pistachio, before finishing crisp and dry. Diam. 12.5% alc. RATING 93 $40 PR

Estate Chardonnay 2020, Yarra Valley Nectarine, melon and fig fruit sit alongside a little vanilla spice and clove. With its bright nectarine fruit, this has good depth and freshness and finishes with a gentle mouth-watering acidity. Screw cap. 13% alc. RATING 93 DRINK 2021-2026 $40 PR

Estate Pinot Noir 2020, Yarra Valley Light cherry red. Black cherries, sweet raspberries, earth and spices like cinnamon and clove can all be found in this wine, that took a while to open up. There is considerable depth and structure on the palate and while approachable now, this could do with another 2 or 3 years in a cool, dark place. Screw cap. 13% alc. RATING 93 DRINK 2022-2026 $40 PR

50th Anniversary Chardonnay 2020, Yarra Valley A bright green gold. Notes of ripe nectarines, melon, grilled nuts and just the right amount of matchstick. The creamily textured and energetic palate finishes dry and chalky, with a burst of acidity that should ensure good ageing potential. Screw cap. 13% alc. RATING 93 DRINK 2021-2016 $50 PR

Estate Reserve Shiraz 2019, Yarra Valley A vibrant, medium crimson purple. Enticing with aromas of red plum, sweet spices and just a hint of fresh vanilla bean. Medium bodied and well put together, this has both elegance and good depth. It's already drinking well now, but with its velvety tannins, this will continue to get better for some time yet. Screw cap. 13% alc. RATING 92 DRINK 2021-2027 $40 PR

Pinot Noir 2020, Yarra Valley A light, very bright, crimson red. Pure strawberry fruit aromas together with a little raspberry and a lick of well-judged vanillin from the 20% new oak. I like the silky mouthfeel and this finishes long with fine, dusty tannins. Screw cap. 13% alc. RATING 91 DRINK 2021-2025 $30 PR

ΨΨΨΨ **Chardonnay 2021, Yarra Valley** RATING 89 DRINK 2021-2023 $30 PR

Kelman Vineyard   ★★★★

2 Oakey Creek Road, Pokolbin, NSW 2320 **Region** Hunter Valley
T (02) 4991 5456 **www**.kelmanvineyard.com.au **Open** Thurs–Mon 10–4
Winemaker Xanthe Hatcher **Est.** 1999 **Dozens** 1300 **Vyds** 9ha
Kelman Vineyard is a community development spread over 40ha, with 9ha under vine. The estate is scattered with traditional country cottages and homesteads; vines, olive and lemon groves meander between the dwellings. Named in honour of William Kelman who travelled to Australia with John Busby (father of James Busby) in 1824, marrying John's daughter Katherine on the ship to Australia. (JH)

ΨΨΨΨ♀ **Blanc de Blancs Chardonnay 2017, Hunter Valley** Exceptional local fizz. Four years on lees. Toasted nuts, gingerbread, nashi pear, sourdough and glazed quince. Detailed and extremely long, this drinks like a grower champagne without the high-acid fidelity. The prototype for the region. I am smitten. The caveat: keep it very cold to harness the intruding dosage. Screw cap. 12.2% alc. RATING 93 $36 NG

Serendipity Vin de Vie Muscat NV, Hunter Valley Black muscat fortified at the advent of fermentation, much akin to a Vin Doux Natural. Older material in the blend imparts complexity, with the average age of all components being 17 years. Spiritous notes of date, sugared plum, clove and cinnamon. While this is fortified, it is far from heavy, unctuous or torrefied, as many Australians can be. Delicious drinking. Screw cap. 19% alc. RATING 92 $45 NG

The Oakey Ridge CSG 2021, Hunter Valley Hunter chardonnay and semillon, with a sluice of gris from the Adelaide Hills. Lightweight, herbal, fresh and versatile, this is an interesting meld. The pungency of the semillon rides above the others aromatically, beaming Thai herb and lemon dew, while finding confluence with cantaloupe and quince. The finish is lanolin waxy and dutifully long. Good drinking. Screw cap. 12.2% alc. RATING 91 DRINK 2021-2026 $26 NG

Shiraz Tempranillo 2019, Hunter Valley This is solid drinking. Prosaic, in the best sense. Pickled cherry, menthol, red plum and a swathe of dusty tannins. The cadence is gentle, but grippy enough to be savoury. Good drinking. Screw cap. 13.7% alc. RATING 91 DRINK 2021-2028 $26 NG

Kennedy

Maple Park, 224 Wallenjoe Road, Corop, Vic 3559 (postal) **Region** Heathcote **T** (03) 5484 8293 **www**.kennedyvintners.com.au **Winemaker** Glen Hayley, Gerard Kennedy **Viticulturist** Barney Touhey **Est.** 2002 **Dozens** 3000 **Vyds** 29.2ha

Having been farmers in the Colbinabbin area of Heathcote for 27 years, John and Patricia Kennedy were on the spot when a prime piece of red Cambrian soil on the east-facing slope of Mount Camel Range became available for purchase. They planted 20ha of shiraz in '02. As they gained knowledge of the intricate differences within the site, further plantings of shiraz, tempranillo and mourvèdre followed in '07. The Shiraz is made in small open fermenters, using indigenous yeasts and gentle pigeage before being taken to French oak for maturation. John and Patricia's geologist son Gerard returned to the family business in '15 and oversees the winemaking and activities in the vineyard. (JH)

🍷🍷🍷🍷🍷 **Pink Hills Rosé 2021, Heathcote** Summer-smart in light copper and orange peel hues, with the scent of red berries, spice and a fleck of pepper. Bone dry, which brings the delicacy of fruit to the forefront, finishing with a nice little sherbety surprise. Screw cap. 13% alc. RATING 93 DRINK 2021-2025 $25 JP ✪

Shiraz 2019, Heathcote Brings together all the Heathcote shiraz qualities we love to see, the deep, brilliant red colour, the intensity of blackberries with lifted spice, the innate balance that comes from the mineral-rich soils. All up, excellent drinking at a great price. Screw cap. 13.5% alc. RATING 93 DRINK 2021-2027 $28 JP

Henrietta Tempranillo 2021, Heathcote A punchy, deep purple-hearted youngster with a lot of go, Henrietta makes quite an entrance. Lively licorice and bush herbs join with ripe, sweet blackberry fruits, pomegranate and savoury woody spice. Flows evenly and long through a full-bodied palate with a lilting peppery thread. Screw cap. 14% alc. RATING 92 DRINK 2022-2028 $24 JP ✪

🍷🍷🍷🍷 **Henrietta Shiraz 2020, Heathcote** RATING 89 DRINK 2021-2025 $24 JP
Henrietta Rosé 2021, Heathcote RATING 88 DRINK 2021-2024 $22 JP

Kerri Greens

38 Paringa Road, Red Hill South, Vic 3937 **Region** Mornington Peninsula **T** (03) 5989 2572 **www**.kerrigreens.com **Open** Sat 11–5, Fri, Sun 12–5 **Winemaker** Tom McCarthy, Lucas Blanck **Viticulturist** Lucas Blanck, Tom McCarthy **Est.** 2015 **Dozens** 1000

Kerri Greens (named after a local surf break) offers excellent and energising wines. Tom McCarthy (son of local Peninsula producers, Kathleen Quealy and Kevin McCarthy) is the lead winemaker at Quealy Wines these days and Lucas Blanck (son of winemaker Frederic, from Domaine Paul Blanck in Alsace) is viticulturist. Since it began in 2013, Tom and Paul have worked tirelessly to bring life back to the various vineyards they manage. Organics, sustainability and treading gently are important considerations. It's also a family business strengthened by their wives, Alyce Blanck and Sarah Saxton, who are very much at the forefront of the business. What's really exciting is that this young quartet is respectful of a wine region that nurtures them, yet not afraid to shake things up. Bravo. (JF)

ŶŶŶŶŶ Ohne Gewürztraminer 2021, Mornington Peninsula Such a contrast to the tighter rendition in '20, yet this is no less fabulous. It's just richer, fleshier and riper, but not heavy. Lychees and musk, poached quinces topped with cinnamon and drizzled with rosewater syrup. Tannins add a slippery, textural coating and grip across the full-bodied palate. Screw cap. 12.5% alc. RATING 95 DRINK 2022-2026 $30 JF ✪

Murra Pinot Noir 2021, Mornington Peninsula Context is everything. This is made to be a vibrant, drink-now red. It's aim is not complexity, but it's a damn delicious drink. Top points for its bright cherry and raspberry flavours, twigs and spice, crunchy poppy acidity and fine-grit tannins. Some Italian-esque bitter herbs and Campari on the finish adds to the mouth-watering effect. Screw cap. 12.2% alc. RATING 95 DRINK 2022-2026 $38 JF

ŶŶŶŶŸ Samphire Sauvignon Blanc 2021, Mornington Peninsula RATING 93 DRINK 2022-2025 $30 JF

Hickson Chardonnay 2021, Mornington Peninsula RATING 93 DRINK 2022-2027 $45 JF

Foothills Pinot Noir 2020, Mornington Peninsula RATING 93 DRINK 2021-2026 $40 JF

Hickson Chardonnay 2020, Mornington Peninsula RATING 93 DRINK 2021-2028 $42 JF

Pinots de Mornington Rosé 2021, Mornington Peninsula RATING 92 DRINK 2021-2023 $30 JF

Lazy Bastard Pinot Noir 2021, Mornington Peninsula RATING 92 DRINK 2021-2025 $35 JF

Pig Face Chardonnay 2020, Mornington Peninsula RATING 92 DRINK 2021-2028 $30 JF

Murra Pinot Noir 2020, Mornington Peninsula RATING 92 DRINK 2021-2025 $34 JF

Duke Chardonnay 2020, Mornington Peninsula RATING 92 DRINK 2022-2027 $62 JF

Pig Face Chardonnay 2021, Mornington Peninsula RATING 91 DRINK 2022-2026 $34 JF

Kerrigan + Berry ★★★★★

PO Box 221, Cowaramup, WA 6284 **Region** South West Australia
T (08) 9755 6046 **www.**kerriganandberry.com.au **Open** 7 days 10–5
Winemaker Michael Kerrigan, Gavin Berry **Est.** 2007 **Dozens** 1500
Owners Michael Kerrigan and Gavin Berry have been making wine in WA for a combined period of over 50 years and say they have been most closely associated with the 2 varieties that in their opinion define WA: riesling and cabernet sauvignon. This is strictly a weekend and after-hours venture, separate from their respective roles as chief winemakers at Hay Shed Hill (Michael) and West Cape Howe (Gavin). They have focused on what is important, and explain, 'We have spent a total of zero hours on marketing research, and no consultants have been injured in the making of these wines'. Exports to the UK, Denmark and Singapore. (JH)

ŶŶŶŶŶ Riesling 2021, Mount Barker What a brilliant wine. Structured, staunch, brawny, powerfully concentrated and very long – this shows the strength of Mount Barker for this style of riesling. It is no shrinking violet. Neither restrained nor delicate; driven by acid. All things in place – a masterstroke. Better for cellaring than drinking now, although it will of course bend to either will. Screw cap. 12% alc. RATING 95 DRINK 2021-2036 $30 EL ✪

Chardonnay 2020, Margaret River As with most great chardonnays from Margaret River in '20, there is an effortlessness about this wine. It is graceful and ever so fine, sure to expand in volume and generosity in the years to come. That briny acidity of Margaret River chardonnays is here, finely knitting the fruit components together. Screw cap. 12% alc. RATING 95 DRINK 2021-2031 $40 EL

Shiraz 2018, Frankland River The vintage was exceptional, giving rise to this fragrant bouquet of spice and a medium-bodied yet intense and elegant palate, finely chiselled black cherry and cedary notes to the finish and aftertaste. Screw cap. 14.5% alc. RATING 95 DRINK 2025-2040 $40 JH

Kersbrook Hill   ★★★☆

1498 South Para Road, Kersbrook, SA 5231 **Region** Adelaide Hills
T (08) 8389 3301 www.kersbrookhill.com.au **Open** 7 days 10–5.30 **Winemaker** Paul Clark, Nigel Nessi **Viticulturist** Paul Clark **Est.** 1998 **Dozens** 8000 **Vyds** 11ha
Paul and Mary Clark purchased what is now the Kersbrook Hill property, then grazing land, in 1997, planting 0.4ha of shiraz on a reality-check basis. Encouraged by the results, they increased the plantings to 3ha of shiraz and 1ha of riesling 2 years later. Yet further expansion of the vineyards has seen the area under vine increased to 11ha, cabernet sauvignon (with 6ha) the somewhat unusual frontrunner. Consultant viticulturist Mark Whisson has been growing grapes in the Adelaide Hills for over 20 years. Exports to the US, Singapore and Hong Kong. (JH)

🍷🍷🍷🍷🍷 **Eliza Jane Shiraz 2018, Barossa Valley** A savoury interpretation of Barossa shiraz that still retains plenty of signature boldness and oomph. Leather, baked earth and smoked meats go head to head with cassis and spice on the bouquet. Kersbrook likes to release reds with age and accordingly they are built for distance around firm, taut structures. Oak also plays a part, too, as tasted here plumping up the middle palate with plenty of warm toastiness picked up from new French oak. Coming together nicely. Screw cap. 14.5% alc. RATING 91 DRINK 2022-2032 $80 JP

🍷🍷🍷🍷 **Riesling 2021, Adelaide Hills** RATING 88 DRINK 2022-2026 $25 JP
The Lindsey Merlot 2017, Adelaide Hills RATING 88 DRINK 2023-2032 $80 JP

Kilgour Wines   ★★★☆

25 McAdams Lane, Bellarine, Vic 3223 **Region** Geelong
T 0448 785 744 **Open** Sat, Public hols & by appt **Winemaker** Alister Timms
Viticulturist Anne Timms **Est.** 1992 **Dozens** 600 **Vyds** 15ha
While this business has roots in the Bellarine Peninsula dating back to 1989, its reappearance in 2017 is a different venture altogether. Anne Timms planted the original vineyard in '89, opening Kilgour Estate. In '10 she sold the 3.2ha title with the Kilgour Estate winery, the winery label and a separate 2ha of vines to David and Lyndsay Sharp who renamed the business Jack Rabbit. Anne Timms retained 8ha of vines surrounding the Jack Rabbit property and for the next 5 years sold the grapes to other wineries. In '17 she retained part of the crop, with Alister Timms (chief winemaker at Shadowfax) making the Kilgour Wines under contract at Shadowfax. (JH)

🍷🍷🍷🍷🍷 **Bellarine Pinot Gris 2021, Geelong** Distinctive pear-drop aromas backed by ripe melon, tarte tatin, sweet apple and honeysuckle. Fills the mouth with flavour and stays long. And that spice? It's a real treat. Screw cap. 13% alc. RATING 90 DRINK 2021-2025 $30 JP

🍷🍷🍷🍷 **Bellarine Pinot Noir 2021, Geelong** RATING 89 DRINK 2022-2026 $40 JP
Bellarine Rosé 2021, Geelong RATING 88 DRINK 2021-2024 $30 JP

Kilikanoon Wines   ★★★★★

30 Penna Lane, Penwortham, SA 5453 **Region** Clare Valley
T (08) 8843 4206 www.kilikanoon.com.au **Open** 7 days 11–5 **Winemaker** Peter Warr, Mercedes Paynter **Viticulturist** Troy van Dulken **Est.** 1997 **Dozens** 100 000 **Vyds** 120ha
Kilikanoon has travelled in the fast lane since winemaker Kevin Mitchell established it in 1997 on the foundation of 6ha of vines he owned with father Mort. With the aid of

investors, its 100000 dozen production comes from 120ha of estate-owned vineyards. A major restructure has been completed with the acquisition of the winery that it had hitherto leased, along with the ownership of the 16.35ha Mount Surmon Vineyard. This very substantial business in the Clare Valley produces 85% red wines, with a further focus on grenache. Kilikanoon accounts for over 35% of the region's production of this variety, with 3 single-vineyard wines and 2 GSM blends. Founder Kevin Mitchell is still involved in the business, providing consultancy advice on sales and marketing. Exports to most markets. (JH)

ＹＹＹＹＹ **Attunga 1865 Shiraz 2019, Clare Valley** Crushed graphite laces blueberries, black cherries, fine white spice and mulberries together. In the mouth the wine is like midnight: deep and endless, the shape of the tannins becoming almost irrelevant as they coat the cheeks in a film of gossamer fine texture. Despite the concentration of flavour here, it is not weighty; displaying finesse and nuance alongside sheer, inarguable depth and magnitude from 157 years of vine age. Imagine the days those vines have seen. Screw cap. 14.5% alc. RATING 97 DRINK 2022-2052 $250 EL

ＹＹＹＹＹ **Tregea Reserve Cabernet Sauvignon 2020, Clare Valley** Concentrated and intense aromatically: this speaks of star anise and crushed peppercorns, blackcurrant pastille and dustings of raw cocoa. In the mouth the wine displays a scintillating show of black fruits and bright, punchy acidity. It swirls and whorls across the palate, and is as impressive for its flavour as it is for its texture; velvety, plush and rippling. More than a handful of reasons to drink this – it's as true to Clare as it is to cabernet, and that's a mighty fine thing. Screw cap. 14.5% alc. RATING 96 DRINK 2022-2037 $96 EL

Ashton 1920 Mataro 2020, Clare Valley Mataro: what a glorious variety. Blood plums and red dirt, earth and berries; it is at once savoury and sweet, always plush, and often relied upon in a blend to provide a stable, plush base of tannins and dense fruit, as it does in this varietal wine. The fruit and the berries come as one package, making for a concentrated, velvety drinking experience. Very impressive. Screw cap. 14% alc. RATING 95 DRINK 2021-2031 $55 EL

Prodigal Grenache 2020, Clare Valley Delicious. Red licorice, aniseed, fennel flower, red apple skins, rhubarb, raspberry and spice galore. This is a beautiful wine! Totally buoyant, plump and pleasurable. Get some. Screw cap. 14.5% alc. RATING 95 DRINK 2021-2031 $40 EL

Covenant Shiraz 2019, Clare Valley Sandalwood and salted licorice rise up out of the glass, fighting for place over the blackberry bramble, blood plum and raspberry coulis. This is a gorgeous, opulent wine of grace and poise. There are layers upon layers of velvety flavour here. Luxurious, sybaritic, and bloody delicious. Screw cap. 14.5% alc. RATING 95 DRINK 2021-2031 $40 EL

Baudinet Blend GSM 2019, Clare Valley GSM is such a brilliant combination of varieties. You get pleasure from all angles: buoyancy, plumpness and clarity from the grenache, mouth-filling roundness from the shiraz, and that plush, earthy base that is mataro. All varieties here perform in each other's presence. This is wonderful – licorice, dark chocolate, raspberry, pomegranate, blueberries, cloves, hung deli meat … it's a feast. Three trophies at the 2021 International Wine Challenge. Screw cap. 14.5% alc. RATING 95 DRINK 2021-2031 $55 EL

Kelly 1932 Grenache 2019, Clare Valley Spicy, plush and succulent, this has an endless array of raspberry, rhubarb, hung deli meat and pink peppercorns, all of it laid on a cloth of svelte tannins. If the way The Duke Reserve Grenache opened up in a decanter is anything to go by, this should not be underestimated … chances are it will escalate in its pleasure-giving properties untold after a decant. Screw cap. 14.5% alc. RATING 95 DRINK 2022-2037 $96 EL

Duke Reserve Grenache 2019, Clare Valley Warmer years suit varieties like grenache. Boiled raspberry humbug, rhubarb, Szechuan peppercorn, curry powder and an array of fresh garden herbs on both the nose and palate. It's a big wine, but there's hedonistic elements that elevate it, untold. No doubt a decant will allow this to open even further. Recommended. Screw cap. 14.5% alc. RATING 94 DRINK 2021-2031 $55 EL

Oracle Shiraz 2018, Clare Valley A fascinating wine: aromatically, this is lush, like chocolate velvet. Sumptuous. In the mouth, however, the wine is lighter, finer, and more savoury than expected, making for extraordinarily engaging drinking. Going back to the nose again, there is antique sideboard, salted licorice, raw cocoa, pastrami and peppercorn. It's got bacon fat, prosciutto and star anise, too. This is spicy, medium weighted, and coming with a swagger of gravitas. Screw cap. 14.5% alc. RATING 94 DRINK 2022-2037 $96 EL

Killibinbin ★★★☆

PO Box 10, Langhorne Creek, SA 5255 **Region** Langhorne Creek
T (08) 85373382 **www**.killibinbin.com.au **Winemaker** Jim Urlwin **Viticulturist** Guy Adams **Est.** 1997 **Dozens** 12 000 **Vyds** 20ha
In late 2010 Guy and Liz Adams (of Metala Vineyards fame) acquired the Killibinbin brand. Production has grown significantly since that time, but the wines continue to be sourced solely from the Metala Vineyards (20ha are dedicated to Killibinbin: 10ha each of shiraz and cabernet sauvignon). Exports to South Korea, Japan, the UK, the US, Canada, the Netherlands, Malaysia, Singapore and Taiwan. (JH)

ΨΨΨΨ♀ **Secrets 2019, Langhorne Creek** A 62/32/6% estate blend of cabernet sauvignon/shiraz/petit verdot. It's supple and smooth, the blackberry and blackcurrant fruit fresh, in best Langhorne Creek style and weight. Extraordinary value. Screw cap. 14.5% alc. RATING 93 DRINK 2022-2032 $15 JH ❂

ΨΨΨΨ **Scream Shiraz 2018, Langhorne Creek** RATING 89 DRINK 2025-2035 $27 JH

Kimbarra Wines ★★★★

422 Barkly Street, Ararat, Vic 3377 **Region** Grampians
T 0428 519 195 **www**.kimbarrawines.com.au **Open** By appt **Winemaker** Peter Leeke, Justin Purser, Adam Richardson **Est.** 1990 **Dozens** 180 **Vyds** 11ha
Peter Leeke has 8.5ha of shiraz, 1.5ha of riesling and 1ha of cabernet sauvignon – varieties that have proven best suited to the Grampians region. The particularly well-made, estate-grown wines deserve a wider audience. (JH)

ΨΨΨΨΨ **Riesling 2021, Great Western** Kimbarra captures the singular purity of Great Western riesling from vintage to vintage. Yet again in '21, it's all about the region's beautiful florals enhanced delicately, perceptively, in intense lime cordial, lemon rind, kaffir lime and green apple. And bringing it all together is bright acidity, piquant and zesty. Screw cap. 11.8% alc. RATING 94 DRINK 2022-2031 $30 JP ❂

ΨΨΨΨ♀ **Shiraz 2020, Great Western** RATING 93 DRINK 2022-2030 $30 JP

Kimbolton Wines ★★★★★

29 Burleigh Street, Langhorne Creek, SA 5255 **Region** Langhorne Creek
T (08) 8537 3002 **www**.kimboltonwines.com.au **Open** 7 days 11–4
Winemaker Contract **Est.** 1998 **Dozens** 2500 **Vyds** 55ha
The Kimbolton property originally formed part of the Potts Bleasdale estate. In 1946 it was acquired by Henry and Thelma Case, grandparents of current owners brother and sister Nicole Clark and Brad Case. The grapes from the vineyard plantings (cabernet sauvignon, shiraz, malbec, fiano, carignan and montepulciano) are sold to leading wineries, with small amounts retained for the Kimbolton label. The name comes from a medieval town in Bedfordshire, UK, from which some of the family's ancestors emigrated. Kimbolton opened its cellar door in Dec '18, constructed from 'a unique mix of high-gloss navy industrial shipping containers' and timber, including a rooftop viewing platform. (JH)

ΨΨΨΨΨ **The Rifleman Cabernet Sauvignon 2019, Langhorne Creek** Excellent, deep crimson colour, the first sign of the quality of the fruit and its relaxed acceptance of the oak. The texture and structure of the palate are faultless, cassis and a black-olive trim gain further traction in the medium–full body of the wine. Decades won't tire it. 160 dozen made. Screw cap. 14.3% alc. RATING 95 DRINK 2025-2045 $60 JH

The Rifleman Shiraz 2019, Langhorne Creek Kept from over extraction, and the luscious fruit takes the oak face on, and doesn't blink. All things good about Langhorne Creek. Screw cap. 14.5% alc. RATING 95 DRINK 2023-2034 $60 JH

Cabernet Sauvignon 2019, Langhorne Creek The youthful colour is a good start. Punches well above its price weight. The fragrant bouquet offers a seamless fusion of fruit and oak, the palate following with alacrity. Blackcurrant/cassis, gently cedary oak, and perfectly balanced and integrated tannins make this a high-quality, all-purpose wine. Screw cap. 14% alc. RATING 94 DRINK 2022-2032 $25 JH ✪

ΨΨΨΨϙ **Single Vineyard M14 Fiano 2021, Langhorne Creek** RATING 93 DRINK 2022-2025 $25 JH ✪

Single Vineyard Brad's Block Montepulciano 2021, Langhorne Creek RATING 93 DRINK 2023-2028 $28 JH

Single Vineyard M18 Carignan 2021, Langhorne Creek RATING 91 DRINK 2022-2027 $28 JH

Shiraz 2019, Langhorne Creek RATING 91 DRINK 2022-2026 $25 JH

King River Estate   ★★★☆

3556 Wangaratta-Whitfield Road, Wangaratta, Vic 3678 **Region** King Valley
T (03) 5729 3689 **www**.kingriverestate.com.au **Open** Fri–Sun & public hols 11–5
Winemaker Dennis Clarke **Est.** 1996 **Dozens** 2000 **Vyds** 13ha
First planted in 1990, King River Estate sits alongside the King River in the heart of the King Valley in Victoria's northeast. The almost 30-year-old vines produce an array of wines which reflect the character and Italian influence of the region. It came under new ownership in '18; it is still very much a family-run business, new investment has reinvigorated the winery and the cellar door experience. Prosecco made its debut in '18, while the Flying Duck range adds some zest to the line-up. Exports to Singapore. (JH)

ΨΨΨΨϙ **Sagrantino 2018, King Valley** The Umbrian grape variety warms to its new King Valley home, revealing some Italian-esque credentials with a light savouriness and medium body, before finishing with a dry astringency. Attractive sage, thyme, black cherry and pastille aromas with some blueberry notes are inviting. Dives right in and explores a range of savoury flavours in addition to fruit, overseen by chewy tannins before finishing firm and dry. Screw cap. 13.5% alc. RATING 90 DRINK 2021-2026 $35 JP

ΨΨΨΨ **Saperavi 2017, King Valley** RATING 89 DRINK 2021-2031 $42 JP
Prosecco 2021, King Valley RATING 88 $24 JP
Flying Duck Pinot Grigio 2021, King Valley RATING 88 DRINK 2021-2025 $22 JP
Flying Duck Rosé 2021, King Valley RATING 88 DRINK 2021-2024 $22 JP
Lagrein 2017, King Valley RATING 88 DRINK 2021-2027 $42 JP

Kirrihill Wines   ★★★★

948 Farrell Flat Road, Clare, SA 5453 **Region** Clare Valley
T (08) 8842 1233 **www**.kirrihill.com.au **Open** By appt **Winemaker** Andrew Locke, Alexandra Wardlaw **Viticulturist** Dick Brysky **Est.** 1998 **Dozens** 55 000 **Vyds** 600ha
The Kirrihill story started in the late '90s. The aim was to build a business producing premium wines from temperate vineyards that represent the unique characters of the Clare Valley. Grapes are sourced from specially selected parcels of Kirrihill's 600ha of vineyards. Andrew Locke, with vintage experience in the Loire Valley, Tuscany, Sonoma Valley and Spain, joined Kirrihill as chief winemaker in '20. Exports to NZ, the USA and the UK. (JH)

🍷🍷🍷🍷🍷 **E.B.'s The Settler Riesling 2021, Clare Valley** The 6th release. Intensely concentrated and palate staining; the palate is littered with green apples, lime and lemon pith, all of it grounded by a minerally/shale base. There's a suggestion of fennel flower and aniseed round the edges of the fruit. A very smart wine. Willowy. Screw cap. 12% alc. RATING 94 DRINK 2021–2036 $35 EL

🍷🍷🍷🍷🍷 **E.B.'s The Squire Shiraz 2020, Clare Valley** RATING 93 DRINK 2022–2032 $65 EL
The Partner Series Shiraz 2019, Clare Valley RATING 93 DRINK 2021–2028 $30 EL
Regional Selection Shiraz 2020, Clare Valley RATING 90 DRINK 2021–2027 $19 EL ✪

Knappstein   ★★★★★

2 Pioneer Avenue, Clare, SA 5453 **Region** Clare Valley
T (08) 8841 2100 www.knappstein.com.au **Open** 7 days 10–4 **Winemaker** Michael Kane, Mike Farmilo (Consultant) **Est.** 1969 **Dozens** 75 000 **Vyds** 114ha
Knappstein's full name is Knappstein Enterprise Winery, reflecting its history before being acquired by Petaluma, then part of Lion Nathan, followed by Accolade. After a period of corporate ownership, Knappstein has now come full circle and is back in private ownership, purchased in '19 by Yinmore Wines. Despite these corporate chessboard moves, wine quality has remained excellent. The wines are produced from the substantial mature estate Enterprise, Ackland, Yertabulti and The Mayor's vineyards. Exports to all major markets. (JH)

🍷🍷🍷🍷🍷 **Ackland Single Vineyard Watervale Riesling 2021, Clare Valley** This is an acid-driven, lean and minerally riesling, with tight lemon, lime and grapefruit. If you thought the Enterprise was taut and terrific, it ain't got nothin' on this. With long sinewy muscles and a tense concoction of fruit on the palate, this is very good, if not a little austere in its youth, currently. Age it. Screw cap. 12% alc. RATING 95 DRINK 2021–2036 $30 EL ✪
Enterprise Vineyard Riesling 2021, Clare Valley The palate here is lean, restrained, minerally and fine, with crushed quartz, saline acidity, jasmine-tea tannins and layers upon layers of citrus pith, zest and flesh. Length of flavour shows the pedigree and ageability of the wine. Very smart indeed. Screw cap. 12% alc. RATING 95 DRINK 2021–2036 $30 EL ✪
Enterprise Vineyard Cabernet Sauvignon 2019, Clare Valley Cassis, salted licorice, cigar box, dark chocolate and blood plums. The nose and the palate are perfectly aligned in this classical, savoury and structural cabernet. Screw cap. 14.5% alc. RATING 94 DRINK 2021–2036 $53 EL

🍷🍷🍷🍷🍷 **Riesling 2021, Clare Valley** RATING 93 DRINK 2021–2031 $22 EL ✪
Insider Riesling 2021, Clare Valley RATING 90 DRINK 2021–2031 $30 EL

Knee Deep Wines   ★★★★

22 Rathay Street, Victoria Park, WA 6100 **Region** Margaret River
T (08) 9755 6776 www.kneedeepwines.com.au **Winemaker** Kate Morgan **Est.** 2000 **Dozens** 5000
Perth surgeon and veteran yachtsman Phil Childs and wife Sue planted their property in Wilyabrup in 2000 to chardonnay, sauvignon blanc, semillon, chenin blanc, cabernet sauvignon and shiraz. The name was inspired by the passion and commitment needed to produce premium wine and as a tongue- in-cheek acknowledgement of jumping in 'boots and all' during a testing time in the wine industry, the grape glut building more or less in tune with the venture. The reins have now passed to the Holden family, Matt and Clair Holden having worked alongside the Childs family for 5 years. Exports to Germany. (JH)

🍷🍷🍷🍷🍷 **Third Rule Chardonnay 2021, Margaret River** Lovely concentration of flavour in the mouth, with layers of yellow peach, red apples, kiwi-fruit acidity and loads of white spice. There's an attractive floral element through the finish, however the experience is bound up in acidity at this inchoate stage. Patience is a virtue, friends. Screw cap. 12% alc. RATING 93 DRINK 2022–2028 $55 EL

Birdhouse Malbec 2020, Margaret River Spiced, nuanced and bright; this is a cool iteration of the variety in a year that is becoming famed for its ability to produce plush, ripe and glossy wines. A decant will assist in bringing out the velvety nature of the fruit, which is hiding beneath a layer of fine tannin and prolific spice. Lovely. Screw cap. 13.5% alc. RATING 92 DRINK 2021–2028 $35 EL

Third Rule Cabernet Sauvignon 2019, Margaret River The '19 vintage was a cool one, and the '19 cabernets from Margaret River are perfumed, delicate and more approachable early. The delicate fruit makes the oak feel heavy handed; all aspects of the wine are coloured by it. While everything is in place and it is clearly well made, the balance of power resides with the oak, not the fruit, and that is a challenging thing to overcome when planning on consuming sooner, rather than later. So, you might have to wait a bit for this one. Screw cap. 13% alc. RATING 92 DRINK 2022–2035 $55 EL

Sauvignon Blanc 2021, Margaret River Light, bright, vibrant and fresh with crunchy layers of apples, lychee, pineapple and even some stone fruit. I'm a fan of lower-alcohol wines (provided it's all been handled well), and this is a good example of the daintiness that is possible within that framework. Screw cap. 11.5% alc. RATING 91 DRINK 2021–2024 $24 EL

Birdhouse Shiraz 2020, Margaret River Likely no surprise, but the fruit and the oak haven't quite come together yet. Having said that, the luscious layers of bright berries show us that all things will be well in a year or so. Very pretty, but get it in a decanter to let the fruit flower and the oak integrate. Screw cap. 14% alc. RATING 91 DRINK 2021–2028 $35 EL

ᵠᵠᵠᵠ **Rosé 2021, Margaret River** RATING 89 DRINK 2022–2023 $24 EL
Birdhouse Cabernet Sauvignon 2020, Margaret River RATING 89 DRINK 2021–2028 $24 EL
Premium Cabernet Sauvignon 2020, Margaret River RATING 89 DRINK 2021–2027 $24 EL

Koomilya ★★★★★

Amery Road, McLaren Vale SA 5171 **Region** McLaren Vale
T (08) 8323 8000 **www.**koomilya.com.au **Open** 7 days 11–4 **Winemaker** Stephen Pannell **Est.** 2015 **Dozens** 2000 **Vyds** 13ha

The Koomilya vineyard is wedged between the original Upper Tintara vineyard planted in 1862, and the Hope Farm or Seaview vineyard established in the early 1850s. More than 15ha of native bush and scrub, with a creek line that flows through the heart of the property, all have a moderating influence on the microclimate of the property. In '12, Stephen and his wife Fiona embarked on rejuvenating it with organic farming, weeding the native bush and removing olive trees to create biochar to return as charcoal to the soil. Plantings of new varieties have followed, with a small set of wines created to specifically reflect the location, accent and circumstances of the seasons throughout each particular vintage. Exports to the UK, the US, Sweden and Singapore. (TL)

ᵠᵠᵠᵠᵠ **Cabernet Touriga 2018, McLaren Vale** This is exceptional, although not for the faint of heart. A mid-weighted and immensely savoury wine that is compact, portentous and so tightly bound to a ferrous orb of tannins that it makes one revel in the anticipation of the next sip. Italian of feel. Steely of resolve. Earthenware, herb, violet, biltong and a dusty swathe of dried plum and tobacco. The tannins are reminiscent of certain Wendouree cuvées or better, great Taurasi. They are a forcefield of enticement, confidence and saliva-sucking moreishness. I want to drink this whole bottle solo, so good is it. A stellar wine hailing from a spellbinding site. Screw cap. 13% alc. RATING 97 DRINK 2022–2033 $70 NG ✿ ♥

ŶŶŶŶŶ JC Block Shiraz 2018, McLaren Vale Jubey and floral. Pomegranate, persimmon, blue- and red-fruit allusions, hung game and ample Asian spice undertones. Best, the tannins! As with all of these Koomilya iterations. Here, a splay of moreish, detailed and utterly precise stitches, like imprints in calf-skin leather across the palate, serve as a weapon to combat any unwanted seam of sweetness. Superlative warm-climate shiraz. Screw cap. 14% alc. RATING 96 DRINK 2021-2038 $115 NG

DC Block Shiraz 2018, McLaren Vale I am detecting some Aussie scrub that I didn't sense when first poured. In the best way! Really aromatic and pulpy, with palate-staining density defied by a lightness of feel. The tannins drive a sumptuous finish, corralling any stray excess. Mulberry, violet, Dr Pepper and a wonderful creaminess that is far from oak-derived. A nostalgic ping with contemporary styling. A manifest of vineyard rejuvenation, historic celebration and future affirmation. Screw cap. 13.5% alc. RATING 95 DRINK 2021-2038 $115 NG

GT Block Shiraz 2018, McLaren Vale The only Block cuvée to be fully destemmed. The tannins, expansive and suede of texture, without the firmer stitch of the DC, or the ferruginous mettle of the JC. Still, ample, impactful and dutifully burly. The aromas disparate across all 3. Here, dark grey silt stone delivers a bright, highly aromatic wine that sits definitely in the savoury, mid-weighted niche. Lilac, musk, grape, spice and pulpy blueberry accents mingle with a judicious reductive clench and a long finish of pastille, Worcestershire and iodine. Elegant and southern Rhône in sensibility. Screw cap. 13.5% alc. RATING 95 DRINK 2021-2038 $115 NG

TGM 2018, McLaren Vale I adore this site, so brilliant are the wines, from the more expensive to expressions such as this: a full-ish weighted, plump, spicy and immensely versatile wine that speaks of a bright future for the Vale once these sort of varieties become the mainstay. Peppery. Floral. Juicy. Spicy. Nothing too sweet. Nothing out of place. Simply a flow of righteousness, manifest as balance and the desire for 4 glasses rather than a single sip. Screw cap. 14% alc. RATING 94 DRINK 2022-2029 $45 NG

Koonara   ★★★★

44 Church Street, Penola, SA 5277 **Region** Coonawarra
T (08) 8737 3222 **www**.koonara.com **Open** Mon–Sun 10–4 **Winemaker** Peter Douglas
Est. 1988 **Dozens** 10000 **Vyds** 9ha
Trevor Reschke planted the first vines on the Koonara property in 1988. Peter Douglas, formerly Wynns' chief winemaker before moving overseas for some years, has returned to the district and is consultant winemaker. After 10 years of organic viticulture practises, Koonara's vineyards in Coonawarra were certified organic in 2017, the first in the region. Exports to Russia and Malaysia. (JH)

ŶŶŶŶŶ Ambriel's Gift Family Reserve Cabernet Sauvignon 2019, Coonawarra Firm, concentrated and engagingly lush … this has a veritable forest of dark berries, shaped by firm structuring tannins and laden with exotic spice. It's classic Coonawarra – the mint, dark choc and blackberry bramble on the nose are a dead giveaway, confirmed in the mouth. A lovely lingering aftertaste offers even more opportunity to taste. Smart. Screw cap. 14% alc. RATING 94 DRINK 2022-2032 $40 EL

ŶŶŶŶŶ Wanderlust Cabernet Sauvignon 2019, Coonawarra RATING 91 DRINK 2022-2032 $28 EL

A Song For Alice Riesling 2021, Coonawarra RATING 90 DRINK 2022-2028 $25 EL

Ezra's Gift Shiraz 2019, Coonawarra RATING 90 DRINK 2021-2031 $40 EL

Angel's Wings Cabernet Shiraz 2016, Coonawarra RATING 90 DRINK 2022-2029 $28 EL

Kooyong ★★★★★

263 Red Hill Road, Red Hill **Region** Mornington Peninsula
T (03) 5989 4444 **www**.kooyongwines.com.au **Open** Mon–Sun 11–5 **Winemaker** Glen
Hayley **Viticulturist** Stuart Marshall **Est.** 1996 **Dozens** 13000 **Vyds** 41.11ha
Kooyong, owned by Giorgio and Dianne Gjergja, released its first wines in 2001. The vineyard
is planted to pinot noir (26.64ha), chardonnay (10.35ha) and, more recently, pinot gris (3ha)
and a little shiraz (0.97ha). In July '15, following the departure of Sandro Mosele, his assistant
of 6 years, Glen Hayley, was appointed to take his place. The Kooyong wines are made at the
state-of-the-art winery of Port Phillip Estate, also owned by the Gjergjas. Exports to the UK,
Canada, Belgium, the Netherlands, Singapore, Hong Kong and Japan. (JH)

🍷🍷🍷🍷🍷 **Farrago Single Block Chardonnay 2020, Mornington Peninsula** Both
single-vineyard chardonnays are on song, as Farrago opens up to a reveal layers
of flavour from stone fruit, citrus to creamy lees with tight yet refreshing acidity
reining everything in. It's luscious without being heavy, with plenty of energy and
drive. This is a touch racier than Faultline, yet both are moreish and satisfying.
Screw cap. 13.5% alc. RATING 96 DRINK 2022–2030 $60 JF ❂
Faultline Single Block Chardonnay 2020, Mornington Peninsula Oh
yeah. This is in a good spot. Tight and linear. It kick starts with a waft of florals,
white stone fruit and no shortage of citrus tones. Superb line and length as the
acidity joins the lees and oak in perfect balance. Screw cap. 13% alc. RATING 96
DRINK 2022–2030 $60 JF ❂
Estate Chardonnay 2020, Mornington Peninsula Totally seductive from the
first sip. An exercise in restraint with a balance of stone fruit and citrus, spice and
oak (a mere 16% new French barriques) and a subtle creamy, nutty lees influence
(on lees 11 months without stirring). Savoury and moreish, yet the acidity is in
charge, pulling everything together seamlessly towards a long finish. Screw cap.
13% alc. RATING 95 DRINK 2022–2028 $42 JF
Estate Pinot Noir 2020, Mornington Peninsula Not the easiest of vintages –
cool, wet and lower yields – yet this wine is easy to get into and enjoy, so in
context, bravo. It's beautifully aromatic with cherries, wood smoke, a hint of meaty
reduction, loads of baking spices and the oak is well integrated. It's lighter framed,
juicy with tangy acidity yet the tannins are finely tuned and persuasive. Drinking
well now and may prove to unfurl and garner more complexity in time, if you can
wait. Screw cap. 12.5% alc. RATING 95 DRINK 2021–2028 $48 JF
Clonale Chardonnay 2021, Mornington Peninsula This first tier for
Kooyong is fabulous. Requisite white stone fruit, citrus and tangy acidity but
it is the depth on the palate and vitality that sets the scene. Grilled nuts, leesy
complexity, moreish and savoury. Spot on. Screw cap. 13.5% alc. RATING 94
DRINK 2022–2027 $34 JF

🍷🍷🍷🍷🍷 **Beurrot Pinot Gris 2021, Mornington Peninsula** RATING 93
DRINK 2022–2025 $32 JF
Massale Pinot Noir 2021, Mornington Peninsula RATING 91
DRINK 2022–2026 $34 JF
Massale Pinot Noir 2020, Mornington Peninsula RATING 90
DRINK 2021–2025 $34 JF
Estate Shiraz 2020, Mornington Peninsula RATING 90 DRINK 2022–2027
$42 JF

Kooyonga Creek ★★★☆

2369 Samaria Road, Moorngag, Vic 3673 **Region** North East Victoria
T (03) 9629 5853 **www**.kooyonga.com.au **Open** Fri–Sun & public hols 11–5 or
by appt **Winemaker** Luis Simian, Barry Saunders **Viticulturist** Barry Nolan **Est.** 2011
Dozens 5000 **Vyds** 7.5ha
When you read the name of this winery, you expect to find it somewhere on or near the
Mornington Peninsula. In fact it's a very long way to North East Victoria, where Barry

and Pam Saunders planted 7.5ha of vineyards on their farm and released the first wines under the name Kooyonga Chapel in '03. They planted a sensibly focused range of shiraz, cabernet sauvignon, chardonnay and sauvignon blanc, with merlot recently grafted over to tempranillo. (JH)

ŸŸŸŸŸ Cabernet Sauvignon 2018, North East Victoria A strong follow-up to the '17 cabernet with a similarly open, earthy, sweet-fruited approach. Dark cherry, blackberry, juniper, aniseed and dried herbs. Generosity is its middle name, with a spicy vanillin oak complexity. Old-school North East Victorian openness and honesty right here. Screw cap. 14.5% alc. RATING 90 DRINK 2021–2030 $22 JP

ŸŸŸŸ Shiraz 2020, Heathcote RATING 89 DRINK 2022–2026 $25 JP
Sauvignon Blanc 2021, North East Victoria RATING 88 DRINK 2022–2024 $22 JP

Kosciuszko Wines

PO Box 57, Campbell, ACT 2612 **Region** Tumbarumba
T 0417 036 436 **www**.kosciuszkowines.com.au **Winemaker** Robert Bruno **Est.** 2007
Dozens 1000
Kosciuszko Wines is the latest wine business venture of the energetic Bill and Maria Mason. Bill has been distributing wine in Canberra since 2004, with a small but distinguished list of wineries, which he represents with considerable marketing flair. In '18 Bill purchased Kosciuszko Wines from founding winemaker Chris Thomas after working with Chris and Kosciuszko Wines for a number of years. Bill sources his fruit from pioneering grapegrower Julie Cullen, from her vineyard in Jingellic Road, Tumbarumba. (JH)

ŸŸŸŸŸ Sangiovese 2021, Tumbarumba A pretty pastel pink, with a fragrance and flavours of Turkish delight, watermelon and strawberries with a hint of fresh herbs. The palate is alive and refreshing acidity keeps this on track to a dry, clean finish. Screw cap. 12.5% alc. RATING 92 DRINK 2021–2022 $27 JF
Sauvignon Blanc 2021, Tumbarumba As refreshing as they come, with its cool lime leaf and fresh basil aromas plus sugar snap, passionfruit pith and lots of citrus zest on the palate, alongside racy lemony acidity. It's a juicy crowd-pleaser, so just chill it right down and enjoy. Screw cap. 11.8% alc. RATING 90 DRINK 2021–2023 $27 JF

Krinklewood Biodynamic Vineyard   ★★★★☆

712 Wollombi Road, Broke, NSW 2330 **Region** Hunter Valley
T (02) 6579 1322 **www**.krinklewood.com **Open** Fri–Mon 10–5 **Winemaker** Valentina Moresco, PJ Charteris (Consultant) **Est.** 1981 **Dozens** 7500 **Vyds** 20ha
Krinklewood is a family-owned certified biodynamic organic winery. Every aspect of the property is managed in a holistic and sustainable way; Rod Windrim's extensive herb crops, native grasses and farm animals all contribute to biodynamic preparations to maintain healthy soil biology. The small winery is home to a Vaslin Bucher basket press and 2 Nomblot French fermentation eggs, a natural approach to winemaking. Exports to Hong Kong. (JH)

ŸŸŸŸŸ Fortified Verdelho 2007, Hunter Valley An impressive fortified. Impressive as much for its rancio complexity, evoking varnish, roasted walnuts and blue cheese, as much as the impeccable poise derived from the high-quality spirit in play and its integration. Excellent. Cork. 17.5% alc. RATING 96 $65 NG ✪

ŸŸŸŸŸ Basket Press Chardonnay 2021, Broke Fordwich RATING 92 DRINK 2021–2028 $55 NG
The Gypsy Sparkling Shiraz 2017, Hunter Valley RATING 91 $50 NG
Wild Chardonnay 2021, Hunter Valley RATING 91 DRINK 2021–2026 $28 NG
Basket Press Semillon 2021, Hunter Valley RATING 90 DRINK 2021–2030 $42 NG

Kurtz Family Vineyards

★★★★

731 Light Pass Road, Angaston, SA, 5353 **Region** Barossa Valley
T 0418 810 982 www.kurtzfamilyvineyards.com.au **Open** By appt **Winemaker** Steve
Kurtz **Viticulturist** Steven Kurtz **Est.** 1996 **Dozens** 3000 **Vyds** 18.1ha
The Kurtz family vineyard is at Light Pass. It has 9ha of shiraz, the remainder planted to
chardonnay, cabernet sauvignon, semillon, sauvignon blanc, petit verdot, grenache, mataro and
malbec. Steve Kurtz has followed in the footsteps of his great-grandfather Ben Kurtz, who
first grew grapes at Light Pass in the '30s. During a career working first at Saltram and then at
Foster's until '06, Steve gained invaluable experience from Nigel Dolan, Caroline Dunn and
John Glaetzer, among others. Exports to the US, Germany and Malaysia. (JH)

ΨΨΨΨΨ **Boundary Row GSM 2019, Barossa Valley** It's a lushly aromatic wine with
super-ripe plum and dark cherry fruit with notes of exotic spice, ginger cake and
earth. Plush, too, on the palate, with great fruit density, sandy tannin for support
and an impressive swagger of black fruits on the finish. Great value. Screw cap.
15% alc. RATING 92 DRINK 2021-2028 $28 DB
Boundary Row Shiraz 2019, Barossa Valley Showing fruit characters of
blackberry, dark plum and blueberry high notes. Hints of deep dark spice, turned
earth, licorice and dark chocolate. Weighty, svelte and broody with some prune
and fig notes coming in on the palate, dense with compact tannins and a graphite-
like sheen. Screw cap. 14.5% alc. RATING 91 DRINK 2021-2028 $28 DB

ΨΨΨΨ **Seven Sleepers Shiraz 2019, Barossa Valley** RATING 89 DRINK 2021-2026
$18 DB ✪
Boundary Row Cabernet Sauvignon Shiraz 2019, Barossa RATING 89
DRINK 2021-2031 $28 DB
Seven Sleepers Cabernet Sauvignon Shiraz Petit Verdot 2019, Barossa
RATING 88 DRINK 2021-2026 $18 DB
Schmick Shiraz 2017, Barossa RATING 88 DRINK 2021-2026 $85 DB

Kyara

★★★★

307 Sawpit Gully Road, Keyneton, SA 5353 **Region** Barossa Valley
T 0408 887 300 www.kyara.com.au **Open** By appt **Winemaker** Jo Irvine **Est.** 2012
Dozens 1200 **Vyds** 4.53ha
Kylie and Leon Pendergast are among the descendants of Eden Valley founder Heinrich
Fiebiger. Their former careers in the fashion accessories industry in Melbourne, which
involved travelling the world promoting products, has left its mark on the slick presentation
of the material explaining their arrival in the Eden Valley, and their business plan. The first
vines were planted on the estate in the 1970s and it's clear from the wines that the vineyard
is mature. Experienced contract winemaker Jo Irvine ensures the vineyard's potential is fully
realised. Exports to Hong Kong. (JH)

ΨΨΨΨΨ **Thistle & Burr Riesling 2018, Eden Valley** A museum release, the steely-eyed
exuberance of youth is tempered a little here, as the wine takes on some toasty,
dried hay-like characters among the lime, grapefruit, floral and crushed-stone
notes. The finish is pure, dry and stoney with a trail of dried grass. Screw cap.
12% alc. RATING 91 DRINK 2021-2030 $35 DB
Thistle & Burr Riesling 2021, Eden Valley The '21 vintage was very strong
in Eden Valley, with steely frames and fragrant, pure lime-juice pulses. Here there
is just a tweak of phenolic grip filling out the palate, which finishes with a blast of
lime and citrus fruits. Screw cap. 12% alc. RATING 90 DRINK 2021-2028 $35 DB

Kyneton Ridge

★★★★

517 Blackhill Road, Kyneton, Vic 3444 **Region** Macedon Ranges
T 0408 841 119 www.kynetonridge.com.au **Open** W'ends & public hols 11–5
Winemaker Patrick Wood, Luke Boucher **Viticulturist** Tom Handyside **Est.** 1997
Dozens 1200 **Vyds** 4ha

Kyneton Ridge is the retirement project of Andrew and Angela Wood, who bought the property in 2019. This is their first foray into wine, although their winemaker son, Patrick, is very much hands on. Originally established by John Boucher and partner Pauline Russell in '97, the Woods have subsequently added nebbiolo, riesling, more chardonnay plus cabernet sauvignon, covering about 4.5ha, while still sourcing shiraz from Heathcote. They have also spent time, energy and finances on renovating the winery and cellar door, then opened a cafe and art space in Dec '21.

♀♀♀♀♀ Shiraz 2020, Heathcote A fantastic red-noir hue immediately entices and the pleasure doesn't stop there. An exuberant wine with a whorl of dark fruits mingling with licorice, oak spices, warm earth, pencil shavings (remember those?) and a distinctive regional gum leaf, menthol note. Full bodied and rich across the palate with plump yet textural tannins. Just a faint green walnut note to the finish, which is not so obvious with food. Screw cap. 14.5% alc. RATING 94 DRINK 2021-2033 $35 JF

♀♀♀♀♀ Skipping Rabbit Pinot Noir 2021, Macedon Ranges RATING 90 DRINK 2022-2025 $28 JF

L.A.S. Vino ★★★★★

PO Box 361 Cowaramup, WA 6284 **Region** Margaret River
T www.lasvino.com **Winemaker** Nic Peterkin **Est.** 2013 **Dozens** 800
Owner Nic Peterkin is the grandson of the late Diana Cullen (Cullen Wines) and the son of Mike Peterkin (Pierro). After graduating from the University of Adelaide with a master's degree in oenology and travelling the world as a Flying Winemaker, he came back to roost in Margaret River with the ambition of making wines that are a little bit different, but also within the bounds of conventional oenological science. The intention is to keep the project small. Achieving 5 stars for the first time this edtion, L.A.S. Vino wins the Companion 2023 Dark Horse Award. Exports to the UK, Belgium, Sweden, Dubai, Singapore and Japan. (JH)

♀♀♀♀♀ Wildberry Springs Chardonnay 2020, Margaret River Fresh curry leaf, white peach, crushed cashew, flat leaf parsley, red apple skins, a whack of pink grapefruit and layers of orchard flowers, gum leaf and licorice. What a cracking wine this is. A kaleidescopic array of fruit, a flinty, wild kind of countenance, and a long, sinuous line of flavour that gives a little 'come hither' at the final turn. Peterkin doesn't make enough of this wine. Or perhaps that's the secret. Screw cap. 14% alc. RATING 97 DRINK 2021-2036 $75 EL ✪

♀♀♀♀♀ CBDB Chenin Blanc Dynamic Blend 2020, Margaret River Taut, textural, tense and almost nervy, the classic waxiness of chenin emerges only on the mid palate and beyond. This speaks of Geraldton wax flower, lanolin, brine, green apples, cheesecloth, a touch of lantana and a sprinkle of grapefruit zest. Long, modern and exciting, it shows chenin in a new light, quite different from the greats of the Loire, but no less profound. Diam. 14% alc. RATING 96 DRINK 2021-2036 $50 EL ✪ ♥
Albino PNO Rosé 2020, Margaret River This is finer and more delicate than the previous release, but with the trademark phenolic shape on the palate. Texturally exciting (fine, talcy, grippy), savoury, spicy and plush. Pomegranate, rockmelon, pink peppercorn, brine, cheesecloth, kiwifruit, red apples, crushed cashew and guava. Really feeling it. Nic Peterkin really is nailing the style here … another wildly impressive release. Screw cap. 13.5% alc. RATING 95 DRINK 2021-2025 $45 EL ♥
The Pirate Blend 2020, Margaret River Midnight purple in the glass and the nose does not disappoint. A constellation of blackberries, pastille, salted licorice, granite, mulberries, blueberries and all sorts of aniseed, arnica and fennel notes. In the mouth it is all that, the acidity a cleansing swoosh that wraps it all up. I see why this has a cult following. Will live for ages, but you should drink it tonight. Diam. 13.5% alc. RATING 95 DRINK 2021-2036 $65 EL

Cabernet Sauvignon 2020, Margaret River Pungent intensity of fruit on the palate; a core of midnight cassis, blackberry, mulberry and graphite. Inky. The tannins are chalky and ripe, and serve to shape the fruit on the palate and through the finish. Super-smart, and quite unique. Not your average cabernet. If you seek something interesting, this is it. Diam. 13.5% alc. RATING 95 DRINK 2021-2036 $75 EL

Granite Grenache 2020, Geographe Super-pale in colour. Maraschino cherries. The power of suggestion is strong but it definitely smells of sun-drenched granite rocks, straw or dry grass, Turkish delight (rosewater and crushed pistachio), strawberries, hung deli meat and peppercorns. This follows on the palate. The finish trails out into a burst of raspberries, petrichor and concrete. As usual, another engaging and unique release from Peterkin – long may they continue. Diam. 13% alc. RATING 94 DRINK 2021-2028 $55 EL

La Kooki Wines

12 Settlers Retreat, Margaret River, WA 6285 **Region** Margaret River
T 0447 587 15 **www.lakookiwines.com.au Winemaker** Eloise Jarvis, Glenn Goodall
Est. 2017 **Dozens** 335
Eloise Jarvis and Glen Goodall have 50 years of winemaking experience between them. They met studying eonology in South Australia in the '90s, and after vintages abroad they settled in WA, Eloise initially working for Cape Mentelle and Glenn for Xanadu, where he remains today as head winemaker. They wanted to create something different, together, drawing on their relationships with local growers to produce drinkable wines that are 'a little bit kooki'. (HT) (JH)

ΨΨΨΨΨ **Boya Chardonnay 2021, Margaret River** Boya means 'stones' in the local Wadandi language. Gingin fruit is fermented wild in barrel with full solids, along with smooth stones collected from the local coast. The barrels are then periodically rolled, agitating the stones within, stirring the lees and creating layers of textural complexity. It's pretty astounding, and the resulting wine picks up the shale and mineral characters of the rocks (suggestive, yes). While the wine is (like the '20) stingingly acidic, it is set against a backdrop of crushed quartz, white peach, brine, green apple skins and pulverised almonds, bringing the picture into focus and balance. It is very smart and very fine. The length of flavour the key. Screw cap. 13% alc. RATING 95 DRINK 2022-2032 $65 EL

Las Piedras Tempranillo 2020, Geographe Vibrant, concentrated and plush, this is shaped by a fortress of savoury tannin on the palate that is at once omnipresent and chalky, earthy and polished (an amalgam of things, all cohesive). The fruit within speaks of mulberries, black cherries and pomegranates. Really smart. Screw cap. 14% alc. RATING 94 DRINK 2022-2028 $40 EL

Local Knowledge Cabernet Sauvignon 2020, Margaret River This is pure. Saline. Inky. Lightweight, yet with gravitas. Detailed, with finesse. It carries on long after the wine has left the mouth. This wine is totally different from everything on the bench beside it. You can really taste the fruit, it isn't sullied by anything. It is crystalline, but shapely – quite a marvel. In Margaret River, there are some producers you can look to for a different perspective, that will show you a 'new way'. La Kooki is fast emerging as one of those, and this is a wine you could start with. In the words of Jay-Z, 'then we gon' keep it in the truest essence of [cabernet]' (he said hip hop. But he meant cabernet). Screw cap. 13.5% alc. RATING 94 DRINK 2022-2036 $40 EL

ΨΨΨΨΨ **Rosé Blonde 2021, Margaret River** RATING 93 DRINK 2021-2024 $28 EL

La Linea

36 Shipsters Road, Kensington Park, SA 5068 (postal) **Region** Adelaide Hills
T (08) 8431 3556 **www.lalinea.com.au Winemaker** Peter Leske **Viticulturist** Peter Leske **Est.** 2007 **Dozens** 4000 **Vyds** 6.64ha

La Linea is a partnership between experienced wine industry professionals Peter Leske (ex-Nepenthe) and David LeMire MW. Peter was among the first to recognise the potential of tempranillo in Australia and his knowledge of it is reflected in the 3 wine styles made from the variety: a dry rosé, a dry red blended from several Adelaide Hills vineyards, and Sureno, made in select vintages from specific sites at the southern end of the Hills. The pair pioneered mencia – the red variety from northwest Spain – in the Hills. They also produce the off-dry riesling 25GR (25g/L RS) under the Vertigo label. Exports to the UK. (JH)

🍷🍷🍷🍷🍷 **Tempranillo Rosé 2021, Adelaide Hills** This has everything you need or want in a good rosé, from bountiful red berries, mid-palate textural complexity and a long-running spiciness across the palate to versatility at the table. Quite an accomplishment. And all of that at a reasonable price. Screw cap. 12.5% alc. RATING 95 DRINK 2021-2025 $24 JP ✪
Mencia 2020, Adelaide Hills Mencia is making itself home in the Hills and McLaren Vale. The Mediterranean variety loves a Mediterranean climate. It fully opens with some air and then wait for the deep spice, dark-berry, cherry and herbal lift. A touch of undergrowth adds a savoury note. Sweeping tannins play across an expansive palate through to a dry finish. Screw cap. 13.5% alc. RATING 95 DRINK 2021-2026 $29 JP ✪

🍷🍷🍷🍷🍷 **Tempranillo 2020, Adelaide Hills** RATING 92 DRINK 2021-2026 $27 JP
Mencia Rosé 2021, Adelaide Hills RATING 90 DRINK 2021-2025 $25 JP
Sureno Tempranillo 2020, Adelaide Hills RATING 90 DRINK 2022-2030 $35 JP

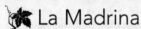 La Madrina ★★★★

206–208 Port Rd, Aldinga, SA 5173 **Region** McLaren Vale
T 0411 809 701 **Open** Fri 5–9, w'ends 12–5 **Winemaker** Gill Gordon-Smith **Est.** 2012 **Dozens** 400
Former overseer of Qantas' Sommelier in the Sky programme, WSET educator Gill Gordon-Smith has been involved in education and mentoring programmes, receiving the Woman of Inspiration Award from Women in Wine in '20. Yet it was Gill's role as a Vinitaly Academy Educator that facilitated her love of things Italian. Gill pined for mid-weighted, savoury and eminently drinkable Italianate expressions when home in McLaren Vale. An Italian Wine Scholar, Gill crafts wines that shimmer with an energy as effusive as her own. Fall from Grace was the first incarnation, sharing the name of the iconoclastic wine store she owned and ran for many years. Today, her succinct swag of minimalist expressions fall under the banner of La Madrina, each a textural potpourri of restrained fruit bound by a herbal sash. (NG)

🍷🍷🍷🍷🍷 **2021 Arneis 2021, McLaren Vale** Gill Gordon-Smith crafts delicious skin-contact wine. Tamarind, orange verbena, tomatillo, ginger chutney, quinine and curry powder. Long, pixelated and immensely saline. Mid weighted, versatile and the sort of wine that draws you back in for another squiz through Alice's looking glass, shade meeting light meeting somewhere in between. Screw cap. 14.5% alc. RATING 91 DRINK 2022-2024 $35 NG
Mazerine Carignan 2021, McLaren Vale A sensuous expression of carignan. Bright without being too jubey. Maraschino cherry, a sluice of smoked biltong, lilac and lots of bergamot. Miraculously succulent for the variety. Asian medicine cabinet opens to lapsang, pickled ume and Asian fantasies. Brilliant drinking in the here and now. Screw cap. 13% alc. RATING 90 DRINK 2022-2024 $30 NG
Rosato Montepulciano 2021, McLaren Vale A pulpy mouthful of intense, sapid-sour cherry nourishment, brimming with the clutch in aldehydic control. Thyme, lavender and Aussie scrub mingling. A whiff of volatility services lift and freshness, given the lack of acidity. pH high. Goodness. I'd chill this and rock it out with antipasti and hard cheeses. A polarising wine, perhaps. But one of immense character. Screw cap. 13.5% alc. RATING 90 DRINK 2022-2024 $30 NG

La Pleiade

M. Chapoutier Australia, 141-143 High Street, Heathcote Vic 3523 **Region** Heathcote
T (03) 9602 1570 **www.**mchapoutier.com.au **Open** Mon–Wed, Fri 10–2 Sat–Sun 10–5
Winemaker Ron Laughton, Michel Chapoutier **Viticulturist** Emily Laughton **Est.** 1998
Dozens 500 **Vyds** 8ha

A joint venture of Michel and Corinne Chapoutier and Ron and Elva Laughton. In spring
'98 a vineyard of Australian and imported French shiraz clones was planted. The vineyard is
run biodynamically and the winemaking is deliberately designed to place maximum emphasis
on the fruit quality. La Pleiade is available for tasting at M. Chapoutier in Heathcote. Exports
to the UK, the US, France, Singapore and Hong Kong. (JH)

ΨΨΨΨΨ Shiraz 2018, Heathcote This is a big wine in every sense of the word, from the
high alcohol, impenetrable black-purple hues to the abundance of generous fruit
and oak. It has eternity in its sights or at least 20+ years ageing potential. Fruitcake,
dried fruits, cassis, baking/woody spices, chocolate, licorice, tar and a wealth of
richness all collide on the palate. It's a little riotous at the moment, the major
players – fruit, oak, tannin, alcohol – all working each other out. They still have a
long way to go. Cork. 15.5% alc. RATING 90 DRINK 2022–2041 $68 JP

La Prova

102 Main Street, Hahndorf, SA 5245 **Region** Adelaide Hills
T (08) 8388 7330 **www.**laprova.com.au **Open** first w'end of the month 11–5 or by appt
Winemaker Sam Scott **Est.** 2009 **Dozens** 5000

Sam Scott's great-grandfather worked in the cellar for Max Schubert and passed his
knowledge down to Sam's grandfather. Sam enrolled in business at university, continuing the
casual retailing with Booze Brothers – which he'd started while at school – picking up the trail
with Baily & Baily. Next came wine wholesale experience with David Ridge, selling iconic
Australian and Italian wines to the trade. This led to a job with Michael Fragos at Tatachilla in
2000 and since then he has been the 'I've been everywhere man', working all over Australia
and in California. He moved to Bird in Hand winery at the end of '06, and from there he
took the plunge on his own account. Exports to the UK and Singapore. (JH)

ΨΨΨΨΨ Nebbiolo Rosato 2021, Adelaide Hills The producer understands nebbiolo
oh, so well. Here, he brings lift and energy, delicacy and strength to a pretty
complex rosato. Red cherry, dried strawberry, almond biscuit and a dash of
pepper are the basis for the exploration. But just look at the tannin and acid
management here: so bright, clean and enduring. Screw cap. 12.8% alc. RATING 95
DRINK 2021–2025 $26 JP ✪ ♥

Pinot Grigio 2021, Adelaide Hills Energy to burn here with an impressive
purity of fruit. Citrus-blossom aromatics fill the glass alongside crab apple, lemon
curd and grapefruit. The line and length, catapulted by the freshest acidity, is
mighty energising. Screw cap. 12.5% alc. RATING 95 DRINK 2021–2024 $26 JP ✪

Fiano 2021, Adelaide Hills A tour de force of winemaking, the bouquet raising
questions despatched to the 4 corners of the field by the palate, with its racy
intensity of lemon and Meyer lemon in the lead; honey, nuts and salt flapping on
the side. Screw cap. 13.3% alc. RATING 95 DRINK 2021–2027 $28 JH ✪

Colpevole Nebbiolo 2019, Adelaide Hills Captures the fineness and floral
beauty of the grape so well. Mid red hues. Black cherry and plum fruits with a
rose petal, floral delicacy on the bouquet. You're hooked. Lays out a persuasive
argument for the grape: supple and fleshy with acid holding true but not intrusive,
and that gorgeous floral/cherry vibrancy and depth. Screw cap. 13.9% alc.
RATING 95 DRINK 2021–2030 $45 JP

Aglianico Rosato 2021, Adelaide Hills Aglianico is a southern Italian variety,
here picked early just as the red fruits start to show, and given minimal skin
contact. It has an ethereal bouquet with savoury red crabapple aromas, and a
deliberately bone dry palate. Will go anywhere. Screw cap. 12.5% alc. RATING 94
DRINK 2021–2027 $26 JH ✪

Sangiovese 2020, Adelaide Hills A fine-edged sangiovese, very smart, with a tickle of the kind of savouriness that winemaker Sam Scott usually seeks. Dark, soused cherries, plum, spice, earth, briar are delivered clean and composed with a light, caper-like lift to finish. Delish. Screw cap. 13.9% alc. RATING 94 DRINK 2021-2026 $26 JP ✪

ΨΨΨΨΨ Piccolino Sangiovese 2019, Adelaide Hills RATING 93 DRINK 2021-2027 $45 JP
Prosecco 2021, King Valley RATING 92 $26 JP
Nero d'Avola 2020, McLaren Vale RATING 92 DRINK 2022-2034 $26 JH

Lake Breeze Wines   ★★★★★

Step Road, Langhorne Creek, SA 5255 **Region** Langhorne Creek
T (08) 8537 3017 www.lakebreeze.com.au **Open** 7 days 10–5 **Winemaker** Greg Follett
Est. 1987 **Dozens** 20000 **Vyds** 90ha
The Folletts have been farmers at Langhorne Creek since 1880, and grapegrowers since the 1930s. Part of the grape production is sold, but the quality of the Lake Breeze wines is exemplary, with the red wines particularly appealing. Best Value Winery in the 2022 Companion. Exports to the UK, the US, Canada, Switzerland, Denmark, Germany, Peru, Singapore, Hong Kong and Japan. (JH)

ΨΨΨΨΨ The Drake Cabernet Sauvignon Shiraz 2016, Langhorne Creek When the wine first enters the mouth you begin to question whether there can be too much of a good thing, until the wine soars on the finish with a satin and velvet stream of incredible purity and length. To be released Sep '22. Screw cap. 14.6% alc. RATING 98 DRINK 2026-2046 $80 JH ✪ ♥
Section 54 Shiraz 2020, Langhorne Creek This is a wonderfully elegant wine with a profusion of red and black berry fruits sustained by its silky mouthfeel, fine tannins a constant thrumming on the finish and aftertaste. Screw cap. 14.5% alc. RATING 97 DRINK 2023-2040 $26 JH ✪
Arthur's Reserve Cabernet Sauvignon Malbec 2019, Langhorne Creek This is an utterly beautiful wine, intensely focused yet silky and elegant. Trophies in '21 may continue to be awarded until May '22 when the wine is released. Screw cap. 14% alc. RATING 97 DRINK 2022-2041 $48 JH ✪ ♥

ΨΨΨΨΨ Old Vine Grenache 2021, Langhorne Creek The brilliantly clear crimson-purple hue announces a beautiful grenache, bursting with juicy red fruits backed up by fine-spun tannins giving a savoury farewell. Screw cap. 14.5% alc. RATING 96 DRINK 2022-2035 $28 JH ✪
Cabernet Sauvignon 2020, Langhorne Creek The crust of tannins and oak that surrounds the polished blackcurrant fruit will soften until its release and continue thereafter for many years. Screw cap. 14% alc. RATING 95 DRINK 2023-2040 $28 JH ✪
Malbec 2020, Langhorne Creek Deep, vibrant purple crimson. Layer upon layer of fruit, satsuma plum, tendrils of licorice and a sprinkle of dark chocolate fruit. Langhorne Creek and malbec walk together. Screw cap. 14.5% alc. RATING 95 DRINK 2022-2040 $30 JH ✪

Lake Cairn Curran Vineyard   ★★★☆

'Park Hill', Leathbridge Road, Welshman's Reef, Vic 3462 **Region** Bendigo
T (03) 5476 2523 www.lakecairncurranvineyard.com.au **Open** By appt
Winemaker Sarah Ferguson, Moorooduc Estate (Richard McIntyre), Kilchurn Wines (David Cowburn) **Est.** 1987 **Dozens** 800 **Vyds** 5.4ha
When Ross and Sarah Ferguson purchased what is now known as Lake Cairn Curran Vineyard in 1999, they acquired not only the vineyard (chardonnay, pinot noir and shiraz), but also a slice of history, evoked by the beautiful labels. The Park Hill homestead dates back to the establishment of the Tarrengower Run in the 1840s, and the mudbrick cellar door is located adjacent to the homestead, overlooking the Cairn Curran Reservoir and Loddon

River Valley. Notwithstanding that, Sarah has a wine science oenology degree from CSU, and having worked several vintages at Moorooduc Estate, makes small batches of wine at the onsite winery. However, Rick McIntyre makes the major table wine releases, David Cowburn of Kilchurn the sparkling wines. (JH)

ΥΥΥΥΥ Shiraz 2019, Bendigo Composed and welcoming in spice-dusted blackberry fruits, fine-ground spices, ripe plums, briar and autumnal dried leaves. Precise tannins tie everything together nicely and carry the wine long. A medium-bodied little charmer. Screw cap. 13% alc. RATING 90 DRINK 2021-2027 $25 JP

ΥΥΥΥ Park Hill Estate Chardonnay 2021, Central Victoria RATING 88 DRINK 2022-2025 $25 JP

Lake Cooper Estate

1608 Midland Highway, Corop, Vic 3559 **Region** Heathcote
T (03) 9387 7657 **www**.lakecooper.com.au **Open** By appt **Winemaker** Paul Boulden, Richard Taylor **Viticulturist** Shane Bartel **Est.** 1998 **Dozens** 11 224 **Vyds** 34ha
Lake Cooper Estate is a substantial venture in the Heathcote region, set on the side of Mount Camel Range with panoramic views of Lake Cooper, Greens Lake and the Corop township. There are plans for the construction of a 300t winery, cellar door, restaurant and accommodation, with a complete overhaul of winemaking practices by the highly experienced Paul Boulden and Richard Taylor. Viticulturist Shane Bartel will oversee new plantings of shiraz and grenache and a move towards sustainable practices in the vineyard. (JH)

ΥΥΥΥΥ Rhapsody Reserve Shiraz 2020, Heathcote The Lake Cooper Estate flagship sourced from the original 1998 vines needs a little time to open. It's still young, feeling its way as it works quite firmly in tannins, resolutely embraced in vanillin oak and oh, so gently releasing ripe black berries, damson plums, aniseed, dark chocolate and earthy ribbons of plushness. Will enjoy a wonderful life ahead. Screw cap. 14.5% alc. RATING 95 DRINK 2022-2033 $100 JP

ΥΥΥΥΥ Shiraz 2020, Heathcote RATING 93 DRINK 2022-2032 $45 JP
Reserve Cabernet Sauvignon 2020, Heathcote RATING 92 DRINK 2022-2030 $45 JP

Lake George Winery

173 The Vineyards Road, Lake George, NSW 2581 **Region** Canberra District
T (02) 9948 4676 **www**.lakegeorgewinery.com.au **Open** Thurs–Sun 10–4
Winemaker Nick O'Leary, Anthony McDougall **Est.** 1971 **Dozens** 2000 **Vyds** 8ha
Lake George Winery was established by legend-in-his-own-lifetime Dr Edgar Riek, who contributed so much to the Canberra District and the Australian wine industry. It has now passed into the hands of Sarah and Anthony McDougall, and the 47yo dry-grown chardonnay, pinot noir, cabernet sauvignon, semillon and merlot plantings have been joined by shiraz, tempranillo, pinot gris, viognier and riesling. The winemaking techniques include basket pressing and small-batch barrel maturation. (JH)

ΥΥΥΥΥ Pinot Noir 2019, Canberra District The Canberra District is not my first port of call for pinot noir. And yet, it can produce such distinct, highly aromatic and lighter-framed wines of great enjoyment, this '19 a case in point. Fragrant and bright with alpine strawberries, red berries, menthol, woodsy spices and ultra-refreshing raspberry-like acidity working alongside chalky tannins. A delicious drink for today. Screw cap. 13% alc. RATING 95 DRINK 2021-2027 $40 JF
Tempranillo 2019, Canberra District This is a light to medium-bodied and juicy red with a freshness that delights, yet it has surprisingly reticent tannins for the variety. Still, it's a joven style, full of mouth-watering acidity, fresh black cherries and some kirsch, cola and red licorice. Drinkability stamped all over this. Screw cap. 12.5% alc. RATING 94 DRINK 2021-2024 $35 JF

♟♟♟♟♀ **Riesling 2021, Canberra District** RATING 92 DRINK 2021–2028 $29 JF
Semillon Sauvignon Blanc 2021, Canberra District RATING 90
DRINK 2021–2023 $26 JF

Lake's Folly ★★★★★

2416 Broke Road, Pokolbin, NSW 2320 **Region** Hunter Valley
T (02) 4998 7507 **www**.lakesfolly.wine **Open** 7 days 10–4 while wine available
Winemaker Rodney Kempe **Est.** 1963 **Dozens** 4500 **Vyds** 13ha
The first of the weekend wineries to produce wines for commercial sale, long revered for its
Cabernet Sauvignon and nowadays its Chardonnay. Just as they should, terroir and climate
produce a distinct wine style. Lake's Folly no longer has any connection with the Lake
family, having been acquired some years ago by Perth businessman Peter Fogarty. Peter's
family company previously established the Millbrook Winery in the Perth Hills and has
since acquired Deep Woods Estate and Evans & Tate in Margaret River, Smithbrook Wines
in Pemberton and Dalwhinnie in the Pyrenees, so is no stranger to the joys and agonies
of running a small winery. Peter has been an exemplary owner of all the brands, providing
support where needed but otherwise not interfering. (JH)

♟♟♟♟♟ **Chardonnay 2021, Hunter Valley** The Hunter's bright beam of fruit: glazed
quince, ginger, white fig, stone and tropical, impeccably harnessed by classy French
oak and its orb of praline and cashew. As savoury as it is impeccably ripe. The
2021 vintage's seam of freshness, imparting tension while towing fine length. The
track record, enviable. The wine in the glass, the reason why. Screw cap. 13.5% alc.
RATING 96 DRINK 2021–2030 $80 NG
Hill Block Chardonnay 2021, Hunter Valley Tangier and more of a nectarine
and white-peach spectrum than that of the home block. Toasted hazelnut, serving
as a moreish curb. Intense, an understatement. A delicious wine, without quite the
expansion, breadth and gentle understated air of the home block. This will grow
in stature, make no mistake. Screw cap. 13.5% alc. RATING 94 DRINK 2021–2029
$90 NG

Landaire at Padthaway Estate ★★★★☆

Riddoch Highway, Padthaway, SA 5271 **Region** Padthaway
T 0417 408 147 **www**.landaire.com.au **Open** Fri–Sun 11–4 **Est.** 2012 **Dozens** 2000
Vyds 200ha
David and Carolyn Brown have been major grapegrowers in Padthaway for 2 decades, David
having had vineyard and farming experience, Carolyn with a background in science. Landaire
evolved from a desire, after many years of growing grapes at their Glendon Vineyard, to select
small quantities of the best grapes to produce wines under their own label. It has proved a
sure-fire recipe for success. The 1850s stables have since been converted into a cellar door,
with accommodation available in the original 1901 shearers' quarters and 1947 cottage. In
2017 Carolyn and David purchased nearby Padthaway Estate and the '18 Eliza Brut Rosé and
'18 Eliza Blanc De Blancs were the first sparkling wines made under their stewardship. Exports
to the UK and Hong Kong. (JH)

♟♟♟♟♟ **Reserve Cabernet Sauvignon 2018, Padthaway** Espresso on the nose,
backed by salted licorice, a whiff of campfire, fresh tobacco leaf and blackberries. In
the mouth, the wine is intensely concentrated, with a pert line of acidity that runs
the length of it. This tastes exactly as the nose suggests … earthy, savoury, sweet,
engaging and delicious. A lovely wine that will live for many years in the cellar.
Cork. 14.5% alc. RATING 95 DRINK 2022–2042 $58 EL
Chardonnay 2020, Padthaway This is creamy, fine and redolent of white
peaches, lemon pith, crushed almonds, red apple skins and some nougat, all of
it stitched together with threads of fine, saline acidity. A wonderful wine. Very
elegant. Screw cap. 12.5% alc. RATING 94 DRINK 2022–2028 $37 EL

♟♟♟♟♀ **Cabernet Sauvignon 2018, Padthaway** RATING 93 DRINK 2022–2032
$40 EL

Lane's End Vineyard

885 Mount William Road, Lancefield, Vic 3435 **Region** Macedon Ranges
T (03) 5429 1760 **www**.lanesend.com.au **Open** By appt **Winemaker** Howard Matthews,
Kilchurn Wines **Est.** 1985 **Dozens** 400 **Vyds** 2ha

Pharmacist Howard Matthews and family purchased the former Woodend Winery in 2000,
with 1.8ha of chardonnay and pinot noir and a small amount of cabernet franc dating back to
the mid '80s. The cabernet franc has been grafted over to pinot noir and the vineyard is now
made up of 1ha each of chardonnay and pinot noir (five clones). Howard has been making
the wines for over a decade. (JH)

L'autre Pinot Noir 2020, Macedon Ranges A delightful drink from start to
finish. It's as fragrant as a bunch of roses and violets with wafts of cherry and spice.
Lighter framed, with juicy tangy fruit across the palate; moreish and savoury with
fine tannins. Spot-on drinking without a second thought. Screw cap. 12.8% alc.
RATING 94 DRINK 2021–2026 $32 JF

Rosé 2021, Macedon Ranges RATING 93 DRINK 2021–2023 $25 JF ○
Chardonnay 2020, Macedon Ranges RATING 93 DRINK 2022–2027 $40 JF
Rosé 2020, Macedon Ranges RATING 92 DRINK 2021–2022 $22 JF ○

Lange Estate

633 Frankland-Cranbrook Road, Frankland River, WA 6396 **Region** Frankland River
T 0438 511 828 **www**.langestate.com.au **Open** By appt **Winemaker** Liam Carmody
and Guy Lyons **Viticulturist** Kim Lange, Lee Haselgrove **Est.** 1997 **Dozens** 7000
Vyds 20ha

The eponymous Lange Estate is owned and run by the family: Kim and Chelsea, their children
Jack, Ella and Dylan, together with parents Don and Maxine. The vineyard is situated in
the picturesque Frankland River, tucked away in the far northwestern corner of the Great
Southern. The vineyard, with an elevation of almost 300m and red jarrah gravel loam soils,
produces wines of great intensity. (JH)

Fifth Generation Cabernet Sauvignon 2020, Frankland River This is
possessed of the intensity we have come to expect from '20. Salted blackberry,
black tea, ferrous and raspberry notes. This is very good, elegant too. The acidity
keeps it fresh, threaded throughout without pomp or impost. Entrenched. Screw
cap. 13.5% alc. RATING 95 DRINK 2022–2036 $50 EL
Providence Road Shiraz 2020, Frankland River Blood plum, kirsch, ferrous
notes and red dirt – these are the regional hallmarks of Frankland River shiraz and
once you smell them, it's hard to see anything else. This is plush and structured,
with a 50/50 split of savoury spice and sweet fruit. Engaging. Elegantly muscled.
Screw cap. 14.5% alc. RATING 94 DRINK 2021–2030 $32 EL

Fifth Generation Riesling 2021, Frankland River RATING 93
DRINK 2022–2032 $40 EL
TSR Cabernet Sauvignon 2020, Frankland River RATING 92
DRINK 2021–2029 $25 EL ○
Providence Road Cabernet Sauvignon 2020, Frankland River RATING 92
DRINK 2022–2028 $32 EL
Providence Road Riesling 2021, Frankland River RATING 91
DRINK 2021–2031 $32 EL

Langmeil Winery

Cnr Langmeil Road/Para Road, Tanunda, SA 5352 **Region** Barossa Valley
T (08) 8563 2595 **www**.langmeilwinery.com.au **Open** 7 days 10–4 **Winemaker** Paul
Lindner **Est.** 1996 **Vyds** 33.12ha

Langmeil Winery, owned and operated by the Lindner family, is home to what may be the
world's oldest surviving shiraz vineyard, The Freedom 1843. It was planted by Christian

Auricht, a blacksmith who fled religious persecution in his native Prussia and sought a new life for his family in Australia. The historic, now renovated, site was once an important trading post and is also the location of the Orphan Bank Vineyard. This plot of shiraz vines, originally planted in the '60s, was transplanted from the centre of Tanunda to the banks of the North Para River in '06. Exports to all major markets. (JH)

ŶŶŶŶŶ **The Freedom 1843 Barossa Shiraz 2019, Barossa Valley** It's a wonderful wine. Calm and very comfortable in its own skin, with rich plum and berry fruits, a lovely textural flow, superfine river-silt tannins and a savoury wash of spicy fruit and finish that carries admirably. Screw cap. 14.5% alc. RATING 96 DRINK 2021-2038 $185 DB

Pure Eden Shiraz 2019, Eden Valley Aromas of red plum, blueberry and boysenberry fruits underscored by hints of spice box, a light cedar nuance, warm earth and roasting meats. Superfine powdery tannins provide gentle support and there is a distinct savoury air to its palate shape, with a toothsome, meaty edge to the fruit profile. A lovely, textural wine. Screw cap. 14.5% alc. RATING 95 DRINK 2021-2036 $185 DB

Pure Eden Shiraz 2018, Eden Valley A picture of grace, the line is finer and more detailed in this lovely Eden Valley wine, than its stablemates from the Barossa Valley floor. The fruits are red and blue with notes of sage, cedar, spice box and olive tapenade. There is a sense of space and clarity to its form, rolling forward propelled by quartz-like acidity and supported by superfine, powdery tannins. Lovely elegant drinking. Screw cap. 14.5% alc. RATING 95 DRINK 2021-2038 $170 DB

The Freedom 1843 Barossa Shiraz 2018, Barossa Valley From vines believed to be planted in 1843. When it comes to these ancient vines, it's often an exercise in texture and fruit density, but there is grace here; there's also a distinct meaty facet that peaks the interest. The fruit is pure and weighty, but not at the expense of detail. Ripe, rich, red and dark fruits abound, the tannin is silky-fine and provides a framework. The finish flows nicely, flush with pure fruit, spice and earthen tones. Screw cap. 14.5% alc. RATING 95 DRINK 2021-2038 $170 DB

25 Year Old Liqueur Tawny NV, Barossa Valley Predominantly shiraz with grenache and muscadelle in the mix. Notes of toffee apple, salted caramel, rich fruitcake, candied nuts, citrus peel and those boozy raisins that my mum slipped in the Christmas pud. Unctuous with a sweet creamy mouthfeel, all the aromas transpose neatly to the palate which is über-luscious with sweetly spiced complexity and a finish that trails off seemingly forever. Screw cap. 21% alc. RATING 95 $40 DB

ŶŶŶŶŶ **Kernel Barossa Cabernet Sauvignon 2019, Barossa Valley** RATING 93 DRINK 2021-2031 $50 DB

Orphan Bank Shiraz 2019, Barossa RATING 93 DRINK 2021-2035 $75 DB

Jackaman's Barossa Cabernet Sauvignon 2018, Barossa Valley RATING 93 DRINK 2021-2035 $75 DB

Wattle Brae Eden Valley Riesling 2121, Barossa Valley RATING 92 DRINK 2021-2030 $30 DB

Black Beauty Barossa Malbec 2020, Barossa Valley RATING 92 DRINK 2021-2030 $30 DB ♥

Hallowed Ground Shiraz 2019, Barossa RATING 92 DRINK 2021-2035 $50 DB

Jackaman's Barossa Cabernet Sauvignon 2019, Barossa Valley RATING 92 DRINK 2021-2035 $75 DB

Orphan Bank Shiraz 2018, Barossa RATING 92 DRINK 2021-2030 $75 DB

Sparkling Shiraz Cuvée NV, Barossa Valley RATING 91 $50 DB

Valley Floor Shiraz 2019, Barossa RATING 91 DRINK 2021-2031 $35 DB

Lark Hill ★★★★★

31 Joe Rocks Road, Bungendore, NSW 2621 **Region** Canberra District
T (02) 6238 1393 **www**.larkhill.wine **Open** Thurs–Mon 11–4 **Winemaker** Dr David
Carpenter, Sue Carpenter and Chris Carpenter **Est.** 1978 **Dozens** 6000 **Vyds** 12ha
The Lark Hill vineyard is situated at an altitude of 860m, offering splendid views of the Lake
George escarpment. The Carpenters have made wines of real quality, style and elegance from
the start, but have defied all the odds (and conventional thinking) with the quality of their
pinot noirs in favourable vintages. Significant changes came in the wake of son Christopher
gaining 3 degrees – including a double in wine science and viticulture through CSU – and
the organic/biodynamic certification of the vineyard and wines in 2003. Lark Hill planted
the first grüner veltliner in Australia in '05 and in '11 purchased 1 of the 2 Ravensworth
vineyards from Michael Kirk, with plantings of sangiovese, shiraz, viognier, roussanne and
marsanne. (JH)

♀♀♀♀♀ **Dark Horse Vineyard Marsanne 2019, Canberra District** A racy style full of
lively acidity yet flavourful with lemon, stone fruit, a touch of burnt butter and a
beeswax character that's appealing. The palate is tight, with a balance of savouriness
to the fruit flavours. Terrific wine and will continue to garner complexity in time.
Screw cap. 12.5% alc. RATING 95 DRINK 2021–2028 $30 JF ✪
Lark Hill Vineyard Grüner Veltliner 2019, Canberra District In 2009, Lark
Hill made Australia's first grüner veltliner and now rightly celebrates a decade on,
as this '19 is singing. Delicate aromas of orange blossom and coriander, flavours
of citrus, a whisper of pepper, cinnamon and lemon cream, with a juiciness across
the palate thanks to its acidity. It has depth, neat phenolics and texture, yet remains
ethereal and refreshingly dry. Screw cap. 12.5% alc. RATING 95 DRINK 2021–2027
$45 JF

♀♀♀♀♀ **Roxanne Petillant Naturel 2020, Hilltops** RATING 92 $30 JF
Lark Hill Vineyard Riesling 2021, Canberra District RATING 92
DRINK 2021–2029 $55 JF
Regional Riesling 2021, Hilltops RATING 91 DRINK 2021–2026 $25 JF
Ley-Line Lark Hill Vineyard Riesling 2019, Canberra District RATING 91
DRINK 2021–2025 $40 JF
Dark Horse Vineyard Sangiovese 2021, Canberra District RATING 90
DRINK 2021–2024 $30 JF
Regional Pinot Noir 2021, Canberra District RATING 90 DRINK 2021–2023
$30 JF
Lark Hill Vineyard Pinot Noir 2019, Canberra District RATING 90
DRINK 2022–2029 $55 JF
Scuro Sangiovese Shiraz 2016, Canberra District RATING 90
DRINK 2021–2025 $45 JF

Laughing Jack ★★★★★

194 Stonewell Road, Marananga, SA 5355 **Region** Barossa Valley
T (08) 8562 3878 **www**.laughingjackwines.com.au **Open** Fri–Sat 10–4
Winemaker Shawn Kalleske **Est.** 1999 **Dozens** 5000 **Vyds** 38.88ha
The Kalleske family has many branches in the Barossa Valley. Laughing Jack is owned by
Shawn, Nathan, Ian and Carol Kalleske, and Linda Schroeter. The lion's share of the vineyard
is planted to shiraz, with lesser amounts of semillon and grenache. Vine age varies considerably,
with old dry-grown shiraz the jewel in the crown. A small part of the grape production is
taken for the Laughing Jack Shiraz. As any Australian knows, the kookaburra is also called the
laughing jackass, and there is a resident flock of kookaburras in the stands of blue and red gums
surrounding the vineyards. Exports to Malaysia and Hong Kong. (JH)

♀♀♀♀♀ **Moppa Hill Gold Seam Cabernet Sauvignon 2019, Barossa Valley** There
is a solid wall of ripe blackberry, blackcurrant and black cherry at this wine's core.
Hints of spice, licorice, dark chocolate and lighter wafts of briar, dried herbs, cedar,
vanillin and earth. A wonderful example of top-drawer Barossa cabernet sauvignon

with impeccable balance, precision and grace; pitch-perfect sinewy tannin support and a gorgeous swell of spicy, pure black fruits on the lengthy finish. Screw cap. 14% alc. RATING 96 DRINK 2022-2042 $40 DB ✪ ♥

Moppa Hill Block 6 Shiraz 2019, Barossa Valley Shawn Kalleske has composed a wonderful contemporary Barossa shiraz here. Compact, with excellent fruit purity, a super-ripe plum and blackberry base and abundant spice and – wonder of wonders – manages to combine both fruit density and a sense of space, finishing savoury, tight of tannin and with a fan of red and black fruits and layered spice. Screw cap. 14.5% alc. RATING 95 DRINK 2022-2035 $40 DB

Greenock Shiraz 2019, Barossa Valley A great example of classic Western Ridge latent power here. Dense blackberry, black cherry and plum characters build in intensity, gather both spice and pace before compressing and accelerating to the exit, framed by superfine tannin before coast slowly into the distance. Lovely stuff. Screw cap. 14.5% alc. RATING 95 DRINK 2022-2038 $50 DB

Carl Albert Moppa Block Shiraz 2019, Barossa Valley Deep red purple in the glass with an inviting nose of ripe plum and berry fruits painted with floral flourishes of violet and jasmine. Plenty of detail and juicy fruit weight on display, layered with spice and judicious cedary oak nuance. Feathery tannins and bright acidity provided the framework and the finish lingers nicely with ripe spicy plum fruits and a slight savoury gait. Cork. 14.5% alc. RATING 95 DRINK 2022-2035 $95 DB

🍷🍷🍷🍷🍷 (4.5) **Jack's Semillon 2021, Barossa Valley** RATING 91 DRINK 2022-2032 $25 DB
Jack's GSM 2019, Barossa Valley RATING 91 DRINK 2022-2028 $25 DB
Jack's Shiraz 2019, Barossa Valley RATING 90 DRINK 2022-2028 $25 DB

Laurel Bank ★★★★☆

130 Black Snake Lane, Granton, Tas 7030 **Region** Southern Tasmania
T (03) 6263 5977 **www**.laurelbankwines.com.au **Open** By appt **Winemaker** Greer Carland **Est.** 1986 **Dozens** 1700 **Vyds** 3.5ha

Laurel Bank was established by Kerry Carland in 1986 but deliberately kept a low profile by withholding release of most of its early wines. When the time came, Kerry entered the Hobart Wine Show in '95 and won the trophy for Most Successful Tasmanian Exhibitor. These days, Kerry's daughter Greer is the extremely qualified winemaker, with a degree in oenology, vintages in Chile, Oregan and Burgundy under her belt and 12 years as senior winemaker at Winemaking Tasmania. She also produces wines for her own label, Quiet Mutiny, on the side. (JH)

🍷🍷🍷🍷🍷 **Cabernet Merlot 2020, Tasmania** It takes grit and talent to achieve ripeness and balance in cabernet and merlot in Southern Tasmania in a vintage as cool as '20. Aggressive fruit thinning was one of many courageous decisions that created this delightful and affordable blend. A core of signature cabernet blackcurrant is perfumed with a wonderful air of violets and structured with an intricate framework of firm, fine and eminently enduring tannins. A benchmark wine with a pedigree and a future at complete odds with its price. Screw cap. 13.9% alc. RATING 95 DRINK 2030-2040 $36 TS

Pinot Noir 2020, Tasmania The detail and attention put into this wine far exceed its price; the quality it delivers in this elegant season follows suit. Morello cherries and wild strawberries are accented by the herbs and spice of 15% whole bunches, well supported by the fine, firm framework of maturation in French oak barrels (30% new). Old-vine integrity (up to 35 years) drives a long and promising finish. Wait. Screw cap. 13.5% alc. RATING 94 DRINK 2028-2035 $36 TS

🍷🍷🍷🍷🍷 (4.5) **Sauvignon Blanc 2021, Tasmania** RATING 93 DRINK 2022-2023 $25 TS ✪
Riesling 2020, Tasmania RATING 91 DRINK 2022-2024 $25 TS

Leconfield

15454 Riddoch Highway, Coonawarra, SA 5263 **Region** Coonawarra
T (08) 8323 8830 **www**.leconfieldwines.com **Open** By appt **Winemaker** Paul Gordon,
Greg Foster **Viticulturist** Bendt Rasmussen **Est.** 1974 **Dozens** 25 000 **Vyds** 43.7ha
Sydney Hamilton purchased the unplanted property that was to become Leconfield
in 1974, having worked in the family wine business for over 30 years until his retirement in
the mid '50s. When he acquired the property, and set about planting it, he was 76 and
reluctantly bowed to family pressure to sell Leconfield to nephew Richard in '81. Richard
has progressively increased the vineyards to their present level, over 75% dedicated to cabernet
sauvignon – for long the winery's specialty. Exports to most major markets. (JH)

ＴＴＴＴＴ **Old Vines Riesling 2020, Coonawarra** Marmalade on buttered toast, spiced
apples, salted citrus and a weighty, almost voluminous countenace about it. It
doesn't billow, like a Clare Valley riesling does, or race like a riesling from the Great
Southern. Rather it has a stately, concentrated and measured presence of flavour in
the mouth that lingers long after the wine has gone. Rich, engaging and sinewy
through the finish. Very smart. Screw cap. 13% alc. RATING 95 DRINK 2022-2037
$28 EL ✪

The Sydney Reserve Cabernet Sauvignon 2017, Coonawarra The
cool '17 vintage has laid the foundation for a wine of detail and weight. It is
layered with graphite tannins, cool mineral acid and dark berry fruits. This is a
traditionally styled Australian cabernet with minty overtones and savoury, leathery
spice. Lovely. Screw cap. 14.5% alc. RATING 95 DRINK 2022-2037 $85 EL

Petit Verdot 2020, Coonawarra Petit verdot doesn't need any encouragement.
It flexes before anyone is even looking, with lavender, potpourri, black fruit and
dark tannins. It is aromatic and brooding, and can be tasted in very tiny amounts
in a blend (3–4% makes itself known). So to experience it solo is something else.
This is lush, pure, glossy, even, with fine shapely tannins and a lingering tail. Really
nice, really well handled. Screw cap. 13.5% alc. RATING 94 DRINK 2022-2032
$32 EL

ＴＴＴＴＹ **Reserve Shiraz 2020, Coonawarra** RATING 93 DRINK 2022-2029 $32 EL
Cabernet Sauvignon 2020, Coonawarra RATING 93 DRINK 2022-2036
$36 EL
Cabernets 2019, Coonawarra RATING 93 DRINK 2021-2041 $32 EL
Shiraz 2020, McLaren Vale RATING 92 DRINK 2021-2028 $28 EL
Syn Rouge Sparkling Shiraz NV, Coonawarra RATING 90 $22 EL
Noble Riesling 2021, Coonawarra RATING 90 DRINK 2022-2028 $32 EL

Leeuwin Estate

Stevens Road, Margaret River, WA 6285 **Region** Margaret River
T (08) 9759 0000 **www**.leeuwinestate.com.au **Open** 7 days 10–5 **Winemaker** Tim
Lovett, Phil Hutchison, Breac Wheatley **Viticulturist** David Winstanley **Est.** 1974
Dozens 50 000 **Vyds** 160ha
This outstanding winery and vineyard is owned by the Horgan family, founded by Denis and
Tricia, who continue their involvement, with son Justin Horgan and daughter Simone Furlong
joint chief executives. The Art Series Chardonnay is, in my (James') opinion, Australia's finest
example based on the wines of the last 30 vintages. The move to screw cap brought a large
smile to the faces of those who understand just how superbly the wine ages. The large estate
plantings, coupled with strategic purchases of grapes from other growers, provide the base for
high-quality Art Series Cabernet Sauvignon and Shiraz; the hugely successful, quick-selling
Art Series Riesling and Sauvignon Blanc; and lower-priced Prelude and Siblings wines.
Exports to all major markets. (JH)

ＴＴＴＴＴ **Art Series Chardonnay 2019, Margaret River** Leeuwin Art Series
Chardonnay on release is an achingly painful thing to drink, because once you've
known the utter pleasure these wines bring at 5 or more years of age, it becomes a
mess of cognitive dissonance to drink them so young. They are closed, taut, coiled,

but more than anything, populated by rippling fruit that undulates untold through the interminably long finish. They typically don't reveal their kaleidoscopic spice and prismatic fruit flavour until a little further down the track. So, all I can humbly do here, is place the vintage in context. Through the lens of the cool year, this glitters with a purity and finesse that is deeply attractive. Aligned in style with the '17. Screw cap. 13.5% alc. RATING 98 DRINK 2022-2042 $138 EL ✪

Art Series Cabernet Sauvignon 2018, Margaret River This was a freak vintage in the hands of many winemakers in WA, capable of power, balance, ripeness and glory. This has pomegranate, red licorice and peppered raspberry. The fruit flavours, while slinky and seductive, are not the major player here. And that is saying something. The key to the brilliance of this wine, like the '14, the '10 and to some extent the '05 before it, is the texture. The tannins. They are tightly woven, very fine and serve to support the fruit and the acid. This wine is built on a stable scaffold of tannin that both cushions the experience and defines it. What a wine. Screw cap. 13.5% alc. RATING 97 DRINK 2022-2042 $79 EL ✪

🍷🍷🍷🍷🍷 **Prelude Vineyards Chardonnay 2020, Margaret River** A second label for a wine of great distinction, and its usual sourcing of fruit from estate and contract-grown vines: purity, intensity and extreme length. Grapefruit speaks louder about the boys in the band. I suppose oak has played some part in shaping the wine, but it isn't obvious. Screw cap. 13.5% alc. RATING 96 DRINK 2025-2040 $38 JH ✪

Prelude Vineyards Cabernet Sauvignon 2019, Margaret River With 2% malbec. Cabernet and malbec are meant to be together. This is vibrant and intense, layered with cassis and pomegranate, licorice, clove, graphite and nori. The layers are sewn together with threads of saline acidity that create structure within the shape provided by the oak. All things in place here – yet another compelling Prelude release from the team at Leeuwin. Unbelievable value for money. Screw cap. 13.5% alc. RATING 95 DRINK 2021-2036 $32 EL ✪

Art Series Shiraz 2019, Margaret River If you've ever watched mercury being poured, you'll understand what I mean when I say that the tannins have a seamless liquidity about them. They shape the fruit and allow it passage over the tongue and into the sunset of its finish. A serious step up in quality and texture from the Siblings Shiraz. The layers of flavour seem never-ending. This wine ages gracefully over the medium term, although my preference is for drinking it within 2–4 years, as I love the vibrancy, detail and poise of it as a young wine. Choose your own adventure. Screw cap. 13.5% alc. RATING 95 DRINK 2021-2031 $41 EL

Art Series Sauvignon Blanc 2021, Margaret River This is extraordinarily elegant, layered with lychee, coriander, passionfruit, hints of jalapeño and shaped by fine, chalky phenolics. Saline acidity threads it all together. Plum Margaret River sauvignon blanc on a good day. Screw cap. 13% alc. RATING 94 DRINK 2021-2028 $31 EL

Lenton Brae Wines ★★★★

3887 Caves Road, Margaret River, WA 6285 **Region** Margaret River
T (08) 9755 6255 **www**.lentonbrae.com **Open** 7 days 10–5 **Winemaker** Ed Tomlinson, Vanessa Carson **Est.** 1982 **Vyds** 7.3ha

The late architect Bruce Tomlinson built a strikingly beautiful winery (heritage-listed by the Shire of Busselton) that is now in the hands of winemaker son Edward (Ed), who consistently makes elegant wines in classic Margaret River style. A midwinter (French time) trip to Pomerol in Bordeaux to research merlot is an indication of his commitment. Exports to the UK. (JH)

🍷🍷🍷🍷🍷 **Wilyabrup Cabernet Sauvignon 2020, Margaret River** Leafy, classical cabernet, here. A dollop (3%) of petit verdot leaves a trace of floral perfume on the nose: violets, potpourri and lavender. In the mouth the wine is very firmly structured, the tannins at this stage lock the fruit in place. The length of flavour tells us more about the wine than the palate does; it unfurls in the mouth and shows pretty, languid fruit. Patience is a virtue, best executed over a number of years. It will live an age. Screw cap. 14.5% alc. RATING 94 DRINK 2022-2037 $80 EL

🍷🍷🍷🍷♀ **Cabernet Sauvignon 2020, Margaret River** RATING 91 DRINK 2021-2031
$38 EL
Southside Chardonnay 2021, Margaret River RATING 90 DRINK 2022-2028
$32 EL
Wilyabrup Chardonnay 2021, Margaret River RATING 90 DRINK 2022-2028
$65 EL

Leo Buring ★★★★☆

Sturt Highway, Nuriootpa, SA 5355 **Region** Clare Valley/Eden Valley
T 1300 651 650 **Winemaker** Tom Shanahan **Est.** 1934
Between 1965 and 2000, Leo Buring was Australia's foremost producer of rieslings, with a
rich legacy left by former winemaker John Vickery. After veering away from its core business
into other varietal wines, it has now refocused on riesling. Top of the range are the Leopold
Derwent Valley and the Leonay Eden Valley rieslings, supported by Clare Valley and Eden
Valley rieslings at significantly lower prices, and expanding its wings to Tasmania and WA. (JH)

🍷🍷🍷🍷🍷 **Leonay DWY17 Riesling 2021, Eden Valley** All the Leonay hallmarks are
here: precision, detail, clarity and drive. What I really love about these wines
is their tubular palate shape of achingly pure, limey fruit, topped with notes
of Christmas lily and stone. The concentration on the palate is impressive, all
compressed lime juice and floral top-notes, the wine coiling at first before
accelerating off across the tongue with a cracking pace, leaving a finish that
lingers beautifully. It's a classic. Screw cap. 11% alc. RATING 97 DRINK 2021-2038
$40 DB ✪ ♥

🍷🍷🍷🍷🍷 **Dry Riesling 2021, Eden Valley** Thoroughly impressive, given the challenging
vintage. This has been extracted with considerable aplomb, from fruit relatively
unscathed. The finish, slightly bitter, but not unattractive. Otherwise, redcurrant,
spearmint, lilac, chilli and a brush of thyme across an effortless finish. Mid
weighted, characterful and altogether, a remarkable effort. The price, a steal. Screw
cap. 13.5% alc. RATING 94 DRINK 2021-2035 $20 DB ✪

Leogate Estate Wines ★★★★★

1693 Broke Road, Pokolbin, NSW 2320 **Region** Hunter Valley
T (02) 4998 7499 **www.**leogate.com.au **Open** 7 days 10–5 **Winemaker** Mark Woods
Est. 2009 **Dozens** 30 000 **Vyds** 127.5ha
Since purchasing the substantial Brokenback Vineyard in 2009, Bill and Vicki Widin have
wasted no time. Initially the Widins leased the Tempus Two winery but prior to the '13
vintage they completed the construction of their own winery and cellar door. They have
also expanded the range of varieties, supplementing the long-established 30ha of shiraz, 25ha
of chardonnay and 3ha of semillon with between 0.5 and 2ha of each of verdelho, viognier,
gewürztraminer, pinot gris and tempranillo. They have had a string of wine show successes
for their very impressive portfolio. In '16 Leogate purchased a 61ha certified organic vineyard
at Gulgong (Mudgee) planted to shiraz, cabernet sauvignon and merlot. Leogate has an
impressive collection of back-vintage releases available on request. Exports to the UK, the US,
Malaysia and Hong Kong. (JH)

🍷🍷🍷🍷🍷 **Museum Release Reserve Semillon 2011, Hunter Valley** Exceptional
semillon from a superlative vintage, at least in these parts. Tightly coiled,
unleashing lemon balm, barley sugar, toasted hazelnut, quinine, buttered toast and
lanolin accents from a spring of talcy, bright acidity. This is hitting middle age,
rather than senescence. Give it another decade to unwind further, or enjoy the
balletic pirouette of fruit, refinement, gentle aged complexity and tensile freshness
now. Screw cap. 11% alc. RATING 97 DRINK 2021-2026 $70 NG ✪

🍷🍷🍷🍷🍷 **Museum Release The Basin Reserve Shiraz 2011, Hunter Valley** This
makes for an interesting counterpoint to the Western Slopes sibling. There is more
tension here. More vibrancy. The fruit, still youthful and sweet. Maraschino cherry,

bergamot, fresh leather and terracotta. The finish unravels with a hint of sous-bois and beef bouillon intimating bottle age, while imparting fine savoury complexity. Screw cap. 14% alc. RATING 96 DRINK 2021–2027 $225 NG

Museum Release Brokenback Vineyard Semillon 2017, Hunter Valley
This is a filigreed, lightweight, almost balletic expression, just pirouetting into adolescence. The sordid career into any mid-life crisis, eons away. And yet, I like the wine here. It will age, sure. But the lemon squash, tonic, citrus balm, Thai herbs and soapy lanolin feel, all attractive. The acidity, arguably better measured than its '11 sibling. A lovely wine now and in the making. Screw cap. 11% alc. RATING 95 DRINK 2021–2029 $30 NG ✪

Museum Release Creek Bed Reserve Semillon 2017, Hunter Valley
This sits nicely in the mouth, idling across an ebb of grapefruit pulp, tonic and lemongrass, juxtaposed against a parry of sandy acidity, a little pucker and an effortless long flow. An exceptional wine for the vintage. Screw cap. 10.8% alc. RATING 95 DRINK 2022–2029 $40 NG

Museum Release Malabar Reserve Shiraz 2017, Hunter Valley Re-release. This is exceptional. The most flamboyant, flirtatious and exotic of scent of all the shiraz cuvées: iodine, blue-fruit aspersions, tapenade, Asian spice and rosewater. Yet the sweet, ferrous terracotta riff of the Hunter is pure and immutable. Lovely wine. Will age exceptionally well. Screw cap. 14.5% alc. RATING 95 DRINK 2022–2030 $80 NG

Museum Release The Basin Reserve Shiraz 2017, Hunter Valley The more I taste across these older releases, the more I am convinced by The Basin. The wines are generally tighter, more detailed, savoury and mid weighted of feel. Hunter sweet earth, terracotta, leather and red cherry. There is a dusty pliancy to this that is attractive. The finish, long and refined. This will age beautifully. Screw cap. 14.5% alc. RATING 95 DRINK 2021–2032 $115 NG

Museum Release Brokenback Vineyard Semillon 2011, Hunter Valley
It is a treat to taste the array of museum-released semillons at this address. Made conventionally, with not a skerrick of skin contact, lees or pressings, the results are pure, immutable of style and inimitably of place. A fine year. A wine to cherish. Lightweight, yet belying the alcohol is the intense quench of lemon drop, citrus balm, barely sugar and brioche. The acidity, a bit perky, but a finely aged regional stalwart. Screw cap. 11% alc. RATING 95 DRINK 2021–2025 $40 NG

Museum Release Western Slopes Reserve Shiraz 2011, Hunter Valley
This has aged well and will continue to do so. There is still sand in an hourglass of autumnal leaves, sandalwood, bing cherry and woodsmoke. There is a little heat across a long, detailed finish. These wines are often glossy and reductive in their youth. Yet age has subsumed this, imparting the unmistakable twang of the Hunter's sweet loam and polished leather. Very good drinking. Screw cap. 14% alc. RATING 95 DRINK 2021–2026 $225 NG

Creek Bed Reserve Chardonnay 2019, Hunter Valley The finest of the chardonnay suite, at least for this warm year. More about toasted nuts, nougat, sexy oak, dried tatami straw and dashi. Some flinty, match-struck reduction, imparting tension. This is, perhaps, the approach to chardonnay that works best in a region that is challenged in its endeavours to grow it. There is no clang of tropical fruits, but a refined drive of complexity and precision. Bravo. Screw cap. 13.5% alc. RATING 94 DRINK 2021–2026 $38 NG

Museum Release Western Slopes Reserve Shiraz 2017, Hunter Valley
Youthful. Ripe. A lot left in the tank, I would suggest burying this for another 5 years. Kirsch, anise, youthful purple-fruit allusions and a latticework of cedar-vanillin oak. The spread of flavours and texture, impressive. Have faith! Screw cap. 14% alc. RATING 94 DRINK 2023–2032 $115 NG

Lerida Estate

87 Vineyards Road, Lake George, NSW 2581 **Region** Canberra District
T (02) 4848 0231 **www**.leridaestate.com.au **Open** 7 days 10–5 **Winemaker** Jacob Law
Viticulturist James Hopper **Est.** 1997 **Dozens** 10000 **Vyds** 19.6ha
Lerida Estate owes a great deal to the inspiration of Dr Edgar Riek; it is planted immediately
to the south of Edgar's former Lake George vineyard. Lerida is planted mainly to pinot noir,
with pinot gris, chardonnay, shiraz, merlot and cabernet franc and viognier also onsite. Michael
and Tracey McRoberts purchased Lerida in 2017 and significant expansion is underway.
They have leased a 20yo shiraz vineyard (4ha) in the heart of Murrumbateman and shiraz
has overtaken pinot noir as the predominant variety produced. The Glen Murcutt–designed
winery, barrel room, cellar door and restaurant have spectacular views over Lake George. (JH)

ŶŶŶŶŶ Cullerin 2019, Canberra District There's a softness and pulpiness at first, then
it starts to expand with a wave of dark fruit and baking spices, with charry oak
and smoky reduction adding to its overall savouriness. It's fuller bodied but reined-
in, with supple tannins and a vitality throughout. Very good drinking now. Screw
cap. 14% alc. RATING 95 DRINK 2021-2028 $38 JF
Shiraz Viognier 2019, Canberra District Outrageous vibrant purple-black
hue and enticing. While it's labelled with viognier it's barely a splash at 1%. A rich,
opulent style but not too weighty, with a core of plump dark fruits plus oak spice
and char. A sweet spot midway, with ripe, velvety tannins holding sway. It's a wine
that offers immediate pleasure but will last some distance. Screw cap. 14.5% alc.
RATING 95 DRINK 2021-2029 $75 JF

ŶŶŶŶ **Pinot Noir Rosé 2021, Canberra District** RATING 88 DRINK 2021-2022
$28 JF

Lethbridge Wines

74 Burrows Road, Lethbridge, Vic 3222 **Region** Geelong
T (03) 5281 7279 **www**.lethbridgewines.com **Open** Mon–Fri 11–4, w'ends 11–5
Winemaker Ray Nadeson, Maree Collis **Est.** 1996 **Dozens** 10000 **Vyds** 7ha
Lethbridge was founded by scientists Ray Nadeson, Maree Collis and Adrian Thomas.
In Ray's words, 'Our belief is that the best wines express the unique character of special
places'. As well as understanding the importance of terroir, the partners have built a unique
strawbale winery, designed to recreate the controlled environment of cellars and caves in
Europe. Winemaking is no less ecological: hand-picking, indigenous-yeast fermentation, small
open fermenters, pigeage (foot-stomping) and minimal handling of the wines throughout
the maturation process are all part and parcel of the highly successful Lethbridge approach.
Ray also has a distinctive approach to full-blown chardonnay and pinot noir. There is also
a contract winemaking limb to the business. Exports to the UK, the US, Denmark, Russia,
Singapore, Thailand, Japan and Hong Kong. (JH)

ŶŶŶŶŶ Dr Nadeson Riesling 2021, Henty With fruit sourced from Drumborg,
winemaker Ray Nadeson is in the riesling zone, and it's quite an intense zone
at that. Concentrated fruit, firmly packed and beautifully fragrant. The palate is
fleshed out in citrus, apple, white nectarine, spice – what spice! – and a touch
of sweetness to allay Henty's strong acidity. Screw cap. 11% alc. RATING 95
DRINK 2022-2027 $38 JP
Pinot Gris 2021, Henty Has the salmon-pink colour of a rosé – and as much
flavour as many. Views on the desirability (or not) of the pink colour are split, with
no likelihood of being resolved any time soon. The bouquet is redolent of spice,
white pepper and wild strawberries. The palate a mirror image. It's not classic,
but as a left-field wine, it is pretty good. From this crusty old barnacle, that's high
praise. Screw cap. 13% alc. RATING 95 DRINK 2022-2026 $38 JH
Chardonnay 2020, Geelong From a difficult year and a small crop comes a
stunning chardonnay, packed in flavour and budding complexity. White stone fruit,
citrus, mandarin rind, mango skin and spice all roam and build on the palate in

tandem with a delicious honeycomb creamy texture. Acidity wields a powerful, invigorating presence. Screw cap. 13.6% alc. RATING 95 DRINK 2022-2026 $55 JP

Allegra Chardonnay 2019, Geelong A difficult vintage but Allegra, which is sourced from the oldest chardonnay vineyard in Geelong at Mt Duneed, shines. A tightly coiled, thrilling chardonnay. White peach, nectarine, flinty grapefruit, lemon curd and nougatine, nutty oak, not to forget the herbs (lemon thyme) and spice, is all here. Length and fine acid drive are impressive. A quiet power lives here. Screw cap. 13.7% alc. RATING 95 DRINK 2022-2027 $110 JP

Mietta Pinot Noir 2019, Geelong From a 'fast and furious' vintage comes a lively, spice-laden, brightly-fruited pinot upbeat in red berries, wild raspberry, exotic spice and a sappy, undergrowth complexity. And that's just the bouquet. Svelte and even, fine in tannins with a most sustained finish with spice and anise in action. Screw cap. 13.5% alc. RATING 95 DRINK 2022-2028 $110 JP

Nebbiolo 2018, Pyrenees RATING 92 DRINK 2022-2028 $55 JP

Indra 2018, Geelong RATING 92 DRINK 2022-2030 $110 JP

Leura Park Estate

1400 Portarlington Road, Curlewis, Vic 3222 **Region** Geelong
T (03) 5253 3180 **www**.leuraparkestate.com.au **Open** Thurs–Sun 11–4
Winemaker Darren Burke **Viticulturist** David Sharp **Est.** 1995 **Dozens** 3000
Vyds 20ha

Leura Park Estate's vineyard is planted to chardonnay (50%), pinot noir, pinot gris, sauvignon blanc, riesling, shiraz and cabernet sauvignon. Owners David and Lyndsay Sharp are committed to minimal interference in the vineyard and have expanded the estate-grown wine range to include Vintage Grande Cuvée. The next step was the erection of a winery for the 2010 vintage, leading to increased production and ongoing wine show success. (JH)

Bellarine Peninsula Pinot Noir 2020, Geelong Looks ahead to a bright future in its tightly coiled youth with a bright intensity of cherry, cranberry fruit and leafy herbs on display. Sinewy across the palate with fine line and length of fruit and vanillin oak before finishing firm. Screw cap. 12.8% alc. RATING 93 DRINK 2022-2028 $42 JP

Limited Release Block 1 Reserve Chardonnay 2020, Geelong From a difficult vintage comes a sophisticated chardonnay, a little restrained maybe compared to previous vintages, but showing some smart oak integration and fine flavour intensity. Fruit moves in the tropical fruit spectrum with peach, melon and nashi pear. Maturation in French oak brings out a textural nougat and almond mealiness, with all components embroidered in lovely lacy acidity. Screw cap. 13.5% alc. RATING 93 DRINK 2022-2026 $45 JP

Bellarine Peninsula Sauvignon Blanc 2020, Geelong Presents with a complex flavour profile: flinty elements, ripe gooseberry, wild herbs, lime pickle. Dry and chalky with tangy gooseberry and green passionfruit flavours, it manages to fit a lot of punch into its modest frame. Screw cap. 11.5% alc. RATING 92 DRINK 2022–2024 $30 JP

Bellarine Peninsula Riesling 2021, Geelong After a difficult '20 vintage, riesling has bounced back in '21 with a more attractive fruit:acid balance and a bright crystalline beauty. Aromas embrace fragrant bath salts, lemons and lime cordial before moving on to a taut and precise palate with plenty of sherbety, lemon jelly-crystal zing. Screw cap. 12.5% alc. RATING 91 DRINK 2022-2026 $35 JP

Cat Out Of The Bag Chardonnay 2020, Geelong Packs a lot of bright energy and clean, solid chardonnay flavour into the price tag. Delivers peach, nectarine, nashi pear and almond-bread aromas, so enticing and inviting. There's a tension playing out across the palate between tight acidity, barrel ferment texture and brisk citrus fruit. Smart wine. Screw cap. 13% alc. RATING 91 DRINK 2022-2024 $25 JP

Bellarine Peninsula Chardonnay 2020, Geelong Impressive varietal clarity here, not to mention cool-climate focus. Brings a range of citrus aromas to the fore led by grapefruit, backed up by peach and apple, but it's the palate that so impresses; so bright and crunchy, the mealy fruit folded into crisp citrus with an enduring honeysuckle finish. Screw cap. 13% alc. RATING 91 DRINK 2022-2027 $35 JP

Vintage Grand Cuvée Pinot Noir Chardonnay 2021, Geelong A sparkling that is striking in salmon pink with a cool, well-composed bouquet in wild strawberries, fresh cut cherries, watermelon and citrus. The drinker can't expect too much autolysis or complexity in such a young vintage, but the fruit quality and freshness is super-attractive. Diam. 12% alc. RATING 90 $35 JP

ΨΨΨΨ **Vintage Grande Sparkling Blanc de Blanc 2021, Geelong** RATING 89 DRINK 2022-2022 $35 JP

Cat Out Of The Bag Rosé Cabernet Sauvignon 2020, Geelong RATING 89 DRINK 2022-2024 $25 JP

Cat Out Of The Bag Shiraz 2020, Geelong RATING 89 DRINK 2022-2024 $28 JP

25 d'Gris Bellarine Peninsula Pinot Gris 2020, Geelong RATING 89 DRINK 2022-2025 $35 JP

Cat Out Of The Bag Pinot Grigio 2020, Geelong RATING 89 DRINK 2022-2024 $25 JP

Bellarine Peninsula Shiraz 2019, Geelong RATING 89 DRINK 2022-2026 $45 JP

Cat Out Of The Bag Sauvignon Blanc 2020, Geelong RATING 88 DRINK 2022-2024 $25 JP

Levrier Wines ★★★★

928 Research Road, Nuriootpa, SA 5355 **Region** Barossa Valley
T (08) 8562 3888 **www**.levrierwines.com.au **Open** By appt **Winemaker** Joanne Irvine
Est. 2017 **Dozens** 3000
'Levrier' is French for greyhound, and Jo Irvine has looked after retired racing greyhounds for 20 years. The wines she now makes on her own account are given the names of famous racing greyhounds. Jo's second career is as a skilled contract winemaker. At 35 she gave up her occupation as a theatre nurse and joined her father Jim Irvine, having enjoyed gap years travelling internationally and doing vintages in the US. She made wines for her father, notably his Grand Merlot, the last vintage in 2014, after which he sold his business. Jo was in no hurry to hang her shingle up until all the pieces were in place: grape supply, winemaking, maturation and packaging. (JH)

ΨΨΨΨΨ **Mosaic Collection Cavall Merlot 2018, Barossa Valley** Pure, fleshy plum fruits cut with baking spice, red licorice, fruitcake, purple flowers and earth. Quite sweetly-fruited and displaying a juicy fruit flow on the palate, with fine, sandy tannin in support and an enduring finish of spiced red cherry and plum fruits. Screw cap. 14.5% alc. RATING 92 DRINK 2021-2028 $60 DB ♥

Meslier Brut Rosé NV, Adelaide Hills Petit meslier is a rare white grape in this country, but it has been known to be a component in some champagnes. Comes into view as a distinctly orange-tinged wine. Bruised apple, poached pear, quince paste, Brazil nut and nougat-rich flavours and complexity. The grape's notable acidity is nicely softened, producing a creamy, long finish. Cork. 12% alc. RATING 90 $50 JP

Liebich Wein ★★★★★

151 Steingarten Road, Rowland Flat, SA 5352 **Region** Barossa Valley
T (08) 8524 4543 **www**.liebichwein.com.au **Open** Wed–Mon 11–5 **Winemaker** Ron Liebich **Est.** 1992 **Dozens** 900 **Vyds** 11.93ha
The Liebich family have been grapegrowers and winemakers at Rowland Flat since 1919, with CW 'Darkie' Liebich one of the great local characters. His nephew Ron began making wine in '69, but it was not until '92 that he and wife Janet began selling wine under the Liebich

Wein label. The business has grown surely but steadily, a new warehouse commissioned in 2008 vastly improving storage and handling capacity. Exports to the UK, Denmark, Germany and Switzerland. (JH)

Rare Fronti 25 NV, Barossa Valley A superb fortified wine produced from red frontignac and aged for 25 years. Rich golden orange in the glass with aromas of marmalade, candied citrus rind, mahogany, toffee apple, honey snaps, cinnamon, leather, brandied fruit, raisins and dried figs and dates. Smooth, intensely concentrated and fresh as a daisy, with excellent fruit richness and complexity, a bright drive and long red-fruited finish. Agglomerate. 18% alc. RATING 95 $65 DB
Rare Tawny 30 NV, Barossa Valley A wonderful tawny hue in the glass with aromas of raisin essence, polished mahogany, candied citrus rind, sweet spices, cinnamon and brandied fruit. Excellent rancio notes and a succulent, sweet finish that shows freshness and a long, long red fruit-cakey finish. Agglomerate. 18% alc. RATING 95 $75 DB
Grand Semillon NV, Barossa Valley Fortified and aged for 15 years. Dark burnished orange in the glass with aromas of candied citrus rind, honeycomb, toffee, salted caramel, dried fruits, brandied figs and roasting nuts. Silky and sumptuous with great complexity and a great sense of freshness to its shape, finishing long and complex with a trail of honeycomb and toffee citrus. Synthetic. 18% alc. RATING 94 $39 DB
Rare Muscat 25 NV, Barossa Valley Sporting a wonderful tawny hue; aromas of floral-flecked essence of raisin with hints of fruitcake, brandied fruit, polished leather and mahogany, marmalade, toffee apple, salted caramel and dried fruit. Sumptuous, concentrated marmalade and dried-fruit characters slide sweetly over the tongue with great concentration, a touch of volatile acidity and a long, long finish. Screw cap. 18% alc. RATING 94 $65 DB

Heritage Release Old Vine Cabernet Shiraz 2012, Barossa Valley RATING 93 DRINK 2022-2026 $58 DB

Lightfoot Wines

717 Calulu Road, Bairnsdale, Vic 3875 **Region** Gippsland
T (03) 5156 9205 **www**.lightfootwines.com **Open** Fri–Sun 11–5 **Winemaker** Alastair Butt, Tom Lightfoot **Viticulturist** Tom Lightfoot **Est.** 1995 **Dozens** 10 000 **Vyds** 29.3ha
Formerly Lightfoot & Sons. Brian and Helen Lightfoot first established a vineyard of predominantly pinot noir and shiraz, with some cabernet sauvignon and merlot, on their Myrtle Point farm in the late '90s. The soils were found to be similar to that of Coonawarra, with terra rossa over limestone. In the early days, most of the grapes were sold to other Victorian winemakers, but with the arrival of Alistair Butt (formerly of Brokenwood and Seville Estate) and sons Tom and Rob taking over the business around '08 (Tom in the vineyard and cellar, Rob overseeing sales and marketing), the focus has shifted to producing estate wines. Cabernet and merlot have since been replaced with more chardonnay, some gamay and pinot grigio, but pinot noir retains the top spot. (TS)

Myrtle Point Vineyard Chardonnay 2021, Gippsland Such an enjoyable, easy to drink wine but with plenty of definition and complexity. Lemony freshness infuses white nectarine and a touch of cedary spice from the oak – 10 months in a mix of barrel sizes (15% new) and perfectly integrated. It feels light and breezy across the palate, then some creamy lees kicks in to bolster it out and lively acidity ensuring the finish lingers. Screw cap. 12.5% alc. RATING 95 DRINK 2021-2029 $30 JF ✪

Myrtle Point Vineyard Rosé 2021, Gippsland RATING 93 DRINK 2021-2023 $25 JF ✪
Home Block Chardonnay 2019, Gippsland RATING 93 DRINK 2021-2027 $60 JF
Chameleon 2021, Gippsland RATING 91 DRINK 2021-2024 $40 JF

Lillydale Estate ★★★★

Davross Court, Seville, Vic 3139 **Region** Yarra Valley
T 0422 962 888 **www.**lillydaleestate.com.au **Winemaker** Franco D'Anna **Est.** 1975
Dozens 2000 **Vyds** 5ha
Lillydale Estate was established in 1975 by Alex White and Martin Grinbergs, fugitives from Carlton & United Breweries, where they were scientists. They were at the forefront of the development of Yarra Valley chardonnay style in the early '80s, but in '94 the winery, brand and vineyards were acquired by McWilliam's. In Aug '12, ownership changed once again when a subsidiary of the very large Wuxi Electronics and Instruments Industry Co. Ltd acquired the property. The intention is to slowly build the brand, protecting the reputation it has gained over the years. (JH)

ΨΨΨΨΨ **Pinot Noir 2021, Yarra Valley** Bright, ruby crimson. From what is shaping up as an excellent vintage for pinot in the Yarra, this smells of freshly picked raspberries, wild strawberry and just a little nutmeg spice from the oak, which is well in balance with the fruit. Full of energy on the palate, with both the wine's bright acidity and velvety tannins providing structure. Screw cap. 13.5% alc. RATING 94 DRINK 2022-2027 $40 PR

ΨΨΨΨΨ **Pinot Noir 2020, Yarra Valley** RATING 93 DRINK 2022-2026 $35 PR

Lillypilly Estate ★★★★★

47 Lillypilly Road, Leeton, NSW 2705 **Region** Riverina
T (02) 6953 4069 **www.**lillypilly.com **Open** Mon–Sat 10–5, Sun by appt
Winemaker Robert Fiumara **Est.** 1982 **Dozens** 11 000 **Vyds** 27.9ha
Botrytised white wines are by far the best offering from Lillypilly, with the Noble Muscat of Alexandria unique to the winery. These wines have both style and intensity of flavour and can age well. Their table wine quality is always steady – a prime example of not fixing what is not broken. Exports to the UK, the US, and Canada. (JH)

ΨΨΨΨΨ **Angela Muscat NV, Riverina** A solera, resplendent with a motherlode of very old base wine hailing from 1986. The result is nothing short of exceptional. The olive rim to the hue and the pine, grape, spice, roasted walnut and varnish rancio complexities do not betray class. Here, delivered in spades. A lilt of volatility only adds to the equation. A stupid price for a fantastic wine. Screw cap. 18% alc. RATING 96 $26 NG
Noble Blend 2021, Riverina Very fine dessert wine. Ginger-spiced complexity, as much as the full kaleidoscope of botrytis riffs: canned peach, dried mango, orange blossom and pineapple chunks. Yet it is the balletic framework of delicate weight and dutiful acidity that is so compelling, imbuing fine detail and exquisite length. Screw cap. 11.5% alc. RATING 95 DRINK 2022-2035 $29 NG

ΨΨΨΨΨ **Noble Sauvignon Blanc 2021, Riverina** RATING 91 DRINK 2021-2028 $29 NG

Lindeman's (Coonawarra) ★★★★★

Level 8, 161 Collins Street, Melbourne, Vic 3000 (postal) **Region** Coonawarra
T 1300 651 650 **www.**lindemans.com **Winemaker** Brett Sharpe **Est.** 1965
Lindeman's Coonawarra vineyards have assumed a greater importance than ever thanks to the move towards single-region wines. The Coonawarra Trio of Limestone Ridge Vineyard Shiraz Cabernet, St George Vineyard Cabernet Sauvignon and Pyrus Cabernet Sauvignon Merlot Malbec are all of exemplary quality. (JH)

ΨΨΨΨΨ **Coonawarra Trio St George Vineyard Cabernet Sauvignon 2019, Coonawarra** Wow – what a wine. Classical, concentrated and almost sturdy, yet it shows a cascade of rippling flavour that flows over the tongue. Interminable and muscly, this is a seriously sophisticated wine that proves the futility of reinventing the wheel. Screw cap. 14% alc. RATING 96 DRINK 2021-2041 $70 EL

Coonawarra Trio Limestone Ridge Vineyard Shiraz Cabernet 2019, Coonawarra The third leg of the Coonawarra Trio tripod, this time the palate is soft, plush and round, no doubt thanks to the large proportion of shiraz. As with all the wines in this range, the oak sits prominently on the nose, but the fruit has such concentration and drive that the oak is consumed on the palate. Another very smart wine, and if you had to rank them in order of drinking windows, this would be first. Screw cap. 13.5% alc. RATING 95 DRINK 2021–2036 $70 EL

Coonawarra Trio Pyrus Cabernet Sauvignon Merlot Malbec 2019, Coonawarra Concentrated, rippling and dense, this is a powerhouse of black fruit flavour, and shows an impressive lineup of exotic spice. At this stage, long, coiled and taut with sinewy tannins that spool out over the finish. This is more of a cellar proposition than a drink-now proposition … classy to the end. Screw cap. 14% alc. RATING 95 DRINK 2022–2042 $70 EL

Lindenderry Estate ★★★★

142 Arthurs Seat Road, Red Hill, Vic 3937 **Region** Mornington Peninsula **T** (03) 5989 2933 **www.**lindenderry.com.au **Open** Sun 12 **Winemaker** Barnaby Flanders **Est.** 1999 **Dozens** 1000 **Vyds** 3.35ha
Lindenderry Estate in Red Hill is a sister operation to Lancemore Hill in the Macedon Ranges and Lindenwarrah at Milawa. It has a 5-star country house hotel, conference facilities, a function area, day spa and restaurant on 16ha of gardens. It also has a little over 3ha of vineyards, planted equally to pinot noir and chardonnay 20 years ago. Notwithstanding the reputation of the previous winemakers for Lindenderry, the wines now being made by Barney Flanders are the best yet. He has made the most of the estate-grown grapes, adding cream to the cake by sourcing some excellent Grampians shiraz. (JH)

ᵀᵀᵀᵀᵀ **Rosé 2021, Macedon Ranges** An attractive pale cherry-bronze hue. Floral and spicy, with fresh basil infusing raspberry and redcurrant flavours, with a hint of fairy floss. There's texture, there's refreshing acidity and a dry finish. Nice one. Screw cap. 13% alc. RATING 94 DRINK 2022–2024 $35 JF

ᵀᵀᵀᵀᵀ **Shiraz 2020, Grampians** RATING 93 DRINK 2023–2030 $55 JF
Pinot Noir 2020, Macedon Ranges RATING 92 DRINK 2022–2026 $55 JF
Chardonnay 2020, Mornington Peninsula RATING 92 DRINK 2022–2027 $55 JF
Pinot Gris 2021, Macedon Ranges RATING 90 DRINK 2022–2023 $40 JF
Pinot Noir 2020, Mornington Peninsula RATING 90 DRINK 2022–2027 $55 JF

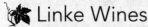 Linke Wines ★★★

60A Seppeltsfield Road, Nuriootpa, SA 5355 **Region** Barossa Valley **T** 0407 025 363 **www.**linkewines.com.au **Winemaker** Brock Harrison **Viticulturist** Scott Linke **Est.** 2002 **Dozens** 5000 **Vyds** 30ha
Linke Wines is a fifth-generation Tanunda-based producer who previously supplied grapes to Barossa Valley wineries such as St Halletts and Langmeil. They have been producing Linke wines since the 2002 vintage from their Stone Well and Dorrien blocks, as well as a dry-grown riesling offering from the cooler climes of the Eden Valley. Shiraz and cabernet sauvignon lie at the heart of their offerings and the wines offer deep, robust drinking in a traditional Barossa style with plentiful rich, dark fruits, spicy oak nuance and classical regional structures. (DB)

ᵀᵀᵀᵀ **Dry Grown Riesling 2021, Eden Valley** Pale straw in the glass with a beautifully perfumed nose of Christmas lilies and orange blossom, flittering over freshly squeezed lime and lemon juice. It's expansive and limey on the palate, with a slight textural tweak to its shape. The wine finishes sapid and pure, with bright acidity and just a smattering of melon and dried herbs on the finish. Screw cap. 12.7% alc. RATING 88 DRINK 2021–2026 $25 DB

Lino Ramble

11 Gawler Street, Port Noarlunga, SA 5167 **Region** McLaren Vale
T 0409 553 448 **www.linoramble.com.au Open** By appt **Winemaker** Andy Coppard
Est. 2012 **Dozens** 3500

After 20 years of working for other wine companies, big and small, interstate and international, Andy Coppard and Angela Townsend say, 'We've climbed on top of the dog kennel, tied a cape around our necks, held our breaths, and jumped'. And if you are curious about the name, the story has overtones of James Joyce's stream of consciousness mental rambles. Exports to Canada and Japan. (JH)

♥♥♥♥♥ Ludo Fiano 2021, McLaren Vale An exuberant fiano, as expressive of candied lemon zest, sea spray, pistachio, quinine, menthol and amaro bitters, as it is idiosyncratic and complex. This sets a very different tone to the regional norm. Textural, of perfect weight and scintillating length. An intriguing drink of chew and flow. Screw cap. 13.1% alc. RATING 93 DRINK 2022-2026 $30 NG

Solitaire Grillo 2020, McLaren Vale I like this. Broader and more textural than other whites in the suite. Almond meal, freshly lain tatami straw, lemon drop, quince paste and the saline wisp of the maritime zone that is the Vale. Long, chewy, pithy and persuasive. Screw cap. 12.8% alc. RATING 93 DRINK 2022-2024 $25 NG ○

Yoyo Pinot Gris 2021, Adelaide Hills A slinky gris, with a spurt of unresolved CO_2 to provide perk and aromatic lift. Nashi pear, baked apple and a sluice of peppery freshness. Gently mid weighted, yet real thrust of fruit and parry of freshness. Lovely drink. Screw cap. 12.4% alc. RATING 92 DRINK 2022-2024 $25 NG ○

Simon Says Saperavi 2021, McLaren Vale As far as saperavi goes, this is handled with aplomb and carnal deliciousness. A big tannic wine, presumably planted to mitigate the excessive fruit to which SA is disposed. Yet there is little in the way of real intrigue. My thinking, focus on Mediterranean varieties. Dark cherry, dill, fennel and cracked pepper. Loads to love despite the outlier status. Screw cap. 14.5% alc. RATING 92 DRINK 2022-2027 $40 NG

Knuckle Bones Nebbiolo 2017, Adelaide Hills Sweet and sappy nebbiolo slung across a spindle of skeletal tannins doused in autumnal complexities with hints of exotica: sandalwood, orange peel, turmeric, clove, campfire and spiced cherry. The bottle age suggests that the time to breach this is nigh. Yet the wine expands and meanders across textures and shifting flavours such that I conclude there is no real rush. Screw cap. 13.2% alc. RATING 92 DRINK 2022-2026 $40 NG

Dot to Dot Arinto 2021, McLaren Vale A Portuguese indigene. Saline, bright and very easy to drink. Lemon drop, a wisp of sea salt, bitter almond and honeydew. Dry and tactile. Pliant and savoury in the mouth, with intensity that belies its light weight. Good length. Prodigious versatility. Screw cap. 12.2% alc. RATING 91 DRINK 2022-2024 $25 NG

Tom Bowler Nero d'Avola 2019, McLaren Vale Hedonic, full weighted and jubey. Grrh! Who wouldn't like this? Few! Loads of whole-berry ammunition fermented wild in older barriques. A slake of tapenade, anise, clove and pepper. Visceral and simple in the best sense. Chill and drain. Screw cap. 14.3% alc. RATING 91 DRINK 2022-2024 $30 NG

Pee Wee Nero d'Avola 2021, McLaren Vale The lighter expression of the 2 iterations of nero, this is what I prefer. Pallid of hue, yet the scape of sour cherry, tamarind, orange verbena and a spindle of bunchy tannins work in the name of freshness. This portends beautifully for the here and now. Whack it in the fridge! Screw cap. 13.5% alc. RATING 90 DRINK 2022-2024 $25 NG

Treadlie Shiraz 2021, McLaren Vale A fun, jubey and joyous mid-weighted expression of shiraz, crafted without oak, acid tweaks and what feels like minimal SO_2. Blueberry, raspberry, nori and a gentle waft of spice and aldehydes. Nothing detracts, however, from the effusive drinkability promoted by an easygoing charm and the benefits of a brisk chill. Screw cap. 12.8% alc. RATING 90 DRINK 2022-2026 $25 NG

♥♥♥♥ Blind Man's Bluff Bastardo 2020, McLaren Vale RATING 89 DRINK 2022-2024 $30 NG

Lisa McGuigan Wines

2198 Broke Road, Pokolbin, NSW 2320 **Region** Various
T 0418 424 382 **www.**lisamcguiganwines.com **Open** By appt **Winemaker** Liz Silkman,
Lisa McGuigan **Est.** 2010 **Dozens** 10 000
Lisa McGuigan is a fourth-generation member of a famous Hunter Valley winemaking
dynasty, started many decades ago by Perc McGuigan and more recently led by Brian
McGuigan. In '99, Lisa started Tempus Two from her garage, and under the McGuigan-
Simeon (now Australian Vintage) umbrella, the volume rose to 250 000 dozen before she left
in '07 to start a retail wine business. In '10 she turned full circle, starting her own business in
the Hunter Valley and using the winemaking skills of Liz Silkman, whom she had headhunted
for Tempus Two, and who is now also chief winemaker at First Creek Wines. Located within
the Blaxland's complex on Broke Road, the VAMP venue and wine room brings together
wine, oysters, art and fashion. (JH)

🍷🍷🍷🍷🍷 **Spartacus Shiraz 2018, Langhorne Creek** Flamboyant. Rich. Powerful
and quintessentially warm-climate South Australia. Christmas cake spice, molten
kirsch and dried fruits. Violet and blueberry. A swathe of vanillin oak tannins
and saline maritime acidity push, pull and reconcile the melee, directing it to a
point of balance and considerable freshness. Screw cap. 14.5% alc. RATING 94
DRINK 2021-2028 $40 NG

🍷🍷🍷🍷🍷 **Maximus Shiraz 2018, Mudgee** RATING 93 DRINK 2021-2026 $35 NG
Renaissance Vermentino 2021, Hunter Valley RATING 92 DRINK 2021-2024
$30 NG
Pinot Gris 2019, Orange RATING 91 DRINK 2021-2022 $35 NG
Botrytis Semillon 2016, Riverina RATING 90 DRINK 2022-2028 $20 NG ✪

🍇 Living Roots

159 Tynan Rd, Kuitpo SA 5201 **Region** Adelaide Hills
T www.livingrootswine.com **Open** By appt **Winemaker** Sebastian Hardy, Anthony
Neilson **Est.** 2016 **Dozens** 400
Summed up perfectly in their own words: 'Living Roots is an urban winery in the Finger
Lakes region of New York and a not-so-urban winery in the Adelaide Hills region of South
Australia. It was founded by husband-and-wife team Sebastian (an Adelaide native and
6th generation winemaker) and Colleen Hardy (a New York native and marketer). The
intercontinental label pays homage to family heritage while also branching out to new
vineyards, styles and techniques. Grapes are sourced from a number of growers, including both
of the Hardys' families, highlighting the natural strengths of each variety and climate in vastly
different corners of the globe: the Finger Lakes and the regions surrounding Adelaide.' Best
New Winery in the Halliday Wine Companion 2023. Exports to the US. (JH)

🍷🍷🍷🍷🍷 **Grenache 2020, McLaren Vale** High-quality wine from start to finish; good
depth to the colour, fragrant berries, flowers and spices on a bouquet that tells you
there is a perfectly proportioned and composed palate, the tannins caressing the
red and purple fruits. Diam. 13.8% alc. RATING 96 DRINK 2022-2030 $34 JH ✪
Montepulciano 2020, Limestone Coast Intense deep purple core; the
bouquet stands aside to leave the exultant power of the sultry black fruits to tell
the tale. A 'no, beg your pardon' full-bodied red wine. Diam. 12.6% alc. RATING 95
DRINK 2025-2040 $34 JH ✪
Pepperberry Shiraz 2018, Adelaide Hills The bouquet exudes licorice,
black cherries and berries, pepper and a waft of cinnamon stick. The freshness
of the long finish is a highlight. Diam. 13.4% alc. RATING 95 DRINK 2023-2038
$34 JH ✪
Coastal Wattle Cabernet Sauvignon 2018, Adelaide There's no doubt
about the quality of the fruit, nor its varietal expression, made with the same deft
touch as all of its siblings. Diam. 14% alc. RATING 94 DRINK 2023-2038 $38 JH

🍷🍷🍷🍷 Lilly Pilly Pinot Noir 2019, Adelaide Hills RATING 93 DRINK 2022-2027
$34 JH
Cabernet Tannat 2020, Adelaide Hills RATING 92 DRINK 2022-2033 $34 JH
Nero d'Avola 2020, McLaren Vale RATING 92 DRINK 2022-2030 $34 JH
Depths of the Earth Red Blend 2019, South Australia RATING 91
DRINK 2022-2026 $24 JH

Liz Heidenreich Wines

PO Box 783, Clare, SA 5453 **Region** Clare Valley
T 0407 710 244 **www.**lizheidenreichwines.com **Winemaker** Liz Heidenreich **Est.** 2018
Dozens 2000 **Vyds** 6ha
In 1866, Liz Heidenreich's great-great-grandfather Georg Adam Heidenreich, a Lutheran
minister, was sent from Hamburg to the Barossa Valley to provide religious care. In 1936,
Liz Heidenreich's grandfather planted vines at Vine Vale; those vines still in production, still
owned and managed by the Heidenreich family. Liz decided to follow her family heritage
and enrolled in a post-graduate winemaking degree course at the University of Adelaide. She
says her spiritual wine homes are the Barossa and Clare valleys. The red wines she makes
are from the family-owned old vines in the Barossa Valley, while her other focus of riesling
comes from the Clare Valley where she makes small parcels of fruit and also undertakes the
contract winemaking of Peter Teakle wines. (JH)

🍷🍷🍷🍷🍷 Watervale Riesling 2021, Clare Valley Cut lime, lemon sherbet, white pepper
and jasmine tea. Plenty going on here. There's an austerity to the acid, which is
a refreshing counterpoint to the voluminous fruit. A beautiful wine. Screw cap.
12.5% alc. RATING 94 DRINK 2022-2032 $25 EL ○

🍷🍷🍷🍷 Watervale Rosé 2021, Clare Valley RATING 90 DRINK 2022-2025 $25 EL

Lloyd Brothers

34 Warners Road, McLaren Vale, SA 5171 **Region** McLaren Vale
T (08) 8323 8792 **www.**lloydbrothers.com.au **Open** 7 days 11–5 **Winemaker** Gonzalo
Sanchez **Est.** 2002 **Dozens** 10 000 **Vyds** 42.4ha
Lloyd Brothers Wine and Olive Company is owned and operated by David and Matthew Lloyd,
third-generation McLaren Vale vignerons. Their 25ha estate overlooks the township, and is
planted to 20ha shiraz, 2.5ha bush-vine grenache and 1ha bushvine mataro (plus 18.9ha of
sauvignon blanc, chardonnay, pinot gris and shiraz in the Adelaide Hills). The shiraz planting
allows the creation of a full range of styles, including Rosé, Sparkling Shiraz, Fortified Shiraz
and Estate Shiraz, along with the White Chalk Shiraz, so named because of the white chalk
used to mark each barrel during the classification process. Exports to the UK. (JH)

🍷🍷🍷🍷 Estate Blend Shiraz Grenache 2020, McLaren Vale Exceptional inaugural
release. More top Côtes du Rhône than SA. Moreish tannins, silty of feel with a
gentle grittiness corralling blue-fruit allusions, beef bouillon, thyme, lavender and a
smear of tapenade across the bolshy finish. Umami aplenty. Savouriness, the modus.
Really very good, although the acidity could be toned. Screw cap. 14.5% alc.
RATING 93 DRINK 2021-2028 $35 NG
Nouveau 2021, McLaren Vale A gently extracted Mediterranean meld, with
whole-berry exuberance contained by some whole-bunch rasp and pliant, yet
gentle, tannins. Red berries, briar and clove. Exceptional early drinking. Loads of
fun, without sacrificing the mettle of a true wine. Seriously dangerous with a chill.
Screw cap. 13.5% alc. RATING 92 DRINK 2021-2023 $28 NG
Sauvignon Blanc 2021, Adelaide Hills Fresh, juicy and ripe. All attractive
qualities in an era of early picking on acidity. Scents of grapefruit, greengage and
lemon myrtle segue to a succulent mid palate and a trail of piquant freshness.
Plenty to like at the price. Screw cap. 13% alc. RATING 91 DRINK 2021-2022
$25 NG
Picpoul Prosecco 2021, Adelaide Hills An immensely pleasurable blend
befitting this sort of swiggable, frothy style made with the Charmat method

(second ferment in tank). Nashi pear, green apple, pine and fennel notes. At once juicy, but also cool of aura. Picpoul's acidity clearly drives this, while prosecco's generous bubble-bath mouthfeel rounds out the edges. As innovative as it is very good drinking. Cork. 12.5% alc. RATING 90 $28 NG

Picpoul 2021, Adelaide Hills RATING 89 DRINK 2021-2023 $25 NG
Pinot Grigio 2021, Adelaide Hills RATING 88 DRINK 2021-2022 $25 NG

Lobethal Road Wines ★★★★

2254 Onkaparinga Valley Road, Mount Torrens, SA 5244 **Region** Adelaide Hills
T (08) 8389 4595 **www.**lobethalroad.com **Open** Thurs–Mon 11–5 **Winemaker** Michael Sykes **Viticulturist** David Neyle **Est.** 1998 **Dozens** 7500 **Vyds** 10.5ha
Dave Neyle and Inga Lidums bring diverse, but very relevant, experience to the Lobethal Road vineyard; the lion's share planted to shiraz, with smaller amounts of chardonnay, tempranillo, sauvignon blanc, graciano, pinot gris and roussanne. Dave has been in vineyard development and management in SA and Tasmania since 1990. Inga has 25+ years' experience in marketing and graphic design in Australia and overseas, with a focus on the wine and food industries. The property is managed with minimal chemical input. Exports to the UK and Switzerland. (JH)

Sauvignon Blanc 2021, Adelaide Hills A star performer for the producer with its zippy, zesty exuberance for life. Aromas of green apple, lantana, lemon, lime and grapefruit and snow pea. A burst of energy on the palate, so zesty and nicely concentrated in flavour. Super-juicy and ready to go. Screw cap. 12.5% alc. RATING 93 DRINK 2021-2025 $25 JP **☉**
Pinot Gris 2021, Adelaide Hills The winemaker regards 2021 as a perfect growing season. It's produced a lovely gris, graceful and fine-featured. White flowers, apple blossom, nashi pear and spice. Boasts a smooth, rolling light texture across the tongue with some brisk, sherbety acidity. Coming together slowly and looking good. Screw cap. 12.8% alc. RATING 92 DRINK 2021-2026 $25 JP **☉**

Rosé 2021, Adelaide Hills RATING 89 DRINK 2021-2024 $25 JP
Chardonnay 2021, Adelaide Hills RATING 88 DRINK 2021-2025 $25 JP
Roussanne 2020, Adelaide Hills RATING 88 DRINK 2021-2024 $25 JP

Logan Wines ★★★★

1320 Castlereagh Highway, Apple Tree Flat, Mudgee, NSW 2850 **Region** Mudgee
T (02) 6373 1333 **www.**loganwines.com.au **Open** 7 days 10–5 **Winemaker** Peter Logan, Jake Sheedy **Viticulturist** Graeme Brown **Est.** 1997 **Dozens** 50 000
Logan is a family-owned and operated business with an emphasis on cool-climate wines from Orange and Mudgee. Owner and head winemaker Peter Logan majored in biology and chemistry at Macquarie University, moving into the pharmaceutical world working as a process chemist. In a reversal of the usual roles, his father encouraged him to change careers and Peter obtained a graduate diploma in oenology from the University of Adelaide in '96. The winery and tasting room are situated on the Mudgee vineyard in Apple Tree Flat. Exports to the EU, Japan and other major markets. (JH)

Vintage M Cuvee 2018, Orange Majority (62%) chardonnay, with descending amounts of pinot noir and meunier; 33 months on lees. Zero dosage. Always a high-quality wine, this vintage is steely and febrile, inducing the saliva while flecking accents of Granny Smith, nashi pear and a sluice of buttered toast across the mid-weighted palate. Long and precise, I'd be drinking this as an aperitif, or ageing for a few years to impart weight to the palate. Cork. 12.5% alc. RATING 94 $40 NG

Shiraz 2019, Orange RATING 93 DRINK 2021-2026 $28 NG
Weemala Riesling 2021, Clare Valley Orange RATING 92 DRINK 2021-2026 $20 NG **☉**

Clementine Pinot Gris 2021, Orange RATING 92 DRINK 2021-2023
$25 NG ❂
Sauvignon Blanc 2021, Orange RATING 92 DRINK 2021-2025 $25 NG ❂
Ridge of Tears Shiraz 2019, Mudgee RATING 92 DRINK 2021-2028 $55 NG
Ridge of Tears Shiraz 2019, Orange RATING 92 DRINK 2022-2030 $55 NG
Cabernet Merlot 2018, Orange RATING 92 DRINK 2022-2027 $28 NG
Weemala Pinot Gris 2021, Orange RATING 91 DRINK 2022-2025 $20 NG ❂
Clementine de la mer 2021, Central Ranges RATING 91 DRINK 2021-2023
$25 NG
Hannah Rosé 2021, Orange RATING 90 DRINK 2021-2022 $25 NG

Lone Palm Vineyard

PO Box 288, Tanunda, SA 5352 **Region** Barossa Valley
T 0411 861 604 **www**.lonepalmvineyard.com.au **Winemaker** Thomas White **Est.** 2019
Dozens 1500 **Vyds** 7ha
Lone Palm has 7ha of shiraz, planted in 1992, at Marananga on the western ridge of the Barossa
Valley. The vineyard gets its name from a single old palm tree next to the original cottage, built
in the late 1800s. The wines are made in a generous style, open-fermented slowly and gently
basket-pressed. The wines are available from the website and www.winesdirect. com.au. (JH)

🍷🍷🍷🍷 Hillside Shiraz 2019, Barossa Valley A muscular, sinewy black-fruited wine
with shades of licorice, earth and cedar/oak spice. Abundant broody blackberry
and black plum fruits on the palate, grippy, gravelly tannin and a spicy, flexing
finish. Screw cap. 14.8% alc. RATING 90 DRINK 2021-2030 $120 DB

Lone Star Creek Vineyard

75 Owens Rd, Woori Yallock, Vic, 3139 **Region** Yarra Valley
T 0414 282 629 **www**.lonestarcreekwines.com.au **Winemaker** Franco D'Anna
Viticulturist Steve Sadlier **Est.** 1997 **Dozens** 800 **Vyds** 22ha
The Lone Star Creek vineyard was established in 1997 by Robin Wood and Gillian Bowers,
who are primarily contract growers; 2017 was the first vintage under their own label. Pinot
noir (52%), pinot gris (23%), chardonnay (15%), sauvignon blanc (5%) and syrah (5%) are
planted. Situated on the border of Woori Yallock and Hoddle's Creek, the cool-climate upper
Yarra fruit was sold to wineries including Hoddle's Creek Estate, so when the time came to
start producing wine under the Lone Star Creek Vineyard label, enlisting Hoddle's Creek's
own Franco D'Anna as winemaker must have seemed an obvious choice. The vineyard is
not subject to strictly organic management, but the philosophy with both the viticulture and
winemaking is one of minimal intervention throughout the entire process. (JH)

🍷🍷🍷🍷🍷 Pinot Noir 2021, Yarra Valley A bright crimson purple. Fragrant and
immediately appealing with its aromas of strawberry puree, raspberries and gentle
spice. The bright, light to medium-bodied palate is well weighted with crunchy
and refreshing tannins, rounding out a wine that will continue to improve over the
next 2-3 years if not longer. A single-vineyard Upper Yarra pinot at this price is a
steal. Screw cap. 12.5% alc. RATING 94 DRINK 2022-2027 $28 PR ❂

🍷🍷🍷🍷 Pet Nat Sauvignon Blanc Pinot Gris 2021, Yarra Valley RATING 93 $28 PR
Pinot Gris 2021, Yarra Valley RATING 92 DRINK 2022-2025 $22 PR ❂
Chardonnay 2021, Yarra Valley RATING 91 DRINK 2022-2027 $28 PR

Lonely Shore

18 Bavin Street, Denmark, WA 6333 (postal) **Region** Denmark
T 0418 907 594 **www**.lonelyshore.com.au **Winemaker** Liam Carmody **Est.** 2014
Dozens 200 **Vyds** 2ha
Liam Carmody's grandmother (Freda Vines) was the author of a historical novel published
in 1958, telling the story of early settlement on the south coast of WA. Liam graduated
from Curtin University in 2003, since working in Sonoma, California, NZ, France, South

Africa and the Mornington Peninsula before settling in Denmark and taking up a full-time winemaking role at Forest Hill. Thus Lonely Shore is very much a busman's holiday. The grapes come from the dry-grown DeiTos Vineyard near Manjimup. (JH)

🍷🍷🍷🍷 **DeiTos Vineyard Pinot Noir 2021, Manjimup** This pinot is routinely different from the pack: dark and brooding, exotic and spicy – and it's got muddy boots. The 20% whole-bunch component brings a real light to the wine, while the grunge and grit found in last year's wine is amplified here, somehow. There's ham hock and blazed maple. It's resinous. Totally delicious in a whole new way. It will split the crowd though. Screw cap. 13% alc. RATING 92 DRINK 2022-2028 $38 EL

Long Gully Estate

100 Long Gully Road, Healesville, Vic 3777 **Region** Yarra Valley
T (03) 9510 5798 **www**.longgullyestate.com **Winemaker** Hamish Smith **Viticulturist** Dan Sergeant **Est.** 1982 **Dozens** 3500 **Vyds** 22ha
Established by Reiner and Irma Klapp in the 1980s, a declining Long Gully Estate was purchased in 2018 by the Magdziarz family in partnership with Vin Lopes. Significant investment in the vineyards, cellar door and the winery followed, with winemakers living onsite in tents during the '19 vintage and relying on fruit from Warramunda and elsewhere for both the '19 and '20 vintages. Plantings of chardonnay, pinot noir, cabernet sauvignon, sauvignon blanc, riesling, shiraz, merlot and viognier have been rescued, with further pinot noir and cabernet added too. '21 represents the first vintage from estate fruit under the new owners. Exports to the UK, Switzerland and Singapore. (TS)

🍷🍷🍷🍷 **Malakov Vineyard Syrah 2020, Pyrenees** Deep, ruby red. Ripe, with aromas of black plum and cherry, subtle spice-rack spices and some black olive tapenade. The palate is rich yet balanced, with fine-grained, plush tannins rounding out a heady and tasty wine that will provide plenty of enjoyment over the next 4–6 years. Screw cap. 14% alc. RATING 93 DRINK 2022-2028 $45 PR
Single Vineyard Shiraz 2020, Yarra Valley A medium cherry red. Red and black fruits are intermingled with freshly crushed black peppercorns, while the medium-bodied and nicely balanced palate has a nice each-way bet between being approachable now but with enough, gently grippy tannins in support that should ensure this will still be looking good 4-6 years, if not longer, from now. Screw cap. 14% alc. RATING 91 DRINK 2023-2027 $38 PR

🍷🍷🍷🍷 **Single Vineyard Pinot Noir 2021, Yarra Valley** RATING 89 DRINK 2023-2027 $38 PR
Single Vineyard Cabernet Sauvignon 2020, Yarra Valley RATING 89 DRINK 2022-2027 $45 PR

Longleat Wines

105 Old Weir Road, Murchison, Vic 3610 **Region** Goulburn Valley
T (03) 5826 2294 **www**.murchisonwines.com.au **Open** W'ends & most public hols 10–5
Winemaker Guido Vazzoler **Est.** 1975 **Dozens** 4000 **Vyds** 8.1ha
Sandra (ex-kindergarten teacher turned cheesemaker) and Guido Vazzoler (ex-Brown Brothers) acquired the long-established Murchison Estate vineyard in 2003 (renaming it Longleat Wines), after living on the property (as tenants) for some years. The mature vineyard has 3.2ha of shiraz, 2.3ha of cabernet sauvignon, 0.8ha each of semillon, sauvignon blanc and chardonnay, and 0.2ha of petit verdot. Exports to Hong Kong. (JH)

🍷🍷🍷🍷 **Zingari Vermentino 2021, Goulburn Valley** Captures the essence of the grape nicely, with its utter liveliness and drink-now appeal. Stone fruits to the fore, with citrus, grapefruit and sweet florals. The palate is super-bright and fresh with pear, nectarine, white peach and zesty acidity. Drink now. Screw cap. 13.5% alc, RATING 89 DRINK 2021-2025 $22 JP
Zingari Grüner Veltliner 2021, Goulburn Valley The Austrian grape likes its new home, revealing its rich, textural qualities as well as its floral musk, honeydew

melon, poached pear and apple flavours. Soft acidity allows the fruit to shine. Screw cap. 13% alc. RATING 88 DRINK 2021-2025 $22 JP

Zingari Sangiovese 2019, Goulburn Valley A mature-tasting sangiovese, medium in weight and showing plum, light spice, dark cherry, chocolate and earth. Tannins are sweet through the middle palate before finishing dry and astringent. Screw cap. 14.5% alc. RATING 88 DRINK 2021-2024 $25 JP

Longview Vineyard   ★★★★★

154 Pound Road, Macclesfield, SA 5153 **Region** Adelaide Hills
T (08) 8388 9694 **www**.longviewvineyard.com.au **Open** Wed–Sun 11–3
Winemaker Peter Saturno, Brian Walsh **Viticulturist** Chris Mein **Est.** 1995
Dozens 22 000 **Vyds** 60ha

With a lifelong involvement in wine and hospitality, the Saturno family has been at the helm of Longview since 2007. Plantings of barbera, grüner veltliner, riesling, pinot noir and new clones of chardonnay and pinot grigio were added to the existing shiraz, cabernet sauvignon, nebbiolo and sauvignon blanc. A new cellar door and kitchen was unveiled in '17, adding to 16 accommodation suites, a popular function room and unique food and wine events in the vineyard. Exports to the UK, Ireland, Canada, Denmark, Finland, Hungary, Germany, Singapore, Thailand, Hong Kong, the US and Sweden . (JH)

ŸŸŸŸŸ **Whippet Sauvignon Blanc 2021, Adelaide Hills** A standout sauvignon blanc from a standout region that is noted for the grape variety. From the more complex end of the spectrum, with layers of tropical fruits and citrus nicely melded to light grassy elements, citrus peel and lime. Concise and complex. Screw cap. 12% alc. RATING 95 DRINK 2021-2025 $25 JP ❂

The Piece Shiraz 2019, Adelaide Hills A most sophisticated Hills shiraz tasted months before release and already in possession of both strength and poise. A great depth of black-hearted fruit is the starting point. It then proceeds to work in layers of spice, coffee-choc oak, cinnamon, cardamom and anise. Strength is applied through a firm tannic base structure. Will age a treat. Diam. 14% alc. RATING 95 DRINK 2022-2029 $100 JP

Macclesfield Grüner Veltliner 2021, Adelaide Hills Engaging aromatics lift from the glass – peach blossom, honeysuckle, melon, citrus and apple. A fine, delicate grüner builds upon a crisp structure, with a touch of light herbal savouriness to close. Grüner clearly loves its new home in the Hills. Screw cap. 12.5% alc. RATING 94 DRINK 2021-2025 $30 JP ❂

ŸŸŸŸŸ **Macclesfield Riesling 2021, Adelaide Hills** RATING 93 DRINK 2021-2027 $30 JP

Fresco 2021, Adelaide Hills RATING 93 DRINK 2021-2023 $40 JP

Macclesfield Cabernet Sauvignon 2020, Adelaide Hills RATING 93 DRINK 2021-2030 $45 JP

Saturnus Nebbiolo 2020, Adelaide Hills RATING 93 DRINK 2021-2031 $50 JP

Juno Nebbiolo Rosato 2021, Adelaide Hills RATING 92 DRINK 2021-2025 $26 JP

Barbera 2020, Adelaide Hills RATING 91 DRINK 2022-2025 $40 JP

Macclesfield Chardonnay 2020, Adelaide Hills RATING 91 DRINK 2021-2027 $45 JP

Macclesfield Syrah 2020, Adelaide Hills RATING 91 DRINK 2021-2027 $45 JP

Queenie Pinot Grigio 2021, Adelaide Hills RATING 90 DRINK 2021-2024 $23 JP

Devils Elbow Cabernet Sauvignon 2020, Adelaide Hills RATING 90 DRINK 2021-2025 $30 JP

Lost Farm Wines

527 Glynburn Road, Hazelwood Park, SA 5063 (postal) **Region** Tasmania
T (08) 8397 7100 **www**.lostfarmwines.com.au **Winemaker** Richard Angove **Est.** 2018
Dozens 2000

Fifth-generation South Australian winemaker and grape grower Richard Angove fell in love
with the Tamar Valley while working vintage in 2008, but it took him a decade to realise his
ambition to work with a small group of growers to produce wines in the region. Sparkling,
pinot noir and a stunning chardonnay are made from well-established vineyards in the
Tamar Valley. (TS)

🍷🍷🍷🍷🍷 **Chardonnay 2020, Tasmania** It has elegance and purity from the first whiff
through to the aftertaste, every component in nuanced balance, in particular
the oak in which the wine was fermented and matured. This sense of calm is
deceptive, because the dominant white peach has a whisper of mandarin within
the citrusy acidity. Screw cap. 13.5% alc. RATING 95 DRINK 2022–2030 $42 JH
Pinot Noir 2020, Tasmania Good colour; a fragrant red flower and berry
bouquet, spices not far away. In its exuberant youth, the montage of red fruits of
every description already has some briary forest floor notes that, here too, will
translate into spices with a few more years in bottle (and, of course, beyond).
Oak is part of the parcel, but doesn't intrude. Screw cap. 13.5% alc. RATING 95
DRINK 2023–2035 $42 JH

Lost Penny

538 Carrara Hill Road, Ebenezer, SA 5355 **Region** Barossa Valley
T 0418 857 094 **www**.lostpennywines.com **Open** By appt **Winemaker** Carol Riebke
Viticulturist Nick Riebke **Est.** 2017 **Dozens** 650 **Vyds** 32.6ha

Sixth-generation Barossan winemaker and grapegrower couple Carol and Nick Riebke bottle
shiraz, cabernet sauvignon and grenache primarily from their estate vineyard in Ebenezer,
passed down through Nick's family since the late 1800s (and in which an 1891 penny was
recently discovered). Carol learnt her craft under Barossa winemaking legend John Glaetzer
before establishing their family brand. 'We're gamblers!' Nick admits. 'It's the risk, the
anticipation and the intrigue about what the next season will bring that keep us coming back
for more!' Exports to Switzerland. (TS)

🍷🍷🍷🍷🍷 **Fire Cart Grenache 2019, Barossa Valley** Pinot-esque in hue. Wonderfully
fragrant and perfumed, with crunch red plum and cherry fruits underscored with
exotic spice, sous bois, ginger cake and softly spoken oak. With a brisk cadence
and spacious air, the Fire Cart trails off nicely with a brisk, acid crunch and a spicy
red-fruit tail. Diam. 14.5% alc. RATING 91 DRINK 2021–2028 $30 DB
Mischief Maker Montepulciano 2020, Barossa Valley Deep purple-red
colour, with bright plummy notes cut with spice, espresso and violets. There is a
youthful exuberance and sense of rawness to this wine; like a horse about to bolt
and chomping on its bit. It provides great fruit-pure drinking and enjoyment with
a bouncy fruit drive. Diam. 15.5% alc. RATING 90 DRINK 2021–2025 $30 DB
Money Garden Cabernet Sauvignon 2019, Barossa Valley This Ebenezer
cabernet sauvignon provides crisply formed, bright red-fruited drinking in a
medium-bodied framework. Red plum, cherry and redcurrant fruits mesh with
baking spice, red licorice and softly spoken oak nuance here, with a liminal, leafy,
sappy edge further in the background. Light, sapid acidity and fine sandy tannin
support wrap things up. Diam. 14.5% alc. RATING 90 DRINK 2021–2028 $30 DB
1891 Penny Shiraz 2019, Barossa Valley Plenty of stuffing here, with deep-
set plum and black fruits acting as the canvas for an array of spice, espresso and
chocolate highlights. Big boned and powerful with a dark, broody gait across
the tongue, fresh acidity and commanding finish. Diam. 15.5% alc. RATING 90
DRINK 2021–2031 $60 DB

🍷🍷🍷🍷 **Almond Row Shiraz 2019, Barossa Valley** RATING 88 DRINK 2021–2028
$30 DB

Lowboi

PO Box 40, Denmark, WA 6333 **Region** Great Southern
T 0438 849 592 **www.**lowboiwines.com.au **Winemaker** Guy Lyons **Est.** 2017
Dozens 400 **Vyds** 3.5ha

In 2017 winemaker Guy Lyons (Forest Hill) and his wife Nicola bought the Springviews vineyard on the south side of the dramatically beautiful Porongurup range in Great Southern and created their brand, Lowboi. Planted in 1985, the vineyard orientation is east-west and was established as a dry-grown site, although irrigation was added in '20 due to constant water pressure in the area. The soils are layered laterite gravels with loam and weathered granite. Planted on the south-facing slope is riesling and Gingin clone chardonnay. Their grüner veltliner comes from the Lyons family farm in Mount Barker. The 'Lowboi' name originates from the farm Lyons' mother grew up on in the Great Southern shire of Tambellup. (EL)

🍷🍷🍷🍷🍷 **Grüner Veltliner 2021, Mount Barker** Grüner is a cool variety – it has the staunch backbone of riesling, yet with a little more meat on its bones. In this case; lavender, orange blossom, Granny Smith apples, chalk and talc. The acidity has race and pace and is of the lemony variety, it really gets things going in the mouth – especially in concert with the phenolics with are decidedly savoury. With plenty of texture, bounce and length, this is yet another smart release from Lowboi. The mineral finish is a highlight … there's a lip-smacking quality to the saline acid that splashes through the mouth. Screw cap. 12.5% alc. RATING 94 DRINK 2021-2031 $32 EL

Riesling 2021, Porongurup Cheesecloth, juniper, green apple skins and spring florals colour this wine. The palate is textural and long, with a fine finish, redolent of crushed chalk and pear skin. Briny acidity laces it all together. It's spicy … there is toasted frangipani tart and exotic market spice. It's all here. Screw cap. 12.5% alc. RATING 94 DRINK 2021-2031 $35 EL

🍷🍷🍷🍷🍸 **Chardonnay 2020, Porongurup** RATING 93 DRINK 2021-2031 $40 EL

Lowestoft

680 Main Road, Berriedale, Tas 7011 **Region** Tasmania
T (08) 9282 5450 **www.**fogarty.wine **Open** By appt **Winemaker** Liam McElhinney
Viticulturist John Fogarty **Est.** 2019 **Dozens** 1250 **Vyds** 3ha

The premium Tasmanian brand of WA-based Fogarty Wine Group, Lowestoft is Tasmania's most exciting new label this year. The group purchased the 3ha Lowestoft vineyard and historic house at Berriedale near Mona just north of Hobart in 2019. Its impressive inaugural release from the same year encompasses sourcing from across Southern Tasmania and the Tamar Valley. Substantial plantings on 2 properties at Forcett and Richmond in the Coal River Valley bring the group's holdings to some 200ha, making this Tasmania's second-largest vineyard owner. Winemaking is conducted at Tasmanian Vintners, the state's biggest contract facility, in which the group purchased a 50% share. Lowestoft is a worthy newcomer to Fogarty's lauded suite of boutique wineries across Western Australia, Lake's Folly in the Hunter Valley and Dalwhinnie in the Pyrenees. (TS)

🍷🍷🍷🍷🍷 **La Maison Pinot Noir 2020, Tasmania** The '20 vintage secures Lowestoft among Tasmania's A-league, but it's going to be a long time before the full magnificence of its flagship is realised. The coiled potential on display here is something to behold, with pristine and precise black and red cherry fruit intricately woven with the perfumed allure of whole bunches and the fine-grained framework of top-class French oak. Brilliant. Screw cap. 13.8% alc. RATING 96 DRINK 2032-2045 $130 TS ♥

Rosé Méthode Traditionnelle Sparkling 2017, Tasmania There's something mighty compelling about the texture and perfume of 100% pinot noir sparkling rosé in Tasmania, seldom achieved outside the A-list of Pipers River. For Lowestoft to attain it in Southern Tasmania is a staggering achievement in itself, to do it on their first attempt is monumental. No surprise that Natalie Fryar is in the wings! Delightful, spicy, lively berry fruits deliver crunch and tang, impeccably framed by the creamy texture of lees age. Outstanding line, length and sheer, bountiful joy. Diam. 12.5% alc. RATING 95 $85 TS

Grand Reserve Méthode Traditionnelle 2016, Tasmania 60/40% pinot noir/chardonnay. This is an elegant and graceful cuvée of pale straw hue. At 6 years of age, primary, crunchy red apple and lemon fruit uphold impressive stamina, beautifully backed by the creamy texture and spicy, toasty allure of lees age. With plenty of endurance tucked into its folds, it will take a good few years in the cellar in its stride. Diam. 12.5% alc. RATING 95 $100 TS

Chardonnay 2020, Tasmania The Fogarty Group has made quite a splash in Tasmania and wines like this make a serious statement about their confidence to play at the top end. The cool '20 season defines impressive flinty, mineral texture and enduring acid drive, energising perfectly ripe white fruits and impeccably integrated oak. Screw cap. 13% alc. RATING 95 DRINK 2022-2026 $75 TS

Pinot Noir 2020, Tasmania Stunning Derwent Valley pinot noir of grace and beauty. Varietally exact red and black cherry fruits are the theme, amplified and never distracted by skilful, subtle work with whole bunches and French oak. Great potential. Purity, class and joy! Screw cap. 13.8% alc. RATING 95 DRINK 2027-2035 $75 TS

Jacoben Single Vineyard Pinot Noir 2020, Tasmania Crafted to an almost identical recipe to Lowestoft's estate pinot, this vineyard delivers a more linear, strict and structured take on the Lower Derwent. Well-focused black and red cherry and berry fruits are confidently supported by fine-grained tannins that promise great things in a decade. Screw cap. 13.8% alc. RATING 94 DRINK 2030-2037 $85 TS

♟♟♟♟♟ **Reserve Brut Méthode Traditionnelle NV, Tasmania** RATING 91 $55 TS

Lyons Will Estate   ★★★★

60 Whalans Track, Lancefield, Vic 3435 **Region** Macedon Ranges
T 0412 681 940 **www.**lyonswillestate.com.au **Open** Sat–Sun 11–5 **Winemaker** Oliver Rapson, Renata Morello **Viticulturist** Oliver Rapson, Renata Morello **Est.** 1996
Dozens 1500 **Vyds** 6.5ha

Oliver Rapson (with a background in digital advertising) and Renata Morello (a physiotherapist with a PhD in public health) believed the Macedon Ranges has the best of both worlds: less than an hour's drive to Melbourne, ideal for pinot and chardonnay and still sparsely settled. The property had 2ha of vines planted in 1996: pinot noir and chardonnay. Over time they have extended the pinot noir to 2ha and the chardonnay to 1.2ha, also planting 1ha each of riesling and gamay. Oliver makes the Pinot Noir and Chardonnay, Renata the Riesling and Gamay. (JH)

♟♟♟♟♟ **Riesling 2021, Macedon Ranges** This is a lovely, enjoyable drink. It sits right. Plenty of flavour though from lemon barley water, mandarin zest, pine lime Splice with some lemon curd. No shortage of mouth-watering acidity either yet the lick of sweetness keeps the palate in check while adding texture. Dangerously gluggable. Diam. 11% alc. RATING 93 DRINK 2021-2021 $37 JF

Pinot Noir 2019, Macedon Ranges This is in a nice spot, with its heady display of florals, spice and cherry compote. It's savoury too, with a meatiness, sappy almost, yet with lots of tannin plumping out the palate. The distinctive menthol character that is part of the wine's DNA is acting as a seasoning and overall, this is thoroughly enjoyable. Diam. 12.8% alc. RATING 92 DRINK 2021-2029 $39 JF

Rosé 2021, Macedon Ranges It's always cheery to see new-vintage rosés appearing around the traps because it signifies summer is on its way. Made from gamay, this cool rendition is an appealing pastel cerise and offers such a spicy, peppery bouquet alongside florals and fresh herbs. It tastes of watermelon and morello cherries, with bracingly fresh acidity driving it. It has a slick of texture and a dab of sweetness, although it's certainly a dry, savoury style. Diam. 13.3% alc. RATING 91 DRINK 2021-2023 $30 JF

M. Chapoutier Australia

141-143 High Street, Heathcote, Vic 3523 **Region** Various
T (03) 5433 2411 **www**.mchapoutieraustralia.com **Open** W'ends 10–5 or by appt
Winemaker Michel Chapoutier **Est.** 1998 **Dozens** 8000 **Vyds** 48ha
M. Chapoutier Australia is the eponymous offshoot of the famous Rhône Valley producer. The business focuses on vineyards in the Pyrenees, Heathcote and Beechworth with collaboration from Ron Laughton of Jasper Hill and Rick Kinzbrunner of Giaconda. After first establishing a vineyard in Heathcote adjacent to Jasper Hill, Chapoutier purchased the Malakoff Vineyard in the Pyrenees to create Domaine Terlato & Chapoutier (the Terlato & Chapoutier joint venture was established in 2000; Terlato still owns 50% of the Malakoff Vineyard). In '09 Michel Chapoutier purchased 2 neighbouring vineyards, Landsborough Valley and Shays Flat; all these are now fully owned by Tournon. (Tournon consists of Landsborough Valley and Shays Flat estates in the Pyrenees and Lady's Lane Estate in Heathcote.) Exports to all major markets. (JH)

🍷🍷🍷🍷🍷 **...Ergo Sum Shiraz 2017, Beechworth** Vegan friendly. A wine that calls for more time in bottle and a decant before broaching. Starts dense and taut, but as it relaxes it loosens up, revealing a cool elegance. Baked plum, red and blue berries with licorice notes, florals and spice slowly transform on the palate into a lightly savoury style, all the while maintaining an even keel of fine tannin and balanced oak. Impressive. Cork. 14% alc. RATING 96 DRINK 2022-2031 $68 JP ✪
Domaine Terlato and Chapoutier L-Block Shiraz 2017, Pyrenees The word 'brooding' comes to mind, not to mention 'complex' and 'textured'. This is one serious shiraz, highlighting Pyrenees dark-fruited intensity hand in hand with wild herbs, mint, earth and spice. Sturdy tannins offer good support. Cork. 14% alc. RATING 94 DRINK 2021-2030 $80 JP

🍷🍷🍷🍷🍷 **Tournon Landsborough Vineyard Viognier 2020, Pyrenees** RATING 91 DRINK 2021-2027 $30 JP
Domaine Terlato and Chapoutier Lieu-Dit Malakoff Shiraz 2018, Pyrenees RATING 91 DRINK 2022-2033 $40 JP
Domaine Terlato and Chapoutier S-Block Shiraz 2017, Pyrenees RATING 91 DRINK 2022-2030 $60 JP
Tournon Landsborough Vineyard Chardonnay 2020, Pyrenees RATING 90 DRINK 2021-2028 $30 JP

Mac Forbes

770 Healesville Koo Wee Rup Rd, Healesville, Vic 3777 **Region** Yarra Valley
T 0484 091 031 **www**.macforbes.com **Open** first Sat of the month 11–4
Winemaker Hannah Hodges **Viticulturist** Owen Littlejohns **Est.** 2004 **Dozens** 8000 **Vyds** 13ha
Mac Forbes cut his vinous teeth at Mount Mary, where he was winemaker for several years before heading overseas in 2002. He spent 2 years in London working for Southcorp in a marketing liaison role, then travelled to Portugal and Austria to gain further winemaking experience. He returned to the Yarra Valley prior to the '05 vintage, purchasing grapes to make his own wines. He has a 2-tier portfolio: first, the Victorian range, employing unusual varieties or unusual winemaking techniques; and second, the Yarra Valley range of multiple terroir-based offerings of chardonnay and pinot noir. Exports to the UK, the US, Canada, Norway, Thailand, Singapore and Hong Kong. (JH)

🍷🍷🍷🍷🍷 **RS5 Riesling 2021, Strathbogie Ranges** 5g/L RS. A very bright, medium green gold. Aromas of jasmine, citrus, honeysuckle, green mango and apricots. Well weighted, gently textured and perfectly balanced, this tastes dry despite the small amount of RS. Finished long with a spicy ginger character. As good as it is now, this will continue to improve for some time yet. Screw cap. 12.5% alc. RATING 95 DRINK 2021-2031 $38 PR
Gladysdale Little Yarra Vineyard Pinot Noir 2019, Yarra Valley A medium cherry crimson. An interesting wine with its aromas of morello cherry, charcuterie,

a touch of freshly cooked rhubarb, bay leaf and the beginnings of some attractive, tertiary forest-floor notes. Cool-fruited (from a warm vintage) this elegant, fine-boned wine has bright, red fruits and finishes savoury and long. Cork. 11.5% alc. RATING 95 DRINK 2022-2028 $75 PR

Woori Yallock Ferguson Chardonnay 2019, Yarra Valley A light, bright green gold. Struck match, white peach and a touch of spice on the nose. Gently and chalky textured, this has a touch of phenolic grip given the wine its structure. Finishes long and should age well. Cork. 11.5% alc. RATING 95 DRINK 2021-2027 $82 PR

EB70 Just Like Heaven Gewürztraminer 2021, Yarra Valley A light lemon gold. Classic aromas of Turkish delight, talc and rosewater. This bone-dry and chalk-textured expression of Gewürztraminer has flavours of green apple, lemon and white pepper. A riesling drinker's gewürztraminer! Diam. 11.5% alc. RATING 94 DRINK 2021-2024 $40 PR

ŶŶŶŶŶ **EB74 After Midnight 2021, Yarra Valley** RATING 93 DRINK 2021-2024 $40 PR

Villages Woori Yallock Chardonnay 2020, Yarra Valley RATING 92 DRINK 2021-2026 $55 PR

Spring Riesling 2021, Strathbogie Ranges RATING 91 DRINK 2022-2029 $33 PR

Macaw Creek Wines   ★★★★

Macaw Creek Road, Riverton, SA 5412 **Region** Mount Lofty Ranges **T** (08) 8847 2657 www.macawcreekwines.com.au **Open** By appt **Winemaker** Rodney Hooper **Est.** 1992 **Dozens** 8000 **Vyds** 10ha

The property on which Macaw Creek Wines is established has been owned by the Hooper family since the 1850s, but development of the estate vineyards did not begin until 1995. The Macaw Creek brand was established in '92 with wines made from grapes from other regions. Rodney Hooper is a highly qualified and skilled winemaker with experience in many parts of Australia and in Germany, France and the US. The wines are certified organic and free of preservatives. Exports to Canada, Sweden, Norway, the Netherlands and Finland. (JH)

ŶŶŶŶŶ **Reserve Shiraz Cabernet Sauvignon 2019, Mount Lofty Ranges** Another side to Mount Lofty with a definite bold, bullish character. Coconut toasty oak and meaty, savoury fermentation characters combine to fill the mouth and then some. Deep, ripe plum, black fruits, licorice, toasted spices, earth and chocolate are dense and tightly focused. Completely fills the mouth with richness and pliable tannins. One to watch and wait for. Screw cap. 14% alc. RATING 92 DRINK 2021-2033 $35 JP

Reserve Cabernet Sauvignon 2019, Mount Lofty Ranges A ripe and luscious chocolate and dark-berried cabernet sauvignon boasting concentrated flavour and a powerful oak presence. Loads of sweet berries, cassis, vanilla, licorice, vanilla and Coconut Rough chocolate American oak here. Fine yet dense tannins aplenty. Still coming together and would appreciate more time. Will have its fans. Screw cap. 13.5% alc. RATING 92 DRINK 2021-2035 $35 JP

ŶŶŶŶ **Tempranillo Rosé 2021, Adelaide Hills** RATING 89 DRINK 2021-2024 $19 JP ✪

Reserve Tempranillo 2019, Clare Valley RATING 88 DRINK 2021-2029 $35 JP

McGlashan's Wallington Estate   ★★★★

225 Swan Bay Road, Wallington, Vic 3221 **Region** Geelong **T** (03) 5250 5760 www.mcglashans.com.au **Open** Thurs–Sun & public hols 11–5, 7 days in Jan **Winemaker** Robin Brockett (Contract) **Est.** 1996 **Dozens** 2500 **Vyds** 12ha

Russell and Jan McGlashan began the establishment of their vineyard in 1996. Chardonnay (6ha) and pinot noir (4ha) make up the bulk of the plantings, the remainder shiraz and pinot gris (1ha each). The wines are made by Robin Brockett, with his usual skill and attention to detail. The cellar door offers food and music, with 4 cottages offering vineyard accommodation. (JH)

🍷🍷🍷🍷🍷 **Bellarine Peninsula Shiraz 2020, Geelong** This is a lively one, exhibiting real energy and verve with its red berries, plums, Middle Eastern spices and surge of pepperiness through to the finish. Plump with a core of sweet, vanillin oak and wild spices, there's plenty to enjoy right here. Screw cap. 13% alc. RATING 91 DRINK 2021–2030 $42 JP
Bellarine Peninsula Rosé 2021, Geelong 50/50% pinot noir/shiraz. Light pink pinot colour, brimming in pinot's cherry, cranberry and strawberry with an underlying influence of shiraz earthiness, and all tied together with a splash of confection and spice. It's got the lot, plus some extra zippy acidity. Screw cap. 12.5% alc. RATING 90 DRINK 2021–2024 $36 JP
Bellarine Peninsula Chardonnay 2020, Geelong A cool, composed chardonnay with aromas of ripe peach, nectarine, lemon butter and lime curd. The palate is full and expressive in yellow peach and baked apple with spicy, toasty oak. Concentrated and layered. Screw cap. 13% alc. RATING 90 DRINK 2022–2027 $40 JP

🍷🍷🍷🍷 **Bellarine Peninsula Pinot Grigio 2021, Geelong** RATING 89 DRINK 2021–2025 $36 JP
Bellarine Peninsula Pinot Noir 2020, Geelong RATING 88 DRINK 2022–2025 $40 JP

McGuigan Wines   ★★★★

447 McDonalds Road, Pokolbin, NSW 2320 **Region** Hunter Valley
T (02) 4998 4111 **www**.mcguiganwines.com.au **Open** 7 days 10–5 **Winemaker** Thomas Jung **Est.** 1992 **Dozens** 4.3 million **Vyds** 2000ha
McGuigan Wines is an Australian wine brand operating under parent company Australian Vintage Ltd. McGuigan represents 4 generations of Australian winemaking and, while its roots are firmly planted in the Hunter Valley, its vine holdings extend across SA, from the Barossa Valley to the Adelaide Hills and the Eden and Clare valleys, into Vic and NSW. McGuigan Wines' processing facilities operate out of 3 core regions: the Hunter Valley, Murray Darling and the Barossa Valley. Exports to all major markets. (JH)

🍷🍷🍷🍷🍷 **Personal Reserve Shiraz 2019, Hunter Valley** A warm year, harnessed with quality oak and fine tannic extraction. The sweet loamy scents of the Hunter, the intro. Dark cherry, mocha oak, lilac, tapenade and root spice, too. The tang across the finish, detracting slightly. Screw cap. 14.5% alc. RATING 92 DRINK 2021–2031 $60 NG
Cellar Select Rosé 2021, Hunter Valley 57%/43% shiraz/tempranillo. 10% barrel fermented. A pallid coral hue. Riffs on powdered musk, orange peel, strawberry and lavender. Fresh, delicate and refined. Easily drunk with a solid chill to mask the faintest lick of sweetness across the finish. Screw cap. 12% alc. RATING 91 DRINK 2021–2022 $22 NG ✪
Bin 9000 Semillon 2021, Hunter Valley The lack of adornment when it comes to Hunter semillon serves this address well. Nothing beyond the average norm, but the result is good. Lemongrass, tonic spritz and citrus balm. Featherweight, but of fine intensity. A bit tangy and sweet across the finish, the denouement. Screw cap. 11% alc. RATING 91 DRINK 2021–2028 $25 NG
The Shortlist Cabernet Sauvignon 2018, Coonawarra This has a classic Coonawarra cab nose: freshly turned earth, mint and cassis bramble. In the mouth it performs exactly as expected, with bright juicy fruit, dusty tannins and firm shape. Screw cap. 14% alc. RATING 90 DRINK 2022–2032 $25 EL

🍷🍷🍷🍷 **The Shortlist Riesling 2021, Eden Valley** RATING 89 DRINK 2021–2028 $25 DB

Cellar Select Carmenère 2021, Murray Darling RATING 89
DRINK 2021-2024 $30 JP
Cellar Select Viognier 2021, Hunter Valley RATING 88 DRINK 2021-2023
$22 NG

McHenry Hohnen Vintners   ★★★★★

10406 Bussell Hwy, Witchcliffe, WA 6286 **Region** Margaret River
T (08) 9757 9600 **www**.mchenryhohnen.com.au **Open** 7 days 10.30–4.30
Winemaker Jacopo Dalli Cani, Henry Wynn **Viticulturist** Mike Sleegers **Est.** 2004
Dozens 7500 **Vyds** 50ha
The McHenry and Hohnen families have a long history of grapegrowing and winemaking
in Margaret River. They joined forces in 2004 to create McHenry Hohnen with the aim
of producing wines honest to region, site and variety. Vines have been established on the
McHenry, Calgardup Brook and Rocky Road properties, all farmed biodynamically. Exports
to the UK, Singapore and Japan. (JH)

🍷🍷🍷🍷🍷 **Calgardup Brook Vineyard Chardonnay 2020, Margaret River** All
single-vineyard chardonnays are made in the same way here, highlighting the
differences in terroir. Where the Burnside is granitic, mineral and fine, this is pithy,
saline and expansive, with layers of cheesecloth and lanolin among the ripe stone
fruit. More volume and density of flavour than the Burnside (neither here nor
there qualitatively, simply an observation), this is sensational. Utterly. Screw cap.
13.5% alc. RATING 97 DRINK 2022-2037 $65 EL ✪
Hazel's Vineyard Chardonnay 2020, Margaret River OK, context: I've
tasted this wine blind in pretty esteemed company (several times), the likes of
Bâtard-Montrachet, Chevalier-Montrachet, Genevrières etc, and while it has come
just under those wines in ranking, it has more than stood its ground, and has
earned my unwavering respect in doing so. Powerful, layered, fragrant, balanced,
rippling and exciting. Back up the car – this is too cheap currently. Screw cap.
13.7% alc. RATING 97 DRINK 2022-2037 $65 EL ✪
Hazel's Vineyard Cabernet Sauvignon 2019, Margaret River In recent
global blind tastings, the McHenry Hohnen Hazel's Vineyard Chardonnay
and Cabernet have both come in the top 5 on my page, among eye-watering
company: Château Lafite, Château Léoville Poyferré, Chevalier-Montrachet,
Les Genevrières and others. The price, when you consider the ability to stand
up alongside these wines is equal to but a penny, tuppence … graphite, cassis,
mulberry, briny acidity and layers of exotic spice. This is a lush superstar wine, and
let me tell you: if McHenry Hohnen isn't on your radar in Margaret River, you
aren't doing it right. Screw cap. 14% alc. RATING 97 DRINK 2022-2038 $70 EL ✪
Rolling Stone 2018, Margaret River 78/16/3/3% cabernet sauvignon/
malbec/merlot/petit verdot. This is closed, restrained and cooling, with layers
of graphite tannins and salty mineral acidity … the fruit is supple and elegant,
defined wholly by blackberries, mulberries and raspberry coulis. This has eons left
in the tank. It would be impatient of you to drink it earlier than '25 (we would
forgive you if you did though, because it is already delicious). Screw cap. 14.4% alc.
RATING 97 DRINK 2022-2042 $135 EL ✪

🍷🍷🍷🍷🍷 **Laterite Hills Chardonnay 2020, Margaret River** Wowsers. This is super-
serious. Unbelievable value for money: scintillating citrus acid line, concentrated,
mouth-staining fruit and complex layers of crushed nuts, creamy tannins … all
wrapped into a long and reverberating tail of flavour. $42: speechless. Screw cap.
13.7% alc. RATING 96 DRINK 2021-2036 $42 EL ✪
Burnside Vineyard Chardonnay 2020, Margaret River Mineral, crunchy
acidity frames lush stone-fruit characters, both aromatically and in the mouth. This
is svelte, classy and spicy, with a granitic backbone of acid structure. If you like this
wine today, you'll be staggered (no hyperbole here) by it in several years' time. Buy
them all by the boot load – they only get better. Screw cap. 13.5% alc. RATING 96
DRINK 2022-2037 $65 EL ✪

Marsanne Roussanne 2021, Margaret River This wine has been doing the rounds at wine shows in '21, and has been picking up golds and favourable comments left, right and centre. I can tell you why: it harnesses the weight, volume and voluptuousness of the 2 varieties, but re-presents them in a restrained and focused way. The phenolics too are ever-present, shapely and balancing. All in all, a class act. Screw cap. 13% alc. RATING 95 DRINK 2021–2027 $42 EL

Grenache 2020, Margaret River The fruit has immediate, scintillating clarity and mouth-watering flavour. Meanwhile, the tannins step in through the finish and close up shop – but after an initial glance through that window, you just know they've got what you want. You must persist. This has ferrous notes, blood, raspberries, plums, a hint of rhubarb, black spice and anise … don't take no for an answer. A firm decant might sort out those tannins. Screw cap. 14.5% alc. RATING 95 DRINK 2021–2031 $45 EL

Hazel's Vineyard Zinfandel 2020, Margaret River This is quite possibly the prettiest, most balanced and most satisfying zinfandel in WA this year. Bitter chocolate, raspberry drops, hints of tar, a touch of licorice and star anise, and all of it shaped by dark, toasty oak. A triumph of diversity here, from red dirts, crushed rocks, gravel, exotic spice and campfire, through to lush blackforest fruit. Another triumph for the Hazel's Vineyard and the hand that shaped this wine. Screw cap. 14.2% alc. RATING 95 DRINK 2022–2032 $55 EL

Apiary Block Chardonnay 2021, Margaret River This is exactly as you'd expect: creamy and rounded (all edges obliterated) from the mlf and concrete, the fruit is nutty and briny and there is a dehydrated orange-zest character that runs through the heart of it. It is textural, slightly chewy, but ultimately soft and pleasurable. A beautiful wine and a completely different take on Margaret River chardonnay. Screw cap. 12.9% alc. RATING 94 DRINK 2022–2026 $35 EL

Sauvignon Blanc 2021, Margaret River This is brilliant. Really good! Snow pea tendril, lemongrass, a touch of bison grass, green apples, nashi pears and a couple of lychees with flakes of sea salt. Yum. Screw cap. 12.4% alc. RATING 94 DRINK 2022–2025 $35 EL

Hazel's Vineyard GSM 2020, Margaret River Smaller berries in '20 means tannins: they create a firm casing around the fruit and really shape the affair through the finish. The layers of dark fruit and spice feel never-ending … a decant will likely assist this in opening up. Screw cap. 14.5% alc. RATING 94 DRINK 2021–2031 $42 EL

McKellar Ridge Wines   ★★★★☆

2 Euroka Avenue, Murrumbateman, NSW 2582 **Region** Canberra District
T 0409 780 861 **www**.mckellarridgewines.com.au **Open** W'ends 10–4
Winemaker John Sekoranja, Marina Sekoranja **Viticulturist** John Sekoranja, Marina Sekoranja **Est.** 2005 **Dozens** 800 **Vyds** 5.5ha
Dr Brian Johnston established McKellar Ridge in 2005 and after 10 years decided it was time to retire. John and Marina Sekoranja worked with Brian for 12 months before purchasing the winery in July '17. Brian continued to provide support as winemaking consultant during vintage while John and Marina completed bachelor of wine science degrees at CSU. The change has seen an increase in the number of wines available, including from Tumbarumba. (JH)

� **Shiraz Viognier 2021, Canberra District** Always a good show of deep plum fruit and spice with the French oak barriques (25% new) adding cedary flavour and support. It's delightfully spicy and a little peppery, with tangy, juicy acidity and tannins holding sway. Another year in bottle will have this in complete harmony, although it is already a smart wine. Screw cap. 13.4% alc. RATING 95 DRINK 2023–2031 $50 JF

♥♥♥♥♡ **Reserve Riesling 2021, Canberra District** RATING 92 DRINK 2022–2031 $35 JF

Merlot Cabernet Franc 2019, Canberra District RATING 90 DRINK 2022–2026 $35 JF

McLaren Vale III Associates ★★★★

86 McMurtrie Rd, McLaren Vale SA 5171 **Region** McLaren Vale
T (08) 8323 7940 **www**.mclarenvaleiiiassociates.com.au **Winemaker** Campbell Greer
Viticulturist Chalk Hill Viticulture **Est.** 1999 **Dozens** 12000 **Vyds** 34ha
McLaren Vale III Associates is a very successful boutique winery owned by Mary and John
Greer and Reg Wymond. An impressive portfolio of estate-grown wines allows them control
over quality and consistency, and thus success in Australian and international wine shows.
The cellar door is due to open in January 2023. Exports to Hong Kong and Singapore. (JH)

ΨΨΨΨΨ **Renaissance Cabernet Sauvignon Merlot 2021, McLaren Vale** A fine nose
here. Warm-climate maritime cabernet epitomised: a saline slick of dried sage,
iodine, bouquet garni and currant. Spearmint, too, from a cooler year. The tannins
unravel nicely across a firm yet poised finish. The oak, nicely nestled; the grape
tannins building across a long finish. Measured, savoury and impressive. Screw cap.
14.5% alc. RATING 93 DRINK 2022-2029 $30 NG
Squid Ink Reserve Shiraz 2020, McLaren Vale A bit tauter, compressed and
more detailed than the most expensive cuvée. A signature burn of heat across the
finish. Iodine and florals define the nose. The palate, rich and typically forceful,
framed by charry oak. Black fruits, anise, clove and Asian spice. Again, these are
not wines that charm. But they impress, nevertheless, by force of sheer flavour
and winemaking artefact. Screw cap. 14.5% alc. RATING 91 DRINK 2021-2032
$65 NG
Giant Squid Ink Reserve Shiraz 2019, McLaren Vale This is the ticket if
one seeks weight, power and amplitude, over finesse and grace. It is impressive in
terms of its sheer extract and force. Black-fruit aspersions, anise, clove, iodine and
a swab of black-olive paste rear across the hot, acidic finish. A wine that bludgeons
rather than caresses, but there is a fan club to be sure. Screw cap. 14.5% alc.
RATING 90 DRINK 2021-2029 $180 NG

ΨΨΨΨ **Pretty Little Thing Rosé 2021, McLaren Vale** RATING 89 DRINK 2021-2022
$35 NG
Squid Ink Sparkling Shiraz NV, McLaren Vale RATING 88 $65 NG

McLeish Estate Wines ★★★★★

462 De Beyers Road, Pokolbin, NSW 2320 **Region** Hunter Valley
T (02) 4998 7754 **www**.mcleishestatewines.com.au **Open** 7 days 10–5
Winemaker Xanthe Hatcher **Viticulturist** Ted Nicolai **Est.** 1985 **Dozens** 8000
Vyds 17ha
Bob and Maryanne McLeish have established a particularly successful business based on estate
plantings. The wines are of consistently high quality, and more than a few have accumulated
show records leading to gold medal–encrusted labels. Xanthe Hatcher (Pooles Rock) took
over the contract winemaking from Andrew Thomas in 2020. Exports to the UK, the US
and Asia. (JH)

ΨΨΨΨΨ **Reserve Merlot 2019, Hunter Valley** This estate makes a fine suite of
Bordeaux varieties. This, no exception. Medium bodied, plummy, earthy and
aromatic, with considerable detail, a mulchy savouriness and a deftly applied lattice
of oak and grape tannins. The finish is long, refined and rewarding. Very good
merlot. Screw cap. 13% alc. RATING 94 DRINK 2021-2029 $65 NG
Cellar Reserve Semillon 2013, Hunter Valley A flaxen meadow of chaff,
lemon trees and dairy. Fine scents. The Hunter in all its glory. A deep yellow, with
green-olive edges. Notes of waxy lanolin, olive, lemon balm and lemon curd. I
wouldn't hold this any further, but the intensity of flavour is impressive. Drink
with relish. Screw cap. 10.5% alc. RATING 94 DRINK 2021-2025 $80 NG

ΨΨΨΨΨ **Reserve Semillon 2021, Hunter Valley** RATING 93 DRINK 2021-2033
$45 NG
Reserve Cabernet Sauvignon 2019, Hunter Valley RATING 93
DRINK 2022-2034 $65 NG

Semillon Sauvignon Blanc 2021, Hunter Valley McLaren Vale RATING 92
DRINK 2021-2024 $25 NG ✪
Cabernet Sauvignon Shiraz 2014, Hunter Valley RATING 92
DRINK 2021-2024 $90 NG
Semillon 2021, Hunter Valley RATING 91 DRINK 2021-2027 $30 NG
Reserve Chardonnay 2016, Hunter Valley RATING 90 DRINK 2021-2024
$45 NG

McPherson Wines

199 O'Dwyer Road, Nagambie, Vic 3608 (postal) **Region** Nagambie Lakes
T (03) 9263 0200 **www**.mcphersonwines.com.au **Winemaker** Jo Nash **Est.** 1968
Dozens 500 000 **Vyds** 262ha

McPherson Wines is, by any standards, a substantial business. Made at various locations from estate vineyards and contract-grown grapes, they represent very good value across a range of labels. Winemaker Jo Nash has been at the helm for many years and co-owner Alistair Purbrick (Tahbilk) has a lifetime of experience in the industry. Quality is unfailingly good. Exports to all major markets. (JH)

🍷🍷🍷🍷♀ **Don't tell Gary 2020, Central Victoria** If you haven't already guessed, Gary is the McPherson accountant. A fun title for a wine that enjoys some pretty schmick and expensive oak which is slurped up easily by this super-generous, ripe shiraz. Over-delivers for the price in deep, dark, sweet berries and plums, earth, dark chocolate, toasted spice and nicely integrated oak that brings warmth and immediate drinkability. Screw cap. 15% alc. RATING 92 DRINK 2022-2028 $24 JP ✪
MWC Cabernet Sauvignon 2019, Victoria Whoa! The palate doesn't compute with the price: it exceeds it. This is one confident, finely tuned cabernet worth getting to know better. It strides into view, raising swirls of autumnal leafiness, black fruits, cinnamon, nutmeg and undergrowth. Tidy and balanced with concentration, it ties the fruit, tannin and oak together, and elegantly so. Smashes it at this price. Screw cap. 13.9% alc. RATING 90 DRINK 2021-2027 $19 JP ✪

🍷🍷🍷🍷 **Andrew's Reserve Shiraz 2020, South Eastern Australia** RATING 89
DRINK 2021-2028 $19 JP ✪
Pickles McPherson Sauvignon Blanc 2021, Victoria RATING 88
DRINK 2022-2023 $15 JP ✪
Aquarius Marsanne Viognier 2021, Central Victoria RATING 88
DRINK 2021-2025 $19 JP
MWC Shiraz Mourvèdre 2019, Victoria RATING 88 DRINK 2021-2025
$19 JP
Jo Nash Single Vineyard Cabernet Sauvignon 2019, Sunbury RATING 88
DRINK 2021-2025 $35 JP
Jo Nash Single Vineyard Pinot Noir 2019, Upper Goulburn RATING 88
DRINK 2021-2023 $35 JP
Jo Nash Single Vineyard Shiraz 2019, Sunbury RATING 88
DRINK 2021-2024 $35 JP

McWilliam's

Jack McWilliam Road, Hanwood, NSW 2680 (postal) **Region** Riverina
T (02) 6963 3400 **www**.mcwilliams.com.au **Winemaker** Russell Cody, Melissa
McWilliam, Jordan Bellato **Viticulturist** Paul Harvey **Est.** 1913 **Vyds** 20ha

McWilliams went into voluntary administration in 2020 and was purchased by Bill Calabria of Calabria wines. McWilliam's Mount Pleasant winery and vineyards were bought by Medich Family Office. The exceptional-value offerings of Hanwood Estate in Griffith remain anchors of the brand. Yet McWilliam's viticultural resources have expanded to include Hilltops, Tumbarumba and Canberra whence wines of considerable detail, cool-climate clarity and exceptional value are crafted under the aegis of chief winemaker, Russell Cody. While the

Single Vineyard suite sets the pace, the 660 range is brilliant, defined by a series of wines that are surely among the country's greatest bargains. The Alternis series, too, as the name implies, is comprised of Mediterranean expressions auguring positively for the brand's future. Exports to the UK, Canada, Singapore and New Zealand. (NG)

🍷🍷🍷🍷🍷 **Eliza Jane Shiraz 2019, Canberra District** An excellent flagship red. Superbly contained yet shapely, with the plummy spicy fruit wound into more savoury flavours: wood spice, pepper berries, ironstone and charcuterie. It's full bodied but there's an evenness and effortlessness across the palate, thanks to beautifully shaped yet fine tannins and its length. Impressive all the way. Screw cap. 14% alc. RATING 96 DRINK 2023–2033 $110 JF

Show Reserve Limited Release Aged 25 Years Muscat NV Amber with olive green rims. Rosewater, lychee, grape spice, clove, tamarind and the fruits and spice sensations of an exotic souk. Viscous, cheek-coating and in all, palate-staining, spiritous and prodigiously intense. An extremely long finish. Very impressive. Screw cap. 18.5% alc. RATING 96 $80 NG

Single Vineyard Shiraz 2019, Canberra District A noir red with a purple tinge to the rim, then a decadent, structured wine follows. A mass of dark plums all spiced up with savoury oak following through on the full-bodied palate. While there's a succulence within, there are also ripe, compact tannins keeping the wine firmly in shape and leading to a slightly drying finish. Screw cap. 14% alc. RATING 95 DRINK 2024–2030 $40 JF

1877 Shiraz 2018, Hilltops No shortage of flavour to this audacious red that will make many sit up and take notice. Why? The palate mainly: full bodied with shapely, savoury, ripe tannins, a depth throughout and terrific length. It's also full of dark fruit, clove and new leather from the French oak, and a touch of meaty, charcuterie reduction adds another layer. There's also a strong ferrous note and good acidity to finish. A smart wine. Screw cap. 14% alc. RATING 95 DRINK 2022–2030 $75 JF

Single Vineyard Cabernet Sauvignon 2018, Hilltops There is a deft touch at this address when it comes to Hilltops cabernet. Some mocha oak here and greater intensity of flavour and structural gristle than the wonderful 660 sibling, yet with no forfeit of flow, detailed tannic latticework or signature sumptuousness of Ribena-esque blackcurrant, bouquet garni and tapenade rolled in to an impressive finish. A little sweet, to be churlish. Yet suave, long and rather classy. Screw cap. 14% alc. RATING 94 DRINK 2022–2032 $40 NG

Show Reserve Limited Release Aged 25 Years Topaque NV A deep mahogany hue with green edges attests to the average 25 years age of the respective components. Walnuts, varnish and molasses. The waft of volatility suffuses energy and a welcome freshness given the sheer density and decadence of the wine. I often prefer Topaque to muscat of this ilk, but not in this instance. Screw cap. 18.5% alc. RATING 94 $80 NG

🍷🍷🍷🍷 **McW Reserve 660 Cabernet Sauvignon 2018, Hilltops** RATING 93 DRINK 2022–2026 $22 NG ✪

McW Reserve 660 Chardonnay 2018, Tumbarumba RATING 93 DRINK 2022–2028 $22 NG ✪

Single Vineyard Revee Estate Pinot Noir 2018, Tumbarumba RATING 93 DRINK 2022–2026 $40 NG

Hanwood Special Reserve 10 Years Old Grand Tawny NV, Riverina RATING 93 $25 NG ✪

Morning Light Botrytis Semillon 2008, Riverina RATING 92 DRINK 2021–2026 $30 NG

Glen 100 Years Vintage Tyrian 2013, Riverina RATING 90 DRINK 2021–2035 $45 NG

Hanwood Estate NV RATING 90 $13 NG ✪

MadFish Wines

137 Fifty One Road, Cowaramup, WA 6284 **Region** Margaret River
T 08 9756 5200 **www**.madfishwines.com.au **Open** 7 days 10–5 **Winemaker** Nic Bowen
Viticulturist Dave Botting **Est.** 1992

Named after a renowned bay in the Great Southern (near Denmark), MadFish was established in 1992 by Howard Park as a standalone brand with a focus on making expressive, affordable, drink-now wines. Sourced from long-term growers in the state's southwest. In its 30 years history it has grown to become a widely recognised and exported wine brand. Today, as always, the wines are made by Nic Bowen and Mark Bailey, and at the same facility. In '07, Gold Turtle was established, projected as a regional (GI specific) tier of wines exclusively for Endeavour Drinks. In the past few years both Gold Turtle and MadFish have expanded to include sparkling wines. Further regional expansion may be imminent. Exports to the UK, US and Sweden. (EL)

TTTTY **Gold Turtle Shiraz 2020, Margaret River** Maraschino cherry, blood plums, raspberries and pomegranate make up the core of this vibrant, fresh, delicious and uncomplicated wine. There is an impressive core of fruit that is quite moreish. Screw cap. 14.5% alc. RATING 91 DRINK 2021-2027 $22 EL **❂**

TTTT **Gold Turtle Pinot Gris 2021, Western Australia** RATING 89
DRINK 2022-2023 $25 EL
Shiraz 2020, Western Australia RATING 89 DRINK 2021-2026 $18 EL **❂**
Rosé 2021, Western Australia RATING 88 DRINK 2021-2023 $18 EL
Gold Turtle Semillon Sauvignon Blanc 2021, Margaret River RATING 88
DRINK 2022-2023 $22 EL
Prosecco 2021, Western Australia RATING 88 DRINK 2021-2023 $23 EL
Riesling 2020, Western Australia RATING 88 DRINK 2021-2026 $18 EL

Main Ridge Estate

80 William Road, Red Hill, Vic 3937 **Region** Mornington Peninsula
T (03) 5989 2686 **www**.mre.com.au **Open** W'ends & public hols 11–5
Winemaker James Sexton **Viticulturist** Linda Hodges **Est.** 1975 **Dozens** 1200
Vyds 2.8ha

Quietly spoken and charming, Nat and Rosalie White founded the first commercial winery on the Mornington Peninsula. It has an immaculately maintained vineyard and equally meticulously run winery. In Dec '15, ownership of Main Ridge Estate passed to the Sexton family, following the retirement of Nat and Rosalie after 40 years. Tim and Libby Sexton have an extensive background in large-scale hospitality, first in the UK, then with Zinc at Federation Square, Melbourne and at the MCG. Son James Sexton is now head winemaker and is nearing completion of his wine science degree studies at CSU. Nat continues as a consultant. (JH)

TTTTT **Chardonnay 2020, Mornington Peninsula** An excellent wine with far more restraint than usual, yet still full of flavour. White peach and preserved lemon, fennel and white pepper, clotted cream and toasted almonds, radicchio and woodsy flavours are all in harmony. Full and fleshy across the palate but not weighed down, as the acidity lifts everything to a long finish. Screw cap. 13% alc. RATING 95 DRINK 2021-2027 $65 JF
Pinot Noir 2020, Mornington Peninsula The '20 vintage was one to make vignerons nervous: cool and wet, resulting in lower yields. Hence the single-site Half Acre and The Acre wines have been declassified to make this wine. And what a wine. A delightful amalgam of bright cherries, raspberries, a hint of menthol, pine needles, dried orange peel and woodsy spices, although it is unencumbered by new oak. The palate is deceptive as it feels light and breezy, refreshing even. The tannins are a strong silk thread weaving everything in place and the acidity is bright to the finishing line. Screw cap. 13% alc. RATING 95 DRINK 2021-2030 $65 JF

Majella

Lynn Road, Coonawarra, SA 5263 **Region** Coonawarra
T (08) 8736 3055 **www**.majellawines.com.au **Open** 7 days 10–4 **Winemaker** Bruce
Gregory, Michael Marcus **Est.** 1969 **Dozens** 30 000 **Vyds** 60ha
The Lynn family has been in residence in Coonawarra for over 4 generations, starting as
storekeepers, later graduating into grazing. The Majella property was originally owned by
Frank Lynn, then purchased in 1960 by nephew George. In '68 Anthony and Brian (the
Prof) Lynn established the vineyards, since joined by Peter, Stephen, Nerys and Gerard.
Bruce Gregory has been at the helm for every wine made at Majella. The Malleea is one of
Coonawarra's classics, The Musician one of Australia's most outstanding red wines selling for
less than $20 (having won many trophies and medals). The largely fully mature vineyards are
principally shiraz and cabernet sauvignon, with a little riesling and merlot. Exports to the UK,
Canada and Asia. (JH)

🍷🍷🍷🍷🍷 **The Malleea 2017, Coonawarra** This is superfine, elegant, concentrated and
restrained, all at once. The most successful cabernet shiraz blends have discernible
features from both varieties; each dovetailed into the grooves of the other. This is a
synchronised ebb and flow of flavour; a seesaw between the mouth-filling softness
of shiraz, and the structured poise of the cabernet. Seamless and quite beautiful.
Screw cap. 14.5% alc. RATING 96 DRINK 2023-2042 $80 EL
GPL68 Cabernet Sauvignon 2017, Coonawarra Love the intensity of
the fruit here – it is traditional. Classically styled cabernet (dense tannins and
endless flavour), with a backlog of black forest fruit that spools out long into
the finish. More years in bottle will allow this to soften even further. A satisfying
wine of grace and poise. Palate staining. Screw cap. 14.5% alc. RATING 96
DRINK 2023-2043 $130 EL

🍷🍷🍷🍷🍷 **Cabernet Sauvignon 2019, Coonawarra** RATING 92 DRINK 2021-2036
$35 EL
Shiraz 2019, Coonawarra RATING 92 DRINK 2022-2035 $35 EL
The Musician Cabernet Shiraz 2020, Coonawarra RATING 90
DRINK 2021-2025 $19 EL ❂

Malcolm Creek Vineyard

33 Bonython Road, Kersbrook, SA 5231 **Region** Adelaide Hills
T (08) 8389 3619 **www**.malcolmcreekwines.com.au **Open** W'ends & publics hols
by appt **Winemaker** Peter Leske, Michael Sykes **Est.** 1982 **Dozens** 800 **Vyds** 2ha
Malcolm Creek was the retirement venture of Reg Tolley, who decided to upgrade his
retirement by selling the venture to Bitten and Karsten Pedersen in '07. The wines are
invariably well made and develop gracefully; they are worth seeking out, and are usually
available with some extra bottle age at a very modest price. Exports to the UK, the US,
Denmark and Malaysia. (JH)

🍷🍷🍷🍷 **Sauvignon Blanc 2021, Adelaide Hills** A deliberate pitch towards a steely,
super-dry sauvignon that works on a tight, acidic structure and a fine citrusy, grassy
edge. The amount of acidity will suit some, less so others. Screw cap. 12.5% alc.
RATING 89 DRINK 2022-2025 $25 JP

Mandala

1568 Melba Highway, Dixons Creek, Vic 3775 **Region** Yarra Valley
T (03) 5965 2016 **www**.mandalawines.com.au **Open** Mon–Fri 11–4, w'ends 10–5
Winemaker Charles Smedley, Don Pope **Est.** 2007 **Dozens** 10 500 **Vyds** 29ha
Mandala is owned by Charles Smedley, who acquired the established vineyard in '07. The
vineyard has vines up to 25 years old, but the spectacular restaurant and cellar door complex
is a more recent addition. The vineyards are primarily at the home base in Dixons Creek, with
chardonnay (9.1ha), pinot noir (6.1ha), cabernet sauvignon (4.4ha), sauvignon blanc (2.9ha),
shiraz (1.7ha) and merlot (0.4ha). There is a separate 4.4ha vineyard at Yarra Junction planted
entirely to pinot noir with an impressive clonal mix. (JH)

🍷🍷🍷🍷🍷 **The Mandala Compass Chardonnay 2020, Yarra Valley** Bright gold with
green tinges. Attractive aromas of struck match, fresh vanilla bean and white
nectarine. Medium bodied. I like the balance of stone fruits, well-handled oak and
fresh acidity. This should age nicely too in the short–medium term. Screw cap.
12.5% alc. RATING 93 DRINK 2021-2025 $60 PR

Rosé 2021, Yarra Valley Blend of 75/25% merlot/pinot noir. A pale, bright
salmon skin. Attractive raspberry, redcurrant and herb aromas. Lively and packed
with red berry, tangerine and orange pith flavours. Finishes, dry and gently grippy.
I imagine it would be an excellent food wine. Screw cap. 13.5% alc. RATING 92
DRINK 2022-2025 $25 PR ✪

Chardonnay 2021, Yarra Valley Bright gold. Apricots, dried pear and a
little fresh vanilla bean can be found in this wine, which has good depth and
and a gentle creaminess through the mid palate. It finishes well and is a wine
to enjoy now and over the next 2 years. Screw cap. 12.3% alc. RATING 92
DRINK 2022-2025 $30 PR

Pinot Noir 2021, Yarra Valley Light, bright, cherry red. Recently bottled,
this is a little reductive at first, but a few minutes air and a good swirl reveal
aromas of strawberries and spiced cherries, leading onto the light to medium-
bodied and gently flavourful palate. Good now, I expect this will flesh out and
become even better in another 6 months or so. Screw cap. 12.8% alc. RATING 92
DRINK 2022-2026 $30 PR

The Mandala Butterfly Cabernet Sauvignon 2019, Yarra Valley A
medium deep, crimson red. There are aromas of blackcurrant pastille, cedar – from
the already well-integrated 40% new French oak – and melted licorice. There's
a hint of tomato leaf too, giving the wine some lift. Medium bodied, elegant
and persistent, with the superfine-grained tannins providing structure. There's a
nice each-way bet here, between enjoying this now or watching it become even
more complex over the next 6 or so years. Screw cap. 13.5% alc. RATING 92
DRINK 2022-2028 $60 PR

Pinot Grigio 2021, Yarra Valley A bright green gold. Aromas of lemon oil,
orange blossom and nashi lead onto the palate, which has good weight and texture.
Finishes clean and relatively long. A convincing and well-priced example. Screw
cap. 13.3% alc. RATING 91 DRINK 2022-2025 $25 PR

Fumé Blanc 2021, Yarra Valley A bright green gold, there's no mistaking the
variety, with its aromas of quince and kiwifruit together with some freshly cut
grass and snow pea tendrils. Mouth-filling and textured, this has plenty of flavour
and the acidity is bright enough to keep the wine nicely balanced. Screw cap.
13% alc. RATING 90 DRINK 2022-2025 $30 PR

The Rock Shiraz 2019, Yarra Valley Medium red. Cranberries and blueberries
on the nose, together with cinnamon, clove and nutmeg. Medium bodied,
this lightly framed and elegant wine has a shy fruit character and finishes with
fine, powdery tannins. A wine to enjoy now and over the next 3–5 or so years.
Screw cap. 13.8% alc. RATING 90 DRINK 2021-2025 $60 PR

🍷🍷🍷🍷 **Shiraz 2020, Yarra Valley** RATING 88 DRINK 2022-2026 $30 PR

Mandoon Estate   ★★★★★

10 Harris Road, Caversham, WA 6055 **Region** Swan District
T (08) 6279 0500 **www**.mandoonestate.com.au **Open** 7 days 10–5 by appt
Winemaker Ryan Sudano, Lauren Pileggi **Est.** 2009 **Dozens** 10 000 **Vyds** 50ha
Mandoon Estate, headed by Allan Erceg, made a considerable impression with its wines
in a very short time. In '08 the family purchased a site in Caversham in the Swan Valley.
Construction of the winery was completed in time for the first vintage in '10. They have also
purchased 20ha in Margaret River. Winemaker Ryan Sudano has metaphorically laid waste
to Australian wine shows with the quality of the wines he has made from the Swan Valley,
Frankland River and Margaret River. (JH)

ΨΨΨΨΨ Reserve Chardonnay 2020, Margaret River Has it both ways: elegance and richness (with intensity and length), and a citrus-blossom fragrance. All of these characters come together, along with white peach and Granny Smith apple, to make magic. Screw cap. 13% alc. RATING 97 DRINK 2022-2032 $59 JH ✪
Reserve Research Station Cabernet Sauvignon 2017, Margaret River The hyper-fragrant bouquet of cassis and spice plays out in leisurely fashion on the palate, as bay leaf and earth notes join hands with the core of the fruit. It's Margaret River's ability to grow cabernet and fully ripen it as 14% alcohol that is so wonderful. Screw cap. 14% alc. RATING 97 DRINK 2025-2042 $84 JH ✪

ΨΨΨΨΨ Reserve Shiraz 2018, Frankland River Bright crimson purple. Full of luscious black cherry fruit, plum and blackberry playing support roles. What in wine show terminology 20 years ago would be Full Bodied Soft Finish (the other class Full Bodied Firm Finish). Oak plays its part, as do ripe tannins. Screw cap. 14.5% alc. RATING 95 DRINK 2023-2043 $55 JH

Mandurang Valley Wines ★★★★

77 Fadersons Lane, Mandurang, Vic 3551 **Region** Bendigo
T 0417 357 688 **www.**mandurangvalleywines.com.au **Open** Mon–Fri by appt. W'ends & public hols 11–5 **Winemaker** Wes Vine, Steve Vine **Est.** 1995 **Dozens** 2500 **Vyds** 3ha
Wes and Pamela Vine planted their first vineyard at Mandurang in '76 and started making wine as a hobby. Commercial production began in '93, and an additional vineyard was established in '97. Wes (a former school principal) became full-time winemaker in '99. Son Steve has progressively taken greater responsibility for the winemaking, while Wes is spending more time developing export markets. Pamela manages the cellar door cafe. (JH)

ΨΨΨΨΨ Riesling 2021, Bendigo Bright as a button. Gentle in grapefruit, lime, apple fruit and preserved-lemon aromas, but opens up on the palate showing some vivacious charm. Smooth, even and crisp with great length sustained by fine, chalky acidity. Screw cap. 12.2% alc. RATING 92 DRINK 2021-2027 $22 JP ✪
Old Vine 2019, Bendigo 60/30/10% cabernet sauvignon/shiraz/malbec. Old Vine is looking composed with typical regional characters and poise. The palate is all about ripe black fruits with bracken, earth, dried herbs, fennel seed, all bundled up in warm, toasty oak and dense tannins. Built for further time in the bottle. Screw cap. 14.5% alc. RATING 90 DRINK 2021-2028 $40 JP

ΨΨΨΨ Merlot 2020, Bendigo RATING 89 DRINK 2021-2027 $26 JP
Riesling 2020, Bendigo RATING 89 DRINK 2021-2024 $22 JP
Shiraz 2018, Bendigo RATING 89 DRINK 2022-2028 $30 JP
GSM 2019, Bendigo RATING 88 DRINK 2021-2028 $30 JP

Manser Wines ★★★★

c/- 3 Riviera Court, Pasadena, SA 5042 (postal) **Region** Adelaide Hills
T 0400 251 168 **www.**manserwines.com.au **Winemaker** Phil Christiansen **Est.** 2015
Dozens 1000 **Vyds** 6ha
Phil Manser has teamed up with brother Kevin and father Bernie to run the family vineyard. The vineyard was established by Tim James, a skilled winemaker with senior winemaking and management roles at Hardys and Wirra Wirra. He planted the vineyard to 4 clones of shiraz, planted randomly throughout the vineyard in '97, a common practice in France. The Mansers acquired the property in '15, Tim remaining an enthusiastic spectator during vintage. They also source fruit from a 65yo vineyard in Blewitt Springs and a third vineyard on the McMurtrie Mile which feeds their One Mad Moment range. Contract winemaker Phil Christiansen looks after the destinies of a considerable number of vineyards throughout McLaren Vale. (JH)

ΨΨΨΨΨ Block 4 Shiraz 2020, Adelaide Hills The high alcohol, it has to be said, is not particularly obvious. It's fully integrated into the wine and the same has to be said for the oak. It's a well-measured wine experience with bramble, blueberry, cassis and bay leaf, with plenty of spice and oak packed tightly by fine tannins. Screw cap. 14.9% alc. RATING 94 DRINK 2022-2033 $65 JP

🍷🍷🍷🍷🍷 Block 4 Shiraz 2019, Adelaide Hills RATING 92 DRINK 2021-2029 $55 JP
Dad's Block Shiraz 2020, Adelaide Hills RATING 90 DRINK 2022-2026
$35 JP

Marchand & Burch

PO Box 180, North Fremantle, WA 5159 **Region** Great Southern
T (08) 9336 9600 **www.**burchfamilywines.com.au **Winemaker** Janice McDonald, Pascal Marchand **Est.** 2007 **Dozens** 2000 **Vyds** 8.46ha
A joint venture between Canadian-born and Burgundian-trained Pascal Marchand and Burch Family Wines. Grapes are sourced from single vineyards and, in most cases, from single blocks within those vineyards (4.51ha of chardonnay and 3.95ha of pinot noir, in each case variously situated in Mount Barker and Porongurup). Biodynamic practices underpin the viticulture in the Australian and French vineyards, and Burgundian viticultural techniques have been adopted in the Australian vineyards (e.g. narrow rows and high-density plantings, Guyot pruning, vertical shoot positioning and leaf and lateral shoot removal). Exports to the UK, the US and other major markets. (JH)

🍷🍷🍷🍷🍷 Mount Barrow Pinot Noir 2020, Mount Barker The Mount Barrow
vineyard has impressive elevation in an area where there isn't much, and it brings poise and detail to the top notes of this wine. It is complex and dense and layered and muscular — all hallmarks of great wines from Mount Barker — and it shows the capacity for longevity that we look for when making assessments about quality. This is structured, powerful, spicy and littered with savoury spice through the long finish. An excellent pinot in an Australian context — as contentious as that is, for a pinot from the west. Screw cap. 14% alc. RATING 95 DRINK 2021-2031 $60 EL
Chardonnay 2020, Mount Barker Creamy and taut, there is a firm undercurrent of salted crushed nuts in here, while the fruit strays to the stone-fruit and apple-and-pear end of the spectrum. Tightly coiled and salty at this stage, we know this wine ages gracefully; perhaps the '20 vintage is guarding it jealously for now. Decant it (please) if you choose to drink it before '25. Screw cap. 13% alc. RATING 94 DRINK 2022-2037 $78 EL

🍷🍷🍷🍷🍷 Villages Pinot Noir 2020, Mount Barker RATING 93 DRINK 2021-2028
$39 EL
Villages Rosé 2021, Western Australia RATING 92 DRINK 2021-2023
$28 EL
Villages Chardonnay 2021, Margaret River RATING 91 DRINK 2022-2028
$42 EL

🍃 Marco Lubiana

60 Rowbottoms Road, Granton, Tas 7030 **Region** Tasmania
T 0429 637 457 **www.**marcolubiana.com.au **Open** Wed–Sun 10–4 **Winemaker** Marco Lubiana **Viticulturist** Marco Lubiana, Steve Lubiana **Est.** 2018 **Dozens** 800 **Vyds** 4ha
Marco Lubiana describes his philosophy as inspired by planet earth, the history of Burgundy and that of his winegrowing family. He discovered the great wines of France and Italy under Michael Andrewartha while working at East End Cellars, before embarking upon an internship in the Côte d'Or during the '19 vintage. He returned home to Granton in the Coal River Valley in '18 to make his first vintage in his parents' winery. His sourcing is from a diverse array of clones exclusively in his parents' biodynamic vineyards in the Derwent and Huon Valleys, and his focus rests entirely on chardonnay and pinot noir as still wines, with barrel-fermented vintage sparkling in the pipeline. Sulphur dioxide is used sparingly — in some cases not at all.

🍷🍷🍷🍷🍷 Lucille Vineyard Pinot Noir 2020, Tasmania A gorgeous pinot of red cherry
and strawberry fruit, built around the bright acidity of the Huon Valley, with

classically silky tannin structure. Old vines imbue impressive length and integrity. The lift of fragrance from judicious whole-bunch fermentation lends a classy air. Diam. 13% alc. RATING 94 DRINK 2021-2030 $50 TS

Marcus Hill Vineyard   ★★★★☆

560 Banks Road, Marcus Hill, Vic 3222 (postal) **Region** Geelong
T 0421 728 437 **www.**marcushillvineyard.com.au **Open** By appt **Winemaker** Chip Harrison **Est.** 2000 **Dozens** 1000 **Vyds** 3ha

In 2000, Richard and Margot Harrison, together with 'gang-pressed friends', planted 2ha of pinot noir overlooking Point Lonsdale, Queenscliff and Ocean Grove, a few kilometres from Bass Strait and Port Phillip. Since then chardonnay, shiraz, more pinot noir, and 3 rows of pinot meunier have been added. The vineyard is run with minimal sprays, and the aim is to produce elegant wines that truly express the maritime site. (JH)

♥♥♥♥♥ Bellarine Peninsula Pinot Meunier 2019, Geelong What a treat to see pinot meunier on the Bellarine Peninsula producing such an accomplished and captivating wine. Heady scent of florals – violet, lilac – with briar, dusty leafiness, dark berries and spice with a touch of musk. It has everything, including firm but fine tannins for some future down time. More, please! Screw cap. 13.5% alc. RATING 95 DRINK 2022-2028 $35 JP ✪

♥♥♥♥♀ Riesling 2020, Geelong RATING 91 DRINK 2022-2028 $25 JP
Bellarine Peninsula Pinot Noir 2019, Geelong RATING 91
DRINK 2022-2026 $35 JP
Bellarine Peninsula Chardonnay 2020, Geelong RATING 90
DRINK 2022-2028 $35 JP

Margan Wines   ★★★★★

1238 Milbrodale Road, Broke, NSW 2330 **Region** Hunter Valley
T (02) 6579 1317 **www.**margan.com.au **Open** 7 days 10–5 **Winemaker** Andrew Margan **Viticulturist** Andrew Margan **Est.** 1996 **Dozens** 25 **Vyds** 100ha

Margan Vineyards was established by Andrew and Lisa Margan in '96. Today it incorporates 2 of the second generation, Alessa and Ollie, as viticulturist and winemaker respectively. Andrew continues to oversee the viticultural and winemaking side; Lisa, the tourism and hatted restaurant. The estate boasts 100ha of vines and the vineyards are largely on the lauded Fordwich Sill, a geological formation dating back 200 million years. They are a meld of old vines (50+ years) planted to traditional varieties including semillon, chardonnay and shiraz, as well as younger plantings of new and exciting varieties albariño and barbera. Field blends of shiraz/mourvèdre and tempranillo/graciano/shiraz are unique to the region. Ollie's minimalist Breaking Ground wines are worthy of attention. Exports to the UK, the US, Canada, Scandinavia, Hong Kong and Singapore. (NG)

♥♥♥♥♥ White Label Fordwich Hill Semillon 2021, Hunter Valley If in doubt about the veracity of terroir, one only has to compare this to its edgier Ceres Hill sibling. Both lightweight, the textural similarities end there. This, more mellifluous. Greater flow, length of finish and ease of drinkability. Aromas of icy pole, lemongrass and tonic. This, too, will grow in stature with time. But it is already delicious. Screw cap. 11.7% alc. RATING 95 DRINK 2023-2036 $35 NG ✪
White Label Ceres Hill Chardonnay 2021, Hunter Valley A tensile, pungently mineral and highly refined chardonnay. A meld of tank and oak ferments, all wild. The purity of fruit, a legacy of a cool and attenuated ripening season. A waft of vanillin oak, subtle and well appointed, frames apricot, nougat, tangerine and cumquat notes. The finish, peppery and long, is almost pixelated, so exquisite is the detail. Among the standout chardonnays of the year. Screw cap. 12% alc. RATING 95 DRINK 2021-2030 $50 NG
White Label Timbervines Chardonnay 2021, Hunter Valley A site planted in 1972, on red volcanic soils. A wine that owes its breadth of texture and sheer intensity, much to them. The cooler reticence of the Ceres Hill in stark contrast.

Peppery again, but more impactful. A marrow of ripe stone fruits, glazed quince, dried mango and classy edges of vanillin oak. I oscillate between the 2 expressions, determined to conclude a victor. This wins by virtue of its strident intensity across the palate. Screw cap. 12% alc. RATING 95 DRINK 2021–2030 $50 NG

Aged Release Timbervines Shiraz 2018, Hunter Valley This is in the throes of ageing well. Plenty of life left. Hunter loam, sweet earth and leather polish. Pickled cherry, clove, violet and a waft of vanillin oak. The finish, strident and long. The acidity, shrill, but the jangles of youth should calm in time. Screw cap. 13.5% alc. RATING 94 DRINK 2021–2033 $75 NG

ᵀᵀᵀᵀᵀ **Semillon 2021, Hunter Valley** RATING 93 DRINK 2022–2031 $22 JH ◐
Breaking Ground Albariño 2021, Hunter Valley RATING 93 DRINK 2021–2024 $28 NG
Breaking Ground Semillon 2021, Hunter Valley RATING 93 DRINK 2021–2029 $28 NG
White Label Ceres Hill Semillon 2021, Hunter Valley RATING 93 DRINK 2022–2035 $35 NG
Botrytis Semillon 2021, Hunter Valley RATING 93 DRINK 2021–2029 $40 NG
Breaking Ground Chardonnay 2021, Hunter Valley RATING 92 DRINK 2021–2027 $28 NG
Breaking Ground Barbera 2021, Hunter Valley RATING 91 DRINK 2021–2024 $28 NG
Breaking Ground Shiraz 2021, Hunter Valley RATING 91 DRINK 2021–2025 $28 NG

Marion's Vineyard   ★★★★

361 Deviot Road, Deviot, Tas, 7275 **Region** Northern Tasmania
T 0437 540 422 **www**.marionsvineyard.com.au **Open** 7 days 11–5 **Winemaker** Cynthea Semmens **Est.** 1979 **Dozens** 3500 **Vyds** 8ha
Marion's Vineyard was established by young Californian couple Marion and Mark Semmens, who purchased a 14ha rundown apple orchard on the Tamar River in 1980. They planted 4ha of chardonnay, pinot noir, cabernet and müller-thurgau, subsequently doubling the size. Daughter Cynthea left Tasmania to ultimately obtain a wine marketing degree from Roseworthy and an oenology degree from CSU. She travelled the world undertaking vintages, gaining invaluable experience. Back in Australia, she worked for Tatachilla and Hardys Tintara when she met husband to be winemaker David Feldheim. They returned to Tasmania in 2010, Cynthea contract-making Marion's Vineyard wines and establishing their own small business Beautiful Isle Wines in '13. In '19, Marion, Cynthea, David and Nick (Cynthea's brother) jointly bought Mark's share of Marion's Vineyard, fulfilling a long-desired succession plan. (JH)

ᵀᵀᵀᵀᵀ **Syrah 2019, Tasmania** Tasmanian syrah is on the rise, and it's still the warmer seasons in which it showcases its finest potential. I love the vibrant purple mood of this vintage, in colour, violet aroma and black cherry and satsuma plum flavour. Glorious white pepper is a wonderful theme, morphing seamlessly with finely textured tannins and lively acidity that carry a long finish in perfect unison. Yet again, Marion's finest wine. Screw cap. 13% alc. RATING 94 DRINK 2024–2029 $55 TS

ᵀᵀᵀᵀᵀ **Chardonnay 2020, Tasmania** RATING 92 DRINK 2030–2036 $50 TS
Cabernet Franc 2019, Tasmania RATING 91 DRINK 2024–2029 $55 TS
Hyperion Syrah Noir 2020, Tasmania RATING 90 DRINK 2022–2025 $40 TS

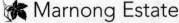 Marnong Estate   ★★★★

2355 Mickleham Road, Mickleham, Vic 3064 **Region** Sunbury
T (03) 9216 3300 **www**.marnongestate.com.au **Open** Fri–Sun 10–4, Mon–Thurs by appt **Winemaker** Sandrine Gimon **Viticulturist** Carl Duncan **Est.** 2016
Dozens 5700 **Vyds** 16.53ha

Marnong Estate is an expansive $35 million property 18km north of Tullamarine airport, overlooking the Macedon Ranges. The 480ha estate is a working farm with Angus cattle. Aside from the restored 19th century homestead, modern facilities include a range of wedding and function venues, restaurant, wine bar, accommodation, farm shop and cellar door. In 2016, the first vines went in following advice from Wine Network Consulting, who continue today with French-born Sandrine Gimon (ex-Rymill Estate, Coonawarra) leading the winemaking. Carl Duncan has come onboard as the full-time vineyard manager. Already, about 16.5ha are under vine including shiraz, chardonnay, pinot noir, montepulciano, pinot grigio, fiano and sangiovese, with more to come; including plans for a winery. (JF)

ŸŸŸŸŸ **Fiano 2021, Sunbury** Young vines at 5 years of age but a wine to watch. Honeysuckle, ginger cream and stone fruit with tinges of citrus. Spicy across the palate with neat acidity and refreshing, yet textural too. Screw cap. 12.5% alc. RATING 92 DRINK 2022-2024 $28 JF
Pinot Grigio 2021, Sunbury You'd have a glass or 2 of this at a barbecue with grilled vegetables or seafood and think all's well. A balance of flavours especially pears and spice to the fore; zesty and vibrant yet soft acidity and an easygoing appeal make this attractive. Screw cap. 13.5% alc. RATING 90 DRINK 2022-2024 $22 JF
Pinot Nero 2021, Sunbury A gentle pinot with its pale ruby hue and delicate aromas, all floral and spicy plus fresh herbs. A lighter-framed palate balanced out with juicy cherries, blood orange and soft tannins. Not complex but delicious nonetheless. For immediate drinking. Screw cap. 12.5% alc. RATING 90 DRINK 2022-2025 $28 JF
Montepulciano 2021, Sunbury One of the joys about this Italian variety,is its wonderful dark purple hue, which immediately entices. Tasted soon after bottling, so it does need more time to settle. Even if the palate is slightly callow and the tannins raw, there's no shortage of jubey bright fruit flavours, some prosciutto and ironstone. A lot to like and more so in the future. Screw cap. 13.5% alc. RATING 90 DRINK 2022-2025 $34 JF

ŸŸŸŸ **Chardonnay 2021, Sunbury** RATING 88 DRINK 2022-2024 $22 JF
Shiraz 2021, Sunbury RATING 88 DRINK 2022-2025 $34 JF

Marq Wines   ★★★★☆

860 Commonage Road, Dunsborough, WA 6281 **Region** Margaret River
T (08) 9756 6227 **www.**marqwines.com.au **Open** Fri–Sun & public hols 10–5,
Mon 10-4 **Winemaker** Mark Warren **Est.** 2011 **Dozens** 2500 **Vyds** 1.5ha
Mark Warren has a degree in wine science from CSU and a science degree from the University of WA; to complete the circle, he is currently lecturing in wine science and wine sensory processes at Curtin University, Margaret River. He also has 27 years' experience in both the Swan Valley and Margaret River, and his current major commercial role is producing the extensive Happs range as well as wines under contract for several other Margaret River brands. When all of this is added up, he is responsible for 60 to 70 individual wines each year, now including wines under his own Marq Wines label. A quick look at the list – Vermentino, Fiano, Wild & Worked Sauvignon Blanc Semillon, Wild Ferment Chardonnay, Rose, Gamay, Tempranillo, Malbec, and Cut & Dry Shiraz (Amarone style) – points to the underlying philosophy: an exploration of the potential of alternative varieties and unusual winemaking methods by someone with an undoubted technical understanding of the processes involved. (JH)

ŸŸŸŸŸ **Cabernet Franq 2020, Margaret River** Pretty, spicy, leafy, plump and delicious cabernet franc. I could smell it all day long. Hard to fathom how this rolls out at just $25, but whatever it is – massive fan. Mark Warren manages a little crunch and grit in the tannins, alongside leafy, varietal fruit – all of it wrapped in a spicy blanket. Lots to like here. Screw cap. 13.9% alc. RATING 94 DRINK 2021-2030 $25 EL ✿

ŸŸŸŸŸ Serious Rosé 2021, Margaret River RATING 93 DRINK 2021-2023 $25 EL ✪
Malbec 2020, Margaret River RATING 93 DRINK 2021-2028 $25 EL ✪
Wild Ferment Chardonnay 2020, Margaret River RATING 93
DRINK 2021-2027 $30 EL
Cut and Dry Shiraz 2020, Margaret River RATING 93 DRINK 2021-2029
$32 EL
Fiano 2021, Margaret River RATING 92 DRINK 2021-2026 $25 EL ✪
Semillon Sauvignon Blanc Verdelho 2021, Margaret River RATING 92
DRINK 2022-2026 $25 EL ✪
Tempranillo 2020, Margaret River RATING 92 DRINK 2022-2028 $30 EL
Epiq Chardonnay 2020, Margaret River RATING 92 DRINK 2021-2028
$55 EL
Epiq Malbec 2020, Margaret River RATING 92 DRINK 2021-2031 $55 EL
Gros Manseng 2021, Margaret River RATING 90 DRINK 2021-2025 $24 EL

Marri Wood Park   ★★★★

28 Whittle Road Yallingup WA 6282 **Region** Margaret River
T 0438 525 580 **www.**marriwoodpark.com.au **Open** 7 days 11–4 **Winemaker** Nic
Peterkin **Viticulturist** Julian Wright **Est.** 1992 **Dozens** 1500 **Vyds** 6ha
Established 1992 in Yallingup, Marri Wood Park is a boutique, family-owned producer with
an impressive range of wines from a bouncy, natty Pet-Nat to the serious classic varieties that
have made the Margaret River region famous. Natalie Wright and her father Julian moved to
Yallingup in 2004 to take over the vineyard that was had been managed for them for 11 years.
Today they have 6.5ha of Demeter-certified, biodynamic vineyards planted to cabernet
sauvignon, sauvignon blanc, chenin blanc and semillon. The emphasis is on an ecologically
beneficial approach to farming that yields top-quality wine grapes, is sustainable and in tune
with the environment. A bright addition to the Margaret River winescape. (DB)

ŸŸŸŸŸ Chenin Blanc 2019, Margaret River Characters of crisp nashi pears, custard
apple, Granny Smith and a waft of apricot come first, followed by hints of
marzipan, white flowers and stone. Clotted cream and lemon curd make an
appearance on the palate which shows sizzling focus, fine phenolic texture and
a wonderful line of porcelain like acided, finishing crisp and long. A wonderful
example of the variety. Screw cap. 13.5% alc. RATING 94 DRINK 2021-2028
$40 DB

ŸŸŸŸŸ Cabernet Sauvignon 2019, Margaret River RATING 93 DRINK 2021-2031
$40 DB
Sauvignon Blanc Semillon 2018, Margaret River RATING 93
DRINK 2021-2031 $28 DB
Crémant Sauvignon Blanc 2016, Margaret River RATING 91 $38 DB
Sauvignon Blanc 2020, Margaret River RATING 91 DRINK 2021-2024
$25 DB

Massena Vineyards   ★★★★★

26 Sturt Street, Angaston, SA 5353 **Region** Barossa Valley
T 0408 821 737 **www.**massena.com.au **Open** By appt **Winemaker** Jaysen Collins
Est. 2000 **Dozens** 5000 **Vyds** 4ha
Massena Vineyards draws upon 1ha each of mataro, saperavi, petite sirah and tannat at
Nuriootpa, also purchasing grapes from other growers. It is an export-oriented business,
although the wines can also be purchased by mail order, which, given both the quality and
innovative nature of the wines, seems more than ordinarily worthwhile. Exports to the US,
Canada, France, Switzerland, Denmark, South Korea, NZ and Hong Kong. (JH)

ŸŸŸŸŸ Verto Shiraz 2019, Barossa Vibrant red purple on the glass, the '19 Verto is
a stunning picture of fruit purity. Blood plum, maraschino cherries and dried
cranberry notes mesh with layers of spice, judicious cedary oak, dark chocolate
and floral tones. Slinky and textural, cascading fine tannin and a vivid acid pulse,

it's a muscular wine with a sense of grace and a lingering, persistent finish. Cork. 14.5% alc. RATING 95 DRINK 2022-2037 $85 DB

Verto Shiraz 2018, Barossa Deeply coloured with aromas of blood plum, blackberry and maraschino cherries. Plenty of spice and depth, with some cedary French oak nuance marching in on the palate, before slowly retreating back behind the wall of dark fruit and firm, sandy tannins. Muscular yet balanced, with impressive presence and flow in the mouth. Cork. 14.5% alc. RATING 95 DRINK 2021-2035 $85 DB

Stonegarden Single Vineyard Grenache 2019, Eden Valley Supple and flexing considerable muscle under all that ripe, spicy blood-plum fruit. Super-compact, fine, black-tea tannin heft, bright mineral cadence and a meaty, savoury flow, it's a serious piece of work from a great vineyard site. Cork. 14.5% alc. RATING 94 DRINK 2022-2032 $85 DB

Stonegarden Single Vineyard Old Vine Shiraz 2018, Eden Valley Plenty going on in this wine. Intense, resonant satsuma plum and macerated berry fruits, deeply cut with exotic spice, meaty facets, turned earth, vanilla bean and dark chocolate. Oak spice sweeps in on the palate, which is opulent and brisk with simmering latent power. Cork. 14.5% alc. RATING 94 DRINK 2021-2031 $70 DB

Mācerō Cabernet Sauvignon 2018, Barossa More often than not, you can forget about herbaceous characters in Barossa cabernet. Try to search for the telltale capsicum notes and you'll send yourself cross-eyed. It's just pure, opulent blackberry and cassis from go to whoa, with abundant spice, dark chocolate and earthy notes and fine tannin support. No shortage of horsepower here. Cork. 14.5% alc. RATING 94 DRINK 2021-2031 $85 DB

ƥƥƥƥƥ **The Moonlight Run 2020, Barossa Valley** RATING 93 DRINK 2022-2030 $35 DB

The Eleventh Hour Shiraz 2019, Barossa Valley RATING 93 DRINK 2021-2030 $45 DB

Stonegarden Single Vineyard Grenache Mataro Shiraz 2018, Eden Valley RATING 93 DRINK 2021-2027 $70 DB

Cellar Blend Shiraz Mataro 2020, Barossa Valley RATING 92 DRINK 2022-2028 $27 DB

Old Vine Semillon Semillon 2021, Barossa Valley RATING 91 DRINK 2022-2028 $23 DB ✪

Regional Selection Old Vine Grenache Mataro 2020, Riverland RATING 91 DRINK 2022-2028 $25 DB

The Twilight Path Primitivo 2020, Barossa Valley RATING 91 DRINK 2021-2027 $30 DB

Maverick Wines ★★★★★

981 Light Pass Road, Vine Vale, Moorooroo, SA 5352 **Region** Barossa Valley
T 0402 186 416 **www.**maverickwines.com.au **Open** Fri–Sun 11–4 **Winemaker** Ronald Brown **Viticulturist** Ronald Brown **Est.** 2004 **Dozens** 6000 **Vyds** 30ha
This is the business established by highly experienced vigneron Ronald Brown. It has evolved, now with 7 vineyards across the Barossa and Eden valleys, all transitioned into biodynamic grape production. The vines range from 40 to almost 150 years old, underpinning the consistency and quality of the wines. Exports to NZ, France, Russian, Thailand and Japan. (JH)

ƥƥƥƥƥ **Ahrens' Creek Ancestor Vine Shiraz 2019, Barossa Valley** One thing that always blows my mind when when I taste wines produced from Ancestor Vines (125+ years old) is their sheer textural volume. Incredible concentration and ripeness here, but with pitch-perfect balance. Plums, spice and all the usual good Barossan stuff is on display, but here we can openly marvel at the textural architecture of old vines and remind ourselves how lucky we are to have such gnarly, old wonders in the ground providing us such joy. Diam. 14.5% alc. RATING 97 DRINK 2021-2041 $320 DB

The Maverick Shiraz Cabernet Sauvignon 2019, Barossa For Maverick Wines' flagship, the aim has always been to highlight the best of the estate's Barossa Valley and Eden Valley holdings. Here it is a fine rendition of the great Australian blend, impressive in both its composition and verve, cutting an elegant line across the palate with perfectly ripe dark and black fruits, perfectly judged oak and a sense of space and detail. A lovely example of great farming, intuitive winemaking and 2 varieties working in harmony. Diam. 14% alc. RATING 97 DRINK 2021–2035 $320 DB ❤

ΨΨΨΨΨ **Ahrens' Creek Cabernet Sauvignon 2019, Barossa Valley** Herbaceous notes begone! Just a solid plinth of blackberry and blackcurrant fruit on display here, with hints of licorice, violets, deep baking spice, pipe tobacco and nary a whisper of oak. There's a toothsome, intense display of fruit here with tight, sandy tannins and a long persistent finish with impressive fruit weight and verve. Diam. 14% alc. RATING 96 DRINK 2021–2036 $150 DB

Shiraz 2021, Barossa Glossy and fleshy with pristine berry and plum fruits, layered with spice, cedar, dark chocolate and earth and dusted with violet high tones. Bright acidity pulses through the wine, providing a swift cadence, and there is a juicy aspect to the lingering finish that is superb. Screw cap. 14.5% alc. RATING 95 DRINK 2022–2035 $50 DB

Eden Regained Shiraz 2020, Barossa Tension, clarity and detail all on song here with ripe damson plum, layered spice, violets and lighter tones of licorice and roasting meats. Composed and graceful with an airy sense of space, fine, ripe cascading tannins and a finish that trails off persistently. Wonderfully elegant drinking. Screw cap. 14% alc. RATING 95 DRINK 2022–2036 $80 DB

Ahrens' Creek Mourvèdre 2020, Barossa Valley It gladdens my heart that mourvèdre, a variety often blended away in the past, is increasingly standing tall on its own. Here, sourced from the ancient vines of the Ahrens' Creek vineyard, it does a sterling job of wooing the wine drinker. Meaty red and dark fruits with that characteristic cacophony of souk-like spice – cinnamon, garam masala, curry leaf – and hints of pressed flowers and soy. Spacious and detailed with a savoury flow, compact tannins and lovely fruit weight. Diam. 14.5% alc. RATING 95 DRINK 2021–2031 $150 DB

Trial Hill Grenache 2020, Eden Valley The vast majority of the Barossa's grenache lies down on the valley floor but those that hail from the cooler climes of the Eden Valley offer finer lines and a redder-fruit spectrum for those in search of transparency of site. Redcurrant and red cherry bound with spice; purple floral notes form in a distinctly pinot-esque palate shape that is tight and airy, with ample drive and detail. Akin to a filigreed line drawing of grenache, and just lovely. Diam. 14.5% alc. RATING 95 DRINK 2021–2031 $150 DB

Barossa Ridge Shiraz 2019, Barossa Valley There is a sense of space and detail in this wine that draws you in to the glass. Medium bodied, with abundant dark summer berry and ripe plummy fruit, sheathed in exotic spice with hints of turned earth, dark chocolate and pressed flowers. Fine acid drive and powdery tannin pressure provide the framework, with a savoury dark-fruit flow on the finish. Diam. 14% alc. RATING 95 DRINK 2021–2031 $150 DB

Ahrens' Creek Shiraz 2019, Barossa Valley I'm liking what I see from the new Maverick releases. Pitch-perfect ripeness, tension and balance with moderate alcohols is a recurring and gleefully accepted theme. Beautifully weighted plumply proportioned plum and dark fruits, plentiful spice and hints of leather, roasting meats and earth. Long and persistent, with impressive composition and purity. Diam. 14% alc. RATING 95 DRINK 2021–2036 $150 DB

Twins Barrel Select The Barossa Shiraz 2021, Barossa Valley A complex and captivating wine showing characters of super-ripe blood plum, exotic spice, pressed purple flowers, licorice, earth and light amaro herb and roasting meat notes. The initial palate flow is quite sweetly-fruited, medium bodied with a swift acid cadence and layers of spice and floral nuance. Compact, fine-grain tannin lends support with a juicy, spiced plum finish. Screw cap. 14.5% alc. RATING 94 DRINK 2022–2032 $50 DB

Barossa Shiraz 2020, Barossa Valley Old-vine, dry-grown Vine Vale fruit with its characteristic high tones and compact, sandy kinetic tannin profile. It's all spiced plummy fruit with a slinky textural flow, bright acidity, floral facets and distinctly savoury palate shape. Delicious drinking now, but will gain complexity with careful cellaring. Screw cap. 14% alc. RATING 94 DRINK 2021–2031 $50 DB

Ahrens' Creek Grenache 2020, Barossa Valley Fragrant plum and red-cherry fruit flow first, cut through with notes of Asian spice, ginger cake, mulberry and pressed flowers. Medium bodied with gentle, sandy tannin tugging at the roof of the mouth, finishing savoury with a plume of spiced plums. Diam. 14.5% alc. RATING 94 DRINK 2021–2031 $150 DB

Eden Regained Shiraz 2019, Barossa A deeply coloured offering with beautifully composed dark plummy fruit, dotted with spice and mulberry lift. There's texture and flow here, with ample sandy tannin and a sapid twang to the acid profile, driving the rich fruit onwards to a persistent, savoury finish. Bright, perfumed and impressive drinking. Diam. 14% alc. RATING 94 DRINK 2021–2030 $80 DB

Max & Me

Eden Valley Hotel, 11 Murray Street, Eden Valley, SA 5235 **Region** Eden Valley **T** 0403 250 331 www.maxandme.com.au **Open** 7 days 12–5 **Winemaker** Philip Lehmann **Viticulturist** Philip Lehmann **Est.** 2011 **Dozens** 900 **Vyds** 10.22ha

Max is the name of a German shepherd / whippet cross purchased by Phil Lehmann from the RSPCA pound and who introduced Phil to his wife to be Sarah during a visit to the Barossa. A dog lover from way back, she fell in love with Max and Phil made it clear she wouldn't get Max unless she married him (Phil). Phil had previously purchased the Boongarrie Estate (on Keyneton Road, at an elevation of 430–460m) with 5.25ha of shiraz and 4.97ha of cabernet sauvignon. They converted the vineyard to (non-certified) organic management, with no herbicides and only copper/sulphur sprays. The benefits are self-evident, reflected in the high quality of the wines made since '11. Sarah manages direct wine sales. The future is for modest growth, planting riesling and grenache. (JH)

Woodcarvers Vineyard Mirooloo Road Riesling 2021, Eden Valley The pale straw-green colour will take years to deepen. An exercise in delicacy from start to finish, the wine melting in the mouth, the aftertaste as clean and fresh as a spring day with a cloudless blue sky. Screw cap. 12.5% alc. RATING 93 DRINK 2022–2032 $30 JH

Boongarrie Vineyard Shiraz 2019, Eden Valley The '19 vintage saw yields drop 0.5t/ha; with small berries and resulted in only a 500L puncheon for their efforts. In its purest form, a wine's release should be an accurate snapshot of a season and we see that here. Medium red in the glass, red cherry and yellow plum fruit, souk-like spice and an airy sense of space. Beguiling. Screw cap. 14.4% alc. RATING 90 DRINK 2021–2026 $60 DB

Maxwell Wines

Olivers Road, McLaren Vale, SA 5171 **Region** McLaren Vale **T** (08) 8323 8200 www.maxwellwines.com.au **Open** 7 days 10–5 **Winemaker** Kate Petering, Mark Maxwell **Est.** 1979 **Dozens** 30 000 **Vyds** 40ha

Maxwell Wines has carved out a reputation as a premium producer in McLaren Vale, making some excellent red wines in recent years. The majority of the vines on the estate were planted in 1972, including 19 rows of the highly regarded reynella clone of cabernet sauvignon. The Ellen Street shiraz block in front of the winery was planted in '53. In a region abounding with first class restaurants (and chefs), Maxwell has responded to the challenge with extensive renovations to the restaurant and cellar door. Kate Petering, formerly chief winemaker at Mount Langi Ghiran, was appointed head winemaker in March '19. Exports to all major markets. (JH) πππππ **Clan Exclusive Nero d'Avola 2020, McLaren Vale** A wine of great promise, combining a heady richness with a pulpy levity. Dark cherry, wood smoke, kirsch, brush, lavender and a cedary, earthen whiff of older oak. Fermentation in ceramic eggs would work better, perhaps. Rich, round and supple, with real vibrato. A joy to drink, portending to the immense future of the variety in these parts. Screw cap. 13.5% alc. RATING 95 DRINK 2021-2025 $36 NG

Small Batch Clan Wine Club Touriga 2019, McLaren Vale Freshly appointed winemaker, Kate Petering, is steering this ship in the right direction: from the antediluvian to the fresh, floral and streamlined styling of the best contemporary Vale wines. Fine aromas that allude to power, latent and behind the scenes, while delivering a floral elegance. Peat, bitter chocolate and crushed black rock, almost llicorella of persuasion. Currant and a verdant whiff of mint and herb, signify cabernet in the mix. A minor player, albeit, the baritone that complements touriga's soprano. Plenty of oak, serving the growing force in the glass well. Salty and long and refined. Delicious wine. Screw cap. 14% alc. RATING 94 DRINK 2021-2027 $55 NG

πππππ **Clan Wine Club Grenache Blanc 2021, McLaren Vale** RATING 93 DRINK 2021-2025 $32 NG

Ellen Street Shiraz 2019, McLaren Vale RATING 93 DRINK 2021-2032 $42 NG

Minotaur Reserve Shiraz 2019, McLaren Vale RATING 93 DRINK 2022-2034 $115 NG

Eocene Ancient Earth Shiraz 2018, McLaren Vale RATING 93 DRINK 2021-2031 $60 NG

Fresca Grenache 2021, McLaren Vale RATING 92 DRINK 2022-2024 $28 NG

Four Roads Grenache 2020, McLaren Vale RATING 92 DRINK 2021-2026 $32 NG

Eight Bells Shiraz 2019, McLaren Vale RATING 92 DRINK 2021-2025 $25 NG ✪

Chardonnay 2020, Adelaide Hills RATING 90 DRINK 2022-2025 $28 JP

Silver Hammer Shiraz 2019, McLaren Vale RATING 90 DRINK 2021-2026 $24 NG

Mayer

★★★★★

66 Miller Road, Healesville, Vic 3777 **Region** Yarra Valley
T (03) 5967 3779 **www**.timomayer.com.au **Open** By appt **Winemaker** Timo Mayer
Est. 1999 **Dozens** 2000 **Vyds** 3ha

Timo Mayer teamed with partner Rhonda Ferguson to establish Mayer on the slopes of Mount Toolebewong, 8km south of Healesville. The steepness of those slopes is presumably 'celebrated' in the name given to the vineyard (Bloody Hill). Pinot noir has the lion's share of the high-density vineyard, with smaller amounts of shiraz and chardonnay. Mayer's winemaking credo is minimal interference and handling, and no filtration. The Empire of Dirt wines are a collaboration between son Rivar Ferguson- Mayer and UK importer Ben Henshaw. Exports to the UK, France, Germany, Denmark, Sweden, Singapore and Japan. (JH)

πππππ **Syrah 2021, Yarra Valley** A wonderful, deep, purple crimson. Smells fabulous – reminiscent of good Cornas, with its aromas of dark fruits, crushed granite, brined black olives, red peppercorns and bay leaf. Backwards and structured on the palate, I'd suggest decanting this if you're going to open a bottle or any time soon, but you'd really want to have some in the cellar to enjoy in 5–10 years, if not longer. Screw cap. 13% alc. RATING 97 DRINK 2023-2032 $55 PR ✪

πππππ **Dr Mayer Pinot Noir 2021, Yarra Valley** A medium, bright crimson red. Raspberries, mountain herbs from 100% whole bunches, and sweet spices as it opens up, all found in this youthful and concentrated wine. You will find pomegranate and blood oranges on the palate, which is also saline and structured.

The tannins are fine, yet tightly wound and this will only get better over the next 5–8 years. Diam. 12.5% alc. RATING 96 DRINK 2022-2030 $60 PR ☉

Bloody Hill Villages Shiraz 2021, Yarra Valley Bright, crimson purple. Redolent of dark cherries, blood plums, a hint of pomegranate, black peppercorns, olives and some floral notes. Medium bodied and delicious straight off the bat, with its dark fruits and chalky, fine tannins. Drink now and over the next 5–8 years. A steal at this price. Diam. 13.5% alc. RATING 95 DRINK 2022-2029 $32 PR ☉

Volcanic Pinot Noir 2021, Yarra Valley At the more delicate end of the Yarra pinot spectrum, but not lacking depth or structure either. There are aromas of cranberries, pomegranate, strawberries and delicate spice. The palate is equally pretty, with fine, chalky tannins rounding out a wine that, while good now, will become even more complex in another 2 or 3 years. Screw cap. 12.5% alc. RATING 95 DRINK 2022-2029 $55 PR

Volcanic Syrah 2021, Yarra Valley This is the first time a wine has been commercially made and released from this vineyard, and what a beauty it is. Brightly coloured, aromas of red and black fruits are complemented by pink peppercorns and Indian spices. Delicious on release – I like how the wine's structure relies as much on its crunchy acidity as it does on the silky tannins. To drink and enjoy now and over the next 6–8 years. Another well-crafted wine from Timo Mayer in '21. Screw cap. 12.5% alc. RATING 95 DRINK 2022-2029 $55 PR

Cabernet 2021, Yarra Valley A saturated crimson purple. Made more in the style of the Loire Valley's Chinon than Australian cabernet sauvignon, there's a lot going on here with its aromas of blackberries and blackcurrants together with salted licorice, black olives and spice-rack spices. Saline on the palate, with good depth of fruit and fine, dusty tannins, this is a wine to be enjoyed with food, now and over the next 5 or so years. Screw cap. 13.5% alc. RATING 95 DRINK 2022-2027 $55 PR

Pinot Noir 2021, Yarra Valley A light, bright crimson red. Gorgeously perfumed with aromas of raspberries, wild strawberries (and I've tasted these, for the record!) and delicate rose petals. Light–medium bodied, this has both delicacy and depth with its red cherry fruit and a gentle savoury edge. It's quite tightly wound and I can see this becoming more complex and filling out over the next 5 or so years. Diam. 13% alc. RATING 95 DRINK 2022-2028 $60 PR

Maygars Hill Winery   ★★★★

53 Longwood-Mansfield Road, Longwood, Vic 3665 **Region** Strathbogie Ranges **T** 0402 136 448 **www.**maygarshill.com.au **Open** By appt **Winemaker** Contract **Est.** 1997 **Dozens** 900 **Vyds** 3.2ha

Jenny Houghton purchased this 8ha property in 1994, planting shiraz (1.9ha) and cabernet sauvignon (1.3ha). The name comes from Lieutenant Colonel Maygar, who fought with outstanding bravery in the Boer War in South Africa in 1901 and was awarded the Victoria Cross. In WWI he rose to command the 8th Light Horse Regiment, winning yet further medals for bravery. The 100th anniversary of Lieutenant Colonel Maygar's death was in 2017. The Shiraz and Cabernet Sauvignon, both in Reserve and standard guise, have been consistently excellent for a number of years. In mid-2021, the winery was sold to established vineyard owners from North East Victoria. (JH)

🍷🍷🍷🍷🍷 **Reserve Cabernet Sauvignon 2020, Strathbogie Ranges** Celebrates just how good, how elegant and successful cabernet can be grown in the Strathbogies with penetrating aromatics, cassis, brambly forest leafy aromas and a light dusting of signature 'bogies bush mint and bay leaf. Plush across the palate delivered with confidence in smart, integrated oak and persistent fine tannins running long and firm, right through to the finish. Screw cap. 13.5% alc. RATING 95 DRINK 2022-2031 $42 JP

🍷🍷🍷🍷🍷 **Shiraz 2020, Strathbogie Ranges** RATING 92 DRINK 2022-2030 $30 JP

mazi wines

5 Wilbala Road, Longwood, SA 5153 **Region** McLaren Vale
T 0406 615 553 **www.**maziwines.com.au **Winemaker** Alex Katsaros, Toby Porter
Est. 2016 **Dozens** 1500

Lifelong friends Toby Porter and Alex Katsaros always talked about making wine together as an adjunct to their day jobs in wine. Toby has been a winemaker at d'Arenberg for 15+ years and Alex had 10 years' experience working with alternative varieties here and abroad. They decided to only make rosé, and more power to them in doing so. McLaren Vale is the sole source for their grapes, focusing on grenache, but they are happy to work with bush-vine mataro. The aim is to produce fresh wines with vibrant fruit, normally by crushing and pressing the grapes for a cool ferment in stainless steel, but maturation in old French oak can (and has) been used to build palate complexity without sacrificing fruit. The derivation of the name is as simple as that of their raison d'être – it is Greek for together. Exports to the US, Singapore and Hong Kong. (JH)

🍷🍷🍷🍷🍷 **Mataro Cinsault Grenache Rosé 2021, McLaren Vale** Arguably one of the finest rosés in the country. The caveat: the lighter hued, herb-doused and gently grippy Provençal style is light years away from most Aussie gear. I prefer it this way. One can push the style to the point of flavourless vapidity, but mercifully, these guys aren't going that way. This is an ode to classicism, the triumvirate of varieties synergistic with the greatest from the south of France, albeit, with some oomph from the Vale. A superlative vintage to boot, exuding scented fruit that is neither too muscular, nor anaemic. Poised. Classy. A musk stick hue. Riffs on glazed red cherry, poached strawberry, Seville orange zest, lavender and thyme. The finish, as reliant on a taper of gentle acidity, as it is on a skein of impeccably tuned phenolics. Long, crunchy and sappy. Superlative rosé here. Screw cap. 12.5% alc.
RATING 95 DRINK 2021-2022 $24 NG ✪

🍷🍷🍷🍷🍷 **Limited Release Rosé 2021, McLaren Vale** RATING 93 DRINK 2021-2022 $44 NG
Grenache Rosé 2021, McLaren Vale RATING 92 DRINK 2021-2022 $25 NG ✪
Mavrodaphne Rosé 2021, McLaren Vale RATING 92 DRINK 2021-2022 $30 NG

Mazza Wines

PO Box 480, Donnybrook, WA 6239 **Region** Geographe
T 0417 258 888 **www.**mazza.com.au **Winemaker** Contract **Est.** 2002 **Dozens** 1000
Vyds 4ha

David and Anne Mazza were inspired by the great wines of Rioja and the Douro Valley, and continue a long-standing family tradition of making wine. They have planted the key varieties of those 2 regions: tempranillo, graciano, bastardo, sousão, tinta cão and touriga nacional. They believe they were the first Australian vineyard to present this collection of varieties on a single site and I am reasonably certain they are correct. Exports to the UK. (JH)

🍷🍷🍷🍷🍷 **Bastardo Rosé 2021, Geographe** Bastardo is a Portugese variety. This is savoury, chewy, meaty and briny, all of which bolt onto the red berry fruit in the mouth. It is medium bodied, dry and a classic food rosé. Very, very good, in what was otherwise a challenging vintage. Screw cap. 13% alc. RATING 93 DRINK 2022-2024 $28 EL
Tempranillo 2019, Geographe The tannins are the feature and the highlight here: they are dusty, chalky and earthy, really shaping the purple fruit in the mouth. This is a savoury, shapely wine, not traditionally fruit driven as we are so conditioned to expect in the New World. We know this wine ages gracefully, give it another year or 2 (if you can) – it'll really start to emerge. Screw cap. 14% alc. RATING 93 DRINK 2024-2031 $30 EL

Graciano 2018, Geographe Formidable, savoury tannins are combined here with salted licorice and blackberry fruit – all things spicy, Mediterranean and reminscent of long-ago holidays. Sigh. The tannins have been admirably reined in, bound tightly to the fruit that pulses in the mouth. Plenty going on in the glass, which wistfully requests a plate of anchovies on toast. Glorious. Total production 33 dozens. Screw cap. 15% alc. RATING 92 DRINK 2021-2028 $35 EL

Touriga Nacional Sousão 2019, Geographe In a word: yum. This is meaty, densely packed with blackberries, cloves and aniseed, layered with ground black pepper and shavings of deli meat. Super-sweet on the nose, not so in the mouth. A wine of interest and rustic charm. 100 dozens made. Screw cap. 14.5% alc. RATING 91 DRINK 2021-2028 $35 EL

Mazzini

131 Lumb Rd, Sutherlands Creek VIC 3331 **Region** Geelong
T 0448 045 845 **www**.mazziniwines.com.au **Winemaker** Ray Nadeson, Duncan Lowe
Est. 2016 **Dozens** 400

Mazzini Wines was established in 2016 by Paul and Karen Marinelli after fostering strong connections with the Geelong wine industry over the last decade. Mazzini Wines doesn't boast the usual winery, vineyard and cellar door but rather operates as a form of négociant/ wine merchant, sourcing fruit from some of the region's most promising individual vineyards and utilising the skills of experienced local winemakers Ray Nadeson and Duncan Lowe. The colourful Mazzini wine labels are a nod to Paul's Italian heritage and the name of his Nonno's street in Mola di Bari in Puglia, Italy. The wines are intended to reflect the hands-on and pure approach to produce he grew up admiring in his family. (JP)

Pinot Noir 2021, Geelong Shimmering in the glass in black cherry-purple hues. Strikes an immediate fresh and elegant poise in aromas of red cherry, raspberry, cranberry fruits with peppery spice. Firm and dry with a juicy acid crunch, it is fleshed out nicely in red berries, rhubarb earthiness, peppercorn and well-judged oak. Screw cap. 12.5% alc. RATING 93 DRINK 2022-2027 $35 JP

Single Vineyard Pinot Gris 2021, Geelong RATING 89 DRINK 2022-2024 $32 JP
Single Vineyard Shiraz 2021, Geelong RATING 88 DRINK 2022-2029 $32 JP
Single Vineyard Chardonnay 2021, Geelong RATING 88 DRINK 2022-2025 $35 JP

MBK

14 Meredyth Street, Millswood, SA 5034 **Region** Barossa Valley
T 0402 114 808 **Winemaker** Steve Baraglia **Est.** 2014 **Dozens** 400

MBK (and parent company, Mabenki) is derived from the names of the three founders: Mario Barletta, Ben Barletta and Kim Falster. Brothers Ben and Mario came from a retail background (Walkerville Cellars, Adelaide), Kim Falster is their wine-loving friend. The company started in 2014, but its genesis was back in 1993, making 'house wine' to sell in the store. They have never missed a vintage, but wines were sold exclusively to a private customer base. The '21 Riesling and '19 Shiraz, sourced from the Clare and Barossa Valleys respectively, represent the first commercial release of the MBK label. (EL)

Watervale Riesling 2021, Clare Valley Scintillating, taut, and extreme knife-edge stuff here. Limes, apples and pears are lit up by pithy, saline acidity. Bright and gorgeous – Clare Valley routinely brings the lovely voluminous base of flavour, while still achieving that almost-austere acid. Awesome. Screw cap. 12% alc. RATING 94 DRINK 2022-2030 $22 EL ☉

Greenock Creek Shiraz 2019, Barossa Valley RATING 91 DRINK 2022-2028 $30 DB

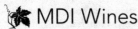

MDI Wines

198 Gertrude St, Fitzroy, Vic 3065 **Region** Murray Darling
T www.mdi.wine **Open** By appt **Winemaker** Kevin McCarthy **Est.** 2022
Dozens 4000

MDI Wines is a celebration of winemaker Kevin McCarthy's enduring love affair with the
people, land and wines of the Murray Darling. His first up-close, hands-on grapes experience
occurred in 2002 when he bought Murray Darling sangiovese to fill otherwise empty tanks
after a disastrously small vintage on the Peninsula at his then winery, T'Gallant. Ever since he
has returned to Mildura to work with growers and winemakers on projects like T'Gallant's
Juliette, Quealy's Fionula and a little-known project, TGQ. With MDI – the name comes from
the postcode for greater Mildura, 3501, which translates in Roman numerals to MMMDI –
he embraces the alternative grape varieties of the region to create approachable skin-contact
wines. In '22, he will release Skin Editions, small-batch wines with a focus on skin contact
made from grapes such as picolit, ansonica, refosco, ribolla and moscato giallo. (JP)

ŸŸŸŸŸ **Sangiovese 2020, Murray Darling** A summer fruit bowl of the freshest red
cherries, raspberries, anise and dusty cacao. The fragrance is mesmerising. Takes a
savoury turn on the palate with an undercurrent of cherry kirsch, salty capers and
earth, against black fruits and a smoky nuttiness. Chalky tannins drive through to
the finish. Diam. 13% alc. RATING 93 DRINK 2022-2025 $25 JP ❂
Pinot Grigio 2021, Murray Darling Honeyed, soft and creamy, it's easy to
interpret this as more in gris territory than grigo. Whatever the camp, it is one
highly individual, expressive grigio in honeysuckle, hay, pear skin and Delicious
apple. Hums along at a fair acidic click, too. Mouth-wateringly good for the price.
Screw cap. 12.5% alc. RATING 90 DRINK 2022-2025 $22 JP

ŸŸŸŸ **Friulano 2021, Murray Darling** RATING 88 DRINK 2022-2024 $25 JP

Meadowbank Wines

652 Meadowbank Road, Meadowbank, Tas 7140 **Region** Southern Tasmania
T 0439 448 151 **www.**meadowbank.com.au **Open** By appt **Winemaker** Peter Dredge
Viticulturist Gerald Ellis **Est.** 1976 **Dozens** 800 **Vyds** 52ha

In 1976, Gerald and Sue Ellis picked the first grapes from their large Glenora property at the
top end of the Derwent River from vines planted 2 years earlier by the previous owner. There
have been 4 major expansions since, most recently a 10ha planting of pinot noir, chardonnay,
syrah and gamay in 2016, lifting the total to 52ha, the major part as fully mature vines.
Meadowbank supplies grapes to 6 or so small wineries and also leases 32ha to Accolade. Peter
Dredge formed a partnership with the Ellis family to relaunch Meadowbank. The wines are
made by Peter at his contract winemaking facility from the portion of vineyard set aside for
the Meadowbank wines. Exports to South East Asia and Taiwan. (JH)

ŸŸŸŸŸ **Riesling 2021, Tasmania** At once exotic yet refined, exuberant yet tense,
immediate yet enduring. A delightful flourish of orange blossom and persimmon
is underlined by wild lemon tension and Derwent Valley drive, impeccably
completed with an invisible lick of sweetness. Remarkable line and length
promise grand things in decades to come. Screw cap. 11.5% alc. RATING 95
DRINK 2026-2038 $36 TS
Blanc de Noirs Sparkling 2018, Tasmania Three years on lees; disgorged
Sept '21. 4g/L dosage. A full straw hue with a faint blush tint anticipates the full
presence and purity of pinot noir, laden with crunchy, spicy red berries of all kinds.
The tension of the Derwent whistles through a tense palate of brittle acid drive,
nicely framed in the creamy texture of barrel fermentation, yet screaming out for
a full decade yet to find peace and calm. Craftsmanship with endurance. Diam.
11.5% alc. RATING 94 $75 TS
Mardi Late Disgorged Sparkling Pinot Noir Chardonnay 2011, Tasmania
Disgorged Sept '21; 3g/L dosage. All the joy of a full decade on lees is generously
thrust forth in a silky palate of butter, vanilla cream, toffee, tarte tatin, preserved

lemon and a nuance of charcuterie. The endurance of this cool season in the deep south charges a taut acid line still confidently present, even within the creamy allure of long age. A sparkling of grand presence, personality, persistence and drive. Diam. 11.5% alc. RATING 94 $120 TS

🍷🍷🍷🍷🍷 Blanc de Blancs 2016, Tasmania RATING 93 $85 TS
Gamay 2021, Tasmania RATING 91 DRINK 2022-2022 $45 TS

Medhurst ★★★★★

24-26 Medhurst Road, Gruyere, Vic 3770 **Region** Yarra Valley
T (03) 5964 9022 **www.**medhurstwines.com.au **Open** Thurs–Mon & public hols 11–5
Winemaker Simon Steele **Est.** 2000 **Dozens** 6000 **Vyds** 12ha

The wheel has come full circle for Ross and Robyn Wilson. Ross was CEO of Southcorp when it brought the Penfolds, Lindemans and Wynns businesses under its banner. Robyn spent her childhood in the Yarra Valley, her parents living less than a kilometre away from Medhurst. The vineyard is planted to low-yielding sauvignon blanc, chardonnay, pinot noir, cabernet sauvignon and shiraz vines. The winery focuses on small-batch production and also provides contract winemaking services. The visual impact of the winery has been minimised by recessing the building into the slope of land and locating the barrel room underground. The building was recognised for its architectural excellence at the Victorian Architecture Awards. The arrival of Simon Steele has enhanced the already considerable reputation of Medhurst. (JH)

🍷🍷🍷🍷🍷 **Estate Vineyard Chardonnay 2021, Yarra Valley** A very bright green gold. Beautifully crafted, you'll find white nectarines, grapefruit pith, orange blossom, jasmine, subtle peony and very subtle struck match. An essay in chardonnay purity, this taut, powerful and beautifully balanced wine tapers into a long, satisfying and saline finish. Screw cap. 13.1% alc. RATING 97 DRINK 2022-2028 $44 PR ✪
Reserve Cabernet 2019, Yarra Valley Only 30 dozen made of this supremely good Yarra Valley cabernet. A deep, plummy crimson purple. Densely packed with dark fruits, spice-rack spices, and already beautifully integrated and well-handled cedary oak. Compact and precise on the palate with dark currants, boysenberry and blood plums. Gently textured, with layered, bright and crunchy tannins, this beauty will still be looking good, in 10, if not 20, years from now. Screw cap. 13.1% alc. RATING 97 DRINK 2023-2036 $90 PR ✪

🍷🍷🍷🍷🍷 **Estate Vineyard Rosé 2021, Yarra Valley** The pale salmon hue reflects whole-bunch pressed cabernet sauvignon and shiraz, fermented off skins. Wafts of perfume float in the air, rose petals to the fore. The unexpectedly intense fruits span spices, light and dark, and small forest berries. Typical Medhurst class. Screw cap. 13% alc. RATING 95 DRINK 2021-2023 $27 JH ✪
YRB 2021, Yarra Valley 50/50% pinot noir/shiraz. A luminous crimson purple. A blend that is totally suited to the Yarra, this has immediate appeal, with its combination of red and black fruits, fresh mountain herbs and some red peppercorns. Medium bodied, this is perfectly weighted, with supple tannins rounding out a wine to be enjoyed now and over the next 3–4 years. Screw cap. 13% alc. RATING 95 DRINK 2022-2026 $44 PR
Estate Vineyard Pinot Noir 2021, Yarra Valley Very bright crimson. Equally bright on the nose with its aromas of wild strawberry, raspberries, crushed violets and a little spice. Delicious straight out of the gate, this balanced and silky smooth wine will still be looking good 5–7 years from now. Screw cap. 13% alc. RATING 95 DRINK 2022-2028 $50 PR
Estate Vineyard Cabernet Sauvignon 2019, Yarra Valley A bright crimson purple, with satsuma plum and blackberry leaf aromatics. From what is shaping up as a great vintage for Yarra cabernet, this simply delicious and fleshy wine has fine, approachable tannins and impressive length. Can be enjoyed with confidence now and over the next 10 years. Screw cap. 13% alc. RATING 95 DRINK 2023-2032 $50 PR

Meerea Park

Pavilion B, 2144 Broke Road, Pokolbin, NSW 2320 **Region** Hunter Valley
T (02) 4998 7474 **www.**meereapark.com.au **Open** 7 days 10–5 **Winemaker** Rhys
Eather **Est.** 1991 **Dozens** 10000

This is the project of Rhys and Garth Eather, whose great-great-grandfather, Alexander
Munro, established a famous vineyard in the 19th century, known as Bebeah. While the
range of wines chiefly focuses on semillon and shiraz, it extends to other varieties (including
chardonnay) and also into other regions. Meerea Park's cellar door is located at the striking
Tempus Two winery, owned by the Roche family, situated on the corner of Broke Road and
McDonald Road. It hardly need be said that the quality of the wines, especially with 5 years'
cellaring, is outstanding. Exports to the UK, the US, Canada and Singapore. (JH)

ΨΨΨΨΨ **Alexander Munro Individual Vineyard Shiraz 2019, Hunter Valley** Deep
crimson-purple hue through to crimson rim. From the third drought vintage in a
row. An earthy bouquet of black fruits and charcuterie, its deep and rich layers of
blackberry and licorice sustained by high-quality tannins, French oak in support.
Screw cap. 14% alc. RATING 96 DRINK 2024–2049 $115 JH

XYZ Semillon 2021, Hunter Valley This wine is still in its infancy, but already
has an abundance of juicy sweet citrus flavours, and a great future. Screw cap.
11% alc. RATING 95 DRINK 2021–2035 $25 JH ❂

Hell Hole Individual Vineyard Semillon 2021, Hunter Valley Some wool
and lanolin aromas are swept away the moment you first taste the lemon curd and
zest on the palate, the DNA of all good young Hunter Valley semillons. Excellent
cellaring prospect. Screw cap. 11% alc. RATING 94 DRINK 2026–2045 $30 JH ❂

Daisy Hill Shiraz 2019, Hunter Valley Nice drinking. A smooth ride. Full
bodied, but less corseted by the oak and extraction of many premium expressions.
Better, the Hunter's sweet red fruits, loam, clove, lacquered cherry, pickled plum
and kirsch are let loose. A touch of vanilla, the framework. Screw cap. 14% alc.
RATING 94 DRINK 2021–2029 $50 NG

Eather & Tedder Great Scot Shiraz 2019, Hunter Valley This is the gentle
face of Hunter Valley shiraz, but don't be fooled by its light, bright colour, nor its
medium body. The third top-quality vintage in a row, its fresh fruits are a light year
away from the earth or leather that used to be the hallmark of the Hunter. Screw
cap. 14% alc. RATING 94 DRINK 2022–2034 $50 JH

ΨΨΨΨΨ **Indie Individual Vineyard Marsanne Roussanne 2021, Hunter Valley**
RATING 93 DRINK 2022–2026 $30 NG

Alexander Munro Individual Vineyard Chardonnay 2021, Hunter Valley
RATING 92 DRINK 2021–2028 $50 NG

XYZ Chardonnay 2021, King Valley RATING 91 DRINK 2021–2026 $25 NG

Aged Release Alexander Munro Individual Vineyard Semillon 2012,
Hunter Valley RATING 91 DRINK 2021–2025 $60 NG

Mercer Wines

426 McDonalds Rd, Pokolbin, NSW 2320 **Region** Hunter Valley
T 1300 227 985 **www.**mercerwines.com.au **Winemaker** Aaron Mercer **Est.** 2020
Dozens 2000

After several years at the bastion of organic Hunter Valley viticulture, Tamburlaine, Aaron
Mercer has set out on his own under the eponymous banner, Mercer Wines. Aaron has been
exposed to a litany of wine styles through his experience across the region, with stints at
Tyrrell's and Brokenwood, in addition to work in France, Germany and California, where he
sourced fruit along the Central Coast from Bien Nacido, Paso Robles and Monterey. Yet it is
the draw of the Hunter, where Mercer was born, that defines his current MO: crafting wines
in small batches to showcase the Hunter's best turf, complemented at times with fruit from
cooler reaches of inter-regional NSW. The range can be purchased via the Mercer website
and at the Small Winemakers Centre, now known as the Wine House Hunter Valley (NG)

ᵀᵀᵀᵀ℧ **Preservative Free Rosé 2021, New South Wales** Shiraz. A pale coral colour. Juicier and slightly more plump and fruitier than its nebbiolo sibling, but no less fresh, frisky, light, evanescent and delicious. Exuberant riffs on musk stick, orange zest and red cherry, befitting its preservative-free idiom. Lip-smacking gear! Screw cap. 12% alc. RATING 91 DRINK 2021-2022 $22 NG ✪

Rouge Preservative Free 2021, New South Wales An intra-state blend of shiraz and montepulciano, made without any SO_2. A mid-weighted feel, pulpy and swiggable. I'd drink this chilled. Shiraz's reductive whiff of iodine melds with the garden herbal lift and ferrous nature of montepulciano. Gentle, mind you. Lithe tannins are soothed by gentle extraction and plenty of sass. Fun drinking. Screw cap. 14% alc. RATING 90 DRINK 2021-2022 $20 NG ✪

Rosato Nebbiolo 2021, Hilltops This is good rosé. Very good, even. Clearly picked early for acid punch and a slaking herbal riff, mingling with orange verbena, pink grapefruit and cumquat notes. Tingly. Long. Juicy enough, mitigating any greenness. I'd like to see half a degree riper, but dangerously drinkable all the same. Screw cap. 12.5% alc. RATING 90 DRINK 2021-2022 $30 NG

ᵀᵀᵀᵀ **Bianco 2021, Hunter Valley** RATING 88 DRINK 2021-2022 $30 NG
Nouveau 2021, Hunter Valley RATING 88 DRINK 2021-2022 $30 NG

Mérite Wines

PO Box 157, Penola, SA 5277 **Region** Wrattonbully
T 0437 190 244 **www**.meritewines.com **Winemaker** Michael Kloak, Colleen Miller
Viticulturist Michael Kloak, Colleen Miller **Est.** 2000 **Dozens** 2000 **Vyds** 45ha
Mérite Wines was established in 2000. It was the end of Mike Kloak and Colleen Miller's protracted search for high-quality viticultural land, with a particular focus on the production of merlot, utilising recently released clones that hold the promise of producing wine of a quality not previously seen. However, it's not a case of all eggs in the same basket; malbec, cabernet sauvignon and shiraz have also been planted. It was not until '13 that the first small amount of wine was made (most of the grapes were, and will continue to be, sold to other winemakers). (JH)

ᵀᵀᵀᵀ℧ **Q Single Vineyard Merlot 2018, Wrattonbully** This is certainly complete and savoury with impressive concentration through the middle palate and finish – an attribute often missing in Australian merlot. The tannins are a highlight; they are fine but gravelly, and give real grip and texture to the palate. Redolent with plums, mulberry, cocoa, licorice and earthy spice. Very smart. Screw cap. 14% alc. RATING 93 DRINK 2021-2031 $32 EL

ᵀᵀᵀᵀ **343 Merlot 2019, Wrattonbully** RATING 88 DRINK 2022-2028 $24 EL

Merricks Estate

97 Thompson Lane, Merricks, Vic 3916 **Region** Mornington Peninsula
T 0419 135 037 **www**.merricksestate.com.au **Open** first w'end of each month & public hols 12–5 **Winemaker** Simon Black (Contract) **Viticulturist** George Kefford **Est.** 1977
Dozens 1800 **Vyds** 4ha
George and Jacky Kefford run Merricks Estate as a weekend and holiday enterprise. It produces distinctive, spicy, cool-climate shiraz, which has accumulated an impressive array of show trophies and gold medals. As the current tasting notes demonstrate, the fully mature vineyard and skilled contract winemaking by Simon Black are producing top class wines. Exports to Hong Kong. (JH)

ᵀᵀᵀᵀᵀ **Chardonnay 2021, Mornington Peninsula** To date, this is the most composed and complete chardonnay from Merricks Estate. Lovely from the start, with its bright straw hue and a glint of green; aromas of ginger flower, creamed honey, white peach, lemon and tangerine. Oak spices kick in and the palate unfurls, layered with flavour but not too much, just right with acidity ensuring it finishes on a high note. Screw cap. 13.5% alc. RATING 95 DRINK 2022-2029 $45 JF

Shiraz 2017, Mornington Peninsula It's full of pepper and spice and all things nice. A neat sync of fruit and savouriness, with a strong iodine and ferrous character adding a layer of intrigue. Grainy tannins and refreshing acidity in check across the medium-bodied palate. Enjoyable to the last drop. Screw cap. 13.5% alc. RATING 95 DRINK 2021–2027 $40 JF

Chardonnay 2020, Mornington Peninsula RATING 93 DRINK 2021–2028 $42 JF
Pinot Noir 2017, Mornington Peninsula RATING 92 DRINK 2021–2025 $45 JF

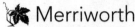 # Merriworth
63 Merriworth Road, Tea Tree, Tas 7017 **Region** Tasmania
T 0406 657 774 **www**.merriworth.com.au **Winemaker** Anna Pooley and Justin Bubb
Viticulturist Mark McNamara **Est.** 2017 **Dozens** 600 **Vyds** 2ha
It was their love of pinot noir that lured Mark McNamara and Kirralee Hatch to Tasmania after several years studying viticulture and winemaking on the Australian mainland. In 2017 they purchased the 2ha Third Child vineyard and renamed it Merriworth. Planted by local John Skinner in 2001 on a hillside overlooking the Jordan River at Tea Tree in the Coal River Valley, the site is home to 9 clones of pinot noir and 3 of riesling, planted on river flats of cracking clay soil and shallow, eroded slopes over dolerite rock. The brand is currently devoted exclusively to riesling and pinot noir from this site. Vibrant, young wines are made with accuracy and precision by Anna Pooley and Justin Bubb.

Estate Riesling 2021, Tasmania A cool season, pristine fruit and acute winemaking make for a delightfully precise riesling. Nuances of rose petal dance over a spine of lemon, lime and Granny Smith apple. Energetic acid drive leads a long finish, brushed with just the right touch of residual sweetness. Screw cap. 12.5% alc. RATING 93 DRINK 2022–2031 $27 TS ✪

Limited WB Pinot Noir 2021, Tasmania RATING 88 DRINK 2022–2022 $36 TS
Estate Pinot Noir 2021, Tasmania RATING 88 DRINK 2022–2024 $39 TS

mesh
40 Eden Valley Road Angaston SA 5353 **Region** Eden Valley
T (08) 8561 3200 **www**.meshwine.com **Winemaker** Robert Hill-Smith, Jeffrey Grosset
Est. 2002 **Dozens** 2000 **Vyds** 12ha
Celebrating its 20th anniversary in '22, mesh is the profound yet unlikely weaving together of the skills, knowledge and ideas of 2 names arguably more obsessive about South Australian riesling than any other: Robert Hill-Smith (fifth-generation at Yalumba) and Clare Valley legend Jeffrey Grosset. Their simple mandate is to champion Eden Valley riesling in a single wine. Fruit is sourced from 2 vineyards planted in 1944 and '82 at 425m elevation. Hill-Smith and Grosset each vinify the same fruit separately, hand picked from alternate rows on the same day. The final blend is determined collaboratively post-vintage, 'amid lively debate.' The result is as legendary as its story anticipates, though unfairly (yet perhaps inevitably) never seems to enjoy quite the limelight enjoyed by Hill-Smith and Grosset's own rieslings. (TS)

Classic Release Riesling 2016, Eden Valley If you need further prodding that riesling is worthy of a place in your cellar, you can always procure a museum release wine such as this stunning '16 from mesh to seal the deal. That initial limey parry-and-thrust focus and velocity has subdued somewhat. The wine takes on notes of oatmeal, beeswax, dried honey and perhaps some soft spice notes that mesh beautifully (see what I did there?) with the existing lime, lemon, grapefruit and blossom characters inherent in the wine. Dry and savoury, with great carry on the finish. We should all be drinking more aged riesling. Screw cap. 12.5% alc. RATING 95 DRINK 2021–2030 $40 DB

Riesling 2021, Eden Valley RATING 93 DRINK 2021–2031 $35 DB

Mewstone Wines

11 Flowerpot Jetty Road, Flowerpot, Tas 7163 **Region** Southern Tasmania
T 0439 367 653 **www**.mewstonewines.com.au **Open** Thurs–Mon 11–4.30
Winemaker Jonathan Hughes **Viticulturist** Luke Andree **Est.** 2011 **Dozens** 5000
Vyds 3.6ha

Brothers Matthew and Jonathan (Jonny) Hughes established Mewstone Vineyard on the banks of the D'Entrecasteaux Channel in 2011. The vineyard is planted on a former cherry orchard, the original 2ha since expanded to 3.6ha consisting mainly of pinot noir (2ha) with 0.7ha each of riesling and chardonnay and a tiny 0.2ha of shiraz. Jonny studied winemaking in NZ before working overseas. Heading home to Tasmania, Jonny settled in as the assistant winemaker at Moorilla Estate for 7 years. With the vineyard established to produce the single-site Mewstone wines, the brothers have embarked on a second label, Hughes & Hughes, which focuses on Tasmania as a whole. Purchasing quality grapes from other local vineyards, this label uses slightly unconventional winemaking techniques that Jonny encountered on his world travels. Small-batch production means he can put maximum effort in. Best New Winery in the Halliday Wine Companion 2019. Exports to Singapore and Italy. (JH)

ŶŶŶŶŶ **Hughes & Hughes Barrel Ferment Flowerpot Riesling 2020, Tasmania**
A totally seductive wine, with a flavour set including fresh ginger, custard apple, and citrus having the last say. Screw cap. 12.4% alc. RATING 95 DRINK 2022-2035 $42 JH
D'Entrecasteaux Channel Chardonnay 2020, Tasmania The complex bouquet and equally complex palate have a generosity beyond the norm for Tasmanian chardonnay. Full mlf the key to the nigh on buttery/toasty flavours and mouthfeel. Screw cap. 12.9% alc. RATING 94 DRINK 2022-2032 $60 JH

Michael Hall Wines

103 Langmeil Road, Tanunda, SA 5352 **Region** Mount Lofty Ranges
T 0448 911 835 **www**.michaelhallwines.com **Open** Fri–Sat 11–5 or by appt
Winemaker Michael Hall **Est.** 2008 **Dozens** 2500

For reasons no longer relevant (however interesting) Michael Hall was once a jewellery valuer for Sotheby's in Switzerland. He came to Australia in 2001 to pursue winemaking – a lifelong interest – and undertook the wine science degree at CSU, graduating as dux in '05. His vintage work in Australia and France is a veritable who's who of producers: in Australia with Cullen, Giaconda, Henschke, Shaw + Smith, Coldstream Hills and Veritas; in France with Domaine Leflaive, Meo-Camuzet, Vieux Telegraphe and Trevallon. He is now involved full-time with his eponymous brand and the wines are as impressive as his experience suggests they should be. Exports to the UK and the US. (JH)

ŶŶŶŶŶ **Pinot Noir 2020, Piccadilly Valley Lenswood** Low rainfall throughout led to a very small crop and a wine of highly concentrated flavour, astonishingly so. Intense aromas of red cherry, redcurrant, fine spices, a hint of red licorice and musk. Draws power as it builds in the mouth. A supple and smooth palate with composed open-weave tannins. Power and grace. Screw cap. 13.5% alc. RATING 96 DRINK 2021-2032 $60 JP ✪
Syrah 2020, Eden Valley Fleshy ripe blood-plum characters underscored by exotic spice, orange blossom, black cherry compote, black pepper and polished leather. Lovely fruit weight and flow, tight granitic tannins, light amaro wafts and a long, black-fruited finish. Screw cap. 13.5% alc. RATING 95 DRINK 2021-2031 $55 DB
Sang de Pigeon Chardonnay 2020, Adelaide Hills Juicy white peach and nectarine characters abound with dots of soft spice, ginger cake, clotted cream, white flowers and softly spoken oak. A splash of lemon enters the fray on the palate, showing lovely clarity and carry, finishing vivid and crisp with a wash of stone fruit and spice. Screw cap. 13.5% alc. RATING 94 DRINK 2021-2027 $32 DB ♥

ŶŶŶŶŸ **Sang de Pigeon Pinot Noir 2020, Adelaide Hills** RATING 93
DRINK 2021-2026 $32 JP

Sang de Pigeon Shiraz 2019, Barossa Valley RATING 93 DRINK 2021-2031 $30 DB
Sauvignon Blanc 2021, Adelaide Hills RATING 91 DRINK 2022-2025 $38 JP
Greenock Roussanne 2021, Barossa Valley RATING 91 DRINK 2021-2026 $45 DB

Michelini Wines

213 Great Alpine Road, Myrtleford, Vic 3737 **Region** Alpine Valleys
T (03) 5751 1990 **www**.micheliniwines.com.au **Open** 7 days, 10–5 **Winemaker** Matt Kilby **Viticulturist** Dino Michelini **Est.** 1982 **Dozens** 12000 **Vyds** 60ha
The Michelini family are among the best-known grapegrowers of the Buckland Valley in North East Victoria. Having migrated from Italy in 1949, they originally grew tobacco, diversifying into vineyards in '82. The main vineyard, on terra rossa soil, is at an altitude of 300m, mostly with frontage to the Buckland River. The Devils Creek Vineyard was planted in '91 on grafted rootstocks with merlot and chardonnay taking the lion's share. A vineyard expansion program has seen the plantings reach 60ha. (JH)

Prosecco NV, Alpine Valleys Fulfils your expectations of prosecco, from the glistening pale colour, persistent mousse and super-fresh apple and lemon aromas through to the sweet sorbety zing on the palate. An easy-drinking prosecco. Crown. 11% alc. RATING 89 $26 JP
Italian Selection Sangiovese 2019, Alpine Valleys Italian by inspiration and in delivery, with a definite savoury edge to this rustic, firm sangiovese. Love the Alpine Valleys herbal thread through this wine, as it meanders around dark cherries, plums, cassia bark and charcuterie, with an enduring earthiness. Medium in body, firm in tannins with a gently tarry edge. It's ready to meet its food match now. Screw cap. 13.5% alc. RATING 88 DRINK 2021-2024 $25 JP

Mike Press Wines

PO Box 224, Lobethal, SA 5241 **Region** Adelaide Hills
T (08) 8389 5546 **www**.mikepresswines.com.au **Winemaker** Mike Press **Est.** 1998
Dozens 12000 **Vyds** 22.7ha
Mike and Judy Press established their Kenton Valley Vineyards in 1998, when they purchased 34ha of land in the Adelaide Hills at an elevation of 500m. They planted mainstream cool-climate varieties (merlot, shiraz, cabernet sauvignon, sauvignon blanc, chardonnay and pinot noir) intending to sell the grapes to other wine producers. Even an illustrious 43-year career in the wine industry did not prepare Mike for the downturn in grape prices that followed and that led to the development of the Mike Press wine label. They produce high-quality sauvignon blanc, chardonnay, rose, pinot noir, merlot, shiraz, cabernet merlot and cabernet sauvignon, which are sold at mouth-wateringly low prices. (JH)

Single Vineyard Pinot Noir Rosé 2021, Adelaide Hills Confection pink hues on this well-priced, attractive young rosé. Boasts plenty of simple, red-fruited appeal: strawberries, cherries, raspberries. Gently creamy to taste. Screw cap. 13% alc. RATING 89 DRINK 2021-2023 $13 JP ○
Single Vineyard Chardonnay 2021, Adelaide Hills A simple, light and ripe style of fruit-driven chardonnay, unoaked. Boasts pear, peach and melon flavours topped with crunchy acidity. All upfront and ready to drink now. Screw cap. 13% alc. RATING 88 DRINK 2021-2023 $13 JP ○
Single Vineyard Sauvignon Blanc 2021, Adelaide Hills Fresh, crisp and varietally true to form with plenty of grapefruit, lime and passionfruit aromas. Smooth and supple across the palate with green mango, melon notes. Soft, sweet finish. Screw cap. 13% alc. RATING 88 DRINK 2021-2023 $13 JP ○

Miles from Nowhere

PO Box 128, Burswood, WA 6100 **Region** Margaret River
T (08) 9264 7800 **www.**milesfromnowhere.com.au **Winemaker** Frederique Perrin, Gary
Stokes **Est.** 2007 **Dozens** 20 000 **Vyds** 46.9ha
Miles from Nowhere is one of the 2 wineries owned by Franklin and Heather Tate. Franklin
returned to Margaret River in 2007 after working with his parents establishing Evans & Tate
from '87 to '05. The Miles from Nowhere name comes from the journey Franklin's ancestors
made over 100 years ago from Eastern Europe to Australia: upon their arrival, they felt they
had travelled 'miles from nowhere'. The plantings include petit verdot, chardonnay, shiraz,
sauvignon blanc, semillon, viognier, cabernet sauvignon and merlot, spread over 2 vineyards
planted over 20 years ago. Exports to the UK, the US, Canada, Asia and NZ. (JH)

Best Blocks Cabernet Sauvignon 2019, Margaret River Salted licorice
and aniseed lace the blackberry fruit. The wine is soft and plump, the oak creates
frame and shape around it in the mouth. There's a gravelly, ferrous character
through the finish which elevates the experience. Screw cap. 14.5% alc. RATING 92
DRINK 2021-2028 $25 EL ✪
Best Blocks Shiraz 2019, Margaret River Juicy, bouncy, spicy and pretty.
Plenty to like here. The fruit, although it spent a not insignificant time in oak,
sings a pure, uncomplicated song. Juicy, concentrated and lovely. Screw cap.
14.5% alc. RATING 91 DRINK 2021-2027 $25 EL

Sauvignon Blanc Semillon 2021, Margaret River RATING 89
DRINK 2022-2024 $15 EL ✪
Best Blocks Chardonnay 2020, Margaret River RATING 89
DRINK 2021-2028 $25 EL
Sauvignon Blanc 2021, Margaret River RATING 88 DRINK 2022-2023
$15 EL ✪

Millbrook Winery

Old Chestnut Lane, Jarrahdale, WA 6124 **Region** Perth Hills
T (08) 9525 5796 **www.**millbrook.wine **Open** Wed–Mon 10–5 **Winemaker** Julian
Langworthy **Viticulturist** John Fogarty **Est.** 1996 **Dozens** 10 000 **Vyds** 8ha
Millbrook is situated in the historic town of Jarrahdale, southeast of Perth. Located at the
picturesque Chestnut Farm, the property backs on to the Serpentine River and is nestled
among jarrah forests. Chestnut Farm dates back to the 19th century, when the original
owner planted an orchard and grapevines in 1865, providing fruit to the local timber-millers
in Jarrahdale. In 1996 Chestnut Farm and Millbrook Winery were bought by Peter and Lee
Fogarty, marking the family's first entry into the wine business. Together with their children
John, Mark and Anna they planted the vineyard. In 2001 a state-of-the-art winery was
completed, including a restaurant. In addition to the 8ha estate, Millbrook draws on vineyards
in prime locations across WA for sauvignon blanc, vermentino, fiano, chardonnay, tempranillo,
grenache, mourvèdre and pedro ximénez. Exports to Malaysia, Hong Kong, Singapore and
Japan. (JH)

Estate Viognier 2021, Western Australia Viognier is one of the key varieties
for Millbrook and it's got a good reputation. It has all the Turkish apricot, red
apple, orchard blossom, frangipani and honeysuckle characters that we associate
with viognier, but it also has a mineral seam of acidity that scrapes through
the wine, keeping things fresh and lively. It's a beautiful wine, again. Screw cap.
13.5% alc. RATING 95 DRINK 2022-2028 $40 EL
Single Vineyard Shiraz 2020, Frankland River Frankland River delivers
characters and textures that you don't get in other parts of WA (or Australia). The
shiraz wines are laden with ferrous, blood, rust, red gravel, and they are evocative
of the vast, open blue skies down there. This wine shows us those parts of itself;
the tannins support the weight of the fruit, the oak imperceptible save for the
texture … testament to the muscle, brawn and might of the fruit. Very smart
indeed. Screw cap. 14.5% alc. RATING 95 DRINK 2021-2031 $35 EL ✪

Limited Release Chardonnay 2020, Geographe This is a big wine: creamy, full bodied, rich, opulent, nutty, dense … all the things. It is old-school, but within that, it is balanced and very satisfying. Horses for courses, this is a glass of largesse; a voluminous wine that will delight many a lover. Screw cap. 14% alc. RATING 94 DRINK 2022-2029 $50 EL

Limited Release Pedro Ximénez NV, Perth Hills Super-fresh, unctuous, and clean as a whistle. Very sweet and quite beautiful, but perhaps lacking in the weight of concentration and intensity that would elevate it overall. The highlight is undoubtedly its freshness. 500ml. Screw cap. 18.5% alc. RATING 94 $60 EL

ΨΨΨΨΩ **Regional Range Fiano 2021, Margaret River** RATING 93 DRINK 2021-2027 $25 EL ✪
Regional Range Viognier 2021, Margaret River Perth Hills RATING 93 DRINK 2021-2027 $25 EL ✪
Single Vineyard Chardonnay 2021, Geographe RATING 93 DRINK 2022-2031 $35 EL
Limited Release Chardonnay 2019, Perth Hills RATING 93 DRINK 2021-2024 $50 JH
Regional Range GSM 2021, Western Australia RATING 92 DRINK 2022-2028 $25 EL ✪
Regional Range GSM 2020, Western Australia RATING 92 DRINK 2025-2035 $25 JH ✪
Regional Range Sauvignon Blanc 2021, Margaret River Geographe RATING 91 DRINK 2021-2023 $25 EL
Regional Range Vermentino 2021, Geographe RATING 90 DRINK 2022-2024 $25 EL
Regional Range Chenin Blanc 2021, Swan Valley RATING 90 DRINK 2021-2030 $25 JH

Millon Wines   ★★★★

48 George Street, Williamstown, SA 5351 **Region** Eden Valley
T (08) 8524 6691 **www**.millonwines.com.au **Winemaker** Angus Wardlaw **Est.** 2013
Dozens 20 000
Millon Wines has 3 vineyards: one in the Eden Valley, the second in the Barossa Valley and the third in the Clare Valley. Winemaker Angus Wardlaw, with a degree in wine science from CSU and experience in the Clare Valley as winemaker at Kirrihill Wines, 'believes the Eden Valley is the future of the Barossa' (see separate entry for his family business, Brothers at War). He makes the Millon wines with a minimalist approach. (JH)

ΨΨΨΨΩ **The Impressionist Riesling 2021, Eden Valley** Pale straw with green flashes in the glass. Aromas of freshly squeezed lime and grapefruit, with some green apple cut and hints of orange and almond blossom and crushed stone. Sapid and brisk, with a lovely crystalline profile and plenty of drive and clarity. Screw cap. 12% alc. RATING 91 DRINK 2021-2031 $18 DB ✪

ΨΨΨΨ **The Impressionist Shiraz 2020, Barossa** RATING 89 DRINK 2021-2016 $18 DB ✪
The Impressionist Pinot Noir 2021, Barossa RATING 88 DRINK 2021-2025 $18 DB
The Impressionist Tempranillo 2021, Barossa RATING 88 DRINK 2021-2026 $18 DB
The Estate Riesling 2021, Eden Valley RATING 88 DRINK 2021-2028 $27 DB

Milton Vineyard

14635 Tasman Highway, Swansea, Tas 7190 **Region** East Coast Tasmania
T (03) 6257 8298 **www**.miltonvineyard.com.au **Open** 7 days 10.30–4.30
Winemaker Anna Pooley, Justin Bubb **Viticulturist** Michael Dunbabin, Robert Elliott
Est. 1992 **Dozens** 11 000 **Vyds** 25ha
Michael and Kerry Dunbabin have one of the most historic properties in Tasmania, dating back to 1826. The property is 1800ha, meaning the vineyard (9ha of pinot noir, 6ha pinot gris, 1.5ha chardonnay, 1ha each of gewürztraminer and riesling, plus 10 rows of shiraz) has plenty of room for expansion. (JH)

TTTT **Reserve Pinot Gris 2021, Tasmania** Boasting a full straw hue with a blush tint, this is a ripe and fleshy gris of accurate pear and grapefruit. Oak fermentation has been well played to build texture that nicely counters both acid zing and bitter phenolic grip, simultaneously building persistence and coherence. Screw cap. 13.4% alc. RATING 90 DRINK 2022–2025 $46 TS

TTTT **Gewürztraminer 2021, Tasmania** RATING 89 DRINK 2022–2022 $28 TS

Miners Ridge

135 Westgate Rd, Armstrong, Vic 3377 **Region** Grampians
T 0438 039 727 **www**.minersridge.com.au **Open** By appt **Winemaker** Adam Richardson **Viticulturist** Andrew Toomey **Est.** 2000 **Dozens** 450 **Vyds** 17ha
Andrew and Katrina Toomey established Miners Ridge Wines in 2000 after many years growing grapes in the Great Western region for other wineries. They decided to take small parcels of their finest fruit and craft a range of wines to reflect their 17ha vineyard site at Armstrong, enlisting experienced local winemaker Adam Richardson (ATR Wines) as their contract winemaker. Their vineyard, nestled on a gentle ridge in the foothills of Victoria's Grampians, takes its name from Chinese gold miners who worked the area's goldfields in the mid 1800s. (JP)

TTTT **Riesling 2021, Grampians** Once again, Grampians riesling rises to the heights many of us know it is capable of. So fine, so delicately floral, in white flowers and in citrus, lime zest, green apple and light spice. Clean, lemon sherbet acidity and crunch through a long, linear finish. Delightful. Trophy Western Victorian Wine Challenge '21 and trophy Ballarat Wine Show '21. Screw cap. 12% alc. RATING 95 DRINK 2022–2028 $25 JP ✪

TTTT **Chardonnay 2021, Grampians** RATING 91 DRINK 2022–2025 $25 JP
Tempranillo 2021, Grampians RATING 90 DRINK 2022–2025 $28 JP

Ministry of Clouds

765 Chapel Hill Road, McLaren Vale, SA 5171 **Region** McLaren Vale
T 0417 864 615 **www**.ministryofclouds.com.au **Open** By appt **Winemaker** Julian Forwood, Bernice Ong **Viticulturist** Richard Leask **Est.** 2012 **Dozens** 5000 **Vyds** 9.6ha
These wines have always been good, but today the best expressions are defined by McLaren Vale, rather than too much external dabbling: detailed wines that are long of limb and vibrant of fruit, dappled with savoury tannins and saline freshness. Clare Valley riesling and Tassie chardonnay are the outliers, dangling from the belt of the Vale's older vines and upper reaches, exciting new varieties including picpoul, mencia and a fringe of cooler Adelaide Hills material. Tim Geddes long made the wines, yet today the team is a triumvirate, with former Wedgetail Estate maker Chris Parsons joining the fray at the new winery. Julian and Bernice craft this and shape that, while Chris is the technical raft. A firm understanding of what varieties grows best where exemplified by 3 new clones of tempranillo, 2 of which are ex-Vega Sicilia. More poignant, one is from their warmer Toro property Pintia. Stay tuned! Exports to the UK, Sweden, Malaysia, Singapore, Hong Kong, South Korea and Thailand. (NG)

TTTT **Kintsugi 2018, McLaren Vale** 85/10/5% grenache, mataro and shiraz. A deliciously spicy and lively bouquet, and a medium-bodied palate travelling along the same pathway to a long and juicy finish. To be gulped, not sipped, thanks to its modest alcohol. Screw cap. 14.2% alc. RATING 97 DRINK 2022-2032 $85 JH ✪

🍷🍷🍷🍷🍷 **Shiraz 2020, McLaren Vale** A wine that is at once complex and fresh, with blackberry, red and black cherry and licorice, aided and abetted by shapely tannins and integrated oak. Screw cap. 14.5% alc. RATING 96 DRINK 2025-2035 $32 JH ✪
Grenache 2020, McLaren Vale Superb colour, vivid and clear; the scented, spicy, flowery bouquet leads a red berry/cherry/piquant palate, savoury elements increasing overall complexity. Screw cap. 14.3% alc. RATING 96 DRINK 2022-2032 $40 JH ✪
Riesling 2021, Clare Valley Pure. Intense. Focused. Long. Lime. Citrus. Apple. All in capital letters. Screw cap. 12.4% alc. RATING 95 DRINK 2021-2031 $32 JH ✪
Grenache Carignan 2021, McLaren Vale Exceptional. Prosaic, I suppose, but the natural buttress of carignan's astringency, wildness and natural acidity obviate Aussie grenache's inherent sweetness. So good! I am having difficult spitting this, such is the first base of saliva-inducing structure. The kirsch, tapenade, white pepper and lavender, a distant second. My favourite wine of the stable. Screw cap. 14.3% alc. RATING 95 DRINK 2021-2026 $32 NG ✪
Grenache 2021, McLaren Vale Expressive. Extremely exotic. Lilac, rosewater, bergamot. The mid palate, defined by a gorgeous pinoté: crunchy red fruits, detail and pin-boned tannins. A tad sweet if picking hairs … delicious! Screw cap. 14.3% alc. RATING 95 DRINK 2021-2028 $40 NG
Chardonnay 2020, Tasmania No new oak, a win-win, reducing the cost price while focusing on the exceptional quality of the fruit. It has drive and complexity, with grapefruit leading the layered fruit, creamy cashew and sustained length. Screw cap. 12.9% alc. RATING 95 DRINK 2021-2031 $48 JH
Onkaparinga Rocks Single Vineyard Shiraz 2019, McLaren Vale A refined nose of oscillating tension and flare: iodine, tapenade, blue-fruit aspersions, but just a glimpse. A smoky underbelly, with the cards played close to the chest. Meaty and firm. Florals, too. McLaren grit, sandy detail and salinity. A bit tangy. This should age well over the mid term. Screw cap. 14.4% alc. RATING 94 DRINK 2021-2028 $65 NG

Minnow Creek   ★★★☆

42 Frontenac Avenue, Panorama, SA 5041 (postal) **Region** McLaren Vale
T 0404 288 108 www.minnowcreekwines.com.au **Winemaker** Tony Walker **Est.** 2005
Dozens 1600
Tony Walker spent 6 years as winemaker at Fox Creek, after 2 previous vintages in Beaujolais and Languedoc. He founded Minnow Creek in 2005, not with any fanfare of (marketing) trumpets, but simply to make very good wines that reflected their place and their variety; the Lopresti family providing many of the grapes for the best red wines of Minnow Creek. (JH)

🍷🍷🍷🍷🍸 **Shiraz 2019, McLaren Vale** Honest regional gear, made very well. Some smoky barrel ferment complexity melded to star anise, clove, fruitcake spice, anise and oodles of blue- and black-fruit references. This will please those seeking honest, well-priced regional representation. Screw cap. 14.5% alc. RATING 91 DRINK 2021-2025 $28 NG

Mino & Co Wines   ★★★☆

113 Hanwood Avenue, Hanwood, NSW 2680 **Region** Riverina
T (02) 6963 0200 www.minoandco.com.au **Open** Mon–Fri 8–4.30, w'ends by appt
Winemaker Sam Trimboli **Est.** 1997 **Dozens** 12375
The Guglielmino family, specifically father Domenic and sons Nick and Alain, founded Mino & Co in 1997. From the outset they realised that their surname could cause problems of pronunciation, so they simply took the last 4 letters for the name of their business. Mino & Co has created 2 brands: Signor Vino and A Growers Touch. Signor Vino covers wines made

from Italian varieties sourced from the Adelaide Hills, Riverina and Riverland. The A Growers Touch brand covers traditional varieties, often with local growers who have been working with the family for over 2 decades. The wines are made at Hanwood Winery (established on what was once a drive-in cinema). Exports to the UK and NZ. (JH)

 Signor Vino Vermentino 2021, Riverina By far the best of this range, this boasts an extra degree of mid-weighted ripeness, mid-palate weight, textural detail and fidelity to variety. A clear skein of saline freshness articulates riffs on white pepper, lemon drop, fennel and raw almond. A fine, long, mineral-driven finish. This has a 'je ne sais quoi' class that belies its affordability. Screw cap. 13.5% alc. RATING 91 DRINK 2021–2024 $18 NG ❂

A Growers Touch Durif 2019, Riverina RATING 89 DRINK 2021–2026 $20 NG

Mr Barval Fine Wines ★★★★★

7087 Caves Road, Margaret River, WA 6285 **Region** Margaret River
T 0407 726 077 **www.**mrbarval.com **Open** 7 days 11–5 **Winemaker** Robert Gherardi
Est. 2015 **Dozens** 1300

Robert Gherardi was born with wine in his blood. As a small boy he'd go to Margaret River to pick grapes with 3 generations of his extended Italian family. The grapes were taken to his grandmother's backyard to begin the fermentation, followed by a big lunch or dinner to celebrate the arrival of the new vintage to be. At 25 he enrolled in the full oenology and viticulture degree. This led to employment at Moss Wood for 4 years, then Brown Hill Estate as assistant winemaker and finally to Cullen for 3 years. Vanya Cullen encouraged him to travel to Barolo and work with Elio Altare for 3 harvests over a five-year period. He returns to Italy each year for his boutique travel business, with customised tours of Barolo, Valtellina and further north. And so he arrived at the name for his winery: Margaret River, Barolo and Valtellina. Exports to Singapore and Hong Kong. (JH)

Cabernet Malbec 2019, Margaret River Savoury, dense and super-spicy, with exotic pan-fried spices (star anise, cinnamon, fennel seeds and licorice root). This has tobacco leaf and saltbush, apple blossom and rhubarb. It is detailed and dark, with admirable depth of flavour that lingers long after the wine has gone. The sweet core of pure fruit comes in right on the back palate. Quite an intriguing wine, one you definitely would/could/should not mindlessly consume. Screw cap. 14.4% alc. RATING 95 DRINK 2022–2036 $40 EL
Giro di Nebbiolo 2019, Margaret River The sweet, bright strawberry characters inherent in the Nebbia have morphed into something decidedly more savoury here. Balsamic poached strawberries in place of fresh, brambly blackberries, enlivening briny acidity and most importantly, grippy, chewy tannins. The tannins are the highlight, and I'm so glad they are. This is malleable, kaleidoscopic and engaging, with tomato, tobacco leaf, dried basil and licorice. The start of the journey. Screw cap. 13.9% alc. RATING 94 DRINK 2022–2032 $65 EL
Riserva Cabernet Sauvignon 2019, Margaret River Star anise, salted licorice, leather strap and raspberry compote. This is supple and lithe, the fruit pliable and lush. Beauty lives here. Screw cap. 14.2% alc. RATING 94 DRINK 2022–2037 $90 EL

Mistral 2021, Margaret River RATING 93 DRINK 2022–2027 $33 EL
Chardonnay 2021, Margaret River RATING 92 DRINK 2022–2028 $45 EL
Nebbia 2021, Margaret River RATING 90 DRINK 2022–2027 $40 EL

Mr Mick ★★★★

7 Dominic Street, Clare, SA 5453 **Region** Clare Valley
T (08) 8842 2555 **www.**mrmick.com.au **Open** 7 days 10–5 **Winemaker** Tim Adams,
Brett Schutz **Est.** 2011 **Dozens** 30 000 **Vyds** 195ha

This is the venture of Tim Adams and Pam Goldsack. The name was chosen to honour KH (Mick) Knappstein, a legend in the Clare Valley and the broader Australian wine community. Tim worked at Leasingham Wines with Mick between 1975 and '86, and knew him well. When Tim and Pam acquired the Leasingham winery in Jan 2011, together with its historic buildings, it brought the wheel full circle. Various commentators (including myself) have used Mick's great one-liner: 'There are only 2 types of people in the world: those who were born in Clare, and those who wish they had been'. Exports to NZ and Taiwan. (JH)

ΨΨΨΨΨ **Riesling 2021, Clare Valley** This delivers a classy and totally inline riesling for $17. That's not bad, considering the wines I used to drink for the same price back in the day. Lemon zest, lime flesh, green apples and a lick of chalk. Everything here, everything good. Screw cap. 12.2% alc. RATING 90 DRINK 2021-2028 $17 EL ❂

Rosé 2021, Clare Valley So it's a little bit sweet, it's got plenty of flavour (think along the lines of raspberry, pomegranate, watermelon and strawberry), it's vibrant and it's uncomplicated. The acid is pert enough to prop it all up, making for some seriously unfettered and delicious summer drinking. Value for money is hard to beat, here. Screw cap. 11.5% alc. RATING 90 DRINK 2022-2023 $17 EL ❂

Shiraz 2018, Clare Valley Surprisingly, 24 months in predominantly American oak has not yielded an oak bomb. Instead, the fruit has enough heft and weight to rise above the oak that encases it, and drives the wine across the mouth – powered by blackberries, cocoa, cassis, jubes and gentle spice. Compelling drinking for the money. Big bang for buck, if big flavour is your proclivity. Screw cap. 14.7% alc. RATING 90 DRINK 2021-2027 $17 EL ❂

ΨΨΨΨ **Grenache 2021, Clare Valley** RATING 89 DRINK 2022-2025 $17 EL ❂
Vermentino 2021, Clare Valley RATING 88 DRINK 2022-2024 $17 EL ❂

Mr Riggs Wine Company ★★★★★

169 Douglas Gully Road, McLaren Flat, SA 5171 **Region** McLaren Vale
T 1300 946 326 **www.**mrriggs.com.au **Winemaker** Ben Riggs **Est.** 2001
Dozens 28 000 **Vyds** 12ha

With over a quarter of a century of winemaking experience, Ben Riggs is well established under his own banner. Ben sources the best fruit from individual vineyards in McLaren Vale, Clare Valley, Adelaide Hills, Langhorne Creek, Coonawarra and from his own Piebald Gully Vineyard (shiraz and viognier). Each wine expresses the essence of not only the vineyard but also the region's terroir. The vision of the Mr Riggs brand is unpretentious and personal: 'To make the wines I love to drink'. He drinks very well. Exports to the US, Canada, Denmark, Sweden, Germany, the Netherlands, Switzerland, Singapore, NZ and Hong Kong. (JH)

ΨΨΨΨΨ **JFR Shiraz 2019, McLaren Vale** A massive wine (and bottle), opaque in colour, and equally densely packed into the mouth, with blackberry, dark chocolate and licorice; oak and ripe tannins filling any chance omission with yet more flavour. Strictly for those who love full-bodied wines. Diam. 14.5% alc. RATING 96 DRINK 2024-2039 $50 JH ❂

Montepulciano d'Adelaide 2020, Adelaide Hills Anyone wondering about the potential of the montepulciano grape in this country need wonder no more. It's in good hands. Ben Riggs combines some Aus-Italian sensibility here, promoting the grape's noteworthy tannin:acid profile with some stellar fruit intensity. Red plums, cherry and dried herbs aplenty, with warm and earthy savoury notes to complete the picture. Goes down very easily. Screw cap. 14.5% alc. RATING 94 DRINK 2021-2028 $30 JP ❂

Sanjo Sangiovese 2020, Adelaide Hills An ultra-fragrant array of raspberry, cherry and allspice scents, the palate living up to the promises of the bouquet with its sour-cherry base note sliding through to the finish and aftertaste. Screw cap. 14.5% alc. RATING 94 DRINK 2023-2028 $35 JH

The Chap 2016, McLaren Vale Coonawarra Ridiculously heavy bottle. Shiraz/cabernet blend. The colour is still a youthful deep crimson, the full-bodied palate still with rampant tannins largely ex fruit, but also oak. Needs 20 years to fully open up. Diam. 14.5% alc. RATING 94 DRINK 2036-2046 $100 JH

🍷🍷🍷🍷🍷 Burnt Block Shiraz 2019, McLaren Vale RATING 93 DRINK 2021-2026 $55 NG
Battle Axe Sparkling Shiraz NV, McLaren Vale RATING 92 $35 NG
Woodside Sauvignon Blanc 2021, Adelaide Hills RATING 92 DRINK 2022-2024 $22 JP ⊙
Yacca Paddock Tempranillo 2021, Adelaide Hills RATING 92 DRINK 2021-2028 $30 JP
Cold Chalk Chardonnay 2020, Adelaide Hills RATING 92 DRINK 2021-2026 $30 JP
Idle Lane Shiraz 2019, McLaren Vale RATING 92 DRINK 2021-2026 $30 NG
Outpost Cabernet 2020, Coonawarra RATING 91 DRINK 2022-2030 $25 EL
Piebald Syrah 2020, Adelaide Hills RATING 91 DRINK 2021-2027 $30 JP
Mr Brightside Preservative Free Shiraz 2021, McLaren Vale RATING 90 DRINK 2021-2023 $22 NG
The Bolter Cabernet Sauvignon 2020, McLaren Vale RATING 90 DRINK 2022-2027 $25 NG
The Bolter Shiraz 2020, McLaren Vale RATING 90 DRINK 2022-2026 $25 NG
The Magnet Grenache 2020, McLaren Vale RATING 90 DRINK 2022-2026 $30 NG

Misty Glen Wines   ★★★

293 Deasys Road, Pokolbin, NSW 2320 **Region** Hunter Valley
T (02) 4998 7781 **www**.mistyglen.com.au **Open** Fri, Sun, Mon 10–4, Sat 10–5
Winemaker Contract **Est.** 1985 **Dozens** 1000 **Vyds** 6.85ha
Vicci Lashmore-Smith and Eric Smith purchased the Wright Family Wines business in Dec 2009. Part of the vineyard dates back to '85, supplemented by an additional 3ha planted between 2000–2002; the varieties planted include chardonnay, cabernet sauvignon, semillon, chambourcin, shiraz and sauvignon blanc. (JH)

🍷🍷🍷🍷 Semillon 2019, Hunter Valley This is a very ripe iteration of the regional flagship. A curb of lemongrass and tonic, indicative of DNA. Otherwise, pineapple chunks, dried mango and glazed stone fruits. Pleasant drinking on the earlier side. I wouldn't be cellaring this. Screw cap. 12.7% alc. RATING 89 DRINK 2021-2025 $30 NG

Mitchell

246 Hughes Park Road, Sevenhill via Clare, SA 5453 **Region** Clare Valley
T (08) 8843 4258 **www**.mitchellwines.com **Open** 7 days 11–5 **Winemaker** Andrew Mitchell, Simon Pringle **Viticulturist** Angus Mitchell **Est.** 1975 **Dozens** 15 000 **Vyds** 70ha
One of the stalwarts of the Clare Valley, established by Jane and Andrew Mitchell, producing long-lived rieslings and cabernet sauvignons in classic regional style. The range now includes very creditable semillon, grenache and shiraz. A lovely old stone apple shed is the cellar door and upper section of the upgraded winery. Children Angus and Edwina are now working in the business, heralding generational changes. Over the years, the Mitchells have established or acquired 70ha of vineyards on 4 excellent sites, some vines over 60 years old; all are managed organically, with biodynamic composts used for over a decade. (JH)

🍷🍷🍷🍷🍷 Sevenhill Vineyard Cabernet Sauvignon 2017, Clare Valley The release window is just about correct here: at 5 years old it has softened considerably from the early, frisky, vivacity that cabernet exudes, and all things have melted into one. The spice, the fruit, the acid and the oak are seamlessly joined, making it difficult to seperate or tease apart. Elegant, mid weight and generally lovely. It has

an heirloom tomato/claret aspect which is most appealing. Screw cap. 13% alc.
RATING 93 DRINK 2022–2029 $30 EL

Pinot Gris 2021, Clare Valley A barrel ferment component is evident both
aromatically and in the mouth, however it's subtle enough to work in concert
with the fruit. Nashi pears, salted lychee and layers of white plum, crushed
limestone and even snow pea tendrils. Lots to like, and framed by soft talcy
phenolics. Very fresh. Screw cap. 13% alc. RATING 92 DRINK 2022–2025 $25 EL ✪

Peppertree Vineyard Shiraz 2017, Clare Valley Bright acidity punctuates
the array of red and purple berries in the mouth, providing structure and a life of
its own. The oak is nicely integrated, as expected after all this time. The wine tails
out elegantly over the finish, showing class and restraint at all times. Screw cap.
14% alc. RATING 91 DRINK 2021–2028 $30 EL

Kinsfolk Grenache 2018, Clare Valley Alpine mountain herbs on the nose,
chaperoned by licorice root and purple berries. In the mouth the wine is fresh
and detailed (not voluminous), the tannins are very fine and chalky. Despite the
sweet fruit, there are shavings of deli meat and pan-fried exotic spice (star anise,
turmeric etc), making for engaging and very pretty drinking. Screw cap. 13.5% alc.
RATING 90 DRINK 2022–2027 $40 EL

🍷🍷🍷🍷 **Watervale Riesling 2021, Clare Valley** RATING 89 DRINK 2023–2036 $25 EL

Mitchell Harris Wines ★★★★★

38 Doveton Street North, Ballarat, Vic 3350 **Region** Pyrenees
T (03) 5331 8931 **www**.mitchellharris.com.au **Open** Sun–Mon 11–5, Tues–Thurs 11–9,
Fri–Sat 11–11 **Winemaker** John Harris **Est.** 2008 **Dozens** 2300
Mitchell Harris Wines is a partnership between Alicia and Craig Mitchell and Shannyn and
John Harris. John, the winemaker, began his career at Brown Brothers, then spent 8 years as
winemaker at Domaine Chandon in the Yarra Valley, cramming in Northern Hemisphere
vintages in California and Oregon. The Mitchell and Harris families grew up in the Ballarat
area and have an affinity for the Macedon and Pyrenees regions. While the total make is not
large, a lot of thought has gone into the creation of each of the wines, which are sourced
from the Pyrenees, Ballarat and Macedon regions. In '12 a multipurpose space was created in
an 1880s brick workshop and warehouse providing a cellar door, bar and education facility.
Exports to Switzerland. (JH)

🍷🍷🍷🍷🍷 **Sabre 2018, Victoria** 78/22% chardonnay/pinot noir. The chardonnay hails
from the Macedon Ranges, the pinot noir is a blend of Henty and Pyrenees. Love
the cut and thrust of this ultra fine, complex sparkling, its cool-climate sourcing
producing a wine of real class. Former Domaine Chandon sparkling winemaker,
John Harris, continues to astound now that he is out on his own. Natural acidity
brings real drive and a strong linear focus. Flinty on the nose with chalky lemon,
apple, stone fruits and nougat, it moves into a complex whole on the palate. Three
years on yeast lees release a lovely nutty intricacy of flavours, spice and texture.
A top Aussie sparkling. Cork. 12% alc. RATING 96 $50 JP ✪ ♥

Wightwick Vineyard Pinot Noir 2021, Ballarat You know when a wine is
good, it has presence. This '21 pinot has it, from the lifted freshness of florals, red
cherries, cranberries, earthy beetroot and whole-bunch herbals, to the cut and
thrust of sapid, fine tannins and flash of dark chocolate and smoky oak to close.
It's a ripper. Screw cap. 12.5% alc. RATING 95 DRINK 2022–2031 $45 JP

🍷🍷🍷🍷🍷 **Wightwick Vineyard Chardonnay 2021, Ballarat** RATING 93
DRINK 2022–2031 $45 JP

Sangiovese 2021, Pyrenees RATING 92 DRINK 2022–2027 $30 JP

Sauvignon Blanc Fumé 2021, Pyrenees RATING 92 DRINK 2022–2027
$30 JP

Pinot Meunier & Sangiovese Rosé 2021, Pyrenees RATING 90
DRINK 2022–2025 $30 JP

Mitchelton

Mitchellstown via Nagambie, Vic 3608 **Region** Nagambie Lakes
T (03) 5736 2222 **www**.mitchelton.com.au **Open** 7 days 10–5 **Winemaker** Andrew
Santarossa **Viticulturist** Andrew Santarossa **Est.** 1969 **Dozens** 35 000 **Vyds** 139ha
Mitchelton was founded in 1969 by Ross Shelmerdine, named after the explorer Thomas
Mitchell, who passed by here. Ross had a splendid vision for the striking winery, restaurant,
now-iconic observation tower and surrounding vineyards. Owned by Gerry Ryan OAM
(founder of Jayco) since 2012, Mitchelton is a destination in its own right, with music concerts
'on the green' hosting such varied luminaries as Dame Kiri Te Kanawa and Jimmy Barnes;
a hotel and spa also opened in 2018. Wine quality has remained consistent over the years,
particularly of the top-tier shiraz. Mitchelton has estate vineyards in both Nagambie and
Heathcote and purchases fruit from growers across Victoria. Exports to Singapore, Indonesia,
South Korea and Vietnam. (JH)

ŸŸŸŸŸ **Single Vineyard Toolleen 2019, Heathcote** Another exciting journey into
Heathcote shiraz territory from a maker who now calls it home, among other
regions. Presents the beauty and strength of the grape, with gorgeous, inviting
blackberry fruits, violet, lifted florals and woodsy spices. The joy here is the balance
achieved, the promotion of fruit set against supporting ribbons of fine tannin.
A fine example of what the region is about. Screw cap. 14.7% alc. RATING 95
DRINK 2021-2031 $50 JP
Spring Single Block Shiraz 2019, Heathcote The Spring Block continues
to excite with a fine follow-up to the '18 vintage. Heathcote characters to the
fore in cassis, blue fruits, dried herbs, woody spice, bracken and briar. Smooth and
supple across the palate, with a lively touch of pepper popping up. In top drinking
form, but there is considerable potential here for ageing. Screw cap. 14.8% alc.
RATING 95 DRINK 2021-2033 $75 JP
Print Shiraz 2019, Heathcote Plenty of changes over the years for the Print
label. Fruit sourcing is now from Heathcote (a good move) and the bottle is
bigger and heavier than ever (reasoning for this is less clear). Plush, deep and
concentrated, it brings Heathcote shiraz into the limelight, dressing it discreetly
in oak and allowing its natural power and elegance to shine. One for the cellar.
Screw cap. 14.8% alc. RATING 95 DRINK 2022-2032 $145 JP
Vine To Wine Arinto 2021, Nagambie Lakes The more you see the
Portuguese white grape, arinto, in Australia, the higher the excitement meter
jumps. It's making itself at home in Nagambie Lakes with its lifted green apple,
lime zest, lemon and pretty floral aromatics. Shows great depth of fruit intensity
for one so young, with lively spice and even livelier bright acidity. Screw cap.
12.5% alc. RATING 94 DRINK 2021-2026 $38 JP

ŸŸŸŸŸ **Blackwood Park Riesling 2021, Nagambie Lakes** RATING 92
DRINK 2021-2027 $28 JP
Shiraz 2020, Heathcote RATING 92 DRINK 2022-2028 $38 JP
Estate Grown Shiraz 2019, Heathcote RATING 92 DRINK 2021-2030 $45 JP
Mourvèdre Rosé 2021, Nagambie Lakes RATING 91 DRINK 2022-2024
$38 JP
Chardonnay 2020, Yarra Valley RATING 90 DRINK 2022-2025 $38 JP

Mitolo Wines

141 McMurtrie Road, McLaren Vale, SA 5171 **Region** McLaren Vale
T (08) 8323 9304 **www**.mitolowines.com.au **Open** Thurs–Mon 10–5 **Winemaker** Ben
Glaetzer **Est.** 1999 **Dozens** 40 000
Mitolo had a meteoric rise once Frank Mitolo decided to turn a winemaking hobby into a
business. In 2000 he took the plunge into the commercial end of the business, inviting Ben
Glaetzer to make the wines. Split between the Jester range and single-vineyard wines, Mitolo
began life as a red wine–dominant brand but now produces a range of varietals. In Nov '17
Mitolo opened their $3 million tasting room, restaurant and event space with a flourish.
Exports to all major markets. (JH)

ŸŸŸŸŸ **Scylla 2021, McLaren Vale** Nero seems sublimely suited to the warmer spots of the Vale, albeit, the vines are young. If this is anything to go by, we have much to look forward to! A sumptuous nose of peppery kirsch, maraschino cherry and tomato bush. The palate, one of a pulpy effusiveness as much as a lithe tannic precision. This is not merely a throwback, but a generously flavoured wine of flavour, texture and imminent drinkability. Really delicious. Screw cap. 14.5% alc. RATING 93 DRINK 2021-2026 $39 NG

Of the Earth Pinot Noir 2021, Adelaide Hills It has been a while since I tasted an Adelaide Hills pinot worth getting excited about. This comes close. A tad green, but I'll give it the benefit of the doubt. It will build in stature. A luminescent ruby. Crunchy red fruits, a sluice of sassafras, garden herb and bright maritime freshness towing it long. A lovely wine. Akin to a cru beaujolais in its current manifest, best drunk cool. Well worth following. Screw cap. 13% alc. RATING 93 DRINK 2021-2029 $69 NG

Angela Shiraz 2019, McLaren Vale Archetypal regional shiraz, with far more detail, aplomb and freshness than in the past. American oak, clear. Maple, vanilla and mocha. And yet the fruit is transparent and vibrant, corralled and shaped, rather than subsumed by it. Violet, iodine, blue and boysenberry and a lovely trail of clove, white pepper and anise. Screw cap. 14.5% alc. RATING 93 DRINK 2022-2032 $39 NG

Jester Shiraz 2020, McLaren Vale A solid house wine with plenty of flavour, good value, nicely managed tannins and a whiff of tradition within a more contemporary-styled package. Dark cherry, plum, lilac, iodine, a smear of olive and a trail of peppery freshness. Thoroughly impressive at the price. Screw cap. 14.5% alc. RATING 92 DRINK 2022-2030 $25 NG ✪

Of the Wind Chardonnay 2021, Adelaide Hills While layers have been built into this with a textural winemaking weave, it lacks flavour. Chablis exceeds this alcohol level and it is considerably chillier. The oak, though, sublime. The lees work, skilful. The bones impressive. Screw cap. 12.5% alc. RATING 91 DRINK 2022-2029 $49 NG

la Spiaggia Sparkling Glera NV, McLaren Vale Glera, otherwise known as prosecco. This is good drinking. The higher acidity from a leaner harvesting window, mopping up the dollop of RS across the finish. A confluence of Granny Smith, baked golden pear and citrus granita. A gently peppery, frothy and effortless flow. Screw cap. 10% alc. RATING 90 $29 NG

Jester Cabernet Sauvignon 2020, McLaren Vale The winemaking at this address has become far more attuned to region, site and style, not to mention contemporary demands for lighter, more vital wines. While this, as with its shiraz brethren, is rich and impactful, there is a welcome freshness. The tannins here, not quite as well shaped. But for the price, savoury and nourishing all the same. Screw cap. 14.5% alc. RATING 90 DRINK 2022-2030 $25 NG

ŸŸŸŸ **Jester Vermentino 2021, McLaren Vale** RATING 88 DRINK 2021-2023 $25 NG

Molly Morgan Vineyard   ★★★☆

496 Talga Road, Rothbury, NSW 2320 **Region** Hunter Valley
T (02) 4930 7695 **www**.mollymorgan.com **Winemaker** Usher Tinkler
Viticulturist Jacob Wiseman **Est.** 1963 **Dozens** 2000 **Vyds** 7.66ha
Established by the Roberts family in 1963, later acquired by a syndicate headed by Andrew Simon of Camperdown Cellars fame. Molly Morgan focuses on estate-grown wines from vines up to 50+ years old (the semillon planted in 1963, shiraz and chardonnay following in stages through to '97). The vineyard is named after an exceptionally resourceful woman who was twice convicted and sent to NSW, married 3 times (the last time when she was 60, her husband aged 31). Out of this improbable background she emerged as a significant benefactor of the sick, earning the soubriquet 'Queen of the Hunter'. (JH)

MoMo Semillon 2018, Hunter Valley An aged release, this semillon is true to form: lightweight yet strident; balletic yet intense of flavour. Lemon curd, sherbet, glazed quince and dried straw, with adolescence dawning and middle age at least several years down the track. Screw cap. 11.5% alc. RATING 93 DRINK 2021–2030 $25 NG ✪

 Rosé 2021, Hunter Valley RATING 89 DRINK 2021–2022 $25 NG

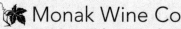

Monak Wine Co

5691 Sturt Highway, Monak, NSW 2738 **Region** Murray Darling
T 418570064 **www**.monakwineco.com.au **Open** By appt **Winemaker** Cindy Heley
Est. 2020
Monak Wine Co. is a relatively new addition to the Murray Darling wine scene (its first vintage was in 2020) but the woman behind it has been making wine in the region for more than 25 years. Owner and winemaker, Cindy Heley, works with local winegrowers and also grows 'hard-to-source varieties'. Her passion lies in the soil and the people of the Murray Darling and she is a strong advocate for highlighting its untapped potential, especially with alternative varieties that thrive in the region's warm, dry conditions. She is particularly interested in viognier, petit verdot and touriga nacional. Production is focused on small-batch winemaking; the first vintage in 2020 crushed just 20t of grapes. Her interest in alternative varieties saw Cindy judge at the 20th Australian Alternative Varieties Wine Show in Mildura in Nov '21. (JP)

 Mon Doyen GSM 2020, Murray Darling 50/30/20% shiraz/grenache/ mourvèdre. This wine is named after the winemaker's late brother, Dean. Magnums of the wine are available, with proceeds going to rural men's mental health. A ripe, impressive wine but one also pretty light on its feet, showing both richness of fruit and aromatic fineness. Layers of cassis, earth, bush mint, aniseed and mourvèdre pepper light up the palate, fully supported by firm, fine tannins. Give it some air to start and enjoy. Screw cap. 14% alc. RATING 90 DRINK 2022–2026 $29 JP

 Mon Cinq Viognier 2020, Murray Darling RATING 89 DRINK 2021–2023 $25 JP

Montague Estate

325 Tom Cullity Drive, Margaret River WA 6280 **Region** Margaret River
T (08) 9755 6995 **www**.montagueestate.com.au **Open** Wed–Sun 11–5
Winemaker Jonathan Mettam **Viticulturist** Tim Quinlan **Est.** 2020 **Dozens** 3475
Vyds 28.5ha
Montague Estate is located in Wilyabrup on what was previously the old Heydon Estate vineyard, and prior to that, Arlewood. The vineyard was planted in 1988 to chardonnay (3.5ha), shiraz (2.8ha), semillon (1.3ha), cabernet sauvignon (1.2ha), sauvignon blanc (0.8ha) and petit verdot (0.4 ha). Tim Quinlan has been looking after the vines there since Heydon Estate days; the wines are made by Jono Mettam. This release is the first under the label, and includes wines made from grapes sourced in Frankland River. (EL)

 Pax Reserve Chardonnay 2021, Margaret River P58 clone. This, like the estate chardonnay, is streamlined. When you consider that the fame and fortune of Margaret River chardonnay is built upon the foundation of the Gingin clone, it is almost scandalous to make a reserve chardonnay from a clone that is anything but. Here we see the potential and the sophistication of the P58 clone in full flight: salted white peach, curry leaves, red apple skins, lemon pith, brine, quartz-like minerality and an array of crushed nuts through the finish. The high acid has a ripe and juicy tang through the finish – just enough to demand another sip. Super-smart and tight. Screw cap. 13.9% alc. RATING 95 DRINK 2022–2032 $65 EL

Viribus Reserve Cabernet Sauvignon 2020, Margaret River This has more horsepower and drive than the estate cabernet, perhaps more traditionally structured, in a cabernet sense. The tannins are chewy and ripe and frame the succulent raspberry/pomegranate/cassis core of fruit – there are shades of salted deli meat and sumac, too. Lashings of exotic spice and leaf: saltbush, bay leaf, tobacco leaf and pink peppercorns. There's a classicism about this wine ... while it's big and ripe, it has balance and finesse courtesy of the briny acidity. It will age gracefully – love to see it again in 5 years. I bet it will be singing. Screw cap. 14.5% alc. RATING 95 DRINK 2022–2037 $80 EL

♀♀♀♀♀ **Chardonnay 2021, Margaret River** RATING 93 DRINK 2022–2030 $38 EL
Tribus GSM 2021, Frankland River Margaret River RATING 93
DRINK 2022–2032 $40 EL
Grenache 2021, Frankland River RATING 93 DRINK 2022–2032 $50 EL
Petit Verdot 2020, Margaret River RATING 93 DRINK 2022–2032 $48 EL
Mataro 2021, Frankland River RATING 92 DRINK 2022–2030 $48 EL
Cabernet Sauvignon 2019, Margaret River RATING 92 DRINK 2022–2030
$38 EL
Sauvignon Blanc Semillon 2021, Margaret River RATING 91
DRINK 2022–2027 $26 EL
Aurum Blanc de Blanc 2019, Margaret River RATING 90 $52 EL
Semillon 2021, Margaret River RATING 90 DRINK 2022–2032 $42 EL

Montalto   ★★★★★

33 Shoreham Road, Red Hill South, Vic 3937 **Region** Mornington Peninsula
T (03) 5989 8412 **www**.montalto.com.au **Open** 7 days 11–5 **Winemaker** Simon Black
Viticulturist Dan Prior **Est.** 1998 **Dozens** 12 000 **Vyds** 47ha
John Mitchell and family established Montalto in '98, but the core of the vineyard goes back to '86. It is planted to pinot noir, chardonnay, pinot gris, riesling, shiraz, tempranillo and sauvignon blanc. Intensive vineyard work opens up the canopy, with yields of 3.7–6.1t/ha. Wines are released in 3 ranges: the flagship Single Vineyard, Montalto estate wines and Pennon Hill. Montalto leases several external vineyards that span the peninsula, giving vastly greater diversity of pinot noir sources and greater insurance against weather extremes. There is also a broad range of clones adding to that diversity. Montalto has hit new heights with its wines from these blocks. Exports to the Philippines, Japan, South Korea, Singapore, Malaysia and Canada. (JH)

♀♀♀♀♀ **Single Vineyard Merricks Block Pinot Noir 2020, Mornington Peninsula**
By some distance, the deepest colour of the quartet in this tasting, and the most powerful, with savoury, foresty texture and structure. The MV6 plum leads the expansive fruit palette, backed up by firm but balanced tannins. Will live long. Screw cap. 13.5% alc. RATING 97 DRINK 2022–2035 $70 JH ✪

♀♀♀♀♀ **Single Vineyard Main Ridge Block Pinot Noir 2020, Mornington
Peninsula** Among the lightest of colours, but – as with all the Montalto pinots – bright and clear, the perfumed red cherry and plum bouquet a striking foreplay to the palate. Screw cap. 13.5% alc. RATING 96 DRINK 2022–2030 $70 JH ✪
Single Vineyard Tuerong Pinot Noir 2020, Mornington Peninsula
Splitting hairs, the colour is the most developed – and lightest – of the 4 Montalto pinots in this tasting, ex whole bunch, and has a highly fragrant fruit expression, spanning the cherry family, and complexed by whole bunch a la Simon Black. Screw cap. 13.5% alc. RATING 96 DRINK 2022–2032 $70 JH ✪
North One Pinot Noir 2020, Mornington Peninsula The bouquet is redolent of warm oriental spices, introducing a supremely elegant palate and its lithe finish. Screw cap. 13.5% alc. RATING 96 DRINK 2022–2030 $90 JH
Estate Chardonnay 2020, Mornington Peninsula When released alongside its single-block siblings, this often turns out as a solid performer, but this vintage, it takes centre stage. Definitely working off a citrus theme, all lemon and grapefruit with some finger-lime juicy acidity; a hint of smoky reduction adds to its

appeal. It's still tight, linear and racy, yet doesn't lack flavour. Screw cap. 13% alc.
RATING 95 DRINK 2021–2028 $45 JF

Single Vineyard Tuerong Syrah 2020, Mornington Peninsula A highly
fragrant bouquet with a poultice of warm Asian spices to choose from, the palate
rippling with fine savoury tannins through the long finish. Screw cap. 13.5% alc.
RATING 95 DRINK 2023–2030 $70 JH

Montara

76 Chalambar Road, Ararat, Vic 3377 **Region** Grampians
T (03) 5352 4798 **www**.montarawines.com.au **Winemaker** Simon Fennell **Est.** 1970
Dozens 3000 **Vyds** 19.2ha
Montara gained considerable attention for its pinot noirs during the '80s and continues
to produce wines of distinctive style under the ownership of no less than 6 siblings of
the Stapleton family. As I (James) can attest from several visits over the years, the view from the
cellar door is one of the best in the Grampians region. Simon Fennell, with an extensive
winemaking history, including assistant winemaker at Best's Wines, and with direct knowledge
of the Grampians region, has replaced long-serving winemaker Leigh Clarnette. Exports to
the US, Canada, Indonesia, Taiwan and Hong Kong. (JH)

🍷🍷🍷🍷🍷 **Museum Release Chalambar Road Shiraz 2010, Grampians** A wine of
soulful depth and impressive intensity, once again clearly expressing the grape in
its western environment. There's power here, too, all within a medium-bodied
frame as it explores scents and flavours of dark, ripe berries, dusty cocoa powder,
baked earth and the Aussie bush with just a touch of eucalyptus. Still youthful, still
gathering pace with a sweet-fruited core that lights up the wine. Still has a way to
go. Cork. 14.8% alc. RATING 96 DRINK 2021–2027 $82 JP

Single Vineyard Shiraz 2020, Grampians Complex and complete red,
sporting a deep spiciness, earth, pepper and dark cherries. Flows natural and long
in total integration, which is remarkable given the amount of new oak involved.
A simple decant will energise and release its beauty. Screw cap. 13% alc. RATING 94
DRINK 2021–2030 $40 JP

🍷🍷🍷🍷♀ **Riesling 2021, Grampians** RATING 92 DRINK 2021–2030 $27 JP
Shiraz 2020, Grampians RATING 90 DRINK 2021–2028 $27 JP

Monteperle Wines

74 God's Hill Road, Lyndoch, SA 5351 **Region** Barossa Valley
T **www**.monteperle.com.au **Open** By appt **Winemaker** Tony Carapetis **Viticulturist**
Advanced Viticulture and Management **Est.** 2017 **Dozens** 60 000 **Vyds** 15.85ha
In 2017, Shenzhen-based Jia Yuan Hua Wines bought the 24.3ha Max's Vineyard in Gods Hill
Road, Lyndoch at the southern end of the Barossa Valley. Tony Carapetis was brought onboard
as chief winemaker and the Monteperle wines made their debut at the China International
Import Expo (CIIE) in '19. Grenache, shiraz, mataro and cabernet sauvignon are planted in
the vineyard and the range features a GSM and Reserve offerings of each of the grape varieties
where they present rich, classically structured Barossa wines focusing on the premium end
of the market. With a production of 60 000 bottles a year, China would have obviously been
the primary market for these wines but they are available in Australia in select outlets. (DB)

🍷🍷🍷🍷♀ **Reserve Shiraz 2018, Barossa Valley** An unashamedly big, bruising, classical
style with intense blackberry and black-plum-jam notes; hints of roasting meats,
clove and baking spice, dark chocolate and loads of toasty oak. Super-concentrated,
with strong grainy tannin and charry black-fruited heft on the finish. Cork.
14.7% alc. RATING 93 DRINK 2021–2035 $185 DB

GSM 2018, Barossa Valley A blend of 48/39/13% grenache/shiraz/mataro.
There is a deep, slightly broody core of fruit here, shaded black and sheathed in
oak spice, earth and Old Jamaica chocolate notes. Composed in a classical style,
with medium-grain tannins, fresh acidity and meaty black fruits on the finish.
Screw cap. 15.2% alc. RATING 91 DRINK 2021–2028 $65 DB

Reserve Mataro 2018, Barossa Valley A muscular, earthy mataro aged for 21 months in 100% new French oak; a wine that appears squarely aimed at the Chinese market. Deep blackberry and dark plum characters with plentiful spice notes and hints of earth, dark chocolate, licorice, polished leather and roasting meats. Dense, rich with strong tannin flex and broody exit. Cork. 15.6% alc. RATING 91 DRINK 2021-2035 $165 DB

Reserve Cabernet Sauvignon 2018, Barossa Valley A concentrated, classically composed Barossa cabernet sauvignon. Fruit notes of rich blackberry, blackcurrant and cassis with hints of tobacco, cedar, vanillin oak spice and licorice. Full bodied, with impressive fruit density, compact chocolatey tannin and a lingering finish of black fruits and French oak spice. Cork. 14.1% alc. RATING 91 DRINK 2021-2035 $185 DB

Monterra

RSD1436 Meadows Road, Willunga, SA 5172 **Region** McLaren Vale
T 0428 581 177 **www.**monterrawines.com.au **Winemaker** Daniel Zuzulo **Est.** 2014
Dozens 20 000 **Vyds** 15ha

Yet another venture by Canadian-born and raised (but long-term McLaren Vale resident) Norm Doole (in partnership with Mike Farmilo and Nick Whiteway). A grapegrower for decades, Norm founded DOWIE DOOLE with Drew Dowie in '95. Monterra, under the wine banner of Field Day, has been a centre of activity in McLaren Vale in recent years. It flew under the radar when established in '14, busy with barrel finance and logistics and Norm Doole's mind-spinning roles with the Willunga Basin Water Company, Southern Adelaide Economic Development Board and Boar's Rock. Wines are made from the Adelaide Hills, McLaren Vale, Barossa Valley and Fleurieu Peninsula. Exports to the US, Hong Kong, Thailand and Singapore. (JH)

Élevage Shiraz Tempranillo 2020, McLaren Vale The fruit is sumptuous and clearly of high quality. I'd like to see bolder winemaking, however. Mocha, menthol, vanilla and coffee grind tannins, all largely oak driven, meld with reductive tension and its notes of iodine and florals. Dark- and blue-fruit aspersions stuffed into the fray, too. A slick, full-bodied wine that will please many. Cork. 14.5% alc. RATING 92 DRINK 2021-2027 NG

Élevage Shiraz 2020, McLaren Vale Floral, concentrated and sweet of fruit. Reliant on a sheen of oak (75% new) and gently extracted tannins for structure. Less of the former and more of the latter would be appreciated. Rich. Plush. Smooth FM in liquid form. Easy-listening sort of stuff. A skein of peppery acidity breaks up the raft of blueberry, nori and kirsch. Screw cap. 14.5% alc. RATING 92 DRINK 2021-2029 NG

Reserve Shiraz 2020, McLaren Vale Restrained for such a warm year. Nice tension, too, across a bow of well-appointed oak (15% new) and dutifully extracted tannins, no matter how conventional the winemaking. Boysenberry, iodine, salumi and faint floral notes. The finish, clove and a spray of pepper. Solid drinking. Screw cap. 14.5% alc. RATING 91 DRINK 2021-2030 $45 NG

Cabernet Sauvignon 2020, McLaren Vale A McLaren Vale set piece, with its display of ripe, rich fruit and commensurate level of cedary oak. Blackberries, plums, nutmeg, cinnamon, and earth, with a gentle leafiness, are varietally on point. Oak steps up on the palate and together with firm, chewy tannins, leads the wine long and strong. Screw cap. 14% alc. RATING 90 DRINK 2021-2027 $30 JP

Sauvignon Blanc 2021, Adelaide Hills RATING 89 DRINK 2021-2023 $30 JP
Mt Pleasant Pinot Noir 2021, Adelaide Hills RATING 88 DRINK 2022-2025 $30 JP
Pinot Grigio 2021, Adelaide Hills RATING 88 DRINK 2021-2024 $30 JP
Vineyard Select No. 1 Shiraz 2018, McLaren Vale RATING 88 DRINK 2021-2024 $25 JP

Moores Hill Estate

3343 West Tamar Highway, Sidmouth, Tas 7270 **Region** Northern Tasmania
T (03) 6394 7649 **www**.mooreshill.com.au **Open** 7 days 11–5 **Winemaker** Julian
Allport **Est.** 1997 **Dozens** 5000 **Vyds** 7ha
The Moores Hill Estate vineyard (owned by winemaker Julian Allport and Fiona Weller plus
Tim and Sheena High) consists of pinot noir, riesling, pinot gris and chardonnay, with a very
small amount of cabernet sauvignon and merlot. The vines are located on a northeast-facing
hillside, 5km from the Tamar River and 30km from Bass Strait. Moores Hill became Tasmania's
first 100% solar-powered winery in '17. All wines are made onsite. (JH)

ŸŸŸŸŸ **Riesling 2021, Tasmania** The long ripening season of the cool 2021 vintage has
built impressive concentration and persistence of flavour, spanning the full riesling
spectrum from Granny Smith apple and lime to more exotic nuances of guava and
frangipani. The tension of the season marks out a taut acid line, interrupted by the
grip and bite of phenolic presence on the finish. Screw cap. 11.5% alc. RATING 91
DRINK 2021-2022 $35 TS
Pinot Noir 2020, Tasmania Judicious use of whole bunches lifts the spicy,
herbal and floral nuances of Tamar Valley pinot. A core of juicy, ripe, red and black
berry fruits is backed a little assertively by firm, slightly coarse tannin grip. Screw
cap. 13.5% alc. RATING 90 DRINK 2024–2027 $40 TS

ŸŸŸŸ **Pinot Gris 2021, Tasmania** RATING 89 DRINK 2021-2022 $35 TS
Chardonnay 2020, Tasmania RATING 88 DRINK 2022-2025 $40 TS

Moorilla Estate

655 Main Road, Berriedale, Tas 7011 **Region** Southern Tasmania
T (03) 6277 9960 **www**.moorilla.com.au **Open** Fri–Mon 12–5 **Winemaker** Conor van
der Reest **Est.** 1958 **Dozens** 11 000 **Vyds** 15.36ha
Moorilla Estate was the second winery to be established in Tasmania in the 20th century.
However, through much of the history of Moorilla Estate, it was the most important
winery in the state, if not in size then as the icon. Production is around 160t/year, sourced
entirely from the vineyards around Moorilla and its St Matthias Vineyard (Tamar Valley).
The winery is part of an overall development said by observers (not Moorilla) to have cost
upwards of $150 million. Its raison d'être is the establishment of Mona, which has the highest
atmospheric environment accreditation of any gallery in the Southern Hemisphere, housing
both the extraordinary ancient and contemporary art collection assembled by Moorilla's
owner, David Walsh, and visiting exhibitions from major art museums around the world.
Exports to South Korea, Hong Kong, Singapore and Taiwan. (JH)

ŸŸŸŸŸ **Muse Cabernet Sauvignon Cabernet Franc 2016, Tasmania** An
impressively affordable introduction to the wonders of Tasmanian cabernet.
Ripeness is always the game in this space, and this is an exemplar. At 5 years of age
its blackcurrant and cassis core is integrating impeccably, with a strong backdrop of
firm, fine tannin structure that promises another decade of potential yet. Screw cap.
14.9% alc. RATING 94 DRINK 2026-2031 $40 TS

ŸŸŸŸŸ **Muse Extra Brut 2016, Tasmania** RATING 93 DRINK 2026-2036 $75 TS
Extra Brut 2009, Tasmania RATING 92 DRINK 2021-2034 $45 TS

Moorooduc Estate

501 Derril Road, Moorooduc, Vic 3936 **Region** Mornington Peninsula
T (03) 5971 8506 **www**.moorooducestate.com.au **Open** 7 days 11–5 **Winemaker** Dr
Richard McIntyre, Jeremy Magyar **Viticulturist** Peninsula Vine Care **Est.** 1983
Dozens 6000 **Vyds** 14ha
Richard McIntyre has taken Moorooduc Estate to new heights, having completely mastered
the difficult art of gaining maximum results from wild-yeast fermentation. Starting with the
2010 vintage, there was a complete revamp of grape sources and hence changes to the tiered

structure of the releases. These changes were driven by the simple fact that the McIntyre vineyard could only yield 1500 dozens, and by leasing additional Mornington Peninsula vineyards the business was able to expand to the 5000-6000 dozen produced annually. Daughter Kate McIntyre MW joined the business full-time after attaining her master of wine in '10. The entry-point wines under the Devil Bend Creek label remain principally sourced from the Osborn Vineyard; the mid-priced Chardonnay and Pinot Noir are now sourced from multiple sites. The single-vineyard Robinson Pinot Noir and Chardonnay, Garden Vineyard Pinot Noir and McIntyre Shiraz are priced a little below the ultimate 'Ducs' (The Moorooduc McIntyre Chardonnay and Pinot Noir). Exports to the UK, the US and Hong Kong. (JH)

♟♟♟♟♟ **Robinson Vineyard Chardonnay 2020, Mornington Peninsula** Such a pristine wine with its definition, purity and superfine acid line. Balanced flavours of grapefruit and nougat. Tangy, flinty and moreish, with terrific length. Impossible to hold back pouring another glass. So don't. Screw cap. 13% alc. RATING 96 DRINK 2022-2028 $60 JF ✪

Chardonnay 2020, Mornington Peninsula A rather tight, linear and super-refreshing chardonnay from a site that often has a bolder expression. I like this a lot. Of course it has flavour, more on a citrus theme, with lemon pith and peel, juicy and zesty across the palate. There's a dab of creamy lees and oak spice adding another layer of depth. Screw cap. 13% alc. RATING 95 DRINK 2022-2028 $40 JF

Pinot Gris On Skins 2020, Mornington Peninsula A tantalising pale orange-pink hue with loads of flavour. It's campari-like in bitterness and flavour with blood orange and zest, making it extra refreshing. It's also spiced with fennel seeds, quinine, sandalwood and the phenolics are just right – giving shape and a pleasant grip to the finish. I love this. Screw cap. 13.5% alc. RATING 95 DRINK 2022-2024 $40 JF

Robinson Vineyard Pinot Noir 2020, Mornington Peninsula A pale ruby hue, but don't let that fool you as there's a heady introduction coming: herbs and exotic spices, warm earth and macerated cherries, with a kiss of sweet cedary oak. Light and fine across the palate, lacy tannins giving a gentle pull to the finish. A gorgeous wine. Screw cap. 13.5% alc. RATING 95 DRINK 2022-2027 $60 JF

The Moorooduc McIntyre Vineyard Pinot Noir 2020, Mornington Peninsula A theme through all of the pinots in '20 at Moorooduc Estate is a gentleness, restraint and here, elegance. The usual varietal charms are at play but dialled down, a light combo of spiced cherries, earth and ironstone with cedary oak. Tannins are fine and lightly grainy, the finish long and feathery light. Delicious drinking now, rather than for the long term. Screw cap. 13.5% alc. RATING 95 DRINK 2022-2027 $80 JF

Pinot Noir 2020, Mornington Peninsula Almost gentle and pretty but that doesn't mean wimpy. It's lightly sappy, with red fruits obviously – cherry to the fore – plus blood orange, exotic spices and a savouriness throughout. Juicy and sweetly-fruited across the palate, with fine tannins and refreshment guaranteed immediately. Screw cap. 13.5% alc. RATING 94 DRINK 2022-2025 $40 JF

The Moorooduc McIntyre Vineyard Chardonnay 2020, Mornington Peninsula The impression is of a wine still coming together. It will. Plenty of flavour with peach, lemon balm, roasted nuts and cedary oak neatly in place. Fleshy and tangy across the palate, with a pleasant savoury edge. Screw cap. 13% alc. RATING 94 DRINK 2023-2028 $80 JF

♟♟♟♟♟ **Garden Vineyard Pinot Noir 2020, Mornington Peninsula** RATING 90 DRINK 2023-2027 $60 JF

Morambro Creek Wines   ★★★★

Riddoch Highway, Padthaway, SA 5271 **Region** Padthaway
T (08) 8723 1065 **www**.morambrocreek.com.au **Winemaker** Ben Riggs **Est.** 1994
Dozens 30 000 **Vyds** 178.5ha
The Bryson family has been involved in agriculture for more than a century, moving to Padthaway in 1955 as farmers and graziers. From the '90s they have progressively established

large plantings of shiraz (88.5ha), cabernet sauvignon (47.5ha), chardonnay (34.5ha) and sauvignon blanc (8ha). The Morambro Creek and Mt Monster wines have been consistent winners of wine show medals. Exports to the UK, the US and other major markets. (JH)

♥♥♥♥♥ **Shiraz 2019, Padthaway** Really full bodied and intense shiraz here. Layer after layer of black fruit, licorice spice and star anise, pouring through the mouth in rivulets of flavour. The tannins are fine and shapely, contributing to the rolling mouthfeel. Quite gorgeous, all things in balance. Screw cap. 14.5% alc. RATING 94 DRINK 2022-2032 $35 EL

♥♥♥♥♀ **Jip Jip Rocks Shiraz 2020, Padthaway** RATING 90 DRINK 2022-2026 $23 EL
Jip Jip Rocks Shiraz Cabernet 2020, Padthaway RATING 90 DRINK 2022-2027 $23 EL

Mordrelle Wines

411 River Road, Hahndorf, SA 5243 **Region** Adelaide Hills
T 0448 928 513 **www.**mordrellewines.com.au **Open** By appt **Winemaker** Martin Moran **Viticulturist** Martin Moran **Est.** 2010 **Dozens** 2000
Based in Hahndorf in the beautiful Adelaide Hills, Mordrelle Wines is owned by Martin Moran together with his wife Michelle and her family, David and Jane Dreckow. The Mordrelle portfolio sources fruit from their own small vineyard in the nearby village of Mylor, as well as pinot noir, syrah, sauvignon blanc, grüner veltliner and a few styles of chardonnay from other Adelaide Hills locations. A special focus has been bottle-fermented Blanc de Blancs with extended time on lees from 5 to 10 years. Martin has also worked on viticulture research projects in Langhorne Creek and (tapping into his Argentinian roots) has made Malbec from there as well as a regional trophy-winning Barbera and other varieties. Mordrelle's labels are created from original artworks painted by Jose Luis Moran, Martin's late father. Exports to Denmark. (TL)

♥♥♥♥♥ **Clone 1654 Basket Press Syrah 2016, Adelaide Hills** We could debate the use of syrah vs shiraz as a descriptor, but suffice to say that this is quite a mouthful of cool-climate florals, ripe fruit and a wealth of spice. Lifted and aromatic, it strolls across the palate at an easy pace providing texture and fine tannins with a nod to smart, toasty oak. Plenty of life and intensity here. Screw cap. 14.5% alc. RATING 95 DRINK 2021-2027 $40 JP
Blanc de Blanc Late Disgorged Chardonnay 2012, Adelaide Hills So fresh! An aged blanc de blancs, 8 years on lees, disgorged on demand and given a crown seal which goes a long way to explaining the vibrancy and complexity to be found in this sparkling. White flowers, lemon, grapefruit and oyster-shell aromas. Bright acidity, intense mousse, clean and brisk across the palate. It's all here. Crown. 12% alc. RATING 94 DRINK 2022-2022 $100 JP

♥♥♥♥♀ **Sauvignon Blanc 2020, Adelaide Hills** RATING 92 DRINK 2021-2025 $30 JP
Blanc de Blancs Reserva Chardonnay 2016, Adelaide Hills RATING 91 $80 JP
Clone 1125 Syrah 2016, Adelaide Hills RATING 91 DRINK 2022-2028 $40 JP
Basket Press Pinot Noir 2020, Adelaide Hills RATING 90 DRINK 2022-2025 $35 JP
The Gaucho Malbec 2020, Langhorne Creek RATING 90 DRINK 2021-2030 $35 JP
Reserva 2019, Adelaide Hills RATING 90 DRINK 2021-2027 $40 JP

Morgan Simpson

PO Box 39, Kensington Park, SA 5068 **Region** McLaren Vale
T 0417 843 118 **www.**morgansimpson.com.au **Winemaker** Richard Simpson **Est.** 1998
Dozens 1200 **Vyds** 17.1ha
Morgan Simpson was founded by SA businessman George Morgan (since retired) and winemaker Richard Simpson, a CSU graduate. The grapes are sourced from the Clos

Robert Vineyard, planted to shiraz (9ha), cabernet sauvignon (3.5ha), mourvèdre (2.5ha) and chardonnay (2.1ha), established by Robert Allen Simpson in 1972. Most of the grapes are sold, the remainder used to provide the reasonably priced, drinkable wines for which Morgan Simpson has become well known: they are available through their website. (JH)

🍷🍷🍷🍷🍷 **Reprieve Shiraz 2018, McLaren Vale** A wine that bridles the sweet fruit and American oak-centric bourbon and vanilla of yore, with a smattering of whole-bunch inclusion, spice and the levity of a more contemporary expression. The oak dominates the nose, before segueing to dark cherry, anise, lilac, bitter chocolate and suede. The finish, sweet of scent and reasonably long of linger. A strong regional expression. Screw cap. 14.2% alc. RATING 91 DRINK 2021–2026 $45 NG

Two Clowns Chardonnay 2019, McLaren Vale A little lacking across the mid palate, but a minor gripe. A little tired, perhaps. But plump and savoury in all. A meld of phenolics and acidity drives this. Far better than what I anticipated. Reminiscent of an easy-goer from the Mâconnais. Best drunk soon. Screw cap. 12% alc. RATING 90 DRINK 2021–2025 $20 NG ✪

Morningside Vineyard

665 Middle Tea Tree Road, Tea Tree, Tas 7017 **Region** Southern Tasmania
T (03) 6268 1748 **Open** By appt **Winemaker** Samantha Connew **Viticulturist** Mark Hoey **Est.** 1980 **Dozens** 600 **Vyds** 2.8ha

The name 'Morningside' was given to the old property on which the vineyard stands because it gets the morning sun first; the property on the other side of the valley was known as Eveningside. Established in 1980 by Peter and Brenda Bosworth, Morningside was acquired by the Melick and Hall families (owners of the adjacent Pressing Matters vineyard) in 2019. Consistent with the observation of the early settlers, the Morningside grapes achieve full maturity with good colour and varietal flavour. (JH)

🍷🍷🍷🍷🍷 **Chardonnay 2020, Tasmania** A year before release, this is tightly coiled chardonnay that rides rails of cool season Coal River Valley acidity. High-tensile lemon and apple fruit is well framed by subtle, high-class French oak. Sam Connew's exacting precision is on full display here, and all it calls for is a decade or 2 to soften. Screw cap. 13.5% alc. RATING 92 DRINK 2030–2040 $49 TS

Morris

Mia Mia Road, Rutherglen, Vic 3685 **Region** Rutherglen
T (02) 6026 7303 www.morriswines.com **Open** Mon–Sun 10–4 **Winemaker** David Morris **Est.** 1859 **Dozens** 100000 **Vyds** 96ha

One of the greatest of the fortified winemakers, ranking an eyelash behind Chambers Rosewood. Morris has changed the labelling system for its sublime fortified wines with a higher-than-average entry point for the (Classic) Liqueur Muscat; Topaque and the ultra-premium wines are being released under the Old Premium Liqueur (Rare) label. The art of these wines lies in the blending of very old and much younger material. These Rutherglen fortified wines have no equivalent in any other part of the world (with the honourable exception of Seppeltsfield in the Barossa Valley). In July 2016 Casella Family Brands acquired Morris after decades of ownership by Pernod Ricard. (JH)

🍷🍷🍷🍷🍷 **Old Premium Rare Topaque NV, Rutherglen** The perpetual understudy to Rutherglen's more celebrated and vivacious muscat, Morris lifts Topaque – aka muscadelle – up to where it belongs, as an equal. The perfume envelops the drinker, the palate astounds in waves of dried fruit, toffee, honey cake, caramel and roasted nuts, luscious but nicely kept trim and clean in neutral spirit. The work of a master. 500ml bottle. Screw cap. 17.5% alc. RATING 98 $90 JP ✪

Old Premium Rare Muscat NV, Rutherglen Each year I reach for superlatives, each year I give up: imagine your favourite dessert and then multiply it tenfold: plum pudding, dark chocolate, sticky date, panforte with fruit peel, caramel sauce, all smoothly honed and lifted by neutral spirit. And the best part is, for all of its lusciousness, it remains attainable. 500ml bottle. Screw cap. 17% alc. RATING 97 $90 JP ✪

ỲỲỲỲ **CHM Charles Henry Morris Shiraz 2018, Rutherglen** Old-school through and through, making a powerful statement about old vines, tradition and endurance. Impenetrable, dark and dense black-garnet hues. It's far from shy but it is balanced (even at 15% alcohol!) with a robust, rich display of fruitcake, cassis, aniseed, clove, nutmeg, a rustic earthiness, coffee and vanilla. Deeply complex tied up in sapid, fine tannins. Just starting life. Screw cap. 15% alc. RATING 95 DRINK 2022-2042 $50 JP

Classic Topaque NV, Rutherglen A well-priced masterpiece. The perfume is both fresh, sweet and savoury. The palate sets the tastebuds alight in honeyed walnuts, butterscotch, malt biscuits and golden raisins, with a nutty rancio lift. Finishes with a clean, tannic splash of muscadelle's signature cold tea. Great value. 500ml. Screw cap. 17.5% alc. RATING 95 $25 JP ✪

CHM Durif 2018, Rutherglen Rhis is in the heroic mould of Rutherglen durif, one that relies on not broaching it too early. Built to last, the base is formed of prominent mocha chocolate oak with overlays of rich, ripe black fruits, spiced plum pudding, tiramisu and a touch of mandarin peel. Tannins are staunch, structure is firm. Potential for ageing is almost endless. Screw cap. 15% alc. RATING 94 DRINK 2022-2036 $60 JP

VP Vintage 2009, Rutherglen Compared to its sibling, the '08 VP, this wine seems markedly younger, fresher and the brandy spirit more obvious. What a difference a year makes. It is still in building mode, but I suspect it will be a more elegant VP, more aromatic, floral and a wine to remember. Screw cap. 19% alc. RATING 94 $25 JP ✪

Classic Muscat, Rutherglen Meets the pricepoint and smashes it with complexity and vibrancy. So much life and energy in this aged muscat, from the lifted aromatics and lusciousness of raisin, orange peel, caramel, mocha-coffee and gentle rancio nuttiness, to the freshness of younger material and clean, neutral spirit. Works a treat. 500ml. Screw cap. 17.5% alc. RATING 94 $25 JP ✪

Moss Brothers ★★★★

351 Herdigan Road, Wandering, WA 6308 **Region** Margaret River
T 0402 275 269 **www**.mossbrotherswines.com.au **Winemaker** Rory Parks **Est.** 1984
Dozens 7000 **Vyds** 16.03ha
This is the reincarnation of the Moss Brothers brand, though not its vineyards, which were acquired by Amelia Park in 2015. It is a parallel business to Trove Estate. Paul Byron and Ralph Dunning are the major forces in both ventures, both with extensive whole-of-business expertise across Australia. Exports to the US. (JH)

ỲỲỲỲ **Fidium Shiraz 2020, Margaret River** Supple, pliable and spicy. Very good. 2020 was a burster year for shiraz in Margaret River. Perhaps the best. This kind of texture and flavour quality is common. A lovely wine. Jubey. Screw cap. 14.5% alc. RATING 94 DRINK 2022-2029 $55 EL

ỲỲỲỲ **Fidium Cabernet Sauvignon 2020, Margaret River** RATING 91 DRINK 2024-2034 $55 EL

Moses Rock Grenache 2021, Geographe RATING 90 DRINK 2022-2028 $32 EL

Moses Rock Cabernet Sauvignon 2020, Margaret River RATING 90 DRINK 2022-2030 $32 EL

Moss Wood ★★★★★

926 Metricup Road, Wilyabrup, WA 6284 **Region** Margaret River
T (08) 9755 6266 **www**.mosswood.com.au **Open** By appt **Winemaker** Clare Mugford, Keith Mugford **Est.** 1969 **Dozens** 11 000 **Vyds** 18.14ha

Widely regarded as one of the best wineries in the region, producing glorious chardonnay, power-laden semillon and elegant cabernet sauvignon that lives for decades. Moss Wood also owns Ribbon Vale Estate, the wines treated as vineyard-designated within the Moss Wood umbrella. Exports to all major markets. (JH)

ŶŶŶŶŶ **Chardonnay 2020, Margaret River** Last year I commented on the 2019 vintage, that it was 'an opulent, luxurious style of chardonnay ... tempered by the cool season'. Be careful what you wish for. Here, through the lens of the warm and ripe '20 vintage, a wine of unbridled, sybaritic luxury is revealed. It has rivulets of flavour tucked in at every possible place, and effortlessly displays the full spectrum of brine, toffee apples, yellow peach, apple skins, some curry leaves and plush, juicy acid. Don't hold it back, and don't wish for the restraint of a cool year – this wine needs to be itself, to be its best. Screw cap. 14% alc. RATING 97 DRINK 2022-2037 $93 EL ❂
Cabernet Sauvignon 2019, Margaret River This is a masterclass in refinement. It is svelte and streamlined, the cool, mineral spool of flavour across the tongue is what the '19 vintage can look like at its most restrained and harnessed. The length of flavour basically flutters out over the finish, so weightless and enduring. The '18 that came before it had a thundering, legendary quality – legs widespread, hands on hips, power pose. This is the creative in the family, the quiet guy. It's intriguing and intelligent and thoughtful ... poignantly red-fruited, spicy and super-supple. I'm descending into hyperbole. It's unnecessary. This is another great Moss Wood release. Screw cap. 14% alc. RATING 97 DRINK 2022-2042 $170 EL

ŶŶŶŶŶ **Ribbon Vale Cabernet Sauvignon 2019, Margaret River** The '18 Ribbon Vale Cabernet Sauvignon almost had me falling off my chair it was so good. This is no different. Like the '18, it is silky, sumptuous and very fine: red fruited, floral, spicy and shaped by fine, chalky tannins. It is a superstar, and at $72, a bargain for the quality you receive. If you're a fan of Moss Wood cabernet, this is the wine you should drink while you wait for the MW to come of age. Screw cap. 14% alc. RATING 96 DRINK 2022-2037 $72 EL ❂
Pinot Noir 2019, Margaret River This wine has a decades-long history of graceful long ageing, so one presumes this vintage will be no different. It has poise, fruit clarity and length. Redcurrants, black cherries, Pink Lady apples, pink peppercorns, jasmine tea tannins and fine, salty acidity. The flavour endures long after the wine has gone. Supple, spicy and layered with red fruits, this is a gorgeous pinot of shape and line. Screw cap. 14% alc. RATING 96 DRINK 2022-2042 $80 EL ♥
Semillon 2021, Margaret River Powerful, dense and almost muscular, this cool-vintage iteration of semillon shows a tight core of apple and lime fruit, wrapped in layers of lemongrass, wisps of jalapeño, coriander root and apple skins. The top notes stray onto the exotic-spice spectrum, with fresh nutmeg, saffron and even za'atar. All this to say, a unique, restrained and precise expression, although a further year in bottle will likely assist in settling some of the early friskiness it has right now. Screw cap. 14.5% alc. RATING 95 DRINK 2022-2032 $46 EL
Ribbon Vale Elsa 2020, Margaret River 90/10% sauvignon blanc/semillon, barrel fermented. The move away from clear juice to slightly cloudy (in 2019) has moved this into big boy's territory, full bodied if you will, but none the worse for that. Screw cap. 14% alc. RATING 95 DRINK 2022-2027 $80 JH
Ribbon Vale Merlot 2019, Margaret River This is supple and lithe; layers of raspberry and cocoa, licorice and clove. In the mouth there is saltbush and bay leaf, and it's beautiful. The structure is fine, it doesn't have that slippery, formless shape that can so afflict merlot from Margaret River. This is Château Lafleur-like in its subtle framework and enduring line. Lovely. Screw cap. 13.5% alc. RATING 95 DRINK 2022-2037 $72 EL

Mount Benson Estate ★★★★

329 Wrights Bay Road, Mount Benson, SA 5275 **Region** Mount Benson
T 0417 996 796 **www**.mountbensonestate.com.au **Open** 7 days 10–5 Sept–Jun
Winemaker Contract **Est.** 1988 **Dozens** 800 **Vyds** 24.2ha
The owners of Mount Benson Estate have one obvious advantage: husband Brian Nitschinsk
served for 39 years in the Australian Navy, retiring as a commander engineer. Figuratively,
Mount Benson (a puny rise measured in only tens of metres) has one foot in the Southern
Ocean and one foot on the ground, so Brian should feel right at home. Wife Carolyn was
a secondary school teacher specialising in art and visual communication. Thus, the cold
windswept landscape of winter is something they can surely cope with. The legacy of
2 generations of the founding Wehl family already demonstrated the ability of the vineyard to
produce shiraz of exceptional quality, cabernet sauvignon not far behind. (JH)

ŸŸŸŸŸ **Reserve Syrah 2019, Mount Benson** The oak is evident here, but not much
can suppress the intensity and concentration of the fruit. Blackberry, blueberry
compote, blood plums, raspberry and cranberry are bolstered by clove, licorice,
red apple skins and shavings of hung deli meat. Very smart. Screw cap. 14.6% alc.
RATING 94 DRINK 2021–2029 $45 EL

ŸŸŸŸŸ **Block 8 Syrah 2018, Mount Benson** RATING 93 DRINK 2021–2028 $35 EL
Syrah Cabernet Sauvignon 2019, Mount Benson RATING 92
DRINK 2022–2029 $35 EL

Mt Bera Vineyards ★★★☆

PO Box 372, Gumeracha, SA 5233 **Region** Adelaide Hills
T (08) 8189 6030 **www**.mtberavineyards.com.au **Winemaker** Jeanneret Wines **Est.** 1997
Dozens 900 **Vyds** 11.63ha
In 2008, Greg and Katrina Horner (plus 4 kids and a growing collection of animals) purchased
Mt Bera from Louise Warner. Both Greg and Katrina grew up on farms, and the 75ha
property, with its homestead built in the 1880s, was irresistible. The property is located in a
sanctuary overlooking the Torrens Valley, looking out to Adelaide, 45 mins drive away. Much of
the production is sold, but the intention is to increase the range and quantity of estate wines.
Exports to the UK. (JH)

ŸŸŸŸŸ **Pinot Gris 2019, Adelaide Hills** A soft light pink blush indicates skin contact
during winemaking, and the lovely textural quality of this wine confirms
it. Distinctly gris-like in scent, the spiced pear, honeysuckle and hay notes
are varietally rich. Fruit flavours are warm and round, the texture more so.
A nice big mouthful of pinot gris right here. Screw cap. 13% alc. RATING 90
DRINK 2021–2024 $30 JP

Mount Eyre Vineyards ★★★★

173 Gillards Road, Pokolbin, NSW 2320 **Region** Hunter Valley
T 0438 683 973 **www**.mounteyre.com **Open** At Garden Cellars, Hunter Valley Gardens
Winemaker Andrew Spinaze, Mark Richardson, Michael McManus **Viticulturist** Neil
Grosser **Est.** 1970 **Dozens** 3000 **Vyds** 25ha
This is the venture of 2 families whose involvement in wine extends back several centuries in
an unbroken line: the Tsironis family in the Peleponnese, Greece; and the Iannuzzi family in
Vallo della Lucania, Italy. Their largest vineyard is at Broke, with a smaller vineyard at Pokolbin.
The 3 principal varieties planted are chardonnay, shiraz and semillon, with smaller amounts of
merlot, chambourcin, verdelho, fiano and nero d'Avola. (JH)

ŸŸŸŸŸ **Three Ponds Fiano 2021, Hunter Valley** The suite of whites here is good.
While I'd like to see this half a degree riper, riding phenolics as much as freshness,
there is ample personality. Bitter almond, fennel, orange blossom, grapefruit and
a candied citrus twist. The finish is a bit tangy, but there is enough weight for
balance and pleasure. A little oak in the mix has helped. Screw cap. 12.5% alc.
RATING 93 DRINK 2021–2027 $33 NG

Grosser Semillon 2021, Hunter Valley A wonderful vintage for whites in the region and this is an example of what it produced. Semillon careening along chalky acid rails flecked with notes of lemongrass, tonic and citrus balm. Long and mellifluous, the acidity juicy rather than hard. A lightweight frame, juxtaposed against precision and intensity. This will make fine old bones. Screw cap. 11.5% alc. RATING 93 DRINK 2021–2035 $35 NG

Chardonnay 2021, Hunter Valley A fine meld of tension and mid-weighted generosity. Canned peach, dried mango, cumquat and nougat. Typical of the riot of fruit exhibited by the Hunter's better examples, strung across a bow of pungent mineral and stylish oak. Screw cap. 13.5% alc. RATING 93 DRINK 2021–2027 $43 NG

Three Ponds Verdelho 2021, Hunter Valley This is impressive. While cases will shift from the cellar door because of fruity riffs on guava and citrus, patchouli and jasmine scents and the sheer exuberance, there is something more serious about it than most. Drier, too. There is a wild fennel note and a white pepper trail of freshness, not dissimilar to quality Soave. Effortless poise. Very good drinking. Screw cap. 13% alc. RATING 92 DRINK 2021–2026 $23 NG ✪

Grosser Fiano 2021, Hunter Valley Of the 2 Mount Eyre fianos, I prefer the Three Ponds. It is juicier and more pleasurable. While this wine's lemon squash, icy pole, nashi pear and grapefruit scents are attractive and nicely melded to a rail of phenolic detail, it would be a vastly better wine a full percentage riper. This said, the finish is long, if not a bit anaemic. Fiano made like a new-wave semillon. A few years of bottle age may well prove me wrong. Screw cap. 11.5% alc. RATING 90 DRINK 2021–2028 $43 NG

♟♟♟♟ **Three Ponds Merlot 2021, Hunter Valley** RATING 89 DRINK 2021–2023 $37 NG

Mount Horrocks ★★★★★

The Old Railway Station, Curling Street, Auburn, SA 5451 **Region** Clare Valley
T (08) 8849 2243 **www.**mounthorrocks.com **Open** W'ends & public hols 10–5
Winemaker Stephanie Toole **Est.** 1982 **Dozens** 3500 **Vyds** 9.4ha
Owner and winemaker Stephanie Toole has never deviated from the pursuit of excellence in the vineyard and winery. She has 3 vineyard sites in the Clare Valley, each managed using natural farming and organic practices. The attention to detail and refusal to cut corners is obvious in all her wines. The cellar door is in the renovated old Auburn railway station. Exports to the UK and other major markets. (JH)

♟♟♟♟♟ **Watervale Riesling 2021, Clare Valley** The scented white flower and lime blossom aromas promise much to come on the palate, and don't deceive. It is utterly delicious, with swathes of lime and pink grapefruit which are fruit-sweet (not RS). Absolutely out of the box. Screw cap. 12.6% alc. RATING 97 DRINK 2021–2036 $37 JH ✪

♟♟♟♟♟ **Cabernet Sauvignon 2020, Clare Valley** This is beautiful. A medium bodied, super-elegant, superfine cabernet. It remains true to its Clare roots with dark chocolate and cocoa scattered throughout the veritable forest of black and purple berries. The acidity is fresh and juicy and countersunk into all aspects of the fruit. In fact, the wine is so seamlessly dovetailed at all junctures (oak, fruit, acid, tannins), that is moves into the supple, slinky, willowy space. This is a truly beautiful wine. Screw cap. 14.3% alc. RATING 96 DRINK 2022–2038 $60 EL ✪

Cabernet Sauvignon 2019, Clare Valley Perfect colour. A polished and elegant wine that is in the heart of the best Clare Valley cabernets, with blackcurrant and cedar marking the bouquet and perfectly balanced medium to full-bodied palate. Its finish and aftertaste are special, too, as is the modest alcohol. Screw cap. 14% alc. RATING 96 DRINK 2025–2039 $60 JH ✪

Nero d'Avola 2020, Clare Valley Sarsaparilla, black cherries, graphite, damp leaves, black pepper, strawberries and pomegranates too. This is elegant, supple, and superfine, with a core of pure fruit that is untouched by tannin, oak, or anything else. Unwavering. The swirling vortex of elements that spiral around it bring the fruit into balance, certainly through the finish. Which is long and again unwavering. Really lovely. Screw cap. 14% alc. RATING 94 DRINK 2022-2030 $45 EL

Mount Langi Ghiran Vineyards   ★★★★★

80 Vine Road, Bayindeen, Vic 3375 **Region** Grampians
T (03) 5359 4400 **www**.langi.com.au **Open** 7 days 10–5 **Winemaker** Adam Louder, Darren Rathbone **Viticulturist** Damien Sheehan **Est.** 1969 **Dozens** 45 000 **Vyds** 65ha
A maker of outstanding cool-climate peppery shiraz, crammed with flavour and vinosity, and very good cabernet sauvignon. The shiraz has long pointed the way for cool-climate examples of the variety. The business was acquired by the Rathbone family group in 2002. The marketing is integrated with the Yering Station and Xanadu Estate wines, a synergistic mix with no overlap. Wine quality is exemplary. Exports to all major markets. (JH)

🍷🍷🍷🍷🍷 **Cliff Edge Shiraz 2020, Grampians** Often cited as a benchmark cool-climate shiraz. There's no denying this is yet another impressive, elegant shiraz from a strong vintage. Boasts refined richness and a depth of flavour that is well-matched to a vivacious personality. Fruit is the star, with flecks of pepper and spice assisted by plump tannins. That's a WOW! Screw cap. 14.5% alc. RATING 96 DRINK 2021-2033 $35 JP ✪
Cliff Edge Cabernet Merlot 2020, Grampians A wine guaranteed to make you smile, highlighting the beauty of Grampians cabernet with a little help from some friendly merlot. Deeply coloured and concentrated in the glass, it launches into a beautifully balanced display of plum, mulberry and cassis, all ripe and warmly spiced with a hint of leafiness. Nicely measured tannins to the finish. Screw cap. 13.5% alc. RATING 95 DRINK 2021-2033 $35 JP ✪

🍷🍷🍷🍷♀ **Cliff Edge Grenache 2020, Grampians** RATING 92 DRINK 2021-2025 $35 JP
Billi Billi Pinot Gris 2021, Grampians RATING 91 DRINK 2021-2024 $20 JP ✪
Cliff Edge Riesling 2021, Grampians RATING 91 DRINK 2022-2027 $25 JP

Mt Lofty Ranges Vineyard   ★★★★★

Harris Road, Lenswood, SA 5240 **Region** Lenswood
T (08) 8389 8339 **www**.mtloftyrangesvineyard.com.au **Open** Fri–Sun & public hols 11–5 **Winemaker** Peter Leske, Taras Ochota **Est.** 1992 **Dozens** 3000 **Vyds** 4.6ha
Mt Lofty Ranges is owned and operated by Sharon Pearson and Garry Sweeney. Nestled high in the Lenswood subregion of the Adelaide Hills at an altitude of 500m, the very steep north-facing vineyard (pinot noir, sauvignon blanc, chardonnay and riesling) is pruned and picked by hand. The soil is sandy clay loam with a rock base of white quartz and ironstone, and irrigation is kept to a minimum to allow the wines to display vintage characteristics. (JH)

🍷🍷🍷🍷🍷 **Home Block Riesling 2021, Lenswood** Compared with the Aspire Riesling, here we see the opposite side of the riesling coin. A classic approach is taken and the fruit is up to the job, in dry lime, lemon, green apple and bright, clean, mineral notes. Taut and dry, with good line and length on show and impressive depth to boot – and it's still early days. Screw cap. 12.5% alc. RATING 95 DRINK 2022-2026 $30 JP ✪
Aspire Pinot Noir 2020, Lenswood A dark, brooding kind of pinot noir. Layers of earth, undergrowth, anise, red berries, violet and baking spices. Loose limbed, it is slowly taking form to reveal a surprising depth of flavour. Sinewy, fine tannins run even through to the finish. This is a wine to savour. Screw cap. 13.5% alc. RATING 95 DRINK 2021-2028 $55 JP
S&G Chardonnay 2020, Lenswood A complex and most convincing premium chardonnay, one that rests its charms on a total purity of fruit. Citrus, nectarines, white peach, lime and nashi pear are juicy and forthright on the palate

against a subtle nougat, leesy background. Complex, yes, but also super-fresh. Screw cap. 13.2% alc. RATING 95 DRINK 2021-2028 $85 JP

Old Pump Shed Pinot Noir 2020, Lenswood Huge drink-me appeal to this wine. Hits the spot time and again, with its ripe summer-pudding strawberry, cherry fruits, musk and baking spices with redcurrant bite. Sour-cherry fruits, lingering and light, together with taut tannins help define the palate. Sets the tastebuds alight. Screw cap. 13.5% alc. RATING 94 DRINK 2022-2026 $35 JP

Aspire Chardonnay 2020, Lenswood A pleasure to delve into this super-smart chardonnay. Layers of lemon and citrus fruits, nectarine, flinty mineral elements and grilled nuts across a taut palate. The sherbet-like zesty acidity raises the bar, lengthening out the palate with toasty oak wafting through to the finish. Screw cap. 13% alc. RATING 94 DRINK 2021-2027 $55 JP

ŢŢŢŢ **Aspire Fumé Blanc 2021, Lenswood** RATING 93 DRINK 2022-2025 $30 JP
S&G Pinot Noir 2020, Lenswood RATING 93 DRINK 2022-2028 $85 JP
Aspire Riesling 2021, Lenswood RATING 92 DRINK 2022-2025 $39 JP
Not Shy Pinot Noir Rosé 2021, Lenswood RATING 90 DRINK 2022-2024 $25 JP
Old Cherry Block Sauvignon Blanc 2021, Lenswood RATING 90 DRINK 2022-2024 $25 JP

Mount Majura Vineyard   ★★★★★

88 Lime Kiln Road, Majura, ACT 2609 **Region** Canberra District
T (02) 6262 3070 **www**.mountmajura.com.au **Open** 7 days 10–5 **Winemaker** Dr Frank van de Loo **Viticulturist** Leo Quirk **Est.** 1988 **Dozens** 5000 **Vyds** 9.3ha

Vines were first planted in 1988 by Dinny Killen on a site on her family property that had been especially recommended by Dr Edgar Riek; its attractions were red soil of volcanic origin over limestone, with reasonably steep east and northeast slopes providing an element of frost protection. The tiny vineyard has been significantly expanded since it was purchased in '99. Blocks of pinot noir and chardonnay have been joined by pinot gris, shiraz, tempranillo, riesling, graciano, mondeuse and touriga nacional. Three single-site tempranillos (Rock Block, Dry Spur and Little Dam) are more recent arrivals. The Mount Majura flagship remains the Canberra District Tempranillo, with volume and quality cementing its place. (JH)

ŢŢŢŢŢ **Riesling 2021, Canberra District** The 8.5g/L RS is perceptible, but so is the (undisclosed) acidity, for they balance each other sufficiently to make this an ideal wine for a sunny day. Minerality is the last piece of the jigsaw. Screw cap. 12% alc. RATING 95 DRINK 2021-2030 $30 JH ✪

Mondeuse 2021, Canberra District Mondeuse is a French variety that I find so appealing, as I do this wine. Firstly, it's refreshing and lively with a core of tangy, juicy, tart raspberries and black cherries with a sprinkle of pepper, fresh herbs and violets. Yet it has a strong savoury element of iodine, prosciutto and meaty reduction, finishing with fine tannins and raspberry-sorbet acidity. Screw cap. 13% alc. RATING 95 DRINK 2023-2028 $34 JF ✪

Dry Spur Tempranillo 2021, Canberra District Of the 3 single-site tempranillos, this stands a little taller and comes across with superb balance and depth. Dark cherries, sarsaparilla, smoky with jamón and other cured meats – or maybe that's just what I want to eat with this super wine. Fuller bodied, savoury tannins then finishes dry and firm. Screw cap. 14% alc. RATING 95 DRINK 2023-2031 $73 JF

Little Dam Tempranillo 2021, Canberra District A structured and serious red with a savoury stamp, even if a core of tangy fruit flecked with spice comes through strongly across the palate. Fuller body, determined tannins, refreshing acidity and terrific length all add up to a top-notch wine. Screw cap. 14% alc. RATING 95 DRINK 2022-2031 $74 JF

ŢŢŢŢ **TSG Tempranillo Shiraz Graciano 2021, Canberra District** RATING 92 DRINK 2022-2028 $38 JF

The Silurian Chardonnay Pinot Noir 2019, Canberra District RATING 91 $34 JF
Chardonnay 2021, Canberra District RATING 91 DRINK 2022-2027 $30 JF
Tempranillo 2021, Canberra District RATING 91 DRINK 2023-2031 $54 JF
Shiraz 2021, Canberra District RATING 91 DRINK 2022-2031 $38 JF
Shiraz 2019, Canberra District RATING 91 DRINK 2023-2029 $38 JH
Graciano 2021, Canberra District RATING 90 DRINK 2023-2030 $34 JF

Mount Mary ★★★★★

Coldstream West Road, Lilydale, Vic 3140 **Region** Yarra Valley
T (03) 9739 1761 **www**.mountmary.com.au **Winemaker** Sam Middleton **Est.** 1971
Dozens 4500 **Vyds** 18ha
Mount Mary was one of the foremost pioneers of the rebirth of the Yarra Valley after 50 years without viticultural activity. From the outset they produced wines of rare finesse and purity. The late founder, Dr John Middleton, practised near-obsessive attention to detail long before that phrase slid into oenological vernacular. He relentlessly strove for perfection and all 4 of the wines in the original Mount Mary portfolio achieved just that (within the context of each vintage). Charming grandson Sam Middleton is equally dedicated. An all-encompassing recent tasting of every vintage of these 4 wines left me in no doubt he is making even better wines since assuming the winemaker mantle in June '11. In '08, Mount Mary commenced a detailed program of vine improvement, in particular assessing the implications of progressively moving towards a 100% grafted vineyard to provide immunity from phylloxera. Part involved a move to sustainable organic viticulture and ongoing use of straw mulch to retain as much moisture as possible in the vineyard. Winery of the Year in the Halliday Wine Companion 2018. Exports to the UK, the US, Denmark, Hong Kong, Singapore and South Korea. (JH)

ΨΨΨΨΨ Quintet 2020, Yarra Valley A blend of 44/30/18/4/4% cabernet sauvignon/ merlot/cabernet franc/malbec/petit verdot. An essay in elegance and understatement. A medium, bright and translucent ruby red, this is beautifully perfumed with aromas of just-ripened blackcurrants, red cherries, rose petals and gentle cedar notes from the oak. The palate is exceptionally pure-fruited and gently textured. The wine finishes with these incredibly silky, long tannins that are in perfect harmony with the fruit and acid. This majestic wine is gorgeous to drink even now but those that still have some in their cellar in 10–15 years (if not longer) will be grateful. Screw cap. 13.2% alc. RATING 98 DRINK 2023-2035 $165 PR ✪ ♥
Chardonnay 2020, Yarra Valley Typically refined and elegant, but isn't stand-offish. The Yarra Valley's calling card of chardonnay is its extreme length, built around natural acidity and citrus zest. Oak is part of the upbringing, but discreet, and the wine has a very long plateau ahead. Screw cap. 13.3% alc. RATING 97 DRINK 2025-2040 $120 JH ✪
Pinot Noir 2020, Yarra Valley Radiant clear crimson. All the red berries of forest and field fill the bouquet and the strikingly fresh palate, which proceeds to expand on the finish with the proverbial peacock's tail on display. Cork. 13.3% alc. RATING 97 DRINK 2025-2035 $165 JH

ΨΨΨΨΨ Triolet 2020, Yarra Valley 62/28/10% sauvignon blanc/semillon/muscadelle. The length of the palate is akin to that of the chardonnay, and the wine's balance guarantees growth in complexity that will build further over the next 5+ years. Green apple, pear and lemon citrus intermingle on an already generous palate. Screw cap. 13% alc. RATING 95 DRINK 2022-2035 $105 JH

Mount Ophir Estate ★★★★★

168 Stillards Lane, Rutherglen, Vic 3685 **Region** Rutherglen
T (02) 6032 8920 **www**.mountophirestate.com.au **Open** W'ends 11–5
Winemaker Nick Brown **Est.** 1891 **Dozens** 270

The Brown family of All Saints Estate and St. Leonards looked to its own backyard in 2017, buying the local National Trust-classified Mount Ophir winery. It was a remembrance of the celebrated history of the Rutherglen wine region which the Browns – Eliza, Angela and Nick – were very much aware of, having grown up nearby. During 1891–1957 when the winery was closed, it is estimated that 600000 gallons of wine were sent from the estate to England. The 3 children of the late Peter Brown (Brown Brothers) have developed accommodation and a stunning location for weddings and events. The purchase was also an opportunity to bring the 1891 brick winery back to life, which is exactly what they did. The property has 3ha of vines dating back to 1995, including shiraz, durif and muscat. (JP)

ŶŶŶŶŶ **Shiraz 2019, Rutherglen** A love letter to the traditional northeastern Victorian shiraz which can be, contrary to some renditions, a medium-bodied celebration of complex fruit and moderate, sympathetic oak, in other words, a wine beyond trends. Baked earth, black fruits, Aussie bush spice, aniseed, cherry kirsch and wood smoke. Taut, woodsy tannins provide cut and structure on what is going to be a long-lived shiraz. Give it the time it deserves. Cork. 14% alc. RATING 95 DRINK 2022-2034 $500 JP

Mt Pilot Estate ★★★★☆

208 Shannons Road, Byawatha, Vic 3678 **Region** North East Victoria
T 0419 243 225 **www.**mtpilotestatewines.com.au **Open** By appt **Winemaker** Marc Scalzo **Est.** 1996 **Dozens** 600 **Vyds** 13ha
Lachlan and Penny Campbell have planted shiraz (7ha), cabernet sauvignon (3ha), viognier (2ha) and durif (1ha). The vineyard is planted on deep, well-drained granitic soils at an altitude of 250m near Eldorado, 20km from Wangaratta and 35km from Beechworth. Exports to Singapore. (JH)

ŶŶŶŶŶ **Durif 2019, North East Victoria** Another salutary lesson in never underestimating the degree of elegance that can be achieved with durif. The grape is very much misunderstood and it's wines like these, with poise and beauty defining the grape's more medium-bodied and spiced side, that will bring a deeper appreciation. And the grape's so-called big tannins are pure silk here. Screw cap. 14.1% alc. RATING 95 DRINK 2021-2028 $30 JP
Cabernet Sauvignon 2018, North East Victoria Heartening to see cabernet sauvignon given its due in the northeast, and explored with terrific precision and concentration. Displays elegance in bright plum, cherry and blackberry aromas with a varietal leafiness. A sweet core of fruit holds the palate. Ripe, dense tannins and a long tail of juicy flavour combine to bring this lovely wine to a neat finish. Screw cap. 14.2% alc. RATING 94 DRINK 2021-2030 $30 JP

ŶŶŶŶ♀ **Shiraz 2018, North East Victoria** RATING 90 DRINK 2021-2028 $30 JP

Mount Pleasant ★★★★★

401 Marrowbone Road, Pokolbin, NSW 2320 **Region** Hunter Valley
T (02) 4998 7505 **www.**mountpleasantwines.com.au **Open** Thurs–Mon 10–4
Winemaker Adrian Sparks, Jaden Hall **Viticulturist** Steve Ferguson **Est.** 1921
Vyds 88.2ha
While the vaunted history of craftsmanship here is indisputable, the reds have ebbed from the reductive tension championed by former Chief Winemaker Jim Chatto, to a more relaxed expression under new maker Adrian Sparks. Sparks seems to have a predilection for mid-weighted, lower-alcohol styles of red, not dissimilar to the great Hunter River Burgundies crafted by Maurice O'Shea. This is a style that is as aspirational today as it was revered then, gleaned from a polyglot of historical vineyards, variable geologies and stylistic patinas, including expressions of the Old Paddock and Rosehill vineyards, in addition to the Mountain series of Medium and Full Bodied Dry Reds. The whites, too, feel less austere. Their fealty to the regional pedigree of steely, long-lived semillon, however, is clear. Winery of the Year in the Halliday Wine Companion 2017. Exports to all major markets. (NG)

ŸŸŸŸŸ **Maurice O'Shea Shiraz 2019, Hunter Valley** The flagship, crafted with the finest fruit from the famed proprietary sites: Old Hill, Old Paddock, Rosehill 1946 and 1965 Vines. As with the other reds in the stable, maker Adrian Sparks has lightened the structural lattices to impart greater freshness and joy. Full and plummy, the wine spent but 10 months in large-format French wood, less than 20% new. The result, almost as pulpy and vital, as it is dense and torqued. Wonderful tannins, alloyed and finely knit. A textural opus. Anise, loamy wet earth scents and flavours of sarsaparilla, clove and cardamom, too. Better after 2 days in the bottle, indicating just how well it will age. Stellar wine. Screw cap. 14% alc. RATING 97 DRINK 2022-2039 $250 NG ♥

ŸŸŸŸŸ **1880 Vines Old Hill Vineyard Shiraz 2019, Hunter Valley** A mid-weighted luncheon danger! Pulpy and fresh, yet dank in the best loamy Hunter art form, with nori, darker cherry, lavender and peppery accents. The tannins, more compact, tenacious, loaded and set to unravel in time. Already a joy to drink, but the vinosity and tannic trajectory, al dente and refined, suggest that it will go a great distance. Screw cap. 14% alc. RATING 96 DRINK 2021-2036 $135 NG
1921 Vines Old Paddock Vineyard Shiraz 2019, Hunter Valley Dark and bracken-like. Cocoa oak, thyme, violet, barbecued meat, olive and dark fruit allusions. This is an incipient module of what it will surely become with patience. Yet a bit clunky. A yeoman, rather than a swan. Drying finish. The acidity, again, trop. I'm giving this the benefit of the doubt, hoping that time works some alchemy and I end up with egg on my face. Screw cap. 14% alc. RATING 96 DRINK 2022-2039 $135 NG
Lovedale Semillon 2014, Hunter Valley Lovedale has a stellar track record as one of the Hunter's greatest semillon sites. Scents of key lime pie, lemongrass, tonic, buttered Wonder bread and citrus curd. Very fine. Pixelated. The mid palate, tightly furled but marked by a chiaroscuro of balletic lightness and ample extract. Plenty of velocity and a long trajectory across the palate. Still an adolescent. Much in store. Screw cap. 12% alc. RATING 96 DRINK 2022-2030 $70 NG ✪
Rosehill Vineyard Shiraz 2019, Hunter Valley This will age very well. Sassafras, thyme, dark cherry, charred meats, clove and iodine. Polished leather, too. The tannic mettle, ferrous and saline; forceful yet highly refined; is the wine's opus. The depth and intensity, too, compelling. The velocity and length, extremely impressive. Expansive. Even better the day after. Screw cap. 14% alc. RATING 95 DRINK 2021-2036 $55 NG
1965 Vines Rosehill Vineyard Shiraz 2019, Hunter Valley Potential energy, rather than kinetic. Despite the moderate alcohol, the fruit feels very ripe, almost straying into grenache territory. The Hunter meets Gigondas! This will deliver far more with belief and patience. Taut. Inchoate. Kirsch, lavender, leather polish, violet, iodine, blueberry, pastis and orange verbena. Firecrackers on the nose. Prodigious extract, yet mid weighted, savoury and quintessentially regional. Bury this and believe! Screw cap. 13.5% alc. RATING 95 DRINK 2022-2033 $135 NG

Mount Stapylton Wines   ★★★★

1212 Northern Grampians Road, Laharum, Vic 3401 **Region** Grampians
T 0429 838 233 **www.**mountstapyltonwines.com.au **Open** By appt **Winemaker** Leigh Clarnette **Viticulturist** Robert Staehr **Est.** 2002 **Dozens** 300 **Vyds** 1.5ha
Mount Stapylton's vineyard is planted on the historic Goonwinnow Homestead farming property at Laharum, on the northwest side of the Grampians, in front of Mount Stapylton. In 2017, the vineyard lease was purchased from founder Howard Staehr by the Staehr family and is now being run as an addition to their mixed farming enterprise. (JH)

ŸŸŸŸŸ **Reserve Shiraz 2019, Grampians** Tasted 5 months before release and, while tight and coiled, this revealed a gentle, developing elegance. Grampians display of spice − clove, aniseed − on full view with black-fruited flavour intensity. Gentle and enticing up front, sinewy tannins take over, providing a firm structure. Should be ready to go come Mar '22. Screw cap. 14% alc. RATING 93 DRINK 2021-2031 $50 JP

Mount Terrible

289 Licola Road, Jamieson, Vic 3723 **Region** Central Victoria
T 0429 406 037 **www**.mountterriblewines.com.au **Open** By appt **Winemaker** John
Eason **Est.** 2001 **Dozens** 350 **Vyds** 2ha
John Eason and Janene Ridley began the long, slow (and at times very painful) business of
establishing their vineyard just north of Mount Terrible in 1992 – hence the choice of name.
In 2001, they planted 2ha of pinot noir (MV6, 115, 114 and 777 clones) on a gently sloping,
north-facing river terrace adjacent to the Jamieson River. DIY trials persuaded John to have
the first commercial vintage in '06 contract-made. He has since made the wines himself in
a fireproof winery built on top of an underground wine cellar. John has a sense of humour
second to none, but must wonder what he has done to provoke the weather gods, alternating
in their provision of fire, storm and tempest. Subsequent vintages have provided some well
earned relief. Exports to the UK. (JH)

ΨΨΨΨΨ Jamieson Pinot Noir 2019, Central Victoria Complex cherry/plum/
spice/earth flavours on a long palate. Screw cap. 13.3% alc. RATING 95
DRINK 2022-2030 $45 JH

Mount Trio Vineyard

2534 Porongurup Road, Mount Barker WA 6324 **Region** Porongurup
T (08) 9853 1136 **www**.mounttriowines.com.au **Open** By appt **Winemaker** Gavin
Berry, Andrew Vesey, Caitlin Gazey **Est.** 1989 **Dozens** 3500 **Vyds** 8.5ha
Mount Trio was established by Gavin Berry, Gill Graham and their business partners shortly
after they moved to the Mount Barker area in late '88. Gavin took up the position of chief
winemaker at Plantagenet, which he held until '04, when he and partners acquired the now
very successful and much larger West Cape Howe. They have increased the estate plantings to
8.5ha with pinot noir (3.4ha), riesling (3.3ha), shiraz (1ha) and chardonnay (0.8ha). Exports
to the UK and Denmark. (JH)

ΨΨΨΨΨ Shiraz 2019, Great Southern Fresh and peppery cool-climate syrah. Layers of
black fruit flavours are shaped by fine tannins and a distinct licorice character that
cools everything down. Remarkably elegant drinking for $23. Bravo. Screw cap.
13.5% alc. RATING 94 DRINK 2028 $23 EL ✪

ΨΨΨΨΨ Riesling 2021, Porongurup RATING 92 DRINK 2021-2031 $23 EL ✪
Home Block Pinot Noir 2020, Porongurup RATING 90 DRINK 2022-2029
$35 EL

Mountadam Vineyards

High Eden Road, Eden Valley, SA 5235 **Region** Eden Valley
T 0427 089 836 **www**.mountadam.com.au **Open** By appt **Winemaker** Caitlin Brown
Viticulturist Caitlin Brown **Est.** 1972 **Dozens** 30 000 **Vyds** 148ha
Founded by the late David Wynn for the benefit of winemaker son Adam, Mountadam
was (somewhat surprisingly) purchased by Möet Hennessy Wine Estates in 2000. In '05,
Mountadam returned to family ownership when it was purchased by David and Jenni Brown
from Adelaide. David and Jenni have worked to bring the original Mountadam property back
together with the purchase of Mountadam Farm in '07 and the High Eden Vineyard from
TWE in '15, thus reassembling all of the land originally purchased by David Wynn in the late
1960s. Exports to the UK, Canada, France, Switzerland, Poland and Hong Kong. (JH)

ΨΨΨΨΨ Riesling 2021, Eden Valley Characters of freshly squeezed lime juice, Christmas
lily, Bickford's lime cordial and grapefruit with wafts of crushed quartz, green
apple and a wisp of cut fennel. Stony, pure and true, with a lovely porcelain acid
drive and focused limey exit. Screw cap. 12.5% alc. RATING 93 DRINK 2022-2032
$28 DB
Chardonnay 2020, Eden Valley I found this wine the more elegant of the
current Mountadam chardonnay triptych. Finer in both aromatic allure and palate
shape. The pure white peach, nectarine and grapefruit notes are all there along

with soft spice, roasted cashews, stone and white flowers, but it's tighter, with fine acidity coiled like a spring and tension and drive to burn. Screw cap. 13.5% alc. RATING 93 DRINK 2022-2028 $28 DB ♥

Pinot Gris 2021, Eden Valley Pale straw in the glass with characters of nashi pear, grapefruit, nectarine, soft spice, clotted cream and stone. Just a tinge of gewürztraminer in the wine adds some textural components and a shimmer of exotic spice/fruit notes … think rose petal and a liminal waft of Turkish delight,. The wine then coils with stony intent and sails off into the distance, a light phenolic and citrus wake marking its passage. Screw cap. 13% alc. RATING 92 DRINK 2022-2025 $28 DB

Five-Fifty Pinot Noir Rosé 2021, Eden Valley Pale, pale pink in the glass with aromas of raspberry, red cherry and pomegranate with hints of white flowers, crushed stone, marzipan and watermelon. Bright, savoury, clean and crisp with excellent tension and a finish that echos with morello cherry and almond paste. Lovely. Screw cap. 14.5% alc. RATING 91 DRINK 2020-2025 $20 DB ✪

Estate Chardonnay 2020, High Eden Pale straw in the glass, we see juicy white peachy fruit along with nectarine and yellow plum. Hints of soft spice, grilled cashews, fig pastry, light struck-flint wafts and vanillin oak complete the picture. Savoury and stony but in an expansive, full-bodied chardonnay style. Screw cap. 13.5% alc. RATING 91 DRINK 2022-2026 $40 DB

Five-Fifty Cabernet Sauvignon 2019, Barossa Awash with red and blackcurrants, dark spice, maraschino cherries, cedar, dark chocolate and dried herbs. Varietal and true with rich black fruits on the palate and a slight meaty edge that adds interest. Compact and pure. Screw cap. 14.5% alc. RATING 90 DRINK 2020-2028 $20 DB ✪

ΨΨΨΨ **Five-Fifty Shiraz 2019, Barossa** RATING 89 DRINK 2022-2028 $20 DB
Five-Fifty Chardonnay 2020, Eden Valley RATING 88 DRINK 2020-2026 $20 DB

Mulline ★★★★★

131 Lumbs Road, Sutherlands Creek, Vic 3331 (postal) **Region** Geelong
T 0402 409 292 **www**.mulline.com **Winemaker** Ben Mullen **Est.** 2019 **Dozens** 1000
This is the venture of Ben Mullen and business partner Ben Hine. Mullen grew up in the Barossa Valley and studied oenology. His journey thereafter was in the purple, working at Yarra Yering, Oakridge, Torbreck and Leeuwin Estate, Domaine Dujac in Burgundy in '13, Craggy Range in NZ ('15), coming back to Geelong as winemaker for Clyde Park in '17–18. Here he made the wine that won the Shiraz Trophy at the National Wine Show (for the '17 vintage) and the Geelong Trophy at the Australian Pinot Noir Challenge. Ben Hine also came from SA, and worked in hospitality for many years before obtaining his law degree; he is working full-time as a lawyer. When they met, it was he who took the running in creating the brand and the business structure behind it. In wine terms, this means a range of single vineyard wines at the top, backed by the Geelong region range (and no wines from elsewhere). Exports to the UK. (JH)

ΨΨΨΨΨ **Single Vineyard Sutherlands Creek Shiraz Viognier 2021, Geelong** A robust, cool-climate shiraz viognier that still retains real elegance. The fragrant perfume rocks in blackberries, plum, lifted baking spices, pepper and bush herbs. Explores real depth on the palate in black fruits, blueberries and lasting red licorice, spice and pepper notes. And it goes and goes. Holds something for now and a lot for later. Screw cap. 13.5% alc. RATING 96 DRINK 2022-2030 $50 JP ✪

Single Vineyard Portarlington Chardonnay 2021, Geelong Not an easy wine to pin down. Is it the Austrian oak? Like previous releases it is complex, firm in structure and carries its maritime credentials proudly, with an intriguing sea-spray quality. Lemon rind, grapefruit, rock pool, green apple and melon introduce the wine, the citrus theme running through to the lemony, brisk acidity that fully wakens the tastebuds. It's just stirring to life and most assuredly, it's a keeper. Screw cap. 13% alc. RATING 95 DRINK 2022-2030 $50 JP

Single Vineyard Sutherlands Creek Chardonnay 2021, Geelong
A fragrant, fresh and lively youngster with well-measured oak that lets the fruit
sing. Grapefruit, lemon, nectarine and white peach fill the bouquet and the palate,
flowing fine in structure and briskly across the tongue by crisp, bright acidity.
A delight now but with a big future ahead. Screw cap. 13% alc. RATING 95
DRINK 2022-2029 $50 JP
Single Vineyard Sutherlands Creek Pinot Noir 2021, Geelong This
pinot from Sutherlands Creek, in the Moorabool Valley, delivers a quiet, almost
understated elegance. Can't miss the whole bunches and what they bring – a
fragrant, gently herbal character – but they are nicely entwined amid the red
cherries, cranberry and brambly fruits, earth and loose-knit tannins. Delicious.
Screw cap. 12% alc. RATING 95 DRINK 2022-2029 $50 JP
Gris 2021, Geelong Pinot Gris. Pale salmon 'eye of the partridge'; complex
and rich poached pear and clove aromas and flavours; fruit sweetness balanced by
savoury notes ex fermentation. Screw cap. 13% alc. RATING 94 DRINK 2022-2025
$32 JH

ŸŸŸŸŸ **Single Vineyard Drysdale Pinot Noir 2021, Geelong** RATING 93
DRINK 2022-2027 $50 JP
Single Vineyard Sutherlands Creek Fumé Blanc 2021, Geelong
RATING 93 DRINK 2022-2026 $50 JP
Syrah 2021, Geelong RATING 91 DRINK 2021-2028 $32 JP
Sauvignon Blanc 2021, Geelong RATING 90 DRINK 2021-2025 $30 JP
Single Vineyard Bannockburn Syrah 2021, Geelong RATING 90
DRINK 2022-2031 $50 JP
Single Vineyard Portarlington Pinot Noir 2021, Geelong RATING 90
DRINK 2022-2028 $50 JP

Munari Wines   ★★★★☆

1129 Northern Highway, Heathcote, Vic 3523 **Region** Heathcote
T 0429 804 360 **www**.munariwines.com **Open** 7 days 11–5 **Winemaker** Adrian Munari
Viticulturist Adrian Munari **Est.** 1993 **Dozens** 3000 **Vyds** 6.9ha
Established on one of the original Heathcote farming properties, Ladys Creek Vineyard is
situated on the narrow Cambrian soil strip 11km north of the town. Adrian Munari has
harnessed traditional winemaking practices to New World innovation to produce complex,
fruit-driven wines that marry concentration and elegance. Wines are produced from estate
plantings of shiraz and cabernet sauvignon. Plantings of merlot, cabernet franc and malbec
have recently been grafted to sangiovese. Exports to the UK. (JH)

ŸŸŸŸŸ **Ladys Pass Shiraz 2019, Heathcote** This is the other side of Heathcote shiraz,
the finer side, the perfumed, velvety textured side that comes fully formed upon
release. Intense dark colour. Ripe fruits gather on the bouquet: black cherry and
plum with an equally dark collection of anise and nutmeg spices. Intrinsically
elegant, the wine moves with poise across the palate, even and balanced. Diam.
14% alc. RATING 95 DRINK 2022-2035 $45 JP

ŸŸŸŸŸ **il Fresco Vermentino 2021, Heathcote** RATING 92 DRINK 2021-2025 $25 JP ❸

Murdoch Hill   ★★★★★

260 Mappinga Road, Woodside, SA 5244 **Region** Adelaide Hills
T (08) 7200 5018 **www**.murdochhill.com.au **Open** Thurs–Mon 11–4
Winemaker Michael Downer **Est.** 1998 **Dozens** 5000 **Vyds** 17.3ha
A little over 20ha of vines have been established on the undulating, gum tree–studded
countryside of Charlie and Julie Downer's 60yo Erika property, 4km east of Oakbank. In
descending order of importance, the varieties planted are sauvignon blanc, shiraz, cabernet
sauvignon and chardonnay. Son Michael, with a bachelor of oenology degree from the
University of Adelaide, is winemaker. Exports to the UK, the US, Canada, Sweden, Norway,
the Netherlands, the UAE, Hong Kong, Taiwan and Singapore. (JH)

ŸŸŸŸŸ The Phaeton Pinot Noir 2021, Piccadilly Valley Just bottled when tasted and a joyous drink, brimming in red fruits and spice. Plenty of life and energy here. Upfront, it delivers a complex set of red cherry, cranberry, plum with potpourri floral/herbals and a splash of musk. A fully integrated, balanced and elegant expression of Piccadilly Valley and Adelaide Hills' pinot, the area's top red variety. Screw cap. 13% alc. RATING 95 DRINK 2022-2030 $53 JP

Apollo Pinot Noir 2021, Piccadilly Valley Developing an established style that is both fragrant, seemingly delicate to start, before it launches into a display of some serious pinot grunt. A bit of a chameleon. Cloudy, crimson-red colour. A super-pretty floral attack on the nose with cranberry, redcurrant, violet and spice. Slips into another gear on the palate, deep and concentrated, with a developing thread of charry, toasty oak. Will reward further with moderate ageing. Screw cap. 13% alc. RATING 95 DRINK 2022-2030 $85 JP

Sauvignon Blanc 2021, Adelaide Hills The white flowers of the bouquet move right towards jasmine, the palate veering left with flecks of grapefruit and snow pea, acidity brightening the finish. Screw cap. 12% alc. RATING 94 DRINK 2022-2025 $25 JH ✪

ŸŸŸŸŸ Limited Release Ridley Pinot x Three 2021, Adelaide Hills RATING 93 DRINK 2022-2026 $36 JP

The Surrey Pinot Meunier 2021, Adelaide Hills RATING 93 DRINK 2022-2026 $40 JP

Limited Release Vis-a-Vis Cabernet Franc 2021, Adelaide Hills RATING 92 DRINK 2022-2028 $40 JP

Syrah 2020, Adelaide Hills RATING 92 DRINK 2022-2028 $30 JP

The Landau Single Vineyard Oakbank Syrah 2020, Adelaide Hills RATING 92 DRINK 2022-2028 $48 JP

Rosé 2021, Adelaide Hills RATING 91 DRINK 2022-2030 $25 JH

The Sulky Riesling 2021, Adelaide Hills RATING 90 DRINK 2022-2025 $36 JP

Murray Street Vineyards ★★★★

37 Murray Street, Greenock, SA 5360 **Region** Barossa Valley
T (08) 8562 8373 **www.**murraystreet.com.au **Open** 7 days 10–5 **Winemaker** Ben Perkins **Est.** 2001 **Dozens** 20000 **Vyds** 105ha

Murray Street Vineyards was founded in 2001 and quickly established itself as a producer of exceptionally good wines. The current winemaker is Ben Perkins, who grew up a stone's throw away in Greenock. The 2 brands of Murray Street and MSV carry the flag, MSV the senior brand. (JH)

ŸŸŸŸŸ Gomersal Shiraz 2019, Barossa Valley From the black cracking clays of the Gomersal plains. The wines from these soils come across as compact and compressed; layers of dark and black fruits, spice and dark chocolate, squeezed into shape by fine, pillowy tannins. They have an expressive palate flow and a sense of latent power, while retaining an air of grace. Savoury and pure. Diam. 14.8% alc. RATING 93 DRINK 2021-2030 $50 DB

Greenock Estate Shiraz 2019, Barossa Valley There's an earthy, ferrous edge to the fruit here, that I often see in the wines of the western ridge. Full, rich and laden with spice, the fruit lies in the dark-plum and black-fruit spectrum with hints of vanillin, licorice, dark chocolate, cedar and deep earthy notes. Compact and savoury, with impressive fruit depth, fine tannin and bright acidity on the finish. Diam. 14.8% alc. RATING 92 DRINK 2021-2030 $50 DB

Greenock Estate Cabernet Sauvignon 2019, Barossa Valley True to its variety there are fruit characters of blackberry, blackcurrant and cassis along with touches of cedar, dried herbs, spice, licorice and a light brushing of capsicum. A purple floral aspect washes in on the palate, which is savoury with sandy tannins and a graceful, medium-bodied air. Diam. 14.5% alc. RATING 92 DRINK 2021-2033 $50 DB

Black Label Shiraz 2019, Barossa Valley Deep red purple in the glass, with plenty of spiced plummy enjoyment, along with hints of earth, violets, licorice and dark chocolate. Medium bodied with a savoury flick of its plummy tail, it's tremendous value at this pricepoint. Screw cap. 14.8% alc. RATING 91 DRINK 2021-2028 $25 DB

Cabernet Shiraz 2019, Barossa Valley An easy-drinking great Australian blend, with a medium-bodied flow of blackberry, black cherry and dark plum fruits, cut with spice, licorice, dark chocolate and softly spoken oak. Spacious with fine, sandy tannin and plenty of appeal. Screw cap. 14.6% alc. RATING 91 DRINK 2021-2028 $35 DB

The Barossa 2019, Barossa Valley Blend of 58/35/7% grenache/mataro/ shiraz. Plenty of spicy, savoury enjoyment here, with composed plum and summer berry fruits dotted with spice, floral and earthen tones. It's at the lighter end of medium bodied. There's detail and an airy sense of grace to its form. Screw cap. 14.8% alc. RATING 91 DRINK 2021-2028 $35 DB

ŸŸŸŸ **Black Label Cabernet Sauvignon 2019, Barossa Valley** RATING 89 DRINK 2021-2028 $25 DB

White Label Semillon 2021, Barossa Valley RATING 88 DRINK 2021-2028 $25 DB

Murrumbateman Winery ★★★★

131 McIntosh Circuit, Murrumbateman, NSW 2582 **Region** Canberra District
T 0432 826 454 **www**.murrumbatemanwinery.com.au **Open** 7 days 10–5
Winemaker Bobbie Makin **Est.** 1972 **Dozens** 3500 **Vyds** 4ha
Draws upon 4ha of estate-grown sauvignon blanc and shiraz. It also incorporates an à la carte restaurant and function room, together with picnic and barbecue areas. (JH)

ŸŸŸŸŸ **Riesling 2021, Canberra District** There's just enough texture and there's the right amount of citrus flavours, with a juiciness throughout that makes this an attractive drink. It's also fresh and lively, so expect to enjoy more than a glass. Screw cap. 11% alc. RATING 92 DRINK 2021-2027 $35 JF

Sangiovese 2021, Hilltops This is a juicy and lighter style with hints of cherries, cranberry tartness and bitter herbs. While it doesn't have complexity, it has raw silk tannins adding some structure, with plenty of refreshment throughout. Screw cap. 13.6% alc. RATING 90 DRINK 2021-2025 $25 JF

Fortified White Starboard NV, Canberra District A deep amber-mahogany colour. It's soft and pulpy with raisins, fruitcake, bitter chocolate and woodsy spices. Spirit is balanced and unobtrusive and it feels soft across the palate. It's not deep or complex but it is enjoyable. 375ml bottle. Screw cap. 18% alc. RATING 90 $34 JF

ŸŸŸŸ **Mollie's Block Sauvignon Blanc 2021, Tumbarumba** RATING 88 DRINK 2021-2022 $35 JF

Muster Wine Co ★★★★

c/- 60 Sheffield Street, Malvern, SA 5061 **Region** Barossa Valley
T 0412 616 340 **www**.musterwineco.com.au **Open** By appt **Winemaker** David Muster
Est. 2007 **Dozens** 2500
Gottfried Muster arrived from Europe with his young family in 1859, settling in the Barossa Valley. Thus direct descendent David Muster was born and bred in the wine purple. This is a virtual winery business; David Muster has been buying and selling wine since 2007. He forages for small batches of wines in the Barossa and Clare valleys, and clearly has developed some very useful contacts, allowing the release of relatively small amounts under each label, sometimes offering very good value. Exports to the US. (JH)

ŸŸŸŸŸ **Polish Hill River Riesling 2021, Clare Valley** The '20 had 2% gewürztraminer in the mix. This is taut, tense and relatively terrific. If there is gewürz in this '21, it is well concealed within the folds of riesling flavours. There are some lychee and dragonfruit characters present among the citrus, apples and white spice, so it is possible. Regardless, a tidy little wine. Screw cap. 10.5% alc. RATING 92 DRINK 2021-2028 $28 EL

Shiraz 2018, Clare Valley Fruit from Armagh. Christmas spice and blood plums on the nose, set against a backdrop of resinous oak. In the mouth, the wine is rich, concentrated and dense. Distinct midnight vibes – broody. Screw cap. 14.4% alc. RATING 92 DRINK 2021-2031 $38 EL

♟♟♟♟ **Grace Under Pressure Blanc de Blancs NV, Mount Gambier** RATING 88 $25 EL

MyattsField Vineyards ★★★★

Union Road, Carmel Valley, WA 6076 **Region** Perth Hills
T (08) 9293 5567 **www.**myattsfield.com.au **Open** Fri–Sun and public hols 11–5
Winemaker Josh Davenport, Rachael Davenport, Josh Uren **Est.** 1997 **Dozens** 4000
Vyds 4.5ha

MyattsField Vineyards is owned by Josh and Rachael Davenport. Both have oenology degrees and domestic and Flying Winemaker experience, especially Rachael. In 2006 they decided they would prefer to work for themselves. They left their employment, building a winery in time for the '07 vintage. Their vineyards include cabernet sauvignon, merlot, petit verdot, shiraz and chardonnay. They also purchase small parcels of grapes from as far away as Manjimup. Exports to Singapore and Taiwan. (JH)

♟♟♟♟♟ **Vermentino 2021, Perth Hills** Pithy, salted lemons and white nectarine – plenty of flavour here. Savoury, spicy and impressive. A really smart wine. Screw cap. 12.6% alc. RATING 94 DRINK 2021-2028 $24 EL ✪

♟♟♟♟♡ **Shiraz Viognier 2019, Perth Hills** RATING 93 DRINK 2021-2030 $26 EL ✪
Joseph Myatt Reserve 2019, Perth Hills RATING 93 DRINK 2021-2031 $45 EL
Shiraz 2020, Perth Hills RATING 91 DRINK 2022-2030 $26 EL
Durif 2020, Perth Hills RATING 90 DRINK 2022-2027 $30 EL
Riesling 2019, Manjimup RATING 90 DRINK 2021-2028 $24 EL

Naked Run Wines ★★★★★

8305 Horrocks Righway, Sevenhill, SA 5453 **Region** Clare Valley/Barossa Valley
T 0408 807 655 **www.**nakedrunwines.com.au **Winemaker** Steven Baraglia **Est.** 2005
Dozens 1500

Naked Run is the virtual winery of Jayme Wood, Bradley Currie and Steven Baraglia; their skills ranging from viticulture through to production, and also to the all-important sales and marketing (and not to be confused with Naked Wines). Riesling and shiraz are sourced from Clare Valley, grenache from the Williamstown area of the Barossa Valley and shiraz from Greenock. (JH)

♟♟♟♟♟ **Place in Time Sevenhill Riesling 2017, Clare Valley** There's a lovely buttered toast character on the nose, however in the mouth the wine is taut and linear, showing drive and compulsion to carry on through the long finish. The acidity pulls a firm and structuring line through the middle palate. Cheesecloth, dried flowers, green apple skins, chalk and curd. Very smart. 108 dozens made. Screw cap. 12% alc. RATING 95 DRINK 2022-2032 $45 EL

♟♟♟♟♡ **The Heroes Cabernet Malbec 2021, Clare Valley** RATING 90 DRINK 2022-2027 $28 EL
The Aldo Grenache 2020, Barossa Valley RATING 90 DRINK 2022-2028 $25 EL

Nannup Estate

Lot 25 Perks Road, Nannup, WA 6275 **Region** Blackwood Valley
T (08) 9756 2005 **www.**nannupestate.com.au **Winemaker** Ryan Aggiss (contract)
Viticulturist Mark Blizard **Est.** 2017 **Dozens** 5000 **Vyds** 14.43ha
Nannup Estate is owned by Mark Blizard and family. The vineyard sits high on the granite
ridges of the Blackwood River escarpment. During the growing season the vines enjoy long
hours of sunshine followed by moderate coastal breezes in the afternoons and cool evenings –
idyllic growing conditions. Abundant water, granite loam soils and low frost and disease
pressure all contribute to reliable quality and consistent vintages. The first 6ha of vines were
planted in '98, with subsequent plantings in '00 and '06. The vineyard now comprises almost
14.5ha of cabernet sauvignon, merlot, chardonnay, tempranillo and malbec. (JH)

Phillip Stanley Cabernet Sauvignon 2019, Blackwood Valley Chocolate-
coated raspberries, licorice, vanilla pod and finely crushed granite. This is fine
and yet plump – a lovely wine which shows the strength of the beautiful (and
I mean totally picturesque and magical) Blackwood Valley wine region. There is
admirable balance here between spice, fruit, oak and acid; all components weaving
in and out of each other, never once colliding. Screw cap. 14% alc. RATING 95
DRINK 2022–2036 $51 EL

Firetower Cabernet Merlot 2020, Blackwood Valley RATING 92
DRINK 2022–2030 $30 EL
Firetower Cabernet Sauvignon 2020, Blackwood Valley RATING 92
DRINK 2022–2032 $30 EL
Rolling Hills Cabernet Sauvignon 2020, Blackwood Valley RATING 92
DRINK 2022–2036 $38 EL
Rolling Hills Malbec 2020, Blackwood Valley RATING 91 DRINK 2024–2029
$38 EL
Phillip Stanley Reserve Chardonnay 2019, Blackwood Valley RATING 91
DRINK 2022–2029 $51 EL
Firetower Shiraz Malbec Tempranillo 2020, Western Australia RATING 90
DRINK 2022–2027 $30 EL
Rolling Hills Tempranillo 2020, Blackwood Valley RATING 90
DRINK 2022–2027 $38 EL
Phillip Stanley Reserve Chardonnay 2020, Blackwood Valley RATING 90
DRINK 2022–2028 $51 EL

Narkoojee

220 Francis Road, Glengarry, Vic 3854 **Region** Gippsland
T (03) 5192 4257 **www.**narkoojee.com **Open** 7 days 10.30–4.30 **Winemaker** Axel
Friend **Viticulturist** Axel Friend **Est.** 1981 **Dozens** 5000 **Vyds** 13.8ha
Narkoojee, originally a dairy farm owned by the Friend family, is near the old gold-mining
town of Walhalla and looks out over the Strzelecki Ranges. The wines are produced from
the estate vineyards, with chardonnay accounting for half the total. Former lecturer in civil
engineering and extremely successful amateur winemaker, Harry Friend, changed horses in
1994 to take joint control of the vineyard and winery with son Axel, and they haven't missed
a beat since; their skills show through in all the wines. (JH)

Reserve Chardonnay 2020, Gippsland This takes pole position of
Narkoojee's '20 chardonnays as it feels much lighter, restrained and refreshing, yet
flavourful. Tangy lemon and white nectarine come spiced up with ginger, the
oak playing its part but unobtrusively adding a lick of sweeter spices on the finish.
Acidity is key to keeping this bopping along nicely. Screw cap. 13% alc. RATING 95
DRINK 2022–2028 $43 JF
Valerie Chardonnay 2020, Gippsland Composed and balanced. It's
full of citrus and white peach, spiced with ginger powder. The oak is well
integrated, while the finish is long and decisive. Screw cap. 13.5% alc. RATING 95
DRINK 2022–2028 $60 JF

Valerie Shiraz 2020, Gippsland There's no denying the fruit quality and depth of flavour here as it has soaked up the French oak (19 months in 50% new oak). An excellent mid red with a purple tinge; loaded with dark fruits, cedary spice, aniseed and earthiness. It's full bodied, with plush tannins yet some grip. Decant it to enjoy now, but it will garner more complexity in time. Screw cap. 14% alc. RATING 95 DRINK 2023-2033 $60 JF

Reserve Chardonnay 2019, Gippsland It's subtle and restrained, which are excellent qualities for a wine that's often brawny. Stone fruit and lemon mingle with the creamy lees and spicy oak. Everything in place and the fine line of acidity extends the palate, ensuring the finish is long. Screw cap. 13.5% alc. RATING 95 DRINK 2021-2027 $43 JF

Valerie Pinot Noir 2020, Gippsland A pale ruby hue and delightfully fragrant with florals, wood spice and all manner of red fruits. Supple and delicate tannins support a light to mid-weight palate, yet sweet fruit comes to the fore, adding an extra burst of flavour. A lovely, composed wine. Screw cap. 13.5% alc. RATING 94 DRINK 2022-2028 $60 JF

ŸŸŸŸŸ **Reserve Maxwell Cabernet 2019, Gippsland** RATING 92 DRINK 2022-2030 $40 JF

Valerie Chardonnay 2019, Gippsland RATING 92 DRINK 2021-2027 $60 JF

Lily Grace Chardonnay 2020, Gippsland RATING 90 DRINK 2021-2025 $29 JF

Francis Road Shiraz 2020, Gippsland RATING 90 DRINK 2023-2030 $30 JF

Nepenthe   ★★★★

93 Jones Road, Balhannah, SA 5242 **Region** Adelaide Hills
T (08) 8398 8899 **www**.nepenthe.com.au **Open** 7 days 10–5 **Winemaker** James Evers **Est.** 1994 **Dozens** 44 000 **Vyds** 93ha

Nepenthe quickly established its reputation as a producer of high-quality wines, but founder Ed Tweddell passed away in 2006 and the business was purchased by Australian Vintage Limited the following year. The winery closed in '09 and winemaking operations transferred to McGuigan Wines (Barossa Valley). The Nepenthe winery has since been purchased by Peter Leske and Mark Kozned, and provides contract winemaking services via their Revenir venture. Nepenthe has 93ha of close-planted vines in the Adelaide Hills, with an exotic array of varieties. Exports to all major markets. (JH)

ŸŸŸŸŸ **Pinnacle Viognier 2020, Adelaide Hills** Quite the charmer, dressed in honeysuckle aromas with stone fruits, pear, citrus and orange peel. Presents a bright-fruited liveliness in the glass finishing with an apricot-pip dryness. Budding complexity. Delicious. Screw cap. 13.5% alc. RATING 93 DRINK 2021-2025 $35 JP

Pinnacle Gewürztraminer 2021, Adelaide Hills Vines grown at high altitude in the Lobethal district which presents a strong, focused gewürz in flavour, with texture and a finish of the brightest acidity. Candied lemon rind, lime curd, rose petal, potpourri and spice. Clean finish and not in the least overblown. Screw cap. 14% alc. RATING 92 DRINK 2021-2025 $35 JP

Altitude Sauvignon Blanc 2021, Adelaide Hills The price is right here and, so too, the flavours on show. Passionfruit, melon, lime and gooseberry fruits. Fleshy and soft to taste with a kick of herbaceousness to close, just in case you don't know what the grape is. Screw cap. 13.5% alc. RATING 90 DRINK 2021-2024 $22 JP

Sauvignon Blanc 2021, Adelaide Hills Part of the Elevation series, grapes were sourced from the cooler, higher parts of the Hills region. A ripe example of sauvignon by any measure, boasting tropical fruits, spiced apple, citrus, gooseberry and lime zest. The palate is crisp, flavoursome and juicy. Good balance here. Screw cap. 13.5% alc. RATING 90 DRINK 2021-2024 $25 JP

Pinnacle Albariño 2021, Adelaide Hills A cool fermentation in stainless steel has helped tame some of the ripe generosity of the fruit, bringing with it peach, nectarine, melon and stewed apple. A rich flavour, well fleshed out and given

extra spark and structure thanks to lively acidity. Screw cap. 14% alc. RATING 90
DRINK 2021–2024 $35 JP

ŶŶŶŶ Pinnacle 2020, Adelaide Hills RATING 89 DRINK 2021–2024 $35 JP
Pinnacle Arneis 2020, Adelaide Hills RATING 88 DRINK 2021–2024 $35 JP

New Era Vineyards   ★★★★

PO Box 391, Woodside SA 5244 **Region** Adelaide Hills
T 0413 544 246 **www**.neweravineyards.com.au **Winemaker** Robert Baxter, Iain Baxter
Viticulturist Bob Baxter, Iain Baxter **Est.** 1988 **Dozens** 1500 **Vyds** 15ha
The New Era vineyard is situated over a gold reef that was mined for 60 years until 1940,
when all recoverable gold had been extracted. The vineyard was mostly contracted to
Foster's and now includes shiraz, pinot noir, cabernet sauvignon, tempranillo, merlot, saperavi,
sangiovese, touriga nacional, nebbiolo, nero d'Avola and chardonnay. Much of the production
is sold to other winemakers in the region. The small amount of wine made has been the
subject of favourable reviews. Exports to Singapore. (JH)

ŶŶŶŶŶ Grüner Veltliner 2021, Adelaide Hills Wild-fermented in both stainless steel
and oak. Some winemaking thought has gone into the making of this grüner,
delivering complex flavours in yellow apple, pear, ginger, lovage and white pepper.
Entwined in a generous palate, textural and long offset by nicely by juicy acidity.
Screw cap. 13% alc. RATING 93 DRINK 2022–2025 $27 JP ✪
Barrel Select Montepulciano 2020, Limestone Coast This Italian red
grape, which rates highly in body, tannin and acidity, is enjoying its new home
in Australia. Deep purple hues with a range of attractive aromas in plum, black
cherry, licorice and olive tapenade, with generous, savoury flavours to follow.
Inky and dense, it's far from shy. Rather, its boldness deserves more time in
bottle to meld with some pretty sturdy tannins. Screw cap. 13.6% alc. RATING 92
DRINK 2022–2028 $40 JP
Barrel Select Touriga Nacional 2019, Langhorne Creek A vintage fortified
that nicely preserves the elegant, aromatic nature of the grape while presenting a
fresh young wine that will benefit from further ageing. A work in progress with
spirit still forming a relationship with the fruit, but give it time. Shows attractive
violet notes with plum, chocolate, blackstrap licorice and spice. Youthful, fresh and
spirity warm. Vinolok. 18.5% alc. RATING 90 $40 JP

ŶŶŶŶ Pinot Grigio 2021, Limestone Coast RATING 89 DRINK 2022–2024 $25 JP
Arneis 2021, Adelaide Hills RATING 89 DRINK 2022–2024 $27 JP
Sangiovese 2020, Adelaide Hills RATING 89 DRINK 2022–2025 $33 JP

Newbridge Wines   ★★★

18 Chelsea Street, Brighton, Vic 3186 (postal) **Region** Bendigo
T 0417 996 840 **www**.newbridgewines.com.au **Open** At Newbridge Hotel, Newbridge
Winemaker Mark Matthews **Viticulturist** Helen Waite **Est.** 1996 **Dozens** 300
Vyds 1ha
The Newbridge property was purchased by Ian Simpson in 1979, partly for sentimental
family history reasons and partly because of the beauty of the property situated on the
banks of the Loddon River. It was not until '96 that Ian decided to plant shiraz. Up to and
including the '02 vintage the grapes were sold to several local wineries. Ian retained the grapes
and made wine in '03, and lived to see that and the following 2 vintages take shape before
his death. The property is now run by his son Andrew, the wines contract-made by Mark
Matthews, supported by Andrew. (JH)

ŶŶŶŶ Shiraz 2019, Bendigo Maturation in a combination of French and American
oak sees the latter making more of an obvious statement in the '19 shiraz with its
strong coconut, high-tannin impact. Equally present is the regional signature of
eucalyptus layered between bracken, earth anise, blue fruits and savoury charcuterie
notes. Each component speaks separately and finds it difficult to meld. Screw cap.
14% alc. RATING 88 DRINK 2022–2026 $25 JP

Nick Haselgrove Wines ★★★★☆

13 Blewitt Springs Road, McLaren Flat, SA 5171 **Region** McLaren Vale
T (08) 8383 0886 **www**.nhwines.com.au **Open** Mon–Sun 10–3 by appt
Winemaker Nick Haselgrove **Est.** 1981 **Dozens** 12 000 **Vyds** 12ha
After various sales, amalgamations and disposals of particular brands, Nick Haselgrove now owns The Old Faithful (the flagship), Blackbilly, Clarence Hill, James Haselgrove and The Wishing Tree brands. Exports to the US, Canada, Hong Kong and Singapore. (JH)

ΨΨΨΨΨ **James Haselgrove Futures Shiraz 2019, McLaren Vale** A burly wine, but the sheath of ground pepper, clove, cardamom, salumi, blue and black fruits, Asian five-spice, anise and root beer is toned by well-applied oak and 28 months' maturation. Therein, serving it well. Each glass reveals more and despite the challenges of the torrid growing season, this is fresh and savoury and rewarding in a bouillon, umami and saline sense. Reminiscent of something from the Rhône, a personal love affair. Very good. Bravo! Screw cap. 14% alc. RATING 96 DRINK 2021-2035 $75 NG ❂

ΨΨΨΨΩ **Clarence Hill Reserve Cabernet Sauvignon 2019, McLaren Vale** RATING 93 DRINK 2022-2032 $65 NG
Clarence Hill Reserve Shiraz 2019, McLaren Vale RATING 93 DRINK 2021-2032 $65 NG
Clarence Hill G.S.M. GSM 2020, McLaren Vale RATING 92 DRINK 2022-2027 $45 NG
Clarence Hill Chardonnay 2021, Adelaide Hills RATING 90 DRINK 2022-2027 $35 NG

Nick O'Leary Wines ★★★★★

149 Brooklands Road, Wallaroo, NSW 2618 **Region** Canberra District
T (02) 6230 2745 **www**.nickolearywines.com.au **Open** By appt **Winemaker** Nick O'Leary **Viticulturist** Nick O'Leary **Est.** 2007 **Dozens** 17 000 **Vyds** 12ha
At the age of 28, Nick O'Leary had been involved in the wine industry for over a decade, working variously in retail, wholesale, viticulture and winemaking. Two years earlier he had laid the foundation for Nick O'Leary Wines, purchasing shiraz from local vignerons (commencing in 2006); riesling following in '08. His wines have had extraordinarily consistent success in local wine shows and competitions since the first vintages, and are building on that early success in spectacular fashion. At the NSW Wine Awards '15, the '14 Shiraz was awarded the NSW Wine of the Year trophy, exactly as the '13 Shiraz was in the prior year – the first time any winery had won the award in consecutive years. (JH)

ΨΨΨΨΨ **Heywood Tempranillo 2021, Canberra District** A new wine and a very welcome one in the classy Nick O'Leary stable. There's more structure to this compared with its sibling, Seven Gates, and more savoury. Pastilles, raspberries and cherries, earthy with baking spices, freshly rolled tobacco and potpourri. Fuller bodied with stealth-like tannins driving long across the palate. Top stuff. Screw cap. 13.5% alc. RATING 96 DRINK 2022-2028 $34 JF ❂
White Rocks Riesling 2021, Canberra District O'Leary's 3 rieslings are basically made the same, it's where the fruit is sourced that makes the big difference. This from the Westering vineyard, one of the oldest riesling sites in the Canberra District, nudging 50 years. The wine's a babe in terms of youth and its charm. Grapefruit and lime, zest and pith, minerally and tight, with ultra-refreshing acidity and a finish that lingers long after the sip has gone. Screw cap. 12% alc. RATING 96 DRINK 2022-2035 $38 JF ❂ ♥
Riesling 2021, Canberra District Always reliable and a very good go-to drink, because it's juicy and refreshing without any brittleness to the acidity. It's also full of freshly squeezed Indian limes and wet pebbles with a touch of lemon curd. The finish is impressively long. Screw cap. 12% alc. RATING 95 DRINK 2021-2029 $25 JF ❂

Seven Gates Tempranillo 2021, Canberra District More depth than a
joven style, yet this retains such a purity of fruit. Red currants and cherries come
infused with sarsaparilla, woodsy spices and turmeric. The medium-bodied palate
delights with bright acidity with some tension throughout and spot-on decisive
tempranillo tannins. Screw cap. 13.5% alc. RATING 95 DRINK 2022-2028 $32 JF ✪
Heywood Red Blend 2021, Canberra District A blend of 40/40/20%
tempranillo/shiraz/sangiovese. This is a ripper. While it charms with upfront fruit
flavours and lots of spice, it's a savoury wine with drinkability writ large. Lighter
framed, juicy, tangy acidity and fine, almost silky, tannins. I'd enjoy this in cool or
warm weather. Screw cap. 13.5% alc. RATING 95 DRINK 2022-2026 $34 JF ✪
Heywood Riesling 2021, Canberra District Comes out punching with apple
and lemon flavours, a waft of blossom and a daikon radish savouriness. It's racy
with bright acidity in the mix and finishes with terrific length. Screw cap. 12% alc.
RATING 95 DRINK 2021-2031 $34 JF ✪

🍷🍷🍷🍷🍷 **Four Miles Sangiovese 2021, Canberra District** RATING 93
DRINK 2022-2026 $32 JF
Chardonnay 2021, Tumbarumba RATING 93 DRINK 2022-2028 $35 JF
Rosé 2021, Canberra District RATING 92 DRINK 2021-2023 $21 JF ✪

Night Harvest   ★★★☆

PO Box 921, Busselton, WA 6280 **Region** Margaret River
T (08) 9755 1521 **www**.nightharvest.com.au **Winemaker** Bruce Dukes, Ben Rector,
Simon Ding **Viticulturist** Andy Ferreira **Est.** 2005 **Dozens** 2000 **Vyds** 300ha
Andy and Mandy Ferreira arrived in Margaret River in 1986 as newly married young
migrants. Their vineyard-contracting business expanded quickly when the region experienced
its rapid growth in the late '90s. They were involved in the establishment of about 300ha of
Margaret River vineyards, many of which they continue to manage today. As their fortunes
grew, they purchased their own property and produced their first wines in '05. Harvesting is
a key part of their business, and currently they harvest fruit from over 100 sites. Hence the
Night Harvest brand was born, and Butler Crest was added as a premium label. Exports to
the US and the UK. (JH)

🍷🍷🍷🍷🍷 **John George Cabernet Sauvignon 2019, Margaret River** Very aromatically
closed and restrained right now, despite almost 20 mins in the glass. In the mouth,
the wine is minty and fresh, with very fine, crumbly tannins that drywall the fruit
into place. A cascade of cassis, mulberries and blackberries huddle within the clos,
telling us that some time in a decanter will really help this to open and blossom.
Screw cap. 14% alc. RATING 91 DRINK 2022-3032 $40 EL

Nikola Estate   ★★★★★

148 Dale Road, Middle Swan, WA 6056 **Region** Swan Valley
T (08) 9374 8050 **www**.nikolaestate.com.au **Open** Thurs–Sun 10–5
Winemaker Damian Hutton, Marcello Fabretti **Viticulturist** Matty Trent **Est.** 2019
Vyds 56ha
While the Nikola brand may be new to the Swan Valley, the Yukich family behind it is anything
but. In late '19, Houghton Estate in the Swan Valley (vineyards, historic cellar door, est 1836,
and the winemaking facility) was purchased by brothers Graeme and third generation Kim
Yukich. Winemaker Damian Hutton has moved from a long history at Millbrook (Fogarty
Group) to assume the mantle at Nikola. The first acquisition of Houghton property by the
Yukich family occurred in 1989 (45ha sold to Mark Yukich, second generation) which
precipitated the formation of Oakover Wines in the '90s. Prior to that, the Yukich Brothers
wine company was formed in '53 by Nikola Yukich. (EL)

🍷🍷🍷🍷🍷 **Gallery Range: The Surrealist 2021, Swan Valley Geographe**
38/24/16/10/7/5% montepulciano/mencia/barbera/grenache/nero
d'Avola/arinto. This is really smart. There's a lot going on, but by virtue of
co-fermentation, the varieties are absolutely and seamlessly integrated. The

Geographe and the Swan are the perfect regions to source these varietals, and this is a wine that both can be proud of. It is bloody, gritty, savoury, salty and yet fresh. The lush purple and red fruit is only half the story; the tobacco leaf, saltbush, brine, clove, nutmeg, star anise and mountain herbs are the other half. Awesome. Screw cap. 15.2% alc. RATING 96 DRINK 2022-2032 $50 EL ✪

Gallery Range: The Minimalist 2021, Geographe This wine is intense. Dark, black, plush, brooding, with taut acid that lasers through the cloud of tannin. The palate is littered with berry fruit that stands guard, maintaining line and order. This has a staunch integrity about it, backed by layers of shaved deli meat, toasted walnuts, crushed graphite and balsamic poached blood plums. It's really good. Screw cap. 14% alc. RATING 95 DRINK 2022-2032 $50 EL

Regional Rosé 2021, Geographe 100% tempranillo. It is pure and plump, dominated by cherry, pomegranate, finely ground pepper, fennel flower and red apples. It's spicy too, a star anise, za'atar character through the finish. Smart wine, smart packaging. All good! Screw cap. 13.4% alc. RATING 94 DRINK 2021-2024 $30 EL ✪

Regional Shiraz 2020, Frankland River French oak (16 months in 30% new) is impactful here, lending the fruit a savoury edge, however nothing is going to smother that dense, muscular and concentrated fruit. Slow ripples of blackberry, raspberry, licorice, red dirt and ferrous notes all coalesce on the palate. Bloody smart for $30. Screw cap. 14.5% alc. RATING 94 DRINK 2021-2031 $30 EL ✪

ɣɣɣɣɣ **Regional Riesling 2021, Frankland River** RATING 93 DRINK 2022-2031 $30 EL

Regional Grenache 2021, Geographe RATING 92 DRINK 2022-2032 $30 EL

Shiraz 2020, Western Australia RATING 92 DRINK 2021-2027 $20 EL ✪

Rare Topaque NV, Swan Valley RATING 92 $50 EL

Regional Chenin Blanc 2021, Swan Valley RATING 91 DRINK 2022-2031 $30 EL

GSM 2021, Western Australia RATING 90 DRINK 2022-2025 $20 EL ✪

Semillon Sauvignon Blanc 2021, Western Australia RATING 90 DRINK 2021-2024 $20 EL ✪

Verdelho 2021, Swan Valley RATING 90 DRINK 2022-2028 $20 EL ✪

919 Wines ★★★★

39 Hodges Road, Glossop, SA 5344 **Region** Riverland
T 0408 855 272 **www.**919wines.com.au **Open** Wed–Sun & public hols 10–5 & by appt
Winemaker Eric Semmler **Viticulturist** Eric Semmler **Est.** 2002 **Dozens** 2500
Vyds 17ha

Eric and Jenny Semmler have been involved in the wine industry since '86 and have a special interest in fortified wines. Eric made fortified wines for Hardys and worked at Brown Brothers. Jenny has worked for Strathbogie Vineyards, Pennyweight Wines and St Huberts. They have planted micro-quantities of varieties for fortified wines: palomino, durif, tempranillo, muscat à petits grains, tinta cão, shiraz, tokay and touriga nacional. They use minimal water application, deliberately reducing the crop levels, and are certified organic. In '11 they purchased the 12.3ha property at Loxton which they now call Ella Semmler's Vineyard. Exports to Sweden. (JH)

ɣɣɣɣɣ **Reserve Touriga Nacional Tempranillo 2021, Riverland** Extraordinarily bright and young, but still with a firm bedrock of tannin grounding it all. '21 was a pretty exceptional vintage; cool (but not cold) with a long, restrained ripening period. This is leading to a bevy of cool, restrained wines being released. What a treat. This has all the hallmarks of the year that birthed it – balanced fruit and alcohol; the oak a structuring element rather than a key feature. Screw cap. 14% alc. RATING 92 DRINK 2022-2028 $40 EL

Reserve Shiraz 2021, Riverland This is super-concentrated and black (but it is balanced, too), with cassis, blackberries, blueberry coulis and black tea. The tannins are plump and cushioning in the mouth, meaning this is a full-bodied, to-the-brim shiraz, that shows the restraint and class of the '21 vintage. A wonderful thing. Screw cap. 14.5% alc. RATING 92 DRINK 2022-2028 $45 EL

Classic Topaque NV, Riverland Average age 10 years. Unctuous and concentrated, this has rich, opulent fruit in the mouth the undulates and courses over the tongue on its way through to the finish. While it doesn't have as many distinct fruit characters as the Tawny, the spirit here is far more integrated, drowned as it has been by the residual. Golden syrup, burnt caramel, toffee apple and molasses. Delicious. 500ml. Screw cap. 19% alc. RATING 92 $42 EL

Reserve Durif 2019, Riverland If ever there was a candidate for American oak, it would be durif. Its big, tannic qualities seem to dovetail nicely with the sweet, cushioned characters that American oak can impart. In this case, the fruit is full of blackberries, mulberries and plums, while 20 months in old and new oak brings sweet vanilla pod and toasted, desiccated coconut. Give it a further year or 2 (or more) as it is a little frisky right now – in time the vibrant, dense primary fruit will hopefully settle into something a little more earthy and savoury, to balance the oak. Screw cap. 16% alc. RATING 91 DRINK 2024-2034 $47 EL

ŶŶŶŶ **Reserve Petit Manseng 2021, Riverland** RATING 89 DRINK 2022-2028 $29 EL
Latin Collection Ruby NV, Riverland RATING 89 DRINK 2021-2026 $20 EL
Latin Collection Lambada NV, Riverland RATING 89 $20 EL
Classic Tawny NV, Riverland RATING 89 $40 EL
Classic Muscat NV, Riverland RATING 89 $42 EL
Durif 2018, Riverland RATING 88 DRINK 2022-2027 $47 EL

Nintingbool ★★★☆

56 Wongerer Lane, Smythes Creek, Vic 3351 (postal) **Region** Ballarat
T 0429 424 399 www.nintingbool.com.au **Winemaker** Peter Bothe **Est.** 1998
Dozens 600 **Vyds** 2ha
Peter and Jill Bothe purchased the Nintingbool property in 1982 and built their home in '84, using bluestone dating back to the gold rush. They established an extensive Australian native garden and home orchard and in '98 diversified by planting pinot noir, with a further planting the following year lifting the total to 2ha. Ballarat is one of the coolest mainland regions and demands absolute attention to detail (and a warm growing season) for success. (JH)

ŶŶŶŶŶ **Shiraz 2019, Ballarat** A black-fruited, savoury expression of shiraz and one that is quite ripe by Ballarat standards. Ripe plum, blackberry, licorice, dark chocolate and brown earth, not to mention eucalyptus and woody spices, are moulded by a leathery, tar character to close. Screw cap. 14% alc. RATING 90 DRINK 2022-2028 $27 JP

ŶŶŶŶ **Blanc de Noir 2019, Ballarat** RATING 88 $35 JP

Noble Red ★★★

13 Eastrow Avenue, Donnybrook, Vic 3064 (postal) **Region** Heathcote
T 0400 594 440 www.nobleredwines.com **Winemaker** Roman Sobiesiak, Katryna Kot
Est. 2002 **Dozens** 1200 **Vyds** 6ha
Roman and Margaret Sobiesiak acquired their property in 2002. It had 0.25ha of shiraz planted in the 1970s. A progressive planting program has seen the area increase to 6ha: shiraz (3.6ha) accounting for the lion's share, the remainder equally split to tempranillo, mourvèdre, merlot and cabernet sauvignon. They adopted a dry-grown approach, which meant slow development during the prolonged drought, but their commitment remains undimmed. Indeed, visiting many wine regions around the world and working within the industry locally has increased their determination. Exports to Poland. (JH)

ŶŶŶŶ **Petit Verdot 2020, Heathcote** A petit verdot with plenty of oomph! It's a big, cuddly wine anyway you look at it, from the high alcohol (which does bring some heat), the inky black colour, the dense fruit and high-tone toasty, coffee-mocha oak. In between, there is actually a fair bit going on, with everything

drawn together by sturdy tannins. Give it some more time. Screw cap. 14.6% alc.
RATING 89 DRINK 2022-2034 $30 JP

Carmenère 2019, Heathcote Launches dark and dense with an arresting
perfume of blue fruits, raspberry, black plum with anise and a touch of pepper.
Maintains the blueberry-choc-peppery intensity across a rich palate with dark
chocolate and tilled earth. Supple tannins do the rest, making this a most enjoyable
foray into carmenère country. Screw cap. 13.3% alc. RATING 89 DRINK 2022-2026
$25 JP

Rosé 2021, Heathcote 50/50% grenache/mourvèdre. Salmon-orange hues
introduce this tasty young rosé showing its grenache credentials early, both
perfume and flavour rich in confection notes with rosehip, musk, red berries,
light spice and earth. Good texture raises its food-pairing possibilities. Screw cap.
12.3% alc. RATING 88 DRINK 2022-2024 $20 JP

BST Shiraz 2020, Heathcote BST? Blood, sweat and tears! A dark, intense
wine that threads a meaty savoury line through the blackberry and plum fruit,
cassia bark, anise and hints of fennel. Framed in warm, toasty oak and sweet spices,
it finishes dry, earthy and just a touch early. Screw cap. 14.3% alc. RATING 88
DRINK 2022-2028 $45 JP

Nocturne Wines ★★★★★

185 Sheoak Dr, Yallingup, WA 6282 **Region** Margaret River
T 0477 829 844 **www.**nocturnewines.com.au **Winemaker** Julian Langworthy **Est.** 2007
Dozens 1300 **Vyds** 8ha

Nocturne Wines create consistently high-quality, limited-quantity wines, which explore
Margaret River's subregions and vineyards. Nocturne started as the side hustle that has evolved
into a fully fledged (and sought after) 'swan' brand. In '16, Julian Langworthy purchased the
Sheoak Vineyard in Yallingup (a former Jimmy Watson–producing vineyard, for the Harvey
River Bridge Estate Cabernet 2010), with its 4ha of mature cabernet sauvignon vines. These
vines are now the backbone of Nocturne's SR Cabernet, and the very essence of the single-
vineyard wine. Produced in maddeningly modest quantities, the Single Vineyard Chardonnay
and Cabernet together make up just over 300 dozen of the total 2000 dozen make. The 2019
SR Rosé (sangiovese/nebbiolo from Carbunup) was awarded the Halliday Wine Companion
Best Rosé 2021. Exports to the UK and Singapore. (EL)

ŶŶŶŶŶ Sheoak Vineyard Cabernet Sauvignon 2020, Margaret River Firmly
placed on the midnight spectrum and twinkling with as many cabernet flavours
as there are stars in the sky. Scintillating. Achingly intense. Totally delicious. Screw
cap. 14% alc. RATING 97 DRINK 2022-2042 $55 EL ✪

Tassell Park Vineyard Chardonnay 2020, Margaret River Toasted curry
leaves, yellow peach, supported by clean and salty minerality (the white sand of
the vineyard is powerfully suggestive) and layers upon layers of rippling flavour.
You should always get to know a wine that you love over a number of days, and
this will show you many sides of its beautiful face over the course of 3 or 4, if you
can stretch it out that long. Screw cap. 13% alc. RATING 97 DRINK 2022-2037
$55 EL ✪

ŶŶŶŶŶ Treeton SR Chardonnay 2020, Margaret River Super-juicy acidity punches
deep into the ripe, concentrated orchard fruit. The texture is wild and shapely and
curvy and fine. What a wine. I mean it. It's salivatingly good. Screw cap. 13% alc.
RATING 96 DRINK 2021-2036 $36 EL ✪

Carbunup SR Sangiovese Nebbiolo Rosé 2021, Margaret River Another
brilliant vintage of this wine. Balanced, layered, exciting, and littered with exotic
spice, this is the full package. As reliable as the sun is hot. Screw cap. 13% alc.
RATING 94 DRINK 2021-2025 $32 EL

Norfolk Rise Vineyard

438 Limestone Coast Road, Mount Benson, SA 5265 **Region** Mount Benson
T (08) 8768 5081 **www**.norfolkrise.com.au **Open** 7 days 11–5 **Winemaker** Nathan
Norman **Viticulturist** George Andrews **Est.** 2000 **Dozens** 20 000 **Vyds** 130ha
Norfolk Rise Vineyard is by far the largest and most important development in the Mount
Benson region. There are 50 blocks of sauvignon blanc, pinot gris, pinot noir, syrah, merlot,
cabernet sauvignon and chardonnay, allowing a range of options in making the 7 single-
variety wines in the portfolio. Previously owned by Kreglinger, of Pipers Brook fame, Norfolk
Rise Vineyard was purchased by the local McBride family in '21. Exports to the US, Canada,
Europe and Asia. (JH)

Maritime Cabernet Sauvignon 2020, Mount Benson Elegant, lightweight
cabernet here, layered with juicy raspberry, pomegrante, and leather-strap
tannins. A savoury finish hints that the life may be on the shorter side, so
enjoying it within 5–7 years is recommended. Screw cap. 14.4% alc. RATING 88
DRINK 2022-2027 $30 EL

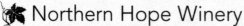 Northern Hope Winery

69 Mount William Road, Lancefield, Vic 3435 **Region** Macedon Ranges
T 0437 984 313 **www**.northernhope.com.au **Open** By appt **Winemaker** Richard
Edwards, Samantha Edwards **Viticulturist** Richard Edwards, Samantha Edwards
Est. 2017 **Dozens** 61 **Vyds** 0.5ha
Originally from the UK and working in digital marketing, Richard and Samantha Edwards
moved to Australia in 2012 and decided to become dedicated vignerons, establishing Northern
Hope winery at Lancefield in '17. The property sits at 750m above sea level, planted to 0.4ha
of pinot noir MV6 and 115 clones, with the same amount of chardonnay to be planted in '23.
Until the site produces fruit, the pinot noir is sourced from a grower in Woodend and the first
wine was made in '19. A Heathcote shiraz is due in mid '23. (JF)

Single Vineyard Pinot Noir 2019, Macedon Ranges This is owners Richard
and Samantha Edwards' first wine. While the core is all dark cherries and woodsy
spices with a touch of eucalyptus, the lasting impression is of a savoury wine.
Fuller bodied, with grainy tannins and the palate bolstered by some radicchio
bitterness, rhubarb and chinotto. Diam. 12.5% alc. RATING 92 DRINK 2021-2029
$44 JF

Nugan Estate

580 Kidman Way, Wilbriggie, NSW 2680 **Region** Riverina
T (02) 9362 9993 **www**.nuganestate.com.au **Open** Mon–Fri 9–4 **Winemaker** Daren
Owers **Est.** 1999 **Dozens** 300
Nugan Estate arrived on the scene like a whirlwind. It is an offshoot of the Nugan Group
headed by Michelle Nugan (until her retirement in Feb '13), inter alia the recipient of an
Export Hero Award in '00. The wine business is now in the energetic hands of Matthew
Nugan. Exports to Denmark, Finland, Ireland, the UK, the US, Canada, NZ, Japan and
Brazil. (JH)

Pinot Grigio 2021, King Valley This is one zesty, energised young grigio with
all the varietal trademarks pear, apple, musk with lemon zest. Palate is supple and
soft with a sweet centre and drizzle of lime. Bright acid crunch to close. Ready to
go. Screw cap. 12.5% alc. RATING 89 DRINK 2021-2024 $22 JP
Frasca's Lane Vineyard Chardonnay 2021, King Valley Nugan creates
wines that are well priced and ready for the glass. Here, we see generous, ripe
stone fruits, spiced apple, white peach and nougat playing to the crowd in a
bright and breezy style of chardonnay. Smooth with added honeysuckle on the
palate. Bright acidity completes this easy-drinking picture. Screw cap. 13.5% alc.
RATING 88 DRINK 2021-2025 $22 JP

O'Leary Walker Wines

7093 Horrocks Highway, Leasingham, SA 5452 **Region** Clare Valley
T 1300 342 569 **www**.olearywalkerwines.com **Open** Mon–Sat 10–4, Sun & public hols
11–4 **Winemaker** David O'Leary, Nick Walker, Jack Walker, Luke Broadbent **Est.** 2001
Dozens 20 000 **Vyds** 45ha
When David O'Leary and Nick Walker took the plunge in 2001 to establish their own
winery and brand, they had more than 30 years' experience as winemakers for some of
Australia's biggest wine groups. Initially the principal focus was on the Clare Valley with 10ha
of riesling, shiraz and cabernet sauvignon as the main plantings. Thereafter attention swung to
the Adelaide Hills where they now have 35ha of chardonnay, cabernet sauvignon, pinot noir,
shiraz, sauvignon blanc and merlot. The vineyards were certified organic in '13. Exports to the
UK, Ireland, Canada, UAE, Asia and Japan. (JH)

TTTTT **The Sleeper Reserve Shiraz 2018, Barossa Valley** A flying start ex high-
quality fruit, and extended time on skins has worked exactly as intended; in the
old wine-show terminology, full bodied, soft finish. A delicious shiraz now or 30
years hence. Diam. 14.5% alc. RATING 98 DRINK 2025-2050 $70 JH ✪

TTTTT **Pinotage 2021, Clare Valley** Plush black and red cherries adorn the front of
the wine, while salted pomegranate, red apples and a wild, earthy element bring
up the rear. The tannins are a highlight, being chewy, malleable and fun. All in all,
this is a bit of a burster. I like it, as will others. Screw cap. 13% alc. RATING 94
DRINK 2022-2029 $30 EL ✪
Polish Hill River Armagh Cabernet Sauvignon 2019, Clare Valley
A highly rated vintage by the winemakers of the Clare Valley. Medium bodied, but
a complex array of blackcurrant fruit, savoury tannins and oak, all merging with
each other from the outset. Screw cap. 14.5% alc. RATING 94 DRINK 2024-2034
$35 JH
Polish Hill River Armagh Shiraz 2019, Clare Valley The fruit is clearly up
to the task here, swallowing up 2 years in French oak (25% new). Licorice, steel
shavings and aniseed colour in the gaps of the generously peppered fruit. Dark,
dense and intense, with a mineral core that balances the Christmas flavours of fig,
quince and nutmeg. Screw cap. 14.5% alc. RATING 94 DRINK 2021-2031 $35 EL

Oakdene

255 Grubb Road, Wallington, Vic 3221 **Region** Geelong
T (03) 5256 3886 **www**.oakdene.com.au **Open** 7 days 10–4 **Winemaker** Robin
Brockett, Marcus Holt **Viticulturist** Sally Enders, Sally Powell **Est.** 2001 **Dozens** 8000
Vyds 32ha
Bernard and Elizabeth Hooley purchased Oakdene in 2001. Bernard focused on planting the
vineyard (shiraz, pinot gris, sauvignon blanc, pinot noir, chardonnay, merlot, cabernet franc and
cabernet sauvignon) while Elizabeth worked to restore the 1920s homestead. Much of the
wine is sold through the award-winning Oakdene Restaurant and cellar door. The quality is
exemplary, as is the consistency of that quality; Robin Brockett's skills are on full display. A new
vineyard (11km from Oakdene) planted in '17 (to shiraz, pinot noir, pinot gris, chardonnay,
sauvignon blanc, merlot, riesling, cabernet franc and cabernet sauvignon) has increased the
plantings from 12ha to 32ha. Export to Hong Kong. (JH)

TTTTT **Liz's Single Vineyard Bellarine Peninsula Chardonnay 2020, Geelong**
Quieter and more fine-boned than the '19 vintage, Liz nevertheless maintains
her usual high level of chardonnay poise and class. Bright and fresh in shades of
citrus – lemon, grapefruit, lime zest – with signature honeysuckle aromas. Walks
a firm, tight line in racy acidity, all the while the citrus, saline, mandarin skin
and gentle oak qualities of the wine are gathering their forces quietly, firmly and
resolutely. This wine intends to be around for a while. Screw cap. 13% alc.
RATING 95 DRINK 2021-2032 $35 JP ✪
Peta's Single Vineyard Bellarine Peninsula Pinot Noir 2020, Geelong
A finer, more delicate pinot noir than the 2019 vintage, but it retains a similar and

singularly impressive wild savouriness. Dusty beetroot, earth, black cherry, anise and wild herb aromas. Fine-edged and sinewy to taste, with an underlying depth of fruit concentration that will build with more time in bottle. Screw cap. 12.7% alc. RATING 94 DRINK 2022–2028 $43 JP

♀♀♀♀♀ **Bellarine Peninsula Chardonnay 2020, Geelong** RATING 92 DRINK 2021–2028 $24 JP ✪
William Single Vineyard Bellarine Peninsula Shiraz 2020, Geelong RATING 92 DRINK 2022–2032 $43 JP
Bellarine Peninsula Rosé 2021, Geelong RATING 91 DRINK 2021–2024 $24 JP
Bellarine Peninsula Pinot Grigio 2021, Geelong RATING 90 DRINK 2022–2024 $24 JP
Bellarine Peninsula Sauvignon Blanc 2021, Geelong RATING 90 DRINK 2022–2024 $24 JP
Bellarine Peninsula Pinot Noir 2020, Geelong RATING 90 DRINK 2021–2027 $24 JP
Bellarine Peninsula Shiraz 2020, Geelong RATING 90 DRINK 2022–2027 $24 JP

Oakover Wines   ★★★★

14 Yukich Close, Middle Swan, WA 6056 **Region** Swan Valley
T (08) 9374 8000 **www.oakoverwines.com.au Open** Wed–Sun 11–4 **Winemaker** Daniel Charter **Est.** 1929 **Dozens** 15 000 **Vyds** 27ha
Oakover Wines is a family-operated winery located in the Swan Valley. Formerly part of Houghton, it came under the Yukich family's control as Oakover Estate in 1990. Prominent Perth funds manager Graeme Yukich and his family have been involved in the region since Nicholas Yukich purchased his first block of land in 1929. In 2002 Oakover Estate became Oakover Wines and is now the third-largest winery in the Swan Valley. Oakover's White Label brand is currently sold in over 500 independent liquor outlets in WA and Vic, with expansion into NSW and Qld planned. Exports to India. (JH)

♀♀♀♀♀ **Chenin Blanc 2021, Western Australia** The fruit is from the Swan Valley – not putting that on the front label is a wasted opportunity, as the region and the variety go hand in glove. Fermented entirely in stainless steel, this is soft, round, plush, pretty, and chalky. With aromas of nashi pear, honeysuckle, honey, beeswax and green apples, it has it all going on. Is there any RS in there? If not, the fruit has such concentration as to appear so. Anyway, chenin always gets better with age, so this one will likely accelerate over the next year or more. A flaming bargain. Screw cap. 10.9% alc. RATING 93 DRINK 2022–2028 $14 EL ✪
Shiraz 2020, Western Australia Fruit from the Swan Valley. It's high-octane alcohol, and high-octane flavour, but for $14 it's very impressive indeed. It is concentrated, vibrant and brooding at once. There's blood, there's a bit of hung deli meat, there's blackberry and there's licorice. Bonza. Fantastic value. Screw cap. 15% alc. RATING 90 DRINK 2022–2027 $14 EL ✪

Oakridge Wines   ★★★★★

864 Maroondah Highway, Coldstream, Vic 3770 **Region** Yarra Valley
T (03) 9738 9900 **www.oakridgewines.com.au Open** 7 days 10–5 **Winemaker** David Bicknell, Tim Perrin **Est.** 1978 **Dozens** 35 **Vyds** 61ha
Winemaker David Bicknell has proved his worth time and again as an extremely talented winemaker. At the top of the Oakridge brand tier is 864, all Yarra Valley vineyard selections, only released in the best years (Chardonnay, Pinot Noir, Syrah, Cabernet Sauvignon); next is the Vineyard Series (the Chardonnay, Pinot Noir and Sauvignon Blanc come from the cooler Upper Yarra Valley; the Shiraz, Cabernet Sauvignon from the Lower Yarra); and the Over the Shoulder range, drawn from all of the sources available to Oakridge (Pinot Grigio, Chardonnay, Pinot Noir, Cabernet Merlot). The estate vineyards are Oakridge Vineyard,

Hazeldene Vineyard and Henk Vineyard. Exports to the UK, the US, Canada, Sweden, Norway, Fiji, Singapore, Hong Kong and Indonesia. (JH)

ΨΨΨΨΨ **864 Single Block Release Drive Block Funder & Diamond Vineyard Chardonnay 2020, Yarra Valley** Rightfully considered one of the great wines of Australia, this brilliant wine – from a cooler year – is another superb rendition. A bright green gold, expect aromas of lemon and pink grapefruit pith, freshly baked ginger-spice biscuits from the beautifully handled and integrated oak as well as jasmine, freshly laundered linen, wet stone and a hint of gunflint. Like many great wines, this balances power and delicacy in equal measure. There's a refreshing limoncello bitterness on the long, super-satisfying finish. Screw cap. 13.5% alc. RATING 98 DRINK 2022-2028 $95 PR ✪ ♥

Horst Riesling 2021, Yarra Valley A pale, lemon gold, this simply beautiful riesling opens with delicate lychee, tangerine and a little fresh, lemon sherbet. Even better on the palate. Bright and energetic, there's subtle orange blossom and feijoa fruit. I love the finely judged tension between the wine's gentle 18g/L RS of sugar and the fine vein of acidity that courses seamlessly through the wine. Screw cap. 11.5% alc. RATING 97 DRINK 2022-2028 $45 PR ✪ ♥

Vineyard Series Henk Chardonnay 2020, Yarra Valley A bright green gold, this is immediately engaging and open with its aromas of white peach, white flowers and preserved lemons. With its superb purity of fruit, I love the way the acidity cuts through the wine, giving it backbone and length. All the 2020 Vineyard Series chardonnays are subtle variations on a theme, with the Henk being my pick today. They all completely over-deliver for the price, too. Screw cap. 12.7% alc. RATING 97 DRINK 2022-2026 $45 PR ✪

Vineyard Series Willowlake Pinot Noir 2020, Yarra Valley Bright ruby. Subtle aromas of cranberries, quince, blood orange, fennel, lavender together with a little vanilla bean. Gently fleshy and compact, this also has excellent depth and concentration. This is deceptive, in that while it's delicious now, the tension between the core of fine tannins and bright acidity gives the wine considerable structure and will reward your patience should you have the necessary restraint. Screw cap. 13.1% alc. RATING 97 DRINK 2022-2026 $45 PR ✪

864 Single Block Release Winery Block Oakridge Vineyard Cabernet Sauvignon 2019, Yarra Valley Made virtually identically to the Original Vineyard Cabernet, this is a totally different, yet equally impressive, beast. A brilliant and bright medium crimson purple. Still a baby, this has a core of concentrated, perfectly pitched cassis fruit, together with some cedar and cigar box and a whiff of gravel and lavender. A touch closed at present, this has terrific purity and depth of fruit on the palate, with everything in place for this to improve for at least the next decade or 2, if not longer! Screw cap. 13% alc. RATING 97 DRINK 2023-2039 $95 PR ✪

ΨΨΨΨΨ **Vineyard Series Hazeldene Chardonnay 2021, Yarra Valley** A superb Hazeldene with white peach, wet stone, fresh mint, white flowers and a hint of macadamia nut. Pure fruited, concentrated and beautifully balanced, this will provide a lot of pleasure now and for years to come. Screw cap. 13.5% alc. RATING 96 DRINK 2022-2029 $45 PR ✪

Vineyard Series Hazeldene Pinot Noir 2020, Yarra Valley A bright ruby red. A very complex and fragrant nose redolent of dark cherry, musk sticks and potpourri. The palate is layered and delicate and I like the tension between the sinewy, long tannins and moreish acidity. A thinking person's pinot. Screw cap. 13.4% alc. RATING 96 DRINK 2022-2026 $45 PR ✪

Vineyard Series Willowlake Chardonnay 2020, Yarra Valley A very bright green gold. Excites from the first, with its aromas of white cut pears, stone fruits and an intriguing, perfectly handled flinty, freshly torched brûlée-top reduction. This has terrific drive and persistence on the palate, and the textured and layered mouth feel is balanced by the wine's perfectly integrated acidity. Screw cap. 13.2% alc. RATING 96 DRINK 2022-2027 $45 PR ✪

Original Vineyard Cabernet Sauvignon 2019, Yarra Valley A wine of medium-deep crimson colour, with gorgeous aromatics including dark cherries, satsuma plums, violets and a gentle waft of cedar from the oak. Classic, medium-bodied and beautifully poised cabernet, with silky long tannins. This should age effortlessly over the next 10–15 years. Screw cap. 13% alc. RATING 96 DRINK 2022-2035 $95 PR

Vineyard Series Willowlake Sauvignon 2020, Yarra Valley Sauvignon blanc. A wine that speaks of its location as much as its variety, with its cool aromas of lemon pith, lemongrass and greengage. Taut, chalky and linear on the palate. Lots to like here. Screw cap. 11.3% alc. RATING 95 DRINK 2022-2027 $30 PR ✪

Vineyard Series Barkala Chardonnay 2020, Yarra Valley A lovely, bright, green gold. Like all the Oakridge '20s, it's worth giving this the time to open up where it reveals grapefruit pith, fennel seeds, fresh nectarine and orange blossom. There's a stoniness to the nicely balanced palate and, like all Oakridge chardonnays, there is plenty of upside for those who buy enough to cellar for the next 5–7 years. Screw cap. 13.4% alc. RATING 95 DRINK 2022-2028 $45 PR

Vineyard Series Henk Pinot Noir 2020, Yarra Valley A bright cherry red. Spiced raspberry jelly and some black cherry fruit. Perfumed with lavender and rosemary notes. There's a core of sweet red fruits which tapers into fine tannins and a refreshing pomegranate-like acidity. It's long, too, and will reward at least another 5 years in the cellar. Screw cap. 14% alc. RATING 95 DRINK 2023-2026 $45 PR

Vineyard Series Oakridge Shiraz 2020, Yarra Valley A medium and bright crimson ruby. This subtle and very well put together wine creeps up on you slowly with its aromas of red fruits, pink peppercorns, mountain herbs and some floral notes. Medium bodied, this has excellent depth and persistence while remaining light on its feet. And it finishes with more than enough fine-grained and persistent tannins to merit seeing how this will evolve over the next 4–6 years, if not longer. Screw cap. 13.5% alc. RATING 95 DRINK 2022-2028 $45 PR

Chardonnay 2021, Yarra Valley A bright green gold. A terrific introduction to Oakridge chardonnays, showing just how good they can be. Classic Bicknell struck match and flint to go with the apple, yellow nectarine and white peach fruit aromas. Tightly wound, this has good depth and will be even better in another six months or so. Excellent value. Screw cap. 12.8% alc. RATING 94 DRINK 2022-2026 $30 PR ✪

Oakway Estate   ★★★★

575 Farley Road, Donnybrook, WA 6239 **Region** Geographe
T (08) 9731 7141 **www.**oakwayestate.com.au **Open** W'ends 11–5 **Winemaker** Tony Davies **Viticulturist** Wayne Hammond, Ria Hammond **Est.** 1997 **Dozens** 1000 **Vyds** 2ha
Ria and Wayne Hammond run a vineyard, beef cattle and sustainable blue-gum plantation in undulating country on the Capel River in the southwest of WA. The grapes are grown on light gravel and loam soils that provide good drainage, giving even sun exposure to the fruit and minimising the effects of frost. The vineyard is planted to shiraz, merlot, cabernet sauvignon, nero d'Avola, malbec, muscat, sauvignon blanc, vermentino and chardonnay, and the wines have won a number of medals. (JH)

🍷🍷🍷🍷🍷 **Los Ninos Single Vineyard Malbec 2020, Geographe** This is a savoury malbec, loaded with blackberry pastille, salted licorice, green peppercorns, fine layers of hung deli meat, shades of pâté and fresh garden herbs. The tannins are fine and minerally, creating a delicate yet firm structure in the mouth. Screw cap. 14% alc. RATING 91 DRINK 2021-2028 $28 EL

Oates Ends

22 Carpenter Road, Wilyabrup, WA 6280 **Region** Margaret River
T 0401 303 144 **www**.oatesends.com.au **Open** By appt **Winemaker** Cath Oates
Viticulturist Russ Oates **Est.** 1999 **Dozens** 2000 **Vyds** 11ha

Cath Oates returned home to Margaret River after an international winemaking career spanning 15 years. The wines are made from the family Wilagri Vineyard, planted in '99 and now owned and managed by viticulturist brother Russ Oates. Oates Ends is the culmination of both of their respective experience and wine philosophies. The vineyard is run on sustainable farming principles (Cath is also chair of AGW's Sustainability Advisory Committee). Sheep are a big part of the vineyard program with winter mowing a given and they are increasingly being relied upon for leaf plucking during the growing season. The name comes from the shed wine made for family and friends in the early 2000s from the ends of the rows the harvesters missed and acknowledges the importance of family farming traditions. Exports to Canada and Singapore. (JH)

♀♀♀♀♀ **Tempranillo 2021, Margaret River** This is super-light in colour, compared with both the other tempranillos on the bench and the '20 vintage before it. This is spicy, herbaceous and also floral: we're talking fennel, licorice root, glacé ginger, raspberry, pomegranate and rose petals. In the mouth the wine is gorgeous – the tannins very fine and quite slinky. Drinks like a pinot. I like it. Screw cap. 13% alc. RATING 94 DRINK 2022-2029 $30 EL ✪

Cabernet Sauvignon 2019, Margaret River Ripe heirloom tomatoes, lavender, blackberry, mulberry, tobacco leaf fresh off the tree and fine white pepper frame the aromatics. In the mouth the wine is delicate; the tannins a subliminal smudge of shape that serve only to caress and cajole the fruit through the long finish. A lovely, elegant wine, and – like the '17 vintage – it speaks with a restrained and soft voice. Screw cap. 13.5% alc. RATING 94 DRINK 2022-2037 $60 EL

♀♀♀♀♀ **Sauvignon Blanc Semillon 2021, Margaret River** RATING 93 DRINK 2022-2025 $25 EL ✪

Chardonnay 2020, Margaret River RATING 93 DRINK 2021-2031 $45 EL
Chardonnay 2021, Margaret River RATING 92 DRINK 2022-2028 $60 EL

Old Plains

71 High Street, Grange, SA 5023 (postal) **Region** Adelaide Plains
T 0407 605 601 **www**.oldplains.com **Winemaker** Domenic Torzi, Tim Freeland
Viticulturist Dom Torzi **Est.** 2003 **Dozens** 4000 **Vyds** 12ha

Old Plains is a partnership between Tim Freeland and Dom Torzi, who have acquired some of the last remaining small parcels of old-vine shiraz, grenache and cabernet sauvignon in the Adelaide Plains region. Wines made from these vines are sold under the Old Plains label. Pinot gris, riesling and a sparkling pinot noir/chardonnay are sourced from the Adelaide Hills and sold under the Longhop brand. Exports to the US and Denmark. (JH)

♀♀♀♀♀ **Power of One Old Vine Shiraz 2019, Adelaide Plains** Vegan friendly. With its open warmth and generosity, you might pick it as Barossan in origin. Delicious and ready to go, there's a lot happening with blackcurrant pastille, chocolate, clove, coffee and earth, coming together in a riot of intense flavour. Spicy tannins are up for the ride. No tabs on itself, just plenty of good, honest drinking. Screw cap. 14.5% alc. RATING 90 DRINK 2021-2026 $35 JP

♀♀♀♀ **Longhop Merlot 2020, Barossa Valley** RATING 89 DRINK 2021-2025 $24 JP
Longhop Pinot Gris 2021, Adelaide Hills RATING 88 DRINK 2021-2024 $20 JP
Longhop Cabernet Sauvignon 2019, Adelaide Plains RATING 88 DRINK 2021-2024 $20 JP

Oliver's Taranga Vineyards ★★★★★

246 Seaview Road, McLaren Vale, SA 5171 **Region** McLaren Vale
T (08) 8323 8498 **www**.oliverstaranga.com **Open** 7 days 10–4 **Winemaker** Corrina
Wright **Viticulturist** Don Oliver **Est.** 1839 **Dozens** 10000 **Vyds** 90ha

William and Elizabeth Oliver arrived from Scotland in 1839 to settle in McLaren Vale. Six
generations later, members of the family are still living on the Whitehill and Taranga farms. The
Taranga property has 15 varieties planted (the lion's share to shiraz and cabernet sauvignon,
with lesser quantities of durif, fiano, grenache, mataro, merlot, sagrantino, tempranillo, mencia,
vermentino and white frontignac). Corrina Wright (the Oliver family's first winemaker)
makes the wines. In '21 the family celebrated 180 years of grapegrowing. Exports to the UK,
the US, Singapore, Hong Kong, Denmark and Finland. (JH)

🏆🏆🏆🏆🏆 **The Banished Fortified Grenache NV, McLaren Vale** Spiritous aromas of
date, cardamom, ginger, mahogany, old stained timber, tobacco and the spices of
a Moroccan souk. A blend with an average age of 20 years, meaning that some
of the wines are considerably older still. Fine depth and spread across the palate.
Turmeric and cardamom linger. Multitudinous and immensely rewarding, albeit,
in small doses. Screw cap. 19% alc. RATING 96 $50 NG ✪

Ruthless Ruth Muscat NV, McLaren Vale Olive edges skirting a mahogany
hue. Scents of molasses, roasted almonds, hazelnuts and walnut, with rancio-
driven closet and old cheese. Brilliant gear! This straddles the edges of overt, fresh
and pointed restraint. Intense, layered and profoundly long. Screw cap. 19% alc.
RATING 96 $60 NG ✪

RW Reserve Grenache 2020, McLaren Vale This is very good. The approach
to grenache at this address has changed, for the better: more ethereal, red-fruited
and finer boned, with a svelte but firm tannic carriage transporting Seville orange,
kirsch, fecund strawberry and the attractively sweet-and-sour pucker of loganberry.
Real succulence, verve and finely defined length. The pantheon is within
sprinting distance. A tad too sweet to warrant a higher score. Screw cap. 14.5% alc.
RATING 94 DRINK 2021-2027 $75 NG

DJ Reserve Cabernet 2019, McLaren Vale It is often difficult to comprehend
that such good cabernet is grown, still, in a growing bastion of Mediterranean
varieties. Led, of course, by grenache. Yet here it is. Mulch, wood sap, cedar oak,
blackcurrant, sage, bayleaf and a swab of black olive, marking the bolshy finish.
Far from a finessed wine, this is nevertheless high on personality. The muscle,
sinew and flesh, all in place. Will age very well. Screw cap. 14.5% alc. RATING 94
DRINK 2022-2037 $75 NG

HJ Shiraz 2019, McLaren Vale At this level, this sort of cedary vanillin oak
works well, galvanising brambly blackberry notes, infused with nori, saline mineral
crunch, anise and smoked pepper. A powerful wine, but the elements are in
synch to meld well with a few years in bottle. For those who like oomph with a
modicum of class. Screw cap. 14.5% alc. RATING 94 DRINK 2022-2034 $75 NG

🏆🏆🏆🏆 **Chica Mencia Rosé 2021, McLaren Vale** RATING 93 DRINK 2021-2022
$27 NG ✪

Small Batch Cadenzia Grenache 2021, McLaren Vale RATING 93
DRINK 2021-2025 $32 NG

Small Batch Sagrantino 2020, McLaren Vale RATING 93 DRINK 2022-2032
$45 NG

Small Batch Brioni's Blend 2021, McLaren Vale RATING 92
DRINK 2021-2025 $32 NG

Small Batch Mencia 2021, McLaren Vale RATING 92 DRINK 2021-2025
$35 NG

Fiano 2021, McLaren Vale RATING 91 DRINK 2021-2023 $27 NG

Shiraz 2020, McLaren Vale RATING 91 DRINK 2021-2025 $30 NG

Oranje Tractor

198 Link Road, Albany, WA 6330 **Region** Great Southern
T 0431 846 412 **www**.oranjetractor.com **Open** Sun 11–5 or by appt **Winemaker** Rob
Diletti, Pamela Lincoln, Marius Mencel **Viticulturist** Murray Gomm **Est.** 1998
Dozens 1000 **Vyds** 3ha

The name celebrates the 1964 vintage orange-coloured Fiat tractor acquired when Murray
Gomm and Pamela Lincoln began the establishment of the vineyard. Murray was born in the
region, but moved to Perth to work in physical education and health promotion. Here he met
nutritionist Pamela, who completed the wine science degree at CSU in 2000, before being
awarded a Churchill Fellowship to study organic grape and wine production in the US and
Europe. The vineyard was certified organic between 2005–2021. They have since dropped the
certification but retained the practice. (JH)

Sauvignon Blanc 2021, Albany Lean and tight, as you'd expect from the
low alcohol, but there is also a lovely, restrained, crushed-shell character here.
Coupled with the very fine saline acidity, this is a delicately poised wine. There's
more flavour here than the fine-boned structure lets on. Screw cap. 11.4% alc.
RATING 92 DRINK 2021-2024 $34 EL

Elixyr Botanica Vermouth 2021, Albany Grassy, herbaceous and reminiscent
of orange-peel essence (plus lemon verbena, beach grass wet with dew, lemon leaf
and cloves) this has an engaging nose, and it was fascinating to see how it opened
up with some air. There's a distinct earl-grey tea character laced through the finish
once it has blossomed and opened up. I can now very much foresee this with
some gin, ice and campari. Screw cap. 17.8% alc. RATING 90 DRINK 2022-2024
$35 EL

Orbis Wines

307 Hunt Road, McLaren Vale, SA 5171 **Region** McLaren Vale
T 0466 986 318 **www**.orbiswines.com.au **Open** By appt **Winemaker** Lauren Langfield,
Nick Dugmore, Samuel Smith **Viticulturist** Richard Leask **Est.** 1960 **Vyds** 26ha

Orbis Wines hail from a site of 32ha at an elevation of 150m, planted in the 1960–70s. The
old-vine shiraz was recently complemented with tempranillo, while grenache, albariño,
montepulciano, nero d'Avola and fiano will soon be coming on steam, making for a
Mediterranean potpourri. Owners Brad Moyes and Kendall Grey's fervent belief that these
varieties will define McLaren Vale's future (as much as shape its present) underlies a holistic
culture in the truest sense: regenerative farming, recycled timber, solar power, polyculture in
the vineyard, the abolishment of heavy machinery and the negation of tin-foil seals and screw
caps, are some of their efforts in the name of bona fide sustainability, carbon neutrality and
the promotion of biodiversity. These ethics are appropriated to minimally invasive harvest
and wine-making practises in the hands of Samuel J Smith and Nick Dugmore, from hand
picking, a reliance on indigenous yeasts and zero sulphur additions. The overarching style is
one of mid-weighted freshness, poise and giddy drinkability. Stay tuned, for the future
is bright. (NG)

Tempranillo Rosé 2021, McLaren Vale A very fine rosé, resplendent with a
lustrous tangerine hue and rails of salty tannins, pliant enough to wind their way
around a densely packed core of musk, bergamot, persimmon and pomegranate.
This drinks like a lighter red such is its versatility, mid weight, freshness and the
whiff of seriousness to its structural latticework. Excellent drinking, far from the
ersatz Provençal blueprint. I love this. Bravo! Screw cap. 12.5% alc. RATING 94
DRINK 2022-2024 $30 NG ✪

The Original Shiraz 2021, McLaren Vale RATING 92 DRINK 2022-2025
$37 NG
Whole Bunch Shiraz 2021, McLaren Vale RATING 92 DRINK 2022-2026
$37 NG

Orlando ★★★★★

Barossa Valley Way, Rowland Flat, SA 5352 **Region** Barossa Valley
T (08) 8521 3111 **www**.pernod-ricard-winemakers.com **Winemaker** Ben Thoman
Est. 1847 **Dozens** 10 000 **Vyds** 14ha

Orlando is the parent who has been separated from its child, Jacob's Creek (see separate entry).
While Orlando is over 170 years old, Jacob's Creek is little more than 45 years old. For what
are doubtless sound marketing reasons, Orlando aided and abetted the separation, but the
average consumer is unlikely to understand the logic and, if truth be known, is unlikely to
care. (JH)

🍷🍷🍷🍷🍷 **Steingarten Riesling 2021, Eden Valley** No longer a single-vineyard wine,
today, it is a blend of 2 separate blocks but retains the name of the famous walled
vineyard. It's still a belter … pristine citrus fruits, a crystalline acid line that crackles
and pulses through the fruit with sapid zeal and focus and a tubular, powerful
palate shape that is much admired. It's a ripper. Screw cap. 11% alc. RATING 96
DRINK 2021-2040 $50 DB ✪
Centenary Hill Shiraz 2017, Barossa Sporting a very glossy, classy aromatic
profile of pristine plum and berry fruits, with a sheen of cedary oak, spice and dark
chocolate. Wonderfully balanced with an elegant, detailed palate shape, fine, sandy
tannin support and a sense of enduring drive and grace. Screw cap. 14.5% alc.
RATING 96 DRINK 2021-2036 $75 DB ✪
Lawson's Shiraz 2019, Padthaway The fruit is pure and bright (blueberries,
raspberry and summer mulberries); the ripe, succulent qualities are amplified by
the foundation of American oak. What really elevates this however, is the pink
peppercorn and dried exotic spice on the mid palate, creating an aura of poise
and detail that is most intriguing. This is gorgeous, all things balanced and in
place. Screw cap. 14.5% alc. RATING 95 DRINK 2022-2037 $75 EL

🍷🍷🍷🍷🍷 **Hilary Chardonnay 2021, Adelaide Hills** RATING 93 DRINK 2022-2028
$35 JP
Cellar 13 2020, Barossa RATING 93 DRINK 2021-2026 $35 DB
Jacaranda Ridge Cabernet Sauvignon 2018, Coonawarra RATING 93
DRINK 2022-2037 $75 EL
Lyndale Chardonnay 2021, Adelaide Hills RATING 92 DRINK 2022-2027
$50 JP
Bungalow Lane 2017, Barossa Valley RATING 92 DRINK 2021-2031 $35 DB

🍇 Ossa Wines ★★★★☆

100 Crossins Road, Swansea, Tas 7190 (postal) **Region** Tasmania
T 0447 404 469 **www**.ossa.wine **Winemaker** Liam McElhinney **Viticulturist** Jay Dillon
Est. 2021 **Dozens** 550 **Vyds** 20ha

Rod and Cecile Roberts retained the best consultants in the state when their 20ha Ossa
vineyard was planted and the first wines made. Winemaking Tasmania is a custom crush and
ferment facility providing birth to bottle care. Their desire for sustainability resulted in an
entirely solar-powered structure; removing noxious plant species, fencing wildlife zones; and
cleaning waterways. The vineyard wasn't in bearing in '20, so they sourced small parcels of
chardonnay (175 dozen), pinot noir (250 dozen) and sparkling (35 dozen), and the first wine
ex the estate Belbrook Vineyard was chardonnay '21 (85 dozen). All of which made the '20
Pinot Noir, winning Best Wine at the Australian Pinot Noir Challenge '21 (and a second
trophy for Best Tasmanian Wine) akin to a fairy tale. (JH)

🍷🍷🍷🍷🍷 **Pinot Noir 2020, Tasmania** Stunning crimson-magenta colour sets the scene
for a perfumed wine of exceptional quality, with ever-changing aromas and
flavours encapsulated in an insistent heartbeat of purity. The mouthfeel, length
and balance of the red and black cherry fruit underpins a wine that is great now,
with spicy complexity just around the corner. Screw cap. 13.5% alc. RATING 98
DRINK 2025-2035 $120 JH ✪

¶¶¶¶¶ Grüner Veltliner 2021, Tasmania RATING 91 DRINK 2022-2022 $60 TS
Méthode Traditionnelle 2016, Tasmania RATING 90 $90 TS
Chardonnay 2020, Tasmania RATING 90 DRINK 2022-2025 $90 TS

Paisley Wines ★★★★

158 Hurns Road, Angaston, SA 5353 **Region** Barossa Valley
T 0491 377 737 **www.**paisleywines.com.au **Winemaker** Derek Fitzgerald **Est.** 2017
Dozens 1800 **Vyds** 5ha
Derek Fitzgerald made wines for nearly 20 years in WA, Langhorne Creek and the Barossa
Valley before gentle persuasion by wife Kirsten led to the decision to make wine on their
own account. The varieties produced are classic Barossa: grenache, mataro and shiraz. Derek
has winkled out some small parcels of grapes from long-proven vineyards up to 70 years old.
Adelaide Hills Fiano completes the range. (JH)

¶¶¶¶¶ **Celtic Maeve Shiraz Cabernet 2019, Barossa Valley** Deep red purple in
the glass with plush satsuma plum and blackberry fruits, cut with dark spice, dark
chocolate, cedar, clove, pepper and leather. Sweetly-fruited, some prune, violets
and oak spice entering on the palate along with assertive talcy tannins and a pure,
glossy fruit-forward finish. Screw cap. 14.5% alc. RATING 93 DRINK 2021-2031
$48 DB
Cashmere Riesling 2021, Eden Valley This vintage will be remembered as
stellar for Eden Valley riesling. This wine sings with the classic aromas of Bickford's
lime cordial and Christmas lily notes along with hints of almond paste, crushed
quartz, orange blossom and stone. Dry, sumptuous and precise with a fine line
and plenty of quartzy acid drive pulsing it along nicely. Lovely stuff. Screw cap.
12.4% alc. RATING 92 DRINK 2021-2031 $30 DB
Denim Mataro 2019, Barossa Valley Excellent aromatic depth and detail with
juicy plum and summer berry fruits, Asian spice, dried citrus rind, jasmine, earth
and roasting meats. The aromas transpose neatly over onto the palate which is pure
of fruit, well-weighted and displays considerable fruit heft. Screw cap. 14.7% alc.
RATING 92 DRINK 2021-2028 $30 DB
Silk Shiraz 2019, Barossa Valley There's substantial fruit weight to this wine
but the addition of some whole bunches lets a little light in, highlighting ripe
plum and blackberry fruits, baking spice, a whiff of choc-mint and gentle oak.
Finishes savoury with an undercoat of exotic spice and amaro herbs and a very
enjoyable fruit flow. Screw cap. 14.7% alc. RATING 92 DRINK 2021-2028 $30 DB

¶¶¶¶ **Linen Fiano 2021, Adelaide Hills** RATING 88 DRINK 2021-2024 $30 DB
Boombox Shiraz 2019, Barossa RATING 88 DRINK 2021-2027 $25 DB
Turntable GSM 2019, Barossa Valley RATING 88 DRINK 2021-2025 $25 DB

Palmer Wines ★★★★

1271 Caves Road, Dunsborough, WA 6281 **Region** Margaret River
T (08) 9756 7024 **www.**palmerwines.com.au **Open** 7 days 10–5 **Winemaker** Mark
Warren, Bruce Dukes, Clive Otto **Est.** 1977 **Dozens** 6000 **Vyds** 51.39ha
Steve and Helen Palmer have mature plantings of cabernet sauvignon, sauvignon blanc, shiraz,
merlot, chardonnay and semillon, with smaller amounts of malbec and cabernet franc. Recent
vintages have had major success in WA and national wine shows. (JH)

¶¶¶¶¶ **The Grandee Reserve Cabernets 2019, Margaret River** 40/30/24/6%
cabernet sauvignon/malbec/merlot/cabernet franc. Biscuity oak frames the
concentrated fruit here, the blend of varieties makes for a balanced and complex
wine. Still 3 years from release at the time of tasting, this has all the hallmarks
required for graceful ageing. We'll give it another go in '24. Screw cap. 14% alc.
RATING 93 DRINK 2024-2039 $42 EL
Cabernet Sauvignon 2019, Margaret River Punchy licorice and blackberry
on the nose, the palate follows in the same vein with beetroot, metal shavings and
exotic spice. The beautiful fruit is enshrouded in oak at this point, contributing to

the overall plushness and density in the mouth. It needs time to come together: it's still very elemental at this stage. Screw cap. 14% alc. RATING 90 DRINK 2024–2036 $35 EL

Krackerjack Bin 618 Cabernet Merlot 2018, Margaret River Leafy, plush and varietal, the palate is cohesive and smooth. The spices here meld seamlessly with the acidity, making for a pretty, easy drink. All good things. Screw cap. 14.3% alc. RATING 90 DRINK 2021–2028 $30 EL

ρρρρ **Krackerjack Bin 218 Shiraz Cabernet 2018, Margaret River** RATING 89 DRINK 2021–2028 $30 EL

Purebred by Bruce Dukes Shiraz 2019, Margaret River RATING 88 DRINK 2024–2029 $40 EL

Paracombe Wines ★★★★

294b Paracombe Road, Paracombe, SA 5132 **Region** Adelaide Hills
T (08) 8380 5058 **www.**paracombewines.com **Open** By appt **Winemaker** Paul Drogemuller **Est.** 1983 **Dozens** 15 000 **Vyds** 22.1ha
Paul and Kathy Drogemuller established Paracombe Wines in 1983 in the wake of the devastating Ash Wednesday bushfires. The winery is located high on a plateau at Paracombe, looking out over the Mount Lofty Ranges, and the vineyard is run with minimal irrigation and hand pruning to keep yields low. The wines are made onsite, with every part of the production process through to distribution handled from there. Exports to the UK, Canada, Denmark, Sweden, Luxembourg and Singapore. (JH)

ρρρρρ **Pinot Blanc 2021, Adelaide Hills** One of those wines you keep returning to, each time discovering something new. It's the saline, oyster-shell and sea-spray quality that is central here: it's so clean and works the tastebuds in unison with honeysuckle, citrus blossom, preserved lemon and spiced apple. Conducts a purity of fruit flavour in tandem with a bright, crisp, lemon pithiness. One to watch. Screw cap. 11% alc. RATING 93 DRINK 2021–2024 $25 JP✪

The Reuben 2017, Adelaide Hills 56/35/7/2% merlot/cabernet sauvignon/ cabernet franc/malbec. The Reuben's lead grape can change from year to year, in '17 it's merlot's moment to take point. Immediately, there is a sense of elegance and fineness with plush plum, mulberry, brambly fruits and gentle spice, herbs. Medium in body, smooth in tannins with restrained, thoughtful oak, it's certainly one tidy wine package for the price. Screw cap. 14.5% alc. RATING 93 DRINK 2021–2027 $27 JP✪

Malbec 2017, Adelaide Hills Malbec is in new territory for the Adelaide Hills. It's settling in nicely. Red plums, raspberry, blueberries and vanilla introduce a friendly, fruit-generous wine. It's all about the fruit, soft and unctuous with a thread of briar and earth running free and long. Delicious. Screw cap. 14.5% alc. RATING 92 DRINK 2021–2029 $32 JP

Pecorino 2021, Adelaide Hills Pecorino is an Italian variety with a great deal to offer in the way of texture and savouriness. Carries plenty of Meyer lemon, grapefruit, quince, baked apple and a summery fruit feel. Tasted before release and firm in structure, there was an emerging supple texture that was most promising, together with a preserved-lemon savouriness. A grape variety to watch. Screw cap. 12.5% alc. RATING 91 DRINK 2021–2025 $25 JP

Pecorino 2020, Adelaide Hills This white Italian variety likes its new home in the Hills. It makes an immediate impact with its textural and savoury liveliness in the glass. Meyer lemon, peach skin, quince and baked apple aromas. A nice counterpoint at play between the firmness of structure and the warmth of the texture across the tongue, ending in a generous savoury quince paste and nutty twist. Screw cap. 13.5% alc. RATING 91 DRINK 2021–2024 $25 JP

Cabernet Franc 2018, Adelaide Hills A nice little surprise packet of a wine, all plums and spices but with an underlying steeliness. I'm immediately thinking further bottle age could be on the cards. Tight as a drum, there are some lovely background aromatics and fruits lining up, waiting for their moment. Let it have its way. Screw cap. 14% alc. RATING 91 DRINK 2021–2027 $32 JP

Montepulciano 2018, Mount Lofty Ranges Bright, iridescent purple catches the eye. This Italian grape is capturing hearts and minds in this country with its open, honest, fruit-forward appeal. Black cherry, plum, prune, tilled earth, aniseed. Italianesque tannic rusticity combined with barely there oak and you have widespread appeal right there. Screw cap. 14.5% alc. RATING 91 DRINK 2021–2024 $33 JP

Caretaker Cabernet Sauvignon 2018, Adelaide Hills Matured 30 months in French oak, endowing this wine with a rich mantle of vanillin, toasty oak which is more than a match for the ripe, blackberry, cassis and spice that runs long and firm in tannins across the palate. Generous now, but with more time on its side. Screw cap. 14% alc. RATING 91 DRINK 2022–2029 $65 JP

Shiraz 2017, Adelaide Hills Fragrant cool-climate shiraz that carries plenty of succulent, ripe plums, earth, licorice and Hills spice. The winemaker has paid attention to the weight of fruit and been even-handed, sparing even, in the delivery of oak. Smart winemaker. Smart wine. Screw cap. 14.5% alc. RATING 91 DRINK 2021–2027 $27 JP

Sauvignon Blanc 2021, Adelaide Hills Impressive freshness and intensity on the nose in bright passionfruit, gooseberry, lime and leafy nettles. The palate's brisk acid crunch is engaging, with a flourish of lemon sherbet zing to close. Perks the tastebuds right up. Screw cap. 12.5% alc. RATING 90 DRINK 2021–2025 $23 JP

Riesling 2021, Adelaide Hills This retains a tight presence in the glass while maintaining charming fragrant appeal. Grapefruit, citrus blossom, lime and green apple, the palate is bright and linear. Made with summer in mind. Screw cap. 12% alc. RATING 90 DRINK 2021–2025 $23 JP

Reserve Pinot Noir 2019, Adelaide Hills Some roasted coffee, mocha, dark cherries, spice and musky aromas offer quite a different, savoury-flecked interpretation of pinot to the Paracombe staple. Dark and herbal, licorice and chocolate move across the palate with an ever-present sturdy tannin savouriness. Screw cap. 13.5% alc. RATING 90 DRINK 2022–2029 $42 JP

💧💧💧💧 **Chardonnay 2021, Adelaide Hills** RATING 89 DRINK 2021–2025 $23 JP
Pinot Gris 2021, Adelaide Hills RATING 89 DRINK 2021–2024 $23 JP
Red Ruby 2021, Adelaide Hills RATING 89 DRINK 2021–2025 $23 JP
Pinot Noir 2021, Adelaide Hills RATING 89 DRINK 2021–2025 $25 JP
Grüner V5 2020, Adelaide Hills RATING 89 DRINK 2022–2025 $25 JP
Tempranillo 2018, Adelaide Hills RATING 89 DRINK 2021–2025 $25 JP
Shiraz Viognier 2016, Adelaide Hills RATING 89 DRINK 2021–2028 $32 JP
Malbec 2019, Mount Lofty Ranges RATING 88 DRINK 2022–2028 $38 JP

Paralian Wines ★★★★★

21 Eden Terrace, Port Willunga, SA 5171 **Region** McLaren Vale
T 0413 308 730 **www**.paralian.com.au **Open** By appt **Winemaker** Skye Salter, Charlie Seppelt **Est.** 2018 **Dozens** 450

Charlie Seppelt and Skye Salter met in '08 working the vintage at Hardys Tintara in McLaren Vale. By the time they took the plunge and established Paralian Wines in '18, they had accumulated 46 vintages between them, albeit for others. The name is a noun for someone who lives by the sea. Charlie's first exposure to McLaren Vale was as a vintage casual at d'Arenberg and it was vinous love at first sight. They headed off overseas, a high point undertaking vintage in Burgundy. He headed back to Australia, she went on to the Languedoc, seemingly ideal, but found it as depressing as Burgundy had been inspirational. They agreed McLaren Vale, and in particular Blewitt Springs, was the place they wanted to make grenache and shiraz with high fragrance and brightness, grenache joining pinot noir as a high-class wine to be enjoyed young or much later. No fining or additions are used other than SO$_2$ and little requirement for new oak. (JH)

🍷🍷🍷🍷🍷 **Springs Hill Vineyard Shiraz 2021, McLaren Vale** An exceptional nose of crushed pepper, dill, clove and a 'je ne sais quoi' peaty wildness reminiscent of Cornas. Long and taut, shimmering with licorice, blue fruits, dried nori accents and the spice elements as they reverberate across the dense, tightly packed palate.

Plenty floral, too. This is an exceptional Blewitt Springs wine. The finish is chewy, pixelated, saline, pithy and so beautifully shaped. This is a very rare occasion when shiraz trumps grenache. Screw cap. 14% alc. RATING 96 DRINK 2022-2032 $42 NG ✪

Marmont Vineyard Grenache 2021, McLaren Vale Very good. The tannins – long limbed, saline, chalky and gritty – the wine's opus. A chastity belt across the mid palate. A timbre of tension plying detail and freshness across notes of kirsch, pink grapefruit pulp, mint, clove and orange peel. The finish, a slow build of furled density and sweetness, giving just enough away for pleasure while promising much more. Screw cap. 14% alc. RATING 95 DRINK 2022-2030 $42 NG

Springs Hill Vineyard Shiraz 2020, McLaren Vale Pulpy. Blewitt Springs florals. Granular, sandy tannins serving as a bow of tension, accentuated further by a gentle reductive clutch. Lilac, iodine, blueberry, anise, a smear of tapenade and some peppery biltong notes. This is the Vale glimpsing the northern Rhône. The acidity, not as fresh. More heft, too. Yet, the tannins are wonderful, serving to assuage the rich flavours as much as corral them. Screw cap. 14% alc. RATING 94 DRINK 2021-2027 $42 NG

ϘϘϘϘϘ **Blewitt Springs Grenache Shiraz 2021, McLaren Vale** RATING 93 DRINK 2022-2032 $36 NG

Bowyer Ridge Vineyard Chardonnay 2021, Adelaide Hills RATING 93 DRINK 2022-2030 $49 NG

Paringa Estate ★★★★★

44 Paringa Road, Red Hill South, Vic 3937 **Region** Mornington Peninsula
T (03) 5989 2669 **www.**paringaestate.com.au **Open** 7 days 11–5 **Winemaker** Lindsay McCall, Jamie McCall **Est.** 1985 **Dozens** 15 000 **Vyds** 30.5ha
Schoolteacher-turned-winemaker Lindsay McCall became known for an absolutely exceptional gift for winemaking across a range of styles but with immensely complex pinot noir and shiraz leading the way. The wines have an unmatched level of success in the wine shows and competitions that Paringa Estate is able to enter; the limitation being the relatively small production of the top wines in the portfolio. His skills are no less evident in contract winemaking for others. But time has passed and son Jamie joined the winemaking team in '12, after completing winemaking and viticulture at the University of Adelaide, Waite Campus. He was put in charge of winemaking at Paringa Estate in '17 following 5 home vintages and one in Oregon, focusing on pinot noir. Exports to the UK, Denmark, Ukraine, Singapore, Japan and Hong Kong. (JH)

ϘϘϘϘϘ **Estate Chardonnay 2020, Mornington Peninsula** I started singing She's So Fine by the Easybeats while tasting this, because obviously this is so fine. Kickstarts with succulent nectarine and lemony flavours, flinty with a hint of complexing lees. Lots of flavour, yet so restrained. A long thread of excellent acidity leads to a lingering finish. Screw cap. 13% alc. RATING 95 DRINK 2022-2028 $45 JF

Robinson Vineyard Pinot Noir 2020, Mornington Peninsula A pale yet bright ruby hue and a beguiling fragrance to follow, with brambly fruit, red cherries and pips, Middle Eastern spices, pepper and whiff of warm earth. Lot of finesse across the palate, with tangy acidity more in charge than the light raw-silk tannins, which means it's also very refreshing. Screw cap. 13% alc. RATING 95 DRINK 2022-2028 $80 JF

The Paringa Single Vineyard Chardonnay 2020, Mornington Peninsula While the chardonnays are my preference this vintage over pinot noirs, this holds a depth of flavour and richness customary of The Paringa, yet retains a tightness and vitality. It's not too big – just right. Stone fruit, Meyer lemon, cedary spicy oak and a luscious infusion of creamy lees. Satisfying. Screw cap. 13% alc. RATING 95 DRINK 2022-2028 $80 JF

ϘϘϘϘϘ **Peninsula Chardonnay 2021, Mornington Peninsula** RATING 93 DRINK 2022-2026 $29 JF

Estate Riesling 2021, Mornington Peninsula RATING 93 DRINK 202–2026
$26 JF
The Paringa Single Vineyard Pinot Noir 2020, Mornington Peninsula
RATING 92 DRINK 2022-2028 $100 JF
Estate Pinot Gris 2021, Mornington Peninsula RATING 90
DRINK 2022-2024 $26 JF
Estate Pinot Noir 2020, Mornington Peninsula RATING 90
DRINK 2022-2026 $65 JF

Parker Coonawarra Estate ★★★★★

15688 Riddoch Highway, Penola, SA 5263 **Region** Coonawarra
T (08) 8737 3525 **www.**parkercoonawarraestate.com.au **Open** 7 days 10–4
Winemaker James Lienert, Andrew Hardy, Keeda Zilm **Est.** 1985 **Dozens** 30 000
Vyds 20ha
Parker Coonawarra Estate is at the southern end of Coonawarra, on rich terra rossa soil
over limestone. Cabernet sauvignon is the dominant variety (17.45ha), with minor plantings
of merlot and petit verdot. It is now part of WD Wines, which also owns Hesketh Wine
Company, St John's Road, Vickery Wines and Ox Hardy. Production has risen substantially
since the change of ownership. Exports to all major markets. (JH)

♥♥♥♥♥ **First Growth 2018, Coonawarra** As true to Coonawarra for its structure,
density and weight, as it is to cabernet for its cassis, blackberries and spice. This is
voluminous, expansive, and eminently classy, with a pedigree of fruit that veritably
floods the palate with flavour. It endures long into the finish, telling us what we
need to know about its capacity for ageing. The tannins too are expertly crafted,
countersunk into the fruit, and at no point intrusive to the experience. Screw cap.
14.5% alc. RATING 97 DRINK 2022-2042 $110 EL ✪ ♥

♥♥♥♥♥ **Kidman Block 2020, Coonawarra** Let us start at the end, for that is where
the tannins show their true colours. This is fine, chalky, almost powdery shiraz,
with layers and layers of flavour settled on one another, like sheets of tissue paper.
The acidity is the thread that binds them, while the fruit flavours are the ink that
transcribes the story. This will be even better in a year or 2, once the tale has had
time to unfold in the glass; for now it is furled, like a sail in storage. Screw cap.
14.5% alc. RATING 95 DRINK 2022-2037 $65 EL
95 Block 2019, Coonawarra 88/12% cabernet/petit verdot. The petit verdot
transforms the aromas into a decidedly blue space – blueberries, potpourri,
lavender, and mulberries. In the mouth, the wine is velvety, cushioned and
plush … it's just wonderful. It is big and concentrated, but there's a cooling,
graphite quality to the tannins that elevate it right out of the park – you've
got to wait for this to emerge through the finish. Make sure you do. Awesome.
Screw cap. 14.5% alc. RATING 95 DRINK 2022-2037 $65 EL
Terra Rossa Cabernet Sauvignon 2019, Coonawarra Garden mint,
eucalypt, blackforest fruits and abundant exotic spice. This is earthy and rich and
loaded with flavour. In the mouth, the muscular tannins become a central part of
the experience, intermeshed with the fruit and shaping the long, trailing finish.
Get this one in a decanter if you're drinking it in the next few years – it will sing.
Screw cap. 14.5% alc. RATING 94 DRINK 2021-2038 $34 EL

Passel Estate ★★★★

655 Ellen Brook Road, Cowaramup, WA 6284 **Region** Margaret River
T (08) 9717 6241 **www.**passelestate.com **Open** 7 days 10.30–5 **Winemaker** Bruce
Dukes **Viticulturist** Andy Ferreira **Est.** 1994 **Dozens** 1500 **Vyds** 6.7ha
Wendy and Barry Stimpson were born in England and South Africa respectively and, during
numerous visits to Margaret River over the years, fell in love with the region's environment.
They made Margaret River home in 2005 and in '11 purchased and expanded the vineyard,
which is planted to shiraz, cabernet sauvignon and chardonnay. Viticulturist Andy Ferreira

manages the vineyard with sustainable practices, keeping yields restricted to 6.5–7t/ha. The very talented and highly experienced contract winemaker Bruce Dukes is responsible for the wines. Exports to Singapore and Hong Kong. (JH)

🍷🍷🍷🍷🍷 **Chardonnay 2018, Margaret River** This is rich, dense chardonnay – heavy, almost. There is no doubting the fruit quality (it speaks in a rumbling baritone of yellow peach, honeydew melon and nectarine). It is so flavoursome as to be opulent. Screw cap. 12.6% alc. RATING 92 DRINK 2021-2030 $42 EL
Chardonnay 2019, Margaret River Concentrated and almost muscular in its structure, this has layers of ripe stone fruit. The mlf contributes a nutty undertow that ties it all together. A smart wine. Screw cap. 12.5% alc. RATING 91 DRINK 2022-2029 $43 EL
Shiraz 2018, Margaret River The '18 vintage was stellar, and produced fruit that was ripe, powerful and balanced. The fruit here falls into that paradigm, however the oak impact is so significant as to smother the beauty of it in the mouth. Thankfully, there is decent length of flavour here, suggesting that perhaps another year or so might be just enough time for that oak to pipe down. A lovely wine, just give it some time. Screw cap. 14.5% alc. RATING 90 DRINK 2022-2028 $39 EL
Lot 71 Reserve Syrah 2017, Margaret River The detailed construction is evident in the glass here – the wine is classily restrained. Overall, the fruit is moving towards the savoury and spicy end of the spectrum, while the oak bolsters it from all sides. The fruit is beautiful, anyone can see that, however the oak feels just a bit too heavy-handed for the delicacies and intricacies of the flavour. Screw cap. 13.5% alc. RATING 90 DRINK 2021-2020 $65 EL

🍷🍷🍷🍷 **Sauvignon Blanc 2020, Margaret River** RATING 89 DRINK 2021-2023 $30 EL

Passing Clouds   ★★★★★

30 Roddas Lane, Musk, Vic 3461 **Region** Macedon Ranges
T (03) 5348 5550 **www.**passingclouds.com.au **Open** 7 days 10–5 **Winemaker** Cameron Leith **Est.** 1974 **Dozens** 5500 **Vyds** 5ha
Graeme Leith and son Cameron undertook a monumental change when they moved the entire operation that started way back in 1974 in the Bendigo region to its new location at Musk, near Daylesford. Graeme has now left the winemaking in the hands of Cameron and Marion, who have made a coup with the establishment of a new train stop (and dedicated platform) at the Passing Clouds cellar door and winery at Musk. The venture is the result of a collaboration between Passing Clouds, Spa Country Railway and the Victorian Regional Development Wine Growth Fund. The development has led to the incorporation of a restaurant (open Mon–Fri) and structured tastings built around the food. Exports to all major markets. (JH)

🍷🍷🍷🍷🍷 **Riesling 2021, Macedon Ranges** This wine should come with a warning: take the rest of the day off and enjoy, for it instils a carefree attitude in the imbiber. Well, it happened to me, all thanks to the racy acidity dashing across the palate alongside a balance of florals, citrus and spice with some talc-like texture. Top-notch, cool and cooling rizza. Screw cap. 11.8% alc. RATING 95 DRINK 2022-2031 $34 JF ✪
Macedon Pinot Noir 2020, Macedon Ranges A refreshingly pure and unadulterated wine that's such a delight to drink. Unencumbered by winemaking artefact, especially oaky flavour as this goes into used French hogsheads, so the fruit and the cool site are the stars. Heady aromas lead the way as a whorl of dark and red cherries lead off on the mid-weighted palate with some forest-floor complexity and exotic spices. The tannins are savoury, the superfine natural acidity is refreshing and ensures the finish is long. In context of the price and quality, this is spot on. Screw cap. 12% alc. RATING 95 DRINK 2022-2026 $28 JF ✪

ŶŶŶŶŶ The Angel 2020, Bendigo RATING 93 DRINK 2025-2040 $53 JF
Graeme's Shiraz Cabernet 2020, Bendigo RATING 92 DRINK 2023-2033
$34 JF
Serpentine Shiraz 2020, Bendigo RATING 92 DRINK 2025-2035 $53 JF
Kilmore Pinot Noir 2020, Macedon Ranges RATING 91 DRINK 2022-2024
$29 JF
Shiraz 2020, Bendigo RATING 91 DRINK 2022-2032 $34 JF
Riesling 2021, Bendigo RATING 90 DRINK 2022-2026 $34 JF
Bridgewater Shiraz 2020, Bendigo RATING 90 DRINK 2022-2033 $44 JF
Estate Pinot Noir 2020, Macedon Ranges RATING 90 DRINK 2022-2027
$47 JF

Patina   ★★★★★

109 Summerhill Lane, Orange, NSW 2800 **Region** Orange
T 0428 662 287 **www**.patinawines.com.au **Open** Sat–Sun 11–5 **Winemaker** Gerald
Naef **Est.** 1999 **Dozens** 2500 **Vyds** 2.8ha

Gerald Naef 's home in Woodbridge in California was surrounded by the vast vineyard
and winery operations of Gallo and Robert Mondavi. It would be hard to imagine a more
different environment than that provided by Orange. Gerald and wife Angie left California in
1981, initially establishing an irrigation farm in northwest NSW. In '01 they moved to Orange
and by '06 Gerald was a final-year student of wine science at CSU. He set up a micro-winery
at the Orange Cool Stores, his first wine the trophy-winning '03 Chardonnay. (JH)

ŶŶŶŶŶ Reserve Chardonnay 2018, Orange Museum release. This is a thrill ride.
'18, clearly a great vintage in these parts. At least in these hands, across this most
chameleonic of varieties. The longest finish. The most pixelated, juicy, complex
and expansive of an impressive chardonnay suite. Nougat, as always. Hazelnut,
orange blossom, honeydew melon, dried tatami and apricot. A gorgeous wine.
Screw cap. 12.7% alc. RATING 96 DRINK 2022-2032 $75 NG ✪
Jezza 2003, Orange Museum release. An even split of cabernet and merlot,
left 20 days on skins, courageous. Scoring wines such as this is unfair, at least from
an aesthetic perspective. Beautiful drinking and a window into the past: a warm
year, well suited. What more do we want? Best, it is not sweet or strung out on
additions and exuberant oak. It just is. A very warm vintage toned by meticulous
attention to detail and rustic, savoury charm. A verdant lilt underlies mocha, cigar
box, bracken, soy and the glorious whiff of autumnal decay. Delicious. Screw cap.
13.2% alc. RATING 96 DRINK 2021-2025 $150 NG
Grand Tawny NV, Orange A fine, resinous blend of deeply aged wines matured
oxidatively. Vinous, forceful and impressionably complex. Think Darjeeling tea-
leaf, orange verbena, cinnamon, turmeric and tamarind. Long and persuasive.
Screw cap. 19.2% alc. RATING 96 NG ✪
Scandalous Riesling 2021, Orange Unadulterated styling, aside from some
skin contact in the press, imparting a skein of white-pepper freshness, offset by a
dollop of sweetness. The perfect amount. A pirouette, rather than a sudden jolt
into the splits. Aussie Kabinett exuding green apple, a hint of grapefruit zest and
a mellifluous, refined finish. Screw cap. 10.7% alc. RATING 95 DRINK 2021-2028
$50 NG
Reserve Chardonnay 2019, Orange I love the savoury stretch of the
chardonnays at this address. The norm of clattering stone fruits, new wood and
reductive handling à l'Australienne can be tiring. Here, a defiant stance that
somehow feels far more intuitive. Natural. Effortless. Drinkable, sumptuous and
detailed. Wines of restraint and a beautiful pulse, the result. The acidity, gorgeous.
Everything done right. A very fine wine in the making. Nougat, blossom, hazelnut
and filigreed precision. Nothing but joy here. Screw cap. 13.2% alc. RATING 95
DRINK 2022-2031 $65 NG
Chardonnay 2016, Orange Museum release. Right in the zone! This will age
further, but I dig where it's at: nougat, creamed cashew and vanilla pod. White
peach, toasted hazelnuts and truffle beyond. The finish, succulent, rather than shrill

and hard like so many. Reminiscent of Meursault, with Aussie derring-do. Screw cap. 12.3% alc. RATING 95 DRINK 2021-2025 $55 NG

🍷🍷🍷🍷♀ Pinot Noir 2018, Orange RATING 92 DRINK 2021-2024 $45 NG
Museum Release Chardonnay 2008, Orange RATING 92 DRINK 2021-2025 $75 NG
Museum Release Cabernet Sauvignon 2006, Orange RATING 92 DRINK 2021-2023 $75 NG
Museum Release Chardonnay 2003, Orange RATING 92 DRINK 2021-2024 $150 NG
Rosé 2021, Orange RATING 91 DRINK 2021-2022 $25 NG

Patrick of Coonawarra

Cnr Ravenswood Lane/Riddoch Highway, Coonawarra, SA 5263 **Region** Coonawarra
T (08) 8737 3687 **www**.patrickofcoonawarra.com.au **Open** 7 days 10–5
Winemaker Luke Tocaciu **Est.** 2004 **Dozens** 5000 **Vyds** 93.5ha
Patrick Tocaciu (who passed away in 2013) was a district veteran, with prior careers at Heathfield Ridge Winery and Hollick Wines. Wrattonbully plantings (almost 55ha) cover all the major varieties, while in Coonawarra the low-yielding Home Block (cabernet sauvignon) is supplemented by a second vineyard of 17.5ha of cabernet and smaller amounts of riesling and sauvignon blanc. Patrick of Coonawarra also carries out contract winemaking for others. Son Luke has taken over in the winery. He has a degree in oenology from the University of Adelaide and vintage experience in Australia and the US. (JH)

🍷🍷🍷🍷🍷 Block 5 Aged Riesling 2014, Coonawarra At 7 years of age this is showing an enthusiastic lemon hue in the glass. On the nose it is layered with lanolin, beeswax, cheesecloth, preserved citrus and brine. In the mouth, the wine has morphed into a nectar-like experience (not sweet, but unctuous). It is opulent and austere at once. A real pleasure. Recommend. Screw cap. 11% alc. RATING 95 DRINK 2022-2037 $45 EL
Home Block Cabernet Sauvignon 2016, Coonawarra As a 6yo wine there is a lot going on here: aged fruit, (domineering) resinous oak and fierce, toasty concentration of flavour. This is savoury to the end of days, with salted licorice, black pepper, blackberry compote, poached rhubarb and black tea, too. Despite the moderate alcohol, this drinks like a big wine, with extraordinary intensity. Sporting a new (and improved) label, this is very good, and stylistically very confident. Screw cap. 13.8% alc. RATING 94 DRINK 2022-2032 $50 EL

🍷🍷🍷🍷♀ P Series by Patrick Sauvignon Blanc 2021, Limestone Coast RATING 90 DRINK 2021-2024 $20 EL✪

Patrick Sullivan Wines

146 Peterson Road, Ellinbank, Vic 3821 **Region** Gippsland
T 0439 729 780 **www**.patricksullivan.com.au **Winemaker** Patrick Sullivan **Est.** 2011
Dozens 2000 **Vyds** 10ha
Patrick Sullivan planted vines at age 15 and headed to London 3 years later. Viticulture studies followed, coupled with working at Vina di Anna, a winery in Sicily, thereafter appointed international wine buyer for Vina di Anna's owner, a London-based wine distribution business. Back in Australia, he became increasingly interested the Baw Baw Shire; winemaker Bill Downie was his guide both there and thereafter in the Yarra Valley. His beliefs and practices took shape over this time, notably sustainability/biodynamics and ultra-close spacing of 7000 vines/ha. In '14 he and wife Megan purchased the 69ha property now called Tumblestone Farm, sitting on red volcanic soil over sandstone at the base of the Strzelecki Ranges. They have planted pinot noir and chardonnay that are still coming into full bearing. In the meantime, he works with chardonnay from the Millstream, Bullswamp and Ada River vineyards. Exports to the UK, the US, Canada, Sweden, Norway, South Korea and Japan. (JH)

🍷🍷🍷🍷🍷 Ada River Chardonnay 2021, Gippsland A powerful wine yet reined in by laser-like and mouth-watering acidity. This is something special. Grapefruit, wood smoke, ginger flower, quinine and lemon peel to the fore. Tension across the palate that plays out to a fineness with great length. Ada River makes my heart skip a beat. Diam. 13.5% alc. RATING 96 DRINK 2022-2031 $85 JF

Bull Swamp Chardonnay 2021, Gippsland A burst of blossom, lemon sorbet, lemon zest and juice, but the ride is all on the palate. Savoury, textural, roasted almonds and lemon curd, lime flavours too. Moreish to the last drop. Very satisfying. If anything, this will benefit with extra bottle age but gee, it's hard to resist now. Diam. 13.5% alc. RATING 96 DRINK 2022-2031 $85 JF

Baw Baw Shire Chardonnay 2021, Gippsland The trio of chardonnays on offer this vintage are made identically, so it is all about sourcing parcels of excellent fruit. While the citrus and white stone-fruit flavours are at play, this works off a savoury riff. Woodsy spices, a layer of creamy lees and grilled nuts; it's moreish, superfine and long thanks to the acidity. Diam. 13.5% alc. RATING 95 DRINK 2022-2029 $65 JF

Patritti Wines

13–23 Clacton Road, Dover Gardens, SA 5048 **Region** Adelaide
T (08) 8296 8261 **www**.patritti.com.au **Open** Mon–Sat 9–5 (7 days Dec)
Winemaker James Mungall, Ben Heide **Est.** 1926 **Dozens** 190 000 **Vyds** 16ha
A family-owned and run business founded by Giovanni Patritti in 1926. Today it has 3 vineyard locations with a mix of old and new plantings. The most historic are patches of grenache (1.3ha), shiraz (0.4ha), muscat gordo (0.5ha), pedro ximénez and palomino (0.25ha combined), all held by a long-term lease from the City of Marion, the oldest vines planted 1906. Today they are encircled by businesses of all kinds, residential housing and scattered remnants of vineyards which are actively protected by most residents and local planning boards. There are 6 ranges of wines. At the head is the Family Range, then follow the Fortified Wines, Urban Vineyard Collection, Discovery Range, Merchant Series and the Lavoro Range. Exports to the UK, Sweden, Germany, Poland, India and Vietnam. (JH)

ΨΨΨΨΨ **Marion Vineyard Grenache Shiraz 2020, Adelaide** Deeply coloured; rich aromas of spicy fruitcake and plum open the door to a beautifully cadenced spray of fresh red and purple fruits, with superfine tannins. Great value. Screw cap. 13.5% alc. RATING 96 DRINK 2022-2033 $40 JH ✪

Paul Conti Wines

529 Wanneroo Road, Woodvale, WA 6026 **Region** Greater Perth
T (08) 9409 9160 **www**.paulcontiwines.com.au **Open** Tues–Sat 11–5 **Winemaker** Jason Conti **Viticulturist** Paul Conti **Est.** 1948 **Dozens** 4000 **Vyds** 11ha
Third-generation winemaker Jason Conti has assumed control of winemaking, although father Paul (who succeeded his own father in 1968) remains involved in the business. Over the years, Paul challenged and redefined industry perceptions and standards. The challenge for Jason is to achieve the same degree of success in a relentlessly and increasingly competitive market environment, and he is doing just that. There are 4 estate vineyards; 3 in Greater Perth, in Carabooda (chenin blanc), at the homestead property in Woodvale (nero d'Avola), and in Mariginiup (shiraz), and one in Wilyabrup in Margaret River (planted to chardonnay, sauvignon blanc, muscat à petit grains, malbec, cabernet sauvignon and shiraz). Exports to Malaysia. (JH)

ΨΨΨΨΨ **Lorenza Sparkling Chenin Blanc NV, Western Australia** Chenin blanc, whether still or sparkling, offers up an array of engaging phenolics and fruit, and it is so here. This has apricots, hessian and green apples, alongside citrus zest, white flowers and fine, diaphanous cheesecloth holding it all together. It's very pretty, with saline through the finish. Screw cap. 12.5% alc. RATING 92 $26 EL

Mariginiup Shiraz 2019, Western Australia Fermented in new and seasoned American and French oak for 12 months. The oak is really impactful, and even a slight backing off would allow some of the fruit to sing more clearly. Here there is poached plum, mulberry, blackberry and aniseed. Saturated and dense.

Big, muscular, old-school style, done well. Screw cap. 14.5% alc. RATING 91
DRINK 2021-2031 $28 EL

ŶŶŶŶ **Tuart Block Chenin Blanc 2021, Western Australia** RATING 88
DRINK 2021-2028 $18 EL
Cabernet Malbec 2019, Margaret River RATING 88 DRINK 2021-2027
$20 EL

Paul Nelson Wines ★★★★★

14 Roberts Road, Denmark, WA 6333 (postal) **Region** Great Southern
T 0406 495 066 **www**.paulnelsonwines.com.au **Open** School hols 11–5
Winemaker Paul Nelson **Est.** 2009 **Dozens** 1500 **Vyds** 2ha
Paul Nelson started making wine with one foot in the Swan Valley, the other in the Great
Southern, while completing a bachelor's degree in viticulture and oenology at Curtin
University. He then worked successively at Houghton in the Swan Valley, Goundrey in Mount
Barker, Santa Ynez in California, South Africa (for 4 vintages), hemisphere-hopping to the
Rheinhessen, 3 vintages in Cyprus, then moving to a large Indian winemaker in Mumbai
before returning to work for Houghton. He has since moved on from Houghton and makes
small quantities of table wines in partnership with his wife Bianca. (JH)

ŶŶŶŶŶ **Karriview Vineyard Chardonnay 2019, Denmark** There's a lot going on
here, and like the brilliant '18 that came before it, this makes a compelling case
for cool-climate chardonnay from Denmark. Complex, endlessly layered, rich and
worked, but with a nuance and finesse that speaks volumes about the vineyard
from whence it came. Curry leaf, crushed nuts, grilled peach, lemon zest, brine,
jasmine tea, aniseed, crushed quartz and fennel flower. Dense, powerful, long. Yes.
Screw cap. 13% alc. RATING 97 DRINK 2021-2036 $65 EL ✪

ŶŶŶŶŶ **Karriview Vineyard Pinot Noir 2019, Denmark** Super-elegant lacy tannins
shape the sweet cherry and cranberry fruit. Counterpoint to the pretty characters
here, there is also olive tapenade and salted heirloom tomato. This has layers of
fine spice; the mineral saline acidity curls and weaves its way across the palate.
This is absolutely delicate, the oak imperceptible, while the length of flavour
persists far beyond what is expected, showing the strength of the combination
of site and handling. Another supreme release. Screw cap. 13.4% alc. RATING 96
DRINK 2021-2036 $65 EL ✪ ♥

Paul Osicka ★★★★★

Majors Creek Vineyard at Graytown, Vic 3608 **Region** Heathcote
T (03) 5794 9235 **www**.paulosickawines.com.au **Open** By appt **Winemaker** Simon
Osicka **Est.** 1955 **Vyds** 13ha
The Osicka family arrived from Czechoslovakia in the early '50s. Vignerons in their own
country, their vineyard in Australia was the first new venture in central and southern Victoria
for over half a century. With the return of Simon Osicka to the family business, there have
been substantial changes. Simon held senior winemaking positions at Houghton, Leasingham,
and as group red winemaker for Constellation Wines Australia, interleaved with vintages in
Italy, Canada, Germany and France, working at the prestigious Domaine Jean-Louis Chave for
the '10 vintage. The fermentation of the red wines has changed from static to open fermenters
and French oak has replaced American. Extensive retrellising of the 65yo estate plantings is
now complete. Installation of a conveyor belt enables 100% berry sorting and eliminates
pumping; installation of new vats is another improvement. Paul Osicka, Simon's father, passed
away in 2019 after 50 vintages and over 60 years of involvement in the vineyards. Exports to
Denmark. (JH)

ŶŶŶŶ **Shiraz 2019, Heathcote** The lively bouquet offers fluttering wafts of spices
crossing into dabs of French oak, but gives little advance notice of the depth and
intensity of the black fruits wrapped in a fine skein of ripe tannins. A Grampians-
like twist is all the better for that in the hands of Simon Osicka. Screw cap.
14.5% alc. RATING 97 DRINK 2022-2040 $38 JH ✪

♟♟♟♟♟ Majors Creek Vineyard Shiraz 2020, Heathcote The wine is deep and rich like the soils from which it hails. Layered regional traits follow from the ripe black fruits and mineral, earthy brightness to generous spice and a fleshy, dense palate supported by firm tannins. It's got a lot of go. There's so much to this wine. Screw cap. 14.5% alc. RATING 95 DRINK 2022–2035 $38 JP

Majors Creek Vineyard Cabernet Sauvignon 2019, Heathcote There was no '20 cabernet, so the '19 vintage was held back an extra year before release. A swish of air really opens it up. First up, cassis, woodsy spice, undergrowth, autumnal leaves and, yes, the subtle hint of familiar Heathcote bush mint and gum leaf. Luscious and ripe, it maintains a medium-bodied weight and concentration guided by supple tannins. Finishes oh so long. Screw cap. 14.5% alc. RATING 95 DRINK 2022–2035 $38 JP

Paulett Wines

752 Jolly Way, Polish Hill River, SA 5453 **Region** Clare Valley
T (08) 8843 4328 **www.**paulettwines.com.au **Open** 7 days 10–5 **Winemaker** Neil Paulett, Jarrad Steele **Viticulturist** Matthew Paulett **Est.** 1983 **Dozens** 35 000 **Vyds** 79.5ha
The Paulett story is a saga of Australian perseverance, commencing with the 1982 purchase of a property with 1ha of vines and a house, promptly destroyed by the terrible Ash Wednesday bushfires the following year. Son Matthew joined Neil and Alison Paulett as a partner in the business some years ago; he is responsible for viticulture on the property holding, much expanded following the purchase of a large vineyard at Watervale. The winery and cellar door have wonderful views over the Polish Hill River region, the memories of the bushfires long gone. Exports to the UK, Denmark, Germany, Singapore, Malaysia and NZ. (JH)

♟♟♟♟♟ Polish Hill River Aged Release Riesling 2017, Clare Valley Buttered toast with marmalade, lemon curd and an array of Asian five-spice and nutmeg. The flavour draw across the palate is long and consistent, leaving deposits of rich flavour as it flows across the tongue. Very smart. Screw cap. 12.8% alc. RATING 95 DRINK 2022–2032 $75 EL

Pauletts 109 Riesling 2021, Clare Valley Savoury, herbal and muscular, this has cheesecloth, salted limes, preserved citrus, green apples and brine. It's full bodied and intense for a riesling, with plenty of heft and flow. Screw cap. 12% alc. RATING 94 DRINK 2022–2032 $75 EL

♟♟♟♟♟ JS Brielle Grenache 2021, Clare Valley RATING 92 DRINK 2022–2030 $52 EL

SHZ 2019, Clare Valley RATING 92 DRINK 2021–2027 $30 EL

109 Reserve Shiraz 2019, Clare Valley RATING 92 DRINK 2022–2032 $120 EL

Polish Hill River Riesling 2021, Clare Valley RATING 91 DRINK 2021–2031 $30 EL

Riesling 2021, Clare Valley RATING 90 DRINK 2021–2028 $25 EL

Rosé Sangiovese 2021, Clare Valley RATING 90 DRINK 2022–2023 $25 EL

Paulmara Estates

144 Seppeltsfield Rd, Nuriootpa, SA 5355 **Region** Barossa Valley
T 0417 895 138 **www.**paulmara.com.au **Open** By appt **Winemaker** Jason Barrette **Viticulturist** Paul Georgiadis **Est.** 1999 **Dozens** 650 **Vyds** 13ha
Born to an immigrant Greek family, Paul Georgiadis grew up in Waikerie, where his family had vineyards and orchards. His parents worked sufficiently hard to send him first to St Peters College in Adelaide and then to Adelaide University to do a marketing degree. He became the whirlwind grower-relations manager for Southcorp, and one of the best-known faces in the Barossa Valley. Paul and wife Mara established a vineyard in 1995, currently planted to shiraz, sangiovese, mataro, nero d'Avola and cabernet sauvignon. Part of the production is sold, and the best shiraz makes the Syna Shiraz ('syna' being Greek for together). (JH)

ΨΨΨΨΨ **APOTIGI Cabernet Sauvignon 2019, Barossa Valley** Inviting aromas of blackberry, cassis and kirsch with hints of baking spice, licorice, dark chocolate and cedar. Mouth-filling and rich with abundant black fruits, laced with tobacco leaf and spice, firm gravelly tannin and a lovely flow and cadence on the long blackberry-dominant finish. Cork. 14.5% alc. RATING 94 DRINK 2021–2038 $100 DB

ΨΨΨΨΨ **MARAnanga Shiraz 2020, Barossa Valley** RATING 92 DRINK 2021–2035 $30 DB
DeNero Nero d'Avola 2020, Barossa Valley RATING 90 DRINK 2021–2026 $22 DB

Paxton

68 Wheaton Road, McLaren Vale, SA 5171 **Region** McLaren Vale
T (08) 8323 9131 **www.**paxtonwines.com **Open** 7 days 10–5 **Winemaker** Dwayne Cunningham, Kate Goodman (Consultant) **Est.** 1979 **Dozens** 32 000 **Vyds** 82.5ha
David Paxton is of one Australia's most successful and respected viticulturists, with a career spanning over 40 years. He started his successful premium grower business in 1979 and has been involved with planting and managing some of the most prestigious vineyards in McLaren Vale, Barossa Valley, Yarra Valley, Margaret River and Adelaide Hills for top global wineries. There are 6 vineyards in the family holdings in McLaren Vale: Thomas Block (25ha), Jones Block (22ha), Quandong Farm (18ha), Landcross Farm (2ha), Maslin (3ha) and 19th (12.5ha). All are certified organic and biodynamic, making Paxton one of the largest biodynamic producers in Australia. Exports to the UK, the US, Canada, Denmark, France, Germany, Sweden, the Netherlands, Russia, Finland, Japan, Malaysia, Singapore, Hong Kong and Taiwan. (JH)

ΨΨΨΨΨ **Quandong Farm Single Vineyard Shiraz 2020, McLaren Vale** A powerful gush of fruit, and even more so tannins, the saving grace being that they are ripe. Bramble, blackberry and dark chocolate are all in the passing parade. Screw cap. 13.5% alc. RATING 95 DRINK 2023–2035 $30 JH ✪
NOW Shiraz 2021, McLaren Vale Deep, bright crimson. No preservative also means no oak, and managing the ferment is not drop-dead easy. This has a run stream of cherry (red and black), plum and blackberry with a smooth gloss of tannins. Well done, indeed. Screw cap. 14% alc. RATING 94 DRINK 2022–2024 $25 JH ✪
Cracker Barrels Shiraz Cabernet Sauvignon 2020, McLaren Vale An older-school expression, perhaps, yet lighter on its feet than in the past. Cabernet's aromas at the fore: sage, tapenade, cassis and garden herb. Cedar oak and well-extracted grape tannins, applied with aplomb, serving as the latticework. The flavours teem long and mercifully refrain from straying into anything sweet or over-extracted. A classic, crafted with style and confidence. Screw cap. 14.5% alc. RATING 94 DRINK 2022–2032 $55 NG

ΨΨΨΨΨ **Quandong Farm Single Vineyard Shiraz 2021, McLaren Vale** RATING 93 DRINK 2022–2030 $30 NG
MV Shiraz 2020, McLaren Vale RATING 93 DRINK 2022–2030 $22 JH ✪
Biodynamic Tempranillo 2021, McLaren Vale RATING 92 DRINK 2021–2024 $25 NG ✪
Queen of the Hive Red Blend 2021, McLaren Vale RATING 92 DRINK 2022–2026 $25 NG ✪
Queen of the Hive Shiraz Mataro 2021, McLaren Vale RATING 92 DRINK 2022–2028 $25 NG ✪
Biodynamic Graciano 2021, McLaren Vale RATING 92 DRINK 2021–2023 $30 NG
Jones Block Single Vineyard Shiraz 2019, McLaren Vale RATING 92 DRINK 2029–2039 $45 JH

AAA Shiraz Grenache 2021, McLaren Vale RATING 91 DRINK 2022-2027 $25 NG
Grenache 2021, McLaren Vale RATING 91 DRINK 2021-2023 $35 NG
AAA Shiraz Grenache 2020, McLaren Vale RATING 90 DRINK 2022-2027 $22 JH

Payne's Rise ★★★★

10 Paynes Road, Seville, Vic 3139 **Region** Yarra Valley
T (03) 5964 2504 **www**.paynesrise.com.au **Open** Thurs–Sun 11–5 **Winemaker** Franco D'Anna (Contract) **Viticulturist** Tim Cullen **Est.** 1998 **Dozens** 2000 **Vyds** 5ha
Tim and Narelle Cullen have progressively established 5ha of cabernet sauvignon, shiraz, pinot noir, chardonnay and pinot gris since '99. They carry out all the vineyard work (Tim is also a viticulturist for a local agribusiness) and are planting new clones and rootstocks with an eye to the future. Narelle is responsible for sales and marketing. The contract-made wines have won both gold medals and trophies at the Yarra Valley Wine Show and the Victorian Wines Show. A recent cellar door and restaurant extension have been added, expanding the original 1860s homestead of the region's first settler, Thomas Payne. (JH)

♀♀♀♀♀ **Anniversary Cabernet Sauvignon 2019, Yarra Valley** Fruit planted in Seville in the Upper Yarra in 1999, hence the anniversary bottling. An impressive bright deep purple colour. Dense, with dark fruit, dark chocolate and a moreish, savoury, meaty edge. Concentrated on the palate, this well-made and -priced medium-bodied wine finishes with classic chewy, gravelly tannins. Screw cap. 13.5% alc. RATING 95 DRINK 2022-2032 $35 PR ✪
Chardonnay 2021, Yarra Valley A very bright green gold. Terrific cool-climate chardonnay from a cool year, with aromas of quince, pear and stone fruits, sitting alongside a little spice from the oak and well-handled gunflint reduction. Elegant and tightly wound, this needs another 3–6 months to fill out and reveal it's full potential. Screw cap. 12.5% alc. RATING 94 DRINK 2021-2027 $30 PR ✪

Peacetree Estate ★★★★

Harmans South Road, Wilyabrup, WA 6280 **Region** Margaret River
T (08) 9755 5170 **Open** 7 days 10–6 **Winemaker** Paul Green, Severine Maudoux (Contract) **Est.** 1995 **Dozens** 1400
Three generations of the Tucker family were involved in the first plantings at Peacetree Estate in 1995; however, it was of olive trees, not vines. One ha each of sauvignon blanc and cabernet sauvignon followed, 0.8ha viognier coming later. For the first 3 vintages the grapes were sold, and in 2001 the Tuckers decided to take the plunge and have the wine bottled under the Peacetree Estate label. (JH)

♀♀♀♀♀ **Reserve Cabernet Sauvignon 2014, Margaret River** Museum release. '14 was a classical vintage in Margaret River, and in the context of cabernet sauvignon, one of the most glorious. While this wine is showing some signs of age, it's in line with what is to be expected of a 7yo cabernet, and the pedigree of the vintage is on show. A beautiful wine, graceful. Screw cap. 14% alc. RATING 94 DRINK 2021-2031 $45 EL

♀♀♀♀♀ **Cabernet Sauvignon Malbec 2020, Margaret River** RATING 93 DRINK 2021-2031 $45 EL
Final Release Cabernet Sauvignon 2018, Margaret River RATING 93 DRINK 2021-2031 $45 EL
Chardonnay 2021, Margaret River RATING 92 DRINK 2022-2028 $40 EL
Seeds and Stems Chenin Blanc 2021, Margaret River RATING 91 DRINK 2021-2031 $28 EL

Peccavi Wines

1121 Wildwood Road, Yallingup Siding, WA 6282 **Region** Margaret River
T 0404 619 861 **www**.peccavi-wines.com **Open** By appt **Winemaker** Bruce
Dukes, Remi Guise, Jeremy Muller, Stuart Watson **Viticulturist** Colin Bell **Est.** 1996
Dozens 6000 **Vyds** 16.5ha

Jeremy Muller was introduced to the great wines of the world by his father when he was
young and says he spent years searching New and Old World wine regions (even looking at
the sites of ancient Roman vineyards in England), but did not find what he was looking for
until one holiday in Margaret River. There he found a vineyard in Yallingup that was available
for sale and he did not hesitate. He quickly put together an impressive contract winemaking
team and appointed Colin Bell as viticulturist. The wines are released under 2 labels: Peccavi
for 100% estate-grown fruit (all hand-picked) and No Regrets for wines with contract-grown
grapes and estate material. The quality of the wines is very good, reflecting the skills and
experience of Bruce Dukes. Exports to the UK, Thailand, Malaysia, Singapore, Japan, Hong
Kong and South Korea. (JH)

🍷🍷🍷🍷🍷 Syrah 2020, Margaret River This is a total pleasure. Spicy, jubilant, layered –
how gorgeous. A whole-bunch/carbonic component has lent a vibrancy and
lift to the fruit that catapults it into the pleasure-sphere. Graphite and crushed
rocks, exotic pan roasted spices, Dutch licorice black cats, red licorice … purity
and finesse here. Bring it on. Screw cap. 14% alc. RATING 95 DRINK 2021-2031
$55 EL

Chardonnay 2019, Margaret River Rich, opulent and powerful, this is a nutty,
ripe fruit-laden wine with unending layers of flavours that undulate over the
long finish. A big wine, a lovely wine – very concentrated. Screw cap. 12.5% alc.
RATING 95 DRINK 2021-2031 $65 EL

The Estate Cabernet Sauvignon 2019, Margaret River Like the cabernet
from Peccavi, the fruit is encased by a wall of tannin, making it prohibitively tight
at this stage. However, the fruit within the clos is generous and pure and decidedly
purple. The wine is delicate overall, for all the talk of tannin, but will endure long
into the future – its slender shape and streaming tannins will fortify it into old age.
Screw cap. 14% alc. RATING 95 DRINK 2022-2037 $150 EL

🍷🍷🍷🍷🍷 The Estate Merlot 2019, Margaret River RATING 93 DRINK 2022-2042
$150 EL

Cabernet Sauvignon 2017, Margaret River RATING 93 DRINK 2023-2033
$75 EL

Peerick Vineyard

★★★★

Wild Dog Track, Moonambel, Vic 3478 **Region** Pyrenees
T (03) 5467 2207 **www**.peerick.com.au **Open** W'ends & public hols 11–4
Winemaker Chris Jessup, Mount Langhi Ghiran (Dan Buckle) **Est.** 1990 **Dozens** 2000

Peerick is the venture of Chris Jessup and wife Meryl. They have mildly trimmed their
Joseph's coat vineyard by increasing the plantings to 5.6ha and eliminating the malbec and
semillon, but still grow cabernet sauvignon, shiraz, cabernet franc, merlot, sauvignon blanc
and viognier. Quality has improved as the vines have reached maturity. Exports to NZ. (JH)

🍷🍷🍷🍷🍷 Reserve Shiraz 2019, Pyrenees A single-vineyard Reserve Shiraz left a
little longer in bottle before release. Unlike its '19 shiraz sibling, there is a little
less viognier and alcohol and a lot more presence. Further ageing is definitely
on its mind. Brings generous Pyrenean wild herbs, bay leaf, gum leaf, black
fruits and licorice together with a dense tannin, charry oak layer and they
remain an emerging force. More time, please. Screw cap. 14.5% alc. RATING 94
DRINK 2022-2031 $39 JP

🍷🍷🍷🍷🍷 Deadly 2021, Pyrenees RATING 91 DRINK 2022-2024 $25 JP

Penfolds

30 Tanunda Road, Nuriootpa, SA 5355 P16 **Region** Barossa Valley
T (08) 8568 8408 **www**.penfolds.com **Open** 7 days 10–5 **Winemaker** Peter Gago
Est. 1844

Penfolds is the star in the crown of Treasury Wine Estates (TWE) but its history predates the formation of TWE by close on 170 years. Its shape has changed in terms of its vineyards, its management, its passing parade of great winemakers and its wines. There is no other single winery brand in the New or the Old World with the depth and breadth of Penfolds. Retail prices range from less than $20 to $950 for Grange, which is the cornerstone, produced every year, albeit with the volume determined by the quality of the vintage, not by cash flow. There is now a range of regional wines of single varieties and the Bin Range of wines that includes both regional blends and (in some instances) varietal blends. Despite the very successful Yattarna and Reserve Bin A Chardonnays, and some impressive rieslings, this remains a red wine producer at heart. Exports to all major markets. (JH)

ҬҬҬҬҬ Reserve Bin A Chardonnay 2020, Adelaide Hills There is a resolute conviction and assuredness to this wine that sets it apart among the greatest and longest-lived of all. A textbook exemplar of Kym Schroeter's wizardry of uniting profound gunflint reduction, high-tensile white fruits and lightening acidity with uber-classy oak that exerts nothing like the presence expected of 86% new barrels. Brilliant, powder-fine mineral texture wraps every detail in seamless unity. For all that there is to astonish about this release, it is its monumental line and sheer, undeviating length that really set it apart. Screw cap. 12.5% alc. RATING 98 DRINK 2030-2045 $125 TS ✪

Yattarna Bin 144 Chardonnay 2019, South Eastern Australia The tension, endurance and sheer molecular detail of Yattarna propels it to the pinnacle of Australia's pointy chardonnay pyramid, and '19 follows in the hallowed footsteps of the sublime '18. This is a vintage that demands a great deal of time to unfurl. Tight, compact, focused and immensely determined, it leads out in its virile youth with the finest struck flint and gunpowder. A pinpoint singularity of white-fruit precision focuses a laser line of pure white acidity that projects from its core through a finish of astounding line, length and promise. Powder-fine, crystalline minerality surges long and strong. Another epic Yattarna. Vintage on vintage, has Yattarna now ascended to become Penfolds' greatest wine of all? Screw cap. 12.5% alc. RATING 98 DRINK 2034-2049 $175 TS ✪ ♥

Superblend 802.A Cabernet Shiraz 2018, South Australia Stature, power and might. The framework of cabernet in the presence of 100% new American oak hogsheads projects a 707esque presence, within which a one-third inclusion of shiraz builds dramatic palate depth and intrigue. It is as if all the grandeur of 707, Grange and 389 have been united in one dramatic whole. The result delivers structural endurance, a grand display of monumental fruit and a line and length that hark back to the glory days of Bin 60A and all the subsequent legends of Penfolds cabernet shiraz. Superblend, A-class indeed! Cork. 14.5% alc. RATING 98 DRINK 2048-2068 $900 TS

Superblend 802.B Cabernet Shiraz 2018, South Australia Matured, fully blended, for 19 months in 54% new French oak hogsheads. Blending just post-harvest is virtually unheard of at Penfolds, and the effect of maturing almost equal proportions of cabernet and shiraz together is a harmony and integration astonishing in a youthful blend of such monumental longevity. The 2 varieties entwine seamlessly with French oak, with the tension of cabernet and the body of shiraz interlocking with dark chocolate and coffee bean. Tannins are superfine and mineral, laying out a trail of longevity that meets every bit of expectation in the grand lineage of Penfolds blends. A world away from Superblend A, yet intrinsically aligned to the very letter of its DNA. The pair beg the question of picking favourites, but for me they are both profoundly unique yet impossible to separate. Ask me again in 2 decades. Screw cap. 14.5% alc. RATING 98 DRINK 2038-2068 $900 TS

G5 NV, South Australia Bookended by the sublime '08 and '18 harvests, the final blend in the G series is a monumental take on Grange. Its black-fruit density and definition are all-encompassing, and it delivers every detail of all there is to love of its 5 component vintages in larger-than-life proportions. Dark chocolate, black olives and coal steam are framed in an impeccably fine lattice of tannins of towering proportions that will see it out for half a century. A fitting crescendo to the G series and a worthy tribute to 70 years of Grange. Cork. 14.5% alc. RATING 98 DRINK 2043-2068 $3500 TS

Bin 707 Cabernet Sauvignon 2019, South Australia Matured 18 months in 100% new American oak hogsheads. Such a bold statement of new American oak seems somehow old-fashioned in this day and age of Australian cabernet, and yet there is a comfortable assurance about the irrefutable Bin 707 model, promising that the woodwork will find its place with sufficient patience. The purity and precision of cassis and blackcurrant fruit on display is something to behold. In inimitable Bin 707 form, new American oak rises to the auspicious occasion, propelling and uplifting to mighty effect and monumental tannin impact. Fruit and oak sit apart for now, but each in their rightful place, and, as ever, promise great things indeed in a very long time to come. Line and length of the highest order confirm it will go the distance without the slightest doubt. Cork. 14.5% alc. RATING 97 DRINK 2049-2069 $650 TS

St Henri Shiraz 2018, South Australia The effortless, unassuming self-assuredness of St Henri holds a unique and beloved place in the assemblage of Penfolds heroes, and '18 marks a particularly special release. Accomplished, spicy, glossy black fruits of grand integrity unfold to magnificent effect in the glass, contrasting a fine-boned frame of rigid yet graceful, powder-fine tannins that carry a finish of long-lingering line and alluring appeal. I look forward to spectating from the sidelines as its fruit slowly unfurls over the decades to come. An adorable St Henri that exemplifies all that this label stands for. Cork. 14.5% alc. RATING 97 DRINK 2028-2058 $135 TS ✪

Grange Bin 95 2017, South Australia The inky density and impenetrable presence that proclaim Grange are irrefutable, even in the cooler '17 season, in which sourcing has been pulled back to the strongholds of the Barossa Valley and McLaren Vale. It's all here: black fruits of every kind, licorice, dark chocolate, coffee bean, coal dust, even a suggestion of fruit-mince spice. A wall of Grange tannins hold back its immense force, as finely engineered as ever. The finish holds motionless for minutes, with a stature and presence possessed only by Grange, yet at every moment upholding statuesque poise, integrity, even tang in this cooler season. Cork. 14.5% alc. RATING 97 DRINK 2037-2052 $950 TS

🍷🍷🍷🍷🍷 **Bin 51 Riesling 2021, Eden Valley** This cascades from the glass in a torrent of lily blossom, talc, fresh lemon, lime and Granny Smith apple. Yet for all its exuberance, it is honed and streamlined like only a cool season can achieve. The palate follows a focused line of magnificent tension, powder-fine mineral structure and the scintillating acid drive of cool nights. The most precise and enthralling Bin 51 of the recent era, irresistible now, and with a grand future before it. Screw cap. 11% alc. RATING 96 DRINK 2021-2041 $40 TS ✪

Bin 389 Cabernet Shiraz 2019, South Australia There is a resolute conviction to Bin 389, a confident assuredness that transcends its seasons like no other wine around it in the Penfolds line-up, its consistency grounded in the almost even marriage of the 2 varieties. The '19 vintage exemplifies this, a seamless harmony between the tension and fine-boned structure of cabernet and the body and depth of shiraz, yet embraced here in seamlessly interlocked harmony. A sea of glorious Penfolds tannins float a finish that is both expansive and far-reaching. Another grand 389 for the cellar! Cork. 14.5% alc. RATING 96 DRINK 2039-2049 $100 TS

Magill Estate Shiraz 2019, Adelaide The exotic spice and plump black fruits that typify the unique Adelaide suburban terroir that is Magill Estate leap from the glass and carry long and strong through a palate of grand stature and structural poise. It's blacker than ever in mood, uniting licorice straps, dark chocolate and coffee bean with a strong tannin frame engineered for the long haul. Luscious and enduring, this is a grand take on Magill. Cork. 14.5% alc. RATING 96 DRINK 2029-2044 $150 TS

Bin 128 Shiraz 2019, Coonawarra I love the bright yet deep and precise satsuma plum core to this release, the way it melds seamlessly with the white pepper that declares Coonawarra shiraz, and the violet lift that elevates the back palate in a wonderful glimmer of cool climate palate fragrance. Magnificent acid line and fine-ground chalk mineral tannins epitomise Coonawarra and declare a long future. I've been avidly following and cellaring Bin 128 for 25 vintages, and this is up there with my favourites. Cork. 14.5% alc. RATING 95 DRINK 2029-2044 $60 TS

RWT Bin 798 Shiraz 2019, Barossa Valley A strong and robust Bin 798 of grand black-fruit impact, framed boldly in French oak tannins of enduring structure. Spicy black fruits of all kinds meet licorice and dark chocolate. Mouth-embracing tannin impact declares both the mood of the drought season and confidently deployed barrels, making for a vintage that commands a long spell in the cellar. Great line and length seal its future. Cork.14.5% alc. RATING 95 DRINK 2039-2059 $200 TS

Bin 23 Pinot Noir 2020, Tasmania Henty Adelaide Hills Bin 23 has defined itself as a true pinot noir rather than just another Penfolds dry red, and '20 confirms it. Leading out with juicy, spicy, engaging berry fruit purity, it pulls into a finely textured tail of herbal intrigue and intricately assembled, fine-grained, mineral tannin structure. Poached strawberries, fresh morello cherries and just-plucked raspberries declare a magnificent and alluring profile, underlined by nuances of rosehip and a glimmer of exotic spice from judiciously played whole-bunch fermentation. Cork. 13.5% alc. RATING 94 DRINK 2022-2027 $50 TS

Bin 311 Chardonnay 2020, Tasmania Adelaide Hills Henty There is an immediacy and an amicable approachability to this vintage, thanks to mid-palate presence, uniting the white peach, lemon and fig of impeccably ripe fruit with the cashew nut of French oak and the subtle struck-flint reductive allure that signs Penfolds chardonnay. Fine-boned structure characterises a long finish, defined by a glorious sweep of brilliantly illuminated, crystalline acidity that spells out medium-term promise. A great 311. Screw cap. 13% alc. RATING 94 DRINK 2021-2027 $50 TS

Bin 138 Shiraz Grenache Mataro 2019, Barossa Valley Bathed in glorious black-fruit depth, this is a blend that leads out with inviting appeal and concludes with the structural framework that declares Penfolds. The dryness of the drought season has been masterfully handled. The tannin sophistication on display here is rarely seen in this blend, a superfine splay of mineral texture that weaves a fabric of endurance, drawing out a finish simultaneously graceful, confident and enticing. Cork.14.5% alc. RATING 94 DRINK 2024-2034 $60 TS

Bin 150 Marananga Shiraz 2019, Barossa Valley Marananga parades its depth, density and gloss to full effect. The dry and warm '19 season builds significant presence of black plum and blackberry fruit, fresh licorice straps and even a spicy fruit compote feel. Firm, fine drying tannins speak both of the season and the house, commanding all the longevity to be expected of both. A powerful if assertive take on Marananga. Screw cap. 14.5% alc. RATING 94 DRINK 2029-2039 $100 TS

Bin 407 Cabernet Sauvignon 2019, South Australia Nuances of menthol and eucalypt not often seen in Bin 407, perhaps the presence of Padthaway taking a stronger lead this vintage? This might also be the explanation, too, for a more saline feel to the palate. All the classic blackcurrant, cassis and roast capsicum expected of Bin 407 hold through a finish of impressive line and length, sustained by strong, fine-grained, mineral tannins. Cork.14.5% alc. RATING 94 DRINK 2029-2039 $110 TS

Penley Estate

McLeans Road, Coonawarra, SA 5263 **Region** Coonawarra
T (08) 7078 1853 **www.**penley.com.au **Open** 7 days 10–4 **Winemaker** Kate Goodman,
Lauren Hansen **Est.** 1988 **Dozens** 48 000 **Vyds** 111ha

In 1988, Kym, Ang and Bec Tolley joined forces to buy a block of land in Coonawarra –
Penley Estate was underway, the amalgamation of a fifth generation wine family Penfold
and Tolley. In 2015 Ang and Bec took full ownership of the company. They made a number
of changes, welcoming general manager Michael Armstrong and, even more importantly,
appointing Kate Goodman as winemaker. Behind the scenes Ang's husband David Paxton,
one of Australia's foremost viticulturists, has been working as a consultant, with improvements
in vineyard performance already evident. In Dec '17, Penley also opened a cellar door in the
main street of McLaren Vale. Exports to all major markets. (JH)

ŸŸŸŸŸ **Helios Cabernet Sauvignon 2020, Coonawarra** Blackberry pie on the
nose, this is concentrated and pure in its expression of both Coonawarra (black
fruit, eucalyptus and ferrous) and exotic spice. On the palate the tannins are
pronounced, and they certainly impact the fruit, but it is clear from the sheer
volume of flavour that swells in the mouth that they will be no match in time.
They will recede into the tidal wave of flavour and serve only to carry and
guide the fruit through the finish, as Helios' chariot drove him across the sky.
Inchoate as this is, it will emerge a superstar. Screw cap. 14% alc. RATING 97
DRINK 2022–2042 $150 EL ✪

ŸŸŸŸŸ **Francis Cabernet Franc 2021, Coonawarra** Juicy, bouncy, stemmy, crunchy
cabernet franc: delicious. Blackberries, eucalyptus, pink peppercorns, red licorice,
brine, bitter dark chocolate and even red snakes. This puts me firmly in mind of a
nouveau wine from Chinon – drink it tonight to experience the joy and X-factor
this wine has to offer. For those who insist on drinking cabernet throughout
summer, this could be the answer. I think it would handle a gentle chill with grace.
Screw cap. 14.5% alc. RATING 95 DRINK 2021–2026 $30 EL ✪

Chertsey 2019, Coonawarra This is lovely. Fresh. Modern. Long. It's a pleasure
to drink (and that's why we're all here, is it not?). Cooling graphite tannins frame
a core of black and purple fruit. Mulberries, blackberries, damsons and star anise.
The shape of the wine patiently tails out over the long finish, spooling out fine
threads of acid as it goes. There's something about this … it's almost crunchy.
It makes for incredibly engaging drinking. Screw cap. 14% alc. RATING 95
DRINK 2022–2037 $75 EL

Steyning Cabernet Sauvignon 2019, Coonawarra This is the sweet,
vibrant, energetic sister to the Chertsey. Tasted side by side, it is a cinch to 'spot
the differences' between them, but it doesn't make one necessarily better or
worse than the other. This is poised and exciting – a cool combination – and
shows a sumptuous spread of ripe berry fruits and fresh exotic spices. Star anise,
blood plums, blackberries, raspberries and fennel seeds are woven into the very
fabric of the wine. Pretty gorgeous stuff here. Screw cap. 14.5% alc. RATING 95
DRINK 2022–2037 $75 EL

Eos Shiraz Cabernet Sauvignon 2019, Coonawarra Like all the Penley reds
submitted this year, this is vibrant and bright on the nose. Brambly blackberries,
mulberries and fresh garden mint adorn the aromas, while in the mouth, the
acidity swooshes in and out of each of the flavours, enlivening them and making
way for the fine tannins: the carriage upon which the experience rides across
the mouth. A modern, concentrated take on the classical Australian blend. Cork.
14% alc. RATING 95 DRINK 2022–2037 $100 EL ♥

Giliam Light Dry Red 2021, Coonawarra Blend of cabernet sauvignon,
merlot and cabernet franc. Vanilla pod, raspberries, strawberries, licorice, a touch of
coconut, red apples, pink peppercorns and mulberries from the bush in summer.
Lots going on, and more of a mouthful than the name suggests. Tannins are plump,
finely knit and omnipresent; they create a shapely tail through the finish. Screw
cap. 14.5% alc. RATING 94 DRINK 2021–2028 $30 EL ✪

Tolmer 2020, Coonawarra Supple, elegant, fine-framed cabernet – hard to see where the 14.5% alcohol is hiding. This is super-pretty, fragrant and lithe, littered with red berries, flowers, blood plums and bay leaves. The palate is a little more substantive and weighty than the Phoenix, but that's to be expected for the extra money. This has presence and poise. Gorgeous. Screw cap. 14.5% alc. RATING 94 DRINK 2021-2031 $30 EL ✪

Penna Lane Wines ★★★★☆

Lot 51 Penna Lane, Penwortham via Clare, SA 5453 **Region** Clare Valley
T 0403 462 431 **www**.pennalanewines.com.au **Open** Fri–Sun 11–5 **Winemaker** Peter Treloar, Steve Baraglia **Est.** 1998 **Dozens** 4500 **Vyds** 4.37ha

Penna Lane is located in the beautiful Skilly Valley, 10km south of Clare. The estate vineyard includes shiraz, cabernet sauvignon and semillon and is planted at an elevation of 450m, which allows a long, slow ripening period, usually resulting in wines with intense varietal fruit flavours. (JH)

🍷🍷🍷🍷🍷 **Watervale Riesling 2021, Clare Valley** Fleshy, plump, pretty riesling with layers of sherbety fresh acid and fruit. Gorgeous. Delicious. Yum. 2021 rocks. Screw cap. 12.5% alc. RATING 95 DRINK 2021-2031 $28 EL ✪

🍷🍷🍷🍷 **Skilly Valley Riesling 2021, Clare Valley** RATING 93 DRINK 2021-2031 $28 EL
Side Track Blewitt Springs Grenache 2021, McLaren Vale RATING 92 DRINK 2021-2024 $35 NG
Shiraz 2020, Clare Valley RATING 91 DRINK 2022-2028 $28 EL
Side Track Rosé Tempranillo 2021, Clare Valley RATING 90 DRINK 2022-2023 $25 EL

Peos Estate ★★★★

1124 Graphite Road, Manjimup, WA 6258 **Region** Manjimup
T (08) 9772 1378 **www**.peosestate.com.au **Open** By appt **Winemaker** Willow Bridge (Kim Horton) **Est.** 1996 **Dozens** 13 000 **Vyds** 37.5ha

The Peos family has farmed in the west Manjimup district for almost a century, the third generation of 4 brothers developing the vineyard from 1996. There are over 37ha of vines including shiraz, merlot, chardonnay, cabernet sauvignon, sauvignon blanc, pinot noir and verdelho. (JH)

🍷🍷🍷🍷🍷 **Four Aces Single Vineyard Pinot Noir 2021, Manjimup** As with the Four Kings Single Vineyard Pinot Noir, this is layered with strawberries and black olive, but has additional spice and tension from additional 2 months in French oak. Both wines are fine boned and more about structure than plushness, but there is plenty of meat on those bones. This has superior silky texture, and an unfurling manner through the finish. Very smart. Screw cap. 14.5% alc. RATING 94 DRINK 2022-2029 $45 EL

🍷🍷🍷🍷 **Four Kings Single Vineyard Pinot Noir 2021, Manjimup** RATING 92 DRINK 2022-2027 $32 EL
Four Aces Single Vineyard Chardonnay 2021, Manjimup RATING 90 DRINK 2022-2028 $35 EL

Pepper Tree Wines ★★★★★

86 Halls Road, Pokolbin, NSW 2320 **Region** Hunter Valley
T (02) 4909 7100 **www**.peppertreewines.com.au **Open** Mon–Fri 9–5, w'ends 9.30–5 **Winemaker** Gwyn Olsen **Est.** 1991 **Dozens** 50 000 **Vyds** 172.1ha

Pepper Tree is owned by geologist Dr John Davis. It sources the majority of its Hunter Valley fruit from its Davis Family Vineyard at Mount View, but also has premium vineyards at Orange, Coonawarra and Wrattonbully. The highly credentialled Gwyn Olsen ('12 Dux, Advanced Wine Assessment Course, AWRI; '14 Young Winemaker of the Year, Gourmet

Traveller WINE; '15 Rising Star of the Year, Hunter Valley Legends Awards; and '15 Len
Evans Tutorial Scholar) has been winemaker since '15. Exports to the UK, Canada, Denmark,
Finland, Singapore and the US. (JH)

ႨႨႨႨႨ **Tallawanta Single Vineyard Shiraz 2011, Hunter Valley** A fascinating
comparison with the other aged re-release, the Coquun. This, more refined. The
tannins, a finer composition of oak and gravelly detail. The sweet terracotta, hoisin
and worn leather, only Hunter. The savoury, moreish and mid-weighted tone, just
as regional. Sous-bois, Asian medicine, tea and smoked biltong. Delicious wine.
Long. Sumptuous and immensely impressive. Screw cap. 14% alc. RATING 97
DRINK 2021-2030 $150 NG ✪

ႨႨႨႨႨ **Single Vineyard Alluvius Semillon 2021, Hunter Valley** A fine Hunter
semillon that is as juicy and optimally ripe – despite its light weight and low
alcohol – as it is pixelated, vibrant and intense because of it. Lanolin, lemon squash,
tonic and galangal notes stream along chalky acid rails. The finish, pointed and
immensely long. Destined for fine things with a decade of patience. Screw cap.
10.5% alc. RATING 96 DRINK 2021-2034 $50 NG ✪

Pump Shed Chardonnay 2020, Wrattonbully This may well be the best
wine under the Pepper Tree banner, tucking in a skein of mineral match-struck
pungency amid folds of stone fruits, nougatine, a waxy mandarin scent with a lick
of quinine to cumquat bitterness to finish. Impressive palate-staining intensity. The
oak, nicely nestled. A countenance of generosity melded with a contemporary
verve. Delicious drinking that is more reminiscent of a flavourful wine from
California than the more linear Aussie norm. Screw cap. 13.8% alc. RATING 96
DRINK 2021-2028 $50 NG ✪

Museum Release Block 21A Single Vineyard Cabernet Sauvignon 2012,
Wrattonbully For a now 10yo wine, this is looking achingly fresh. The glorious
'12 vintage has morphed into a graceful rendition of itself – the tannins, on release
fine and closely knit, have melted into the backdrop of the fruit. They shape the
flavours, and give the tongue something to tease once the wine has gone, but
they do not intrude. Tobacco leaf, fresh leather, cassis coulis and blackcurrant
bramble. This is beautiful, the experience drinking it – zen. The drinking window
is conservative, for it shows no signs of slowing down. Screw cap. 14% alc.
RATING 96 DRINK 2022-2037 $90 EL

Single Vineyard Alluvius Semillon 2011, Hunter Valley A stunning iteration
of aged semillon. From a fine vintage, to boot. This feels uber-ripe and weighty,
waxy and layered as it entices the next glass. Yet, low of alcohol and gentle of
extract, the wine's mouthfeel is a paradox. The magic of age, if you will! Ginger
crystals, tangerine, glazed quince, mango and peat, akin to a fine whisky. This is
what it is all about! Screw cap. 10.8% alc. RATING 96 DRINK 2021-2024 $85 NG

Coquun Premium Shiraz Blend 2011, Hunter Valley A museum release
from a distinguished vintage, this is drinking very well. There is no mistake about
its origin, as the warm loamy scents of sweet earth and worn leather flow across
a finely tuned palate, still sweet of fruit and jubilant of life. Inimitably Hunter.
Tertiary suggestions of mulch, dried porcini, soy and dashi make for a savoury
conversation with the palate. An exceptionally fine regional expression, aged and
ready to drink. Screw cap. 14% alc. RATING 96 DRINK 2021-2030 $135 NG

Coquun Premium Shiraz Blend 2019, Hunter Valley A bright vermilion
sheen. Less earthy and firm than its Tallawanta sibling, this mid-weight remains
firmly in the luncheon 'Hunter burgundy' mould. Lively, with the tangy acidity
more synergistic with the jubey blue fruits, anise, root spice and clove of the
profile. Almost drinks like something from the Loire, which, when good, drinks
like something from Burgundy. This is sap, crunch and plenty of pop. A revitalising
salve. Brilliant work! Screw cap. 13.8% alc. RATING 95 DRINK 2022-2029 $90 NG

Museum Release Single Vineyard Strandlines Cabernet Shiraz 2012,
Wrattonbully The museum release program at Pepper Tree allows us real insight
into the quality of the premium wines at their first release. The colour has moved
to a deep garnet, while the fruit has morphed over time from vibrant blue fruits,

to licorice, earthy flavours, peppered with graphite, arnica, amaro herbs and mint. The finish is decidedly flavoured with blueberry skin, but mostly licorice: the spicy, mint and aniseed character you are left with after eating too much of it. A decant is advised, it opens even as I write. Screw cap. 14% alc. RATING 95 DRINK 2022-2032 $90 EL

Tallawanta Single Heritage Vineyard Shiraz 2019, Hunter Valley I like the shift in this vintage from the reductive, more glossy styles of the recent past to the mid-weighted digestive expressions that are inimitably Hunter. One of the region's oldest sites. Damson plum, blueberry, sassafras, Asian spice and the signature terracotta/loam/petrichor notes of the Hunter. A little less acidity would be nice, but a fine wine all the same. This will age very well. Screw cap. 13.8% alc. RATING 94 DRINK 2022-2034 $130 NG

PepperGreen Estate ★★★☆

13 Market Place, Berrima, NSW 2577 **Region** Southern Highlands
T (02) 48771070 **www**.peppergreenestate.com.au **Open** Wed–Mon 10–5
Winemaker Balog Brothers (Contract) Kiri Irving (Contract) **Viticulturist** Ben Brazenor **Est.** 2016 **Dozens** 3750 **Vyds** 16ha
Established in 2016 in the bucolic Southern Highlands town of Berrima, PepperGreen Estate's proprietary vineyard is tucked away in nearby Canyonleigh at 700m elevation, complete with olive oil processing and a high-quality tasting room that serves modern cuisine. Pinot noir, shiraz, riesling and chardonnay are all grown on the estate's holdings as the owners endeavour to appropriate ideal grape varieties to the cool climate of the region. As it stands, the traditionally crafted sparkling wines show promise, having spent extended time on lees to impart a toasty complexity and creamy generosity to the twang of the cooler zone. (NG)

99999 **Tempranillo 2019, Orange** A full-weighted, compact wine, framed by sweet (presumably American) mocha-bourbon oak. It all works rather well. Darker-fruit allusions, a swab of anise and a lilt of violet. Already approachable, this offers considerable pleasure. Screw cap. 14.5% alc. RATING 90 DRINK 2021-2024 $32 NG

Petaluma ★★★★★

254 Pfeiffer Road, Woodside, SA 5244 **Region** Adelaide Hills
T (08) 8339 9390 **www**.petaluma.com.au **Open** 7 days 10–5 **Winemaker** Teresa Huezenroeder **Viticulturist** Mike Harms **Est.** 1976 **Dozens** 130000 **Vyds** 240ha
The Petaluma range has been expanded beyond the core group of Croser sparkling, Clare Valley Riesling, Piccadilly Valley Chardonnay and Coonawarra Merlot. Newer arrivals of note include Adelaide Hills Viognier and Shiraz. The plantings in the Clare Valley, Coonawarra and Adelaide Hills provide a more than sufficient source of estate-grown grapes for the wines. A new winery and cellar door opened in 2015 on a greenfield site with views of Mount Lofty. In '17 Petaluma (along with all wine brands owned by Lion Nathan) was acquired by Accolade. Exports to all major markets. (JH)

99999 **Croser Pinot Noir Chardonnay 2017, Piccadilly Valley** A traditional-method blend of 59/41% pinot noir/chardonnay. Abundant white peach and nectarine fruits, blanched almonds and a long, well-balanced finish. Looks as if it will handsomely repay a few more years on lees (preferably) or just with time in bottle. Diam. 13% alc. RATING 96 $42 JH ❂

Croser Pinot Noir Chardonnay 2018, Piccadilly Valley 76/24% pinot noir/chardonnay. On lees for 3+ years. With master sparkling maker Teresa Heuzenroeder at the helm, Croser is looking fresh and vital while making an impressive complex statement. A brilliant aperitif-style sparkling in its lifted bouquet of lemon butter and dusty apple blossom florals, with melon and stone fruits. Nicely textured and long on the palate with that continuing citrus line of flavour, enlivened by a soft, nougat, nutty complexity. Diam. 13% alc. RATING 95 $42 JP

Hanlin Hill Riesling 2021, Clare Valley The '21 vintage was a godsend for almost all regions in South Australia, and the rieslings from this vintage are typified by balance and restraint across the board. In many cases, the wines produced this year are among the finest in decades – no small feat. This wine is generous and plump in the mouth, littered with green apples, ripe limes, nashi pears and juniper berries, punctuated by pockets of juicy, salty acidity. The wine is glorious now, but it will age gracefully too. Screw cap. 13.5% alc. RATING 95 DRINK 2021-2031 $36 EL

B&V Vineyard Shiraz 2019, Adelaide Hills Generosity is this wine's middle name, from the ripe, persistent tannins and the black-hearted fruit and spice to the well-laid coffee-mocha oak. Fragrant and complex in dark spice, licorice, nutmeg, blackberry, loamy earth and toasty oak, it goes on to form a solid tannin base on the palate with an impressive intensity. If you can, give it more time in the bottle. Screw cap. 14.5% alc. RATING 95 DRINK 2022-2030 $52 JP

ŸŸŸŸ♀ **Croser NV, Adelaide Hills** RATING 93 $30 JH
White Label Sauvignon Blanc 2021, Adelaide Hills RATING 93
DRINK 2022-2024 $30 JP
White Label Cabernet Sauvignon 2019, Coonawarra RATING 91
DRINK 2022-2029 $30 EL
Merlot 2019, Coonawarra RATING 90 DRINK 2022-2029 $68 EL

Peter Drayton Wines ★★★★☆

Ironbark Hill Vineyard, 694 Hermitage Road, Pokolbin, NSW 2321 **Region** Hunter Valley **T** (02) 6574 7085 **www.**pdwines.com.au **Open** 7 days 10–5 **Winemaker** Damien Stevens, Peter Drayton **Est.** 2001 **Dozens** 20 000 **Vyds** 16.5ha
Owned by Peter and Leesa Drayton. The estate plantings include shiraz, chardonnay, semillon, cabernet sauvignon, tempranillo, merlot, verdelho and tyrian. Peter is a commercial/ industrial builder, so constructing the cellar door was a busman's holiday. The vineyard features an atmospheric function venue and wedding chapel set among the vines, with events organised and catered for by Enzo Weddings. Exports to Vietnam and Hong Kong. (JH)

ŸŸŸŸŸ **TJD Reserve Semillon 2014, Hunter Valley** A fine vintage in these parts. Many reds, massacred by ambition. The whites on the other hand, svelte, intense of tatami straw, nectarine, citrus curd, barley sugar and Thai herbal accents. Beautifully detailed. Riper and weightier than the regional norm. A gorgeous outlier portending well. Euro of styling. Would be better even more textural. Nouveau Hunter of feel. Very good. Screw cap. 13% alc. RATING 95 DRINK 2021-2025 $80 NG

ŸŸŸŸ♀ **TJD Reserve Semillon 2015, Hunter Valley** RATING 93 DRINK 2021-2026 $80 NG
Wildstreak Semillon 2021, Hunter Valley RATING 91 DRINK 2021-2026 $45 NG

Peter Lehmann ★★★★★

Para Road, Tanunda, SA 5352 **Region** Barossa Valley
T (08) 8565 9555 **www.**peterlehmannwines.com **Open** By appt **Winemaker** Nigel Westblade, Tim Dolan, Brett Smith, Brooke Blair **Viticulturist** Jade Rogge **Est.** 1979 **Dozens** 750 000
The seemingly indestructible Peter Lehmann (the person) died in June 2013, laying the seeds for what became the last step in the sale of the minority Lehmann family ownership in the company. The Hess Group of California had acquired control in '03 (leaving part of the capital with the Lehmann family) but a decade later it became apparent that Hess wished to quit its holding. Various suitors put their case forward but Margaret Lehmann (Peter's widow) wanted ongoing family, not corporate, ownership. Casella thus was able to make the successful bid in Nov '14, followed by the acquisition of Brand's Laira in Dec '15. Exports to the UK, the US and Canada. (JH)

🍷🍷🍷🍷🍷 VSV Hurn Shiraz 2019, Eden Valley While full bodied and still needing time, this has a certain elegance and balance to its spicy, savoury black fruits and velvety tannins. Screw cap. 14.5% alc. RATING 95 DRINK 2024-2039 $60 JH

H&V Riesling 2021, Eden Valley Pale straw in the glass with aromas of freshly squeezed limes, Granny Smith apple crunch, Bickford's lime cordial and hints of orange blossom, crushed quartz and lighter notes of almond paste and fennel. Expansive and concentrated on the palate with a core of limey fruit pulsing through the wine. The light tweak of phenolics adds texture and appeal and a crisp line of acidity provides propulsion across the tongue. Good stuff in a strong vintage. Screw cap. 11.5% alc. RATING 94 DRINK 2021-2031 $25 DB ✪

8 Songs Shiraz 2018, Barossa If you seek a generously proportioned Barossan shiraz; one that retains its sense of place with just a sprinkle of contemporary flair, the 8 Songs is a good bet. It's a deep red purple in the glass, with heady aromas of black plum, cherry and blueberry, underscored by baking spice, dark chocolate and lovely French oak. Weighty with a velvety flow, fine, gypsum-like tannins and no shortage of pure horsepower on the exit. Bold yet fleshy and graceful. No mean feat! Impressive stuff. Screw cap. 14.5% alc. RATING 94 DRINK 2021-2035 $45 DB

Mentor Cabernet 2018, Barossa This impressive, pure-fruited Mentor release will win the hearts of those who prefer their cabernet sauvignon to speak more of fruit intensity and less of herbaceous nuance. A densely packed blackberry, cassis and kirsch-like fruit profile, cut through with deep spice, dark chocolate, espresso, licorice and earth. Impressive fruit density with a bristling, muscular framework and chewy, blackberry-rich finish that lingers nicely. Screw cap. 14.5% alc. RATING 94 DRINK 2021-2035 $45 DB

🍷🍷🍷🍷 H&V Tempranillo 2021, Barossa Valley RATING 91 DRINK 2022-2028 $25 DB

H&V Pinot Gris 2021, Eden Valley RATING 91 DRINK 2021-2025 $25 DB

Portrait Riesling 2021, Eden Valley RATING 90 DRINK 2021-2028 $20 DB ✪

The Barossan Grenache 2020, Barossa RATING 90 DRINK 2022-2030 $25 JH

Peter Teakle Wines   ★★★☆

31 Whillas Road, Port Lincoln, SA 5606 **Region** Southern Eyre Peninsula
T 0499 235 527 **www.**peterteaklewines.com **Open** W'ends 11–5 **Winemaker** Liz Heidenreich **Viticulturist** Andrew Blackberry **Est.** 2017 **Dozens** 2200 **Vyds** 5.19ha
Peter Teakle worked for over 40 years for his family company, Collotype Wine Labels, recipient of a number of industry awards. His first venture outside of label printing was managing a vineyard on Akuna Station in the Riverland for many years. In early '16 he purchased the former Dellacolline Estate at Port Lincoln and has spent the intervening time in rehabilitating the rundown vineyard, doubling its size to 12ha. For the time being, the grapes are hand-picked and transported to O'Leary Walker Wines in the Clare Valley, where Liz Heidenreich makes the wines. (JH)

🍷🍷🍷🍷 Estate Shiraz 2018, Limestone Coast Very concentrated and dense, perhaps a little too much for balance, but you've got to hand it to the fruit, it has punch and personality. Weight and depth, too. An impressive wine in terms of its bounty of flavour. If you are partial to the super-ripe, dense styles, then you should give this a go. You'll love it. Screw cap. 15% alc. RATING 90 DRINK 2022-2032 $50 EL

Pewsey Vale Vineyard   ★★★★★

Eden Valley Road, Eden Valley, SA 5353 **Region** Eden Valley
T (08) 8561 3200 **www.**pewseyvale.com **Open** By appt **Winemaker** Louisa Rose
Est. 1847 **Dozens** 20 000 **Vyds** 65ha
Pewsey Vale was a famous vineyard established in 1847 by Joseph Gilbert. It was appropriate that when the Hill-Smith family began the renaissance of the Eden Valley plantings in 1961, it should do so by purchasing Pewsey Vale and establishing 50ha of riesling. In '77 the Riesling

also finally benefited from being the first wine to be bottled with a Stelvin screw cap. While public reaction forced the abandonment of the initiative for almost 20 years, Pewsey Vale never lost faith in the technical advantages of the closure. A quick taste (or better, a share of a bottle) of 5-7yo Contours Riesling will tell you why. Exports to all major markets. (JH)

🍷🍷🍷🍷🍷 **Prima 25GR Riesling 2021, Eden Valley** I've always enjoyed the Prima. Those fresh lime and crunchy apple notes are there, sluiced with soft spice and heady blossom notes, but I love the dance between sweetness and acid, the tension and the tempering effect of the acidity on the perception of sweetness. It's about balance and the Prima gets it right, especially in the impressive 2021 vintage. Screw cap. 9% alc. RATING 95 DRINK 2021–2031 $30 DB ✪

1961 Block Single Vineyard Estate Riesling 2020, Eden Valley Aromas of freshly squeezed lime juice with notes of lemon myrtle, almond blossom, crushed stone and perhaps a vague honeysuckle note further in the distance. It's a purely focused wine; quartzy and sapid with wonderful clarity, detail and drive. Screw cap. 12.5% alc. RATING 95 DRINK 2021–2035 $35 DB ✪

10 Years Cellar Aged The Contours Museum Reserve Single Vineyard Estate Riesling 2012, Eden Valley This contour-planted (1965) block of riesling, high in the Eden Valley has been the source of many a riesling epiphany. Pale to mid straw in the glass, with aromas of Bickford's lime, grapefruit pith, lemon zest. There's a complex array of underlying characters: preserved lemon, kaffir lime, beeswax, dried honey, lemon curd, crushed quartz, sage, soft spice, pressed flowers and almond paste. Toasty, long of finish and still boasting plenty of zesty drive, detail and clarity, it's just wonderful drinking. Screw cap. 12.5% alc. RATING 95 DRINK 2021–2028 $51 DB

🍷🍷🍷🍷🍷 **Single Vineyard Estate Riesling 2021, Eden Valley** RATING 93 DRINK 2021–2031 $26 DB ✪

Pfeiffer Wines   ★★★★★

167 Distillery Road, Wahgunyah, Vic 3687 **Region** Rutherglen
T (02) 6033 2805 **www.**pfeifferwines.com.au **Open** Mon–Sat 9–5, Sun 10–5
Winemaker Jen Pfeiffer, Chris Pfeiffer **Viticulturist** Paul Heard, Mick Patford **Est.** 1984
Dozens 20 000 **Vyds** 33ha

Family-owned and run, Pfeiffer Wines occupies one of the historic wineries (built in 1885) that abound in North East Victoria, which is worth a visit on this score alone. In 2012, Chris Pfeiffer was awarded an Order of Australia Medal (OAM) for his services to the wine industry. Both hitherto and into the future, Pfeiffer's Muscats, Topaques and other fortified wines are a key part of the business. The arrival of daughter Jen, has dramatically lifted the quality of the table wines, led by the reds. Chris Pfeiffer celebrated his 40th vintage in '13, having well and truly set the scene for supremely gifted daughter Jen to assume the chief winemaking role. Exports to the UK, the US, Canada, Belgium, Hong Kong and Singapore. (JH)

🍷🍷🍷🍷🍷 **Rare Muscat NV, Rutherglen** Few winemakers can enter into the rarefied Rare classification of muscat. Pfeiffer Wines, here boasting an average of 25 years, brings a fresh, fruity and floral input on what remains a luscious, concentrated fortified. Dark amber in hue. Walnut kernel, toasted hazelnut, blackstrap licorice, fig, treacle and rose petal bring a luxurious richness in aroma and taste, enhanced and brought to life with energy by the blender's art. Lives long. 500ml. Screw cap. 17.5% alc. RATING 97 $130 JP ✪

Rare Topaque NV, Rutherglen Just gaining entry to a state of complexity and absolute lusciousness is one thing, smashing the category with a vibrant freshness is another. The Pfeiffer style is quite distinctive, the cold-brew-coffee aromas so characteristic, joined by almond nougat, Christmas cake, prune, burnt butter and Saunders' malt extract. Winds and glides its way through the mouth, intensely sweet but also cleanly delivered. Lovely. 500ml. Screw cap. 17.5% alc. RATING 97 $130 JP ✪

ΨΨΨΨΨ Grand Muscat NV, Rutherglen It is a work of art to see the progression in concentration and richness from the Classic classification to Grand. Everything here is lifted a notch, all the while keeping an enviable freshness. The average age is 18–20 years. Malt leads with dried fruits, fruitcake, treacle with the presence of spice and nuts bringing that extra dimension. Superb. Screw cap. 17.5% alc. RATING 96 $85 JP

Grand Topaque NV, Rutherglen Average age is 18 years and it's another exciting journey into the beauty of an aged Topaque. Malt extract, coffee, licorice and prune. It presents so fresh, so luscious and smooth. It is sweet but it's a relative sweetness (263g/L) when compared with its Grand Muscat sibling. Screw cap. 17.5% alc. RATING 96 $85 JP

Rare Tawny NV, Rutherglen A veritable army of Portuguese and French grape varieties have gone into the making of this wine, which has an average age of 25 years. So smooth, so fresh and, above all, so complex in dried fruit, walnut, toffee and orange peel, panforte and fig. Controlled, balanced spirit is a big part of its huge appeal. Screw cap. 20% alc. RATING 96 $95 JP

Seriously Fine Pale Dry Apera NV, Rutherglen Jen Pfeiffer practises a dying winemaking art with gusto. More power to her, as she delivers one super-refreshing, dry and sultry apera. One whiff of the almond, orange peel, salted butter and nutty flor aromas gets the saliva working. A touch of lime-rich marmalade and salted nuts on the palate with plenty of tang, and it's an irresistible force. 500ml bottle. Screw cap. 16% alc. RATING 95 $29 JP ✪

Classic Muscat NV, Rutherglen Classic sets the standard, the house style for most Rutherglen makers, and this sets it very high indeed. Aromas of wet rose petal, orange peel, dried fruit and butterscotch. Sets the scene for a sweet (261g/L), clean and fresh fortified that offers amazing quality for the price. 500ml. Screw cap. 17.5% alc. RATING 95 $35 JP ✪

Classic Rutherglen Topaque NV, Marginally drier (248g/L) than the Classic Muscat and gives the strong impression of being younger and fresher than its sibling. It isn't. Average age remains 12-13 years. Golden syrup, salted caramel and orange peel are the trademarks for this house's Topaque, together with a bright freshness and long finish. Another winner from master fortified makers Chris and Jen Pfeiffer. 500ml. Screw cap. 17.5% alc. RATING 95 $35 JP ✪

Seriously Nutty Medium Dry Apera NV, Rutherglen A blend of palomino and monbadon, aged oxidatively for up to 30 years. A work of art by any reckoning, not to mention patience. A wine to get lost in, with layers of roasted nutty flor yeast, dried fruits, honey, apricot and orange peel, all brought to a vibrant liveliness with dry, clean acidity. 500ml. Screw cap. 21.5% alc. RATING 95 $50 JP

Pierro ★★★★★

Caves Road, Wilyabrup via Cowaramup, WA 6284 **Region** Margaret River
T (08) 9755 6220 **www**.pierro.com.au **Open** 7 days 10–5 **Winemaker** Dr Michael Peterkin **Est.** 1979 **Dozens** 10000 **Vyds** 7.85ha
Dr Michael Peterkin is another of the legion of Margaret River medical practitioner-vignerons; for good measure, he married into the Cullen family. Pierro is renowned for its stylish white wines, which often exhibit tremendous complexity; the Chardonnay can be monumental in its weight and texture. That said, its red wines from good vintages can be every bit as good. Exports to the UK, Denmark, Belgium, Russia, Malaysia, Indonesia, Hong Kong, Singapore and Japan. (JH)

ΨΨΨΨΨ Chardonnay VR 2018, Margaret River This is a thundering wine of booming power and length. It is characteristic of the '18 vintage of course, but few people were able to extract this reverberating density of flavour. It is long. It is nuanced. It is not restrained. It is awesome. For all of the complexity and beauty of Pierro Chardonnay, it appears positively fine boned and delicate when tried alongside this VR. The length here is a tour de force … it spools flavour, endlessly. It stains the mouth with it. Screw cap. 14% alc. RATING 98 DRINK 2022-2042 $125 EL ✪

ㅜㅜㅜㅜㅜ **Chardonnay 2020, Margaret River** In a word: beautiful. The warm year has produced a wine of effortless purity, underscored by a river of creamy, nutty texture, redolent of almond meal, briny acidity and pan-roasted exotic spice. This will live an age in the cellar, but it is so gorgeous now, it will be lucky to make it that far. A true classic. Screw cap. 13.5% alc. RATING 96 DRINK 2022–2042 $110 EL
Cabernet Sauvignon Merlot L.T.Cf. 2018, Margaret River All things on paper here speak of restraint: the responsibly weighted glass, low percentage of new oak, time in oak, a balance of varieties … and in the mouth all is confirmed. This is elegant and layered flavour in every part of the mouth. It creeps up on you, and lingers long after it has gone. This is a wonderful wine, and evidence that restraint was possible in the wonderful '18 vintage. Superb. Screw cap. 14% alc. RATING 96 DRINK 2021–2036 $48 EL ❂
Reserve Cabernet Sauvignon Merlot 2018, Margaret River As ever, this is delicate and poised, a most elegant expression of cabernet. The fruit is decidedly red – peppered with Szechuan peppercorn, pomegranate molasses, raspberry and even cocoa dust (unusual for Margaret River, but certainly present here). The endurance of flavour through the finish is admirable. A fitting tribute to a beautiful vintage. Screw cap.14% alc. RATING 96 DRINK 2022–2042 $95 EL
L.T.C. Semillon Sauvignon Blanc 2021, Margaret River Routinely one of the great sauvignon blends of the region, and this vintage is no exception. This is intensely concentrated in the mouth; finger lime, banana, guava, red apples, pink grapefruit, peach … the parade marches on. This feels marginally more tropical and opulent than years gone by: no bad thing. The '21 seems built on pleasure. Suffice to say, another excellent release. Screw cap. 13.5% alc. RATING 95 DRINK 2021–2031 $40 EL
Nunc Tempus Est Chenin Blanc 2020, Margaret River Effortless, with green apples, nashi pear, summer apricots, lanolin and cheesecloth, and fine, lemon pith acid. The Pierro 'nuts' are in there too (all the whites have a creamy, nutty character; it makes them what they are). A beautiful wine. Totally graceful. Screw cap. 13% alc. RATING 95 DRINK 2021–2036 $40 EL

Pike & Joyce   ★★★★★

730 Mawson Road, Lenswood, SA 5240 **Region** Adelaide Hills
T (08) 8389 8102 **www.**pikeandjoyce.com.au **Open** 7 days 11–4 **Winemaker** Steve Baraglia, Andrew Kenny **Est.** 1998 **Dozens** 5000 **Vyds** 18.5ha
This is a partnership between the Pike family (of Clare Valley fame) and the Joyce family, related to Andrew Pike's wife, Cathy. The Joyce family have been orchardists at Lenswood for over 100 years and also have extensive operations in the Riverland. Together with Andrew they have established a vineyard planted to sauvignon blanc (5.9ha), pinot noir (5.73ha), pinot gris (3.22ha), chardonnay (3.18ha) and semillon (0.47ha). The wines are made at the Pikes' Clare Valley winery. Exports to the UK and other major markets. (JH)

ㅜㅜㅜㅜㅜ **The Kay Reserve Chardonnay 2020, Adelaide Hills** A nicely captured, pristine chardonnay with a compact citrusy nose, grapefruit and nectarine with added barrel ferment mealy complexity. Oak is integrated and taut throughout, finishing with a mango-skin tang. Screw cap. 13% alc. RATING 95 DRINK 2022–2029 $65 JP
W.J.J. Reserve Pinot Noir 2020, Adelaide Hills Clear, welcoming hue; a warm bouquet of dark cherries, spice and a background of forest floor, the palate building on the bouquet with a seductive, juicy mix of ripe fruit, discreet tannins and French oak. All in balance, all in harmony. Screw cap. 13.5% alc. RATING 95 DRINK 2022–2038 $65 JH
Vintage Sparkling Chardonnay Pinot Noir 2016, Adelaide Hills With 4.5 years on lees, you can begin to appreciate the inherent power in this sparkling, the complexity, while also maintaining a great freshness. Flinty, lemon butter, grapefruit, honeydew melon aromas. Zesty on the plate with a pronounced citrus intensity backed by a soft nutty autolysis. Brisk acidity to close. Crown. 12% alc. RATING 94 $65 JP

🍷🍷🍷🍷🍷 **Séparé Grüner Veltliner 2021, Adelaide Hills** RATING 93 DRINK 2022–2024 $25 JP ✪
Beurre Bosc Pinot Gris 2021, Adelaide Hills RATING 92 DRINK 2022–2024 $25 JP ✪
Innesti Nebbiolo 2020, Adelaide Hills RATING 92 DRINK 2023–2031 $40 JP
Clonal Selection 114 Pinot Noir 2020, Adelaide Hills RATING 92 DRINK 2022–2025 $50 JP
Méthode Cuve Pinot Noir Rosé 2021, Adelaide Hills RATING 91 $30 JP
Descente Sauvignon Blanc 2021, Adelaide Hills RATING 91 DRINK 2022–2025 $25 JP
Sirocco Chardonnay 2020, Adelaide Hills RATING 91 DRINK 2025–2030 $32 JH
Céder Riesling 2021, Adelaide Hills RATING 90 DRINK 2023–2028 $30 JP
Vue du Nord Pinot Noir 2021, Adelaide Hills RATING 90 DRINK 2022–2026 $32 JP
Clonal Selection 777 Pinot Noir 2020, Adelaide Hills RATING 90 DRINK 2022–2024 $50 JP

Pikes ★★★★★

233 Polish Hill River Road, Sevenhill, SA 5453 **Region** Clare Valley
T (08) 8843 4370 **www**.pikeswines.com.au **Open** 7 days 10–4 **Winemaker** Andrew Pike **Viticulturist** Andrew Pike **Est.** 1984 **Dozens** 50 000 **Vyds** 130ha

Pikes is a family affair, established in the '80s by Andrew, Neil and Cathy Pike with support from their parents Merle and Edgar. A generation on, Neil Pike has retired after 35 years as chief winemaker and Andrew's sons Jamie and Alister have come on board (Jamie to oversee sales and marketing, Alistair to run the craft brewery that opened in '14). The award-winning Slate restaurant opened in '18, alongside a new tasting room. Riesling inevitably makes up half of all plantings; shiraz, cabernet, sangiovese, pinot grigio and tempranillo dominate the other half. Pikes' flagship wines are the Merle Riesling and EWP Shiraz, named after Merle and Edgar, and only made in exceptional vintages. Exports to Hong Kong, Canada, Ireland, Singapore, Poland, Japan, Sweden, Malaysia, Taiwan, NZ, the UK, Cyprus, the Philippines, France and the US. (TS)

🍷🍷🍷🍷🍷 **The Merle Riesling 2021, Clare Valley** The nose here is littered with characters that take some time to unpick: green pineapple, green and red apple skins, white peach, lemon zest, lime flesh and beeswax. Layers of white pepper, crushed chalk and hints of garden mint round this out. It's incredibly detailed and interesting, not to mention long. Screw cap. 11.5% alc. RATING 95 DRINK 2021–2036 $55 EL

Il Premio Sangiovese 2020, Clare Valley Raspberry essence, white pepper, bramble and spice is backed by salty acidity and fine, structuring tannins. This is delicious. Australian sangiovese at its best. What a supple, slinky little number. Big yes. Screw cap. 14% alc. RATING 95 DRINK 2022–2037 $72 EL

The E.W.P. Shiraz 2020, Clare Valley Wow – loads of fresh shaved deli meat here, with black cherries, kirsch, clove, star anise, pink peppercorn and licorice. In the mouth, the wine is pert and finer than expected from the meaty introduction, yet it does not waver from its savoury roots. Very good, very long, and more-ish for its bacon fat and maple vibes. Like it. Screw cap. 14% alc. RATING 95 DRINK 2022–2032 $72 EL

🍷🍷🍷🍷🍷 **Traditionale Riesling 2021, Clare Valley** RATING 93 DRINK 2021–2031 $26 EL ✪
The Hill Block Cabernet 2020, Clare Valley RATING 92 DRINK 2022–2035 $72 EL
The Assemblage Shiraz Grenache Mourvèdre 2019, Clare Valley RATING 91 DRINK 2021–2028 $25 EL
Luccio Fiano 2021, Clare Valley RATING 90 DRINK 2021–2023 $24 EL
Eastside Shiraz 2020, Clare Valley RATING 90 DRINK 2022–2027 $28 EL

Pimpernel Vineyards

6 Hill Road, Coldstream, Vic 3770 **Region** Yarra Valley
T 0407 010 802 **www**.pimpernelvineyards.com.au **Open** by appt **Winemaker** Damien
Archibald, Mark Horrigan **Viticulturist** Damien Archibald **Est.** 2001 **Dozens** 3000
Vyds 6ha

Mark Horrigan's love affair with wine started long before he had heard about either the
Yarra Valley or his family's links, centuries ago, to Condrieu, France. In '01 he and wife Fiona
purchased a property in the Yarra Valley on which they have built a house, planted a vineyard,
and established a capacious winery designed by WA architect Peter Moran. In the course of
doing so they became good friends of near-neighbour the late Dr Bailey Carrodus; some of
the delphic labelling of Pimpernel's wines is pure Carrodus. Exports to Japan. (JH)

Whole Bunch Shiraz 2019, Yarra Valley Bright crimson red with wild
berries, white and black pepper, star anise and violet aromatics. The wood is
sitting discreetly in the background and there's excellent flow on the palate, with
the wine's concentration and silky mouthfeel balanced by the gently chewy,
yet fine and persistent tannins. A keeper. Screw cap. 14.8% alc. RATING 95
DRINK 2022-2032 $90 PR

Pinot Noir Four 2019, Yarra Valley RATING 93 DRINK 2022-2019 $90 PR
Estate Pinot Noir 2019, Yarra Valley RATING 91 DRINK 2021-2026 $60 PR
Shiraz 2019, Yarra Valley RATING 91 DRINK 2022-2030 $60 PR

Pindarie

946 Rosedale Road, Gomersal, SA 5352 **Region** Barossa Valley
T (08) 8524 9019 **www**.pindarie.com.au **Open** 7 days 11–5 **Winemaker** Peter Leske
Viticulturist Wendy Allan **Est.** 2005 **Vyds** 36ha

Owners Tony Brooks and Wendy Allan met at Roseworthy College in 1985. Tony was the
6th generation of farmers in SA and WA, and was studying agriculture; NZ-born Wendy was
studying viticulture. On graduation, Tony worked overseas managing sheep feedlots in Saudi
Arabia, Turkey and Jordan; Wendy worked for the next 12 years with Penfolds, working her
way up to become a senior viticulturist. She also studied viticulture in California, Israel, Italy,
Germany, France, Portugal, Spain and Chile, working vintages and assessing vineyards for wine
projects. In '01, she completed a graduate diploma in wine business. The cellar door and the
Grain Store cafe (winner of Australian tourism awards in '13 and '14 as well as Hall of fame
for SA Tourism) has panoramic views. Exports to Taiwan and Singapore. (JH)

Western Ridge Shiraz 2020, Barossa Valley Dense, compact aromatic
profile of blackberry and black cherry, black licorice, dark chocolate, coal dust,
clove and earth. Impressive fruit density and heft with classic, compact Western
Ridge tannins and sprightly acidity, finishing dry and talcy. Screw cap. 14.5% alc.
RATING 93 DRINK 2021-2031 $30 DB
Small Block Montepulciano 2020, Barossa Valley Vivid purple red in the
glass with aromas of juicy blueberry, mulberry and blackberry fruits. Abundant
spice, floral and chocolatey tannin nuance here and while the young vines lack
the carry of their older and wiser siblings, they more than make up for it with
juicy, youthful exuberance. Good drinking. Screw cap. 14.5% alc. RATING 91
DRINK 2021-2026 $30 DB

Pine Drive Vineyards

PO Box 1138, Nuriootpa, SA 5355 **Region** Barossa Valley
T 0404 029 412 **www**.pinedrivewineyards.com **Open Winemaker** Joanne Irvine
Viticulturist Matthew Grayson **Est.** 1962 **Dozens** 100 **Vyds** 8.5ha

Pine Drive Vineyards is a fledgling wine label established by Matthew Grayson and Bernadette
Stewart, a Queenslander and a Canadian, who met in Qatar and whose mutual love of wine
saw them relocate to the Barossa Valley, purchasing a property in between the northern
subregions of Moppa and Ebenezer. Their 8.5ha of shiraz vines, some planted in 1964, lie on

the famous rolling Moppa sand dunes that Max Schubert was fond of when he crafted the early vintages of Grange Hermitage. This is a young winery, with only a single shiraz offering to date, but it's an impressive wine and other wines will join the fold in the near future. One to watch. (DB)

♥♥♥♥♥ The Pine Drive Shiraz 2019, Barossa Valley Bright red purple in the glass with wonderfully perfumed ripe fruits along the lines of satsuma plum, blackberry and black cherry. Hints of violets, licorice, earth, dried cranberry, baking spice and dark chocolate combine with fine, sandy tannins and a swift, minerally acid cadence providing the pulse. A lovely, savoury contemporary Barossa shiraz. Screw cap. 14.4% alc. RATING 94 DRINK 2022-2028 $50 DB

Pinelli Wines

30 Bennett Street, Caversham, WA 6055 **Region** Swan District
T (08) 9279 6818 **www.**pinelliwines.com.au **Open** Mon–Sat 9–5, Sun & public hols 10–5 **Winemaker** Robert Pinelli, Daniel Pinelli **Est.** 1980 **Dozens** 17 000 **Vyds** 9.78ha
Domenic and Iolanda Pinelli emigrated from Italy in the mid '50s. With the benefit of 20 years' experience gained with Waldeck Wines he purchased a 2.8ha vineyard in '80. It became the site of the Pinelli family winery, cellar door and home vineyard, subsequently significantly expanded, with cabernet sauvignon, colombard, merlot and shiraz. Son Robert, has been the winemaker at Pinelli for over 20 years. His brother Daniel obtained his oenology degree from CSU in '07. He graduated with distinction, and was awarded the Domaine Chandon Sparkling Wine Award for best sparkling wine production student. (JH)

♥♥♥♥♡ La Tavola Shiraz 2020, Western Australia The fruit is from the Swan Valley, which (in my opinion) should be declared loudly on the front label. As one of Australia's oldest wine regions, the Swan Valley has plenty to be proud of. Not the least of which, is its ability to produce ripe, concentrated shiraz in a style very different to that of other regions. This is uncomplicated, littered with blackberries, mulberries, star anise, some warm spice (think cinnamon, cardamom and the like) and cloves. Swan Valley represent. Screw cap. 14% alc. RATING 91 DRINK 2021-2027 $20 EL ✪
Grand Tawny NV, Swan Valley Spiced fig, dark chocolate, quince, star anise and cigar box/tobacco. In the mouth this is sweet (of course), with lacings of bitter almonds, toffee and exotic spice. The bitterness through the finish is a little distracting to the display of fruit flavour on show, although it does even out over the finish. Give it some time. It's a little disjointed, the spirit not fully integrated into the fruit, yet. 375ml. Screw cap. 18.5% alc. RATING 90 $60 EL

♥♥♥♥ Breanna Rosé 2021, Swan Valley RATING 89 DRINK 2022-2023 $22 EL
Reserve Shiraz 2020, Western Australia RATING 89 DRINK 2021-2027 $26 EL
Reserve Verdelho 2021, Swan Valley RATING 88 DRINK 2022-2025 $18 EL
Reserve Durif 2020, Swan Valley RATING 88 DRINK 2022-2027 $32 EL

Pipan Steel

583 Carrolls Road, Mudgegonga, Vic 3737 **Region** Alpine Valleys
T 0418 679 885 **www.**pipansteelwines.com.au **Open** By appt **Winemaker** Paula Pipan, Daniel Balzer **Viticulturist** Radley Steel, Paula Pipan **Est.** 2008 **Dozens** 230 **Vyds** 0.4ha
Paula Pipan and Radley Steel are passionate about nebbiolo, the grape that hails from Piedmont, Italy. Their search for suitable land took them to a hillside of decomposed granite soil in Mudgegonga in North East Victoria in the foothills of the Australian Alps. And so Pipan Steel was born. Under the sponsorship of Tyrrell's Wines winemaker, Andrew Spinaze, Paula was accepted into the wine degree at CSU. Radley, a sports medicine practitioner, moved his practice to North East Victoria and became the viticulturist. Three nebbiolo clones were sourced from Gruppo Matura in Italy, each clone is vinified separately, and each wine spends time in large, seasoned French oak for 2 years and then another 2 year in bottle before release. (JP)

ᵀᵀᵀᵀᵀ III Nebbiolo 2017, Alpine Valleys Blend 3 is a mix of 43/41/16% clone 9/10/7. While individual clones bring their own strengths, it's not surprising to see a blend of those strengths make the biggest impact. Blend 3 is a fine tannin-edged combination of aromatics and fruit intensity, so fresh and vital at 5yo! Potential+ for further ageing. Screw cap. 14.1% alc. RATING 95 DRINK 2022-2032 $49 JP
IX Nebbiolo 2017, Alpine Valleys Clone 9 takes centre stage here. Paula Pipan regards this as the 'luscious, generous' clone. Looking a little coy but opens with air to reveal pinot-like flair in red cherry, redcurrant, anise and rose with a touch of wood smoke. Building in volume as it opens, with almost lush tannins by nebbiolo standards. You can sense this wine is growing all the while and will love some time in the dark. Screw cap. 14.2% alc. RATING 95 DRINK 2021-2032 $49 JP

ᵀᵀᵀᵀᵀ X Nebbiolo 2017, Alpine Valleys RATING 93 DRINK 2021-2030 $49 JP
VII Nebbiolo 2017, Alpine Valleys RATING 92 DRINK 2021-2032 $49 JP

Pipers Brook Vineyard ★★★★★

1216 Pipers Brook Road, Pipers Brook, Tas 7254 **Region** Northern Tasmania
T (03) 6382 7555 **www**.kreglingerwineestates.com **Open** By appt **Winemaker** Luke Whittle **Viticulturist** Kym Ayeliffe **Est.** 1974 **Dozens** 70 000 **Vyds** 176.51ha
The Pipers Brook empire has almost 200ha of vineyard supporting the Ninth Island, Pipers Brook and Kreglinger labels with the major focus, of course, being on Pipers Brook. Fastidious viticulture and a passionate winemaking team along with immaculate packaging and enterprising marketing create a potent and effective blend. Pipers Brook operates a cellar door at the winery and is owned by Belgian-owned sheepskin business Kreglinger, which has also established the large Norfolk Rise Vineyard at Mount Benson in SA (see separate entry). Exports to the UK, the US and other major markets. (JH)

ᵀᵀᵀᵀᵀ Kreglinger Brut Rosé 2017, Tasmania Traditional method, aged 44 months on lees with 7.5g/L dosage. The pinot noir of the old vines of the Kreglinger vineyard has always been something to behold, and never has it looked more precise nor more graceful than this. Delectable red cherry and wild-strawberry fruit seduces from the outset, graced with the signature Turkish delight of Pipers River, but it's the creamy, silky texture of barrel and lees work that really sets apart this sublime creation. Cork. 12.5% alc. RATING 96 $75 TS ✪ ♥
Kreglinger Brut Rosé NV, Tasmania Traditional method, aged 12+ months on lees in bottle. 8g/L dosage. A brand-new rosé landing between the sublime Ninth Island and Kreglinger Vintage Brut comes with palpable anticipation, and every detail of hope has been realised here. It takes mighty talent to tone Pipers River pinot noir to such elegance, while drawing out incredible texture that's more than just silky and creamy. The fingerprints of the legendary Natalie Fryar are all over this wine. Diam. 12.5% alc. RATING 95 $40 TS
Kreglinger Vintage Brut 2017, Tasmania Traditional method, 60/40% pinot noir/chardonnay. Aged 44 months on lees; 6.25g/L dosage. The powerful '17 season in Pipers River delivers considerable presence and character of a panoply of fruit from apple and pear, to spicy berries and cherries. The precision of this outfit delivers impressive tension and line, while building all the creaminess and silkiness of barrel fermentation. It's compelling from the outset, and will evolve to wonderful places over the coming years. Cork. 12.5% alc. RATING 94 $60 TS
Pinot Gris 2021, Tasmania West Tamar gris can tend towards excessive richness and ripeness, while the naturally high malic acidity of Pipers Brook can be confrontingly steely. The ideal middle ground of blending both is exemplified here. Perfectly ripe, spicy pear energised by delightfully lively lemon-juice acidity carries with great line and energy. Spicy yet vibrant, fleshy yet zesty, making for eminent dexterity on the dining table. Screw cap. 13.5% alc. RATING 94 DRINK 2022-2023 $35 TS
Sauvignon Blanc 2021, Tasmania Old-vine fruit depth, cool season tension and masterfully deployed woodwork unite in a sophisticated sauvignon engineered

for the cellar. Characteristic gooseberry, lantana and passionfruit are here in full measure, nicely contrasting the hazelnut cream of 8 months in French oak barrels, but it's the racy lemon-and-lime-juice spine and the way it tussles with creamy barrel ferment texture that really delivers excitement here. Do not underestimate its longevity, and do not dare open a bottle for at least 5 years, preferably 10. Screw cap. 12.5% alc. RATING 94 DRINK 2031-2041 $35 TS

Rosé 2021, Tasmania Is there any finer recipe for Australian rosé than Pipers River pinot noir in a cool season? Such is its delectable Turkish delight fragrance and wild strawberry and morello cherry fruit that everything else seems incidental – a monumental suggestion for a delicate rosé that's spent 6 months in barrel. Impeccably crafted and irresistible from the outset – but don't underestimate the endurance of that soaring acid line. Screw cap. 13.5% alc. RATING 94 DRINK 2022-2026 $50 TS

ＹＹＹＹＹ **Ninth Island Sparkling Rosé NV, Tasmania** RATING 93 $25 TS ✪
Gewürztraminer 2021, Tasmania RATING 93 DRINK 2022-2026 $35 TS
Riesling 2021, Tasmania RATING 93 DRINK 2026-2036 $35 TS
Pinot Noir 2020, Tasmania RATING 93 DRINK 2027-2035 $50 TS
Kreglinger Brut NV, Tasmania RATING 92 $35 TS
Chardonnay 2020, Tasmania RATING 92 DRINK 2030-2040 $45 TS
Ninth Island Sparkling NV, Tasmania RATING 91 $25 TS

Pirathon ★★★★

979 Light Pass Road, Vine Vale, SA 5352 **Region** Barossa Valley
T www.pirathon.com **Open** By appt **Winemaker** Adam Clay **Viticulturist** Tony Marshall **Est.** 2005 **Dozens** 9000 **Vyds** 22ha
Pirathon primarily focuses on full-bodied Barossa Valley shiraz from the north-western districts of Greenock (contract-grown) and Maranaga (estate-grown). A new 480t winery was completed in '21. Exports to all major markets. (JH)

ＹＹＹＹＹ **Gold Shiraz 2019, Barossa Valley** Notes of blackberry, blood plum and black cherry are underscored by licorice, clove, cinnamon, violets, dark chocolate and vanillin oak. The fruit has sucked up the oak nicely here and flows with medium body on the palate, finishing with some whole-grain tannin grit and a savoury, cassis-like flourish. Screw cap. 14.5% alc. RATING 91 DRINK 2022-2030 $100 DB
Blue Shiraz 2020, Barossa Valley Purple red in the glass with an exuberant nose of juicy satsuma plum, jasmine, Asian spice, cherry pie and licorice. There's a slurpy edge to this one, with heady ripe plum and black fruits, abundant spice, fine tannin and brisk line. Good juicy drinking and great value. Screw cap. 14.5% alc. RATING 90 DRINK 2022-2026 $18 DB ✪

ＹＹＹＹ **Silver Shiraz 2019, Barossa Valley** RATING 89 DRINK 2022-2026 $27 DB
Bronze Label Shiraz 2019, Barossa Valley RATING 88 DRINK 2022-2028 $22 DB

Pirie Tasmania ★★★★

1a Waldhorn Drive, Rosevears, Tas 7277 **Region** Northern Tasmania
T (03) 6335 5480 **www.tamarridge.com.au/pirie Open** 7 days 10–5 **Winemaker** Tom Wallace **Est.** 2004 **Vyds** 82.9ha
Andrew Pirie has had a lifetime of experience growing grapes and making wine in Northern Tasmania. He established Pipers Brook Vineyard in 1974, and was responsible for making it the best-known Tasmanian winery in the 1980s and much of the '90s, before he relinquished what was then part-ownership. The cellar door is now located at the spectacularly situated Rosevears Vineyard, which is also home to Estelle Restaurant, with its panoramic views over the Tamar River. Some will no doubt find it ironic that one of Rosevears' attractions is said to be eco-retreats. This is peripheral to the quality of the wines, which has always been very good. Exports to the UK, the US and other major markets. (JH)

🍷🍷🍷🍷🍷 **Traditional Method 2017, Tasmania** A chardonnay and pinot noir blend from the Tamar Valley, 3 years on tirage/lees. Overall, very fresh and has a clearly defined trail of stone fruits going through the mid-palate, brioche on the finish. Cork. 12% alc. RATING 95 $40 JH

🍷🍷🍷🍷🍷 **Traditional Method NV, Tasmania** RATING 91 $32 TS

Pirramimma   ★★★★

Johnston Road, McLaren Vale, SA 5171 **Region** McLaren Vale
T (08) 8323 8205 www.pirramimma.com.au **Open** Mon–Fri 9.30–4.30, w'ends & public hols 11–5 **Winemaker** Geoff Johnston **Viticulturist** Andrew Johnston **Est.** 1892 **Dozens** 50 000 **Vyds** 91.5ha
A long-established, family-owned company with outstanding vineyard resources, which it is using to full effect. A series of intense old-vine varietals includes semillon, sauvignon blanc, chardonnay, shiraz, grenache, cabernet sauvignon and petit verdot, all fashioned without over-embellishment. Wines are released in several ranges: Pirramimma, Stock's Hill, White Label, ACJ, Katunga, Eight Carat and Gilded Lilly. Exports to all major markets. (JH)

🍷🍷🍷🍷🍷 **ACJ 2018, McLaren Vale** 83/17% cabernet/petit verdot. Plenty of oak framework, imparting mocha, coffee grind and cinnamon. Cassis, black olive, sage and bay leaf stuffed within. The finish, vacillating between the refined tannic grain and the saline waft of these parts. Plenty to like here. Screw cap. 14.5% alc. RATING 94 DRINK 2022-2035 $100 NG

🍷🍷🍷🍷🍷 **Ironstone Malbec 2018, McLaren Vale** RATING 93 DRINK 2022-2028 $70 NG
War Horse 2017, McLaren Vale RATING 93 DRINK 2021-2034 $100 NG
Ironstone Old Bush Vine Grenache 2019, McLaren Vale RATING 91 DRINK 2021-2028 $70 NG
Old Bush Vine Grenache 2019, McLaren Vale RATING 90 DRINK 2021-2027 $35 NG
Ironstone 2019, McLaren Vale RATING 90 DRINK 2022-2034 $70 NG

Pizzini   ★★★★★

175 King Valley Road, Whitfield, Vic 3768 **Region** King Valley
T (03) 5729 8278 www.pizzini.com.au **Open** 7 days 10–5 **Winemaker** Joel Pizzini **Viticulturist** David Morgan **Est.** 1980 **Dozens** 30 000 **Vyds** 75ha
The Pizzini family have been grapegrowers in the King Valley for over 40 years. Originally, much of the then riesling, chardonnay and cabernet sauvignon grape production was sold, but since the late '90s the focus has been on winemaking, particularly from Italian varieties. Pizzini's success has enabled an increase vineyard in holdings to 75ha, with 30ha of sangiovese, 20ha of pinot grigio, 13ha of prosecco, 2.5ha each of brachetto, arneis and verduzzo, 2ha each of nebbiolo and colorino and 0.5ha of teroldego. Exports to the UK and Japan. (JH)

🍷🍷🍷🍷🍷 **Coronamento Nebbiolo 2016, King Valley** That scent! It captures the essence of what we love about nebbiolo: the rose petals, violets, acacia and dark cherry is a thoroughly compelling perfume. Works its charm with an underlying power and intensity. Cherry and cranberry red fruits join a herbal and floral infusion of red licorice, anise and potpourri, earth and wood smoke. Firm, savoury tannins guide the palate long. An Australian nebbiolo of real class, and it's only just starting its journey. Screw cap. 13.8% alc. RATING 96 DRINK 2022-2032 $140 JP
Attento Pinot Grigio 2021, King Valley Attento means 'careful' in Italian, and fruit was sourced from the Whitlands subregion at 800m elevation, with the intention of making a grigio for bottle ageing. From a top year comes a top wine, complex and presenting a serious side to grigio, with aromas of honeysuckle, hay, apple and a burst of citrus in lemon zest and grapefruit. Expands on the palate running deep, showing a touch of almond-edge savouriness and creaminess, then comes the acid tang. Brilliant. Screw cap. 12.7% alc. RATING 95 DRINK 2022-2028 $55 JP

Per gli Angeli 2012, King Valley Dried and semi-pressed, then macerated; the process is repeated up to 5 times, before a 2-year ferment and 7 years' maturation. A significant price rise for the '12 vintage, indicative of the time and care taken to create this little 'for the angels' beauty. Golden syrup and burnt orange hues. A world of intriguing scents awaits, of orange rind, dried fruits, toffee and honey. Sustained force of flavour and texture with the added discreet charm of mocha oak. Delightfully Italian-esque in style. Where's the almond biscotti? 375ml bottle. Screw cap. 14% alc. RATING 95 DRINK 2021-2023 $125 JP

Pietra Rossa Sangiovese 2019, King Valley Celebrates what we love about the sangiovese grape from an immediate red-fruit and spice intensity through to a warm, textural mouthfeel and light savouriness. That's a lot to pack into the price. Black cherry, raspberry, pomegranate, potpourri, thyme aromas and flavours aplenty. Flavours envelop the tastebuds, moving in time with gentle oak. Savoury tannins bring added character to this impressive, well-priced sangiovese. Screw cap. 13.8% alc. RATING 94 DRINK 2021-2029 $28 JP ○

Il Barone 2019, King Valley Beechworth 48/22/18/7/5% cabernet sauvignon/shiraz/sangiovese/nebbiolo/teroldego. A busy wine to be sure, with 5 strong personalities combining their strengths and that's exciting in itself, challenging traditional red blends and drinkers' attitudes. Sour cherry, rhubarb, plum, saltbush, eucalyptus, earth, game and so much more. It's one busy, interesting, excitingly different wine. Gotta love it. Screw cap. 13.8% alc. RATING 94 DRINK 2022-2033 $55 JP

Rubacuori Sangiovese 2016, King Valley An exploration of sangiovese as a medium-aged, complex, savoury wine, one we don't see often enough in Australia. Strong varietal credentials with aromas of tilled earth, leather, maraschino cherry, anise, espresso coffee. The mid palate, expansive and savoury, opens on to a world of sinewy, dry tannins with an oh, so Italian astringent finish. Does the grape proud. Screw cap. 13.8% alc. RATING 94 DRINK 2021-2028 $140 JP

ŶŶŶŶŶ **Riesling 2021, King Valley** RATING 93 DRINK 2021-2031 $22 JP ○
Forza di Ferro Sangiovese 2019, King Valley RATING 92 DRINK 2022-2034 $55 JP
Pinot Grigio 2021, King Valley RATING 91 DRINK 2021-2024 $22 JP ○
Rosetta Sangiovese Nebbiolo Rosé 2021, King Valley RATING 90 DRINK 2021-2025 $22 JP
Verduzzo 2021, King Valley RATING 90 DRINK 2022-2024 $28 JP
Teroldego 2021, King Valley RATING 90 DRINK 2022-2028 $28 JP

Place of Changing Winds ★★★★☆

Waterloo Flat Road, Bullengarook, Vic 3437 **Region** Macedon Ranges
T www.placeofchangingwinds.com.au **Open** By appt **Winemaker** Remi Jacquemain, Robert Walters, Tom Trewin **Viticulturist** Remi Jacquemain, Robert Walters, Tom Trewin **Est.** 2012 **Dozens** 1000 **Vyds** 3.1ha
This extraordinary high-density vineyard is slotted between Mount Macedon and Mount Bullengarook. It's the brainchild of the committed and obsessive Robert Walters. Through his many connections and much research comes Place of Changing Winds, known as Warekilla in the local Wurundjeri language. It's a rocky site at 500m elevation, surrounded by forest. The whole farm covers 33ha but vines comprise just 3.1 ha, planted to 44000 vines. A high-density site of pinot noir and chardonnay, ranging from 12500 to 33000 vines/ha: there is nothing like this in Australia, or even in Burgundy (where 10000 vines is deemed high density). No expense has been spared. The site is organically certified and the level of detail is nothing short of extraordinary. Best New Winery 2022. Exports to France, Sweden, Spain, the UK, Malaysia and Singapore. (JF)

ŶŶŶŶŶ **Second Bottling Syrah 2019, Heathcote** The first incarnation (Colbinabbin Vineyard Syrah 2019) was released in '21. This second bottling has come together beautifully, revealing a more savoury outlook with a composed, medium-bodied structure. It's peppery and spicy, with hints of bay leaves mingling with the red-fruit spectrum. Detailed, fine tannins are a feature and it finishes long and convincingly. Diam. 13% alc. RATING 95 DRINK 2022-2033 $48 JF

ŸŸŸŸ♀ **Colbinabbin Vineyard Marsanne 2019, Heathcote** RATING 92 DRINK 2021-2026 $42 JF

PLAN B! WINES   ★★★★

Freshwater Drive, Margaret River, WA 6285 **Region** Western Australia
T 0413 759 030 **www.**planbwines.com **Winemaker** Vanessa Carson **Est.** 2003
Dozens 35 000 **Vyds** 40ha
Plan B is owned and run by wine consultant Terry Chellappah 'between rocking the bass guitar and researching bars'. He says he is better at one than the other. Plan B has been notably successful, with significant increases in production. Winemaker Vanessa Carson has made wine in Margaret River and Frankland Valley, as well as in Italy and France. Exports to the EU, Singapore, Hong Kong, Malaysia, Fiji and Indonesia. (JH)

ŸŸŸŸ♀ **The Next Hundred Years Syrah 2020, Frankland River** With 2% barrel-fermented viognier. Savoury, meaty and slick, as many shiraz viogniers can be. The ironstone gravels of Frankland River impart a ferrous/blood character on the wines, which is evident here through the finish. Structured and firm, this is very good because it plays within a medium-bodied frame, while having very good flavour concentration. Not an easy thing to achieve! Screw cap. 14.5% alc. RATING 93 DRINK 2022-2029 $40 EL
Mental Blanc 2021, Frankland River Despite all the hoo-hah on the back label of the bottle about Mental Blancs and pearly whites, the wine in the glass is very good. Structural and chalky with taut acidity that shapes the citrus fruit. Long and reminiscent of crushed shells and brine. Smart. Screw cap. 13.5% alc. RATING 92 DRINK 2021-2025 $25 EL ✪
DR Riesling 2021, Great Southern Chalky, fine phenolics encase a taut core of citrus fruit. Some green leafy characters woven through the finish (Thai basil, coriander). Pretty. Screw cap. 12% alc. RATING 90 DRINK 2021-2031 $29 EL
Modern White Chardonnay Viognier 2021, Margaret River Viognier at 8% is a major player here, contributing white flowers, apricots, a touch of hessian, sandalwood and green apples to the orchard fruit that emerges so effortlessly in Margaret River chardonnay. There is frisky phenolic presence through the finish (as there is in the Minor Chardonnay), however here, it works in a spicy, attractive sort of way. Intriguing. Screw cap. 13% alc. RATING 90 DRINK 2022-2028 $25 EL

ŸŸŸŸ **Ferguson Valley Tempranillo Rosado 2021, Geographe** RATING 89 DRINK 2021-2023 $25 EL
Frespañol Shiraz 2020, Frankland River RATING 89 DRINK 2025-2030 $25 JH
Minor Chardonnay 2021, Margaret River RATING 88 DRINK 2022-2028 $25 EL
The Next Hundred Years Riesling 2021, Great Southern RATING 88 DRINK 2022-2029 $40 EL
Modern Red 2019, Great Southern RATING 88 DRINK 2023-2035 $25 JH

Plantagenet   ★★★★★

45 Albany Highway, Mount Barker, WA 6324 **Region** Mount Barker
T (08) 9851 3111 **www.**plantagenetwines.com **Open** 7 days 10–4.30 **Winemaker** Luke
Eckerseley, Chris Murtha **Viticulturist** Jordan Ellis **Est.** 1968 **Dozens** 30 000
Vyds 126ha
Plantagenet was established by Tony Smith, who continues to be involved in its management over 45 years later, notwithstanding that it has been owned by Lionel Samson & Son for many years. He established 5 vineyards: Bouverie in 1968 (sold in 2017), Wyjup in '71, Rocky Horror 1 in '88, Rocky Horror 2 in '97 and Rosetta in '99. These vineyards are the cornerstones of the substantial production of the consistently high-quality wines that

have always been the mark of Plantagenet: highly aromatic Riesling, tangy citrus-tinged Chardonnay, glorious Rhône-style Shiraz and ultra-stylish Cabernet Sauvignon. Exports to the UK, Canada, the US, Japan and South Korea. (JH)

🍷🍷🍷🍷🍷 **Wyjup Collection Riesling 2021, Mount Barker** And here we are, at the pinnacle riesling for Plantagenet: the single-vineyard expression. This is restrained and pithy in this cool year, showing a mineral seam of acidity that courses and flows through every aspect of the wine. Very, very classy, with a lingering spool of flavour through the finish that remains long after the wine is gone. Screw cap. 13% alc. RATING 94 DRINK 2022-2035 $45 EL

🍷🍷🍷🍷🍷 **Lancaster Shiraz 2019, Great Southern** RATING 93 DRINK 2022-2030 $45 EL
Wyjup Collection Cabernet Sauvignon 2019, Mount Barker RATING 93 DRINK 2022-2037 $80 EL
Angevin Riesling 2021, Great Southern RATING 92 DRINK 2022-2032 $32 EL
Wyjup Collection Chardonnay 2020, Mount Barker RATING 92 DRINK 2022-2028 $45 EL
Wyjup Collection Pinot Noir 2020, Mount Barker RATING 92 DRINK 2022-2028 $70 EL
Wyjup Collection Shiraz 2019, Mount Barker RATING 91 DRINK 2022-2032 $80 EL
Three Lions Riesling 2021, Great Southern RATING 90 DRINK 2022-2029 $23 EL
York Chardonnay 2020, Great Southern RATING 90 DRINK 2022-2027 $40 EL
Aquitaine Cabernet Sauvignon 2019, Great Southern RATING 90 DRINK 2022-2028 $45 EL

Poacher's Ridge Vineyard ★★★★★
1630 Spencer Road, Narrikup, WA 6326 **Region** Mount Barker
T (08) 9857 6066 **www**.poachersridge.com.au **Open** Fri–Sun 10–4 **Winemaker** Robert Diletti **Viticulturist** Alex Taylor **Est.** 2000 **Dozens** 1000 **Vyds** 6.9ha
Alex and Janet Taylor purchased the Poacher's Ridge property in 1999. It had previously been used for cattle grazing. The vineyard includes shiraz, cabernet sauvignon, merlot, riesling, marsanne, viognier and malbec. Winning the Tri Nations 2007 merlot class against the might of Australia, NZ and South Africa with its '05 Louis' Block Great Southern Merlot was a dream come true. And it wasn't a one-time success – Poacher's Ridge Merlot is always at, or near, the top of the tree. Exports to Singapore and Japan. (JH)

🍷🍷🍷🍷🍷 **Riesling 2021, Great Southern** Cheesecloth, citrus zest and Golden Delicious apples on the nose. In the mouth the wine is taut and austere, with bracing acidity that bands across the tongue. A couple of extra years under the belt will assist with melting acid into the fruit, as it becomes a graceful middle-aged wine. Screw cap. 12.5% alc. RATING 90 DRINK 2023-2033 $28 EL
Shiraz 2020, Great Southern Fruit from Sophie's Yard on the estate. Aromatically very restrained, the palate yields a cool-climate, pepper-laden spread of blueberries, blackberries and clove. The oak is dusty and savoury, making an impact thorough the finish. Screw cap. 14.7% alc. RATING 90 DRINK 2021-2028 $34 EL

Pt. Leo Estate ★★★★★
3649 Frankston-Flinders Road, Merricks, Vic 3916 **Region** Mornington Peninsula
T (03) 5989 9011 **www**.ptleoestate.com.au **Open** 7 days 11–5 **Winemaker** Tod Dexter (Consultant) **Est.** 2006 **Dozens** 600 **Vyds** 20ha
Pt. Leo Estate is owned by one of Australia's wealthiest families, headed by octogenarian John Gandel and his wife Pauline. Thirty years ago they purchased 20ha of land on the wild side

of the Mornington Peninsula. They added parcels of land, created a lake at the entrance of the property, and in 2006 planted a 20ha vineyard. It is now also the site of a 16ha sculpture park featuring works by international and Australian artists. A cellar door and restaurant opened in Oct '17 and the fine dining restaurant, Laura, opened in Mar '18. A third space, the Wine Terrace, has since been added. Ainslie Lubbock (ex Attica and The Royal Mail Hotel) oversees service alongside head sommelier Amy Oliver (ex Cutler + Co, Rockpool) and culinary director Joseph Espuga. (JH)

ΨΨΨΨΨ Reserve Chardonnay 2019, Mornington Peninsula Give this air time, as it keeps unfurling and revealing more and more as a result. A powerful wine, intensely flavoured with layers of smoky sulphides, savoury and citrusy, tight with mouth-watering acidity. Moreish to the very end. Screw cap. 14% alc. RATING 95 DRINK 2022-2029 $86 JF
Reserve Pinot Noir 2019, Mornington Peninsula There's a bit more rev to the reserve this vintage, in its flavour profile and shape. Loads of spiced cherries, rhubarb, menthol, some meaty reduction and a fair whack of smoky, toasty oak also lends a savoury element with a slight drying sensation to the tannins. It opens up and keeps surprising at every sip. Screw cap. 14% alc. RATING 95 DRINK 2023-2033 $86 JF

ΨΨΨΨΨ Pinot Gris 2021, Mornington Peninsula RATING 93 DRINK 2022-2025 $34 JF
Rosé 2021, Mornington Peninsula RATING 90 DRINK 2022-2023 $34 JF

Politini Wines ★★★

65 Upper King River Road, Cheshunt, Vic 3678 **Region** King Valley
T (03) 5729 8277 **www**.politiniwines.com.au **Open** 7 days 11–5 **Winemaker** Luis Simian **Est.** 1989 **Dozens** 6500 **Vyds** 15.15ha
The Politini family have been grapegrowers in the King Valley supplying major local wineries since 1989, selling to Brown Brothers, Miranda and the Victorian Alps Winery. In '00 they decided to move into winemaking, and have steadily increased their wine production to its present level. They have also planted pinot gris, sangiovese, vermentino, nero d'Avola and grecanico (garganega) to accompany the previously planted cabernet sauvignon, shiraz, merlot and sauvignon blanc. Luis Simian is a winemaker with a significant track record of success in many places, including Chile. Exports to Hong Kong. (JH)

ΨΨΨΨ Prosecco NV, King Valley a fresh, vibrant sparkling personality. The scent of fresh-cut apples, pear and citrus greets the drinker. A touch of lemon zest lifts the palate together with crunchy, bright acidity. Perfect lazy afternoon drinking. Crown. 10.5% alc. RATING 89 DRINK 2022-2022 $22 JP
Cabernet Sauvignon 2018, King Valley An aged cabernet from the King Valley is an unusual sight. You might argue that it could have rewarded an earlier release, but it definitely still manages to fit a lot into a smart pricepoint. The perfume is edged in leather and earth with a big dollop of ripe berries and spice. Cabernet's noted tannins hold the line firm on the palate with bitter chocolate and woodsy spice notes, and generous sweet fruit flavours. Ready to go. Screw cap. 14% alc. RATING 88 DRINK 2022-2025 $28 JP

Pontifex Wines ★★★★

PO Box 161, Tanunda, SA 5352 **Region** Barossa Valley
T 0418 811 066 **www**.pontifexwines.com.au **Winemaker** Peter Kelly **Est.** 2011
Dozens 2000 **Vyds** 7ha
Sam Clarke is the son of David and Cheryl Clarke, founders of Thorn-Clarke Wines, a leading Barossa Valley winery (see separate entry). Thus it was easy for the family to meet Sam and wife Helen's wish to buy a 6ha slice of shiraz planted in 1991. For good measure, Peter Kelly (Thorn-Clarke's winemaker) is the winemaker for the venture. After 6 years, Pontifex (as the new venture was named on its birth in '11) planted a hectare of mourvèdre

and grenache on the rich Bay of Biscay soils of the Krondorf district. They also purchase old-vine grenache. (JH)

🍷🍷🍷🍷 **Shiraz 2019, Barossa Valley** Primary-fruit characters of crunchy blueberry and ripe plums, cut with spice, violets, licorice and dark chocolate. Weight and concentrated, the tannins come across as a little pixelated and there's a touch of heat on the finish, but drinks well regardless. Screw cap. 14.9% alc. RATING 91 DRINK 2022-2032 $40 DB

GSM 2019, Barossa Valley Macerated summer berry fruits, red plums and red cherry, cut with ginger spice and earth; a medium-bodied flow across the palate with sandy tannin grip and a medium-length finish. Screw cap. 14.9% alc. RATING 90 DRINK 2022-2030 $40 DB

Ponting

169 Douglas Gully Road, Blewitt Springs SA 5171 **Region** McLaren Vale
T 0439 479 758 **www**.pontingwines.com.au **Winemaker** Ben Riggs **Est.** 2020
Dozens 9500

The Ponting label falls under the aegis of Three Kings Wine Merchants, a collaboration between winemaker Ben Riggs and the former Australian cricket captain, Ricky Ponting. A tensile Chardonnay and a Pinot Noir, hewn of cooler-climate Tasmanian fruit as an homage to the cricketing Taswegian's involvement, are exceptions to the South Australian sourcing pervasive across the line-up: an Adelaide Hills Sauvignon Blanc, a McLaren Vale Shiraz, a Langhorne Creek Cabernet and at the pointy end, the Ponting 366 cuvée, a blend of Shiraz from the Vale and Cabernet from Coonawarra. (NG)

🍷🍷🍷🍷🍷 **366 Shiraz Cabernet Sauvignon 2018, McLaren Vale Coonawarra** Bottle weighs over 1.9kg when full. There must be a quip in there about rivalling Ponting's Kookaburra back in the day … The impact of McLaren Vale is clear in this wine, lending a concentrated, creamy and totally saturated dark fruit character to the overall, deftly fitting into the Coonawarra grooves of blue fruit and fine, ferrous tannins. In the mouth the wine is heady and dense, it hasn't even started to open up yet; it is clear the evolution will be slow. Screw cap. 14.5% alc. RATING 94 DRINK 2022-2042 $125 EL

🍷🍷🍷🍷 **Rianna Rosé 2021, Fleurieu** RATING 92 DRINK 2021-2023 $25 JH ✪
The Pinnacle Shiraz 2018, McLaren Vale RATING 92 DRINK 2021-2028 $26 NG
First Session Sauvignon Blanc 2021, Adelaide Hills RATING 91 DRINK 2021-2024 $26 JP
127 Shiraz 2019, Barossa RATING 91 DRINK 2021-2028 $38 DB

Pooles Rock

576 De Beyers Road, Pokolbin, NSW 2320 **Region** Hunter Valley
T (02) 4993 3688 **www**.poolesrock.com.au **Open** 7 days 10–5 **Winemaker** Xanthe Hatcher **Est.** 1988 **Vyds** 14.6ha

Pooles Rock was founded, together with the Cockfighter's Ghost brand, in 1988 by the late David Clarke OAM, and acquired by the Agnew family in '11 (who also own the neighbouring Audrey Wilkinson). Pooles Rock sources fruit from a number of wine regions, although its essential operations are based in the lower Hunter. Over time, the emphasis has become one of site-specific iterations across 3 tiers: Single Vineyard (proprietary Hunter fruit), Premiere (externally sourced fruit from as far afield as South Australia and Tasmania) and Museum Releases (aged wines, incorporating all sources). The style is one of optimal ripeness, plump palate weight and precise structural latticework. Exports to the US and Canada. (NG)

🍷🍷🍷🍷 **Single Vineyard Semillon 2011, Hunter Valley** Superb aromas of candied citrus, glazed quince, buttered toast and lemon curd. Long and febrile of feel, despite the bottle maturation. This sits at a strident middle age, with plenty more to come. The finish is immense. Intense, despite the balletic weight, this drives across the palate as much as it coats it in doing so. A bit tangy, but … it makes one salivate in preparation for the next glass. Screw cap. 12% alc. RATING 96 DRINK 2022-2030 $75 NG ✪

Single Barrel Chardonnay 2021, Hunter Valley The most subdued, layered and confidently reticent of this estate's wines, white or red. Not made so differently to the Premiere, but the oak is finer, the fruit more concentrated without being overt and the intensity, compelling. A small quantity devoted to a single new puncheon. Pain grillé, ginger, fresh dough, nougatine and white peach. Pithy and mineral. Long and refined. Very good. Screw cap. 13% alc. RATING 94 DRINK 2025-2029 $65 NG

🍷🍷🍷🍷🍷 **Shiraz 2011, Hunter Valley** RATING 93 DRINK 2022-2026 $90 NG
Premiere Chardonnay 2021, Hunter Valley RATING 90 DRINK 2022-2028 $40 NG

Pooley Wines   ★★★★★

Butcher's Hill Vineyard, 1431 Richmond Road, Richmond, Tas 7025 **Region** Tasmania **T** (03) 6260 2895 **www**.pooleywines.com.au **Open** 7 days 10–5 **Winemaker** Anna Pooley, Justin Bubb **Viticulturist** Hannah McKay **Est.** 1985 **Dozens** 8500 **Vyds** 18ha
Pooley Wines is a glowing exemplar of a boutique Tasmanian family estate. Three generations of the family have been involved in its development, with the little hands of the fourth generation now starting to get involved. The heart of production has historically been the glorious Campania vineyard of Cooinda Vale (after which the brand was originally named), planted to 12ha of chardonnay, pinot noir, riesling and pinot grigio, with new plantings currently underway. In 2003, the family planted pinot noir and pinot grigio (and more recently chardonnay, riesling and syrah, bringing plantings to 6ha) at Belmont Vineyard near Richmond, renamed Butcher's Hill. A cellar door was established in the heritage-listed sandstone barn and coach house of the distinguished 1830s convict-built Georgian home, standing in pride of place on the heritage property. In 2017 the family acquired the nearby 1830s Prospect House and refurbished it into a glorious private hotel. Wine quality has risen to dramatic effect, no small feat while doubling production, since the return to Tasmania of Anna Pooley and husband Justin Bubb to establish the winemaking arm of the estate in 2012. Riesling, pinot noir and chardonnay now rank among Tasmania's finest. Conversion to organic viticulture is currently underway, with a goal of achieving certification by the 2026 vintage. Pooley is the Wine Companion 2023 Winery of the Year. Exports to the UK, the US and Sweden. (TS)

🍷🍷🍷🍷🍷 **Jack Denis Pooley Pinot Noir 2020, Tasmania** This 33% whole-bunch pinot has depth beyond that of its siblings. It's full-on forest floor, full-on savoury spices, with tannins made to measure, but all bow down to the primacy of the dark berry fruit of the impossibly long finish. World class. Screw cap. 13.1% alc. RATING 99 DRINK 2022-2037 $140 JH ✪ ♥
Butcher's Hill Pinot Noir 2020, Tasmania Vivid crimson purple, slightly deeper than that of its siblings. The bouquet is extremely complex, with satsuma plum, dark cherry and a crescendo of spices, the palate as elegant as it is intense, and throwing in a pinch of savoury tannins. Screw cap. 13.1% alc. RATING 97 DRINK 2022-2035 $70 JH ✪
Cooinda Vale Pinot Noir 2020, Tasmania Although there's only 15% whole bunches, it makes its presence felt right from the first whiff, the first sip, like a Rubik's Cube in the hands of an expert. Satisfyingly elegant. Screw cap. 13.2% alc. RATING 97 DRINK 2022-2035 $70 JH ✪

🍷🍷🍷🍷🍷 **Margaret Pooley Tribute Riesling 2021, Tasmania** My Tasmanian riesling of the year last year was no one-hit wonder. The '21 is another vintage of profound purity and enduring longevity. The micro-engineering at play here is something to behold, with the puncheon fermentation and dribble of RS creating no distraction whatsoever, rather serving to launch its fruit to dramatic lengths and breathtaking heights. A soaring tribute to the endurance of Tasmanian riesling. Screw cap. 12.8% alc. RATING 96 DRINK 2026-2046 $80 TS ♥

Cooinda Vale Chardonnay 2020, Tasmania Identical vinification to Butcher's Hill except a 20-day (not 22) ferment. This has more intensity, more length, more grapefruit, but still has the finesse and balance of its Butcher's Hill sibling. Screw cap. 13.2% alc. RATING 96 DRINK 2022-2035 $65 JH ✪

Butcher's Hill Riesling 2021, Tasmania 2g/L RS. A cool summer and a sunny autumn with cool nights are an exciting recipe for riesling. Crystalline purity of radiant, mineral acidity drives a core of pure lemon, lime and Granny Smith apple. I love the way old oak puncheons (rather than sugar) have been masterfully deployed to tone structure and build the finish. Line and length are unrelenting, promising a huge future. Screw cap. 13% alc. RATING 95 DRINK 2022-2036 $65 TS

Butcher's Hill Chardonnay 2020, Tasmania A wine of purity, elegance and finesse, making light work of its new oak. It is at the dawn of what will be a long life, its balance a guarantee of the good things to come. Screw cap. 13.3% alc. RATING 95 DRINK 2023-2033 $65 JH

Cooinda Vale Oronsay Pinot Noir 2020, Tasmania It's a tremendous endorsement of the confidence of these well-established vines that fruit and place speak louder even than 100% whole bunches and 50% new French oak. Testimony, likewise, to sensitivity and no small amount of wizardry in the winery. The grip and structure set it off for a long life indeed. Exotic spice holds grand persistence amid well-honed cherry and plum fruit. Screw cap. 12.6% alc. RATING 95 DRINK 2030-2040 $120 TS

Poonawatta   ★★★★★

1227 Eden Valley Road, Flaxman Valley, SA 5235 **Region** Eden Valley
T 0448 031 880 **www.**poonawatta.com.au **Open** Wed–Mon 11–4.30
Winemaker Andrew Holt, Christa Deans, Harry Mantzarapis **Viticulturist** Andrew Holt
Est. 1880 **Dozens** 1800 **Vyds** 4ha
The Poonawatta story is complex, stemming from 0.8ha of shiraz planted in 1880. When Andrew Holt's parents purchased the Poonawatta property, the vineyard had suffered decades of neglect and the slow process of restoration began. While that was underway, the strongest canes available from the winter pruning of the block were slowly and progressively dug into the stony soil, establishing the Cuttings Block over 7 years, and the yield is even lower than that of the 1880 Block. The Riesling is produced from a separate vineyard planted by the Holts in the 1970s. Grenache was planted in 2019. Exports to France, the US, Canada, Malaysia and Denmark. (JH)

♟♟♟♟♟ **Valley of Eden Riesling 2021, Eden Valley** A lovely little off-dry example of the region's famous grape variety. Lime, citrus and grapefruit notes, crushed stone and orange blossom all catch the eye (nose?). The crisp, crystalline acidity tempers the 15g/L RS here, so we'll call it just off-dry. We'll also call it delicious. Screw cap. 11% alc. RATING 92 DRINK 2021-2031 $30 DB

The Eden Reserve Riesling 2021, Eden Valley Expansive notes of fresh lime, yellow plum and Granny Smith apples along with hints of soft spice, stone, cut fennel and nectarine. Quite textural in the mouth, some dried herbs swooping in to join the crisp lime and citrus notes, a quartz-like acid cadence driving proceedings along nicely. Screw cap. 12% alc. RATING 92 DRINK 2021-2031 $44 DB

The Eden Riesling 2021, Eden Valley Characters of freshly squeezed lime and grapefruit, with hints of Christmas lily, yellow plum, fennel, soft spice and crushed quartz. It's quite yellow-fruited and expansive. You get the feeling that it wants to broaden, but that crisp acidity whips it back in focus, finishing long, dry and flush with pure citrus and peachy fruit. Screw cap. 12% alc. RATING 92 DRINK 2021-2031 $44 DB

1919 Mark Bartholomaeus Shiraz 2019, Eden Valley Slightly shy fruit aromas of rich blackberry and dark plum are joined by hints of licorice, dark chocolate, oak spice and a cedary sheen. Pure fruit on the palate, with a vivid acid line driving the black-fruit core along nicely, grainy in tannin and rich in cassis and kirsch-like notes. Cork. 14.5% alc. RATING 90 DRINK 2021–2031 $70 DB

The Cuttings Shiraz 2018, Eden Valley Aromas of blackberry, black cherry and plum are joined by hints of baking spice, tobacco leaf, black pepper, licorice and cedary oak. Expansive, brightly edged with fine acid and tannin and leaves a lingering trail of cassis and oak spice. Screw cap. 14.5% alc. RATING 90 DRINK 2021–2031 $55 DB

♥♥♥♥ **1858 South Rhine Estate Grenache 2019, Eden Valley** RATING 89 DRINK 2021–2026 $70 DB

Tempus on Uva Cutis Single Vineyard 2019, Eden Valley RATING 89 DRINK 2021–2031 $70 DB

🍇 Poppelvej ★★★★

185 Almond Grove Road, Willunga South, SA 5172 **Region** McLaren Vale
T 0431 432 570 **www**.poppelvej.com **Open** By appt **Winemaker** Uffe Deichmann
Est. 2016 **Dozens** 4500

Poppelvej is the name of the street where winemaker Uffe grew up. It is a benevolent confluence of Danish winemaker with an inquisitive mind, Adelaide Hills and McLaren Vale fruit and minimalist handling. The culture here is one of early picking for freshness, zero additions (other than minimal sulphur dioxide for psychological reassurance) and little messing about. The wines are turbid, as they are neither fined nor filtered, firmly in the natural camp and for those accustomed to little but conventional winemaking, potentially challenging. Yet the modus here is one of textural detail and imminent drinkability which, for those with eyes, palates and minds wide open, may be a reinvigorating force. Exports to Denmark, the US, South Korea, Thailand and Hong Kong. (NG)

♥♥♥♥♥ **Semi Divine Lagrein 2021, Adelaide Hills** This is delicious. The inky and sumptuous characteristics of this variety, indigenous to Alto Adige, suffuse generosity and freshness. A captivating nose of alpine herb, dark foresty fruits, pastille and clove. Pulpy, but with a carriage of svelte tannins. Juicy and limpid, but oh, so vital. Diam. 13% alc. RATING 93 DRINK 2021–2024 $33 NG

Zoonotic Spillover Mourvèdre 2021, McLaren Vale This is also delicious! It sits pretty on the right side of fresh and pulpy, without being green or anaemic. Riffs on sour cherry, boysenberry, anise, clove and sassafras. I'd be ripping this from the fridge to drink cold. A quasi-Mediterranean-accented Beaujolais sort of wine, brimming with energy and moxie. Diam. 11.5% alc. RATING 92 DRINK 2021–2023 $33 NG

Only Shallow Viognier 2021, Adelaide Hills On skins for 99 days, fermented wild, minimal sulphur, unfined and unfiltered. A wine to light up a party of wine folk. Not necessarily for the uninitiated, but for those keen to dabble in the eccentricities of les vins naturels d'Australie. Here is a ticket! A turbid navel orange of hue. Vivid scents of citrus verbena, mandarin, geranium, curry powder, chamomile, dried straw, ginger and apricot. A revitalising drink, with or without food, such is its freshness and chewy nourishment. Diam. 10% alc. RATING 92 DRINK 2021–2025 $35 NG

Rookie Grenache 2021, McLaren Vale Like a raspberry, ripe strawberry, licorice and white pepper-doused smoothie, with a nerve of frisky tannins pulsating throughout. Drink cool, with gusto and with eyes and mind wide open. Screw cap. 12.5% alc. RATING 91 DRINK 2021–2022 $33 NG

Dead Ohio Sky 2021, McLaren Vale Mourvèdre rosé. Turbid. For those willing to explore an alternative to safe convention sans prejudice, there is plenty to like, at least for a nerd: sapid notes of musk stick, tangerine, tomatillo, chilli, orange peel, ginger and dried hay, unravel across a firm phenolic thread and some acetic perk. This is not a rosé for sipping, but a contemplative vino da meditazione for the table. There is little primary fruit here, but ample texture and oodles of intrigue. Diam. 12% alc. RATING 90 DRINK 2021–2023 $30 NG

Vicissitudes of Life Pinot Noir 2021, Adelaide Hills 50% whole bunches, imparting a febrile edginess and salty crunch, the frame within which strawberry, root spice and floral notes lie. Not complex, but something to wash the day away with. Diam. 12.5% alc. RATING 90 DRINK 2021-2023 $33 NG

Port Phillip Estate ★★★★★

263 Red Hill Road, Red Hill, Vic 3937 **Region** Mornington Peninsula
T (03) 5989 4444 **www.**portphillipestate.com.au **Open** 7 days 11–5 **Winemaker** Glen Hayley **Est.** 1987 **Dozens** 7000 **Vyds** 21.04ha
Port Phillip Estate has been owned by Giorgio and Dianne Gjergja since 2000. The ability of the site to produce outstanding syrah, pinot noir and chardonnay, and very good sauvignon blanc, is something special. In July '15, following the departure of winemaker Sandro Mosele, his assistant of 6 years, Glen Hayley, was appointed to take his place. The futuristic, multi-million-dollar restaurant, cellar door and winery complex, designed by award-winning Wood/ Marsh Architecture, overlooks the vineyards and Westernport Bay. Exports to Canada. (JH)

🍷🍷🍷🍷🍷 **Sauvignon 2021, Mornington Peninsula** The fruit is gently whole-bunch pressed to old French barriques, fermented wild and left on lees for a couple of months, which explains the excellent texture, complexity and even flow of this wine. It's subtle and savoury, with flinty sulphides but includes grapefruit and pith, white stone fruit and rocket. This is a sauvignon I'd gladly drink anytime. Screw cap. 13.5% alc. RATING 95 DRINK 2022-2025 $27 JF ✪

Salasso Rosé 2021, Mornington Peninsula A light and enticing copper hue. When slightly chilled, this rosé means summer in a glass. Really lovely aromatics; all florals and red berries, quite spicy too. Starts fruit-sweet on the palate then savouriness takes over all the way to a dry, fresh finish. Excellent rosé in anyone's book. Screw cap. 13% alc. RATING 95 DRINK 2021-2023 $27 JF ✪

Amber Pinot Gris 2021, Mornington Peninsula I'm not sure if winemaker Glen Hayley is turning into a hipster or if there's another reason for this terrific wine. Its pale cherry-terracotta hue entices immediately; rosehips, poached quince, chinotto and blood orange – lots going on aroma and flavour-wise. The palate is composed with delicate phenolics, with just some chew and shape to the finish. Fresh all the way through. Bravo. Screw cap. 12.5% alc. RATING 95 DRINK 2022-2024 $32 JF ✪

Pinot Noir Shiraz 2021, Mornington Peninsula This rendition is exactly what the style should be about, which is a vibrancy of fruit and freshness. Spiced plums and cherries with lots of savoury inputs some woodsy spices, herbs and a succulence across the light- to mid-weighted palate. Textural tannins and juicy acidity to close. Good one Glenn (Hayley, winemaker). Screw cap. 13% alc. RATING 95 DRINK 2022-2026 $34 JF ✪

Balnarring Chardonnay 2020, Mornington Peninsula It's racy, citrusy – especially pink grapefruit – and it's spicy, with an appealing fennel aroma. There's more to come in time as it's still tightly wound, led by acidity making it intense and linear, yet oh, so refreshing. Screw cap. 12.5% alc. RATING 94 DRINK 2021-2028 $36 JF

Red Hill Pinot Noir 2020, Mornington Peninsula Like its Balnarring sibling, this is a fragrant and delicate wine, although there's more tannin structure and savouriness here. A good combo of red cherries and rhubarb, oak spice and wood smoke, a touch autumnal and a vibrancy throughout. Just medium bodied. Subtle, yet a persistent finish makes this a compelling drink for today. Screw cap. 12.5% alc. RATING 94 DRINK 2021-2028 $38 JF

Morillon Single Block Pinot Noir 2020, Mornington Peninsula Serious and structured yet tightly composed with wafts of whole-bunch fragrance, soused cherries with all manner of baking spices and a hint of pepper in the mix. Menthol and bitter herbs. Blood orange and peel. A touch lean but it has bright acidity making it compelling. Screw cap. 12.5% alc. RATING 94 DRINK 2022-2028 $60 JF

ŸŸŸŸŸ **Pinot Nouveau Pinot Noir 2021, Mornington Peninsula** RATING 93
DRINK 2021-2025 $27 JF ✪
Quartier Pinot Gris 2021, Mornington Peninsula RATING 93
DRINK 2022-2025 $28 JF
Balnarring Pinot Noir 2020, Mornington Peninsula RATING 93
DRINK 2021-2026 $38 JF
Tuerong Shiraz 2020, Mornington Peninsula RATING 93 DRINK 2021-2028
$38 JF
Quartier Pinot Gris 2020, Mornington Peninsula RATING 92
DRINK 2022-2025 $26 JH
Morillon Single Block Chardonnay 2020, Mornington Peninsula
RATING 92 DRINK 2022-2028 $55 JF
Quartier Chardonnay 2021, Mornington Peninsula RATING 91
DRINK 2022-2025 $29 JF
Red Hill Chardonnay 2020, Mornington Peninsula RATING 91
DRINK 2022-2026 $36 JF
Quartier Pinot Noir 2021, Mornington Peninsula RATING 90
DRINK 2022-2025 $29 JF

Precious Little Wine ★★★★

Peninsula Providore, 2250 Bull Creek Rd, Tooperang, SA 5255 **Region** South Australia
T 0417 212 514 **www**.preciouslittlewine.com.au **Open** Mon–Fri 10–4, w'ends 11–4
Winemaker Marty O' Flaherty **Viticulturist** Adam Smith **Est.** 2016 **Dozens** 600
Precious Little is the side project of mates Marty O'Flaherty and Adam Smith. Ex-chef
Marty is winemaker for Atkins Family and Fox Gordon Wines, having cut his winemaking
teeth at Zilzie in Victoria before working across South Australia and as far afield as Piedmont.
Clare Valley boy Adam has 20 years of experience as an independent viticultural consultant
and a grower liaison officer, now enjoying the challenge of seeking out exciting parcels for
Marty to transform into small-batch wines. Current sourcing is from growers in the Barossa
Valley, Langhorne Creek and Adelaide Hills. Wines can be tasted at the nearby Peninsula
Providore. (TS)

ŸŸŸŸŸ **Grenache 2021, Langhorne Creek** Royal purple hue. It's a good wine, but
didn't need the shiraz tannins. Will repay 10 years minimum in bottle. Screw cap.
14.5% alc. RATING 92 DRINK 2023-2034 $30 JH
Marananga Shiraz 2020, Barossa Valley There's plenty of generous,
enveloping plummy fruit on display here, sheathed in baking spice, chocolate and
a lick of cedary, vanillin oak. Great fruit weight with fine tannin, cedary oak and a
bright line. Screw cap. 15% alc. RATING 91 DRINK 2021-2030 $45 DB
Riesling 2021, Clare Valley Super-pretty nose here! Spring florals, citrus
blossom, apples, limes and lychees. In the mouth the wine performs exactly as the
nose has promised, making for delicious summer drinking. Screw cap. 12.5% alc.
RATING 90 DRINK 2021-2028 $25 EL

Pressing Matters ★★★★★

665 Middle Tea Tree Road, Tea Tree, Tas 7017 **Region** Southern Tasmania
T 0474 380 109 **www**.pressingmatters.com.au **Open** Thurs–Sun 10–4 by appt
Winemaker Samantha Connew **Viticulturist** Mark Hoey **Est.** 2002 **Dozens** 2600
Vyds 7.3ha
Greg Melick wears more hats than most people manage in a lifetime. He is a major general
(the highest rank in the Australian Army Reserve) a top level barrister (senior counsel) and has
presided over a number of headline special commissions and enquiries into subjects as diverse
as cricket match–fixing and the Beaconsfield mine collapse. More recently he became deputy
president of the Administrative Appeals Tribunal and chief commissioner of the Tasmanian
Integrity Commission. Yet, if asked, he would probably nominate wine as his major focus
in life. Having built up an exceptional cellar of the great wines of Europe, he has turned his
attention to grape growing and winemaking, planting almost 3ha of riesling at his vineyard

in the Coal River Valley. It is on a perfect north-facing slope, and the Mosel-style rieslings are making their mark. His multi-clone pinot noir block (just over 4ha) is also striking gold. Exports to the US, Singapore and Hong Kong. (JH)

🍷🍷🍷🍷🍷 **R139 Riesling 2021, Tasmania** Acidity is the secret to all things sweet, and the cool '21 harvest was idyllic for wines of this ilk. Pale straw green; it leaps from the glass with brilliant purity of white lily fragrance, Granny Smith apple, lime and lemon. Not a molecule out of place. Sublime line and length. Irresistibly seductive right away, with decades of potential yet. 375mL. Screw cap. 7.5% alc. RATING 96 DRINK 2022-2051 $39 TS ✪ ♥
R69 Riesling 2021, Tasmania Medium-sweet rieslings rank among the greatest whites in the world and Tasmania doesn't make nearly enough of them. Pinpoint purity of preserved lemon and lime and apple blossom carry with brilliantly illuminated clarity, from the first fragrant whiff of the bouquet to the last whisper of elongated persistence. As ever, acidity is the hero, and the cool '21 season delivered magnificently. Drink or hold, you can't lose. Screw cap. 9% alc. RATING 95 DRINK 2022-2041 $39 TS
Cuvée C Pinot Noir 2020, Tasmania A selection of the top 6 barrels of its estate pinot, Pressing Matters' flagship delivers more black fruit depth, spice and character, infused with the same enduring longevity. Black cherries and blackberries are woven into a tapestry of confident, fine-grained tannins and energetic acid drive. Patience. Screw cap. 13.2% alc. RATING 95 DRINK 2030-2040 $150 TS
Pinot Noir 2020, Tasmania Floral, precise and fine boned, this is an intricately crafted pinot noir built for the cellar. A core of elegant, accurate red cherry fruits are lifted by subtle rose-petal perfume and spicy allure, presumably of a touch of whole-bunch inclusion. Firm, confident, fine-ground tannins are accentuated by bright, cool-season acidity, together promising grand endurance. Screw cap 13% alc. RATING 94 DRINK 2030–2040 $69 TS

R9 Riesling 2021, Tasmania A touch of RS does marvellous things in lifting the exoticism of orange-blossom fragrance, tying down unwieldy, cool-season acidity and drawing out magnificent persistence. A compelling core of crunchy Granny Smith apple and pitch-perfect lime and lemon are charged with tremendous stamina. Screw cap. 11.8% alc. RATING 94 DRINK 2026-2041 $39 TS

🍷🍷🍷🍷🍷 **R0 Riesling 2021, Tasmania** RATING 93 DRINK 2031-2041 $39 TS

Primo Estate   ★★★★★
McMurtrie Road, McLaren Vale, SA 5171 **Region** McLaren Vale
T (08) 8323 6800 **www**.primoestate.com.au **Open** 7 days 11–4 **Winemaker** Joseph Grilli, Daniel Grilli, Tom Garrett **Est.** 1979 **Dozens** 30 000 **Vyds** 34ha
Joe Grilli has always produced innovative and excellent wines. The biennial release of the Joseph Sparkling Red (in its tall Italian glass bottle) is eagerly awaited, the wine immediately selling out. The vineyard includes plantings of colombard, shiraz, cabernet sauvignon, riesling, merlot, sauvignon blanc, chardonnay, pinot gris, sangiovese, nebbiolo and merlot. Also highly regarded are the vintage-dated extra virgin olive oils. Exports to all major markets. (JH)

🍷🍷🍷🍷🍷 **Pecorino 2021, Adelaide Hills** The highly floral bouquet is left on the wayside by the richness and succulence (not sweetness) of the palate. It strikes a further blow with its titanium backbone of acidity. Screw cap. 12.5% alc. RATING 96 DRINK 2021-2025 $28 JH ✪
Joseph The Fronti NV, McLaren Vale Superlative, managing to capture the decadent richness of the style as much as an uncanny detail, freshness and drinkability. Muscat, the grape. Frontignan, a town in the Languedoc. Scents of the Moroccan souk: incense, cardamom, orange peel, cinnamon and grape spice. Mahogany. Decay. Turkish delight. Liquid promise. It's all here. Take a whiff and recline. Screw cap. 17% alc. RATING 96 $50 NG ✪

Zamberlan Cabernet Sauvignon Sangiovese 2020, McLaren Vale Made using the Ripasso method of fermenting the wine over the skins of the Primo flagship Joseph Moda, honouring late wife Dina's father, Rinaldo Zamberlan. Such an unusual wine will always attract attention, but this doesn't need a head start. It's medium bodied, and has intensity and texture without any aggressive tannins, just a world of exotic spices woven through its black fruits. Screw cap. 13.5% alc. RATING 95 DRINK 2025-2030 $40 JH

Joseph Moda Cabernet Sauvignon Merlot 2019, McLaren Vale The oak on this powerful expression – uber-ripe and saturated with cassis, dark fruit accents, licorice, bay leaf and clove – works much better than its nebbiolo sibling. American and French, the oak bridles the fruit while augmenting the sheer extract and impact. The grape tannins are a screen of pixelated, chewy, mocha detail. This may be akin to eating wine, but for those who dig an Amarone style, this is a dream. An enigmatic wine of great character. Screw cap. 14.5% alc. RATING 95 DRINK 2021-2032 $90 NG

Joseph Clarendon Nebbiolo 2019, McLaren Vale It must be the virtues of site to bestow nebbiolo at a mere 13%. Yet there is no dearth of ripeness, celebrated with red and dark cherry, licorice stick, bergamot and rosewater notes. A quilt of tannins is thrown across the mouth. The oak, assertive. A bit too much mocha and coffee-grind tannins for this taster. A very modern idiom, if compared to Piedmont. Larger-format older wood, better for this variety. Nevertheless, an impressive wine. Screw cap. 13% alc. RATING 94 DRINK 2021-2028 $90 NG

ΨΨΨΨ **Joseph d'Elena Pinot Grigio 2021, Adelaide Hills** RATING 92 DRINK 2021-2024 $35 NG

Il Briccone Shiraz Sangiovese 2020, McLaren Vale RATING 92 DRINK 2021-2026 $28 NG

Prince Albert ★★★★

100 Lemins Road, Waurn Ponds, Vic 3216 **Region** Geelong
T 0412 531 191 **www.**princealbertvineyard.com.au **Open** By appt **Winemaker** Fiona Purnell, David Yates **Est.** 1975 **Dozens** 350 **Vyds** 2ha
The original Prince Albert vineyard operated from 1857 to 1882, and was re-established on the same site by Bruce Hyett in 1975 (Bruce passed away in Feb 2013, aged 89). In '07 Dr David Yates, with a background based on a degree in chemistry, purchased the pinot noir-only venture. David is committed to retaining certified organic status for Prince Albert, and sees no reason to change the style of the wine, which he has always loved. Exports to the UK. (JH)

ΨΨΨΨΨ **Pinot Noir 2016, Geelong** The Prince Albert style is to show pinot as an aged wine, a rarity in these times. As such, it takes a moment to adjust to these more mature flavours: earth, undergrowth, black cherry, plum, anise and a fleck of truffle. Savoury, smoky oak offers a gentle persuasion and nothing more. It's in the dark-and-brooding school of pinot and it's drinking well now. Screw cap. 14.5% alc. RATING 92 DRINK 2021-2028 $50 JP

Principia ★★★★★

139 Main Creek Road, Red Hill, Vic 3937 **Region** Mornington Peninsula
T (03) 5931 0010 **www.**principiawines.com.au **Open** By appt **Winemaker** Darrin Gaffy **Viticulturist** Darrin Gaffy **Est.** 1995 **Dozens** 750 **Vyds** 3.5ha
Darrin Gaffy's guiding philosophy for Principia is minimal interference, thus the vines (3ha of pinot noir and 0.5ha of chardonnay) are not irrigated and yields are restricted to 3.75t/ha or less. All wine movements are by gravity or by gas pressure, which in turn means there is no filtration, and both primary and secondary fermentation are by wild yeast. 'Principia' comes from the word 'beginnings' in Latin. Exports to Japan and Hong Kong. (JH)

ΨΨΨΨΨ **Chardonnay 2020, Mornington Peninsula** There's never any doubt that this has personality and a load of flavour. Stone fruit, melon with a splash of lemon, almond meal and creamy lees with the French oak, 20% new, neatly tucked into its shape. Sure there are some woodsy spices, a touch of butterscotch for this has body, but also good definition. If you like a chardonnay with a bit more oomph, this fits the bill superbly. Screw cap. 13.4% alc. RATING 95 DRINK 2022–2027 $45 JF

Pinot Noir 2020, Mornington Peninsula Alas, no Altior – the flagship – made in '20, but this is no slouch. It feels cool and refreshing across the palate. It's a lighter wine and compelling. Cherries, pips, blood orange juice and zest with a pleasant chinotto and bitter radicchio flavour in between. Fine tannins and plenty of tangy acidity keep this buoyant and highly drinkable now. Screw cap. 13% alc. RATING 95 DRINK 2022–2027 $45 JF

Kindred Hill Pinot Noir 2020, Mornington Peninsula Oh yeah. This is good. A whorl of exotic spices infusing the dark cherries and blood-orange flavours. It entices more as it builds across the structured palate, but it's not weighty, with the oak nestled well into wine's body. It's lifted with raw silk tannins and lithe acidity with a succulence all the way through. Screw cap. 13.2% alc. RATING 95 DRINK 2022–2030 $60 JF

Printhie Wines ★★★★★

208 Nancarrow Lane, Nashdale, NSW 2800 **Region** Orange
T (02) 6366 8422 **www.**printhiewines.com.au **Open** Fri–Sat 10–5, Sun–Thurs 11–4
Winemaker Drew Tuckwell **Viticulturist** Dave Swift **Est.** 1996 **Dozens** 20 000
Vyds 32ha

Owned by the Swift family, brothers Edward and David took over from their parents Jim and Ruth Swift in the early 2000s. Together the family have clocked up almost 20 years of commercial wine production and the vineyards are now reaching a good level of maturity at 25 years. The 32ha of estate vineyards are planted between 630–1070m elevation, including Orange's highest vineyard nat 1070m. Winemaker Drew Tuckwell has been at Printhie since 2007 and has over 20 years of winemaking experience in Australia and Europe. Exports to Singapore, Canada and the Philippines. (JH)

🍷🍷🍷🍷🍷 **Swift Blanc de Blancs 2011, Orange** A late-disgorged wine based on the cool '11 vintage. A whopping decade on lees, with an intriguing dosage (4.75g/L) comprised of barrel-fermented chardonnay and a dollop of brandy spirit. This will age further in bottle. Already toasty, creamy and broad, exuding riffs of orange blossom, quince, raw pistachio, nashi pear and brioche. The finish, long, detailed and vibrant. Thoroughly convincing. Screw cap. 11.5% alc. RATING 96 $120 NG

Swift Cuvée Brut NV, Orange The 9th disgorgement of this NV wine; 8 years on lees; 75/25% chardonnay/pinot noir. Dosage 5.5g/L. Could be lower, but an excellent segue into a fine range. A broad style which, if it weren't for the softer acidity, is synonymous with high-quality champagne. Doughy. Stone and autumnal fruit inflections, citrus and a skein of juicy, altitudinal acidity pulling it as long as it is broad. Cork. 12% alc. RATING 95 $50 NG

Swift Vintage Brut 2013, Orange 80/20% chardonnay/pinot noir. A warmer vintage amplified by an ambitious 7 years on lees. Perhaps the dosage could be lower, yet the equation works very well. Impeccably poised between a gentle stream of acidity, toasty complexity, ripe apple, nashi pear and jasmine. Dosage of barrel-fermented chardonnay, older reserve wines and a dash of brandy, parlaying additional intrigue. I'd drink this on the younger side with food and ample chill. Cork. 12% alc. RATING 94 $65 NG

Topography Pinot Gris 2021, Orange Very good. Unctuous, weighty and slippery of feel. Alsatian of styling. Light years away from the stuff picked on acidity. Marzipan, tarte tatin, spiced pear, quince and cinnamon stick. The sole caveat: could use more phenolics to bolster the structural latticework. Excellent, full-throttle gris all the same. Screw cap. 14.3% alc. RATING 94 DRINK 2021–2025 $30 NG ✪

🍷🍷🍷🍷🍸 **Swift Blanc de Noirs 2017, Orange** RATING 93 $85 NG
Swift Rosé Brut NV, Orange RATING 93 $50 NG

Topography Sauvignon Blanc 2021, Orange RATING 93 DRINK 2021-2025 $30 NG

Topography Chardonnay 2021, Orange RATING 93 DRINK 2021-2028 $38 NG

Topography Shiraz 2019, Orange RATING 93 DRINK 2021-2028 $38 NG

Topography Pinot Meunier 2021, Orange RATING 92 DRINK 2021-2023 $38 NG

Mountain Range Pinot Gris 2021, Orange RATING 91 DRINK 2021-2023 $24 NG

Snow Line Three Pinots Rosé 2021, Orange RATING 91 DRINK 2021-2022 $30 NG

Mountain Range Cabernet Sauvignon 2019, Orange RATING 91 DRINK 2021-2024 $24 NG

Mountain Range Sauvignon Blanc 2021, Orange RATING 90 DRINK 2021-2022 $24 NG

Project Wine

83 Pioneer Road, Angas Plains, SA 5255 **Region** South Australia
T (08) 8537 0600 **www**.projectwine.com.au **Winemaker** Peter Pollard **Est.** 2001
Dozens 155 000

Originally designed as a contract winemaking facility, Project Wine has developed a sales and distribution arm that has rapidly developed markets both domestic and overseas. Located in Langhorne Creek, it sources fruit from most key SA wine regions, including McLaren Vale, Barossa Valley and Adelaide Hills. The diversity of grape sourcing allows the winery to produce a wide range of products under the Drop Zone, Tail Spin, Pioneer Road, Parson's Paddock and Bird's Eye View labels. Exports to the UK, NZ, Switzerland, Canada and Japan. (JH)

🍷🍷🍷🍷🍷 **Drop Zone Riesling 2021, Clare Valley** The '21 vintage is a beautiful prism. Through this looking glass, we see the effects of a restrained and cool year – effortless acidity, voluminous fruit and presence in the mouth, offered with tension and very fine phenolics. Green apple skins, lime flesh and a hint of kiwi. Gorgeous stuff here. Screw cap. 13% alc. RATING 93 DRINK 2022-2029 $27 EL ✪

🍷🍷🍷🍷 **Drop Zone Montepulciano 2021, Adelaide Hills** RATING 89 DRINK 2022-2025 $27 JP

Drop Zone Tempranillo 2020, Adelaide Hills RATING 89 DRINK 2022-2024 $27 JP

Protero

60 Olivers Road, McLaren Vale SA 5171 **Region** Adelaide Hills
T (08) 8323 8000 **www**.protero.com.au **Open** By appt **Winemaker** Stephen Pannell
Est. 1999 **Dozens** 3000 **Vyds** 13.2ha

Stephen and Fiona Pannell first discovered the nebbiolo growing outside Gumeracha in the northern Adelaide Hills in 2004. Planted in '99, the vineyard, on a western-facing slope, is home to 5 clones of nebbiolo that Stephen has worked with since '05. Surrounded by native bush, the vineyard has been surrounded by fire twice in 20 years and survived twice (including a week after the Pannells bought the property in Dec '19). They have since removed chardonnay, pinot noir, merlot and viognier from the vineyard and planted barbera, dolcetto, gewürztraminer, pinot gris and riesling. Nebbiolo remains a passion, but Stephen poses the questions each year: what is Australian nebbiolo? 'We shouldn't attempt to replicate the wines of Piedmont, but rather create a unique style of nebbiolo that speaks of our place.' (TL)

🍷🍷🍷🍷🍷 **Gumeracha Nebbiolo 2019, Adelaide Hills** This is very good. The best expression from this site yet. The right weight, the right degree of sap, parry of fruit and ebb of spindly, fine-boned tannins melded with maritime freshness. Complementary oak. Kudos! Nothing particularly profound, mind you. Langhe sort of gear. But the caress of promise, fealty to variety and savoury righteousness is enough to get me reaching for another glass. Screw cap. 14.5% alc. RATING 94 DRINK 2021–2027 $38 NG

🍷🍷🍷🍷🍷 Aromatico 2021, Adelaide Hills RATING 93 DRINK 2021–2025 $30 NG
Grigio Nero Pinots 2021, Adelaide Hills RATING 92 DRINK 2021–2024 $28 NG
Gumeracha Barbera 2019, Adelaide Hills RATING 92 DRINK 2021–2024 $38 NG

Provenance Wines   ★★★★★

100 Lower Paper Mills Road, Fyansford, Vic 3221 **Region** Geelong
T (03) 5222 3422 **www.**provenancewines.com.au **Open** 7 days 11–5 summer, Thurs–Mon 11–5 winter **Winemaker** Scott Ireland, Sam Vogel **Viticulturist** Blake Tahapehi
Est. 1997 **Dozens** 6500 **Vyds** 14.2ha
In 1997 when Scott Ireland and partner Jen Lilburn established Provenance Wines, they knew it wouldn't be easy starting a winery with limited capital and no fixed abode; notwithstanding Scott's 20+ years' experience operating contract wine services. He says he met so many dedicated small winemakers that he was hooked for life. In '04 Scott moved to Austins & Co as winemaker while continuing to grow the Provenance business, developing key relationships with growers in Geelong, the ultra-cool Macedon, Ballarat and Henty. In '16, Scott's long-term assistant winemaker, Sam Vogel, stepped up to join the business as a partner and they took a long-term lease of 25% of the Fyansford Paper Mill, refurbishing the heritage-listed 1870s local bluestone buildings, providing excellent cellaring conditions. Exports to Malaysia and Hong Kong. (JH)

🍷🍷🍷🍷🍷 Chardonnay 2020, Henty A stunning follow-up to the '19 that proves the capacity of Henty to produce complex chardonnays that soar. Cool and composed with bright citrus, green apple, quince and white-nectarine aromas. Contained and almost Chablis-like with its innate quiet power and delicate palate enhanced by a thread of nougat textural softness. That's a wow. Screw cap. 12.8% alc. RATING 95 DRINK 2021–2030 $52 JP
Pinot Noir 2019, Geelong Brings together in the glass the strengths of Geelong pinot noir, including a dried sage, saline, maritime-climate quality that so impresses. Black cherry, aniseed, fennel seed and leafy aromas. Fine tannin edge through to the finish. Elegance in the glass. Screw cap. 13.2% alc. RATING 95 DRINK 2022–2028 $52 JP
Pinot Noir 2019, Henty A gentle hand has guided this delicate pinot noir which is restrained and coiled even as a 3yo. Fragrant in aromatic spice, dried flowers, violets, cherry and plum. Precision plus on the palate. So elegant and fine. Screw cap. 13% alc. RATING 95 DRINK 2022–2028 $52 JP

🍷🍷🍷🍷🍷 Western Districts Rosé 2021, Geelong RATING 93 DRINK 2021–2025 $27 JP ✪
Golden Plains Chardonnay 2020, Western Victoria RATING 93 DRINK 2021–2027 $34 JP
Pinot Noir 2019, Ballarat RATING 93 DRINK 2022–2028 $52 JP
Pinot Gris 2021, Henty RATING 92 DRINK 2021–2025 $32 JP
Riesling 2021, Henty RATING 92 DRINK 2022–2033 $32 JP
Golden Plains Pinot Noir 2020, Western Victoria RATING 90 DRINK 2022–2024 $34 JP
Nebbiolo 2019, Geelong RATING 90 DRINK 2022–2032 $38 JP
Regional Selection Pinot Noir 2019, Macedon Ranges RATING 90 DRINK 2022–2026 $52 JP

Punch   ★★★★★

10 Scott Street, St Andrews, Vic 3761 **Region** Yarra Valley
T 0424 074 234 **www.**punched.com.au **Open** W'ends 12–5 **Winemaker** James Lance
Viticulturist James Lance **Est.** 2004 **Dozens** 1800 **Vyds** 3.25ha

In the wake of Graeme Rathbone taking over the brand (but not the real estate) of Diamond Valley, James and Claire leased the vineyard from James' parents David and Catherine Lance, including the 0.25ha block of close-planted pinot noir. In all, Punch has 2.25ha of pinot noir (including the close-planted), 0.8ha of chardonnay and 0.4ha of cabernet sauvignon. When the '09 Black Saturday bushfires destroyed the crop, various grapegrowers called offering assistance, which led to the purchase of the grapes used for that dire year and the beginning of the 'Friends of Punch' wines. Exports to Singapore.(JH)

ΨΨΨΨΨ **Lance's Vineyard Close Planted Pinot Noir 2019, Yarra Valley** A very bright, medium, crimson red. Lifted and aromatic with exotic forest-floor fruits, ferrous notes, pomegranate and whole-bunch-derived dried herbs and fennel seeds. The equally impressive palate is concentrated, layered and effortless. This is a pleasure to drink, even now. Ripe, fine and persistent tannins make for a wine that will provide years of enjoyment, but you will need to be quick: only 80 dozen were made. Screw cap. 14% alc. RATING 96 DRINK 2022–2037 $80 PR

ΨΨΨΨΨ **Lance's Vineyard Cabernet Sauvignon 2019, Yarra Valley** RATING 93 DRINK 2022–2029 $45 PR
Lance's Vineyard Chardonnay 2019, Yarra Valley RATING 93 DRINK 2021–2025 $45 PR
Lance's Vineyard Pinot Noir 2019, Yarra Valley RATING 92 DRINK 2022–2032 $55 PR

Punt Road   ★★★★★

10 St Huberts Road, Coldstream, Vic 3770 **Region** Yarra Valley
T (03) 9739 0666 **www**.puntroadwines.com.au **Open** 7 days 10–5 **Winemaker** Tim Shand, Travis Bush **Est.** 2000 **Dozens** 20 000 **Vyds** 65.61ha
Punt Road is owned by the Napoleone family, third-generation fruit growers in the Yarra Valley. Their vineyard in Coldstream is one of the most historic sites in Victoria, first planted to vines by Swiss immigrant Hubert De Castella in 1860. The Napoleone Vineyard was established on the property in 1987. Chief winemaker Tim Shand joined the winery in 2014 and has established a reputation for consistent quality of all the Punt Road wines. The 2 main ranges are Punt Road and Airlie Bank, plus a small production of single-vineyard 'Block' wines, only available at cellar door, made only in the best vintages. Exports to the US, UK, Canada, Sweden, Denmark, Singapore and Sri Lanka.(JH)

ΨΨΨΨΨ **Napoleone Vineyard Block 18 Gamay 2021, Yarra Valley** A really vibrant, light and appealing crimson purple. Crunchy raspberries, cranberries and pomegranate seeds on the nose, while the palate is equally vibrant with sweet fruit and a long chalky finish. Serve cool for the perfect summer red. Screw cap. 13.5% alc. RATING 93 DRINK 2021–2024 $28 PR
The Holy Quinity 2020, Yarra Valley A blend of 60% cabernet with the balance coming from merlot, malbec, petit verdot and cabernet franc. A bright, medium ruby red. Freshly cooked strawberries and ripe red cherries, together with lifted purple flowers and some oak-derived spice notes. Medium bodied and gently textured, the tannins are pliant and persistent, giving this wine an each-way bet between being approachable now, but knowing it will improve over the next 5–8 years. Screw cap. 13% alc. RATING 93 DRINK 2022–2030 $85 PR
Airlie Bank Sauvignon Blanc 2021, Yarra Valley A light green gold. Aromas of passionfruit and lemon pith, nashi pear and fresh guava are all present in this subtle and beautifully put together Yarra sauvignon blanc. Dry, chalky textured and refreshing, this will be at peak now and over the next 12–24 months. Screw cap. 11% alc. RATING 92 DRINK 2021–2021 $22 PR ✪
Airlie Bank Gris Fermented On Skins 2021, Yarra Valley A bright copper colour. Attractive aromas of apricot kernel, strawberries, musk sticks and rose petals, while the palate is dry with a reasonably long, chalky finish. Screw cap. 12% alc. RATING 91 DRINK 2021–2023 $22 PR ✪

Garden Red 2021, Yarra Valley Equal parts grenache, gamay and cabernet franc. A really bright crimson purple. Dark fruits, mountain herbs and violets pervade this new and interesting blend. Medium–full bodied, this richly fruited wine has good depth and structure, with chalky tannins rounding out and good each-way bet between drinking now or watching it soften and mature over the next 5 years. Screw cap. 12.5% alc. RATING 91 DRINK 2021–2025 $22 PR ❂

Block 1 Pinot Noir 2020, Yarra Valley A light, bright cherry red. A little reduction. Lots of bright, mainly red fruits, with lifted, floral and spicy whole-bunch aromas. Crunchy and gentle on the palate, this builds nicely in the glass and can be enjoyed now and over the next 2–5 years. Screw cap. 12.5% alc. RATING 91 DRINK 2021–2026 $40 PR

Yarra Cuvée Chardonnay Pinot Noir NV, Yarra Valley 80/20% chardonnay/pinot noir. Charmat method. 6g/L dosage. A pale, bright green gold. Excellent bang for your buck here. Citrus, honey, some red fruits and just enough freshly baked biscuits to make it interesting. The palate is just dry enough, finishing clean and crisp. Cork. 12.5% alc. RATING 90 $22 PR

Napoleone Vineyard Block 11 Cabernet Sauvignon 2020, Yarra Valley A bright scarlet red. Lots of reds fruits such as satsuma plums and raspberries, together with some attractive floral notes and a waft of lemon thyme. Compact and fleshy, with plummy, crunchy cranberry fruit and the gently cedary oak already well integrated into the wine. There are firm tannins on the finish, suggesting this should age well in the medium term. Screw cap. 13.4% alc. RATING 90 DRINK 2021–2028 $85 PR

🍷🍷🍷🍷 **Airlie Bank Pinot Noir 2021, Yarra Valley** RATING 89 DRINK 2021–2025 $22 PR
Airlie Bank Cabernet Franc 2021, Yarra Valley RATING 88 DRINK 2021–2025 $22 PR
Napoleone Vineyard Pinot Noir 2021, Yarra Valley RATING 88 DRINK 2021–2026 $32 PR

Pure Vision Organic Wines ★★★

PO Box 258, Virginia, SA 5120 **Region** Adelaide Plains
T 0412 800 875 **www**.purevisionwines.com.au **Winemaker** Joanne Irvine, Ken Carypidis **Est.** 2001 **Dozens** 18 000 **Vyds** 55ha
The Carypidis family runs 2 brands: Pure Vision and Nature's Step. The oldest vineyards were planted in 1975; organic conversion began in 2009. Growing grapes under a certified organic regime is much easier if the region is warm to hot and dry, conditions unsuitable for botrytis and downy mildew. You are still left with weed growth (no herbicides are allowed) and powdery mildew (sulphur sprays are permitted), but the overall task is much simpler. The Adelaide Plains, where Pure Vision's vineyard is situated, is such a region. Ken Carypidis has been clever enough to secure the services of Joanne Irvine as co-winemaker. Exports to Singapore and Hong Kong. (JH)

🍷🍷🍷🍷 **Nature's Step Organic Wild Ferment Pinot Grigio 2021, Adelaide Plains** A golden–blush colour introduces a soft and approachable young grigio nicely aromatic in honeysuckle, Golden Delicious apple, pear and white peach. Mild in flavour, nicely refreshing in soft acidity, it's a drink-now proposition. Screw cap. 12.5% alc. RATING 88 DRINK 2022–2023 $15 JP ❂

Cabernet Sauvignon 2020, Adelaide Plains Oak enjoys a background presence with black spiced fruits holding centre stage. For the price, there is a lot on offer from the fragrant violets, black fruits, anise and leafy appeal of the bouquet, to the nicely integrated palate. Firm, drying tannins to close. Screw cap. 14.5% alc. RATING 88 DRINK 2022–2024 $17 JP ❂

Purple Hands Wines

24 Vine Vale Road, Tanunda, SA 5352 **Region** Barossa Valley
T 0401 988 185 **www.**purplehandswines.com.au **Winemaker** Craig Stansborough
Viticulturist Craig Stansborough **Est.** 2006 **Dozens** 3000 **Vyds** 14ha
The finely honed, contemporary Barossa wines of Purple Hands are borne out of a
partnership between Mark Slade and winemaker Craig Stansborough. Their home estate, the
Stansborough vineyard, lies in the far south of the Barossa Valley and is planted with shiraz,
montepulciano and aglianico. They also source grenache from the Zerk vineyard and cabernet
sauvignon from the Woodlands vineyard, both in the south of the valley near Lyndoch. The
range includes pinot blanc, pinot gris and several red blends – one a mix of funky Italian
varieties, the other the more traditional GSM. Purple Hands captures the purity and elegance
that is possible when the raw materials are in good hands. (DB)

ŸŸŸŸŸ **Grenache 2020, Barossa Valley** A springtime basket of red flowers and fruits
fill the senses, with a bright, almost tangy, back-palate and finish. Purple Hands
at its best – and happiest. Screw cap. 14% alc. RATING 96 DRINK 2022-2032
$30 JH ✪

ŸŸŸŸŸ **Colours of the South Pinot Blanc 2021, Barossa Valley** RATING 93
DRINK 2021-2026 $28 DB
Shiraz 2020, Barossa Valley RATING 93 DRINK 2021-2029 $30 DB
Colours of the South Pinot Gris 2021, Adelaide Hills RATING 92
DRINK 2021-2025 $28 DB
Colours of the South Mourvèdre 2020, Barossa Valley RATING 92
DRINK 2021-2028 $28 DB
Colours of the South Rosso 2020, Barossa Valley RATING 92
DRINK 2021-2026 $28 DB
Mataro Grenache Shiraz 2020, Barossa Valley RATING 92
DRINK 2021-2028 $30 DB
Shiraz 2019, Barossa Valley RATING 92 DRINK 2021-2028 $30 DB
Old Vine Grenache 2020, Barossa Valley RATING 91 DRINK 2021-2025
$30 DB

Pyren Vineyard

Glenlofty-Warrenmang Road, Warrenmang, Vic 3478 **Region** Pyrenees
T (03) 5467 2352 **www.**pyrenvineyard.com **Winemaker** Leighton Joy, Brock Alford
Viticulturist Graeme Mills **Est.** 1999 **Dozens** 10 000 **Vyds** 28.3ha
Brothers Brian and Leighton Joy planted 15ha of shiraz, 5ha of cabernet sauvignon, 3.2ha of
sauvignon blanc, 2.5ha of cabernet franc, 0.6ha of malbec and 0.2ha of petit verdot on the
slopes of the Warrenmang Valley near Moonambel in 1999. Yield is restricted to between 3.7t
and 6.1t/ha. Exports to the UK. (JH)

ŸŸŸŸŸ **Reserve Cabernet 2020, Pyrenees** Tasted before release and already a
singularly impressive young cabernet, proudly displaying regional menthol and
bay-leaf terroir characters, an attractive feature bringing a potent sense of the land
from which it comes. Impressive concentration of cassis, loganberry, dried herbs,
bracken, earth and toasted spices, which stays with you for a long, long time. A
figurative heavyweight dressed in a literally medium-weight body. Diam. 13.5% alc.
RATING 95 DRINK 2022-2033 $60 JP

ŸŸŸŸŸ **Union 2020, Pyrenees** RATING 93 DRINK 2022-2034 $60 JP
Earthscape Shiraz 2020, Pyrenees RATING 92 DRINK 2022-2032 $40 JP
Little Ra Ra Roopa 2021, Pyrenees RATING 90 DRINK 2021-2025 $30 JP

Quarisa Wines

743 Slopes Road, Tharbogang, NSW 2680 (postal) **Region** South Australia
T (02) 6963 6222 **www.**quarisa.com.au **Winemaker** John Quarisa **Est.** 2005

John Quarisa has had a distinguished career as a winemaker spanning over 20 years, working for some of Australia's largest wineries including McWilliam's, Casella and Nugan Estate. He was also chiefly responsible in 2004 for winning the Jimmy Watson Trophy (Melbourne) and the Stodart Trophy (Adelaide). John and Josephine Quarisa have set up a very successful family business using grapes from various parts of NSW and SA, made in leased space. Production has risen in leaps and bounds, doubtless sustained by the exceptional value for money provided by the wines. Exports to NZ, Canada, the US, the UK, Ireland, Scandinavia, Poland, Japan, South Korea, Malaysia, Indonesia, Hong Kong, Singapore and Thailand. (JH)

ΨΨΨΨ **Mrs Q Sangiovese 2021, Adelaide Hills** This sangiovese is living life large. There's no denying the generosity on hand; the deep, inky colour, the powerful flavour base ripe in black fruits and plums with a persistent spicy thread of aniseed, clove and cacao. That said, it's nicely controlled by a fine but firm tannin presence. Screw cap. 14.8% alc. RATING 89 DRINK 2022–2026 $19 JP ✪
Q Malbec 2021, Riverina There is an impressive flow of blueberry, mulberry and iodine here, lit by blazing florals. This is packed with flavour while offering the sort of oomph that the shopper in this zone is all over. Screw cap. 14% alc. RATING 88 DRINK 2021–2026 $17 NG ✪
Johnny Q Petite Sirah 2020, Riverina A monster truck! Inky, opaque and foreboding of density. Purple fruits, lavender and lilac. Huge, palate-staining tannins. Some mocha-bourbon oak, augmenting the impact. Far from finessed, complex or discreet, yet if big flavour at a price is the MO, look no further. Screw cap. 14.5% alc. RATING 88 DRINK 2021–2028 $17 NG ✪

Quarry Hill Wines   ★★★☆

2181 Barton Highway, Jeir, NSW 2582 **Region** Canberra District
T (02) 6223 7112 **www.**quarryhill.com.au **Winemaker** Alex McKay **Est.** 1999
Dozens 650 **Vyds** 4.5ha
Dean Terrell is the ex-vice chancellor of the Australian National University and a professor of economics. The acquisition of the property, originally used as a quarry for the construction of the Barton Highway and thereafter as a grazing property, was the brainchild of his family, who wanted to keep him active in retirement. The vineyard was established in 1999, with further plantings in 2001 and '06. There are 2ha of shiraz, 1ha of sauvignon blanc and 0.25ha each of savagnin, sangiovese, tempranillo, grenache, pinot noir and sagrantino. Only part of the production is released under the Quarry Hill label; grapes are also sold to wineries, including Clonakilla and Collector Wines. (JH)

ΨΨΨΨΫ **Lost Acre Tempranillo 2021, Canberra District** This joven style spends a mere 2 months in old French oak. It's awash with dark cherries, licorice, cola and lots of baking spices. Jubey and juicy across the mid-weighted palate, yet plenty of steadfast gritty tannins and fresh acidity to close. Best with food. Screw cap. 13% alc. RATING 90 DRINK 2022–2025 $27 JF

Quattro Mano   ★★★☆

PO Box 189, Hahndorf, SA 5245 **Region** Barossa Valley
T 0430 647 470 **www.**quattromano.com.au **Open** By appt **Winemaker** Anthony Carapetis, Christopher Taylor, Philippe Morin **Est.** 2006 **Dozens** 2500 **Vyds** 3.8ha
Anthony Carapetis, Philippe Morin and Chris Taylor have collective experience of over 50 years working in various facets of the wine industry, Philippe as a leading sommelier for over 25 years, and founder and director of French Oak Cooperage, Anthony and Chris as winemakers. The dream of Quattro Mano began in the mid '90s, becoming a reality in '06. (It's unclear how 3 equals 4.) They produce an eclectic range of wines, tempranillo the cornerstone. It's an impressive, albeit small, business. Exports to the US and Japan. (JH)

ΨΨΨΨΫ **La Reto Tempranillo 2019, Barossa Valley** Red and black cherry fruits with a splash of damson plum, hints of brown spices, cola, violets, mulberry and earth. There's a meaty edge to the wine on the palate, tight of tannin and plenty

of drive, with a red-fruited and savoury finish. Screw cap. 14.5% alc. RATING 91
DRINK 2022-2028 $28 DB

🍷🍷🍷🍷 **Novillo Tempranillo 2019, Barossa Valley** RATING 88 DRINK 2022-2028
$19 DB

Quealy Winemakers

62 Bittern-Dromana Road, Balnarring, Vic 3926 **Region** Mornington Peninsula
T (03) 5983 2483 **www**.quealy.com.au **Open** 7 days 9–5 **Winemaker** Kathleen Quealy,
Tom McCarthy **Viticulturist** Lucas Blanck, Kevin McCarthy **Est.** 1982 **Dozens** 8000
Vyds 8ha
Kathleen Quealy and Kevin McCarthy were among the early waves of winemakers on
the Mornington Peninsula. They successfully challenged the status quo – most publicly by
introducing Mornington Peninsula pinot gris/grigio. Behind this was improvement and
diversification in site selection, plus viticulture and winemaking techniques. The estate
plantings are 2ha each of pinot noir, pinot gris and friulano, as well as smaller plots of riesling,
chardonnay and moscato giallo. Their leased vineyards are established on what are premium
sites for pinot gris and pinot noir. These are now single-vineyard wines: Musk Creek,
Campbell & Christine and the newer Tussie Mussie Vineyard. Son Tom stepped up as head
winemaker in '19. Lucas Blanck manages the certified organic estate vineyards; the leased
vineyards are moving towards 100% organic management. Exports to Japan and Taiwan.(JH)

🍷🍷🍷🍷🍷 **Balnarring Vineyard Pinot Grigio 2021, Mornington Peninsula** There's
great tension between the acidity and the restrained flavours racing through
this delicious wine. Loads of citrus, juice and zest, with some lemon thyme
and a thirst-quenching saline sensation across the palate. Screw cap. 12.8% alc.
RATING 95 DRINK 2022-2025 $35 JF ✪
Feri Maris Single Block Pinot Grigio 2021, Mornington Peninsula It's
a refined, textural pinot grigio in the style of the finest Italians. Quince, not-
quite-ripe pears, lemon cream, daikon and tonic water with tangy acidity that
tempers the texture to keep it smooth and fine. Screw cap. 13% alc. RATING 95
DRINK 2022-2026 $40 JF
Musk Creek Pinot Gris 2021, Mornington Peninsula A compelling wine.
Textural, lightly phenolic, an array of spices, especially star anise, with cinnamon
mixed with creamed honey. There's a leesy, ginger fluff–cake element, making it feel
even more luscious. Screw cap. 13.8% alc. RATING 95 DRINK 2022-2028 $40 JF
**Tussie Mussie Vineyard Late Harvest Pinot Gris 2021, Mornington
Peninsula** An attractive straw-gold colour, with florals, toffee and malt alongside
peaches, apricot juice and kernel, with no shortage of spice. Deliciously sweet yet
everything kept very tidy, thanks to the acidity. 375ml bottle. Screw cap. 10.2% alc.
RATING 95 DRINK 2022-2027 $40 JF

🍷🍷🍷🍷🍷 **Balnarring Vineyard Friulano 2021, Mornington Peninsula** RATING 92
DRINK 2022-2027 $30 JF
Pobblebonk Field Blend 2021, Mornington Peninsula RATING 92
DRINK 2022-2024 $35 JF
Musk Creek Pinot Noir 2020, Mornington Peninsula RATING 90
DRINK 2022-2025 $45 JF

Quiet Mutiny

10 Elaine Cresecent, West Hobart, Tas, 7000 (postal) **Region** Tasmania
T 0410 552 317 **www**.quietmutiny.wine **Winemaker** Greer Carland **Est.** 2017
Dozens 400
Owner and winemaker Greer Carland grew up on the Laurel Bank family property, learning
to prune vines at an early age. She completed her oenology degree at the University of
Adelaide in 2000 and, after a few years of international vintages in Chile, France and the US
and a short stint in WA, she returned to Tasmania in '04. For the next 12 years she worked
with Julian Alcorso at Winemaking Tasmania, also making the Laurel Bank wines. In '16 she

left to focus on making the family wines at Laurel Bank and to start her own label. The name Quiet Mutiny is a reference to Australia's first female pirate. Cartland intends to secure land and establish a vineyard for Quiet Mutiny with her viticulturist husband Paul Smart. (JH)

🍷🍷🍷🍷🍷 **Charlotte's Elusion Rosé 2021, Tasmania** The full, spice-driven allure of and juicy berry-fruit mood of meunier is well contrasted with the tension of crunchy Tasmanian acidity. With a medium crimson-copper hue, this is a rosé of full-flavour impact, with just the right phenolic bite to tone supple fruit sweetness. Screw cap. 13% alc. RATING 90 DRINK 2022-2022 $35 TS

🍷🍷🍷🍷 **Venus Rising Pinot Noir 2020, Tasmania** RATING 88 DRINK 2022-2024 $49 TS

R. Paulazzo

852 Oakes Road, Yoogali, NSW 2680 **Region** Riverina
T 0412 696 002 **www.**rpaulazzo.com.au **Winemaker** Rob Paulazzo **Est.** 2013
Vyds 12ha

Rob Paulazzo began winemaking in 2000 and covered a lot of ground before establishing his eponymous Riverina business. In Australia he worked for McWilliam's and Orlando, in NZ for Giesen. He also completed 4 vintages in Burgundy, plus vintages in Tuscany, the Napa Valley and Niagara Peninsula in Canada. In addition to the family's vineyard, established over 80 years ago, Rob also sources fruit from Hilltops, Tumbarumba, Orange and Canberra District. (JH)

🍷🍷🍷🍷🍷 **M-2305 Chardonnay 2019, Tumbarumba** This is very good, transcending the paint-by-numbers approach of too many overly lean, contemporary chardonnays. Partial mlf. I prefer the effects of complete malolactic and a bit more phenolic chew, yet this is streamlined, pungently mineral and impressively long. The sub-alpine freshness jettisoning notes of white nectarine, pink grapefruit, curd, flint and oatmeal about the mouth. Best, the acidity is juicy, pulling the saliva from the back of the mouth with a confident cadence seen only in better examples, grown in the right places. Screw cap. 13% alc. RATING 93 DRINK 2021-2028 $30 NG
Reserve Cabernet Sauvignon 2019, Hilltops Subtle scents of crushed currant, green olive and bay leaf. There is a cool aura to this. Sage-strewn tannins, a bit gristly and in need of toning, mark a firm finish. A little time in the cellar will sort it out. This will mature nicely across the medium term. Screw cap. 14% alc. RATING 93 DRINK 2022-2031 $35 NG
V-8109 Syrah 2019, Canberra District Rob Paulazzo has gleaned ample experience in foreign lands. And it shows. The quality of hand-picked fruit; nicely extracted tannins of detail, mettle and sap; judicious bunchy complexity (25%) and 12 months in assorted French oak formats (20% new), all serve as a clear conduit for the Canberra District's DNA of iodine, blue fruits, tapenade, tar and assorted spice. Poised. Elegant, even. Lovely freshness and length. A bit reductive, but nothing an aggressive decant won't fix. This is good drinking. Screw cap. 14% alc. RATING 92 DRINK 2021-2027 $30 NG
F-1366 Botrytis Semillon 2019, Riverina Scents of bitter almond, tangerine, green mango, lemon balm and quinine. The pedal is firmly on the brakes of restraint. Suitably fresh, too, for a luscious style. Screw cap. 11% alc. RATING 92 DRINK 2021-2026 $27 NG
Grand Vintage Pinot Noir Chardonnay 2018, Tasmania Blend of 58/42% pinot noir/chardonnay. Traditionally crafted, with 3 years on lees. Red apple, currant, jasmine and oodles of saline acidity are welded to a creamy nougatine core. More an aperitif style than a rich one, the only caveat is the pokey dosage. It could be lower and the wine even brisker. Screw cap. 12.5% alc. RATING 91 $35 NG

🍷🍷🍷🍷 **Reserve Shiraz 2019, Hilltops** RATING 89 DRINK 2021-2026 $35 NG

Rahona Valley

3/48 Collins Road, Dromana **Region** Mornington Peninsula
T 359892254 **www.**rahonavalley.com.au **Open** Sat–Sun 12–5 **Winemaker** Natalie Fryar,
Alisdair Park **Est.** 1991 **Dozens** 2200 **Vyds** 8.4ha
The Rahona Estate vineyard was planted in 1991 and is one of the older and more interesting
small vineyards on the Mornington Peninsula, on a steep north-facing slope of a secluded
valley in the Red Hill area known for its ancient red basalt soils. The Pinot Noir is produced
from a single 1.6ha vineyard, consisting of 5000 close-planted vines. Rahona Valley also
produce sparkling wines made in the traditional method. Toby Pieters and Dianne Gardiner
made a 'vine change' to Rahona Valley in July '14, moving from an inner city suburb of
Melbourne to Red Hill on the Mornington Peninsula. (JH)

ŶŶŶŶŶ **Trinity 2021, Mornington Peninsula** A trio of pinot gris, riesling and
gewürztraminer come together to create this harmonious wine. Nothing overt,
all tangy juicy fruit, spice and pears, poached apple and musk. It's light yet viscous,
with a touch of creaminess across the palate. Not complex, but a thoroughly
satisfying drink nonetheless. Screw cap. 13% alc. RATING 93 DRINK 2022-2025
$30 JF
Abel Riesling 2021, Tasmania A livewire of lime and lemon flavours, all juice
and zest, with ultra-racy acidity out front. Thankfully, there's a smidge of leesy
texture and creaminess to shape the palate and act as a counterpoint. Screw cap.
13% alc. RATING 93 DRINK 2023-2033 $35 JF
Sparkling Rosé NV, Mornington Peninsula Pinot noir leads this assemblage,
followed by chardonnay and pinot meunier. On lees for 20 months, disgorged
Dec '20. A pale pastel pink with a slight copper blush. It's nicely weighted and
fruited, with a touch of cherries and strawberry shortcake. Soft and dryish on the
finish. Screw cap. 12.5% alc. RATING 90 $30 JF
Sauvignon Blanc 2021, Mornington Peninsula A mix of citrus and
tropical fruits, but not mawkish. Good acidity driving this, with some texture
across the palate. Refreshing and uncomplicated. Screw cap. 13% alc. RATING 90
DRINK 2022-2024 $30 JF

ŶŶŶŶ **Cuvée Blanc NV, Mornington Peninsula** RATING 89 $38 JF
Pinot Gris 2021, Mornington Peninsula RATING 89 DRINK 2022-2024
$30 JF
Mary's Block Pinot Gris 2019, Mornington Peninsula RATING 88
DRINK 2021-2023 $25 JF
Pinot Noir 2019, Mornington Peninsula RATING 88 DRINK 2022-2025
$50 JF
Mary's Block Gewürztraminer 2018, Mornington Peninsula RATING 88
DRINK 2021-2024 $30 JF

Ravenscroft Vineyard

274 Spring Creek Road, Stanthorpe, Qld 4380 **Region** Granite Belt
T (07) 4683 3252 **www.**ravenscroftvineyard.com **Open** Fri–Sun 10–4.30
Winemaker Mark Ravenscroft, Caitlin Hawkes Roberts, Nick Roberts **Viticulturist**
Mark Ravenscroft, Caitlin Hawkes Roberts, Nick Roberts **Est.** 2002 **Dozens** 1000
Vyds 1.5ha
Mark Ravenscroft was born in South Africa and studied oenology there. He moved to
Australia in the early '90s, and in '94 became an Australian citizen. His wines come from estate
plantings of verdelho, pinotage and albariño, supplemented by contract-grown grapes from
other vineyards in the region. The wines are made onsite. (JH)

ŶŶŶŶ **Sangiovese 2021, Granite Belt** A nicely composed expression of sangiovese's
red-fruit mood, transposed onto a backdrop of the tense acid structure of 950m
elevation in Stanthorpe, supported by finely structured tannins. It will appreciate
time to soften. Screw cap. 13.3% alc. RATING 89 DRINK 2026-2029 $35 TS

Pinot Grigio 2021, Granite Belt Tropical overtones suggest banana esters, which detract from varietal pear notes. Nicely textured acidity carries a bright but short finish. Screw cap. 12% alc. RATING 88 DRINK 2022-2022 $28 TS

Raven Rosé 2021, Granite Belt A rosé of predominantly sangiovese, boasting a medium crimson tone. It's clean, spicy and bone dry, with red berry fruits tensioned with a taut line of Granite Belt acidity. It concludes short, but the decision not to bolster it with sweetness was correct. Screw cap. 12.5% alc. RATING 88 DRINK 2022-2022 $28 TS

Ravensworth

312 Patemans Lane, Murrumbateman, ACT 2582 **Region** Canberra District
T (02) 6226 8368 **www.**ravensworthwines.com.au **Open** By appt in Sept
Winemaker Bryan Martin **Viticulturist** Bryan Martin **Est.** 2000 **Dozens** 8000
Vyds 3.4ha

Ravensworth is led by innovative winemaker Bryan Martin, his wife Jocelyn, plus his brother David. Bryan takes an organic approach, eschewing chemicals, preventing soil compaction and allowing the vines to thrive in what he describes as 'natural forestry principles'. The vineyard comprises mostly shiraz, riesling and sangiovese with marsanne, roussanne and viognier plus recent plantings of gamay, chardonnay, savagnin, ribolla gialla and nebbiolo. He also sources fruit for Ravensworth's other labels including the Regional. In '20, a winery and cellar were completed, the latter made with straw bales and filled with large-format oak, Italian amphorae, ceramic eggs and concrete vessels: all expressing Bryan's desire to experiment and craft minimum-intervention wines with texture. A second generation has come on board with son Lewis enrolling in winemaking at CSU in '21. (JF)

🍷🍷🍷🍷🍷 **Murrumbateman Riesling 2021, Canberra District** Such a yin-and-yang wine, as it has texture and depth yet is spritely and vibrant. There's so much flavour and delight, with its infusion of lemonade (without the sweetness), ginger beer and daikon, as this dips into savoury territory; a citrusy tang then a fine line of acidity pulling it altogether to form a complete wine. Refreshing, complex and utterly delicious. Screw cap. 11.5% alc. RATING 95 DRINK 2021-2028 $30 JF ❂

Pinot Gris 2021, Canberra District If you want pinot gris that's dilute of colour and without tannin, leave now. If you like it full of flavour, texture and complexity, then come join the party. This is fab and yes, it is an amber wine. It's a pale orangey pink and tastes of negroamaro, with lots of pink grapefruit, ginger-poached pears, Sichuan pepper (without the numbing effect) and a dusting of baking spices. The palate is alive with fine phenolics and acidity. It's a vim-and-vigour drink. Screw cap. 12.5% alc. RATING 95 DRINK 2021-2025 $30 JF ❂

The Long Way Around Tinto 2021, Swan Valley Hilltops Blend of 90yo grenache from the Swan Valley (65%), with tempranillo/graciano from Hilltops and a little monastrell from Ricca Terra Farm in the Riverland. Yep, long way around. A very good Iberian outcome. It's super-savoury, even if it has a core of dark red fruit plus pomegranate juice. Earthy, with lots of Middle Eastern spices from sumac to a more complex ras el hanout, with grainy and lightly if pleasantly drying tannins. It gets better and better in the glass; moreish with every sip. Screw cap. 14% alc. RATING 95 DRINK 2022-2026 $32 JF ❂

The Long Way Around Malbec et al 2021, Margaret River The et al is cabernets franc and sauvignon which undergo carbonic maceration to lighten up the malbec. As a result, it's meaty and floral, savoury without forfeiting malbec's dark cherry-fruit profile with its stony, slatey, tarry notes. Full bodied and shapely, with ripe tannins and utterly compelling. This might be a one-off which is a shame, because it's bloody good. Screw cap. 13.5% alc. RATING 95 DRINK 2022-2028 $38 JF

Project C Reduction Big Thick Barrels Chardonnay 2021, Tumbarumba Made with reduction in mind, in a 2000L new foudre. Flinty and funky and very slinky across the palate. Lemon and wood smoke, radish and quinine, this is complex and mouth-watering. It's on a tight leash that will loosen with a bit more time. But gee it's compelling now. Alas 150 magnums only, as with all Project C wines this vintage. Screw cap. 12.5% alc. RATING 95 DRINK 2022-2030 $90 JF

**Project C Oxidation Skinny Little Barrels Chardonnay 2021,
Tumbarumba** Project C, as in chardonnay, made in 3 styles (reductive, oxidative and on skins). This is the oxidative iteration. Maybe this will be the most 'out there' wine for those unfamiliar with the style. For those who are on board – rock on. It's a mid gold hue, full of lemon barley water, a peach-fuzz texture, with crunchy acidity and a nice length of tannin. Wood smoke and woodsy spices with the palate super-tight and linear with pleasant oxidative notes. Screw cap. 12.5% alc. RATING 95 DRINK 2022-2024 $90 JF

Project C Skins Amphora Chardonnay 2021, Tumbarumba A slightly cloudy straw hue is a dead giveaway this has spent time on skins. It's very good. There's a lemon twist of flavour, Angostura bitters and lemon barley water. Savoury and moreish with mouth-watering acidity and chewy tannins throughout but nicely placed and succulent. Screw cap. 12.5% alc. RATING 95 DRINK 2022-2026 $90 JF

The Grainery 2019, Canberra District Three Rhône rangers, marsanne, viognier and roussanne, come together exceptionally well through a combination of top-notch fruit, some whole-bunch pressing to demi-muid and ceramic eggs, some skin contact or whole-cluster ferments – a bit of everything really. The end result, a harmony of texture with a depth of flavour. There's stone fruit, spiced pears and butter lemon curd on toast, with phenolics that add shape and structure. Delicious drinking from go to whoa. Screw cap. 13% alc. RATING 95 DRINK 2021-2029 $42 JF

The Long Way Around Bianco 2021, Swan Valley Hilltops Bianco makes a welcome return with 60% trebbiano again coming from the Swan Valley, with new additions of 30/10% fiano/pinot grigio for good measure, both from Hilltops. It's rather racy, with its citrus flavours and lemony acidity with some melon. A trickle of tannin adds to the pleasing texture. The label says it's an 'everyday rustic white … drink it outta anything safe & watertight.' Good advice. Screw cap. 13.5% alc. RATING 94 DRINK 2022-2026 $32 JF

Grüner Veltliner 2021, Hilltops It's really good. While aromas of stone fruit, lime zest, ginger spice and florals entice, this is all about the palate. Texture is key, with lovely poached quince and ripe peach-like phenolics mingling with some creamy nuances; there's also quinine and fine acidity throughout. For the inaugural release, it's impressive and delicious. Alas, not much made – a measly 60 dozen. Fingers crossed Bryan Martin has access to the fruit again. Screw cap. 13% alc. RATING 94 DRINK 2021-2025 $36 JF

ɸɸɸɸɸ **Regional Sangiovese 2021, Canberra District** RATING 92 DRINK 2022-2026 $30 JF

Regional Montepulciano 2021, Hilltops RATING 92 DRINK 2022-2026 $38 JF

Barbera Nebbiolo 2021, Hilltops RATING 90 DRINK 2022-2024 $30 JF

Redbank ★★★★

1597 Snow Road, Milawa, Vic 3678 **Region** King Valley
T (08) 8561 3200 www.redbankwines.com **Open** 7 days 10–5 **Winemaker** Dave Whyte
Viticulturist Michael Murtagh **Est.** 2005 **Dozens** 33 000 **Vyds** 20ha
The Redbank brand was for decades the umbrella for Neill and Sally Robb's Sally's Paddock. The brand was acquired by Hill-Smith Family Vineyards in 2005, leaving the Robbs with the winery, surrounding vineyard and the Sally's Paddock label. Local winegrowers – the Ross, Judd and Murtagh families – purchased the brand in Aug '18 and have launched a new cellar door venture under the umbrella of Milawa Providore. Redbank purchases grapes locally from the King Valley and Whitlands as well as further afield. Exports to all major markets. (JH)

ɸɸɸɸɸ **Prosecco 2021, King Valley** The region's favourite sparkling fuses a touch of Italian-style citrus rind savouriness with outright varietal liveliness in apple, pear and honeysuckle flavours. Zippy and brisk, this is what we expect and want from the sparkling. Chill and go. Crown. 11% alc. RATING 91 $25 JP

Ellora Brut Cuvée 2016, King Valley 70/30% chardonnay/pinot noir. Bottle fermented, 3 years on lees. An engaging sparkling that offers plenty of cool-climate character in lemon, nectarine, wild herbs, spice and honeysuckle. Gentle autolysis-derived complexity offers hints of savoury yeast-driven Vegemite. Stays super-fresh with fine acid tingle to close. Cork. 12% alc. RATING 90 $28 JP

Pinot Grigio 2021, King Valley The merest hint of a blush colour and, yes, you know you are in grigio country. An excellent follow-up to the '20 release with just a touch of sweetness. Honeysuckle, apple blossom, apple, cut pear and lemon drop/ pastille. Throws sparks on the palate, the acidity and zesty citrus notes joining up and running long. Screw cap. 12.8% alc. RATING 90 DRINK 2021-2023 $25 JP

ᵀᵀᵀᵀ **Sunday Morning Prosecco NV, King Valley** RATING 89 $23 JP
Sunday Morning Prosecco Rosé NV, King Valley RATING 89 $23 JP
Emily Chardonnay Pinot Noir NV, King Valley RATING 88 $23 JP
Pinot Grigio 2021, Victoria RATING 88 DRINK 2021-2023 $20 JP
Sauvignon Blanc 2021, Victoria RATING 88 DRINK 2021-2025 $25 JP

Red Edge ★★★★

54 Golden Gully Road, Heathcote, Vic 3523 **Region** Heathcote
T 0407 422 067 **www.**rededgewine.com.au **Open** Mon–Fri 9–5, Sat 10–4.30 by appt **Winemaker** Peter Dredge, Will Dredge **Viticulturist** Peter Dredge **Est.** 1971
Dozens 1500 **Vyds** 14ha
Red Edge's vineyard dates back to 1971 and the renaissance of the Victorian wine industry. In the early '80s it produced the wonderful wines of Flynn & Williams, and was rehabilitated by Peter and Judy Dredge, producing 2 quite lovely wines in their inaugural vintage and continuing that form in succeeding years. Exports to the US and Canada. (JH)

ᵀᵀᵀᵀᵀ **71 Block Shiraz 2017, Heathcote** There's a wealth of ripe plum and blackberry fruit here, so smooth, so spiced and juicy, so Heathcote. Fills the mouth and makes for a rich, ripe expression with woodsy spice, licorice and dark chocolate. The palate arcs long with sturdy tannins in tow. Released as a 4yo wine, it's got a long journey ahead. Screw cap. 14.6% alc. RATING 94 DRINK 2021-2032 $70 JP

ᵀᵀᵀᵀᵀ **Cabernet Sauvignon 2017, Heathcote** RATING 92 DRINK 2021-2028 $25 JP ✪
Shiraz 2017, Heathcote RATING 90 DRINK 2021-2027 $40 JP

Redesdale Estate Wines ★★★☆

PO Box 35, Redesdale Vic 3444 **Region** Heathcote
T 0408 407 108 **www.**redesdale.com **Open** By appt **Winemaker** Alan Cooper
Est. 1982 **Dozens** 1000 **Vyds** 4ha
Planting of the Redesdale Estate vines began in 1982 on the northeast slopes of a 25ha grazing property fronting the Campaspe River on one side. The rocky quartz and granite soil meant the vines had to struggle and the annual yield is little more than 1.2t/acre. The vineyard property has since been sold, allowing Peter and Suzanne Williams more time to market their wines. (JH)

ᵀᵀᵀᵀᵀ **La Scassatina 2016, Heathcote** Cabernet sauvignon/cabernet franc/shiraz. Comes fully formed as a 6yo wine, with a glimpse of savouriness among the ripe, generous black fruits and spice. Deep red-garnet hues. Lifted aromatics of rose petal, blackcurrant, plum, sage, thyme and dusty earthiness. Cuts a trim figure on the palate, firm and elegant with a bacon smokiness that fits in well as a feature of its development in bottle. Screw cap. 14% alc. RATING 91 DRINK 2022-2026 $35 JP

RedHeads Wine

258 Angaston Road, Angaston, SA 5353 **Region** South Australia
T (08) 8562 2888 **www.**redheadswine.com **Open** Fri–Sat 12–5 or by appt
Winemaker Alex Trescowthick, Darren Harvey **Est.** 2003 **Dozens** 25 000 **Vyds** 8ha
RedHeads was established by Tony Laithwaite in McLaren Vale and has since moved to the
Barossa Valley. The aim was to allow winemakers working under corporate banners to produce
small-batch wines. The team 'liberates' premium parcels of grapes from large companies 'a few
rows at a time, to give them the special treatment they deserve and to form wines of true
individuality and character. It's all about creating wines with personality, that are made to be
enjoyed.' Exports to most major markets. (JH)

Esule Cabernet Franc Cabernet Sauvignon 2019, McLaren Vale Straight
out of the gates, the nose is treated to bright floral-flecked red cherry and dark
plum fruits with some mulberry and crunchy cranberry lift, before showing hints
of spice, violets, tobacco leaf, light wafts of amaro herbs and softly spoken French
oak nuance. Sprightly and medium bodied in the mouth, the aromas transpose
neatly over onto the palate which has a lovely cadence, light, fine tannin support
and finely composed fruit weight on the exit, closing pure, savoury and moreish.
Cork. 15% alc. RATING 93 DRINK 2021–2027 $50 DB

Dogs of the Barossa Shiraz 2019, Barossa Valley Delivers robustly
flavoured, classically structured Barossan comfort immediately upon opening.
Deeply coloured, with abundant dark berry and plum fruits, cut with spice, dark
chocolate and a fair lick of French and American oak. Full bodied and opulent
with ripe, fine-grained tannin and bright acidity providing the framework for the
rich fruit, with just a touch of alcohol warmth on the lingering finish. There is a
lot of enjoyment here. Cork. 15% alc. RATING 92 DRINK 2021–2030 $50 DB

Dan'Jango Shiraz 2020, Barossa Valley Vibrant red-purple hue, with
enticing, floral-flecked fruit notes of satsuma plum and ripe summer berry fruits,
hints of exotic spice, orange blossom, ginger cake, rum-and-raisin chocolate and
softly spoken coconut oak nuance. The wine is pure of fruit, with a lovely flow
across the palate, leaving a trail of spicy plummy fruit, the gentle tug of a curtain
of sandy tannin and a distinct floral flick of the tail. Great value for money and
excellent drinking here. Screw cap. 14.5% alc. RATING 91 DRINK 2021–2028
$30 DB

Whip-Hand Cabernet Sauvignon 2019, Barossa Valley A deeply coloured
Barossa cabernet in the classic vein. Aromas of blackberry, kirsch and cassis abound,
with some mulberry high tones to brighten things up. It sits at the lighter end of
full bodied, with loose-knit blackberry, cassis and hints of licorice, baking spice,
espresso, dark chocolate and vanillin oak notes. The wine drifts off with fine,
gypsum-like tannins and gently spiced berry fruits. Comforting and classically
composed drinking. Cork. 14.5% alc. RATING 91 DRINK 2021–2029 $50 DB

Wilson Gunn Bellum Cabernet Shiraz 2019, Barossa Valley Coonawarra
Bright red-purple hue, with aromas of ripe summer berry fruits, dark plum and
black cherry, purple floral tones and spicy oak. Full bodied, yet bright in acidity,
with a swift cadence across the palate before resolving with fine, sandy tannin
grip, bright fruit and a crisp twang of G&T-like acidity. Enjoyable cross-regional
drinking. Screw cap. 14.5% alc. RATING 90 DRINK 2021–2026 $30 DB

Redman

14830 Riddoch Highway, Coonawarra, SA 5263 **Region** Coonawarra
T (08) 8736 3331 **www.**redman.com.au **Open** Mon–Fri 9–5, w'ends 11–4
Winemaker Bruce Redman, Daniel Redman **Viticulturist** Malcolm Redman, Michael
Redman **Est.** 1966 **Dozens** 18 **Vyds** 34ha
Redman has been making wine in Coonawarra for over 110 years – and Coonawarra cabernet
for 50 years. Brothers Bruce (winemaker) and Mal (general manager) and Bruce's sons Dan
(winemaker and marketer) and Mike (assistant winemaker and cellar hand), represent the
fourth and fifth generations of the family business. Their prestige cuvée is The Redman, a

blend of cabernet sauvignon, shiraz and merlot. Exports to the UK, Japan, Taiwan and South Korea.(JH)

ϙϙϙϙϙ **The Last Row Limited Release Shiraz 2019, Coonawarra** The fruit here is very pretty: intense and concentrated, with layers of berries and exotic spice jostling for pole position. The oak is nicely matched to the fruit: it supports but doesn't obscure, rather, shapes the wine through the finish, allowing the fruit to carry long. Smart. Screw cap. 13.9% alc. RATING 92 DRINK 2021-2031 $35 EL
Cabernet Sauvignon 2019, Coonawarra Blackberries, salted licorice, aniseed and raspberry aromas, the palate follows with blood plum. This is pliable, -shaving tannins that course over the palate. Elegant and fine boned. Restrained and understated. Gorgeous. Screw cap. 13.5% alc. RATING 91 DRINK 2021-2028 $30 EL
Cabernet Sauvignon Merlot 2019, Coonawarra The oak is impactful on the palate and through the finish, lending an earthy texture to the mouthfeel. Blood plum, sticky/sweet balsamic, blackberry and mulberry all jostle for supremacy. Eventually a graphite character emerges and carries the fruit through the finish. Screw cap. 13.5% alc. RATING 90 DRINK 2021-2029 $35 EL

ϙϙϙϙ **Shiraz 2019, Coonawarra** RATING 88 DRINK 2021-2027 $20 EL

Reillys Wines ★★★★☆

Cnr Leasingham Road/Hill Street, Mintaro, SA 5415 **Region** Clare Valley
T (08) 8843 9013 **www.reillyswines.com.au Open** 7 days 10–4 **Winemaker** Justin Ardill
Viticulturist Rob Smyth **Est.** 1994 **Dozens** 25000 **Vyds** 115ha
Established in 1993 by Justin and Julie Ardill. Justin hand made the first vintage in '94 on the verandah of the heritage-listed Reillys Cottage – built in 1856 by Irish shoemaker Hugh Reilly from local slate – which today serves as their cellar door and restaurant. Justin continues to use the same traditional winemaking techniques of prolonged open fermentation, hand plunging and barrel maturation. The wines are made from estate vineyards (the oldest planted in 1919). Exports to Canada, Malaysia, Singapore, NZ and Hong Kong. (JH)

ϙϙϙϙϙ **The Dancer Limited Release Cabernet Sauvignon 2018, Clare Valley** Concentrated and dark, with a cassis-compote character in the mouth that lingers long after the wine has gone. The American oak contributes a decided softness and cushion to the finish, giving the fruit a soft landing, and drawing it to a long, lingering close. This is plush, lush and long with a distinct elegance and polish. Very smart. Screw cap. 14.5% alc. RATING 95 DRINK 2022-2038 $65 EL

ϙϙϙϙϙ **Moonvine Limited Release Cabernet Shiraz 2018, Clare Valley Barossa Valley** RATING 92 DRINK 2024-2034 $50 EL
Watervale Riesling 2021, Clare Valley RATING 90 DRINK 2022-2029 $28 EL
Dry Land Shiraz 2018, Clare Valley RATING 90 DRINK 2022-2030 $38 EL

Renzaglia Wines ★★★★☆

38 Bosworth Falls Road, O'Connell, NSW 2795 **Region** Central Ranges
T (02) 6337 5756 **www.renzagliawines.com.au Open** By appt **Winemaker** Mark Renzaglia, Sam Renzaglia **Viticulturist** Mark Renzaglia **Est.** 2017 **Dozens** 2500
Vyds 3ha
American Mark Renzaglia and his Australian wife Sandy planted their first vineyard in 1997 to 1ha of chardonnay, cabernet sauvignon and merlot. Mark made small quantities of his own wines while working as a vineyard manager and winemaker at Winburndale Wines for 11 years. The original plantings now make up the estate Bella Luna Vineyard, to which shiraz, viognier, tempranillo and grenache have been added in recent years. He also manages a vineyard in the middle of the famous Mount Panorama race circuit and has access to the grapes from the 4ha Mount Panorama Estate. Son Sam has since joined the business too, and a new winery and cellar door have been constructed. Winner of the Companion's Dark Horse Award in 2022. Exports to the US. (JH)

ΨΨΨΨ **Murnang White di Renzo 2021, Orange** 45/32/17/6% sauvignon/arneis/
gewürztraminer/chardonnay. An iconoclastic quasi-field blend that is the sort
of drink I reach for in a hope that is seldom fulfilled. Until now! Fermented in
concrete. Kept on lees for several months. Delicious! Nicely viscous, but fresh
and aromatic to boot. Jasmine, orange verbena, lychee, ginger, cardamom and
grape spice. Spicy. Long of finish and exquisitely dangerous. Screw cap. 12.2% alc.
RATING 93 DRINK 2021-2024 $30 NG

Chardonnay di Renzo 2021, Orange An easygoing, round and generous
chardonnay in the intensely flavoured house style. Nothing too lean or linear here.
Better because of it. Honeydew melon, peach, nougat, cashew and apricot. The
di Renzo series is hewn of purchased fruit, albeit, made in the same unfettered
approach as all wines here. The barrel regime, just right. The tension, perfect
for the mid-weighted style. The feel, one of everyday pleasure, belying a reliable
exactitude. Screw cap. 12% alc. RATING 92 DRINK 2021-2025 $35 NG

Riesling di Renzo 2021, Orange The fruit, partially botrytised, wild fermented
in tank, muted with some balancing RS and left on lees for textural complexity,
for several months. Juicy. Far from the austere Australian norm. Riffs on quince,
candied lemon rind, dried apricot, citrus verbena, frangipani and jasmine. A
skein of juicy acidity drives the length and palpable sense of dryness, but it is
the succulence that proves so winning. Lovely drinking. Screw cap. 11% alc.
RATING 92 DRINK 2021-2026 $35 NG

Rural Method di Renzo 2021, Orange Made in the ancient fashion, in which
the primary fermentation is finished in bottle, with cap sealed. Thus, the fizz.
Several months on lees. Strawberry Fields. A little Jumping Jack Flash, manifest as
perk and froth. The fizz, jubilant, before segueing to a creamy finish, reminiscent
of Exile on Mainstreet's Loving Cup. As great and rakishly confident as that album
is, it is pretty loose. Like this wine. Good times! Crown seal. 12.5% alc. RATING 91
$32 NG

Sauvignon Blanc 2021, Orange Made in a fashion that is so far from the
shrieking early-harvested norm, that it makes me happy. Fresh, sure, but the
emphasis here is on a plump mid palate, textural interest and ripe fruit suggestive
of kiwi, bath salts, hedgerow, saltbush, pickled chilli and curry leaf. Very good
drinking. Screw cap. 12.3% alc. RATING 91 DRINK 2021-2023 $25 NG

Nuovo di Renzo 2021, Orange 25/20/20/19/10/6% barbera/primitivo/
shiraz/nebbiolo/pinot noir/cabernet. This has nothing to do with varietal makeup,
subsumed by a sloshy, joyous style. Right up the sommelier alley. As much as a
richer rosé as it is a light, frisky and pulpy red. Point being, chill this! Fecund
strawberry, bergamot and sassafras notes are bound by a gentle twine of herbal,
whole-bunchy tannins. Easy drinking, in the best sense. Screw cap. 12.3% alc.
RATING 91 DRINK 2021-2023 $32 NG

Cabernet Merlot 2019, Central Ranges Not quite the success of the previous
vintage at this level. Gently mid weighed, leafy and a tad green. The tannins,
unresolved, feeling as if the picking date was hastened. Blackcurrant, tomato leaf,
capsicum and a smattering of thyme, mint and other garden herbs dousing the
finish. This has its charms, best enjoyed young. Screw cap. 13.2% alc. RATING 91
DRINK 2021-2024 $25 NG

Rosé di Renzo 2021, Orange A copper pink with rusty edges. Majority pinot,
with a dollop (15%) of gewürztraminer serving a spicy, floral lift. The former,
fermented wild in large-format wood; the latter, in tank. Fecund strawberry, grape
spice and bitters melded with blood-orange amaro and root spice. Gently slippery.
Nicely fresh. Almost a light-weighted red, really. Versatile drinking. Screw cap.
12.8% alc. RATING 90 DRINK 2021-2022 $32 NG

Shiraz 2019, Central Ranges This address provides very solid drinking for
the price and at the higher end, wines of a palpable purity and fealty to site:
decomposed granitic turf in a cooler zone. Blueberry, pepper grind, iodine
and clove scents. Some anise and tar at the finish. A little reductive tension,
not astray. Mid weighted, savoury and ready. Screw cap. 14% alc. RATING 90
DRINK 2021-2025 $25 NG

Reschke Wines

CW Wines, 7089 Riddoch Highway, Padthaway, SA 5271 **Region** Coonawarra
T (08) 8239 0500 **www.cwwines.com Winemaker** Ben Wurst (Contract) **Est.** 1998
Dozens 25 000 **Vyds** 155ha
The Reschke family has been a landowner in Coonawarra for 100 years, with a large holding
that is part terra rossa, part woodland. Cabernet sauvignon (with 120ha) takes the lion's share
of the plantings, with merlot, shiraz and petit verdot making up the balance. In 2020, Reschke
was purchased by Coonawarra-based CW Wines. Exports to the UK, Canada, Germany,
Malaysia, Japan and Hong Kong. (JH)

ŢŢŢŢŢ Vitulus Shiraz 2020, Coonawarra Gorgeous. Oak is evident, but the fruit has
so much exuberant concentration that it hardly matters. This is a deeply satisfying
rendition of Coonawarra shiraz. The brightness of the fruit is almost addictive,
and very attractive. Hedonistic, but classy. Screw cap. 14.5% alc. RATING 95
DRINK 2021-2031 $30 EL ✪
Bull Trader Shiraz 2020, Coonawarra This is a bright, super-pretty, sweetly-
fruited and gently spicy wine that shows the modern side of Coonawarra. The
vinification is by no means groundbreaking, but the jubilant expression of fruit
in the glass is. This is delicious, verging on uncomplicated, and just a total delight.
What fun for $20! Screw cap. 14.5% alc. RATING 94 DRINK 2021-2027 EL ✪
Vitulus 2019, Coonawarra Dark, salted cassis and blackberry. In the mouth
the wine is laced with a fine mineral seam of graphite tannins and saline acidity.
This is very elegant, while also managing to convey great concentration of fruit.
All things in balance, a classy wine to the end. Screw cap. 14.5% alc. RATING 94
DRINK 2022-2037 $30 EL ✪
Bos Cabernet Sauvignon 2014, Coonawarra This has certainly softened in
its old(er) age, but is showing few signs of slowing down. As we expect from older
cabernet, the tannins have melted into the fruit, akin to the way marbled fat melts
into the flesh of a good Wagyu steak. The fruit is fleshy, dark and layered with
spice: licorice root, star anise, clove and peppercorns, with a smattering of cigar
box, tobacco leaf and freshly grated nutmeg. The chalky and very fine tannins are
a highlight. Screw cap. 14.5% alc. RATING 94 DRINK 2022-2029 $45 EL

ŢŢŢŢŢ Empyrean Cabernet Sauvignon 2010, Coonawarra RATING 92
DRINK 2022-2037 $120 EL
Bull Trader Cabernet Sauvignon 2019, Coonawarra RATING 91
DRINK 2022-2031 $20 EL ✪
Bull Trader Cabernet Sauvignon Merlot 2019, Coonawarra RATING 91
DRINK 2022-2029 $20 EL ✪
R-Series Sauvignon Blanc 2021, Limestone Coast RATING 90
DRINK 2022-2024 $16 EL ✪

Ricca Terra

PO Box 305, Angaston, SA 5353 **Region** Riverland
T 0411 370 057 **www.riccaterra.com.au Winemaker** Ashley Ratcliff **Est.** 2017
Dozens 10 000 **Vyds** 80ha
Ricca Terra is the venture of Ashley and Holly Ratcliff. Ashley began his journey in wine in
1992 when he joined Orlando as a viticulturist, thereafter moving to Yalumba where he was
winery manager for the vast Riverland winery and technical manager until '16. He was the
recipient of 4 major state and federal industry awards, all focusing on viticulture in drought-
prone regions. So when he and Holly purchased an 8ha vineyard in the Riverland, it presented
the opportunity to plant varieties such as the rare ancient Balkan variety slankamenka bela.
There are now 80ha of varieties. The wines are hand picked into 0.5t bins and chilled for
12 hours before transfer to the winery in the Barossa Valley. Exports to the UK, the US,
Canada and Belgium. (JH)

ŢŢŢŢŢ Aglianico 2021, Riverland Spicy, savoury, sweet and lush, this is a goodie. There
are layers of deli meat, blackberry, glacé cherry and star anise. The tannins hold and

shape the affair in the mouth. Really good value for money. Screw cap. 14.3% alc. RATING 92 DRINK 2022–2027 $27 EL

Small Batch Nero d'Avola 2021, Riverland Nero has the propensity to taste sweet, such is the cascade – nay, the waterfall – of black and red berry fruits in the mouth. Here, it is an avalanche of sweet fruit, red snakes and raspberries, saved by a rush of savoury tannin that ducks in right behind it. It's delicious. It's delightful. You could chill it, if you want. Screw cap. 14.5% alc. RATING 92 DRINK 2022–2026 $27 EL

Bullets Before Cannonballs 2021, Riverland Tempranillo, shiraz, lagrein and lambrusco. Juicy, black and brooding, this does a really good job of carrying oodles of black fruit within a medium-bodied frame. It's deceptively light, for all the flavour that is crammed in. Licorice, blackberries, star anise, black pepper, plums and resin. Lush and lively. Super-smart for the money. Screw cap. 14.5% alc. RATING 91 DRINK 2022–2027 $23 EL ✪

22 Degrees Halo Kaleidoscope of Mayhem Rosé 2021, Riverland Grenache, mataro, nero d'Avola. Spicy, juicy and layered with medicinal strawberries, amaro/mountain herbs, some shaved deli meat, and ras el hanout … lots going on. Screw cap. 13.2% alc. RATING 90 DRINK 2022–2024 $20 EL ✪

Small Batch Arinto 2021, Riverland Portuguese variety. This is cool. It has a real bitter/phenolic character that laces throughout the wine, but it is offset by the lush green fruit (apples, melons and white currant) and perky citrus acidity. Serving this cold is going to add a whole 'nother element into the mix, and pairing it with food yet another elevation. Screw cap. 12.8% alc. RATING 90 DRINK 2022–2025 $27 EL

Small Batch Fiano 2021, Riverland Crunchy apples and pears dominate this wine, while the oak softens the texture in the mouth and brings with it some soft spice through the finish. Eminently smashable. Screw cap. 12.4% alc. RATING 90 DRINK 2022–2025 $27 EL

Soldiers' Land 90 Year Old Vines Grenache 2021, Riverland Pretty fierce (muscular) tannin and acid intersect in the back of the mouth; it stops just short of jarring. Meanwhile, the fruit that precedes it is fresh and lush. The jam donut vibe to the raspberries is attractive. Spicy and full. Plenty to grab on to. Screw cap. 15.5% alc. RATING 90 DRINK 2022–2028 $30 EL

🍷🍷🍷🍷 **22 Degrees Kaleidoscope of Mayhem Blanc 2021, Riverland** RATING 89 DRINK 2022–2025 $20 EL
Bronco Buster 2021, Riverland RATING 89 DRINK 2022–2025 $23 EL
Colour of Calmness Rosé 2021, Riverland RATING 89 DRINK 2022–2023 $23 EL
Terra do Rio Arinto 2021, Riverland RATING 89 DRINK 2022–2025 $30 EL

Richard Hamilton ★★★★

439 Main Road, McLaren Vale, SA 5171 **Region** McLaren Vale
T (08) 8323 8830 **www.**richardhamiltonwines.com **Open** Mon–Fri 10–5, w'ends & public hols 11–5 **Winemaker** Paul Gordon, Greg Foster **Viticulturist** Lee Harding **Est.** 1972 **Dozens** 25 000 **Vyds** 40.46ha

Richard Hamilton has outstanding estate vineyards, some of great age, all fully mature. An experienced and skilled winemaking team has allowed the full potential of those vineyards to be realised. The quality, style and consistency of both red and white wines has reached a new level; being able to keep only the best parcels for the Richard Hamilton brand is an enormous advantage. Exports to the UK, the US, Canada, Denmark, Sweden, Germany, Belgium, Malaysia, Vietnam, Hong Kong, Singapore, Japan and NZ. (JH)

🍷🍷🍷🍷🍷 **Farm Twelve Single Vineyard Mourvèdre 2020, McLaren Vale** It is always exciting to taste mourvèdre/mataro, by far the best among the established varieties in the region alongside grenache. Its wines, rich, ferrous and savoury. Sadly, most of it was pulled up. Good aromas of tar, pulled pork, clove and polished leather. The tannic growl binds the scents, fast and furiously, to the firm finish. This is clunky in

its youth, but I have confidence that it will come good with patience. Screw cap.
14.5% alc. RATING 92 DRINK 2021-2027 $38 NG

Burton's Vineyard Old Vine Grenache 2020, McLaren Vale Cherry cola,
tangerine, sassafras and raspberry bon-bons exploding across the palate. Juicy, with
a tannic framework that corrals any excess. The acidity could be a little easier
on the mouth, but solid drinking all the same. Screw cap. 14.5% alc. RATING 91
DRINK 2021-2026 $38 NG

Les Collinnes Pinot Gris 2021, Adelaide Hills Evidence of just how much
better gris is at this sort of pricing than chardonnay, which requires costlier
intervention. The colour, an honest 'gris' onion skin. Aromas, à point: spiced
apple, Asian pear slushy and some lanolin-cinnamon barrel-inflected spice with
a phenolic grip across the finish. Nicely done. Screw cap. 12% alc. RATING 90
DRINK 2021-2023 $24 NG

ҮҮҮҮ **Little Road Shiraz 2020, McLaren Vale** RATING 88 DRINK 2021-2027
$24 NG

Hut Block Cabernet Sauvignon 2020, McLaren Vale RATING 88
DRINK 2022-2029 $26 NG

RidgeView Wines ★★★★★

273 Sweetwater Road, Pokolbin, NSW 2320 **Region** Hunter Valley
T (02) 6574 7332 **www.**ridgeview.com.au **Open** Thurs–Sun 10–5 **Winemaker** Darren
Scott, Gary MacLean, Mark Woods **Viticulturist** Darren Scott **Est.** 2000 **Dozens** 3000
Vyds 15ha

Ridgeview is an insider's secret, brimming with a solid suite of wines and some exceptional
aged releases and older cellar stock. The address also boasts the funkiest retro label in all of
the Hunter. In 2020 Ridgeview purchased a neighbouring property, Eagle's Nest, planted to
chardonnay, sangiovese, verdelho and shiraz. In lieu of the expansion, a new winery is slated
for completion in '23. This will complement the established restaurant and its holistic culture
of wines, local produce and herbs, all grown at the estate. (NG)

ҮҮҮҮҮ **Impressions Semillon 2010, Hunter Valley** Among the very finest aged
Hunter semillons tasted. A superlative wine. Aged characteristics and depth of fruit
find confluence with an underbelly of waxy freshness. This runs on, despite its
aged embellishments: truffle, lemon butter, brioche, peat and bees wax. A stunning
drink, it would be a shame to miss it. A regional totem. Screw cap. 11.5% alc.
RATING 97 DRINK 2021-2026 $50 NG ✪ ♥

ҮҮҮҮҮ **Impressions Effen Hill Vineyard Shiraz 2015, Hunter Valley** An aged
release from a challenging year. But this has blossomed. A penumbra of cherry
cola and tamarind, tucked behind a veneer of leather and the fecund earth of the
Hunter. Lacking the concentration of its '17 sibling, but more than making up for
it with a digestible, mid-weighted drinkability. Poised, sappy, long and absolutely
delicious. My sort of wine. Screw cap. 13.5% alc. RATING 96 DRINK 2021-2025
$45 NG ✪

Impressions Effen Hill Vineyard Shiraz 2017, Hunter Valley Museum
release. This has aged very well. Distinctly regional with its stamp of sweet loam,
terracotta, mulch and leather armchair, mingling amid scents of yeast extract,
Asian spice, clove and anise. A warm year. The tannins, a bit twiggy and spiky.
But otherwise, a pleasurable drink exuding tertiary complexities, while emitting a
beam of freshness suggestive of years of life left. Screw cap. 14.5% alc. RATING 94
DRINK 2021-2030 $60 NG

Rieslingfreak ★★★★★

103 Langmeil Road, Tanunda, SA 5352 **Region** Clare Valley
T 0439 336 250 **www.**rieslingfreak.com **Open** Sat 11–4 or by appt **Winemaker** John
Hughes, Belinda Hughes **Viticulturist** Richard Hughes **Est.** 2009 **Dozens** 7500
Vyds 40ha

The name of John Hughes' winery leaves no doubt about his long-term ambition: to explore every avenue of riesling, whether bone-dry or sweet, coming from regions across the wine world, albeit with a strong focus on Australia. The wines made from his Clare Valley vineyard offer dry (No. 2, No. 3, No. 4 and No. 10), off-dry (No. 5 and No. 8), sparkling (No. 9) and fortified (No. 7) styles. Exports to the UK, the US, Canada and Hong Kong. (JH)

♀♀♀♀♀ No. 2 Riesling 2021, Clare Valley Crushed rock minerals are peppered into the fine, saline fruit. This is elegant and restrained, with layers of subtle flavour that reveal themselves over the course of drinking. What a wonderful wine – minerally and taut, with chalky phenolic structure that binds the fruit in place. While this is not the most complex wine in the line-up, it has so many different facets of flavour that it is impossible to underestimate. Just wait for the length of flavour to recede: you'll be waiting a while. Screw cap. 10.5% alc. RATING 96 DRINK 2021-2041 $37 EL ❂

No. 4 Riesling 2021, Eden Valley Citrus pith and lime flesh dominate the very fine aromatics. On the palate, I am carried away on a sea of flavour, only just resurfacing through the finish to appreciate what has just occurred. Generous fruit ebbs and flows across the tongue, the acidity is threaded in and out in a fine, saliva-inducing web. On closer inspection there is white pepper, aniseed and fennel flower too. Another masterful release, at once voluminous and restrained, certainly enduringly long. The price is mind-blowing. This is the fine, delicate, spicy wine in the line-up. Screw cap. 11% alc. RATING 95 DRINK 2021-2036 $27 EL ❂

No. 12 Riesling 2021, Eden Valley A new wine to mark the excellent '21 vintage, widely regarded as being the best Eden Valley vintage since '02. Fruit is sourced from Flaxman Valley and the regional stamp of chalky, mineral precision is all over it. This is restrained to the max – fine, tense and layered with rivulets of flavour that spool out over the long finish. What a sensational wine – more savoury and salted than plush and plump. Like the Eden Valley itself, this has a superbly rocky countenance; it takes me there. Epic stuff. Screw cap. 11% alc. RATING 95 DRINK 2021-2041 $37 EL

No. 3 Riesling 2021, Clare Valley Saffron and turmeric lace the aromatics, straying into the pink peppercorn and aniseed space. On the palate the wine is rich and intense, a very different shape to its peers, and all the better for it – its identity is clear and pronounced. Salted lemon, lime, crunchy green apple and white peach, too. Super-pleasurable and multidimensional. Astounding price. Screw cap. 11% alc. RATING 94 DRINK 2021-2036 $27 EL ❂

♀♀♀♀♀ No. 10 Zenit Riesling 2021, Eden Valley Clare Valley RATING 93 DRINK 2021-2036 $45 EL

Rileys of Eden Valley   ★★★★

PO Box 71, Eden Valley, SA 5235 **Region** Eden Valley
T (08) 8564 1029 **www**.rileysofedenvalley.com.au **Winemaker** Peter Riley, Jo Irvine (Consultant) **Est.** 1982 **Dozens** 2000 **Vyds** 11.24ha
Rileys of Eden Valley is owned by Terry and Jan Riley with son Peter, who, way back in 1982, purchased 32ha of a grazing property that they believed had potential for quality grape production. The first vines were planted in that year and now extend to over 11ha. In '98 Terry retired from his position (professor of Mechanical Engineering) at the University of South Australia, allowing him to concentrate on the vineyard and, more recently, winemaking activities, but the whole family (including granddaughter Maddy) have been involved in the development of the property. It had always been intended that the grapes would be sold, but when not all the grapes were contracted in '06, the Rileys decided to produce some wine. (JH)

♀♀♀♀♀ Old Vine Riesling 2021, Eden Valley Pure and true aromas of freshly squeezed lime juice, orange blossom, crushed stone and just a waft of cut fennel. A liminal note of dried herbs joins the chorus on the palate which is dry, crisp and shows pristine and swift acid drive. Screw cap. 11.5% alc. RATING 91 DRINK 2021-2031 $25 DB

Maxiumus Shiraz 2018, Eden Valley A densely proportioned example of Eden Valley shiraz showing rich fruit characters of blackberry, cassis and macerated plums along with hints of baking spice, turned earth, licorice and high-cocoa dark chocolate. Intense, broody and chewy on the palate with deep-set black fruits, abundant spice, fine, tannin and a sense of latent power. Screw cap. 15% alc. RATING 91 DRINK 2021-2031 $60 DB

The Engineer Merlot 2018, Eden Valley A plush, leafy-edged example of the variety showing fruit characters of deep plum and macerated summer berry fruits along with notes of cassis, baking spice, chocolate and earth. Supple, velvety and broody on the palate with a deep, resonant, earthy mood. Screw cap. 14.5% alc. RATING 90 DRINK 2021-2028 $25 DB

Ringbolt ★★★★

40 Eden Valley Road, Angaston, SA 5353 (postal) **Region** Margaret River
T www.smithswinestore.com.au **Winemaker** Heather Fraser **Est.** 2001 **Dozens** 20000
Ringbolt was established as a brand in 2001 and the cabernet grapes were initially sourced, picked and made in Margaret River at the old Watershed site, prior to being shipped off for maturation at the Yalumba cellars in Barossa. The wines enjoyed a blistering run of show success, and have typically attained very high scores from critics, and received gold medals and trophies at shows over the years since its inception. At an RRP of $28, but often available for just over $20, it is an impressive, concentrated, well-made example of Margaret River cabernet sauvignon. Exports to the US, the UK and NZ. (EL)

🍷🍷🍷🍷♀ **Cabernet Sauvignon 2020, Margaret River** We all know the many accolades this wine has attracted in the past. Interestingly, the fruit is sourced from Margaret River but it's made at Yalumba in SA. The South Australian penchant for American oak (rare in WA) shows, lending the wine a plush bed of texture. The succulent fruit is sensational, thanks to the brilliant '20 vintage, making for yet another satisfying release from Ringbolt. Screw cap. 14% alc. RATING 93 DRINK 2021-2028 $28 EL

Riposte ★★★★★

PO Box 256, Lobethal, SA 5241 **Region** Adelaide Hills
T 0412 816 107 www.timknappstein.com.au **Winemaker** Tim Knappstein **Est.** 2006 **Dozens** 14000
Tim Knappstein is a third-generation vigneron, his winemaking lineage dating back to 1893 in the Clare Valley. He made his first wines at the family's Stanley Wine Company and established his own wine company in the Clare Valley in 1976. After the sale of that company in '81, Tim relocated to Lenswood in the Adelaide Hills to make cool-climate wines led by pinot noir and chardonnay. His quest has now been achieved with consistently excellent wines reflected in the winery's 5-star rating since the Wine Companion 2012. Exports to the UK, the US, Canada, Switzerland, Denmark, Germany, Indonesia, Japan and Hong Kong. (JH)

🍷🍷🍷🍷🍷 **The Dagger Pinot Noir 2021, Adelaide Hills** The complete package here, immediately appealing and bright. Wrapped in perfectly ripe cherry fruits, bramble, plum, violet and dried herbs. Beautifully detailed, assisted by integrated oak, crunchy acid bite and leafy, savoury tannins. Impressive depth. Screw cap. 13.5% alc. RATING 95 DRINK 2022-2028 $24 JP ✪

The Foil Sauvignon Blanc 2021, Adelaide Hills Plenty of passionfruit, peach, lime, herbs, grass and cut apple here, combining the 2 halves – tropical and herbal – of the sauvignon personality beautifully. Acidity, smooth and bright, aids the delivery of these elements on the palate. Well sustained and with depth of flavour. Screw cap. 12.5% alc. RATING 95 DRINK 2022-2024 $24 JP ✪

The Scimitar Single Vineyard Riesling 2021, Clare Valley Raised in the Clare Valley, Tim Knappstein is a master riesling maker. His and his son's skills are in evidence here, with a masterclass in riesling celebrating purity of fruit and fantastic line and length. Lime juice, apple blossom, Golden Delicious apple and white peach are concentrated with flavours running deep. Linear and sleek in fine, chalky acidity and grapefruit pith. Stunning. Screw cap. 11.5% alc. RATING 95 DRINK 2021-2031 $24 JP ✪

The Stiletto Pinot Gris 2021, Adelaide Hills Embraces an almost Alsatian mentality in the delivery of this pinot gris with some deep-running layers of spice. Vibrant and enticing. Trademark apple, pear, lemon drop, dried fruit, bergamot and spice. Smooth and even with great persistence. Fine and elegant. Screw cap. 12.5% alc. RATING 95 DRINK 2021-2024 $24 JP ✪

The Katana Single Vineyard Chardonnay 2020, Adelaide Hills All class here, with the experienced hand of winemaker, Tim Knappstein, in evidence. Ripe, well-composed stone fruits, citrus, lime zest, nougat, jasmine with grilled-nut qualities of barrel fermentation, open and bright. Smooth, flavoursome and long through the finish. On point and delicious. Screw cap. 13% alc. RATING 95 DRINK 2022-2026 $29 JP ✪

ŸŸŸŸŸ **The Sabre Pinot Noir 2020, Adelaide Hills** RATING 93 DRINK 2022-2025 $38 JP

Rising ★★★★

Yow Yow Rising, St Andrews, Vic 3761 **Region** Yarra Valley
www.risingwines.com.au **Winemaker** Anthony Fikkers **Est.** 2017 **Dozens** 2500
Anthony Fikkers crafts wines that express the power of the Rising Vineyard, while also coaxing out the elegance that the Yarra Valley is renowned for. Anthony's philosophy of minimal intervention but maximum attention to detail allows each of the wines to fully express its origins. (JH)

ŸŸŸŸŸ **Cabernet Franc 2021, Yarra Valley** A brightly coloured wine with aromas of ripe plums, dried flowers and some black pepper, while the palate is textured and a touch saline. Silky yet persistent tannins round out a flavourful wine to be enjoyed in the short–medium term. Screw cap. 13% alc. RATING 92 DRINK 2022-2027 $35 PR

Chardonnay 2021, Yarra Valley Brightly coloured, this restrained wine has aromas of just-ripened white peach, tangerine peel, lemon oil and a hint of struck match, while the palate is balanced, equally restrained and long. Finishes gentle and long. Like a few of the '21s which haven't been in bottle long, this should look even better with another 6 months or so of bottle age. Screw cap. 12.5% alc. RATING 91 DRINK 2022-2025 $30 PR

Gamay 2021, Yarra Valley Bright crimson. Fragrant with red cherries and raspberries, along with dried mountain herbs and pepper from 100% whole bunches. Brightly-fruited, crunchy and refreshing, this is ideally suited to being served slightly chilled and in its youth. Screw cap. 13% alc. RATING 91 DRINK 2022-2025 $35 PR

Pinot Noir 2021, Yarra Valley A light cherry red, this has aromas of red cherry and strawberry fruit, a little white pepper and an earthy nuance. Medium bodied, with a solid core of fruit. Once the tannins (which are quite firm and solid at present) settle down and the wine opens up a little, this will look even better. Screw cap. 13% alc. RATING 91 DRINK 2023-2026 $35 PR

Bad Earth Light Dry Red 2021, Yarra Valley A blend of pinot noir and shiraz. A medium and bright crimson. Red and black fruits, along with crushed green peppercorns and some whole-bunch-derived aromas of dried rosemary and lavender can be found in this medium-bodied, relatively soft and easy-drinking red. Screw cap. 13% alc. RATING 90 DRINK 2022-2026 $28 PR

ŸŸŸŸ **Chardonnay 2020, Yarra Valley** RATING 88 DRINK 2021-2023 $32 PR

Risky Business Wines

PO Box 6015, East Perth, WA 6892 **Region** Various
T 0457 482 957 **www**.riskybusinesswines.com.au **Winemaker** Andrew Vesey
Viticulturist Rob Quenby **Est.** 2013 **Dozens** 8900
The name Risky Business is decidedly tongue-in-cheek because the partnership headed by
Rob Quenby has neatly side-stepped any semblance of risk. The grapes come from vineyards
in Great Southern and Margaret River that are managed by Quenby Viticultural Services.
Since the batches of wine are small, the partnership is able to select grapes specifically suited
to the wine style and price. So there is no capital tied up in vineyards, nor in a winery – the
wines are contract-made. In '18 Risky Business expanded its operations to Victoria's King
Valley, making Italian-style Prosecco, Grigio and Sangiovese. Exports to Japan. (JH)

🍷🍷🍷🍷🍷 **Prosecco NV, King Valley** Stays true to its award-winning style which
celebrates the grape's laser-like purity of flavour. Citrus blossom, lemon sorbet,
mandarin peel and green apple aromas. Super-clean sherbety acidity – it positively
tingles – with citrus and green apple intensity. Does the grape proud. Crown.
10.5% alc. RATING 95 $25 JP ✪

🍷🍷🍷🍷🍷 **Shiraz Grenache Tempranillo 2020, Margaret River** RATING 92
DRINK 2022-2028 $25 EL ✪

Rivendell Winery Estate

1172 Wildwood Road, Yallingup Siding, WA 6282 **Region** Margaret River
T (08) 9755 2000 **www**.rivendellwinery.com.au **Open** Fri–Sun 11–5 **Winemaker** Julian
Langworthy **Viticulturist** John Fogarty **Est.** 1987 **Dozens** 2500 **Vyds** 3.5ha
Rivendell was established in 1987 by a local Margaret River family and became recognised for
its gardens, restaurant and wines. The property was purchased by private investors in '04 (who
established Howling Wolves in this location). The ensuing 11 years saw changing ownership of
the property by a number of different parties. Fast forward to '15, and Darryn and Silje (Celia)
Gruenthal joined Danny and Corinne Gruenthal (Darryn's parents) in full ownership of the
property. After a few years of extensive renovations, '18 was their first release of wine under
the Rivendell label. The vineyard on the property is planted mostly to cabernet sauvignon,
while the fruit for the remainder of the wines is purchased from local growers. Wines are
currently sold only in WA. (EL)

🍷🍷🍷🍷🍷 **Cabernet Sauvignon 2020, Margaret River** This is lush and plush, and lays
out a heady combination of firm but fine tannins, red and purple berries and
pan-fried toasted spices. This is really delicious and perfectly approachable now,
with enough structure to show its integrity. Screw cap. 14.5% alc. RATING 92
DRINK 2022-2032 $32 EL
Sauvignon Blanc Semillon 2021, Margaret River Green apple skins, snow
peas, passionfruit and cheesecloth in abundance. This is crunchy and bright, with a
seam of mineral acidity that laces the affair together. Typical Margaret River SBS:
S for smart. Screw cap. 12.5% alc. RATING 90 DRINK 2022-2023 $22 EL
Tempranillo Shiraz 2020, Margaret River Frankland River Blackberries,
plums, salted deli meat and leather strap on the nose; in the mouth the fruit is
here, but it is driven by firm tannins. This is a common story in '20 reds from WA,
although the quality is generally excellent and likely long-lived. Here the wine
is concentrated and ripe, however the tannins will need either a further year or
2 in bottle to start to soften, or certainly an hour or so in a decanter. Screw cap.
14.5% alc. RATING 90 DRINK 2022-2028 $36 EL

🍷🍷🍷🍷 **Sauvignon Blanc Semillon 2020, Margaret River** RATING 89
DRINK 2021-2023 $22 EL
Ex Fida Fiducia Cabernet Sauvignon Shiraz 2019, Margaret River
RATING 89 DRINK 2021-2026 $22 EL

RiverBank Estate

126 Hamersley Road, Caversham, WA 6055 **Region** Swan Valley
T (08) 9377 1805 **www**.riverbankestate.com.au **Open** Wed–Sun & public hols 10–4
Winemaker Troy Overstone **Est.** 1982 **Dozens** 4500 **Vyds** 12ha
RiverBank Estate was first planted on the fertile banks of the Swan River in 1982 and has
grown to encompass 12ha of mature, low-yielding vines (18 varieties), the wines made onsite.
The property was purchased by the Lembo family in 2017 and has been rebranded into
3 wine ranges: On The Run, Rebellious and Eric Anthony. RiverBank was named Best Small
Wine Producer of the Year '19 by Ray Jordan and Best Small Cellar Door in the Swan Valley
'19 by Peter Forrestal of Gourmet Traveller. Exports to Azerbaijan and Maldives. (JH)

PPPPP **Rebellious Tempranillo 2021, Swan Valley** With 5% malbec; the tempranillo
co-fermented with 8% vermentino (skins), co-planted in the vineyard. Bacon
fat, maple and violets are the introduction while the palate is saturated in red
licorice, raspberries and black cherries. It's juicy and bright and delicious. The
tannins are ever present, but not overbearing. Screw cap. 14% alc. RATING 94
DRINK 2022-2027 $25 EL ✪

PPPPP **Eric Anthony Cabernet Malbec 2019, Swan Valley Geographe**
RATING 92 DRINK 2021-2031 $35 EL
Rebellious Chenin Blanc 2021, Swan Valley RATING 91 DRINK 2021-2028
$25 EL
Eric Anthony Chardonnay 2021, Margaret River RATING 91
DRINK 2022-2028 $35 EL
Bossman Malbec Shiraz 2018, Geographe Swan Valley RATING 91
DRINK 2022-2037 $80 EL
Rebellious Grenache Shiraz Malbec 2021, Swan Valley RATING 90
DRINK 2022-2028 $25 EL

Riversdale Estate

222 Denholms Road, Cambridge, Tas 7170 **Region** Southern Tasmania
T (03) 6248 5555 **www**.riversdaleestate.com.au **Open** Thurs–Sun 10–5
Winemaker Jasper Marais **Viticulturist** Ian Roberts, Rainier Roberts **Est.** 1991
Dozens 9000 **Vyds** 37ha
Ian Roberts purchased the Riversdale property in 1980 while a university student. He says
he paid a record price for the district. The unique feature of the property is its frontage to
the Pittwater waterfront, which acts as a buffer against frost and also moderates the climate
during the ripening phase. It is a large property with 37ha of vines and one of the largest olive
groves in Tasmania, producing 50 olive-based products. Five families live permanently on the
estate, providing all the labour for the various operations, which also includes luxury French
Provincial-style cottages overlooking the vines, a French bistro, an orangery (where high tea
is served) and a cellar door. Wine quality is consistently good and can be outstanding. (JH)

PPPPP **Coal River Valley Riesling 2021, Tasmania** An enticing exoticism is lifted by
all the best attributes of botrytis – orange blossom, apricot, loquat and fig, along
with a subtle palate viscosity and not a hint of the bitterness that all too often
sneaks in. A touch of sweetness has been played to masterful effect, leaving the final
impression to a long tail of perfectly ripe yet energetic and lithe acidity. Drink it
now or in a decade or more. Screw cap. 12% alc. RATING 95 DRINK 2022-2036
$39 TS
Centaurus Pinot Noir 2020, Tasmania The best reserve-style pinots
distinguish themselves from their estate counterparts not by more volume or
impact but through greater polish, purity, texture and fragrant allure. There's
a compelling elegance at play here, unashamedly red-fruited and wonderfully
floral and light on its feet, from start to enduring finish. Fine-grained mineral
tannins and lively acidity are pitched perfectly to the restrained mood of this cool
season. Very much more Chambolle-Musigny than Gevrey-Chambertin and
I love it for that! Screw cap. 13% alc. RATING 95 DRINK 2022-2030 $62 TS

Musca Syrah 2019, Tasmania This is the biggest Tasmanian wine of the shelves this year, with a ripeness to rival the Barossa, yet upholding an integrity and a coherence that correlate to supreme balance. A warm season has drawn out black fruits of all kinds, even licorice and high-cocoa dark chocolate, allusions rarely heard in these parts. Fine, mineral, peppery tannins and a determined line of focused acidity keep a long finish on the straight and true. Screw cap. 14.5% alc. RATING 95 DRINK 2024-2034 $60 TS

Crater Chardonnay 2020, Tasmania RATING 93 DRINK 2025-2030 $62 TS
Coal River Valley Syrah 2019, Tasmania RATING 93 DRINK 2022-2027 $42 TS
Pictor Winter Harvest Riesling 2021, Tasmania RATING 93 DRINK 2022-2051 $60 TS
Blanc de Blanc 2016, Tasmania RATING 92 $52 TS
Coal River Valley Pinot Gris 2021, Tasmania RATING 92 DRINK 2022-2023 $36 TS
Coal River Valley Chardonnay 2020, Tasmania RATING 91 DRINK 2023-2025 $40 TS
Crux NV, Tasmania RATING 90 $38 TS
Coal River Valley Pinot Noir 2019, Tasmania RATING 90 DRINK 2024-2026 $42 TS

Rob Dolan Wines

21-23 Delaneys Road, South Warrandyte, Vic 3134 **Region** Yarra Valley
T (03) 9876 5885 www.robdolanwines.com.au **Open** 7 days 10–5 **Winemaker** Rob Dolan, Adrian Santolin **Viticulturist** Maris Feldgen **Est.** 2010 **Dozens** 30 000 **Vyds** 25ha
Rob Dolan has been making wine in the Yarra Valley for over 30 years and knows its every nook and cranny. In '11 he was able to purchase the Hardys Yarra Burn winery at an enticing price. It is singularly well equipped and, in addition to making the excellent Rob Dolan wines there, he conducts an extensive contract winemaking business. Business is booming, production having doubled, with exports driving much of the increase. Exports to the UK, the US, Canada, Malaysia, Singapore, Hong Kong and Thailand. (JH)

White Label Pinot Noir 2020, Yarra Valley A nice, bright crimson red signalling a vibrant wine with aromas of fresh raspberries, some spice from 10% whole bunches and a gentle lick of well-handled oak. Equally fresh on the palate, this silky textured and refreshing wine finishes with long chalky tannins. Screw cap. 13% alc. RATING 93 DRINK 2021-2025 $38 PR
White Label Chardonnay 2020, Yarra Valley Immediately appealing with its aromas of stone fruits, ripe Golden Delicious apples and a little fresh vanilla bean. There's a light creaminess to the palate, which is balanced, taut and long for a wine at this modest price. Screw cap. 13% alc. RATING 92 DRINK 2021-2026 $35 PR

Robert Channon Wines

32 Bradley Lane, Amiens, Qld 4352 **Region** Granite Belt
T (07) 4683 3260 www.robertchannonwines.com **Open** Mon, Tues & Fri 11–4, w'ends 10–5 **Winemaker** Paola Cabezas, Ash Smith, Robert Channon **Viticulturist** Clark Strudwick **Est.** 1998 **Dozens** 2500 **Vyds** 8ha
Peggy and Robert Channon have established verdelho, chardonnay, pinot gris, shiraz, cabernet sauvignon and pinot noir under permanent bird protection netting. The initial cost of installing permanent netting is high but in the long term it is well worth it: it excludes birds and protects the grapes against hail damage. Also, there is no pressure to pick the grapes before they are fully ripe. (JH)

Verdelho 2021, Granite Belt A clean, fresh and fruit-focused take on Robert Channon's signature wine, capturing a nicely toned point in verdelho's ripening curve. Star fruit and nashi pear are accented with a compelling hint of white pepper. A focused and long finish is well honed by finely textured phenolic bite and vibrant acidity. Screw cap. 14% alc. RATING 91 DRINK 2022-2022 $30 TS

🍷🍷🍷 **Pinot Shiraz 2021, Granite Belt** RATING 89 DRINK 2024-2028 $30 TS
Reserve Cabernet Sauvignon 2021, Granite Belt RATING 89
DRINK 2026-2029 $35 TS
Singing Lake Chardonnay Verdelho 2021, Granite Belt RATING 88
DRINK 2022-2022 $30 TS
Albariño 2021, Granite Belt RATING 88 DRINK 2022-2022 $65 TS

Robert Johnson Vineyards ★★★★

33 Onkaparinga Valley Road, Verdun, SA, 5245 **Region** Eden Valley
T (08) 8359 2600 **www**.robertjohnsonvineyards.com.au **Open** W'ends and public hols
11–5 **Winemaker** Robert Johnson **Est.** 1997 **Dozens** 3000 **Vyds** 3.86ha
The home base for Robert Johnson is a 12ha vineyard and olive grove purchased in 1996, with 0.4ha of merlot and 5ha of olive trees. The olive grove has been rehabilitated, and 2.1ha of shiraz, 1.2ha of merlot and a small patch of viognier have been established. Wines made from estate-grown grapes are released under the Robert Johnson label; these are supplemented by Alan & Veitch wines, made from grapes purchased from the Sam Virgara vineyard in the Adelaide Hills, and named after Robert Johnson's parents. A new cellar door opened in '20, located in an old church in Verdun. Exports to the US and Poland. (JH)

🍷🍷🍷🍷 **Viognier 2021, Eden Valley** Light straw in the glass with aromas of ripe
apricot, nectarine and peach along with hints of soft spice, honeysuckle, stone, clotted cream and almond blossom. There's some slinky texture on the palate along with bright acidity and a lovely wash of apricot, nectarine and spice on the exit. Lovely. Screw cap. 13.5% alc. RATING 93 DRINK 2022-2028 $40 DB
Shiraz 2019, Eden Valley Deep in colour and packed full of ripe black cherry, blackberry and satsuma plum, with hints of baking spice, blackberry jam, graphite, licorice, violets and earth. Pure dark fruits on the palate with a savoury palate shape and dark, broody notes on the finish. Screw cap. 14.5% alc. RATING 90
DRINK 2022-2028 $30 DB

🍷🍷🍷 **Shiraz Viognier Rosé 2021, Eden Valley** RATING 89 DRINK 2022-2026 $26 DB

Robert Oatley Vineyards

Craigmoor Road, Mudgee, NSW 2850 **Region** Mudgee
T (02) 9433 3255 **www**.robertoatley.com.au craigmoor.com.au **Open** Thurs–Mon from
11am **Winemaker** Larry Cherubino **Est.** 2006 **Vyds** 155ha
Robert Oatley Vineyards, founded by the late Robert (Bob) Oatley AO BEM in 2006, is a family-owned winery led by his eldest son Sandy Oatley who, with his father, brother and sister, planted the first Oatley vineyards in the late '60s. The Robert Oatley brand has a trio of labels producing wines from Margaret River, Great Southern and McLaren Vale: the Signature Series, particular vineyard sites with Finisterre and the best of the best barrels under The Pennant. Previously based in Margaret River, the cellar door is now in Mudgee, where the family also produce wines for Mudgee labels, Montrose and Craigmoor. Other Robert Oatley brands include Yves, Wild Oats, Wildflower, Four In Hand, pocketwatch and Hancock & Hancock from vineyards across NSW, Vic, SA and WA. Exports to the UK, the US and Canada. (JH)

🍷🍷🍷🍷🍷 **Robert Oatley The Pennant Cabernet Sauvignon 2018, Frankland**
River Concentrated and bloody, this has grit and depth; it is a pool of flavour that glimmers with blackberry, licorice, mulberry and raspberry. There is menthol and layers of exotic spice. This is a bit of a ball tearer: big, moving to robust, and resinous. Midnight. Black. The dead of night. The hour before dawn. Screw cap.
14.5% alc. RATING 96 DRINK 2022-2042 $105 EL

Robert Oatley The Pennant Chardonnay 2020, Margaret River This is rich, cushioned and opulent, with custard powder, yellow peach, Golden Delicious apples and shortcrust pastry. There is no way you could mistake this as being from anywhere other than Margs, such is the voluminous folds of flavour, in combination with briny, pink-grapefruit acidity. Very smart, and absolutely a style. Screw cap. 12.5% alc. RATING 95 DRINK 2022-2030 $95 EL

Robert Oatley Limited Release Shiraz 2018, Barossa Larry Cherubino heads to the Barossa and Eden Valleys to source fruit for this deeply flavoured, limited release wine. Glossy and elegant, the wine resonates with ripe satsuma plum and black berry fruits and classy French oak nuance. The Barossa Valley provides the richness and horsepower and the cooler Eden Valley the graceful line. tight fine tannin and drive. A wonderfully balanced and textural release. Screw cap. 14.5% alc. RATING 95 DRINK 2021-2035 $70 DB

Robert Oatley Limited Release Cabernet Sauvignon 2018, Barossa A beautifully composed cabernet. Densely packed blackberry, black cherry and cassis are supported by notes of deep spice, thyme, bay leaf, espresso and cedary French oak. The mouthfeel is luscious and textured with wonderful flow, fruit density, graceful line and tightly packed gypsum-like tannins. The finish, long and pure, is awash with black fruits, cedar and spice. Wonderfully balanced and a wine with a bright future in the cellar. Screw cap. 14.5% alc. RATING 95 DRINK 2021-2040 $70 DB

Robert Oatley The Pennant Cabernet Sauvignon 2018, Margaret River There can't be too many more 2018s to be released on to the market – this must be among the very last. It is savoury, dense and ripe; the concentrated flow of flavour shows the flux between sweet and savoury fruit, all of it framed within spicy oak. This is a big wine, muscly and tense. Give it some further time to stretch out – it needs it. Will go the distance, though. Screw cap. 14% alc. RATING 95 DRINK 2024-2042 $105 EL

Robert Oatley Finisterre Chardonnay 2019, Margaret River This is very fine, generous, spicy Margaret River chardonnay: salted yellow peaches, lemon zest and crushed white pepper coalesce in the mouth the form a sleek whole. Three more years and this wine will really shine. Screw cap. 12.5% alc. RATING 94 DRINK 2021-2031 $40 EL

Robert Oatley Limited Release Shiraz 2017, Barossa A mix of Barossa Valley and Eden Valley fruit that provides an insight into fruit source and the fine art of blending. The fruit from the valley floor provides the lavish dark-fruit density, fine, ripe tannin heft and raw horsepower, all dark and brooding; the Eden Valley component supplies red-fruited high tones, fine acidity and a sense of grace. Together, they make quite a wine; elegant and opulent in equal measure, with classy French oak and wonderful balance and flow. Screw cap. 14.5% alc. RATING 94 DRINK 2021-2038 $70 DB

♀♀♀♀♀ **Robert Oatley Finisterre Grenache 2019, McLaren Vale** RATING 93 DRINK 2021-2025 $40 NG

Robert Oatley Finisterre Shiraz 2018, McLaren Vale RATING 93 DRINK 2021-2028 $40 NG

Robert Oatley Limited Release Cabernet Sauvignon 2017, Barossa RATING 93 DRINK 2025-2038 $70 DB

Robert Oatley Signature Series GSM 2019, McLaren Vale RATING 92 DRINK 2021-2024 $24 NG ✪

Robert Oatley Signature Series Chardonnay 2021, Margaret River RATING 90 DRINK 2021-2026 $24 EL

Robert Oatley Signature Series Shiraz 2019, McLaren Vale RATING 90 DRINK 2021-2024 $24 NG

Robin Brockett Wines

43 Woodville St, Drysdale, Vic 3222 (postal) **Region** Geelong
T 0418 112 221 **www**.robinbrockettwines.com **Winemaker** Robin Brockett **Est.** 2013
Dozens 400

Robin Brockett is chief winemaker at Scotchmans Hill, a position he has held for over 30 years, making consistently very good wines through the ebbs and flows of climate. In 2013 he took the first steps towards the realisation of a 35-year dream of making and selling wines under his own label. He put in place an agreement to buy grapes from the Fenwick (2ha) and Swinburn (1ha) vineyards, and in '13 made the first wines. Robin is one of the most experienced winemakers in the Geelong region. (JH)

Swinburn Vineyard Bellarine Peninsula Chardonnay 2020, Geelong The fineness and purity of fruit is something to behold — so clean, so stylish. Fresh zesty lemon, lime peel, nectarine, white peach, almond and slate. Restrained oak influence only helps to accentuate the fruit more, with a touch of nougat-soft mouthfeel before bracing brisk acidity to close. Screw cap. 13% alc. RATING 95 DRINK 2021–2030 $40 JP

Swinburn Vineyard Bellarine Peninsula Pinot Noir 2019, Geelong RATING 92 DRINK 2022–2027 $42 JP

Rockcliffe

18 Hamilton Road, Denmark, WA 6333 **Region** Great Southern
T 0419 848 195 **www**.rockcliffe.com.au **Open** 7 days 11–5 or by appt
Winemaker Elysia Harrison, Mike Garland, Neil Miles **Viticulturist** Elysia Harrison, Mike Garland, Neil Miles **Est.** 1990 **Dozens** 30 000 **Vyds** 11ha

The Rockcliffe winery and vineyard business, formerly known as Matilda's Estate, is owned by citizen of the world Steve Hall. The wine ranges echo local surf place names, headed by Rockcliffe itself but extending to Third Reef and Quarram Rocks. Over the years, Rockcliffe has won more than its fair share of trophies and gold and silver medals in wine shows. Exports to the UK, Canada, Malaysia, Singapore, Thailand, Japan and Taiwan. (JH)

Nautica Chardonnay 2019, Great Southern At this stage, the tightly coiled acidity that is achieved so effortlessly in Frankland, in combination with the taut linearity of clone 96 have joined forces to create a wine of singular, javelin-like speed, ferocity and direction. This will come into its own in time, once the fruit and acid have softened together, however right now it is a formidable thing. The component that has undergone mlf goes a long way towards softening the impact, and is most appreciated. Screw cap. 13% alc. RATING 91 DRINK 2022–2032 $100 EL

Zi No Zinfandel Nouveau 2021, Western Australia Super-vibrant in the glass and in the mouth, this drinks like spiced lolly water. No hard edges, and just enough interest and minerality to make one think, 'hey, I might just put this in the fridge for a while.' Fun, flirty summer drinking here. Limited release. Screw cap. 13.5% alc. RATING 90 DRINK 2021–2023 $35 EL

Third Reef Chardonnay 2020, Denmark Citrus blossom, beach sand, nectarine, green apple, cheesecloth and toasty oak spice. In the mouth the wine is peachy, creamy, round and soft. Flowing, formless and plush, with plenty of pleasure and flavour. Screw cap. 12.5% alc. RATING 90 DRINK 2021–2028 $30 EL

Third Reef Rosé 2021, Great Southern RATING 88 DRINK 2021–2022 $28 EL

Single Site Riesling 2021, Great Southern RATING 88 DRINK 2021–2031 $40 EL

Rogers & Rufus

40 Eden Valley Road, Angaston, SA 5353 **Region** Barossa Valley
T (08) 8561 3200 **www**.rogersandrufus.com **Winemaker** Sam Wigan **Est.** 2009
This is a decidedly under-the-bedcover partnership between Robert Hill-Smith and his immediate family, and Rupert and Jo Clevely – Rupert is the former Veuve Clicquot director in Australia but now runs gastro pub group Geronimo Inns in London. Late in 2008, the Hill-Smiths and Clevelys decided (in their words) 'to do something fun together with a serious dip at Euro-styled dry and savoury delicate rosé using 3 site-specific, old, low-yielding, dry-grown grenache sites from the Barossa floor'. (JH)

Grenache of Barossa Rosé 2021, Barossa Valley Bright raspberry, cranberry and redcurrant notes with a splash of strawberries and cream for good measure. A touch of cream, soft spice and white flowers come in on the palate which finishes dry and moreish. Screw cap. 11.5% alc. RATING 89 DRINK 2021-2025 $23 DB

Rogue Vintner

324 Koornang Road, Carnegie, Vic 3163 (postal) **Region** Various
T 0423 216 632 **www**.roguevintner.com **Winemaker** Matt Herde **Est.** 2019
Dozens 1500
A multi-regional wine brand created and led by wine marketer Matt Herde, sourced from regions including Langhorne Creek, McLaren Vale, the Great Southern and Margaret River. Exports to the US and Norway. (EL)

Permission to Pivot Cabernet Sauvignon 2020, Great Southern This is sweet-fruited and tannic, a devilish combination, holding both shape and form all the way through the finish. Nicely handled. Screw cap. 14.5% alc. RATING 92 DRINK 2022-2032 $28 EL

Permission to Pivot L.S.D. Riesling 2021, Great Southern RATING 89 DRINK 2022-2025 $23 EL

Rogues Lane Vineyard

370 Lower Plenty Road, Viewbank, Vic 3084 (postal) **Region** Heathcote
T 0413 528 417 **www**.rogueslane.com.au **Winemaker** Wild Duck Creek (Liam Anderson) **Est.** 1995 **Dozens** 240 **Vyds** 3.2ha
Philip Faure grew up in South Africa and studied agriculture at Stellenbosch University. After migrating to Australia and spending some time in the IT industry, Philip found his way to Heathcote, purchasing Rogues Lane Vineyard in 2015. The low-yielding vineyard, planted in 1995 and made up of 95% shiraz and 5% malbec, has seen 'an enormous amount of work'. Philip produced his first wine in '17. (JH)

Shiraz 2019, Heathcote Makes a statement upfront about the power and intensity of Heathcote shiraz. It has to be said that it's a positive thing to behold in the glass, even at 15% alcohol, because it remains in balance. Blueberry, red fruits and spiced plums join on a palate that is ripe, luscious and totally mouth-filling. Woody spice and oak play a supportive background role. A long life awaits. Screw cap. 15% alc. RATING 90 DRINK 2021-2029 $50 JP

Ros Ritchie Wines

Magnolia House, 190 Mount Buller Road, Mansfield, 3722 **Region** Upper Goulburn
T 0448 900 541 **www**.rosritchiewines.com **Open** Fri 5-8, w'ends & public hols 11-4
Winemaker Ros Ritchie **Est.** 2008 **Dozens** 2000 **Vyds** 7ha
Ros Ritchie was winemaker at the Ritchie family's Delatite winery from 1981 to 2006, but moved on to establish her own winery with husband John in '08 on a vineyard near Mansfield. They became shareholders in Barwite Vineyards in '12 (planted to chardonnay, pinot noir, riesling and pinot gris) and in '14 established their new winery there. Apart from gewürztraminer (grown at Dead Man's Hill Vineyard), they work with local growers, foremost

the Kinlock, McFadden, Timbertop and Baxendale vineyards, the last planted by the very experienced viticulturist Jim Baxendale (and wife Ruth) high above the King River Valley. All vineyards are managed with minimal spray regimes. The cellar door is located at the historic Magnolia House at Mansfield, open on select weekends, hosting seasonal wine dinners and special events. (JH)

ΨΨΨΨΨ **Barwite Vineyard Riesling 2021, Upper Goulburn** Ros Ritchie established her early reputation on the almost fragile beauty of her rieslings. Super-cool-climate riesling remains one of her great strengths. Longevity is assured with the '21 with its filigree-fine lemony acidity a firm basis for floral citrus blossom, lime and lemon aromas and a palate that is crisp, dry and imbedded with a gentle spice which lifts the whole wine. Screw cap. 11.9% alc. RATING 95 DRINK 2022–2031 $27 JP ✪

ΨΨΨΨΨ **Devil's River Cabernet Merlot 2019, Upper Goulburn** RATING 93 DRINK 2022–2030 $38 JP
Dead Man's Hill Vineyard Gewürztraminer 2021, Upper Goulburn RATING 92 DRINK 2022–2026 $16 JP ✪
Dead Man's Hill Vineyard Reserve Gewürztraminer 2019, Upper Goulburn RATING 92 DRINK 2022–2026 $22 JP ✪
Cuvée 2015, Upper Goulburn RATING 90 $40 JP
Dead Man's Hill Vineyard Gewürztraminer 2016, Upper Goulburn RATING 90 DRINK 2022–2024 $29 JP

Rosabrook Margaret River Wines   ★★★★

1390 Rosa Brook Road, Rosabrook WA 6285 **Region** Margaret River
T (08) 9368 4555 **www.rosabrook.com.au Winemaker** Severine Logan
Viticulturist Murray Edmonds **Est.** 1980 **Dozens** 12 000 **Vyds** 25ha
The original Rosabrook estate vineyards were established between 1984 and '96. In later years Rosabrook relocated to a more eastern part of the Margaret River wine region. Warm days and cool nights, influenced by the ocean, result in slow, mild-ripening conditions. Exports to the US, Sweden, the UAE, Japan and Hong Kong. (JH)

ΨΨΨΨΨ **Lamarque Reserve Sauvignon Blanc 2020, Margaret River** If you've ever had the pleasure of meeting winemaker Severine Logan, you will encounter a feisty, uncompromising and whipcrack smart French woman – her way is evident in this wine. This is long, expertly constructed and complex, with a saline acid thread woven through every aspect of the fruit. Super-smart wine here. Screw cap. 13% alc. RATING 94 DRINK 2021–2030 $28 EL ✪

ΨΨΨΨΨ **Shiraz 2020, Margaret River** RATING 93 DRINK 2021–2027 $26 EL ✪
Dear Father Reserve Cabernet Sauvignon 2019, Margaret River RATING 93 DRINK 2021–2031 $35 EL
Single Vineyard Estate Chardonnay 2017, Margaret River RATING 92 DRINK 2020–2030 $45 EL
Rosé 2021, Margaret River RATING 91 DRINK 2021–2022 $26 EL
Chardonnay 2021, Margaret River RATING 90 DRINK 2021–2026 $26 EL

Rosby   ★★★☆

122 Strikes Lane, Mudgee, NSW 2850 **Region** Mudgee
T 0419 429 918 **www.rosby.com.au Open** Thurs–Mon 10–4 **Winemaker** Tim Stevens
Viticulturist Gerald Norton-Knight **Est.** 1995 **Dozens** 1500 **Vyds** 8ha
Gerald and Kay Norton-Knight have shiraz and cabernet sauvignon established on what is a truly unique site in Mudgee. Many vignerons like to think that their vineyard has special qualities, but in this instance the belief is well based. The vineyard is situated in a small valley with unusual red basalt over a quartz gravel structure, encouraging deep root growth, making the use of water far less critical than normal. Tim Stevens of Huntington Estate has purchased some of the ample production and makes the Rosby wines. A rammed-earth cellar door has

recently been completed at Rosby and there is an art gallery and sculpture garden onsite, too. (JH)

ΥΥΥΥΥ Cabernet Sauvignon 2019, Mudgee Hand harvested. French oak (25% new). Things done right. Full weighted, with strong varietal traits edging their way across a beam of mocha/cedar oak: cassis, mulberry leaf, mint, sage and mulch. Honest, solid drinking. Screw cap. 14.2% alc. RATING 90 DRINK 2021-2028 $40 NG

Rosenthal Wines   ★★★★☆

24 Rockford Street, Denmark, WA 6333 **Region** Great Southern
T 0432 312 918 **www.**rosenthalwines.com.au **Winemaker** Luke Eckersley, Coby Ladwig
Est. 2001 **Dozens** 35 000 **Vyds** 40ha
The original Rosenthal Vineyard (Springfield Park) was established in 1997 just north of Manjimup, by Dr John Rosenthal. In 2012 Coby Ladwig and Luke Eckersley acquired the business and relocated it to Mount Barker. Both have a sound knowledge of vineyards throughout the southwest of WA. The fruit for Rosenthal wines is sourced from their leased vineyard in Mount Barker, plus growers in Frankland River and Pemberton. Exports to the UK, India and the Philippines. (JH)

ΥΥΥΥΥ Collector Cabernet Sauvignon 2020, Mount Barker Intensely ripe, muscular cabernet here. The fruit shows a spectrum of blood plum, salted blackberries, chocolate-coated licorice, raspberry, damson and szechuan peppercorns. The tannins trail out over a long finish, showing its capacity to age in the cellar. If you choose to drink this in the short term (perfectly valid: the fruit is beautiful), you must decant it, to afford it every opportunity to open up. Screw cap. 14.4% alc. RATING 95 DRINK 2022-2037 $90 EL
Richings Chardonnay 2021, Pemberton This is nice. Super-saline and slippery; salted pineapple, just-ripe yellow peach, freshly picked and muddled curry leaves and red apples. On the palate there's a lemon-oil and cheesecloth character, making for sophisticated, soothing and engaging drinking. Screw cap. 13.3% alc. RATING 94 DRINK 2021-2031 $60 EL
Richings Cabernet Sauvignon 2020, Frankland River Chocolatey oak cups the black and red fruit. The carriage of flavour across the mouth is aided in no small part by the very fine, pervasive tannins. The wine is plump, savoury and a little bit chewy – all good things. Its greatest days are ahead of it. Screw cap. 14.5% alc. RATING 94 DRINK 2021-2036 $60 EL
Collector Chardonnay 2020, Mount Barker Sophisticated and powerful, this has rich tropical fruit, underpinned by green-apple acidity. Guava, salted pineapple and a slice of kiwi, along with that salivating curry-leaf character that comes from solids in the ferment. Lovely stuff. Screw cap. 12.9% alc. RATING 94 DRINK 2022-2029 $90 EL

ΥΥΥΥΥ Richings Riesling 2021, Mount Barker RATING 93 DRINK 2021-2036 $35 EL
The Marker Pinot Noir 2021, Pemberton RATING 91 DRINK 2022-2028 $40 EL
Richings Shiraz 2020, Frankland River RATING 91 DRINK 2021-2028 $60 EL

Rosily Vineyard   ★★★★☆

871 Yelverton Road, Wilyabrup, WA 6284 **Region** Margaret River
T (08) 9755 6336 **www.**rosily.com.au **Open** Sat or by appt **Winemaker** Peter Stanlake
Est. 1994 **Dozens** 6000 **Vyds** 12.28ha
Ken Allan and Mick Scott acquired the Rosily Vineyard site in 1994 and the vineyard was planted over 3 years to sauvignon blanc, semillon, chardonnay, cabernet sauvignon, merlot, shiraz, grenache and cabernet franc. The first crops were sold to other makers in the region, but by '99 Rosily had built a 120t capacity winery. It has gone from strength to strength, all of its estate-grown grapes being vinified under the Rosily Vineyard label, the wines substantially over-delivering for their prices. The vineyard was certified organic (ACO) in May '17. (JH)

🍷🍷🍷🍷🍷 **Reserve Chardonnay 2020, Margaret River** Golden in the glass; tropical and rich in the mouth. This is layered with yellow peach, red apple skins, curry leaf and loads of brine ... an interesting white currant character and a hint of salted pear. The finish is decidedly salty – a telltale sign that we're in Margaret River, baby. Very smart; a nod to the more opulent styles that are possible in the region, that are increasingly rare. Screw cap. 13% alc. RATING 95 DRINK 2022-2032 $60 EL

Reserve Cabernet Sauvignon 2019, Margaret River This is supple, elegant and spicy, with layers of raspberry compote, black licorice, pomegranate and blackberry. The oak and fruit are perfectly in balance here, the overall effect being very smooth and silky, moving to willowy. These '19s may not live as long as some of the neighbouring vintages, but they will be widely loved for their perfume, class and poise. Screw cap. 14% alc. RATING 94 DRINK 2022-2038 $60 EL

🍷🍷🍷🍷🍷 **Chardonnay 2021, Margaret River** RATING 92 DRINK 2022-2027 $28 EL
Cabernet Sauvignon 2019, Margaret River RATING 92 DRINK 2022-2032 $28 EL
Semillon 2021, Margaret River RATING 90 DRINK 2022-2028 $28 EL
The Cartographer 2020, Margaret River RATING 90 DRINK 2022-2032 $25 EL

Ross Hill Wines ★★★★★

134 Wallace Lane, Orange, NSW 2800 **Region** Orange
T (02) 6365 3223 **www.**rosshillwines.com.au **Open** 7 days 10.30–5 **Winemaker** Luke Steele **Viticulturist** Scott Burke, Peter Robson **Est.** 1994 **Dozens** 25 000 **Vyds** 18.2ha
Peter and Terri Robson planted chardonnay, merlot, sauvignon blanc, cabernet franc, cabernet sauvignon and pinot noir on north-facing slopes of the Griffin Road Vineyard in 1994. In '07 their son James and his wife Chrissy joined the business and the Wallace Lane Vineyard (pinot noir, sauvignon blanc and pinot gris) was planted. The vines are now mature and the winery was NCOS Certified Carbon Neutral in '13. The Barrel & Larder School of Wine and Food (WSET Levels 1 and 2) operates from the extended cellar door. Exports to Germany, Singapore and Hong Kong. (JH)

🍷🍷🍷🍷🍷 **The Griffin Cabernet Sauvignon Merlot Cabernet Franc 2018, Orange** An archetypal bordeaux blend, treated with empathy and respect. They are not always synergistic, my heart tells my brain. But there is both soul and intelligence here. Mid weighted. Digestible. The oak and acid meld, a finely balanced lattice across which cassis, sage, mint, mulberry leaf and a smattering of garden herb are splayed. This is a lovely wine that will benefit with an aggressive decant or extended cellaring. Screw cap. 14.5% alc. RATING 94 DRINK 2022-2033 $95 NG

🍷🍷🍷🍷🍷 **Pinnacle Series Griffin Road Vineyard Sauvignon Blanc 2021, Orange** RATING 93 DRINK 2021-2026 $35 NG
Pinnacle Series Pinot Gris 2021, Orange RATING 93 DRINK 2021-2025 $35 NG
Pinnacle Series Griffin Road Vineyard Shiraz 2019, Orange RATING 92 DRINK 2021-2029 $50 NG
Maya Chardonnay 2021, Orange RATING 91 DRINK 2021-2025 $25 NG
Lily Sauvignon Blanc 2021, Orange RATING 90 DRINK 2021-2022 $25 NG
Monocle Riesling 2021, Orange RATING 90 DRINK 2021-2027 $30 NG

Rouleur ★★★★☆

80 Laurens Street, North Melbourne, Vic 3051 **Region** Various
T 0419 100 929 **www.**rouleurwine.com **Open** By appt **Winemaker** Matthew East
Est. 2015 **Dozens** 2500
Owner Matt East's interest in wine began at an early age while he was growing up in the Yarra Valley and watching his father plant a vineyard in Coldstream. Between Feb '99 and Dec '15 his day job was in sales and marketing, culminating in his appointment in '11 as national sales

manager for Wirra Wirra (which he had joined in '08). Following his retirement from that position, he set in motion the wheels of Rouleur. He lives in Melbourne, with the Yarra in easy striking distance for sourcing fruit and making wine (at Yering Farm in Coldstream). He also makes wines from McLaren Vale, with that fruit cold-freighted to Coldstream. Back in Melbourne he has transformed a dilapidated milk bar in North Melbourne into his inner-city cellar door. Exports to Hong Kong, Singapore and Switzerland. (JH)

ㅜㅜㅜㅜㅜ **Chardonnay 2021, Yarra Valley** A wine with textural verve and phenolic persuasion. The oak, beautifully appointed. Candied quince, cherry plum, tangerine and chalk. Racy, yet chewy and saliva inducing. This is a delicious wine that retains freshness without sacrificing personality. Screw cap. 12.9% alc. RATING 95 DRINK 2022-2030 $34 NG ✪
Grenache 2020, McLaren Vale 50% whole bunches delivering whiffs of amaro, sandalwood and mescal. Yet this spicy, herbal, campfire element melds impeccably with the sapid red cherry succulence, fecund strawberry, white pepper and clove to follow. A lovely wine. Best drunk on the earlier side such is the bunchy pinosity, but the tannins are lithe and sinuous, serving to corral any excess and drive a good 5 years of cellaring. Screw cap. 14.3% alc. RATING 94 DRINK 2021-2026 $33 NG

ㅜㅜㅜㅜㅜ **Strawberry Fields Pinot Meunier 2021, Yarra Valley** RATING 93 DRINK 2022-2025 $34 NG
Shiraz 2020, McLaren Vale RATING 93 DRINK 2021-2026 $33 NG
Pinot Noir 2021, Yarra Valley RATING 92 DRINK 2022-2030 $34 NG

Rowlee   ★★★★

19 Lake Canobolas Road, Nashdale, NSW 2800 **Region** Orange
T (02) 6365 3047 **www.**rowleewines.com.au **Open** Wed–Sat 10–5 **Winemaker** Nicole Samodol, James Manny **Est.** 2000 **Dozens** 7000 **Vyds** 8ha
Rowlee's vineyard (chardonnay, pinot noir, pinot gris, riesling, sauvignon blanc, gewürztraminer and Italian varieties arneis and nebbiolo) was planted over 20 years ago by Nik and Deonne Samodol in the high-altitude (950m) cool climate of Orange. Their daughter, Nicole Samodol, and her partner James Manny 'combine European wine growing heritage with New World practices' to make the wines in 3 ranges: Rowlee, Single Vineyard and R-Series. The wines are available from the cellar door, specialist wine retailers and restaurants. (JH)

ㅜㅜㅜㅜㅜ **Single Vineyard Arneis 2021, Orange** Green apple skin, lime and citrus blossom. Fresh and mid weighted of mouthfeel. Versatile by virtue of texture and overall neutrality which, in this instance, is a positive. Meaning a wine that does not get in the way with food or vibe. The acidity is a bit shrill, but very pleasing drinking in all. Screw cap. 13.3% alc. RATING 93 DRINK 2022-2026 $38 NG
Single Vineyard Chardonnay 2021, Orange Barrel fermented under the aegis of what feel like ambient yeasts. Stirred regularly, conferring an element of roasted hazelnut confit to nougatine, glazed quince and peaches in syrup. At once slender, taut and flinty; but on the other hand, equipped with plenty of flavour. Fine punchy length. Screw cap. 12.6% alc. RATING 93 DRINK 2022-2028 $50 NG
Single Vineyard Pinot Gris 2021, Orange Good gris. Potentially very good. If only the weight and extract was notched up a degree to embrace ripeness and phenolics, over acidity. The oak element evinces structural mettle and some textural interest. A mid-weight wine that yearns to be drunk at a heavier-weight class. Marzipan, spiced pear and baked apple. An undesirable sweet/sour sauvignon-like tang. Solid length. On the cusp of real merit. Screw cap. 13% alc. RATING 92 DRINK 2022-2027 $35 NG
Single Vineyard Pinot Noir 2021, Orange A pallid ruby segues to high-toned scents of red cherry, root spice, bergamot and ume, with a sinewy realm of tannins, gentle but spiky, suggestive of early harvesting. These find confluence with high-quality French barriques (9 months). A pleasant wine with plenty of verve and easy-drinking appeal. Screw cap. 12.4% alc. RATING 92 DRINK 2022-2026 $50 NG

Single Vineyard Gewürztraminer 2021, Orange The scents of lychee, frangipani and citrus blossom here are gorgeous. And yet the framework is delicate and fragile, verging on feeble. This wine needs to be brought to its natural leitmotif: one of unctuous texture, minimal acidity and full-throttle flavour. It is on these attributes, chew and amp, that great gewürz. rides. A pretty halfway house. Screw cap. 11.9% alc. RATING 91 DRINK 2022–2024 $35 NG
Single Vineyard Riesling 2021, Orange Nothing particularly striking about the winemaking, although the wine differentiates itself by virtue of its juicy acidity and balletic poise. Scents of tarte tatin, crystallised ginger and jasmine. Prosaic, but gentle on the gums and effortless. Palpably natural, the skein of acidity tows a dainty texture to a long, seamless finish. Screw cap. 11.8% alc. RATING 91 DRINK 2022–2030 $35 NG

Rudderless Wines

Victory Hotel, Main South Road, Sellicks Hill, SA 5174 **Region** McLaren Vale
T (08) 8556 3083 **www**.rudderlesswines.com.au **Open** 7 days **Winemaker** Peter Fraser, Shelley Torresan **Viticulturist** Jock Harvey **Est.** 2004 **Dozens** 550 **Vyds** 2ha
It's a long story how Doug Govan, owner of the Victory Hotel (circa 1858), came to choose the name Rudderless for his vineyard. The vineyard is planted on 2 levels (in '99 and '03) to a complex mix of shiraz, graciano, grenache, malbec, mataro and viognier. It surrounds the hotel, which is situated in the foothills of the Southern Willunga Escarpment as it falls into the sea. The wines are mostly sold through the Victory Hotel, where the laid-back Doug keeps a low profile. (JH)

🍷🍷🍷🍷 **Grenache Shiraz Mataro 2020, McLaren Vale** A fine meld of Mediterranean goodness. Sumptuous, forward and spicy. Spiced cherry, star anise, rhubarb, salumi, rooibos and sangria. Polished, smooth and impeccably weighted. Poised to please a crowd. A skein of spicy freshness keeping the finish long and intriguing. Screw cap. 13.8% alc. RATING 93 DRINK 2022–2028 $35 NG
Sellicks Hill Malbec 2020, McLaren Vale A polished, floral and medium-bodied wine with a frame of immaculately applied cedar oak. Violet, boysenberry and a sluice of cherry liqueur. The finish, shimmering with cedar, vanilla and pithy, early picked blue fruits. Already delicious. Screw cap. 13.5% alc. RATING 92 DRINK 2022–2032 $35 NG

Running With Bulls

40 Eden Valley Road, Angaston SA 5353 **Region** Barossa Valley
T (08) 8561 3200 **www**.runningwithbulls.com.au **Winemaker** Sam Wigan **Est.** 2008
Dozens 19 000
Running With Bulls is the Hill-Smith Family's foray into value- and flavour-packed, Spanish-inspired wines under the helmsmanship of winemaker Sam Wigan. These 'alternative' (or 'appropriate' varieties) are well suited to the Barossa Valley. Running With Bulls have consistently released excellent wines every year – full of character and inherent drinkability while remaining strong to their Barossa roots. Think contemporary riffs on tempranillo and garnacha (grenache) and you are on the right track. They suggest their red wines, with their light tannin loads, can be enjoyed in the warmer months. (DB)

🍷🍷🍷🍷 **Garnacha 2021, Barossa Valley** A pinot-esque and wonderfully perfumed Barossa garnacha (grenache) with vibrant aromas of red and yellow plum, mulberry, watermelon, strawberry and raspberry, with hints of Asian spice, ginger cake, cola and violets. Fleshy and juicy, with a spacious mouthfeel, loads of crunchy red and blue fruits, abundant spice, bright line and gypsum-like tannins. Super-value juicy drinking. Screw cap. 14.5% alc. RATING 92 DRINK 2021–2026 $23 DB ✪
Tempranillo 2021, Barossa Valley Bright red purple in the glass, with oodles of spicy, plummy fruit immediately jumping out. Hints of brown spices, cola, licorice, blueberry danish, maraschino cherries and earth. Plenty of bright acid

crunch, tight, gritty tannin grip and cola-infused back fruits on the medium-length finish. Screw cap. 14% alc. RATING 91 DRINK 2022-2028 $23 DB ✪
Tempranillo 2020, Barossa Valley Dark plum and black cherry with hints of dark chocolate, deep spice, cola, pressed flowers and turned earth. Plenty of moody dark fruits, substantial grainy tannin and a finish that sings of earthen tones and dark spice. Screw cap. 14% alc. RATING 90 DRINK 2021-2026 $23 DB

Russell & Suitor

1866 Pipers River Road, Lower Turners Marsh, Tas 7267 **Region** Various
T 0400 684 654 **www.**russellandsuitor.com.au **Winemaker** Alex Russell
Viticulturist Alex Russell **Dozens** 6000 **Vyds** 14.43
Winemaker and owner Alex Russell is based in Tasmania's Pipers River, where he produces the cool-climate varieties of chardonnay, pinot noir, riesling and sauvignon blanc, under the label Russell & Suitor. He also has a significant focus on alternative varieties under his Alejandro, Franca's Vineyard and Plums & Roses labels (saperavi, durif, vermentino, lagrein, arneis, nero d'avola, montepulciano, etc), making an extensive range of wines out of his Renmark property in South Australia. Russell began his winemaking career at Angove, Zilzie and the Riverland Vine Improvement Committee nursery in the early 2000s, which led him to Spain, where he worked with a colleague from his Zilzie days. This inspired in Russell a need to explore varieties usually planted in Australia for the purposes of fortified wine production; hence Alejandro was born. (EL)

🍷🍷🍷🍷🍷 **Alejandro Sagrantino 2021, Victoria** Juicy, jubey, fleshy and pert, with very fine, talcy tannins that hold the whole affair together. Raspberry and rhubarb. The acidity is the star here – it spears through the mid-weight fruit and props the tent up with freshness. Nice. Screw cap. 14.5% alc. RATING 91 DRINK 2021-2027 $24 EL
Alejandro Saperavi 2020, Murray Darling The density and saturation of colour in this glass is precisely what you'd expect of a grape with flesh as dark as its skin. Saperavi hails from Georgia originally, but there are small plantings here in Australia. This is an unencumbered expression of black fruit, sweet vanilla pod, blackcurrant pastille, jubes and a hint of licorice. It's floral, pretty and longer than expected. Red apples, perhaps? Quite lovely! Screw cap. 15% alc. RATING 91 DRINK 2021-2026 $24 EL
Son of a Bull Riesling 2021, Tasmania A late-harvested riesling of tremendous concentration, energised by the tension of Pipers River in the cool, slow ripening 2021 season. With a bright straw-green hue, it's brimming with baked apple, spice and lime. Phenolic bitterness marks a finish of medium persistence. Screw cap. 12% alc. RATING 90 DRINK 2022-2026 $29 TS

🍷🍷🍷🍷 **Plums & Roses 2021, South Eastern Australia** RATING 88 DRINK 2021-2024 $18 EL
Alejandro Durif 2020, Riverland RATING 88 DRINK 2022-2027 $24 EL

Rusty Mutt

PO Box 724 MSC, Torrens Park, SA 5062 **Region** McLaren Vale
T (08) 7228 6183 **www.**rustymutt.com.au **Winemaker** Scott Heidrich **Est.** 2009
Dozens 1500
Scott Heidrich lived in the shadow of Geoff Merrill for 20 years, but has partially emerged into the sunlight with his virtual micro-winery. Back in 2006, close friends and family (Nicole and Alan Francis, Stuart Evans, David Lipman and Phil Cole) persuaded Scott to take advantage of the wonderful quality of the grapes that year and make a small batch of shiraz. The wines are made at a friend's micro-winery in McLaren Flat. The name Rusty Mutt comes from Scott's interest in Chinese astrology and feng shui; Scott was born in the year of the dog with the dominant element being metal, hence Rusty Mutt. What the ownership group doesn't drink is sold through fine wine retailers and selected restaurants, with a small amount exported to the UK. (JH)

ΨΨΨΨ♀ **Original Shiraz 2018, McLaren Vale** A rich, highly traditional shiraz that will
have many fans. Dark brooding fruits, charred and sweet mocha-smoky oak and
an earthy scent of crushed black rocks and menthol. Long of finish by force of
personality alone. Screw cap. 14.5% alc. RATING 90 DRINK 2022-2028 $35 NG

Rymill Coonawarra   ★★★★☆

110 Clayfield Road, Glenroy, SA 5277 **Region** Coonawarra
T (08) 8736 5001 **www**.rymill.com.au **Open** 7 days 10–5 **Winemaker** Lewis White
Viticulturist Martin Wirper **Est.** 1974 **Dozens** 25 000 **Vyds** 140ha
The Rymills are descendants of John Riddoch and have long owned some of the finest
Coonawarra soil, upon which they have grown grapes since 1970. In '16, the Rymill family
sold the business, but the management, vineyard and winery teams remained in place, with
new capital financing improvements in the vineyards and cellar. The winery building also
houses the cellar door and art exhibitions, which, together with viewing platforms over the
winery, make it a must-see destination for tourists. Exports to all major markets. (JH)

ΨΨΨΨΨ **The Surveyor Cabernet Sauvignon 2019, Coonawarra** Dark, brooding
and resinous, the tannins are omnipresent and scattered across a bedrock of black
berries and exotic spice. It's all going on here. Diam. 14.5% alc. RATING 95
DRINK 2022-2042 $90 EL

Classic Release Cabernet Sauvignon 2019, Coonawarra Blackberry
pie (crust and all), licorice, cassis, star anise, bramble, garden mint, cigar box and
tobacco leaf. In the mouth the wine is ultra-concentrated, firm and structured.
This pays homage to both the variety and the region. It offers truth from every
angle, leaving no lingering doubt about where this could possibly have come from,
and what grape it is. It has a long life ahead of it. Screw cap. 15% alc. RATING 94
DRINK 2022-2036 $32 EL

Classic Release Shiraz 2019, Coonawarra This is a wonderful wine. The
black fruit is concentrated and dense, packed into the oak structure. It's all there,
but it's in balance. The tannins are a highlight through the finish: they're fine
and chalky, and provide a bit of chew and bounce. Nice. Screw cap. 14.5% alc.
RATING 94 DRINK 2021-2028 $32 EL

ΨΨΨΨ♀ **Riddoch Run Block 1 Cabernet Sauvignon 2019, Coonawarra** RATING 92
DRINK 2022-2032 $60 EL

SHZ 2020, Coonawarra RATING 90 DRINK 2022-2027 $25 EL

St Aidan   ★★★★

754 Ferguson Road, Dardanup, WA 6236 **Region** Geographe
T (08) 9728 3007 **www**.saintaidan.com.au **Open** Mon–Fri 11–4, Sat–Sun 11–5
Winemaker Mark Messenger (Contract) **Viticulturist** Mary Smith **Est.** 1996
Dozens 1500 **Vyds** 2.6ha
Phil and Mary Smith purchased their property at Dardanup in 1991, a 20-min drive from
the Bunbury hospital where Phil works. They first ventured into Red Globe table grapes,
planting 1ha in '94–05, followed by 1ha of mandarins and oranges. With this experience, and
with Mary completing a TAFE viticulture course, they extended their horizons by planting
1ha each of cabernet sauvignon and chardonnay in '97, 0.5ha of muscat in '01, and semillon
and sauvignon blanc thereafter. (JH)

ΨΨΨΨ♀ **Ferguson Tempranillo 2020, Geographe** An eminently drinkable, crowd-
pleasing tempranillo, with just enough tannic structure and spice complexity to
keep things interesting. Mulberries, hung deli meat, some star anise and a load of
raspberry, licorice and dark choc. Really smart. Screw cap. 14.5% alc. RATING 91
DRINK 2022-2028 $25 EL

Ferguson Cabernet Sauvignon 2019, Geographe Cabernet from
Geographe has a distinct chocolate character to it, making for creamy, round,
comforting cabernets. This is no exception to that rule. The fruit is weighted by

blackcurrant, mulberry, black tea, licorice and raspberry, backed by toasty oak. Welcoming. Screw cap. 14% alc. RATING 91 DRINK 2021-2028 $35 EL

🍷🍷🍷🍷 **Sparkling Chardonnay 2019, Geographe** RATING 89 $28 EL
Chardonnay 2020, Geographe RATING 89 DRINK 2022-2027 $35 EL
Cassie Moscato 2021, Geographe RATING 88 DRINK 2022-2023 $21 EL

Saint & Scholar
Maximilian's Restaurant, 15 Onkaparinga Valley Road, Verdun, SA 5245
Region Adelaide Hills
T (08) 8388 7777 www.saintandscholar.com.au **Open** Fri–Sun 11–4
Winemaker Stephen Dew **Est.** 2018 **Dozens** 12000 **Vyds** 50ha
Owned by Ed Peter, Dirk Wiedmann and Reid Bosward, Saint and Scholar is a substantial newcomer with 50ha of shiraz, pinot noir, pinot gris, chardonnay and sauvignon blanc. It has a large cellar door in Maximilian's Restaurant in Verdun. Winemaker Stephen Dew is the Saint, Reid Bosward (winemaker at Kaesler) is the Scholar. Stephen Dew has worked vintages at Domaine Prieure-Roch owned by Henri Frederic Roch, a co-director of Domaine de la Romanée-Conti (by virtue of the Roch family ownership of 50% of Domaine). Henri Frederic is a natural winemaker and having tasted Roch's wines in his winery in Burgundy, I (James) can attest that his wines reflect his beliefs. Reid Bosward has worked 30 harvests over 25 years in Bordeaux (the Lurton family), Minervois, Moldova, South Africa and Spain. He is the Scholar and absolutely not a natural winemaker, just a very good one. Exports to all major markets (JH)

🍷🍷🍷🍷🍷 **Pinot Gris 2021, Adelaide Hills** Adelaide Hills producers are talking up '21 as a 'once in a lifetime vintage'. Lightly spiced and delicately flavoured with pear, apple and lingering honeysuckle. There's texture and a hint of savouriness enlivened by fresh acidity. All spiced up and ready to meet its food match. Screw cap. 13% alc. RATING 90 DRINK 2021-2025 $25 JP

🍷🍷🍷🍷 **Sauvignon Blanc 2021, Adelaide Hills** RATING 88 DRINK 2021-2024 $25 JP
Pinot Noir 2019, Adelaide Hills RATING 88 DRINK 2021-2025 $30 JP

St Hallett
St Hallett Road, Tanunda, SA 5352 **Region** Barossa Valley
T (08) 8563 7070 www.sthallett.com.au **Open** 7 days 10–5 by appt **Winemaker** Helen McCarthy **Est.** 1944 **Dozens** 210000
St Hallett sources all grapes from within the Barossa GI and is synonymous with the region's icon variety – shiraz. Old Block is the ultra-premium leader of the band (using old-vine grapes from Lyndoch and Eden Valley), supported by Blackwell (Greenock, Ebenezer and Seppeltsfield). The winemaking team continues to explore the geographical, geological and climatic diversity of the Barossa, manifested through individual processing of all vineyards and single-vineyard releases. In '17, St Hallett was acquired by Accolade. Exports to all major markets. (JH)

🍷🍷🍷🍷🍷 **Old Block Shiraz 2017, Barossa** Elegant and perfumed wine, reflecting the cool vintage to best effect. Black cherry and berry, long and supple in the mouth, with some cedary oak and finely wrought tannins. Always a classy wine, the first vintage put St Hallett on the road to where it is today. Screw cap. 14.7% alc. RATING 97 DRINK 2023-2041 $160 JH

🍷🍷🍷🍷🍷 **Blackwell Shiraz 2019, Barossa** Bright-rimmed crimson purple. A perfectly balanced and poised medium-bodied shiraz, with a lustrous, succulent palate and a texture akin to Thai silk, tannins sufficient for the job and no more. Screw cap. 14.5% alc. RATING 96 DRINK 2025-2042 $55 JH ✪
Mighty Ox Shiraz 2019, Barossa From the dry and low-yielding '19 vintage and packaged in a 'Barossa stubby' (a magnum, to the uninitiated), the '19 Mighty Ox provides all you could want from a Barossa shiraz. Plushly fruited with

lashings of satsuma plum and blackberry characters, deep layered spice, turned earth, roasting meats and dark chocolate. It's concentrated, yet there is detail and clarity to its form and a sense that it is very comfortable in its own skin, with a fresh, pure-fruited finish that lingers persistently. Screw cap. 15% alc. RATING 96 DRINK 2021-2035 $210 DB

Higher Earth Syrah 2019, Eden Valley I've been impressed in recent years by the quality of St Hallett's forays into the Eden Valley and their take on syrah from the higher ground. From the dry and low-yielding '19 vintage, the picture is again one of elegance and grace. The fruit is more in the spectrum of black cherry and dark plum, with plentiful spice, purple floral high-tones and crushed-quartz tannins, impressive detail and clarity, and a finish that lingers nicely with memories of cherry and spice. Screw cap. 14.5% alc. RATING 95 DRINK 2021-2035 $60 DB

St Huberts

Cnr Maroondah Highway/St Huberts Road, Coldstream, Vic 3770 **Region** Yarra Valley **T** (03) 5960 7096 **www**.sthuberts.com.au **Open** 7 days 10–5 **Winemaker** Greg Jarratt **Est.** 1966 **Vyds** 20.49ha

The St Huberts of today has a rich 19th-century history, not least in its success at the 1881 Melbourne International Exhibition, which featured every type of agricultural and industrial product. The wine section alone attracted 711 entries. The Emperor of Germany offered a Grand Prize, a silver gilt epergne, for the most meritorious exhibit in the show. A St Huberts wine won the wine section, then competed against objects as diverse as felt hats and steam engines to win the Emperor's Prize, featured on its label for decades thereafter. Like other Yarra Valley wineries, it dropped from sight at the start of the 20th century, was reborn in 1966 and, after several changes of ownership, became part of what today is TWE. The wines are made at Coldstream Hills but have their own, very different, focus. St Huberts is dominated by cabernet and the single-vineyard roussanne. Its grapes come from warmer sites, particularly the valley floor (part owned and part under contract). (JH)

ΨΨΨΨΨ **Pinot Noir 2020, Yarra Valley** Brightly coloured with red fruits and attractive herbal, sage leaf and spice notes. The palate is bright and relaxed with a little sour cherry fruit and gentle barrel-ferment characters, giving this easygoing wine plenty of drink-now appeal. Screw cap. 13% alc. RATING 90 DRINK 2021-2026 $33 PR

ΨΨΨΨ **The Stag Pinot Noir 2020, Yarra Valley** RATING 89 DRINK 2021-2025 $24 PR
The Stag Tempranillo Shiraz 2020, Victoria RATING 88 DRINK 2021-2025 $20 PR

St Hugo

2141 Barossa Valley Way, Rowland Flat, SA 5352 **Region** Barossa Valley **T** (08) 8115 9200 **www**.sthugo.com **Open** Fri–Mon 10.30–4.30 **Winemaker** Peter Munro **Est.** 1983 **Dozens** 50 000 **Vyds** 57ha

This is a stand-alone business within Pernod Ricard, focused on the premium and ultra-premium end of the market, thus differentiating it from Jacob's Creek. There is a restaurant with kitchen garden, and self-catering accommodation is available in a 19th-century stone cottage. Exports to the UK, Singapore and NZ. (JH)

ΨΨΨΨΨ **Barossa Grenache Shiraz Mataro 2021, Barossa Valley** Vivid red purple in the glass, super-ripe plum and blueberry notes are lead by wafts of frangipani over a base of exotic spice, amaro herbs, licorice, earth and cherry danish. A very modern, juicy take on the classic blend, with pure, juicy fruit, tight ripe tannin and a finish that lingers beautifully. It's just great, spicy drinking. Screw cap. 14.5% alc. RATING 96 DRINK 2022-2032 $50 DB ✪

Cabernet Sauvignon 2019, Coonawarra This is massive, the oak a central part of the experience right now. However, at the time of tasting, this wine still has a year and a bit to go before release. The time will be crucial for the ample black and red fruit to soak up that oak, step up on its shoulders and ride the chariot with muscle and power. Concentrated and focused; this will be great in time. The Feb '23 release date: well judged. Screw cap. 14% alc. RATING 96 DRINK 2023-2043 $50 EL ✪

Vetus Purum Cabernet Sauvignon 2015, Coonawarra This is a dense, muscular wine of swathe and swagger. It doesn't hold back on anything at all: fruit volume, oak and intensity are all dialled up to 10. But in this land of saturation and high volume, there is a zen, there is balance, and there is peace. So, if aged cabernet is something you love but don't get to drink often enough (for one reason or another), you might like to try this. Age has hardly made a stamp upon it. Screw cap. 14.2% alc. RATING 96 DRINK 2022-2042 $240 EL

Riesling 2021, Eden Valley The stellar '21 Eden Valley vintage keeps on delivering, with its pristine rieslings packed to the brim with juicy, freshly squeezed lime characters and high tones of Christmas lilies and orange blossom. There is a wonderful velocity to this current release, with the porcelain acidity providing a cracking cadence for the fruit. There's a sapid sense of umami here too; akin to the savoury ache of letting a flake of sea salt dissolve on your tongue. The wine's clarity and drive is most impressive indeed. Screw cap. 11% alc. RATING 95 DRINK 2021-2035 $40 DB

Single Vineyard Cabernet Sauvignon 2018, Coonawarra This intensity, this density of texture, is what put Australia on the map internationally. The way it feels is both comforting and satisfying. It's not made in the modern style of Australian cabernet – it is firmly placed in the old-school – but there is significant charm there. Classical and concentrated, the tannins are so finely knit that the webbing is almost opaque, the fruit caught in it speaks of poached plums, summer figs, blackcurrant pastille and licorice. This will absolutely evolve gracefully in the cellar, but if you're drinking it now you must decant it. Screw cap. 14% alc. RATING 95 DRINK 2022-2037 $80 EL

Barossa Shiraz 2019, Barossa Valley St Hugo has always been one of the most dependable brands on the market for consistency, quality and all-round drinking enjoyment when you creep into that mid-tier price bracket. It again delivers the goods in '19, with a wine featuring wonderfully detailed plummy fruits, cut through with spice, earth and cocoa powder and dotted with floral nuance and softly spoken oak. The tannins are fine and ripe, the fruit is pure and endearing and the finish lingers in a vapor trail of plum, earth and spice. Screw cap. 14.5% alc. RATING 94 DRINK 2021-2035 $50 DB

Single Vineyard Barossa Shiraz 2018, Barossa Valley Deep red purple in the glass. Awash with ripe red and dark plum fruits, blueberry and boysenberry, with notes of purple flowers, spice, chocolate and softly spoken oak. There's a lovely fruit flow and medium-weighted purity to the palate with tight, savoury tannins and an elegant line to the prolonged finish. Screw cap. 14% alc. RATING 94 DRINK 2021-2025 $80 DB

ＹＹＹＹＹ **Cabernet Shiraz 2019, Coonawarra Barossa Valley** RATING 93 DRINK 2021-2032 $50 DB

Chardonnay 2021, Eden Valley RATING 92 DRINK 2022-2026 $40 DB

St Johns Vineyards ★★★★

Unit 3, 2 Smeaton Way, Rockingham WA 6168 **Region** Margaret River
T 0438 668 681 **www.stjohnswine.com.au Winemaker** Andrew Dawson **Est.** 1997
Dozens 70 000 **Vyds** 100ha
St Johns Vineyards (previously Latitude 34 Wine Co) was established in 1997 with their first vineyards in the Blackwood Valley (83ha), followed in '98 by the St Johns Brook Vineyard in Yallingup (37ha). A 1200t winery with temperature-controlled wine storage was built in 2004. The wines are released under the St Johns Brook, Optimus, The Blackwood and Crush labels. Exports to Thailand, the UK, Poland and Hong Kong. (JH)

ŸŸŸŸŸ St Johns Brook Reserve Chardonnay 2020, Margaret River Concentrated and intense, with a veritable orchard of peaches, pears and nectarines, all of it fenced in by briny acidity and toasty oak. Smart. Love the concentration of flavour on the mid palate. Screw cap. 13.5% alc. RATING 94 DRINK 2022-2029 $60 EL
St Johns Brook Reserve Shiraz 2020, Margaret River This is great. The fruit is concentrated and red, littering the palate with raspberry, mulberry and blueberries. The oak is present, it shapes the fruit, and it leaves a trail of flavour through the finish. Very good – quite big, and the length of flavour is long. A lovely wine. Screw cap. 14.5% alc. RATING 94 DRINK 2022-2029 $60 EL

ŸŸŸŸŸ St Johns Brook Reserve Cabernet Sauvignon 2019, Margaret River RATING 92 DRINK 2022-2032 $60 EL
St Johns Brook Single Vineyard Chardonnay 2020, Margaret River RATING 91 DRINK 2022-2029 $34 EL
St Johns Brook Single Vineyard Shiraz 2020, Margaret River RATING 91 DRINK 2021-2027 $34 EL
St Johns Brook Single Vineyard Cabernet Sauvignon 2019, Margaret River RATING 91 DRINK 2021-2031 $34 EL
St Johns Brook Recolte Cabernet Sauvignon 2020, Margaret River RATING 90 DRINK 2021-2027 $24 EL
St Johns Brook Recolte Shiraz 2020, Margaret River RATING 90 DRINK 2021-2027 $24 EL

St Leonards Vineyard ★★★★

St Leonards Road, Wahgunyah, Vic 3687 **Region** Rutherglen
T 1800 021 621 **www.**stleonardswine.com.au **Open** Thurs–Sun 10–5 **Winemaker** Nick Brown, Chloe Earl **Est.** 1860 **Dozens** 3500 **Vyds** 12ha
An old favourite, with a range of premium wines cleverly marketed through an attractive cellar door and bistro at the historic winery on the banks of the Murray. It is run by Eliza Brown (CEO), sister Angela (online communications manager) and brother Nick (vineyard and winery manager). They are perhaps better known as the trio who fulfil the same roles at All Saints Estate. Exports to the US, the Philippines and Hong Kong. (JH)

ŸŸŸŸŸ Cabernet Franc 2021, Rutherglen Captures the grape variety perfectly! The winemaker allows the grape full rein here and the result is a lovely thing to behold and taste. The wine is ablaze in red plum, raspberry and black cherry fruits with a herbal infusion of thyme and pepper, finishing with a dash of rose petal. A long finish, aided and abetted by bright acidity and tannins. More please. Screw cap. 13.5% alc. RATING 92 DRINK 2021-2025 $35 JP
Hip Sip Muscat NV, Rutherglen Smart packaging, hip name and a mighty tasty, fresh and youthful muscat is responsible for reaching out to a younger fortified-drinking audience. A timely reflection on the beauty of the style with an abiding floral charm. Rose oil infiltrates every space with dried fruit, fig and orange peel with a sweet golden syrup harmony. Fresh, lively and a smart price. 350ml. Screw cap. 17.5% alc. RATING 92 $22 JP ✪
Hip Sip Tawny NV, Rutherglen This amber-coloured tawny carries both freshness and richness in flavour: prune, dried fruit, walnut and burnt toffee. Smooth palate texture follows with bright, clean spirit leading the way. 350ml bottle. Vinolok. 17.5% alc. RATING 92 $22 JP ✪

ŸŸŸŸ The Doctor Durif 2019, Rutherglen RATING 89 DRINK 2021-2032 $30 JP
Rosé 2021, Rutherglen RATING 88 DRINK 2021-2024 $30 JP
Shiraz 2017, Rutherglen RATING 88 DRINK 2021-2026 $35 JP

Salena Estate ★★★

837 Bookpurnong Road, Bookpurnong, SA 5333 **Region** Riverland
T (08) 8584 1333 **www.**salenaestate.com.au **Open** Mon–Fri 9–4, Sat–Sun 11.30–4
Winemaker Mark Thwaites **Est.** 1998 **Dozens** 200 000 **Vyds** 208ha

This business encapsulates the once hectic rate of growth across the entire Australian wine industry. Its 1998 crush was 300 tonnes, and by '01 it was processing around 7000 tonnes. It is the venture of Bob and Sylvia Franchitto; the estate named after their daughter. Exports to Canada, Sweden, Indonesia, Taiwan, Singapore, South Korea, Hong Kong and Japan. (JH)

🍷🍷🍷🍷 **Expression Touriga Nacional 2020, Riverland** Cassis, poached plums, warm fruit and super-ripe (close to overripe) characters through the finish. Christmas cake and glacé cherries. Cinnamon. Screw cap. 14.5% alc. RATING 88 DRINK 2022-2026 $30 EL

Salo Wines ★★★★★

28 Dorothy Street, Healesville, Vic 3777 (postal) **Region** Yarra Valley
T (03) 5962 5331 **www**.salowines.com.au **Winemaker** Steve Flamsteed, Dave Mackintosh **Est.** 2008 **Dozens** 250
Business partners Steve Flamsteed and Dave Mackintosh say that Salo means dirty and a little uncouth, which with the Australian sense of humour, can be used as a term of endearment. They wish to keep their wines a little dirty by using hands-off, minimal winemaking to make more gritty, textured wines. Exports to Hong Kong. (JH)

🍷🍷🍷🍷🍷 **Chardonnay 2021, Yarra Valley** A really vibrant green gold. Pure fruited with seductive nashi pear, almond skin and subtle wet rock and gun flint. Gently creamy but with racy, fresh acidity too. It's an excellent combination, making it delicious as a young wine but with the potential to age well too. Tops. Screw cap. 13% alc. RATING 96 DRINK 2022-2028 $40 PR ☉

Salomon Estate ★★★★★

Braeside Road, Finniss, SA 5255 **Region** Southern Fleurieu
T 0417 808 243 **www**.salomonwines.com **Open** By appt **Winemaker** Bert Salomon, Simon White **Viticulturist** Simon White **Est.** 1997 **Dozens** 7000 **Vyds** 12.1ha
Bert Salomon is an Austrian winemaker with a long-established family winery in the Kremstal region, not far from Vienna. He became acquainted with Australia during his time with import company Schlumberger in Vienna; he was the first to import Australian wines (Penfolds) into Austria, in the mid '80s, and later became head of the Austrian Wine Bureau. He was so taken by Adelaide that he moved his family there for the first few months of each year, sending his young children to school and setting in place an Australian red winemaking venture. He is now a full-time travelling winemaker, running the family winery in the Northern Hemisphere vintage and overseeing the making of the Salomon Estate wines. Exports to all major markets. (JH)

🍷🍷🍷🍷🍷 **Finniss River Braeside Vineyard Peninsula Cabernet Sauvignon 2019, Fleurieu** Blackcurrant fruit is joined by notes of oak and a whisper of olive tapenade. The mouthfeel of this elegant and medium-bodied cabernet is superb, its freshness doubtless amplified by its modest alcohol, the tannins likewise as the long finish lingers in the mouth. Screw cap. 13.5% alc. RATING 95 DRINK 2025-2038 $36 JH
Finniss River Sea Eagle Vineyard Peninsula Shiraz 2019, Fleurieu A very expressive bouquet yields immediate waves of licorice, dark earth, leather and black fruits, oak peeping through the curtains. It works very well indeed, picked at (true) optimum maturity, the result a wine of finesse and elegance. Screw cap. 14% alc. RATING 95 DRINK 2025-2039 $40 JH
Wildflower Peninsula Syrah-V 2020, Fleurieu Well, 7.5% viognier certainly lifts the floral notes of the bouquet and takes its vibrant colour right through to the rim. It is an opulent, fleshy wine that coats every corner of the mouth, not for the first time outside the more elegant restraint of some of its siblings. Screw cap. 14.5% alc. RATING 94 DRINK 2024-2035 $32 JH

🍷🍷🍷🍷🍷 **Norwood Peninsula Heritage Red 2020, Fleurieu** RATING 93 DRINK 2024-2034 $26 JH ☉

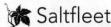 ## Saltfleet

3 Jamieson Street, Moana, SA 5169 **Region** McLaren Vale
T 0427 674 077 **www**.saltfleetwines.com **Winemaker** Jonny Cook, Kyle Egel **Est.** 2021
Dozens 200

Saltfleet is a micro-operation created by a couple of young surfers with their gaze on a future built on the right grapes, rather than the wrong ones. Saltfleet is focused on fruit from lauded sites, non-invasive handling and pulpy, effusively energetic wines with a winning immediacy and mouth-watering deliciousness. The winsome approach is built on hand harvesting, semi-carbonic fermentations smattered with a seasoning of whole bunches, gentle extractions, a short élevage in used wood and minimal adds (other than psychologically reassuring dollops of sulphur dioxide). The results are impressive. (NG)

ŸŸŸŸ♀ Touriga Nacional 2021, McLaren Vale Floral, mid weighted of feel, fleet of freshness and sumptuous of texture. Lilac, boysenberry, white pepper and clove, spruced long across a timbre of gentle oak and maritime saltiness. Crunchy, addictive and beautifully poised to the effect of dangerous drinkability. Screw cap. 14% alc. RATING 92 DRINK 2022–2026 $35 NG

ŸŸŸŸ Grenache 2021, McLaren Vale RATING 89 DRINK 2022–2024 $35 NG

Saltram

Murray Street, Angaston, SA 5353 **Region** Barossa Valley
T (08) 8561 0200 **www**.saltramwines.com.au **Open** Thurs–Mon 10–5 **Winemaker** Alex MacKenzie **Est.** 1859 **Dozens** 150 000

There is no doubt that Saltram has taken strides towards regaining the reputation it held 30 or so years ago. Grape sourcing has come back to the Barossa Valley for the flagship wines. The red wines, in particular, have enjoyed great show success over the past decade with No. 1 Shiraz and Mamre Brook leading the charge. Exports to all major markets. (JH)

ŸŸŸŸŸ Mr Pickwick's Limited Release Particular Tawny NV, Barossa Valley Head-spinning complexity with detailed red fruits, mince pies, baking spice, roasting nuts, candied citrus rind and earth. Incredibly fresh and vivid with a finish that just keeps on going. Just lovely. Cork. 19.5% alc. RATING 96 $75 DB ✪

ŸŸŸŸ♀ Mamre Brook Cabernet Sauvignon 2020, Barossa Valley RATING 92 DRINK 2021–2032 $38 DB
Mamre Brook Shiraz 2018, Barossa RATING 92 DRINK 2021–2030 $38 DB
Pepperjack Sangiovese 2021, McLaren Vale Padthaway Barossa RATING 91 DRINK 2021–2028 $30 DB
Pepperjack Grenache 2020, Barossa RATING 91 DRINK 2021–2028 $28 DB
Pepperjack Scotch Fillet Graded Shiraz 2020, McLaren Vale RATING 91 DRINK 2021–2028 $35 DB
Pepperjack Grenache Rosé 2021, Langhorne Creek RATING 90 DRINK 2022–2027 $30 DB
Barossa Shiraz Cabernet 2020, Barossa Valley RATING 90 DRINK 2021–2028 $29 DB
Pepperjack Cabernet Sauvignon 2020, Barossa RATING 90 DRINK 2021–2028 $30 DB
Pepperjack Porterhouse Graded Shiraz 2020, Langhorne Creek RATING 90 DRINK 2021–2029 $35 DB

Samson Tall

219 Strout Road, McLaren Vale, SA 5171 **Region** McLaren Vale
T 0488 214 680 **www**.samsontall.com.au **Open** 7 days 11–5 **Winemaker** Paul Wilson
Est. 2016 **Dozens** 500

Paul Wilson and Heather Budich purchase grapes from local growers, making the wine in a small winery on their property. The cellar door is a small church built in 1854, the winery and church (with a small historic cemetery) surrounded by gardens and a vineyard. Paul has learned his craft as a winemaker well; all of the wines are well made and the grapes well chosen. (JH)

🍷🍷🍷🍷🍷 **Mataro Cinsault Rosé 2021, McLaren Vale** Very good. Less flirtatious than its grenache sibling. More earthenware, savoury, herbal, ferrous and firm of tannic twine. Fresh as. To use the clichéd term 'food wine' undersells this. This is a mid-weighted rosé of chew over mere zip, punching with the country's finest. Screw cap. 12% alc. RATING 95 DRINK 2021–2022 $25 NG ✪ ♥
Hatwell Vineyard Grenache 2019, McLaren Vale Museum Release. Shadowing nebbiolo's tannic twine and accents of mint, red fruits and sandalwood, this sits in a savoury, mid-weighted zone. Clove, camphor and root spice. Beginning to glimpse forest floor, this will unravel further in the short term. Well worth following. Screw cap. 14.5% alc. RATING 95 DRINK 2022–2025 $60 NG
Grenache 2020, McLaren Vale A very modest price for a meld of fruit of this pedigree: Hatwell, Slate Creek and Marmont sites, 78, 110 and 80 years of age, respectively. A warm year, to be sure. But the twine of 30% whole bunches and properly extracted tannins, manages to corral most of the excess. Fine tannins! Blood plum, fecund strawberry, white pepper. A tad sweet. A bit lactic. Big oak (1500L foudre for 12 months) not only the righteous way but – in a region where too many handle grenache in used barriques – the courageous choice. Fine drive and sinuous length from a producer nudging the pantheon, if not already in it. Screw cap. 14.5% alc. RATING 94 DRINK 2021–2027 $30 NG ✪

🍷🍷🍷🍷🍷 **Hatwell Vineyard Grenache 2020, McLaren Vale** RATING 93 DRINK 2021–2024 $60 NG
Grenache Blanc Picpoul 2021, McLaren Vale RATING 92 DRINK 2021–2024 $25 NG ✪
Grenache Rosé 2021, McLaren Vale RATING 92 DRINK 2021–2022 $25 NG ✪
Shiraz 2020, McLaren Vale RATING 92 DRINK 2021–2025 $30 NG
Tempranillo Grenache 2020, McLaren Vale RATING 91 DRINK 2021–2025 $30 NG

Samuel's Gorge   ★★★★☆

193 Chaffeys Road, McLaren, SA 5171 **Region** McLaren Vale
T (08) 8323 8651 **www.gorge.com.au Open** 7 days 11–5 **Winemaker** Justin McNamee, Riley Harrison **Est.** 2003 **Dozens** 5000 **Vyds** 10ha
After a wandering winemaking career in various parts of the world, Justin McNamee became a winemaker at Tatachilla in '96, where he remained until '03, leaving to found Samuel's Gorge. He established his winery in a barn built in 1853, part of the old Seaview Homestead. The historic property was owned by Sir Samuel Way, variously Chief Justice of the South Australian Supreme Court and Lieutenant Governor of the state. The grapes come from small contract growers spread across the ever-changing (unofficial) subregions of McLaren Vale and are basket-pressed and fermented in old open slate fermenters lined with beeswax. Exports to the UK, Singapore and New Zealand. (JH)

🍷🍷🍷🍷🍷 **Kaleidoscope Horizons 2019, McLaren Vale** 55/26/19% grenache/graciano/tempranillo. This is full, thirst-slaking and immaculately put together. It does not aspire to what its Mosaic of Dreams sibling is not. A bit sweet of fruit, but the cracked pepper and sour cherry elements confer a welcome spice and an amaro bitterness and savouriness. The tannins across the cheeks and tongue, lithe and long-limbed. I'd like some more extraction to mitigate the sweetness. But very good, all the same. Screw cap. 14.5% alc. RATING 95 DRINK 2021–2026 $75 NG
Shiraz 2020, McLaren Vale Very good proprietary shiraz. Weighty, but svelte and stylish, the French oak (15% new) and the period in it (18 months) both well placed, serving to harness lively florals, dark cherry, dried nori, clove and anise. Nicely structured and fresh of feel as a result. Very good drinking. Screw cap. 14% alc. RATING 94 DRINK 2021–2030 $40 NG

Mosaic of Dreams Grenache Mourvèdre Syrah 2019, McLaren Vale
A quintessential southern Rhône blend. The Vale's future. Red cherry, raspberry liqueur, bergamot, pepper, clove, olive, thyme and sassafras. The oak, apparent. Reliant a bit too much on oak and pulpiness rather than extraction of grape tannins. Needs a bit more courage. Delicious on the cooler side. Screw cap. 14.5% alc. RATING 94 DRINK 2021-2027 $75 NG

ŸŸŸŸŸ **Mourvèdre 2020, McLaren Vale** RATING 93 DRINK 2021-2028 $40 NG
Comet Tail Sparkling Shiraz 2018, McLaren Vale RATING 92 $50 NG
Tempranillo 2021, McLaren Vale RATING 92 DRINK 2021-2024 $40 NG
Grenache 2020, McLaren Vale RATING 92 DRINK 2021-2024 $40 NG

Sandalford ★★★★★

3210 West Swan Road, Caversham, WA 6055 **Region** Swan Valley
T (08) 9374 9374 **www**.sandalford.com **Open** 7 days 10–5 **Winemaker** Hope Metcalf
Est. 1840 **Dozens** 60 000 **Vyds** 106.5ha
Sandalford is one of Australia's oldest and largest privately owned wineries. In '70 it moved beyond its original Swan Valley base, purchasing a substantial property in Margaret River that is now the main source of its premium grapes. Wines are released under the 1840 (Swan Valley), Element, Winemakers, Margaret River and Estate Reserve ranges with Prendiville Reserve at the top. There is a second cellar door at 777 Metricup Road in Wilyabrup. Exports to all major markets. (JH)

ŸŸŸŸŸ **1840 Shiraz 2019, Swan Valley** It's satisfying to see producers proudly proclaiming the Swan Valley on the front label. As Australia's second-oldest wine region, the history there spans 2 centuries. Shiraz is one of the key red varieties grown (along with grenache) and this 1840 does Swan Valley shiraz justice. Concentrated, shapely, lush and long, this is a brilliant and opulent iteration of shiraz, the warmth of the sunshine over the Swan on show. All things tucked away and in place (oak, tannins and acid). Screw cap. 14.5% alc. RATING 95 DRINK 2021-2031 $50 EL
Prendiville Reserve Chardonnay 2020, Margaret River Concentrated, intense and long. What this wine lacks in complexity, it gains in power. It is raw and dense, with layer upon layer of orchard fruit, laced together with taut briny acidity. Very smart. Screw cap. 13.5% alc. RATING 94 DRINK 2022-2029 $75 EL
Estate Reserve Wilyabrup Vineyard Cabernet Sauvignon 2019, Margaret River With 5/3% malbec/merlot. Aromatically reticent at this early stage, however in the mouth there is hung deli meat, red berry fruits and a fortification of toasty, resinous oak. All things in place, and built for the long haul. Screw cap. 14.5% alc. RATING 94 DRINK 2021-2036 $45 EL

ŸŸŸŸŸ **Prendiville Reserve Cabernet Sauvignon 2019, Margaret River** RATING 93 DRINK 2023-2033 $120 EL
1840 Cabernet Merlot 2019, Swan Valley RATING 92 DRINK 2021-2031 $50 EL
Estate Reserve Wilyabrup Vineyard Shiraz 2019, Margaret River RATING 91 DRINK 2021-2027 $35 EL
Cabernet Merlot 2020, Margaret River RATING 90 DRINK 2021-2028 $22 EL
Estate Reserve Wilyabrup Vineyard Chardonnay 2020, Margaret River RATING 90 DRINK 2021-2027 $35 EL

Sandhurst Ridge ★★★★

156 Forest Drive, Marong, Vic 3515 **Region** Bendigo
T (03) 5435 2534 **www**.sandhurstridge.com.au **Open** 7 days 11–5 **Winemaker** Paul
Greblo **Viticulturist** George Greblo **Est.** 1990 **Dozens** 3000 **Vyds** 7.3ha
The Greblo brothers (Paul is the winemaker, George the viticulturist) began the establishment of Sandhurst Ridge in 1990, planting the first 2ha of shiraz and cabernet sauvignon. Plantings have increased to over 7ha, principally cabernet and shiraz but also a little merlot, nebbiolo

and sauvignon blanc. As the business has grown, the Greblos have supplemented their crush with grapes grown in the region. Exports to Malaysia and Taiwan. (JH)

ΤΤΤΤΤ **Fringe Shiraz 2020, Bendigo** In eye-catching deep purple hues. A bold personality here, laden with dark cherry, plum, dried herbs, nutmeg, licorice and some well-integrated oak and tannins. Ready to go. Top value for money. Screw cap. 14.6% alc. RATING 90 DRINK 2021–2025 $25 JP
Reserve Shiraz 2019, Bendigo The Reserve makes a bold statement of power and generosity, not to mention colour, which is almost black. Chocolate, cigar box, cassis, fruitcake, spice and licorice flavours are dense and savoury. Unrestrained ripe tannins and sweet vanillin oak guide the wine to a lasting finish. Screw cap. 15.5% alc. RATING 90 DRINK 2021–2030 $60 JP

ΤΤΤΤ **Sauvignon Blanc 2021, Bendigo** RATING 88 DRINK 2021–2024 $20 JP
Italiano Nebbiolo Cabernet Sauvignon Sangiovese 2020, Bendigo RATING 88 DRINK 2021–2025 $30 JP

Sanguine Estate

77 Shurans Lane, Heathcote, Vic 3523 **Region** Heathcote
T (03) 5433 3111 **www.**sanguinewines.com.au **Open** W'ends & public hols 10–5
Winemaker Mark Hunter **Viticulturist** Mark Hunter **Est.** 1997 **Dozens** 15 000
Vyds 28ha

The Hunter family – parents Linda and Tony, their children Mark and Jodi and their respective partners Melissa and Brett – have 21.5ha of shiraz and a 'fruit salad block' of chardonnay, viognier, verdelho, merlot, tempranillo, petit verdot, lagrein, nebbiolo, grenache, cabernet sauvignon and cabernet franc. Low-yielding vines and the magic of the Heathcote region have produced Shiraz of exceptional intensity, which has received rave reviews in the US and led to the 'sold out' sign being posted almost immediately upon release. With the ever-expanding vineyard, Mark has become full-time vigneron and winemaker, and Jodi has taken over from her father as CEO and general manager. (JH)

ΤΤΤΤΤ **Inception Shiraz 2019, Heathcote** A hot season brought harvest earlier than normal in '19, but had no impact on the poise and elegance delivered in this wine. It's a beauty. Impressive depth of colour (as usual), opens to reveal fragrant musky, violet, spice and black fruits. Fruit power is well managed by the vibrant spice and oak integration and fine tannins. A joy to behold. Screw cap. 14.8% alc. RATING 96 DRINK 2021–2033 $40 JP ✪
Progeny Shiraz 2020, Heathcote A beacon in a difficult vintage. Progeny retains its well-known vibrancy and immediate drinking appeal. Deep, dense purple hues introduce lifted aromas of blackberry, briar, earth and violet. The winemaker believes that although there is less than 2% viognier, it makes its presence felt. I believe him. There is an aromatic appeal to this wine where the fruit is allowed free rein, with just a nod to French oak (20% new). The result is a wine of flavour and depth. Screw cap. 14.8% alc. RATING 95 DRINK 2021–2030 $25 JP ✪

ΤΤΤΤΤ **Music Festival Shiraz 2020, Heathcote** RATING 90 DRINK 2021–2025 $30 JP
Robo's Mob Shiraz 2019, Heathcote RATING 90 DRINK 2021–2028 $33 JP

Santa & D'Sas

2 Pincott Street, Newtown, Vic 3220 **Region** Various
T 0417 384272 **www.**santandsas.com.au **Winemaker** Andrew Santarossa, Matthew Di Sciascio **Est.** 2014 **Dozens** 9000

Santa & D'Sas is a collaboration between the Santarossa and Di Sciascio families. Andrew Santarossa and Matthew Di Sciascio met while studying for a bachelor of applied science (wine science). Wines are released under the Valentino label (fiano, sangiovese and shiraz), are dedicated to Matthew's father; the remaining wines simply identify the region and variety. (JH)

TTTTT **Prosecco NV, King Valley** A '21-based NV blend of prosecco from the Aussie home of the grape. So, so easy to love. This prosecco shines with the kind of purity of fruit that invites another sip. Making the most of their Italian heritage, the winemakers celebrate prosecco's inviting aperitif-style drinking in chalky lemon aromas and flavours, crunchy apple freshness and brisk acidity. Crown. 11% alc. RATING 94 $24 JP ✪

TTTTY **D'Sas Prosecco 2021, King Valley** RATING 92 $32 JP
D'Sas Pinot Gris 2021, King Valley RATING 90 DRINK 2022-2024 $32 JP

Santarossa Wine Company   ★★★★

1 The Crescent, Yea, Vic 3717 (postal) **Region** Various
T 0419 117 858 **www**.seaglasswines.com.au **Winemaker** Andrew Santarossa **Est.** 2007
Vyds 16ha
Santarossa Vineyards started out as a virtual winery business owned and run by 3 brothers of Italian heritage. It is now solely owned by winemaker Andrew and wife Megan Santarossa. Yarra Valley wines appear under the Better Half label, while the Sea Glass range explores the many different terroirs of the Mornington Peninsula. (JH)

TTTTY **Sea Glass Chardonnay 2020, Mornington Peninsula** It's hard to know how this wine is going to play out: it's nervy and tightly wound with a noose of acidity holding firm. Some stone fruit and citrus, a hint of lees and sulphides pop out from time to time. On that note, it needs more time. Screw cap. 13.3% alc. RATING 90 DRINK 2022-2027 $45 JF

TTTT **Sea Glass 2020, Mornington Peninsula** RATING 88 DRINK 2021-2024 $45 JF

Santolin Wines   ★★★★☆

c/- 21-23 Delaneys Road, South Warrandyte, Vic 3134 **Region** Yarra Valley
T 0402 278 464 **www**.santolinwines.com.au **Winemaker** Adrian Santolin **Est.** 2012
Dozens 1000
Adrian Santolin grew up in Griffith, NSW, and has worked in the wine industry since he was 15. His wife Rebecca has worked in marketing roles at various wineries. Together, they moved to the Yarra Valley in '07. Adrian's love of pinot noir led him to work at wineries such as Wedgetail Estate, Rochford, De Bortoli, Sticks and Rob Dolan Wines. In '12 his dream came true when he was able to buy 2t of pinot noir from the Syme-on-Yarra Vineyard, increasing production in '13 to 4t, split between chardonnay and pinot noir. Exports to the UK, the US and Hong Kong. (JH)

TTTTT **Gladysdale Chardonnay 2020, Yarra Valley** An impressive wine from the first, with its aromas of stone fruits, grilled nuts and discreet, well-judged struck match. There are white nectarines and grapefruit pith on the mouth-watering palate, and I like the touch of grip on the long finish, derived, most probably, from one barrel that was a whole-berry ferment. A lovely effort. Screw cap. 12.9% alc. RATING 96 DRINK 2022-2027 $45 PR ✪

Sapling Yard Wines   ★★★★

56 Wallace Street, Braidwood, NSW 2622 **Region** Canberra District
T 0410 770 894 **www**.saplingyard.com.au **Open** Sat-Sun 11-4 by appt
Winemaker Carla Rodeghiero, Malcolm Burdett **Est.** 2008 **Dozens** 1800 **Vyds** 1.2ha
Carla Rodegheiro and Andrew Bennett work full-time in the pharmaceutical clinical research and building industries respectively. Carla started out as a microbiologist working as a locum in hospitals in Australia and London. While in London, she also worked evenings in a wine bar in Carnaby Street, where she tasted a 1993 Mount Langi Ghiran Shiraz and vowed to one day make a wine of similar remarkable quality. In '97 she began a wine science degree at CSU, completing the last residential term in 2004 (with 9-week-old daughter Mia in

tow), having worked vintages in the Hunter Valley, Orange, Macedon Ranges and Willamette Valley, Oregon. In '08 Carla and Andrew planted a 1.2ha vineyard at Braidwood to pinot noir, riesling, pinot blanc and tempranillo but they also continue to source their best grapes from the Canberra District. (JH)

ΨΨΨΨΨ Pirouette Chardonnay 2021, Tumbarumba It's a very good wine. It has a richness, creaminess and spicy, cedary oak from the winemaking inputs yet the acidity and quality of Tumbarumba fruit keeps this in check. Hints of citrus, stone fruit and lemon verbena with a smidge of complex sulphides giving it a savoury overlay. Screw cap. 12.8% alc. RATING 94 DRINK 2022-2027 $38 JF

ΨΨΨΨΨ Entrechat 2019, Canberra District RATING 93 $38 JF
Rosé Sur Lie 2021, Hilltops RATING 90 DRINK 2022-2023 $27 JF
The Four Pinots 2021, Southern New South Wales RATING 90 DRINK 2022-2024 $27 JF

Savaterre   ★★★★★

929 Beechworth-Wangaratta Road, Everton Upper, Vic 3678 **Region** Beechworth
T (03) 5727 0551 **www.**savaterre.com **Open** By appt **Winemaker** Keppell Smith
Est. 1996 **Dozens** 2500 **Vyds** 8ha

Keppell Smith embarked on a career in wine in 1996, studying winemaking at CSU and (at a practical level) with Phillip Jones at Bass Phillip. He has established 8ha of chardonnay and pinot noir (close-planted at 7500 vines/ha), shiraz and sagrantino on the 40ha Savaterre property, at an elevation of 440m. Organic principles govern the viticulture and the winemaking techniques look to the Old World rather than the New. Smith's stated aim is to produce outstanding individualistic wines far removed from the mainstream. Exports to France, UAE and Singapore. (JH)

ΨΨΨΨΨ Pinot Noir 2018, Beechworth Take a deep breath, inhale; the scent of mountain wildflowers, violet, crushed raspberry and cherry is enthralling, addictive even. Intense and tight on the palate, it opens to layers of clean, bright red and black fruits, enhanced by savoury spice, warm background oak and ripe, textural tannins. A savoury ferrous, mineral finish offers yet another layer on this most complex pinot. Outstanding. Screw cap. 13.5% alc. RATING 97 DRINK 2022-2030 $75 JP ✪ ♥

ΨΨΨΨΨ Chardonnay 2019, Beechworth Close planted (8000 vines/ha) and organically farmed, the Savaterre vineyard produces sublime chardonnays of depth and concentration. Here's a wine to get easily lost in, with its distinctive mineral intensity and aromas of nectarine, peach skin, preserved lemon, grapefruit and cashew. Brimming with ripe fruit, freshness, focused acidity and a creamy lusciousness. Boasts a lovely elegance that never tires. Screw cap. 13.5% alc. RATING 95 DRINK 2022-2031 $85 JP
Shiraz 2018, Beechworth Early days still for this little beauty, which brings a stalky wild edge to cool-climate Beechworth shiraz. Stems bring a complexity and structure; they're both here contributing to the wine. Aromas of blue and red fruits, with green twig, leaf, earth and smoky charcuterie notes. The palate is dense and tight in sturdy tannins with a strong savoury bent. A wine for further ageing. Screw cap. 13.5% alc. RATING 95 DRINK 2022-2034 $75 JP
Maurizio Sagrantino 2018, Beechworth The high priest of tannin, the sagrantino grape is transformed by Keppell into a plush, focused, savoury, full-bodied, fine (and firm) tannic young wine, worthy of extended time in the cellar. A striking herbal thread blends in with black fruits, plum, bramble, bracken, earth and truffle which, in itself, is a complex grouping and so very different. You are not in comfortable ol' shiraz territory anymore; it's a pretty exciting place to be. Screw cap. 13.6% alc. RATING 95 DRINK 2022-2034 $85 JP

Savitas Wines

Level 8, 420 King William Street, Adelaide, SA 5000 (postal) **Region** Barossa Valley
T 0438 803 876 **www.**savitaswines.com **Winemaker** Matt O'Leary **Est.** 2015
Dozens 3000 **Vyds** 13.6ha
Chief winemaker Matt O'Leary has had a long and successful career in South Australia, including 18+ years with Wolf Blass, working with both red and white wines, reaching the role of senior winemaker. His knowledge has been of prime importance in securing the intake of additional varieties to supplement the annual intake of grapes as the Savitas Wines business grows. (JH)

ŸŸŸŸŸ Alainn Fion Chardonnay 2018, Adelaide Hills In purity and precision – not to mention deliciousness – Àlainn Fion lives up to its Gaelic name of 'beautiful wine'. Layers of stone fruit, cumquat, grapefruit peel and citrus join bright lemony acidity. Gentle spice and restrained oak connect on the palate with a saline juiciness. Delightful. Screw cap. 13% alc. RATING 95 DRINK 2022-2025 $45 JP

ŸŸŸŸŸ Alainn Fion Chardonnay 2019, Adelaide Hills RATING 91 DRINK 2022-2025 $45 JP

SC Pannell

60 Olivers Road, McLaren Vale, SA 5171 **Region** McLaren Vale
T (08) 8323 8000 **www.**pannell.com.au **Open** 7 days 11–4 **Winemaker** Stephen Pannell
Est. 2004 **Dozens** 15 000 **Vyds** 9ha
The only surprising piece of background is that it took (an admittedly still reasonably youthful) Steve Pannell and wife Fiona so long to cut the painter from Constellation/ Hardys and establish their own winemaking and consulting business. Steve radiates intensity and his extended experience has resulted in wines of the highest quality, right from the first vintage. The Pannells have 2 vineyards in McLaren Vale, the first planted in 1891 with a precious 3.6ha of shiraz. The future for the Pannells is limitless, the icon status of the label already well established. Exports to the UK, the US, Sweden and Singapore. (JH)

ŸŸŸŸŸ Aglianico 2020, McLaren Vale A warmer year like this seems to have proven beneficial to this sturdy, ferruginous and late-ripening variety. Make no mistake, it is as emblematic of our vinous future as grenache, despite being a relative arriviste. If you like savoury wines laden with dried tobacco, graphite, black cherry and licorice, harnessed by tannins of mettle and stridency like few others, here's your ticket to ride! Screw cap. 14% alc. RATING 96 DRINK 2021-2030 $42 NG ✪
Old McDonald Grenache 2020, McLaren Vale A more successful vintage across the elevated sands of Blewitt Springs than Clarendon. Delicious wine. Kirsch, thyme, dried rosemary, lavender, mint and florals, tiptoeing along a balance beam of fibrous tannins and saline freshness. Nothing drying. A squeaky pucker to the finish. Aussie sweet fruit, to be sure. But tamed. Long, flowing and sandy of aura. Bravo! Screw cap. 14% alc. RATING 95 DRINK 2021-2030 $60 NG
Oliver's Road Aglianico 2018, McLaren Vale This estate is investing a great deal into the future of this prodigious variety, responsible for some of Italy's most age-worthy, sturdy and complex wines. Less dense than the expression from the home block, but no less ferrous, firm, full or impressive. More of the redder fruit spectrum with a slake of dried tobacco, sage, mulch and black olive-doused tannins directing a long, savoury and effusively energetic finish. A delicious wine auguring so well for a future in the Vale. Screw cap. 14% alc. RATING 94 DRINK 2021-2027 $42 NG

ŸŸŸŸŸ Basso Garnacha 2020, McLaren Vale RATING 93 DRINK 2021-2025 $28 NG
Smart Clarendon Grenache 2020, McLaren Vale RATING 93 DRINK 2021-2028 $60 NG
The Vale 2019, McLaren Vale RATING 93 DRINK 2021-2028 $42 NG
Tempranillo Touriga 2020, McLaren Vale RATING 92 DRINK 2021-2026 $32 NG

Scarborough Wine Co

179 Gillards Road, Pokolbin, NSW 2320 **Region** Hunter Valley
T (02) 4998 7563 **www**.scarboroughwine.com.au **Open** Thurs–Mon 10–5
Winemaker Ian Scarborough, Jerome Scarborough **Est.** 1985 **Dozens** 25 000 **Vyds** 47ha
Ian Scarborough honed his winemaking skills during his years as a consultant, and has
brought all those skills to his own label. The Scarborough family acquired a portion of the
old Lindemans Sunshine Vineyard (after it lay fallow for 30 years) and have planted it with
semillon and chardonnay. (JH)

ŸŸŸŸŸ **Keepers of the Flame Chardonnay 2019, Hunter Valley** A bridle between
Scarborough's signature behemoths and a more contemporary lineage of flint,
mineral and welcome freshness. Tangerine, apricot, glazed quince, white nectarine
and peat. The finish, intense and forceful, as to be expected, serving to drive
impressive length. Screw cap. 14% alc. RATING 93 DRINK 2021-2027 $90 NG
The Obsessive Old North Vineyard Shiraz 2019, Hunter Valley Time
should mould this into something more suave, shapely and refined. Now, in the
grip of jangly youth and firm, oaky edges. Mocha and pine. Dark cherry, sassafras,
licorice and kirsch, beyond. Needs patience. Screw cap. 14.5% alc. RATING 92
DRINK 2023-2030 $60 NG

ŸŸŸŸ **The Obsessive The Cottage Vineyard Semillon 2021, Hunter Valley**
RATING 88 DRINK 2021-2028 $30 NG
Yellow Label Chardonnay 2019, Hunter Valley RATING 88
DRINK 2021-2026 $25 NG

Scarpantoni Estate

Scarpantoni Drive, McLaren Flat, SA 5171 **Region** McLaren Vale
T (08) 8383 0186 **www**.scarpantoniwines.com **Open** Mon–Fri 9–5, w'ends & public
hols 11.30–4.30 **Winemaker** Michael and Filippo Scarpantoni, David Fleming **Est.** 1979
Dozens 37 000 **Vyds** 40ha
Scarpantoni has come a long way since Domenico Scarpantoni purchased his first vineyard
in 1958. He worked for Thomas Hardy at its Tintara winery, then as vineyard manager for
Seaview Wines and soon became one of the largest private grapegrowers in the region. The
winery was built in '79 with help from sons Michael and Filippo, who continue to manage
the company. Exports to the UK and other major markets. (JH)

ŸŸŸŸŸ **Montepulciano 2021, McLaren Vale** By far the best wine in this suite,
attesting to the promise of sturdy, late-ripening Italian varieties in the region,
particularly when endowed with ferrous tannins – lithe and drawn gently – and
saline freshness. This stands out like the proverbial promised land. Macerated
cherry, clove, beef bouillon, lilac and licorice strap. But it is the mould of pulpy,
impeccably extracted whole berries and the intuitive varietal DNA, structured and
pointed in the right direction, that win me over. Screw cap. 14% alc. RATING 94
DRINK 2021-2028 $25 NG ✪

ŸŸŸŸŸ **Nero d'Avola 2021, McLaren Vale** RATING 91 DRINK 2021-2024 $25 NG

Schild Estate Wines

1095 Barossa Valley Way, Lyndoch, SA 5351 **Region** Barossa Valley
T (08) 8524 5560 **www**.schildestate.com.au **Open** Fri–Mon 10–4 **Winemaker** Scott
Hazeldine **Viticulturist** Michael Schild **Est.** 1998 **Dozens** 40 **Vyds** 134ha
Ed Schild is a Barossa Valley grapegrower who first planted a small vineyard at Rowland Flat
in 1952, steadily increasing his vineyard holdings over the next 50 years to their present level.
The flagship wine is made from 170+yo shiraz vines on the Moorooroo Vineyard. Exports to
all major markets. (JH)

ŸŸŸŸ **Moorooroo Shiraz 2019, Barossa Valley** High-toned and perfumed with
hints of violets and jasmine hovering over the ripe plum and dark berry compote

notes. Plenty of spicy nuance, hints of licorice, dark chocolate and turned earth. Medium bodied, with a sense of grace and elegance to its form; fine tannins and stony acidity shape the fruit nicely and the wine finishes savoury and long. Screw cap. 14.5% alc. RATING 95 DRINK 2021-2032 $199 DB

🍷🍷🍷🍷🍷 **Edgar Schild Reserve Old Bush Vines Grenache 2020, Barossa Valley** RATING 93 DRINK 2021-2031 $40 DB
Pramie Narrow Road Vineyard Shiraz 2019, Barossa Valley RATING 93 DRINK 2024-2034 $50 JH
Lorraine Schild Cabernet Sauvignon 2020, Barossa Valley RATING 92 DRINK 2021-2035 $40 DB
Old & Survivor Vine Grenache 2020, Barossa Valley RATING 91 DRINK 2021-2028 $43 DB

Schoolhouse Wines

4 Nelson Street, Stepney, SA 50969 **Region** Coonawarra
T (08) 8362 6135 **www.cwwines.com Open** Mon–Fri 9–5 **Winemaker** Ben Wurst
Est. 2020 **Dozens** 5000
Schoolhouse is the top brand of the large wine enterprise CW Wines, a business with a host of local and SA labels. Coonawarra shiraz and cabernet sauvignon are Schoolhouse's mainstays, with a Limestone Coast sauvignon blanc featuring in the second tier Headmaster range. The wines are crafted by Ben Wurst, who has worked in the region for close to 20 years. (JF)

🍷🍷🍷🍷🍷 **Shiraz 2019, Coonawarra** Impossibly blue and bright on the nose – blackberry pie, blueberry and fresh bay leaf. In the mouth the wine is satisfying and fresh, almost uncomplicated in its expression of succulent, saturated fruit flavour. It is velvety and full. The length is very good, it shows promise for the years ahead. Screw cap. 14.5% alc. RATING 95 DRINK 2022-2037 $80 EL

🍷🍷🍷🍷🍷 **Headmaster Sauvignon Blanc 2021, Coonawarra** RATING 91 DRINK 2021-2024 $55 EL
Cabernet Sauvignon 2019, Coonawarra RATING 91 DRINK 2022-2031 $80 EL

Schubert Estate

26 Kensington Road, Rose Park, SA 5067 **Region** Barossa Valley
T (08) 8431 1457 **www.schubertestate.com Open** Mon–Fri 9–5 **Winemaker** Matt Reynolds **Est.** 2000 **Dozens** 4200 **Vyds** 14ha
Founders Steve and Cecilia Schubert sold their business to Mrs Sofia Yang and Mrs Lin Tan in 2019. It was agreed that the Schuberts would guide the new owners into the business as they came to grips with running a small but ultra-successful high-end wine business. They aim to continue making the Goose-yard Block and the Gander on the premises with plans for a larger winery and to have other wines in an expanded portfolio contract-made elsewhere. In 2016 Schubert Estate opened a cellar door in Adelaide in a renovated stone villa. Exports to Germany, Malaysia, South Korea and Hong Kong. (JH)

🍷🍷🍷🍷🍷 **Goose-yard Block Shiraz 2018, Barossa Valley** An unashamedly big, bold style of wine and a delicious one at that. Fruit characters of black cherry, plum and blackberry fruits with some date and fig notes providing the bass. Layers of licorice and spice, chocolatey tannins, fresh line and some nice detail for such a weighty wine. A touch of alcohol is noticeable, but that comes with the territory. Screw cap. 15.5% alc. RATING 95 DRINK 2021-2031 $160 DB
The Gander Reserve Shiraz 2016, Barossa Valley Deep crimson in colour with a wave of blackberry and blackcurrant fruit straight out of the glass. The oak is quite percussive with its spicy, cedary heft and there are hints of blackstrap licorice, dark chocolate, dried dates, leather and earth in the mix. Full bodied, with concentrated black fruits, plenty of French oak, tight ripe tannins and a lingering, powerful finish. Flexes hard. Cork. 15.5% alc. RATING 95 DRINK 2021-2035 $258 DB

Schwarz Wine Company

PO Box 779, Tanunda, SA 5352 **Region** Barossa Valley
T 0417 881 923 **www.**schwarzwineco.com.au **Open** At Vino Lokal, Tanunda
Winemaker Jason Schwarz **Est.** 2001 **Dozens** 5000

The economical name is appropriate for a business that started with 1t of grapes making 2 hogsheads of wine in 2001. Shiraz was purchased from Jason Schwarz's parents' vineyard in Bethany, the vines planted in 1968; the following year half a tonne of grenache was added, once again purchased from the parents. In '05, grape sale agreements with another (larger) winery were terminated, freeing up 1.8ha of shiraz and 0.8ha of grenache. From this point on things moved more quickly: in '06 Jason formed a partnership (Biscay Road Vintners) with Peter Schell of Spinifex, giving them total control over production. Exports to the UK, the US, France, Denmark, Singapore and Japan. (JH)

TTTTT **The Schiller Single Vineyard Shiraz 2019, Barossa Valley** Aromas of deep spice notes sheathing super-ripe blackberry, black cherry and plum fruits along with hints of licorice, dark chocolate, espresso and vanillin oak. Rich and mouth filling, with impressive fruit weight and purity. Gorgeous tannins fade back into the fruit, providing ample support and a finish that lingers admirably. A very impressive, textural wine that shows grace and power in equal measure. Screw cap. 14.8% alc. RATING 95 DRINK 2021-2038 $80 DB

TTTTY **Meta Grenache 2021, Barossa Valley** RATING 93 DRINK 2021-2026 $38 DB
Meta Mataro 2021, Barossa Valley RATING 93 DRINK 2021-2028 $38 DB
Nitschke Block Single Vineyard Shiraz 2020, Barossa Valley RATING 93 DRINK 2021-2035 $50 DB
The Grower Shiraz 2020, Barossa Valley RATING 92 DRINK 2021-2028 $30 DB
Rosé 2021, Barossa Valley RATING 91 DRINK 2021-2024 $28 DB
The Grower GSM 2020, Barossa Valley RATING 90 DRINK 2021-2026 $30 DB

Scion

74 Slaughterhouse Road, Rutherglen, Vic 3685 **Region** Rutherglen
T (02) 6032 8844 **www.**scionwine.com.au **Open** 7 days 10–4.30 **Winemaker** Rowly Milhinch **Est.** 2002 **Dozens** 2500 **Vyds** 4.85ha

Self-taught winemaker Rowly Milhinch is a descendant of GF Morris, one of Rutherglen's most renowned vignerons of the mid-19th century. Rowly aspires to make contemporary wines 'guided by a creative interpretation of traditional Rutherglen varietals, durif a specialty'. The wines are made from the estate Linlithgow Vineyard and the revitalised 1.48ha Terravinia Vineyard managed by Rowly. (JH)

TTTTY **Fortrose 2019, Rutherglen** The winemaker chooses not to label this wine durif because he wishes the drinker to keep an open mind: this is to be applauded. The grape is often portrayed as a monster red, yet it can be far from it. Here, we see an elegance that deserves serious attention; dark-fruited, blueberry, oak spice and rosemary aromas with a lilting floral thread. The essence of the grape is explored: its black heart and firm tannins delivered with fineness and all within a medium-bodied, complex wine. Durif can be beautiful. Here's the proof. Screw cap. 13.4% alc. RATING 93 DRINK 2021-2029 $35 JP

Sutherland Vineyard Shiraz 2019, Heathcote Boy, it's got a lot of charm. While restrained on the bouquet, it lights up the palate in brilliant aromatics and a lovely black and blue berry intensity. Looking elegant and filigree fine in sunny tannins, the winemaker showed enviable restraint in letting the fruit sing. Screw cap. 14% alc. RATING 92 DRINK 2022-2029 $36 JP

Rosé 2021, Rutherglen Who knew durif could inspire such a fine-featured rosé, so delicate and pretty? It's a welcome revelation for some red wine drinkers, I'm sure, to see that light copper blush, to smell the floral aromatics, the cherry, plum and stewed rhubarb. It fairly dances on the palate, crisp, easy and fresh. Screw cap. 12.4% alc. RATING 90 DRINK 2021-2024 $28 JP

Syrah 2019, Rutherglen The winemaker likes to take preconceptions and turn them on their head. Herewith, Rutherglen shiraz shows its more genteel side, polished and charming. It certainly makes an impression hosting heady aromatics, red berries, dried herbs, all corralled nicely by well-mannered oak. Sneaks up on you and then you are hooked. Screw cap. 13.6% alc. RATING 90 DRINK 2021-2028 $36 JP

Muscat Nouveau 2019, Rutherglen From the creative brain of winemaker Rowly Milhinch, an ancestor of pioneering Australian vigneron, G. F Morris. A vintage muscat that captures the freshness and floral beauty of the grape (and vintage) with a light dusting of neutral spirit. Brings honeyed raisins, rose petal and a glacé-pear sweet intensity, while remaining light on its feet, clean and bright. A new look for a trad style. 500ml. Screw cap. 16.9% alc. RATING 90 $32 JP

Scorpo Wines

23 Old Bittern-Dromana Road, Merricks North, Vic 3926 **Region** Mornington Peninsula **T** (03) 5989 7697 **www.**scorpowines.com.au **Open** first w'end each month or by appt **Winemaker** Paul Scorpo **Est.** 1997 **Dozens** 6000 **Vyds** 17.3ha
Paul Scorpo has a background as a horticulturist and landscape architect, working on major projects ranging from private gardens to golf courses in Australia, Europe and Asia. His family has a love of food, wine and gardens, all of which led to them buying a derelict apple and cherry orchard on gentle rolling hills between Port Phillip and Western Port bays. They have established pinot noir (10.4ha), pinot gris and chardonnay (3.2ha each) and shiraz (0.5ha). Exports to Japan. (JH)

ＹＹＹＹＹ **Eocene Single Vineyard Chardonnay 2020, Mornington Peninsula** While there are layers of flavour and a depth to this, it doesn't come across as too big or too much of a good thing, but just right. Citrus and stone fruit, spice and a subtle oak influence, long and pure across the palate, coming out rather savoury. Moreish, with great definition. Screw cap. 13% alc. RATING 96 DRINK 2022-2030 $75 JF ❂
Rosé 2021, Mornington Peninsula Is it the aroma or texture that make this such a compelling drink? Well, probably both. It's an attractive pale coppery pink for starters. Wafts of black pepper, aniseed and red cherries with watermelon and rind which set things rolling. It's juicy, tangy and vibrant, yet there's texture too, and lithe, light tannins. This is a top-notch, totally delicious rosé. Screw cap. 13.4% alc. RATING 95 DRINK 2021-2023 $28 JF ❂
Aubaine Chardonnay 2021, Mornington Peninsula Oh yeah. Rock solid chardonnay from a lovely vintage. Everything just so – the citrus flavours, spice, a dash of quality oak, the layer of creamy lees – not too much – and finishes with fine acidity. This glides across the palate leaving a desire for another glass. Screw cap. 13.2% alc. RATING 95 DRINK 2022-2028 $32 JF ❂
Noirien Pinot Noir 2021, Mornington Peninsula A very classy Noirien that perfectly matches savoury attributes to the excellent fruit within. Dark cherries, all spiced up with some tart rhubarb and blood orange, fresh herbs and chinotto. Unencumbered by new oak, but the palate is shapely, the tannins persuasive and the acidity humming. Screw cap. 13.6% alc. RATING 95 DRINK 2022-2021 $32 JF ❂
Old Cherry Orchard 10K Single Vineyard Pinot Noir 2020, Mornington Peninsula A deceptive wine as its light ruby hue and delicate aromas bely the power it holds and the definition of the savoury yet raw silk-like tannins. Sweet red cherries, tart rhubarb, spices befitting a souk and acidity tightly holding everything in place. Screw cap. 13.5% alc. RATING 95 DRINK 2022-2035 $110 JF

ＹＹＹＹＹ **Aubaine Chardonnay 2020, Mornington Peninsula** RATING 93 DRINK 2021-2026 $32 JF
Bestia Pinot Grigio Tradizionale 2020, Mornington Peninsula RATING 93 DRINK 2021-2024 $45 JF
Pinot Gris 2019, Mornington Peninsula RATING 93 DRINK 2022-2024 $35 JF
Pinsanto Late Harvest Pinot Gris 2019, Mornington Peninsula RATING 90 DRINK 2021-2023 $33 JF

Scotchmans Hill

190 Scotchmans Road, Drysdale, Vic 3222 **Region** Geelong
T (03) 5251 3176 **www**.scotchmans.com.au **Open** 7 days 11.30–4 **Winemaker** Robin
Brockett, Marcus Holt **Est.** 1982 **Dozens** 50 000 **Vyds** 80ha
Established in 1982, Scotchmans Hill has been a consistent producer of well-made wines
under the stewardship of long-term winemaker Robin Brockett and assistant Marcus Holt.
The wines are released under the Scotchmans Hill, Cornelius, Jack & Jill and Swan Bay labels.
A change of ownership in '14 resulted in significant vineyard investment. Exports to Asia. (JH)

🍷🍷🍷🍷🍷 **Bellarine Peninsula Shiraz 2019, Geelong** Spectacularly deep colour with
a crimson rim. Typical Scotchmans Hill vinification: whole bunches and whole
berries, cold soak, wild ferment, new and used French oak. The wonder of
cool-grown shiraz with attention to detail from start to finish, part the mouth-
watering spice and black pepper, licorice and blackberry flavours, part the texture
and structure. Irresistible Australian shiraz. Screw cap. 14.5% alc. RATING 98
DRINK 2024-2049 $42 JH ✪ ♥

🍷🍷🍷🍷🍷 **Bellarine Peninsula Pinot Noir 2020, Geelong** Bright colour sets the tone
for a deliciously scented bouquet of cherry blossom, wafts of red berry fruits and
gentle but persistent spices. The palate is lively and juicy, the aftertaste fresh. Screw
cap. 13% alc. RATING 96 DRINK 2022-2030 $42 JH ✪
**Cornelius Norfolk Vineyard Bellarine Peninsula Pinot Noir 2019,
Geelong** The Norfolk vineyard produces another delight of a pinot noir, utterly
scrumptious a good 9 months before release, which bodes well. A seamless
combination of lively cherry, plum, dried herbs, violets and gracious oak. Tannins
run smooth and friendly. Presents a false sense of modesty because its pinot
concentration runs very deep. Screw cap. 13.5% alc. RATING 95 DRINK 2022-2029
$72 JP
**Cornelius Airds Vineyard Bellarine Peninsula Chardonnay 2019,
Geelong** Continues on from the excellent '18 vintage with another stellar
performance. A succulent and seamless rendition, bursting in citrus energy with
nectarine, green apple and mealy notes. Gently spiced oak comes into play, too,
lending texture. Finishes with a saline bright acidity. All class. Screw cap. 13% alc.
RATING 95 DRINK 2022-2029 $75 JP
**Cornelius Kincardine Vineyard Bellarine Peninsula Chardonnay 2019,
Geelong** Love the individuality of the single-vineyard releases, Kincardine
presenting a warm, creamy and complex interpretation of the grape. Stone fruits,
pear skin, nougat, cumquat and honeysuckle. The palate is beautifully composed,
with some nutty notes adding extra depth. Screw cap. 13.5% alc. RATING 95
DRINK 2022-2029 $75 JP
Cornelius Strathallan Vineyard Bellarine Peninsula Syrah 2019, Geelong
Tasted well before release and already there was the Strathallan approachability and
generosity of fruit on display. The friendly one is quite the personality in upfront
spices and ripe fruits, with layers of smart, toasty, smoky oak and smooth, tight
tannins, all quite seamless. Just goes on and on. Screw cap. 14%. alc. RATING 95
DRINK 2022-2030 $75 JP
**Cornelius Sutton Vineyard Bellarine Peninsula Chardonnay 2019,
Geelong** Sutton has slurped up 18 months in oak and come out the other side
nicely integrated, sporting bright citrus and stone-fruit generosity. It is impeccably
contrasted with tightly wound, lemony acidity. Promises endurance. Screw cap.
13% alc. RATING 95 DRINK 2022-2029 $75 JP
Cornelius Single Vineyard Bellarine Peninsula Pinot Gris 2020, Geelong
A rich complexity immediately, with the scent of spiced apple, pear, spice and
ginger snaps. Rolls out smooth across the tongue, with plenty of weight and
flavour concentration. A thread of citrus and sweet grapefruit weaves its way
through. Screw cap. 12.5% alc. RATING 94 DRINK 2022-2025 $38 JP
**Cornelius Kirkcaldy Vineyard Bellarine Peninsula Pinot Noir 2019,
Geelong** Each Cornelius single-vineyard wine enjoys a singular personality.

Kirkcaldy brings precision and fineness to pinot noir, a quiet, restrained approach that will reward with further time in bottle. A host of florals, of violet and cranberry join dark cherry, spice and discreet oak. Sinewy tannins address this fine-edged pinot noir as it closes. This pinot won't be rushed. Screw cap. 13.5% alc. RATING 94 DRINK 2022–2028 $72 JP

Seabrook Wines

1122 Light Pass Road, Tanunda, SA 5352 **Region** Barossa Valley
T (08) 8563 0368 **www**.seabrookwines.com.au **Open** Thurs–Mon 11–5
Winemaker Hamish Seabrook **Est.** 2004 **Dozens** 3000 **Vyds** 10.1ha
Hamish Seabrook is the youngest generation of a proud Melbourne wine family once involved in wholesale and retail distribution, and as leading show judges of their respective generations. Hamish too, is a wine show judge but was the first to venture into winemaking, working with Best's and Brown Brothers in Victoria before moving to SA with wife Joanne. In 2008 Hamish set up his own winery on the family property in Vine Vale, having previously made the wines at Dorrien Estate and elsewhere. Here they have shiraz (4.4ha), cabernet sauvignon (3.9ha) and mataro (1.8ha), and also continue to source small amounts of shiraz from the Barossa, Langhorne Creek and Pyrenees. Exports to Hong Kong. (JH)

🍷🍷🍷🍷🍷 **The Judge Riesling 2021, Eden Valley** Another cracking riesling from the superb '21 Eden Valley vintage. Aromas of freshly squeezed lime with hints of lemon zest, freshly cut fennel, crushed quartz, rose petals and Christmas lilies. Great citrus fruit carry across the palate, cut with white florals and stone with vivid acidity and a pristine, dry, stony finish. Screw cap. 11.5% alc. RATING 93 DRINK 2021–2028 $28 DB

The Gambler Mataro 2021, Barossa Valley Deep red-purple hue with notes of jasmine-speckled satsuma plum and macerated summer berries, underscored by exotic spice, ginger cake, tangerine rind, brandied fruit, earth and licorice. Perfumed in the mouth too, with a plume of exotically spiced plum and cherry fruits, tight tannin and a meaty facet to the rich, lingering finish. A lot to like here. Screw cap. 14% alc. RATING 93 DRINK 2022–2032 $29 DB

The Architect Cabernet Sauvignon 2015, Coonawarra Burnished red in the glass with complex aromas of black and red currants, polished leather, mahogany, briar, mushroom broth, red licorice and earth. Graceful red fruits with spicy sour-cherry zing, powdery tannins and a long, complex finish. Screw cap. 15.1% alc. RATING 93 DRINK 2022–2032 $80 DB

Lineage Cabernet Malbec 2019, Barossa Valley A deeply coloured wine with a slab of opulent blackberry and mulberry fruit with hints of deep spice, turned earth, licorice and cedar. It shows impressive balance and flow with rich fruit, gravelly tannin pull and is flush with juicy dark fruit on the finish. Screw cap. 14% alc. RATING 92 DRINK 2021–2028 $22 DB ✪

Lineage Mataro Rosé 2021, Barossa Valley Pale copper-tinged pink in the glass, with aromas of delicate redcurrant, raspberry and strawberry fruit with hints of soft spice, watermelon, almond blossom and stone. Flush with red fruits and a little slinky texture to boot, the wine finishes crisp with fresh acidity and a white blossom, strawberry flourish. Screw cap. 12.5% alc. RATING 91 DRINK 2021–2023 $22 DB ✪

Tiger Moth Marshall Montepulciano 2020, Adelaide Hills Dark summer berry and satsuma plum notes combine with spice, licorice, purple flowers, roasting meats and earth. There's a graphite depth on the palate, crunchy acidity and no shortage of assertive tannin making its presence felt behind the dark fruits. Screw cap. 14.5% alc. RATING 90 DRINK 2022–2028 $29 DB

The Triple Threat Grenache Shiraz Mataro 2018, Barossa Valley Grenache from the Barossa's western ridge blended with shiraz and mataro from the region's eastern slopes. Fragrant aromas of ripe plum and summer berry fruits merge with notes of Asian spice, dark chocolate and Barossa earth. Plush in the mouth with gentle tannin grip, bright acidity and a plume of spiced plum fruit on the finish. Screw cap. 14.5% alc. RATING 90 DRINK 2021–2025 $29 DB

ΨΨΨΨ **Lineage Pinot Grigio 2021, Adelaide Hills** RATING 89 DRINK 2021-2023
$22 DB

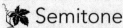

Semitone ★★★☆

Ingliston Road, Ballan, Vic 3342 **Region** Victoria
T 0400 514 613 **Winemaker** David Garner **Est.** 2017 **Dozens** 100
It all started with 0.5t of Pyrenees cabernet sauvignon back in the 2017 vintage, hence the
name Semitone. What started off as a curiosity and passion for winemaking, coupled with
opportunity and shadowing of a number Victorian winemakers, this teacher–come–amateur–
winemaker is now in his fifth vintage of making ultra-small batches of wine from predominantly
(at this stage) Western Victorian vineyards in the Pyrenees, Geelong and Grampians regions.
Production grew to 1t/year in the subsequent vintages culminating in a 3t production from the
amazing 2021 vintage in Victoria, in time for the first commercial release. (JP)

ΨΨΨΨΨ **Cabernet Sauvignon 2019, Pyrenees** A statuesque young cabernet of some
poise and elegance, a reminder of just how suited the Pyrenees region is to
this variety. Opens with aromas of blackberry, plum, violets and an aniseed-led
spiciness. A plush, sweet-fruited palate embraces equally a leafiness and a dried
herbal character. Well-integrated oak completes this attractive, well-priced wine.
Screw cap. 14.2% alc. RATING 90 DRINK 2021-2027 $25 JP

ΨΨΨΨ **Shiraz 2020, Pyrenees** RATING 88 DRINK 2021-2026 $25 JP

Semprevino ★★★★

271 Kangarilla Road, McLaren Vale, SA 5171 **Region** McLaren Vale
T 0417 142 110 **www**.semprevino.com.au **Winemaker** Russell Schroder **Est.** 2006
Dozens 800
Semprevino is the venture of Russell Schroder and Simon Doak, who became close friends
while at Monash University in the early 1990s – studying mechanical engineering and science
respectively. Russell is the prime mover, who, after working for CRA/Rio Tinto for 5 years,
left on a 4-month trip to Western Europe and became captivated by the life of a vigneron.
Returning to Australia, he enrolled in part-time wine science at CSU, obtaining his wine
science degree in 2005. Between '03 and '06 he worked vintages in Italy and Victoria, coming
under the wing of Stephen Pannell at Tinlins (where the Semprevino wines are made). (JH)

ΨΨΨΨΨ **GSM 2020, McLaren Vale** This is good. Reminiscent of quality Côtes du
Rhône, with a swirl of purple fruits and florals, sluiced with Mediterranean
herb, iodine and some smoked-meat extract. The tannins, gently fibrous against
the effortless flow of fruit. An acceptable whiff of reduction, imparts tension.
Mid weighted, plump and extremely versatile. Screw cap. 14.6% alc. RATING 93
DRINK 2021-2026 $26 NG ✪
Shiraz 2020, McLaren Vale A warm year has produced a capacious, large-
framed wine. To its credit, there is nothing jammy or untowards about it. Smoky
to be sure, with an astute selection of wood to assist in reining in the cavalcade of
purple fruits, barbecue, tapenade and dried nori accents. The hot-year tannins are
drying across the finish, but good drinking in all. Screw cap. 15% alc. RATING 91
DRINK 2022-2026 $35 NG

Seppelt ★★★★★

36 Cemetery Road, Great Western, Vic 3377 **Region** Great Western
T (03) 5361 2239 **www**.seppelt.com.au **Open** 7 days 10–5 **Winemaker** Clare Dry
Est. 1851 **Vyds** 648ha
Seppelt once had dual, and very different, claims to fame. The first was as Australia's foremost
producer of both white and red sparkling wine, the former led by Salinger, the latter by Show
Sparkling and Original Sparkling Shiraz. The second claim, even more relevant to the Seppelt
of today, was based on the small-volume superb red wines made by Colin Preece from the
1930s through to the early '60s. These were ostensibly Great Western–sourced but – as the

laws of the time allowed – were often region, variety and vintage blends. Two of his labels (also of high quality) were Moyston and Chalambar. Preece would have been a child in a lolly shop if he'd had today's viticultural resources to draw on, and would have been quick to recognise the commitment of the winemakers and viticulturists to the supreme quality of today's portfolio. Ararat businessman Danial Ahchow has leased the cellar door and surrounds, including the underground drives. Winemaker Clare Dry took over from Adam Carnaby from the '21 vintage. (JH)

ŸŸŸŸŸ Drumborg Vineyard Pinot Noir 2020, Henty Deeper hue than the Pinot Meunier, with more purple. This is a ravishing wine, the bouquet expressive, the palate explosive, with a profusion of red and blue berries, rhubarb and spice, given texture and structure by savoury tannins and a nudge of oak. Screw cap. 13% alc. RATING 97 DRINK 2022–2032 $45 JH ✪

ŸŸŸŸŸ Drumborg Vineyard Riesling 2021, Henty A new senior winemaker (Clare Dry) and a top vintage combine to produce a fully formed classic Drumborg Riesling. Tasted just 10 days after bottling and it was already in scintillating form. Can't wait to see how this progresses over the decade. Palest lemon in colour and a mere 11% alcohol belies the depth and beauty of this wine; its alluring florals of white flowers and spring blossom, of fresh-cut citrus, lime zest and musk. It all rolls into a textural, juicy, lemony-fresh, lightly spiced wonder with life assured for a decade and more. Screw cap. RATING 96 DRINK 2021–2034 $40 JP ✪

St Peters Shiraz 2020, Grampians St Peters continues its drive for greater elegance while retaining a serious degree of complexity. Not all that easy to achieve in the '20 vintage, but it's there in the glass, a vibrantly fresh and fragrant Grampians shiraz. Blackberry, cassis, licorice and lifted woody spices steal your attention. A palate, sinewy in tannin and structure, delves deeper into the rich resource of fruit, aided and abetted by smoky, intriguing oak. Fab drinking now and so much more to give. Screw cap. 14.5% alc. RATING 95 DRINK 2021–2034 $80 JP

Mount Ida Shiraz 2019, Heathcote A contemplative wine for sure, one that would appreciate some more time in bottle before broaching. Has all the elements for a fine, generous Heathcote shiraz circling, coming together nicely. Spicy, perfumed, complex and welcoming in cherry plum, dark berries, dark chocolate, anise and cacao. Immaculate tannin structure, firm and incisive. Stays with you on the finish. Screw cap. 14% alc. RATING 95 DRINK 2022–2032 $55 JP

Seppeltsfield   ★★★★★

730 Seppeltsfield Road, Seppeltsfield, SA 5355 **Region** Barossa Valley
T (08) 8568 6200 **www.seppeltsfield.com.au Open** 7 days 10.30–5 **Winemaker** Fiona Donald, Charlie Seppelt, Matthew Pick, Henry Slattery **Viticulturist** Kingsley Fuller
Est. 1851 **Dozens** 50 000 **Vyds** 648ha
The historic Seppeltsfield property and its bounty of old fortified wines was originally established by the Seppelt family in 1851. Later acquired by Foster's Group (now Treasury Wine Estates), Seppeltsfield returned to private ownership in 2007 with Warren Randall now owning in excess of 90% of its capital. Randall, former sparkling winemaker for Seppelt Great Western in the '80s, has led a revival of Seppeltsfield, gradually restoring the heritage-listed property. The estate's 1888 gravity cellar is back in full operation and a tourism village has been established. Randall has also slowly pieced together the largest premium, privately owned vineyard holding in the Barossa – enabling Seppeltsfield to complement its treasure trove of fortifieds with table wine releases. The 100 Year Old Paras have no parallel anywhere else in the world and the conjunction of 100 years of devoted stewardship (think former cellarmaster James Godfrey) and climate, terroir and varieties have had an outcome that can never, ever, be duplicated. Exports to the UK, South East Asia, Hong Kong, Scandinavia, Japan, South Korea, Canada and the US. (JH)

ŸŸŸŸŸ 100 Year Old Para Vintage Tawny 1922, Barossa Valley There's no surprise that this release easily lives up to its 100-point rating. The heady bouquet (as usual) is followed by a palate of pure joy; as it enters the mouth, the viscous big bass drum beats with every known spice, and every known preserved and dried fruit. Then the finish has the acidity to provide balance, but the sometimes searing spear of volatile acidity doesn't heat the aftertaste. In the world of wine, no other winery makes a vintage-dated 100yo release of truly extraordinary complexity. Cork. 21.4% alc. RATING 100 $1500 JH ♥

Para 21 Year Old Tawny 2001, South Australia Medium tawny in the glass with amber flashes and notes of roasting nuts, candied citrus rinds, burnt toffee, butterscotch, brandy snaps, rancio and Christmas cake, with layers and layers of spice below. Unctuous, with head-spinning complexity and length of finish, with a seam of freshness that drives the flavours across the tongue and off into the distance. Screw cap. 20.4% alc. RATING 97 $95 DB ✪

⛃⛃⛃⛃⛃ **Para Rare Tawny NV** Average age of at least 15 years. Deep–mid tawny with amber shades and green flashes at the edge. Rich fruitcake characters along with layers of spice, candied citrus peel, toffee, roasting nuts, dried and liqueur fruit, rancio, mahogany, polished leather and salted caramel. Fresh as a daisy on the palate, with superb detail, drive and a finish that lingers wonderfully packed with candied fruit and spice. Screw cap. 20.6% alc. RATING 96 $80 DB

No. EC3 Tinta Cão Tinta Amarela Touriga 2020, Barossa An unqualified success: elegant, fresh and perfectly balanced. Ready whenever you are. Screw cap. 14% alc. RATING 95 DRINK 2022-2035 $50 JH

No. EC403 Grenache Shiraz Mataro 2020, Barossa Deeply coloured; the expressive bouquet is a delight, as is the depth of the black berry and cherry flavours on the palate, all achieved with great balance. Barossa Valley on its best behaviour. Screw cap. 14.5% alc. RATING 95 DRINK 2025-2045 $50 JH

Para Grand Tawny NV, South Australia Para Grand Tawny is composed of individual blending of parcels for an average blended age of 10 years. Amber-flecked mahogany in the glass with notes of fruit cake, roasting nuts, toffee, candied citrus rind, caramel, rancio and brandied fruits. Fresh, long and complex with a finish that trails away slowly, leaving a wake of candied and liqueured fruits along with the mahogany tones of extended ageing. Screw cap. 20.2% alc. RATING 95 $40 DB

Serafino Wines   ★★★★★

Kangarilla Road, McLaren Vale, SA 5171 **Region** McLaren Vale
T (08) 8323 0157 www.serafinowines.com.au **Open** Mon–Fri 10–4.30, w'ends & public hols 10–4.30 **Winemaker** Michelle Heagney **Est.** 2000 **Dozens** 30000 **Vyds** 121ha
After the sale of Maglieri Wines to Beringer Blass in 1998, Maglieri founder Serafino (Steve) Maglieri acquired the McLarens on the Lake complex originally established by Andrew Garrett. The operation draws upon over 120ha of shiraz, cabernet sauvignon, chardonnay, merlot, semillon, barbera, nebbiolo, sangiovese, and grenache; part of the grape production is sold. Serafino Wines has won a number of major trophies in Australia and the UK, Steve Maglieri awarded a Member of the Order of Australia in Jan '18. Exports to the UK, the US, Canada, Hong Kong, Malaysia and NZ. (JH)

⛃⛃⛃⛃⛃ **Reserve Grenache 2020, McLaren Vale** Largely sourced from 60-100yo vines in Blewitt Springs and McLaren Flat; the estate bush-vine planting adding mid-palate strength. Essence of McLaren Vale grenache; scented red fruits and hints of musk, supple texture and a long, lifted finish. Screw cap. 14.5% alc. RATING 95 DRINK 2023-2035 $40 JH

Vintage Fortified Shiraz 2006, McLaren Vale Impressive material. Mottled crimson, with garnet edges. A kaleidoscope of complexities from the beef bouillon, yeast stock, hoisin and five-spice at first glimpse, to the dark spiced fruits and sweet mocha of the underbelly. This is in a nice place. It will age further, but I would suggest from this point, give or take another 8 years, is the optimal window. Cork. 18% alc. RATING 95 $50 NG

Cabernet Sauvignon 2019, McLaren Vale Bordeaux's maritime climate for cabernet sauvignon is replicated in McLaren Vale, albeit in a warmer mode, providing a generous style that doesn't lose the variety's signature of blackcurrant, nor the region's lick of dark chocolate. This is an inviting medium- to full-bodied wine, the contributions of tannins and French oak dextrously handled. Bargain. Screw cap. 14.5% alc. RATING 94 DRINK 2024-2034 $28 JH ✪

🍷🍷🍷🍷🍷 Terremoto Syrah 2018, McLaren Vale RATING 93 DRINK 2022-2030 $120 NG
Reserve Grenache 2021, McLaren Vale RATING 92 DRINK 2021-2026 $40 NG
Malpas Vineyard 2020, McLaren Vale RATING 92 DRINK 2022-2032 $45 NG
Shiraz 2019, McLaren Vale RATING 92 DRINK 2024-2034 $28 JH
Bellissimo Sangiovese 2021, McLaren Vale RATING 91 DRINK 2021-2024 $25 NG
Shiraz 2020, McLaren Vale RATING 91 DRINK 2021-2027 $28 NG

Serengale Vineyard ★★★★★

1168 Beechworth-Wangaratta Road, Everton Upper, Vic 3678 **Region** Beechworth
T 0428 585 348 **www**.serengalebeechworth.com.au **Open** By appt **Winemaker** Gayle Taylor **Viticulturist** Serena Abbinga, Gayle Taylor **Est.** 1999 **Dozens** 1000 **Vyds** 7ha
Gayle Taylor and Serena Abbinga established their business in 1999. Gayle had worked in the wine industry for over 20 years, while Serena was seeking to return to North East Victoria after many years living and working in inner city Melbourne. A 3-year search culminated in the acquisition of a 24ha property in the Everton Hills. In the early years they concentrated on planting the 7ha vineyard, with 2.6ha of merlot, 1.2ha chardonnay, 1ha each of cabernet sauvignon, shiraz and pinot gris, and 0.2ha of prosecco. In '15 the winery was completed, and the first vintage made. While Gayle is winemaker and Serena estate manager, their hands-on approach means there's a fair degree of job sharing. (JH)

🍷🍷🍷🍷🍷 Row 16 Chardonnay 2019, Beechworth More structured, with a clean and linear mouthfeel, than the standard chardonnay, Row 16 embraces a mineral, flinty interpretation of the grape with almost chablis-like precision. Nougat, spiced apple, white peach and grapefruit concentrated flavours. Pure, fresh acidity is nicely integrated. Screw cap. 13.8% alc. RATING 96 DRINK 2021-2029 $62 JP ✪
Chardonnay 2019, Beechworth An impressive wine giving full expression to Beechworth chardonnay with its noteworthy quiet power and intensity. Layer upon layer of citrus, grapefruit, mandarin skin, nectarine and white peach with a pinch of oak spice and grilled hazelnuts. Textural and bright and yet with so much hidden in reserve. Screw cap. 13.8% alc. RATING 95 DRINK 2021-2028 $52 JP
Chardonnay 2018, Beechworth The epitome of Beechworth class, this top chardonnay reaches out and pulls you in close. Neatly composed, its fragrance is high in white flowers, summer stone fruit, mandarin and quince. With energy to burn, it wields impressive fruit concentration in tandem with bright acidity as it roams long across the palate. With such drinkability now, it may prove a challenge to age. Screw cap. 13.4% alc. RATING 95 DRINK 2021-2028 $46 JP

🍷🍷🍷🍷 Cabernet Merlot 2019, Beechworth RATING 89 DRINK 2021-2026 $42 JP

Serrat ★★★★★

115 Simpsons Lane, Yarra Glen, Vic 3775 **Region** Yarra Valley
T (03) 9730 1439 **www**.serrat.com.au **Winemaker** Tom Carson, Kate Thurgood
Viticulturist Tom Carson, Kate Thurgood **Est.** 2001 **Dozens** 1000 **Vyds** 3.5ha
Serrat is the family business of Tom Carson (after a 12-year reign at Yering Station, now running Yabby Lake and Heathcote Estate for the Kirby family) and wife Nadège. They have close planted (at 8800 vines/ha) 1.2ha of pinot noir, 0.85ha of shiraz, 0.6ha of chardonnay, 0.4ha of grenache, 0.28ha of nebbiolo and 0.3ha in total of barbera, grenache blanc and malbec. Most recent has been the establishment of an esoteric mix of 0.1ha each of malbec, nebbiolo, barbera and grenache. The vineyards are undergoing organic conversion. As well as being a consummate winemaker, Tom has one of the best palates in Australia and a deep understanding of the fine wines of the world, which he and Nadège drink at every

opportunity (when they aren't drinking Serrat). Tom Carson is the Halliday Wine Companion 2023 Viticulturist of the Year. Exports to Hong Kong. (JH)

♀♀♀♀♀ Shiraz Viognier 2021, Yarra Valley A vibrant crimson purple. A truly wonderful set of wines from Tom Carson in '21, cementing (not that it's needed) his place as one of Australia's best winemakers and the Serrat vineyard as a great, modern-day site. Seductive aromas of cherry plums, dark cherries and raspberries, graphite, sandalwood incense and star anise. Even better on the palate, which is creamy textured, bright, crunchy and perfectly balanced. The tannins are silken and long. This seriously good and gorgeous wine can be enjoyed now and over the next 10–15 years, if not longer. Screw cap. 13.5% alc. RATING 98 DRINK 2022-2033 $48 PR ❂ ♥

Grenache Noir 2021, Yarra Valley A light, bright crimson purple. Pretty and perfumed with aromas of black cherries, raspberries, strawberries, lilacs, thyme and just a hint of bay leaf. Perfectly weighted, this is simultaneously intense, silky and light on the palate. A gorgeous wine that finishes with bright acidity and very fine, gently chalky tannins. Remarkable to think that a grenache of this quality can be made in the Yarra. Screw cap. 14% alc. RATING 97 DRINK 2022-2031 $45 PR ❂ ♥

Pinot Noir 2021, Yarra Valley A brilliant, medium-deep crimson. There's a lot going on here from the outset, with its wild, briary, red fruits, a ferrous character, violets, rose petals and a hint of sweet spice. Medium bodied, the palate is multi layered with fine, persistent and chalky tannins providing considerable backbone and structure. Tightly coiled at the moment, but bear in mind it has just recently been bottled. This will look even better in just a few months and will continue to improve for years to come. Screw cap. 13% alc. RATING 97 DRINK 2022-2031 $45 PR ❂

♀♀♀♀♀ Fourre-Tout 2021, Yarra Valley Fourre-Tout is a French word meaning 'catch-all' and the '21 is a blend of 80/15% barbera/nebbiolo, with a little grenache and pinot noir making up the remainder. A deep, vibrant, crimson purple. Opens up with unctuous blueberries, satsuma plums, violets and mountain herbs. Smells super. And it tastes as good as it smells, with its core of densely packed red and black fruits, plum skins, refreshing acidity and very fine, chalky tannins. Delicious now, I've got no doubt this also has the potential to become more complex over at least the next 5 years. Screw cap. 13% alc. RATING 96 DRINK 2022-2029 $45 PR ❂

Chardonnay 2021, Yarra Valley A very bright green gold. Restrained, with aromas of pink grapefruit, Beurre Bosc pears, jasmine and wet stone. Concentrated and intense but not remotely heavy, there's a steeliness here that's in total harmony with the fruit. Excellent now, this will only open up and become more complex over the next 3–5 years, if not longer. Screw cap. 13.5% alc. RATING 96 DRINK 2022-2028 $45 PR ❂

Sevenhill Cellars   ★★★★☆

111c College Road, Sevenhill, SA 5453 **Region** Clare Valley
T (08) 8843 5900 **www.**sevenhill.com.au **Open** 7 days 10–5 **Winemaker** Will Shields
Est. 1851 **Dozens** 25 000 **Vyds** 96ha
One of the historical treasures of Australia; the oft-photographed stone wine cellars are the oldest in the Clare Valley and winemaking has been an enterprise within this Jesuit province since 1851. All the wines reflect the estate-grown grapes from old vines. In recent years, Sevenhill Cellars has increased its vineyard holdings from 74ha to 96ha and, naturally, production has risen. Exports to Switzerland, South Korea, Indonesia, Malaysia, Papua New Guinea, Singapore, NZ and Hong Kong. (JH)

♀♀♀♀♀ Open Range Grenache 2020, Clare Valley Pert, lifted and vibrant grenache, this has spice aplenty, with layers of flavour and texture to spare. Raspberry, sarsaprilla, even hints of chinotto emerge in the mouth, all of it coming

together and tailing out over a long finish. Screw cap. 14% alc. RATING 95
DRINK 2022-2032 $80 EL

27 Miles Riesling 2021, Clare Valley The wine is super delicate, restrained
and taut. It doesn't have the plump generosity of the Inigo, but the key indicator
of quality is to be found in the length of flavour. While very quiet, it is
enduring. A layered wine of tension and poise. Screw cap. 11% alc. RATING 94
DRINK 2021-2031 $50 EL

Spire's Lament Viognier 2020, Clare Valley Aromatically, this is the pure
essence of apricots. In the mouth: apricots, red apples, fine white spice, crushed
cashews, custard and little hints of turmeric and star anise. A gorgeous wine and a
brilliant example of viognier. Screw cap. 13.5% alc. RATING 94 DRINK 2022-2027
$45 EL

Inigo Cabernet Sauvignon 2019, Clare Valley Cassis, red apples, blackberry
pie and pomegranates. This is laden with aromas and spice: pink peppercorn,
licorice and dark cocoa. The palate is concentrated and lithe, the wine lingering
long after it is gone. The tannins are interesting: very fine, quite grippy, and they
ride in tandem with the fruit, steering it through the long finish. Screw cap.
14% alc. RATING 94 DRINK 2022-2036 $28 EL ✪

ㅜㅜㅜㅜㅜ **Inigo Riesling 2021, Clare Valley** RATING 93 DRINK 2021-2031 $25 EL ✪
Thatch and Clay Touriga 2020, Clare Valley RATING 93 DRINK 2021-2029
$50 EL
Quarry Road Cabernet Malbec 2019, Clare Valley RATING 92
DRINK 2021-2031 $45 EL
Inigo Grenache 2021, Clare Valley RATING 91 DRINK 2022-2028 $28 EL
Inigo Shiraz 2019, Clare Valley RATING 91 DRINK 2021-2028 $28 EL

Seville Estate   ★★★★★

65 Linwood Road, Seville, Vic 3139 **Region** Yarra Valley
T (03) 5964 2622 **www.**sevilleestate.com.au **Open** 7 days 10–5 **Winemaker** Dylan
McMahon **Est.** 1972 **Dozens** 8000 **Vyds** 12ha
Seville Estate was founded by Dr Peter and Margaret McMahon in 1972. After several changes
of ownership, Yiping Wang purchased the property in early '17. Yiping's supportive yet
hands-off approach has allowed winemaker and general manager Dylan McMahon (grandson
of founder Peter McMahon) to steer the ship. The estate has expanded to encompass
the neighbouring vineyard and property (formerly Ainsworth Estate). This extra land has
allowed for replanting original vine material grafted onto rootstock to preserve the original
1972 clones and safeguard the future of this unique property. Seville Estate also has luxury
accommodation with the original homestead and 3 self-contained apartments. Exports to the
US and Canada. (JH)

ㅜㅜㅜㅜㅜ **Old Vine Reserve Pinot Noir 2021, Yarra Valley** A bright, medium, crimson
purple. A special wine from the first whiff, there are aromas of red and black fruits,
floral notes, spice-rack spices together with complex ferrous notes. Concentrated
but pure, structured and balanced. A special wine in the making and one of the
very best '21 Yarra pinots I tasted for this year's Companion. So long. Drink a
bottle now but worth putting some away to enjoy 10–15 years from now. Screw
cap. 13% alc. RATING 97 DRINK 2022-2035 $90 PR ✪

Reserve Chardonnay 2021, Yarra Valley A deepish bright green gold. A
superb Yarra chardonnay – power without weight. Lemon oil, melon, spices, a
nougat nuttiness and ginger. A rich, complex, yet focused and structured mouthful,
becoming fleshier and more open the longer it sits in the glass. Worth decanting
or giving it some air in the glass, but know that this will continue to improve
and become more complex in the bottle over the next 5–10 years. Screw cap.
12.6% alc. RATING 97 DRINK 2022-2028 $90 PR ✪

Old Vine Reserve Shiraz 2020, Yarra Valley A brilliant crimson magenta.
Beautifully perfumed and pure. Redolent of raspberry coulis, peony, Asian spices
and potpourri. Supremely elegant and structured, there's a gentle meatiness to

go with the pure red fruits. The tannins are silky and persistent. Finishes very long and too good to spit! Screw cap. 13% alc. RATING 97 DRINK 2023-2029 $90 PR ✪

Dr McMahon Pinot Noir 2020, Yarra Valley A deep, bright crimson. A powerhouse of a wine that has loads of dark, morello cherry, star anise, cedar from new oak and dried roses from the whole bunches (which are present, but by no means totally dominate the wine). Densely packed on the firmly structured palate, with dark fruits and some black olive tapenade. Needs time – in a good way. This is really pushing the boundaries and I'd love to taste this again in 10, if not 20 years. Screw cap. 13.5% alc. RATING 97 DRINK 2025-2035 $175 PR

ΨΨΨΨΨ **Chardonnay 2021, Yarra Valley** An effortless wine that has power but doesn't feel as if it's been 'made' or forced in any way. Subtle stone fruits, spice and a mineral note that follows onto the palate, which is simultaneously generous yet restrained; the acidity in total harmony with the fruit. In a word – lovely. Screw cap. 12.8% alc. RATING 96 DRINK 2022-2029 $55 PR ✪

Dr McMahon Shiraz 2019, Yarra Valley A bright, medium, crimson purple. Super-aromatic with red and black fruits, pink peppercorns and cedar from new oak. Textured, structured and balanced, there's an elegance to this wine, despite its inherent power. There's plenty of fine-grained and chewy tannins and it will be fascinating to see how this develops as the whole bunches become more integrated and the tannins soften. Screw cap. 13% alc. RATING 96 DRINK 2025-2035 $175 PR

Single Vineyard Series Seville Chardonnay 2021, Yarra Valley A bright green gold. Immediately appealing with its aromas of jus- ripened white peach, together with some orange blossom and a little struck match. A good balance: relaxed and approachable now, but not lacking structure or backbone. Screw cap. 12.5% alc. RATING 95 DRINK 2022-2027 $40 PR

Single Vineyard Series Seville Pinot Noir 2021, Yarra Valley A very light but very bright crimson. A lovely, pure-fruited pinot nose with strawberry, raspberry fruit and just a little spice. Ripe, poised, balanced and long. Good now, this will only improve over the next 5-8 years. Screw cap. 13% alc. RATING 95 DRINK 2022-2030 $45 PR

Shiraz 2020, Yarra Valley A fabulous deep, bright crimson purple. Densely packed with dark fruits, black peppercorns, olive tapenade and some intriguing iodine notes. A rich but balanced mouthful; juicy, yet structured. Fine, long-chained tannins round out a super wine that can be enjoyed now or cellared for at least another 10 years. Screw cap. 13.5% alc. RATING 95 DRINK 2022-2032 $55 PR

Single Vineyard Series Gembrook Pinot Noir 2021, Yarra Valley A gorgeous light bright crimson purple. Pretty from the get go. Aromas of red fruits, dried rose petals and a touch of bitter orange. Just bottled and still quite tightly wound, there's a core of red berry fruits, crunchy tannins and acidity that bodes well for this wine's future. Screw cap. 13% alc. RATING 94 DRINK 2023-2028 $45 PR

Riesling 2020, Yarra Valley A deepish bright green gold. Influenced by winemaker Dylan McMahon's love of German and Alsatian riesling, this is a no-holes-barred approach, which is reflected in the wine's aroma and palate. Ripe, citrus and mandarin peel, spice; a touch exotic in a good way. A textured, mouth-filling but still vibrant and structured wine that finishes with grippy phenolics that would make this a terrific food wine. Screw cap. 11.6% alc. RATING 94 DRINK 2022-2030 $40 PR

Sew & Sew Wines ★★★☆

97 Pennys Hill Road, The Range, SA 5172 **Region** McLaren Vale
T 0437 763 139 **www**.sewandsewwines.com.au **Open** By appt **Winemaker** Jodie Armstrong **Viticulturist** Jodie Armstrong **Est.** 2015 **Dozens** 3500

Winemaker and viticulturist Jodie Armstrong has worked in the wine industry for more than 20 years. She sources grapes from the vineyards that she manages, her in-depth knowledge of these vineyards allowing her to grow and select premium fruit. She makes the wines in friends' wineries 'where collaboration is a source of inspiration'. Exports to Denmark, Canada and Fiji. (JH)

🍷🍷🍷🍷 **Sashiko Series Nero 2020, McLaren Vale** A play on the usual GSM with mataro (aka mourvèdre) joined by nero d'Avola playing the role of shiraz and aglianico assuming a savoury, tannic third party. It is an enticing blend in black cherry, spiced plum and red licorice, spiced up through the middle palate and finishing fresh and juicy. Screw cap. 14% alc. RATING 92 DRINK 2021–2028 $25 JP ☺

🍷🍷🍷 **Sashiko Series GSM 2020, McLaren Vale** RATING 89 DRINK 2021–2028 $25 JP
Sashiko Series Blanc de Blancs NV, Adelaide Hills RATING 88 $25 JP
Sashiko Series Sauvignon Blanc 2021, Adelaide Hills RATING 88 DRINK 2021–2025 $25 JP
Sashiko Series Pinot Gris 2021, Adelaide Hills RATING 88 DRINK 2021–2025 $25 JP

Shadowfax Winery   ★★★★★

K Road, Werribee, Vic 3030 **Region** Port Phillip
T (03) 9731 4420 **www.**shadowfax.com.au **Open** Wed–Mon 11–5 **Winemaker** Alister Timms **Viticulturist** Ko Hironaka **Est.** 2000 **Dozens** 10 000 **Vyds** 28ha
Once an offspring of Werribee Park and its grand mansion, Shadowfax is now very much its own master. It has 10ha of mature vineyards at Werribee; plus 5ha of close-planted pinot noir, 5ha of chardonnay and 2ha of pinot gris at the Little Hampton Vineyard in Macedon; and 3ha of pinot noir, 2ha of chardonnay and 1ha of gewürztraminer elsewhere in Macedon. Alister Timms, with degrees in science (University of Melbourne) and oenology (University of Adelaide) became chief winemaker in '17 (replacing long-serving winemaker Matt Harrop). Exports to the UK and the US. (JH)

🍷🍷🍷🍷🍷 **Minnow Roussanne 2021, Port Phillip** Mmm, this is probably the finest Minnow Roussanne to date. Heady aromas of ginger flower and honeysuckle, mandarin, white stone fruit and pear, all in perfect proportion. A drizzle of honey and ginger, plus some cinnamon with fluffy creamy lees filling out the finely tuned palate. The lemon acidity takes it to a long finish. Screw cap. 13% alc. RATING 95 DRINK 2022–2025 $28 JF ☺
Pinot Gris 2021, Macedon Ranges Gosh, I'd swear there's gewürztraminer in the mix given the lychee aroma and flavour – most unusual yet appealing, too. That adds to delicious flavours of baked apple and pear crumble, ginger cream and tangy lemon sauce. The palate is luscious without being heavy. It finishes convincingly. Screw cap. 13% alc. RATING 95 DRINK 2021–2025 $30 JF ☺
Chardonnay 2021, Geelong While Shadowfax's Macedon Ranges chardonnays often steal the limelight, when Geelong is good it is very, very good. This being a case in point. A wave of white nectarine, grapefruit and lemon layered with zest, ginger cream, woodsy spices plus vanillin toasty oak, not too much, set the richer scene. However, the saline-like acidity is pure, long and reins everything back into a svelte shape. Screw cap. 13% alc. RATING 95 DRINK 2022–2029 $35 JF ☺
Pinot Noir 2020, Macedon Ranges A light, bright, enticing ruby hue and so aromatic: florals, damp forest floor, spiced macerated cherries and a pepperiness too, with a hint of meaty reduction. Lighter framed with fine tannins and while this is overall savoury, it's led more by refreshing acidity, rendering it a vivacious wine. Made from a blend of fruit off 4 single-vineyard sites and in this vintage, very much the sum of its parts – and shining as a result. Screw cap. 13% alc. RATING 95 DRINK 2021–2028 $35 JF ☺

Minnow Grenache Mataro 2021, Port Phillip An even split between the varieties and they are good friends as each complements the other, resulting in a balanced, complete wine in the drink-me-now category. It's such a great mix because it's floral and spicy, full of juicy, red berries, sarsaparilla, cherry cola and meaty charcuterie characters. Plenty of refreshing perky acidity and grainy, light tannins to guide across the mid-weighted palate. Screw cap. 13% alc. RATING 94 DRINK 2022-2028 $28 JF ✪

♟♟♟♟♙ **Gewürztraminer 2021, Macedon Ranges** RATING 93 DRINK 2021-2024 $30 JF
Chardonnay 2020, Macedon Ranges RATING 93 DRINK 2021-2030 $35 JF
Minnow Rosé 2021, Port Phillip RATING 92 DRINK 2021-2023 $26 JF
Little Hampton Pinot Noir 2020, Macedon Ranges RATING 92 DRINK 2023-2033 $65 JF
Pinot Noir 2021, Geelong RATING 91 DRINK 2023-2031 $35 JF
Nebbiolo 2020, Pyrenees RATING 91 DRINK 2023-2028 $35 JF
Straws Lane Pinot Noir 2020, Macedon Ranges RATING 90 DRINK 2023-2030 $65 JF

Shaw + Smith   ★★★★★

136 Jones Road, Balhannah, SA 5242 **Region** Adelaide Hills
T (08) 8398 0500 **www**.shawandsmith.com **Open** 7 days 11–5 **Winemaker** Adam Wadewitz, Martin Shaw **Viticulturist** Murray Leake **Est.** 1989 **Vyds** 62ha
Cousins Martin Shaw and Michael Hill Smith MW already had unbeatable experience when they founded Shaw + Smith as a virtual winery in 1989. In '99 Martin and Michael purchased the 36ha Balhannah property, building the superbly designed winery in '00 and planting more sauvignon blanc, shiraz, pinot noir and riesling. It is here that visitors can taste the wines in appropriately beautiful surroundings. The 20ha Lenswood Vineyard, 10km northwest of the winery, is mainly planted to chardonnay and pinot noir. Exports to all major markets. (JH)

♟♟♟♟♟ **Sauvignon Blanc 2021, Adelaide Hills** A model of consistency over 32 vintages, Shaw + Smith Sauvignon Blanc continues to lead the way in '21 with a combination of fruit intensity and a seeming lightness of being. It's told in 2 parts; the first is exuberant tropicals, citrus and herbal interplay, but it quickly moves into a state of serious intensity, filigree acidity and mealy texture. That lasting impression saturates the tastebuds and stays with you. Screw cap. 12% alc. RATING 96 DRINK 2021-2023 $30 JP ✪ ♥
Riesling 2021, Adelaide Hills This is one of those sneaky wines that manage to hide their qualities until the finish and aftertaste, when all heaven breaks free. Its mix of lime, lemon, Granny Smith apple and white peach all demand a place. Screw cap. 12% alc. RATING 96 DRINK 2023-2041 $35 JH ✪
Lenswood Vineyard Chardonnay 2020, Adelaide Hills Offers a journey into the deep heart of Adelaide Hills chardonnay country, which is both filigree fine and powerful. Quite the winemaking statement in what was a difficult year. Expect citrus, flint, grapefruit pith and bite, peach skin and nectarine. Arrives with both texture and length, beautifully detailed and enhanced by lemony bright acidity. Early days for this lip-smacking, gorgeous thing. Screw cap. 13.5% alc. RATING 96 DRINK 2022-2031 $93 JP ♥
Balhannah Vineyard Shiraz 2019, Adelaide Hills Spellbinding in its classy elegance. This one is for those who wonder how good cool-climate Adelaide Hills shiraz can be. It rolls, seamless, across the tongue with little gems of fennel seed, pomegranate, bergamot and anise left along the way, as the wine delivers plush fruit and a quiet but resounding tannic drive. Excellence in the glass. Screw cap. 13.5% alc. RATING 96 DRINK 2022-2031 $93 JP
Pinot Noir 2021, Adelaide Hills Arrives as a fully fledged pinot noir, complex and intriguing. Starts with a wealth of dark fruits, forest floor, bracken, earthy notes and woodsy spice, before launching into a sweeping, textural palate, glossy and

even. Oak adds some extra creamy, spicy complexity and, boy, it runs long. Screw cap. 13.5% alc. RATING 95 DRINK 2022-2029 $52 JP

Shiraz 2020, Adelaide Hills In other marketing hands there might have been the urge to call this syrah, such is the elegance and fine detail in the '20. But these vinous characters are also true of shiraz, too. In the glass, it is all cool-climate Aussie shiraz: laden with spice, blue and black fruits, a touch of peppery lift and bitter herbal savouriness and supple tannins that first helps glide and then smack the lips as it nears the finish. Fab energy and drive. Screw cap. 14% alc. RATING 95 DRINK 2022-2030 $52 JP

Shaw Family Vintners ★★★☆

369 Myrtle Grove Road, Currency Creek, SA 5214 **Region** Currency Creek
T (08) 8555 4215 **www.**shawfamilyvintners.com **Open** Mon–Fri 9–5 **Winemaker** Brie Overcash, Brooke Blair **Est.** 2001 **Dozens** 60000 **Vyds** 414ha
Shaw Family Vintners was established in the early '70s by Richard and Marie Shaw and sons Philip, Nathan and Mark when they planted shiraz at McLaren Flat. Extensive vineyards were acquired and developed in McLaren Vale (64ha) and Currency Creek (350ha), and a winery at Currency Creek. In Apr '17 the winery, vineyards, stock and brands were purchased by Casella Family brands and are now managed by the next generation of Casella and Shaw families. Exports to the UK, the US and Canada. (JH)

♥♥♥♥♀ **Stonemason Shiraz 2019, Currency Creek** Wow. Finding wines at this price and quality – we are in unicorn land. Luscious notes of black cherry and dark chocolate have balanced, ripe tannins to provide texture and structure. Screw cap. 14.5% alc. RATING 90 DRINK 2022-2025 $15 JH ✪

♥♥♥♥ **The Josephine Pinot Gris 2021, Adelaide Hills** RATING 89 DRINK 2021-2022 $17 JH ✪
True Colours Riesling 2021, Clare Valley RATING 89 DRINK 2022-2024 $17 JH ✪
Moonraker Merlot 2019, McLaren Vale RATING 89 DRINK 2021-2024 $22 JH

Sherrah Wines ★★★★

148 McMurtrie Rd, McLaren Vale SA 5171 **Region** McLaren Vale
T 0429 123 383 **www.**sherrahwines.com.au **Open** Fri–Mon 11–5 **Winemaker** Alex Sherrah **Est.** 2016 **Dozens** 3000
Alex Sherrah's career started with a bachelor of science in organic chemistry and pharmacology, leading him to travel the world, to return home broke and in need of a job. Time spent as a cellar rat at Tatachilla and a graduate diploma in oenology at Waite University were followed by a job at Kendall Jackson's Napa Valley crown jewel, Cardinale, making ultra-premium bordeaux blends. Stints at Knappstein and O'Leary Walker followed, punctuated by vintages in Burgundy and Austria. At the end of 2011 he moved to McLaren Vale and Coriole, where he became senior winemaker in '12, remaining there for 6 years, before moving on to head up winemaking at Haselgrove, his present day job. He says ' I believe in balance, a great wine should have no sharp edges, it should have beautiful smooth curves from front to back.' Exports to the US and Luxembourg. (JH)

♥♥♥♥♀ **Fiano 2021, McLaren Vale** Delicious! Drinks like lemon Kool-Aid with a briny twist, a whiff of wild fennel, jasmine and orange blossom. Best, the texture. Mid weighted, layered and bright. This sits pretty. Screw cap. 12.5% alc. RATING 93 DRINK 2021-2023 $30 NG
Nero d'Avola 2021, McLaren Vale Crunchy, lip smacking and juicy all at once. Delicious, mid weighted of feel and exuberant! Red fruits, root spice and a fine twine of pin-bone tannins, herbal and moreish, sewing it all together. Screw cap. 14% alc. RATING 93 DRINK 2021-2024 $30 NG
Skin Party Fiano 2021, McLaren Vale A great vintage, a solid wine. The phenolic pickup, perfectly attuned to this easy-drinking style, etching it with

texture as much as riffs on wild ginger, quince, turmeric and orange zest. Long, vibrant and impeccably detailed. Very good drinking. Screw cap. 12% alc. RATING 93 DRINK 2021-2024 $30 NG

Shiraz 2020, McLaren Vale Solid. Violets, a smear of furikake, menthol, olive and smoky oak where, presumably, the fermentation finished. Round, rich and relatively juicy for the vintage. Drying, robust tannins mark the finish. Screw cap. 14% alc. RATING 91 DRINK 2021-2025 $30 NG

Preservative Free Grenache 2021, McLaren Vale From 3 plots, 2 of old bush vines. Separate whole-berry ferments promote a jubey, soft, semi-carbonic aura of rosewater, Cherry Ripe and anise flavours. Some bunches were added to impart a spicy riff, but the vibe is one of irreverent gulpability, demanding a serious chill. Screw cap. 14.2% alc. RATING 90 DRINK 2021-2022 $25 NG

🍷🍷🍷🍷 **Red et Al Grenache Shiraz Nero d'Avola 2020, McLaren Vale** RATING 89 DRINK 2021-2023 $30 NG

Grenache Rosé 2021, McLaren Vale RATING 88 DRINK 2021-2022 $25 NG

Shingleback ★★★★☆

3 Stump Hill Road, McLaren Vale, SA 5171 **Region** McLaren Vale
T (08) 8323 7388 **www**.shingleback.com.au **Open** 7 days 10–5 **Winemaker** John Davey, Dan Hills **Viticulturist** Paul Mathews, John Davey **Est.** 1995 **Dozens** 150000 **Vyds** 120ha
Brothers Kym and John Davey planted and nurture their family-owned and sustainably managed vineyard on land purchased by their grandfather in the '50s. Shingleback has been a success story since its establishment. Its 120ha of estate vineyards are one of the keys to that success, which includes winning the Jimmy Watson Trophy in 2006 for the '05 D Block Cabernet Sauvignon. The well-made wines are rich and full-flavoured, but not overripe (and hence, not excessively alcoholic). Exports to NZ, Canada, the US, the UK, Singapore, Cambodia and Vietnam. (JH)

🍷🍷🍷🍷🍷 **Davey Estate Single Vineyard Shiraz 2019, McLaren Vale** A compellingly endowed shiraz which has managed to emerge from its oak womb with a supple, seductive medium-bodied palate that has an energetic savoury finish, which is the high point of the wine. Three trophies McLaren Vale Wine Show '20. Screw cap. 14% alc. RATING 95 DRINK 2024-2034 $25 JH ✪

🍷🍷🍷🍷🍷 **The Bio Project Fiano 2021, McLaren Vale** RATING 93 DRINK 2022-2029 $25 JH ✪

D Block Reserve Cabernet Sauvignon 2019, McLaren Vale RATING 93 DRINK 2021-2032 $55 NG

NX Gen Grenache 2021, McLaren Vale RATING 91 DRINK 2021-2024 $25 NG

The Bio Project Tempranillo Blend 2020, McLaren Vale RATING 91 DRINK 2021-2025 $25 NG

Shirvington ★★★★

107 Strout Road, McLaren Vale, SA 5171 **Region** McLaren Vale
T (08) 8323 7649 **www**.shirvington.com **Open** Thurs–Mon 11–4 **Winemaker** Kim Jackson **Viticulturist** Peter Bolte **Est.** 1996 **Dozens** 950 **Vyds** 23.8ha
The Shirvington family began the development of their McLaren Vale vineyards in '96 under the direction of viticulturist Peter Bolte and now have almost 24ha under vine, the majority to shiraz and cabernet sauvignon, with small additional plantings of grenache and mataro. A substantial part of the production is sold as grapes, the best reserved for the Shirvington wines. Exports to the US. (JH)

🍷🍷🍷🍷 **Row X Row Riesling 2021, Clare Valley** Riesling Australiana. Candied lemon peel, cumquat, talc, bath salts and Rose's Lime. Impressionable. Exuberant. Tangy, racy and long, without being brittle or mouth-puckeringly dry. Fun. Screw cap. 11.5% alc. RATING 88 DRINK 2022-2028 $25 NG

Shoofly | Frisk

PO Box 119, Mooroolbark, Vic 3138 **Region** Various
T 0405 631 557 **www.**shooflywines.com **Winemaker** Ben Riggs, Garry Wall, Mark
O'Callaghan **Est.** 2003 **Dozens** 20 000
This is a far-flung, export-oriented, business. It purchases a little over 620t of grapes each
vintage, the lion's share (surprisingly) riesling (250t), followed by shiraz (200t) and chardonnay
(50t); the remainder is made up of pinot noir, gewürztraminer, merlot, dolcetto and muscat
gordo blanco. Ben Riggs makes Shoofly Shiraz and Chardonnay at Vintners McLaren Vale;
Frisk Riesling and Prickly Riesling is made by Garry Wall at King Valley Wines. The bulk of
exports go to the US, Canada, Ireland and South Korea. (JH)

ŸŸŸŸ **Shoofly Shiraz 2020, South Australia** Tanned hide, star anise, chocolate, red
earth, hung deli meat and blackberries. This is a savoury, spicy wine with more
secondary and tertiary characters than expected for its recent vintage. The finish
rounds out a touch rugged, but plenty of varietal typicity for the money. Screw
cap. 14.5% alc. RATING 88 DRINK 2022-2024 $17 EL ✪

Shut the Gate Wines

8453 Main North Road, Clare, SA 5453 and SA Snowy Mountains Berridale,
39 Jindabyne Road, Berridale, NSW 2628 **Region** Clare Valley
T (08) 8843 4114 **www.**shutthegate.com.au **Open** Clare Valley, 7 days 10–4.30,
Snowy Mountains, 7 days 10–5 **Winemaker** Contract **Est.** 2013 **Dozens** 6000
Shut the Gate is the venture of Richard Woods and Rasa Fabian, which took shape after
5 years' involvement in the rebranding of Crabtree Watervale Wines, followed by 18 months
of juggling consultancy roles. During this time Richard and Rasa set the foundations for
Shut the Gate; the striking and imaginative labels (and parables) catching the eye. The engine
room of the business is the Clare Valley, where the wines are contract-made and the grapes
for many of the wines are sourced. They have chosen their grape sources and contract
winemakers with considerable care. (JH)

ŸŸŸŸŸ **For Love Single Site Tempranillo 2020, Clare Valley** Blackberry coulis,
raspberry and red licorice; the palate powered by a track of savoury, almost chalky
tannin. Deli meat and black cherries come in through the finish – this is earthy
and fruit-driven at once. Quite delicious. The highlight is certainly the tannins;
they are chewy and omnipresent and really shape the fruit. Screw cap. 13.5% alc.
RATING 92 DRINK 2022-2028 $32 EL

The White Deer Pinot Gris 2021, Hilltops Upfront florals mingle with an
estery/yeasty note but also stone fruit, apple compote and baking spices. The
palate has good weight and texture, yet finishes fresh and lively. Screw cap. 13% alc.
RATING 91 DRINK 2021-2023 $25 JF

For Love Sauvignon Blanc 2021, Adelaide Hills Juniper, lemongrass, green
apple skins and a little flick of cassis. Gorgeous. In the mouth the wine is saline,
fine, pretty and restrained; an ode to the wonderful year that birthed it. Screw cap.
12% alc. RATING 91 DRINK 2021-2024 $29 EL

The Forager Shiraz 2019, Clare Valley Concentrated black and red fruits, plus
spice; damsons, raspberries, licorice, mulberries, clove, aniseed and black pepper.
It's very smart – all this for $28. It's a goodie. Screw cap. 14.5% alc. RATING 91
DRINK 2021-2028 $28 EL

Fur Elise Grenache Rosé 2021, Clare Valley Raspberries, watermelon,
pomegranate and red apples. This is a dark colour for a rosé, and brings back fond
memories of the Rose of Virginia. In the mouth this is sweet and littered with
fruit, the finish closing out into a crunchy, refreshing place (some tart rhubarb for
good measure). Uncomplicated, but satisfying. Screw cap. 12% alc. RATING 90
DRINK 2022-2023 $25 EL

Rosie's Patch Watervale Riesling 2021, Clare Valley Tight, citrussy riesling
with a core of green apple and lime. Uncomplicated, pure drinking, here. Screw
cap. 12% alc. RATING 90 DRINK 2021-2027 $25 EL

For Love Watervale Riesling 2021, Clare Valley Cheesecloth, apple skins and layers of citrus zest and pith. Light, bright and breezy – a beautiful summer wine. Screw cap. 12% alc. RATING 90 DRINK 2021-2028 $29 EL
For Love Fiano 2021, Wrattonbully Green apples, lychee, jasmine flowers and pea tendrils. This is clean and green and bright, a testament to the freshness and finesse of the '21 vintage. Lovely persistence through the finish. Screw cap. 12.5% alc. RATING 90 DRINK 2022-2025 $29 EL

ŢŢŢŢ **Blossom 24GRS Riesling 2021, Clare Valley** RATING 89 DRINK 2022-2025 $25 EL

Shy Susan Wines

Billy Button Wines, 11 Camp Street, Bright, Vic 3741 **Region** Tasmania
T 0434 635 510 **www**.shysusanwines.com.au **Open** 7 days 11–6 **Winemaker** Glenn James **Est.** 2015 **Dozens** 300
'Shy Susan (Tetratheca gunnii) is a critically endangered wildflower endemic to a tiny part of Tasmania. Her survival depends completely on a little native bee, who alone is capable of pollination. Their fate is forever entwined.' After working with Tasmanian fruit for nearly 2 decades Glenn James and Jo Marsh have released a range of unique wines from some of Tasmania's most exciting vineyards. Their initial release includes Riesling, a Sylvaner Riesling blend, Gewürztraminer, Chardonnay, Pinot Noir and an Amphora Shiraz. Select small parcels of fruit are crafted to reflect variety, vineyard and the stylistic approach forged from Glenn's skill and experience. Jo Marsh is owner and winemaker of Billy Button Wines (see separate entry). (JH)

ŢŢŢŢ **Chardonnay 2019, Tasmania** Powerful, nutty oak takes the lead, with generous white peach and lemon fruit carrying long amid racy Tasmanian acidity. It's buttery and voluptuous. Power over precision, with certain appeal for those who love chardonnay in this shape. Screw cap. 13% alc. RATING 89 DRINK 2021-2022 $55 TS
Pinot Noir 2019, Tasmania Exotic spice and macerated berry fruits frame a bouquet of lifted musk fragrance. The palate leads out red-fruited and tangy, but immediately loses momentum, lacking fruit persistence to support its finely textured tannin tail. Screw cap. 14% alc. RATING 88 DRINK 2021-2021 $65 TS

Sidewood Estate

6 River Road Hahndorf, SA 5125 **Region** Adelaide Hills
T (08) 8388 1673 **www**.sidewood.com.au **Open** Mon–Sun 11–5 **Winemaker** Darryl Catlin **Viticulturist** Mark Vella **Est.** 2004 **Vyds** 90ha
Sidewood Estate was established in 2004. It is owned by Owen and Cassandra Inglis who operate it as a winery and cidery. Situated in the Onkaparinga Valley, the vines weather the cool climate of the Adelaide Hills. Significant expenditure on regeneration of the vineyards was already well underway when Sidewood invested over $12 million in the expansion of the winery, increasing capacity from 500t to 2000t each vintage and implementing sustainable improvements including 100kW solar panels, water treatment works and insulation for the winery. The expansion includes new bottling and canning facilities capable of handling 6 million bottles of wine and cider annually. A multimillion-dollar restaurant, cellar door and cidery was opened in 2020. Wines are released under the Sidewood Estate, Stablemate and Mappinga labels. Exports to the UK, the US, Canada, the Netherlands, Malaysia, Thailand, Vanuatu, Singapore and Japan. (JH)

ŢŢŢŢŢ **Abel Pinot Noir 2019, Adelaide Hills** A light and open-weaved single-clone pinot. Bright brick red colour, a little shy to the nose, though thoroughly enticing, perhaps because of it. Shag-pile carpet softness on the palate offers a gentle feel, before you notice its fruit-driven acidity in a delicate wave of subtle and sophisticated pinot. As alluring as pinot can be. Screw cap. 12.5% alc. RATING 96 DRINK 2020-2025 $40 TL ✪

Sauvignon Blanc 2021, Adelaide Hills What do we ask of sauvignon blanc? We ask for this: a wine that combines tension and energy with simply joyous, live-for-the-moment fruit intensity. Kaffir lime, lemon zest, grapefruit, nettle and lemongrass moments dart in, out and around zippy acidity. Scintillating. Trophy Perth Royal Wine Awards 2021. Screw cap. 12% alc. RATING 95 DRINK 2021-2024 $22 JP ✪

Ironstone Barrels The Old China Hand Syrah 2019, Adelaide Hills A single PT15 clonal selection from the estate's Echunga vineyard, offering dark and intense aromatics like sarsaparilla and roasted beetroot. Then prepare for intense dark chocolate and prune flavours and textures; these build concentration, but don't deter the wine's natural dark fruit and acidity. Plenty of excitement to experience in this outing. Screw cap. 14.5% alc. RATING 95 DRINK 2021-2027 $50 TL

Mappinga Shiraz 2019, Adelaide Hills Adelaide Hills shiraz kicks goals. Another fine example here, one with density and concentration. A ripe, dark-fruited expression that slides effortlessly between Aussie bush, briar, spearmint and black fruits on the one hand and earthy savouriness with layered toasty oak on the other. Sturdy tannins add some kick and grip. Will evolve handsomely in the bottle. Screw cap. 14.5% alc. RATING 95 DRINK 2021-2029 $65 JP

Late Disgorged Isabella Rosé 2015, Adelaide Hills A salmon-pink colour, this has a gentle toasty complexity on show, laid across a palate of ripe, red fruits, grilled almond and biscuit. Dry and invigorating in its clean acid finish. Diam. 12% alc. RATING 94 $35 JP

Mappinga Chardonnay 2020, Adelaide Hills Makes an immediate creamy, buttery, complex impression with summery stone-fruit intensity, biscuit spice, nougat and citrus. The oak is well integrated, providing a background hum and vanillin creaminess. Plenty of flavour right here, and the price makes it a steal. Screw cap. 12.5% alc. RATING 94 DRINK 2021-2026 $25 JP ✪

Oberlin Pinot Noir 2020, Adelaide Hills Alluring bouquet, quite lovely, in violet aromatics, musk, black cherry, mulberry, sappy bracken and lively pinot spice. We could debate the quantity of whole bunches – they are evident – but they become another interesting, complex layer in this lean, sinewy young wine. Screw cap. 12% alc. RATING 94 DRINK 2021-2029 $45 JP

🍷🍷🍷🍷🍷 **Cassandra Late Disgorged Blanc de Blancs 2016, Adelaide Hills** RATING 93 $55 JP
Pinot Gris 2021, Adelaide Hills RATING 93 DRINK 2021-2024 $24 JP ✪
Shiraz 2020, Adelaide Hills RATING 93 DRINK 2021-2029 $26 JP ✪
Pinot Noir Chardonnay NV, Adelaide Hills RATING 92 $22 JP ✪
Abel Pinot Noir 2020, Adelaide Hills RATING 91 DRINK 2021-2028 $45 JP

Sieber Wines   ★★★☆

82 Sieber Road, Tanunda South, SA 5352 **Region** Barossa Valley
T (08) 8562 8038 **www.sieberwines.com Open** 7 days 11–4 **Winemaker** Tony Carapetis
Viticulturist Ben Sieber **Est.** 1999 **Dozens** 7500 **Vyds** 18ha
Richard and Val Sieber are the third generation to run Redlands, the family property, traditionally a cropping and grazing farm. They have diversified into viticulture with shiraz (14ha) occupying the lion's share, the remainder split between viognier, grenache and mourvèdre. Exports to Canada. (JH)

🍷🍷🍷🍷 **Ernest Shiraz 2020, Barossa Valley** Jasmine-dusted rich dark satsuma plum and blackberry fruits with hints of dark spice, pressed flowers, licorice, smoky charcuterie and coal dust. Medium bodied, with compact drying tannins, black fruit profile and a graphite note on the finish. Screw cap. 14.1% alc. RATING 89 DRINK 2022-2028 $25 DB

Piper Lilli Viognier 2021, Barossa Valley An interesting little frizzante viognier that took me by surprise on the first sip. There's a lively spritz apparent in the glass and characters of tropical and citrus fruits, clotted cream, lemon sherbet and the characteristic waft of apricot. It's sweet and bouncy, maybe a touch sugary but heck, ice cold, bare foot on the lawn? You get the picture. Screw cap. 6% alc. RATING 88 $18 DB

GSM 2020, Barossa Valley Bright red in the glass with characters of ripe plum, red cherry and raspberry fruits, cut through with hints of gingerbread, exotic spice, tropical flowers, red licorice and earth. Medium bodied with floral, musky notes, ripe red fruits and gingery spice trailing off slowly. Screw cap. 15% alc. RATING 88 DRINK 2022-2027 $20 DB

Shiraz Mataro 2019, Barossa Valley Moody dark and black fruits with an undercurrent of roasting meats, dark spice, salted licorice, pressed flowers and turned earth. The floral elements picks up on the palate, as does the coal-dust broodiness and chewy tannin, finishing dark and dry. Screw cap. 14.4% alc. RATING 88 DRINK 2022-2027 $20 DB

Cabernet Shiraz 2019, Barossa Valley Crunchy and floral with vibrant mulberry, red plum and red cherry fruits along with hints of ginger spice, cola, red licorice, purple flowers and earth. Floral, ripe and mucky in the mouth with a jasmine-infused finish. Screw cap. 13.3% alc. RATING 88 DRINK 2022-2027 $40 DB

Silent Noise

44 Hamilton Road, McLaren Flat, SA 5171 **Region** McLaren Vale
T (08) 8383 0533 www.silentnoisewine.com.au **Open** Mon–Fri 9–4.30, w'ends & public hols 11–4 **Winemaker** Charlie O'Brien **Est.** 2016 **Dozens** 2000 **Vyds** 0.2ha
Charlie O'Brien is the son of Helen and Kevin O'Brien, founders of Kangarilla Road. As a small child (a photo on the website says it all) he revelled in the noise of vintage, the 'silent noise' that of the wine when bottled. Since leaving school at the end of 2016 he worked vintages at Gemtree and Yangarra Estate in McLaren Vale, Pikes in the Clare Valley, Pike & Joyce in the Adelaide Hills, Moss Wood in Margaret River, as well as Paul Mas in the Languedoc and Château Haut-Bailly in Bordeaux. The world is his oyster. Exports to the UK, Denmark and NZ. (JH)

🍷🍷🍷🍷🍷 **MF Grenache 2021, McLaren Vale** A sappy and delicious expression, beaming sandalwood, tamarind, woodsmoke and a carnal clove to cherry underbelly. The 15% whole bunches is responsible for the modicum of mescal-peppery complexity and an additional parry to the tannins, extracted across an apposite 3 weeks. Long-limbed and chewy, the tannins make the wine. A nicely crafted, visceral and highly contemporary expression that resounds with the urgency of now. The linger, impressive. Screw cap. 14% alc. RATING 94 DRINK 2021-2025 $35 NG

🍷🍷🍷🍷🍷 **FO Shiraz 2021, McLaren Vale** RATING 93 DRINK 2021-2024 $35 NG
SGZ 2020, McLaren Vale RATING 93 DRINK 2021-2025 $35 NG
Cloudy but Fine Primitivo Under Flor 2020, McLaren Vale RATING 92 DRINK 2022-2028 $40 NG
Chardonnay 2020, Adelaide Hills RATING 90 DRINK 2021-2025 $40 JP

Silkwood Estate

2280 Channybearup Road, Pemberton, WA 6260 **Region** Pemberton
T (08) 9776 1584 www.silkwoodestate.com.au **Open** Fri–Mon & public hols 10–4
Winemaker Michael Ng **Viticulturist** Joel Stefanetti **Est.** 1998 **Dozens** 20 000
Vyds 25ha
Silkwood Wines has been owned by the Bowman family since 2004. The vineyard is patrolled by a large flock of guinea fowl, eliminating most insect pests and reducing the use of chemicals. In '05 the adjoining vineyard was purchased, lifting the estate plantings to 23.5ha, which include shiraz, cabernet sauvignon, merlot, sauvignon blanc, chardonnay, pinot noir, riesling and zinfandel. The cellar door, restaurant and 4 luxury chalets overlook the large lake on the property. Exports to Malaysia and Singapore. (JH)

🍷🍷🍷🍷🍷 **The Walcott Chardonnay 2021, Pemberton** Savoury, worked and driven by oak and acid at this point. The fruit is reminiscent of white peaches and green apples, the oak is pervasive throughout every aspect of the wine, without actually being 'woody'. The highlight is undoubtedly the finish, lingering and concentrated. Screw cap. 13.5% alc. RATING 90 DRINK 2022-2028 $30 EL

The Bowman Chardonnay 2021, Pemberton There's a lot going on here. It's edgy and plump, there is salted peach and apples and plenty of brine. The acid and the oak/tannin have a bit of an awkward intersect at this stage; it's not quite come together yet, although that's hardly surprising given it is so young. Give it a year or 2 to sink into itself. Screw cap. 13.5% alc. RATING 90 DRINK 2022-2028 $55 EL

The Walcott Cabernet Sauvignon 2020, Pemberton Fine but firm tannins shape the dark berries and spicy fruit. The length doesn't linger as long as one would hope, but everything is in place. This is elegant, medium-bodied, herbal (think Amaro, not green) cabernet. Screw cap. 13.5% alc. RATING 90 DRINK 2022-2032 $30 EL

ŸŸŸŸ **The Bowers Chardonnay 2021, Pemberton** RATING 88 DRINK 2022-2027 $21 EL

Silver Lining ★★★★

60 Gleneagles Road, Mount Osmond, SA 5064 **Region** Adelaide Hills
T 0438 736 052 **www.**silverliningwine.com.au **Winemaker** Leigh Ratzmer, Marty Edwards **Viticulturist** Vitiworks, Simon Tolley **Est.** 2020 **Dozens** 1200
The name alone says a lot about the positive and life-affirming attitude of this venture by Marty Edwards, whose love of the Adelaide Hills was nurtured by his family's pioneering involvement with The Lane Vineyard in Hahndorf. They have all left that business now but after being diagnosed with Parkinson's Disease in 2012, Marty (previously an elite navy clearance diver) decided he still had a lot more to give. He focused on his health and young family, but couldn't give up his passion for Hills vineyards and wines. Silver Lining Wines was the result, with proceeds going to Parkinson's Disease research with the aim of helping others on the same challenging journey as this inspiring vigneron. Exports to the UK. (TL)

ŸŸŸŸŸ **Sauvignon Blanc 2021, Adelaide Hills** Bristles with Adelaide Hills sauvignon blanc zesty swagger: kaffir lime leaf, grapefruit, nectarine and white peach with a splash of passionfruit. Energy to burn on the palate, with super bright limey acidity and citrus zestiness. Hits the sauvignon spot. Screw cap. 12.5% alc. RATING 92 DRINK 2021-2025 $25 JP **●**

Chardonnay 2021, Adelaide Hills Less fruit forward and more a partnership of fruit and oak, producing a savoury-edged, textural chardonnay. Combines succulent Hills' stone fruit, lime and citrus with nougat and almond meal. Preserved lemon savouriness on the finish is super tasty. Screw cap. 12.7% alc. RATING 92 DRINK 2021-2028 $30 JP

Silver Spoon Estate ★★★★

503 Heathcote-Rochester Road, Heathcote, Mount Camel, Vic 3523 **Region** Heathcote
T 0412 868 236 **www.**silverspoonestate.com.au **Open** Fri–Sun & public hols 10.30–5 or by appt **Winemaker** Peter Young **Est.** 2008 **Dozens** 1500 **Vyds** 22ha
When Peter and Tracie Young purchased an existing shiraz vineyard on the top of the Mount Camel Range in 2008, they did not waste any time. They immediately planted a second vineyard, constructed a small winery and in '13 acquired a neighbouring vineyard. The estate name comes from the Silver Spoon fault line that delineates the Cambrian volcanic rock from the old silver mines on the property. Peter became familiar with vineyards when working in the '70s as a geologist in the Hunter Valley and he more recently completed the master of wine technology and viticulture degree at the University of Melbourne. (JH)

ŸŸŸŸŸ **The Hallmark Shiraz 2018, Heathcote** Striking in deep purples and in a lifted, aromatic fragrance that really leaps from the glass. The maker has channelled Heathcote generosity and created a wine of some class. Ripe in blackberry, blue fruits, violet, anise and earthy nuance, The Hallmark is built on a solid core of fruit,

integrated oak and fine tannins. Screw cap. 15% alc. RATING 95 DRINK 2021-2030
$68 JP

🍷🍷🍷🍷⚲ **The Fandango Dry Red 2019, Heathcote** RATING 90 DRINK 2021-2028
$25 JP

Silverstream Wines   ★★★★☆
241 Scotsdale Road, Denmark, WA 6333 **Region** Denmark
T (08) 9848 2767 **www.**silverstreamwines.com **Open** By appt **Winemaker** Michael
Garland **Est.** 1997 **Dozens** 2500 **Vyds** 9ha
Tony and Felicity Ruse have 9ha of chardonnay, merlot, cabernet franc, pinot noir, riesling and
viognier in their vineyard 23km from Denmark. The wines are contract-made and, after some
hesitation, the Ruses decided their very pretty garden and orchard more than justified opening
a cellar door, a decision supported by the quality of the wines on offer at very reasonable
prices. Exports to the UK, Singapore and Japan. (JH)

🍷🍷🍷🍷⚲ **Reserve Chardonnay 2011, Denmark** Golden in colour in '21, the wine is
rich with Golden Delicious apples, lemon oil, vermouth (Martini Bianco), bitter
walnuts, alpine herbs and vanilla Tina wafers. This has a lot going for it, but it's at
its peak currently: another 12-18 months from now and the characters may start to
turn. Perfect if you want to drink aged chardonnay NOW – and you didn't even
have to age it yourself. Bingo. Screw cap. 14% alc. RATING 91 DRINK 2021-2023
$45 EL
Single Vineyard Reserve Cabernet Franc 2012, Denmark Matured for
18 months in seasoned French oak. This has all the savoury development you'd
expect from a wine 9 years of age. Olive tapenade, mulberry compote, stewed
rhubarb, fennel seeds and clove. It is graceful and engaging, but drink it now,
because it is at its peak. Screw cap. 14% alc. RATING 90 DRINK 2021-2025 $40 EL

🍷🍷🍷🍷 **Blanc de Blancs NV, Great Southern** RATING 88 $35 EL

Singlefile Wines   ★★★★★
90 Walter Road, Denmark, WA 6333 **Region** Great Southern
T 1300 885 807 **www.**singlefilewines.com **Open** 7 days 11–5 **Winemaker** Mike
Garland, Coby Ladwig, Patrick Corbett **Est.** 2007 **Dozens** 10 000 **Vyds** 3.75ha
In 1986, Phil Snowden and his wife Viv moved from South Africa to Perth, where they
developed their successful multinational mining and resource services company, Snowden
Resources. Following the sale of the company in 2004, they turned their attention to their
long-held desire to make and enjoy fine wine. In '07 they bought an established vineyard
(planted in '89) in the beautiful Denmark subregion. They pulled out the old shiraz and
merlot vines, kept and planted more chardonnay and retained Larry Cherubino to set up
partnerships with established vineyards in Frankland River, Porongurup, Denmark, Pemberton
and Margaret River. The cellar door, tasting room and restaurant are strongly recommended.
The consistency of the quality of the Singlefile wines is outstanding, as is their value for
money. Exports to the US, Singapore, Japan and Hong Kong. (JH)

🍷🍷🍷🍷⚲ **The Vivienne Chardonnay 2019, Denmark** Bright straw-green hue; a
complex bouquet encompassing citrus and toasted macadamia nuts, thence to
a long grapefruit and mineral-accented finish. Time is on its side. Screw cap.
12.9% alc. RATING 96 DRINK 2023-2032 $100 JH
Riesling 2021, Great Southern Fresh and lively; a delicious array of lime,
lemon and passionfruit to open proceedings on the palate and bouquet; steely
acidity runs throughout, but does so without disturbing the peace. Changes will
emerge down the track, but don't hesitate to drink it tonight. Screw cap. 11.9% alc.
RATING 95 DRINK 2021-2031 $25 JH ✪
Single Vineyard Shiraz 2020, Frankland River Bright colour. A tightly
framed array of blackberry and dark chocolate flavours and savoury ripe

tannins, all in harmonious balance and length. Screw cap. 14.5% alc. RATING 95
DRINK 2025–2040 $39 JH

Family Reserve Single Vineyard Chardonnay 2020, Denmark Filled with
peach, fig and almond flavours; entering maturity, and still needing more time
to build on its long finish. Screw cap. 13.4% alc. RATING 95 DRINK 2024–2029
$60 JH

ΨΨΨΨΨ **Single Vineyard Riesling 2021, Mount Barker** RATING 92 DRINK 2023–2030
$35 JH

Sister's Run   ★★★★

PO Box 148, McLaren Vale, SA 5171 **Region** South Australia
T (08) 8323 8979 **www**.sistersrun.com.au **Winemaker** Elena Brooks **Est.** 2001
Sister's Run is now part of the Brooks family empire, the highly experienced Elena Brooks
making the wines. The Stiletto and Boot on the label are those of Elena, and the motto 'The
truth is in the vineyard, but the proof is in the glass' is, I (James) would guess, the work of
marketer extraordinaire husband Zar Brooks. Exports to all major markets. (JH)

ΨΨΨΨΨ **Bethlehem Block Gomersal Cabernet Sauvignon 2019, Barossa Valley**
Unctuous blackberry fruit leads the charge here with hints of blackcurrant jelly,
blackstrap licorice, dark chocolate, cedar, oak spice and a blast of choc-mint
on the back end. There's oodles of black-fruited entertainment here; it's supple
and ripe, the tannins are superfine, sinking way back into the fruit and it flows
nicely across the tongue. Good-value drinking. Screw cap. 14% alc. RATING 92
DRINK 2021–2028 $23 DB ✪

Calvary Hill Lyndoch Shiraz 2019, Barossa Valley Ginger-spiced, ripe
red and dark plum fruits wash over a backdrop of Asian spice, milk chocolate,
jasmine and earth, for a most enticing first sniff. The fruit attack on the palate
fans out nicely and shows plummy exuberance, packed with exotic spice, earth,
softly spoken oak and pressed flowers. The wine tightens on the exit and the
acidity kicks in brightly as the tail lights fade. Screw cap. 14.5% alc. RATING 91
DRINK 2021–2028 $23 DB ✪

ΨΨΨΨ **Epiphany Shiraz 2019, McLaren Vale** RATING 88 DRINK 2021–2024 $23 NG

Sittella Wines   ★★★★★

100 Barrett Street, Herne Hill, WA 6056 **Region** Swan Valley
T (08) 9296 2600 **www**.sittella.com.au **Open** Tues–Sun & public hols 11–4
Winemaker Colby Quirk, Yuri Berns **Est.** 1998 **Dozens** 15 000 **Vyds** 25ha
Simon and Maaike Berns acquired a 7ha block (with 5ha of vines) at Herne Hill, making
the first wine in 1998 and opening a most attractive cellar door facility. They also own the
Wildberry Estate Vineyard in Margaret River. Plantings in Margaret River have increased
with new clones of cabernet sauvignon, cabernet franc, P95 chardonnay and malbec. New
clones of tempranillo and touriga nacional have also been added to the Swan Valley plantings.
Consistent and significant wine show success has brought well-deserved recognition for the
wines. Exports to Japan. (JH)

ΨΨΨΨΨ **Pedro Ximénez NV, Swan Valley** This is gorgeous. The old material enriches
the foundations, while the top notes remain fresh and vibrant. Quince, fig, loquat,
cumquat, date and star anise are the stars here. The length of flavour lingers
and curls in the mouth, while all components are beautifully integrated. Coffee
grounds, toffee and caramel. Smooth to the very last drop. 350ml. Screw cap.
18.5% alc. RATING 96 $50 EL ✪

Show Reserve Liqueur Verdelho NV Dried quince, fig, date, boot polish,
salted licorice strap and star anise – all of it whirling about in the glass and then
the mouth. Coffee grounds, espresso, dark chocolate, resin and molasses (even
hashish, at a push). This is exceptional, and the sugar, fruit and spice are all in

balance. Really expertly crafted. Worth every precious penny. 350ml. Screw cap. 19% alc. RATING 96 $80 EL

Marie Christien Lugten Grand Vintage 2016, Pemberton 60/40% pinot noir/chardonnay. Left 5 years on lees and 4 years in bottle. Dosage 7g/L. This is, and always has been a powerful, muscular wine that speaks of structure and shape – a wine of substance. This is one of the best releases of this wine to date, perhaps the very best, due to the fact that all elements are balanced – it's a high-octane wine in sparkling terms, but a brilliant version of that. Fresh, nutty, savoury, layered. It's classy. 250 dozen. Diam. 12.5% alc. RATING 95 $50 EL

Grand Vintage Late Disgorged 2009, Pemberton 50/50% pinot noir/chardonnay. On lees for 12 years. The first release. In the mouth this has a superfine mousse, and is laden with cheesecloth, crushed nuts (walnuts, almond meal and more), double cream, brine and salted citrus. There is a voluminous, generosity of fruit here, meaning you can drink this now with pleasure – it's more than ready. It'll make you stop and think as you drink … a wonderful thing. 10 dozen made. Cork. 12.5% alc. RATING 95 $120 EL

Berns Reserve Buckshot Ridge Cabernet Sauvignon 2020, Margaret River Concentrated and pert. This is alive, bright and medium bodied, layered with perfumed cassis, raspberry dust and licorice root. A beautiful cabernet that can, and should, be drunk in the short–medium term. Not that it won't age gracefully (it will), but the vibrancy of fruit is so attractive, now. There is no right or wrong answer in terms of 'when to drink' a wine, each of our palates differ, however the freshness of this wine is irresistible to me. Screw cap. 14.5% alc. RATING 95 DRINK 2022-2032 $60 EL

Museum Release Silk 2015, Swan Valley Verdelho, chenin blanc and chardonnay. The nose is an amalgam of cheesecloth, lanolin, summer apricots, kiwifruit, poached green apples and white peeper. In the mouth the wine is texturally creamy and complex … a really engaging and kaleidoscopic wine that has both poise and volume. Verdelho is a variety in use far less often than it once was, which is a damn shame when you see it like this. Glorious. Screw cap. 13.5% alc. RATING 95 DRINK 2022-2037 $35 EL ✪

Avant-Garde Dry Rosé 2021, Swan Valley Old vine Swan Valley grenache for rosé feels decadent or excessive, not sure which. Regardless; raspberries, bramble, spice, red licorice and briny acidity course through the wine, tumbling over themselves for dominance in the mouth. Rose petals, crushed pistachios, red apples and more. The varietal characters of the grenache really shine here, the heat of the Swan has imbued it with concentration and life. Super-smart first release. Screw cap. 13% alc. RATING 94 DRINK 2021-2025 $25 EL ✪

Avante-Garde Series Tempranillo Touriga 2021, Swan Valley Yum. Spicy, mid weight, delicious. Do you need more? The wild ferment has afforded the wine a structural complexity and softness, everything was hand picked, hand sorted and matured in seasoned oak. At no point does the oak get in the way of the fruit, and from every angle there is ease, flow and range of flavour. This is flexible, pliable, awesome. Yes. Screw cap. 14% alc. RATING 94 DRINK 2022-2027 $40 EL

Show Reserve Liqueur Muscat NV, Swan Valley Viscous, thick, glistening, intense and totally delicious. If you want to drink more fortified, but aren't sure when: pour it over vanilla ice cream for dessert, or chill it and have it after dinner in summer, or have it with with duck parfait and bread; the options are limitless. This has enough spice and structure to suit a plethora of situations. All things in balance. 375ml. Cork. 18.5% alc. RATING 94 $44 EL

🍷🍷🍷🍷 **Reserve Wilyabrup Chardonnay 2021, Margaret River** RATING 93 DRINK 2022-2029 $40 EL

Avant-Garde Series Blanc de Noirs 2016, Pemberton RATING 92 $75 EL

Silk 2021, Swan Valley RATING 92 DRINK 2022-2042 $18 EL ✪

Tinta Rouge 2021, Swan Valley RATING 92 DRINK 2022-2026 $20 EL ✪

Avant-Garde Series Chenin Blanc 2021, Swan Valley RATING 92 DRINK 2021-2036 $25 EL ✪

Reserve Single Vineyard Cabernet Malbec 2020, Margaret River
RATING 92 DRINK 2022-2032 $35 EL
Grand Vintage Blanc de Blancs 2016, Pemberton RATING 91 $50 EL
Grand Vintage Rosé 2016, Pemberton RATING 91 $50 EL
Cuvée Blanc NV, Pemberton RATING 91 $34 EL
Coffee Rock Shiraz 2020, Swan Valley RATING 91 DRINK 2022-2032 $60 EL
Chenin Blanc Brut NV, Swan Valley RATING 90 $25 EL
Avant-Garde Cherry Bomb Nouveau Rouge 2021, Swan Valley
Pemberton RATING 90 DRINK 2021-2024 $30 EL
El Vivero Blanco 2021, Swan Valley RATING 90 DRINK 2022-2026 $33 EL
A-G Rare Series Golden Mile Grenache 2021, Swan Valley RATING 90
DRINK 2022-2027 $40 EL

Six Acres ★★★★

20 Ferndale Road, Silvan, Vic 3795 **Region** Yarra Valley
T 0408 991 741 **www.sixacres.com.au Open** By appt **Winemaker** Ralph and Aaron
Zuccaro **Viticulturist** Ralph Zuccaro **Est.** 1999 **Dozens** 800 **Vyds** 1.64ha
Nestled in the southern hills of the Yarra Valley, Six Acres boutique winery and vineyard is
owned and worked by the Zuccaro family. Planted in 1999 by Ralph and Lesley Zuccaro, the
vineyard (pinot noir, cabernet sauvignon and merlot) is dry grown in deep red volcanic soil,
with yields kept low to encourage balance and concentration within the grapes. Currently
biologically farmed, the family's goal is to move towards organic/sustainable grape growing.
The small size of the property means that the whole family is involved in the minimal
intervention winemaking process. A visit to Six Acres will likely involve being greeted by a
Zuccaro family member as they emerge from the rows of vines or from the barrel shed. All
wines are vegan. (JH)

ৢৢৢৢৢ **Spectrum Syrah Shiraz 2020**, Yarra Valley A light crimson cherry colour.
An attractive lighter summer syrah that could be served lightly chilled. There are
aromas of raspberries, strawberries and pomegranate. Fresh, bright and crunchy
on the palate, with some blood orange fruit and very gentle tannins. Screw cap.
13.8% alc. RATING 91 DRINK 2021-2023 $24 PR
Spectrum Pinot Noir 2021, Yarra Valley A bright cherry red. High toned
with red fruits and a touch of spice. Totally suited to being served lightly
chilled, with its cranberry fruit and crunchy, light tannins. Screw cap. 12.6% alc.
RATING 90 DRINK 2022-2026 $24 PR
Pinot Noir 2019, Yarra Valley A light, bright crimson. Lifted with aromas
of cherries and rose petals from the well-handled and already integrated whole
bunches. Pomegranate notes on the gently fleshy palate, finishing with fine-
grained and persistent tannins. Screw cap. 13.5% alc. RATING 90 DRINK 2021-2025
$30 PR
Black Label Pinot Noir 2018, Yarra Valley A deepish cherry brick red.
Showing some secondary characters with bracken, wood spices and dark cherries.
Ripe on the palate, this sweetly-fruited wine is already nearing its peak but there is
more than enough tannin to suggest that it will hold if not improve over the next
3–5 years. Diam. 14% alc. RATING 90 DRINK 2021-2026 $59 PR

ৢৢৢৢ **Spectrum Pinot Noir 2020**, Yarra Valley RATING 89 DRINK 2021-2025
$24 PR
White Label Fiano 2020, Heathcote RATING 88 DRINK 2021-2023 $25 PR
Bianco Blanc 2019, Heathcote Yarra Valley RATING 88 DRINK 2021-2022
$24 PR

Sixty Eight Roses ★★★★

68 Chilton Road, Berri, SA 5343 **Region** Riverland
T 0416 983 720 **www.sixtyeightroses.com.au Winemaker** Eric Semmler
Viticulturist John Koutouzis **Est.** 2020 **Dozens** 250 **Vyds** 8ha

Named for the roses dotting the property Theodora and George Koutouzis have farmed since the 1970s. Originally from Greece, they met in Australia, raised a family of 4 and the Berri farm, rich with rows of orchards of apricots, pears and plums, and grapevines. Their son John is behind the Sixty Eight Roses wine label, which began in earnest in 2020 with the inaugural release of a 2019 syrah off vines planted by his parents, 48 years ago. He's dreaming big. Plantings of alternative varieties are underway and certified organics is part of the story. (JF)

Syrah 2020, Riverland Blackberry, star anise, roasted vanilla pod and jasmine tea. The palate is filled to the brim with quince and fig, black cherry and spice. The alcohol quietly threatens to reveal itself, but pipes down in the nick of time. A juicy, flavoursome, spice-laden and, dare I say, muscular wine, that trails fine-grit tannins across the tongue. Smart. Screw cap. 15.5% alc. RATING 90 DRINK 2021-2030 $30 EL

Tempranillo 2020, Riverland Super-ripe and juicy – the tannins really wrap around the mouth, and are absorbed into the jubey fruit. The alcohol threatens to reveal itself through the finish, but those tannins really mop it all up. Screw cap. 15% alc. RATING 90 DRINK 2021-2028 $32 EL

Skillogalee

Trevarrick Road, Sevenhill via Clare, SA 5453 **Region** Clare Valley
T (08) 8843 4311 **www**.skillogalee.com.au **Open** 7 days 9.30–5 **Winemaker** Kerri Thompson **Viticulturist** Brendan Pudney **Est.** 1989 **Dozens** 15 000 **Vyds** 51ha
David and Diana Palmer established Skillogalee in 1989. In 2002 the Palmers purchased next-door neighbour Waninga Vineyard with 30ha of 30-year-old vines, allowing an increase in production without any change in quality or style. David and Diana retired in July 2021, selling Skillogalee to the Clausen family. Talented winemaker Kerri Thompson (Wines by KT), who has long consulted to the Palmer family while making her own wines at Skillogalee, took over in the cellar from the 2022 vintage. Exports to the UK, Switzerland, Malaysia, Vietnam, Thailand and Singapore.

Trevarrick Single Contour Riesling 2021, Clare Valley '21 was a pristine vintage, producing wines just like this: so perfumed, lemon sherbet and citrus pith frill the edges of lime flesh, juniper berry and elderflowers. In the mouth the wine touches high notes of pure and crystalline fruit. It is spicy, fine and tense with layers of saline acidity. Worth the wait. Screw cap. 12% alc. RATING 96 DRINK 2021-2036 $53 EL ○

Gewürztraminer 2021, Clare Valley RATING 93 DRINK 2022-2029 $29 EL
Cabernet Malbec Rosé 2021, Clare Valley RATING 92 DRINK 2021-2024 $24 EL ○
Basket Pressed The Cabernets 2017, Clare Valley RATING 92 DRINK 2020-2030 $35 EL

Small Island Wines

Drink Co, Shop 10, 33 Salamanca Place, Hobart, Tas 7004 **Region** Southern Tasmania
T 0414 896 930 **www**.smallislandwines.com **Open** Mon–Sat 10–8 **Winemaker** James Broinowski **Est.** 2015 **Dozens** 750 **Vyds** 4ha
Tasmanian-born James Broinowski completed his bachelor of viticulture and oenology at the University of Adelaide in 2013. He was faced with the same problem as many other young graduates wanting to strike out on their own: cash. While others in his predicament may have found the same solution, his was the first wine venture to successfully seek crowdfunding. The first year ('15) allowed him to purchase pinot noir from Glengarry in the north of the island, making 2100 bottles of pinot noir that won a gold medal at the Royal International Hobart Wine Show '16; and 200 bottles of rosé that sold out in 4 days at the Taste of Tasmania Festival '15. In '16 he was able to buy pinot from the highly rated Gala Estate on the east coast and back up the '15 purchase from the Glengarry Vineyard with a '16 purchase. It looks very much like a potential acorn to oak story, for the quality of the wines is seriously good. (JH)

Patsie's Blush Rosé 2021, Tasmania 100% pinot noir. Elegant rosé of structure over aroma or flavour. A pretty, pale salmon hue matches the rose-gold foil of its label. Subtle strawberry hull is energised by the bright acidity of the cool 2021 harvest, eloquently toned by the soft, silky influence of old-barrel fermentation. A class act, let down only by a short finish. Screw cap. 13.5% alc. RATING 92 DRINK 2022-2022 $35 TS

Riesling 2021, Tasmania 6.1g/L RS. A generous and ripe riesling that brims with the exuberance of guava, baked apple and spice, over a core of lemon and lime tension. Full and fleshy, it boldly and unashamedly contrasts phenolic grip with taut acid line, tactically toned by a lick of residual sweetness, carrying the finish long and strong. A versatile style to drink over the short term. Screw cap. 13.5% alc. RATING 91 DRINK 2022-2025 $35 TS

Black Label Pinot Noir 2020, Tasmania The island may be small, but the 2 sites united here are far distant, melding the dark fruits and spice of the Tamar with the crunchy red berries of the Tasman Peninsula. Whole bunches bring exoticism, pepper and spice to the party, while bright acidity and furry tannins offer medium-term potential. Screw cap. 13.5% alc. RATING 91 DRINK 2024-2027 $45 TS

Glengarry Single Vineyard Pinot Noir 2020, Tasmania I love the cool touch of the 2020 harvest in the Tamar, exemplified here in crunchy cherry and spicy wild strawberries. Whole bunches lend their touch of floral perfume and herbal interest. Bright acid line directs a finish of medium persistence, marked by furry tannins. Screw cap. 13.5% alc. RATING 91 DRINK 2023-2025 $45 TS

Pinot Gris 2021, Tasmania RATING 89 DRINK 2022-2023 $35 TS

Saltwater River Single Vineyard Pinot Noir 2020, Tasmania RATING 89 DRINK 2024-2026 $45 TS

🌿 Small Victories Wine Co ★★★★

3–5 Tanunda Road, Nuriootpa, SA, 5355 **Region** Barossa Valley
T (08) 8568 7877 **www.**smallvictorieswine.com **Open** Fri–Mon 11–4 **Winemaker** Julie Ashmead **Est.** 2021

Sisters-in-law Jules and Bec Ashmead work at Elderton as winemaker (Jules) and production/logistics (Bec). The decision to create Small Victories came about after the constant search for wines that were interesting and a little different. In the end, they made their own, sourcing fruit from Elderton (shiraz, grenache, mataro and carignan) and from growers in the Adelaide Hills and Ricca Terra in the Riverland. The wines are made at Elderton. Sales from the wines support 2 local charities, Variety and Trees For Life. The label has a strong focus on sustainability, including environmentally friendly packaging, lightweight bottles and recycled cardboard cartons. And the reason for the name? The 2 friends believe in celebrating our small victories each day. (JP)

Shiraz 2021, Eden Valley Vibrant and vivid characters of super-ripe plums with high tones of raspberry and blueberry, hints of exotic spice, musk, jasmine and licorice. Boisterous and exuberant with super-pure fruit and chalky tannins. Put simply, it's about plummy joyful consumption without pretence. Screw cap. 14.5% alc. RATING 93 DRINK 2022-2026 $27 DB ✪

Vermentino 2021, Riverland Pretty gorgeous, really. Nashi pears, crunchy summer apples, juniper and little pockets of cassis and white currant. The mid palate loops and curls around the mouth, leaving swathes of refreshing, saline acid and vibrant fruit through the finish. Delicious. Screw cap. 12.5% alc. RATING 93 DRINK 2021-2024 $27 EL ✪

Old Vine Grenache 2021, Barossa Valley Fragrant and perfumed with juicy satsuma plum notes encircled in gingerbread, exotic spice and floral edging. Pretty on the palate too, with a lovely juicy fruit flow, fine billowing tannins and bright acid cadence. Great vibrant drinking. Screw cap. 14.5% alc. RATING 93 DRINK 2021-2028 $48 DB

Rosé 2021, Barossa Valley This mataro/grenache blend is pale copper in the glass. Bright aromas of raspberry, redcurrants and strawberry, with hints of cream, soft spice and white flowers. Refreshing and crisp with a dry, savoury swish to its tail and a vivid line across the palate. Screw cap. 13% alc. RATING 91 DRINK 2021-2025 $27 DB

Sangiovese 2021, Adelaide Hills Bright and pretty with notes of red cherry, redcurrant and a splash of cranberry. Hints of amaro herbs, spice, marzipan, candied citrus rind, pressed flowers and red licorice. Light in body with a sense of space and detail, lovely crunchy fruit and a pulsating line, it's great-value drinking. Screw cap. 14% alc. RATING 91 DRINK 2021-2016 $27 DB

Pinot Gris 2021, Adelaide Hills Vegan friendly. A bit of a long, slow reveal to this delicate, young wine, so don't over-chill. Pretty florals, honeysuckle, spiced apple, citrus and musk aromas. Clean purity of fruit and brisk acidity fairly bounce across the palate. Energy to burn. Screw cap. 12.7% alc. RATING 90 DRINK 2021-2024 $27 JP

Smidge Wines

150 Tatachilla Road, McLaren Vale, SA 5171 **Region** McLaren Vale
T 0419 839 964 **www**.smidgewines.com **Open** second w'end of each month, 12–5
Winemaker Matt Wenk **Est.** 2004 **Dozens** 8000 **Vyds** 4.1ha
Smidge Wines is owned by Matt Wenk and Trish Callaghan. In '13, Matt retired from Two Hands where he was a winemaker and plans to increase production of Smidge to 8000 dozen came to fruition over the next few years. Smidge owns the vineyard in Willunga that provides the grapes for all the cabernet sauvignon releases and some of the McLaren Vale shiraz. The vision is to build a modern customised facility on the Willunga property. The Magic Dirt wines are made from the same clone, in the same way, the purpose to show the impact of terroir on each wine. Pedra Branca wines are limited-quantity project wines, and St Brioc Wine Co. (www.stbriocwineco.com.au) is Matt's newest label. Exports to the UK, the US and South Korea. (JH)

ΨΨΨΨΨ **Grand Muscat Blend 1 NV, Rutherglen** A deep crimson, with a sunset orange glint. Mahogany, coffee bean, mocha, turmeric, grape spice and date, laced with tamarind and the spices of the souk. An endless finish that never slips into torrefaction, nor does it become cloying. Screw cap. 17% alc. RATING 96 $85 NG

ΨΨΨΨΨ **Pedra Branca Saperavi 2020, McLaren Vale** RATING 93 DRINK 2021-2026 $45 NG
Pedra Branca VP 2019, McLaren Vale RATING 93 $45 NG
The Ging Shiraz 2018, McLaren Vale RATING 92 DRINK 2021-2028 $28 NG
St Brioc Wine Co. Sauvignon Blanc 2021, Adelaide Hills RATING 91 DRINK 2021-2025 $28 NG

Smith & Hooper

Caves Edward Road, Naracoorte, SA 5271 **Region** Wrattonbully
T (08) 8561 3200 **www**.smithandhooper.com **Open** By appt **Winemaker** Heather Fraser **Est.** 1994 **Dozens** 15 000 **Vyds** 62ha
Smith & Hooper can be viewed as simply one of many brands within the Hill-Smith family financial and corporate structures. However, it is estate-based, with cabernet sauvignon and merlot planted on the Hooper Vineyard in 1994; and cabernet sauvignon and merlot planted on the Smith Vineyard in '98. Spread across both vineyards are 9ha of trial varieties. Exports to all major markets. (JH)

ΨΨΨΨΨ **Merlot 2019, Wrattonbully** Layers of sweet fruit drive the palate, which is kept on track by very fine tannins and pert acidity. Compelling drinking for the price. Screw cap. 14.5% alc. RATING 90 DRINK 2021-2027 $21 EL ✪

ΨΨΨΨ **Cabernet Sauvignon Merlot 2019, Wrattonbully** RATING 89 DRINK 2022-2027 $21 EL

Smithbrook

Smithbrook Road, Pemberton, WA 6260 **Region** Pemberton
T (08) 9750 2150 **www**.smithbrook.wine **Open** By appt **Winemaker** Ben Rector
Est. 1988 **Dozens** 10 000 **Vyds** 57ha
The picturesque Smithbrook property is owned by Perth businessman Peter Fogarty and
family, who also own Lake's Folly in the Hunter Valley, Deep Woods Estate in Margaret River
and Millbrook in the Perth Hills. Originally planted in the 1980s and one of the first in the
Pemberton region, the Smithbrook Vineyard covers over 57ha of the 110ha property and
focuses on sauvignon blanc, chardonnay and merlot. (JH)

❦❦❦❦❦ **The Yilgarn Blanc de Blancs 2017, Pemberton** Traditional method; on lees
for 36 months, less than 2g/L RS. Cheesecloth, green apple, lemon zest and briny
acidity work in concert to create a gently complex and quite gorgeous sparkling.
The phenolics through the finish are a little tart/coarse, but we'll overlook
it, in favour of the pleasure delivered by the whole package. Cork. 12.5% alc.
RATING 91 $35 EL
Chardonnay 2020, Pemberton Crushed almond, walnut, salted white peach
and a hint of curry leaf. In the mouth the texture is admirable – creamy and fine.
The acidity is coiled and the fruit is intense. A lovely wine, especially for the price.
Screw cap. 13% alc. RATING 91 DRINK 2021-2027 $25 EL
Single Vineyard Nebbiolo 2019, Pemberton Savoury salted tomato, dried
rose petals and wet asphalt – all the good nebbiolo things on the nose here. In
the mouth the wine is lovely; it's vibrant and fresh at its core, although not hugely
complex. Medium flavour concentration on the palate, which flows through to
the moderately long finish, but really a very good iteration of nebbiolo. Screw cap.
14% alc. RATING 90 DRINK 2022-2027 $25 EL

❦❦❦❦ **Single Vineyard Merlot 2020, Pemberton** RATING 89 DRINK 2022-2027
$25 EL
Single Vineyard Pinot Noir 2021, Pemberton RATING 88 DRINK 2022–2027
$25 EL

Snake + Herring

3763 Caves Road, Wilyabrup, WA 6284 **Region** Margaret River
T 0427 881 871 **www**.snakeandherring.com.au **Open** 7 days 11–5 summer,
(11–4 winter) **Winemaker** Tony Davis **Est.** 2010 **Dozens** 12 000
Tony (Snake) Davis and Redmond (Herring) Sweeny both started university degrees before
finding that they were utterly unsuited to their respective courses. Having stumbled across
Margaret River, Tony's life changed forever; he enrolled at the University of Adelaide,
thereafter doing vintages in the Eden Valley, Oregon, Beaujolais and Tasmania, before
3 years at Plantagenet, next Brown Brothers, then a senior winemaking role at Yalumba, a
6 year stint designing Millbrook Winery in the Perth Hills and 4 years with Howard Park
in Margaret River. Redmond's circuitous course included a chartered accountancy degree
and employment with an international accounting firm in Busselton, and the subsequent
establishment of Forester Estate in '01, in partnership with Kevin McKay. Back on home turf,
he is the marketing and financial controller of Snake + Herring. Exports to the US. (JH)

❦❦❦❦❦ **Cannonball Cabernet Sauvignon Merlot Petit Verdot 2020, Margaret
River** This is very good. It is concentrated and intense, with supple black fruit and
a wall of firm yet malleable tannin. It's chewy and generous, with enough savoury
spice through the finish to really elevate the experience. It'll live for some time.
Screw cap. 14% alc. RATING 95 DRINK 2022-2038 $45 EL
**The Distance Black Betty Yallingup Cabernet Sauvignon 2020,
Margaret River** This is concentrated and intense, like black pepper, licorice and
salted cassis. It's blackberries and fresh leather strap, the tannins are fine and chewy.
Very good. Not as long as I expected, but exceptionally delicious nonetheless.
Screw cap. 14% alc. RATING 95 DRINK 2022-2032 $90 EL

Outshined Wilyabrup Cabernet Sauvignon 2020, Margaret River This is inky, cassis laden and littered with blackcurrant pastille. The tannins are open weave and pervasive, and shape the fruit in the mouth. This is an elegant, full expression of cabernet, with fine, chalky bones. There's pomegranate molasses and mulberry in there too somewhere … yum. Very smart. Screw cap. 14% alc. RATING 94 DRINK 2022-2032 $33 EL

Cannonball Cabernet Sauvignon Merlot Petit Verdot 2019, Margaret River Aromatic and leafy, with lavendar, cassis and mulberry on the nose. In the mouth, layers of licorice, raspberry compote, red apples and star anise compete for attention: it is soft, cushy and seamless. Quite lovely indeed. Creamy. Screw cap. 14% alc. RATING 94 DRINK 2021-2031 $45 EL

The Distance Black Betty Yallingup Cabernet Sauvignon 2019, Margaret River Pungent cassis and chocolate on the nose; concentrated and densely packed with flavour on the palate. The tannins are very fine and shapely, they suspend the flavours motionless. Very big, it demands a decant, or some years in the cellar to show its best. The wine was in the glass 30 mins and the difference in that time was monumental. Screw cap. 14% alc. RATING 94 DRINK 2022-2036 $90 EL

♟♟♟♟♟ **Calypso Cabernet Franc Merlot 2020, Margaret River** RATING 93 DRINK 2022-2032 $45 EL

Corduroy Karridale Chardonnay 2020, Margaret River RATING 93 DRINK 2021-2028 $45 EL

Business Time Shiraz 2020, Frankland River RATING 93 DRINK 2022-2032 $55 EL

Business Time Syrah 2019, Frankland River RATING 93 DRINK 2021-2029 $55 EL

Bizarre Love Triangle Pinot Gris Gewürztraminer Riesling 2021, Great Southern RATING 92 DRINK 2021-2025 $29 EL

Sabotage Riesling 2021, Great Southern RATING 92 DRINK 2021-2028 $25 EL ✪

Tough Love Chardonnay 2020, Margaret River RATING 92 DRINK 2021-2026 $25 EL ✪

Wide Open Road Pinot Noir 2021, Great Southern RATING 91 DRINK 2022–2027 $25 EL

Dirty Boots Cabernet Sauvignon 2020, Margaret River RATING 92 DRINK 2022-2028 $25 EL ✪

Perfect Day Sauvignon Blanc Semillon 2021, Margaret River RATING 91 DRINK 2021-2025 $25 EL

Redemption Shiraz 2020, Great Southern RATING 91 DRINK 2022-2028 $25 EL

Hallelujah Chardonnay 2020, Porongurup RATING 91 DRINK 2021-2028 $45 EL

Tainted Love Syrah Rosé 2021, Margaret River RATING 90 DRINK 2022-2023 $25 EL

Vamos Tempranillo 2020, Margaret River RATING 90 DRINK 2022-2027 $25 EL

Dirty Boots Cabernet Sauvignon 2019, Margaret River RATING 90 DRINK 2021-2027 $25 EL

🌱 Solum Wines   ★★★★

193 Seventh Avenue, Rosebud, Vic 3939 (postal) **Region** Mornington Peninsula **T** 0413 050 416 **www.**solumwines.com.au **Winemaker** Ryan Horaczko **Viticulturist** Ryan Horaczko **Est.** 2020 **Dozens** 225

Ryan Horaczko's first foray into wine began while working at his father's burgeoning booze shop. As it turned out, he had a knack for tasting and started to get more serious before travel took him to some of the world's great wine regions. He enrolled in the bachelor of agriculture and technology – viticulture and winemaking at Melbourne Polytechnic in 2017. There he met chardonnay and pinot noir specialist Darrin Gaffy, from Principia winery, a former Dark Horse Winery Of The Year winner, and the rest is history. Ryan now works part-time at Principia. While he loves syrah, sourcing some from Quartz Hill in the Pyrenees, co-owned by Darrin's sister, he lives on the Peninsula and has taken on a lease of a 0.8ha vineyard. He is set to release a chardonnay too. (JF)

ΨΨΨΨΨ Pinot Noir 2020, Mornington Peninsula Take a bow, young Ryan Horaczko – your first pinot under your own label and it's a little beauty. Nothing complicated, just gentle winemaking with good fruit. Subtle aromas of cherries, wood spice, turmeric and fennel. The palate at ease with its mid weight, textural light tannins and bright acidity. A terrific drink-now option. Screw cap. 13% alc. RATING 94 DRINK 2022-2025 $35 JF

ΨΨΨΨΨ Syrah 2020, Pyrenees RATING 92 DRINK 2022-2030 $35 JF

Sons of Eden ★★★★★

Penrice Road, Angaston, SA 5353 **Region** Barossa Valley
T (08) 8564 2363 **www.**sonsofeden.com **Open** 7 days 11–6 **Winemaker** Corey Ryan
Viticulturist Simon Cowham **Est.** 2000 **Dozens** 9000 **Vyds** 60ha
Corey Ryan and Simon Cowham both learnt and refined their skills in the vineyards and cellars of Eden Valley. Corey is a trained oenologist with over 20 vintages under his belt, having cut his teeth as a winemaker at Henschke. Thereafter he worked for Rouge Homme and Penfolds in Coonawarra, backed up by winemaking stints in the Rhône Valley and in '02 he took the opportunity to work in NZ for Villa Maria Estates. In '07 he won the Institute of Masters of Wine scholarship. Simon has had a similarly international career covering such diverse organisations as Oddbins, UK, and the Winemakers' Federation of Australia. Switching from the business side to grape growing when he qualified as a viticulturist, he worked for Yalumba as technical manager of the Heggies and Pewsey Vale vineyards. Exports to the UK, the US, Germany, Switzerland, Hong Kong, the Philippines and Taiwan. (JH)

ΨΨΨΨΨ Zephyrus Shiraz 2019, Barossa Deeply coloured; a finely structured wine of great class as befits the vintage, the whole bunches lifting the red-fruit aromatics on the predominantly blackberry/black cherry foundations. Screw cap. 14.5% alc. RATING 97 DRINK 2025-2039 $45 JH ✪
Autumnus Shiraz 2016, Eden Valley An epic display of fruit concentration. Black plum, cherry and berry fruits are layered with spice and hints of dark chocolate, tamari, cedar, pipe tobacco, cola, choc-mint, black-olive tapenade and oodles of oak spice. That spicy, cedar oak flares on the palate but it just melts into the hedonistic, concentrated fruit beautifully. Super-plush, with ripe long-chain tannins. The wine finishes with substantial fruit horsepower and sarsaparilla-like spice. Impressive and heady drinking. Cork. 14.5% alc. RATING 97 DRINK 2021-2038 $350 DB

ΨΨΨΨΨ Notus Grenache 2021, Barossa Valley Bright ruby with purple flashes in the glass and aromas of finely poised red cherry, red plum and macerated raspberry fruits, cut with gingery spice, floral high tones and all the vibrancy and verve you'd expect from a top-flight grenache. Medium bodied, pure fruit edged with exotic spice, powdery tannin support and a bright line equals a sense of effortless drinkability. Screw cap. 14.5% alc. RATING 96 DRINK 2022-2032 $54 DB ✪
Marschall Shiraz 2020, Barossa Valley You get a generous bang for your buck with this elegant, medium-bodied shiraz, supple and fresh, with finely strung tannins and oak. Screw cap. 14.5% alc. RATING 95 DRINK 2023-2040 $29 JH ✪
Romulus Old Vine Shiraz 2019, Barossa Valley A deep and concentrated shiraz that flexes considerable muscle yet retains a sense of elegance. Super-deep blackberry and black cherry notes with hints of baking spice, licorice, dark chocolate, crème de cassis and roast meats. Impressive fruit weight and density, tightly packed tannins and a meaty, blackberry fruited finish of considerable length. Screw cap. 14.5% alc. RATING 95 DRINK 2022-2038 $80 DB

Stauros Old Vine Mourvèdre 2016, Barossa Valley It's immediately broody and meaty from first sniff. Black cherry and deep-black plum fruits cut through with notes of exotic spice, veal jus, cassis and earth. There is initially a soft, open-knit fruit attitude that swells and compacts with great meaty purity, with layers of complexity and firm, superfine feathery tannins providing a sound frame for the savoury, spiced plummy fruits. Complex and enchanting drinking. Screw cap. 14.5% alc. RATING 95 DRINK 2021-2035 $130 DB

Freya Riesling 2021, Eden Valley A mouth-watering and lip-smacking riesling that reflects the punctilious vinification in its freshness and finesse, citrusy acidity drawing out the long finish. Screw cap. 12.5% alc. RATING 94 DRINK 2021-2030 $25 JH ✪

Cirrus Single Vineyard Riesling 2021, High Eden The outstanding '21 vintage delivers yet again, providing laser-like precision, pure limey fruit and sapidity. There's wonderful tension here between the fresh lime juice and blossom notes and the porcelain-like acid structure. Light phenolics add gentle texture and luff its sails but then that lip-smacking acidity powers through, finishing crisp, dry and limey. Screw cap. 12% alc. RATING 94 DRINK 2021-2030 $56 DB

Kennedy GSM 2020, Barossa Valley Ripe plummy goodness from the first sip, with light floral facets flitting around above the fruit, which sits on a base of exotic spice, earth, kirsch and roasting meats. Superfine sandy tannins lend support. It has a lively line, great balance and presents both super drinking and great value. Screw cap. 14.5% alc. RATING 94 DRINK 2022-2032 $30 DB ✪

Sorby Adams Wines   ★★★☆

759 Light Pass Road, Angaston, SA 5353 **Region** Eden Valley
T (08) 8564 2435 www.sorbyadamswines.com **Open** By appt **Winemaker** Simon Sorby Adams **Viticulturist** Simon Sorby Adams **Est.** 2004 **Dozens** 15000 **Vyds** 15ha
In 1996 Simon Sorby Adams purchased a 3.2ha vineyard that had been planted by Pastor Franz Julius Lehmann (none other than Peter Lehmann's father) in 1932. Peter Lehmann always referred to it as 'Dad's Block'. Simon added 0.25ha of viognier, which, as one might expect, is used in a shiraz viognier blend. Most recent plantings are of shiraz, riesling, cabernet sauvignon and traminer. Nonetheless, the top red wines, The Family Shiraz and The Thing Shiraz, need no assistance from viognier. Simon also purchased the Jellicoe Vineyard at Mount McKenzie in 2006. Exports to the UK, Germany, Sweden, Singapore and Hong Kong. (JH)

🍷🍷🍷🍷🍷 **Jellicoe Riesling 2021, Eden Valley** A delightfully fragrant riesling from the excellent 2021 vintage in Eden Valley. The palest of straw, with green flashes in the glass. Aromas of juicy, freshly squeezed lime and Bickfords lime cordial, with hints of Christmas lily, almond blossom, wet stone and some cut fennel further in the distance. Textural and juicy with crisp acidity and pure limey fruit on the finish. Screw cap. 11% alc. RATING 91 DRINK 2021-2027 $24 DB

🍷🍷🍷🍷 **Jazz Pinot Rosé 2021, Eden Valley** RATING 89 DRINK 2021-2025 $24 DB
Margret Pinot Gris 2021, Eden Valley RATING 88 DRINK 2021-2023 $24 DB

Soul Growers   ★★★★★

218 Murray Street, Tanunda, SA 5352 **Region** Barossa Valley
T (08) 8523 2691 www.soulgrowers.com **Open** By appt **Winemaker** Paul Heinicke, Stuart Bourne **Est.** 1998 **Dozens** 10000 **Vyds** 4.85ha
Friends and partners Paul Heinicke, Stuart Bourne (winemaker, ex Château Tanunda) Tom Fotheringham (sales and marketing, ex Penfolds) first met while all working at Barossa Valley Estate. Soul Growers source from multi-generational family growers (13 in total) in Moppa, Ebenezer, Kalimna, Vine Vale, Eden Valley and Nuriootpa with pocket-handkerchief vineyard blocks of mataro at Nuriootpa and grenache at Krondorf. Exports to the UK, Singapore and Malaysia. (JH)

ΨΨΨΨΨ El Mejor 2019, Barossa Valley Cabernet sauvignon, mourvèdre and shiraz.
A wine deeply infused with blackberry, cassis and plum-compote characters,
studded with star anise, baking spice, licorice, dark chocolate and a fair lick of
cedary oak. Mouth-filling and confident in its gait across the palate, with densely
packed fine tannins, bright line and a sour cherry/ macerated berry fruit flourish
on the finish, that trails off showing spice and cedar. Cork. 14% alc. RATING 94
DRINK 2021-2035 $110 DB

ΨΨΨΨΨ Slow Grown Shiraz 2019, Barossa Valley RATING 92 DRINK 2021-2028
$60 DB
The Debutant 2021, Barossa Valley RATING 91 DRINK 2021-2023 $25 DB
**Soul Sister Rosé Cabernet Sauvignon Mourvèdre Shiraz 2021, Barossa
Valley** RATING 91 DRINK 2021-2023 $28 DB
Cellar Dweller Cabernet Sauvignon 2019, Barossa Valley RATING 90
DRINK 2021-2028 $60 DB

South by South West   ★★★★☆

2/12 Wrigglesworth Drive, Cowaramup, WA 6284 (postal) **Region** Margaret River
T 0438 001 181 **www**.southbysouthwest.com.au **Winemaker** Livia Maiorana
Viticulturist Pete Schiller **Est.** 2016 **Dozens** 7000 **Vyds** 2ha
Livia (Liv) Maiorana and Mijan (Mij) Patterson, engineer and graphic designer, share a love of
travel. They embarked on a 'wine odyssey' to study the cycle of winemaking in different wine
regions around the world. 'We learned from masters of the craft at some of the biggest and
smallest players in California, Italy, France and British Columbia. We learned about terroirs
and varietals, viticultural practices, cultural winemaking tricks and techniques. We drank a lot
of wine'. They make the South by South West wines in small batches, the grapes sourced from
multiple districts within the Margaret River (Carbunup, Wilyabrup, Wallcliffe and Karridale).
Exports to Singapore. (JH)

ΨΨΨΨΨ Chardonnay 2021, Margaret River Hand picked, whole-bunch pressed
straight to oak for wild ferment. Matured on full solids for 9 months. Bâtonnage
was conducted regularly and mlf occurred in some barrels. For all the work,
the cool year has kept this totally in line. It's like a picture of opulence, without
actually being opulent. Kind of like a brilliant outdoor fresco. It has crushed nuts,
briny acid, toasty oak, salted peach … it's all there, but it's restrained. Very smart
and well handled. Delicious. Screw cap. 12.5% alc. RATING 94 DRINK 2022-2029
$45 EL

ΨΨΨΨΨ Pinot Noir 2021, Pemberton RATING 93 DRINK 2022-2028 $35 EL
Sangiovese 2021, Margaret River RATING 91 DRINK 2022-2027 $35 EL
Arancia 2021, Geographe RATING 90 DRINK 2022-2025 $25 EL
Rosso Bianco 2021, Pemberton Margaret River RATING 90
DRINK 2022-2024 $35 EL

Southern Vales   ★★★★

PO Box 521, McLaren Vale SA 5171 **Region** McLaren Vale
T 419980380 **www**.southernvaleswine.com.au **Winemaker** Mike Farmilo **Est.** 2012
Dozens 17000 **Vyds** 4.5ha
The Southern Vales winery in McLaren Vale was originally a regional cooperative, or shared
production facility for grape growers to make wine from their own fruit, much in the way of
the European model. Built in 1896, the large facility produced wines for domestic sales and
export, until its sale in the mid 1990s. Subsequently, the brand went into hibernation. In 2012,
it was purchased by 2 local families with winemaker Mike Farmilo at the helm. The fruit
is proprietary sourced as well as purchased. The wines are corpulent, rich and heady. Shiraz is
the mainstay. (NG)

ΨΨΨΨΨ Ten Plus Shiraz 2017, McLaren Vale Impressive intensity of aromas of molten
black rock, dark-fruit aspersions, Asian five-spice, licorice straps and clove. The

palate, weighty and powerful, is bridled by firm cedar-mocha oak tannins that while edgy, are sure to be sublimated by the wine's forcefield in a few years. Palate-staining extract. Fine length and plenty of promise. Screw cap. 15% alc. RATING 93 DRINK 2021-2029 $65 NG

Encounter Shiraz 2017, McLaren Vale Solid wines here, with significantly more time in the cellar pre-release than those of the neighbours. Sweet cherry aromas laced with anise, clove and lavender. Kirsch, across the finish. Sappy, forceful and ready to drink. Yet the style here never stoops into excessive extraction or jamminess. A bit hot across the Adam's apple, but such was the vintage. Screw cap. 15% alc. RATING 91 DRINK 2021-2025 $35 NG

Spence ★★★★☆

760 Burnside Road, Murgheboluc, Vic 3221 **Region** Geelong
T (03) 5265 1181 **www.**spencewines.com.au **Open** first Sun each month
Winemaker Peter Spence, Scott Ireland **Est.** 1997 **Dozens** 1300 **Vyds** 3.2ha
Peter and Anne Spence were sufficiently inspired by an extended European holiday – which included living on a family vineyard in Provence – to purchase a small property and establish a vineyard and winery. They have planted 3.2ha on a north-facing slope in a valley 7km south of Bannockburn, the lion's share to 3 clones of shiraz (1.83ha), the remainder to chardonnay, pinot noir and viognier. The vineyard attained full organic status in 2008, since then using only biodynamic practices. (JH)

�♙ **Chardonnay 2020, Geelong** Carries plenty of flinty complexity ahead of nectarine, peach, citrus and mealy leesy characters. Juicy and forthright on the palate, with a little more oak-led grilled nuts and toast before a smooth finish. Pretty stylish. Screw cap. 13% alc. RATING 90 DRINK 2021-2027 $35 JP

♙♙♙♙ **Pinot Noir 2020, Geelong** RATING 88 DRINK 2021-2024 $35 JP

Spinifex ★★★★★

PO Box 511, Nuriootpa, SA 5355 **Region** Barossa Valley
T (08) 8564 2059 **www.**spinifexwines.com.au **Open** At Vino Lokal, Tanunda
Winemaker Peter Schell **Viticulturist** Peter Schell **Est.** 2001 **Dozens** 6000 **Vyds** 12ha
Peter Schell and Magali Gely are a husband-and-wife team from NZ who came to Australia in the early '90s to study oenology and marketing at Roseworthy College. They have spent 4 vintages making wine in France, mainly in the south where Magali's family were vignerons for generations near Montpellier. The focus at Spinifex is the red varieties that dominate in the south of France: mataro (more correctly mourvèdre), grenache, shiraz and cinsault. The wines are made in open fermenters, basket pressed, with partial wild (indigenous) fermentation and relatively long post-ferment maceration. This is a very old approach, but nowadays à la mode. Exports to the UK, Canada, Belgium, Singapore, Hong Kong and NZ. (JH)

♙♙♙♙♙ **Single Vineyard Moppa Shiraz 2019, Barossa Valley** From the deep colour and vivid crimson edge through to the finish, this wine sings a song of purity and intensity. The black fruits, the background of earth, oak and lifted spice simply serve to throw you back to shiraz of great quality, thanks to the skill of winemaker Peter Schell. Screw cap. 14.5% alc. RATING 97 DRINK 2025-2050 $60 JH ✪

♙♙♙♙♙ **Single Vineyard Moppa Grenache 2020, Barossa Valley** It's all red plum and cherry fruit with a splash of raspberry coulis, along with hints of spice, ginger cake, earth and stone. It's concentrated but 40% whole bunches in the ferment opens the wine up beautifully, highlighting the crunchy, pure fruit, fine sandy tannin and savoury palate shape. Wonderful drinking. Screw cap. 14.7% alc. RATING 96 DRINK 2021-2031 $45 DB ✪

Bête Noir 2019, Barossa Valley It's elegant yet powerful, with ripe blackberry, licorice and a touch of plum. However long you wait, it will be there waiting for you. Bargain. Screw cap. 14.5% alc. RATING 96 DRINK 2024-2049 $39 JH ✪

Dominion Shiraz 2019, Barossa Valley As with all of Pete's wines, the leitmotif is fruit purity writ large. Here it's juicy damson plum and black cherries sheathed in purple floral flecks that I often see in wines from the foot of the eastern range. Deep spice, a touch of polished leather, fine long-chain tannins that cascade through the wine and a simmering sense of latent power. It's a wine of great depth but there is a sense of grace present also, which is a wonderful thing. Screw cap. 14.5% alc. RATING 96 DRINK 2021-2038 $60 DB ✪

Bête Noir 2020, Barossa There is a beautifully pure, stony sense of calm and detail to this wine, with composed blackberry and cherry fruits, deep spice and meaty facets. It has brightness and clarity, not at the expense of fruit depth. Bright acidity provides the pulse and tannins akin to powdered granite give savoury support. It's great drinking. Screw cap. 14.5% alc. RATING 95 DRINK 2022-2036 $45 DB

Syrah 2021, Barossa Deep purple red in the glass, it's a rollicking, crunchy, bright and sapid ride with a gorgeous plume of plummy fruit, cut with spice and floral nuance, whole-bunch amaro notes and a sense of space, clarity and detail that brings a smile to the face. Such a wonderful drink and great value. Screw cap. 14% alc. RATING 94 DRINK 2022-2029 $30 DB ✪

ΨΨΨΨ **Luxe 2021, Barossa** Winemaker Pete Schell is a fan of Bandol rosés and the Luxe is a tip of the hat to the rosé styles of the Mediterranean. This year, a blend of 68/26/6% mataro/cinsault/vermentino. Red cherry, watermelon and pomegranate with hints of soft spice, crushed rock, blood orange and wild herbs. Slinky and textural with crisp acidity and a wicked stony, savoury finish. Screw cap. 12.5% alc. RATING 93 DRINK 2021-2024 $35 DB ♥

Spring Spur   ★★★

52 Fredas Lane, Tawonga, Vic 3697 **Region** Alpine Valleys
T (03) 5754 4849 **www.**springspurwine.com.au **Open** Thurs–Mon 8–6
Winemaker Alex Phillips **Est.** 2017 **Dozens** 80
Alex Phillips was born and raised in South Africa. She graduated cum laude from the University of Stellenbosch in '13, where she was awarded the prestigious Prof PA van der Bijl medal and crowned Best Academic Student: Viticulture and Oenology. After mentoring under celebrated winemaker Adam Mason at Mulderbosch Vineyards, she launched into vintages across the world before finding her feet as assistant winemaker at Billy Button Wines in the Alpine Valleys of North East Victoria. It is here she found love; not only in the picturesque winemaking region itself but in her fiancé, Lin. The pair live on Spring Spur – a beautiful working horse property in the Kiewa Valley, where Alex brings Spring Spur wines to life. (JH)

ΨΨΨΨ **Gewürztraminer 2021, King Valley** Quite a developed, rich gewürz so early on, but brim full in rosewater, lychee, lime cordial flavour. The floral and spice intensity on this wine is quite an outstanding feature. It's big on texture and phenolics with clean, bright acidity. Only modest ageing required. Screw cap. 13.8% alc. RATING 89 DRINK 2021-2025 $32 JP

Vermentino 2021, King Valley Displays gentle florals, melon and citrus aromas. Lightly textured on the palate with a noticeable sweetness with lemon and barley notes. Unpretentious and easy. Screw cap. 12.5% alc. RATING 88 DRINK 2021-2024 $32 JP

Pinotage 2021, Alpine Valleys Dense, dark purple in hue. The scent of sweet plums, raspberry syrup, violet and eucalyptus immediately sets the scene for a highly approachable wine. It's a bit of fun, too. Pinotage is often compared to Aussie shiraz in boldness of flavour and ripeness. It's all here and then some, while retaining a medium-bodied, easy-going attitude. Early drinking recommended. Screw cap. 14% alc. RATING 88 DRINK 2022-2025 $38 JP

Spring Vale Vineyards

130 Spring Vale Road, Cranbrook, Tas 7190 **Region** East Coast Tasmania
T (03) 6257 8208 **www.**springvalewines.com **Open** 7 days 11–4 **Winemaker** Barry
Kooji **Viticulturist** Tim Lyne **Est.** 1986 **Dozens** 15000 **Vyds** 32.5ha
Lyn and Rodney Lyne have progressively established pinot noir (19ha), chardonnay (4ha),
pinots gris and meunier (3ha each), syrah (2ha), sauvignon blanc (1ha) and gewürztraminer
(0.5ha) since 1986. The nearby Melrose Vineyard was purchased in 2007. Son Tim, armed
with a degree in viticulture and a MBA, is now general manager and viticulturalist. Exports
to Russia and Hong Kong. (JH)

👑👑👑👑👑 **Family Selection Pinot Noir 2018, Tasmania** A selection of the 7 best barrels
of estate pinot noir, released a year later at more than 2.5 times the price. A serious
step up, too. Depth of red and black cherry fruit is accented with East Coast black
pepper, confidently supported by toasty French oak. It will appreciate time to
harmonise, boasting the fine-grained tannin profile, tangy acidity and lingering
persistence to go the distance. Screw cap. 13.5% alc. RATING 94 DRINK 2025–2028
$125 TS

👑👑👑👑👑 **Rosé 2021, Tasmania** RATING 92 DRINK 2022–2026 $30 TS
Gewürztraminer 2021, Tasmania RATING 91 DRINK 2022–2022 $45 TS
Estate Pinot Noir 2019, Tasmania RATING 91 DRINK 2022–2024 $48 TS
Family Selection Blanc de Blanc 2016, Tasmania RATING 90 $85 TS

Springs Road Wines

761 Playford Highway, Cygnet River, Kangaroo Island, SA 5233 **Region** Kangaroo Island
T 0499 918 448 **www.**springsroad.com.au **Open** 7 days 12–5 Oct–Apr, Wed–Mon
12–4 May–Sept **Winemaker** Joch Bosworth **Viticulturist** Joch Bosworth **Est.** 1994
Dozens 4000 **Vyds** 11ha
Springs Road runs east-west across the northern part of Kangaroo Island. The Springs Road
vineyards were established in 1994 on a small sheep property about 7km west of Kingscote
and are now owned and operated by Joch Bosworth and Louise Hemsley-Smith from Battle
of Bosworth in McLaren Vale (see separate entry). Small quantities of Chardonnay, Shiraz,
Cabernet Sauvignon and a Cabernet Sauvignon Shiraz blend are made from the very low-
yielding 20yo vines. The vineyards have been managed organically since Louise and Joch
took over in 2016, and are awaiting certification. The wine label is adapted from Louis de
Freycinet's 1808 map of Southern Australia, 'Terre Napoléon'. Exports to Hong Kong. (JH)

👑👑👑👑👑 **Little Island Red 2021, Kangaroo Island** A powerful, yet inherently full-
bodied wine, with blackberry to the fore. Needs time, but has balance and will
repay extended cellaring. Screw cap. 14.5% alc. RATING 94 DRINK 2025–2040
$25 JH ✪

👑👑👑👑👑 **Chardonnay 2021, Kangaroo Island** RATING 92 DRINK 2022–2026 $35 JH

Staniford Wine Co

20 Jackson Street, Mount Barker, WA 6324 **Region** Great Southern
T 0405 157 687 **www.**stanifordwineco.com.au **Open** By appt **Winemaker** Michael
Staniford **Est.** 2010 **Dozens** 500
Michael Staniford has been making wine in Great Southern since '95, principally as senior
winemaker for Alkoomi at Frankland River, with additional experience as a contract
maker for other wineries. The business is built around single-vineyard wines; in particular
a Chardonnay from a 25+yo vineyard in Albany and a Cabernet Sauvignon from a 20+yo
vineyard in Mount Barker. The quality of these 2 wines is every bit as one would expect.
Michael plans to introduce a Riesling and a Shiraz with a similar individual vineyard origin,
quality being the first requirement. (JH)

👑👑👑👑👑 **Reserve Chardonnay 2018, Great Southern** Rich, toasty, taut, tense,
expansive, voluminous and generally brilliant. Really well done. The length

of flavour is the final clincher. Very smart. Screw cap. 14% alc. RATING 95
DRINK 2021-2031 $47 EL

ŸŸŸŸŸ Reserve Cabernet Franc 2016, Mount Barker RATING 91 DRINK 2022-2036
$34 EL

Stanton & Killeen Wines ★★★★★

440 Jacks Road, Murray Valley Highway, Rutherglen, Vic 3685 **Region** Rutherglen
T (02) 6032 9457 **www**.stantonandkilleen.com.au **Open** Mon–Sat 9–5, Sun & public
hols 10–5 **Winemaker** Faustine Ropars **Est.** 1875 **Dozens** 10 000 **Vyds** 34ha
In 2020, Stanton & Killeen celebrated its 145th anniversary. The business is owned and run by
7th-generation vigneron Natasha Killeen and her mother and CEO, Wendy Killeen. Fortifieds
are a strong focus for the winery with around half of its production dedicated to this style.
Their vineyards comprise 14 varieties, including 7 Portuguese cultivars used for both fortified
and table wine production – 2 additional Portuguese varieties are planned for future planting.
A vineyard rejuvenation program has been implemented since '14, focusing on sustainable
and environmentally friendly practices. Exports to the UK, Switzerland, Taiwan and Hong
Kong. (JH)

ŸŸŸŸŸ Grand Muscat, Rutherglen Feel the weight, taste the complexity and
concentration. This is a mighty fine Grand Muscat (average age 12–15 years), and
so, so luscious. It moves like silk, seamless in treacle, soused prune, raisin, honeyed
figs, dried fruits and the deep nuttiness of walnut with caramel. The mix of age
and youth in the blending process is exemplary. 500ml bottle. Screw cap. 18.5% alc.
RATING 96 $105 JP
Fortitude Durif 2019, Rutherglen Yes, it's a Rutherglen durif. No, it's not
turned up to 11. In fact, it's an excellent study in how to contain the grape's
inherent power while also bringing to light its more aromatic, spice-laden, berry-
chocolate and rosemary and pepper side. And there's more where that came from,
in this delightfully complex and complete wine. Screw cap. 13.8% alc. RATING 95
DRINK 2022-2033 $38 JP
Jack's Block Shiraz 2019, Rutherglen Looking good and in great shape,
despite the hot vintage conditions, Jack's Block is mighty flavoursome. Deep red
garnet, the bouquet shines in ripe dark plum, black fruits, licorice, cedary oak and
the kind of baked-earth notes so familiar to Rutherglen shiraz. The palate is laid
out on long, supple tannins. Mouth-filling and impressive, Jack's Block is named
in honour of a Rutherglen winemaking legend. Screw cap. 14.3% alc. RATING 95
DRINK 2022-2034 $50 JP
Vintage Fortified 2018, Rutherglen A mix of 5 Portuguese traditional port
varieties and durif (a Rutherglen favourite), brings a certain distinctive North
East Victorian feel to this vintage fortified. It carries on the fine tradition set by
generations of Stanton & Killeen winemakers. A brilliant and well-judged blend.
Arrives with speed, a rush of sweet, nutty, savoury scents of anise, woodsy spices,
blackberry, black cherry, licorice and chocolate panforte. Gathers pace on the
palate, sped along with bright, brisk neutral spirit. Still feeling its way. Do not
disturb for 10 years, at least!! Cork. 18% alc. RATING 95 $22 JP ✪
Grand Topaque NV, Rutherglen The Grand classification starts to get serious
indeed in both age, complexity and lusciousness. Aromatic intensity of soused
raisins, fruitcake, toffee, touch of molasses, espresso coffee and then that lilting
thread – just there in the background – of fish oil (a good thing!). That's a big, fat
yum! Screw cap. 18.5% alc. RATING 95 $105 JP
Arinto 2021, Rutherglen S&K are making a name for their promotion of
Iberian grape varieties. Here, Portugal's arinto speaks loudly, without the presence
of oak, in citrus, green apple, orange peel with musk. Shows a clean, dry pair of
heels. Screw cap. 13% alc. RATING 94 DRINK 2022-2025 $30 JP ✪

ŸŸŸŸŸ Alvarinho 2021, Rutherglen RATING 93 DRINK 2022-2028 $30 JP
Classic Muscat NV, Rutherglen RATING 92 $38 JP
Classic Topaque NV, Rutherglen RATING 91 $38 JP

Star Lane Winery

51 Star Lane, Wooragee, Vic 3747 **Region** Beechworth
T 0427 287 268 **www**.starlanewinery.com.au **Open** By appt **Winemaker** Liz Lord
Barnes **Viticulturist** Brett Barnes **Est.** 1997 **Dozens** 1500 **Vyds** 6ha

Star Lane is the venture of Brett and Liz Barnes, and Rex Lucas. Both families have small vineyards, the Barnes's with merlot and shiraz, and Rex's with sangiovese and nebbiolo. Liz is the winemaker and has received encouragement and assistance from Rick Kinzbrunner; Brett is overall vineyard manager. (JH)

🍷🍷🍷🍷🍷 **Amphora Nebbiolo 2019, Beechworth** Complex and yet so immediately vibrant and juicy. This is one of those wines where the more you look, the more you find something intriguing. Brings together the grape's wonderful aromatics of rose petal, anise, red licorice and rosehip in tandem with cranberry, cherry and spices. Nebbiolo was made for maturation in amphora, its notable tannins slowly yielding while retaining a forceful structure for ageing. A match made in heaven. Screw cap. 14.2% alc. RATING 95 DRINK 2022-2029 $55 JP

🍷🍷🍷🍷🍷 **Merlot 2019, Beechworth** RATING 92 DRINK 2022-2027 $45 JP
Shiraz 2019, Beechworth RATING 90 DRINK 2022-2027 $50 JP

Stargazer Wine

37 Rosewood Lane, Tea Tree, Tas 7017 **Region** Tasmania
T 0408 173 335 **www**.stargazerwine.com.au **Open** By appt **Winemaker** Samantha Connew **Viticulturist** Samantha Connew, Bryn Williams **Est.** 2012 **Dozens** 1800 **Vyds** 3ha

Samantha Connew obtained a postgraduate diploma of oenology and viticulture from Lincoln University, Canterbury, NZ, before moving to Australia. Here she undertook the Advanced Wine Assessment course at the Australian Wine Research Institute in 2000, was chosen as a scholar at the '02 Len Evans Tutorial, won the George Mackey Award for the best wine exported from Australia in '04 and was awarded International Red Winemaker of the Year at the International Wine Challenge, London in '07. After a highly successful and lengthy position as chief winemaker at Wirra Wirra, Sam moved to Tasmania (via the Hunter Valley) to make the first wines for her own business, something she said she would never do. The emotive name (and label) is in part a tribute to Abel Tasman, the first European to sight Tasmania before proceeding to the South Island of NZ, navigating by the stars. Exports to the UK, the US, Singapore, Japan and Hong Kong. (JH)

🍷🍷🍷🍷🍷 **Coal River Valley Riesling 2021, Tasmania** This is a glorious wine; the bouquet and fore palate are full of Rose's lime juice that has a siren allure, but it's the soaring finish and aftertaste that send all the senses into overdrive, with a quivering line of acidity within its fruit. Screw cap. 12% alc. RATING 97 DRINK 2022-2036 $35 JH ☺
Palisander Vineyard Coal River Valley Riesling 2020, Tasmania Utterly exceptional riesling that could only come from Tasmania. The scented white flower and citrus blossom bouquet yields to a palate with mouth-watering grapefruit and lime, surrounded by endless crystalline acidity that creates balance now or in a decade or more. Screw cap. 13% alc. RATING 97 DRINK 2025-2040 $42 JH ☺
Palisander Vineyard Coal River Valley Pinot Noir 2020, Tasmania Perfect clarity and colour; a vibrant pinot that caresses the mouth with its red cherry, wild strawberry, pomegranate flavours and gossamer tannins. Utterly delicious, yet there's more to come as exotic spices start to play. Screw cap. 13.5% alc. RATING 97 DRINK 2024-2030 $55 JH ☺

🍷🍷🍷🍷🍷 **Tupelo 2021, Tasmania** A 51/34/15% blend of pinot gris, riesling and gewürztraminer. Eight hours of skin contact; wild-yeast ferment in used oak; 15% of the riesling component was fermented on skins; on lees for 3 months with lees stirring. A very good outcome for a daunting vinification of a daunting blend, that has avoided a phenolic trap. Screw cap. 12.5% alc. RATING 95 DRINK 2022-2030 $35 JH ☺

Single Vineyard Derwent Valley Chardonnay 2020, Tasmania A little hesitant on the bouquet, perhaps, but leaps with the grapefruit and lemon of the vibrant, finely strung and very long palate, the aftertaste bringing even more facets into play. High-quality Tasmanian chardonnay. Screw cap. 13.5% alc. RATING 95 DRINK 2022-2032 $55 JH

Steels Gate

1974 Melba Highway, Dixons Creek 3775 Vic **Region** Yarra Valley
T (03) 5965 2155 **www.**steelsgate.com.au **Open** Fri–Sun 11–5.30 **Winemaker** Brad Atkins, Matthew Davis **Viticulturist** Matthew Davis **Est.** 2010 **Dozens** 2500 **Vyds** 7ha
Brad Atkins and Matthew Davis acquired a 2ha vineyard of 25–30yo dry-grown chardonnay and pinot noir in 2009. For reasons unexplained, the owners have a particular love of gates, and as the property is at the end of Steels Creek, the choice of Steels Gate was obvious. The next step was to engage French designer Cecile Darcy to create what is known today as the Steels Gate logo. (JH)

Melba Block Shiraz 2018, Yarra Valley There's a real drive to this fine-featured shiraz. Brisk tannins lead the charge, good line and length assured across the palate of black fruits, woody spice, vanilla pod and toasty oak. Balance all the way. Diam. 14% alc. RATING 91 DRINK 2021-2030 $45 JP
Pinot Noir 2019, Yarra Valley All dressed up and ready to impress with smart winemaking on display, highlighting the summer red berry power of ripe fruit. It's utterly delicious. Upbeat entry with said red berries on full display, with lively spice, pastille and spice. A touch of chocolate panforte goes hand in hand with supple, even-handed tannins, as it rolls easily across the tongue. Diam. 13.2% alc. RATING 90 DRINK 2021-2025 $35 JP

Melba Block Chardonnay 2019, Yarra Valley RATING 89 DRINK 2021-2028 $35 JP
Melba Block Cabernets 2018, Yarra Valley RATING 89 DRINK 2021-2028 $45 JP

Stefani Estate

735 Old Healesville Road, Healesville, Vic 3777 **Region** Yarra Valley
T 0492 993 446 **www.**stefaniwines.com.au **Open** Thurs–Fri by appt, Sat–Sun 11–5
Winemaker Peter Mackey **Est.** 1998 **Dozens** 5730 **Vyds** 18ha
Stefano Stefani came to Australia in '85. Business success has allowed him and his wife Rina to follow in the footsteps of his grandfather, who had a vineyard and was an avid wine collector. The first property they acquired was at Long Gully Road in the Yarra Valley, planted to pinot grigio, cabernet sauvignon, chardonnay and pinot noir. The next was in Heathcote, where they acquired a property adjoining that of Mario Marson (ex Mount Mary), built a winery and established 14.4ha of shiraz, cabernet sauvignon, merlot, cabernet franc, malbec and petit verdot. In '03 a second Yarra Valley property was acquired and dijon clones of chardonnay and pinot noir were planted; that vineyard is currently undergoing organic conversion. In addition, 1.6ha of sangiovese have been established, using scion material from the original Stefani Vineyard in Tuscany. (JH)

The Gate Shiraz 2018, Yarra Valley A very youthful and deep crimson purple. Aromas of ripe, juicy cranberries. fresh red plum and well-handled cedar oak that will settle down in time. Medium–full bodied, this has a core of concentrated, dark, briary fruits and there are enough ripe and persistent tannins to suggest this will age well over the next decade. Diam. 14.2% alc. RATING 96 DRINK 2022-2028 $65 PR ✪

The View Vineyard Pinot Noir 2019, Yarra Valley RATING 92 DRINK 2021-2027 $65 PR
Riserva Sangiovese 2018, Yarra Valley RATING 92 DRINK 2022-2028 $90 PR

The View Vineyard Pinot Noir 2021, Yarra Valley RATING 90
DRINK 2021–2026 $35 PR
Boccallupo Sangiovese 2020, Yarra Valley RATING 90 DRINK 2022–2025
$35 PR
The View Vineyard Chardonnay 2019, Yarra Valley RATING 90
DRINK 2022–2024 $65 PR

Stefano Lubiana

60 Rowbottoms Road, Granton, Tas 7030 **Region** Southern Tasmania
T (03) 6263 7457 **www**.slw.com.au **Open** Wed–Sun 11–4 **Winemaker** Steve Lubiana
Est. 1990 **Vyds** 25ha
Monique and Steve Lubiana moved to the banks of the Derwent River in '90 to to make
high-quality sparkling wine. They built a gravity-fed winery and the winemaking approach
has been based on attention to detail within a biodynamic environment. The first sparkling
wines were made in '93 from the initial plantings of chardonnay and pinot noir. Over the
years they have added riesling, sauvignon blanc, pinot gris and merlot. The Italian-inspired
Osteria restaurant is based on their own biodynamically produced vegetables and herbs,
the meats (all free-range) are from local farmers and the seafood is wild-caught. In '16, the
Lubianas purchased the Panorama Vineyard, first planted in 1974. Exports to the UK, Sweden,
Singapore, Indonesia, South Korea, Japan, Taiwan and Hong Kong. (JH)

🍷🍷🍷🍷🍷 **Collina Chardonnay 2019, Tasmania** Tasmania is yet to realise its full potential
to craft graceful, enduring chardonnay, making wines that exemplify this all the
more outstanding. Beckoning and enticing with subtle lemon blossom fragrance
and pristine white peach flavour, this is an immaculately engineered wine of
breathtaking purity and structure, for the long haul. Oak is masterfully played
to elongate and texturise, adding but a whisper of flavour and aroma. Screw cap.
13% alc. RATING 96 DRINK 2029–2039 $100 TS
Chicane Malbec 2018, Tasmania An exceptional wine wherever grown and
made – but Tasmania? Malbec? This is extraordinary, with depth, richness and
ripeness plus black pepper, spice and fine-spun tannins for good measure. Cork.
13.5% alc. RATING 96 DRINK 2023–2028 $55 JH ✪
Pinot Noir 2020, Tasmania There is something compelling about the coiled
reticence of a cool season on the Derwent. Intricately structured with fine-boned
tannins and nicely toned acid drive, this is a vintage for the cellar. There is much
more integrity, persistence and definition wrapped in its folds than first glances
suggest. Its elegant rose petal and red cherry fruit will emerge in time. Patience
will be rewarded. Screw cap. 13% alc. RATING 95 DRINK 2030–2038 $62 TS
Collina Chardonnay 2020, Tasmania After the elegant poise of the '19
vintage, '20 represents a chardonnay of confidence and presence. It brims with
tangy grapefruit, crunchy white peach, succulent white nectarine and fig. Sweet,
ripe, fleshy fruit is well energised by the tension of southern Tasmanian acidity,
gently supported by creamy French oak. It holds impressive line and length. This
is the vintage to drink while '19 waits in the cellar. Screw cap. 13% alc. RATING 94
DRINK 2022–2027 $100 TS
Sauvignon Blanc 2020, Tasmania If you're like me and love enduring,
structured whites over flamboyant exoticism, this is the sauvignon for you. Steve
Lubiana has stripped his sauvignon back to racing spec, hitting new heights in
the racy '20 season. It's all about flinty tension and lightly oaked texture. Deadly
serious, it's poised to unravel monumentally over the next 2 decades. Screw cap.
13% alc. RATING 94 DRINK 2030–2040 $33 TS
Riesling 2020, Tasmania The cool '20 vintage has set off a steely riesling of
structure, focus and endurance. Still emphatically youthful at a full 2 years of age,
it projects beautiful purity of kaffir lime, Granny Smith apple and the memory of
lemon blossom. Cool acid drive and phenolic grip are well framed on a long finish
of body and texture, beautifully toned by wild fermentation in large-format oak
barrels. Screw cap. 12.5% alc. RATING 94 DRINK 2025–2040 $33 TS

Chardonnay 2020, Tasmania Textbook Tasmanian chardonnay that epitomises the tension and purity of a cool season in the Derwent Valley. Pitch-perfect white peach and lemon, framed in classy, toasted cashew nut French oak. A wonderfully crystalline finish of natural acid line. Give it time for oak to tuck into its pristine fruit. Screw cap. 13% alc. RATING 94 DRINK 2025-2035 $58 TS

Syrah 2020, Tasmania Real depth belies such a cool season. Blackberries, black pepper, licorice, even coal dust. Yet at every moment savoury, linear and finely woven, with plenty of air space. Firm, fine, peppery, mineral tannins lay out a long and rigid finish that demands patience and promises greatness. Screw cap. 13.5% alc. RATING 94 DRINK 2030-2040 $62 TS

ŢŢŢŢŢ **Blanc de Blanc 2015, Tasmania** RATING 92 $58 TS
Primavera Pinot Noir 2020, Tasmania RATING 92 DRINK 2022-2025 $40 TS

Stella Bella Wines   ★★★★★

205 Rosabrook Road, Margaret River, WA 6285 **Region** Margaret River
T (08) 9758 8611 **www.**stellabella.com.au **Open** 7 days 10–5 **Winemaker** Luke Jolliffe, Jarrad Olsen **Est.** 1997 **Dozens** 40 000 **Vyds** 55.7ha
This enormously successful winemaking business produces wines of true regional expression with fruit sourced from the central and southern parts of Margaret River. The company owns and operates 6 vineyards, and also purchases fruit from small contract growers. Substantial quantities of wine covering all styles and pricepoints make this an important producer for Margaret River. Exports of Stella Bella, Suckfizzle and Skuttlebutt labels to all major markets. (JH)

ŢŢŢŢŢ **Luminosa Chardonnay 2020, Margaret River** A very complex wine of immediate power, with a deliberately funky bouquet, then changing tack with the glorious purity and focus of the palate, white peach, grapefruit, cashew and almond combining in a single stream of joy. Screw cap. 13.6% alc. RATING 98 DRINK 2021-2030 $70 JH ✪ ♥

Luminosa Cabernet Sauvignon 2019, Margaret River You've got to love a premium cabernet at 13.9% – it's the sweet spot. Aromatically, the nose is laden with a sumptuous spread of forest fruits, star anise, fennel, maraschino cherry and even cocoa. In the mouth the wine is succulent and sleek, screaming past with the speed and slipstream of an F1 car – there's so much horsepower under the hood here that it's hard to compete. Mouth-filling, complete, elegant (owing to the relatively low alcohol) and already on the way to seamless: like the doppler effect in play, the reverberations of flavour are felt long after the wine has gone. Screw cap. 13.9% alc. RATING 97 DRINK 2022-2042 $90 EL ✪

ŢŢŢŢŢ **Suckfizzle Chardonnay 2020, Margaret River** Flinty, pithy, mineral and sumptuous. This is an expansive chardonnay of pristine poise and length. I love it. So much. But then again, all the chardonnays that the Stella Bella team have been putting out of late have been just like this: powerful and driven, but endlessly nuanced and detailed. The acid, although high, is perfectly nailed. Screw cap. 13.6% alc. RATING 96 DRINK 2022-2037 $80 EL

Suckfizzle Cabernet Sauvignon 2019, Margaret River A luminescent ruby hue all but shimmers in the light. The fruit in this glass is scintillatingly pure, the acidity threaded through is briny and enlivening. The tannins provide shape and support as the carriage of flavour makes its way over the tongue, hinting at the capability of this wine to age over the coming years. Quite gorgeous now though, I bet many don't make it past middle age. Screw cap. 14.1% alc. RATING 96 DRINK 2022-2039 $65 EL ✪

Shiraz 2020, Margaret River This wine is gorgeous. There is hung deli meat, pomegranate, raspberry, licorice, aniseed, fennel flower, briny acidity and shapely tannins. The flavour left lingering in the mouth once the wine is gone is sweet and chewy, both great things. Complex, slightly savoury, sweet, balanced and a bit spicy. A beauty. Screw cap. 14% alc. RATING 95 DRINK 2021-2028 $36 EL

Suckfizzle Sauvignon Blanc Semillon 2020, Margaret River Suckfizzle is routinely one of the great examples of oaked sauvignon blanc/semillon to emerge from WA in any given year. With a proven track record for brilliance in the cellar, it has earned its place as a serious part of a complex meal. This powerful example from the ripe '20 vintage tells us why: intense sugar snap pea and grapefruit on the nose and palate, with shell, stone fruit and spice. The toasty oak really rides the fruit at this stage, however I suggest you purchase this now but don't touch it – it needs time to settle. And settle it will. Screw cap. 13.4% alc. RATING 95 DRINK 2024–2036 $45 EL

Chardonnay 2020, Margaret River The chardonnays under the Stella Bella label are capable of statuesque poise and precision – they are truly wonderful. This is a little snippet of what is on show in the Suckfizzle and Luminosa chardonnays, and it carries all the same DNA and sumptuous flavour. Utterly delicious. Screw cap. 13.5% alc. RATING 95 DRINK 2021–2035 $38 EL

Cabernet Sauvignon 2019, Margaret River With 5% malbec. Stunningly pure and detailed nose, layered with cassis, raspberry, licorice, pomegranate and black pepper. In the mouth the wine is shaped by fine yet firm tannins, that allow the fruit to drape and trail through the finish. The texture of those tannins is a highlight: chalky, a touch grippy, and almost a little bit chewy. Very smart. Screw cap. 14.3% alc. RATING 95 DRINK 2021–2036 $38 EL

Sauvignon Blanc 2021, Margaret River Fruit from Karridale, and how we love Karridale. Cool and wet most of the time, grapes from this area often exhibit bright natural acid and plenty of delicacy and nuance; this is no exception. Like biting into a crunchy green apple with a few flakes of sea salt still on your lips, the texture on the palate is finely structured and chalky, and it drags the fruit out over the long finish. More mineral and spicy than it is punchy and obvious. Class act. Screw cap. 12.6% alc. RATING 94 DRINK 2021–2026 $25 EL ✪

Steve Wiblin's Erin Eyes ★★★★☆

58 Old Road, Leasingham, SA 5452 **Region** Clare Valley
T 0418 845 120 **www**.erineyes.com.au **Winemaker** Steve Wiblin **Est.** 2009
Dozens 2500

Steve Wiblin became a winemaker accidentally when he was encouraged by his mentor at Tooheys Brewery, who had a love of fine art and fine wine. Because Tooheys owned Wynns and Seaview, the change in career from beer to wine was easy. He watched the acquisition of Wynns and Seaview by Penfolds and then Seppelt, before moving to Orlando. He moved from the world of big wineries to small when he co-founded Neagles Rock in 1997. In 2009 he left Neagles Rock and established Erin Eyes explaining, 'In 1842 my English convict forebear John Wiblin gazed into a pair of Erin eyes. That gaze changed our family make-up and history forever. In the Irish-influenced Clare Valley, what else would I call my wines but Erin Eyes?' (JH)

♟♟♟♟♟ **Pride of Erin Single Vineyard Reserve Riesling 2021, Clare Valley** Finer and more restrained than the Emerald Isle Riesling – the spices and layers are dovetailed into the acidity and phenolic texture more seamlessly here. Very long, refined and saline. Quite beautiful. Screw cap. 11.5% alc. RATING 95 DRINK 2021–2036 $35 EL ✪

♟♟♟♟♟ **Emerald Isle Riesling 2021, Clare Valley** RATING 93 DRINK 2021–2031 $25 EL ✪
Blarney Stone Shiraz 2019, Clare Valley RATING 92 DRINK 2021–2028 $30 EL
Shamrock Malbec 2019, Clare Valley RATING 91 DRINK 2022–2029 $30 EL

Sticks

3/436 Johnston St, Abbotsford, Vic 3067 **Region** Yarra Valley
T (03) 9224 1911 **www**.sticks.com.au **Winemaker** Anthony Fikkers **Est.** 2000
Dozens 15 000

One of many labels under the Joval Wine Group, headed by John Valmorbida, with a strong link to the Australian food-and-wine scene thanks to his Italian family heritage. The Valmorbida family is behind a host of successful enterprises including wine distribution, importing Italian comestibles, retail and of course their own wine labels. The Sticks brand is all about offering entry-level yet fresh and simple everyday wines sourced from Yarra Valley floor sites at Coldstream, Dixon's Creek and Yarra Glen. The core comprises pinot grigio, chardonnay, pinot noir and cabernet sauvignon. In 2019, Anthony Fikkers took over as chief winemaker. Exports to Hong Kong, the UK and the US. (JF)

🍷🍷🍷🍷🍷 **Rosé 2021, Yarra Valley** A bright salmon colour. Cherry, tangerine and a touch of florals make for an attractive nose that follows through onto the palate which is dry, well weighted, refreshing and long. Good stuff. Screw cap. 12.5% alc. RATING 92 DRINK 2021–2023 $24 PR ✪

Stilvi

PO Box 116, Dromana, Vic 3936 (postal) **Region** Mornington Peninsula
T 0408 811 072 **www**.stilviwines.com.au **Open** By appt **Winemaker** Tim Elphick
Est. 2020 **Dozens** 400

Tim Elphick calls Stilvi his Peninsula passion project. That is, small-batch winemaking, both modern and ancient techniques from skin contact to clay vessels, all in a bid to create interesting wine and conversation. It's early days, with Tim sourcing fruit from various sites, mostly pinot gris, with pinot noir and chardonnay soon to be added. After 11 years as winemaker at Portsea Estate, he quit in '21 to concentrate on Stilvi, which means 'shimmering light' or 'shine' in Greek. As it turns out, one of his favourite Greek rock bands, Pyx Lax, released an album called Stilvi in '98. The wine is a delightful collaboration with his teenage daughter Kalypso, who designed the labels. (JF)

🍷🍷🍷🍷🍷 **Pinot Gris 2021, Mornington Peninsula** A pale copper hue; a very attractive wine with lots of flavour but not at all big or too rich – in other words, just right. Expect poached pears and apple, smoky spicy aromas, a creaminess across the palate and a gentle tannic pull on the finish. Rather delicious. Screw cap. 12.3% alc. RATING 93 DRINK 2022–2024 $33 JF

🍷🍷🍷🍷 **Skin Contact Pinot Gris 2021, Mornington Peninsula** RATING 88 DRINK 2022–2023 $35 JF

Stockman's Ridge Wines

21 Boree Lane, Lidster, NSW 2800 **Region** Orange
T (02) 6365 6212 **www**.stockmansridge.com.au **Open** Mon 12–5, Fri 11–5, Sat 11–8, Sun 11–5 **Winemaker** Will Rickard-Bell **Viticulturist** Jonathan Hambrook **Est.** 2002
Dozens 2500 **Vyds** 5ha

Stockman's Ridge is a handy operation in Orange, providing a swag of well-crafted wines from the usual cadre of varieties. The dark horses are the grüner veltliner and zinfandel, grown at circa 800m elevation. The 'groovy grüner' (as American sommeliers called it in the late '90s when its fashionability rose to a crescendo) is pungent and fresh, an easy hop, skip and a jump for riesling drinkers. Zinfandel may seem idiosyncratic, but after years in the United States, I can attest to its veracity. Neighbour David Lowe also crafts a fine example, suggesting the suitability of zin to Orange's higher reaches and strong diurnal shifts. Live music happens of a weekend and accommodation is available at the on-site Swagman Homestead. Exports to the US. (NG)

🍷🍷🍷🍷🍷 **Outlaw Grüner Veltliner 2021, Orange** An intriguing dry white, reminiscent of a modern Soave as much as a grüner. Ripe quince, preserved Meyer lemon and tangerine. Glossy. The acidity is lowish for the variety, but a peppery perk services definition and decent length. Nice drinking. Screw cap. 12.8% alc. RATING 90 DRINK 2021–2023 $40 NG

Stomp Wine

504 Wilderness Road, Lovedale, NSW 2330 **Region** Hunter Valley
T 0409 774 280 **www**.stompwines.com.au **Open** Thurs–Mon 10–5
Winemaker Michael McManus **Est.** 2004 **Dozens** 1000
After a seeming lifetime in the food and beverage industry, Michael and Meredith McManus moved to full-time winemaking. They set up Stomp Winemaking, a contract winemaker designed to keep small and larger parcels of grapes separate through the fermentation and maturation process, thus meeting the needs of boutique wine producers in the Hunter Valley. The addition of their own Stomp label is a small but important part of their business. (JH)

ŸŸŸŸŸ Limited Release Fiano 2021, Hunter Valley A great grape done justice. Excellent aromas: lemon pith, fennel and white pepper. As much textural intrigue as there is freshness. Skinsy and moreish. Resolute length and energy. Bravo! I'll like to taste this again in a few years. Riveting potential. Screw cap. 12.5% alc. RATING 94 DRINK 2021–2026 $28 NG ✪

ŸŸŸŸŸ Chardonnay 2021, Hunter Valley RATING 93 DRINK 2021–2028 $28 NG
Semillon 2021, Hunter Valley RATING 90 DRINK 2021–2028 $26 NG

Stonefish

3739 Caves Road, Wilyabrup, WA 6280 **Region** Margaret River
T (08) 9755 6774 **www**.stonefish.wine **Open** Thurs–Fri 11–4, Sat 11–5, Sun 11–4
Winemaker Contract, Peter Papanikitas **Est.** 2000 **Dozens** 20 000 **Vyds** 58ha
Peter Papanikitas has been involved in various facets of the wine industry for the past 30+ years. Initially his contact was with companies that included Penfolds, Lindemans and Leo Buring, then he spent 5 years working for Cinzano, gaining experience in worldwide sales and marketing. In '00, he established Stonefish, a virtual winery operation, in partnership with various grape growers and winemakers, principally in the Barossa Valley and Margaret River, who provide the wines. The value for money has never been in doubt but Stonefish has moved to another level with its Icon and Reserve wines. Exports to Thailand, Vietnam, Indonesia, the Philippines, the Maldives, Singapore, Fiji and Hong Kong. (JH)

ŸŸŸŸŸ Kudos Cabernet Sauvignon 2020, Margaret River Sweet vanillin oak encases the aromatics and leads with a confident and plump foot first. In the mouth the wine is plush and concentrated, almost effortless in its display of forest berries and exotic spice. The oak again struts through the finish, however the sweetness of it makes for a luscious kind of drinking – it avoids being intrusive. Perhaps drinking this in the short term will bring much enjoyment, especially after a decant. It'll cellar well, though. Diam. 14.6% alc. RATING 94 DRINK 2022–2032 $88 EL

ŸŸŸŸŸ Nero Old Vines Shiraz 2018, Barossa Valley RATING 93 DRINK 2022–2032 $50 DB
Reserve Chardonnay 2020, Margaret River RATING 92 DRINK 2021–2027 $42 EL
Concerto Shiraz 2017, Barossa Valley RATING 91 DRINK 2022–2032 $44 DB

Stonehaven

7089 Riddoch Highway, Padthaway, SA 5271 **Region** Padthaway
T (08) 8765 6140 **www**.stonehavenwines.com.au **Open** 7 days 10–5 **Winemaker** Grant Semmens, Leisha Slattery, Sean Carney **Est.** 1998 **Dozens** 500 000 **Vyds** 400ha
Stonehaven was established by Constellation Brands in 1998. By 2011, the winery – built in '98 at a cost of more than $33 million – was in mothballs. The business changed hands a few

times over the following decade and in '21, Stonehaven was purchased by Coonawarra-based CW Wines, owner of Reschke, Ulithorne and Schoolhouse brands. The brand is expected to be relaunched and the facilities to form 'the cornerstone' of CW Wines' operations. Exports to all major markets. (JH)

🍷🍷🍷🍷 **Stepping Stone Shiraz 2020, Limestone Coast** Delicious. It's spicy, juicy and a little bit fruit-sweet with plenty of plump, plush fruit to keep things joyful. It's not complex, but there's a really satisfying backdrop of exotic spice and soft tannins to engage. At $13, you'd be pretty happy with this, I should imagine. Screw cap. 14.5% alc. RATING 89 DRINK 2022–2024 $13 EL ✪

Stonehurst Cedar Creek ★★★★

1840 Wollombi Road, Cedar Creek, NSW 2325 **Region** Hunter Valley
T (02) 4998 1576 **www**.stonehurst.com.au **Open** Mon–Thurs 11–3, Fri–Sun 10–5
Winemaker Daniel Binet **Viticulturist** Daryl Heslop **Est.** 1995 **Dozens** 4000
Vyds 6.5ha

Stonehurst Cedar Creek has been established by Daryl and Phillipa Heslop on a historic 220ha property in the Wollombi Valley, underneath the Pokolbin Range. The vineyards (chambourcin, semillon, chardonnay and shiraz) are organically grown. A substantial part of the business, however, is the six self-contained cottages on the property. (JH)

🍷🍷🍷🍷🍷 **Reserve Shiraz 2019, Hunter Valley** A mid-weighted and pithy wine, with a line of earthen tannins framing sweet cherry, anise and terracotta accents. Matured 22 months in American and Hungarian oak adds a vanillin accent, without obfuscating the sweet tilled-earth notes of the Hunter. This is delicious, savoury drinking. Screw cap. 12.5% alc. RATING 93 DRINK 2022–2030 $35 NG

Mrs. Collins Chardonnay 2021, Hunter Valley An attractive, immensely flavourful mid-weighted chardonnay. Cedar-vanillin oak finds a nourishing confluence with praline and toasted hazelnut, white peach and nectarine. A creamy and texturally comforting finish for those seeking flavour after years of linear styles. Screw cap. 13% alc. RATING 92 DRINK 2022–2027 $30 NG

Stoney Rise ★★★★★

96 Hendersons Lane, Gravelly Beach, Tas 7276 **Region** Northern Tasmania
T (03) 6394 3678 **www**.stoneyrise.com **Open** Thurs–Mon 10–5 **Winemaker** Joe Holyman **Est.** 2000 **Dozens** 2000 **Vyds** 7.2ha

The Holyman family had been involved in vineyards in Tasmania for 20 years, but Joe Holyman's career in the wine industry – first as a sales rep, then as a wine buyer and more recently working in wineries in NZ, Portugal, France, Mount Benson and Coonawarra – gave him an exceptionally broad-based understanding of wine. In '04, Joe and wife Lou purchased the former Rotherhythe Vineyard, which had been established in '86, and set about restoring it to its former glory. There are 2 ranges: the Stoney Rise wines, focusing on fruit and early drinkability; and the Holyman wines – with more structure, more new oak and the best grapes, here the focus is on length and potential longevity. Exports to the UK, the Netherlands, Singapore and Japan. (JH)

🍷🍷🍷🍷🍷 **Holyman Pinot Noir 2020, Tasmania** It's intense and has impressive length; the savoury rumble is, of course, ex the whole bunches, imparting notes of spice and forest floor. Screw cap. 11.5% alc. RATING 95 DRINK 2025–2035 $60 JH

Holyman Project X Pinot Noir 2018, Tasmania Exceptionally vivid colour for a 4yo pinot, and pulls no punches. There's excellent plum and morello cherry fruit, and it carries 100% new oak with ease. Not everybody's favourite, but it should flourish with 5+ years in bottle. Screw cap. 12% alc. RATING 95 DRINK 2028–2038 $90 JH

Pinot Noir 2020, Tasmania A powerful wine that makes a mockery of its very low alcohol, other than the savoury whipcord that runs through the palate. Demands food. Screw cap. 11.5% alc. RATING 94 DRINK 2024–2034 $32 JH

🍷🍷🍷🍷🍷 **Yes Miss Pinot Noir 2021, Tasmania** RATING 93 DRINK 2026–2029 $40 JH

Stonier Wines

Cnr Thompson's Lane/Frankston-Flinders Road, Merricks, Vic 3916
Region Mornington Peninsula
T (03) 5989 8300 **www**.stonier.com.au **Open** 7 days 11–5 **Winemaker** Michael
Symons, Will Byron **Viticulturist** Luke Buckley **Est.** 1978 **Dozens** 35 000 **Vyds** 17ha
Stonier has embarked on a serious sustainability program that touches on all aspects of its
operations. It is one of the few wineries in Australia to measure its carbon footprint in detail,
using the officially recognised system of the Winemaker's Federation of Australia. It has created
a balanced ecosystem in the vineyard by strategic planting of cover crops and reduction of
sprays; and its need to irrigate. All wines are estate-grown and made with a mix of wild yeast
(from initiation of fermentation) and cultured yeast (added towards the end of fermentation
to ensure that no RS remains), and almost all are destemmed to open fermenters. All have
a 2-stage maturation – always French oak and variable use of barriques and puncheons for
the first stage. Justin Purser takes over as head winemaker from '22. Exports to all major
markets (JH)

W-WB Pinot Noir 2021, Mornington Peninsula Smoky, twiggy, bitter herbs,
rhubarb liqueur and all the complexity that comes from whole bunches are
complementary to the dark cherries, spice and woodsy flavours. A structured palate
with textural, furry tannins and a fragrant lift throughout. Screw cap. 13.8% alc.
RATING 97 DRINK 2022-2035 $90 JF ✪ ♥

Gainsborough Park Vineyard Chardonnay 2021, Mornington Peninsula
I can't recall a better, more focused Gainsborough Park Vineyard Chardonnay.
This is smokin'. Tight and linear with excellent fruit clarity; the lemon flavours
enhanced by creamy lees and moreish sulphides. Superfine acidity guides it to a
long finish. Screw cap. 13.5% alc. RATING 96 DRINK 2022-2031 $45 JF ✪
KBS Vineyard Chardonnay 2021, Mornington Peninsula Comes packed
with flavour, complexity and depth, yet fantastic acidity to drive this. Grapefruit,
Meyer lemon and lemon balm to the fore, building on the fine palate before
meeting up with a touch of delicate oak spice, nutty lees and a flourish of
savouriness. Moreish and impossible to resist a second glass. Screw cap. 13.5% alc.
RATING 96 DRINK 2022-2031 $50 JF ✪
Reserve Chardonnay 2021, Mornington Peninsula The Reserve is always
a blend of the best vineyards. It's not necessarily better than the single-site
wines – although it can be – it's a different expression. In this excellent vintage,
it's complex and pure. Certainly a core of citrus and stone fruit, but the layering
effect from oak, lees and a touch of flint give this a distinct savoury outlook.
It is a great shame the '21 wines are winemakers Michael Symons and Will
Byron's last, although they can leave on a high. Screw cap. 13.5% alc. RATING 96
DRINK 2022-2031 $50 JF ✪
Georgica Vineyard Pinot Noir 2021, Mornington Peninsula Merron's
vineyard was recently sold and renamed Georgica. As usual, no new oak used and
the fruit clarity shines through. A heady fragrance delights, so too, sweet cherries,
a dash of kirsch, some pips and woodsy spices, yet all glossy and detailed across
the medium-bodied palate. Superfine tannins and acidity to close. Beautiful wine.
Screw cap. 13.8% alc. RATING 96 DRINK 2022-2031 $55 JF ✪
Reserve Pinot Noir 2021, Mornington Peninsula Fragrant, lightly stemmy
and herbal (but not green), with flavours of red cherries, chinotto, blood
orange and sandalwood. Fleshy fruit across the fuller-bodied palate with raw
silk tannins holding sway. Incredibly refreshing now, but will garner even more
complexity in time. Screw cap. 13.8% alc. RATING 96 DRINK 2022-2035 $60 JF ✪
KBS Vineyard Pinot Noir 2021, Mornington Peninsula A composed yet
charming drink. Plenty of savoury fruit-derived tannin and refreshing acidity, so
there's a depth and structure within plus sweet, ripe black cherries, kirsch and
baking spices. It's a mouth-watering style and approachable now, but will reward
the patient, too. Screw cap. 13.5% alc. RATING 96 DRINK 2022-2033 $65 JF ✪
Windmill Vineyard Pinot Noir 2021, Mornington Peninsula The palest
ruby colour of all the pinots, but it has plenty of depth and structure. Archetypal

Mornington Peninsula flavours – the dark cherries, the blood orange and earthy notes, with a touch of turmeric and sandalwood. Supple tannins and tangy, bright acidity work across the fuller-bodied palate. It finishes convincingly and confidently. Screw cap. 13.8% alc. RATING 95 DRINK 2022-2034 $65 JF

Stormflower Vineyard ★★★★☆

3503 Caves Road, Wilyabrup, WA 6280 **Region** Margaret River
T 0421 867 488 **www**.stormflower.com.au **Open** 7 days 11–5 **Winemaker** Joel Page
Viticulturist Joel Page **Est.** 2007 **Dozens** 2800 **Vyds** 9ha
Stormflower Vineyard was founded by David Martin, Howard Cearns and Nic Trimboli, 3 friends better known as co-founders of Little Creatures Brewery in Fremantle. They thought the location of the vineyard (planted in the mid '90s) was ideal for producing high-quality wines. They pulled out one-third of the vines planted in the wrong way, in the wrong place, leaving almost 10ha of cabernet sauvignon, shiraz, chardonnay, sauvignon blanc, semillon and chenin blanc in place. Now the sole owner, David Martin is the driving force in the vineyard, with a family background in agriculture. The vineyard, certified organic by NASAA in '16, is managed using natural soil biology and organic compost. A new winery was completed just in time for the '20 vintage, with all wines now made onsite. (JH)

ΨΨΨΨΨ **Wilyabrup Chardonnay 2020, Margaret River** Acid freaks will be delighted to know that this wine carries 10.8g/L of acid, which is tempered by 3g/L of RS. Mlf was blocked, driving that acid deeper into the palate. Powerfully concentrated fruit (ripe summer peach and all things orchard), slick from the little bit of RS that remains, and vibrantly alive, jolted awake like an early morning ocean swim – that acid. The work in the winery has imparted a curry leaf and toasted-spice character that lingers. All in all, pretty awesome. Screw cap. 13.3% alc. RATING 95 DRINK 2021-2031 $50 EL

ΨΨΨΨΨ **Wilyabrup Cabernet Shiraz 2020, Margaret River** RATING 93 DRINK 2021-2027 $28 EL
Wilyabrup Shiraz 2019, Margaret River RATING 91 DRINK 2021-2027 $40 EL
Sauvignon Blanc 2021, Margaret River RATING 90 DRINK 2021-2024 $30 EL

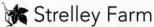 Strelley Farm ★★★★

Level 1, 5 Ord Street, West Perth, WA 6872 (postal) **Region** Tasmania
T (08) 9282 5417 **www**.https://strelleyfarm.wine/ **Winemaker** Liam McElhinney
Viticulturist John Fogarty, Christian De Camps **Est.** 2021 **Vyds** 36ha
Strelley Farm is the commercial range of the Fogarty Group's significant Tasmanian development. Fruity and bold, the initial release comprises chardonnay, pinot gris, sauvignon blanc, rosé, pinot noir, sparkling white and rosé and pét nat white and rosé. Sourcing spans all the major growing areas of Tasmania, with a particular focus to date on the Tamar Valley, Coal River Valley and East Coast. The Strelley Farm vineyard itself comprises 36ha (and counting) on 170ha of land. The range is line priced at $30 but discounted as low as $19 in the chain stores. A cellar door is scheduled to open near Richmond in the Coal River Valley in 2023. (TS)

ΨΨΨΨΨ **Strelley Farm Estate Pinot Noir 2019, Tasmania** Bright, clear crimson; a fragrant, perfumed bouquet with red fruits and spices galore, the palate elegant and fine boned. Red fruits are again leading the band, with trumpets of spices providing a resounding finish and aftertaste – opening the full peacock's tail. Screw cap. 13.5% alc. RATING 96 DRINK 2022-2031 $40 JH ❸

ΨΨΨΨ **Pinot Gris 2021, Tasmania** Confidently orbiting at the richer end of the gris universe, this is a full and fleshy rendition, loaded with ripe pear, honey and mixed spice. Fruit sweetness, integrated acidity and firm phenolic bite unite to find balance, if not grace. Screw cap. 13% alc. RATING 88 DRINK 2022-2022 $30 TS

Pinot Noir 2020, Tasmania 65/35% East Coast/Coal River Valley; matured 10 months in 20% new French oak barrels and puncheons. Fruity and bold, Strelley Farm is the Fogarty Group's commercial Tasmanian range. Accurate red and black cherry fruits are framed in tangy acidity and fine-grained tannins, concluding short and a touch sweet. Screw cap. 13.5% alc. RATING 88 DRINK 2022-2022 $30 TS

Studley Park Vineyard

5 Garden Terrace, Kew, Vic 3101 (postal) **Region** Port Phillip
T (03) 9852 8483 **www.studleypark.com.au** **Winemaker** Llew Knight (Contract)
Est. 1994 **Dozens** 500 **Vyds** 0.5ha
Geoff Pryor's Studley Park Vineyard is one of Melbourne's best kept secrets. It is on a bend of the Yarra River barely 4km from the Melbourne CBD, on a 0.5ha block once planted to vines, but for a century used for market gardening, then replanted with cabernet sauvignon. A spectacular aerial photograph shows that immediately across the river, and looking directly to the CBD, is the epicentre of Melbourne's light industrial development, while on the northern and eastern boundaries are suburban residential blocks. (JH)

Rosé 2020, Port Phillip A bright, light orange. Cherry, blood orange and gentle spice aromas lead onto the dry and well-balanced palate, before closing with gently grippy tannins which should make this a treat with grilled lamb cutlets and barbecued salmon or tuna this summer. Screw cap. 12.5% alc. RATING 90 DRINK 2021-2022 $20 PR ✪

Sunshine Creek

350 Yarraview Road, Yarra Glen, Vic 3775 **Region** Yarra Valley
T (03) 9882 1800 **www.sunshinecreek.com.au** **Winemaker** Chris Lawrence
Viticulturist Andrew Smith **Est.** 2009 **Dozens** 7000 **Vyds** 20ha
Packaging magnate James Zhou commissioned Mario Marson to find an appropriate vineyard. They discovered Martha's Vineyard; the excellent site compensating for the need to change the existing spur-pruned vineyard to vertical shoot position for increased quality and hand-picking. In '11, Andrew Smith was appointed vineyard manager to change the focus of management to sustainability and minimal interference. In '14 winemaker Chris Lawrence joined the team and an onsite winery (capable of handling 275t) was completed prior to the '16 vintage. In '17 there was a changing of the guard in the winery as Mario decided to concentrate solely on his Vinea Marson brand and Chris took on the role of chief winemaker. Exports to Hong Kong and Japan. (JH)

Ulysses Cabernets 2019, Yarra Valley 93/3/3/1% cabernet/merlot/petit verdot/malbec. A vibrant crimson purple. Dark cherry and black plums intermingle with sage and olive tapenade, along with classic cigar-box aromas from the well-handled oak. Equally good on the palate, this medium- to full-bodied wine has energy, structure and freshness. Good now, this will only get better over the next 5–10 years. Diam. 13.5% alc. RATING 95 DRINK 2023-2029 $45 PR

Cabernets 2019, Yarra Valley RATING 92 DRINK 2023-2029 $45 PR
Shiraz 2019, Heathcote RATING 90 DRINK 2021-2027 $45 PR
Shiraz 2019, Yarra Valley RATING 90 DRINK 2022-2025 $45 PR

Surveyor's Hill Vineyards

215 Brooklands Road, Wallaroo, NSW 2618 **Region** Canberra District
T (02) 6230 2046 **www.survhill.com.au** **Open** W'ends & public hols
Winemaker Brindabella Hills (Dr Roger Harris), Greg Gallagher (sparkling) **Est.** 1986
Dozens 1000 **Vyds** 10ha
Surveyor's Hill Vineyards is on the slopes of the eponymous hill, at 550m-680m above sea level. It is an ancient volcano, producing granite-derived, coarse-structured (and hence well drained) sandy soils of low fertility. This has to be the ultimate patchwork-quilt vineyard with 1ha each of chardonnay, shiraz and viognier; 0.5ha each of roussanne, marsanne, aglianico, nero

d'Avola, mourvèdre, grenache, muscadelle, moscato giallo, cabernet franc, riesling, semillon, sauvignon blanc, touriga nacional and cabernet sauvignon. (JH)

🍷🍷🍷🍷🍷 **Hills of Hall Cabernets 2018, Canberra District** 75/25% cabernets sauvignon/franc. While the fruit is on the riper side of the spectrum, the colour remains a deep bright garnet and the wine just shy of medium bodied. Cassis, pastilles, tapenade and licorice root form the main flavour profile, while the supple tannins work towards a gentle finish. Screw cap. 14.2% alc. RATING 91 DRINK 2021–2027 $28 JF

Hills of Hall Tinto 2018, Canberra District A blend of 58/32/10% tempranillo/graciano/grenache. It's a rich yet medium-bodied style with some cherry, maraschino and dried plum accents, although it's more a savoury wine. Licorice, cedary oak spices and warm earth add much to the enjoyment. Screw cap. 13.7% alc. RATING 90 DRINK 2021–2023 $28 JF

🍷🍷🍷🍷 **Cabernet Franc 2021, Canberra District** RATING 88 DRINK 2021–2022 $22 JF

Sussex Squire Wines   ★★★★

293-295 Spring Gully Road, Gillentown, SA 5453 **Region** Clare Valley
T 0458 141 169 www.sussexsquire.com.au **Open** Sun–Thurs 11–4, Fri–Sat 11–5
Winemaker Daniel Wilson, Mark Bollen **Viticulturist** Mark Bollen **Est.** 2014
Dozens 1200 **Vyds** 8ha
There's a long family history attached to this wine business, beginning with Walter Hackett (1827–1914), a Sussex farmer; followed by Joseph Hackett (1880–1958), Joseph Robert Hackett (1911–98) and now fourth generation Mark and Skye Bollen. Mark and Skye returned to the Clare Valley after 25 years working in other pursuits and in '14 purchased 5ha of shiraz, which is now dry-grown and organically managed. 0.5ha each of nero d'Avola, sangiovese, mataro, grenache and malbec have also been added. They have a flock of Black Suffolk sheep that roam the vineyard during winter to provide natural weed control and fertilise the soil. (JH)

🍷🍷🍷🍷🍷 **JRS The Sussex Squire Barrel Selection Cabernet Sauvignon 2018, Clare Valley** Chocolatey and dense, this has mulberries, blackberries, rhubarb and strawberries. In the mouth the wine is astoundingly intense – like when you poach raspberries to make coulis, and reducing the liquid content is part of the process … this is concentrated and essence-like, the fruit becoming almost pure in its piercing (tart?) song through the finish. Quite individual. Quite impressive. Screw cap. 14.5% alc. RATING 93 DRINK 2022–2037 $75 EL

The Prancing Pony Single Vineyard Polish Hill River Riesling 2021, Clare Valley Tangy lime and citrus populate the nose, there is a bath salts/pithy/ briny undertow that keeps the bright fruit on track. In the mouth, the palate is voluminous and pillowed, with layers of taut acidity and chalky phenolics. The acidity is perhaps a little tart, however the length of flavour is lingering and elegant. Screw cap. 10.5% alc. RATING 91 DRINK 2021–2036 $30 EL

The Darting Hare Single Vineyard Sangiovese 2020, Clare Valley Cherries, raspberries, and all the spice and life we look for in sangiovese. Perhaps this is lacking the structural pertness that makes the Italian iterations so balanced (of plump fruit and firm tannins), however – all else is there in spades. Lovely wine. Screw cap. 14% alc. RATING 90 DRINK 2021–2027 $30 EL

The Partnership Shiraz Mataro 2019, Clare Valley 60/40% shiraz/mataro makes for a plush, plump, rounded wine with no hard edges. Layers of hung deli meat and mulberries, plums and blackberries. Uncomplicated spicy drinking, here. Screw cap. 14.5% alc. RATING 90 DRINK 2021–2027 $40 EL

The Raging Bull Single Vineyard Malbec 2019, Clare Valley Green peppercorns, raspberry coulis and apple skins dominate the aromas here. In the mouth the wine performs just as expected: it's fruit driven, spicy and slightly medicinal. Well played. Screw cap. 14.2% alc. RATING 90 DRINK 2021–2028 $40 EL

JRS The Sussex Squire Barrel Selection Shiraz 2018, Clare Valley Two of the best new French oak barrels, matured for 24 months. That's a long time in new oak, and the impact is clear on the nose. There's a distinct pine-needle character that laces through the black and blue fruits, which translates to the palate also. The concentration of flavour is admirable, however the oak really does distract from that beautiful fruit. Perhaps it will come together in a few years time. Screw cap. 14.5% alc. RATING 90 DRINK 2021–2032 $75 EL

🍷🍷🍷🍷 **Thomas Block Single Vineyard Shiraz 2019, Clare Valley** RATING 89 DRINK 2021–2029 $40 EL

Sutton Grange Winery ★★★★★

Carnochans Road, Sutton Grange, Vic 3448 **Region** Bendigo
T (03) 8672 1478 **www.**suttongrange.com.au **Open** W'ends 11–5 **Winemaker** Chris Smailes **Est.** 1998 **Dozens** 6000 **Vyds** 12ha

Sutton Grange, a 400ha property, in the foothills of Leanganook near Harcourt, combines a horse training facility with grape growing and winemaking, as well as a venue for corporate events. This multi-functional enterprise was acquired in '96 by Peter Sidwell, a Melbourne businessman with horseracing and breeding interests. The wine side of the business dates back to '98 and a chance lunch at the property with modern-day Bendigo wine pioneer, Stuart Anderson (founder Balgownie) and local winemaker, Alec Epis. Vines went in soon after, with Stuart Anderson's Burgundy-born son-in-law, Gilles Lapalus, installed as winemaker in '01. He introduced biodynamics to the property and planted Italian varieties suited to a changing climate. The experienced wine-making hand of Melanie Chester (ex Seppelt) from '15 took the Sutton Grange name to greater heights, regularly winning major trophies and accolades, most notably for her Syrah. In '22 Mel passed the baton to Chris Smailes, (ex Blue Pyrenees Estate). Exports to the UK, the US, Canada and Switzerland. (JP)

🍷🍷🍷🍷🍷 **Fairbank Rosé 2021, Central Victoria** A blend of cabernet sauvignon, shiraz, sangiovese and viognier. A wine with a big following and it's easy to see why. Copper pink tea rose hues are easy on the eye, the perfumed strawberry, raspberry fruit, bracken and light musk aromas and flavours equally inviting. Restrained and composed, with great balance. Screw cap. 12.5% alc. RATING 95 DRINK 2022–2024 $35 JP ✪ ♥

Fairbank Syrah 2020, Central Victoria A collaborative project following the disastrous spring frosts in '19 that wiped out the '20 crops. In keeping with the Fairbank Syrah style, we see an elegant expression of the grape, deep and engaging in black fruits, blueberry, pepper, spice and chocolate. Juicy fruit on the palate is nicely wrapped in fine tannins, driving the wine towards a smooth finish. Screw cap. 13.5% alc. RATING 95 DRINK 2022–2032 $35 JP ✪

🍷🍷🍷🍷🍷 **Fairbank Ancestrale Sparkling Rosé 2021, Central Victoria** RATING 90 $40 JP

Fairbank Field Blend 2021, Bendigo RATING 90 DRINK 2022–2024 $35 JP

Sweetwater Wines ★★★★★

117 Sweetwater Road, Belford, NSW 2335 **Region** Hunter Valley
T (02) 4998 7666 **www.**sweetwaterwines.com.au **Winemaker** Bryan Currie **Est.** 1998 **Vyds** 16ha

Sweetwater Wines is a single-vineyard winery making semillon, shiraz and cabernet sauvignon, the wines made by Andrew Thomas from 2003 to '16 and all stored in a temperature-controlled underground wine cellar that is part of the very large ornate house and separate guest accommodation built on the property. The reason for the seemingly unusual focus on cabernet sauvignon (true, second to shiraz) is the famed red volcanic soil over limestone. Exports to Hong Kong. (JH)

🍷🍷🍷🍷🍷 **Single Estate Semillon 2021, Hunter Valley** This is excellent. Fidelitous to the lanolin, grapefruit and lemon balm-doused nervy Hunter archetype, this lightweight also expresses whiffs of white pepper, sugar snap pea and a verdant undercarriage, not dissimilar to white bordeaux or quality Austrian grüner veltliner. Tensile, nicely chewy and very long, this is a beauty. Screw cap. 11% alc. RATING 95 DRINK 2021-2033 $27 NG ✪

Cabernet Sauvignon 2010, Hunter Valley An aged release of purity, immense vibrancy and the pleasures of a hearth, fire and creased leather armchair, incarnate as liquid. An opportunity, too, to relish a wine at an apogee of complexity and mid-weighted drinkability. Sweet loamy earth, varnish, camphor, mulch, Cuban cigar and tinderbox, with an ineffable sweetness that defies obvious descriptives, lingering long. Thoroughly rewarding. Screw cap. 13% alc. RATING 95 DRINK 2021-2024 $90 NG

Shiraz 2006, Hunter Valley A museum release, strongly reminiscent of the wines of my childhood. Nostalgic and warm. American oak (60%), the provocateur, splaying mocha and coconut shavings across an orb of darker fruits, root beer, anise and that unique Hunter sensibility of savouriness, defined as much by camphor, loam and sweet earth, as it is by an aura of digestibility. Sweet, tactile and very long. Works well. Screw cap. 14% alc. RATING 95 DRINK 2021-2026 $90 NG

Swinging Bridge   ★★★★☆

701 The Escort Way, Orange, NSW 2800 **Region** Orange
T 0447 416 295 **www**.swingingbridge.com.au **Open** Mon–Sun by appt
Winemaker Tom Ward **Viticulturist** Tom Ward **Est.** 1995 **Vyds** 6ha

Swinging Bridge Estate was established in '95 by the Ward and Payten families. Tom and Georgie Ward took the helm in '08. The label had its founding in Canowindra with initial plantings of chardonnay and shiraz. Today, Swinging Bridge has a variety of ranges on offer, including a number of Reserve wines, the Experimental Series, Winemaker Series and Estate Series. Tom's pursuit of premium grapes resulted in a number of wines made from grapes grown on Peter and Lee Hedberg's Hill Park Vineyard (planted in 1998). Hill Park Vineyard is now the permanent home of Swinging Bridge. Tom was a Len Evans scholar in 2012 and has been president of NSW Wine since '13. (JH)

🍷🍷🍷🍷🍷 **Hill Park Block 7 Chardonnay 2019, Orange** These single-block wines are largely made the same way, give or take minute shifts of oak influence (20-25% new here). This exercise is all about texture. Stone-fruit inflections and some almond-meal lees, a given. Talcy, chewy phenolic grip. A long drive across the palate. Strident and confident, auguring for optimal drinking across the mid term. The most Euro of feel. Screw cap. 12.9% alc. RATING 95 DRINK 2021-2030 $80 NG

by Tom Ward Eliza Riesling 2021, Orange Light–mid weighted, the intensity of lime cordial, beeswax, blossom, green apple, camphor and quinine notes, riveting. The acidity is tingly, juicy and palpably natural. A dash of RS, the balletic balance beam that softens the acidity without detracting from perceivable dryness and vitality. Australian riesling that achieves a rare feat: deliciousness in youth. Screw cap. 12.8% alc. RATING 94 DRINK 2021-2029 $30 NG ✪

by Tom Ward #003 Amber 2021, Orange A blend of gris, gewürztraminer and riesling, each fermented spontaneously on skins. The rosewater, lychee and grape spice of gewürz at the fore. Some nashi pear and ginger, too. Yet the light- to gently mid-weighted palate defers to riesling's acid sparkle for perk and drive and the time on skins for a refined, salty, raspy sinew to corral the melee and pull it taut and long. This is very good. Uber-versatile at the table. Orange wine for the uninitiated, perhaps. The skinsy detail is of a diplomatic level. Nicely honed and refined, rather than brazen and extreme. Screw cap. 12.4% alc. RATING 94 DRINK 2021-2024 $35 NG

🍷🍷🍷🍷🍸 **by Tom Ward #009 Gamay 2021, Orange** RATING 93 DRINK 2021-2024 $35 NG

Caldwell Lane Block D Chardonnay 2019, Orange RATING 93 DRINK 2021-2029 $65 NG

Caldwell Lane Block A Chardonnay 2019, Orange RATING 92 DRINK 2021-2028 $65 NG

Swings & Roundabouts

2807 Caves Road, Yallingup, WA 6232 **Region** Margaret River
T (08) 9756 6640 **www.**swings.com.au **Open** 7 days 10–5 **Winemaker** Brian Fletcher
Est. 2004 **Dozens** 10 000 **Vyds** 5ha

The Swings & Roundabouts name comes from the expression used to encapsulate the eternal balancing act between the various aspects of grape and wine production. Swings aims to balance the serious side with a touch of fun. The wines are released under the Swings & Roundabouts and Backyard Stories labels. The arrival of Brian Fletcher as winemaker has underwritten the quality of the wines. He has never been far from the wine headlines, with over 35 years of experience making wine all over the world. Exports to the US, Canada and Japan. (JH)

Backyard Stories Chardonnay 2020, Margaret River Complex and densely flavoured, this is almost a behemoth of a wine, showing the full spectrum of spicy orchard fruits, curry leaf, grated nutmeg, brine, red apple skins, pink grapefruit and cheesecloth. Long, satisfying and impressive. Screw cap. 13% alc. RATING 94 DRINK 2021-2031 $50 EL

Backyard Stories Cabernet Sauvignon 2019, Margaret River Juicy and supple, the fruit here shows a balance between plush, ripe and just al dente fruit. Cassis, raspberry and pomegranate make up the bulk of the profile, while the finish is peppered with graphite, red apples and licorice. Screw cap. 14.5% alc. RATING 94 DRINK 2021-2031 $55 EL

Backyard Stories Chenin Blanc 2021, Margaret River RATING 91 DRINK 2022-2032 $34 EL

Backyard Stories Pinot Noir 2021, Mount Barker RATING 91 DRINK 2022-2028 $45 EL

Backyard Stories Chardonnay 2021, Margaret River RATING 91 DRINK 2022-2028 $50 EL

Backyard Stories Pinot Noir Chardonnay NV, Margaret River RATING 90 $45 EL

Shiraz 2020, Margaret River RATING 90 DRINK 2022-2025 $24 EL

Swinney

325 Frankland-Kojonup Road, Frankland River, WA 6396 **Region** Frankland River
T (08) 9200 4483 **www.**swinney.com.au **Winemaker** Rob Mann **Viticulturist** Rhys Thomas **Est.** 1998 **Dozens** 2500 **Vyds** 160ha

The Swinney family (currently parents Graham and Kaye, and son and daughter Matt and Janelle) has been resident on their 2500ha property since it was settled by George Swinney in 1922. In the '90s they decided to diversify and now have 160ha of vines across 4 vineyards, including the Powderbark Ridge Vineyard in Frankland River (planted in '98, purchased in partnership with former Hardys winemaker Peter Dawson). The lion's share goes to shiraz (67ha) and cabernet sauvignon (48ha), followed by riesling, semillon, pinot gris, gewürztraminer, viognier, vermentino and malbec. They also pushed the envelope by establishing grenache, tempranillo and mourvèdre as bush vines, a rarity in this part of the world. Exports to the UK, Singapore and Hong Kong. (JH)

Farvie Syrah 2020, Frankland River An utterly gorgeous nose awaits. Ferrous, blood plum, rust, pastrami, blackberries in summer, black cherries and mulberries too. '20 was warm and yields were low. Across the board, berries were small. An odd observation perhaps, until you encounter the tannins. This is concentrated and textured, with fine-grit tannins that shape the palate and encase the fruit. It insists on a decant as it's tight as a drum currently – you will miss the complete spectrum of texture if you decide to wade right in. This is a monumental wine of gravitas and poise, the flavour all clustered on the back palate. I suspect we haven't seen the best of it yet. Screw cap. 14% alc. RATING 97 DRINK 2022-2042 $150 EL ✪

Mourvèdre Syrah Grenache 2020, Frankland River The mourvèdre just has such beautiful tannins and shape. Gloriously earthy, gravelly yet fine, it underpins the success of the other varieties and lends a real chew to the overall. Beautiful, supple, vibrant. With muscle. Screw cap. 14% alc. RATING 96 DRINK 2021–2031 $42 EL ✪ ♥

Farvie Grenache 2020, Frankland River This region's '20 reds are, on the whole, totally sensational, as this is. But they are fortified at this early stage by a fortress of tannin. When reviewing the Swinney Grenache, it took a full 24 hrs for the wine to show what I knew it had in it all along: supple, slinky, fleshy grenache fruit. This, too, is extraordinarily reticent to open up at this stage, even after an hour in the glass, with repeat swirling events. Tight doesn't cover it. This may be a profound wine, judging by its length and detailed construction, but it will require patience. Screw cap. 14% alc. RATING 96 DRINK 2025–2045 $150 EL ♥

Grenache 2020, Frankland River This is muscly grenache, with brawn and heft. The tannins, while gravelly and pervasive, serve to structure the wine in the mouth and through the finish. Fair warning: I was stumped by this wine upon initial opening: the tannins are firm. But give it some time in a decanter (an hour or so should do it, for me it was overnight in the bottle, on the kitchen bench) and they dissolve into the fruit, allowing it to sing, as it should. A stellar wine – I'm so glad I waited. Screw cap. 14% alc. RATING 95 DRINK 2022–2032 $42 EL

Syrah 2020, Frankland River Sweet, perfumed black fruit on the nose is laced with blood and rust, serving up a potently engaging mix of characters that demand a second and third look. In the mouth the fruit is concentrated and dense, with very finely woven tea-like tannins that distinctly express graphite and coal dust … a lot going on. Screw cap. 14% alc. RATING 94 DRINK 2021–2028 $42 EL

Symphonia Wines ★★★★

1699 Boggy Creek Road, Myrrhee, Vic 3732 **Region** King Valley
T (02) 4952 5117 **www**.symphoniafinewines.com.au **Open** By appt **Winemaker** Lilian Carter **Est.** 1998 **Dozens** 1500 **Vyds** 28ha

Peter Read and his family are veterans of the King Valley, commencing the development of their vineyard in 1981. After extensive trips to both Western and Eastern Europe, Peter embarked on an ambitious project to trial a series of grape varieties little known in this country. Current owners Peter and Suzanne Evans are committed to continuing Peter Read's pioneering legacy, making arneis, petit manseng, pinot grigio, savagnin, tannat, tempranillo and saperavi. Exports to the UK. (JH)

🍷🍷🍷🍷🍷 **Prosecco NV, King Valley** Charmet method, 7g/L RS. Brings the clean, fresh, joie de vivre that prosecco drinkers want first and foremost. Fantastic aperitif style bursting in lemon pith, fresh cut apple, citrus and nashi pear. Plenty of tang and lightly savoury. Crown. 11.2% alc. RATING 93 $28 JP

Royal Late Harvest Manseng 2021, King Valley 17g/L RS. The producer's second dessert-style manseng, quite complex and compelling. Brings together quince, lime marmalade, spiced apple and attractive fragrant florals and spice. Concentrated and fresh, with a nice touch of lemon barley lusciousness, it flows with textural slide through to the finish. Screw cap. 8.1% alc. RATING 91 DRINK 2022–2025 $45 JP

Manseng 2021, King Valley Brings both ripe stone and tropical fruits to the fore, together with a distinctive waxy edge. Fills the mouth with flavour, fleshy in texture and is developing quite a richness and spiciness. Demands to be matched with Thai food. Screw cap. 13.5% alc. RATING 90 DRINK 2022–2025 $28 JP

Pinot Grigio 2021, King Valley A neat, crisp grigio which plays to the inherent strengths of the grape: clean, assertive acidity and subtle fruit with some real zip to close. Packs some tart and tang in Nashi pear, green apple and citrus with chalky texture on the palate. Crunchy acidity all the way to the finish. Screw cap. 12% alc. RATING 90 DRINK 2022–2024 $28 JP

🍷🍷🍷🍷 **Pinot Trois Rosé 2021, King Valley** RATING 89 DRINK 2022–2024 $28 JP
La Solista Tempranillo 2019, King Valley RATING 89 DRINK 2022–2025 $28 JP
Arneis 2021, King Valley RATING 88 DRINK 2022–2024 $28 JP

Symphony Hill Wines

2017 Eukey Road, Ballandean, Qld 4382 **Region** Granite Belt
T (07) 4684 1388 **www.**symphonyhill.com.au **Open** 7 days 10–4 **Winemaker** Abraham
de Klerk **Viticulturist** Abraham de Klerk **Est.** 1999 **Dozens** 6000 **Vyds** 3.5ha
Ewen Macpherson purchased an old table-grape and orchard property in 1996. A partnership
with his parents, Bob and Jill Macpherson, led to development of the vineyard while Ewen
completed his bachelor of applied science in viticulture (2003). The vineyard (now much
expanded) was established using state-of-the-art technology. (JH)

ＹＹＹＹＹ **Wild Child Viognier 2021, Granite Belt** The apricot-kernel signature of
viognier is well framed in the spicy, nutty mood of fermentation and 4 months'
maturation in old French oak barrels. Vanilla custard flavours and texture contrast
just the right amount of phenolic crunch and draw out a long finish. Well played,
Symphony Hill! Screw cap. 13.4% alc. RATING 92 DRINK 2023–2026 $65 TS
Reserve Cabernet Sauvignon 2019, Granite Belt Symphony Hill's flagship
unites the depth and breadth of fully ripe cabernet with the high-altitude energy
of the Granite Belt. Impressive depth of colour heralds mulberry and cassis fruit,
framed in dark chocolate oak. Hot alcohol clashes with firm acidity on the
finish, and will appreciate time to integrate. Screw cap. 14.8% alc. RATING 91
DRINK 2026–2034 $95 TS
Reserve Petit Verdot 2019, Granite Belt A full, vibrant purple hue proclaims
signature petit verdot. A compact, tense palate is packed with tiny blackcurrants
and blackberries, confidently framed in firm, fine tannins. New oak (50% for
12 months) lends impressive support. One for the cellar. Screw cap. 14.3% alc.
RATING 90 DRINK 2029–2034 $65 TS

ＹＹＹＹ **Vermentino 2021, Granite Belt** RATING 89 DRINK 2022–2022 $30 TS
Reserve Graciano 2019, Granite Belt RATING 89 DRINK 2024–2029 $65 TS
Reserve Verdelho 2021, Granite Belt RATING 88 DRINK 2022–2022 $45 TS

Syrahmi

2370 Lancefield-Tooborac Road, Tooborac, Vic 3523 **Region** Heathcote
T 0407 057 471 **www.**syrahmi.com.au **Open** By appt **Winemaker** Adam Foster
Est. 2004 **Dozens** 2400 **Vyds** 0.8ha
Adam Foster worked as a chef in Victoria and London before moving to the front of house
and becoming increasingly interested in wine. He then worked as a cellar hand with a who's
who in Australia and France, including Torbreck, Chapoutier, Mitchelton, Domaine Ogier,
Heathcote Winery, Jasper Hill and Domaine Pierre Gaillard. He became convinced that
the Cambrian soils of Heathcote could produce the best possible shiraz, and since '04 has
purchased grapes from the region, using the full bag of winemaking techniques. In '17, 0.8ha
of shiraz (3 clones) were planted at 8888 vines/ha at Tooborac, with a winery completed in
time for the '19 vintage. Exports to the US, Japan and Hong Kong. (JH)

ＹＹＹＹＹ **La La Shiraz 2016, Heathcote** By any reckoning this is a daring wine –
100% whole bunches, 44 months in new oak – yeah, that's out there! And the
name? That, too! The winemaker is pushing himself and his grapes in pursuit
of an exciting journey of discovery, one of complexity and longevity. Bottle
ageing before release allows for a wine in symmetry and balance, and it shines.
Fragrant, lifted perfume in anise, bush leaves, cassis, dark chocolate and game –
it's a moveable, ever-changing feast of scents. Heathcote shiraz seduces the
palate, its lush black fruits, deep-seated spices and savoury depth framed in warm,
toasty oak and taut, sturdy tannins. Spectacular. Screw cap. 13.8% alc. RATING 96
DRINK 2022–2036 $200 JP
Garden of Earthly Delights Pinot Noir 2020, Macedon Ranges Adam
Foster reaches out across the Heathcote border to neighbours in the Macedon
Ranges for this alluring pinot whose aromas are every inch as captivating as
its taste. Fragrant in lifted violet notes, cherry, wild strawberry and dried herbs.

Carries well across the palate, gaining depth and concentration, and aided by brisk, sinewy tannins. Screw cap. 12.8% alc. RATING 95 DRINK 2022–2027 $55 JP

ŸŸŸŸŸ **Garden of Earthly Delights Chardonnnay 2020, Macedon Ranges**
RATING 93 DRINK 2022–2028 $55 JP
Mourvèdre 2019, Heathcote RATING 92 DRINK 2022–2029 $45 JP
Garden of Earthly Delights Sangiovese 2019, Heathcote RATING 91
DRINK 2022–2029 $45 JP
Grenache 2019, Heathcote RATING 90 DRINK 2022–2032 $45 JP

T'Gallant

1385 Mornington-Flinders Road, Main Ridge, Vic 3928 **Region** Mornington Peninsula
T (03) 5931 1300 **www.**tgallant.com.au **Open** 7 days 9–5 **Winemaker** Tom Shanahan
Est. 1990 **Vyds** 8ha
Husband-and-wife winemakers Kevin McCarthy and Kathleen Quealy carved out such an important niche market for the T'Gallant label that in 2003, after protracted negotiations, it was acquired by Beringer Blass (now part of TWE). The acquisition of a 15ha property and the planting of 8ha of pinot gris gave the business a firm geographic base, as well as providing increased resources for its signature wine. (JH)

ŸŸŸŸŸ **Cyrano Pinot Noir 2020, Mornington Peninsula** This hits the spot with its restraint, vibrancy and refreshing tangy tartness across the lighter-framed palate, alongside supple tannins. In between is a mix of gently spiced cherries, cranberries, woodsy spices and a subtle savouriness. Screw cap. 13% alc. RATING 90 DRINK 2021–2026 $28 JF

Tahbilk

254 O'Neils Road, Tabilk, Vic 3608 **Region** Nagambie Lakes
T (03) 5794 2555 **www.**tahbilk.com.au **Open** Mon–Fri 9–5, Sat–Sun 10–5
Winemaker Alister Purbrick, Alan George, Brendan Freeman **Viticulturist** Richard Flatman **Est.** 1860 **Dozens** 120 000 **Vyds** 221.5ha
In 2020, Tahbilk celebrated its 160th birthday. For 5 generations, the Purbrick family have tended vines and protected the delicate watering holes and landscape of their property outside Nagambie. The winery should be visited at least once by every wine-conscious Australian. It produces marsanne and a range of reds made very much as they were by the late, great Eric Purbrick. The family has moved fast in securing a more sustainable future, re-establishing natural wetlands, revegetating 160ha of land with indigenous trees and plants, achieving carboNZero certification in '16 and beginning the journey in '21 to convert its vineyards to accredited organic. In '22, Alister Purbrick stepped down as CEO but will continue to be involved on industry boards. Tahbilk is a founding member of Australia's First Families of Wine and was the Companion's Winery of the Year in '16. (JP)

ŸŸŸŸŸ **1860 Vines Shiraz 2018, Nagambie Lakes** A picture of effortless elegance. As always, it benefits from a splash of air to fully open and reveal, fully pliant in ripe fruit – cassis, black berries, plum – and cinnamon spice before launching into baked earth, leather, savoury truffle and undergrowth. Oak is measured, tannins are fine and polished, fanning out across the palate. Everything is in its place. A fine wine boasting a mature confidence. Screw cap. 14% alc. RATING 97 DRINK 2022–2044 $325 JP ♥

ŸŸŸŸŸ **BDX Blend Old Block Vines 2019, Nagambie Lakes** I like to think that this is a birthday present to wine drinkers, an incredibly well-priced cabernet blend, from a company which recently celebrated its 160th birthday. It's also a statement wine; it says 'look at what cabernet sauvignon and friends can do in the Nagambie Lakes', a region more often associated with shiraz. It's a star performance. Intriguing and complex, it immediately makes an impact with lifted aromas of blackberry, dark spices, an autumnal leafiness and dusty earth encased in violet aromatics. Fills the mouth with flavour and a fine, trimmed elegance. Everything is in place. It's a limited, one-off release and a gem. Screw cap. 14% alc. RATING 96 DRINK 2022-2034 $67 JP ✪

Eric Stevens Purbrick Cabernet Sauvignon 2018, Nagambie Lakes
Some years it is the ESP Shiraz that shines the brightest, and some years it is the ESP Cabernet. The '18 vintage was such a year for cabernet, producing impressive depth of flavour, concentration and, above all, elegance. Leafy black fruit, clove, anise and sweet earth scents. Boasts depth, length and firm line as fine tannins guide the palate, embracing intense fruit, spice and a touch of cigar box complexity. Screw cap. 14.5% alc. RATING 96 DRINK 2022-2035 $72 JP ✪

Marsanne 2021, Nagambie Lakes The Nagambie Lakes shared the great vintage for whites, and Tahbilk didn't miss out here, oozing with honeysuckle, lime and custard apple, the signature of acidity neatly tying the parcel up for now or in a decade or 2. It's a deadset gold medal. Screw cap. 13% alc. RATING 95 DRINK 2025-2031 $20 JH ✪

Viognier 2021, Nagambie Lakes The perfection of the growing season has provided a luxurious wine, packed with flavours spanning ripe stone fruits through to shafts of fresh ginger, and a sprightly mouthfeel. Breaks all the rules of convention. Screw cap. 13.5% alc. RATING 95 DRINK 2021-2024 $21 JH ✪

Grenache Mourvèdre Rosé 2021, Nagambie Lakes Boasts concentrated flavour and a degree of complexity not generally seen at this price. Morello cherry, raspberry, rose and cardamom spice up this confection-pink rosé. Juicy energy in the mouth. Flavour is intense and runs deep, with a firm tannin grip as company. A rosé to savour. Screw cap. 13% alc. RATING 95 DRINK 2021-2026 $22 JP ✪

Cane Cut Marsanne 2019, Nagambie Lakes One of the many faces of marsanne, which once again reveals the delicate beauty and quiet strength of the grape. Light golden hues introduce a concentrated perfume of jasmine, citrus blossom, cumquat, stone fruit and mandarin rind. Runs long and smooth across the palate, luscious and so, so moreish. 500ml bottle. Screw cap. 11% alc. RATING 95 DRINK 2022-2025 $26 JP ✪

Eric Stevens Purbrick Shiraz 2018, Nagambie Lakes Delivers aromas of ripe black fruits, plum, chocolate, earth and Aussie bush. The palate is mapped out in firm, fine tannins, nicely balanced with a light leathery, woodsy savouriness. As always, warm and complex. Screw cap. 14.5% alc. RATING 95 DRINK 2022-2035 $72 JP

Museum Release Marsanne 2016, Nagambie Lakes A fabulous follow-up vintage to the excellent '15, encapsulating all the beauty of the Rhône grape that comes with bottle age. The characters we see in youth remain: the honeysuckle, jasmine florals and citrus force. Built around them are complexing additions through age, of hay, almond meal, pear skin and apricot nut. Acidity is firm but also soft. Stunning value, as always. Screw cap. 13% alc. RATING 95 DRINK 2022-2031 $26 JP ✪

1927 Vines Marsanne 2016, Nagambie Lakes 1927 Vines is a fine example of the amazing versatility of the marsanne grape. It is probably its purest expression, capturing its essential beauty early and then allowing bottle age to bring complexity. From '16 we see lovely florals emerging on the bouquet, showing signature honeysuckle, grilled grapefruit and almond development. Belies its age with a youthful energy and drive across the palate, lively acidity matched by a soft texture. By no means at its peak. Screw cap. 10.5% alc. RATING 95 DRINK 2022-2030 $47 JP

1927 Vines Marsanne 2015, Nagambie Lakes 1927 Vines was an epiphany, inspired by the beauty that comes to bottle-aged Hunter semillon. A steely, pure backbone of clean acidity is the vehicle for the grape's underrated versatility and charm. Honeysuckle, apple blossom, white peach, honeycomb and hay mingle in the glass. Six years old and still fresh, it tingles on the palate with lemon zest, grapefruit and dusty apple brightness. Texture is developing and the long, apricot nut finish is something that stays with you. Still a pup. Screw cap. 11% alc. RATING 95 DRINK 2021-2035 $47 JP

Talbots Block Wines

62 Possingham Pit Road, Sevenhill, SA 5453 **Region** Clare Valley
T 0403 517 401 **www.**talbotsblock.com.au **Open** By appt **Winemaker** Contract
Est. 2011 **Dozens** 1000 **Vyds** 5ha

Alex and Bill Talbot started their journey to wine in 1997 while working and living at Woomera in the SA desert. They purchased land in the Sevenhill area of the Clare Valley and dreamed of some day making wine for their friends. They then moved to various places in Asia, including Kuala Lumpur, Jakarta and Singapore, their minds always returning to their Sevenhill vineyard. They now live in the house they built high on the block, with views across the vineyard, and have the opportunity to tend the vines whenever they please. Initially the grapes were sold but since '12 they have kept enough of the production to have around 1000 dozen made across their 2 distinctly different shiraz styles. The labels are striking and evocative. (JH)

♀♀♀♀♀ **The Sultan Shiraz 2018, Clare Valley** Matured for 20 months in a combination of French (30% new) and American oak. The flagship wine, and generally released 3-4 years from harvest. For all the time spent in oak, the concentrated ripe fruit has sucked it all into a swirling vortex of black and red berries, whorls of exotic market spice and a swoosh of bright acid. This is really, really lovely. Screw cap. 14.2% alc. RATING 95 DRINK 2021-2035 $39 EL

Talisman Wines

Wheelman Road, Wellington Mill, WA 6236 **Region** Geographe
T 0401 559 266 **www.**talismanwines.com.au **Open** By appt **Winemaker** Peter Stanlake
Viticulturist Victor Bertola **Est.** 2009 **Dozens** 3000 **Vyds** 9ha

Kim and Jenny Robinson began the development of their vineyard in 2000 and now have cabernet, shiraz, malbec, zinfandel, chardonnay, riesling and sauvignon blanc. Kim says that 'after 8 frustrating years of selling grapes to Evans & Tate and Wolf Blass, we decided to optimise the vineyard and attempt to make quality wines'. The measure of their success has been consistent gold-medal performance (and some trophies) at the Geographe Wine Show. They say this could not have been achieved without the assistance of vineyard manager Victor Bertola and winemaker Peter Stanlake. (JH)

♀♀♀♀♀ **Ferguson Valley Riesling 2021, Geographe** '21 was a cool season in WA, and that is immediately evident on the nose here. Finely crushed white pepper, juniper, hints of star anise, lemon zest, apple skin and lychee (if you really look hard enough). In the mouth the wine goes lightly, tiptoeing across the tongue through to a delicate finish. Very pretty, very fine, very quiet. Screw cap. 11.7% alc. RATING 93 DRINK 2021-2028 $25 EL ✪

Ferguson Valley Cabernet Malbec 2020, Geographe This is pure, layered and very elegant. At this early stage in its life, it is recommended that you exercise some restraint and allow the wine some time, either in a decanter or in a cellar. Cassis, garden mint, dark chocolate and licorice combine to sing a pure and unfettered song of Geographe. Screw cap. 14% alc. RATING 93 DRINK 2022-2031 $30 EL

Gabrielle Ferguson Valley Chardonnay 2020, Geographe The acidity afforded by the elevation of the vineyard is always a highlight of this wine. It pierces through the rich, ripe fruit and creates structure and intensity in the mouth. This year, the fruit has a very salty, banana character that I haven't noticed in previous vintages, however the winemaking and acidity do their parts to resurrect the wine through the finish. Very smart, nutty, complex and long chardonnay. Screw cap. 13.8% alc. RATING 93 DRINK 2021-2031 $40 EL

Ferguson Valley Malbec 2020, Geographe Blood plum, cassis, raspberry, licorice, pink peppercorns and just a little herbal lift (fresh garden basil, or perhaps bay leaf). Supple, elegant and restrained. Closes with a very delicate finish. Screw cap. 14.3% alc. RATING 92 DRINK 2021-2031 $35 EL

Aged Release Riesling 2011, Geographe Golden in the glass, with hints of honeysuckle, honeycomb, brine, salted preserved lemons, cheesecloth and apple pie. In the mouth the wine is savoury and toasty, with layer upon layer of brie rind, cheesecloth, dough and white plums. The finish is silky and spiced, although stops short of the thundering reverberations that were expected. Screw cap. 13% alc. RATING 90 DRINK 2022-2025 $35 EL

Talits Estate

722 Milbrodale Road, Broke Fordwich, NSW 2330 **Region** Broke Fordwich
T 0404 841 700 **www.**talitsestate.com.au **Open** Fri–Sun & public hols 10–5
Winemaker Daniel Binet **Viticulturist** David Grosser **Est.** 2011 **Dozens** 1700 **Vyds** 8ha
Gayle Meredith is the owner of this 4ha vineyard in the Broke Fordwich subregion of the Hunter Valley, resplendent with stellar accommodation and a forward-thinking mindset driven by winemaker, Daniel Binet. This manifests as a suite of wines stamped with a welcome savouriness. The hark back to a past, defined as much by the quintessential Hunter twang of sweet earth as it by the uncanny regional blend of pinot noir and shiraz, is captivating. The quest for savoury, versatile expressions is also iterated across innovative work with sangiovese, admirably homegrown rather than outsourced to cooler zones. (NG)

Blanc de Blancs 2013, Hunter Valley An aspirational fizz with 7 years on lees, yet assembled with apero styling in mind. A mid-weighted, creamy expression serving as an intrepid balancing act of minimal dosage, crisp green–apple accents and a waft of brioche. An exercise in how to make fizz in a region as warm as this. Bravo. Diam. 12.5% alc. RATING 93 $40 NG
The Forbidden Fruit Pinot Noir Syrah 2019, Hunter Valley A fidelitous iteration of a domestic classic, with the savoury balm of a French hand. Intense Asian spice, boysenberry compote, dark plum, sassafras and a curb of dusty, earthenware Hunter tannins. Mid weighted, fresh and ready, yet the intensity belies the versatile, easygoing subtleties. This is delicious. Cork. 13.5% alc. RATING 93 DRINK 2022-2030 $48 NG

Village Wine Chardonnay 2021, Hunter Valley RATING 88 DRINK 2022-2027 $35 NG

Tallarook

140 Ennis Road, Tallarook, Vic 3659 **Region** Upper Goulburn
T (03) 5793 8344 **www.**tallarookwines.com.au **Open** By appt **Winemaker** Terry Barnet
Est. 1987 **Dozens** 1200
Tallarook has been established on a property between Broadford and Seymour. Since 1987, 11ha of vines have been planted, mainly to chardonnay, shiraz and pinot noir, but with significant amounts of marsanne, roussanne and viognier. The second label, Terra Felix, was sold in '05, and the quality of the Tallarook wines has risen significantly. The '07 vintage was destroyed by frost, an unfortunately common story. Exports to the UK and Germany. (JH)

Pinot Gris 2021, Orange Gris with ample skin contact, imparting a mid coral hue with onion-skin rims. Delicious aromas of redcurrant, nashi pear, musk stick and rosehip. The texture, a satisfying conflation of grape skin chewiness and juicy, saline freshness. Versatile drinking in spades. Screw cap. 12.5% alc. RATING 91 DRINK 2021-2023 $30 NG

Taltarni

339 Taltarni Road, Moonambel, Vic 3478 **Region** Pyrenees
T (03) 5459 7900 **www.**taltarni.com.au **Open** Wed–Sun 11–5 **Winemaker** Robert Heywood, Peter Warr, Ben Howell **Est.** 1969 **Dozens** 80 000 **Vyds** 78.5ha
The American owner and founder of Clos du Val (Napa Valley), Taltarni and Clover Hill (see separate entry) has brought the management of these 3 businesses and Domaine de Nizas (Languedoc) under the one roof, the group known as Goelet Wine Estates. Taltarni is

the largest of the Australian ventures, its estate vineyards of great value and underpinning the substantial annual production. Insectariums are established in permanent vegetation corridors, each containing around 2000 native plants that provide a pollen and nectar source for the beneficial insects, reducing the need for chemicals and other controls of the vineyards. Taltarni celebrates 45 years of winemaking in 2022. Exports to all major markets. (JH)

ϢϢϢϢϢ **Old Vine Estate Cabernet Sauvignon 2020, Pyrenees** Sourced from the original cabernet sauvignon vines planted in the late '60s and, once again, doesn't disappoint. One sip and you're in, seduced by the grace and beauty. Cassis, dark plums, bay leaf, spice and a gentle dusting of vanillin oak prevail, ably assisted by fine, lithe tannins. Elegance in the glass. Screw cap. 14% alc. RATING 96 DRINK 2022-2033 $45 JP ✪

Old Vine Estate Shiraz 2020, Pyrenees Oozes class. Pyrenees shiraz celebrated for its elegance right here, with fruit and oak in harmony. Damson plum, black cherry, crushed violets, cinnamon and fennel with signature notes of regional Aussie bush. Fully sustained in fine, lithe tannins. One for the cellar. Screw cap. 14.5% alc. RATING 95 DRINK 2022-2033 $50 JP

Estate Shiraz 2019, Pyrenees A wine built for further time in the cellar, such is its power and intensity. Dense purple garnet hues. The mourvèdre brings an added aromatic lift to the bouquet together with dark cherry, plum, chocolate and earth. The palate follows suit, strapped to sturdy, smooth tannins. Drives deep through to the finish. Screw cap. 14.5% alc. RATING 95 DRINK 2022-2032 $45 JP

ϢϢϢϢϢ **Brut 2016, Pyrenees** RATING 92 $26 JP
Blanc de Blancs 2017, Pyrenees RATING 90 $26 JP
Mourvèdre 2021, Pyrenees RATING 90 DRINK 2022-2024 $26 JP
GSM 2020, Pyrenees RATING 90 DRINK 2021-2024 $26 JP

Tamar Ridge ★★★★★

1a Waldhorn Drive, Rosevears, Tas 7277 **Region** Northern Tasmania
T (03) 6330 0300 **www**.tamarridge.com.au **Open** 7 days 10–5 **Winemaker** Tom Wallace, Anthony De Amicis **Est.** 1994 **Vyds** 130ha
Since the Brown Family Wine Group (then Brown Brothers) acquired Tamar Ridge and its sister brands of Pirie and Devil's Corner in '10, it has tactically honed each of the 3 labels to increasingly play to its strengths. For Tamar Ridge, this means a strategic focus on pinot noir, sourced from its magnificent and substantial Kayena Vineyard, tucked into a fold of the Tamar River in the north of the Tamar Valley. Single Vineyard and experimental Research Series pinot noirs are exciting indicators of the direction of evolution of the brand under talented winemaker Tom Wallace. He is also responsible for riesling, sauvignon blanc and pinot gris from the same site, supplemented a little by vineyards in the proximity of its cellar door at Rosevears, north of Launceston. Exports to all major markets. (JH)

ϢϢϢϢϢ **Tamar Ridge Single Block Pinot Noir 2020, Tasmania** Aromatic and powerful, with layers of dark cherry and plum fruit, and positive tannins. Built to go the distance, but its balance makes it an each-way proposition. Screw cap. 11.5% alc. RATING 95 DRINK 2022-2033 $100 JH

Tamar Ridge Pinot Noir 2019, Tasmania Typical deep colour; a highly expressive and fragrant bouquet of spiced plum, forest floor and charcuterie lays down the path for the palate, with whole-bunch savoury notes alongside a rich core of juicy plum and berry flavours. Great value. Screw cap. 13% alc. RATING 95 DRINK 2021-2029 $34 JH ✪

Tamar Ridge Research Series Pinot Noir 2020, Tasmania Light scarlet hue. Blends elegance with complexity, totally correct choice of used oak (none new) allowing the juicy small red and blue fruits free rein. Screw cap. 11.5% alc. RATING 94 DRINK 2021-2029 $50 JH

Tambo Estate

96 Pages Road, Tambo Upper, Vic 3885 **Region** Gippsland
T 0418 100 953 **www**.tambowine.com.au **Open** Thurs–Sun 11–5 **Winemaker** Alastair
Butt **Viticulturist** Bill Williams **Est.** 1994 **Dozens** 1940 **Vyds** 5.11ha

Bill and Pam Williams returned to Australia in the early '90s after 7 years overseas, and began
the search for a property which met the specific requirements for high-quality table wines
established by Dr John Gladstones in his masterwork Viticulture and Environment. They
chose a property in the foothills of the Victorian Alps on the inland side of the Gippsland
Lakes, with predominantly sheltered, north-facing slopes. They planted a little over 5ha: 3.4ha
to chardonnay, as well as a little cabernet sauvignon, pinot noir and sauvignon blanc. They are
mightily pleased to have secured the services of Alastair Butt (one-time winemaker at Seville
Estate). (JH)

ΨΨΨΨΨ **Lakes Cabernet Sauvignon 2019, Gippsland** What's pleasing about this
is the subtlety and gentleness throughout. It's lovely to drink, with its delicate
flavours of currants, blueberries and blackberries, pastille and licorice with a
smattering of woodsy spices and tapenade. Medium bodied, with fine tannins
and nothing else to consider except to pour it. Screw cap. 13.8% alc. RATING 94
DRINK 2021-2029 $28 JF ○

ΨΨΨΨΨ **Malakoff Shiraz 2018, Pyrenees** RATING 92 DRINK 2021-2028 $28 JF
Merrill Chardonnay 2019, Gippsland RATING 91 DRINK 2021-2026 $28 JF
Bumberrah Station Chardonnay 2018, Gippsland RATING 90
DRINK 2021-2024 $22 JF

Tapanappa ★★★★★

15 Spring Gully Road, Piccadilly, SA 5151 **Region** Piccadilly Valley
T (08) 7324 5301 **www**.tapanappa.com.au **Open** 7 days & public hols 11–4
Winemaker Brian Croser **Est.** 2002 **Dozens** 2500 **Vyds** 16.7ha

Tapanappa was founded by Brian Croser in 2002. The word Tapanappa is probably derived
from the local Aboriginal language and likely translates to 'stick to the path'. Through
Tapanappa, Brian is continuing a career-long mission of matching the climate, soil and
geology of distinguished sites to the right varieties, and then developing and managing the
vineyards to optimise quality. Tapanappa is dedicated to producing unique 'wines of terroir'
from its 3 distinguished sites in SA with its winery located in the heart of the Piccadilly Valley.
The brand's components are the Whalebone Vineyard at Wrattonbully (planted to cabernet
sauvignon, shiraz and merlot in 1974), the Tiers Vineyard at Piccadilly in the Adelaide Hills
(chardonnay) and the Foggy Hill Vineyard on the southern tip of the Fleurieu Peninsula (pinot
noir). Exports to Canada, Europe, Sweden, the UK, Hong Kong, Japan and the UAE. (JH)

ΨΨΨΨΨ **Tiers Vineyard Chardonnay 2020, Piccadilly Valley** Tiers brings its A game
to the '20 vintage release. In a difficult year, it manages to shine as bright as ever.
Combines power and elegance, no easy thing, from the lifted perfume of white
flowers and citrus to the fine-edged palate, walking a precise, graceful line. Do
not over chill, or that grace is muted. Power stems from the harmonious interplay
of fruit, oak and acidity, working as one. Screw cap. 13.9% alc. RATING 96
DRINK 2021-2030 $90 JP
Single Vineyard Riesling 2021, Eden Valley Typically fragrant Eden Valley
riesling aromas – they really are quite distinctive – in apple blossom, musk and
white flowers, with lemon and lime zest. A delicate youngster, filigree fine acidity
offsets a citrus-dominated, lively palate. Effortless in its beauty. Screw cap. 13% alc.
RATING 95 DRINK 2022-2031 $35 JP ○
Tiers Vineyard Chardonnay 2021, Piccadilly Valley A chardonnay
masterclass from a master that brings complexity and concentration with an utterly
irresistible liveliness. Beautifully worked flinty aromas, grapefruit, lime zest, stone
fruits and nougat. Superfine sherbet-like acidity works the tastebuds alongside a
wealth of citrus and stone fruits with terrific concentration and weight. Screw cap.
13.4% alc. RATING 95 DRINK 2022-2031 $110 JP

Chardonnay 2020, Piccadilly Valley From a year of frost and fire comes, according to Brian Croser, a 'miracle'. The '20 offers a celebration not only of fruit but life, a beauty of a chardonnay fresh and immediate in appeal but oh so capable of a much longer time in bottle. Flashes of honeysuckle, citrus, nectarine, apple and a whisper of mango skin wrapped around brisk acidity. But there's more to the palate: it's creamy and leesy, textural and long, but not heavy in the least. Screw cap. 13.9% alc. RATING 95 DRINK 2021-2030 $39 JP

Foggy Hill Vineyard Pinot Noir 2020, Fleurieu The '20 vintage was cooler than average, a welcome indicator of pinot quality. Elegance and detail go hand in hand here. Chalky in texture, taut in structure indicate it's early days for this pinot, but then you meet the depth of fruit – black cherry, cranberry, pomegranate – and accompanying aromatics and spice, and there is plenty to enjoy right now. Cork. 13.8% alc. RATING 95 DRINK 2022-2031 $55 JP

Whalebone Vineyard Cabernet Shiraz 2018, Wrattonbully 86/14% cabernet sauvignon/shiraz. A ripe year has undoubtedly imparted more warmth and roundness to this wine, but it remains resolutely medium bodied and finely tuned. Fragrant with cabernet's wild berries, violet and bush herbs in the lead role. Comes together seamlessly to taste, a perfect specimen of the great Aussie red blend, with even a touch of local menthol on the finish as proof. Cork. 14.2% alc. RATING 95 DRINK 2022-2034 $55 JP

Tiers Vineyard 1.5m Chardonnay 2021, Piccadilly Valley This wine is regularly defined by its racy acidity, making it a different personality to its Tiers sibling. If you love acidity – and I do – it's a perfect foil for the wine's bright lemon, grapefruit, apple fruit juiciness. It's also a marker for some further extended ageing. Expect a linear palate enhanced in aromatic florals, nougat, almond bread and a budding texture. It's all here, you just need time. Screw cap. 13.4% alc. RATING 94 DRINK 2022-2034 $55 JP

Tiers Vineyard 1.5m Chardonnay 2020, Piccadilly Valley This young chardonnay vineyard, just 13 years old, is starting to fully express itself. It's a little racy in a chablis kind of way, sporting brisk acidity and keen, juicy fruit. Opens with aromas of lemon blossom, all lemony clean and bright. Nougat, Granny Smith apple and lemon rind busy the palate, oak is worked into the budding almond mealy, textural mouthfeel. Comes to a taut close. Give it time, it will be rewarded. Screw cap. 13.9% alc. RATING 94 DRINK 2022-2030 $55 JP

Whalebone Vineyard Merlot Cabernet Franc 2018, Wrattonbully A warm year and a generous expression of fruit which sets the scene for some enjoyable drinking. Redcurrant, black cherry, fennel seed, red licorice, raspberry and pepper work with sinewy tannins and vanillin oak to reveal a complex whole. Finishes firm and would love more time in bottle. Cork. 13.9% alc. RATING 94 DRINK 2022-2033 $90 JP

🍷🍷🍷🍷 **Chardonnay 2021, Adelaide Hills** RATING 93 DRINK 2022-2027 $45 JP

Tar & Roses ★★★★★

61 Vickers Lane, Nagambie, Vic 3608 **Region** Nagambie Lakes
T (03) 5794 1811 **www**.tarandroses.com.au **Open** first w'end each month 10–4
Winemaker Narelle King **Est.** 2006 **Dozens** 40 000

Tar & Roses produces wines inspired by the classic Mediterranean varietals and was named after the signature characteristics of nebbiolo. The name also ties back to the winemaking team behind the venture, the legendary Don Lewis and his winemaking partner Narelle King. Narelle is carrying on the Tar & Roses tradition after Don's passing in 2017. Exports to the UK, the US, Canada, Singapore, Japan and NZ. (JH)

🍷🍷🍷🍷🍷 **Lewis Riesling 2021, Central Victoria** So much budding complexity waiting to break through, with lifted floral aromatics, lemon, lime, citrus peel and a touch of exotic lemongrass. Concentrated on the palate, saturated in citrus intensity and length with a ribbon of apply spice with bright acidity that keeps on going. Wow! Screw cap. 13% alc. RATING 95 DRINK 2021-2028 $26 JP ✪

Nebbiolo 2020, Heathcote Some Australian producers understand the nebbiolo grape better than others. Narelle King has a sensitive approach, allowing a sense of power to pervade her wines while also searching for the inner fineness. The aromatics of rose petal and cherry mix with earth, mineral and spice. Elegance is delivered through fleshy red fruits and anise. The tannin isn't shy, but it's not supposed to be. A convincing wine in every respect. Screw cap. 13.5% alc. RATING 95 DRINK 2021-2035 $50 JP

Sangiovese 2021, Central Victoria Thoughts immediately rush to pizza, it's that kind of sangiovese. Gets the tastebuds singing with the first rush of black cherry scents with redcurrant, thyme and pepper. Seriously smashable with its vibrancy, its mix of dark chocolate, cola, cherry, licorice and light savouriness running across the palate. Plenty of charm. Screw cap. 13.5% alc. RATING 94 DRINK 2021-2028 $27 JP ✪

ＹＹＹＹＹ **Pinot Grigio 2021, Central Victoria King Valley** RATING 93 DRINK 2021-2024 $24 JP ✪
Rosé Mediterraneo 2021, Strathbogie Ranges Heathcote RATING 91 DRINK 2021-2024 $26 JP
Trust Pet Nat 2021, Central Victoria RATING 90 DRINK 2022-2022 $25 JP

TarraWarra Estate ★★★★★

311 Healesville-Yarra Glen Road, Yarra Glen, Vic 3775 **Region** Yarra Valley **T** (03) 5957 3510 **www.**tarrawarra.com.au **Open** Tues–Sun 11–5 **Winemaker** Clare Halloran, Adam McCallum **Viticulturist** Stuart Sissins **Est.** 1983 **Dozens** 9000 **Vyds** 28ha

TarraWarra is, and always has been, one of the top-tier wineries in the Yarra Valley. Founded by Marc Besen AC and wife Eva Besen AO, it has operated on the basis that quality is paramount, cost a secondary concern. The creation of the TarraWarra Museum of Art (twma.com.au) in a purpose-built building provides another reason to visit; indeed, many visitors come specifically to look at the ever-changing displays in the Museum. Changes in the vineyard include the planting of shiraz and merlot, and in the winery, the creation of a 4-tier range: a deluxe MDB label made in tiny quantities and only when the vintage permits; the single-vineyard range; a Reserve range; and the 100% estate-grown varietal range. Exports to France and Vietnam. (JH)

ＹＹＹＹＹ **Cellar Release Reserve Chardonnay 2012, Yarra Valley** If you wish to see the extreme length and longevity of Yarra Valley chardonnay, go no further. This lovely self-possessed wine is on its plateau of perfection, and will hold its form for years (5+) to come. The freshness of its finish and lingering aftertaste is its ace in the hole. Screw cap. 12.8% alc. RATING 97 DRINK 2021-2027 $60 JH ✪

ＹＹＹＹＹ **Late Disgorged Vintage Reserve Blanc de Blanc 2010, Yarra Valley** Traditional method; disgorged May '21. This is a remarkable wine, a one-off that has handsomely repaid the decision to defer disgorgement for a decade. The bright straw-green colour signals an elegant, finely strung array of white flowers on the bouquet, moving to white peach, citrus and brioche on the palate. The overall balance and length are perfect. Diam. 12.8% alc. RATING 96 DRINK 2021-2026 $70 JH ✪

Reserve Chardonnay 2020, Yarra Valley A bright and medium-deep green gold. Aromas of yellow stone fruits, acacia, orange blossom and fresh vanilla bean are all present on the nose of this complex and powerful wine. The palate is rich and textured, yet equally refined and balanced. Finishes long and satisfying. Screw cap. 13% alc. RATING 96 DRINK 2021-2026 $65 PR ✪

J Block Shiraz 2019, Yarra Valley A deep, almost opaque purple red. A slightly atypical but nonetheless super-impressive and accomplished Yarra shiraz with its Crozes-Hermitage-like aromas of dark fruits, freshly hung meat, black olive, and both white and black pepper. The viognier provides just the right amount of lifted violets. Medium bodied and seductively textured, with superfine tannins in support, this is a wine that can be enjoyed now and over the next 5–10 years. Screw cap. 13.6% alc. RATING 96 DRINK 2022-2031 $40 PR ✪

Barbera 2020, Yarra Valley A deep, crimson plummy red. A convincing and appealing barbera from the start, with its aromas of dark morello cherry, fresh plum, sage and thyme. Totally delicious on the palate too. Ripe and rich, but not heavy, with fine-grained tannins rounding out a wine that can be enjoyed now and over the next 3–5 years. Would be fantastic with a bowl of pasta! Screw cap. 14% alc. RATING 95 DRINK 2022-2027 $35 PR ✪

I Block Pinot Noir 2020, Yarra Valley A medium-deep and bright cherry-crimson red. Fragrant with raspberries, satsuma plum, purple flowers and a little oak-derived nutmeg. Focused with a tight core of fruit, this well-put-together wine finishes with ripe, powdery tannins and, as good as this is now, this will look even better in 4–6 years. Screw cap. 13.5% alc. RATING 95 DRINK 2022-2028 $45 PR

Tarrawatta

102 Stott Highway, Angaston, SA 5353 **Region** Eden Valley
T 0447 117 762 **www.**tarrawattawine.com.au **Winemaker** Craig Isbel
Viticulturist Nick Radford **Est.** 2017 **Dozens** 1700 **Vyds** 9.3ha
Tarrawatta's inaugural Shiraz and Grenache immediately secured its place among the who's who of the Barossa, making this one of the most exciting newcomers in the 2022 Companion. Devoted exclusively to red wines, fruit is currently sourced entirely from the estate Ambervale vineyard in the northern Eden Valley. First planted in the mid 1800s, today the site boasts mostly dry-grown shiraz, cabernet sauvignon and a little grenache, with vines dating from 1968. A second site is earmarked for planting. Nick Radford oversees the vineyards and management of the estate, with Izway's Craig Isbel taking care of winemaking. The estate is owned by the Goldin Group, alongside Sloan Estate in the Napa and 3 Bordeaux château, including Château Le Bon Pasteur in Pomerol. Exports to Hong Kong. (TS)

♀♀♀♀♀ **Ambervale Shiraz 2019, Eden Valley** Aged in French oak for 23 months. There's a lovely purple sheen to the hue in the glass as the wine shows characters of deep, spicy black fruits, sheathed in cedary oak, licorice and dark chocolate. Impressive fruit flow and presence on the palate; balance and composition all in check, ripe tannin support and a graceful and long curtain call. Elegant drinking and a great prospect for the cellar. Screw cap. 14.9% alc. RATING 95 DRINK 2021-2035 $50 DB

♀♀♀♀♀ **Ambervale Cabernet Sauvignon 2019, Eden Valley** RATING 91 DRINK 2021-2031 $50 DB
Ambervale Grenache 2019, Eden Valley RATING 91 DRINK 2021-2030 $50 DB

Tasmanian Vintners

63 Kennedy Drive, Cambridge, Tas 7170 **Region** Southern Tasmania
T 0429 215 680 **www.**tasvintners.wine **Winemaker** Liam McElhinney
Viticulturist Christian de Camps **Est.** 2019 **Vyds** 200ha
Tasmanian Vintners (TV) is a joint company owned 50/50% by Tasmanian businessman Rod Roberts and the Fogarty Wine Group, which acquired the assets of Winemaking Tasmania from the administrator of that business. TV will continue to process grapes and wine for a broad range of smaller Tasmanian producers, and also buy their excess fruit and assist them to market their wines. TV is well set up for small-batch production with Liam McElhinney as winemaker and responsible for business operation. Fogarty Wine Group (in its own right) has a number of other rapidly developing major projects in Tasmania. (JH)

♀♀♀♀♀ **Artisan Riesling 2017, Tasmania** Pale quartz green. Just delicious. While still in its infancy, its long-life-giving acidity is now cocooned by a fine-spun shroud of lime, lemon and apple fruit, the balance impeccable, the length ditto. Screw cap. 12.5% alc. RATING 95 DRINK 2022-2027 $40 JH

ΨΨΨΨΨ James Busby Vineyard Series Pinot Noir 2019, Tasmania RATING 93
DRINK 2021-2029 $40 JH
Beyond The Wilderness Pinot Noir 2019, Tasmania RATING 91
DRINK 2022-2027 $25 JH
Beyond The Wilderness Chardonnay 2019, Tasmania RATING 90
DRINK 2023-2027 $25 JH

Tatler Wines

477 Lovedale Road, Lovedale, NSW 2321 **Region** Hunter Valley
T (02) 4930 9139 **www.**tatlerwines.com **Open** 7 days 10–5 **Winemaker** Daniel Binet
Est. 1998 **Dozens** 6000 **Vyds** 15ha

Tatler Wines is a family-owned company headed by Sydney hoteliers, brothers Theo and Spiro
Isak (Isakidis). The name comes from the Tatler Hotel on George Street, Sydney, which was
purchased by father James (Dimitri) Isak in 1974 and operated by the family until its closure
in '86. In '98 the Tatler name was reborn with the purchase of a 40ha property in Lovedale.
The vineyard is planted to 7ha of chardonnay and 4ha each of semillon and shiraz, and the
wines are made onsite in the recently renovated winery. Exports to the US. (JH)

ΨΨΨΨΨ **Shiraz 2018, McLaren Vale** Well-made, highly regional shiraz. Corpulent and
precise, with boysenberry, molten raspberry and Christmas cake, dried fruits and
spices teeming across a full-weighted palate. Malty oak and saline freshness, tidy up
the finish. Screw cap. 14.5% alc. RATING 93 DRINK 2021-2026 $52 NG
Non Pariel Shiraz 2014, Hunter Valley Here, new French barriques for a
whopping 18 months. A softer, larger-format embellishment suits this region
better. Soy, hoisin, dark cherry, cedar and vanilla. There is such beautiful fruit
behind it all. The challenge is drawing it out from amid the oak shards. Time may
tell a different story. Screw cap. 14.5% alc. RATING 92 DRINK 2021-2028 $100 NG
Riesling 2021, Adelaide Hills Lime blossom, pink grapefruit pulp and lemon
peel. Lightweight and plenty fresh, with a talcy curb of texture, melding effortlessly
with the variety's telltale acidity. A lick of sweetness tones the finish nicely. Screw
cap. 12% alc. RATING 91 DRINK 2021-2026 $29 NG
Dimitri's Paddock Chardonnay 2019, Hunter Valley A mid-weighted
chardonnay that unravels across a beam of tangy acidity and a nudge of vanillin
oak. Ripe and reflective of the warmer year. Tangerine, canned peach and
pineapple chunks. The sweetness of fruit expands across a finish of considerable
length. Good drinking. Screw cap. 13.5% alc. RATING 91 DRINK 2021-2025
$30 NG
Archie's Paddock Shiraz 2017, Hunter Valley A capacious, extremely ripe
wine that almost manages to placate any excess with well-placed oak and a
peppery underbelly. Dark cherry, tar, anise, mocha and a whiff of American oak's
coconut chips. Forceful and long. The ripeness lingers as an afterburner across my
Adam's apple. Screw cap. 14.8% alc. RATING 91 DRINK 2021-2024 $36 NG
Pinot Gris 2021, Orange An attractive onion-skin hue suggesting that the wine
has not been overly messed with. The aromas, indicative of earlier harvesting: nashi
pear, green apple, sugar snap pea and white pepper. A waft of gentle sweetness and
phenolic chew mitigate any overt greenness while playing a card of diversity at the
table. Screw cap. 12.5% alc. RATING 90 DRINK 2021-2023 $30 NG
**The Butler Brother's Blend Cabernet Sauvignon Shiraz Merlot 2018,
Hunter Valley** This is developing nicely, with the caveat of spiky acidity marking
the finish. Malt chocolate, spearmint, menthol, bracken, currant, dried tobacco
and a verdant underbelly of herb. Good drinking. Screw cap. 14% alc. RATING 90
DRINK 2021-2024 $29 NG

Taylors ★★★★★

89A Winery Road, Auburn, SA 5451 **Region** Clare Valley
T (08) 8849 1111 www.taylorswines.com.au **Open** Mon–Fri 9–5, w'ends 10–4
Winemaker Mitchell Taylor, Adam Eggins, Phillip Reschke, Chad Bowman, Thomas
Darmody **Viticulturist** Peter Rogge **Est.** 1969 **Dozens** 250 000 **Vyds** 400ha
The family-founded and owned Taylors continues to flourish and expand – its vineyards are
now by far the largest holding in the Clare Valley. Over the years there have been changes
in terms of the winemaking team and the wine style and quality, particularly through the
outstanding St Andrews range and more recently, The Visionary Cabernet Sauvignon and The
Pioneer Shiraz. With each passing vintage, Taylors is managing to do for the Clare Valley what
Peter Lehmann did for the Barossa Valley. Recent entries in international wine shows have
resulted in a rich haul of trophies and gold medals for wines at all pricepoints. A founding
member of Australia's First Families of Wine, the family celebrated 50 years in '19. Exports
(under the Wakefield brand due to trademark reasons) to all major markets. (JH)

ŸŸŸŸŸ **St Andrews Riesling 2021, Clare Valley** Wow – what a beautiful wine.
This is restrained and delicate, with layers upon layers of citrus blossom, nashi
pears, Granny Smith apples, lime flesh and juniper berries, all of it coalescing and
swirling on the palate as the tide eddies the shore. It is plump, after all of that – it
has shape and generosity and volume. The acidity is salty and bright, urging the
fruit through the long finish and encouraging it even further into the memory.
What a wine. Screw cap. 12% alc. RATING 96 DRINK 2021–2036 $43 EL ✪
The Pioneer Exceptional Parcel Release Shiraz 2017, Clare Valley A cool
array of black cherries, blueberries and mulberries adorn both the nose and palate,
however the oak prematurely interrupts the party in the mouth, laying down a
foundation of firm, stringy characters. The fruit, it is clear, is utterly beautiful. A
thing to behold. The oak will hopefully learn to play nicely in the years to come.
Screw cap. 14.5% alc. RATING 95 DRINK 2022–2042 $275 EL

ŸŸŸŸŸ **St Andrews Cabernet Sauvignon 2019, Clare Valley** RATING 93
DRINK 2022–2037 $75 EL
St Andrews Shiraz 2019, Clare Valley RATING 92 DRINK 2022–2037 $75 EL
The Visionary Exceptional Parcel Release Cabernet Sauvignon 2017,
Clare Valley RATING 92 DRINK 2022–2037 $275 EL
Winemaker's Project Shiraz 2019, Limestone Coast Clare Valley
RATING 91 DRINK 2021–2028 $25 EL
Jaraman Pinot Noir 2019, Yarra Valley RATING 91 DRINK 2021–2027
$34 EL
Masterstroke Cabernet Shiraz 2017, Clare Valley RATING 91
DRINK 2021–2028 $60 EL
Taylor Made Seasoned French Oak Shiraz 2020, Clare Valley RATING 90
DRINK 2021–2027 $25 EL
Winemaker's Project Cellar Selection Cabernet Sauvignon 2020,
Limestone Coast Clare Valley RATING 90 DRINK 2022–2027 $25 EL
St Andrews Chardonnay 2020, Clare Valley RATING 90 DRINK 2022–2027
$43 EL

Tellurian ★★★★★

408 Tranter Road, Toolleen, Vic 3551 **Region** Heathcote
T 0431 004 766 www.tellurianwines.com.au **Open** W'ends 11–4.30 or by appt
Winemaker Tobias Ansted **Est.** 2002 **Dozens** 7000 **Vyds** 32ha
The vineyard is situated on the western side of Mount Camel at Toolleen, on the red
Cambrian soil that has made Heathcote one of the foremost regions in Australia for the
production of shiraz (Tellurian means 'of the earth'). Viticultural consultant Tim Brown not
only supervises the certified organic Tellurian estate plantings, but also works closely with the
growers of grapes purchased under contract for Tellurian. Further plantings on the Tellurian
property in 2011 introduced small parcels of grenache, mourvèdre, carignan, nero d'Avola,

marsanne, viognier, fiano, riesling and grenache gris to the 20ha of shiraz. Exports to the US, and Singapore. (JH)

ŶŶŶŶŶ **Marsanne 2021, Heathcote** Marsanne, like its sibling Rhône grapes (both white and red), is naturally attuned to the Heathcote landscape. It gets to showcase its richness and textural qualities here, its honeysuckle lifted florals, leatherwood honey and spice with exotic Asian pear, quince paste, baked apple and peach. A warm, waxy mouthfeel is freshened by crisp, clean acidity. The grape shows its versatility yet again. Screw cap. 13.5% alc. RATING 95 DRINK 2022-2027 $30 JP ✪
Tranter Shiraz 2019, Heathcote Another strong, composed, concentrated Tranter shiraz from what was an extended vintage which allowed for extra hang time. A mighty tidy shiraz, in striking deep purple hues with lifted aromatics melding with black berries, licorice, chocolate and Aussie bush notes. Taut, fine tannins are in perfect balance. Screw cap. 14.6% alc. RATING 95 DRINK 2021-2031 $44 JP
Sommet Shiraz 2019, Heathcote The Sommet block comprises 35 rows of vines on 500+ million year-old Cambrian soils. The maker confidently lets the complexity of the fruit do all the talking. Density, precision and complexity work hand in hand with florals, fine ground spices, bay leaf, black cherry, blackberry and earth carried by fine tannins to a resounding, long finish. Screw cap. 14.5% alc. RATING 95 DRINK 2021-2031 $85 JP

ŶŶŶŶ♀ **GSM 2020, Heathcote** RATING 93 DRINK 2021-2028 $30 JP
Marsanne 2020, Heathcote RATING 91 DRINK 2021-2026 $30 JP

Tempus Two Wines   ★★★★

Cnr Broke Road/McDonalds Road, Pokolbin, NSW 2321 **Region** Hunter Valley
T (02) 4993 3999 **www.**tempustwo.com.au **Open** 7 days 10–5 **Winemaker** Andrew Duff **Est.** 1997 **Dozens** 55 000 **Vyds** 120ha
Tempus Two is a mix of Latin (Tempus means time) and English. It has been a major success story: production was just 6000 dozen in 1997 with sales increasing by over 140% in the last 5 years. Its cellar door and restaurant complex (including the Oishii Japanese restaurant) are situated in a striking building. The design polarises opinion; I (James) like it. Exports to all major markets. (JH)

ŶŶŶŶ♀ **Copper Series Vermentino 2021, Hunter Valley** Saline, chalky and nobly bitter, with grapefruit pulp, preserved lemon and apricot meandering to a long finish. Dry, fresh and very drinkable. Screw cap. 12% alc. RATING 91 DRINK 2021-2024 $30 NG
Uno Shiraz 2018, Hunter Valley A rich, throaty wine with beef stock, dark macerated cherry, lilac and the sweet earthenware scents of the Hunter. Mid weighted and savoury of feel, the tannins unravel nicely. The finish, sound if not a bit tangy. The mid palate, hollow. Time may bestow the benefit of the doubt. Screw cap. 14.5% alc. RATING 91 DRINK 2022-2030 $75 NG
Wilde Chardonnay 2021, Hunter Valley Good drinking at the price. Contemporary flint and pungent mineral undertones find an effortless confluence with the Hunter's gong of dried mango, canned pineapple and peach. Bright, of ample fruit and taut, all at once. The oak, nestled. The finish pushy and vibrant. Screw cap. 13% alc. RATING 90 DRINK 2021-2026 $30 NG
Copper Shiraz 2019, Barossa Valley A deeply coloured and highly perfumed offering here, as the Hunter-based Tempus Two take on a parcel of Barossa shiraz. Aromas of bright satsuma plum and black cherry fruits with hints of blackstrap licorice, crème de cassis, earth and warm spice. Mid weighted, with a broody fruit flow, plenty of drive and a finish that fans out with black forest fruits and spice. Screw cap. 15% alc. RATING 90 DRINK 2021-2028 $35 DB

Tenafeate Creek Wines

1071 Gawler-One Tree Hill Road, One Tree Hill, SA 5114 **Region** Mount Lofty Ranges
T (08) 8280 7715 **www.tcw.com.au Open** Fri–Sun & public hols 11–5
Winemaker Larry Costa, Michael Costa **Est.** 2002 **Dozens** 3000 **Vyds** 1ha
Larry Costa, a former hairdresser, embarked on winemaking as a hobby in 2002. The property,
with its 1ha of shiraz, cabernet sauvignon and merlot, is situated on the rolling countryside
of One Tree Hill in the Mount Lofty Ranges. The business grew rapidly, with grenache,
nebbiolo, sangiovese, petit verdot, chardonnay, semillon and sauvignon blanc purchased to
supplement the estate-grown grapes. Michael Costa, Larry's son (with 18 vintages under
his belt, mainly in the Barossa Valley, with Flying Winemaker stints in southern Italy and
Provence), has joined his father as co-owner of the business. The red wines have won many
medals over the years. (JH)

🍷🍷🍷🍷🍷 **Museum Release One Tree Hill Basket Press Shiraz 2013, Mount Lofty
Ranges** One Tree Hill vineyard sits close to the boundary of the Adelaide Hills
and the Barossa Valley. The '13 shiraz offers a taste of both, with a fullness of
flavour and body and a fineness of tannins and structure. Looking good at 8 years
old, it's powering along, fuelled by bright, ripe fruit, earth, woodsy spices and
smoky, toasty oak. Still youthful, still in development mode. Brilliant. Screw cap.
14.5% alc. RATING 95 DRINK 2021–2033 $70 JP
Judgement Shiraz 2016, Adelaide Produced only in 'exceptional' years,
Judgement Shiraz arrives as a complex 5yo, but can still look forward to many
years ahead in bottle. Flavour, oak and tannin have melded with time producing a
charming elegance. Brings a swathe of ripe red and black berries in tandem with
chocolate, coffee grounds, anise and Asian spice. Sapid fine tannins to the fore.
Screw cap. 15% alc. RATING 94 DRINK 2021–2036 $100 JP

🍷🍷🍷🍷🍷 **One Tree Hill Basket Press GSM 2020, Mount Lofty Ranges** RATING 92
DRINK 2021–2026 $30 JP
Sauvignon Blanc 2021, Adelaide Hills RATING 91 DRINK 2021–2024 $25 JP
One Tree Hill Basket Press Shiraz 2018, Mount Lofty Ranges RATING 90
DRINK 2021–2028 $30 JP

Terindah Estate

90 McAdams Lane, Bellarine, Vic 3223 **Region** Geelong
T (03) 5251 5536 **www.terindahestate.com Open** Sat–Sun 11–4 **Winemaker** Tim
Byrne **Est.** 2003 **Dozens** 3000 **Vyds** 5.6ha
Retired quantity surveyor Peter Slattery bought the 48ha property in 2001, intending to plant
the vineyard, make wine and develop a restaurant. He has achieved all of this (with help from
others, of course), planting shiraz, pinot noir, pinot gris, picolit, chardonnay and zinfandel.
Picolit is most interesting: it is a highly regarded grape in northern Italy, where it makes small
quantities of high-quality sweet wine. It has proven very temperamental here, as in Italy, with
very unreliable fruit set. In the meantime, he makes classic wines of very high quality from
classic grape varieties – not wines for sommeliers to drool over because they're hip. Exports
to Canada. (JH)

🍷🍷🍷🍷🍷 **Blanc de Blanc Chardonnay 2017, Geelong** Complex sparkling of floral
and citrus, carrying a layer of yeasty complexity, grilled nuts and toast, courtesy
of 3 years on lees. The palate is clean, assertive and crisp in cumquat, mandarin,
citrus and tarte tatin with hints of sweet lemon drop Super fresh and lively. Cork.
11.8% alc. RATING 93 $47 JP
Single Vineyard Bellarine Peninsula Shiraz 2020, Geelong A ripping
wine that delivers a lot of maritime-climate punchy, ripe black and red fruits.
They are joined by briar, bracken and an earthy savouriness that persists long in
tandem with spice. Glides with poise to the finish. Screw cap. 14% alc. RATING 91
DRINK 2021–2030 $44 JP
Single Vineyard Bellarine Peninsula Chardonnay 2019, Geelong Vegan
friendly. Sports a sunny disposition, the bright and breezy aromas and flavours

of the Mendoza clone are a real attraction. Lemon drop, mango, white peach and quince scents fill the senses. Mendoza brings a warm, textural glow to the chardonnay, it's immediately drink-me material, soft and plentiful. Brings a lot to the pricepoint. Screw cap. 12.5% alc. RATING 90 DRINK 2021-2026 $37 JP

Single Vineyard Bellarine Peninsula Zinfandel 2019, Geelong Meets many of the expectations we have when we see the word zinfandel. That is, it's high in alcohol, super generous in fruit flavour, dense and thick with a full sheen of toasty oak. However, there is also a firmness in tannins here that brings all of these abundant charms into balance. Screw cap. 15.5% alc. RATING 90 DRINK 2021-2027 $47 JP

ㅇㅇㅇㅇ **Single Vineyard Bellarine Peninsula Pinot Grigio 2021, Geelong** RATING 89 DRINK 2021-2025 $32 JP

Single Vineyard Bellarine Peninsula Pinot Gris 2021, Geelong RATING 89 DRINK 2021-2025 $32 JP

Single Vineyard Bellarine Peninsula Rosé 2021, Geelong RATING 89 DRINK 2021-2024 $32 JP

Single Vineyard Bellarine Peninsula Chardonnay 2020, Geelong RATING 88 DRINK 2021-2024 $32 JP

Terre à Terre ★★★★★

15 Spring Gully Rd, Piccadilly SA 5151 **Region** Piccadilly Valley
T 0400 700 447 **www.terreaterre.com.au Open** At Tapanappa Wed–Sun 11–4
Winemaker Xavier Bizot **Viticulturist** Xavier Bizot **Est.** 2008 **Dozens** 4000
Vyds 20ha

It would be hard to imagine 2 better-credentialled owners than Xavier Bizot (son of the late Christian Bizot of Bollinger fame) and wife Lucy Croser (daughter of Brian and Ann Croser). 'Terre à terre' is a French expression meaning down to earth. The close-planted vineyard is on a limestone ridge, adjacent to Tapanappa's Whalebone Vineyard. The vineyard area has increased, leading to increased production (the plantings include cabernet sauvignon, sauvignon blanc, cabernet franc and shiraz). In '15, Terre à Terre secured the fruit from one of the oldest vineyards in the Adelaide Hills, the Summertown Vineyard, which will see greater quantities of Daosa and a Piccadilly Valley pinot noir. Wines are released under the Terre à Terre, Down to Earth, Sacrebleu and Daosa labels. Exports to the UK, the US, Canada, Japan and Hong Kong. (JH)

ㅇㅇㅇㅇㅇ **Crayeres Vineyard Sauvignon Blanc 2021, Wrattonbully** This is a marvel. It has all of the sophistication and line of the Down to Earth Sauvignon Blanc, but it works within a startlingly streamlined framework of phenolics. This is slippery and supple in texture, with rivulets of flavour that ripple and course through the mouth, long after the wine has left. We are lucky to have the quality of sauvignon blanc that we do here in Australia and this is one of the very best. An amazing display of class. Screw cap. 12.8% alc. RATING 97 DRINK 2022-2032 $50 EL ✪ ♥

ㅇㅇㅇㅇㅇ **Down to Earth Sauvignon Blanc 2021, Wrattonbully** Totally sophisticated; the fruit here is completely at one with the oak, which, save for the textural impact of soft, round shape, is largely invisible. This has persistent flow of flavour across the palate, trailing into a long and languid finish. Juniper, cassis, green apple skins, snow pea florals, brine, jasmine tea and blackberry bramble. Really smart. Restrained and seamless. Screw cap. 12.8% alc. RATING 95 DRINK 2022-2028 $32 EL ✪

Crayeres Vineyard Reserve 2018, Wrattonbully 58/31/11% cabernet sauvignon/shiraz/cabernet franc. This wine is routinely firm on release. The tannins are firm, but as ever, superfine; they shape the fruit in the mouth and carry it across the tongue through into the long finish. They will surely fortify the wine for the long future it has ahead of it. Elegant plus. Cork. 14.5% alc. RATING 95 DRINK 2022-2042 $90 EL

Daosa Blanc de Blancs 2017, Piccadilly Valley After more than 4 years on lees, expect a quality sparkling exploring some of chardonnay's hidden depths. Layers of flavour and texture here, quince, zesty lemon, grapefruit, apple, almond and a citrus pith and peel intensity. Boasts roundness and weight, with bright acidity and verve right through to the finish. Another impressive release. Diam. 13.2% alc. RATING 95 $90 JP

Daosa Natural Reserve NV, Piccadilly Valley Traditional method, 72/28% pinot noir/chardonnay; low dosage (7g/L), disgorged June '21. Complex floral and citrus aromas introduce this charmer with pastry and yeasty notes in support. With input from reserve wines – '17 and '18 reserve chardonnay and pinot noir, aged in old barrels – the palate delves into mandarin, cumquat, nougat and toast, in harmony with a surge in tangy acidity. Great balance and length on display. Diam. 12.9% alc. RATING 94 $50 JP

Tertini Wines

Kells Creek Road, Mittagong, NSW 2575 **Region** Southern Highlands
T (02) 4878 5213 **www.**tertiniwines.com.au **Open** 7 days 10–5 by appt
Winemaker Jonathan Holgate **Est.** 2000 **Dozens** 5500 **Vyds** 7.9ha
When Julian Tertini began the development of Tertini Wines in 2000, he followed in the footsteps of Joseph Vogt 145 years earlier. History does not relate the degree of success that Joseph had, but the site he chose then was, as it is now, a good one. Tertini has pinot noir and riesling (1.8ha each), cabernet sauvignon and chardonnay (1ha each), arneis (0.9ha), pinot gris (0.8ha), merlot (0.4ha) and lagrein (0.2ha). Winemaker Jonathan Holgate, who is responsible for the outstanding results achieved at Tertini, presides over High Range Vintners, a contract winemaking business also owned by Julian Tertini. Exports to Asia. (JH)

Private Cellar Collection Riesling 2019, Southern Highlands This is very good, playing the textural card of a warm, dry year to its advantage, affirming phenolics over acidity in an ersatz Alsatian mould. The wine, lightweight and dutifully vibrant, is nevertheless deft of feel. Lime curd, quince paste, ginger candy and a waxy lanolin feel across a forceful, dry finish sets this up for a diversely set table. Screw cap. 11.8% alc. RATING 93 DRINK 2021-2028 $42 NG

Shiraz 2018, Hilltops A deep crimson. A fine nose of violet, bramble, tar, pepper grind and black to blue fruits. Loads of smoked meats, anise and clove too, with a swab of black olive tapenade. Density, without heaviness. A spicy pliancy to the tannins. A suave understated nature, too, without being demure. Classy. This is very good drinking for this sort of money. Screw cap. 14.1% alc. RATING 93 DRINK 2021-2025 $28 NG

Noble Viognier 2019, Hilltops Pineapple chunk, mango chutney, orange blossom and grape spice in abundance. The finish, a cacophony of sweet versus sour, suggestive of the finest marmalade running riot through the mouth across a lightweight frame. This is fun. Good domestic sticky. Screw cap. 11% alc. RATING 93 DRINK 2021-2030 $30 NG

Private Cellar Collection Chardonnay 2019, Southern Highlands Dried mango, peach syrup and other sweet stone- and tropical-fruit references. Some lees-derived oatmeal and almond powder. Creamed cashew and nougatine, too. Solid length, albeit, a bit hollow across the mid-palate. Time may shift this equation. Screw cap. 13% alc. RATING 92 DRINK 2021-2025 $48 NG

Private Cellar Collection Corvina 2018, Hilltops This is good. While I suggest the oak regime be altered, its drying tannins cannot temper the stream of lilac, pepper, pastille, anise and cherry amaro. 15% of the material was dried on trays, to concentrate the fruit and shift the composition of the tannins. An homage to the Veneto, whence this fine variety hails. A wine destined for the table. Diam. 14% alc. RATING 92 DRINK 2021-2025 $42 NG

Private Cellar Collection Nebbiolo 2019, Hilltops A solid effort, with sandalwood, sweet cherry, mulch and woodsmoke notes unravelling across a bridge of shifty tannins. The mid palate needs some filling. A bit hollow. A good drink,

auguring for a bright future with the variety in these parts. Screw cap. 14.5% alc.
RATING 91 DRINK 2021-2026 $45 NG

**Private Cellar Collection Refosco dal Peduncolo Rosso 2019, Southern
Highlands** I remember the first time I went to Friuli when I drank refosco from
a tap, so pervasive is the variety across simple bars to top tables. Lithe, peppery
and red-fruited, it is akin to an alpine beaujolais. This, more ambitious. Darker
of fruit tones and plenty reductive. Brambly and forceful, with a piney vegetal
inflection to the finish. This needs time, perhaps. Screw cap. 13.8% alc. RATING 90
DRINK 2021-2028 $65 NG

ΨΨΨΨ **Rosé 2021, Southern Highlands** RATING 89 DRINK 2021-2022 $32 NG
Prosecco 2021, Hilltops RATING 88 DRINK 2021-2023 $29 NG
Yaraandoo Vineyard Riesling 2019, Southern Highlands RATING 88
DRINK 2021-2025 $35 NG

🍇 Téssera Wines

4 McCallum Court, Strathalbyn, SA 5255 **Region** Adelaide Hills
T 0403 716 785 **www.**tesserawines.com.au **Open** By appt **Winemaker** Peter Lesk,
Phil Christiansen **Viticulturist** Jed Hicks, Arthur Loulakis, Ross McMurtrie **Est.** 2019
Dozens 1552
Téssera Wines started life in 2015 sourcing grapes from its local area around Strathalbyn on
the Fleurieu Peninsula. The word 'tessera' means 'four' in Greek and refers to the 4 close
friends who founded the company. As sales have increased, sourcing of grapes has broadened
to include McLaren Vale and the Adelaide Hills. Red wines are made by Phil Christiansen in
McLaren Vale, whites by the Australian Society of Viticulture and Oenology Winemaker of
the Year '20, Peter Leske. The company focuses on small-batch, quality wines that remain true
to the varietal integrity of the grapes sourced. Exports to Papua New Guinea. (JP)

ΨΨΨΨΨ **Middle Child Cabernet Sauvignon 2019, McLaren Vale** Smart wine,
serving to harness the heat, weight and potential ripeness of the vintage with savvy
extraction, the clip of American oak's suede, mocha, and bourbon-doused tannin
and the seaside riffs of iodine and saltbush. Varietal currant, tapenade and dried
herbs driven long. Screw cap. 14.6% alc. RATING 93 DRINK 2021-2032 $29 NG
Hulah Hoop Rosé Tempranillo 2021, Adelaide Hills Dressed in tea-rose-
pink hues and sitting in the floral, redcurrant–cherry spectrum, this rosé is one
smart drink. Captures both the dryness and the creamy palate we enjoy so much
in modern rosé, all encased in cool, fine-edged, red-fruited and lightly sweet spiced
flavours. Screw cap. 12.5% alc. RATING 92 DRINK 2022-2024 $27 JP
Chaste Shiraz 2019, McLaren Vale Consummate craftsmanship at this address.
A shiraz from a hot year that serves up savoury riffs on plum, licorice, tapenade
and mocha oak. There is an uncanny refinement here, as with all the wines. Sure,
there is some heat packed across the finish. But each rivet serves a greater weld.
Good drinking. Screw cap. 14.6% alc. RATING 92 DRINK 2021-2028 $29 NG
Good Oil Shiraz Cabernet 2019, McLaren Vale This is good for the
price. The coconut, bourbon and mocha accents and the sweet tannic frame of
American oak suits this hot year well. A fine nose of maritime salinity melds with
dried sage, thyme, Chinese herb, tea and damson plum. Forceful and carrying some
heat. But in all, well crafted. Screw cap. 14.5% alc. RATING 92 DRINK 2021-2030
$29 NG
Foxtrot Reserve Pinot Noir 2016, Adelaide Hills I wouldn't age this any
longer, but it offers good insight into the carnal complexities of pinot after some
patience: root spice, orange peel, sandalwood, dried porcini and wet autumnal
leaves. A hint of sour cherry lingers, but this is an exercise in drinking a wine at its
zenith. Really delicious and fine drinking now. Screw cap. 13.9% alc. RATING 92
DRINK 2021-2023 $45 NG

Teusner

95 Samuel Road, Nuriootpa, SA 5355 **Region** Barossa Valley
T (08) 8562 4147 **www.teusner.com.au** **Open** By appt **Winemaker** Kym Teusner
Est. 2001 **Dozens** 30 000 **Vyds** 120ha

Teusner is a partnership between former Torbreck winemaker Kym Teusner and Javier Moll, and is typical of the new wave of winemakers determined to protect very old, low-yielding, dry-grown Barossa vines. The winery approach is based on lees ageing, little racking, no fining or filtration and no new American oak. As each year passes, the consistency, quality and range of the wines increases; there must be an end point, but it's not easy to guess when, or even if, it will be reached. Exports to the UK, the US, Canada, the Netherlands, Malaysia, Singapore, Japan and Hong Kong. (JH)

MC Sparkling Shiraz 2017, Barossa Valley That bright purple spume of bubbles that erupts when you first pour a glass is quite something, huh. Deep notes of plum, cherry and black fruits, dotted with exotic spice, charcuterie, licorice, milk chocolate and earthen tones. It's like the pure dark fruit envelops you when you take a sip, with comforting fruit sweetness, an expansive palate shape and a super-plummy, meaty-edged exit. Great drinking. Crown. 14% alc. RATING 95 $65 DB ♥

Avatar 2020, Barossa Valley Good colour; a blend of grenache, mataro and shiraz matured in used oak. An instantly appealing bouquet with bright polished fruits turns right on the palate with spicy and savoury embellishments that provide flavour balance and very good mouthfeel. Screw cap. 14.5% alc. RATING 95 DRINK 2022-2030 $40 JH

Albert Museum Release Shiraz 2010, Barossa Valley Still deeply coloured with aromas of rich plum and blackberry fruits and hints of deep spice, licorice, chocolate, cassis, earth and vanillin oak. In a wonderful spot at the moment, still fruit-sweet and rich with fine tannin, softly spoken oak and a comforting fruit flow and lingering finish. Screw cap. 14.5% alc. RATING 94 DRINK 2022-2028 $85 DB

The G Grenache 2021, Barossa Valley RATING 93 DRINK 2022-2028 $32 DB

The Gentleman Cabernet Sauvignon 2020, Barossa RATING 93 DRINK 2021-2030 $27 DB ✪

The Wark Family Shiraz 2020, Barossa Valley RATING 93 DRINK 2021-2030 $30 DB

Salsa Rosé 2021, Barossa Valley RATING 91 DRINK 2021-2024 $23 DB ✪

Thalia

680 Main Road, Berriedale, Tas 7011 **Region** Tasmania
T 08 9282 5417 **www.thalia.wine** **Winemaker** Liam McElhinney **Viticulturist** John Fogarty, Christian De Camps, Fred Peacock **Est.** 2021 **Dozens** 2000 **Vyds** 3ha

Thalia is the entry-level non-vintage brand of the Fogarty Wine Group's Tasmanian sparkling operation, sister label to its more premium Lowestoft brand. Pinot noir takes the lead in each blend, supported largely by chardonnay, sourced from across the length and breadth of Tasmania, with a reserve cuvée hailing exclusively from a cool, coastal site on the Tasman Peninsula. A serious newcomer to the Tasmanian sparkling set, crafting cuvées of this calibre in an inaugural release is no simple undertaking, and it's no surprise that Tasmanian sparkling queen Natalie Fryar is consulting on the sidelines. Watch this space. (TS)

Thalia Rosé NV, Tasmania 70/30% pinot noir/chardonnay. A serious newcomer to the sparkling rosé set, this vibrant and fresh young thing is an altogether different recipe to Thalia blanc. Racy, young Coal River Valley pinot noir makes for an energetic spine of crunchy strawberry hull and lemon, with an air of rose petals. An elegant apéritif, unashamedly all about primary fruit over texture or complexity, yet still achieving a classy mouthfeel and inherent balance. Diam. 12.5% alc. RATING 91 $40 TS

NV, Tasmania The new-entry cuvée for the Fogarty Group's Tasmanian sparkling operation is crisp, fresh and fruity, built around cool, Tasman Peninsula pinot noir. Crunchy red apples, strawberries and lemons are the theme. Clean, precise and well put together, this is a well-balanced apéritif, more about fruit than texture or complexity. It will appreciate a little bottle age to build depth. Diam. 12.5% alc. RATING 90 $40 TS

ΨΨΨΨ   **Reserve Cuvée NV, Tasmania** RATING 89 $50 TS

The Bridge Vineyard   ★★★

Shurans Lane, Heathcote, Vic 3552 **Region** Heathcote
T 0417 391 622 **www**.thebridgevineyard.net.au **Open** By appt **Winemaker** Lindsay Ross **Est.** 1997 **Dozens** 1000 **Vyds** 4.75ha
This venture of former Balgownie winemaker Lindsay Ross and wife Noeline is part of a broader business known as Winedrops, which acts as a wine production and distribution network for the Bendigo wine industry. The wines are sourced from long-established vineyards, providing shiraz (3.5ha), malbec and viognier (0.5ha each) and sangiovese (0.25ha). The viticultural accent is on low cropping and thus concentrated flavours, the winemaking emphasis on finesse and varietal expression. (JH)

ΨΨΨΨ   **Knots Rose Lashing Arinto 2021, Heathcote** This high-acid Portuguese white grape is certainly full of bracing lemony acidity. However, it's nicely offset by a dry savouriness of preserved lemon, bruised apple, quince and poached pear. Almost demands to be enjoyed with food. Screw cap. 13% alc. RATING 88 DRINK 2021–2025 $30 JP
Shurans Lane Shiraz 2019, Heathcote In keeping with the generous fruit and oak nature of the Shurans Lane Shiraz style, the '19 launches into a deep, dark world of blackberry, cassis, woody spice, earth, leather and dark chocolate. Toasty oak and sturdy tannins accompany the fruit every step of the way. Diam. 14.5% alc. RATING 88 DRINK 2022–2032 $50 JP
Altus Shiraz 2019, Heathcote A high alcohol, funky ride of a shiraz that veers down some heavy, savoury layers of smoked meats and game with a touch of feral wildness before landing on a plush, soft cushion of sweet black fruits, spice and dusty oak. Diam. 15% alc. RATING 88 DRINK 2022–2032 $80 JP

The Cutting   ★★★

439 Stonewell Road, Tanunda, SA, 5352 **Region** Barossa Valley
T 0467 596 340 **www**.the-cutting.com.au **Open** By appt **Winemaker** Belinda van Eyssen **Viticulturist** Daniel McDonald **Est.** 2017 **Dozens** 90 **Vyds** 5ha
Viticulturist Daniel McDonald and partner winemaker Belinda van Eyssen launched The Cutting in 2018 on their Stonewell vineyard, bought by Daniel's parents in his birth year of '80 and planted in '98. An initial resolve to remain grapegrowers was thwarted by the temptation to make their own wines, inspired by other winemakers (to whom they were selling) producing single-vineyard wines from the site. Belinda gained winemaking experience in her home town of Cape Town, as well as in Portugal, France, California and NZ. Vinification and maturation in French oak barrels are carried out in a micro-winery in a shed on site, 54m from the vineyard ('10 seconds by tractor!'). (TS)

ΨΨΨΨ   **Shiraz 2020, Barossa Valley** Plenty of black cherry and blackberry fruits with brown spice notes, licorice, crème de cassis, amaro herbs, violets and earth. Spacious with a savoury line and a finish that I wanted to carry further. Screw cap. 14% alc. RATING 89 DRINK 2022–2027 $38 DB
The Outlier Grenache 2021, Barossa Valley A light pinot-esque hue with aromas of red cherry, dried cranberry, raspberry and red plum. Notes of exotic spice, red licorice, amaro herbs, ginger cake and earth. There's a light bunchy, curry leaf note on the palate which is airy, vivid in its drive and stony in a savoury kind of way. Screw cap. 14% alc. RATING 88 DRINK 2022–2026 $38 DB

The Flying Winemaker

801 Glenferrie Road, Hawthorn, Vic 3122 (postal) **Region** Various
T 0413 960 102 **www**.eddiemcdougallwines.com.au **Winemaker** Eddie McDougall,
Lilian Carter **Viticulturist** Eddie McDougall, Lilian Carter **Est.** 2007 **Dozens** 1000
The Flying Winemaker is the brainchild of Eddie McDougall, award-winning winemaker,
wine judge, columnist and TV personality. Eddie's winemaking credentials extend over a
decade of experience with some of the world's most influential wineries. He has made wines
with the likes of Vietti (Barolo), Mas de Daumas Gassac (Languedoc), Deep Woods Estate
(Margaret River), Giant Steps (Yarra Valley) and O'Leary Walker (Clare Valley). Eddie holds
a bachelor of international business from Griffith University and a post-graduate diploma
of wine technology and viticulture from the University of Melbourne. He spearheaded the
acquisition of Wairarapa's Gladstone Vineyard in '18, where he took on the role of CEO and
chief winemaker. Exports to NZ, Hong Kong, Macau, Singapore, Taiwan, the UK, Philippines
and the US. (JH)

Pinot Grigio 2021, King Valley The winemaker catches the King Valley grigio
style very well, pursuing a brisk, cool-climate line and length fleshed delicately in
green apple, honeysuckle, hay and clean herbals. Provides both a soft mid-palate
texture and brisk acidic finish. Screw cap. 13% alc. RATING 90 DRINK 2022-2024
$20 JP ✪

Prosecco NV, King Valley RATING 89 $22 JP

 ## The Group

822 George Street, Chippendale, NSW 2008 (postal) **Region** South Australia
T 1800 819 341 **www**.thegroupwines.com.au **Winemaker** Marnie Roberts **Est.** 2020
Dozens 6000
The Group is an enterprising collective of around 100 growers and their support networks,
showcasing wines from what are dubbed 'Australia's leading wine regions'. With supply chains
established to large retailers, The Group is a strategic response to the restrictive impingements
of bushfires and Covid-19 on fruit quality and passage to market. To date, under the aegis of
winemaker Marnie Roberts, McLaren Vale Grenache and Shiraz, alongside Adelaide Hills
Pinot Noir, are the focus. The modus operandi is not only to support the livelihood of the
growers, but to ensure that their collective expertise and wisdom are shared in order that
the vineyards thrive and prosper for posterity's sake. (NG)

The Fever 2018, McLaren Vale Blend of merlot, mourvèdre and cabernet.
This is my sort of wine. Sophisticated. Poised. Versatile. Everyday. An uncanny
blend that seems to suit the turf beautifully. Mid weighted of feel, with savoury
fruit over sweet. Herbal inflections melding effortlessly with a band of firm,
juicy tannins. This smells southwestern French, before a night in the decanter
emancipates the Aussie fruit. I preferred it before the decant, the sappy, plummy
essence of the merlot ruling the aromatic roost. Cabernet and mourvèdre cleaving
structure and an earthen mettle to tone. Drink in big glasses. Filled. Screw cap.
14.1% alc. RATING 93 DRINK 2021-2027 $34 NG
The Murder Shiraz 2017, McLaren Vale Clearly sourced from fine sites and
old vines, such as the vinous marrow and sap. And yet, again, the alcohol is far
reaching, the fruit a bit stewed and the freshness, a tad lacking. This said, it billows
across the palate akin to something from a warm region, while suggesting a deft
touch defined by saline acidity, detailed tannins and sensitive oak handling. A wine
that glimpses very bright future releases, without quite realising their promise as
yet. Screw cap. 14.9% alc. RATING 90 DRINK 2021-2026 $34 NG

The Quiver Grenache 2019, McLaren Vale RATING 88 DRINK 2021-2024
$34 NG

The Hairy Arm ★★★★

18 Plant Street, Northcote, Vic 3070 **Region** Victoria
T 0409 110 462 **www.**hairyarm.com **Open** By appt **Winemaker** Steven Worley
Viticulturist Steven Worley **Est.** 2004 **Dozens** 1000 **Vyds** 3ha

Steven Worley graduated as an exploration geologist, then added a master of geology degree, followed by a postgraduate diploma in oenology and viticulture. Until Dec '09 he was general manager of Galli Estate Winery. The Hairy Arm started as a university project in '04, and has grown from a labour of love to a commercial undertaking. Steven has an informal lease of 2ha of shiraz at Galli's Sunbury vineyard, which he manages, and procures 1ha of nebbiolo from the Galli vineyard in Heathcote. Exports to the UK, Canada and Hong Kong. (JH)

🍷🍷🍷🍷 **Merrifolk Cote Nord Syrah 2020, Yarra Valley** A bright crimson cherry. Black plum and peppercorns along with some savoury, black olive and bay leaf. Full of flavour, there are some plum skins on the palate and the tannins are fine and chalky. An impressive, well-priced wine for early- to mid-term drinking. Screw cap. 14% alc. RATING 93 DRINK 2022-2028 $26 PR ✪
Valhalla Nebbiolo 2020, Yarra Valley A bright, medium ruby. Raspberry compote, aniseed and a hint of rose petal can be found in this juicy, very drinkable and well-priced Yarra nebbiolo. Screw cap. 14% alc. RATING 91 DRINK 2022-2026 $26 PR

The Happy Winemaker ★★★★

16 Maddern Street, Black Hill, Vic 3350 **Region** Victoria
T 0431 252 015 **www.**thehappywinemaker.com.au **Winemaker** Jean-Paul Trijsburg
Est. 2015 **Dozens** 700 **Vyds** 1ha

Jean-Paul Trijsburg graduated with an agronomy degree from the Wageningen University in the Netherlands and followed this with a joint MSc in viticulture and oenology in Montpellier, France and Geisenheim, Germany. In between degrees he headed to Burgundy in 2007 and says, 'I started out picking grapes in Nuits-Saint-Georges, but somehow I ended up in the winery within a week'. The experience left him with a love of all things French, but he went on to work in wineries in Pomerol, the Rheingau, Rioja, Chile and South Africa. Since '12, he has called Australia home, having worked for Hanging Rock Winery in the Macedon Ranges and Lethbridge Wines in Geelong. He and wife Jessica live in Ballarat and, following the arrival of their second son, Jean-Paul runs a nearby 1ha vineyard of pinot noir and is an at-home dad for their children, Jessica working at a local health service. Jean-Paul moved from his garage-cum-winery to Hanging Rock for the '19 vintage (and ongoing thereafter). Additional grapes come from Heathcote, Bendigo and Ballarat. (JH)

🍷🍷🍷🍷 **Grenache Rosé by Jean-Paul 2021, Heathcote** Wild fermentation in 5-8yo French barriques. Lights up in vibrant red berries – cherry, raspberry and macerated strawberries – with spice and a hint of musk. The winemaker likes to build texture into his wines, but this has something else, a concentration of flavour that runs deep and fresh and bright and long. Delicious. Screw cap. 12.5% alc. RATING 94 DRINK 2022-2024 $25 JP ✪

🍷🍷🍷🍷 **Mistelle Rouge by Jean-Paul NV, Victoria** RATING 93 DRINK 2022-2022 $40 JP
Mount Alexander Riesling by Jean-Paul 2021, Bendigo RATING 92 DRINK 2022-2027 $25 JP ✪
Granite Shiraz by Jean-Paul 2020, Bendigo RATING 91 DRINK 2022-2028 $32 JP
Mount Alexander Pinot Gris by Jean-Paul 2021, Bendigo RATING 90 DRINK 2022-2025 $25 JP
Pinot Rosé by Jean-Paul 2021, Strathbogie Ranges Ballarat RATING 90 DRINK 2022-2024 $25 JP

The Islander Estate Vineyards

78 Gum Creek Road, Cygnet River, SA 5223 **Region** Kangaroo Island
T (08) 8553 9008 **www**.iev.com.au **Open** Thurs–Tues 12–5 **Winemaker** Jacques
Lurton, Yale Norris **Viticulturist** Jacques Lurton, Yale Norris **Est.** 2000 **Dozens** 8000
Vyds 10ha

Jacques Lurton established a close-planted vineyard with principal varieties cabernet franc, shiraz and sangiovese; and lesser amounts of grenache, malbec, semillon and viognier. The wines are made and bottled at the onsite winery. The property was ravaged by the terrible Jan '20 bushfire which consumed the entire vineyard, its infrastructure, the house, the laboratory and the office, which became the sacrificial lamb slowing the fire sufficiently to allow the protection of the winery and its stock of bottled wine. Business partner Yale Norris cut back every vine down to 20cm hoping that shoots would appear. If the regeneration ceases, the entire vineyard will be pulled out and replanted. Exports to the UK, Ireland, the US, Canada, France, Switzerland, Germany, Abu Dhabi, Hong Kong and Taiwan. (JH)

🍷🍷🍷🍷🍷 **Boundary Track Shiraz 2018, Kangaroo Island** Still holding a crimson edge to the hue, it is a beautifully made wine with silky tannins and fruit freshness, the oak playing a nigh on unseen hand. One glass insists on another. Screw cap. 13.5% alc. RATING 96 DRINK 2028–2048 $75 JH ✪

The Independence Malbec 2016, Kangaroo Island Deep crimson-purple hue, showing no sign of age. An alluring, expressive bouquet with licorice, polished leather, eastern spices, dried plum and earth all calling out. The palate tucks in behind that array, giving substance and cedary oak tannins on the long, perfectly balanced finish. Diam. 14.5% alc. RATING 96 DRINK 2022–2036 $150 JH

The Cygnet Shiraz 2017, Kangaroo Island Matured in new 600L French demis for 24 months. The quality of the oak is clearly good and is still to pull its head in, but will certainly do so as part of a long future. It's an elegant wine and already attractive, with more in store as the oak diminishes. Diam. 14.5% alc. RATING 95 DRINK 2025–2040 $150 JH

The Red Shiraz 2021, Kangaroo Island The crimson magenta hue is striking. Positively juicy, with black cherry and plum fruit; tannin extract minimal. Altogether unusual wine, and it would be interesting to buy 6 or so bottles and track its development over the next 5 years or more. Screw cap. 14% alc. RATING 94 DRINK 2023–2028 $25 JH ✪

Pinot Gris 2021, South Australia While the back label shows South Australia, the winery says Adelaide Hills is the region, and the wine in the mouth is emphatically cool grown. Its exceptional power and texture is derived from wild ferment of the pressings in used French oak, the balance cool-fermented in stainless steel. Screw cap. 12.5% alc. RATING 94 DRINK 2022–2027 $30 JH ✪

Sauvignon Blanc 2021, Kangaroo Island Pale quartz green. Classic sauvignon blanc flavours, ranging from snow pea to wild herbs to gooseberry. No compromises needed – nor used. Revels in the exceptional vintage, flawless mouthfeel and balance. Screw cap. 13% alc. RATING 94 DRINK 2022–2023 $30 JH ✪

The King's Creed

169 Douglas Gully Road, Blewitt Spings SA 5171 **Region** McLaren Vale
T 0439 479 758 **www**.threekingswinemerchants.com.au **Winemaker** Ben Riggs
Est. 2020

The King's Creed label falls under the aegis of Three Kings Wine Merchants, a collaboration between winemaker Ben Riggs, former Wallaby Nathan Sharpe and ex-LVMH marketeer, David Krenich. With no cellar door, sales rely on an online shopping portal, drawing on a broad network of celebrity support. The wines are largely reliant on McLaren Vale and Langhorne Creek sources, marked with salubrious oak and plenty of extract at the pointy end of the hierarchy. (NG)

🍷🍷🍷🍷🍷 **Rosé 2021, Fleurieu** No mention of the variety, but the wine has attitude. The winemaker is the ubiquitous Ben Riggs, who has invested the wine with crisp, crunchy crabapple and wild strawberry flavours. I'd cheerfully have a second glass of this at my local Chinese restaurant. Screw cap. 13% alc. RATING 91 DRINK 2021-2022 $25 JH

Shiraz 2019, McLaren Vale An easygoing sassy shiraz, designed for imminent drinking. Dark fruits, spice and licorice. The tannins, suave, gently grippy and well aligned to the plump fruit, directing it nicely. The winemaking hand, gentle and diplomatically applied, promoting poise and versatility at the table. Well done. Screw cap. 14.5% alc. RATING 90 DRINK 2021-2025 $25 NG

♀♀♀♀ **Limited Batch Pinot Grigio 2021, Adelaide Hills** RATING 88 DRINK 2021-2024 $24 JP
Limited Batch Chardonnay 2020, Adelaide Hills RATING 88 DRINK 2021-2025 $25 JP

The Lake House Denmark ★★★★

106 Turner Road, Denmark, WA 6333 **Region** Denmark
T (08) 9848 2444 **www.lakehousedenmark.com.au Open** 7 days 10–5
Winemaker Harewood Estate (James Kellie) **Est.** 1995 **Dozens** 8000 **Vyds** 5.2ha
Garry Capelli and Leanne Rogers purchased the property in 2005 and have restructured the vineyard to grow varieties suited to the climate – chardonnay, pinot noir, semillon and sauvignon blanc – incorporating biodynamic principles. They also manage a couple of small family-owned vineyards in Frankland River and Mount Barker with a similar ethos. The top wines are released under the Premium Reserve and Premium Block ranges. The combined cellar door, restaurant and gourmet food emporium is a popular destination. Exports to Singapore. (JH)

♀♀♀♀♀ **Premium Reserve Single Vineyard Riesling 2021, Porongurup** The plump fruit here is very attractive: salty, fine, layered, floral and generally pretty gorgeous. Sherbety acidity backs the fruit, giving it a tingle and lift. Screw cap. 12.5% alc. RATING 92 DRINK 2021-2031 $40 EL
Merum Shiraz Cabernet 2020, Frankland River This has spent time in oak, which gives it the plush landing through the finish. For this aspect, it is a lush, concentrated wine, however the sweet oak does do more than its fair share of the lifting in the sweetness department. Anyway, good value for $25! Screw cap. 14.5% alc. RATING 91 DRINK 2022-2029 $25 EL
Premium Reserve Single Vineyard Cabernet Sauvignon 2019, Frankland River 24 months in French oak (50% new) dominates the fruit, but the fruit has very good density and concentration. This is brooding, dark and resinous, with layers of spice and tannin. Perhaps the oak will recede in a few years, perhaps it won't, but certainly if you're a lover of the style, then this one is for you. All things are well handled otherwise. Screw cap. 14.5% alc. RATING 91 DRINK 2022-2039 $59 EL
Premium Block Selection Cabernet Merlot 2020, Great Southern The tannins here are gravelly yet fine, forming the bedrock of the wine, rooted in to which is the black brooding fruit. Plentiful in flavour and tannin. Screw cap. 14.5% alc. RATING 90 DRINK 2022-2028 $29 EL
Premium Reserve Single Vineyard Chardonnay 2020, Denmark The impact of oak on this wine is strong, and emerges through the finish to imprint itself on the final lingering memory of sweet, toasty, vanilla oak. The fruit beneath it is citrusy, lean and bright: the acidity that weaves in and out is juicy and ripe. All in all, an amalgam of components that perhaps time will stitch together. Screw cap. 13.5% alc. RATING 90 DRINK 2022-2028 $49 EL
Merum Reserve Shiraz Cabernet 2020, Frankland River The fruit profile here is very similar to the Merum Shiraz Cabernet, however it appears the oak is the defining difference. The French oak here makes for spicy drinking, potentially setting back the drinking window a year or 2 from now. There is a fair bit of fire and warmth through the finish, inhibiting the graceful flow of the black fruit. Screw cap. 14.5% alc. RATING 90 DRINK 2023-2029 $32 EL

Merum Reserve Shiraz 2019, Frankland River The time (22 months) spent in oak is evident on the nose, lending the affair an aniseed and licorice spice note that coats the fruit. Concentrated blackberries and spice on the palate: plenty of flavour. Give it another year for the oak to recede a little more, otherwise this is very smart. Screw cap. 14.5% alc. RATING 90 DRINK 2022–2028 $32 EL

Merum Reserve Chardonnay 2019, Great Southern A tropical nose of nectarine, pineapple, guava and melon backed by toasty, spicy oak. In the mouth the wine has plump texture and intense fruit, however the oak plays a very dominant role in proceedings at this stage. It cloaks the finish. Screw cap. 14% alc. RATING 90 DRINK 2021–2028 $32 EL

ΨΨΨΨ **Single Vineyard Selection Semillon Sauvignon Blanc 2021, Frankland River** RATING 88 DRINK 2022–2023 $25 EL
Premium Reserve Single Vineyard Shiraz 2020, Frankland River RATING 88 DRINK 2022–2028 $49 EL

The Lane Vineyard ★★★★★

5 Ravenswood Lane, Balhannah, SA 5244 **Region** Adelaide Hills
T (08) 8388 1250 **www**.thelane.com.au **Open** 7 days 10–5 **Winemaker** Turon White
Viticulturist Jared Stringer **Est.** 1993 **Dozens** 25 000 **Vyds** 75ha
The Lane Vineyard is one of the Adelaide Hills' elite wine tourism attractions, with a cellar door and restaurant that offers focused tastings by region and style, with endless views. Established by the Edwards family in '93, it was acquired by the UK's Vestey Group in '12, following their establishment of Coombe Farm in the Yarra Valley. Four distinct tiers of single-vineyard wines are produced at The Lane; the entry-level Lane series from the Adelaide Hills, the Provenance range from in and around the Adelaide Hills and the top-tier Estate and Heritage ranges from their Hahndorf estate vines. Exports to the UK, Canada, South East Asia, Sweden and Norway. (JH)

ΨΨΨΨΨ **Heritage Chardonnay 2020, Adelaide Hills** Has what its sibling Beginning lacks – finesse and precision in line, length and balance. White peach and apple take the knee to pink grapefruit, the finish fresh and clean. Screw cap. 13.1% alc. RATING 96 DRINK 2027–2032 $100 JH

Heritage Shiraz Viognier 2019, Adelaide Hills A very classy wine, full bodied yet supple, with a well-balanced array of black and purple fruits. 1307 bottles made. Screw cap. 14% alc. RATING 96 DRINK 2024–2044 $120 JH

Provenance Pinot Noir 2021, Adelaide Hills Lithe and tangy with super-bright acidity, it explores both crunchy cherry, berry, pomegranate fruits and a herbal, earthiness with plenty of flesh and jaunty tannins. So much energy, potential, too. Screw cap. 13.2% alc. RATING 95 DRINK 2022–2027 $50 JP

Shiraz 2020, Adelaide Hills Sometimes back labels can be useful for vinification information, and once in a blue moon are as accurate as this 'Aromas of forest fruits and clove followed by flavours of plum, black pepper and charcuterie with a silky texture and fine tannins.' Precisely. Screw cap. 13.8% alc. RATING 95 DRINK 2022–2035 $30 JH ◐

Gathering Single Vineyard Sauvignon Blanc Semillon 2020, Adelaide Hills A single-site expression that raises the bar for the classic white bordeaux style in this country, with a heightened intensity and clean pure flavour. Watch out Margaret River! Citrus blossom, nettle, grapefruit rind and herbs bring great carry to the bouquet. The influence of oak brings a mealy, spicy contribution to the palate of white nectarine and peach. This is one complex wine. Screw cap. 12.5% alc. RATING 94 DRINK 2021–2027 $40 JP

ΨΨΨΨΨ **Sauvignon Blanc 2021, Adelaide Hills** RATING 93 DRINK 2022–2024 $25 JP ◐
Provenance Cabernet Franc 2021, Adelaide Hills RATING 93 DRINK 2022–2026 $40 JP

Beginning Single Vineyard Chardonnay 2020, Adelaide Hills RATING 93
DRINK 2025-2030 $50 JH
19th Meeting Single Vineyard Cabernet Sauvignon 2019, Adelaide Hills
RATING 93 DRINK 2021-2027 $65 JP
Reunion Single Vineyard Shiraz 2019, Adelaide Hills RATING 93
DRINK 2021-2029 $65 JP
LDR 2021, Adelaide Hills RATING 92 DRINK 2022-2031 $30 JP
Provenance Gamay 2021, Adelaide Hills RATING 92 DRINK 2022-2026
$50 JP
Provenance Syrah 2020, Adelaide Hills RATING 91 DRINK 2022-2027
$40 JH
Rosé 2021, Adelaide Hills RATING 90 DRINK 2021-2025 $25 JP
Provenance Sangiovese 2021, Adelaide Hills Fleurieu RATING 90
DRINK 2022-2028 $40 JP

The Other Wine Co

136 Jones Road, Balhannah, SA 5242 **Region** South Australia
T (08) 8398 0500 **www.theotherwineco.com Open** At Shaw + Smith **Winemaker** Matt
Large **Viticulturist** Murray Leake **Est.** 2015 **Dozens** 5000
This is the venture of Michael Hill Smith and Martin Shaw, established in the shadow of Shaw
+ Smith but with an entirely different focus and separate marketing. The name reflects the
wines, which are intended for casual consumption; the whole focus being freshness combined
with seductive mouthfeel. The concept of matching variety and place is one without any
particular limits and there may well be other wines made by The Other Wine Co in years to
come. Exports to the UK, Canada and Germany. (JH)

Pinot Gris 2021, Adelaide Hills A full-on spring-blossom aroma sets the scene
for this aromatic gris that fairly bounces with energy. Apple blossom, honeysuckle,
fresh-cut pear and lemon zest aromas draw you in. Jumps with bright upfront
acidity and lemon drop/pastille confection, pear and spiced apple. An exuberant
youngster when first tasted, but there's plenty of time to settle and work on that
budding textural component. Screw cap. 13.5% alc. RATING 92 DRINK 2021-2024
$26 JP
Barbera 2021, Adelaide Hills One of the darkest, most opaque Australian
barberas you'll come across. It's one deeply layered wine in dark fruits, bramble,
licorice and earth with sappy notes, too. Assertive in sturdy tannins and bold to
taste, it is host to both complexity and richness. Love to see how it ages. Screw cap.
14.5% alc. RATING 92 DRINK 2022-2028 $35 JP
Ricca Terra Farms Arinto 2021, Riverland Winemaker Matt Large considers
the Portuguese grape, with its high acidity, to be highly suited to a warm climate
like the Riverland. Skin contact is on display here in this restrained, elegant
white with its warm, textural intrigue dressed in bright citrus, apple, ginger snap
and spice. Acidity is nicely tamed bringing a tight finish. Screw cap. 13% alc.
RATING 90 DRINK 2022-2024 $26 JP

The Pawn Wine Co.

10 Banksia Road, Macclesfield, SA 5153 **Region** South Australia
T 0438 373 247 **www.thepawn.com.au Winemaker** Tom Keelan **Viticulturist** Tom
Keelan **Est.** 2004 **Dozens** 10 000 **Vyds** 35ha
The Pawn Wine Co. began as a partnership between Tom Keelan and Rebecca Willson
(Bremerton Wines) and David and Vanessa Blows. Tom was for some time manager of
Longview Vineyards at Macclesfield in the Adelaide Hills, and consulted to the neighbouring
vineyard, owned by David and Vanessa. In '02 Tom and David decided to make some small
batches of Petit Verdot and Tempranillo at Bremerton, where Tom was vineyard manager. In
'17 Tom and Rebecca purchased David and Vanessa's share. David still supplies grapes to the
Pawn Wine Co., and Tom works very closely with David and his 3 sons to produce food-
friendly wines that reflect their origins. Exports to the UK and NZ. (JH)

ŶŶŶŶŶ **Fiano 2021, Langhorne Creek** Fiano is a difficult customer at the best of times, but here it roars defiantly, its depth and power driving the palate through the finish and lingering aftertaste. Screw cap. 12% alc. RATING 94 DRINK 2021–2031 $26 JH ☺

ŶŶŶŶŶ **Shiraz 2019, Adelaide Hills** RATING 92 DRINK 2021–2025 $40 JP
El Desperado Sauvignon Blanc 2021, Adelaide Hills RATING 90 DRINK 2021–2023 $20 JP ☺
Chardonnay 2018, Adelaide Hills RATING 90 DRINK 2021–2025 $36 JP

The Ridge North Lilydale ★★★

106 Browns Road, North Lilydale, Tas, 7268 **Region** Northern Tasmania
T 0408 192 000 **www**.theridgenorthlilydale.com **Open** Sun 10.30–5 Oct–May
Winemaker Harry Rigney, Susan Denny **Viticulturist** Harry Rigney, Susan Denny
Est. 2013 **Dozens** 1000 **Vyds** 2ha
This venture marks the return to Tasmania of husband and wife Harry Rigney and Susan Denny after more than 30 years on the east coast of the mainland. In his mid-20s Harry was the sole recipient of the prized Menzies Scholarship to undertake his master's degree at Harvard, becoming a highly acclaimed specialist in taxation law (while continuing to this day to play his electric guitar in a rock band). Susan completed a fine arts degree in the '70s (dux of her year) then moving into Applied Arts inter alia mastering oxy and electric welding. She also saw her father Tim's scientific, engineering and agricultural innovations trail-blaze the world's lavender industry. So, they were equipped to purchase a 20ha property with north-facing slopes at an altitude of 350m and planted a 2ha close-planted 6000 vine vineyard in 2013/14. It earned them the title of Best Small Vineyard Tasmania '17. The winery was sold to new owners in 2022. (JH)

ŶŶŶŶ **Tasmanian Traditional 2017, Tasmania** 58/38/4% chardonnay/pinot noir/ meunier. Aged 38 months on lees. This is a sparkling of concentration and tension. Grapefruit, peach and strawberries are well supported by the toasty, spicy complexity and creamy texture of lees age. A touch of phenolic bitterness clips the finish. Diam. 13.5% alc. RATING 89 $67 TS

The Story Wines ★★★★★

170 Riverend Road, Hangholme, Vic 3175 **Region** Grampians
T 0411 697 912 **www**.thestory.com.au **Open** By appt **Winemaker** Rory Lane
Est. 2004 **Dozens** 2500
Over the years I have come across winemakers with degrees in atomic science, doctors with specialties spanning every human condition, town-planners, sculptors and painters; Rory Lane adds yet another to the list: a degree in ancient Greek literature. He says that after completing his degree and 'desperately wanting to delay an entry into the real world, I stumbled across and enrolled in a postgraduate wine technology and marketing course at Monash University, where I soon became hooked on … the wondrous connection between land, human and liquid'. Vintages in Australia and Oregon germinated the seed and he zeroed in on the Grampians, where he purchases small parcels of high-quality grapes. He makes the wines in a small factory where he has assembled a basket press, a few open fermenters, a mono pump and some decent French oak. Exports to the UK. (JH)

ŶŶŶŶŶ **Syrah 2019, Grampians** Has built on its layers of savoury and spicy cool-grown shiraz flavours over the past year, adding weight and depth but without compromising its freshness. The lingering aftertaste is special, throwing up sparklets of blackberry and blackcurrant. Screw cap. 13.5% alc. RATING 97 DRINK 2023–2040 $30 JH ☺

ŶŶŶŶŶ **Westgate Vineyard Shiraz 2020, Grampians** Intense, deep purple-red colour, a good indication of what follows. Lane has worked ripeness and richness into a smooth result: blood plum, black fruits, chocolate, licorice and signature Grampians pepperiness. Tannins are firm and free flowing. Finishes with a touch of amaro

bitters. Complex and still so very young. Screw cap. 13.5% alc. RATING 96
DRINK 2022-2035 $75 JP ✪
Super G Grenache Syrah Mourvèdre 2021, Grampians Another love
letter from the maker to the Rhône varieties he loves best out of the Grampians.
Delightfully open, honest and plush in lifted violet, red licorice, ripe dark fruits,
bracken and tilled earth. The star is the spice that binds: the peppery, clove and
cinnamon with a dash of menthol that sends it – together with firm tannins –
off into a world of its own. Screw cap. 14% alc. RATING 95 DRINK 2022-2031
$30 JP ✪

The Wanderer ★★★★☆

2850 Launching Place Road, Gembrook, Vic 3783 **Region** Yarra Valley
T 0415 529 639 **www**.wandererwines.com **Open** By appt **Winemaker** Andrew Marks
Est. 2005 **Dozens** 500
The Wanderer wines are a series of single-vineyard wines made by Andrew Marks, winemaker
and viticulturalist at Gembrook Hill Vineyard. Andrew spent 6 years as a winemaker with
Penfolds before returning to Gembrook Hill in 2005. He has worked numerous vintages in
France and Spain including Etienne Sauzet in Puligny Montrachet in '06 and more recently
over 10 vintages in the Costa Brava, Spain. Andrew seeks to achieve the best expression of his
vineyards through minimal handling in the winery. In '12 he founded The Melbourne Gin
Company. (JH)

🍷🍷🍷🍷🍸 **Upper Pinot Noir 2020, Yarra Valley** Pale terracotta. Earthy with
some reduction which opens up with air to reveal orange peel and aromas
including ginger and juniper. Light–medium bodied, this sinewy, savoury and
interesting wine finishes with gently grippy tannins. Diam. 13% alc. RATING 90
DRINK 2021-2025 $55 PR

The Willows Vineyard ★★★★☆

310 Light Pass Road, Light Pass, SA 5355 **Region** Barossa Valley
T (08) 8562 1080 **www**.thewillowsvineyard.com.au **Open** Wed–Mon 10.30–4.30
Winemaker Peter Scholz **Est.** 1989 **Dozens** 6000 **Vyds** 42.74ha
The Scholz family have been grapegrowers for generations and they have over 40ha of
vineyards, selling part of the crop. Current-generation winemaker Peter Scholz makes rich,
ripe, velvety wines, some marketed with some bottle age. Exports to the UK, Canada,
Switzerland and NZ. (JH)

🍷🍷🍷🍷🍷 **G Seven Shiraz 2020, Barossa Valley** Vibrant in both its purple splashed hue
and the purity of its fruit. Juicy plum with a touch of blueberry coming through
with plentiful spice, violet and dark chocolatey nuance. Lifted and succulent
with grippy, gypsum-like tannins, bright acidity and an impressive long balanced
finish. Delicious now but has the architecture to age well in the cellar. Screw cap.
14.6% alc. RATING 95 DRINK 2021-2038 $40 DB
Bonesetter Shiraz 2019, Barossa Valley The flagship wine of The Willows
Vineyard is densely proportioned, with opulent blackberry, black cherry and dark
plum fruits along with hints of espresso, cedary oak, baking spice, licorice and dark
chocolate. Powerful and thick-shouldered palate with an intense, concentrated fruit
profile, firm, fine tannins and a classical Barossan form that bodes well for its future
in the cellar. Cork. 14.8% alc. RATING 94 DRINK 2021-2035 $65 DB

🍷🍷🍷🍷🍸 **G Seven Mataro 2021, Barossa Valley** RATING 93 DRINK 2022-2028
$32 DB
Old Vine Semillon 2021, Barossa Valley RATING 92 DRINK 2021-2031
$20 DB ✪
Riesling 2021, Barossa Valley RATING 91 DRINK 2021-2031 $18 DB ✪
G Seven Grenache 2021, Barossa Valley RATING 90 DRINK 2022-2027
$32 DB

Thick as Thieves Wines

355 Healesville-Kooweerup Road, Badger Creek, Vic 3777 **Region** Yarra Valley
T 0417 184 690 **www**.tatwines.com.au **Open** By appt **Winemaker** Syd Bradford
Viticulturist Syd Bradford **Est.** 2009 **Dozens** 2000 **Vyds** 1.5ha

Syd Bradford is living proof that small can be beautiful and, equally, that an old dog can learn
new tricks. A growing interest in good food and wine might have come to nothing had it
not been for Pfeiffer Wines giving him a vintage job in 2003. In that year he enrolled in the
wine science course at CSU; he then moved to the Yarra Valley in '05, gaining experience at a
number of wineries including Coldstream Hills. In '09 he came across a small parcel of arneis
from the Hoddles Creek area, and Thick as Thieves was born. These days Syd farms 1.5ha of
his own pinot noir (MV6 and Abel clones) and purchases other varieties from both the Yarra
and King Valleys. The techniques used could only come from someone who has spent a long
time observing and thinking about what he might do if he were calling the shots. Exports
to Japan. (JH)

🍷🍷🍷🍷🍷 **Another Bloody Chardonnay 2021, Yarra Valley** Leaps out of the glass
with attractive aromas of pink grapefruit pith, lemon oil, white peaches and an
undercurrent of cashew and flint. Loads of flavour, but equally this is poised and
very well balanced, finishing minerally and long. A very accomplished wine. Screw
cap. 12.7% alc. RATING 96 DRINK 2022-2027 $37 PR ☻

The Aloof Alpaca Arneis 2021, Yarra Valley Used 24-hour pre-fermentation
skin contact (old is new), wild-yeast barrel fermentation and lees contact. Every bit
as powerful and complex as the variety – and its vinification – suggests. Difficult
to be dogmatic about the outcome, but at $25 there's room for debate and little or
no downside. Screw cap. 12.5% alc. RATING 94 DRINK 2022-2026 JH ☻

Limited Release Syrah 2021, Yarra Valley Matured in seasoned French
hogsheads and puncheons. Vibrant crimson purple. Alluring, this opens with ripe,
black plums, black olives and pink peppercorns. The palate is plushly fruited with
immediate appeal, but then manages to finish balanced and refreshing and with
fine, chalky tannins. Screw cap. 12.8% alc. RATING 94 DRINK 2022-2031 $45 PR

🍷🍷🍷🍷🍷 **Purple Prose Gamay 2021, King Valley** RATING 93 DRINK 2022-2026
$37 PR

Limited Release Pinot Syrah 2021, Yarra Valley RATING 92
DRINK 2022-2026 $45 PR

Thistledown Wines

c/- Revenir, Peacock Road North, Lenswood, SA 5240 **Region** South Australia
T 0424 472 831 **www**.thistledownwines.com **Winemaker** Giles Cooke MW **Est.** 2010
Dozens 10 000

Thistledown is a conflation of wisdom, foresight and strident confidence; an assemblage of
talent, superb old-vine sites and remarkable wines that have, with a few others, established a
firmament at the top of the grenache totem in this country. Giles Cooke and Fergal Tynan –
each a Master of Wine, historian and lover of the world's finest grenache – became tired of
international stereotypes of Australian wine. With vast experience respectively making and
selling wines from Spain, they began to carve out a niche defined by filigreed precision,
thirst-slaking tannins and crunchy red fruit elements under the local guidance of maker Peter
Leske. These are small-batch micro-ferments handled in the right vessels and extracted with
aplomb. They unravel as exquisite expressions of grenache to be sure, but also handy shiraz
and chardonnay, sourced across McLaren Vale, Barossa and the Eden Valley. Exports to the UK,
the US, Canada, Ireland, the Netherlands, Denmark, Czech Republic, Poland, Malta, South
Korea, Singapore and NZ. (NG)

🍷🍷🍷🍷🍷 **Our Fathers Just Like Heaven Roussanne 2021, McLaren Vale** A not-for-
profit label with all proceeds going towards mental health charities. Exceptional
wine, here! Riffs on Asian pear, rooibos, quince, preserved lemon, hazelnut and
dried herb, whisk me to Avignon and environs. Like an unctuous Meursault,
with a Mediterranean sheen. Viscous and detailed of phenolics, yet paradoxically

taut, with a slippery mineral underbelly propelling it to scintillating length. We should be proud of wines like this coming from these shores. Screw cap. 14% alc. RATING 97 DRINK 2021-2028 $30 NG ✪

Sands of Time Single Vineyard Blewitt Springs Grenache 2021, McLaren Vale Raspberry, lilac and rosehip behind. The tannins, a saline scape of bridling force that stretch from the attack to the long, chalky finish. Delicious. Concrete ferment, layered bunches and destemmed material to promote perfume and a mescal whiff of the best parts beyond a border of control. Saliva-sapping energy. Screw cap. 14.5% alc. RATING 97 DRINK 2022-2031 $90 NG ✪

♱♱♱♱♱ **She's Electric Old Vine Single Vineyard Grenache 2021, McLaren Vale** The Vagabond is superlative, but this is extraordinary! The tannins, taut, febrile and wound across a spool of sage, thyme and blood orange zest. The drive of red cherry, rhubarb and Mediterranean herb is palate staining, without ever reneging on its sandy, vibrant and effortless hand. Incredibly complex. Scintillating length. Kerpow! Screw cap. 14.5% alc. RATING 96 DRINK 2022-2028 $65 NG ✪

The Quickening Shiraz 2020, Barossa A striking wine, as juicy as quicksilver on the first whiff and taste, before the spicy, savoury whole-bunch nuances come into play. Has the X-factor. Screw cap. 14.5% alc. RATING 96 DRINK 2022-2040 $50 JH ✪

Bachelor's Block Ebenezer Shiraz 2020, Barossa Valley Subdued aromas of blueberry, licorice, clove, dried nori, sassafras and kirsch. Plenty of oomph. But classy. No jam, or overt angles. The acidity, briny. The tannins, an immaculate sheath, as polished as it is detailed, articulating the fruit and spicy underbelly as a long, chinotto-soused finish. This opens up nicely with time, becoming floral. But still a nascent proposition, needing a whack into a decanter. Superlative, full-bodied shiraz, for those who appreciate structure and refinement. Diam. 14.5% alc. RATING 96 DRINK 2022-2030 $80 NG

Sands of Time Single Vineyard Blewitt Springs Grenache 2020, McLaren Vale Fermented wild, with attenuated maceration in eggs and the inclusion of 30% whole bunches imparting turmeric, sandalwood, cardamon scents and finely wrought, granular tannins akin to nebbiolo. Real pinosity and sap to this. Succulent notes of kirsch, fecund strawberry and anise. A parry of tension and thrust of gentle sweetness. Remarkable freshness. A wine that places domestic grenache among the world's best. Screw cap. 14.5% alc. RATING 96 DRINK 2022-2028 $80 NG

Our Fathers Shiraz 2018, Barossa Made to the exactitude that one expects from this address, with all profits imparted to mental-health causes. While the region cannot deliver the finesse, mid-weighted balletic energy and complexity, perhaps, of the northern Rhône, it can deliver vinous fortitude and a latent power that, in the right hands, has its own stamp of elegance without straying into the galumphing, sweet, clumsily oaked grind of so many. Here, a prime example. Violet, crushed black rock, mace, pepper grind, salumi, clove, lilac and five spice. A textural thread, of detailed complexity woven very long. Superlative! Screw cap. 14% alc. RATING 96 DRINK 2021-2028 $50 NG ✪

The Vagabond Old Vine Blewitt Springs Grenache 2021, McLaren Vale Such a fine vintage, reverberating across such a great wine. Pithy cherry, cranberry, raspberry bon-bon, anise, thyme and basil. The leitmotif, the thrust of a superbly extracted tannic kit, sandy and pixelated, juxtaposed against the parry of fruit so refined that one can only believe. Screw cap. 14.5% alc. RATING 95 DRINK 2022-2026 $60 NG

This Charming Man Single Vineyard Clarendon Grenache 2021, McLaren Vale Pickled cherry, ume, lavender, rhubarb and poached plum. A waft of menthol, too, but nothing intrusive. The Smart vineyard is high and cool. Characterful, while pushing the svelte tannic line of grit and paradoxical elegance that mark the region's finest wines. All, let's face it, grenache. This is stellar. It grows in stature as it unravels and beams clove, white pepper and violet across a brilliant finish of real pizazz. Diam. 14.5% alc. RATING 95 DRINK 2022-2028 $80 NG

The Vagabond Old Vine Blewitt Springs Grenache 2020, McLaren Vale
A wine that sits below the single-vineyard hierarchy albeit can, at times, equal
if not better them. Raspberry liqueur, anise, white pepper, lilac and orange zest.
Gorgeous aromatics framed by herb-doused tannins. Pinosity and grip. Flare and
excitement. Length of finish eased across a throttle of dangerous drinkability.
Screw cap. 14.5% alc. RATING 95 DRINK 2021-2026 $65 NG

**This Charming Man Single Vineyard Clarendon Grenache 2020,
McLaren Vale** When siphoning amidst the pantheon of the country's greatest
grenache it is important to take time to let wines unwind. And so it is that I write
on the 2nd day after opening. Was clunky. Now, a swan! From the cherished Smart
Family vineyard. Cherry amaro, bergamot, thyme, lavender and a whiff of mint,
rather than (mercifully) eucalyptus. Some malty oak could be shifted. Sweeter
than the '19, with a skein of freshness and bunchy (20%) tannins tucking in the
exuberance. Expansive. The broader of the siblings. Long and juicy. Delicious.
14.5% alc. RATING 95 DRINK 2022-2032 $90 NG

Thorny Devil Old Vine Grenache 2021, McLaren Vale While this doesn't
quite have the thrust of its more expensive siblings, the shimmy of florals and
red-fruited fragrances, juxtaposed against a veil of diaphanous tannins, sandy and
detailed, is impressive. Crunchy and tensile – although a little looser around the
seams, for imminent pleasure – and thoroughly impressive. Screw cap. 14% alc.
RATING 94 DRINK 2021-2025 $32 NG

Thomas St Vincent   ★★★★☆
PO Box 633, McLaren Vale, SA 5171 **Region** McLaren Vale
T 0438 605 694 **www**.thomasstvincent.com **Winemaker** Gary Thomas **Est.** 2016
Dozens 240
Owner and winemaker Gary Thomas is the only vigneron I (James) know of who is a
ruthless critic of his own wines. He explains he has come from a writing background in the
(unspecified) media and has had a passion for Rhône wines since the mid-1980s. He made
his way 'to the cool heart of McLaren Vale's Blewitt Springs, and its old vines, dry-grown on
sand for flavour and purity. Wines in small batches, extended ferments, subtle blends, reflecting
the terroir and the season. Bottled without fining or filtration. As wines used to be made.' He
makes his wines at McLaren Vale winery La Curio. (JH)

🍷🍷🍷🍷🍷 **Blewitt Springs Fleurieu Septentrionale Rouge 2019, McLaren Vale**
A mourvèdre-dominated blend inspired by the wilds of the southern Rhône.
Australian sweetness of fruit mopped up by the ferrous, tobacco-doused leathery
tannins of the grape. Meat stock, pepper, clove, lapsang, tamarind, sandalwood
and an attractive smokiness. A lovely point to be released, with the whiff of time
encroaching in the best sense. Delicious! As with all these wines, I'd like the acidity
to be more in tune with the rugged intuitions of the blend. This said, immensely
satisfying. Screw cap. 14.5% alc. RATING 95 DRINK 2021-2027 $39 NG

🍷🍷🍷🍷🍷 **Septentrionale Blewitt Springs 2021, Fleurieu** RATING 93
DRINK 2021-2027 $27 NG ✪
Blewitt Springs Provencale Rosé 2021, Fleurieu RATING 90
DRINK 2021-2022 $27 NG

Thomas Wines   ★★★★★
28 Mistletoe Lane, Pokolbin, NSW 2320 **Region** Hunter Valley
T (02) 4998 7134 **www**.thomaswines.com.au **Open** 7 days 10–5 **Winemaker** Andrew
Thomas **Viticulturist** Andrew Thomas **Est.** 1997 **Dozens** 10 000 **Vyds** 6ha
Andrew Thomas moved to the Hunter Valley from McLaren Vale to join the winemaking
team at Tyrrell's Wines. After 13 years, he left to undertake contract work and to continue
the development of his own label. He makes single-vineyard wines, underlining the subtle
differences between the various subregions of the Hunter. The major part of the production
comes from long-term arrangements with growers of old-vine semillon and shiraz. The

acquisition of Braemore Vineyard in Dec '17 was significant, giving Thomas Wines a long-term supply of grapes from one of the Hunter Valley's most distinguished semillon sites. The quality of the wines and the reputation of Andrew Thomas have never been higher. Exports to Japan. (JH)

🍷🍷🍷🍷🍷 **Braemore Individual Vineyard Semillon 2021, Hunter Valley** Pungent lemongrass and lemon aromas carry through in a high-fidelity replay on the long palate with its glittering acidity. Screw cap. 11% alc. RATING 96 DRINK 2026–2036 $35 JH ✪
Braemore Cellar Reserve Semillon 2016, Hunter Valley An exquisite wine that suggests the style here was finer boned and less overt of fruit, in the past. Barley water, lemon oil and a strong waft of peat, not dissimilar to great aged champagne or Laphroaig. Lightweight and skeletal, yet of immense thrust, intensity of extract, drive and length. A bit tangy, to be churlish. Nevertheless, an indomitable wine worthy of much attention. Screw cap. 10.8% alc. RATING 96 DRINK 2021–2026 $65 NG ✪
Will's Hill Shiraz 2019, Hunter Valley This is lovely drinking. Mid weighted and juicy of feel. A shift away from the glossier, more reductive expressions of the past, to a wine that is immensely pure, effusive of energy and deliciousness. Wild strawberry, clove, a whiff of vanilla and a diaphanous spread of fine-boned tannins, gentle oak and dutiful acidity. Screw cap. 13.6% alc. RATING 94 DRINK 2021–2026 $30 NG ✪

🍷🍷🍷🍷🍷 **The O.C. Individual Vineyard Semillon 2021, Hunter Valley** RATING 93 DRINK 2021–2026 $28 NG
Herlestone Shiraz 2019, Hunter Valley RATING 93 DRINK 2022–2028 $30 NG
Synergy Vineyard Selection Shiraz 2020, Hunter Valley RATING 91 DRINK 2021–2023 $25 NG
Two of a Kind Shiraz 2020, Hunter Valley McLaren Vale RATING 91 DRINK 2021–2024 $25 NG
Sweetwater Individual Vineyard Shiraz 2020, Hunter Valley RATING 91 DRINK 2021–2025 $35 NG

Thompson Estate   ★★★★★

Tom Cullity Drive, Wilyabrup, WA 6284 **Region** Margaret River
T (08) 9755 6406 **www**.thompsonestate.com **Open** 7 days 10.30–4.30 **Winemaker** Paul Dixon **Est.** 1994 **Dozens** 10 000 **Vyds** 38ha
Cardiologist Peter Thompson planted the first vines at Thompson Estate in '97, inspired by his and his family's shareholdings in the Pierro and Fire Gully vineyards and by visits to many of the world's premium wine regions. Two more vineyards (both planted in '97) have been purchased, varieties include cabernet sauvignon, cabernet franc, merlot, chardonnay, sauvignon blanc, semillon, pinot noir and malbec. Thompson Estate wines are made onsite at its state-of-the-art winery. Exports to the UK, Canada, Belgium, the Netherlands, Denmark, Finland, Singapore and Hong Kong. (JH)

🍷🍷🍷🍷🍷 **The Specialist Cabernet Sauvignon 2018, Margaret River** Bright crimson purple; the colour is indicative of the great vintage, but that's just the start. This is a perfect rendition of cabernet sauvignon à la Margaret River, with a full-bodied well of cassis and blackcurrant, tapenade with powerful – but appropriate and not grippy – tannins that underwrite the long-term future of this great cabernet. Screw cap. 14.5% alc. RATING 97 DRINK 2025–2050 $90 JH ✪

🍷🍷🍷🍷🍷 **Chardonnay 2020, Margaret River** Grapefruit is the leader of the fruit pack, though white peach and nectarine are also involved, along with some French oak spice. The overall line and length is very good. Screw cap. 13.3% alc. RATING 96 DRINK 2023–2035 $50 JH ✪
Cabernet Sauvignon 2019, Margaret River 86.5/6/5.5/2% cabernet sauvignon/cabernet franc/malbec/merlot. Classical, supple and silky. The red fruits

are on show here, backed by a wall of crafted oak. The oak provides structure but also rigidity, the waves of flavour crash against it in the mouth. The acidity is finely woven into the fruit, stitched with invisible thread. Screw cap. 14% alc. RATING 95 DRINK 2021-2036 $50 EL

Thorn-Clarke Wines ★★★★★

266 Gawler Park Road, Angaston, SA 5353 **Region** Barossa
T (08) 8564 3036 **www.**thornclarkewines.com.au **Open** Fri–Sun 10–5 by appt
Winemaker Peter Kelly **Viticulturist** Steve Fiebiger **Est.** 1987 **Dozens** 90 000
Vyds 222ha
Established by David and Cheryl Clarke (née Thorn), and son Sam, Thorn-Clarke is one of the largest family-owned estate-based businesses in the Barossa. Their winery is close to the border between the Barossa and Eden valleys and 3 of their 4 vineyards are in the Eden Valley. The fourth vineyard is at St Kitts, at the northern end of the Barossa Ranges. In all 4 vineyards careful soil mapping has resulted in matching of variety and site, with all the major varieties represented. The quality of grapes retained for the Thorn-Clarke label has resulted in a succession of trophy and gold medal–winning wines at very competitive prices. Exports to all major markets. (JH)

🍷🍷🍷🍷🍷 **Sandpiper Riesling 2021, Eden Valley** The floral bouquet is shy, the palate anything but. It explores the world of citrus fruits and adds some tropicals. An interplay between piercing acidity and fruit sweetness draws out the length of the palate and adds to the overall enjoyment, acidity having the last word. Screw cap. 11.5% alc. RATING 95 DRINK 2021-2031 $25 JH ✪
William Randell Shiraz 2018, Barossa Deeply coloured and chock-full of flavours ex blackberry fruit, plum, oak and ripe tannins. Remarkably, it doesn't wilt under the load of its alcohol and all of the above, even with a savoury twist on the finish. Cork. 14.9% alc. RATING 95 DRINK 2025-2040 $70 JH
William Randell Cabernet Sauvignon 2018, Eden Valley This estate-grown icon of the Thorn-Clarke stable sets the scene with deep crimson-purple colour and a polished interplay between cassis, savoury and cedary aromas, supported by fine-spun tannins that create both texture and structure. Cork. 14.7% alc. RATING 95 DRINK 2023-2033 $70 JH
Ron Thorn Single Vineyard Shiraz 2017, Barossa A deeply-fruited, classic shiraz from vineyards at the region's northern extreme, St Kitts and Milton Park in the Eden Valley. Saturated red hue with aromas of macerated black fruits, plums, deep spice, licorice, dark chocolate, tobacco leaf and American oak. That oak comes charging in on the palate, but there is ample fruit weight to support it. Firm, compact tannin provides a base and it's in the classic, muscular Barossan mould. Cork. 14.5% alc. RATING 94 DRINK 2021-2035 $110 DB

🍷🍷🍷🍷♀ **Varietal Collection Chardonnay 2020, Eden Valley** RATING 92 DRINK 2021-2026 $30 DB
Varietal Collection Pinot Gris 2021, Eden Valley RATING 90 DRINK 2021-2023 $30 DB
Shotfire Shiraz 2019, Barossa RATING 90 DRINK 2025-2035 $35 JH

Three Dark Horses ★★★★

307 Schuller Road, Blewitt Springs, SA 5171 **Region** McLaren Vale
T 0405 294 500 **www.**3dh.com.au **Winemaker** Matt Broomhead **Viticulturist** Matt Broomhead **Est.** 2009 **Dozens** 5000 **Vyds** 8.9ha
Three Dark Horses is the project of former Coriole winemaker Matt Broomhead. After vintages in southern Italy (2007) and the Rhône Valley, he returned to McLaren Vale in late 2009 and, with his father Alan, buys quality grapes, thanks to the many years of experience they both have in the region. The third dark horse is Matt's grandfather, a vintage regular. They are expanding the plantings with grenache blanc, clairette and touriga nacional, and reworking some of the shiraz vines planted in 1964. Part of the vineyard is sand soil–based

interspersed with ironstone, a highly desirable mix for shiraz and cabernet sauvignon. Exports to NZ. (JH)

ＹＹＹＹＹ **Grenache Touriga 2020, McLaren Vale** At this price, the wine is very good – not merely in a domestic sense, but in an international one. Jubey. Ripe. Savoury. Round. Floral. Fresh. The reductive hand, a little out of the holster. Touriga, floral and peppery. The grenache, warm and soothing and finer boned. Delicious drinking. The tannins and acidity, a finessed patina. Screw cap. 14.5% alc. RATING 93 DRINK 2021-2026 $25 NG ✪

Basket Pressed Shiraz 2021, McLaren Vale A tightly packed palate is furled across vanillin oak and moreish, spice-clad grape tannins. Clove, anise, reductive elements, lilac, dried seaweed and blue fruits. This unravels nicely, drinking very well already. Screw cap. 14.5% alc. RATING 92 DRINK 2022-2027 $28 NG

Shiraz 2020, McLaren Vale A torrid year, but harnessed beautifully. At this pricing tier, impregnable. Oodles of blue fruits, iodine, clove, salumi, tapenade and white-pepper-laced freshness hit the varietal high points. A bit reductive/neoprene, but this has become the Australian means of mitigating low acidity while imparting a sense of tension. Impressive within the constructs. Screw cap. 14.5% alc. RATING 92 DRINK 2021-2027 $25 NG ✪

Preservative Free Shiraz 2021, McLaren Vale This address provides stellar value. The wines, inevitably delicious. Archetypal gently extracted shiraz, sans SO_2. Wild fermented. Playing the sassy florals of partial carbonic influence with aplomb. Pithy blue fruits, a waft of spice and a frame of the right sort of gently applied oak, this goes down with very little effort after a brisk chill. Best enjoyed in its fruity primacy. Screw cap. 14.5% alc. RATING 91 DRINK 2022-2024 $22 NG ✪

ＹＹＹＹ **Chardonnay 2020, McLaren Vale** RATING 89 DRINK 2021-2025 $20 NG
Grenache 2020, McLaren Vale RATING 89 DRINK 2021-2025 $25 NG

3 Drops ★★★★★

PO Box 1828, Applecross, WA 6953 **Region** Mount Barker
T 0417 172 603 **www**.3drops.com **Winemaker** Robert Diletti (Contract) **Est.** 1998
Dozens 3500 **Vyds** 21.5ha

3 Drops is the name given to the Bradbury family vineyard at Mount Barker. The name reflects 3 elements: wine, olive oil and water – all of which come from the substantial property. The vineyard is planted to riesling, sauvignon blanc, semillon, chardonnay, cabernet sauvignon, merlot, shiraz and cabernet franc, and irrigated by a large wetland on the property. 3 Drops also owns the 14.7ha Patterson's Vineyard, planted in 1982 to pinot noir, chardonnay and shiraz. Exports to South Korea and Hong Kong. (JH)

ＹＹＹＹＹ **Riesling 2021, Great Southern** A pale quartz green hue foretells a wine of unbridled intensity; aromas of white flowers, passionfruit and Granny Smith apple open proceedings on a palate of vibrant drive and intensity. Rose's lime juice with soaring acidity drive the seemingly endless flavours demanding an extra glass (or 2). Screw cap. 12% alc. RATING 96 DRINK 2021-2031 $26 JH ✪

Shiraz 2019, Great Southern Bright crimson-purple hue. A lively, fresh and juicy medium-bodied wine, its spicy red and black cherry fruits and fine tannins holding hands as they dance along the palate without a care in the world. There's every reason to drink it forthwith, but it will wait patiently for those wishing to cellar it for 5 or so years. Screw cap. 14.5% alc. RATING 95 DRINK 2022-2030 $28 JH ✪

Merlot 2020, Great Southern A fragrant and pure expression of a good merlot clone, grown in a climate that is perfect for it. An armful of red fruits and roses fill this medium-bodied wine, sufficient tannins also contributing (not distracting). Screw cap. 14% alc. RATING 94 DRINK 2022-2035 $27 JH ✪

Pinot Noir 2020, Great Southern The colour is superb, deep yet bright, and signals a wine that will be long lived, but there isn't a hint of over-extraction. Rob Diletti has unlocked the key to making high-quality pinot noir in the Great

Southern. The abundant red and black cherry and berry fruits will live for many years, opening the jar of spices of all kinds that are still lurking in the backdrop. Screw cap. 14% alc. RATING 94 DRINK 2022-2030 $32 JH

🍷🍷🍷🍷♀ **Sauvignon Blanc 2021, Great Southern** RATING 92 DRINK 2021-2024 $24 JH ✪
Chardonnay 2020, Great Southern RATING 92 DRINK 2021-2028 $30 JH
Cabernet Franc 2019, Great Southern RATING 92 DRINK 2021-2027 $27 JH
Cabernets 2020, Great Southern RATING 91 DRINK 2021-2031 $27 EL

3 Oceans Wine Company   ★★★☆

Cnr Boundary Road/Bussell Highway, Cowaramup, WA 6284 **Region** Margaret River
T (08) 9756 5656 **www.**3oceanswine.com.au **Open** Thurs–Mon 10–5
Winemaker Jonathan Mettam **Est.** 1999 **Dozens** 145 000
After a period of spectacular growth and marketing activity, Palandri Wine went into voluntary administration in Feb '08. In Jun '08, the Ma family, through their 3 Oceans Wine Company Pty Ltd, acquired the Palandri winery, its Margaret River vineyard and 347ha of the Frankland River vineyards. In Oct '08, 3 Oceans also amassed the Palandri and Baldivis Estate brands. The arrival of COVID-19 and collapse of the Chinese markets for all Australian wines has led to a restructure and lower profile of the business' activities. Exports to the UK, Singapore and Japan. (JH)

🍷🍷🍷🍷♀ **The Explorers Cabernet Sauvignon 2020, Margaret River** Concentrated, tannic and layered with fruit and spice. Not as long as one would hope, from the bombasity of fruit initially, but plenty of satisfaction here. Screw cap. 14.3% alc. RATING 92 DRINK 2021-2031 $45 EL

🍷🍷🍷🍷 **The Explorers Chardonnay 2020, Margaret River** RATING 89 DRINK 2021-2027 $40 EL

Tillie J   ★★★★

305 68B Gadd Street, Northcote, Vic 3070 (postal) **Region** Yarra Valley
T 0428 554 311 **www.**tilliejwines.com.au **Winemaker** Natillie Johnston
Viticulturist Natillie Johnston **Est.** 2019 **Dozens** 200
Mark my (James') words. Tillie Johnston is going to become a great winemaker. She began her career in 2012, one of the vintage crew at Coldstream Hills, and says her love for pinot noir began there. She then spent 4 of the next 8 years drifting between the Northern and Southern hemispheres unerringly picking the eyes out of an all-star cast of wineries: Leeuwin Estate, Brokenwood, Cristom (Oregon), Keller (Rheinhessen), Framingham (Marlborough) and Yarra Yering. Since then, she's been assistant winemaker at Giant Steps to Steve Flamsteed and Jess Clark. In '19 she was offered the opportunity to buy 2t of grapes from Helen's Hill of whatever variety she chose which was, of course, pinot noir. It came in 2 parcels: one Pommard and 943, hand-picked, whole bunches and destemmed; the second 777, Selectiv' harvested, 100% whole berries. Seven barriques: one new, 6 used. (JH)

🍷🍷🍷🍷♀ **Pinot Noir 2021, Yarra Valley** A light, bright cherry red. Initially a little reductive, but blows away to reveal an attractive, brightly-fruited wine with red cherries, cranberries and gentle spice notes. Red-fruited on the palate, this delicately framed and nicely put-together wine builds in the glass and finishes with fine gently grippy tannins and a refreshing, bitter amaro note. Screw cap. 13% alc. RATING 92 DRINK 2021-2026 $42 PR

Tim Adams ★★★★☆

156 Warenda Road, Clare, SA 5453 **Region** Clare Valley
T (08) 8842 2429 **www**.timadamswines.com.au **Open** 7 days 10–4.30 **Winemaker** Tim Adams, Brett Schutz **Viticulturist** Mick Plumridge **Est.** 1986 **Dozens** 60 000
Vyds 195ha

Tim Adams and partner Pam Goldsack preside over a highly successful business. Having expanded the range of estate plantings with tempranillo, pinot gris and viognier, the business took a giant step forward in '09 with the acquisition of the 80ha Leasingham Rogers Vineyard from CWA, followed in '11 by the purchase of the Leasingham winery and winemaking equipment (for less than replacement cost). The winery is now a major contract winemaking facility for the region. Exports to the UK, Sweden, Denmark, the Netherlands, South Korea, Taiwan, Hong Kong, Singapore and NZ. (JH)

🍷🍷🍷🍷🍷 **Skilly Ridge Riesling 2021, Clare Valley** This is an interesting wine: it has a preserved citrus austerity initially, but the wine quickly morphs into a toasty, rounded, opulent space which is littered with cheesecloth, baked pie crust, Golden Delicious apples and nashi pear. The length of flavour endures long after the wine is gone, making for a rather sumptuous drinking experience. I keep expecting the toastiness to lose its form through the finish, but it doesn't. It's very impressive. Screw cap. 11.5% alc. RATING 95 DRINK 2021-2031 $30 EL ✪

🍷🍷🍷🍷½ **Heinrich Fiano 2021, Clare Valley** RATING 93 DRINK 2022-2032 $30 EL
Ladera Tempranillo 2020, Clare Valley RATING 92 DRINK 2022-2032 $40 EL
Schaefer Shiraz 2015, Clare Valley RATING 92 DRINK 2021-2031 $40 EL
Skilly Ridge Riesling 2019, Clare Valley RATING 91 DRINK 2021-2031 $30 EL
Riesling 2021, Clare Valley RATING 90 DRINK 2021-2028 $24 EL

Tim Gramp ★★★☆

1033 Mintaro Road, Watervale, SA 5452 **Region** Clare Valley
T (08) 8843 0199 **www**.timgrampwines.com.au **Open** W'ends 12–4 **Winemaker** Tim Gramp **Viticulturist** Tim Gramp **Est.** 1990 **Dozens** 6000 **Vyds** 16ha

Tim Gramp has quietly built up a very successful business, and by keeping overheads to a minimum, provides good wines at modest prices. Over the years, estate vineyards (shiraz, riesling, cabernet sauvignon, grenache and tempranillo) have been expanded significantly. Exports to Malaysia and Taiwan. (JH)

🍷🍷🍷🍷 **Watervale Riesling 2021, Clare Valley** Talcy and fine with zesty bath salts on the nose, citrus pith and lavender through the finish. The palate is littered with lime kasundi and spice, but it doesn't quite hit the high notes promised by the aroma. Nonetheless, a lovely wine! Screw cap. 12.5% alc. RATING 88 DRINK 2021-2028 $22 EL

Tim McNeil Wines ★★★☆

71 Springvale Road, Watervale, SA 5452 **Region** Clare Valley
T (08) 8843 0040 **www**.timmcneilwines.com.au **Open** Sat–Sun & public hols 11–5
Winemaker Tim McNeil **Est.** 2004 **Dozens** 1500 **Vyds** 2ha

When Tim and Cass McNeil established Tim McNeil Wines, Tim had long since given up his teaching career, graduating with a degree in oenology from the University of Adelaide in '99. He then spent 11 years honing his craft at important wineries in the Barossa and Clare valleys. In Aug '10 Tim McNeil Wines became his full-time job. The McNeils' 16ha property at Watervale includes mature dry-grown riesling. The cellar door overlooks the riesling vineyard, with panoramic views of Watervale and beyond. Exports to Canada. (JH)

🍷🍷🍷🍷½ **Watervale Riesling 2020, Clare Valley** Marmalade, citrus, galangal and sandalwood. This is savoury, secondary and sort of exotic on the nose, with a cheesecloth/brine palate. Breadth and weight here. The acidity is the highlight, saline and flowing. Screw cap. 12.5% alc. RATING 90 DRINK 2022-2028 $32 EL

Tim Smith Wines

996 Light Pass Road, Vine Vale, SA 5352 **Region** Barossa Valley
T 0416 396 730 **www**.timsmithwines.com.au **Open** By appt **Winemaker** Tim Smith
Est. 2001 **Dozens** 6000 **Vyds** 1ha

After many years working at Barossa producers such as Yalumba, St Hallett, Charles Melton
and Château Tanunda, today Tim Smith plies his vinous craft from his shed in Vine Vale at the
foot of the eastern range of the Barossa Valley. Making wines under his own label since 2002,
it was perhaps Tim's time working harvest for Chapoutier, Gabriel Meffre and Domaine du
Mandeville in France's Rhône valley, that have most strongly shaped where Tim's wines are
today. Intuitive, considered winemaking, a knack for sourcing exceptional grapes from across
the Barossa and an ability to make those wines sing clearly of their place is no mean feat, but
Smith consistently achieves great results, year in, year out. Exports to South Korea, the US, the
UK, Ireland and Denmark. (DB)

ΨΨΨΨΨ **Riesling 2021, Eden Valley** A wonderfully fragrant Eden Valley riesling from
the strong '21 vintage. Classic regional aromas of freshly squeezed lime juice
and Bickfords lime cordial with hints of Christmas lily, frangipani, almond paste
and wet stone. These aromas transpose pitch-perfect on to the crisp, dry palate.
It displays wonderful fruit purity, drive and tension, finishing with a stony, fresh
lime blast and a cleansing, moreish appeal. Such great value. Screw cap. 11.5% alc.
RATING 94 DRINK 2021-2031 $28 DB ☻
Grenache 2020, Barossa Valley Tim Smith gets grenache. Early picked for
natural acidity and a gentle hand in the cellar brings out the variety's spice and
sense of space. Pure, snappy-edged red and dark fruits, cut with spice, ginger cake,
cola and earthy nuance. Bright, light, savoury and effortlessly drinkable. Screw cap.
14.4% alc. RATING 94 DRINK 2021-2028 $42 DB

ΨΨΨΨΨ **Bugalugs Barossa Grenache 2021, Barossa Valley** RATING 93
DRINK 2021-2027 $28 DB
Bugalugs Barossa Shiraz 2020, Barossa Valley RATING 92
DRINK 2021-2027 $28 DB
Viognier 2021, Eden Valley RATING 91 DRINK 2021-2028 $28 DB

Tinklers Vineyard

★★★★☆

Pokolbin Mountains Road, Pokolbin, NSW 2320 **Region** Hunter Valley
T (02) 4998 7435 **www**.tinklers.com.au **Open** 7 days 10–5 **Winemaker** Usher Tinkler
Est. 1946 **Dozens** 7000 **Vyds** 41ha

Three generations of the Tinkler family have been involved with the property since 1942.
Originally a beef and dairy farm, vines have been both pulled out and replanted at various
stages and part of the adjoining 80+yo Ben Ean Vineyard has been acquired. Plantings include
semillon (14ha), shiraz (11.5ha), chardonnay (6.5ha) and smaller areas of merlot, muscat and
viognier. The majority of the grape production is sold to McWilliam's and Tyrrell's. Usher
was chief winemaker at Pooles Rock and Cockfighter's Ghost for over 8 years, before taking
on full-time responsibility at Tinklers. See also Usher Tinkler Wines. Exports to Sweden and
Singapore. (JH)

ΨΨΨΨΨ **School Block Semillon 2021, Hunter Valley** This is a benchmark expression.
A filigreed, cooler vintage. Very good! Gin-and-tonic aromas muddled with
rosemary, thyme and lemongrass. The acidity, juicy. A rail of phenolic pucker, an
augment of complexity. This is a sinuous balancing act of the right degree of
ripeness, immaculate detail and impressive length. A thoroughbred at a bargain
price. Screw cap. 11% alc. RATING 94 DRINK 2021-2029 $25 NG ☻

ΨΨΨΨΨ **Poppys Vineyard Chardonnay 2021, Hunter Valley** RATING 93
DRINK 2021-2029 $40 NG
U and I Shiraz 2019, Hunter Valley RATING 93 DRINK 2021-2029 $60 NG
Hill Chardonnay 2021, Hunter Valley RATING 91 DRINK 2021-2029 $30 NG
Tempranillo Rosé 2021, Hunter Valley RATING 90 DRINK 2021-2022
$25 NG

Tokar Estate

6 Maddens Lane, Coldstream, Vic 3770 **Region** Yarra Valley
T (03) 5964 9585 **www.tokarestate.com.au Open** 7 days 10.30–5 **Winemaker** Martin
Siebert **Est.** 1996 **Dozens** 5000 **Vyds** 12ha
Leon Tokar and wife Rita dreamed of a weekender and hobby farm and it was largely by
chance that in '95 they found a scruffy paddock fronting onto Maddens Lane. By the end of
the day they had signed a contract to buy the property, following in the footsteps of myself
(James) and then wife Suzanne, 10 years earlier when we also signed a contract to purchase
what became Coldstream Hills on the day we first set foot on it (albeit several years after we
first saw it). The Tokars wasted no time and by '99, had planted their 12ha vineyard and built
a Mediterranean-inspired cellar door and restaurant. Martin Siebert has been winemaker for
many years, making consistently good wines and, with son Daniel Tokar as general manager,
has full responsibility for the day-to-day management of the business. Exports to the UK,
Canada and Malaysia. (JH)

ŶŶŶŶŸ **Shiraz 2020, Yarra Valley** A medium crimson purple. Aromas of blackberries,
black peppercorns and fresh licorice with the oak discreetly in the background.
The palate is ripe and quite firm, with an intriguing salted-black-licorice character.
Finishes with some cedar and firm, persistent tannins. Screw cap. 14% alc.
RATING 92 DRINK 2021-2025 $30 PR
Pinot Noir 2020, Yarra Valley Red fruits of all kinds and a hint of
whole-bunch savoury and spicy notes. Screw cap. 13.5% alc. RATING 90
DRINK 2021-2026 $30 JH

ŶŶŶŶ **Carafe & Tumbler Pinot Shiraz 2020, Yarra Valley** RATING 89
DRINK 2021-2026 $30 JH
Cabernet Sauvignon 2020, Yarra Valley RATING 88 DRINK 2022-2027
$30 PR

Tolpuddle Vineyard

37 Back Tea Tree Road, Richmond, Tas, 7025 **Region** Southern Tasmania
T (08) 8155 6003 **www.tolpuddlevineyard.com Winemaker** Adam Wadewitz, Martin
Shaw **Viticulturist** Carlos Souris, Murray Leake **Est.** 1988 **Dozens** 2800 **Vyds** 28ha
If ever a winery was born with blue blood in its veins, Tolpuddle would have to be it. The
vineyard was established in 1988 on a continuous downhill slope facing northeast; in '06
it won the inaugural Tasmanian Vineyard of the Year Award. Michael Hill Smith MW and
Martin Shaw are joint managing directors. David LeMire looks after sales and marketing;
Adam Wadewitz, one of Australia's brightest winemaking talents, is senior winemaker.
Vineyard manager Carlos Souris loses nothing in comparison, with over 30 years of grape
growing in Tasmania under his belt and an absolutely fearless approach to making a great
vineyard even greater. Wines can be tasted at Shaw + Smith in the Adelaide Hills. Exports to
the US, the UK, Canada, Denmark, Japan and Singapore. (JH)

ŶŶŶŶŶ **Chardonnay 2020, Tasmania** The concentration from a small crop contrasts
the tension of this cool site with grand stature and presence. The carefully tuned
gunflint of barrel fermentation backs a core of pure grapefruit and lemon, backed
emphatically with crystalline acidity and the finely textured, creamy structure of
lees age and bâtonnage. Dreamy line and length. Screw cap. 13% alc. RATING 96
DRINK 2021-2030 $93 TS
Pinot Noir 2020, Tasmania Somewhat turbid, though the hue is good after
aeration. The bouquet brings red fruits and a spicy, savoury palate. Very likely
going through a phase, but a question mark on turbidity. Screw cap. 13% alc.
RATING 94 DRINK 2025-2035 $93 JH

Tomboy Hill

204 Sim Street, Ballarat, Vic 3350 (postal) **Region** Ballarat
T (03) 5331 3785 **Winemaker** Scott Ireland, Sam Vogel (Contract) **Est.** 1984
Dozens 500 **Vyds** 3.6ha
Former schoolteacher Ian Watson seems to be following the same path as Lindsay McCall of Paringa Estate (also a former schoolteacher) in extracting greater quality and style than any other winery in their respective regions. Since 1984, Ian has patiently built up a patchwork quilt of small plantings of chardonnay and pinot noir. In the better years, single-vineyard Chardonnay and/or Pinot Noir are released; Rebellion Chardonnay and Pinot Noir are multi-vineyard blends, but all 100% Ballarat. After difficult vintages in '11 and '12, Tomboy Hill has been in top form since '15. (JH)

ŸŸŸŸŸ **MacKenzie's Picking Pinot Noir 2020, Ballarat** Fragrant in cherries, bergamot, mandarin skin and spice, it hosts a supple, concentrated palate. Red cherry flavour is enhanced by shaded autumnal characters delivered clean and fresh, with a shot of brisk acidity. Screw cap. 13% alc. RATING 95 DRINK 2021-2030 $60 JP
The Tomboy Pinot Noir 2020, Ballarat From a very small vintage comes a finely tuned, cool-climate pinot noir that is decidedly plush in woodsy red berries and warm, vanillin oak. Spice plays a significant role, as it curls and spikes its way through the wine. Texture, too, that elicits a full mouthful of flavour. Screw cap. 13% alc. RATING 95 DRINK 2021-2030 $75 JP

Tomich Wines

87 King William Road, Unley, SA 5061 **Region** Adelaide Hills
T (08) 8299 7500 **www**.tomich.com.au **Open** Mon–Fri 9–5 **Winemaker** Randal
Tomich **Viticulturist** Randal Tomich **Est.** 2002 **Dozens** 40 000 **Vyds** 85ha
Patriarch John Tomich was born on a vineyard near Mildura, where he learnt firsthand the skills and knowledge required for premium grape growing. He went on to become a well-known Adelaide ear, nose and throat specialist. Taking the wheel full circle, he completed postgraduate studies in winemaking at the University of Adelaide in 2002 and embarked on the master of wine revision course from the Institute of Masters of Wine. His son Randal is a cutting from the old vine (metaphorically speaking), having invented new equipment and techniques for tending the family's vineyard in the Adelaide Hills, resulting in a 60% saving in time and fuel costs. Exports to Cambodia, the UK, Canada, India and the US. (JH)

ŸŸŸŸŸ **Woodside Vineyard Pinot Grigio 2021, Adelaide Hills** Adelaide Hills grigio is getting a reputation for a charming fineness and a lightness of touch with the grigio grape. It's explored here with an enticing, delicate perfume of spring blossom, honeysuckle, pear skin and freshly baked biscuits. Superfine acidity brings the palate alive. Beautiful brightness and balance. Delightful. Screw cap. 12.5% alc. RATING 94 DRINK 2021-2025 $25 JP ✪

ŸŸŸŸŸ **Woodside Vineyard Sauvignon Blanc 2021, Adelaide Hills** RATING 90 DRINK 2021-2024 $25 JP

Topper's Mountain Wines

13420 Guyra Road, Tingha, NSW 2369 **Region** New England
T 0411 880 580 **www**.toppers.com.au **Open** By appt **Winemaker** Jared Dixon, Glen
Robert **Viticulturist** Mark Kirkby **Est.** 2000 **Dozens** 1200 **Vyds** 9.79ha
Topper's Mountain is named after brothers Edward and William Topper, who were employees of George Jr and Alwyn Wyndham (sons of George Wyndham, founder of Wyndham Estate). They previously owned 'New Valley Station', which included the present day 'Topper's Mountain'. These days, Topper's Mountain is owned by Mark Kirkby. Planting began in the spring of 2000 with the ultimate fruit salad trial of 15 rows each of innumerable varieties and clones. The total area planted was made up of 28 separate plantings, many of these with only 200 vines in a block. As varieties proved unsuitable, they were grafted over to those that

held the most promise. Thus far, gewürztraminer and sauvignon blanc hold most promise among the white wines, the Mediterranean reds doing better than their French cousins. The original 28 varieties are now down to 16; chardonnay, gewürztraminer, sauvignon blanc, tempranillo, shiraz and merlot are the commercial varieties, the remainder in the fruit salad block still under evaluation. In Feb '19 a bushfire destroyed 90% of the vineyard, hours before harvest was due to begin. Exports to the UK, Germany, Singapore and Japan. (JH)

♥♥♥♥♥ Gewürztraminer 2020, New England A stellar achievement in the face of great adversity: bushfires not too far away, and heat. Yet the exotic DNA is firmly intact, with grape spice, rosewater, lychee and cardamom smeared across phenolic rails, chewier perhaps than normal. Consistently one of the finest iterations of this exuberant variety in the country. Screw cap. 13% alc. RATING 93 DRINK 2021-2025 $35 NG

Nebbiolo 2016, New England I have followed the evolution of this cuvée for a time, enjoying the small shifts in style and most of all, the better tannin management and concentration that seem to have come with lower yields and better vineyard supervision. A bit hot, but make no mistake: it IS inimitably nebbiolo. Good nebbiolo, too. Fine scents of campfire, sandalwood, red cherry, mint, bracken and varnish. The tannins, an impressive fibrous spread, spindly and edgy and ripe. The finish, long and pulsating. Released in the right zone, I'd drink this over the earlier to medium term. Screw cap. 15% alc. RATING 93 DRINK 2021-2026 $45 NG

Wild Ferment Touriga & Tintas 2017, New England This is a soulful wine with an intriguing nose: rustic, but with ample charm. Pickled cherry, beet, clove, tobacco leaf, anise, turmeric, mint and tamarind. It makes we want to visit Iberia on my imaginary carpet. I'd be drinking this imminently, although it's certainly not going to crash within the next year or so. A minor gripe, the tannins. While a cool, measured year, I'd like a little more. Screw cap. 13% alc. RATING 92 DRINK 2021-2024 $40 NG

♥♥♥♥ Pinot Noir M.T. Brut Nature Pinot Noir 2016, New England RATING 88 $45 NG

Torbreck Vintners   ★★★★★

348 Roennfeldt Road, Marananga, SA 5352 **Region** Barossa Valley
T (08) 8562 4155 **www**.torbreck.com **Open** 7 days 10–5 by appt **Winemaker** Ian Hongell, Scott McDonald **Viticulturist** Nigel Blieschke **Est.** 1994 **Dozens** 70 000 **Vyds** 112ha
Torbreck Vintners was already one of Australia's best-known producers of high-quality red wine when, in Sept 2013, wealthy Californian entrepreneur and vintner Peter Kight (of Quivira Vineyards) acquired 100% ownership of the business. Talented winemaker Ian Hongell joined the team in '16. Shiraz (and other Rhône varieties) is the focus, led by The Laird, RunRig, The Factor and Descendant. Wines are unfined and unfiltered. Exports to all major markets. (JH)

♥♥♥♥♥ The Laird 2017, Barossa Valley Single-vineyard shiraz. The Spinal Tap effect is in full force here, with everything turned up to eleven. Impenetrable purple red in the glass, showing characters of head-spinning purity and heft; black plum, blackberry and prune notes mesh with shades of deep, exotic spice, Dutch blackstrap licorice, crème de cassis, roasting meats, espresso, graphite, cedar and polished mahogany. Profound fruit depth and purity with melt-in-the-mouth, mineral-edged tannins and a finish that carries long and proud with a solid rush of black plum and cherry compote, spice and chocolate. If you are after a powerful shiraz with finesse, this is your benchmark. Cork. 15.5% alc. RATING 98 DRINK 2026-2046 $800 DB ♥

♥♥♥♥♥ The Factor 2019, Barossa Valley 100% shiraz. Glossy red purple in the glass with characters of ripe satsuma plum and macerated summer berry fruits, Asian five-spice, cedar, licorice and Old Jamaica chocolate. Fruit weight, purity and intensity perfectly on point here, tannins too, fine and long. There just seems to be so much packed into the wine yet everything is in proportion and true. Power with grace. Cork. 15% alc. RATING 96 DRINK 2021–2035 $130 DB

Les Amis Grenache 2019, Barossa Valley Quite open-knit and welcoming; awash with red plum and raspberry fruit notes, cut with exotic spice, gingerbread, sarsaparilla, star anise and earth. A wine of detail, finesse and tension. I often say I'm not a fan of new oak and grenache, and more often than not the Les Amis proves me wrong. It's done it again. Wonderful. Cork. 15% alc. RATING 96 DRINK 2021–2035 $200 DB

RunRig 2019, Barossa Valley Shiraz with 1.5% viognier. Impenetrable purple red in the glass, with layers of dense dark plum and blackberry fruit of considerable purity and heft. Notes of blackforest cake, Old Jamaica chocolate, cedar, turned earth, crème de cassis and kirsch. Big, bold and balanced with a velvety flow, firm fine tannin and long dark finish of warmth and classic Barossan fruit weight. Cork. 15% alc. RATING 96 DRINK 2021–2031 $300 DB

Hillside Vineyard Shiraz Roussanne 2020, Barossa Valley Co-fermentation dialling the colour saturation up to Spinal Tap levels here. Intense and pure black cherry, plum and blackberry fruits are cut with deep spice, licorice and earth. Weighty and concentrated with a toothsome, muscular frame, deep resonant black fruits, assertive fine tannin and simmering latent power on the finish. There's a lot of fruit heft and bang for your buck here. Cork. 15% alc. RATING 95 DRINK 2021–2031 $33 DB ✪

The Gask 2020, Eden Valley Wonderfully bright purple red in the glass with aromas of blood plum, exotic spice, purple flowers, earth, licorice and dark chocolate. It's a beautifully composed, glossy, contemporary take on Eden Valley shiraz, impressive in its fruit purity and detail, fine tannin framework and its inherent drinkability and cellaring potential. Superb balance too, with not a peep from that alcohol content; it's all about fruit and place. Cork. 15% alc. RATING 95 DRINK 2021–2035 $80 DB

Hillside Vineyard Grenache 2019, Barossa Valley Airy and elegant red cherry and red plum characters mesh seamlessly with notes of gingerbread, souk-like spice, red licorice, purple flowers and earth. It sits comfortably at the lighter end of medium bodied, detailed, confident and flagrantly expressive with initially reticent tannins providing gentle support, superb fruit clarity and a balanced, spicy finish that lingers nicely, leaving memories of red plum and spice. Cork. 15% alc. RATING 95 DRINK 2021–2031 $80 DB

The Growers' Cut Shiraz 2019, Barossa Valley I think things have changed a bit at Torbreck in recent years. There was always a distinct thumbprint of house style. That seems less obvious now; place and fruit purity shine through brightly. Here's a good example. Super-ripe, concentrated plum fruits with sub-regional nuance of ironstone, Asian spice and earth; a brightness of line and fine tannic intensity that bodes very well for a long future. A stunner. Screw cap. 15% alc. RATING 95 DRINK 2021–2041 $80 DB

Descendant 2019, Barossa Valley Shiraz co-fermented with 7% viognier. Vibrant purple red, with a gentle layer of apricot and stone fruit sheathing the impressively pure plummy shiraz beneath. Silky, superfine pillowy tannins and a compact, powerful fruit canvas that holds true throughout, showing balance, poise and considerable latent power and cellaring potential. Cork. 15% alc. RATING 94 DRINK 2021–2035 $130 DB

The Steading 2020, Barossa Valley 65/20/15% grenache/shiraz/mataro. A beautifully composed take on the humble GSM blend, with the trademark Torbreck purity, gloss and contemporary swagger. No variety trying to assert its dominance here; all fitting together perfectly for an impressively balanced wine that shows detailed plum and spice notes, fine ripe tannin and a sense of being very comfortable in its own skin. Pour me another glass. Cork. 15% alc. RATING 94 DRINK 2021–2031 $40 DB

The Pict 2019, Barossa Valley Savoury, meaty and layered with exotic spice and black fruits, the Pict represents a Barossa mataro of some serious stature and heft. Dotted with herbal nuance, deep, dark earthy tones, notes of polished leather and bitter chocolate all set against a canvas of ripe, assertive tannin and dark cocoa, and spicy oak. Impressive stuff. Cork. 15% alc. RATING 94 DRINK 2021-2031 $130 DB

Torzi Matthews Vintners

Cnr Eden Valley Road/Sugarloaf Hill Road, Mt McKenzie, SA 5353 **Region** Eden Valley **T** 0412 323 486 **www**.torzimatthews.com.au **Open** By appt **Winemaker** Domenic Torzi **Est.** 1996 **Dozens** 3000 **Vyds** 10ha
Domenic Torzi and Tracy Matthews, former Adelaide Plains residents, searched for a number of years before finding a block at Mount McKenzie in the Eden Valley. The block they chose is in a hollow; the soil is meagre but they were in no way deterred by the knowledge that it would be frost-prone. The result is predictably low yields, concentrated further by drying the grapes on racks, thus reducing the weight by around 30% (the Appassimento method is used in Italy to produce Amarone-style wines). Newer plantings of sangiovese and negroamaro, and an extension of the original plantings of shiraz and riesling, have seen the wine range increase. Exports to the UK and Denmark. (JH)

ΨΨΨΨΨ **Vigna Cantina Prosecco NV, Barossa** Base vintage '21 produced in the Charmat method. Pale straw in the glass with a lively mousse and characters of crunchy green apple, nashi pear, melon and a splash of lime with hints of white flowers, dried herbs, marzipan and soft spice. Clean, crisp and steely with a swift cadence and dry, persistent finish. Cork. 12% alc. RATING 90 $28 DB
Vigna Cantina Negro Amaro 2020, Barossa Valley A wonderfully airy and spacious negroamaro with characters of red plum and cherry, amaro herbs, spice and red flowers. Sports a bright acidity and a sapid, savoury lean. I hate that saying 'food wine' but this will be like another implement at the dinner table. Buon appetito! Screw cap. 14% alc. RATING 90 DRINK 2021-2028 $28 DB
Vigna Cantina Sangiovese 2020, Barossa Valley I'm a fan of Dom Torzi's Vigna Cantina wines focussing on Italian grape varieties for their detailed and spacious palate shapes. Coming from good Calabrian bloodstock, I trust him in such matters. Airy and zesty with bright red fruits, just the right amount of amaro herbs and spice, and a brisk cadence on the finish. Screw cap. 14% alc. RATING 90 DRINK 2021-2026 $28 DB

ΨΨΨΨ **Schist Rock Single Vineyard Shiraz 2021, Eden Valley** RATING 89 DRINK 2021-2028 $28 DB
Francesca Grillo Collina Calcarea Syrah 2021, Barossa RATING 88 DRINK 2021-2024 $38 DB

Totino Estate

982 Port Road, Albert Park, SA 5014 (postal) **Region** Adelaide Hills
T (08) 8349 1200 **www**.totinowines.com.au **Winemaker** Don Totino, Damien Harris **Est.** 1992 **Dozens** 15 000 **Vyds** 29ha
Don Totino migrated from Italy in 1968, and at the age of 18 became the youngest barber in Australia. He soon moved on, into general food and importing and distribution. Festival City, as the business is known, has been highly successful, recognised by a recent significant award from the Italian government. In '98 he purchased a rundown vineyard at Paracombe in the Adelaide Hills, since extending the plantings to 29ha of chardonnay, pinot grigio, sauvignon blanc, sangiovese and shiraz. Various family members, including daughter Linda, are involved in the business. Exports to Italy. (JH)

ΨΨΨΨ **Francesco Riserva Shiraz 2018, Adelaide Hills** Super generous across the board, in fruit intensity, oak contribution and tannin deployment. A little overwrought in what the Hills usually delivers ripeness-wise, in bold black-fruit aromas with stewed plums, dark chocolate, heavy woodsy spices and cedary, toasty oak. Meaty and complex on the palate, dense and ripe in muscular tannins and chocolatey, spiced oak, it delivers some punch on the palate. Cork. 14.9% alc. RATING 89 DRINK 2022-2034 JP

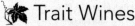 # Trait Wines

256 Carters Road, Burnside, WA 6285 (postal) **Region** Margaret River
T 0438 808 678 **www**.traitwines.com **Winemaker** Theo Truyts **Viticulturist** Theo
Truyts **Est.** 2019 **Dozens** 500 **Vyds** 2.7ha

Vigneron Theo Truyts (originally from Lesotho in Southern Africa) and his wife Clare
Trythall (born in Japan to English and Welsh parents, grew up in Singapore and went on to
become an ER doctor) purchased their Margaret River vineyard in 2019 (planted in 1988).
After grafting a substantial block of sauvignon blanc to chardonnay, the majority of the
vineyard is now chardonnay (100% Gingin clone) with the remainder made up of sauvignon
blanc, semillon and chenin. The key wines in their first release were a chardonnay and a white
field blend. They also source chenin blanc and grenache from bush vines in Geographe. (EL)

Chardonnay 2020, Margaret River Creamy and nutty and exuding aromas
of nougat, marzipan and vanilla pod. In the mouth the wine is enveloping and
cushioned … marvellous and plump and beautiful. The acidity, although high
(thanks to the clone) is juicy and gives a chewy aspect to the wine which is most
welcome. A brilliant first release. Screw cap. 13% alc. RATING 95 DRINK 2022-2032
$89 EL

Grenache 2021, Geographe Very pale in colour, delicate summer strawberries,
pastrami, petrichor, briny acidity and a creaminess threaded into the finish. The
acidity is salty and bright. 5 barrels, unfined and unfiltered. Screw cap. 12.5% alc.
RATING 94 DRINK 2021-2029 $39 EL

Chenin Blanc 2021, Margaret River RATING 91 DRINK 2021-2031 $33 EL
Sauvignon Blanc 2021, Margaret River RATING 90 DRINK 2022-2028
$33 EL

Trentham Estate

6531 Sturt Highway, Trentham Cliffs, NSW 2738 **Region** Murray Darling
T (03) 5024 8888 **www**.trenthamestate.com.au **Open** 7 days 10–5 **Winemaker** Anthony
Murphy, Shane Kerr, Kerry Morrison **Est.** 1988 **Dozens** 60 000 **Vyds** 38.66ha

Remarkably consistent tasting notes across all wine styles from all vintages attest to the
expertise of ex-Mildara winemaker Tony Murphy, a well-known and highly regarded
producer. The estate vineyards are on the Murray Darling. With an eye to the future, but also
to broadening the range of the wines on offer, Trentham Estate is selectively buying grapes
from other regions with a track record for the chosen varieties. In 2018 Trentham Estate
celebrated its 30th anniversary. Exports to the UK, Belgium, Sweden and Japan. (JH)

Cellar Reserve Verdejo 2021, Murray Darling Yet another convincing
example of a new variety to the Murray Darling, destined for big things. Youthful
green-yellow hue with a delightful bunch of spring flowers and honeysuckle-led
perfume, with citrus and spice. The palate is crisp and even, nicely fleshed out
through the middle with a bright acid crunch. Screw cap. 12.5% alc. RATING 90
DRINK 2022-2025 $28 JP

The Family Vermentino 2021 Murray Darling Vermentino is a natural grape
choice in the Murray Darling, holding its acidity in the warmth while delivering
a quality wine. This is an excellent example. Tahitian lime, grapefruit and green-
apple brightness on the bouquet – quite summery and fresh. Keeps to the theme
on the palate, with an added touch of almond. So crisp and fresh. Delightful!
12.5% alc. RATING 90 DRINK 2021–2024 $18 JP

Reserve Shiraz 2018, Heathcote Exudes Heathcote ripeness and signature
red fruits, blueberries and plummy fruits running long over a supple palate. Fine
spices, licorice and chocolate mix with a well-placed layer of toasty oak on the
palate, bringing everything together rather nicely. Screw cap. 14.5% alc. RATING 90
DRINK 2021-2026 $28 JP

Estate Noble Taminga 2015, Murray Darling Trentham Estate has been
a firm believer in the taminga grape, created for Australian conditions by the

CSIRO, with one parent being gewürztraminer. Gewürz certainly pops its floral and spicy head up in this botrytised sweetie, with its distinctly lantana, potpourri florals and lychee lifted aromatics. Honeyed spice and ginger play on the sweet palate, which is nicely balanced by crisp acidity. 375ml. Screw cap. 10.5% alc. RATING 90 DRINK 2022–2025 $18 JP ✪

⛊⛊⛊⛊ The Family Sangiovese Rosé 2021, Murray Darling RATING 88
DRINK 2021–2022 $18 NG
Estate Shiraz 2020, Murray Darling RATING 88 DRINK 2021–2025 $18 JP
Reserve Cabernet Sauvignon 2019, Coonawarra RATING 88
DRINK 2021–2026 $28 JP

Trevelen Farm

506 Weir Road, Cranbrook, WA 6321 **Region** Great Southern
T 0418 361 052 **www**.trevelenfarm.com.au **Open** 7 days 10–4.30 **Winemaker** James Kellie **Est.** 1993 **Dozens** 3000 **Vyds** 6.5ha
In 2008 John and Katie Sprigg decided to pass ownership of their 1300ha wool, meat and grain producing farm to son Ben and wife Louise. However, they have kept control of the 6.5ha of sauvignon blanc, riesling, chardonnay, cabernet sauvignon and merlot planted in 1993. When demand requires, they increase production by purchasing grapes from growers in Frankland River. Riesling remains the centrepiece of the range. Exports to the US. (JH)

⛊⛊⛊⛊⛊ Estate Riesling 2021, Great Southern Citrus pith, chalk and plenty of green apple skins. This is fine and firm and taut, with plenty of flavour on the mid palate to offer pleasurable drinking in the short term. Screw cap. 12% alc. RATING 90 DRINK 2022–2029 $25 EL
Estate Aged Release Riesling 2012, Great Southern Getting on in age and colour, this has a golden hue, and is imbued with honeysuckle, passionfruit, cheesecloth and lemon curd. Aged riesling is a marvel, however this, while lovely, tails out over the finish to a very quiet close. Perhaps lacking the fruit volume to see it out over the years, but there are some gorgeous aged characters that absolutely redeem it and bring joy: lanolin, Geraldton wax florals and gentle incense spice. Screw cap. 12% alc. RATING 90 DRINK 2022–2025 $60 EL
Estate Aged Release Riesling 2006, Great Southern Dehydrated grapefruit, cheesecloth, a touch of kerosene, white pepper and a distinct dough character. Plenty of toast and grapefruit the mouth. This is round and soft and full, tailing out to a moderate finish. The consistency of flavour on the palate is a highlight. Screw cap. 11% alc. RATING 90 DRINK 2022–2026 $60 EL

Trifon Estate Wines

PO Box 258, Murchison, Vic 3610 **Region** Central Victoria
T (03) 9432 9811 **www**.trifonestatewines.com.au **Winemaker** Glenn Eberbach, Amelie Mornex **Viticulturist** Sam Gallo, Ben Rose (consultant) **Est.** 1998 **Dozens** 90 000
Vyds 312ha
Trifon Estate has flown under the radar since it was established in 1998. Since that time 312ha of vines have been planted to 16 varieties, the lion's share to shiraz (83.26ha), cabernet sauvignon (47.93), merlot (42.74), chardonnay (38.79ha) and sauvignon blanc (23.76ha). Exports to Hong Kong, Taiwan, Japan, South Korea, the US and the UK. (JH)

⛊⛊⛊⛊⛊ Lagoon View Museum Release Semillon 2012, Central Victoria A bottle-aged semillon is a rarity in these parts, but as it hits 10 years old, this semillon – with a touch of off-dry sweetness (7.5g/L) – sings. Lemon butter, toast, barley sugar, lime rind and lemon balm make an immediate impact aroma-wise. Light on its feet, it combines a warm texture with bright, lively acidity, all the while, bottle-aged characters maintain a complex hold on the palate. Delicious. Screw cap. 12.5% alc. RATING 92 DRINK 2022–2025 $25 JP ✪

🍷🍷🍷🍷 **Humble Vine Cabernet Sauvignon 2018, Central Victoria** RATING 88
DRINK 2022-2025 $22 JP
Humble Vine Chardonnay 2018, Central Victoria RATING 88
DRINK 2022-2024 $22 JP

tripe.Iscariot   ★★★★★

20 McDowell Road, Witchcliffe, WA 6286 **Region** Margaret River
T 0414 817 808 **www**.tripeiscariot.com **Winemaker** Remi Guise **Est.** 2013
Dozens 800

This has to be the most way-out winery name of the century. It prompted me (James) to email South African–born and trained winemaker Remi Guise asking to explain its derivation. He courteously responded with a reference to Judas as 'the greatest black sheep of all time', and a non-specific explanation of 'tripe' as 'challenging in style'. He added, 'I hope this sheds some light, or dark, on the brand'. The wines provide a better answer, managing to successfully harness highly unusual techniques at various points of their elevage. His day job as winemaker at Naturaliste Vintners, the large Margaret River contract winemaking venture of Bruce Dukes, provides the technical grounding, allowing him to throw the 'how to' manual out of the window when the urge arises. His final words on his Marrow Syrah Malbec are: 'So, suck the marrow from the bone, fry the fat, and savour the warm, wobbly bits'. (JH)

🍷🍷🍷🍷🍷 **Absolution Wilyabrup Chenin Blanc 2020, Margaret River** The Absolution chenins are all made in the same fashion, but from different growing areas. This is the roundest and most obvious of the 3 chenins, but it is, at this stage, the most pleasurable. Apricots, tangelos, green apples and lemons. This has chalky phenolics that shape and caress the fruit, with a swathe of exotic spice through the finish. Drink it in a couple of years and your pleasure will be amplified. Screw cap. 12.5% alc. RATING 95 DRINK 2022-2036 $32 EL ✪
Brawn Chardonnay 2020, Margaret River I'm not alone in struggling with Remi Guise's winery name nor that of this wine, which is elegant almost to the point of delicate – except, that is, for the length and persistence of its stone and citrus fruits, length without even a scintilla of extraction. Screw cap. 12.8% alc. RATING 95 DRINK 2021-2029 $42 JH
Absolution Karridale Chenin Blanc 2020, Margaret River Scintillating acidity swarms around the green apples, nutmeg, brine, apricots and citrus pith. The wine shows its absolute best after a few years in bottle. If you can bear to hang onto some for at least 3 years, you won't regret it. Screw cap. 12% alc. RATING 94 DRINK 2022-2036 $32 EL
Aspic Grenache Rosé 2020, Margaret River Brilliant intensity of flavour in the mouth. This is staunch, intense, structured and long. There is the classic acid line that we have come to expect from Remi Guise, and it punctuates voluminous fruit that billows in the mouth. Cheesecloth and berries though the finish. Staunch and impressive. Screw cap. 13% alc. RATING 94 DRINK 2021-2025 $32 EL
Kroos Chenin Blanc 2019, Margaret River The Kroos sees no skin time, unlike the Absolution chenins. The vineyard canopy is managed differently as well – more leaves retained to minimise light throughout the season, impacting acidity and aromatics. As we have come to expect from Guise, the acidity is pronounced, and due to the oak, one must wait for the finish or aftertaste in order to experience the chenin spice and texture. This takes a long time, because the wine itself is very long. A thought-provoking wine indeed. I want to see this in 5 years. Screw cap. 12.8% alc. RATING 94 DRINK 2021-2036 $45 EL

Trofeo Estate   ★★★★★

85 Harrisons Road, Dromana, Vic 3936 **Region** Mornington Peninsula
T (03) 5981 8688 **www**.trofeoestate.com **Open** 7 days 10–5 **Winemaker** Richard Darby
Est. 2012 **Dozens** 7500 **Vyds** 18.5ha

This property has had a chequered history. In the 1930s Passiflora Plantations Company was set up to become Australia's leading exporter of passionfruit and associated products.

By '37, 120ha was covered with 70000 passionfruit vines and a processing factory was in operation. The following year a disease devastated the passionfruit and the company went into receivership. In '48 a member of the Seppelt family planted a vineyard on the exact site of Trofeo Estate and it was thereafter acquired by leading Melbourne wine retailer and wine judge, the late Doug Seabrook, who maintained the vineyard and made the wine until the vines were destroyed in a bushfire in '67. In '98 it was replanted but passed through several hands and fell into and out of neglect until the latest owner, Jim Manolios, developed the property as a restaurant, vineyard and winery with pinot noir (8.2ha), chardonnay (5ha), shiraz (2.5ha), pinot gris (1.6ha) and cabernet sauvignon (1.2ha). All Trofeo Estate wines are matured in terracotta amphorae, imported from Chianti, Italy. (JH)

ŸŸŸŸŸ **Aged in Terracotta Shiraz 2019, Mornington Peninsula** This comes dripping in dark fruits and spice with an attractive meaty reduction adding to the savoury profile. Full-bodied, juicy and tangy with fine sandpaper tannins creating more texture. A very good Peninsula shiraz. Screw cap. 14% alc. RATING 95 DRINK 2022-2029 $34 JF ✪

The Chosen Few Aged In Terracotta Amphorae Shiraz 2019, Mornington Peninsula The outstanding dark purple hue really sets the scene. Enchanting aromas of florals, plums and baking spices, earthy and savoury with some grit to the tannins but well placed with a slight green edge to the finish. Medium-bodied, finely tuned and always a captivating wine. Cork. 13.7% alc. RATING 95 DRINK 2022-2028 $58 JF

ŸŸŸŸŸ **Aged In Terracotta Amphorae Single Block Pinot Noir 2020, Mornington Peninsula** RATING 93 DRINK 2022-2026 $49 JF

The Chosen Few Aged In Terracotta Amphorae Pinot Noir 2020, Mornington Peninsula RATING 93 DRINK 2022-2026 $58 JF

Aged in Terracotta Amphorae Rosé 2021, Mornington Peninsula RATING 92 DRINK 2022-2024 $28 JF

Aged in Terracotta Amphorae Cabernet Sauvignon 2019, Mornington Peninsula RATING 92 DRINK 2022-2025 $39 JF

Blanc de Noir 2017, Mornington Peninsula RATING 92 DRINK 2022-2024 $45 JF

Aged in Terracotta Amphorae Pinot Noir 2020, Mornington Peninsula RATING 91 DRINK 2022-2026 $36 JF

The Chosen Few Aged In Terracotta Amphorae Cabernet Sauvignon 2019, Mornington Peninsula RATING 90 DRINK 2022-2025 $46 JF

Tumblong Hills ★★★★

1149 Old Hume Highway, Gundagai, NSW 2722 **Region** Gundagai
T 0401 622 808 **www.**tumblonghills.com **Open** Thurs–Sun 11–4 **Winemaker** Simon Robertson **Viticulturist** Simon Robertson **Est.** 2009 **Dozens** 10000 **Vyds** 200ha
This large vineyard was established by Southcorp Wines in the '90s, as part of 'Project Max', an initiative to honour Max Schubert of Penfolds Grange fame. It was acquired in '09 by business partners Danny Gilbert, Peter Leonard and Peter Waters. They were able to secure the services of viticulturist and general manager Simon Robertson, who knew the vineyard like the back of his hand, his experience stretching across the wine regions of Southern New South Wales. In '11, investors Wang Junfeng and Handel Lee came onboard. While shiraz and cabernet sauvignon remain the 2 most significant varieties, nebbiolo, barbera, sangiovese and fiano are increasingly important. (JH)

ŸŸŸŸŸ **Table of Plenty Fiano 2021, Gundagai** Honeysuckle, stone fruit and Mediterranean herbs offer varietal context. The palate soft and giving with texture in the mix and lemon sherbet acidity keeping it fresh and lively. Screw cap. 12.5% alc. RATING 90 DRINK 2022-2023 $19 JF ✪

Table of Plenty Nebbiolo Rosé 2021, Gundagai A light copper blush sets the scene. Strawberries, blood orange and raspberry-like acidity with a slip of texture add to the appeal. Screw cap. 13.5% alc. RATING 90 DRINK 2022-2023 $19 JF ✪

Chardonnay 2021, Tumbarumba A clear-cut case for immediate drinkability. It's tight, light and bright, with its lemon flavouring and racy acidity. What it lacks in complexity, it makes up with energy, drive and guaranteed refreshment. Screw cap. 12.4% alc. RATING 90 DRINK 2023-2026 $29 JF

J Block Cuvée 2019, Gundagai A vibrant dark red, purple-tinged hue. Aromas of lavender, warm earth and baking spices, while the fuller-bodied palate is infused with very ripe sweet fruit, licorice and cedary oak. Tannins are plush and it's accessible now – best drunk in the short term. Definitely a party pleaser. Screw cap. 14.5% alc. RATING 90 DRINK 2021-2025 $32 JF

🍷🍷🍷🍷 **Chenin Blanc 2021, Gundagai** RATING 89 DRINK 2022-2023 $27 JF
Track Winding Back Shiraz 2019, Gundagai RATING 89 DRINK 2022-2025 $22 JF
Shiraz 2019, Gundagai RATING 89 DRINK 2022-2025 $27 JF

Turkey Flat ★★★★★

67 Bethany Road, Tanunda, SA 5352 **Region** Barossa Valley
T (08) 8563 2851 **www.turkeyflat.com.au Open** 7 days 11–5 **Winemaker** Mark Bulman
Est. 1990 **Dozens** 20000 **Vyds** 47.83ha
The establishment date of Turkey Flat is given as 1990 but it might equally have been 1870 (or thereabouts), when the Schulz family purchased the Turkey Flat Vineyard; or 1847, when the vineyard was first planted – to the very old shiraz that still grows there today and the 8ha of equally old grenache. Plantings have since expanded significantly, now comprising shiraz (24ha), grenache (10.5ha), cabernet sauvignon (5.9ha), mourvèdre (3.7ha) and smaller plantings of marsanne, viognier and dolcetto. The business is run by sole proprietor Christie Schulz. Exports to the UK, the US and other major markets. (JH)

🍷🍷🍷🍷🍷 **Grenache 2020, Barossa Valley** For this price, it's astounding that the lion's share of the grenache in this wine hails from 100+yo estate-grown vines; we are indeed a lucky country. A vibrant red-fruited aromatic blast with hints of ginger cake, cola, exotic spice, purple flowers and light Turkish delight lift. Juicy and pure, yet with a stony, savoury lean on the finish. Consistently delightful drinking and a regional classic. Screw cap. 14.1% alc. RATING 95 DRINK 2021-2028 $45 DB

Butchers Block Shiraz 2020, Barossa Valley Fragrant and lifted ripe plum and dark berry fruits with hints of exotic spice, violets, chocolate and underlying wafts of roasting meats, pressed flowers and light amaro herbs. The addition of a small amount of whole bunches to the ferment seems to open the wine up and let a little more light in, along with spice and textural elements. Pure of fruit with long, sandy tannins and a juicy finish, the Butchers Block provides excellent value and delicious drinking. Screw cap. 14.1% alc. RATING 94 DRINK 2021-2026 $25 DB ✪

🍷🍷🍷🍷 **Rosé 2021, Barossa Valley** RATING 92 DRINK 2021-2024 $25 DB ✪

Turners Crossing Vineyard ★★★★

747 Old Bridgewater-Serpentine Road, Serpentine, Vic 3517 **Region** Bendigo
T 0427 843 528 **www.turnerscrossing.com.au Winemaker** Adam Marks, Rob Ellis, Cameron Leith **Est.** 1999 **Dozens** 4000 **Vyds** 42ha
This outstanding, mature vineyard was named to remember the original landholder, Thomas Turner. During the 1800s, farmers and gold rush prospectors crossed the Loddon River beside the property, at what became known as Turners Crossing. During the Gold Rush period European settlers in the area started to plant vineyards, trusting that Bendigo's terroir would reveal itself as a suitable site on which to grow grapes. And they were right to be so confident. Its alluvial composition of rich limestone soils and Mediterranean climate make it a happy home for viticulture in particular. Turners Crossing Vineyard now spans 42ha of mature vines. The vineyard is virtually pesticide and chemical free; warm days and cool nights allow the grapes to ripen during the day and the vines to recover overnight. The vineyard bears shiraz, cabernet sauvignon, viognier and picolit (a rare white Italian variety). Exports to the UK, Canada and Vietnam. (JH)

ỶỶỶỶỢ **The Crossing Shiraz 2019, Bendigo** The Crossing style is now established. It's a vehicle for Bendigo shiraz in all of its well-built, oak-framed, deep dark-berried, earthy intensity, with a display of local Aussie bush, bay leaf and eucalyptus. In other words, it's pretty chock-full of goodness. Diam. 14.9% alc. RATING 91 DRINK 2021-2035 $60 JP

Shiraz Viognier 2019, Bendigo Rob Ellis does a mighty job exploring the beauty of the blend with a wine of elegance and depth. Hosts a beautiful purple hue and fragrance, with lifted floral aromatics courtesy of the viognier and shiraz-led spicy lift with summer berries. A fully energised wine, fresh in plum flavours, bay leaf and spice complexity and fine tannins. Screw cap. 14.5% alc. RATING 90 DRINK 2021-2026 $25 JP

ỶỶỶỶ **Picolit 2019, Bendigo** RATING 89 DRINK 2021-2024 $50 JP

Turon Wines

1760 Lobethal Road, Lobethal, SA 5241 **Region** Adelaide Hills
T 0423 956 480 **www**.turonwines.com.au **Open** By appt **Winemaker** Turon White
Est. 2013 **Dozens** 800 **Vyds** 2ha
This is the venture of husband-and-wife team Turon and Alex White. Turon realised the potential of the ever varying site climates within the Adelaide Hills. His overseas winemaking experience while completing his degree was appropriately lateral, with vintage winemaking at Argyle in Oregon and at Kovács Nimród in Eger, Hungary. Out of this has come a minimal-intervention approach to winemaking. Selecting the right site, soil and meso climate within the region is crucial in allowing the wines to reach their full potential. That said, experimentation of method is also of prime importance in understanding the potential of terroir and variety. They have built a winery at their property in Lenswood and turned it into a co-operative winery from the outset, where young winemakers can work together, sharing equipment, resources and knowledge. As it is, it was one of the top new wineries in the Wine Companion 2019. (JH)

ỶỶỶỶỢ **Artist Series Chardonnay 2021, Lenswood** So juicy and lively, just what you expect from a young Adelaide Hills chardonnay which has been given full rein to express its fruit quality with some masterful oak handling playing a support role. Impressive poise, too. Citrus to the fore, with Delicious apple, nashi pear, white nectarine and a savoury touch of almond kernel, finely structured with good acid line and length. Delicious. Screw cap. 13.5% alc. RATING 92 DRINK 2022-2026 $32 JP

Artist Series Balhannah Syrah 2020, Adelaide Hills A spice-laden array of dark berry fruits, lifted florals, licorice and cassia bark. Palate is bright and elegant, held firmly in place by fine, even tannins. Excellent drinking now and with so much potential for further ageing. Screw cap. 13.9% alc. RATING 91 DRINK 2022-2029 $32 JP

Artist Series Field Blend 2021, Adelaide Hills A blend of sauvignon blanc, pinot blanc and riesling. A different field blend mix to the previous release, with only sauvignon blanc remaining a constant. It tends to take over on the bouquet with its exuberant grassy, gooseberry and passionfruit notes, but its friends hold more sway on the palate, producing lively citrus, nashi pear notes with an attractive creaminess. Screw cap. 12.5% alc. RATING 90 DRINK 2022-2024 $25 JP

Artist Series Rosé 2021, Adelaide Hills Pinot meunier is highly underrated as the basis of a rosé, as this expressive little charmer shows. So lively in summer-pudding berries and brambly fruits, with ruby grapefruit citrusy acidity bringing some crunch and brightness. Screw cap. 11.8% alc. RATING 90 DRINK 2022-2024 $25 JP

ỶỶỶỶ **Artist Series Blanc de Noirs 2021, Adelaide Hills** RATING 88 $32 JP
Artist Series Pinot Noir 2021, Lenswood RATING 88 DRINK 2022-2026 $32 JP

Twinwoods Estate

Brockman Road, Cowaramup, WA 6284 **Region** Margaret River
T 0419 833 122 **www**.twinwoodsestate.com **Winemaker** Deep Woods Estate (Julian
Langworthy), Aldo Bratovic **Est.** 2005 **Dozens** 2500 **Vyds** 8.5ha
This is a winery that was bound to succeed. It is owned by the Jebsen family, for many years
a major player in the importation and distribution of fine wine in Hong Kong, more recently
expanded into China. Jebsen invested in a NZ winery, following that with the acquisition of
this vineyard in Margaret River in 2005. It brings together senior Jebsen managing director
Gavin Jones, and peripatetic winemaker Aldo Bratovic, who began his career decades ago
under the tutelage of Brian Croser. The quality of the wines I (James) have tasted fully lives up
to what one would expect. (I tasted the wines without any knowledge of the background of
Twinwoods.) Exports to Denmark, Germany, Singapore, Taiwan, Hong Kong and NZ. (JH)

** TTTT Chardonnay 2019, Margaret River** Creamy, nutty, and mostly restrained
chardonnay here. The steel shavings through the finish make for minerally
impressions, otherwise the density of the Margaret River fruit is on show. Screw
cap. 13% alc. RATING 89 DRINK 2021-2027 $25 EL

Two Hands Wines

273 Neldner Road, Marananga, SA 5355 **Region** Barossa Valley
T (08) 8562 4566 **www**.twohandswines.com **Open** 7 days 11–5 **Winemaker** Richard
Langford **Viticulturist** Travis Coombe **Est.** 1999 **Dozens** 55 000 **Vyds** 40ha
The 'hands' in question were originally those of founders Michael Twelftree and Richard
Mintz, Michael in particular having extensive experience in marketing Australian wine in the
US (for other producers). Grapes are sourced from the Barossa Valley (where the business has
40ha of shiraz), McLaren Vale, Clare Valley, Eden Valley, the Adelaide Hills and Heathcote. The
emphasis is on sweet fruit and soft tannin structure, all signifying the precise marketing strategy
of what is a very successful business. In '15, Two Hands embarked on an extensive planting
programme using vines propagated from a number of vineyards (including Prouse Eden Valley,
Wendouree 1893, Kaelser Alte Reben, Penfolds Modbury, Kays Block 6, Kalimna 3C), as well
as a high-density 1.4ha clos (a walled vineyard) with bush vines trained to stakes, known as
echalas, in the style of terraced vineyards in the Northern Rhône Valley. Exports to all major
markets. (JH)

TTTTT Bella's Garden Shiraz 2020, Barossa Valley Two Hands' Garden Series sees
them embark on a regional road-trip around 5 famous Australian wine regions
before they settle back to their home turf of the Barossa Valley with the Bella's
Garden. Like their McLaren Vale release it's a 'best of' the famous subregions, with
many familiar names. Fragrant, plush and supple with a distinct contemporary feel,
it's an excellent example of a modern Barossa style that will please many drinkers.
Diam. 14.2% alc. RATING 94 DRINK 2021-2031 $65 DB
Charlie's Garden Shiraz 2020, Eden Valley The Garden Series provides
a deep dive into regionality in Australia and the Charlie's Garden, way up on
Mengler's Hill, has always been a firm favourite. Red and dark berry fruits are set
against a spicy frame that is flecked with violets and purple floral facets. There's a
keen sense of space and savoury sway here, with a lovely Eden Valley acidity and
cadence driving the fruit forwards. Diam. 14.2% alc. RATING 94 DRINK 2021-2031
$65 DB
Samantha's Garden Shiraz 2020, Clare Valley The Samantha's Garden
represents a snapshot of Clare Valley shiraz in the regional context of their Garden
Series of wines. It's a pretty-smelling little thing. Blackberry and satsuma plum fruit
for sure, but there's a violet sheen to its aromas and a meaty facet that draws the
drinker in. The fruit weight is impressive, as is the wine's detail and tannin profile,
muscling up on the finish with compact tannin heft. Diam. 14.4% alc. RATING 94
DRINK 2021-2031 $65 DB

ᵀᵀᵀᵀᵀ Lily's Garden Shiraz 2020, McLaren Vale RATING 93 DRINK 2021-2030
$65 DB
Max's Garden Shiraz 2020, Heathcote RATING 93 DRINK 2021-2030
$65 DB
Angels' Share Shiraz 2021, McLaren Vale RATING 92 DRINK 2021-2031
$32 DB
Brave Faces Grenache Mourvèdre Shiraz 2021, Barossa Valley
RATING 92 DRINK 2021-2027 $32 DB
Gnarly Dudes Shiraz 2021, Barossa Valley RATING 92 DRINK 2021-2030
$32 DB
Harriet's Garden Shiraz 2020, Adelaide Hills RATING 92 DRINK 2021-2030
$65 DB

2 Mates
160 Main Road, McLaren Vale, SA 5171 **Region** McLaren Vale
T 0411 111 198 **www.**2mates.com.au **Winemaker** Mark Venable, David Minear
Viticulturist Ben Glaetzer **Est.** 2005 **Dozens** 250 **Vyds** 20ha
The 2 mates are Mark Venable and David Minear, who say, 'Over a big drink in a small bar in
Italy a few years back, we talked about making "our perfect Australian shiraz". When we got
back, we decided to have a go.' The wine ('05) was duly made and won a silver medal at the
Decanter World Wine Awards in London, in some exalted company. Eleven years on, they hit
the rarefied heights of 97 points for their $35 The Perfect Ten Shiraz 2016. (JH)

ᵀᵀᵀᵀᵀ The Next Level Shiraz 2020, McLaren Vale If you are after a rich, hedonistic
shiraz that somehow remains fresh despite its decadence, here is your ticket. Palate-
staining dark fruits, a vinous carriage of pepper, licorice and clove, a swathe of
salty freshness and a bristle of firmly applied mocha oak tannins. There is nothing
innovative here. Just a tried-and-true approach to making what is for many
drinkers a classic, full-bodied regional expression. Screw cap. 14.9% alc. RATING 92
DRINK 2022-2035 $35 NG

Two Rivers
2 Yarrawa Road, Denman, NSW 2328 **Region** Hunter Valley
T (02) 6547 2556 **www.**tworivers.com.au **Open** 7 days 11–4 **Winemaker** Liz Silkman
Viticulturist Brett Keeping **Est.** 1988 **Dozens** 10 000 **Vyds** 67.5ha
Two Rivers has long been a staple of the Upper Hunter Valley landscape. In recent times,
under winemaker Liz Silkman, a slick suite of wines has been crafted, nurtured stylistically
over several vintages. Ownership of the brand shifted – from the Tullochs, to a collaborative
partnership between Ross Crump, along with Colin Peterson of the eponymous Petersons
wine label – just in time for the 2022 vintage. It is envisaged that the Denman vineyard
and abutting cellar-door facility will remain, while premium red wine production will be
increased to leverage a second cellar door in Pokolbin. Farming is conventional yet the style is
one that reaps a plump approachability from regional staples, including lees-inflected semillon,
tropical-accented chardonnay and nourishing shiraz with a whiff of reductive polish. (NG)

ᵀᵀᵀᵀᵀ Museum Release Stone's Throw Semillon 2018, Hunter Valley Barley
sugar, tonic, citrus balm … the usual. What makes this wine impressive is just how
detailed the structural latticework is, juxtaposed against the teeming intensity of
fruit. The finish, long and racy. Lemon lozenge, apricot and quince, emerging from
the density. This casts an optimistic veil across a long future. Screw cap. 11% alc.
RATING 95 DRINK 2022-2032 $50 NG
Yarrawa Road Chardonnay 2021, Hunter Valley A wine of impressive
poise, intensity and restraint, subdued by classy oak. A vibrato of brassy stone
fruits, toasted nuts and nougat, shimmering behind the veneer. The length, very
impressive. The Hunter penchant for ripe fruit and concentration, beautifully
articulated. An impressive wine with a bright future across the mid term. Screw
cap. 13% alc. RATING 94 DRINK 2021-2028 $50 NG

🍷🍷🍷🍷🍷 Stone's Throw Semillon 2019, Hunter Valley RATING 93 DRINK 2021-2031
$50 NG
Museum Release Stone's Throw Semillon 2017, Hunter Valley RATING 93
DRINK 2021-2026 $50 NG
Vigneron's Reserve Chardonnay 2021, Hunter Valley RATING 90
DRINK 2021-2026 $30 NG

Tyrrell's Wines   ★★★★★

1838 Broke Road, Pokolbin, NSW 2321 **Region** Hunter Valley
T (02) 4993 7000 **www**.tyrrells.com.au **Open** Mon–Sun 9–4 by appt
Winemaker Andrew Spinaze, Mark Richardson, Chris Tyrrell **Viticulturist** Andrew
Pengilly **Est.** 1858 **Dozens** 220 000 **Vyds** 364ha
One of the most successful family wineries, a humble operation for the first 110 years of its
life that has grown out of all recognition over the past 40 years. Vat 1 Semillon is one of
the most dominant wines in the Australian show system and Vat 47 Chardonnay is one of the
pacesetters for this variety. Tyrrell's has an awesome portfolio of single-vineyard semillons
released when 5–6 years old. Its estate plantings include over 100ha in the Hunter Valley and
26ha in Heathcote. In Dec '17 Tyrrell's purchased the 13.5ha Stevens Old Hillside Vineyard
on Marrowbone Road; 6.11ha are planted to shiraz, including a 1.1ha block planted in 1867,
the balance planted in 1963, notably to shiraz and semillon. There are 11 blocks of vines older
than 100 years in the Hunter Valley and the Tyrrell family owns 7 of those blocks. A founding
member of Australia's First Families of Wine. Exports to all major markets. (JH)

🍷🍷🍷🍷🍷 Single Vineyard Stevens Shiraz 2018, Hunter Valley The regional magic
allows the power of this great shiraz to come from 13.5% alc. and neutral oak.
It's Hunter Valley to its bootlaces, with decades to come, a steal in these days
of $300+ wines coming from everywhere. Screw cap. 13.5% alc. RATING 97
DRINK 2023-2058 $50 JH ✪
Single Vineyard Belford Semillon 2017, Hunter Valley I need to turn the
music down. Take a breath. Strap in for a fidelitous ride across the ebbs and flows
of Hunter regality, when I taste this suite of semillon. The top-drawer, with few
peers. Belford, a little more reticent and stonier than its Stevens brethren. Talc, wet
pebbles strewn across a stream, lemongrass and citrus balm. But the texture, the
opus. Still in need of time. Taut, linear and of pixelated detail and precision. Wait
with bated breath. Screw cap. 11% alc. RATING 97 DRINK 2021-2030 $45 NG ✪
Vat 1 Semillon 2017, Hunter Valley While I enjoy the open-knit approaches
to crafting semillon across the region, this remains the bulletproof benchmark.
Even here, there have been endeavours towards greater accessibility, with some
lees inflection. A meld of the finest dry-grown plots conferring a carapace of talc,
sandy mineral and effusive acidity that is, to be frank, indomitable. Descriptives,
ineffable. The length, justifiable. Bury this. Screw cap. 11.5% alc. RATING 97
DRINK 2021-2035 $105 NG ✪

🍷🍷🍷🍷🍷 Vat 47 Chardonnay 2021, Hunter Valley This stands aloft. Regal in a Hunter
sense, without any forfeit of the regional signature of tangy stone fruits and white-
fig riffs. Nougat and cashew, pinioned amid a steelier framework. This drives long.
Thoroughly impressive. Screw cap. 13.5% alc. RATING 96 DRINK 2021-2033
$100 NG
Single Vineyard HVD Semillon 2017, Hunter Valley Lightweight. A skitter
of lemon zest, tamarind and quince, bulwarked with a talcy mineral pungency
and a juicy acid kit. Long, tactile and pummelling of intensity. This is a late-
released Hunter semillon, barely nudging middle age. Strap yourself in, turn Eddie
Van Halen up to full volume and get ready. Stevens, the exuberant. Belford, the
intellectual nerd. This, the louche with class. Screw cap. 10.5% alc. RATING 96
DRINK 2021-2029 $45 NG ✪
Johnno's Semillon 2021, Hunter Valley The vineyard for this wine was
planted in 1908, the wine made in the method of that time – basket pressed,
the juice only partly clarified. While the acidity provides the spine of the wine,

it has more texture than almost all of its peers. Screw cap. 11% alc. RATING 95 DRINK 2025-2036 $75 JH

Single Vineyard Stevens Semillon 2017, Hunter Valley Light sand and red clay, the origin. A richer give than the meagre white sands of Belford, its majestic sibling. All the better for youthful exuberance, without quite the tactile feel and tensile vibrancy. Optimal drinking! Apricot pith, quince, quinine and citrus balm. Taut, but a far more open weave across the mid palate than others in the family. This, the crowd favourite. Visceral and absolutely delicious. Screw cap. 11% alc. RATING 95 DRINK 2021-2026 $45 NG

HVD Chardonnay 2021, Hunter Valley Planted in 1908. Dry grown on sandy soils. Likely the oldest chardonnay vineyard in the country. Taut and leesy. White fig, cantaloupe, peach and a drift of barrel-inflected nougat. Fine thrust of acidity and parry of fruit, the jangle ricocheting long. A very fine, chiselled and classy style, defined as much by flare as its understated reticence. Screw cap. 12.5% alc. RATING 94 DRINK 2021-2032 $90 NG

Single Vineyard Old Hut Shiraz 2019, Hunter Valley A mid ruby. Digestible and mid weighted, the signatures of the Hunter. Sweet loam and terracotta aromas, the calling card. Larger oak and judicious extraction, the conduits. Sarsaparilla, bergamot, violet, sweet red and black cherry and a sluice of anise. More intensity than the Mother, with similar sap, a bit more flare and greater pinosity. Screw cap. 13.5% alc. RATING 94 DRINK 2021-2033 $65 NG

Ulithorne   ★★★★☆

85 Kays Road, Blewitt Springs, SA 5171 **Region** McLaren Vale
T 0406 336 282 **www**.ulithorne.com.au **Open** By appt **Winemaker** Matthew Copping **Est.** 1971 **Dozens** 2500 **Vyds** 7.2ha
Ulithorne produces small quantities of red wines from selected parcels of grapes from its estate vineyard in McLaren Vale, planted in 1950 by Bob Whiting. The small-batch, high-quality wines are influenced by Ulithorne's associate Laurence Feraud, owner of Domaine du Pegau of Châteauneuf-du-Pape. The business was sold to CW Wines in Dec '20. Exports to the UK, Canada, Sweden, Malaysia and Hong Kong. (JH)

♥♥♥♥♥ **Frux Frugis Shiraz 2018, McLaren Vale** Blewitt Springs fruit. Micro-fermented in new and used French wood after hand harvesting. The right portions of each, judging by a finely hewn bridle of tannins, controlling and directing the fray. As far as warm-climate shiraz goes, this is good. Contemporary in terms of lifted florals and a modicum of tension. Avuncular in terms of weight, power and the armchair you'll need to settle into after drinking it. Finishes with a dose of heat. Screw cap. 14.5% alc. RATING 95 DRINK 2021-2034 $120 NG

Avitus Shiraz 2018, McLaren Vale Some of the more delicate varieties and blends suffer from the indomitable oak handling here. But this – dense, burly, rich and brimming with darker fruit tones, licorice strap, smoked meats, clove and alternate spices flowing from attack to finish – relishes it. A unashamedly big wine, of poise, power and precision. Screw cap. 14.5% alc. RATING 94 DRINK 2021-2028 $80 NG

Paternus Shiraz 2018, McLaren Vale A classy wine. Elevated floral aromas, a lightness of being, gritty sandy tannins and for those seeking heft, plenty of extract and French oak. Raspberry bon-bon, blueberry, anise, lavender, clove and thyme. A wine that bridles power for the punter with a refined tannic kit, a treat for the experienced imbiber. Long and forceful. Screw cap. 14.5% alc. RATING 94 DRINK 2021-2030 $80 NG

♥♥♥♥♀ **Prospera Shiraz 2018, McLaren Vale** RATING 92 DRINK 2021-2027 $50 NG
Epoch Rosé 2021, McLaren Vale RATING 91 DRINK 2021-2022 $25 NG
Chi Grenache Shiraz 2019, McLaren Vale RATING 91 DRINK 2021-2027 $50 NG
Paternus Cabernet Shiraz 2019, Coonawarra McLaren Vale RATING 91 DRINK 2021-2028 $80 NG

Unicus Shiraz 2018, McLaren Vale RATING 91 DRINK 2021-2026 $85 NG
Specialist Tempranillo Graciano Garnacha 2021, McLaren Vale
RATING 90 DRINK 2021-2024 $35 NG
Dona Shiraz 2019, McLaren Vale RATING 90 DRINK 2021-2025 $25 NG
Magnum Opus Nero d'Avola 2019, McLaren Vale RATING 90
DRINK 2021-2023 $35 NG
Dona Shiraz Greanche 2018, McLaren Vale RATING 90 DRINK 2021-2026
$25 NG

Ulupna Winery   ★★★★

159 Crawfords Road, Strathmerton, Vic 3641 **Region** Goulburn Valley
T (03) 9533 8831 **www**.ulupnawinery.com.au **Open** By appt **Winemaker** Vio Buga,
Viviana Ferrari **Est.** 1999 **Dozens** 35 000 **Vyds** 22ha
Ulupna started out as a retirement activity for Nick and Kathy Bogdan. The vineyard on
the banks of the Murray River is planted to shiraz (50%), cabernet sauvignon (30%) and
chardonnay (20%); the plantings allowing for expansion in the years ahead. The wines are
made under the direction of Vio Buga, who also designed and planted the vineyard. Exports
to Hong Kong, South Korea and Singapore. (JH)

ŸŸŸŸŸ **Royal Phoenix Single Vineyard Cabernet Sauvignon 2019, Goulburn**
Valley Deep purple garnet in hue, the aromas are immediately spicy and black-
fruited in intensity. Handles the high alcohol quite well, matching the richness and
background oak. All tied neatly together through the finish. Screw cap. 15% alc.
RATING 92 DRINK 2021-2029 $55 JP
Single Vineyard 2019, Goulburn Valley Ripeness and richness work together
to produce a very smooth result. Classic black fruits on show with plum, chocolate,
licorice and spice. Well composed on the palate, supple in tannin and boasting
a light savoury earthy and meaty twist that blends in well. Cork. 13.8% alc.
RATING 91 DRINK 2021-2029 $27 JP

ŸŸŸŸ **Cellar Reserve Shiraz Cabernet 2019, Goulburn Valley** RATING 89
DRINK 2021-2026 $32 JP
Limited Edition Shiraz 2019, Goulburn Valley RATING 88 DRINK 2021-2025
$32 JP
Royal Phoenix Single Vineyard Shiraz 2013, Goulburn Valley RATING 88
DRINK 2021-2023 $55 JP

Uplands   ★★★☆

174 Richmond Road, Cambridge, Tas 7170 **Region** Southern Tasmania
T 0419 390 015 **www**.uplandsvineyard.com.au **Open** By appt **Winemaker** Tasmanian
Vintners **Viticulturist** Fred Peacock **Est.** 1998 **Dozens** 80 **Vyds** 0.5ha
Michael and Debbie Ryan bought the historic Uplands House (1823) in 1998 and decided to
plant the front paddock with chardonnay, joining the grape growing trend in the Coal River
Valley of Southern Tasmania. The vineyard is planted with the 2 most suitable clones for the
area, 8127 for sparkling and the Penfold clone for their still chardonnay. (JH)

ŸŸŸŸŸ **Blanc de Blancs 2018, Tasmania** Aged 3 years on lees; disgorged Sept '21;
6.5g/L dosage. Compelling, elegant and high-tensile Tasmanian sparkling, uniting
the depth and concentration of a well-established vineyard (celebrating its 20th
birthday this vintage) with the pristine precision of vinification by the smart
Tasmanian Vintners outfit. All the tension and energy of cool chardonnay defines a
laser-aligned palate of linear drive, fixed with tremendous endurance. Wait. Diam.
12% alc. RATING 93 $50 TS

ŸŸŸŸ **Coal River Valley Chardonnay 2020, Tasmania** RATING 88
DRINK 2022-2027 $35 TS

Upper Reach

77 Memorial Avenue, Baskerville, WA 6056 **Region** Swan Valley
T (08) 9296 0078 **www**.upperreach.com.au **Open** 7 days 11–5 **Winemaker** Derek
Pearse **Est.** 1996 **Dozens** 4000 **Vyds** 8.45ha
This 10ha property on the banks of the upper reaches of the Swan River was purchased by
Laura Rowe and Derek Pearse in 1996. The original 4ha vineyard was expanded and plantings
now include chardonnay, shiraz, cabernet sauvignon, verdelho, semillon, merlot, petit verdot
and muscat. 90% of grapes are estate-grown; all wine is vinified on site. The restaurant has
recently been revamped and the cellar door has received a string of Gourmet Traveller WINE
awards since 2013. (JH)

ŸŸŸŸŸ Tempranillo 2020, Swan Valley Black cherries, black pepper, earthy, chewy
tannins and a spicy line of acidity that courses through the wine. It's very ripe –
and pretty fierce at this young age – but nothing that a quick decant won't fix.
Lovely stuff. Screw cap. 14% alc. RATING 92 DRINK 2022-2027 $35 EL
Reserve Shiraz 2019, Swan Valley This is a high-octane wine. The fruit has
a medicinal edge to it, otherwise showing abundant blackberries and spice. The
impact of the oak is intense and shapely: it firmly cups the fruit, ushering it across
the palate and into the finish. Decant this to encourage it out of its shell – it needs
it. Screw cap. 14.5% alc. RATING 91 DRINK 2021-2031 $50 EL
Reserve Cabernet Sauvignon 2018, Margaret River Leafy, minty and
layered with licorice, black olive and clove, the aromas couldn't hide their Margaret
River roots if they tried. Cassis, rhubarb and aniseed in the mouth, this is elegant
and fine. '18 was a glorious vintage in Margaret River, one of the best, and it
yielded wines of power, poise and longevity. This will likely see out the medium
term with grace. A decant is recommended if drinking before '23. Screw cap.
14% alc. RATING 91 DRINK 2022-2032 $50 EL

Usher Tinkler Wines

97 McDonalds Road, Pokolbin, NSW 2320 **Region** Hunter Valley
T 02 4998 7069 **www**.ushertinklerwins.com **Open** 7 days 10–5 **Winemaker** Usher
Tinkler **Est.** 2014 **Dozens** 10 000 **Vyds** 22ha
Usher Tinkler is the progeny of 3 generations of Hunter farming, setting out on his own
after first making wine (of sorts) in the family bathtub. His nemesis, boring wines. Like
other aesthetic forms of expression, Tinkler strives for emotional connection with the end
consumer. Set in the original Pokolbin church built in 1905, Tinkler's tasting room is as
iconoclastic as it is brimming with a sense of place. Much like his wines: the Nose to Tail
series tweaks Hunter classics into an easygoing vibe of idiosyncratic blends, while the Usher
Tinkler Reserve wines are firmly of place, melding the Hunter's proclivity for bright fruit
and its shiraz's earthen terracotta accent, with quality oak and stridently extracted structural
latticework. They age well. (NG)

ŸŸŸŸŸ Reserve Chardonnay 2021, Hunter Valley A wine that successfully placates
the intensity of the Hunter's fruit, with some wild-yeast lanolin, umami and
funk, melded to a kit of classy oak. Restraint defines the nose. Dried hay and
porcini. Then the party starts. Long, filigreed and brimming with nectarine riffs.
A very impressive chardonnay for the region. Screw cap. 12.5% alc. RATING 94
DRINK 2021-2028 $55 NG

ŸŸŸŸŸ Reserve Shiraz 2019, Hunter Valley RATING 93 DRINK 2021-2030 $75 NG

Utopos

PO Box 764, Tanunda, SA 5352 **Region** Barossa Valley
T 0409 351 166 **www**.utopos.com.au **Winemaker** Kym Teusner **Est.** 2015
Dozens 1500 **Vyds** 20ha
The fates were kind when Neil Panuja, a friend of Kym Teusner's from 'the big smoke', said
he had the wish to get into fine-wine production and asked that Kym keep an eye out for

something special. Shortly thereafter, a vineyard that Kym had coveted from his beginnings in the Barossa Valley came onto the market. The 20ha vineyard was duly acquired, Kym investing in a small share. The vineyard is perched on Roenfeldt Road at one of the highest points of the boundary between Greenock and Marananga. The depleted stony soils consistently produce low yields of high-quality grapes that loudly proclaim their Barossan origin. The X-factor is the site-driven savoury balance that Kym says he always longs for. The name they have given the business is the root word of Utopia. Everything is just so right: great vineyard, great winemaker, great story, great packaging. (JH)

ΤΤΤΤΤ **Grenache 2021, Barossa Valley** Bright red purple in the glass with aromas of juicy plum, red cherry fruits, exotic spice, gingerbread, violets, earth and red licorice. The fruit weight is spot on, pure yet with a distinct sense of space. The aromas transpose over onto the palate, which shows a chalky tannin texture and shimmering acid line. It's a cracker. Screw cap. 14.5% alc. RATING 96 DRINK 2022-2032 $70 DB ☻

Shiraz 2019, Barossa Valley Deep red purple in the glass, with a perfumed cascade of satsuma plum and macerated blackberry characters, underscored by hints of baking spice, licorice, dark chocolate, vanilla and cedar. The balance is impeccable, with great fruit purity and detail throughout its length; the classy, cedary cut of French oak perhaps a little more noticeable on the palate. Deep, resonant and long, with über-ripe tannins and a sense of brightness to its form. Cork. 14.5% alc. RATING 96 DRINK 2021-2038 $70 DB ☻

Cabernet Sauvignon 2019, Barossa Valley Kym Teusner is a dab hand at coaxing terrific wines out of some of the best vineyards the Barossa has to offer. Pure, balanced and true to both its region and variety, the wine offers gorgeous blackberry and plum fruits, cut through with baking spice, licorice and earth. Pitch-perfect fruit intensity and weight, fine chocolatey tannins and a supple, bright-eyed finish that trails off with detail and clarity. Cork. 14.5% alc. RATING 95 DRINK 2021-2038 $70 DB

Utter Wines   ★★★★

2427 Maroondah Highway, Buxton, Vic 3711 **Region** Upper Goulburn
T 0411 550 519 **www**.riverhousewineandtruffles.com.au **Open** By appt
Winemaker Adrian Utter, Robert Utter **Viticulturist** Adrian Utter **Est.** 2012
Dozens 500 **Vyds** 2ha

Agronomist and viticulturist Adrian Utter and his father, Robert, farm a family property at Buxton in the Acheron River Valley, in the Murrindindi area of the Goulburn Valley. Initial plantings of grape vines have expanded slowly to just under 2ha of high-density vines, with further gradual expansion planned. The Utters believe the high continentality of the mountain valley, with cool nights and warm days, allows longer ripening, preserving the vibrancy of the fruit. Sustainability guides vineyard practices, promoting biodiversity and maintaining plant health. The complete process from planting to bottling is performed by Adrian and Robert. The farm also supports a productive truffiere (Buxton Black Truffles) and beef cattle production. (JP)

ΤΤΤΤΤ **Syrah 2020, Upper Goulburn** With 1% viognier. Maintains the lively spiciness of the previous release together with a big, juicy mouthful of ripe black and red berries, pomegranate and Dutch licorice. Still coming together but the taut palate – led by fine, grainy tannins – bodes well. Diam. 13.6% alc. RATING 94 DRINK 2022-2026 $35 JP

ΤΤΤΤΤ **Pinot Noir 2020, Upper Goulburn** RATING 92 DRINK 2022-2026 $35 JP

Vanguardist Wines   ★★★★★

121A Radford Road, Seppeltsfield, SA 5355 **Region** Barossa Valley
T 0487 193 053 **www**.vanguardistwines.com **Open** By appt **Winemaker** Michael John Corbett **Viticulturist** Michael John Corbett **Est.** 2014 **Dozens** 2000 **Vyds** 7.5ha

Vanguardist Wines maker, Michael John Corbett, draws on established sources across South Australia to craft a delicious swag of Mediterranean-inspired wines of textural intrigue. A card of neutral wood, ambient ferments and plenty of whole-bunch is dealt with a deft hand. The results, often compelling. Corbett's opus is grenache, specifically Blewitt Springs grenache, hewn of the region's low-yielding elevated old vineyards. His ripeness barometer challenges notions of what is optimal, flirting with marginal levels of alcohol on the lower side. Quantities are small, selling out fast. Exports to France, Hong Kong and NZ. (NG)

♟♟♟♟♟ **Grenache 2020, McLaren Vale** I have always appreciated the style here: a pinosity of red fruits with a firm yet svelte etching of nebbiolo-esque bristly tannins. Sometimes, though, the ripeness was on the south side of ideal. Not this year! This sits pretty on a dial between elegance and sappier fruit, still defined by signature fine-boned tannic latticework and saline freshness. Darker cherry, anise, mint, thyme, rosemary and sandalwood. A whiff of orange zest, too. This address is now at the top of the stylistic totem pole and one of the few true regional benchmarks. Diam. 14.1% alc. RATING 96 DRINK 2021-2027 $56 NG ✪
Blewitt Springs Mourvèdre 2020, McLaren Vale This is among the very finest iterations of this great variety in the country, if not the finest. Still, I'd like to see firmer tannins and a more brooding veil of herb and smoked meat, rather than the pulpy blue fruits of whole-berry fermentation. A fine ferrous bow of tannins, all the same. Anise, white pepper and lavender, too. Given mourvèdre's reductive tendencies, for now at least, it is worth decanting it aggressively or having a sip, re-corking and waiting for the next day. Screw cap. 14.1% alc. RATING 95 DRINK 2021-2028 $56 NG
Vin Doux Naturel Grenache 2020, McLaren Vale A delicious fortified expression of a guise seldom seen in Australia. The ferment was muted before it began, in the traditional deep Mediterranean tradition. This serves to promote the quality of the spirit and the grapey, spicy element of grenache. I love this! Visceral, warm and nourishing. Weighty, but so contagiously delicious that it is difficult to spit. Kirsch, clove, molten earth and a sweet rasp of spiritous tannins. Chill and drink lustfully. Screw cap. 17% alc. RATING 95 $80 NG

♟♟♟♟♟ **La Petite Vanguard Grenache 2021, McLaren Vale** RATING 91 DRINK 2022-2025 $30 NG
La Petite Vanguard Blewitt Grenache Mourvèdre 2021, McLaren Vale RATING 90 DRINK 2022-2026 $13 NG ✪

Varney Wines   ★★★★★

62 Victor Harbor Road, Old Noarlunga, SA 5168 **Region** McLaren Vale
T 0450 414 570 **www**.varneywines.com.au **Open** Thurs–Mon 11–5 **Winemaker** Alan Varney **Est.** 2017 **Dozens** 1500

Alan Varney's Australian career grew out of a vintage stint with d'Arenberg into an 11-year employment, much of it as senior winemaker. He says that this period meant he came to be friends with many of the best local growers in McLaren Vale, the Adelaide Hills and Langhorne Creek. The d'Arenberg vintage typically included making 9 varieties, some mainstream, some alternative. He is a brilliant winemaker, saying, 'I am not afraid to step out of the box and go with my intuition … I only use old seasoned oak with no fining or filtration.' His ability to draw the varietal heart of each wine he makes with alcohol levels between 12% and 14% is extraordinary. He has built an environmentally sensitive winery alongside wife Kathrin's restaurant, Victor's Place, overlooking the Onkaparinga Gorge. Varney Wines were the Wine Companion 2021 Best New Winery. (JH)

♟♟♟♟♟ **GSM 2019, McLaren Vale** Best GSM in the land? Very possibly. Suave, taut, streamlined, savoury. Wonderfully pliant and spicy, with a seasoning (15%) of whole bunches. Mourvèdre's hung game, to kick off. Clove, anise, pepper, blue and black fruits, cardamom and violet, otherwise. Measured, compact and dense. Perfectly extracted. Each tannin a finely wrought rivet, serving to weld a superb wine of precision and latent force. Screw cap. 14% alc. RATING 96 DRINK 2021-2027 $32 NG ✪

GSM 2020, McLaren Vale As Rhône-like as it gets. Grenache (55%), the kirsch, sandalwood and white pepper. Shiraz (25%), the florals and salumi. But there is far more to this: old vines, propitious siting and the confidence to extract with an MO of savoury complexity and strident tannins that ready one for the fifth glass rather than one sip … before lights out. Screw cap. 14.2% alc. RATING 95 DRINK 2021-2028 $32 NG ✪

Fiano 2019, Langhorne Creek Alan Varney certainly knows what he's doing. The scented, slightly peppery bouquet is a logical forerunner to the skilfully engineered, grapefruit-accented palate. A wine to stand tall with any food style. Screw cap. 12.4% alc. RATING 95 DRINK 2021-2024 $28 JH ✪

🍷🍷🍷🍷🍷 **Expressions of Interest Mencia 2021, McLaren Vale** RATING 93 DRINK 2021-2025 $35 NG
Grenache 2021, McLaren Vale RATING 93 DRINK 2021-2029 $35 NG
Chardonnay 2020, Adelaide Hills RATING 93 DRINK 2021-2026 $32 NG
Entrada Grenache Mourvèdre Touriga 2021, McLaren Vale RATING 92 DRINK 2021-2024 $25 NG ✪
Chardonnay 2021, Adelaide Hills RATING 92 DRINK 2021-2028 $32 NG
Fiano 2020, Langhorne Creek RATING 92 DRINK 2021-2024 $28 NG
Shiraz 2020, McLaren Vale Adelaide Hills RATING 92 DRINK 2021-2028 $42 NG
Cabernet Sauvignon 2019, Adelaide Hills RATING 92 DRINK 2021-2026 $58 NG
Entrada Rose of Grenache 2021, McLaren Vale RATING 91 DRINK 2021-2022 $25 NG
Entrada Verdelho 2021, Langhorne Creek RATING 90 DRINK 2022-2024 $25 JH

Vasse Felix   ★★★★★

Cnr Tom Cullity Drive/Caves Road, Cowaramup, WA 6284 **Region** Margaret River
T (08) 9756 5000 **www.**vassefelix.com.au **Open** 7 days 10–5 **Winemaker** Virginia Willcock **Viticulturist** Bart Molony **Est.** 1967 **Dozens** 150 000 **Vyds** 330ha
Vasse Felix is Margaret River's founding wine estate, established in 1967 by regional pioneer Dr Tom Cullity. Owned and operated by the Holmes à Court family since '87, Paul Holmes à Court has brought the focus to Margaret River's key varieties of cabernet sauvignon and chardonnay. Chief Winemaker Virginia Willcock has energised the winemaking and viticultural team with her no-nonsense approach and fierce commitment to quality. Vasse Felix has 4 scrupulously managed vineyards throughout Margaret River that contribute all but a small part of the annual production. Wines include icons Tom Cullity (cabernet blend) and Heytesbury Chardonnay as well as Cabernet Sauvignon, Chardonnay, Sauvignon Blanc Semillon and Shiraz; Filius Chardonnay and Filius Cabernet Sauvignon; Classic Dry White and Classic Dry Red, plus limited quantities of Cane Cut Semillon and Blanc de Blancs. Exports to all major markets. (JH)

🍷🍷🍷🍷🍷 **Tom Cullity Cabernet Sauvignon Malbec 2018, Margaret River** This wine is the benchmark of the latent power, grace and inherent balance of the '18 vintage in Margaret River. Texturally similar to the classically sophisticated '14 vintage, but with far greater density and weight. Here, the savoury tannins are countersunk into the fruit already: shapely, firm, chewy, malleable – everywhere and nowhere at once. Waves of blood plum, cassis, blackberry, pomegranate, juniper, raspberries, saltbush, bay leaf and salted red licorice crash against the rocks, as kelp, nori, iodine, red gravel and brine ride the smaller sets out the back. Sensational. Astounding. A wine for the ages. Screw cap. 13.5% alc. RATING 99 DRINK 2022-2052 $190 EL ✪ ♥

Heytesbury Chardonnay 2020, Margaret River In warmer vintages like '20, the Heytesbury chardonnay has extension and flex on release, billowing with flavour and pleasure, with the oak seeming to be enveloped by it early on. So goes the story here: like the '18 (on release) this is a scintillating show of powerful fruit, juicy mineral acidity and layers of crushed rocks, petrichor, nori, summer fig and salted yellow peaches. A superstar wine – it's closed now though: patience or a decant is recommended. Screw cap. 13.5% alc. RATING 97 DRINK 2022-2037 $100 EL ✪

Chardonnay 2020, Margaret River The '20 vintage was made for the Vasse Felix chardonnay style. This is seamless, concentrated, floral, intense, so smart that it elicited a little chuckle upon tasting. Notes of peach and apple skin (of course) backed by jacaranda flowers, curry leaf, brine, crispy nori and pan fried nuts. What a wine. And what a bargain for this pedigree – so classy it's ridiculous. Screw cap. 13% alc. RATING 96 DRINK 2021-2036 $44 EL ✪

Syrah 2020, Margaret River Iridescent in the glass, and all silky flow on the palate. This vintage was responsible for a tranche of wines that taste, frankly, effortless. This is one of those wines. Gorgeous, with all the push and pull of exotic spice, Chambord, orange zest and crispy nori you could possibly want. Glorious. Screw cap. 14% alc. RATING 95 DRINK 2021-2031 $37 EL

Filius Chardonnay 2020, Margaret River The immediacy of the complexity of the bouquet and the juicy white peach that floods the palate leave no room for discussion. This is a perfect rendition of a drink-now chardonnay of the highest quality within its station of life (and price). Screw cap. 13% alc. RATING 94 DRINK 2021-2030 $29 JH ✪

Filius Sauvignon Blanc Semillon 2020, Margaret River You can be assured that when Virginia Willcock turns her mind to something, it's going to be good. Sauvignon blanc here – a component has been fermented on skins, which layers the wine with an extra spicy sumthin sumthin. This is a serious, bordeaux blanc style, and at a very low price to match. So smart! Screw cap. 13% alc. RATING 94 DRINK 2021-2026 $29 EL ✪

Sauvignon Blanc 2020, Margaret River Field mushrooms and sea salt, guava and crushed lychee, nashi pear and Golden Delicious apples. So much going on, and from so many different angles: this is complex, textural, layered and long. This style will not be for everyone, although if you love chardonnay this will firmly be in your ballpark. The Campari/orange-zest character that comes from skin contact can be addictive – it's here, if you look closely. I'd like to see this in 5 and 10 years. Screw cap. 13% alc. RATING 94 DRINK 2021-2031 $33 EL

Cabernet Sauvignon 2019, Margaret River The '19 vintage was cool, largely responsible for a tranche of very precise, perfumed cabernet sauvignons. Aniseed, kelp, bitter chocolate, blackberry and all things midnight. Rich and savoury – the fruit is bolstered by firm graphite tannins. The length of flavour, coupled with Willcock's proven pedigree in this field, tell us what we want to know about longevity: always back bluechip. The fruit is encased in tannin right now: if you plan to drink in the short term, you must decant. This will go far. Screw cap. 14.5% alc. RATING 94 DRINK 2021-2036 $52 EL

Vella Wines

147B Sheoak Hill Road, Mount Torrens, SA 5244 (postal) **Region** Adelaide Hills **T** 0499 998 484 **www.**vellawines.com.au **Winemaker** Henry Borchardt, Franco D'Anna, Daryl Catlin **Viticulturist** Mark Vella, Vitiworks **Est.** 2013 **Dozens** 1000 **Vyds** 10ha
Mark Vella was blooded at Bloodwood Estate in 1995 (an appalling but inevitable pun). Over the following 22 years Mark has plied his trade as viticulturist in Orange, the Hunter Valley and now (and permanently) the Adelaide Hills. He manages to avoid conflicts of interest in running his vineyard management company, Vitiworks, and pinpointing outstanding parcels of fruit for the Vella brand. A broader conflict (which is in fact no conflict at all) comes from his 12 years of vineyard management, supplying contract-grown fruit for more than 40 of the leading wine producers in SA. He uses Andre Bondar to make his Chardonnay, Franco D'Anna his Pinot Noir, and Daryl Catlin his Pinot Blanc blend. (JH)

Troublemaker Pinot Blanc Pinot Gris Gewürztraminer 2019, Adelaide Hills What a little charmer! With pinot blanc in lead position, the result is a textural, nicely restrained wine, ripe in honeysuckle, stewed apple and pear with a tickle of gewürz spice. Screw cap. 13% alc. RATING 89 DRINK 2021-2025 $25 JP

Dirt Boy Pinot Noir 2019, Adelaide Hills A soft, warm-hearted pinot noir that will be a crowd pleaser. Ripe and forward in red cherry, plum and musk, with a layer of light spice running free. Nice creaminess on the palate. Screw cap. 13% alc. RATING 89 DRINK 2021-2025 $32 JP

Victory Point Wines

92 Holben Road, Cowaramup, WA 6284 **Region** Margaret River
T 0417 954 655 **www.**victorypointwines.com **Open** Wed–Sun 11–4 **Winemaker** Mark Messenger (Contract) **Viticulturist** Colin Bell **Est.** 1997 **Dozens** 2500 **Vyds** 13.7ha
Judith and Gary Berson have set their sights high. They established their vineyard without irrigation, emulating those of the Margaret River pioneers (including Moss Wood). The fully mature plantings comprise 4.2ha of chardonnay and 0.4ha of pinot noir; the remainder bordeaux varieties with cabernet sauvignon (6.2ha), cabernet franc (0.5ha), malbec (1.7ha) and petit verdot (0.7ha). The cellar door overlooks the 20+yo vineyard. (JH)

🍷🍷🍷🍷🍷 **Rosé 2021, Margaret River** Slickly made, with a blend of pinot noir, cabernet franc and malbec. A luxuriantly rich rosé, but remains nimble on its feet as the bevy of red fruits roll along the tongue. Top-class match for Asian food. Screw cap. 13.5% alc. RATING 95 DRINK 2021-2023 $25 JH ✪

Pinot Noir 2020, Margaret River '20 is shaping up to be such an effortless vintage (for us drinkers, anyway). This is silken and plush, laden with ripe red cherries, redcurrants, pomegranates and summer strawberries. Routinely a wonderful wine and this vintage is no exception. Screw cap. 13.5% alc. RATING 95 DRINK 2021-2031 $55 EL

Cabernet Franc 2020, Margaret River In the popular modern approach of minimum intervention and sustainable practises, partly in the vineyard, partly in the winery. The result is a seductive wine only just reaching medium-bodied status, fermentation techniques pitched to gentle extraction, temperature control and limited time in wood or tank. Screw cap. 14% alc. RATING 94 DRINK 2023-2035 $35 JH

The Mallee Root Cabernet Sauvignon Petit Verdot Cabernet Franc 2019, Margaret River The heady aromatics of the petit verdot lend lashings of blueberries and potpourri to the nose here. On the palate this is silky, saturated in ripe fruit and layered with exotic market spices. Licorice, aniseed and fennel flowers linger through the finish, adorning the resplendent red fruit. Quite gorgeous. At this price, a steal. Screw cap. 14% alc. RATING 94 DRINK 2021-2029 $29 EL ✪

Cabernet Sauvignon 2019, Margaret River Another wonderful cabernet release from Victory Point. Where the '18 was dense and concentrated, this is supple and elegant, showing very pretty layers of cassis, bitter cocoa, raspberry licorice and briny acidity. Drink this while you wait for the '18 to gather momentum. Screw cap. 14% alc. RATING 94 DRINK 2022-2037 $55 EL

Chardonnay 2018, Margaret River Fabulous intensity of flavour – this really dives deep and goes long on the palate. Yellow and white peach, brine, curry leaf and all the good things we want to see in high-quality chardonnay, with some red apple skins and crushed cashew for good measure. Great length of flavour, no shortage of heft. Screw cap. 13% alc. RATING 94 DRINK 2020-2030 $45 EL

🍷🍷🍷🍷🍷 **Chardonnay 2019, Margaret River** RATING 90 DRINK 2022-2032 $55 EL

Vigena Wines

210 Main Road, Willunga, SA 5172 **Region** McLaren Vale
T 0433 966 011 **Open** By appt **Winemaker** Ben Heide **Est.** 2010 **Dozens** 20000 **Vyds** 15.8ha

Vigena Wines is principally an export business. In recent years the vineyard has been revitalised, with one significant change: chardonnay has been grafted to shiraz, giving the business a 100% red wine focus. Exports to Singapore and Hong Kong. (JH)

🍷🍷🍷🍷🍷 **Cabernet Sauvignon 2020, McLaren Vale** This is by far the best wine of the suite, at least in its current equilibrium of force and intensity of cassis and black olive flavours, supported by a verdant chassis and cylinders of vanilla-pod oak and saline freshness. Perfectly varietal. Undeniably classy. The structural mettle, no matter how strong, feels suited to the quality of fruit and scattered herbal notes. While I have said that some wines will come around at this address, this is already delicious. No doubt it will become even more so after a decade. Cork. 14.5% alc. RATING 96 DRINK 2022-2035 $65 NG ✪
Limited Edition Shiraz 2020, McLaren Vale Built like a classed growth from Bordeaux, from extraction, weight and pricey oak regime. Capacious, sure, but there is rationale and balance. Beautifully extracted grape tannins, lithe and grippy, coating the sides of the tongue and cheeks. Boysenberry, white pepper and iodine. The oak is unrelenting, but there is so much behind it that I have little doubt it will cellar well. Not my sort of drink, but it is impressive. Cork. 15% alc. RATING 95 DRINK 2023-2035 $79 NG

🍷🍷🍷🍷🍷 **Cabernet Sauvignon Shiraz 2020, McLaren Vale** RATING 93 DRINK 2023-2035 $55 NG

Vigna Bottin ★★★★☆
192 Main Road, Willunga SA 5172 **Region** McLaren Vale
T 0414 562 956 **www.**vignabottin.com.au **Open** Fri 11–4, Sat–Sun 11–5
Winemaker Paolo Bottin **Est.** 2006 **Dozens** 1500 **Vyds** 15.22ha
The Bottin family migrated to Australia in 1954 from Treviso in northern Italy where they were grapegrowers. The family began growing grapes in McLaren Vale in '70, focusing on mainstream varieties for sale to wineries in the region. When son Paolo and wife Maria made a trip back to Italy in '98, they were inspired to do more, and, says Paolo, 'my love for barbera and sangiovese was sealed during a vintage in Pavia. I came straight home to plant both varieties in our family plot. My father was finally happy!' They now trade under the catchy phrase 'Italian Vines, Australian Wines'. (JH)

🍷🍷🍷🍷🍷 **Fiano 2021, McLaren Vale** I enjoy tasting this family's wines. Each year, an incremental ascendancy of quality and integrity: hand picked, partially wild fermented on skins for 10 days to impart flavour and textural moxie, a bit of barrel, blending and time on lees with some stirring. This brims with pear, wild fennel, raw almond and citrus verbena. The finish, salty and firm, the phenolics directing the intense wave of flavour. As prescient as it is fine drinking. Screw cap. 12.8% alc. RATING 95 DRINK 2021-2025 $27 NG ✪

🍷🍷🍷🍷🍷 **Vermentino 2021, McLaren Vale** RATING 93 DRINK 2021-2024 $27 NG ✪
Sangiovese Rosato 2021, McLaren Vale RATING 92 DRINK 2021-2023 $27 NG
Sangiovese 2019, McLaren Vale RATING 92 DRINK 2021-2026 $32 NG
Compare's Shiraz 2019, McLaren Vale RATING 90 DRINK 2021-2028 $27 NG

Vignerons Schmölzer & Brown ★★★★★
39 Thorley Road, Stanley, Vic 3747 **Region** Beechworth
T 0411 053 487 **www.**vsandb.com.au **Winemaker** Tessa Brown, Jeremy Scholzer
Viticulturist Tessa Brown **Est.** 2014 **Dozens** 1800 **Vyds** 2ha
Winemaker and viticulturist Tessa Brown graduated from CSU with a degree in viticulture in the late '90s and undertook postgraduate winemaking studies at the University of Adelaide in the mid '00s. In '09, Mark Walpole showed Tessa and partner Jeremy Schmölzer a property that he described as 'the jewel in the crown of Beechworth'. When it came onto the market

unexpectedly in '12, they were in a position to jump. They have planted chardonnay, shiraz, riesling and nebbiolo. By sheer chance, just across the road from Thorley was a tiny vineyard, a bit over 0.4ha, with dry-grown pinot and chardonnay around 20 years old. When they realised it was not being managed for production, they struck up a working relationship with the owners, getting the vineyard into shape and making their first Brunnen wines in '14. The Obstgarten wines come from a small, high-altitude riesling vineyard in the King Valley. Exports to the UK and Hong Kong. (JH)

ΨΨΨΨΨ Obstgarten T Riesling 2021, King Valley T stands for trocken, meaning dry in the German riesling classification. With 6–8g/L RS, this is not necessarily as dry as Australians would consider it, but the high acidity is definitely softened and the result is quite a stunning display of precision with clear, bright lemon zest, grapefruit, green apple and white flowers with sherbety, bright acidity. Screw cap. 11.5% alc. RATING 95 DRINK 2021-2032 $35 JP ✪
Berrern Pinot Noir 2020, Yarra Valley Coming out of its shell and in possession of the most alluring perfume in cherry, redcurrant, musk and pomegranate. A touch of spice brightens, while the sinewy tannins drive the wine with energy and elan. Screw cap. 13% alc. RATING 95 DRINK 2021-2026 $45 JP
Halbinsel Shiraz 2020, Mornington Peninsula The winemakers advise that the wine will fully open when allowed to breathe for an hour or 2. There's no denying this is a wine of reserved power and beauty, certainly in the red fruits, spice and pepper department. Lifted and enhanced in fine, filigreed tannins. A modern cool-climate shiraz that shows how it's done. Screw cap. 13% alc. RATING 95 DRINK 2021-2032 $45 JP

ΨΨΨΨΩ Peebee Shiraz 2020, Heathcote RATING 92 DRINK 2021-2028 $45 JP
Somerset Chardonnay 2020, Goulburn Valley RATING 91 DRINK 2021-2027 $34 JP
Halbinsel Rosé Pinot Gris 2020, Mornington Peninsula RATING 91 DRINK 2021-2024 $36 JP
Pret-a-Blanc 2021, King Valley RATING 90 DRINK 2021-2025 $30 JP
Pret-a-Rouge 2019, Beechworth RATING 90 DRINK 2021-2024 $30 JP

Vinaceous Wines ★★★★

49 Bennett Street, East Perth, WA 6004 (postal) **Region** Western Australia
T (08) 9221 4666 **www.**vinaceous.com.au **Winemaker** Gavin Berry, Michael Kerrigan
Est. 2007 **Dozens** 8000
This somewhat quirky venture was the baby of wine marketer Nick Stacy, Michael Kerrigan (winemaker/partner Hay Shed Hill) and Gavin Berry (winemaker/partner West Cape Howe). Nick Stacy separated from the business in Aug '20 (John Waldron, managing partner of Risky Business Wines, has since stepped in), taking the Reverend V and Clandestine Vineyards brands with him. Fruit is now all sourced from Margaret River and Great Southern. The wines are of seriously good quality and equally good value. Exports to the UK, the US, Canada, South America, Denmark, Finland, Indonesia, the Philippines, Thailand, Singapore and Hong Kong. (JH)

ΨΨΨΨΩ Pétillant Naturel Arneis Pinot Gris 2021, King Valley 54/30/16% arneis/ pinot grigio/gewürztraminer. Bottled before this wine's first and only fermentation is fully complete. Pale lemon dusty/cloudy hues. A well-executed Pét Nat bursting in flavour and just a hint of wildness. Fills the senses with a perfume of honeysuckle, apple, mandarin skin and spice. A tension-strong sparkling bringing lemon pie, grapefruit, lime and a light herbal savouriness to the palate. Definitely makes a lasting impression. Crown. 12.5% alc. RATING 91 $30 JP
Snake Charmer Shiraz 2019, Frankland River Typically dark fruit flavours from the Frankland River region. This expresses as a fleshy, soft, supple, sweet and round core, with flavours of raspberry lollies, summer blackberry, raspberry, red licorice and vanilla pod colouring the edges of this bouncy little wine. Not

complex or robust, but delicious and juicy early drinking. Screw cap. 14.5% alc.
RATING 91 DRINK 2021-2026 $25 EL

ŶŶŶŶ Crafted by Hand Fiano 2020, Mount Barker RATING 89 DRINK 2021-2023
$28 EL
Voodoo Moon Malbec 2019, Margaret River RATING 88 DRINK 2021-2027
$25 EL

Vinden Wines   ★★★★★

138 Gillards Road, Pokolbin, NSW 2320 **Region** Hunter Valley
T 0488 777 493 **www.**vindenwines.com.au **Open** 7 days 10–5 **Winemaker** Angus
Vinden **Viticulturist** Angus Vinden **Est.** 1998 **Dozens** 6000 **Vyds** 22ha

Angus Vinden may be young in the context of regional winemakers, but he lacks neither
moxie nor experience. A second-generation farmer with 22ha under vine, Angus' deft touch
is due as much to his regional nous as to the mentorship of Glen Howard and the influence of
his backyard sites. A traditional suite of semillon and shiraz galvanises the crowd at the Vinden
cellar door, but for those seeking intrigue there are exciting tremors beyond. With the use of
amphorae, long macerations and whole-bunch fermentations across varieties that augur well
for the future, the atmosphere at Vinden is one of febrile excitement, strung across a bow of
great possibility and high expectations. The tempranillos are possibly the finest in the country.
Full and plump, but savoury and marked by a detailed tannic mettle and Hunter earthiness.
The chenin, electrifying. Stay tuned! Exports to the UK, the US and Singapore. (NG)

ŶŶŶŶŶ The Vinden Headcase Somerset Vineyard Reserve Tempranillo 2019,
Hunter Valley Make no mistake, the tempranillo at this address shows great
promise across cuvées, even in riper years such as this. Lilac, damson plum, Asian
medicine cabinet whiffs, liniment and garden herb. The tannins, beautifully refined.
The acidity, dutiful. The choice of oak, savvy. The American segment lending as
pliant a coconut sweetness to the fray as much as it is, paradoxically, the reason for
the wine's tension and savouriness. Diam. 14% alc. RATING 95 DRINK 2021-2027
$60 NG
Aged Release Reserve Semillon 2016, Hunter Valley A fine aged example.
Lemon balm, barley candy, ginger crystal and heavily buttered white bread, like
an old-school Japanese kissaten. Creamy, yet fresh. Lightweight and of immaculate
precision, yet intense despite it all. Good drinking. Screw cap. 10.8% alc.
RATING 95 DRINK 2021-2025 $60 NG
Somerset Vineyard Fountainhead Shiraz 2021, Hunter Valley I am liking
the '21s from the producer. Fine. Detailed. Fresh. Fidelitous to the Hunter scents
of sweet earth and its mid-weighted digestibility. Done right, with a smidgeon of
whole bunches (10%) and fermentation in concrete. A good vintage. Very good.
For reds, as much as whites. Pulpy at first glimpse, before the wine leans into
a peppery freshness across a long finish marked by root spice and lithe, herbal
tannins. . Screw cap. 13% alc. RATING 94 DRINK 2022-2030 $60 NG
Somerset Vineyard Grand Reserve Tempranillo 2018, Hunter Valley This
is very good. The 40 months in larger-format French and American wood, perfect
for the style. Full, but savoury. Oodles of mocha and bourbon oak, a harmonious
conduit to dark cherry, sandalwood, raspberry and thyme. Wonderful length, the
oak serving to palate the sweetness of the region to beautiful effect. Tangy acidity,
the caveat. Diam. 13.9% alc. RATING 94 DRINK 2022-2028 $70 NG

ŶŶŶŶŶ The Vinden Basket Press Shiraz 2021, Hunter Valley RATING 93
DRINK 2021-2026 $40 NG
Somerset Vineyard Chardonnay 2021, Hunter Valley RATING 93
DRINK 2021-2027 $55 NG
Somerset Vineyard Single Barrel Chardonnay 2021, Hunter Valley
RATING 93 DRINK 2021-2026 $55 NG
Lignée Semillon Sauvignon Blanc 2021, Hunter Valley Orange RATING 93
DRINK 2021-2026 $75 NG

The Vinden Headcase Single Barrel Shiraz 2017, Hunter Valley
RATING 93 DRINK 2021-2027 $60 NG
The Vinden Headcase Nouveau Shiraz 2021, Hunter Valley RATING 92
DRINK 2021-2023 $30 NG
Experimental Release Shiraz Gamay Noir 2021, Hunter Valley RATING 92
DRINK 2021-2023 $35 NG
Experimental Release Somerset Vineyard Semillon 2021, Hunter Valley
RATING 92 DRINK 2021-2025 $35 NG
Pokolbin Blanc 2021, Hunter Valley RATING 92 DRINK 2021-2024 $35 NG
The Vinden Headcase Experimental Release Gewürztraminer 2021,
Hunter Valley RATING 92 DRINK 2021-2024 $35 NG
The Vinden Headcase Somerset Vineyard Semillon 2021, Hunter Valley
RATING 92 DRINK 2021-2028 $35 NG
Somerset Vineyard Single Barrel Chenin Blanc 2021, Hunter Valley
RATING 92 DRINK 2021-2026 $55 NG
Somerset Vineyard Reserve Semillon 2021, Hunter Valley RATING 92
DRINK 2021-2028 $60 NG
Spinning Away Rosé 2021, Hunter Valley RATING 91 DRINK 2020-2022
$30 NG
Lignée Rosé 2021, Hunter Valley Orange RATING 90 DRINK 2021-2023
$75 NG
Lignée Shiraz Pinot Noir 2021, Hunter Valley Orange RATING 90
DRINK 2021-2024 $95 NG

Vinea Marson   ★★★★☆

411 Heathcote-Rochester Road, Heathcote, Vic 3523 **Region** Heathcote
T 0430 312 165 **www**.vineamarson.com **Open** W'ends **Winemaker** Mario Marson
Est. 2000 **Dozens** 2500 **Vyds** 7.12ha
Owner-winemaker Mario Marson spent many years as the winemaker and viticulturist
with the late Dr John Middleton at the celebrated Mount Mary. Mario has over 35 years of
experience in Australia and overseas, having undertaken vintages at Isole e Olena in Tuscany
and Piedmont and at Domaine de la Pousse d'Or in Burgundy, where he was inspired to
emulate the multi-clonal wines favoured by these producers, pioneered in Australia by John
Middleton. In '99 he and his wife, Helen, purchased the Vinea Marson property on the eastern
slopes of the Mount Camel Range. They have planted shiraz and viognier, plus Italian varieties
of sangiovese, nebbiolo, barbera and refosco dal peduncolo. Marson also sources northeastern
Italian varietals from Porepunkah in the Alpine Valleys. (JH)

🍷🍷🍷🍷🍷 Sangiovese 2018, Heathcote Tasted a good 8 months before release and
it was nicely integrated and resoundingly excellent drinking already. It augurs
well for a bright future. Briar, pepper, black cherry and kirsch aromas lead into a
lightly savoury, medium-bodied palate with Heathcote sweet earth and minerality
contributing a natural balance and flow. Boasts a touch of an Italian-inspired dry,
firm finish. Diam. 14% alc. RATING 95 DRINK 2022-2035 $42 JP

🍷🍷🍷🍷🍷 Friulano #7 2019, Alpine Valleys RATING 93 DRINK 2022-2029 $30 JP
Prosecco 2021, Alpine Valleys RATING 92 $28 JP
Grazia 2019, Alpine Valleys RATING 92 DRINK 2022-2029 $32 JP
Shiraz Viognier 2018, Heathcote RATING 92 DRINK 2022-2034 $42 JP
Nebbiolo 2017, Heathcote RATING 91 DRINK 2022-2032 $46 JP
Rosato 2019, Heathcote RATING 90 DRINK 2021-2024 $30 JP

Vinifera Wines   ★★★★

194 Henry Lawson Drive, Mudgee, NSW 2850 **Region** Mudgee
T (02) 6372 2461 **www**.viniferawines.com.au **Open** Sun–Fri 11–4, Sat 10–5
Winemaker Lisa Bray, Jacob Stein **Viticulturist** Paul Stig **Est.** 1994 **Dozens** 1200
Vyds 11ha

Having lived in Mudgee for 15 years, Tony McKendry (a regional medical superintendent) and wife Debbie succumbed to the lure of winemaking; they planted their small (then 1.5ha) vineyard in 1995. In Debbie's words, 'Tony, in his spare 2 minutes per day, also decided to start Wine Science at CSU in 1992'. She continues, 'He's trying to live 27 hours per day (plus we have 4 kids!). He fell to pieces when he was involved in a severe car smash in 1997. Two months in hospital stopped his full-time medical work, and the winery dreams became inevitable'. Financial compensation finally came through and the small winery was built. The now-expanded vineyard includes 3.25ha each of chardonnay and cabernet sauvignon, 1.5ha of tempranillo and 1ha each of semillon, grenache and graciano. (JH)

ΨΨΨΨΨ **Organic Semillon 2021, Mudgee** With 5% sauvignon. Some skin contact and 9 months in American oak, to boot. Not really the right oak for this sort of thing, but the wine's idiosyncrasies win me over by virtue of the additional textural detail and intensity of flavour. That herbs, tonic, a squeeze of lemon and an inconspicuous – but still palpable – waft of vanilla. Long and chewy, in a way that suggests further intrigue will come with patience. Screw cap. 11.5% alc. RATING 92 DRINK 2022-2030 $25 NG

Rosé 2021, Mudgee A mid coral, with complex notes of redcurrant, tomato bush, orange pastille and strewn garden herb. Crunchy and intense of flavour, this gently mid-weighted rosé has plenty of appeal, fine length and expansive sweetness of fruit, suggesting substantial versatility at the table. Screw cap. 12.5% alc. RATING 91 DRINK 2021-2022 $28 NG

Organic Reserve Cabernet Sauvignon 2017, Mudgee This full-bodied wine has oodles of personality, brimming with Aussie menthol, clove, black currant, cinder box, dried sage and tomato leaf-lain tannins. There is plenty of push to the fruit, but not a great deal of refinement to the tannins. Time should serve this characterful wine well. Screw cap. 14% alc. RATING 91 DRINK 2022-2030 $40 NG

Reserve Chardonnay 2021, Mudgee Stone fruits, cantaloupe and nougatine to praline creaminess. I'd prefer this at full flavour amplitude, rather than the tensile, cool-climate framework that it plies. A wine of precision, considerable textural detail and sneaky length. Screw cap. 12.5% alc. RATING 90 DRINK 2021-2026 $35 NG

ΨΨΨΨ **Organic Graciano 2019, Mudgee** RATING 88 DRINK 2022-2025 $50 NG

Vino Intrepido ★★★★

22 Compton Street, Reservoir, Vic, 3078 (postal) **Region** Victoria
T 0488 479 999 **www.**vinointrepido.com **Winemaker** James Scarcebrook **Est.** 2016
Dozens 850
Before the grape crush took hold, James Scarcebrook started out in wine retail, working his way from cellar door assistant to marketing coordinator at Domaine Chandon in the Yarra Valley and most recently in sales with leading importers. A love of Italian varieties had been cemented earlier when he took off overseas for 16 months in '11 after finishing a master of wine business at Adelaide University. Then in '16, a small parcel of Heathcote sangiovese morphed into the inaugural Vino Intrepido. Dedicated solely to Italian varieties with fruit sourced mostly from Victorian growers, the range has expanded to include vermentino, friulano, fiano, nero d'Avola and nebbiolo. (JF)

ΨΨΨΨΨ **Grey Matter Ramato Pinot Grigio 2021, Nagambie Lakes** Ramato comes from the word rame, meaning copper. Skin contact brings an eye-catching bright copper tinge to the wine, together with a creamy mouthfeel which, at times, feels more gris than grigio. A minor point, because this wine nails the brief with a subtle flair. Good depth of baked apple, poached pear, musk and some delicious spiciness. Screw cap. 13% alc. RATING 90 DRINK 2021-2024 $28 JP

Nero's Fiddle Mildura Nero d'Avola 2021, Murray Darling The Sicilian red grape is enjoying its time in this country. This is the third release of Nero's Fiddle, with fruit sourced from the Chalmers family at Merbein. A mighty tasty young red in bold black cherry, plum, licorice, confection notes and dried herbs.

The sweet core of fruit explodes in the mouth, aided and abetted by juicy, ripe tannins. Screw cap. 12.5% alc. RATING 90 DRINK 2021-2025 $28 JP

Wolf In Sheep's Clothing Pinot Gris 2021, Mornington Peninsula A wine full of texture and flavour, with the fruit soaking up the oak easily. Flavours of spiced pears and apples, a hint of lemon curd and clotted cream. Pleasing to the last drop. Screw cap. 13% alc. RATING 90 DRINK 2021-2024 $28 JF

ΨΨΨΨ **The Sharpest Thorn Rosé 2021, Heathcote** RATING 89 DRINK 2021-2024 $28 JP
A Pound of Flesh Skin Contact Vermentino 2021, Nagambie Lakes RATING 88 DRINK 2021-2024 $28 JP

Vino Volta

184 Anzac Road, Mount Hawthorn, WA 6016 **Region** Swan Valley
T 0427 614 610 **www.**vinovolta.com.au **Open** By appt **Winemaker** Garth Cliff
Est. 2018 **Dozens** 1800

Garth Cliff was winemaker at Houghtons in the Swan Valley for 10 years prior to starting Vino Volta with his partner Kristen McGann in Jan '19. Vino Volta largely focuses on chenin blanc (they make 4 styles) and grenache from the Valley. Chenin blanc is in a revival phase currently, much of it thanks to Cliff, culminating in the inaugural nationwide Chenin Blanc Challenge in '20, held in the Swan Valley. Together they have also started their own wine import portfolio called Wine Terroirists, calling on McGann's long experience in the trade. Cliff is an active (in every sense) member of the Swan Valley Winemakers Association and a tireless proponent for the region. Exports to Singapore. (EL)

ΨΨΨΨΨ **Pezzonovante Grenache 2021, Swan Valley** Reductive upon opening. Superfine boned and taut, with layers of spice and acid, couched in a muscular framework. This is a more complete iteration of Swan Valley grenache, satisfying and complex in the mouth. There is salted heirloom tomato, blackberry bramble, black tea, jasmine tea pearls, raspberry compote and poached rhubarb. It has fennel and star anise and a multitude of other exotic spice characters, all of it united by a thread of bacon fat and blood laced throughout. Slam dunk. Screw cap. 13.5% alc. RATING 95 DRINK 2022-2032 $48 EL
La Chingadera Tempranillo Grenache Touriga 2020, Western Australia In stroll the cool-kid regions: Fruit was sourced from across Margaret River, Geographe, Swan Valley and Frankland River. Epic tension and concentration in the mouth. This is savoury and sweet, with layers of spice (star anise, licorice root, aniseed, black pepper, tobacco leaf), fruit (blackberry, blood plum, raspberry) and flowers (violets, lavender and black rose petals). Another cool release of La Chingadera. Screw cap. 14% alc. RATING 94 DRINK 2022-2030 $35 EL

ΨΨΨΨΟ **Post Modern Seriousism Grenache 2021, Swan Valley** RATING 93 DRINK 2022-2029 $30 EL
Nothing Wrong With Old Skool Chenin Blanc 2021, Swan District RATING 92 DRINK 2022-2032 $30 EL
Different Skins Frontignac Gewürztraminer 2021, Perth Hills Swan Valley RATING 92 DRINK 2022-2028 $35 EL
Funky And Fearless Chenin Blanc 2021, Swan Valley RATING 92 DRINK 2022-2032 $35 EL

Vintage Longbottom

15 Spring Gully Road, Piccadilly, SA 5151 **Region** Adelaide Hills
T (08) 8132 1048 **www.**vintagelongbottom.com **Winemaker** Matt Wenk **Est.** 1998
Dozens 48 000 **Vyds** 94.9ha

Kim Longbottom has moved her wine business from Padthaway to the Adelaide Hills, where Tapanappa has taken on the responsibility of making 3 tiers of wines. At the top is Magnus Shiraz from Clarendon and Blewitt Springs; the middle is the H Range from the McLaren Vale floor districts; and there is a sparkling range from the Adelaide Hills. Her daughter Margo brings experience in fashion, digital marketing and business administration. Exports to the UK, the US, Canada, Denmark, Singapore, Hong Kong and NZ. (JH)

🍷🍷🍷🍷🍷 **H Sauvignon Blanc 2021, Adelaide Hills** The Longbottoms don't choose to employ the word fumé to describe this style of sauvignon, but it's certainly imbued with a light woody smokiness that is very attractive. It helps define the wine and its depth of flavour. White peach, lime, grapefruit and white florals edge into a soft mid-palate texture. Oak softens the grape's aggressive herbals while enhancing its length. Screw cap. 12.1% alc. RATING 95 DRINK 2021–2026 $25 JP ✪

🍷🍷🍷🍷🍷 **Henry's Drive Shiraz Grenache Mourvèdre 2020, McLaren Vale** RATING 92 DRINK 2021–2025 $40 NG
Henry's Drive Shiraz Cabernet Sauvignon 2020, McLaren Vale RATING 92 DRINK 2021–2030 $40 NG
H Medium Dry Red 2020, McLaren Vale RATING 91 DRINK 2021–2025 $25 NG

Vinteloper

Lot 100 - 68 Chambers Road, Hay Valley, SA 5252 **Region** Adelaide Hills
T 0491 334 795 **www.**vinteloper.com.au **Open** Thurs–Sun 11–5 **Winemaker** David Bowley **Est.** 2008 **Dozens** 1500 **Vyds** 10.85ha
In David Bowley's words, 'Vinteloper is a winery started by a guy who decided, on instinct, to skip through his own daisy fields.' Vineyards and wineries had permeated David's mind before he left school, so it was inevitable that he would obtain his oenology degree at Adelaide University (in 2002). After several years training in both Australia and France, with some of the biggest and smallest players in the game, he founded Vinteloper in 2008. Wife Sharon draws the unique labels. Vinteloper continues to handcraft wines styled with a light touch and upbeat aromatics. Exports to the UK, the US, Canada, South Korea, Singapore, Japan and NZ. (JH)

🍷🍷🍷🍷🍷 **Chardonnay 2021, Adelaide Hills** A bit of a deceptive wine, subtle and restrained, you sense it is building slowly, methodically, into quite a complex beauty. Carries grapefruit, lemon, green apple and a finely tuned touch of spice and floral honeysuckle. Oak is discreet, just allowing a soft creaminess with a bite of almond skin poking through. Excellent depth and length. Give it time. Screw cap. 13% alc. RATING 93 DRINK 2022–2028 $36 JP
Shiraz 2020, Adelaide Hills A textural, spicy feast with lashings of dark cherries, plum, wild herbs, anise and well-placed vanillin oak. Fine line and length across the palate which opens up nicely, warmly in savoury tannins and generous flavour. Finishes trim and clean. No shortage of cool Hills personality here. Screw cap. 14% alc. RATING 93 DRINK 2022–2028 $33 JP
Pinot Pinot Rosé 2021, Adelaide Hills 70/30% pinot noir/pinot gris. Subtle, dusty tea-rose pink in colour. The addition of pinot gris brings with it a lifted honeysuckle presence to the aromas of red cherry, cranberry and dried herbs, not to mention a solid textural feel to the palate. Altogether, this is a rosé that is ready for anything, with food or without. Screw cap. 11.9% alc. RATING 92 DRINK 2021–2025 $27 JP
Pinot Noir 2021, Adelaide Hills There is a real youthful energy to this youngster, together with a serious dark side. Quite the chameleon. Soft red and cloudy in the glass with dried herbs, undergrowth, beetroot-earthiness and sour-cherry perfume, it then proceeds to launch into a lively onslaught of cherry, cranberry and pomegranate, with bitter chocolate and spice. Sinewy and detailed in fine tannins. Screw cap. 13.5% alc. RATING 92 DRINK 2022–2028 $37 JP
Touriga Nacional 2020, Langhorne Creek Immediately, irresistibly Langhorne Creek with its dense flavours and generosity. The Portuguese grape clearly loves its new home. Robust and forthright in blueberry, plum and chocolate with lilting aromatic bergamot and violet aromatics, the maker has done a mighty good job of controlling the grape's notable tannins. They are firm but not intrusive. Love to see how it ages. Screw cap. 13.5% alc. RATING 92 DRINK 2022–2030 $29 JP

Skins Black Label Pinot Gris 2021, Adelaide Hills A strong blush colour. Quite a delicate and refined gris with gentle florals – orange blossom, honeysuckle, acacia – moving in tandem with citrus, apple, green mango and pear. There's energy and freshness aplenty, not to mention potential. Nicely tuned to a delicate refrain. Screw cap. 12.5% alc. RATING 91 DRINK 2021–2026 $29 JP

ΨΨΨΨ **Watervale Riesling 2021, Clare Valley** RATING 89 DRINK 2021–2027 $29 EL

Vintners Ridge Estate ★★★★

Lot 18 Veraison Place, Yallingup, Margaret River, WA 6285 **Region** Margaret River
T 0417 956 943 **www.**vintnersridge.com.au **Open** By appt **Winemaker** Flying Fish Cove (Simon Ding) **Viticulturist** Andy Ferreira **Est.** 2001 **Dozens** 250 **Vyds** 2.1ha
When Maree and Robin Adair purchased the Vintners Ridge Vineyard in 2006 (cabernet sauvignon), it had already produced 3 crops, having been planted in Nov '01. The vineyard overlooks the picturesque Geographe Bay. (JH)

ΨΨΨΨΨ **Cabernet Sauvignon 2020, Margaret River** The low-yielding '20 was a cracking vintage in Margaret River. Ripe, powerful and graceful, not unlike '18. This wine is perfect testament to that – balanced fruit ripeness with chewy, shapely tannins and refreshing briny acidity that courses through the mouth. All things in place; pity we have to wait for release in 2023! Screw cap. 14.2% alc. RATING 92 DRINK 2023–2031 $27 EL

Voyager Estate

41 Stevens Road, Margaret River, WA 6285 **Region** Margaret River
T (08) 9757 6354 **www.**voyagerestate.com.au **Open** Wed–Sun 10–5 **Winemaker** Travis Lemm **Est.** 1978 **Dozens** 40 000 **Vyds** 112ha
Voyager Estate is located on Stevens Road in the Boodjidup Valley, which is emerging as hallowed ground (Leeuwin, the western neighbour, Xanadu's Stevens Road vineyard and the vineyards of Voyager Estate complete the trinity of prestige in this neck of the woods). The estate was established in 1978 by viticulturist Peter Gherardi, and later purchased and expanded by Michael Wright in '91. Michael's daughter, Alexandra Burt, has been at the helm since '05. The vineyard and winery are undergoing transition to certified organic status (due for completion in '23) and there is extensive clonal and varietal experimentation in the estate vineyards. The grounds are well known for their immaculate year-round grooming, as is the lavish, high-ceiling tasting room, home to an award-winning restaurant with a rolling, seasonal degustation of local produce. Exports to all major markets. (EL)

ΨΨΨΨΨ **MJW Cabernet Sauvignon 2018, Margaret River** The tannins require us to start at the finish, as they close around the fruit. However, they are superfine, pumice-like, and shape the red fruit in the mouth. This is a sophisticated, powder-fine cabernet that shows the power and might of the '18 vintage, albeit in its inherently restrained manner. This is svelte and it will live an age. Decanting essential. Screw cap. 14% alc. RATING 97 DRINK 2022–2042 $180 EL

ΨΨΨΨΨ **MJW Chardonnay 2020, Margaret River** Inchoate, powerful, raw and dense. At this point, the '20 vintage is on parade; the acidity which backs to fruit is juicy and lip smacking. The marriage of the Dijon and Gingin clones is not yet seamless, but given the pedigree of this wine, it will be, given time. Screw cap. 13% alc. RATING 95 DRINK 2022–2042 $110 EL

Cabernet Sauvignon 2018, Margaret River The calling card for this wine has long been the soft tannins, and it is recommended, if you have the patience, to hold for at least 5 years to allow them to melt into the fruit. As it stands, the powerful '18 vintage is on show, making for one of the more robust and intense iterations of this wine. Screw cap. 14% alc. RATING 95 DRINK 2022–2037 $85 EL

Chardonnay 2020, Margaret River This vintage in Margaret River has produced a tranche of effortless wines: powerful, ripe and with bright acidity. As ever, this is classy to the max – creamy, taut, restrained, nutty and super-fresh; all of it wrapped in a web of saline acidity and glossy phenolics. Screw cap. 14% alc. RATING 94 DRINK 2022-2032 $50 EL

Walsh & Sons

4/5962 Caves Road, Margaret River, WA 6285 **Region** Margaret River
T (08) 9758 8023 **www**.walshandsons.com.au **Open** Wed–Sun 11–5 **Winemaker** Ryan Walsh, Freya Hohnen **Est.** 2014 **Dozens** 1500 **Vyds** 20ha
The name Walsh & Sons has a Burgundian twist, the only difference is that Walsh & Sons would be Walsh et Fils. The analogy continues: the sons Roi and Hamish (Ryan Walsh and Freya Hohnen their parents) are in turn from McHenry Hohnen, of Margaret River blue blood wine aristocracy. Ryan and Freya have had a Burgundian family association having made wine for McHenry Hohnen from 2004 to '12, and over that time visiting/working for wineries in France, Spain, Switzerland and the US. At present, part of the crop from their 11ha Burnside Vineyard (where they base themselves) and the Walsh 7ha Osmington Vineyard is sold to McHenry Hohnen, Yalumba and Domain & Vineyards. The Burnside Vineyard is in biodynamic conversion. Exports to the US. (JH)

🍷🍷🍷🍷🍷 **Roi Cabernet Sauvignon 2020, Margaret River** Unfined, unfiltered, and – like all the wines from Walsh & Sons – super-charming, a bit rustic, and wildly attractive. Not your average. So, to the wine: this has cassis, double cream, hung deli meat, Szechuan peppercorns, cooling, mineral acidity and chalky/graphite tannins. Lovely, gentle, persistent flavour through the finish reinforces the beauty of this wine. Cork. 13.5% alc. RATING 94 DRINK 2021-2031 $50 EL

🍷🍷🍷🍷🍷 **Little Poppet White 2021, Margaret River** RATING 93 DRINK 2021-2025 $28 EL
Remi Rosé 2021, Margaret River RATING 92 DRINK 2022-2024 $28 EL
Riesling 2021, Frankland River RATING 91 DRINK 2022-2027 $25 EL
Westside Malbec 2020, Frankland River RATING 90 DRINK 2021-2028 $28 EL

Wangolina

8 Limestone Coast Road, Mount Benson, SA 5275 **Region** Mount Benson
T (08) 8768 6187 **www**.wangolina.com.au **Open** 7 days 11–4 **Winemaker** Anita Goode **Est.** 2001 **Dozens** 4000 **Vyds** 11ha
Four generations of the Goode family have been graziers at Wangolina Station, but Anita Goode broke with tradition by becoming a vigneron. She originally planted sauvignon blanc, shiraz, cabernet sauvignon and semillon, later adding pinot gris, grüner veltliner, and malvasia istriana. (JH)

🍷🍷🍷🍷🍷 **A Series Lagrein 2020, Limestone Coast** Wow! Beetroot on the nose is immediate and earthy. It is black as spades in the glass, with anise and fresh leather. In the mouth the wine is intense, rich, and a little bit leafy, with black olive, bay leaf and mulberry. Screw cap. 14% alc. RATING 91 DRINK 2022-2027 $28 EL
Spectrum Mt Benson Syrah 2018, Mount Benson Brilliant intensity and concentration of flavour, the tannins that shape this wine are a real highlight: chewy, supple and ripe. The oak is a little domineering, and detracts from the sumptuous display of fruit, but it will hopefully be washed into the ocean of flavour that currently dominates the wine. Only time will tell. Good length through the finish hints that we may have our wish granted. Time is on our side. Screw cap. 13.5% alc. RATING 91 DRINK 2022-2037 $50 EL

🍷🍷🍷🍷 **A Series Grüner Veltliner 2021, Mount Benson** RATING 89 DRINK 2022-2028 $28 EL
Montepulciano 2021, Limestone Coast RATING 89 DRINK 2022-2026 $28 EL
Moscato 2021, Limestone Coast RATING 89 DRINK 2022-2024 $20 EL

Wantirna Estate

10 Bushy Park Lane, Wantirna South, Vic 3152 **Region** Yarra Valley
T (03) 9801 2367 **www.**wantirnaestate.com.au **Winemaker** Maryann Egan, Reg Egan
Est. 1963 **Dozens** 700 **Vyds** 4.2ha

Reg and Tina Egan were among the early movers in the rebirth of the Yarra Valley. The vineyard surrounds the house they live in, which also incorporates the winery. These days Reg describes himself as the interfering winemaker but in the early years he did everything, dashing from his legal practice to the winery to check on the ferments. Today much of the winemaking responsibility has been transferred to daughter Maryann, who has a degree in wine science from CSU. Both have honed their practical skills among the small domaines and châteaux of Burgundy and Bordeaux, inspired by single-vineyard, terroir-driven wines. Maryann was also winemaker for many years in Domaine Chandon's infancy. Exports to Thailand and Hong Kong. (JH)

ʕʕʕʕʕ **Amelia Cabernet Sauvignon Merlot 2019, Yarra Valley** Traditionally cabernet merlot on the label, but actually a blend of 45% cabernet, 45% field blend of merlot and cab franc, with 10% petit verdot. A deep crimson purple. Super-impressive with blackcurrant, cedar from well-handled oak and just a touch of cigar leaf. Textured and richly flavoured, with dark fruits on the palate as well as some savoury black olive/tapenade flavours. The tannins are satiny and integrated. Enjoy this with richly flavoured food now or watch is slowly unfurl over the next 10–15 years. Screw cap. 13% alc. RATING 95 DRINK 2023-2033 $75 PR

ʕʕʕʕʕ **Isabella Chardonnay 2020, Yarra Valley** RATING 92 DRINK 2022-2027 $75 PR

Waratah Hills Vineyard

20 Cottmans Road, Fish Creek, Vic 3959 **Region** Gippsland
T (03) 5683 2441 **www.**waratahhills.com.au **Open** Fri-Sun 11–5 **Winemaker** Marcus Satchell **Viticulturist** Georgia Roberts **Est.** 1997 **Dozens** 900 **Vyds** 4ha

Melbourne-based business partners and friends, Oliver and Brooke Smith, Paul and Tanya Smith and Charlie and Hayley Blomley bought Waratah Hills cellar door in Aug '20. Oliver's brother Ben lives on site to manage the business. Viticulturist Georgia Roberts is reinvigorating the vineyards, including re-trellising the 1.2ha of chardonnay and 2.8ha of pinot noir. The plan is to plant another 4ha of the aforementioned varieties to double the production of single-vineyard wines yet remain a boutique producer. A commercial kitchen has been added to expand the casual dining experience, with a focus on pairing wine and food.

ʕʕʕʕʕ **Chardonnay 2019, Gippsland** Chardonnay appears the star in the range. This has a certain presence and definition. It's superfine and long, spearheaded by mouth-watering acidity taking the citrus flavours, creamy lees and spice for a joy ride. It has good tension and energy. A touch short on the finish, but definitely a wine to watch. Screw cap. 13% alc. RATING 93 DRINK 2022-2028 $60 JF
Alexandra Blanc de Noirs South Sparkling 2015, Gippsland A straw-gold hue, with a bronze blush points to the pinot noir base, with spice and slight red-fruit accents too. Some complexity via dough/yeasty autolysis and good acidity, keeping this lively. Diam. 11.5% alc. RATING 91 $70 JF
Pinot Noir 2019, Gippsland The colour is advanced, yet a neatly tuned wine with its gentle sway of red berries, cherries and pips plus a distinct flavour of Zucca Rabarbaro (an Italian rhubarb liqueur). It's lightly spiced, peppery with some bush mint. While it has plenty of flavour, it works off a more mid-weighted palate. There's a slight grip to the tannins and a charred radicchio bitterness to the finish, which is complementary. Screw cap. 13% alc. RATING 90 DRINK 2022-2025 $85 JF
Ignatius South Pinot Noir 2017, Gippsland The advanced hue is a concern, although there's a pale ruby centre; aromas and flavours of whole bunches in the ferment adding a floral, spicy and stemmy edge. Rhubarb compote, morello cherries and lots of cinnamon, star anise and pepper, too. Some grip to the tannins, plenty of fresh acidity and while it's not a big wine, it feels supple. Many will baulk at the price. Screw cap. 13% alc. RATING 90 DRINK 2022-2025 $105 JF

Warner Glen Estate

PO Box 383, Mount Barker, WA 6324 **Region** Margaret River
T 0457 482 957 **www.**warnerglenwines.com.au **Winemaker** Various **Viticulturist** Glen
Harding **Est.** 1993 **Dozens** 6000 **Vyds** 34.6ha
Warner Glen Estate is a partnership of 5 WA families, led by viticulturist Glen Harding. The
Jindawarra Vineyard, just south of Karridale, is only 6km from the Southern Ocean and 4km
from the Indian Ocean; it avoids extreme high temperatures as a result of the cooling sea
breezes. It is planted to shiraz, chardonnay, sauvignon blanc, pinot noir, viognier and pinot
gris. Cabernet sauvignon is sourced from the Warner Glen-managed vineyard at Wilyabrup.
Wines are released under the Warner Glen Estate, Frog Belly and Smokin' Gun labels. Exports
to Switzerland. (JH)

⚕⚕⚕⚕ **Chardonnay 2021, Margaret River** Green apple, nashi pear, white peach,
nectarine and lemons. Uncomplicated, pure chardonnay. Screw cap. 12% alc.
RATING 89 DRINK 2022-2027 $20 EL

Warramunda Estate

860 Maroondah Highway, Coldstream, Vic 3770 **Region** Yarra Valley
T 0412 694 394 **www.**warramundaestate.com.au **Open** Fri–Sun 10–5
Winemaker Robert Zak-Magdziarz **Viticulturist** Dan Sergeant **Est.** 1998 **Dozens** 6000
Vyds 25.2ha
The Magdziarz family acquired Warramunda from the Vogt family in 2007, producing their
first vintage in '13. The Magdziarz family have built on the existing solid foundations with a
deep respect for the surrounding landscape and a vision for terroir-driven wines. Viticulture
follows biodynamic principles, vines are unirrigated and wines are all naturally fermented with
wild yeast. Second label Liv Zak (named for daughter Olivia, studying viticulture, winemaking
and business at Charles Sturt university) was launched in '15. Exports to the UK, the US,
Canada and Japan. (JH)

⚕⚕⚕⚕⚕ **The Compass Series Cabernet Merlot Cabernet Franc 2019, Yarra
Valley** A deep, vibrant crimson purple. Impressive from the outset, with aromas of
black plums, dark cherries, blackberries, cedar and fresh vanilla bean. Unctuously
flavoured, yet very well balanced, there is a core of perfectly ripened dark fruits
and this finishes long and seductive with very fine and persistent tannins. Good
now and in the medium term. Diam. 14% alc. RATING 95 DRINK 2022-2031
$120 PR

⚕⚕⚕⚕⚕ **Coldstream Syrah 2020, Yarra Valley** RATING 92 DRINK 2022-2022 $55 PR
Liv Zak Sparkling Rosé 2020, Yarra Valley RATING 91 $38 PR
Coldstream Pinot Noir 2020, Yarra Valley RATING 90 DRINK 2022-2028
$55 PR

Water Wheel

Bridgewater-Raywood Road, Bridgewater-on-Loddon, Vic 3516 **Region** Bendigo
T (03) 5437 3060 **www.**waterwheelwine.com **Open** Mon–Fri 9–5, w'ends 12–4
Winemaker Bill Trevaskis, Amy Cumming **Est.** 1972 **Dozens** 35000 **Vyds** 136ha
Peter Cumming, with more than 2 decades of winemaking under his belt, has quietly built
on the reputation of Water Wheel year by year. The winery is owned by the Cumming
family, which has farmed in the Bendigo region for more than 50 years, with horticulture
and viticulture special areas of interest. Over half the vineyard area is planted to shiraz (75ha),
followed by chardonnay and sauvignon blanc (15ha each), cabernet sauvignon and malbec
(10ha each) and smaller plantings of petit verdot, semillon, roussanne and grenache. Water
Wheel continues to make wines that over-deliver at their modest prices. Exports to the UK,
the US and Canada. (JH)

⚕⚕⚕⚕⚕ **Viognier 2020, Bendigo** Aromas of bright ginger, honeysuckle, apricot
and yellow peach with orange peel, showing some pretty inviting complexity.
Viscous with weight and a warm creaminess across the palate. A rare example

of this variety from the Bendigo region. Screw cap. 14.4% alc. RATING 93
DRINK 2021–2026 $24 JP ✪
Kettle of Fish Red 2021, Bendigo Blend of primitivo/shiraz/grenache. Young
and juicy, all the way from the black cherry, pepper and woody spice to the supple,
linear tannins and neat finish. Deceptively long, strong finish. Reinforces the need
for, and enjoyment to be found in, these early-drinking, easygoing and well-made
young reds. Diam. 13% alc. RATING 90 DRINK 2022–2025 $30 JP

♥♥♥♥ **Memsie Homestead Shiraz 2019, Bendigo** RATING 89 DRINK 2021–2025
$13 JP ✪
Baringhup Shiraz 2019, Bendigo RATING 89 DRINK 2021–2032 $26 JP
Chardonnay 2021, Bendigo RATING 88 DRINK 2022–2025 $18 JP
Malbec 2020, Bendigo RATING 88 DRINK 2021–2026 $22 JP
Shiraz 2019, Bendigo RATING 88 DRINK 2021–2029 $18 JP

Waterton Hall Wines   ★★★☆

61 Waterton Hall Road, Rowella, Tas 7270 **Region** Northern Tasmania
T 0417 834 781 **www**.watertonhall.com.au **Open** By appt **Winemaker** Tasmanian
Vintners **Est.** 2006 **Dozens** 1800 **Vyds** 10.1ha
The homestead that today is the home of Waterton Hall Wines was built in the 1850s.
Originally a private residence, it was modified extensively in 1901 by well known neo-gothic
architect Alexander North and ultimately passed into the ownership of the Catholic church
from '49–96. Together with various outbuildings it was variously used as a school, a boys'
home and a retreat. In 2002 it was purchased by Jennifer Baird and Peter Cameron and in
'15 passed into the family ownership of 'one architect, one farmer, one interior designer, one
finance director and one labradoodle'. Their real names are David and Susan Shannon, John
Carter and Belinda Evans (the dog's name is Bert.) Susan and John are sister and brother. (JH)

♥♥♥♥♀ **Tamar Valley Viognier 2020, Tasmania** It's a challenge to ripen viognier
in Tasmania, but here's evidence of its potential, provided yields are managed
stringently (just 108 dozen bottles were made from 0.15ha). Crunchy apricot and
grapefruit carry tension and bite, nicely shaped by 7 months' maturation in old
oak barrels with regular bâtonnage. It holds good persistence and strong potential.
A little phenolic bitterness may assimilate with maturity. Screw cap. 12.6% alc.
RATING 91 DRINK 2023–2027 $40 TS

♥♥♥♥ **The Barn Pinot Noir 2021, Tasmania** RATING 89 DRINK 2026–2031 $38 TS
Chardonnay 2021, Tasmania RATING 88 DRINK 2022–2023 $38 TS

Watkins   ★★★★

59 Grants Gully Road, Chandlers Hill, SA, 5159 **Region** Langhorne Creek
T 0422 418 845 **www**.watkins.wine **Open** Fri–Sat 11–6, Sun 11–5 **Winemaker** Sam
Watkins **Est.** 2019 **Dozens** 6500 **Vyds** 150ha
Sibling trio Ben, Sam and Jo Watkins, under the guidance of parents David and Ros Watkins,
have established Watkins as a new label based at their Chandlers Hill winery and cellar door.
They are tapping into their well-established estate vineyards there and in Langhorne Creek:
both regions' vines are maritime influenced, with afternoon sea breezes tempering summer
ripening temperatures. The top-of-the-ridge cellar door overlooks rolling hillside vines on
one side and St Vincent Gulf on the other. Winemaker Sam Watkins has worked in Napa
Valley, USA, and Porto, Portugal, as well as Orange, NSW, Coonawarra, Barossa and McLaren
Vale, SA. Brother Ben is commercial director, and sister Jo is brand director and cellar door
manager. (TL)

♥♥♥♥♀ **Limited Bright Red Grenache Sangiovese 2021, Langhorne Creek** An
interesting cross between a rosé and a light dry red. It's not sweet, yet is all about
red berry and pomegranate seeds that have a biting freshness. The colour alone
will drive sales at high speed. Screw cap. 13.5% alc. RATING 90 DRINK 2022–2022
$20 JH ✪

Shiraz 2020, Langhorne Creek There's plenty to chew on in this supple, rich, warmly-accented wine which will repay cellaring as it slims down with age in bottle. Screw cap. 14% alc. RATING 90 DRINK 2024–2034 $20 JH ✪

♟♟♟♟ Cabernet Sauvignon 2020, Langhorne Creek RATING 89 DRINK 2022–2025 $20 JH
Extra Brut Blanc de Blanc 2021, Langhorne Creek RATING 88 $25 JH
Limited Wild Sauvignon Blanc 2021, Fleurieu RATING 88 DRINK 2022–2022 $20 JH

WayWood Wines   ★★★★☆

67 Kays Road, McLaren Vale, SA 5171 **Region** McLaren Vale
T (08) 8323 8468 **www.**waywoodwines.com **Open** By appt **Winemaker** Andrew Wood
Viticulturist Andrew Wood **Est.** 2005 **Dozens** 1500 **Vyds** 3ha
This is the culmination of Andrew Wood and Lisa Robertson's wayward odyssey. Andrew left his career as a sommelier in London and retrained as a winemaker, working in Portugal, the UK, Italy and the Granite Belt (an eclectic selection), settling in McLaren Vale in early '04. Working with Kangarilla Road winery for the next 6 years, while making small quantities of shiraz, cabernets and tempranillo from purchased grapes, led them to nebbiolo, montepulciano and shiraz. Exports to Canada. (JH)

♟♟♟♟♟ LBVP Shiraz 2017, McLaren Vale The late-bottled (LB) evolution of '17 VP, decanted to 100L barrels in '19 for a further 2 years' maturation. Very smart. The spirit impeccably embedded into the fray of dark cherry, camphor, raspberry bon-bon and molten black rock. A tautly arched bow of gritty, seamlessly melded tannins, corrals any excess. The finish, endless. Excellent domestic fortified. Screw cap. 19% alc. RATING 97 $40 NG ✪

♟♟♟♟♟ Carignan 2019, McLaren Vale RATING 93 DRINK 2021–2025 $25 NG ✪
Shiraz 2019, McLaren Vale RATING 92 DRINK 2021–2028 $25 NG ✪
Reserve Tempranillo 2017, McLaren Vale RATING 92 DRINK 2021–2027 $50 NG

Weathercraft Wine   ★★★★☆

1241 Beechworth-Wangaratta Road, Everton Upper, Vic 3678 **Region** Beechworth
T (03) 5727 0518 **www.**weathercraft.com.au **Open** By appt **Winemaker** Raquel Jones
Viticulturist Raquel Jones **Est.** 1998 **Dozens** 1800 **Vyds** 4ha
In 2016, Raquel and Hugh Jones discovered a vineyard 10min out of Beechworth, neighbouring the likes of Gianconda and Castanga. It had an immaculate 20yo of shiraz, planted in 1998, with fruit sold to Yalumba (for a single-vineyard shiraz) as well as to smaller producers. Raquel and Hugh retained some of the shiraz and have since added tempranillo, albariño, grenache and monstrell, a nod to Raquel's Spanish heritage. Biological farming and soil health is a priority for them and the preference is for traditional, low-intervention winemaking, including the use of amphora. (JH)

♟♟♟♟♟ Amphora Blanco 2021, Beechworth Albariño/chardonnay blend. A revelation! The use of amphora opens up not only complexity and the textural possibilities of albariño and chardonnay, but performs it with a streamlined, seamless beauty. Grapefruit, lemon zest, tangerine, white nectarine and saline aromas. Time in amphora has knitted the whole piece together. Stunning! Screw cap. 12% alc. RATING 96 DRINK 2021–2026 $38 JP ✪ ♥
Pinot Gris 2021, Alpine Valleys Striking exotic, complex aromas: spiced apple, white peach, mango, talc and musk. The soft, gentle mouthfeel is a feature, together with a delicious spiciness before finishing clean. Easy to love. Screw cap. 13% alc. RATING 94 DRINK 2021–2025 $25 JP ✪

♟♟♟♟♟ Chardonnnay 2019, Beechworth RATING 93 DRINK 2021–2025 $34 JP
Reserve Syrah 2019, Beechworth RATING 93 DRINK 2022–2030 $45 JP
Rosé 2021, Beechworth RATING 90 DRINK 2021–2024 $25 JP

Welland

Lot 1 Welland Road, Nuriootpa, SA 5355 **Region** Barossa Valley
T 0438 335 510 **www**.wellandwines.com **Winemaker** Soul Growers
Viticulturist Amanda Mader **Est.** 2017 **Dozens** 5000 **Vyds** 1.7ha
Surrounded by the sprawling northern expanse of the township of Nuriootpa and destined
to be sold for development, the 1923-planted Welland shiraz vineyard was rescued in 2017 by
a group of friends led by Ben and Madeleine Chapman. The neglected vineyard of 30 rows
was resurrected in '19 with new trellising, irrigation and replanting of dead vines. Fruit from
the site is supplemented by shiraz and cabernet sauvignon from other vineyards around the
Barossa and Eden valleys. Contract winemaking is handled by the talented team at Soul
Growers. Exports to Singapore. (TS)

¶¶¶¶¶ **Old Hands Cabernet Sauvignon 2019, Barossa** Awash with blackberry
and blackcurrant jube notes with hints of licorice, cocoa powder, dark chocolate,
violet, briar and earth. Cedary notes kick in on the palate which shows lovely
blackcurrant intensity, fine, compact tannins and a sapid, cassis-rich finish. Screw
cap. 14.5% alc. RATING 91 DRINK 2021-2030 $70 DB

¶¶¶¶ **Old Hands Shiraz 2019, Barossa Valley** RATING 89 DRINK 2021–2031
$70 DB
Valley & Valley Cabernet Sauvignon 2020, Barossa RATING 88
DRINK 2021-2028 $30 DB
Valley & Valley Shiraz 2020, Barossa RATING 88 DRINK 2021-2026 $30 DB

Wellington & Wolfe

3 Balfour Place, Launceston, Tas 7250 **Region** Tasmania
T 0474 425 527 **www**.wellingtonwolfe.com **Winemaker** Hugh McCullough **Est.** 2017
Dozens 250
There are many routes to winemaking, and a master's degree in modern history from Scotland
is among the more unusual. Hugh McCullough came to love wine through hospitality work
to fund his studies, ultimately culminating in a master's in viticulture and oenology, focusing
on sparkling and aromatic wine production. Vintages in Oregon, Washington, the Barossa
and Tasmania followed, finally settling in Launceston with his partner winemaker Natalie
Fryar (Bellebonne), establishing Wellington & Wolfe in '17. The aromatic expression, depth of
flavour and racy acidity of Tasmanian riesling are his first love: second label Wolfe at the Door
was introduced in '20 to showcase the 'supporting' varietals. Production is tiny and fruit is
sourced from growers in Pipers River and the Tamar Valley. (TS)

¶¶¶¶¶ **Riesling 2021, Tasmania** Hugh McCullough is becoming ever more refined in
the art of upholding the delicacy and detail in riesling, and this is his finest estate-
grown release yet. Skin contact, old barrels, wild ferment, bâtonnage and just the
slightest drop of RS are all played with masterful sensitivity to build harmony
and beauty. But the real game here is pristine Tamar fruit: floral, tropical, racy
and downright delicious. Irresistible now, and with plenty of mileage in the tank.
Screw cap. 12% alc. RATING 95 DRINK 2021-2031 $38 TS
Eylandt Off Dry Riesling 2021, Tasmania The fragrant, spicy elegance
of the cool '21 season in Pipers River is electric, and it's testimony to Hugh
McCullough's dexterity that he's successfully deployed every trick in the book to
achieve balance, without for a moment interrupting purity or crystalline linearity.
A few hours of skin contact and cool fermentation (12 degrees) energise kaffir
lime, Granny Smith apple and lemon fruit accented with white pepper. Texture
and body derive equally from maturation and bâtonnage, mlf and 35g/L RS. Huge
potential. Screw cap. 8.5% alc. RATING 94 DRINK 2026-2041 $50 TS

¶¶¶¶¶ **Wolfe at the Door RGG White Blend 2021, Tasmania** RATING 92
DRINK 2021-2023 $28 TS
Pinot Meunier 2021, Tasmania RATING 91 DRINK 2021-2022 $30 TS

West Cape Howe Wines

Lot 14923 Muir Highway, Mount Barker, WA 6324 **Region** Mount Barker
T (08) 9892 1444 **www.**westcapehowewines.com.au **Open** Mon–Fri 10–5, w'ends
11–4 **Winemaker** Gavin Berry, Caitlin Gazey **Viticulturist** Rob Quenby **Est.** 1997
Dozens 60000 **Vyds** 310ha

West Cape Howe is owned by a partnership of 4 WA families, including those of Gavin Berry
and Rob Quenby. Grapes are sourced from estate vineyards in Mount Barker and Frankland
River. The Langton Vineyard (Mount Barker) has 100ha planted to cabernet sauvignon, shiraz,
riesling, sauvignon blanc, chardonnay and semillon; the Russell Road Vineyard (Frankland
River) has 210ha. West Cape Howe also sources select parcels of fruit from valued contract
growers. Best Value Winery Wine Companion 2016. Exports to the UK, the US, Denmark,
Switzerland, South Korea, Singapore, Japan and Hong Kong. (JH)

ȲȲȲȲȲ **Riesling 2021, Mount Barker** Ticks each and every box along the journey,
starting with the quartz-green colour, then the flowery and fragrant aromas telling
of the citrus-accented palate gathering drive as it explores lime and passionfruit. All
throughout the line of acidity provides cohesion. Screw cap. 12.5% alc. RATING 95
DRINK 2021-2032 $22 JH ✪
Sauvignon Blanc 2021, Mount Barker First up are juicy tutti-frutti
aromas, flavours and feel until the crisp finish. Screw cap. 12.5% alc. RATING 94
DRINK 2021-2023 $22 JH ✪
Shiraz 2019, Frankland River A small portion finishes its ferment in new oak
barriques; matured in new and used French oak. You have to wonder how any
new-oak expenditure could be justified by the giveaway price. Unbeatable now or
for later consumption, with its spicy black fruits and precise tannin control. Screw
cap. 14.5% alc. RATING 94 DRINK 2022-2037 $22 JH ✪

ȲȲȲȲȲ **Riesling 2021, Porongurup** RATING 93 DRINK 2021-2031 $30 EL
Hanna's Hill Cabernet Malbec 2019, Frankland River RATING 92
DRINK 2021-2031 $22 EL ✪
Tempranillo 2020, Frankland River Perth Hills RATING 91 DRINK 2022-2027
$22 EL ✪
Styx Gully Chardonnay 2020, Mount Barker RATING 91 DRINK 2021-2027
$30 EL
Pinot Noir 2020, Mount Barker RATING 90 DRINK 2022-2027 $22 EL
Karri Oak Pinot Noir 2020, Mount Barker RATING 90 DRINK 2021-2031
$30 EL

Whicher Ridge

200 Chapman Hill East Road, Busselton, WA 6280 **Region** Geographe
T 0448 531 399 **www.**whicherridge.com.au **Open** Thurs–Mon 11–5 **Winemaker** Cathy
Howard **Viticulturist** Neil Howard **Est.** 2004 **Dozens** 2500 **Vyds** 9ha

It is hard to imagine a founding husband-and-wife team with such an ideal blend of viticultural
and winemaking experience accumulated over a combined 40+ years. Cathy Howard (née
Spratt) was a winemaker for 16 years at Orlando and St Hallett in the Barossa Valley, and at
Watershed Wines in Margaret River. She now has her own winemaking consulting business
as well as making the Whicher Ridge wines. Neil Howard's career as a viticulturist began in
the Pyrenees region with Taltarni and Blue Pyrenees Estate, then he moved to Mount Avoca
as vineyard manager for 12 years. When he relocated to the west, he managed and developed
a number of vineyards throughout the region. Whicher Ridge's Odyssey Creek Vineyard at
Chapman Hill in Geographe supplies sauvignon blanc and cabernet sauvignon, as well as a
little viogner, malbec, mataro and petit verdot. Shiraz and cabernet are also sourced from
a leased vineyard in Margaret River. Exports to Singapore. (JH)

ȲȲȲȲȲ **Odyssey Garden Cabernet Sauvignon 2019, Geographe** Cabernet from
Geographe excels at chocolate, mulberry and sweet, plush tannins. All that here,
folded into a medium-weight body and stretched out over the finish. Lovely.
Screw cap. 14% alc. RATING 91 DRINK 2021-2031 $25 EL

Whispering Brook

Rodd Street, Broke, NSW 2330 **Region** Hunter Valley
T (02) 9818 4126 **www**.whispering-brook.com **Open** Thurs–Sun 10.30–5 and by appt
Winemaker Susan Frazier, Adam Bell **Viticulturist** Adam Bell, Neil Grosser **Est.** 2000
Dozens 1100 **Vyds** 3ha

It took some time for partners Susan Frazier and Adam Bell to find the property on which they established their vineyard over 20 years ago. It has a combination of terra rossa loam soils on which the reds are planted, and sandy flats for the white grapes. A trip to Portugal in '07 inspired the planting of Portuguese varieties, including touriga and arinto, alongside Hunter staples, shiraz and semillon. The partners have also established an olive grove and accommodation for up to 18 guests in the large house set in the vineyard, offering vineyard and winery tours. (JH)

♛♛♛♛♛ Semillon 2021, Hunter Valley I love this vintage for wines of both colours: cool, attenuated and herbal complexity, its tattoo. The best wines, way beyond mere citrus balm and acid. Lightweight, yet a fine thrust of nettle, lemon squash, white pepper grind, dill, Thai herb and icy pole. The acidity, fine boned and juicy. The finish, taut, yet with nothing brittle, hard, or out of place. Very long. A fine wine that will reward mid- to longer-term cellaring. Screw cap. 10.5% alc. RATING 95 DRINK 2022–2034 $35 NG ✪

♛♛♛♛♛ Single Vineyard Limited Release Arinto 2021, Hunter Valley RATING 93 DRINK 2021–2023 $40 NG
Basket Pressed Touriga Nacional 2019, Hunter Valley RATING 93 DRINK 2022–2026 $65 NG
Red Earth Mosaic 2018, Hunter Valley RATING 93 DRINK 2021–2026 $65 NG
Basket Pressed Merlot Cabernet 2017, Hunter Valley Hilltops RATING 93 DRINK 2021–2026 $65 NG
Museum Release Single Vineyard Semillon 2016, Hunter Valley RATING 93 DRINK 2021–2024 $50 NG

🍇 Whistle and Hope Wines

5 Warby St, Wangaratta, Vic 3677 (postal) **Region** Nagambie Lakes
T 0407 749 441 **Winemaker** Matt Kilby **Est.** 2017 **Dozens** 360

Matt Kilby worked his first vintage in 2005 at Dominion Wines in the Strathbogie Ranges, followed by stints at Tahbilk and then 10 years at Mitchelton, completing his winemaking degree at CSU along the way and travelling overseas to work vintage in the Mosel. Matt is now winemaker at Michelini Wines in the Alpine Valleys, running Whistle & Hope alongside. The first releases have been rieslings, and during '22 he will bottle a '21 Heathcote shiraz and hopes to pursue a Yarra Valley cabernet sauvignon, too. He says 'I want to target varieties and regions that interest me. I believe that Victoria has the capacity to successfully grow any variety when matched with the right site.' (JP)

♛♛♛♛ Riesling 2019, Goulburn Valley Rich in apple blossom, honeysuckle and citrus zest aromas, this 3yo riesling is drinking well and would be suited to a good food match. A preserved-lemon savouriness adds a touch of the exotic flavour-wise, together with Gala apple, grapefruit pith and a lemony bright upfront acidity. Coming together. Screw cap. 12% alc. RATING 88 DRINK 2022–2025 $24 JP

Whistler Wines

241 Seppeltsfield Road, Stone Well, SA 5352 **Region** Barossa Valley
T (08) 8562 4942 **www**.whistlerwines.com **Open** 7 days 10.30–5 **Winemaker** Michael J. Corbett, Adam Hay **Viticulturist** Martin Pfeiffer **Est.** 1997 **Dozens** 7500 **Vyds** 14.2ha

Whistler was established in '99 by brothers Martin and Chris Pfeiffer but is now in the hands of the next generation, brothers Josh and Sam Pfeiffer. Josh took over the winemaking and viticulture in '13 and has incorporated the sustainable approach of organic and biodynamic techniques. Sam has stepped into the general manager role, largely focused on sales and marketing. Whistler maintains the traditional Estate range of wines as well as the fun, easy drinking 'next gen' range, which has more adventurous labelling and names. Exports to Norway, Hong Kong, Canada, the US, Denmark, Mauritius and South Korea (JH)

🍷🍷🍷🍷 **Get In My Belly Grenache 2021, Barossa Valley** Pure plummy joy here with hints of souk-like spice, pressed flowers, amaro-esque herbs, gingerbread and cola. Spacious and airy in the mouth with an exotic spicy edge to the pure plummy fruit and a wicked chalky, savoury finish. Screw cap. 13.9% alc. RATING 94 DRINK 2021-2025 $40 DB

🍷🍷🍷🍷 **Shock Value SMG 2021, Barossa Valley** RATING 93 DRINK 2021-2024 $25 DB ✪
Thank God It's Friday Shiraz 2020, Barossa Valley RATING 92 DRINK 2021-2030 $28 DB
Estate Cabernet Sauvignon 2020, Barossa Valley RATING 92 DRINK 2021-2030 $40 DB
Estate Shiraz 2020, Barossa Valley RATING 92 DRINK 2021-2030 $60 DB
Shiver Down My Spine Shiraz 2020, Barossa Valley RATING 91 DRINK 2021-2028 $40 DB
Dry As A Bone Rosé 2021, Barossa Valley RATING 90 DRINK 2021-2022 $28 DB
Estate Riesling 2021, Barossa Valley RATING 90 DRINK 2021-2025 $28 DB

Whistling Eagle Vineyard ★★★★☆

2769 Heathcote-Rochester Road, Colbinabbin, Vic 3559 **Region** Heathcote
T (03) 5432 9319 www.whistlingeagle.com **Open** By appt **Winemaker** Ian Rathjen **Viticulturist** Ian Rathjen **Est.** 1995 **Dozens** 950 **Vyds** 40ha
This is a remarkable story. Owners Ian and Lynn Rathjen are farmers living and working on the now famous Cambrian red soil of Heathcote. Henning Rathjen was lured from his birthplace in Schleswig Holstein by the gold rush, but soon decided farming provided a more secure future. In 1858 he made his way to the Colbinabbin Range, and exclaimed, 'We have struck paradise.' Among other things, he planted a vineyard in the 1860s, expanding it in the wake of demand for the wine. He died in 1912, and the vineyards disappeared before being replanted in '95, with 20ha of immaculately tended vines. The core wine is Shiraz, with intermittent releases of Sangiovese, Viognier, Cabernet Sauvignon and Semillon. (JH)

🍷🍷🍷🍷🍷 **Eagles Blood Shiraz 2018, Heathcote** A cult wine among some shiraz lovers, Eagles Blood brings the essence of Heathcote to the glass with its complexity, cool savouriness and trademark spice. Midnight blue-purple hues. Cacao, dried herbs, blackberries, dark cherry-juice aromas and a touch of bush mint. Lovely balance here, everything is on its place including woodsy tannins. There's a freshness, too. Nice attention to detail on display. Screw cap. 14.5% alc. RATING 95 DRINK 2021-2030 $60 JP

🍷🍷🍷🍷 **Arinto 2021, Heathcote** RATING 91 DRINK 2021-2026 $30 JP
Sangiovese 2019, Heathcote RATING 91 DRINK 2021-2027 $30 JP

Wicks Estate Wines ★★★★★

21 Franklin Street, Adelaide, SA 5000 (postal) **Region** Adelaide Hills
T (08) 8212 0004 www.wicksestate.com.au **Winemaker** Adam Carnaby **Est.** 2000 **Dozens** 25 000 **Vyds** 53.96ha
Tim and Simon Wicks had a long-term involvement with orchard and nursery operations at Highbury in the Adelaide Hills prior to purchasing their property at Woodside in '99. They planted fractionally less than 54ha of sauvignon blanc, shiraz, chardonnay, pinot noir, cabernet sauvignon, tempranillo and riesling. Wicks Estate has won more than its fair share of wine show medals over the years, the wines priced well below their full worth. Exports to the US, Singapore and Hong Kong. (JH)

🍷🍷🍷🍷🍷 **Chardonnay 2021, Adelaide Hills** With ex-Seppelt winemaker Adam Carnaby at the helm, expectations are high. They are met in full with this terrific, fully-energised young chardonnay. Polished and focused in citrus and stone fruits, it shows additional complex ferment-derived characters as it works its way across the palate briskly. One more-ish chardonnay! Screw cap. 12.5% alc. RATING 95 DRINK 2022-2028 $25 JP ○

C.J. Wicks Shiraz 2019, Adelaide Hills A lovely dedication to C.J. Wicks, dressed in the most brilliant, vibrant purple hues. Comes alive in the glass, brimming in dark plum, black cherry and spiced fruit from go to whoa. So much poise and energy, you almost forget the tannin structure, which is fine and even throughout. Plenty of class right here. Screw cap. 14% alc. RATING 95 DRINK 2021-2029 $45 JP

Sauvignon Blanc 2021, Adelaide Hills There's a lot of flavour here for such a small price. Has a foot in both sauvignon worlds, with an array of dusty herbals, gooseberry, Tahitian lime, green-skinned passionfruit and mango skin. Crisp acid crunch to close. Plenty to enjoy here. Does proud by the grape and the region. Screw cap. 12.5% alc. RATING 94 DRINK 2021-2025 $20 JP ○

🍷🍷🍷🍷 **Cabernet Sauvignon 2019, Adelaide Hills** RATING 93 DRINK 2021-2029 $25 JP ○

Riesling 2021, Adelaide Hills RATING 92 DRINK 2021-2027 $20 JP ○
Pinot Noir 2021, Adelaide Hills RATING 91 DRINK 2022-2026 $25 JP
C.J. Wicks Cabernet Sauvignon 2019, Adelaide Hills RATING 91 DRINK 2021-2029 $45 JP

Wignalls Wines   ★★★☆

448 Chester Pass Road (Highway 1), Albany, WA 6330 **Region** Albany
T (08) 9841 2848 **www.**wignallswines.com.au **Open** Thurs–Mon 11–4
Winemaker Rob Wignall, Michael Perkins **Est.** 1982 **Dozens** 7000 **Vyds** 18.5ha
While the estate vineyards have a diverse range of sauvignon blanc, semillon, chardonnay, pinot noir, merlot, shiraz, cabernet franc and cabernet sauvignon, founder Bill Wignall was one of the early movers with pinot noir, producing wines that, by the standards of their time, were well in front of anything else coming out of WA (and up with the then limited amounts being made in Victoria and Tasmania). The establishment of an onsite winery and the assumption of the winemaking role by son Rob, with significant input from Michael Perkins, saw the quality and range of wines increase. Exports to Denmark, Japan and Singapore. (JH)

🍷🍷🍷🍷 **Cabernet Merlot 2020, Great Southern** The difference that 30 minutes in the glass has made, tells us a lot about this wine. On opening, the oak presented a varnishy and metallic ring, which distracted from the display of fruit beneath. As it was the last on the bench, it had the chance to open up – and it needed it. Uncomplicated, bright fruit, perfectly in line with the pricepoint. The oak is still assertive, but it's manageable. Screw cap. 14% alc. RATING 89 DRINK 2021-2028 $19 EL ○

Shiraz 2020, Great Southern Spicy, juicy and bright. There is an element of deli meat in here, shaped by fine tannins, giving a little extra edge of interest to the fruit. Screw cap. 13.4% alc. RATING 89 DRINK 2021-2027 $29 EL

Single Vineyard Pinot Noir 2020, Albany Layers of plums, cherries and licorice here. The texture is a highlight, the tannins are slinky and supple and shapely. The alcohol is a bit of a concern though – 15.1% starts to rear up through the finish – but the fruit is nicely in line. Screw cap. 15.1% alc. RATING 89 DRINK 2022-2027 $35 EL

Chardonnay 2019, Albany Crushed nuts, orchard fruit and briny acidity. A smart wine, that is looking better a year on. Screw cap. 14.2% alc. RATING 89 DRINK 2021-2026 $35 EL

Willoughby Park

678 South Coast Highway, Denmark, WA 6333 **Region** Great Southern
T (08) 9848 1555 **www**.willoughbypark.com.au **Open** Thurs–Sun 11–5
Winemaker Elysia Harrison **Est.** 2010 **Dozens** 13 000 **Vyds** 19ha
Coming from a rural background, Bob Fowler had always hankered for a farming Life. He and his wife Marilyn purchased the former West Cape Howe winery and surrounding vineyard in '10. In '11 Willoughby Park purchased the Kalgan River Vineyard and business name, and winemaking operations were transferred to Willoughby Park. There are now 3 labels: the Kalgan River and Ironrock single-vineyard ranges, and Willoughby Park, the Great Southern brand for estate and purchased grapes. (JH)

🍷🍷🍷🍷 **Ironrock Kalgan River Riesling 2021, Great Southern** Spicy, layered and taut, this has oodles of salted citrus and white orchard fruit. The cool vintage has imbued the wine with delicacy and restraint, very positive attributes when overlaid onto the powerful fruit. Screw cap. 12.5% alc. RATING 91 DRINK 2021-2031 $35 EL
Kalgan River Riesling 2021, Great Southern Bright and pert, this has all the cut citrus, green apple and salty acidity you could ask for from a Great Southern riesling. The finish has a distinct steeliness about it, the fruit is the highlight. Screw cap. 12.5% alc. RATING 90 DRINK 2021-2028 $32 EL

Willow Bridge Estate

178 Gardin Court Drive, Dardanup, WA 6236 **Region** Geographe
T (08) 9728 0055 **www**.willowbridge.com.au **Open** 7 days 10.30–4.30
Winemaker Kim Horton **Est.** 1997 **Dozens** 25 000 **Vyds** 59ha
Jeff and Vicky Dewar have followed a fast track in developing Willow Bridge Estate since acquiring the spectacular 180ha hillside property in the Ferguson Valley. Chardonnay, semillon, sauvignon blanc, shiraz and cabernet sauvignon were planted, with merlot, tempranillo, chenin blanc and viognier following. Many of its wines offer exceptional value for money. Kim Horton, with 25 years of winemaking in WA, believes that wines are made in the vineyard; the better the understanding of the vineyard and its unique characteristics, the better the wines reflect the soil and the climate. Exports to the UK and other major markets. (JH)

🍷🍷🍷🍷 **Gravel Pit Shiraz 2020, Geographe** From the site of gravel once excavated from local roads, its deep colour and full-bodied palate replete with firm tannins typical of this site. 12 months' maturation in French oak (35% new) has added its weight to an altogether compelling wine, with a very long life ahead. Screw cap. 14.2% alc. RATING 96 DRINK 2025-2045 $30 JH ❂
Black Dog Shiraz 2018, Geographe Meaty, dense, savoury and full bodied, this is more in balance than it used to be and is all the better for it. It is a proud display of the intensity and concentration that Geographe is so capable of. The ripe, malleable, chewy tannins are the final indicator of quality. Cigar box, tobacco leaf, black tea, salted licorice, resin, char, blackberry compote and even cassis. Super good stuff here. Screw cap. 14% alc. RATING 96 DRINK 2022-2037 $65 EL ❂
GSM 2021, Geographe Willow Bridge are the masters of plush, pliable, supple wines that are fresh and affordable. Fruit rides the chariot and lashes the horses (tannins) … it forges a path across the tongue leaving a trail of berries, spice and exotic flavours in its wake. This is, and always was, about the fruit. Long live the fruit. Hyah. Screw cap. 14.5% alc. RATING 95 DRINK 2022-2028 $25 EL ❂

🍷🍷🍷🍷 **Solana 2020, Geographe** RATING 93 DRINK 2025-2030 $30 JH
Dragonfly Shiraz 2020, Geographe RATING 92 DRINK 2022-2027 $22 EL ❂
G1-10 Chardonnay 2021, Geographe RATING 90 DRINK 2022-2027 $30 EL

Willow Creek Vineyard

166 Balnarring Road, Merricks North, Vic 3926 **Region** Mornington Peninsula
T (03) 5931 2502 **www**.rarehare.com.au **Open** 7 days 11–5 **Winemaker** Geraldine
McFaul **Viticulturist** Robbie O'Leary, Ant Davenport **Est.** 1989 **Dozens** 6000
Vyds 11ha

Significant changes have transformed Willow Creek. In '08, winemaker Geraldine McFaul,
with many years of winemaking in the Mornington Peninsula under her belt, was appointed
and worked with viticulturist Robbie O'Leary to focus on minimal intervention in the
winery; in other words, to produce grapes in perfect condition. In '13 the Li family arrived
from China and expanded its portfolio of hotel and resort properties in Australia by
purchasing Willow Creek, developing the luxury 46-room Jackalope Hotel, the Rare Hare
and Doot Doot Doot restaurants, a cocktail bar and tasting room. (JH)

ᵭᵭᵭᵭᵭ Chardonnay 2020, Mornington Peninsula A classy chardonnay coming
across as well composed and beautifully balanced. A core of succulent fruit, from
white nectarine to lots of citrus. It's walking a tightrope of acidity but it's not a
lean offering, as there's subtle creamy, leesy flavouring and oak spice that allows the
palate to build. Savoury and moreish too. One of the finest from this region in a
difficult vintage. Screw cap. 13% alc. RATING 95 DRINK 2021–2028 $45 JF

ᵭᵭᵭᵭᵭ Pinot Noir 2020, Mornington Peninsula RATING 92 DRINK 2021–2028
$45 JF

Wills Domain

Cnr Abbeys Farm Road/Brash Road, Yallingup, WA 6281 **Region** Margaret River
T (08) 9755 2327 **www**.willsdomain.com.au **Open** 7 days 10–5 **Winemaker** Richard
Rowe **Viticulturist** Ernie Lepidi **Est.** 1985 **Dozens** 20000 **Vyds** 20ha

When the Haunold family purchased the original Wills Domain Vineyard in '00, they were
adding another chapter to a family history of winemaking stretching back to 1383 in what
is now Austria. Their Yallingup vineyard is planted to shiraz, semillon, cabernet sauvignon,
sauvignon blanc, chardonnay, merlot, petit verdot, malbec, cabernet franc and viognier. The
onsite restaurant has won numerous accolades. Exports to the US. (JH)

ᵭᵭᵭᵭᵭ Paladin Hill Matrix 2020, Margaret River 63/29.5/7.5% cabernet sauvignon/
malbec/petit verdot. This is a sensational wine, as was the previous vintage. Seen
through the lens of the marvellous '20 season, this is succulent, flavoursome, supple
and downright delicious. The acidity is slightly tart (on my page refreshing, but we
are all different) but it punches through the walls of fruit and gives handholds for
the next part of the climb. The tannins are fine and chewy, and the oak – where
is it? Imperceptible. Awesome. Screw cap. 14% alc. RATING 96 DRINK 2022–2042
$110 EL

**Cuvée D'Elevage Vintage Chardonnay Pinot Noir 2015, Margaret
River** 74 months on lees. Disgorged Nov '21. A pale lemon yellow in the
glass – impressive after all this time. On the nose, there is freshly scraped vanilla
pod, apple pie (shortcrust pastry and all), custard, lemon curd and preserved
lemons. In the mouth this is taut and complex, with layers of plush citrus fruits
and brioche, all of it melting in to one over the course of drinking. The phenolics
take some time to emerge through the finish, and even these are fine. The mousse
is energetic and a little expansive. All in all, extremely smart. Airy. Cork. 12% alc.
RATING 95 $85 EL

Paladin Hill Chardonnay 2021, Margaret River The concentrated and
focused power of the Gingin clone comes to the fore here: '21 was a cool,
challenging season, and it birthed an unpredictable tranche of wines. Glimmers
of brilliance, like this, shine through a clouded (sometimes very literally) sky. This
is tight, floral and citrus, layered with brine, toasty oak and curry leaves. Very
pretty – there's a saltbush thing happening here too, which lends the wine a herbal,
coastal character through the finish. Fresh and alive. Screw cap. 13% alc. RATING 95
DRINK 2022–2032 $85 EL

Eightfold Cabernet Sauvignon 2020, Margaret River Wills Domain are really hitting a purple patch. The wines are brilliant. This Eightfold cabernet is juicy and concentrated, with a salivating undercurrent of briny acidity that sparks life and light into the supple red fruits that flow above it. What pleasure this is, and really important to try after the Mystic Spring cabernet, which is also very good, however the oak and fruit is more serious here. A real step up, and worth every penny. Screw cap. 13.7% alc. RATING 95 DRINK 2021-2031 $39 EL

Paladin Hill Shiraz 2020, Margaret River This is utterly delicious. Succulent red fruit is padded down by plump tannins that cushion the affair. It is supple and it is spicy, the juicy acid a little prominent at this stage. Total pleasure awaits. Screw cap. 14% alc. RATING 95 DRINK 2022-2037 $85 EL

Mystic Spring Cabernet Sauvignon 2020, Margaret River Super-bright and delicious. This has supple redcurrant, wine gums, pomegranate and raspberry fruit, backed by salted licorice, a sheet of nori and crushed black pepper. Concentrated and lively, this is a compelling way to spend $25. Screw cap. 13.8% alc. RATING 94 DRINK 2021-2031 $25 EL ○

Eightfold Chardonnay 2021, Margaret River RATING 93 DRINK 2022-2028 $39 EL

Eightfold Shiraz 2020, Margaret River RATING 93 DRINK 2021-2029 $39 EL

Cuvée D'Elevage Chardonnay Pinot Noir 2020, Margaret River RATING 92 $39 EL

Eightfold Semillon 2021, Margaret River RATING 92 DRINK 2021-2027 $35 EL

Mystic Spring Sauvignon Blanc 2021, Margaret River RATING 92 DRINK 2021-2024 $25 EL ○

Mystic Springs Semillon Sauvignon Blanc 2021, Margaret River RATING 91 DRINK 2021-2024 $25 EL

Cuvée D'Elevage Blanc de Blanc 2021, Margaret River RATING 90 $39 EL

Mystic Spring Rosé 2021, Margaret River RATING 90 DRINK 2021-2022 $25 EL

Mystic Spring Shiraz 2020, Margaret River RATING 90 DRINK 2021-2027 $25 EL

Willunga 100 Wines ★★★★

PO Box 2239, McLaren Vale, SA 5171 **Region** McLaren Vale
T 0417 401 856 **www**.willunga100.com **Winemaker** Tim James, Mike Farmilo, Skye Salter **Est.** 2005 **Dozens** 9500 **Vyds** 19ha

Willunga 100 is owned by Liberty Wines (UK), sourcing its grapes from McLaren Vale (it owns a 19ha vineyard in Blewitt Springs). The winemaking team is decidedly high powered with the hugely experienced Tim James and Mike Farmilo the conductors of the band. The focus is on the diverse districts within McLaren Vale and dry-grown bush-vine grenache. Exports to the UK, Canada, Singapore, Hong Kong and NZ. (JH)

Trott Vineyard Blewitt Springs Grenache 2021, McLaren Vale A stark contrast of terroir's nuances with the Smart site, this is pithy and firm of texture, like biting into hard-skinned, juicy berries. Tactile and pliant. Raspberry, poached and macerated in liqueur, orange peel and star anise. Floral and beautifully fitted, without any forfeit of savouriness. Long and al dente tannic of texture, there is loads to love here. Grenache of a high order and pedigree. Screw cap. 14.5% alc. RATING 94 DRINK 2022-2029 $45 NG

Tempranillo 2021, McLaren Vale RATING 92 DRINK 2022-2027 $25 NG ○

Smart Vineyard Clarendon Grenache 2021, McLaren Vale RATING 92 DRINK 2022-2027 $45 NG

Grenache 2021, McLaren Vale RATING 90 DRINK 2022-2027 $25 NG

Grenache Rosé 2021, McLaren Vale RATING 90 DRINK 2021-2022 $25 NG

Windance Wines

2764 Caves Road, Yallingup, WA 6282 **Region** Margaret River
T (08) 9755 2293 **www**.windance.com.au **Open** 7 days 10–5 **Winemaker** Tyke
Wheatley **Viticulturist** Tyke Wheatley **Est.** 1998 **Dozens** 4500 **Vyds** 9ha
Drew and Rosemary Brent-White founded this family business, situated 5km south of
Yallingup. Cabernet sauvignon, shiraz, sauvignon blanc, chardonnay, merlot, grenache, semillon
and grenache have been established. The estate wines are all certified organic. Daughter
Billie and husband Tyke Wheatley now own the business: Billie, a qualified accountant, was
raised at Windance and manages the business and the cellar door; and Tyke (with winemaking
experience at Picardy, Happs and Burgundy) has taken over the winemaking and manages
the vineyard. (JH)

🍷🍷🍷🍷🍷 Glen Valley Shiraz 2020, Margaret River Inky, vibrant and succulent. This
is a bit of a belter, with layers of raspberry tart, blackberry bramble, blueberries,
summer fig, blood orange and loads of spice (aniseed, star anise, Szechuan
peppercorn and more). The little brother to this wine – the Windance Shiraz –
was awarded 4 gold medals at wine shows around the country: this is that wine,
just bigger, with more volume and more flavour. It's an opulent wine. Screw cap.
14% alc. RATING 95 DRINK 2021-2029 $42 EL
Cabernet Merlot 2020, Margaret River An ultra-rich full-bodied blend
that needs time to settle down, but has the balance to give confidence that it
will happen for the patient drinker – and the price is decidedly right. Screw cap.
14% alc. RATING 94 DRINK 2029-2039 $29 JH ✪

🍷🍷🍷🍷🍷 Cabernet Sauvignon 2020, Margaret River RATING 93 DRINK 2021-2031
$34 EL
Glen Valley Rosé 2021, Margaret River RATING 92 DRINK 2021-2023
$26 EL
Glen Valley Cabernet Sauvignon 2020, Margaret River RATING 92
DRINK 2023-2035 $55 JH
Glen Valley Blanc de Blancs 2019, Margaret River RATING 90 $35 EL
Sauvignon Blanc Semillon 2021, Margaret River RATING 90
DRINK 2021-2023 $21 EL ✪
Glen Valley Riesling 2021, Mount Barker RATING 90 DRINK 2021-2027
$29 JH

Windows Estate

4 Quininup Road, Yallingup, WA 6282 **Region** Margaret River
T (08) 9756 6655 **www**.windowsestate.com **Open** 7 days 10–5 **Winemaker** Chris
Davies **Viticulturist** Chris Davies **Est.** 1999 **Dozens** 2000 **Vyds** 7ha
Chris Davies planted the Windows Estate vineyard (cabernet sauvignon, shiraz, chenin blanc,
chardonnay, semillon, sauvignon blanc and merlot) in 1996, at the tender age of 19. He has
has tended the vines ever since, gaining organic certifcation in '19. Initially selling the grapes,
Chris moved into winemaking in '06 and has had considerable show success for the
consistently outstanding wines. Exports to the UK, the US and Italy. (JH)

🍷🍷🍷🍷🍷 La Fenêtre Chardonnay 2018, Margaret River Through the lens of the ripe,
powerful and graceful '18 vintage, one would expect that this wine would blow
your socks off. Actually, it is incredibly restrained and fine, with a tension and line
that carve a track across the tongue. This is saline, mineral, expansive and exciting.
If you buy one chardonnay this year that isn't one of the 'big guys', this has to be
it. Sadly only 600 bottles made – get on their mailing list. Utterly glorious. Screw
cap. 13.5% alc. RATING 97 DRINK 2021-2036 $85 EL ✪
Petit Lot Basket Pressed Syrah 2018, Margaret River The still brilliant
crimson hue introduces a vibrant medium-bodied shiraz with its dancing array
of red cherry, plum and blackberry fruits; acidity and fine, spicy tannins complete
a very beautiful wine. Drink whenever the mood strikes, but be careful when
pouring it. Screw cap. 14% alc. RATING 97 DRINK 2021–2030 $39 JH

♟♟♟♟♟ **Petit Lot Chenin Blanc 2020, Margaret River** This vintage in Margaret River was warm, short and low yielding, producing wines of intense concentration like this one: deeply flavoured, layered and very long. The juicy acid gives a lick of moreishness through the enduring finish. Very smart, again. Screw cap. 12% alc. RATING 96 DRINK 2021-2036 $39 EL ✪

Petit Lot Chardonnay 2020, Margaret River Incredibly aromatic: pink grapefruit, lavender, fennel flower, white peach, musk stick, preserved lemon, crushed cashew and ocean spray all rise up as one from the glass. On the palate the acidity is taut and alive – it drags saliva from the back of the mouth and inundates the senses in a wave of saline, crushed rocks and shell. This is a hugely powerful, intense wine; the Dijon clones have had a distinct impact on the line and tension, giving it a unique combination of punch and elegance. Screw cap. 13.5% alc. RATING 96 DRINK 2021-2031 $50 EL ✪

Petit Lot Basket Pressed Cabernet Sauvignon 2018, Margaret River As usual, this is leafy and floral and very pretty aromatically, with cassis, bay leaf, raspberry and anise. The palate is medium weight and elegant. The drive and power from the '18 vintage is harnessed by a thumping cadence and a long finish. Instead of being beefy and big, this is super-long and layered. It's not an obvious wine; rather, it has restraint and intrigue. Beautiful, supple and tense. Screw cap. 14% alc. RATING 95 DRINK 2020-2035 $48 EL

Petit Lot Malbec 2018, Margaret River This has oodles of blackberries and raspberries, aniseed and pepper wafting out of the glass. Concentrated and intense, with a purity and finesse on the palate that complements its muscly tannin profile. A seriously pretty and seriously structured wine that shows the strength of Margaret River malbec. A variety to watch in this region. This wine sells out in a minute, and it is obvious why. Lovely. Screw cap. 14% alc. RATING 95 DRINK 2020-2030 $50 EL

Wine Architect

38a Murray Street, Tanunda, SA 5352 **Region** Adelaide Hills
T 0439 823 251 **www.**winearchitect.com.au **Open** Wed–Thurs 2–6, Fri 2–late, or by appt **Winemaker** Natasha Mooney **Viticulturist** Natasha Mooney, Caj Amadio **Est.** 2006 **Dozens** 3000
This is a reasonably significant busman's holiday for Natasha Mooney, a well-known and highly talented winemaker whose 'day job' (her term) is to provide winemaking consultancy services for some of SA's larger wineries. This allows her to find small, unique parcels of grapes that might otherwise be blended into large-volume brands. She manages the arrangements so that there is no conflict of interest, making wines that are about fruit and vineyard expression. She aims for mouthfeel and drinkability without high alcohol, and for that she should be loudly applauded. Wines are released under La Bise (named for the southerly wind that blows across Burgundy) and The Thief? labels. (JH)

♟♟♟♟♟ **La Bise Rosé Grenache 2021, Adelaide Hills** Grenache blended with 15% pinot gris. A good rosé is a work of art. La Bise is a serious practitioner and it shows, in a wine of grace and charm, not to mention subtle flavour depth. Striking ruddy pink in colour. Gently scented dusty cherry, macerated strawberry, musk and dried herbs. Doesn't rush things on the palate, offering a dry, textural style with a crunchy red-fruit core. Of serious intent. Screw cap. 12.5% alc. RATING 94 DRINK 2021-2024 $22 JP ✪

♟♟♟♟♟ **La Bise Whole Bunch Pressed Pinot Gris 2021, Adelaide Hills** RATING 92 DRINK 2021-2023 $22 JP ✪

La Bise Sangiovese 2020, Adelaide Hills RATING 91 DRINK 2021-2028 $25 JP

The Thief? Shiraz 2020, Barossa Valley RATING 91 DRINK 2021-2018 $28 DB

The Thief? Shiraz 2019, Barossa Valley RATING 91 DRINK 2021-2028 $28 DB

Wine Unplugged

2020 Upton Road, Upton Hill, Vic 3664 (postal) **Region** Victoria
T 0432 021 668 **www**.wineunplugged.com.au **Winemaker** Callie Jemmeson, Nina
Stocker **Est.** 2010 **Dozens** 5000

Nina Stocker and Callie Jemmeson believe that winemaking doesn't have to have barriers:
what it does need is quality, focus and a destination. With a strong emphasis on vineyard
selection and a gentle approach to their small-batch winemaking, the wines are a true
reflection of site. The wines are released under the Pacha Mama, La Vie en Rose, Cloak &
Dagger, Motley Cru and Harvest Moon labels. (JH)

🍷🍷🍷🍷🍷 **Pacha Mama Chardonnay 2021, Yarra Valley** A bright green gold. An
attractive and vibrant nose with white stone fruits, a little green mango and
lemongrass. With its good drive and persistence, this really well-weighted wine
has nectarine fruit and finishes long and satisfying. Excellent value. Screw cap.
13.3% alc. RATING 94 DRINK 2021–2025 $32 PR

🍷🍷🍷🍷🍷 **Pacha Mama Chardonnay 2020, Yarra Valley** RATING 93 DRINK 2021–2025
$32 PR
Cloak & Dagger Prosecco 2021, Victoria RATING 92 $27 JP
Pacha Mama Pinot Gris 2021, North East Victoria RATING 92
DRINK 2021–2024 $29 JP
Pacha Mama Foraged Sangiovese Pinot Noir Syrah 2021, Victoria
RATING 92 DRINK 2022–2025 $35 JP
Cloak & Dagger The Dagger Pinot Grigio 2021, King Valley RATING 91
DRINK 2021–2024 $27 JP
Pacha Mama Pinot Noir 2020, Yarra Valley RATING 91 DRINK 2021–2025
$28 PR
Cloak & Dagger The Cloak Sangiovese 2021, North East Victoria
RATING 90 DRINK 2022–2024 $29 JP
Pacha Mama Little Petal Pinot Noir Pinot Gris 2021, Victoria RATING 90
DRINK 2021–2025 $35 JP

Wines by KT ★★★★

20 Main North Road, Watervale, SA 5452 **Region** Clare Valley
T 0419 855 500 **www**.winesbykt.com **Open** Thurs–Mon 11–4 **Winemaker** Kerri
Thompson **Est.** 2006 **Dozens** 4500 **Vyds** 9ha

KT is winemaker Kerri Thompson. Kerri graduated with a degree in oenology from
Roseworthy Agricultural College in '93, and thereafter made wine in McLaren Vale, Tuscany,
Beaujolais and the Clare Valley, becoming well known as the Leasingham winemaker in the
Clare Valley. She resigned from Leasingham in '06 after 7 years at the helm, and after a short
break became winemaker at Crabtree. Here she is also able to make Wines by KT, sourcing
the grapes from 2 local vineyards, one biodynamic, the other farmed with sulphur and copper
sprays only. (JH)

🍷🍷🍷🍷🍷 **Melva Wild Fermented Riesling 2021, Clare Valley** 15th consecutive release
of the Melva. 5g/L R.S. Barrel and lees work is evident on the nose, in the form
of cheesecloth, brine, citrus pith, saltbush and beeswax. On the palate the wine is
everything we want from 2021: pert, classy and totally restrained … super-smart.
This is sensational. Screw cap. 12% alc. RATING 94 DRINK 2021–2036 $34 EL
Peglidis Vineyard Watervale Riesling 2021, Clare Valley Austere on the
nose, like tumbled river stones, shale and citrus pith. On the palate, the wine is
lingering and willowy, shaped by chalky phenolics. This has real flow and rhythm;
the length of flavour tells us all we need to know about its ability to age. Not
voluminous like the other rieslings in the collection – this is pure, taut and super-
long. Screw cap. 12% alc. RATING 94 DRINK 2022–2036 $38 EL

🍷🍷🍷🍷🍷 **5452 Watervale Shiraz 2020, Clare Valley** RATING 93 DRINK 2021–2031
$29 EL
5452 Watervale Riesling 2021, Clare Valley RATING 92 DRINK 2021–2036
$25 EL ✪

Wirra Wirra Vineyards

255 Strout Road, McLaren Vale, SA 5171 **Region** McLaren Vale
T (08) 8323 8414 **www**.wirrawirra.com **Open** Mon–Sat 10–5, Sun & public hols 11–5
Winemaker Paul Smith, Tom Ravech, Kelly Wellington, Grace Wang **Viticulturist** Anton
Groffen **Est.** 1894 **Dozens** 140 000 **Vyds** 21.5ha

Wirra Wirra has established a formidable reputation. The wines are of exemplary character,
quality and style; The Angelus Cabernet Sauvignon and RWS Shiraz battling each other for
supremacy, with The Absconder Grenache one to watch. Long may the battle continue under
managing director Andrew Kay and the winemaking team of Paul Smith, Tom Ravech and
Kelly Wellington, who forge along the path of excellence first trod by the late (and much loved)
Greg Trott, the pioneering founder of modern-day Wirra Wirra. Its acquisition of Ashton Hills
in '15 added a major string to its top-quality bow. Exports to all major markets. (JH)

99999 **The Holy Thirst Cabernet Sauvignon Shiraz 2018, McLaren Vale** The
archetypal Australian blend, or at least our interpretation: a generous core of
shiraz tucked between cabernet's astringent seams and a savoury orb of currant,
green bean, graphite and sage. The tannins, managed impeccably: oak and grape.
Seamless. The oak, well coopered and perfectly toasted for the material on hand,
too. This will age beautifully. Screw cap. 14.5% alc. RATING 95 DRINK 2022-2033
$125 NG
Church Block Cabernet Sauvignon Shiraz Merlot 2019, McLaren Vale
This satisfies all the criteria for a blend such as this: bright colour and fresh
black and red fruits, undaunted by the extended time in barrel, and satisfying
ripe tannins. And a gold-plated bargain. Screw cap. 14.5% alc. RATING 94
DRINK 2022-2039 $22 JH ◐
The Angelus Cabernet Sauvignon 2019, McLaren Vale A fine, savoury
cabernet scent: cassis, mulberry leaf, bouquet garni, green olive and pencil lead.
The tannins, an oscillating current of pliancy and freshness, corralling and shaping
the forceful fruit. A spray of maritime saltiness across the finish. The acidity, a
tad shrill. Fine drinking all the same. Will age very well. Screw cap. 14% alc.
RATING 94 DRINK 2022-2034 $70 NG

99999 **The Absconder Grenache 2020, McLaren Vale** RATING 93
DRINK 2021-2028 $70 NG
RSW Shiraz 2019, McLaren Vale RATING 93 DRINK 2022-2029 $70 NG
Chook Block Shiraz 2019, McLaren Vale RATING 93 DRINK 2022-2030 $150
NG
Hiding Champion Sauvignon Blanc 2021, Adelaide Hills RATING 92
DRINK 2021-2024 $26 JP
Woodhenge Basket-Pressed Shiraz 2019, McLaren Vale RATING 92
DRINK 2021-2032 $38 NG
Scrubby Rise Sauvignon Blanc 2021, Adelaide Hills RATING 90
DRINK 2021-2023 $18 JP ◐
The Lost Watch Riesling 2021, Adelaide Hills RATING 90 DRINK 2022-2026
$26 JP

Wise Wine

237 Eagle Bay Road, Eagle Bay, WA 6281 **Region** Margaret River
T (08) 9750 3100 **www**.wisewine.com.au **Open** Sun–Fri 9–5, Sat 9–6
Winemaker Andrew Siddell, Matt Buchan, Larry Cherubino (Consultant) **Est.** 1986
Dozens 10 000 **Vyds** 2.5ha

Wise Wine, headed by Perth entrepreneur Ron Wise, has been a remarkably consistent
producer of high-quality wine. The vineyard adjacent to the winery (2ha of cabernet
sauvignon and shiraz, and 0.5ha of zinfandel) in the Margaret River is supplemented by
contract-grown grapes from Pemberton, Manjimup and Frankland River. The value for
money of many of the wines is extraordinarily good. Exports to Switzerland, the Philippines
and Singapore. (JH)

ΨΨΨΨΨ Eagle Bay Chardonnay 2020, Margaret River This is pristine, driven and pure, with a creamy, crushed-nut undertow beneath the fruit. It billows and undulates and it's awesome. This is a routinely great wine and the '20 continues form. You better get used to it. Screw cap. 13.2% alc. RATING 96 DRINK 2022-2037 $65 EL ✪

Eagle Bay Cabernet Sauvignon 2019, Margaret River A wonderful character that I often notice in Margaret River cabernet is nori. Kelp. It's coastal, it's briny and it's fresh, but it also contributes to the umami vibe of the wine. This has it in spades, both aromatically and in the mouth. It is backed by cassis, pomegranate, saltbush and licorice. This is a supple, undulating wine of prismatic shape and spice. Drink it now, sure (decant it), but it will gracefully grow into old age as well. I almost forgot to add (!) that the tannins are a major highlight; fine, chewy and shapely. Screw cap. 14% alc. RATING 96 DRINK 2022-2037 $85 EL

Leaf Cabernet Sauvignon 2020, Margaret River '20 was an extraordinary vintage: short and fast, and with excellent quality, if tiny yields. This is polished and ripe, with layers of spice and fruit, cupped by the toasty oak. Brilliant now, but will be even better in 5 years, I'd wager. The aftertaste is a highlight; succulent, persistent and just a little bit chewy. Gorgeous. Screw cap. 14.2% alc. RATING 95 DRINK 2021-2036 $45 EL

Leaf Cabernet Malbec 2020, Margaret River At this stage, this wine is every bit as bright and vibrant as you could possibly hope for: the colour, iridescent. A dazzling array on both nose and mouth of raspberries, cassis, red apples, red licorice and pomegranates. The oak and tannins are still trying to settle down into the bed of plush fruit. Give it another year – it's still super-frisky right now – but it's very good. It may even be great. Screw cap. 14.5% alc. RATING 94 DRINK 2022-2036 $45 EL

Leaf Malbec 2020, Margaret River This is classy. There is the expected array of red and black berries, littered with Szechuan peppercorns and shaped by cool, mineral tannins. This rides a wave of undulating spice and flavour. It is nuanced and dappled and exciting. Screw cap. 14.5% alc. RATING 94 DRINK 2021-2031 $45 EL

ΨΨΨΨΨ Leaf Riesling 2021, Porongurup RATING 93 DRINK 2021-2031 $30 EL
Eagle Bay Wilyabrup Shiraz 2019, Margaret River RATING 92 DRINK 2023-2029 $85 EL
Leaf Pinot Noir 2020, Great Southern RATING 90 DRINK 2022-2027 $45 EL

Witches Falls Winery   ★★★☆

79 Main Western Road, Tamborine Mountain, Qld 4272 **Region** Queensland
T (07) 5545 2609 **www.**witchesfalls.com.au **Open** Mon–Thurs 10–4, Fri–Sun 10–5 by appt **Winemaker** Jon Heslop, Allan Windsor, Ren Dalgarno **Est.** 2004 **Dozens** 12000 **Vyds** 10.5ha

Witches Falls is the venture of Jon and Kim Heslop. Jon has a deep interest in experimenting with progressive vinification methods in order to achieve exceptional and interesting results. He has a degree in applied science (oenology) from CSU and experience working in the Barossa and Hunter valleys, as well as at Domaine Chantal Lescure in Burgundy and with a Napa-based winegrower. Witches Falls' grapes are sourced from the Granite Belt (in addition to its 0.4ha of estate pecorino and some fruit from South Australia). Exports to Singapore and Taiwan. (JH)

ΨΨΨΨ Wild Ferment Touriga 2021, Riverland Spicy on the front, rounded and sweetly fruited on the end, this is a juicy, fruity quaffer of finely textured structure. Nicely composed mouthfeel, it's shame its fruit doesn't carry the persistence, depth or complexity to take it to the next level. Screw cap. 13.9% alc. RATING 89 DRINK 2022-2023 $40 TS

Wild Ferment Arinto 2021, Riverland The Portuguese white grape arinto upholds plenty of natural acidity, giving it zest and structure even in the Riverland. Tropical fruits make for a simplistic feel, but grapefruit tang brings control to a long finish. The creamy, biscuity mood of wild fermentation and a spell in oak barrels lends lovely texture and flow. Screw cap. 12.7% alc. RATING 88 DRINK 2022 $38 TS

Prophecy Syrah 2019, Granite Belt A tangy and savoury take on Granite Belt shiraz, with vibrant if slightly shrill natural acidity and a fine-grained web of confident tannins. Nuanced with sarsaparilla and cola, its fruit expression has been quashed by oak influence. Screw cap. 13.3% alc. RATING 88 DRINK 2024-2029 $64 TS

Wolf Blass ★★★★★

97 Sturt Highway, Nuriootpa, SA 5355 **Region** Barossa Valley
T (08) 8568 7311 **www**.wolfblass.com **Open** Wed–Mon 10–4.30 **Winemaker** Chris Hatcher, Steven Frost **Est.** 1966
The Wolf Blass wines are made at all pricepoints, ranging through Red, Yellow, Gold, Brown, Grey, Black, White and Platinum labels covering every one of the main varietals. In '16, a new range of wines labelled BLASS was introduced. The style and range of the wines continue to subtly evolve under the leadership of chief winemaker Chris Hatcher. Exports to all major markets. (JH)

🍷🍷🍷🍷🍷 **Platinum Label Medlands Vineyard Shiraz 2018, Barossa Valley** Limited Release. Vibrant hue. Any thought of blockbuster is instantly dismissed with the first taste. It is an elegant medium-bodied wine, albeit with a compelling blend of blackberry, spice and plum. The oak integrated, tannins perfectly pitched behind the fruit. Gold medals Barossa and Royal Adelaide Wine Shows 2020. Screw cap. 14.5% alc. RATING 97 DRINK 2028-2048 $200 JH

🍷🍷🍷🍷🍷 **Black Label Cabernet Sauvignon Shiraz 2018, Barossa Valley Langhorne Creek McLaren Vale** Deeply coloured, this is full bodied, with firm tannins running through the length of the palate, trading blows with the blackberry and blackcurrant fruit, the ultimate balance calling an end to the battle. But it needs time – lots of it. Screw cap. 14.5% alc. RATING 96 DRINK 2028-2043 $130 JH
Grey Label Cabernet Shiraz 2019, Langhorne Creek Takes Wolf Blass back to its origins and does so with aplomb, the fruit flavours sit lively, fresh and long. Yes, tannins and oak do their stuff (barrel ferment is part of this), but not at the expense of the fruit. Complexity and balance go hand in hand. Screw cap. 14.5% alc. RATING 95 DRINK 2022-2034 $45 JH
Grey Label Shiraz 2019, McLaren Vale Deeply coloured; typical opulent Blass style, ripe blend of black fruits plus McLaren Vale's gift of dark chocolate. The tannins are rounded and sewn into the fabric of the palate. Screw cap. 14.5% alc. RATING 94 DRINK 2022-2032 $45 JH

Wood Park ★★★★☆

17 Milawa-Bobinawarrah Rd, Milawa, Vic 3678 **Region** King Valley
T (03) 5727 3778 **www**.woodparkwines.com.au **Open** 7 days 10–5 **Winemaker** John Stokes **Viticulturist** John Stokes **Est.** 1989 **Dozens** 12 000 **Vyds** 16ha
With a background in environmental science, John Stokes planted his first vines at Wood Park in 1989 in the back paddocks of his grazing property at Bobinawarrah in the hills of the Lower King Valley, east of Milawa. The surrounding hill country has been excluded from grazing since the time of the first vine plantings. Natural regeneration, additional native plantings and 3 large dams have enhanced biodiversity. The vineyard is managed with minimal chemical use. Winemaking includes open ferments, hand plunging and French oak. Wood Park also sources fruit from sites in the King and Alpine Valleys, ranging from 250–800m elevation. The mix of mainstream and alternative varieties includes tempranillo, sangiovese and roussanne. He is probably best known for his cabernet shiraz blend. (JP)

🍷🍷🍷🍷🍷 **Reserve Zinfandel 2019, King Valley** Shares the same DNA as primitivo and is definitely a hard one to understand. John Stokes does a mighty job taming the alcohol richness while elevating fruit intense in blackberry, cinnamon, chocolate, panforte and five-spice. It's a generous wine, but beautifully trimmed in savoury, ripe tannins. Runs long in the mouth. Screw cap. 14.5% alc. RATING 95 DRINK 2021-2032 $45 JP

ŸŸŸŸŸ Reserve Tempranillo 2015, King Valley RATING 93 DRINK 2021-2027 $55 JP
Reserve Cabernet Sauvignon 2019, King Valley RATING 92
DRINK 2023–2029 $45 JP
Chardonnay 2020, Alpine Valleys RATING 92 DRINK 2022-2030 $32 JP
Whitlands Pinot Noir 2019, King Valley RATING 92 DRINK 2022-2026 $30 JP
Whitlands Pinot Gris 2021, King Valley RATING 91 DRINK 2021-2026
$26 JP
The Tuscan 2019, King Valley RATING 91 DRINK 2021-2027 $29 JP
Pinot Noir Rosé 2021, King Valley RATING 90 DRINK 2021-2024 $26 JP

Woodgate Wines   ★★★★

43 Hind Road, Manjimup, WA 6258 **Region** Manjimup
T (08) 9772 4288 **www**.woodgatewines.com.au **Open** Fri–Sun 12.30–5, Mon–Thurs
by appt **Winemaker** Mark Aitken **Viticulturist** Mark Aitken **Est.** 2006 **Dozens** 1000
Vyds 5ha
Woodgate is the family business of Mark and wife Tracey Aitken. Mark became a mature-age
student at Curtin University, obtaining his oenology degree in 2001 as Dux, earning a trip
to Bordeaux to undertake vintage, returning to work at Manjimup's Chestnut Grove winery
from '02. In '05 he and Tracey began their own contract winemaking business, as well as
making wine for their Woodgate brand. Most of the grapes come from the estate plantings
of cabernet sauvignon, chardonnay, sauvignon blanc, pinot noir and merlot, supplemented
by grapes from a leased vineyard. The name of the sparkling wine, Bojangles, reflects the
extended family's musical heritage, which stretches back 3 generations and includes vocalists,
guitarists, pianists, a trumpeter, a saxophonist, 2 drummers and a double bass player. (JH)

ŸŸŸŸŸ The Black George Single Vineyard Pinot Noir 2019, Pemberton
Pemberton and pinot noir are a really great fit. There is always, no matter the
producer, a distinct olive tapenade (green or black, depending the site) and
summer strawberry character. In this glass, these flavours are offset by very fine
tannins and saline, rhubarb acidity. The texture is a standout: silky and supple.
Screw cap. 14% alc. RATING 93 DRINK 2022-2028 $48 EL
The Black George Single Vineyard Cabernet Franc 2019, Pemberton
Broody, tannic, leafy and dark. A wine of sumptuous favour intensity, but elegance
and line, as well. Very smart, and lovely to see so much flavour at 13.6% alc. – the
sweet spot. Screw cap. 13.6% alc. RATING 92 DRINK 2021-2031 $48 EL
Fiano 2021, Manjimup A green and herbal rendition of fiano – not pejorative
descriptors in this case. This has coriander, green apple, garden mint and chalk
through the finish. Leafy, and likely even more refreshing straight out of the fridge.
Screw cap. 12.8% alc. RATING 90 DRINK 2021-2026 $22 EL
Tempranillo 2020, Manjimup Lighter in colour than many on the table, this
is littered with a selection of sliced meats, black forest berries and earthy tannins;
salted plums play a big role in the mouth. Overall the wine is salty and savoury,
with a core of fruit that is uncomplicated by tannins or oak. A lovely wine. Screw
cap. 14% alc. RATING 90 DRINK 2022-2027 $35 EL

Woodhaven Vineyard   ★★★★

87 Main Creek Road, Red Hill, Vic 3937 **Region** Mornington Peninsula
T 0421 612 178 **www**.woodhavenvineyard.com.au **Open** By appt **Winemaker** Lee
Ward, Neil Ward **Est.** 2003 **Dozens** 250 **Vyds** 1.6ha
Lee and Neil Ward spent 2 years looking for a suitable site on the Mornington Peninsula,
ultimately finding one high on Red Hill. They decided from the outset to be personally
responsible for all aspects of growing the grapes and making the wines, relying on the advice
readily given to them by George and Ruth Mihaly of Paradigm, David and (the late) Wendy

Lloyd of Eldridge, John and Julie Trueman of Myrtaceae and Nat and Rose White, formerly of Main Ridge. They grow the vines organically and biodynamically; it took 8 years to produce their first 2 barrels of wine in '10. In '13 the 0.8ha each of pinot noir and chardonnay finally produced more than one barrel of each wine. (JH)

ŸŸŸŸ♀ **Desailly Chardonnay 2019, Mornington Peninsula** Mid gold with bright green tinges. The aromas are all embracing: ripe stone fruit, quince, oak spices and buttered toast. Full bodied, rich and luscious with lots of creamy lees-infused flavours. Yet the neat acidity keeps this in check, adding a buoyancy and freshness across the palate. To date, the best Desailly I've tasted. Screw cap. 13.5% alc. RATING 92 DRINK 2021-2026 $60 JF

Pinot Noir 2019, Mornington Peninsula There's a bright ruby hue and the wine is youthful and still tightly wound. It opens up to reveal cherries, root vegetables with wood char and warm spices, especially sarsaparilla. It's medium bodied, definitely in the savoury spectrum, with an astringency to the finish. The raspy tannins are largely oak derived, and indeed the oak needs to settle into the body of the wine – give it time. Screw cap. 13.3% alc. RATING 90 DRINK 2022-2028 $50 JF

Woodlands ★★★★★

3948 Caves Road, Wilyabrup, WA 6280 **Region** Margaret River
T (08) 9755 6226 **www**.woodlandswines.com **Open** 7 days 10–5 **Winemaker** Stuart Watson **Viticulturist** Jaden McLean **Est.** 1973 **Dozens** 15 000 **Vyds** 26.5ha
Founders David Watson and wife Heather had spectacular success with the cabernets he made in 1979 and the early '80s. Commuting from Perth on weekends and holidays, as well as raising a family, became all too much and for some years the grapes from Woodlands were sold to other Margaret River producers. With the advent of sons Stuart and Andrew (Stuart primarily responsible for winemaking), the estate has bounced back to pre-eminence. The wines come in 4 price bands, the bulk of the production under the Chardonnay and Cabernet Merlot varietals, then a series of Reserve and Special Reserves, then Reserve de la Cave and finally Cabernet Sauvignon. The top end wines primarily come from the original Woodlands Vineyard, where the vines are almost 50 years old. Exports to the UK, the US, Sweden, Denmark, Finland, South Korea, Mauritius, Indonesia, Malaysia, the Philippines, Singapore and Japan. (JH)

ŸŸŸŸŸ **Xavier Cabernet Sauvignon 2018, Margaret River** If you haven't had the pleasure of drinking one of these cabernets as an older wine, you may not get the full scope of the young wine on release. Here, today, it is tightly coiled, spicy and concentrated. The savoury, biscuity oak we often associate with good quality bordeaux is here in spades, and it encases the kaleidoscopic flavours that lie possible beyond. However, in 10 years, this wine transforms into a powerful and expansive wine of depth, grace and evocation. From one of Margaret River's greatest all-time vintages, this is a wine for the ages. Screw cap. 13.5% alc. RATING 98 DRINK 2022-2052 $179 EL ✪ ♥

ŸŸŸŸŸ **Margaret 2018, Margaret River** 80/10/10% cabernet sauvignon/merlot/malbec. Rooted in the very fabric of this wine is a savoury lining of spice. It is inescapable, and it's what makes this wine a wonder. Is it better than the great '14? Hard to say – the '14 was pretty amazing. But this has all the ripe power and concentration of the vintage. The pure 'cabernosity' of this wine is a thing to marvel at. I keep coming back to the savoury layers – they are a defining characteristic of the house style. Screw cap. 13.5% alc. RATING 96 DRINK 2022-2042 $70 EL ✪

Woodlands Brook Vineyard Chardonnay 2021, Margaret River Savoury, framed by toasted oak, and layered with preserved citrus, yellow peach and Pink Lady apples. There is a creamy, crushed-nut undercurrent to this which balances the taut acidity and the firm oak, bringing all things into perspective and balance. Opulent and very smart. Screw cap. 12.5% alc. RATING 95 DRINK 2022-2032 $55 EL

Emily 2020, Margaret River 45/45/8/1/1% cabernet franc/merlot/malbec/ cabernet sauvingon/petit verdot. This is kaleidoscopic. Where last year was restrained, supple, and red fruited, this is dark, brooding, concentrated, spicy and exotic. The fruit maintains a pure core, but it is buried deep beneath layers of savoury tannin (normal and expected from this vintage), resinous oak, and an array of tobacco leaf, star anise, fennel seed, black peppercorn, salted licorice and hung deli meat in the background. It has tremendous staying power; the longer it is open, the more it opens up (no surprise there), but it does indicate that time in the cellar will be its friend. A superb wine. Screw cap. 13.5% alc. RATING 95 DRINK 2022-2042 $59 EL

Clémentine 2019, Margaret River 54/22/18/5/1% cabernet sauvignon/ merlot/malbec/cabernet franc/petit verdot. Savoury, dense and packed with flavour, this has cassis, tobacco, Szechuan peppercorns, bramble and even shades of pomegranate. The highlight, however, is the tannin profile: it is absolutely everywhere in the mouth, giving the wine substance and chew. This is clearly a wine that will perform well in the cellar, should you choose to do that. Otherwise, drinking it now will provide much pleasure, if you decant it. Screw cap. 13.5% alc. RATING 95 DRINK 2022-2036 $49 EL

Woods Crampton

P O Box 417, Hamilton, NSW 2303 **Region** Various
T 0417 670 655 **www.**woods-crampton.com.au **Winemaker** Nicholas Crampton, Aaron Woods **Est.** 2010 **Dozens** 11 000
This is one of the most impressive ventures of Nicholas Crampton (his association with McWilliam's is on a consultancy basis) and winemaking friend Aaron Woods. The 2 make the wines at the Sons of Eden winery with advice from Igor Kucic. The quality of the wines and the enticing prices have seen production soar from 1500 to 11 000 dozen, with every expectation of continued success. Exports to the UK, Canada, Denmark, Switzerland, Russia, Singapore, Hong Kong and NZ. (NG)

Single Vineyard Shiraz 2020, Eden Valley Bright red purple in the glass with vibrant, juicy characters of satsuma plum and blueberry fruits, layered with exotic spice, amaro herbs, berry danish, milk chocolate and licorice. It's a slurpy, medium-bodied kind of style with plush ripe fruit and plenty of spice and inherent drinkability. Screw cap. 14.5% alc. RATING 92 DRINK 2022-2028 $28 DB

Dry Riesling 2021, Eden Valley Tightly bound aromatics that reveal focused lime and grapefruit characters with a little time in the glass. Hints of orange blossom, crushed quartz and lighter notes of marzipan become apparent with time. The wine shows a brisk cadence and a clean, dry finish with plenty of steely lime and citrus notes. Screw cap. 12.2% alc. RATING 91 DRINK 2021-2030 $21 DB ❂

Shiraz 2021, Barossa A deeply coloured, contemporary Barossa shiraz showing characters of sweet ripe plum, baking spice, salted licorice, earth and blackberry jam. Juicy and unctuous with fine tannin and a crème de cassis-like finish. Screw cap. 14.5% alc. RATING 90 DRINK 2022-2027 $21 DB ❂

Elephant In The Room Fantabulous Chardonnay 2020, Adelaide Hills The name and the label are quite eye-catching. The former is said to represent 'big wines with lots of flavour and smooth, cream oak finishes.' In reality, the elephant is probably generous by Adelaide Hills' standards but less so outside the region. Fruit-driven, it moves to a tropical fruit beat with plenty of peach, pear, melon and stone fruits, with a most arresting smoky oak influence. Plush and full of flavour, it remains well balanced by juicy acidity. Screw cap. 13.5% alc. RATING 90 DRINK 2021-2025 $22 JP

Elephant In The Room Splendiferous Shiraz 2020, Barossa Bright red with purple flashes and aromas of ripe plums and summer berry fruits undercut with hints of Asian spice, jasmine, red licorice, kirsch, vanilla bean and mulberry. Sweetly fruited and juicy with a flash of tangy acidity and spicy dark and red berry throughout its length. Screw cap. 14.5% alc. RATING 90 DRINK 2022-2028 $22 DB

Woodside Park Vineyards ★★★★

27 Croydon Road, Keswick, SA 5035 **Region** Adelaide Hills
T (08) 7070 1401 **www**.cloudbreakwines.com.au **Winemaker** Simon Greenleaf, Randal
Tomich **Est.** 1998 **Dozens** 10 000 **Vyds** 17ha
Woodside Park Vineyards is a joint venture between Randal Tomich and Simon Greenleaf,
who share a friendship of over 20 years. Woodside specialises in cool-climate wines (released
under the Cloudbreak label), grown on the Tomich family's Woodside Park Vineyard.
Simon has been producing wines from the Tomich vineyards since 2005 and has a strong
understanding of the site and fruit quality. Randal has had more than 20 years' experience in
winemaking, specialising in vineyard development and establishes vineyards for brands across
Australia and California, US. The Woodside Park vineyards include chardonnay, sauvignon
blanc, pinot noir, grüner veltliner, riesling, gewürztraminer and shiraz. Exports to the US and
South East Asia. (JH)

ΥΥΥΥΥ Cloudbreak Chardonnay 2021, Adelaide Hills A harmonious, low-fi
Hills chardonnay that plays its cards close to its chest. Dusty lemon, cumquat,
grapefruit pith float from the glass. Soft acidity and mouthfeel conspire to give the
appearance of a lighter framed chardonnay but there is depth here, a resonance of
almond mealiness, citrus and mineral brightness all the more persuasive through
well-managed oak. A flinty, smoky finish makes for a more-ish wine. Diam.
13% alc. RATING 92 DRINK 2021-2021 $35 JP
Cloudbreak Pinot Gris 2021, Adelaide Hills Brings some cool-climate tang
to the grape variety and attractive acid crispness, too. Explores the finer side of gris
with delicate fuji apple, citrus and nashi pear aromas that translate into a lightly
spiced, citrus-based palate with depth and developing texture. Screw cap. 13% alc.
RATING 92 DRINK 2021-2024 $35 JP

ΥΥΥΥ Cloudbreak Pinot Noir 2021, Adelaide Hills RATING 89 DRINK 2021-2025
$35 JP

Woodstock ★★★★

215 Douglas Gully Road, McLaren Flat, SA 5171 **Region** McLaren Vale
T (08) 8383 0156 **www**.woodstockwine.com.au **Open** 7 days 11–4 **Winemaker** Ben
Glaetzer **Est.** 1905 **Dozens** 22 000 **Vyds** 18.44ha
The Collett family is among the best known in McLaren Vale, the late Doug Collett AM was
known for his World War II exploits flying Spitfires and Hurricanes with the RAF and RAAF,
returning to study oenology at Roseworthy Agricultural College and rapidly promoted to take
charge of SA's largest winery, Berri Co-operative. In 1973 he purchased the Woodstock estate,
built a winery and in '74 he crushed its first vintage. Son Scott Collett, once noted for his
fearless exploits in cars and on motorcycles, became winemaker in '82 and has won numerous
accolades; equally importantly, he purchased an adjoining shiraz vineyard planted circa 1900
(now the source of The Stocks Shiraz) and a bush-vine grenache vineyard planted in '30.
In '99 he joined forces with Ben Glaetzer, passing responsibility for winemaking to Ben, but
retaining responsibility for the estate vineyards. Exports to most major markets. (JH)

ΥΥΥΥΥ Audacity Rosé 2021, McLaren Vale Langhorne Creek A 65/25/7/3%
blend of vermentino/grenache/mataro/shiraz. Some bloom and red berry
scents on the bouquet are followed by a palate that is not only fresh, but adds
flavours of pomegranate and forest strawberries. Screw cap. 11.5% alc. RATING 93
DRINK 2021-2023 $24 JH
Sauvignon Blanc 2021, Adelaide Hills My, it certainly packs a lot of cool-
climate sauvignon pleasure into the pricepoint. Fabulous value for money here.
Ripe tropical fruits mingle with grapefruit, lime, apple and lantana. The palate
is the key to this wine, it brings both depth of flavour, texture and a fruit-tingle
sweet spot, all the while gracefully rolling along via juicy acidity to the finish.
Screw cap. 13% alc. RATING 90 DRINK 2021-2025 $19 JP ✪
Cabernet Sauvignon 2017, McLaren Vale This cuvée has long offered value
for those seeking a saline, maritime cabernet made in an older-school mould. New

and used American and French oak impart considerable oaky astringency, riffs on cedar, chocolate and bourbon. Blackcurrant, sage and spearmint. Undeniable varietal character, plenty of oomph and a certain rustic charm. Screw cap. 14.5% alc. RATING 90 DRINK 2021-2026 $26 NG

ŢŢŢŢ   **Shiraz 2019, McLaren Vale** RATING 88 DRINK 2021-2025 $26 NG
Pilot's View Shiraz 2017, McLaren Vale RATING 88 DRINK 2021-2025 $38 NG

Woody Nook   ★★★★

506 Metricup Road, Wilyabrup, WA 6280 **Region** Margaret River
T (08) 9755 7547 **www**.woodynook.com.au **Open** 7 days 10–4.30 **Winemaker** Digby Leddin, Courtney Dunkerton **Viticulturist** Digby Leddin **Est.** 1982 **Dozens** 8000 **Vyds** 14.23ha

Woody Nook, with a backdrop of 18ha of majestic marri and jarrah forest, doesn't have the high profile of the biggest names in Margaret River but it has had major success in wine shows over the years. It was founded by Jeff and Wynn Gallagher in 1978 and purchased by Peter and Jane Bailey in 2000, with Jeff and Wynn's son Neil involved in the vineyards and winery until very recently. Major renovations by the Bailey family transformed Woody Nook with a new winery, a gallery tasting room for larger groups and an alfresco dining area by the pond. Exports to the UK, Singapore and Malaysia. (JH)

ŢŢŢŢŢ   **Single Vineyard Fumé Blanc 2021, Margaret River** The fruit is clearly concentrated and intense, while the oak is very impactful, both on the nose and in the mouth. This is in line with the vibe in Margaret River at the moment – it's very good, but it's overt. If you love oak and love sauv blanc, you'll love this. It's done well. Screw cap. 13.8% alc. RATING 92 DRINK 2021-2031 $28 EL
Chenanigans 2021, Margaret River Unfined, unfiltered, cloudy in the glass. Micro-trial batch of 293 bottles. It's good! Salty, textural, pithy, plenty of apples and spice. It's very oaky (no surprise given the stats), but the fruit holds it, and the oak doesn't impact the finish (the death-knell for any oaked wine). So: I'd say the trial is a success, although a second vintage, in the same (by then 1yo seasoned) barrel, will likely allow the fruit to sing a little more clearly. Diam. 13.5% alc. RATING 90 DRINK 2021-2028 $36 EL
Limited Release G & T 2019, Margaret River 60/40% tempranillo/graciano. The marriage of 2 very tannic varieties has birthed a very tannic baby – no surprises there, but the fruit has lovely ebb and flow in the mouth. The wine won't be for everyone, as the structure is staunchly firm and savoury, but if you're a fan of tannin and rustic Spanish wine vibes, then this will likely be right up your alley. Screw cap. 14% alc. RATING 90 DRINK 2021-2028 $28 EL
Single Vineyard Cabernet Merlot 2019, Margaret River Matured for 18 months in a combination of French (15% new) and Hungarian (12.5% new) oak. As expected, the impact of the oak on the wine is immediate on the nose: biscuit and oatmeal overlay the fruit. In the mouth, the purity of the dark berry fruit is there to be witnessed, escaping the shackles that bind it. Good length of flavour through the finish. Screw cap. 13.5% alc. RATING 90 DRINK 2021-2031 $36 EL
Gallagher's Choice Cabernet Sauvignon 2018, Margaret River Matured for 20 months in 28.5% new French oak, the balance seasoned French and Hungarian. The fruit is plush and dense, however the oak sadly swamps it. While oak will certainly assist in fortifying a wine into its future, the match of oak and fruit here feels adjunct, rather than seamless. The fruit carries all the DNA of the powerful '18 vintage. Waiting until '23 to drink this may assist in the absorption process. Diam. 15.5% alc. RATING 90 DRINK 2023-2033 $65 EL

ŢŢŢŢ   **Kelly's Farewell Semillon Sauvignon Blanc 2021, Margaret River** RATING 88 DRINK 2021-2023 $24 EL

Word Play

41 Jenke Road, Marananga, SA 5355 **Region** Barossa Valley
T 0499 618 260 **www**.wordplaywines.com.au **Open** By appt **Winemaker** Fiona Donald,
Matthew Pick **Viticulturist** Matthew Pick, Fiona Donald **Est.** 2015 **Dozens** 350
Vyds 6ha

Wordplay Wines is the side project of Seppeltsfield winemakers Matthew Pick and Fiona
Donald. Their compact range consists of just 1500 bottles each of Shiraz and Cabernet
Sauvignon from their 4ha Jenke Road Block vineyard planted in 1999 in Marananga, and
1100 bottles of Yarra Valley Pinot Noir. This little operation is quite a contrast to their
day jobs, where they have enjoyed long and varied careers making wines for larger brands
including Hardys, Barossa Valley Estate, Penfolds, Château Reynella, Leasingham, Leo Buring
and Yalumba. First released in 2018, their reds are generous, characterful and age-worthy. (TS)

TTTTT **An Anagram Shiraz 2018, Barossa Valley** Juicy blackberry and blood plum
are underscored by dark chocolate, brown spice, licorice, blueberry pie and mocha.
Impressive fruit weight and elegant line, cascading tannin support and a graceful,
lengthy finish. Screw cap. 14.8% alc. RATING 94 DRINK 2022-2035 $90 DB

TTTTY **41 Across Cabernet Sauvignon 2018, Barossa Valley** RATING 93
DRINK 2022-2032 $75 DB

Wren Estate

389 Heathcote-Rochester Road, Mt Camel, Vic 3523 **Region** Heathcote
T (03) 9972 9638 **www**.wrenestate.com.au **Open** Mon–Thurs by appt, Fri 12.30–5.30,
w'ends & public hols 10.30–5.30 **Winemaker** Michael Wren **Est.** 2017 **Dozens** 10 000
Vyds 14.5ha

Owner and winemaker Michael Wren has been making wine for over 18 years across multiple
continents. For 10 years he was a Flying Winemaker for one of Portugal's top wineries,
Esporao, and was particularly struck by the use of lagares for top-quality wines. Lagares are
low, wide, open red-wine fermenters that allow foot treading (or stomping) with the level
little more than knee deep. The consequence is the very soft, yet high, extraction of colour,
flavour and soft tannins. The vineyard (of 14.5ha) sits in a 52ha property and was planted in
'02, the shiraz with 16 different clone and rootstock combinations, giving Michael priceless
information on the vagaries of the site. Each block is picked, fermented and aged separately,
the best in a limited release single-block series. All the premium wines are individually barrel
selected. Exports to the US. (JH)

TTTTT **I'm So Ronely Shiraz 2019, Heathcote** Winemaker Michael Wren looks
to the prettiest wines of all the shiraz he sees each vintage, for his heart-wearing
homage to Rhône syrah. Invariably, Ronely shines. The '19 keeps to the style,
radiant with such energy and life. Aniseed, blackberry, blueberry, cinnamon, a
touch of pepper and a layer of lively spices awaits. Plush and seamless, it lets loose
on the palate and just keeps going, smoothly, resolutely towards a dry, amaro-like
finish. Delicious. Screw cap. 14.2% alc. RATING 95 DRINK 2022-2029 $40 JP

TTTTY **The Game's Afoot Shiraz 2019, Heathcote** RATING 93 DRINK 2022-2032
$29 JP
Block 8 Shiraz 2018, Heathcote RATING 92 DRINK 2022-2035 $198 JP
Syrahphim Shiraz 2020, Heathcote RATING 90 DRINK 2022-2024 $35 JP
Elementary Shiraz 2019, Heathcote RATING 90 DRINK 2022-2033 $75 JP

Wynns Coonawarra Estate

77 Memorial Drive, Coonawarra, SA 5263 **Region** Coonawarra
T (08) 8736 2225 **www**.wynns.com.au **Open** 7 days 10–5 **Winemaker** Sue Hodder,
Sarah Pidgeon **Viticulturist** Ben Harris **Est.** 1897

Privileged to own the longest-established vineyards in the region, first planted by visionary
pioneer John Riddoch in 1891, Wynns Coonawarra Estate still resides in the fabled

triple-gabled winery that he built on Memorial Drive. Large-scale production has not prevented Wynns (an important part of TWE) from producing excellent wines covering the full price spectrum from the bargain-basement Riesling and Shiraz through to the deluxe John Riddoch Cabernet Sauvignon and Michael Shiraz. Even with steady price increases, Wynns offers extraordinary value for money and its Black Label Cabernet Sauvignon is a mainstay of many Australian cellars. Investments in rejuvenating and replanting key blocks – and skilled winemaking – have resulted in wines of far greater finesse and elegance. Exports to the UK, the US, Canada and Asia. (JH)

Davis Single Vineyard Cabernet Sauvignon 2019, Coonawarra The last bottling of wine from the Davis vineyard was in '08. The aromas here are impossibly bright and deep. Blackberry and raspberry, blood and ferrous, creamy blackberry pie – crust as well. The acidity is saline and fresh. This is astoundingly beautiful. Driven by fruit and powered by a thundering undercurrent of soft tannin, this will surely live into its third decade with ease, and likely still retain some of the vibrancy. Inchoate though it is, a star is on the rise. Screw cap. 13.8% alc. RATING 97 DRINK 2022-2052 $90 EL ✪

John Riddoch Limited Release Cabernet Sauvignon 2019, Coonawarra Like the '18 that preceded it, this is a wine of stature, precision and endurance. The tannins are fine and omnipresent, but then a cabernet without tannins would be like a person without purpose. This is direct, forthright and confident, with a core of pure, soft and unfettered berry fruits that cascade over the tongue and trail through the interminable finish. The piercing intensity of fruit on the middle palate echoes in the mouth. Truly, sublime. Screw cap. 13.5% alc. RATING 97 DRINK 2022-2052 $150 EL ✪

Michael Limited Release Shiraz 2019, Coonawarra If this doesn't set your heart aflutter, I don't know what will. Featherlight and concentrated at once, this has tissue paper-fine layers of black cherry, blueberry, graphite, licorice, chalk and ferrous notes. The acidity is flowing and ripe, weaving the layers of flavour together; the oak, invisible. Another beautiful release, with undulating length through the finish. I bet it'll live an elegant age. Screw cap. 14% alc. RATING 97 DRINK 2022-2052 $150 EL ✪

Shiraz 2020, Coonawarra RATING 91 DRINK 2021-2028 $20 EL ✪
The Siding Cabernet Sauvignon 2020, Coonawarra RATING 90 DRINK 2021-2028 $20 EL ✪
Cabernet Shiraz Merlot Malbec 2019, Coonawarra RATING 90 DRINK 2021-2027 $20 EL ✪

Xanadu Wines ★★★★★

316 Boodjidup Road, Margaret River, WA 6285 **Region** Margaret River
T (08) 9758 9500 **www.**xanaduwines.com **Open** 7 days 10–5 **Winemaker** Glenn Goodall, Brendan Carr, Steve Kyme, Darren Rathbone **Viticulturist** Suzie Muntz
Est. 1977 **Dozens** 45 000 **Vyds** 82.8ha

Xanadu Wines was established in 1977 by Dr John Lagan and was purchased by the Rathbone family in 2005. Together with talented winemaker Glenn Goodall and his team, they have significantly improved the quality of the wines. The vineyard has been revamped via soil profiling, improved drainage, precision viticulture and reduced yields. The quality of the wines made since the acquisition of the Stevens Road Vineyard in '08 has been consistently outstanding. Glenn Goodall is the Wine Companion 2023 Winemaker of the Year. Exports to most major markets. (JH)

Stevens Road Chardonnay 2020, Margaret River This wine is pristine, and routinely defined by acid on release. It is soft, pithy and lush (that acid), and it is met by white peach and nectarine, red apple and lime flesh. Brine, cheesecloth and little pockets of pop-rock vibrancy. This is a beautiful wine, but it is even better with some age. The temptation to drink them young however, is overwhelming. Screw cap. 13% alc. RATING 97 DRINK 2022-2037 $80 EL ✪

Reserve Chardonnay 2020, Margaret River The problem with Xanadu Reserve Chardonnay is that it is delicious on release. But that has nothing on what it morphs into, with age. This is a wine that is all too often overlooked (not in the show system, granted) by collectors, because too few people have been privy to the wines in their middle age. A problem emerges: the wines are drunk too early and don't get the opportunity to show their full potential. This is crystalline, pure – almost austere – toasty and spiced, with layers of undulating flavour through the fine, spooling finish. A monumental wine of endless potential. Screw cap. 13% alc. RATING 97 DRINK 2022-2042 $110 EL ✪

Stevens Road Cabernet Sauvignon 2019, Margaret River Scintillating, pure, creamy, salty and layered, this is every bit as impressive as I expected it to be. Expectations can occasionally be cumbersome, in that they have the ability to get in the way of accurate and present assessment. But in this case, the reality exceeds the expectation, leaving only good things in its wake. The cooler year is viewed here through perfectly ripe fruit, and has imparted a freshness to the acidity that only serves to highlight the pristine character of the wine. Hyperbole aside: it's very, very excellent. The tannins are like silk. Screw cap. 14% alc. RATING 97 DRINK 2022-2042 $80 EL ✪

Reserve Cabernet Sauvignon 2019, Margaret River Sometimes, you gotta start at the end of a wine, rather than the front. Usually it is because the wine is so long, that the first flavours are long forgotten. Such is life, here. The tannins, which are laced like a fine silky web through the finish, capture the pure fruit on the mid palate and coax it through the mouth. Caught also, like fine droplets of dew in a spider's web, are pockets of spice which add pop and thrill to the overall. Another scintillating and pure cabernet release from the team at Xanadu. Screw cap. 14% alc. RATING 97 DRINK 2022-2042 $110 EL ✪

♟♟♟♟♟ **DJL Malbec 2020, Margaret River** This was a ripping little vintage. 'Little' is not intended in a pejorative – it was generally brutally low yielding, due to dry conditions at the end of '19 resulting in a small crop of small berries. This in turn lends a firmness to the tannins. This is no problem for a naturally tannic variety like malbec, that simply takes it in its stride. This wine is polished, glossy, ripe, saturated in black and purple fruit flavours and propped up by a fine mineral seam of saline acidity. Bring it on. Screw cap. 14% alc. RATING 95 DRINK 2021-2031 $28 EL ✪

DJL Shiraz 2020, Margaret River A supremely delicious and pure wine that unapologetically displays the finesse and slink that is possible with the variety, when handled this way. A lot of words to tell you: this is a wonderful wine, and ridiculous(ly good) value for money. Screw cap. 14% alc. RATING 95 DRINK 2021-2028 $28 EL ✪

Cabernet Sauvignon 2020, Margaret River Perfumed, pure and very pretty. The 3 'p's for success. In the mouth the wine is all that the nose promised, the very fine tannins curve and shape the fruit. Very smart. Tasted alongside wines 3+ times the price of this and it still held its own. The finish is creamy and svelte. Screw cap. 14% alc. RATING 95 DRINK 2022-2036 $40 EL

Chardonnay 2021, Margaret River The combination of Xanadu's staunch approach to mlf (it's banned) in chardonnay, together with the cooler '21 vintage, had my mouth puckering in anticipation. I needn't have bothered. This is acidic, sure, but in a taut, pert way, rather than an upfront, pushy manner. The fruit that resides within is redolent of white peach and red apples, and the oak, as always, is slotted in carefully behind it all, framing the wine and shaping the carriage across the palate. This is pure and streamlined. It's becoming a habit at Xanadu. Screw cap. 13% alc. RATING 94 DRINK 2022-2032 $40 EL

Chardonnay 2020, Margaret River There's nothing accidental about this wine. It's been assembled from the copious viticultural resources and with tight control of oak handling. Balance, length and freshness are its aces in the hole. Screw cap. 13% alc. RATING 94 DRINK 2022-2032 $40 JH

XO Wine Co

13 Wicks Road, Kuitpo, SA 5172 **Region** Adelaide Hills
T 0402 120 680 **www**.xowineco.com.au **Winemaker** Greg Clack, Kate Horstmann
Est. 2015 **Dozens** 1800

Greg Clack spent 11 years in McLaren Vale with Haselgrove Wines. In 2014 he took himself
to the Adelaide Hills as chief winemaker at Chain of Ponds – this remains his day job, nights
and days here and there devoted to XO. Kate has a degree in viticulture and oenology and
a masters in wine business. XO's raison d'être revolves around small-batch, single-vineyard
wines chiefly made from grenache, barbera, chardonnay and gamay. The winemaking
minimises wine movements, protecting freshness. (JH)

Single Vineyard Small Batch Barbera 2021, Adelaide Hills A bold,
deeply coloured and flavoured interpretation of the grape. Ripe, too, in black
cherry, black licorice, blackberry, dried herbs and tar. The palate offers quite a
mouthful of flavour, enhanced by firm tannins. Screw cap. 14% alc. RATING 93
DRINK 2022-2026 $32 JP

Cherry Pie Light Red 2021, Adelaide Hills 35/22/21/18/4% pinot noir/
barbera/tempranillo/dolcetto/grenache. The use of 100% carbonic maceration
on pinot noir and dolcetto is made for this style of light dry red. It brings an
extra level of liveliness and plummy sweet fruits to the fore. Ripe in black cherry,
plum, spice and pepper with a touch of tasty amaro and firm tannins to close. Fab
drinking early. Screw cap. 13% alc. RATING 92 DRINK 2021-2024 $24 JP ✪

Single Vineyard Small Batch Grenache 2021, McLaren Vale With 10/1%
touriga/shiraz. Grenache and touriga enjoy each other's company which makes
you wonder why we don't see more of these blends. A touch of touriga with
its blueberry, violet and mintiness livens and lifts its black-fruited, spicy buddy
enormously. A tight ball of ripe, sweet-fruited energy on the palate, soft and
plummy, makes for excellent drinking young. Screw cap. 14.5% alc. RATING 92
DRINK 2022-2028 $32 JP

Single Vineyard Small Batch Pinot Noir 2021, Adelaide Hills This is a
subtle expression, combining intense red fruits in cranberry, cherry and redcurrant
with an infusion of stalky herbal leafiness and undergrowth. Firm tannins drive
the energy of this wine on the palate, ensuring further ageing potential. Screw cap.
13.5% alc. RATING 92 DRINK 2021-2027 $32 JP

Single Vineyard Small Batch Tempranillo 2021, Adelaide Hills Captures
the joy and liveliness of the grape nicely. No problem with colour here, it's deepest
purple. No problem either with bouquet, which is exuberant in red licorice, dark
cherries, plum and Mediterranean dried herbs. Fruit powers through the palate,
assisted by fine, firm tannins. Screw cap. 14% alc. RATING 92 DRINK 2022-2025
$32 JP

Single Vineyard Small Batch Chardonnay 2020, Adelaide Hills Vegan
friendly. Strong regional expression here with elements of nectarine, citrus,
mandarin and complex leesy almond nougat. Juicy and upfront, it settles into
a taut, structural wine still in building mode. Give it a little more time to fully
open up and do the big reveal. Screw cap. 13% alc. RATING 92 DRINK 2021-2026
$32 JP

Single Vineyard Small Batch Nebbiolo 2020, Adelaide Hills This looks to
the grape's savoury side, while maintaining a youthful buoyancy. Lights the glass
up in crushed raspberry hues with the lifted fragrance of red cherries and plums,
almost pinot-esque. Cherries fill the mouth, spiced plums, violets, vanilla pod.
More flavour than texture at this point with solid tannins cruising to the finish.
Screw cap. 14% alc. RATING 90 DRINK 2021-2027 $45 JP

Games Night Sauvignon Blanc 2021, Adelaide Hills RATING 89
DRINK 2021-2023 $24 NG

Games Night Rosé Grenache Barbera 2021, Adelaide RATING 88
DRINK 2021-2024 $24 NG

Single Vineyard Small Batch Chardonnay 2021, Adelaide Hills RATING 88
DRINK 2021-2024 $24 JP
Single Vineyard Small Batch Fiano 2021, Adelaide Hills RATING 88
DRINK 2021-2024 $27 JP

Yabby Lake Vineyard ★★★★★

86-112 Tuerong Road, Tuerong, Vic 3937 **Region** Mornington Peninsula
T (03) 5974 3729 **www**.yabbylake.com **Open** 7 days 10–4 **Winemaker** Tom Carson,
Chris Forge, Luke Lomax **Est.** 1998 **Dozens** 3350 **Vyds** 50ha
This high-profile wine business was established in 1998 by Robert and Mem Kirby of Village
Roadshow. The vineyard enjoys a north-facing slope, capturing maximum sunshine while
also receiving sea breezes. In the midst of conversion to organic viticulture, the main focus is
on 25ha of pinot noir, 14ha of chardonnay and 8ha of pinot gris; 3ha of shiraz, merlot and
sauvignon blanc take a back seat. The arrival of the hugely talented Tom Carson as group
winemaker in '08 added lustre to the winery and its wines, making the first Jimmy Watson
Trophy–winning pinot noir in '14 and continuing to blitz the Australian wine show circuit
with single-block pinot noirs. Exports to the UK, Canada, Sweden and Hong Kong. (JH)

🍷🍷🍷🍷🍷 Single Vineyard Pinot Noir Rosé 2021, Mornington Peninsula There's
a coppery tinge to the light ruby hue; a joyous mix of raspberries, chinotto,
cranberry tartness, watermelon and a touch of spice yet savoury through and
through. The palate is refreshing with red apple and juicy acidity, plus the right
amount of feathery tannins to give it shape. Nice one. Screw cap. 12.5% alc.
RATING 95 DRINK 2021-2023 $30 JF ✪
Single Vineyard Syrah 2020, Mornington Peninsula If pinot noir is your
go-to red on the Peninsula, this syrah just might convince you otherwise, as it's
an elegant and perfectly poised wine. A neat combo of dark plums, fragrant with
red licorice, a hint of menthol and woodsy spices. Sitting comfortably on medium
bodied, with beautiful textural tannins unfurling all the way through. Screw cap.
13.5% alc. RATING 95 DRINK 2022-2033 $36 JF

🍷🍷🍷🍷🍷 Single Vineyard Cuvée Nina 2018, Mornington Peninsula RATING 93
$45 JF
Red Claw Pinot Noir 2020, Mornington Peninsula RATING 93
DRINK 2025-2030 $30 JH
Red Claw Shiraz 2020, Heathcote RATING 91 DRINK 2022-2025 $28 JP
Red Claw Chardonnay 2020, Mornington Peninsula RATING 91
DRINK 2021-2025 $28 JF
Cuvée Nina Rosé NV, Mornington Peninsula RATING 90 $36 JF
Single Vineyard Pinot Gris 2021, Mornington Peninsula Blueberry, dark
plum and black cherry fruit of considerable extract with hints of espresso, oak
spice, olive tapenade, vanillin and dark chocolate. Svelte with a graceful fine, ripe
powdery tannin and a velvety flow of dark and blue fruits on the exit. Screw cap.
14.5% alc. RATING 90 DRINK 2021-2025 $33 JF

Yal Yal Estate ★★★☆

21 Yal Yal Road, Merricks, Vic 3916 **Region** Mornington Peninsula
T 0416 112 703 **www**.yalyal.com.au **Open** Fri–Sun 10–5 **Winemaker** Rollo
Crittenden **Est.** 1997 **Dozens** 2500 **Vyds** 7ha
In 2008 Liz and Simon Gillies acquired a vineyard in Merricks, planted in 1997 to 1.6ha of
chardonnay and a little over 1ha of pinot noir. It has since been expanded to 7ha, half devoted
to chardonnay, half to pinot noir. The Yal Yal Estate cellar door was launched in Mar '21. (JH)

🍷🍷🍷🍷🍷 Winifred Pinot Noir 2020, Mornington Peninsula Longevity is not going
to be the Peninsula's trademark of '20, but drinkability seems to be, with some
wines. Winifred is the estate flagship, a barrel selection that incorporate 25% new
French oak, and it has a bit more depth yet is still defined by the refreshing, lively
characters of vintage. Expect some macerated red cherries dipped in baking spices,

rhubarb and a hint of chinotto. Really tangy acidity, brisk even, with sinewy tannins working across a lighter– to medium-bodied palate. This is pleasing to drink. Screw cap. 13.5% alc. RATING 93 DRINK 2021-2027 $45 JF

ŸŸŸŸ **Yal Yal Rd Pinot Noir 2020, Mornington Peninsula** RATING 88 DRINK 2021-2024 $32 JF

Yalumba ★★★★★

40 Eden Valley Road, Angaston, SA 5353 **Region** Eden Valley
T (08) 8561 3200 **www.**yalumba.com **Open** 7 days 11–4 **Winemaker** Louisa Rose (chief), Kevin Glastonbury, Sam Wigan, Heather Fraser, Will John **Est.** 1849
Dozens 930 000 **Vyds** 180ha
Owned and run by the Hill-Smith family, Yalumba has a long commitment to quality and great vision in its selection of vineyard sites, new varieties and brands. It has always been a serious player at the top end of full-bodied Australian reds and was a pioneer in the use of screw caps. It has a proud history of lateral thinking and rapid decision-making by a small group led by Robert Hill-Smith. The synergy of the range of brands, varieties and prices is obvious, but it received added lustre with the creation of The Caley. A founding member of Australia's First Families of Wine. Exports to all major markets. (JH)

ŸŸŸŸŸ **The Virgilius Viognier 2019, Eden Valley** Yalumba has firmly positioned itself at the pointy end of the Australian viognier hierarchy with its Virgilius. It's a style more in line with the wines of the northern Rhône than the usual overtly apricotty numbers we often see from the Antipodes. Steely and textural with savoury-shaped stone fruits and a light dusting of apricot and citrus fruits, along with notes of marzipan, dried honey and light ginger spice. It boasts a savoury, stony palate shape and a light tweak of phenolics on the finish, which is fruit-pure and enduring. Screw cap. 13% alc. RATING 97 DRINK 2021-2027 $50 DB ✪ ♥

The Menzies Cabernet Sauvignon 2017, Coonawarra An icon in Australian wine, Yalumba's Coonawarra-born Menzies Cabernet Sauvignon has long stood at the pointy end of our country's fine-wine pyramid, and I'm sure many will fondly remember occasions when a well-cellared example of the Menzies has knocked their socks off. Nothing's changed, perhaps the oak has been dialled back a little, but that classic, herbal-flecked blackberry and blackcurrant fruit at its core is all elegance and latent power. Fine spice and graphite-like tannins lay down layers on the palate. The finish is long and with impeccable balance, trailing off with a vapour trail of blackcurrant, cedar and olive tapenade. It's a classic. Cork. 14.5% alc. RATING 97 DRINK 2021-2041 $60 DB ✪ ♥

ŸŸŸŸŸ **Vine Vale Grenache 2020, Barossa Valley** A wonderful, bunchy grenache that ticks all the boxes. Red fruited and fragrant with a deep seam of souk-like spice and gingerbread, notes of macerated raspberry and strawberry, a splash of soy, dried herbs, pressed flowers and lighter meaty tones. Medium bodied with a pure, savoury fruit flow that makes the wine seem very comfortable in its own skin. Balanced tannins and on-point acidity provide structure and cadence. Effortless drinking. Screw cap. 14% alc. RATING 96 DRINK 2021-2031 $40 DB ✪

The Signature Cabernet Sauvignon Shiraz 2018, Barossa There is a resonance and depth to this release that I really like. Wonderfully pure and concentrated blackberry and plum fruits, layered with spice, dark chocolate, earth, cedar and oak nuance. Succulent and sinewy in the mouth, it flexes considerable muscle, yet remains purely fruited and approachable even at this stage of its evolution. Rich and balanced with fine, ripe tannin and plenty of energy for such depth of fruit. Lovely. Cork. 14.5% alc. RATING 96 DRINK 2021-2050 $65 DB ✪

The Cigar Cabernet Sauvignon 2019, Coonawarra Expressive, leafy-edged fruit characters of blackberry and blackcurrant with hints of briar, licorice, dark soy, Old Jamaica chocolate, tobacco and clove. Fleshy and sweetly fruited with grippy, sandy tannins, bright acidity and a lingering trail of cassis and spice on the finish. Screw cap. 13.5% alc. RATING 94 DRINK 2021-2036 $35 DB

Shiraz Viognier 2018, Eden Valley Red purple in the glass, with perfumed satsuma plum fruit, along with hints of red cherry, exotic spice, light amaro and violet notes, raspberry licorice and earth. Lovely medium-bodied fruit sashays across the palate, pure and true with fine, gypsum-like tannin and a sapid flick to its tail. Lovely drinking. Screw cap. 14.5% alc. RATING 94 DRINK 2021-2031 $40 DB

Steeple Vineyard Light Pass 2017, Barossa Valley Blueberry, dark plum and black cherry fruit of considerable extract, with hints of espresso, oak spice, olive tapenade, vanillin and dark chocolate. Svelte with a graceful fine, ripe powdery tannin and a velvety flow of dark and blue fruits on the exit. Diam. 14.5% alc. RATING 94 DRINK 2021-2023 $80 DB

Yangarra Estate Vineyard ★★★★★

809 McLaren Flat Road, Kangarilla SA 5171 **Region** McLaren Vale
T (08) 8383 7459 **www.**yangarra.com.au **Open** Mon–Sat 11–5 **Winemaker** Peter Fraser
Viticulturist Michael Lane **Est.** 2000 **Dozens** 15 000 **Vyds** 100ha

This is the Australian operation of Jackson Family Wines, one of the leading premium wine producers in California, which in 2000 acquired the 172ha Eringa Park Vineyard from Normans Wines (the oldest vines dated back to 1923). The renamed Yangarra Estate Vineyard is the estate base for the operation and has moved to certified biodynamic status with its vineyards. Peter Fraser has taken Yangarra Estate to another level altogether with his innovative winemaking and desire to explore all the possibilities of the Rhône Valley red and white styles. Thus you will find grenache, shiraz, mourvèdre, cinsault, carignan, tempranillo and graciano planted, and picpoul noir, terret noir, muscardin and vaccarese around the corner. The white varieties are roussanne and viognier, with grenache blanc, bourboulenc and picpoul blanc planned. Then you see ceramic eggs being used in parallel with conventional fermenters. Peter was named Winemaker of the Year in the Wine Companion 2016. Exports to the UK, the US and other major markets. (JH)

ŸŸŸŸŸ **Roux Beaute Roussanne 2020, McLaren Vale** Arguably the finest white wine in the Vale. A few contenders. A lustrous deep yellow. Saline, as is so much in these parts. Then a decompression of rooibos, the ripest lemon that sits as a figment of the imagination, raw pistachio and green olive-brine martini. Thick, intense, powerful and yet, tiptoeing across a drawbridge of phenolics, almost the daintiest powerhouse that I've pirouetted with. Screw cap. 13.5% alc. RATING 97 DRINK 2022-2037 $65 NG ✪

Ovitelli Grenache 2020, McLaren Vale Always an exciting proposition. A transparent grenache of pixelated precision. As reminiscent of its nebbiolo brethren as it is of pinot. A shimmering red-fruited veil. Gritty, attenuated tannins derived from old vines (1946) and a long, gentle agitation in ceramic eggs. Like biting into the juiciest raspberry that bridles the perfect edge of ripeness, before sucking on sandstone. Long is an understatement. This is among Australia's greatest wines from the country's finest cultivar. Screw cap. 14.5% alc. RATING 97 DRINK 2022-2032 $75 NG ✪ ♥

High Sands Grenache 2019, McLaren Vale This is the benchmark of the region on many levels, made in a denser fashion, perhaps, than its siblings. Yet this vintage feels more elegant. The fruit, crunchy and of the red spectrum. The acidity, salty. The tannins, lithe and slinky with the embellishment of oak an accent of intrigue, rather than a jarring dialect. Resinous. Powerful. Yet pixelated of detail as it strides to a long finish clad with thyme, orange verbena and a whiff of cedar. Screw cap. 14.5% alc. RATING 97 DRINK 2023-2035 $250 NG

ŸŸŸŸŸ **Ovitelli Blanc 2020, McLaren Vale** 50/25/12/9/4% grenache blanc/ roussanne/clairette/piquepoul/bourboulenc, all of the southern Rhône and well at home here. Taut, salty and nascent of feel. Then, an explosion with air. Loads in store. Lanolin, sea salt, skinsy quince notes, nashi pear, baked apple and preserved Moroccan lemon. Yet it is the texture that compels, from the first rail of chew, to the last lattice of saliva-sucking bite and pithy mealiness. Stay tuned. This is only

the beginning of the ascension. Screw cap. 13% alc. RATING 96 DRINK 2022-2035
$65 NG ✪

Ironheart Shiraz 2019, McLaren Vale Density and pliancy, the calling cards.
All offset by the juiciest red cherry–skinned tannins flecked with violet, blueberry,
rose petal and spice here directing the fray. Tactile barely describes this, so moreish
and conducive to the next glass, as it draws the saliva in preparation. Screw cap.
14.5% alc. RATING 96 DRINK 2022-2034 $125 NG

King's Wood Shiraz 2020, McLaren Vale I like this. A wine that embraces a
more medium-bodied, compact and restrained archetype, defined by spicy lithe
grape tannins as much as McLaren Vale fruit. Green olive tapenade, clove, pepper
grind and salumi mingle with succulent red cherry, mescal and blue-fruit allusions.
The tannins, a spindle of spicy, pithy chewiness, attenuated and polymerised by
gentle agitation in French foudres for 16 months. A strong regional statement.
Screw cap. 14.5% alc. RATING 95 DRINK 2022-2032 $65 NG

Hickinbotham Clarendon Grenache 2020, McLaren Vale Gorgeous.
Pinosité in spades. Noble bitterness. Lavender and white pepper. Pink grapefruit
pulp and sapid, sour-cherry accents. Like the most glorious amaro with a slice
of Sicilian orange, this plays a finessed card of consummate elegance, racy length,
crunchy saline tannins and latent power. Brethren to Ovitelli in terms of shape,
if not a bit looser and more flamboyant at the seams. A belly dancer in a souk
of carnal desire. Scintillating, uber-aromatic grenache. Screw cap. 14.5% alc.
RATING 95 DRINK 2022-2030 $75 NG

Roussanne 2021, McLaren Vale Sea spray, rooibos, quince and lemon pith.
Stone fruits tucked amid the fray. A fine, textural, forceful and filigreed finish,
marked by a burst of fruit weight. 13% alc. RATING 94 DRINK 2022-2030 $35 NG

GSM 2020, McLaren Vale An excellent GSM thanks to maker Pete Fraser's
erudition when it comes to the Rhône. A spice rub of complexity galvanises the
fruit, without overwhelming it. The overall effect is one of freshness, detail, pangs
for the Mediterranean and a delicious, full-weighted and savoury gulpability rather
than the norm of pulpy, sweet fruit. Charcuterie, clove, thyme, rosemary, ume,
turmeric, raspberry, sandalwood and scrub. A wonderful spread of umami warmth
across the nourishing finish. An enticing day-to-day proposition. Screw cap.
14% alc. RATING 94 DRINK 2022-2027 $35 NG

Yarra Burn   ★★★★

60 Settlement Road, Yarra Junction, Vic 3797 **Region** Yarra Valley
T 131 492 **www.**yarraburn.com.au **Winemaker** Ed Carr, Ella Hoban **Est.** 1975
At least in terms of name, this is the focal point of Accolade's Yarra Valley operations. However,
the winery was sold and the wines are now made elsewhere. The Upper Yarra vineyard largely
remains. (JH)

🍷🍷🍷🍷🍷 **Prosecco 2021, King Valley** The Charmat method and 5% 'other' grapes
produce this attractive young prosecco. Fresh and vibrant on the bouquet in
fresh-cut free apple, pear, lemon zest. Fills out on the palate cushioned by a splash
of sugar (9.7g/L) and gentle creaminess. Good balance and length here. Cork.
12% alc. RATING 93 $26 JP ✪

Pinot Noir Chardonnay Pinot Meunier 2017, Yarra Valley 45/35/20%
pinot noir/chardonnay/pinot meunier. Matured 30 months on lees. Transfer
method. A light, bright green gold. Red-fruited, with some gentle breadiness and
a creamy, peach yoghurt nuance. Good depth and persistence on the even palate
which finishes dry and nicely long. Cork. 12.7% alc. RATING 91 $30 PR

🍷🍷🍷🍷 **Pinot Noir Chardonnay Pinot Meunier 2019, Victoria** RATING 89 $25 JP

Yarra Edge

455 Edward Road, Chirnside Park, Vic 3116 **Region** Yarra Valley
T 0428 301 517 **www.**yarraedge.com.au **Winemaker** Dylan McMahon
Viticulturist Lucan Hoorn **Est.** 1983 **Dozens** 3500 **Vyds** 12.73ha
Yarra Edge was established by the Bingeman family in 1983, who were advised and guided by
John Middleton (of Mount Mary). The advice was, of course, good and Yarra Edge has always
been able to produce high-quality fruit if the vineyard was properly managed. Up to '98 the
wines were made onsite under the Yarra Edge label, but in that year the vineyard was leased by
Yering Station, which used the grapes for their own wines. Subsequently the vineyard received
minimal care until it was purchased by new owners in 2013, who set about restoring it to its
full glory. This has been achieved with Lucas Hoorn (formerly of Hoddles Creek Estate and
Levantine Hill) as full-time vineyard manager and Dylan McMahon as contract winemaker,
the wines made at Seville Estate. The quality of the wines speaks for itself. (JH)

ŸŸŸŸŸ **Amnis Cabernet Malbec 2019, Yarra Valley** 10% malbec and matured in
barriques (25% new) for 18 months. A deepish plummy red. With its aromas
of dark cherry and blackcurrant fruit, cedar and tobacco, as well as some dried
oregano and thyme, there's quite a bit going on here. Medium–full bodied, the
concentrated and well-weighted palate gives way to some serious, yet balanced,
fine-grained tannin. Screw cap. 13.2% alc. RATING 94 DRINK 2023-2030 $89 PR

ŸŸŸŸŸ **Rose Nebbiolo 2021, Yarra Valley** RATING 91 DRINK 2021-2023 $25 PR

Yarra Yering

4 Briarty Road, Gruyere, Vic 3770 **Region** Yarra Valley
T (03) 5964 9267 **www.**yarrayering.com **Open** 7 days 10–5 **Winemaker** Sarah Crowe
Est. 1969 **Dozens** 5000 **Vyds** 40ha
This high-profile wine business was established in 1998 by Robert and Mem Kirby of Village
Roadshow. The vineyard enjoys a north-facing slope, capturing maximum sunshine while
also receiving sea breezes. In the midst of conversion to organic viticulture, the main focus is
on 25ha of pinot noir, 14ha of chardonnay and 8ha of pinot gris; 3ha of shiraz, merlot and
sauvignon blanc take a back seat. The arrival of the hugely talented Tom Carson as group
winemaker in '08 added lustre to the winery and its wines, making the first Jimmy Watson
Trophy–winning pinot noir in '14 and continuing to blitz the Australian wine show circuit
with single-block pinot noirs. The Halliday Wine Companion 2023 named Yarra Yering the
Winery of the Year, and the Yarra Yering Dry Red No. 1 2019 the Wine of the Year. Exports
to the UK, Canada, Sweden and Hong Kong. (JH)

ŸŸŸŸŸ **Carrodus Cabernet Sauvignon 2020, Yarra Valley** A deep crimson purple.
An incredibly complex nose with its core of fresh blackcurrant and cherry as well
as cassis, graphite, bay leaf, black olive and cedar from the perfectly handled and
already integrated oak. Darkly fruited on the palate, this iron fist in a velvet glove
textured and structured wine is worth every cent of its lofty asking price. Screw
cap. 13.5% alc. RATING 98 DRINK 2022-2035 $275 PR ♥
Dry Red No. 1 2020, Yarra Valley 60/20/15/5% cabernet sauvignon/
merlot/malbec/petit verdot. A deep, bright crimson-purple hue. Essence of
great cabernet with its core of blackcurrant and boysenberry fruit, as well as a
complex assortment of cardamom, coriander seed, black tea and gentle, fresh
tobacco leaf. Just as good on the detailed, layered and persistent palate. There is a
coolness and restraint to the cassis fruit that builds, culminating in a long, chalky
tannin finish. A complete and beautiful wine. Screw cap. 13.5% alc. RATING 97
DRINK 2022-2035 $120 PR ✪
Underhill 2020, Yarra Valley A very bright, medium crimson purple. A
riotous amalgam of aromas including blueberries, potpourri, licorice root,
Szechuan pepper and caraway seeds. Medium bodied and elegant, this has terrific
viscosity and the tannins are oh, so powdery and fine. Gorgeous now and over
the next 10 years or longer. Screw cap. 13.5% alc. RATING 97 DRINK 2022-2035
$120 PR ✪

ꢁꢁꢁꢁꢁ **Dry Red No. 3 2020, Yarra Valley** 35/35/12/7/6/5% touriga nacional/
tinta cão/tinta amarela/tinta roriz/alvarelhão/sousão. This one-of-a-kind wine is
beautifully perfumed with mountain herbs, lavender, rosemary and briary red fruits.
Beautifully balanced and proportioned on the palate and immediately appealing
with its gentle texture, refreshing acidity and superfine tannin structure. Screw cap.
13.5% alc. RATING 96 DRINK 2021-2029 $105 PR

Dry Red No. 2 2020, Yarra Valley Shiraz with 3% mataro and 1% viognier, the
latter added as skins to some of the fermenters. A deep crimson red. Concentrated
with redcurrants, satsuma plums and blackberries, along with fennel seed, olive
tapenande, dark chocolate powder and a little fresh vanilla from the oak. A
complete wine on the palate with its dark sour-cherry fruit, a slight savoury edge
and firm, very fine tannins providing the structure for this to age well into the
decade and beyond. Screw cap. 13.5% alc. RATING 96 DRINK 2022-2032 $120 PR

Carrodus Pinot Noir 2020, Yarra Valley A medium-deep crimson purple.
Focused with strawberries and other red fruits, along with a little spice from the
well-handled oak. On the palate this has real power and density, with a core of
sweet, darker fruits and savoury, ripe and long tannins. A serious wine built for the
long haul. Screw cap. 13% alc. RATING 96 DRINK 2023-2030 $275 PR

Light Dry Red Pinot Shiraz 2021, Yarra Valley A gorgeous bright crimson
purple, this just beckons to be smelled. A pure and fruit-driven wine, redolent of
wild briary red fruits and spice-rack spices. Medium bodied, there is a delicious
juiciness to this wine, but equally, there is extract and concentration. Despite
how good this is now, it should age effortlessly for the next 5–8 years. Screw cap.
14% alc. RATING 95 DRINK 2021-2028 $95 PR

Chardonnay 2020, Yarra Valley A bright green gold. Aromas of grapefruit
pith, lemon zest and fresh ginger are all present in this fruit-focused, single-
vineyard wine. A wine of purity and finesse on the palate, there's also good
extract and weight, finishing pithy and long. Screw cap. 13% alc. RATING 95
DRINK 2021-2028 $110 PR

Pinot Noir 2020, Yarra Valley Restrained, with fresh cherries, rhubarb and a
subtle floral/Szechuan spice. Medium bodied, elegant and composed, there is a
tight core of fruit and excellent length of flavour. Finishes with very fine-grained
tannins and will look even better in 6–12 months. Screw cap. 13% alc. RATING 95
DRINK 2022-2028 $110 PR

Carrodus Chardonnay 2020, Yarra Valley A deepish bright green gold. A
powerhouse Yarra chardonnay with ripe stone fruits, custard apple, spice and gentle
reduction. Creamily textured, it also has great drive and acidity. Screw cap. 13% alc.
RATING 95 DRINK 2021-2028 $160 PR

Agincourt Cabernet Malbec 2020, Yarra Valley A deep crimson red.
Fragrant with darker red fruits, freshly hung meat and a lifted floral, herbal
character from the malbec. An open, confident, bright and quite delicious Yarra
cabernet. Screw cap. 23.5% alc. RATING 94 DRINK 2021-2028 $105 PR

Yarrabank

38 Melba Highway, Yarra Glen, Vic 3775 **Region** Yarra Valley
T (03) 9730 0100 **www.**yering.com **Open** Mon–Fri 10–5, Sat–Sun 10–6
Winemaker Brendan Hawker, James Oliver, Darren Rathbone **Viticulturist** Rod
Harrison **Est.** 1993 **Dozens** 2000 **Vyds** 4ha
The highly successful Yarrabank was established as a joint venture between the French
Champagne house Devaux and Yering Station in 1993. Until '97 the Yarrabank Cuvée Brut
was made under Claude Thibaut's direction at Domaine Chandon, but thereafter the entire
operation has been conducted at Yarrabank and the venture is now owned solely by Yering
Station. There are 4ha of dedicated vineyards at Yering Station planted to pinot noir and
chardonnay, the balance of the intake comes from growers in the Yarra Valley and southern
Victoria. Exports to all major markets. (JH)

ꢁꢁꢁꢁꢁ **Brut Rosé 2013, Yarra Valley** Traditional method and disgorged June '21. Pale-
ish salmon, with no pink lift, but the wine is very rich and complex, with fraises

des bois, studded with spices and an auto-suggestion of hot smoked salmon, and not the least problematic. Diam. 13% alc. RATING 95 $40 JH

♥♥♥♥ Brut Rosé 2015, Yarra Valley RATING 89 $40 PR

Yarradindi Wines   ★★★★★

1018 Murrindindi Road, Murrindindi, Vic 3717 **Region** Upper Goulburn
T 0438 305 314 **www.**mrhughwine.com **Winemaker** Hugh Cuthbertson **Est.** 1979
Dozens 90 000 **Vyds** 70ha
Murrindindi Vineyards was established by Alan and Jan Cutherbertson as a minor diversification from their cattle property. Son Hugh Cutherbertson (with a long and high-profile wine career) took over the venture and in '15 folded the business into his largest customers to create Yarradindi Wines. The fortified wines, under the Mr Hugh label, are crafted from a solera system started in the 1880s by Melbourne wine merchant W.J. Seabrook. Exports to the UK. (JH)

♥♥♥♥♥ Mr Hugh Sipping Bliss Aperitif NV This is a taste of history. Golden amber-brown hue, it shimmies in the glass. The aromas and flavours are intoxicating in hazelnut, dried fruits, burnt toffee, salted nuts and gingerbread. Complex, intense but beautifully fresh and alive. Sipping bliss indeed. 500ml. Screw cap. 18% alc. RATING 95 $65 JP
Mr Hugh Sipping Bliss Digestif NV Another wonderfully evocative and smoothly delivered reminder of a style of fortified that is sadly losing ground among Australian makers and drinkers. This is a call to arms, to engage in its complex array of tastes, of silky caramels and dripping molasses, golden walnuts and dried fruits, orange rind and coffee. What a delight! 500ml. Screw cap. 18% alc. RATING 95 $65 JP

♥♥♥♥♀ Mr Hugh Shiraz 2021, Mornington Peninsula RATING 90 DRINK 2022-2025 $45 JP
Mr Hugh Yea Valley Vineyard Riesling 2021, Central Victoria RATING 90 DRINK 2022–2028 $42 JP

YarraLoch   ★★★★

11 Range Road, Gruyere Vi 3770 **Region** Yarra Valley
T 0407 376 587 **www.**yarraloch.com.au **Open** By appt **Winemaker** Contract **Est.** 1998
Dozens 2000 **Vyds** 6ha
This is the ambitious project of successful investment banker Stephen Wood. He has taken the best possible advice and has not hesitated to provide appropriate financial resources to a venture that has no exact parallel in the Yarra Valley or anywhere else in Australia. Six hectares of vineyards may not seem so unusual, but in fact he has assembled 3 entirely different sites, 70km apart, each matched to the needs of the variety/varieties planted on that site. Pinot noir is planted on the Steep Hill Vineyard with a northeast orientation and a shaley rock and ironstone soil. Cabernet sauvignon has been planted at Kangaroo Ground with a dry, steep northwest-facing site and abundant sun exposure in the warmest part of the day, ensuring full ripeness. Merlot, shiraz, chardonnay and viognier are planted at Upper Plenty, 50km from Kangaroo Ground. This has an average temperature 2°C cooler and a ripening period 2-3 weeks later than the warmest parts of the Yarra Valley. (JH)

♥♥♥♥♀ Single Vineyard Pinot Noir 2019, Yarra Valley A bright and quite deep crimson red. An impressive core of darker fruits, including dark cherry and blueberries, with the oak sitting discreetly in the background. Medium–full bodied, there is both enough stuffing and tannins for this to soften and become more complex over the next 5–8 years. Screw cap. 13.5% alc. RATING 92 DRINK 2022-2028 $40 PR
Single Vineyard Chardonnay 2019, Yarra Valley A light, bright gold with green tinges. Ripe yellow peaches intermingled with some vanilla bean, honeycomb and almonds. Textured and rich with flavours of ripe stone

fruits, before finishing moderately long. Screw cap. 13.5% alc. RATING 90
DRINK 2021-2024 $40 PR

ŸŸŸŸ **La Cosette Pinot Noir 2019, Yarra Valley** RATING 89 DRINK 2022-2026
$30 PR

Yarran Wines ★★★★
178 Myall Park Road, Yenda, NSW 2681 **Region** Riverina
T (02) 6968 1125 **www.**yarranwines.com.au **Open** Mon–Sat 10–5 **Winemaker** Sam
Brewer **Est.** 2000 **Dozens** 20000 **Vyds** 30ha
Lorraine Brewer (and late husband John) were grapegrowers for over 30 years and when son
Sam completed a degree in wine science at CSU. The majority of the grapes from the estate
plantings are sold but each year a little more has been made under the Yarran banner; along
the way a winery with a crush capacity of 150t has been built. Sam decided to take the plunge
in '09 and concentrate on the family winery. The majority of the grapes come from the
family vineyard but some parcels are sourced from growers, including Lake Cooper Estate in
the Heathcote region. Over the past 3 years Sam has focused on improving the quality of the
estate-grown grapes, moving to organic conversion. Yarran was the Wine Companion 2021
Dark Horse of the Year. Exports to Canada and Singapore. (JH)

ŸŸŸŸŸ **A Few Words Pétillant Naturel Montepulciano 2021, Riverina** Among
the finest pet nats tasted from these shores. Made in the most authentic manner,
or méthode ancestrale, as it is known, in which the first ferment simply finishes in
bottle. An incantation of picked cherry, ume and shiso. A turbid, elemental beauty.
A textural source of immense nourishment and pleasure. A fine amaro bitterness,
marking the frothy finish. Screw cap. 13% alc. RATING 93 $25 NG ✪
A Few Words Montepulciano Rosé 2021, Riverina Very good rosé. Picked
early. The bunches shaded by savvy vine training. pH tweaks, thus, minimal. A mid
coral with copper seams. Red fruits, musk and a savoury umami note, ferrous and
meaty. Fine intensity and length, here. Thoroughly impressive and worth seeking
out. Screw cap. 12.5% alc. RATING 90 DRINK 2021-2022 $20 NG ✪

Yarrh Wines ★★★★
440 Greenwood Road, Murrumbateman, NSW 2582 **Region** Canberra District
T (02) 6227 1474 **www.**yarrhwines.com.au **Open** Fri–Sun 11–5 **Winemaker** Fiona
Wholohan **Est.** 1997 **Dozens** 2000 **Vyds** 6ha
Fiona Wholohan and Neil McGregor are IT refugees; both now work full-time running the
Yarrh Wines Vineyard and making the wines. Fiona undertook the oenology and viticulture
course at CSU and has also spent time as an associate judge at wine shows. They spent
5 years moving to a hybrid organic vineyard with composting, mulching, biological controls
and careful vineyard floor management. The vineyard includes cabernet sauvignon, shiraz,
sauvignon blanc, riesling, pinot noir and sangiovese. They have recently tripled their sangiovese
plantings with 2 new clones. Yarrh was the original Aboriginal name for the Yass district. (JH)

ŸŸŸŸŸ **Riesling 2021, Canberra District** A lovely wine in anyone's book. The combo
of grapefruit juice, finger-lime pop and a squirt of lemon juice gives this a head
start in the refreshment stakes. A touch of white pepper, bath salts and brisk acidity
completes the story. Screw cap. 11.5% alc. RATING 91 DRINK 2021-2027 $30 JF
Sangiovese 2021, Canberra District Tasted soon after bottling and with more
time to settle, this will be something. A pale ruby with juicy, tangy and oh, so
sweet cherry flavours. Enough spice, including oaky woodsy ones, to add another
layer of complexity. Tannins are surprisingly supple and un-sangiovese-like in way,
yet overall, it's a lovely drink. Screw cap. -% alc. RATING 91 DRINK 2023-2026
$32 JF
Shiraz 2021, Canberra District This was tasted soon after bottling; it is gangly
and reductive. Lots of oak char and wood smoke infusing the core of very good
dark fruit, sprinkled with baking spices and pepper. Tannins firm and a touch raw,

yet the wine should settle down well in time, ultimately changing the outcome.
Screw cap. -% alc. RATING 90 DRINK 2023-2028 $35 JF

Year Wines

PO Box 638, Willunga, SA 5172 **Region** McLaren Vale
T 0434 970 162 **www.**yearwines.com.au **Winemaker** Luke Growden, Caleigh Hunt
Est. 2012 **Dozens** 600
A suite of easygoing, texturally interesting, finely hewn wines, crafted with minimal fussing:
quality fruit, hand harvesting, wild fermentations and gentle extractive techniques. As
impressive is the championing of the right varieties for the land from the layered fiano,
textural grenache and smattering of ersatz field blends, these are wines that augur well for
the present and even brighter for the future. The style here is one of considered immediacy,
to contemplate briefly before drinking with gusto. Exports to the US and Singapore. (NG)

Sausage in Bread 2021, McLaren Vale Carbonic and pulpy of feel without
straying from the zone of savoury detail, nor my will to have another glass.
Beautifully articulated. Mid weighted of feel. Sapid sour cherry, red pastille, rosehip,
lilac and bergamot. Just enough tannic twine to sustain poise and refreshment
factor. A gorgeous drink, best drunk lustfully with a solid chill. Screw cap.
12.4% alc. RATING 91 DRINK 2022-2024 $25 NG
Noodle Juice 2021, McLaren Vale Equal parts (48%) grillo and riesling,
with a dollop of muscat à petit grains. This is loads of fun. Reminiscent of thirst-
slaking wines of the Languedoc, served as an apero in the louche bars of Sète. The
makeup, starkly different. Lime cordial, lemon drop, grape, spiced quince and leesy
almond meal. The balance between texture, fruit and freshness, apposite. Delicious
swigging. Ready now. Screw cap. 12.3% alc. RATING 91 DRINK 2022-2024
$26 NG

YEATES

138 Craigmoor Road, Mudgee, NSW 2850 **Region** Mudgee
T 0427 791 264 **www.**yeateswines.com.au **Open** Thurs–Mon 11–5 **Winemaker** Jacob
Stein **Viticulturist** Alexander (Sandy) Yeates **Est.** 2010 **Dozens** 300 **Vyds** 11.5ha
The Yeates family purchased the 20ha Mountain Blue Vineyard in Mudgee in '10 from
Foster's, who in turn purchased it from Rosemount (the shiraz and cabernet were the source
of Rosemount's single-vineyard Mountain Blue label). Planted in 1968, these are some of the
oldest vines in Mudgee. The vineyard has been managed organically since '13 and the vines
and wines have flourished under this management regimen. Riesling and albariño have since
been established too. A new cellar door and accommodation were constructed in '20. (JH)

Riesling 2021, Mudgee Made by Jacob Stein, a man with a masterly stroke
with riesling, the cool vintage is clear. Jasmine, spa salts and lemon zest twirl about
a bright, high-acid pulse. Lightweight, tensile and a bit sour at this nascent state.
The intensity and focus is so clear, however, that I don't doubt it will age well
across the mid term. Screw cap. 11.5% alc. RATING 91 DRINK 2022-2030 $30 NG

Yelland & Papps

279 Nuraip Road, Nuriootpa, SA 5355 **Region** Barossa Valley
T 0408 628 494 **www.**yellandandpapps.com **Open** By appt **Winemaker** Michael and
Susan Papps **Est.** 2005 **Dozens** 4000 **Vyds** 2ha
Michael and Susan Papps (née Yelland) set up this venture after their marriage in 2005. It
is easy for them to regard the Barossa Valley as their home because Michael has lived and
worked in the wine industry in the Barossa Valley for more than 20 years. He has a rare
touch, producing consistently excellent wines, but also pushing the envelope; as well as using
a sustainable approach to winemaking with minimal inputs, he has not hesitated to challenge
orthodox approaches to a number of aspects of conventional fermentation methods. Exports
to Norway. (JH)

🍷🍷🍷🍷🍷 Second Take Mataro 2020, Barossa Valley Very good purple hue, bright crimson on the rim. The most substantial of the 3 wines profiled, yet isn't the least bit extractive. Spice, black pepper and cinnamon punctuate the plum that fills the mouth, aided by a gloss of superfine tannins. Screw cap. 13% alc. RATING 95 DRINK 2022-2035 $45 JH

Second Take Shiraz 2020, Barossa Valley Spectacular depth of colour given its low alcohol and 50% whole-bunch fermentation; 3.55 pH and 5.84g/L acidity (conventional levels) provide the answer. Black spices drive the bouquet, the palate with red and black cherry fruit. It's vibrantly fresh and zesty, yet there are tannins to provide texture. Screw cap. 12.2% alc. RATING 94 DRINK 2022-2029 $45 JH

🍷🍷🍷🍷🍷 Second Take Grenache 2020, Barossa Valley RATING 93 DRINK 2022-2025 $45 JH

Yering Station ★★★★★

38 Melba Highway, Yarra Glen, Vic 3775 **Region** Yarra Valley
T (03) 9730 0100 **www**.yering.com **Open** Mon–Fri 10–5, Sat–Sun 10–6
Winemaker Brendan Hawker, James Oliver, Darren Rathbone **Viticulturist** Rod Harrison **Est.** 1988 **Dozens** 60 000 **Vyds** 112ha
The historic Yering Station (or at least the portion of the property on which the cellar door and vineyard are established) was purchased by the Rathbone family in 1996; it is also the site of Yarrabank. A spectacular and very large winery was built, handling the Yarrabank sparkling and the Yering Station table wines, immediately becoming one of the focal points of the Yarra Valley – particularly as the historic Château Yering, where luxury accommodation and fine dining are available, is next door. Exports to all major markets. (JH)

🍷🍷🍷🍷🍷 Reserve Shiraz Viognier 2020, Yarra Valley Co-fermented with 2.3% viognier. Red and black fruits, together with a panoply of spice aromas, ranging from pink peppercorns to more exotic spice rack spices. Comfortable in its own skin, this strikes the perfect balance between having excellent depth and concentration while remaining elegant and pure. Really fine yet persistent tannins round out a wine that's sure to provide plenty of enjoyment over the next 8–15 years. Screw cap. 14.3% alc. RATING 96 DRINK 2023-2030 $130 PR

Reserve Chardonnay 2020, Yarra Valley A bright green gold. Aromas of freshly picked white peach, green mangoes, some star anise and discreetly handled wood that is already well integrated. This has real drive on the palate, with flavours of nectarine and grapefruit pith. Finishes chalky and long. An excellent expression of Yarra chardonnay that will reward at least another 5 years, if not more, in the cellar. Screw cap. 13% alc. RATING 95 DRINK 2021-2027 $130 PR

PDC Shiraz 2020, Yarra Valley With 5% viognier. A medium and bright crimson purple. Aromas redolent of cranberry raisins, raspberries and lifted violets from the viognier. Medium bodied and very nicely put together, this elegant wine is gentle and creamy textured and finishes long with very fine, supple tannins. Screw cap. 14.3% alc. RATING 94 DRINK 2021-2027 $70 PR

🍷🍷🍷🍷🍷 Pinot Noir 2021, Yarra Valley RATING 93 DRINK 2022-2027 $40 PR
Shiraz Viognier 2020, Yarra Valley RATING 91 DRINK 2022-2026 $40 PR
Village Chardonnay 2021, Yarra Valley RATING 90 DRINK 2021-2024 $28 PR
Village Pinot Noir 2021, Yarra Valley RATING 90 DRINK 2022-2025 $28 PR
Village Pinot Noir 2020, Yarra Valley RATING 90 DRINK 2021-2027 $28 JH
GSM 2020, Yarra Valley RATING 90 DRINK 2021-2026 $40 PR

Yeringberg ★★★★★

810 Maroondah Highway, Coldstream, Vic 3770 **Region** Yarra Valley
T (03) 9739 0240 **www**.yeringberg.com.au **Open** By appt **Winemaker** Sandra de Pury
Viticulturist David de Pury **Est.** 1863 **Dozens** 1500 **Vyds** 12ha

A 19th century Yarra Valley pioneer, Yeringberg's renaissance began when the third generation wine grower, Guill and Katherine de Pury began replanting vines in 1969, making their first commercial wine in '74. Since '08, the wines have been made by daughter Sandra while her brother, David, who has a PhD in plant physiology, manages the vineyards and Yeringberg's grass-fed lamb and cattle. Committed to the future, a new winery is in design phase and a new vine program began in '20 to mitigate against climate change and phylloxera, establishing 2 new vineyard sites on south- and east-facing slopes. The future could not be more exciting for one of the Yarra's oldest and most important producers. Exports to the UK, the US, Switzerland and Hong Kong. (PR)

ŶŶŶŶŶ **Yeringberg 2020, Yarra Valley** A blend of 61/10/10/10/9% cabernet sauvignon/cabernet franc//merlot/petit verdot/malbec. A medium and bright ruby red. Even in a cooler year, this always great wine delivers the goods. Aromas of subtle cranberry, blackberries and brambly blackberry leaf, together with a little clove and fresh vanilla bean from the well-handled oak. Medium bodied and beautifully poised, this has fine, elegant tannins contributing to a wine that, as delicious as it is now, boasts a track record that means you can cellar it for as long as you have the patience to do so. An under-priced icon wine. Screw cap. 13% alc. RATING 97 DRINK 2022-2035 $95 PR ✪

ŶŶŶŶŶ **Chardonnay 2020, Yarra Valley** A bright, medium green gold. Lovely aromatics with yellow peach and nectarine fruit as well as subtle oatmeal and grilled nuts. Orange blossom and a hint of matchstick too. Textured and bright in the mouth, I like the touch of grip on the long and satisfying finish. Screw cap. 12.5% alc. RATING 96 DRINK 2022-2028 $65 PR ✪
Viognier 2020, Yarra Valley A bright green gold. Relatively restrained, with white stone fruits, apricot kernel, honey and a little ginger and nutmeg spice. Rich and textured without a hint of oiliness, this finishes long. Bright acidity rounds out a wine that can be enjoyed over the next 2–3 years. One of the better Australian viogniers I've tasted. Screw cap. 14.5% alc. RATING 95 DRINK 2022-2025 $40 PR
Marsanne Roussanne 2020, Yarra Valley A deepish gold with green tinges. Honeyed with apricot skins, melon and fig fruit along with a little orange blossom and jasmine. There's a lot going on here! Really mouth-filling and textured, but equally importantly, this quite delicious wine finishes refreshing and long. Screw cap. 13% alc. RATING 95 DRINK 2022-2026 $65 PR ♥

Yes said the seal   ★★★★☆

1251-1269 Bellarine Highway, Wallington, Vic 3221 **Region** Geelong
T (03) 5250 6577 **www.yessaidtheseal.com.au Open** 7 days 10–5 **Winemaker** Darren Burke **Viticulturist** David Sharp **Est.** 2014 **Dozens** 1200 **Vyds** 8ha
This is the newest venture of David and Lyndsay Sharp, long-term vintners on Geelong's Bellarine Peninsula. It is situated onsite at the Flying Brick Cider Co's Cider House in Wallington. The estate vineyard includes 3ha of pinot noir, 2ha each of chardonnay and shiraz and 1ha of sauvignon blanc. (JH)

ŶŶŶŶŶ **The Bellarine Shiraz 2019, Geelong** A well-integrated and serious young shiraz just starting out on what should prove a productive, long journey. Captivating aromas of spice, black cherry, musk and fresh-cut wild herbs. The palate is laid out beautifully, thoughtfully, in fine tannins with a core of plush, ripe fruit and gentle oak. Cool-climate generosity, yes, but with a real sense of elegance. Screw cap. 14% alc. RATING 95 DRINK 2022-2027 $42 JP
The Bellarine Rosé 2021, Geelong Shiraz rosé. A striking, serious rosé as always, with shiraz turned up full volume, bursting in red-fruited flavour, wild herbs, musk and plenty of old zip and zing. Bold and delicious. Screw cap. 12.5% alc. RATING 94 DRINK 2022-2024 $35 JP

ŶŶŶŶŶ **Reserve Blanc de Blanc 2018, Geelong** RATING 93 $45 JP
The Bellarine Pinot Noir 2020, Geelong RATING 90 DRINK 2022-2026 $42 JP

Z Wine ★★★★★

Shop 3, 109-111 Murray Street, Tanunda, SA 5352 **Region** Barossa Valley
T (08) 8563 3637 **www**.zwine.com.au **Open** Sun–Thurs 10–8, Fri–Sat 10–late
Winemaker Janelle Zerk **Est.** 1999 **Dozens** 10000
Z Wine is the partnership of sisters Janelle and Kristen Zerk, whose heritage dates back
5 generations at the Zerk Vineyard in Lyndoch. Vineyard resources include growers that
supply old-vine shiraz, old bush-vine grenache and High Eden riesling. Both women have
completed degrees at the University of Adelaide (Janelle winemaking and Kristen wine
marketing). Janelle also has vintage experience in Puligny-Montrachet, Tuscany and Sonoma
Valley. Wines are released under the Z Wine, Rustica and Section 3146 labels. Z Wine's
cellar door is in the main street of Tanunda. Exports to the US, Singapore, NZ, Taiwan and
Hong Kong. (JH)

🍷🍷🍷🍷🍷 **Roman Old Vine GSM 2021, Barossa Valley** The colour is fresh and full, the
perfumed aromas and flavours of all manner of cinnamon spice, through licorice,
dark chocolate, and velvety blackberry on the palate and into the lingering, bright
finish. Screw cap. 14.5% alc. RATING 96 DRINK 2022-2041 $40 JH ✪
August Old Vine Grenache 2021, Barossa Valley Old vines, modern
grenache style, picked while all the perfume and exotic spices of grenache are in
high relief throughout the long palate. Best of all is the absence of heat on the
juicy finish. Screw cap. 14.5% alc. RATING 95 DRINK 2023-2031 $35 JH ✪
Saul Riesling 2021, Eden Valley Scents of citrus, apple, white peach and
powder puff float in the glass, giving way to the more direct mix of lime and
lemon on the long travel through to the finish and aftertaste of the palate. High-
quality wine. Screw cap. 11.5% alc. RATING 95 DRINK 2023-2036 $35 JH ✪
Julius Shiraz 2020, Barossa Valley Bright red with purple flashes in the glass
and characters of satsuma plum, red cherry and macerated raspberries along with
spice, smoked meats, mocha coffee and dark chocolate. The rich fruit hangs off an
impressive scaffold of fine tannin; bright acidity drives the wine to a long finish.
Detailed and delicious drinking, with a lovely flow of fruit and great balance.
Screw cap. 14.5% alc. RATING 95 DRINK 2022-2038 $70 DB
Julius Barossa Valley Shiraz 2013 A cellar release from a warm and dry, low-
yielding year. Rich blackberry, black cherry and plum fruits are beginning to be
embraced by the complex characters of bottle age – mahogany, polished leather,
gentle cedar, licorice, pressed flowers and baking spice. Calm and composed
with a lovely confident flow of fruit, spicy, leathery nuance and cascading tannin
drifting down on the long persistent finish. Screw cap. 14.5% alc. RATING 95
DRINK 2022-2030 $150 DB
Saul Night Havest Riesling 2021, Eden Valley I was looking forward to
Zerk's flagship Saul riesling from the outstanding '21 Eden Valley vintage and
it didn't disappoint. Tightly coiled and running on rails it's a picture of linear
precision and focus, crisp lime and citrus notes with hints of Christmas lily, cut
fennel and stone. Sizzling line, a light twist of sapid, phenolic goodness on the exit
and a finish that powers off into the distance. Screw cap. 11.5% alc. RATING 94
DRINK 2022-2035 $35 DB
Plowman Dry Grown Shiraz 2019, Barossa Valley Deeply coloured with
spiced plum, black cherry and blueberry notes cut with baking spice, licorice,
mocha and earth. Full bodied and richly proportioned, grippy, ripe tannin, dense
cassis and plum fruits, abundant spice and a concentrated finish of some length.
Diam. 14.5% alc. RATING 94 DRINK 2022-3025 $120 DB

🍷🍷🍷🍷🍷 **Rohrlach Survivor Vine Grenache 2020, Barossa Valley** RATING 93
DRINK 2023-2030 $120 JH
Poole Old Vine Shiraz 2018, Barossa Valley RATING 93 DRINK 2022-2035
$120 DB
Audrey Cabernet Sauvignon 2019, Barossa Valley RATING 92
DRINK 2022-2032 $35 DB
Mae Riesling 2021, Eden Valley RATING 90 DRINK 2022-2032 $28 DB

Laverin Old Vine Bonvedro 2021, Barossa Valley RATING 90
DRINK 2022-2027 $30 DB
Hedley Shiraz 2019, Barossa Valley RATING 90 DRINK 2022-2028 $35 DB
Franz Cabernet Shiraz 2019, Barossa Valley RATING 90 DRINK 2022-2030
$60 DB

Zagora ★★★

8 The Parade West, Kent Town, SA 5067 (postal) **Region** South Australia
T 1300 559 463 **www**.zagoraestatewines.com **Winemaker** Peter Pollard **Est.** 2001
Dozens 5000
Zagora was established in 2001, drawing on purchased fruit from South Australia's premium
regions, mitigating the overheads of vineyard ownership while offering winemaker Peter
Pollard the opportunity to craft impressively poised wines marked by ample flavour and
delectable value. Few heads are turned or envelopes pushed, but for around $20, the straight-
shooting McLaren Vale shiraz and firmer, more savoury cabernet sauvignon, are hard to
beat. (NG)

 Shiraz 2018, McLaren Vale It would be churlish to pull this wine apart, so
good is its value. Exeptionally made, with economising steps along the way. Yet
one would not know it, so polished is the texture, well embedded the American
oak and seamless the tangy finish. Vibrant florals, purple fruits a whiff of barbecued
meat and a white-pepper trail. Screw cap. 14.5% alc. RATING 88 DRINK 2021-2025
$18 NG

Zarephath Wines ★★★★

424 Moorialup Road, East Porongurup, WA 6324 **Region** Porongurup
T (08) 9853 1152 **www**.zarephathwines.com.au **Open** Mon–Sat 10–5, Sun 10–4
Winemaker Robert Diletti **Est.** 1994 **Dozens** 1500 **Vyds** 8.9ha
The Zarephath vineyard was owned and operated by Brothers and Sisters of The Christ
Circle, a Benedictine community. In '14 they sold the property to Rosie Singer and her
partner Ian Barrett-Lennard, who live on the spot full time and undertake all the vineyard
work, supplemented by the local Afghani community during vintage and pruning. They have
diverse backgrounds, Ian's roots in the Swan Valley, while Rosie has worked in various aspects
of fine arts, first in administration and thereafter as a practising visual artist with galleries in
north Queensland and regional WA. (JH)

 Pinot Noir 2019, Porongurup This wine carries all of the luscious ripe
raspberry aromatics that are common in pinot from the area; they morph on the
palate in a cascade of red licorice, white pepper, anise and olive tapenade. This is
a super-pretty wine, with fine chalky tannins that shape it as it rides out into the
sunset/finish. Screw cap. 13% alc. RATING 93 DRINK 2021-2031 $35 EL

Zerella Wines ★★★★☆

182 Olivers Rd, McLaren Vale, SA 5171 **Region** McLaren Vale
T (08) 8323 8288/0417 766 699 **www**.zerellawines.com.au **Open** Thurs–Mon 11–4
Winemaker Jim Zerella **Viticulturist** Jim Zerella **Est.** 2006 **Dozens** 2500 **Vyds** 58ha
Ercole Zerella left Campania in southern Italy in 1950 to seek a better life in SA. With a
lifetime of farming and grape growing, the transition was seamless. Ercole's son Vic followed
in his father's footsteps, becoming an icon of the SA farming and wine industries. He founded
Tatachilla, where his son Jim began as a cellar hand, eventually controlling all grape purchases.
While working there, Jim purchased land in McLaren Vale and, with help from family and
friends, established what is now the flagship vineyard of Zerella Wines. When Tatachilla was
purchased by Lion Nathan in 2000 he declined the opportunity of continuing his role there
and by '06 had purchased 2 more vineyards, and become a shareholder in a third. These all
now come under the umbrella of Zerella Wines, with its 58ha of vines. Exports to the UK
and Canada. (JH)

ŸŸŸŸŸ **Oliveto Single Vineyard Mataro 2020, McLaren Vale** This is very good. Aromatic precision and burliness. As mataro should be. A savoury sheath of saddle leather, smoked meat, iodine, terracotta and blood. The tannins, firm, ferruginous and expansive. The oak, well nestled. This exemplifies just how superior these later ripening Mediterranean cultivars are in our torrid climates. A very good wine that will only get better such is this family's strident progress. Screw cap. 14.5% alc. RATING 95 DRINK 2021-2030 $60 NG

Home Block Single Vineyard Shiraz 2018, McLaren Vale Very good. The mechanics, alloyed to site and purpose: a full-weighted wine exuding blueberry, iodine, white pepper, charcuterie, lavender and a smear of black olive. Clearly a lovely vintage for this wine, although the acidity is a bit shrill. Screw cap. 14% alc. RATING 94 DRINK 2021-2030 $60 NG

ŸŸŸŸŸ **La Gita Nero d'Avola 2020, McLaren Vale** RATING 93 DRINK 2021-2023 $35 NG

Olivers Road Grenache 2020, McLaren Vale RATING 93 DRINK 2021-2026 $60 NG

Packing Shed Grenache Mataro Shiraz 2020, McLaren Vale RATING 92 DRINK 2021-2025 $30 NG

La Gita Etrurian 2017, McLaren Vale RATING 92 DRINK 2021-2024 $60 NG

La Gita Fiano 2021, McLaren Vale RATING 91 DRINK 2021-2023 $30 NG

La Gita Arneis 2019, McLaren Vale RATING 90 DRINK 2021-2024 $30 NG

Zilzie Wines   ★★★★★

544 Kulkyne Way, Karadoc, Vic 3496 **Region** Murray Darling
T (03) 5025 8100 **www**.zilziewines.com **Open** By appt **Winemaker** Jonathan Creek
Viticulturist Andrew Forbes, Steven Forbes **Est.** 1999 **Vyds** 700ha
The Forbes family has been farming since the early 1900s. Zilzie is currently run by Roslyn Forbes and sons Steven and Andrew, the diverse range of farming activities now solely focused on grap egrowing from substantial vineyards. Having established a dominant position as a supplier of grapes to Southcorp, Zilzie formed a wine company in '99 and built a winery in 2000, expanding it to its current capacity of 60000t. The wines consistently far exceed expectations, that consistency driving the substantial production volume in an extremely competitive market. The business includes contract processing, winemaking and storage; the winery is certified organic. Exports to the US, Singapore, South Korea, Indonesia and Malaysia. (JH)

ŸŸŸŸŸ **Platinum Edition Arinto 2021, Riverland** A mild summer in the Riverland has delivered a beauty of a wine. Arinto, the Portuguese white grape, brings forth its lemon citrus tang in spades here with pear, spice and apple. Acidity is keen, delicious and super-dry. Screw cap. 12.5% alc. RATING 95 DRINK 2021-2025 $35 JP ❂

Limited Edition Riesling 2020, Clare Valley A barrel-fermented riesling that explores the richness that lies within the grape when this method is used. Mid yellow in hue with lifted aromas of honeysuckle, white flowers, musk, citrus and orange peel. Richness and texture roll through the palate, delivering concentrated lime cordial, nougat and vanilla pod, all to the tune of zesty acidity. Screw cap. 14% alc. RATING 95 DRINK 2021-2026 $60 JP

Limited Edition Shiraz 2018, McLaren Vale This has muscle, but it also has a core of ripe, plush fruit. It offers a smorgasbord of richness from woodsy spices, oak and lots of tannin. Yet it has come together well. It also has an appealing savoury edge. Yes, full bodied, and not at all shy in an era where the Vale is heading towards more refinement. Or should be. Cork. 14.5% alc. RATING 95 DRINK 2022-2030 $70 JF

Limited Edition Shiraz 2020, McLaren Vale Barossa Valley A complex and fragrant expression of shiraz which is undoubtedly ripe but manages it particularly well. A thread of aromatic dark fruit and spice – plum, black cherry, licorice, earth, vanilla and baking spices – runs gently, with some elegance and power across the palate. Impressive. Screw cap. 14.8% alc. RATING 94 DRINK 2022-2030 $70 JP

🍷🍷🍷🍷🍷 **Platinum Edition Grenache 2020, Barossa** RATING 91 DRINK 2022–2026 $35 JP
Platinum Edition Cabernet Sauvignon 2019, McLaren Vale RATING 91 DRINK 2021–2025 $45 JP

Zitta Wines ★★★☆

3 Union Street, Dulwich, SA 5065 (postal) **Region** Barossa Valley
T 0419 819 414 **www**.zitta.com.au **Winemaker** Angelo De Fazio **Viticulturist** Angelo B De Fazio **Est.** 1864 **Dozens** 3200 **Vyds** 28ha

Owner Angelo De Fazio says that all he knows about viticulture and winemaking came from his father (and generations before him). It is partly this influence that has shaped the label and brand name: Zitta is Italian for 'quiet', and the seeming reflection of the letters of the name Zitta on the label is in fact nothing of the kind, turn the bottle upside down, and you will see it is the word 'Quiet'. The Zitta vineyard dates back to 1864, with a few vines remaining from that time, and a block planted with cuttings taken from those vines. Shiraz dominates the plantings (24ha), the balance made up of grenache and a few mataro and nero d'Avola vines. The property has 2 branches of Greenock Creek running through it and the soils reflect the ancient geological history of the site, in part with a subsoil of river pebbles, reflecting the course of a long-gone river. Exports to Denmark, Sweden and Norway. (JH)

🍷🍷🍷🍷🍷 **Single Vineyard Bernardo Greenock Shiraz 2019, Barossa Valley** Deep, resonant black fruits with hints of baking spice, dark chocolate, ironstone, licorice and cedar. Plenty of heft and power with a broody black-fruit profile, ripe, grainy tannin and flexes with a long, sinewy finish. Screw cap. 14.9% alc. RATING 91 DRINK 2021–2031 $55 DB

🍷🍷🍷🍷 **Union Street GSM 2019, Barossa Valley** RATING 89 DRINK 2021–2027 $35 DB
Union Street Shiraz 2019, Barossa Valley RATING 88 DRINK 2021–2028 $35 DB

Zonte's Footstep ★★★★☆

The General Wine Bar, 55a Main Road, McLaren Flat, SA 5171 **Region** McLaren Vale
T (08) 7286 3083 **www**.zontesfootstep.com.au **Open** Mon–Sat by appt **Winemaker** Brad Rey **Viticulturist** Brad Rey **Est.** 2003 **Dozens** 20 000 **Vyds** 214.72ha

Brad Rey is the kingpin of a small group of winemakers and wine marketers who in 2003 decided it was time to do their own thing in McLaren Vale. Scott Collett's family are multi-generation grape growers and makers; Anna Fisher provides business management skills; and the Heath family own the 215ha organically run vineyards in the Finniss River district whence the grape requirements of Zonte's organic wines are supplied. This sees an extraordinary varietal range of 24 different wines using all the classic northern European varieties of shiraz, viognier, cabernet sauvignon, malbec, pinot noir, sauvignon blanc and chardonnay, as well as the Mediterranean varieties of vermentino, pinot grigio, glera, grenache, sangiovese, lagrein, tempranillo and montepulciano. Exports to the US, Canada, Ireland, Belgium, Finland, Sweden, Denmark, Thailand, Singapore, South Korea and Hong Kong.

🍷🍷🍷🍷🍷 **Violet Beauregard Malbec 2021, Langhorne Creek** Standard no-frills vinification, but this is a wine that is anything but standard. Its depth and breadth of dark berry fruits, licorice, spice and plum coat the palate with flavours that draw you back up repeatedly. Wonderful stuff: hail the vintage! Screw cap. 14% alc. RATING 95 DRINK 2022–2032 $30 JH ✪

🍷🍷🍷🍷🍷 **Age of Enlightenment Shiraz 2019, McLaren Vale** RATING 93 DRINK 2022–2030 $75 NG
Z-Force Shiraz 2018, McLaren Vale RATING 93 DRINK 2022–2032 $75 NG
Scarlet Ladybird Rosé 2021, Fleurieu RATING 92 DRINK 2022–2023 $25 JH ✪
Dusk Till Dawn Chardonnay 2021, Adelaide Hills RATING 92 DRINK 2022–2028 $35 JP

Index

Wineries are arranged alphabetically under geographical
indications (see page 8), to help you find a wine or winery if
you're looking locally or on the road. If you are hoping to
visit, the following key symbols will be of assistance.

♀ **Cellar door sales**

🍴 **Food:** lunch platters to à la carte restaurants

🛏 **Accommodation:** B&B cottages to
luxury vineyard apartments

♫ **Music events:** monthly jazz in the vineyard
to spectacular yearly concerts

Barossa Valley (SA) continued

Wolf Blass 703 ♀ ⑪

Word Play 709 ♀

Yelland & Papps 721 ♀

Z Wine 724 ⓠ ♀ ⑪

Zitta Wines 727

Beechworth (Vic)

A. Rodda Wines 66

Bowman's Run 126 ♀

Eldorado Road 234 ♀

Fighting Gully Road 244 ♀

Giaconda 266 ♀

Indigo Vineyard 325 ⓠ ♀ ⊨ ⑪

James & Co Wines 331 ♀ ⑪

Savaterre 563 ♀

Serengale Vineyard 574 ♀ ⊨

Star Lane Winery 603 ⓠ ♀ ⑪

Vignerons Schmölzer & Brown 677

Weathercraft Wine 689 ♀

Bendigo (Vic)

Balgownie Estate 93 ♀ ⑪

BlackJack Vineyards 121 ♀

Glenwillow Wines 275 ♀

Harcourt Valley Vineyards 289 ⓠ ♀ ⑪

Lake Cairn Curran Vineyard 365 ♀ ⑪

Mandurang Valley Wines 403 ⓠ ♀ ⑪

Newbridge Wines 458 ♀

Sandhurst Ridge 560 ♀ ⊨

Sutton Grange Winery 615 ⓠ ♀ ⑪

Turners Crossing Vineyard 664

Water Wheel 687 ♀

Blackwood Valley (WA)

Nannup Estate 456

Broke Fordwich (NSW)

Talits Estate 623 ♀ ⊨

Canberra District (NSW)

Capital Wines 150 ⓠ ♀

Clonakilla 176 ♀ ⑪

Collector Wines 183 ♀ ⑪

Eden Road Wines 230 ♀ ⑪

Helm 301 ♀

Lake George Winery 366 ⓠ ♀ ⊨ ⑪

Lark Hill 370 ♀ ⑪

Lerida Estate 376 ⓠ ♀ ⑪

McKellar Ridge Wines 396 ♀ ⑪

Mount Majura Vineyard 446 ♀ ⊨

Murrumbateman Winery 454 ⓠ ♀ ⑪

Nick O'Leary Wines 459 ♀

Quarry Hill Wines 523

Ravensworth 527

Sapling Yard Wines 562 ♀ ⑪

Grampians (Vic)

Clarnette 175

Fallen Giants 239 ♀ ⑪

Grampians Estate 277 ♀ ⑪

Kimbarra Wines 353 ♀

Miners Ridge 425 ♀ ⊨ ⑪

Montara 435 ⚱ ⑪

Mount Langi Ghiran Vineyards 445 ⚱ ♀ ⑪

Mount Stapylton Wines 449

The Story Wines 644 ♀

Granite Belt (QLD)

Ballandean Estate Wines 94 ⚱ ♀ ⑪

Banca Ridge 95 ⚱ ♀ ⑪

Hidden Creek 307 ♀ ⊨ ⑪

Ravenscroft Vineyard 526 ⚱ ♀ ⑪

Robert Channon Wines 541 ⚱ ♀ ⑪

Symphony Hill Wines 619 ♀

Great Southern (WA)

Castelli Estate 153 ⚱ ♀ ⊨ ⑪

Forest Hill Vineyard 250 ⚱ ♀ ⑪

Lowboi 390

Marchand & Burch 404

Oranje Tractor 471 ♀

Paul Nelson Wines 482 ♀

Rockcliffe 544 ⚱ ♀ ⑪

Rosenthal Wines 547

Singlefile Wines 587 ♀

Staniford Wine Co 601 ♀

Trevelen Farm 661 ♀

Willoughby Park 695 ⚱ ♀ ⑪

Great Western (Vic)

ATR Wines 87 ⚱ ♀ ⑪

Best's Wines 112 ⚱ ♀ ⊨ ⑪

Black & Ginger 120

Seppelt 571 ⚱ ♀

Greater Perth (WA)

Paul Conti Wines 481 ♀ ⑪

Gundagai (NSW)

Tumblong Hills 662 ♀

Heathcote (Vic)

Armstead Estate 84 ♀

Bull Lane Wine Company 138

Burke & Wills Winery 140 ⚱ ♀

Cavalry Wines 155

Condie Estate 186 ♀

Domaine Asmara 207 ♀ ⊨

Ellis Wines 235 ♀

Farmer & The Scientist 241

Heathcote Estate 297

Heathcote Winery 298 ♀ ⑪

Humis Vineyard 320 ♀

Idavue Estate 323 ⚱ ♀ ⑪

Henty (Vic)

Hilltops (NSW)

Hunter Valley (NSW)

Manjimup (WA)

Margaret River (WA)

Mornington Peninsula (Vic)

South Australia continued

The Group 638

The Other Wine Co 643 ♀

The Pawn Wine Co. 643

Thistledown Wines 646

Zagora 725

South West Australia

Kerrigan + Berry 350 ♀ ⫙

Southern Eyre Peninsula (SA)

Peter Teakle Wines 495 ⚬ ♀ ⊨ ⫙

Southern Fleurieu (SA)

Salomon Estate 557 ♀

Southern Highlands (NSW)

Centennial Vineyards 156 ⚬ ♀ ⫙

Cherry Tree Hill 166 ♀ ⫙

PepperGreen Estate 493 ⚬ ♀ ⫙

Tertini Wines 634 ♀

Southern New South Wales

Corang Estate 188 ♀

Strathbogie Ranges (Vic)

Baddaginnie Run 91

Fowles Wine 253 ⚬ ♀ ⫙

Maygars Hill Winery 413 ⚬ ♀ ⊨

Sunbury (Vic)

Craiglee 193 ♀

Marnong Estate 406 ♀ ⊨ ⫙

Swan District (WA)

Mandoon Estate 402 ⚬ ♀ ⊨ ⫙

Pinelli Wines 501 ♀ ⫙

Swan Hill (VIC)

Andrew Peace Wines 76 ♀ ⫙

Swan Valley (WA)

Corymbia 191 ♀

Faber Vineyard 239 ♀ ⫙

Harris Organic 292 ♀

Houghton 315 ♀ ⫙

John Kosovich Wines 337 ♀

Nikola Estate 460 ⚬ ♀ ⫙

Oakover Wines 466 ⚬ ♀ ⫙

RiverBank Estate 540 ⚬ ♀ ⫙

Sandalford 560 ⚬ ♀ ⫙

Sittella Wines 588 ♀ ⫙

Upper Reach 671 ♀ ⫙

Vino Volta 682 ♀

Tumbarumba (NSW)

Kosciuszko Wines 359 ♀

Upper Goulburn (VIC)

Delatite 214 ◔ ♀ ⑪
Gioiello Estate 271
Ros Ritchie Wines 545 ◔ ♀ ⑪
Tallarook 623
Utter Wines 672 ♀
Yarradindi Wines 719

Various

Allegiance Wines 71 ♀
Clandestine 173
Fourth Wave Wine 252
Handpicked Wines 287 ◔ ♀ ⑪
Lisa McGuigan Wines 383 ♀ ⑪
M. Chapoutier Australia 392 ♀
Risky Business Wines 539
Rogue Vintner 545
Rouleur 548 ◔ ♀
Russell & Suitor 551
Santa & D'Sas 561
Santarossa Wine Company 562
Shoofly | Frisk 582
The Flying Winemaker 638
Woods Crampton 706

Victoria

B Minor 91
Carlei Estate | Carlei Green
    Vineyards 151 ◔ ♀ ⑪
Semitone 571
The Hairy Arm 639 ♀
The Happy Winemaker 639
Vino Intrepido 681
Wine Unplugged 700

Western Australia

Battles Wine 104
Byron & Harold 142
Cherubino 167
PLAN B! WINES 505
Vinaceous Wines 678

Wrattonbully (SA)

Mérite Wines 419
Smith & Hooper 593 ♀

Yarra Valley (Vic)

Alkimi Wines 67
Allinda 72
Ben Haines Wine 110
Bicknell fc 114
Bird on a Wire Wines 119
Buttermans Track 141 ♀
Centare 155
Chandon Australia 161 ♀ ⑪

Acknowledgements

It goes without saying that it takes a cast of thousands to create a project of this magnitude, and this year, all the more. So thanks to an ever-growing and immensely talented team.

This book is the shared labour and passion of an expanding tasting team, each of whom is deserving of having their name on the cover. The mandate of delivering the most up-to-date reviews calls for a punishing tasting and writing schedule. Turning a mountain of thousands of tasting samples into articulate reviews is hardly the idyllic life that a wine writer is imagined to lead! Each and every one of these pages is a testimony to the devotion and talent of these eight incredible individuals.

The unique and distinctive voice of each taster coming to life on these pages loud, clear and captivating is an inspiration to me, second only to seeing the finest wines and wineries of the year rise to the top. Erin, you bring wine to life like nobody else. Ned, your vocabulary ever captivates and challenges me. Jane, I love that you can simultaneously make wine no-nonsense and fun. Jeni, you make wine real and keep us all honest. Dave, every review articulates your deep connection with the Barossa. Philip, you have brought the Yarra to life with your insights this year. And James, you are the master of capturing a wine authoritatively, concisely and eloquently.

The true credit for pulling this edition together is again due to Emily Lightfoot, our talented and tireless Tasting Manager, who achieved the impossible of assembling countless pieces of this vast puzzle, while ever refining an endlessly complex process. She remained the hero of the tasters for her brilliance and patience. Her name is every bit deserving of front-cover status, too.

At Hardie Grant, my thanks always to founder Sandy Grant for his support and leadership; and to the dedicated HGX team, who are responsible for the day-to-day operations of the Companion online and in print, as well as the annual judging and awards presentation. It is very much a team effort, led by Nick and Jac Hardie-Grant, weaving together the expertise of Shana Rohn and Haydn Spurrell in marketing, Uno de Waal in product, Anna Webster, Amelia Ball, J'aime Cardillo and Olivia Campbell in editorial, Glenn Moffatt in design, Amy Banks, Ellen Arcus, Katrina Butler, Nicole Prioste and Claire Teisseyre in commercial, Christine Dixon and Sammi Gui in finance and Emily Lightfoot in tasting. Particular thanks to Katrina and Olivia for additional support in the final hectic weeks of this book.

My thanks also to the Hardie Grant Books team; to Roxy Ryan, managing director; Anna Collett, senior editor; Brooke Munday, project editor; Lucy Pijnenburg, editor; Megan Ellis, typesetter; and Kasi Collins and the rest of the Hardie Grant Books marketing team.

Personal thanks from me to Rachael, Linden, Huon and Vaughn Stelzer for your patience and support. Ned's thanks go to Matilda, Jack, Don and Dianne Goodwin, and to Gregory and Gaye Ross, for receiving so many deliveries on his behalf. Erin's heartfelt thanks and gratitude go to Wendy Roach, whose friendship and commitment to routine are treasured. And to Jesse, without whom, all is lost.

Dave thanks Jen for her patience and support, his neighbours Emily, Matt, Lynne and Tim for the use of their recycling bins and Dudley the dog for not knocking over any bottles this year.

Jeni, to GT, always.

Philip's heartfelt thanks go to Melanie, Chris and Sebastian and to Emily for always being on top of everything and making his first year go so smoothly!

Emily, to Alice, Jack and Tom Percival.

James' thanks go to Beth (Queen Bee, who has been by his side for 22 years) and Jake (Go Go Girl, 14 years), for their unwavering attention to detail that cannot be overemphasised; and to Emily Lightfoot for her patience and calm throughout.

Finally, to the wineries who sent wines and answered our calls for wine and vintage background, this edition owes its existence to you all.

Artist's Note

The artwork for the cover was created with the celebration of Country in mind. It was painted in acrylic on a gesso ground, with a touch of collage and wabi sabi.

The idea that Country is alive appeals to me. I've been painting it for years now, and I've always thought of it as living and breathing – static but moving, dancing and singing. When I think of Country I think of the joy of the land. And as we know, the terroir gives us many pleasures in a bottle.

As such, the connection between wine and Country are inseparable.

Cheers,
David Lancashire AGI.